MANAGING SERVICES MARKETING
TEXT AND READINGS

Third Edition

MANAGING SERVICES MARKETING
TEXT AND READINGS
Third Edition

John E. G. Bateson
London Business School

THE DRYDEN PRESS
Harcourt Brace College Publishers

Fort Worth   Philadelphia   San Diego   New York   Austin   Orlando   San Antonio
Toronto   Montreal   London   Sydney   Tokyo

Acquisitions Editor   Lyn Hastert
Developmental Editor   Iva Foster
Art Director   Jeanette Barber
Marketing Manager   Lisé Johnson
Publisher   Carl Tyson
Editor-in-Chief   Lyn Hastert
Director of Editing, Design, and Production   Dine Southworth
Project Management   Seaside Publishing Services
Text Type   10/12 Garamond

Address for orders:
The Dryden Press
6277 Sea Harbor Drive
Orlando, FL 32887-6777
1-800-782-4479 or 1-800-433-0001 (in Florida)

Address for editorial correspondence:
The Dryden Press
301 Commerce Street, Suite 3700
Fort Worth, TX 76102

ISBN: 0-03-098666-4

Library of Congress Catalog Card Number: 94-73629

Printed in the United States of America

5 6 7 8 9 0 1 2 3 4 0 6 9 9 8 7 6 5 4 3 2 1

The Dryden Press
Harcourt Brace College Publishers

To Dori, who brought joy back to my world.

THE DRYDEN PRESS SERIES IN MARKETING

PREFACE

Managing Services Marketing, Third Edition is designed for an advanced MBA course in the marketing of services and executive programs geared to managers in service firms.

Every textbook on marketing should be based upon services with a couple of chapters at the end on "the special case of goods." Chapter 1 gives ample macroeconomic data suggesting that the service sector is becoming the primary source of wealth, trade, and growth throughout the developed world. Even this data under-represents the impact on consumers. The proportion of purchasing effort focused on goods is declining rapidly due to the impact of a number of forces: the commoditization of branded goods; the shattering of the mass market into a mosaic of millions of pieces and the resultant growing power of the trade.

By comparison, the purchasing of service is becoming increasingly complex. The global communications network will soon provide home shopping, video on demand, and thanks to digital compression, up to 240 channels of television. In other sectors, the world is being colonized by the multi-site, service firms. Diplomatic relations with China may vary, but the McDonalds close to Tiananman Square is the worlds biggest with 28,000 square feet of space, more than 700 seats, and a staff of 900. The restaurant is not only changing consumer habits but is also changing the work ethic of its staff. Recently Union Bank of Switzerland rated the cost of living in various worldwide sectors using the Big Mac Scale: percentage of the weekly wage needed to buy a Big Mac.

Economic prosperity means that service transactions are becoming a trade-off between the benefits obtained and the cost incurred in terms of time and control, with price becoming irrelevant. Services provide opportunities to both generate and consume discretionary time. Services also require the giving up of that sense of control that is becoming a key decision criterion after time and before price.

Economists and consumers know we are in a service world and the marketing textbooks should reflect this. This textbook is dedicated exclusively to the problems of marketing services.

The title of the textbook reflects its orientation. It is concerned with the management problems of services marketing managers. The concepts and tools developed in the package goods and industrial marketing areas apply to services. The problems of services marketing, however, are more complex. The service product is more difficult to design, and introducing marketing orientation into a firm dominated by operations is more difficult.

This textbook is divided into three parts. Part One covers the basic building blocks that are needed before going on to consider the management of the services experience in part Two. Part Three adopts a firmwide viewpoint and discusses alternative ways service firms can compete.

PART ONE

The four chapters in Part One cover the service consumer, the service operation, and the service provider. A chapter devoted to understanding consumer behavior is not unexpected in a marketing book, but one on operations management is surprising. Because the operation is the product, it is important to understand not only the needs of the consumer but also the needs of the operation. Equally important is the understanding of the service providers, their motivations, and their role.

Chapter 1 provides an overview of the theoretical framework of the textbook, as well as background on the importance of services. Chapter 2, the consumer chapter, builds on the experiential nature of the service product to suggest that a number of emerging theories from environmental psychology may provide additional insights into the consumer choice process.

Chapter 3 opens with an operation management perspective, and sets forth the requirements for an efficient operation. These requirements are then compared with the operational demands of service, and several major threats to efficiency are identified. A number of concepts and theories, which are developed in operations management to overcome these problems, are then described. Throughout the textbook the emphasis is on understanding the operation and its interdependence with marketing.

Chapter 4 focuses on the service providers, those individuals who sit on the boundaries of the service firm and provide day-to-day contact with consumers. They are the product for many service firms and yet they are often at the bottom of the organizational hierarchy. Because of their low position in the hierarchy, they are sometimes caught between the consumer and the firm and have to resolve the conflicts produced.

PART TWO

These four chapters deal with the creation and management of the service experience, which constitutes the product the consumer buys. The complexity of the service product is one of the key differentiating features of service marketing. The creation of experiences (service) that take place in real time, poses many problems that differ from those faced in the creation of mere physical good. Chapter 5 deals with the configuration of the operation and the environment. chapter 6 discusses the design of human resource policies necessary to successfully motivate the contact personnel. In particular, it deals with who uses and how to use empowerment and enforcement.

A unique characteristic of services is that consumers are part of the production process and actually co-produce their own experience. Chapters 7 and 8 look at pricing and communication from this perspective. Instead of looking at the traditional theories in both areas, they look instead at how these traditional tools can influence consumer behavior in the service experience.

PART THREE

This part takes the much broader perspective of the services firm and discusses alternative competitive strategies. chapter 9 provides an overview for this section of the book and provides a framework of different kinds of competition: for share, reach, and geography. By far the most complex is competition for share, and ideas in Chapter 9 are developed in the rest of the chapters.

Chapter 10 discusses customer retention as a competitive strategy. Chapter 11 shows how service recovery can be used competitively. Chapters 12 and 13 look at the related topics of service quality and creating customer focus.

ACKNOWLEDGMENTS

There is a myth that business academics walk the cloister of their universities seeking inspiration, and then when that inspiration strikes, they dash to the nearest office and write a book. The truth is far more painful and complex. This textbook represents the compilation of 16 years of work in the services. Over those years I have attended conferences, written papers and most importantly, taught service marketing to MBAs and executives every year. How is it possible to thank all of the people who have contributed to the development of my thinking? Clearly it is not possible and I am left with the unenviable task of naming names and, worse still, omitting others. To those of you not mentioned explicitly, blame only the fact that it is impossible to capture 16 years of one's professional life in a few short lines.

I am indebted to all of the faculty members using the book throughout the world who have taken the time to share their feedback with me. I thank the following people who provided critical reviews of the second edition: Lawrence Cunningham, University of Colorado, Denver; Kirk Davidson, Mount St. Mary's College; Bill Hess, University of California; Ken Kendall, Washing State University; and Leo Renaghan, Cornell University. I am particularly indebted to Doug Hoffman whose enthusiasm for the textbook reignited my own. As a contributing author to this book he provided insights, material, and the beginning of the new structure.

To Earl Sasser, Daryl Wykoff, and Christopher Lovelock, from whom I took my first courses in services at the Harvard Business School, thanks for sowing the seeds that grew into my burning interest in the service.

To Eric Langeard and Pierre Eiglier, truly the pioneers who led the way, thanks for showing me the power of conceptualization in services.

To the Marketing Science Institute, whose Consumer Service Project nurtured my interest in services, supported my first ideas, and created in Christopher Lovelock, Eric Langeard, and Pierre Eiglier a great team of project colleagues, I extend my gratitude.

To the services marketing class of the London Business School and the Stanford Business School, thank you for your patience. What you don't know is that I learned as much from you as you did from me!

To Leonard Berry, Valerie Zeithaml, Greg Upah, Ven Venkatesen, Mary Jo Bitner, Bernard Booms, Ben Schneider, Christian Grönroos, Dick Chase, Carol Congram, and all the other who attended those early American Marketing Association service marketing conferences, thanks for the company. If one is going to wander into the wilderness of a new area and be a pioneer, it is good to have friends around to protect your back.

Finally, I am immensely grateful to Lyn Hastert and Iva Foster for their work on the third edition; to Marilyn Livingstone, Morgen Witzel, and Rachael Young for their patience and preparation of the manuscript.

John E.G. Bateson
London
June 1995

ABOUT THE AUTHOR

John E.G. Bateson is a Senior Vice President with Gemini Consulting. He was Associate Professor of Marketing at the London Business School, England, and a visiting associate professor at the Stanford Business School. Prior to teaching, he was a brand manager with Lever Brothers and marketing manager with Philips.

Dr. Bateson holds an undergraduate degree from Imperial College, London, a master's degree from London Business School, and a doctorate in marketing from the Harvard Business School. He has published extensively in the services marketing literature including the *Journal of Marketing Research*, the *Journal of Retailing*, *Marketing Science*, and the *Journal of Consumer Research*. He is also the author of *Marketing Public Transit: A Strategic Approach* (Praeger).

Dr. Bateson was actively involved with the formation of the services of the division of the American Marketing Association. He served on the Services Council for Four years and has chaired sessions of the AMA Services Marketing Conferences. He also serves on the Steering committee of the Marketing Science Institute. Dr. Bateson consults extensively in the services sector.

TABLE OF CONTENTS

MANAGING SERVICES MARKETING
TEXT AND READINGS

Third Edition

PART ONE

THE BASIC
BUILDING BLOCKS

CHAPTER 1

INTRODUCTION

THE SERVICE REVOLUTION

THE SERVICE ECONOMY

Services permeate every aspect of our lives. We use transportation services when we travel, often to and from work; when we travel away from home, we use restaurant services to feed us and hotels to put roofs over our heads. At home, we rely on services such as electricity and telephone; at work, we need postal, courier, and maintenance services to keep our work places running. We use the services of hairdressers to maintain our personal self-image, and our employers use the services of public relations and advertising firms to maintain their corporate images. Lawyers, doctors, dentists, stockbrokers, and insurance agents look after our personal and financial health. In our leisure time, we use a battery of services ranging from cinemas to swimming pools to Disney-style theme parks for amusement and relaxation. And when we do buy goods, such as a new car or a washing machine, we often still rely on services to keep them running and repair them when they break down.

Services allow us to budget our time as well as our money. We use some services to generate increased discretionary time so as to buy other services. A family might, for example, eat at McDonald's in order to save the time that would have been spent cooking a meal at home. That "extra" time might then be "spent" at a cinema or at a theme park, using another service to provide recreation. A company might buy a service, such as advertising or research or catering, rather than spending its own valuable time in the field, and then be free to concentrate on its core business.

Many of these services have always been present to some degree, but the complexity and diversity of services has increased dramatically over the past century. Contrary to popular belief, services, not manufactured goods, have fueled modern economic growth. The Industrial Revolution of the eighteenth century involved changes not only in production, but also in financial structures and in transportation and communication networks. It is no coincidence that two of the biggest service sectors, banks and railroads, boomed at the same time as the Industrial Revolution. Without the emergence of these and other services, the economic benefits of large-scale production units could never have been realized.[1]

Economic growth has in its turn fueled the growth of the service sector, as increasing prosperity means that companies, institutions, and individuals increasingly have become willing to trade money for time and to buy services rather than spend time doing things for themselves. New technology has led to considerable changes in the nature of many services and in the development of new services. Higher disposable incomes have led to a proliferation of personal services, particularly in the entertainment sector. Growth has meant an increase not only in the overall volume of services, but in the variety and diversity of services offered.

The result has been phenomenal growth in service industries, shown clearly in economic and trade statistics. In economic terms, the service sector now accounts for 58 percent of worldwide gross national product (GNP); in 1980, service business worldwide was valued at $350 billion, and accounted for 20 percent of all world trade, while by 1992 that figure had nearly trebled to $1,000 billion.[2] All of the developed economies now have large service sectors, and Japan and Germany in particular have service economies at least as developed as that of the United States. Many service firms now operate internationally, and exports of services are also increasing. The United States remains the world's leading service exporter, with exports valued at $148.5 billion, or 10.5 percent of total worldwide service exports in 1991; service imports amounted to $100 billion in the same year. Given that the American balance of payments deficit in manufactured goods is nearly $130 billion a year, the $50 billion trade surplus in services is obviously vital to the American economy.[3]

The difference in trade figures shows distinctly the growing importance of services and the parallel decline of manufacturing. In 1970, manufacturing accounted for 26 percent of American gross domestic product (GDP); by 1991, it accounted for only 21 percent. Even more dramatic declines can be seen in the other two traditional manufacturing nations: In the former West Germany, manufacturing as a percentage of GDP fell from 41 percent in 1970 to 28 percent in 1991, and in Japan the figures show a drop from 36 percent to 29 percent. Yet the idea that an economy cannot survive without relying on manufacturing to create wealth continues to dominate business and political thinking in the West. *The Economist* noted in 1993: "That services cannot thrive without a strong manufacturing 'base' is a claim rarely challenged. The opposite argument—that manufacturing needs services—is hardly ever put."[4]

In fact, the American economy is becoming heavily reliant on services; it is hard to avoid the conclusion that it is services, not manufacturing, which are the real creators of wealth in America. In 1993, services accounted for 74 percent of American GNP.[5] Services also provide the bulk of employment. In 1900, 30 percent of the United States' work force was employed in the service sector; by 1984, service industries employed 74 percent of the work force; and by 1992, that figure had risen to nearly 80 percent. At the same time, the proportion of the work force engaged in agriculture declined from 42 percent to just 3 percent.[6] In 1948, 20.9 million people were employed in goods production of all kinds in America, and 27.2 million in services; by 1992, employment in goods production was 19.9 million (with no increase in over two decades), while service employment (including wholesale and retail trade and financial services) had risen to 81.1 million, far more than the total number of people employed in all sectors 30 years earlier.[7]

The service industries not only have grown in size, they also have absorbed all the jobs shed by traditional industries, such as agriculture, mining, and manufacturing, along the way. The Bureau of Labor Statistics expects service occupations to account for *all* net job growth through the year 2005. And the same pattern is being repeated in the European Community and Japan. In 1990, services accounted for 58 percent of GDP in Japan and 60 percent of total GDP in the European Community. The service sector employs 133 million people, or 60 percent of the work force, in the European Community, while industrial employment has declined steadily to 32 percent. Only in Japan has industrial employment continued to increase.[8]

Even these numbers conceal the true contribution of services to economic growth, since service employees on the direct payroll of goods companies are counted as goods industry employees. The service division of IBM, one of the largest worldwide service organizations, is counted as being in the goods, not the service, sector because IBM's core business is computers and electronics. A truer picture can be obtained by looking at the combination of people employed formally in the services sector—such as independent architectural or accounting firms, for example—and people employed in the same jobs, but working for firms based in goods sectors. Ginzberg and Vojta state that the number of the latter rose from 4.7 million to 12.7 million between 1948 and 1978. They go on to suggest that the value added to the economy by these producer services alone exceeded the value added by all of manufacturing in 1977; and this is without counting the formal service sector and its value.[9]

One of the consequences of this change has been an alteration in the shape of the work force itself. Ginzberg and Vojta point out how the bulk of new jobs creat-

FIGURE 1.1   Service Economics and Employment

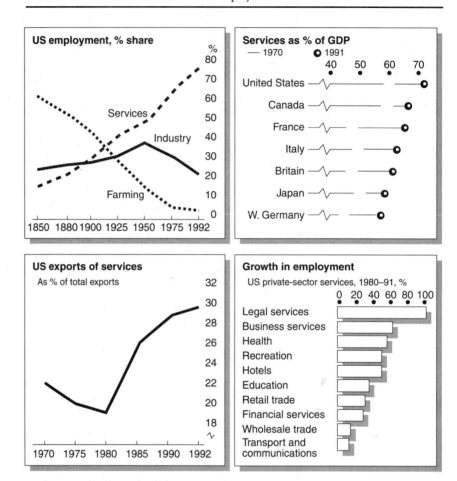

SOURCE: *The Economist*, February 20, 1994, 20.

ed in the previous 30 years were white-collar jobs, in higher-level professional, technical, administrative, and sales positions. Not all service jobs are necessarily white-collar jobs, but Ginzberg and Vojta contend that, in the United States, as services have replaced goods as the most dominant force in the economy, "human capital" has replaced physical capital as the important source of investment. "Americans must unshackle themselves from the notion," the authors declare, "that goods alone constitute wealth, whereas services are nonproductive and ephemeral. At the same time, they should act on Adam Smith's understanding that the wealth of a nation depends on the skill, dexterity, and knowledge of its people."[10]

SERVICE AT THE FIRM LEVEL

Interest in the problems of marketing in service organizations is growing rapidly. This may be explained in part by rising levels of competition in many parts of the service sector. Services marketing emerged late because of a perceived lack of need for it in times when demand exceeded supply and competitive pressures were few. Now, however, competition is increasing and consumers are demanding more and better services. Growing sophistication among consumers means that service standards are changing steadily, and there were fears that American service firms were failing to keep up. An article in *Time* magazine in 1987 warned that national disenchantment with services was reaching near-epidemic proportions, and that bad service even could damage the country's economic position abroad; at the time, Japanese banks were making serious inroads into the U.S. market at the expense of their "sloppy" American competitors.[11] The article cited Quinn and Gagnon who warned: "While there is still time, it is essential to take a hard look at how we think about services, how we manage them, and how much they contribute to the nation's public health."[12]

American firms—of all kinds, not just pure service firms—face a challenge, in the words of Henkoff, to treat service as "the ultimate strategic imperative, a business challenge that has profound implications for the way we manage our companies, hire employees, develop careers, and craft policies."[13] It seems clear that this challenge is being met. Again, in Henkoff's words, product quality is no longer a source of competitive advantage. Henkoff (1994) cites one American CEO as saying: "Everyone has become better at developing products. The one place you can differentiate yourself is in the service you provide."[14]

There are numerous examples of firms using the "service imperative" to differentiate themselves from the market and to increase profits. In the highly competitive, low margin auto insurance market, one company, Progressive Corp., has made policyholder service a major part of its competitive strategy. Four years ago, Progressive introduced its Immediate Response Program, where clients who need to make claims can contact the company at any time of day or night. Progressive representatives make contact with 80 percent of clients who have been involved in accidents within nine hours of the event; sometimes they arrive at the scene of the accident. Most claims are settled in less than a week. Automated claims-management systems streamline the process and keep costs down. Customers are impressed by the service, and Progressive's profits are increasing at a rate of 20 percent a year.[15]

It is clear that services in America are no longer manufacturing's poor cousin. Services provide the bulk of the country's wealth and are an important source of employment and exports. American companies have woken up to the potential of using service as a source of competitive advantage, both at home and abroad. Since the last edition of this book, one of the companies profiled in it, catalogue retailers Lands' End, have begun successfully exporting their brand of service to the UK. There are countless other examples of American firms using the service imperative to drive their businesses forward to profit and growth. And the service boom looks set to continue; it seems likely that by the time the twenty-first century arrives, there will be no successful business that does not make service the foundation of its competitive strategy.

WHAT IS A SERVICE?

It is extremely difficult to define a pure good or a pure service. A pure good implies that the consumer obtains benefit from the good alone, without any added value from service; concurrently, a pure service assumes that there is no "goods" element to the service which the customer receives. In reality, most services contain some goods element. At McDonald's the customer receives a hamburger; the bank provides a bank statement; the garage that repairs cars adds new parts to those cars, and so on. And most goods offer some service—even if it is only delivery. Increasingly, firms in the goods sectors are using service offerings as a way of differentiating their products from those of their competitors. The goods/service dichotomy is a subtly changing spectrum, with firms moving their position within that spectrum over time.[16] In fact, an exact definition of services is not really necessary in order to understand services and the marketing problems associated with them. That there are different problems associated with the two is readily apparent; Mills and Moberg describe two factors which set service *operations* apart from goods operations, namely differences in process and differences in output.[17] It is probably of greater practical value to focus on these kinds of differences rather than on ultimate definitions. Certainly the line between goods and services can be drawn in different places for different companies. James L. Schorr, who went from Procter & Gamble to be vice president of marketing for Holiday Inns, provides his own rough definition:

> Simply defined, in our terms, a product is something a consumer purchases and takes away with him or consumes, or otherwise uses. If it is not physical, not something that they can take away or consume, then we call it a service.[18]

When asked which he was selling in the hotel business, however, Schorr's answer put the goods/service dichotomy firmly in the realms of the theoretical:

> What I am really selling, in terms of what people are buying, is a hotel experience. I'm selling the room, the way they treat you at the front desk, the way the bellman treats you, the way the waitress treats you—it's all mixed together in a consumer's mind when he makes a hotel decision.[19]

Another good example of a goods/service dichotomy is Domino's Pizza, the national home-delivery pizza chain. Domino's sells a product that is clearly visible (and indeed, edible), but an important element in Domino's business was its home-delivery service, which originally guaranteed that the customer's pizza would arrive within 30 minutes of the order being placed. Is the customer buying a good or a service? Clearly, in practical terms, he or she is buying both. The service offering, which is what any marketing proposition must consider, is a mix of services and goods.

We still can speak of goods and services, and, indeed, this book will continue to use them, but the word *service* should be read with the following caveat: *to the extent that the benefits are delivered to the consumer by a service rather than a good.* As will become apparent when our basic model is developed, there is an implicit assumption made here that service benefits are delivered through an interactive experience involving the consumer to a greater or lesser extent. In real terms, however, it is necessary to remember that the *product* delivered to the consumer is usually a bundle of benefits that can include, as in the Holiday Inn example above, both goods and services in a variety of combinations.

CLASSIFICATION OF SERVICES

Even more contentious than the goods/service dichotomy is the question of classification of services. Classification has a long tradition within science; of all classification systems, perhaps the most powerful is the periodic table of elements developed by Mendeleyev to analyze elements in chemistry. By classifying the properties of the elements, the Russian chemist was able to show that the elements could be organized into groups having common properties. This schematic representation was sufficiently powerful to allow scientists to identify "missing" elements that were later formally discovered. Subsequent developments in atomic physics were able to verify the entire table using the subatomic characteristics of the individual elements.

Those classifications for services which have emerged so far compare poorly with such a benchmark. Most of these schemes attempt to combine organization with classification, and they are not based on empirically testable properties of services. As with the goods/services dichotomy, they tend to focus on opposites and produce categories such as people-based versus equipment-based (services that are delivered by people or by machines), high-contact versus low-contact, individual versus collective. In each set, many examples can be produced that fit cleanly into neither category but are somewhere in the middle.

Too many of these classifications focus on the operational aspect of services and fail to take the marketing problems into account. For example, one traditional dichotomy is that of for-profit versus not-for-profit services. The not-for-profit sector of the economy is huge, particularly if the various levels of government are included, but many not-for-profit organizations share common problems with their for-profit brethren, far more so than with other not-for-profit organizations. For example, a not-for-profit health-care chain has more in common with a for-profit health-care chain, such as Humana, than with a government department. Such a distinction is of little value when assessing the marketing problems of the organizations concerned. In fact, virtually all of this book is as relevant to not-for-profit organizations as it is to for-profit businesses.

Lovelock argues that classification schemes can only be of value if they offer strategic insights into the services themselves. It is important, he says, for such schemes to highlight the characteristics that certain types of service have in common, and to analyze the implications of these common factors for marketing managers. Lovelock suggests that the following questions be asked to determine which category a service fits into:

1. What is the nature of the service act?
2. What type of relationship does the service organization have with its customers?
3. How much room is there for customization and judgment on the part of the service provider?
4. What is the nature of demand and supply for the service? and
5. How is the service delivered?[20]

The thrust of Lovelock's argument is that services should be considered not for the factors that set them apart, but for the factors that draw them together. His concern is less to provide an organizational schema than to provide a series of guidelines for marketing managers. Identifying factors that different types of service have in common helps marketing managers to better understand their products, their organizations, and the relationships their organizations have with their customers.

> Recognizing that the products of service organizations previously considered as "different" actually face similar problems or share certain characteristics in common can yield valuable managerial insights. Innovation in marketing, after all, often reflects a manager's ability to seek out and learn from analogous situations in other contexts.[21]

Commonalities, rather than differences, between services are the focus of this book. Zeithaml, Parasuraman, and Berry sum up four common factors that characterize all services: *intangibility, inseparability of production and consumption, heterogeneity,* and *perishability.* Services are said to be intangible because they are performances rather than objects, and they cannot be touched or seen in the same manner as goods; rather, they are experienced, and consumers' judgments about them tend to be more subjective than objective. Inseparability of production and consumption refers to the fact that whereas goods are first produced, then sold, and then consumed; services are sold first and then produced and consumed at one and the same time. A passenger on an airplane first purchases a ticket and then flies, consuming the in-flight service as it is produced. Heterogeneity refers to the potential for variability in the performance of services and problems of lack of consistency that cannot be eliminated in services as they frequently can be with goods. Finally, perishability means that services cannot be saved; unused capacity in services cannot be claimed, and services themselves cannot be inventoried.[22]

THE BASIC MODEL

All products, be they goods or services, deliver a bundle of benefits to the consumer. The *benefit concept* is the encapsulation of these benefits in the consumer's mind. For a detergent brand, such as Tide, that benefit concept might simply be cleaning; the consumer wants clean clothes and buys a product that will achieve this goal. On a more detailed level, this benefit concept might include attributes built into the product that go beyond the powder or liquid itself; extending the benefit concept might produce attributes such as cleanliness, whiteness, or even parenthood. The determination of what constitutes the bundle of benefits purchased by the consumer is at the heart of marketing, and it transcends any distinction between goods and services.

When a consumer purchases a service, he or she purchases an *experience* created by the delivery of that service. In other words, services deliver a bundle of benefits to the consumer through the experience that is created for that consumer. The way in which the consumer receives the benefits package is thus very different for services than for goods. With goods, the benefits package is intimately connected to the actual goods and remains a part of it, generally disappearing once the good has been consumed or is not being used.

With services, however, the different parts of the bundle of benefits can come from a variety of sources at once. The model of the *servuction system,* shown below, illustrates this simply and effectively. First, we break the service firm into two parts, that which is visible to the consumer and that which is not. The invisible portions of the firm—the kitchen in a restaurant, or the room-cleaning department of a hotel—affect the visible part of the organization, which is, in turn, broken into two parts, the inanimate physical environment in which the service encounter takes place and the contact personnel who actually provide the service.

Finally, the model suggests that Customer A, who is purchasing the service, also will be affected by Customer B, who is in contact with the service organization at the same time. In practical terms, customers in a restaurant may find their service experience spoiled if other customers are loud or rude; conversely, passengers on an airline may come away with a favorable outlook on the service they have just received if they were sitting next to an interesting fellow passenger who made stimulating conversation and helped pass the time.

The benefits package, therefore, is derived from an interactive process or experience. The visible components of the organization are supported by the invisible components that provide the administration and maintenance of the physical facilities; further, as service usually is delivered to groups of customers simultaneously, benefits are derived from interaction with other customers.

The servuction system model not only shows the different elements of the service experience, but it shows how the service experience as a whole is created. If services are experiences, as has been demonstrated above, then it is inappropriate to speak of *delivering* them, a term that in some way implies their transportation. The servuction system model, first developed by Langeard and Eiglier, shows how consumers interact with the visible part of the system and with other consumers to create the service experience. The whole of the servuction system creates the experience, and the experience, in turn, creates the benefit to the consumer.[23]

FIGURE 1.2 The Servuction Service Model

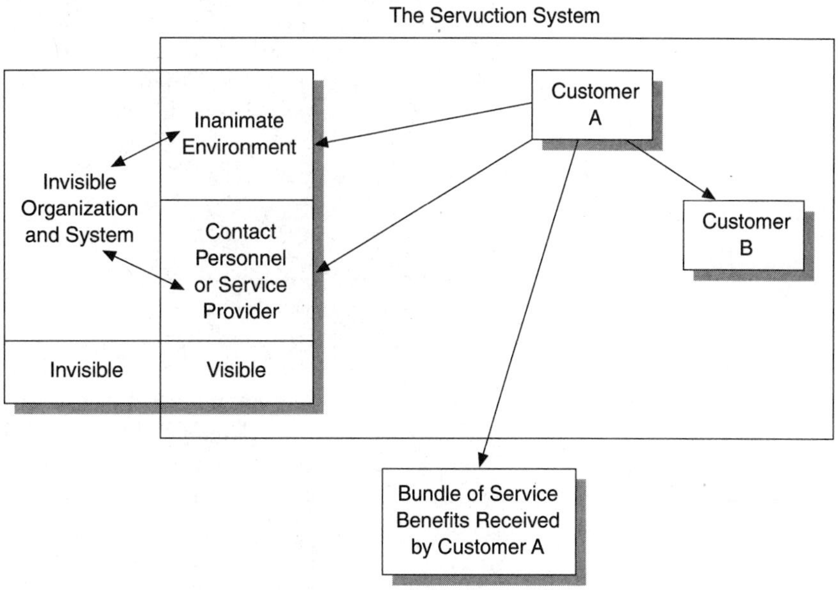

The Servuction System

Invisible | Visible

Invisible Organization and System

Inanimate Environment

Contact Personnel or Service Provider

Customer A

Customer B

Bundle of Service Benefits Received by Customer A

Such a simple perspective has profound implications. Looking at the model, we can draw a number of conclusions about services in general, conclusions that are of direct importance to the problems of services marketing.

SERVICES CANNOT BE INVENTORIED

Perhaps the most far-reaching implication of the servuction system model is that, in order to receive the benefit, the consumer must be part of the system. It is thus impossible to inventory services. For example, a British Airways' flight from London to New York that leaves this morning has empty seats, while the afternoon flights are over-booked. The flight experience of the passengers cannot be moved from morning to afternoon; their decisions to fly at a particular time of day are part of their own decision-making process and are outside the airline's ability to control.

Some service firms find it is possible to inventory part of the service process. McDonald's, for example, can inventory hamburgers for a limited period of time. However, a McDonald's outlet cannot inventory the entire service experience. Spare capacity in the system on a Thursday evening cannot be saved for the Friday evening peak, nor can the hamburgers.

This inability to inventory creates profound difficulties for marketing. In goods, the ability to create an inventory of the good that eventually will be purchased by the consumer means that production and consumption of the good can be separated in time and space. A good can be produced in one locality in the United States and transported for sale in another; a good can be produced in January and not released into the channels of distribution until June. Most services, however, are consumed at the point of production. From a goods-marketing manager's point of view, concerns about when and where the consumer consumes the product

SERVICES IN ACTION 1.1

THE AMERICAN AUTOMOBILE ASSOCIATION

The American Automobile Association (AAA) can claim to be one of the largest service organizations in the world, with more than 30 million members in the United States and Canada. Though its members still refer to it as "the auto club," the AAA prefers to describe itself as a travel service organization.

As a non-profit firm, the AAA exists solely to provide service to its members. The spectrum of services provided is considerable, ranging from roadside emergency service to travel advice, auto insurance, road safety schemes, and even driving lessons and driver education courses. The AAA itself is actually an umbrella group of some 159 regional organizations, all of which have considerable leeway in their ability to configure services to meet local demand.

The regional organizations first must operate global AAA services, such as breakdown assistance and insurance (the AAA regularly inspects member organizations to ensure that these services are provided according to a standard), and then provide local programs to meet other traveler requirements. Travel advice, for example, is provided by more than a thousand regional offices across North America. However, while these services account for a great deal of the AAA's business with its customers, the core service and the principal reason why people join and remain members of the AAA is the roadside emergency service.

When planning a roadside emergency service, regional organizations have a number of factors to coordinate. Local population, geography, climate, and traffic patterns all play a part in the incidence of demand. However, demand is never predictable, as no one, not even the customer, knows exactly when the customer's car is going to break down.

When a breakdown does occur, the customer may not be aware of the cause of the failure. Nor can the customer usually move a vehicle to a place of the AAA's choice. Finally, the customer may be under considerable stress, particularly if the weather is bad or if it is late at night. The service will be perceived from the customer's viewpoint not only on the basis of whether or not the car was repaired, but how long the service took to arrive, and on the helpfulness and courtesy of the service personnel both on the telephone and with the recovery vehicle.

The challenge to AAA organizations is thus to configure a service that is capable of meeting the demands of individual members, regardless of all other variables. The exact nature of these variables never can be known until the actual moment of service.

are important in understanding consumer behavior and motivation, but are largely irrelevant in day-to-day operations.

The existence of inventory also greatly facilitates quality control in goods-producing organizations. Statistical sampling techniques can be used on warehouse stock to select individual items for testing, to the point of destruction if necessary. The sampling process can be set up to ensure minimum variability in the quality of the product released for distribution. Quality-control systems also provide numerical targets against which managers can work. It is thus possible for Procter & Gamble to produce tens of millions of packages of Tide that are all essentially identical. James L. Schorr, speaking about the differences between Procter & Gamble and Holiday Inns, notes: "A major difference between product marketing and services marketing is that we can't control the quality of our product line as well as a P&G control engineer on a production line can control the quality of his product. When you buy a box of Tide, you can reasonably be 99 and 44/100 percent sure that the stuff will work to get your clothes clean. When you buy a Holiday Inn room, you're sure at some lesser percentage that it will work to give you a good night's sleep."[24]

Finally, in goods-producing businesses, inventory performs the function of separating the marketing and production departments. In many organizations, stock actually is sold at a transfer price from one department to another. The two parts of the firm have what amounts to a contract on quality and volumes. Once this contract has been negotiated, each department is able to work relatively independently of the other. In service firms, however, marketing and operations constantly are interacting with one another—owing to the inability to inventory the product.

SERVICES ARE TIME DEPENDENT

In theory, a marketing manager in a service firm does not care when people consume a service because they are part of the system while they are consuming it.

The American Automobile Association offers a 24-hour roadside emergency service to its members across the United States. Because drivers may have an emergency at any time, the AAA cannot "plan ahead"; service is delivered when the customer asks for it. Nor can Domino's Pizza make and deliver its pizzas ahead of time; service delivery is confined to the narrow space of time between the customer placing the order and the firm's delivery.

In aggregate terms, customers often tend to utilize a service more frequently at certain peak times. In these cases, generating further customer demand can be more of a disadvantage than an advantage, placing strain on contact staff and resources and creating a poor customer experience through overcrowding of the physical site. Restaurants may experience a rush of customers at lunch time, filling the site to capacity, and then can be nearly empty for the rest of the afternoon; holiday resorts may be booked full in summer and stand empty all winter. One service which suffers especially from this peak time phenomenon is public transit. Transit services in many large cities are full to capacity at morning and evening rush hours, often causing delays due to overcrowding and breaking down of over-stressed equipment. For the large part of the middle of the day, however, transit facilities are heavily underutilized. In these cases, marketing efforts can attempt to move customer demand out of peak times and into slack times. This kind of movement can be very profitable.[25]

SERVICES ARE PLACE DEPENDENT

Where the service experience takes place is also largely dependent on the consumer. The AAA is perhaps an extreme example of this; when a customer calls for roadside emergency service, that service has to be delivered wherever the customer is; the customer cannot move his or her vehicle to a place of the AAA's choosing. Again, Domino's Pizza undertakes to provide a pizza delivered to the place of the customer's choosing, usually a private residence. All that the service provider can do in each case is try to ensure that the service operation is widespread enough to cover the areas where service demand is likely.

Even when customers come into a shop or to an airport for service, hence narrowing the geographical focus of the service experience, the service organization still is required to provide products across a variety of locations. McDonald's cannot follow the lead of Ford or Procter & Gamble and build a huge capital-intensive factory

SERVICES IN ACTION 1.2

DOMINO'S PIZZA

Domino's Pizza is a pizza-delivery chain consisting of about 5,000 stores, based mostly in the United States. About 70 percent of the locations are franchises, nearly all owned by former Domino's employees who purchased a franchise with the company's assistance. Unlike other pizza chains, Domino's has no sit-down restaurant facilities. The target market consists of people who are, for one reason or another, unwilling to go out for a meal and prefer to have food delivered to them at a time and place of their choosing.

Domino's original aim was to narrow the market still further, and to concentrate on people who prefer pizza to other forms of fast food. The only thing on the original menu besides pizza was soft drinks. Generally speaking, however, fast-food customers are expecting the service as much as the food itself (i.e., they want "fast" as well as "food"). In order to secure its market position, Domino's offered delivery within 30 minutes of the time the order was placed, with the customer receiving the pizza free if the delivery took longer.

The operation was designed to meet this goal. Individual stores were built according to the same design, and simple, efficient internal systems were instituted. Domino's employees fell into five basic categories: drivers, order-takers, pizza-makers, oven-tenders, and routers, the last having responsibility for ensuring that orders and deliveries were matched correctly. The object was to achieve an assembly-line-style production in which the customer is involved directly only at two points, the initial order and the moment of delivery.

If one part of the organization breaks down, then the entire service operation can be in jeopardy. Because of limited customer contact, there is little room for service personnel to attempt to reassure customers or offer them alternative services. If the pizza arrived late, giving away a free product costs the firm money and might not always mollify a hungry customer. The actual delivery process was particularly important because a cooked pizza rapidly grows cold and inedible. Small matters, such as finding traffic-free routes to allow drivers to avoid congestion, were crucial to operations.

Establishing this type of service operation requires strict control, first when establishing the location of a store and determining its service radius, and then over employee training, product quality, operations, and routing. Constant monitoring of both customer satisfaction and employee performance establishes whether or not the service goal is being met.

to produce 1 billion hamburgers a year in Michigan, because the consumers who want food are scattered all over the world. The huge factory has to be broken up into what Levitt (1972) calls "factories in the field."[26] Each service location has to be its own factory, and, in the instance of delivered services, such as the AAA's repair service, the factory in the field literally extends down to the scale of the repairperson and a van.

CONSUMERS ARE ALWAYS INVOLVED IN THE FACTORY

As the servuction model clearly demonstrates, consumers are an integral part of the service process. Their participation may be active or passive, but their role cannot be ignored. Put simply, the role of the consumer in the factory has four principal ramifications for services marketing:

☐ If we change the factory, then we have to change consumer behavior.

☐ If we change the benefit concept, then we have to change the factory.

☐ Everyone who comes into contact with the consumer is delivering the service.

☐ Everything that comes into contact with the consumer is delivering the service.

CHANGES IN THE FACTORY MEAN CHANGES IN CONSUMER BEHAVIOR

Logically, if changes are made in the factory and the consumer is involved in the factory, then consumer behavior will have to be changed as well. Changes made to the visible part of the service firm at the least will be apparent to the consumer and may affect his or her decision-making and purchasing processes; and, frequently, changes will demand that the consumer alter his or her behavior.

Lovelock and Young[27] cite the change from full-service to self-service gas stations as one example of how changes in the factory necessitate changes in consumer behavior. The switch to self-service was made largely for operational reasons, to save on labor costs and to increase profitability, and the gas station owners assumed that by keeping prices down they would continue to attract customers who valued price over service quality. However, the behavioral change required from full-service (wait in the car and be warm and comfortable while an attendant pumped the gas) to self-serve (get out of the car no matter what the weather and handle a dirty, smelly gas pump) was one that some consumers were not willing to make. In order to get consumers to accept self-service stations, gas station owners had to make a number of other amendments to the stations, such as better equipment and weather protection. Even so, some consumers still prefer not to use self-serve stations.

Similar examples abound in other services, particularly those where the customer comes to a set location, such as a store or restaurant, in order to receive service. Changes in the layout of a bank, for example, or in the table arrangement of a restaurant, can affect consumers. Banks in particular believe that they can substitute products for personal service, with technological improvements such as automatic tellers; more than half of all of Citibank's customers in the New York area say they now no longer have any need to go into the bank to transact their business.[28] In this case, changes in the factory have met with customer approval and the customers have altered their behavior accordingly. On the other hand, in the airline industry it has long been known that, in the event of a crash, fatalities can be reduced sharply by having passengers sit facing backwards rather than facing forwards. But even this simple change in the layout of a service operation can affect passenger behavior, and so far no airline has been able to risk flying aircraft with backward-facing passenger seats.

CHANGES IN THE BENEFIT CONCEPT MEAN CHANGES IN THE FACTORY

Changes in the benefit concept mean alterations in the factory for both goods and services. A goods firm might have to change its factory procedures, developing new specifications and re-tooling to produce a different product. Most of these changes will be invisible to the consumer, who only will see the different benefits package in the finished product. With services, changes in the benefit concept usually mean change in both the visible and invisible parts of the factory. This is particularly important when considering start-ups and their attendant potential problems. Shostack notes that structural changes to service operations fall into one of two categories, being either changes to the *complexity* of the services or changes to the *divergence* of the services. Changes in the benefits concept can result in services becoming either more or less divergent or complex.[29]

Shostack cites changes in barbering services through the 1970s as an example of a service becoming both more diverse and more complex. Barbers began adapting techniques borrowed from women's hair salons, transforming themselves into "hair stylists" and offering both a broader range of services other than just basic hair-cutting. In the process, they tapped into a new market segment—men willing to pay higher prices for a more elaborate service than that offered by old-fashioned barbers.[30] Changing benefits concepts can result in changes to the factory which are off-putting to customers—witness the quiet family restaurant that transforms itself into an up-scale cafe, alienating its family customers—but they can also be used to re-position the service operation into a new market.

The involvement of the consumer in the factory is one of the most important aspects of services marketing. Consumer behavior in the service process becomes the core of any marketing analysis. Understanding consumer behavior and consumer decision-making processes will be discussed in much greater detail in Chapter 2, but it is important to understand from the very beginning that the experiential nature of services requires a different perspective for consumer behavior. The focus here must be on an understanding of *evaluation* processes as well as *choice* processes; theories must address the interactive nature of services and the involvement of the consumer in the production process.

One idea, discussed in more detail in Chapter 2, is that consumers will have a script for frequently used services. That script is analogous to a theatrical script, and governs the experience in much the same way. Consumers may have a wide variety of scripts to cover the different kinds of service encounters that they might have in the course of a day: putting gas in the car, eating a meal, buying a ticket and riding on a train, or using operator assistance to make a long-distance telephone call. But, although consumers themselves will have different scripts for different services, a group of consumers coming to use the same service will not necessarily have homogenous scripts. A wide variety of variables can affect the script, as well as consumer expectations.[31]

The relationship between changes in the benefits concept, changes in the factory, and the changes in consumer behavior raise real issues for innovation and for the relationship between marketing and operations in service organizations. Innovation coming from either the factory or the consumer implies major changes in the consumer script, which in turn implies changes for the contact personnel. Trade-offs then have to be made between operational efficiency and marketing effectiveness, a series of choices that will be discussed in greater detail in Chapter 3. Strategic changes that are made to increase the efficiency of the operating system often can reduce the quality of the product; part of the marketing challenge is to find ways of improving the efficiency of the servuction system while, at the same time, improving the service experience for customers.

EVERYONE AND EVERYTHING THAT COMES INTO CONTACT WITH THE CONSUMER IS DELIVERING THE SERVICE

The servuction system is a simple model, but identifying that model in practice turns out to be more difficult than it first appears. Many firms underestimate the number of points of contact between them and their customers. Many forget or underestimate the importance of telephone operators or accounting departments. The AAA delivers service principally through its roadside repair people who come out to repair the stranded motorist's car. But the AAA also has to pay attention to the service offered by its telephone operators, who are the first personnel to come into contact with a frequently agitated motorist, and dispatchers, who the customer does not see at all but who are responsible for ensuring the repair people get to the motorist in time.

One way of assessing the level of contact between customers and the service organization is to understand the process through which the organization delivers service to the customers. Chapter 4 describes the key figures in this system: the boundary-spanning personnel who link the customer with the organization and deliver the service. Chapter 5 then looks at the service process in some detail, and introduces the use of flowcharts to analyze both the complexity and diversity of a service and to create a service blueprint that plugs gaps and controls implementation. Mapping out current levels of customer contact can help show deficiencies in the service organization and point the way toward improvement.[32]

CONTACT PEOPLE ARE PRODUCTS

Just as customers are part of the service process, so contact personnel are part of the experience. Unlike goods, contact personnel are not inanimate objects, and being human, they exhibit variances that cannot be controlled by the service process. The feelings and emotions of contact personnel are apparent to the customer and can affect the service experience for better or for worse.

Robert L. Catlin, a senior vice president with N. W. Ayer ABH International in New York, describes his business as "dealing with something that is primarily provided by people—to people. Your people are as much your product in the consumer's mind as any other attribute of that service. People's performance day in and day out fluctuates up and down. Therefore, the level of consistency that you can count on and try to communicate to the consumer is not a certain thing."[33] Surly or unhappy employees can affect the customers with whom they come into direct contact and also can affect other employees. On the other hand, a bright, well-motivated employee can create a more pleasant service experience for everyone who comes into contact with that person. Certainly a large percentage of consumer complaints about service focus on the action or inaction of employees. Critics of service quality have focused on "robotic" responses by staff and on staff who have been trained to use technology, but have no training in how to deal with different types of customers.[34]

Contact personnel are frequently in positions that cause personal stress, which adds a further complication to the service process (Chapter 4). Marketing can play a role in this area and can help to ameliorate stress, which can lead to excessive turnover in both staff and customers, and should be involved in discussions about the human resources policies that are used to manage contact personnel (Chapter 6).

SERVICES CANNOT BE QUALITY CONTROLLED AT THE FACTORY GATE

One of the most frequently stressed differences between goods and services is the lack of ability to control service quality before it reaches the consumer. Service encounters occur in real time, and consumers already are involved in the factory; if something goes wrong during the service process, it is too late to institute quality-control measures before the service reaches the customer. Indeed, the customer or another customer may be part of the quality problem. If, in a restaurant, something goes wrong during a meal, that service experience for a customer is bound to be affected; the manager cannot logically ask the customer to leave the restaurant, re-enter, and start the meal over again.

Almost by definition, therefore, it is impossible for a service to achieve 100 percent perfect quality on an ongoing basis. Manufacturing operations also may have problems achieving this sort of target, but they can isolate mistakes and correct them over time, as mistakes tend to be recurring parts of the process. Many errors in service operations are one-offs; in the restaurant above, the waiter who drops a plate creates a technical problem that neither can be foreseen nor corrected ahead of time. Interestingly enough, such mistakes often can be used to create customer satisfaction by recovering the situation in an excellent fashion. Chapter 11, which discusses service recovery, develops this logic and shows how recovery can become a competitive advantage.

Chapter 12 focuses on the problems of service quality and suggests that the key may be to build quality into all the processes of the firm. Since mistakes cannot be corrected as they occur, the only answer is to attempt to eradicate them at the source. Again, as the consumer is both part of the process and the person who ultimately determines service quality, understanding consumer behavior must be a basic part of the quality process. Service quality is an integrated function, which needs inputs from all parts of the service organization.

A DIFFERENT CONCEPT OF MARKETING AS AN ORGANIZATIONAL FUNCTION

This chapter has outlined some of the factors which characterize services marketing in general, and some of the problems which service marketers face. Marketing, it is clear, plays a very different role in service-oriented organizations than it does in pure goods organizations. The servuction system model shows how closely interwoven the different components of the service organization are; the invisible and visible parts of the organization, the contact personnel and the physical environment, the organization and its customers, and, indeed, customers themselves are all bound together by a complex series of relationships.

Accordingly, the marketing department must maintain a much closer relationship with the rest of the service organization than is customary in many goods businesses. The concept of operations being responsible for producing the product and marketing being responsible for selling it, which is starting to disappear in goods firms in any case, cannot work in service firms. Channels of distribution are either very short—from the kitchen to the dining room in our restaurant example—or nonexistent, with production and consumption being simultaneous. Gronroos argues that marketing is a key function in the service sector: "Even if the term *marketing* is not used in connection with the activities in the buyer/seller interaction, managing these activities is a marketing function."[35] Blois suggests that consumers' perceptions of a service are tightly linked to the organization, are adopted by the service firm, and that the two questions of how consumers perceive services and how marketing fits into the service organization cannot be logically separated.[36] The role of marketing in the service firm will be discussed in more detail in Chapter 13.

SUMMARY OF THE BOOK

This book is divided into three parts. Part I covers the basic building blocks of services marketing, key concepts that need to be understood before going on to consider the management of the service experience in Part II. Part III takes a broader perspective and considers the various ways service firms try to create competitive advantage.

PART I: BASIC BUILDING BLOCKS

The first three chapters focus on the services consumer, the services operation, and the service provider. The consumer is, of course, important, and it is vitally necessary to understand the consumer and to gain insights into consumer behavior. The second is equally important because, in services, operations *is* the product. It is therefore important to understand the needs of the operation as well as the needs of the consumer. Every company faces a trade-off between consumer needs, technology, and economics, but the servuction system model implies that this trade-off is more pronounced for service firms. If the provider is the product, then a deep understanding of the role and motivation of service providers is a necessary building block.

Chapter 2 builds on the experiential nature of the service product to suggest that a number of emerging theories may provide additional insights into the consumer choice and evaluation processes. These include the dramaturgical perspective as well as role theory and script theory. The perceived control theory, which suggests that, in any situation, individuals like to feel in control, is also discussed.

Chapter 3 then turns to the perspective of operations management and seeks to determine the requirements for an efficient operation. These requirements are compared with the operational demands of services, which allows the identification of several major threats to operational efficiency. A number of concepts and theories that have been developed in operations management to overcome these problems are described. Throughout this chapter, the emphasis is on understanding the service operation and on coming to terms with its interdependence with marketing.

Chapter 4 looks at the final element of the service experience, the service provider. This chapter discusses the key role that the service provider can play, not only as part of an operation, but as an individual. However, such roles are extremely stressful since they are boundary-spanning roles, bridging the gap between the environment and the firm. The role stress and conflict caused by boundary-spanning are described, as are the strategies adopted by contact personnel to overcome that stress.

PART II: MANAGING THE SERVICE EXPERIENCE

The four chapters in this section describe the service marketing mix, the variables available to the firm to manage the service experience. "Product policy" issues discussed in Chapters 5 and 6 include the configuration of the operation, both the physical environment and the people who provide the service. The complexity of the service product is one of the key differentiating features of service marketing, as the creation of a real-time experience poses many problems that differ significantly from the problems arising from the creation of a mere physical good.

Chapter 5 focuses on the configuration of the operating system, and uses processes, flowcharting, and process re-engineering as a framework. It also discusses the physical environment that has to be created in order to house the operating system.

Chapter 6 looks at the human resources policies of the service firm as being the key means of influencing the service provider. In particular, it looks at two emerging issues, empowerment and enfranchisement. Varying degrees of empowerment have been shown to be highly motivating for service providers. In the retail area, firms such as Nordstrom have combined empowerment with payment by results in order to enfranchise their employees.

Chapters 7 and 8 cover the problems of service pricing and service communication strategy. In these chapters, there is a sizable overlap with existing models and theories in marketing. The emphasis in these chapters is on the unique characteristics of the service communications and pricing processes and how these influence the service experience. Chapter 7 shows how the management of expectations is crucial to service communications and how misdirected communications can have a noticeable effect on services and on customers. Communications, moreover, can be aimed at employees as well as external customers. Chapter 8 focuses on the three characteristics of services that affect pricing; the nature of service costs, time-dependent capacity, and the role of the customer as part of the process.

PART III: COMPETING AS A SERVICE FIRM

This section of the book refocuses on the higher levels of the firm and discusses the potential sources of competitive advantage for the service firm. The topics covered include the competition for space or sites as firms spread geographically and internationally; this section discusses the role of franchising in this type of competition. Competition to attract different consumer segments to the same service site and competition by offering more services through the same sites are also covered in Chapter 9.

Customer retention as a service strategy is discussed in Chapter 10. It argues that for many service businesses, the customer base is the strongest competitive advantage. If this is accepted, then marketing should focus on existing customers, not new customers, and this chapter describes how that focus can be achieved.

A competitive strategy based on service recovery is described in Chapter 11. No service business can deliver 100 percent of the time. Failure, however, can be turned to advantage if correct recovery plans are in place. Enhanced levels of customer satisfaction often can be the result.

Service quality as a way of competing has been a popular topic in the last three to five years. A successful quality program touches every part of the organization and can have a profound effect on consumers. Chapter 12 describes a service quality model and shows how it can be applied.

Finally, Chapter 13 takes up the question of building customer focus into the service organization as a way of competing. This chapter discusses how marketing often can be sidelined in service businesses, and goes on to outline the actions necessary to re-establish customer focus.

NOTES

1. See Dorothy I. Riddle (1986), "Service-Led Growth," *International Trade 1991/92* (Westpoint, CT: Praeger, 1993); GATT publication. GATT acknowledge that it is difficult to estimate precisely the total value of the service production worldwide as some countries do not report statistics on many service items and many service transactions are not registered; the real figure is probably well over $1,000 billion.

2. *Ibid.*

3. *International Trade 1991/92* (1993).

4. *The Economist,* February 20, 1992.

5. See Ronald Henkoff, "Service Is Everybody's Business," *Fortune,* June 27, 1994, 26–31.

6. See Peter Mills, *Managing Service Industries* (Cambridge, MA: Ballinger, 1986), 3.

7. *Statistical Abstract of the United States,* 1993.

8. Sernos, *Annual Statistics 1990,* Eurostat, 1993.

9. Eli Ginzberg and George J. Vojta, "The Service Sector of the U.S. Economy," *Scientific American* vol. 244, no. 3 (March 1981): 31–39.

10. Ginzberg and Vojta, "The Service Sector," 31–39.

11. Stephen Koepp, "Pul—eeze! Will Somebody Help Me?" *Time,* February 2, 1987, 28–34.

12. James Quinn and Christopher Gagnon, "Will Services Follow Manufacturing into Decline?" *Harvard Business Review* (November–December, 1986): 95.

13. Henkoff, "Service Is Everybody's Business," 26.

14. *Ibid.,* 27.

15. *Ibid.*

16. The idea of a goods/service spectrum has existed for many years (see John M. Rathmell, *Marketing in the Services Sector* [Cambridge, MA: Winthrop, 1974]; and Lynn G. Shostack, "Breaking Free from Product Marketing," *Journal of Marketing* 41 (April 1977): 73–80. In fact, any attempt to define this spectrum leads to more examples which are exceptions than which fit the rule.

17. Peter K. Mills and Dennis J. Moberg, "Perspectives on the Technology of Service Operations," *Academy of Management Review* vol. 7, no. 3 (1982): 467–478.

18. Gary Knisely, interviewing James L. Schorr in *Advertising Age,* January 15, 1979, 10–13.

19. *Ibid.*

20. Christopher H. Lovelock, "Classifying Services to Gain Strategic Marketing Insights," *Journal of Marketing* vol. 47 (Summer 1983): 9–20.

21. *Ibid.*

22. Valarie A. Zeithaml, A. Parasuraman, and Leonard L. Berry, "Problems and Strategies in Services Marketing," *Journal of Marketing* vol. 49 (1985): 33–46. The authors include a review of previous literature on the characteristics of services.

23. The servuction system model originally was developed by Eric Langeard and Pierre Eiglier in an article published in a French journal. More detailed descriptions of the model appear in E. Langeard, J. Bateson, C. Lovelock, and P. Eiglier, *Marketing of Services: New Insights from Consumers and Managers* report no. 81-104 (Cambridge, MA: Marketing Sciences Institute, 1981); and in Pierre Eiglier and Eric Langeard, *Servuction* (Paris: McGraw-Hill, 1987), Chap. 1.

24. Knisely, *Advertising Age,* 12.

25. Langeard, et al., "Marketing of Services."

26. Theodore Levitt, "Production-Line Approaches to Services," *Harvard Business Review* 50, no. 5 (September–October, 1972): 41–52.

27. Christopher H. Lovelock and Robert F. Young, "Look to Consumers to Increase Productivity," *Harvard Business Review* (May–June, 1979): 168–178.

28. Koepp, "Pul—eeze!" 28–34.

29. G. Lynn Shostack, "Service Positioning through Structural Change," *Journal of Marketing* vol. 51 (January 1987): 34–43. Shostack's ideas will be discussed in more detail in Chapter 5.

30. *Ibid.*

31. Michael R. Solomon, Carol Surprenant, John A. Czepiel, and Evelyn G. Gutman, "A Role Theory Perspective on Dyadic Interactions: The Service Encounter," *Journal of Marketing* vol. 49 (Winter 1985): 99–111.

32. Shostack, "Breaking Free," 73–80.

33. Knisely, *Advertising Age,* 11.

34. Koepp, "Pul—eeze!" 28–34.

35. Christian Gronroos, "Designing a Long-Range Marketing Strategy for Services," *Long-Range Planning* vol. 13 (1980): 36–42.

36. K. J. Blois, "The Structure of Service Firms and Their Marketing Policies," *Strategic Management Journal* vol. 4 (1983): 251–261.

CHAPTER 2

UNDERSTANDING THE SERVICE CONSUMER

CHAPTER OVERVIEW

The heart of the marketing concept lies in consumer orientation. As marketers, we are required to understand our consumers and to build our organizations around them. This requirement is particularly important for services, which in the past have tended to be operations dominated rather than marketing led.

Today it is more important than ever to understand consumers, and to understand how consumers choose between alternative services offered to them and how they evaluate these services once they have received them. Understanding the link between choice and evaluation processes is particularly important, as satisfied customers are necessary for repeat business.

THE THREE-STAGE MODEL OF SERVICES CONSUMER BEHAVIOR

To market services effectively, marketing managers need to understand the thought processes used by consumers during each of the three stages of purchase: the prepurchase choice between alternatives, the consumers' reactions during consumption, and the postpurchase evaluation of satisfaction. In the first stage, the objective is to understand why a consumer chooses to use a particular service or service outlet. In the second stage, it is necessary to understand consumers' reactions to the interactive process; and, in the last stage, we need to understand the sources of customer satisfaction or dissatisfaction.

THE PREPURCHASE STAGE

The prepurchase stage refers to all consumer activities occurring before the acquisition of the service. This stage begins when an individual realizes a need or problem. The recognition of a problem demands a solution from the individual, and it usually implies a potential purchase. The individual then searches for relevant information from both internal and external sources, arrives at a set of solutions to the recognized problem, and, finally, selects the option that he or she considers to be most satisfactory.

For example, consider a consumer trying to decide which restaurant to go to for lunch. The first question to be considered might be "What is the occasion?" It is often possible to segment consumers into homogenous groups based on the occasion of the purchase. Clearly, in our example, the choice of restaurant will be different if our consumer is planning to eat alone and in a hurry rather than have a business lunch with colleagues and a client. Often, the same individuals who eat in McDonald's at lunch eat in a French restaurant in the evening.

Once the occasion for a meal has been specified, the next question becomes "Which restaurants are on the list?" Similar questions can be posed for other services. For banking, this question might become "Which brands in which locations are on the list?" It is clear that in all consumer decision making, consumers seldom consider all feasible alternatives. Instead, they have a limited list of options chosen on the basis of past experience, convenience, and knowledge. This list often is referred to by theorists as the evoked set—the set of "brands" that will be evoked by the consumer and from which the choice will be made.

Even if the occasion and the evoked set have been specified, the consumer still has to choose from that set a specific restaurant to go to for lunch. We can never truly know the thought process used by the individual when making that choice. As will be discussed later, however, we need a model on which to structure our thinking and to guide our market research.

THE CONSUMPTION STAGE

An important outcome of the prepurchase stage is a decision to buy a certain brand of the service category. This decision is accompanied by a set of expectations about the performance of the product. In the case of goods, the consumer then uses the product and disposes of any solid waste remaining. The activities of buying, using, and disposing are grouped together and labeled as the *consumption process.*[1]

For services, this stage is more complex. The servuction system concept introduced in Chapter 1 suggests that the benefits bought by a customer consist of the experience that is delivered through an interactive process. Even when a service is rendered to an individual's possession (e.g., auto repair) rather than to the individual's person, the service production/consumption process often involves a sequence of personal interactions (face-to-face or by telephone) between a customer and a service provider.[2]

Furthermore, interactions between the customer and the company's facilities and personnel are also inevitable. It is from these interpersonal and human–environment interactions that the service experience is acquired. "Differences in kind"[3] between the services- and goods-purchasing processes can be attributed largely to this extended client–company interface.

Perhaps the most important outcome of the prepurchase stage is the contradiction of the idea that post-choice evaluation occurs only at a certain point in time after use.[4] The *use* of goods is virtually free from any kind of direct-marketer influences. An individual customer can choose when, where, and how he or she will use a good. On the other hand, service firms play an active role in the customer consumption activities because services are produced and consumed simultaneously. No service can be produced or used with either the customer or the service firm absent. Due to the extended service delivery process, some authors have hypothesized that post-choice evaluation occurs both during and after, rather than just after, the use of services. Customers evaluate the service while they are interacting with the service provider.

From a marketer's point of view, this opens up the prospect of being able to influence that evaluation directly. The restaurant manager who visits diners' tables and asks, "How is the meal?", is able to catch problems and change evaluations in a way that the manufacturer of a packaged good never could.

POSTPURCHASE EVALUATION

Customer satisfaction is the key outcome of the marketing process. It is an end in itself, but it is also the source of word-of-mouth recommendations and thus can stimulate further purchases. As will be discussed later, there is considerable evidence to suggest that buying service represents a major risk to the consumer, and this makes word-of-mouth recommendation very valuable. But how is this satisfaction created? A number of approaches have been suggested, but perhaps the simplest and most powerful is the disconfirmation of expectations model. The concept of this model is straightforward. Consumers evaluate services by comparing the service they perceive they have received with their expectations. If the perceived service is equal to or better than the perceived service, then the consumer is satisfied.

It is crucial to point out that this entire process takes place in the mind of the consumer. It is perceived service which matters, *not* the actual service. Once this simple idea is established, two subsidiary questions emerge: what is it that drives expectations, and what is it that drives perceptions?

The nature and source of expectations have been the subject of much recent theoretical and empirical research. Current thinking discriminates between at least two standards of service delivery expectations that have been referred to as *will expectations* and *should expectations*.[5] Other researchers have used different terminology to make similar distinctions between types of expectations. Parasuraman, et al., in Article 2.1 refer to three levels of expectations: desired expectations, predicted service expectations, and adequate service expectations.

Will expectations correspond with what consumers believe will happen during subsequent contacts with the service delivery system. In contrast, *should expectations* represent a normative standard that corresponds roughly to "what ought to happen" in subsequent encounters.[6]

According to Article 2.1, customer *should* (or desired service) expectations and *will* (or predicted service) expectations are based on past experience, word-of-mouth communications, and explicit and implicit service promises made by the organization. Additionally, should (or desired) expectations also are based on enduring service requirements and personal needs. This covers factors such as the consumer's personal service philosophy.

FIGURE 2.1 Nature and Determinants of Customer Expectations of Service

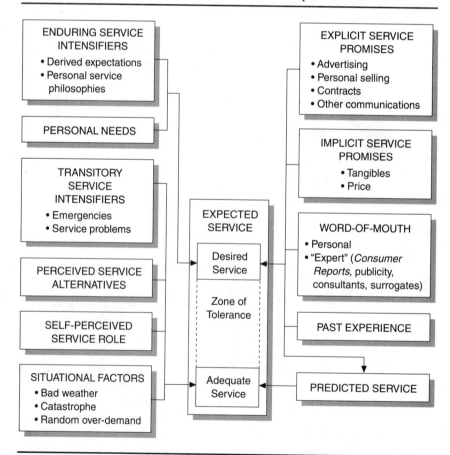

SOURCE: Adapted from V. Zeithaml, L. Berry, and A. Parasuraman, "The Nature and Determinants of Customer Expectations of Service," *Journal of the Academy of Marketing Science,* Winter, 1993, 1–12.

Will (or predicted) expectations are subject to updating after each service encounter.[7] Each time the consumer is involved in a particular service encounter, the consumer updates his or her prediction of what the next service encounter will be like. *Should* expectations are more stable and change only when they have been exceeded during service delivery. Unfortunately, an unusually successful service encounter can create higher should expectations, as indeed can a competitive offering of higher performance.

Article 2.1 introduces the additional idea of an *adequate service* standard. Although customers hope to realize their service desires, they recognize that this is not always possible. Thus, they hold another, lower expectation for the threshold of acceptable service. This standard is hypothesized to be influenced by personal service alternatives, situational factors, and predicted service. In addition, the authors suggest that two other factors influence the adequate service standard: self-perceived service roles and transitory service intensifiers. The latter are short-term individual factors that lead the customer to a heightened sensitivity to service. The former represent the degree to which the customers perceive they can influence the level of service they receive.

The nature of service perceptions in turn are driven not merely by the technical quality of the service. Technical quality is important, and can be thought of as the reality that is measurable using a stopwatch or television camera. It is the real and objective world in which the operations people of the service firm operate. Unfortunately, it is the consumer's perceptions of that reality that are crucial. Waiting time in a bank may well have been reduced by 30 seconds, but there is no reason why consumers should perceive the difference when past experience may have shown them that there is always a long wait. Further, the staff members may be surly and rude and this will be reflected in the perception of service time. Many things can interfere with the perception (see Article 5.1).

Many factors can influence a consumer's perceptions of service, including most of those hypothesized to influence expectations: word-of-mouth, advertising, and past experience. To these must be added the full complement of the servuction system. The dress and behavior of the contact personnel, the physical environment, and the other customers are all bound to have an impact on how the service experience is perceived.

As noted earlier, the consumption of goods can be divided into three activities: buy, use, and dispose. The three activities occur in a definite buy–use–dispose order and have clear boundaries between them. The customer buys a box of detergent at a supermarket, uses it at home in the washing machine, and disposes of the empty box after the detergent is used up.

This scenario does not apply to the consumption of services, however. First of all, there does not exist a clear-cut boundary or definite sequence between acquisition and use of services because there is no transfer of ownership. Because of the prolonged interactions between the customer and the service provider, the production, acquisition, and use of services often become entangled and appear as a single process.[8] Furthermore, the concept of disposition is obviously irrelevant because of the intangibility and experiential nature of services.

In short, the postchoice evaluation of services is a complex process. It begins soon after the customer makes the choice of the service firm he or she will be buying and continues throughout the consumption and postconsumption stages. The evaluation is influenced by the unavoidable interaction of a substantial number of social, psychological, and situational variables. Service satisfaction relies not only on the properties of the four elements of the servuction system—contact personnel,

FIDELITY INVESTMENTS

Fidelity Investments is a high-volume investment house which, since 1986, has offered a toll-free telephone dealing service on a 24-hour, 7-days-a-week basis. Fidelity's basic operation revolves around providing information about certain investment products to its customers and potential customers and then inviting them to purchase those products either by telephone or in person through Fidelity's network of offices.

Many of Fidelity's clients are individuals with money to invest in stocks or other investment products. The clients themselves lack the time and facilities, particularly the technology, to monitor the markets and make buying decisions. Fidelity provides that service for them and with the service comes a form of security for the customer, who knows that his investment funds are in safe hands. In effect, Fidelity does the job a client cannot do herself.

Fidelity's position is that it has no direct control over the products it sells, but can only configure them into packages which make them more desirable to customers. Part of that package is the service that Fidelity itself can offer. For investment customers, factors such as accurate information, instant communications, and investment security are of prime importance.

To meet the first two demands, Fidelity has invested heavily in systems, including automated telephone services, computerized information management, technical support for customers who use home computers, and even telecommunications devices for the deaf. The basic telephone dealing service offers fast communication, promising that the telephone will be answered within three rings, and connection will be made at all times to a licensed dealer who can provide information and arrange trades.

The "Black Friday" stock market crash of October 1987 changed the nature of the service operation. Whereas the telephone system normally logged 80,000 to 100,000 calls per day, by the end of that particular day, nearly 600,000 calls had been logged. In this case, Fidelity's customers suddenly perceived the risk to their investments to be high, and equated security with direct communication links to the investment firm. Customer expectations and perceptions had changed overnight. The problem for Fidelity Investments on Black Friday became one of adapting its existing service operations to provide a different, more intense service experience.

physical support and environment, clients, and internal organization system—but also on the synchronization of these elements in the service production/consumption process.

The success or failure of a service firm can be at least partly attributed to management's ability or inability to manipulate the customer experience as the output of a collection of interpersonal interactions (client versus client, client versus employee) and human–environment interactions (employee versus working environment and supporting facilities, customer versus service environment and supporting facilities).

MODELS OF THE CONSUMERS' DECISION-MAKING PROCESS

In both the prepurchase choice and postconsumption evaluation, the consumer must be using a process or model to make his or her decision. There are many versions of those models, but it is important to point out before going further that no model is wholly correct. The consumer's mind is still closed to us; it is a "black box" that remains sealed. We can observe inputs to the box and the decisions taken as a result, but we never can know how the process truly happens.

Why then bother with such models? The problem remains that the heart of marketing is consumer orientation. Whether marketing managers like it or not, every time they make marketing decisions they are basing them on some model of how the consumer will behave. Quite often these models are implicit and seldom are shared with others, representing in effect the marketing manager's own experience. However, every time a price is changed, a new product is launched, or advertising is shown, some assumption has been made about how the consumer will react.

Models therefore are needed as a way of structuring marketing decisions. They may not be totally real, but many are the result of much research in marketing and psychology and they allow us at least to make logical deductions about consumer behavior when making marketing decisions. Models also can provide frameworks and formats for the structuring of market research, which is the core of the marketing process.

Since all the perspectives to be described here have both strengths and weaknesses, they therefore should be considered as complementary rather than mutually exclusive. Some, such as the risk-taking perspective and the multiattribute model, are more relevant to the prepurchase choice process. Others are more powerful when trying to understand customer satisfaction: these include the control and script theory models. Managerial insights can be developed more effectively through a combination of these various perspectives.

THE CONSUMER AS A RISK TAKER

The concept of perceived risk as an explanation for customer purchasing behavior was first suggested in the 1960s.[9] The central theory is that consumer behavior involves risk in the sense that any action of a consumer will produce consequences that he or she cannot anticipate with any certainty, and some of which are likely to be unpleasant. Bauer, who first suggested this idea, proposed that perceived risk is actually composed of two structural dimensions:

☐ Consequence, the degree of importance and/or danger of the outcomes derived from any consumer decision.

☐ Uncertainty, the subjective possibility of occurrence of these outcomes.

As the idea was developed, four types of perceived risk were identified based on four different kinds of outcomes: financial, performance, physical, and social.[10] Performance risk relates to the idea that the item or service purchased will not perform the task for which it was purchased. Financial risk assumes there may be financial costs if the purchase goes wrong or fails to operate. The physical risk of a purchase can emerge if something does go wrong and injury is inflicted on the purchaser. Social risk suggests that there might be a loss of personal social status associated with a particular purchase (a fear that one's peer group will react negatively, e.g., "Who bought *this*?").

A number of authors have shown that services have a higher perceived risk of purchase than goods, for several reasons. Much already has been made of the fact that it is extremely difficult to standardize the service product.[11] Since a service is an experience involving highly complex interactions, it is not surprising that it is very difficult to replicate the experience from customer to customer or from day to day. As a result of this, however, the customer may find that it is difficult to predict

SERVICES IN ACTION 2.2

RIVERSIDE METHODIST HOSPITAL

Hospitals are unique among service providers in that they provide services that most people need, but not everyone necessarily wants. Relatively few people use the services of a hospital out of pure choice.

A number of factors set hospitals apart. In the first place, levels of risk are higher; a poor service choice can endanger health or life, not just create an unpleasant impression of the experience. Second, because many patients lack proper knowledge about how a hospital functions and the nature of the treatment they are receiving, even a merely unpleasant service experience can be genuinely frightening.

Riverside Methodist Hospital in Columbus, Ohio, is a part of U.S. Health Corporation, a small for-profit hospital chain. A key part of Riverside's competitive strategy revolves around changing the image of the hospital and the service experience in the eyes of patients and potential patients. Reducing the patient's sense of inferiority changes the nature of patient evaluation of the experience before, during, and after the hospital visit.

Understanding patient demands is an important part of this strategy. First, not all patients are the same, and the needs of different groups can contain important variables. For example, the presence of a large Honda automobile plant nearby means that the hospital regularly takes in Japanese-speaking patients and visitors. On a different scale, Riverside Methodist has developed the Elizabeth Blackwell Centre, a separate facility dealing specifically with women's needs for health care.

Once patients are in the hospital, the principal objective is to reduce patient anxiety and insecurity. The physical facilities of the hospital, the attitude and demeanor of nursing and medical staff, and the perceived quality and frequency of care all can have an impact, as can more peripheral factors, such as frequency and duration of family visits to patients. The question is not one of improving patient care, but of improving patient perception of care by making an otherwise unpleasant experience as comfortable as possible.

---

precisely the quality of the service he or she will be buying. The fact that Brown's Auto Repair shop did a good tune up for your neighbor does not mean it will perform to the same level for you. Perceived risk, therefore, may be high.

Other authors have argued that the higher risk level is due to the very limited information available before the purchase decision is made. Parasuraman, Zeithaml, and Berry,[12] for example, draw on economics literature to suggest three different properties of goods and services:

☐ *Search attributes* are those that can be evaluated before purchase.

☐ *Experience attributes* are those that cannot be evaluated until after a service has been received.

☐ *Credence attributes* are those that cannot be evaluated confidently, even immediately after receipt.

Because of the nature of services, it is often extremely difficult for consumers to evaluate a service objectively before it is bought. Services thus have very low search attributes. Rather, a large proportion of the properties of the service (how friendly are the air hostesses and hosts of a particular airline?) can only be discovered by consumers after the consumption of the service and are thus experience attributes. Finally, some of the properties of many services (how well a car has been repaired by the garage) may not be assessed even after the service is completed and are thus credence attributes.

The involvement of the consumer in the "production process" of services is another source of increased perceived risk. Unlike goods, which can be purchased and taken away, services cannot be taken home and used in private where the buyer's mistakes will not be visible. Instead, the consumer must take part in the ritual of the service itself. To be part of such a process and not to know exactly what is going on clearly increases the uncertainty about the consequences, particularly the social consequences of doing the wrong thing.

RISK-REDUCTION STRATEGIES FOR CONSUMER SERVICES

If we start from the premise that consumers do not like taking risks, then it would seem obvious that they will try when possible to reduce risk during the purchase process. Much research has been done on how consumers will attempt to reduce high perceived risk.

One strategy is for a consumer to be brand- or store-loyal; having been satisfied in one high risk purchase, consumers are less likely to experiment with others. This is an obvious trade-off between the risk inherent in returning to one possibly uncertain service business and the even greater risk of trying something new.

Research also has shown that, in the area of communications, word-of-mouth references often take on increased importance over company-controlled communication. A reference from a friend becomes more important when the purchase to be made has a greater risk. For example, a visit to a new hairdresser can be stressful since the outcome of the service will be highly visible. That stress can be reduced by a prior recommendation from someone whose judgment the consumer trusts. The consumer then will feel more confident about the outcome. Article 7.1 empirically tests these ideas and shows that consumers do use different information search procedures for goods and services. This provides the basis of the discussion of services communications strategies.

Similarly, there is some evidence to suggest that opinion leaders play an important role in the purchase of services. An opinion leader in a community is an individual who is looked up to for advice. Within the perceived risk framework, an opinion leader can be viewed as a source of reduced social risk. The consumer, referred to above, who visited a hairdresser for the first time may feel uncertain about the quality of the outcome. However, the consumer may be reassured by the fact that the friend who recommended the service is well-known to have good judgment in such matters, and will tell others in his or her social group this fact. In this way, the opinion leader's judgment partially substitutes for the consumer's own.

RISK-REDUCTION STRATEGIES FOR INDUSTRIAL AND PROFESSIONAL SERVICES

A number of authors have used the risk idea to study the purchase of industrial services. Their approach is summarized in Table 2.1. This model considers the risk-reduction strategies available through reducing uncertainty and/or consequences.

TABLE 2.1   Risk-Reduction Strategies for Industrial and
Professional Services

	Uncertainty	**Consequences**
External	Reputation Advertising References Articles	Pilot projects Investigations
Internal	Past experiences	The decision-making unit

The vertical axis focuses on how the reduction of uncertainty or consequences is to occur, breaking it down into sources internal to the firm and those that are external.

Minimizing uncertainty requires the collection of information. That information can come from both inside and outside the organization. Information can be of a general nature, such as an appraisal of a "general reputation," or as specific as a reference from a current user of the service.

Strategies for reducing consequence also can involve internal and external approaches. External reduction of consequences is relatively straightforward. It can involve, for example, the minimization of the financial consequences by making financial purchases small. This implies trials and pilot projects for professional service firms. Such a strategy also can be thought of as one of the key reasons for using multiple sources, since in this way the consequences of the failure of any one supplier is minimized.

The reduction of consequences internally can be used as an explanation of the buying committee or decision-making unit (DMU). This unit often consists of a formal or informal committee involved in the purchase of goods or services in organizations. The rational explanation for the emergence of such committees is the need to assemble interested parties with relevant information or expertise. Users need to be involved, as do engineering, finance and other relevant departments within the firm.

From the risk perspective, however, a different explanation can be hypothesized. It is the committee, or DMU, that makes the decision, and therefore it suffers the consequences of a bad decision. An individual DMU member , if necessary, can deny involvement in the decision or at least claim that involvement was only minor. Alternatively, each member of the committee, in turn, can claim, for example, that they wanted to buy professional services from firm X, but were overruled when the service of firm Y was contracted.

Recognizing this risk perspective, it is important for the supplier to offer as many opportunities as possible for the client to reduce risk. Competitively, it could be argued that the client will choose the supplier with the lowest risk. This implies either low consequences or low uncertainty. Buying from a well-known firm can help, but clients always are seeking for other ways to reduce their risk.

THE CONSUMER AS A RATIONAL MATHEMATICIAN

Marketing theorists have made extensive use of multiattribute models to simulate the evaluation process of the purchase of tangible goods. According to these models, a number of salient attributes or dimensions are employed by consumers as the basic references for the evaluation of a service. Consumers compute their preference for the service by combining the scores of the product on each individual attribute.

In the prepurchase evaluation process consumers are assumed to create a table similar to that shown in Table 2.2. This example uses the choice of an airline for travel across the North Atlantic. Across the top of the table are two types of variables. The first is the evoked set of brands that will be evaluated. Generally, this evoked set will, for various reasons, be less than an exhaustive list of all possible brands; in this case, it includes British Airways (BA), United, American, and El Al. (This evoked set idea was discussed earlier.) The second type of variable is an importance rating with which the consumer is supposed to rank the various attributes that constitute the vertical axis of the table. In Table 2.2, the consumer rates safety as the most important attribute, followed by time of flight, and so on. To complete the table, the consumer rates each brand on each attribute. This particular consumer gives BA top marks for safety, time of flight, type of aircraft and cabin crew, but perceives the airline to be less good on lounge facilities.

Given such a table, various choice processes have been suggested with which the consumer can use the table to make a decision. The *linear compensatory model* proposes that the consumer creates a global score for each brand or airline by multiplying the rating of the airline on each attribute by the importance attached to that attribute and adding the scores together. British Airways would score 10 x 10 (safety) plus 9 x 9 (time of flight) plus 10 x 8 (aircraft), and so on. The result of such a process would be that British Airways would be chosen with a score of 384, followed by El Al (383), United (365), and American (358).

Perhaps the most intriguing process that has been suggested is the *lexicographic model*. This rather pedantic term in fact describes lazy decision makers who try to minimize the effort involved. They look at each attribute in turn, starting with the most important, and try to make a decision. The individual whose preferences are shown in Table 2.2 would look first at safety and rule out El Al. Next, time of flight would rule out BA. The choice is thus reduced to American and United; type of aircraft does not help, as it produces a tie in the scoring. Managerially, this highlights a key problem, since consumers cannot actually make a choice based on aircraft type, but managers cannot change aircraft type either, since they then no longer would be at parity. The type of aircraft thus becomes a minimum requirement. Finally, the choice can be made in favor of United based on the next attribute, flight time. Thus, a different decision rule results in a different choice; United under the lexicographic model and BA under the linear compensatory model.

The same kind of model can be applied to the postpurchase evaluation process. In this case, the brands are replaced by two columns. The first is the score expected by the consumer on each attribute. The second is the perceived score on each

TABLE 2.2   A Typical Multiattribute Choice Matrix

| Attributes | Evoked Set of Brands | | | | Importance Weights |
	British Airways	United	American	El Al	
Safety	10	10	10	9.9	**10**
Time of flight	9	10	10	9.0	**9**
Type of aircraft	10	8	8	10.0	**8**
Flight time	9	9	8	9.0	7
Cabin crew	10	8	8	10.0	**6**

attribute obtained by the consumer after purchase. The satisfaction score then is derived by creating a global score of the comparisons between perceptions and expectations weighted by the importance of each attribute. This is shown in Table 2.3.

In this example, the customer has chosen to fly on British Airways using the multiattribute choice matrix shown in Table 2.2 and a linear compensatory model. The expected levels on each attribute therefore are taken from that matrix. This is, in fact, a gross oversimplification of the expectation. There are many sources of expectation, as was discussed earlier. However, there must be a link between the choice process and the satisfaction process. The multiattribute model implies a ranking of different choices, and such a ranking must include an expectation that the brand or service can satisfy an individual's needs on a particular attribute. That expectation, developed for the choice process, in some way must be carried over into the satisfaction process. In reality, the flight was delayed and the cabin crew was not very helpful under the circumstances. The consumer therefore downgraded his evaluation on those attributes.

Given the popularity of the multiattribute models, it is not unexpected that they have been used to describe and explain the consumers' service decision processes. The merit of these multiattribute models lies in their simplicity and explicitness. The attributes identified cover a wide range of concerns related to the service experience, and are understood easily by service managers. The tasks for management when using this model are relatively straightforward.

First, it is necessary to identify the criteria used by consumers. This often can be done using focus groups during which customers are asked to talk about a particular service. The kinds of words consumers use and the dimensions they use for choice and evaluation become apparent. Importance scores, evoked sets, and brand scores are elicited directly. It should be stressed that such a model must be thought of at the individual level, for groups of consumers cannot be combined for these purposes. Different consumer segments can be created, however, by combining individuals into rate attributes with the same importance weights.

Once managers understand the process, there are obvious actions that can be taken to improve the firm's competitive positions, through improving the firm's share of consumers' choices. If the service package does not contain the appropriate mixture of attributes, then clearly a new service ought to be developed. To return to our airline example, if consumers' demand an executive cabin, this ought to be built into the aircraft and the system.

Alternatively, advertising can be used to stress a particular attribute on which the firm's service appears to be weak in the mind of the consumers. An airline may have had a bad punctuality record in the past but still may be perceived as punc-

TABLE 2.3   A Postpurchase Evaluation Model for a Flight Taken on British Airways

Attributes	Expected Score	Perceived Score	Importance Weights
Safety	10	10.0	**10**
Time of flight	10	9.5	**9**
Type of aircraft	10	10.0	**8**
Flight time	9	9.0	7
Cabin crew	10	8.0	**6**

tual by consumers. If necessary, advertising also can be used to try to reduce the attribute scores obtained by competitors by engaging in competitive advertising. For example, Federal Express, when it was first launched, featured the results of market research regarding "on-time delivery," which showed that it outperformed existing competitors.

The same logical process can be applied to managing customer satisfaction. Since satisfaction is the result of the comparison of expectations with perceptions, two different routes are open to improve satisfaction. Consumer perceptions of service can be improved by stressing in communications how good the service is, relative to the competition, on key attributes. Alternatively, care can be taken in communications to ensure the accuracy of customers' expectations on the same key attributes. Returning to the Federal Express example, care would need to be taken when advertising to ensure that a clear distinction was made between Priority Service (guaranteed overnight delivery) and Standard Air (second-day delivery).

SHORTCOMINGS OF THE MULTIATTRIBUTE MODEL FOR SERVICES

Although the multiattribute model has been used widely in the analysis of services, it does have a number of shortcomings that are specific to services. The first shortcoming of such models is that they adopt a static perspective on an experience which consists of a series of dynamic interactions. A defect in one aspect of the service encounter may affect adversely the customers' perceptions on a wide array of attributes and thus there is no way to find and tackle the real source of the problem.

For instance, a crowded bank may not only give its customers a perception of a poor service environment, but also may jeopardize the relationship between the tellers and the customers. The customers may feel that the tellers are unfriendly and unhelpful when actually they are trying to speed up their work pace to cope with the large crowd of customers.

On the other hand, the tellers may feel that the customers are too demanding of tellers when they are working under pressure. In this case, it may not be the best strategy for the management of the bank to focus solely on training and regulating their tellers' manner and behavior; rather, the managers also may have to tackle in some way the real source of the trouble, the crowded environment.

In a similar way, researchers in the area of human touch have demonstrated the existence of a "Midas touch."[13] In a library setting, researchers manipulated whether or not the librarian touched borrowers' hands when they checked out the books. They controlled for the sex of the librarian and the borrower, and the touch was so casual that only 57 percent of the respondents who actually had been touched claimed that they had when asked. Intercepted after leaving the library, respondents were asked for their evaluation of the librarian and the library environment and their own emotional state. All of those touched, independent of whether or not they noticed it, responded more positively on all scales. A single touch, therefore, was able to influence apparently concrete attributes of the environment as well as customers' emotional states.

RELATING CONSUMERS' ATTRIBUTES TO MANAGERIAL ACTIONS

The second major shortcoming is the lack of correspondence between a service company's effort to improve its operational standards (e.g., increase the number of branches of a bank) and its customers' rating of the service attributes (e.g., convenience). One reason for this is that the attributes are often abstract in nature, such as reliability or friendliness. Secondly, the attributes are rarely under the full control of the service organization. The service delivery process is open to the influence of the customers and to environmental factors that are predominantly beyond the service manager's control.

As a response to the insufficiency of the multiattribute-type models, theorists recently have proposed a number of new perspectives on the service encounter. New concepts, originally developed in various disciplines of the behavioral sciences, have been suggested.

THE CONSUMER AS A SEARCHER FOR CONTROL

The concept of control has drawn considerable attention from psychologists. They argue that, in modern society where people no longer have to bother about the satisfaction of primary biological needs, the need for control over situations in which one finds oneself is a major force driving human behavior.[14] Rather than being treated as a service attribute, as implied by multiattribute models, perceived control can be conceptualized as a super-factor, a global index which summarizes an individual's experience in the service. The basic premise of this perspective is that, during the service experience, the higher the level of control over the situation perceived by the consumers, the stronger will be their satisfaction with the service. A similar positive correlation is proposed between the service providers' experience of control and their job satisfaction (see Article 2.2).

In a slightly different way, it is equally important for the service firm itself to maintain control of the service experience. If the consumer gets too much control, then the economic position of the firm may be affected as consumers tip the value equation in their favor, to such an extent that the firm may begin losing money. On the other hand, if the service employees take control, then the consumers may become unhappy and leave. Even if this does not happen, if the employees take too much control, the operation efficiency of the firm may be impaired. This three-cornered fight between the firm, the employees, and the consumers is described in Figure 2.2.

Services can be thought of as the exchange of cash and control by the consumer in exchange for benefits, with each party seeking to gain as much advantage as possible. But it would appear that no one can truly win such a contest. In fact, the concept of control is much broader than implied. Behavioral control, the ability to control what actually is going on, is only part of the idea. Much work has been done to suggest that cognitive control is also important. Thus, when consumers perceive they are in control, or at least that what is happening to them is predictable, the effect can be the same as that achieved by behavioral control. In other words, it is the *perception* of control that is important, not the reality.

Managerially, this raises a number of interesting ideas. The first is the value of information given to the consumers during the service experience, in order to increase their sense that they are in control and that they know what will happen next. This is particularly important for professional service firms, which often assume that simply because they are doing a good job, their clients will be happy. They forget that their clients have not heard from them for over a month and are frantic from lack of information. It is equally important to the airline that delays the flight after boarding, but fails to let the passengers know what is happening. In the same way, if the firm is due to make changes to the operation which will have an

FIGURE 2.2 The Perceived Behavioral Control Conflicts in the Servic

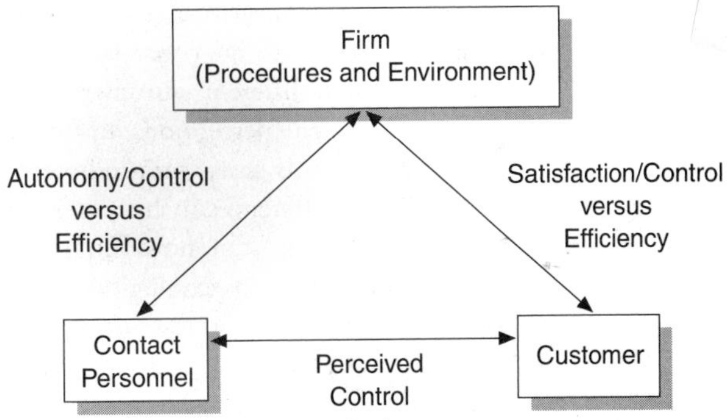

SOURCE: John G. Bateson, "Perceived Control and the Service Encounter," in John A. Czepiel, Michael R. Solomon, and Carol F. Suprenant, eds., *The Service Encounter* (Lexington, MA: Heath, 1985), 67–82.

impact on the consumers, it is important that those consumers are forewarned. If not, they may perceive themselves to be "out of control" and may be dissatisfied with the service received to the extent that they may change suppliers.

The control perspective raises interesting issues about the trade-off between predictability and choice. Operationally, one of the most important strategic issues is the amount of choice to give to the consumer. Since both choice and predictability (standardization) can contribute to a sense of control, it is crucial to determine which is the more powerful source of control for the relevant consumers.

THE CONSUMER AS AN ACTOR WITHIN A SCRIPT

A number of alternative theories within psychology and sociology can be brought together under the idea of a *script* and a *role*. A role is generally defined as "a set of behavior patterns learned through experience and communication, to be performed by an individual in a certain social interaction in order to attain a maximum effectiveness in goal accomplishment."[15] The principal idea proposed is that, in a service encounter, customers will perform roles, and their satisfaction is a function of "role congruence"—whether or not enacted behaviors by customers and staff are consistent with the expected roles (see Article 2.3).

This role congruence thus focuses on the postpurchase phase of a service encounter. Since the described interaction is two-way, role congruence is expected to exert an impact on the customer as well as on the service provider. In other words, the satisfaction of both parties is likely when the customer and the service provider enact behaviors consistent with each other's role expectation; otherwise, both performers may be upset by the interaction.

The key managerial tasks implied by role theory perspectives are (1) the design of roles for the service encounter that are acceptable and able to fulfill the needs of both customers and service providers, and (2) the communication of these roles to both the customers and the employees, so that both of them have a realistic perception of their own role as well as that of their partners in the interactions.

Role is assumed to be extra-individual. Every individual is expected to display the same predetermined set of behaviors when he or she takes up a certain role, either as a customer or as a service provider. Role theory is not concerned directly with the perception of the participants in the service encounter, and is therefore incompatible with the concepts of service evaluation and customer satisfaction. For example, two different customers, one introvert and one extrovert, may have completely different perceptions and evaluations of interactions with the same chatty provider. In this case, intra-individual variables have to be employed in order to explain the differences in customer evaluation and satisfaction.

The role idea can, however, be adapted for use in service situations. This adaption draws on the psychological idea of a script. The script theory and role theory perspectives appear, on the surface, to be extremely similar. Script theory argues that rules, mostly determined by social and cultural variables, exist to facilitate interactions in daily repetitive events, including a variety of service experiences.[16] These rules shape the expectation of the participants in this type of event.

Furthermore, the rules have to be acknowledged and obeyed by all participants if satisfactory outcomes are to be generated; if one participant deviates from the rules, the other co-actors will be uncomfortable. Therefore, a satisfied customer is unlikely with a dissatisfied service provider, while a dissatisfied customer is unlikely a satisfied service provider.

Figure 2.3 shows a script developed by one researcher for the process of going for a job interview at the end of an MBA program. Through individual interviews, it was possible to develop a script for what had become a frequently occurring experience for many MBAs.

Despite the similarity of the role theory and script theory perspectives, two basic differences exist between them. First, the script theory perspective has a wider range of concerns (e.g., the impact of the service setting) and hence is concerned with the whole service experience rather than only with the interpersonal service encounter. Second, scripts are by definition intra-individual and are a function of the individual's experience and personality. Part of the job of the service provider is to uncover the script and either enact it, if appropriate, with the customer, or to revise it with the customer. On the other hand, the content of a role is defined in a more objective sense, by means of a social position or title (doctor, waiter) rather than the perception and cognition of an individual. Part of the job of the service provider who has a defined role is to manage the customers' expectations by educating them about the service process.

THE CONSUMER AS A PARTIAL EMPLOYEE

A more radical view of consumers' behavior in services is to consider them as partial employees. Consumers derive the benefit they receive from service from an interactive experience of which they are part. Following the script analogy, consumers *must* obey the script, otherwise they will negate the entire experience. Classic examples of this occur when "novice consumers" appear in services. Foreign tourists who are on their first visit to McDonald's or the tourist new to a bank do not know the script. As a result, they can impair the experience, not only for themselves, but also for those people trying to serve them and for other customers.

Such a perspective opens up an opportunity for marketing to improve the profitability of service firms in nontraditional ways. At the heart of marketing is the idea that consumer behavior can be changed to induce more consumers to buy and/or each consumer to buy more. In service a third option appears—to change the consumers' behavior as a partial employee. This can involve asking consumers to do

FIGURE 2.3 A Script for an MBA Job Interview

As a business student in your final semester at the University of Wisconsin-Madison, you are using the business placement office in your search for a permanent position after graduation. Earlier this semester, you checked the master list of firms that would be recruiting at Wisconsin, and chose a group of companies to interview whose requirements matched your qualifications. Also at that time, you picked up a supply of computerized interview request forms at the placement office.

Shortly after the recruiters from one of the firms you had selected were scheduled to be on campus, you carefully prepared a college interview form and an interview request form in order to obtain an interview with that company. Since the firm was one in which you were especially interested, you used one of your priorities. Exactly seven days before the firm's visit, you turned one of these forms in at the placement office.

The next day, you checked the company's interview schedule to confirm that you had an appointment. Over the next several days, you researched the firm, using materials available in the placement office and from other sources. Based on this information, you prepared a list of questions for the interviewer, and formulated your answers to the questions you expected to be asked.

You purchased a good business suit to wear to the interview, and the day before your appointment, you assembled all the materials you wanted to take with you, including a copy of your resume. That evening, you attended a pre-interview reception at the Union-South which was sponsored by the firm. At the reception, you had an opportunity to talk with some of the company's representatives, and you expressed your enthusiasm for the firm.

On the day of the interview, you dressed appropriately and arrived at the placement office about 15 minutes before your appointment. You checked "Today's Interviews" for the location of your interview, and wrote down the name, title, and address of the recruiter you would meet. You were pleased to discover that your interviewer was Mr. James Moore, with whom you had talked at the previous evening's reception.

You then found a seat outside the interview room, and waited for Mr. Moore to call you. At exactly the scheduled time, he emerged from the interview room with another student. After bidding good-bye to the previous interviewee, he called your name, and you stood up, shook hands, and then followed Mr. Moore into the interview room. During the next half-hour, you responded to his questions about your career goals and accomplishments, and asked him several questions about the company. Finally, you thanked the recruiter for the opportunity to talk, and left the interview room as Mr. Moore welcomed the next student on his schedule.

You immediately found a quiet spot to sit and collect your thoughts about the meeting. You made notes about the critical points that had been discussed, and the instructions Mr. Moore had given you for following up on the preliminary interview. You also noted your impressions of the firm, and your feelings about further pursuing employment opportunities there.

That evening, you composed a formal letter of thanks to Mr. Moore, expressing your continued interest in a position with the company, and briefly summarizing the main points discussed in the interview. You then began the tedious wait to hear about the firm's decision, hoping you would be invited for a second interview. You decided that if you had not heard within a reasonable interval, you would follow up with a letter or phone call to Mr. Moore.

SOURCE: Ruth A. Smith, "An Investigation of the Measurement and Explanatory Potency of Cognitive Scripts as an Element in Satisfaction with Services," unpublished doctoral dissertation (Madison, WI: University of Wisconsin, 1983). Reprinted with permission.

SERVICES IN ACTION 2.3

SAFEWAY

Point-of-sale scanning devices, or scanners, are the latest innovation in supermarket store technology. Scanners, which read a bar code on the back of each item and compute the price automatically, are now in use by nearly all large supermarket chains. Stores have noticed considerable increases in the number of customers processed per hour (and hence profitability) and considerable decreases in line-ups waiting to be served at check-outs. There was some initial public opposition to the scanners, which meant that they could not actually see checkers inputting the price, and people expressed fears that they could be overcharged without their knowing it. By and large, however, scanners have been accepted by the public.

In September 1990, Safeway stores in Maryland took the innovation a step further and introduced do-it-yourself checkers for grocery-store customers. Instead of waiting while a checker ran each item through the scanner, shoppers now were invited to use the scanners themselves at check-out points. Safeway maintained the original system of staffed check-outs, but set up several lanes to allow those shoppers who wished to check themselves through.

Each self-check-out machine comes with a video terminal, a keyboard, and a bar scanner with a simple set of controls. The system has advantages over the staffed check-outs in that customers can see prices much more easily. Customers also can subtotal at will, keeping a running tab on how much their order is before actually paying. Once the order has been run through the scanner and totaled, customers then take their receipt to a central cashier booth to pay before leaving the store.

Customer reactions so far have been mixed. Some customers expressed satisfaction when making a quick purchase of a few items, but maintained the system would be cumbersome when making a large grocery purchase. Others expressed worry about the difficulties of simultaneously running groceries through the scanner and looking after small children.

One customer complained that Safeway was now making him do the work normally done by staff but still was charging the original price, and suggested that the service he now received was worth less: "Safeway should give me a ten percent discount now, since I'm doing all the work." Another customer complained that the routine of buying groceries had been disturbed, and while scanning her own groceries she had no opportunity to write out the check to pay for them. This operation normally was performed while the staff manning the original check-outs were running the groceries through the scanner.

Many people appeared to miss the personal touch of having staff serve them at the check-outs. Safeway's answer to this has been to have a cashier appear on the check-out video screen at the end of each transaction, to thank the customer for his or her patronage.

more work, as with self-service gas stations for example, or just asking them to behave differently during the interaction with the firm. Consumers, for example, might be asked to behave differently by using a single line for customers to wait in, which "snakes" as those seen in amusement parks, rather than using multiple lines, which can cause anger in a consumer who gets stuck in one line that is moving more slowly than another.

CONSUMER BEHAVIOR AND MANAGEMENT DECISIONS

A number of authors have pointed out an analogy between marketing and warfare. The enemy is the competition. The market is the battlefield; but what are the weapons? At one level, they can be thought of as the elements of the marketing mix; product, price, promotion, and channels. At a much more basic level, firms compete with their knowledge of the consumers. The competitor that best understands the consumer wins.

As mentioned earlier, all marketing managers have models of consumers, but they do not always make these models explicit. The purpose of this chapter has been to suggest a number of alternative models, each of which can be used in conjunction with others. These models permeate the remainder of this book, and it is important that they are understood before proceeding further. The next chapter, for example, reconciles the conflicting needs of operational efficiency and marketing effectiveness by using a deep understanding of the consumer. Chapter 5 on configuring the operation draws upon the models suggested here, particularly when considering the design of the physical environment.

Chapter 6 revisits many of these themes from the perspective of the service provider. Although employees can be viewed from the organizational behavior perspective, they also can be viewed as partial consumers who are part of the servuction process. Chapter 7 draws directly on both the models of consumer choice and evaluation to position the role of communications. Finally, Chapter 12 approaches quality from the consumer's perspective and suggests the first cause of a quality problem may be an inappropriate model of consumer behavior.

CHAPTER 2 READINGS

The readings in this chapter highlight a number of different perspectives on the behavior of consumers within the service experience. Article 2.1 looks at the whole area of consumer expectations of the service they will receive. It defines three different expectation levels, as well as discussing the probable antecedents of each.

In Article 2.2, the theory surrounding the perceived-control idea is introduced. The perspective encompasses more than the consumer, and the service encounter is conceptualized as a "fight for control" among the service consumer, the service provider, and the service organization. In Article 2.3, Soloman and his colleagues develop in detail the application of role theory and script theory. They use theories to develop a series of propositions about services marketing.

QUESTIONS

1. Apply the role theory, script theory, and perceived-control concepts to a common service of your choice. What insights could you give that would be useful to management?

2. What are the implications of script theory and perceived-control theory for the design and introduction of a new form of home banking that allows customers to access their accounts from a personal computer in their own homes?

3. Describe two or three instances of a service experience with which you were dissatisfied. Interpret your dissatisfaction using script theory or perceived-control theory.

4. Imagine tourists encountering a McDonald's for the first time. How would they learn the script? What are the clues that would allow them to deduce what to do?

5. "The art of being a tourist is to go some place where you don't know the script." Discuss this statement and suggest why people might want to pursue this art.

6. Collect two or three print advertisements for services. What are they promising? What expectations are they raising in the mind of the consumer? In the context of the disconfirmation model of satisfaction, is the firm wise to raise such expectations?

7. For a service experience with which you are familiar, write a role specification for the actions and behaviors expected of you as a consumer.

NOTES

1. F. Nicosia and R. N. Mayer, "Toward a Sociology of Consumption," *Journal of Consumer Research* 3(2) (1976): 65–75.

2. Christopher Lovelock has argued for a distinction between services performed to oneself versus those performed to one's possessions (C. Lovelock, "Classifying Marketing Services to Gain Strategic Insights," *Journal of Marketing* vol. 47 (Summer 1983): 9–20.

3. Alan Andreson, "Consumer Research in the Service Sector" in L. Berry, G. L. Shostack, and G. Upah, eds., *Emerging Perspectives on Services Marketing* (Chicago, IL: American Marketing Association, 1984): 63–64.

4. Raymond Fisk, "Towards a Consumption/Evaluation Process Model for Services," in J. Donnelly and W. George, eds., *Marketing of Services* (Chicago, IL: American Marketing Association, 1981), 191.

5. William Boulding, Ajay Kabra, Richard Staelin, and Valerie A. Zeithaml, "A Dynamic Process Model of Service Quality: From Expectations to Behavioral Intentions," *Journal of Marketing Research* 30 (February 1993): 7–27.

6. *Ibid.*

7. *Ibid.*

8. Bernard Booms and Jody Nyquist, "Analyzing the Customer/Firm Communication Component of the Services Marketing Mix," in J. Donnelly and W. George, eds., *Marketing of Services* (Chicago, IL: American Marketing Association, 1984), 172; and Fisk, "Towards a Consumption/Evaluation Process Model," 191.

9. D. Guseman, "Risk Perception and Risk Reduction in Consumer Services," in James H. Donnelly and William R. George, eds., *Marketing of Services* (Chicago, IL: American Marketing Association, 1981), 200–204; and R.A. Bauer, "Consumer Behavior as Risk Taking," in R. S. Hancock, ed., *Dynamic Marketing for a Changing World* (Chicago, IL: American Marketing Association, 1960), 389–398.

10. L. Kaplan, G. J. Szybillo, and J. Jacoby, "Components of Perceived Risk in Product Purchase: A Cross-Validation," *Journal of Applied Psychology* 59 (1974): 287–291.

11. Guseman, "Risk Perception and Risk Reduction," 200–204.

12. A. Parasuraman, V. Zeithaml, and L. Berry, "A Conceptual Model of Service Quality and Its Implications for Future Research," *Journal of Marketing* 49 (Fall 1985): 41–50.

13. Jeffrey Fisher, Martin Rytting, and Richard Neslin, "Hands Touching Hands: Affective and Evaluative Effects on Interpersonal Touch," *Sociometry* 39, no. 4 (1976): 416–421.

14. John E. G. Bateson, "Perceived Control and the Service Encounter," in John A. Czepiel, Michael R. Soloman, and Carol F. Surprenant, eds., *The Service Encounter* (Lexington, MA: Lexington Books, 1984), 67–82.

15. Michael R. Soloman, Carol F. Surprenant, John A. Czepiel, and Evelyn G. Gatman, "A Role Theory Perspective on Dyadic Interactions: The Service Encounter," *Journal of Marketing* 1, 49 (Winter 1985): 99–111.

16. Ruth A. Smith and Michael Houston, "Script-Based Evaluations of Satisfaction with Services," in L. Berry, G. L. Shostack, and G. Upah (eds.), *Emerging Perspectives in Services Marketing* (Chicago, IL: American Marketing Association, 1982), 59–62.

THE NATURE AND DETERMINANTS OF CUSTOMER EXPECTATIONS OF SERVICE

Valerie A. Zeithaml
Schmalensee Zeithaml

Leonard L. Berry
Texas A&M University

A. Parasuraman
Texas A&M University

A conceptual model articulating the nature and determinants of customer expectations of service is proposed and discussed. The model specifies three different types of service expectations: desired service, adequate service, and predicted service. Seventeen propositions about service expectations and their antecedents are provided. Discussion centers on the research implications of the model and its propositions.

> Levels of expectation are why two organizations in the same business can offer far different levels of service and still keep customers happy. It is why McDonald's can extend excellent industrialized service with few employees per customer and why an expensive restaurant with many tuxedoed waiters may be unable to do as well from the customer's point of view. Davidow and Uttal (1989, p. 84).

Customer expectations are pretrial beliefs about a product (Olson and Dover 1979) that serve as standards or reference points against which product performance is judged. According to the Gaps Model of service quality (Parasuraman, Zeithaml, and Berry 1985, 1988; Zeithaml, Berry, and Parasuraman 1988), customer assessments of service quality result from a comparison of service expectations with actual performance. While the importance of expectations has been acknowledged in previous research on service quality (e.g., Gronroos 1982) and customer satisfaction (e.g., Oliver 1981a), many research questions about the role of expectations in service evaluation remain to be answered.

Among the research areas to be addressed are the nature of service expectations and their key antecedents. In the first area, research is needed to define and delineate the types of expectations that customers hold for services. For instance, are these expectations best conceptualized as predictions or are they ideal standards? In the second area, research is required to identify and understand key factors affecting service expectations. What factors most influence the formation of service expectations? What role do these factors play in changing expectation levels? This article addresses these and related issues.

THEORETICAL BACKGROUND

Customer expectations have been investigated in a number of research settings (see Winer 1985) but have received the most thorough treatment in the customer satisfaction and dissatisfaction (CS/D) and service quality literatures. In these literatures, consensus exists that expectations serve as standards with which subsequent experiences are compared, resulting in evaluations of satisfaction or quality. Consensus on other issues—the specific nature of the expectation standard, the number of standards used, and the sources or antecedents of expectations—has not yet been reached.

Journal of the Academy of Marketing Science Volume 21, Number 1, pages 1–12. Copyright © 1993 by Academy of Marketing Science. All rights of reproduction in any form reserved. ISSN 0092-0703.

43

EXPECTATIONS-AS-PREDICTIONS STANDARD

In the dominant paradigm in the CS/D literature, expectations are viewed as predictions made by customers about what is likely to happen during an impending transaction or exchange. According to Oliver (1981b, p. 33), "It is generally agreed that expectations are consumer-defined probabilities of the occurrence of positive and negative events if the consumer engages in some behavior." Miller (1977) called this standard the *expected standard,* defined it as an objective calculation of probability of performance, and contrasted it with three other types of expectations (to be described later). Swan and Trawick (1980) and Prakash (1984) termed this standard *predictive expectations,* defined as estimates of anticipated performance level.

While the predictions paradigm dominates, considerable disagreement about standards has characterized the CS/D literature. Researchers have often departed from the prediction paradigm, arguing that alternative standards exist. Empirical support for distinctions between expectations-as-predictions and other standards has been offered (Gilly 1979; Gilly, Cron, and Barry 1983; Swan and Trawick 1980).

EXPECTATIONS-AS-IDEAL STANDARD

A normative standard of expectations has been proposed by a variety of researchers. Miller (1977) proposed *ideal expectations,* defined as the "wished for" level of performance. Swan and Trawick (1980) proffered a standard they termed *desired expectations,* defined as the level at which the customer wanted the product to perform. Prakash (1984) formulated *normative expectations,* i.e., how a brand should perform in order for the consumer to be completely satisfied. More generally, several researchers (Westbrook and Reilly 1983; Woodruff, Cadotte, and Jenkins 1983, 1987; Sirgy 1984) argued that CS/D is more likely to be determined by how well focal brand performance fulfills innate needs, wants, or desires of consumers, rather than how performance compares with prepurchase predictions. Kahneman and Miller (1986, p. 136) claim that each stimulus (e.g., a service encounter) is "interpreted in a rich context of remembered and construed representations of what it could have been, or should have been."

The expectations construct has been viewed as playing a key role in customer evaluation of service quality (Gronroos 1982; Lehtinen and Lehtinen 1982; Parasuraman, Zeithaml, and Berry 1985, 1988; Brown and Swartz 1989). Its meaning in the service quality literature is similar to the ideal standard in the CS/D literature. Expectations are viewed as desires or wants of consumers, i.e., what they feel a service provider should offer rather than would offer (Parasuraman, Zeithaml, and Berry 1988).

OTHER EXPECTATION STANDARDS

Several other expectation standards have been proposed and tested empirically in CS/D research. Woodruff, Cadotte, and Jenkins (1983) augmented earlier conceptualizations by proposing that customers rely on standards that reflect what the focal brand should provide to meet needs and wants, but that these expectations are constrained by the performance customers believe is possible based on experiences with real brands. They called these expectations *experience-based norms* because they captured both the ideal and realistic aspects of expectations. Miller (1977) also proposed *minimum tolerable expectations,* defined as the lower level of performance acceptable to the consumer, and *deserved expectations,* reflecting the consumers' subjective evaluation of their own product investment. Finally, Prakash (1984) proposed a standard called *comparative* expectations, consumer expectations from other similar brands.

EXPECTATIONS: SINGLE STANDARD VERSUS MULTIPLE STANDARDS

Recent conceptualizations of CS/D (Oliver 1985; Wilton and Nicosia 1986; Forbes, Tse, and Taylor 1986; Tse and Wilton 1988) have held that CS/D is a post-choice process involving complex, simultaneous interactions that may involve more than one comparison standard. Kahneman and Miller (1986, p. 136) contend that "A number of representations can be recruited in parallel, by either a stimulus event or an abstract probe such as a category name, and a norm is produced by aggregating the set of recruited representations." Empirical work has supported this view. As previously noted, Prakash (1984) documented three types of expectations: predictive, normative, and comparative.

Cadotte, Woodruff, and Jenkins (1987) proposed and tested alternative CS/D models involving different standards of comparison. Their *product-norm* model and *best-brand norm* model were consistently better than the brand expectation (prediction) model at explaining variation in satisfaction feelings and total model fit. These different norms were moderately correlated, suggesting that they share a common core but that each also has a unique component.

Using path analysis, Tse and Wilton (1988) found support for the influence of both predicted and ideal expectations. They concluded that:

> the results suggest that more than one comparison standard may be involved in CS/D formation because both expectation (prediction) and ideal relate individually to satisfaction . . . expectations and ideal appear to represent different constructs contributing separately to the CS/D formation process. The single-standard model fails to represent the underlying processes adequately in comparison with a multiple-standard paradigm (p. 209–210).

EXPECTATIONS: ANTECEDENT FACTORS

One relatively unexplored area of research involves the sources of consumer expectations. Cadotte, Woodruff, and Jenkins (1987) discussed experience as a source of the expectation norm and pointed out that focal brand expectations may be but one of several norms that operate. They suggest that the norm may also be derived from the typical performance of a particular brand (the favorite brand, the last-purchased, the most popular brand). A second possibility is that the norm might be an average performance believed typical of a group of similar brands (a product-type norm). They found that these norms, which they called *product norm* and *best-brand norm,* were consistently better at explaining variation in satisfaction than prediction of focal brand performance.

Beyond the specification of experience as influencing expectations, research in marketing on the antecedents of expectations has been limited. Oliver (1980a) ascribed expectations to three factors: the product itself, the context, and individual characteristics. Parasuraman, Zeithaml, and Berry (1985) acknowledged the importance of external company communications to customers in shaping expectations. Literature on other consumer behavior topics, such as search for information about quality, has yielded some sources that may be relevant in the formation of expectations. These include external sources such as direct inspection of a product (Beales et al. 1981) and personal consumer characteristics (Winer 1985).

GAPS IN THE EXPECTATIONS LITERATURE

The expectations component of the disconfirmation paradigm has been conceptualized in a variety of ways in the CS/D literature, with expectations-as-predictions being the dominant conceptualization. Research attempts to ascertain the appropriateness of these conceptualizations for understanding CS/D have been, for the most part, empirical, focusing on the ability of competing models to explain the variance in CS/D. This empirical research has provided several important insights about customer satisfaction: a variety of expectation standards exist, disconfirmation of expectations (rather than the expectations themselves) influences the satisfaction process, and focal brand predictions may not be the standard that customers use. However, a comprehensive theoretical framework that captures and explicates these results and integrates the different types of comparison standards remains to be developed.

Several CS/D researchers, after conducting empirical investigations grounded in the extant disconfirmation paradigm, have issued calls for more theoretical work in this area. For example, Cadotte, Woodruff, and Jenkins (1987) state: "Additional work is needed to refine and expand the conceptualizations of norms as standards" (p. 313). Tse and Wilton (1988) echo this need by pointing out that "Researchers have not converged on the exact conceptualization of the comparison standard and disconfirmation constructs" (p. 204).

Another gap in existing literature involves delineation of the antecedents of expectations. With the possible exception of customer experience, these sources have not been identified and discussed in detail. Furthermore, antecedents of customer expectations of service are as yet unspecified, although the services marketing literature suggests several distinguishing characteristics of service that may complicate the expectations formation process. These include customer involvement in the service production process and product intangibility (see Zeithaml, Parasuraman, and Berry 1985).

In the same literature, Parasuraman, Zeithaml, and Berry (1985) defined service quality as the comparison between customer expectations and perceptions of service. Their definition of expectations was broad and general—expectations are customer desires—and did not stipulate the antecedents or norms of expectations used by customers in assessing service quality. In other words, what is the relationship among the different standards of expectation and perceived service? Do different expectations standards exist for perceived service quality as they appear to for customer satisfaction?

Another unresolved question concerns the relationship between the core constructs of customer satisfaction and perceived service quality. While many academics and practitioners use the constructs interchangeably, and while both constructs invoke the disconfirmation paradigm, some researchers (e.g., Parasuraman, Zeithaml, and Berry 1988) suggest that a distinction exists.

The research reported in this paper is an attempt to explore these knowledge gaps, better understand expectations as they pertain to customer assessment of service quality, and extend the theoretical work that exists in the customer satisfaction literature.

RESEARCH METHODOLOGY

Exploratory research was required to develop an understanding of different types of customer expectations and their sources. Focus group interviews with customers of various service industries were conducted to provide input for a conceptual model of customer expectations of service. The approach used is consistent with procedures recommended for marketing theory development by several scholars (Deshpande 1983; Peter and Olson 1983; Zaltman, LeMasters, and Heffring 1982).

SERVICE CATEGORIES INVESTIGATED

The exploratory research design for this study was chosen to include contexts where different sources and types of customer expectations might exist. First, "pure services" (e.g., insurance) may generate different expectations than services associated with tangible products (e.g., equipment repair). Second, business customers' expectations might differ from those of end customers. Third, experienced and inexperienced customers could have differing expectations because of varying levels of familiarity with the service (Parasuraman, Zeithaml, and Berry 1985). Because the sources and types of expectations could differ in important ways within these three comparison pairs, respondents for the focus groups were chosen to represent each of them.

A total of eight sponsoring firms from the insurance, business equipment repair, truck rental and leasing, automobile repair, and hotel industries were selected. Customers of five of these firms (three insurance firms, an automobile repair firm, and a hotel chain) were chosen to represent the end-customer or consumer segment. Customers of the remaining firms (one each from insurance, business equipment repair, and truck rental and leasing) were chosen to represent the business-customer segment.

Sixteen focus group interviews were held, four each for the following cells: business customer/pure service; business customer/product-related service; end customer/pure service; end customer/product-related service. In each of these four cells, two of the focus group interviews were with experienced customers and two were with inexperienced customers.

Experienced and inexperienced customers of each firm were defined using the firm's operationalization of these segments. Distinctions between experienced and inexperienced customers were typically made on the basis of number of service contacts within a certain time period.

The selection of a diverse set of service categories for the focus groups was motivated by a desire to generate insights that would transcend specific services, consistent with Lovelock's (1983) call for more cross-industry research in the services sector. Moreover, the selected industries vary along key criteria used by Lovelock (1983) to classify services. For instance, in terms of the nature and results of the service act (one of several two-dimensional classification schemes proposed by Lovelock), business equipment repair, automobile repair, and truck rental and leasing would represent "tangible" actions directed at "physical possessions;" hotel services would represent "tangible" as well as "intangible" actions directed at "people's bodies and minds;" and insurance would represent "intangible" actions directed at "physical possessions and intangible assets."

CONDUCTING OF FOCUS GROUPS

The 16 focus group interviews were held in Atlanta, Chicago, Seattle, Rochester (NY), and Dallas to provide geographical balance. The groups were formed in accordance with guidelines traditionally followed in the marketing research field (Bellenger, Bernhardt, and Goldstucker 1976). Field research companies in the various locations were hired to recruit and screen participants for the focus groups. Participants were chosen from customer lists provided by the sponsor firms in accordance with criteria pertaining to customer experience. The average number of participants per group was nine. All interviews were conducted in the focus-group facilities of the research companies, but were moderated by the researchers.

Because the focus groups were exploratory, and intended as an aid in generating constructs and hypotheses, they were conducted in a non-directive and unstructured fashion as recommended by Calder (1977). Broad, open-ended questions were posed (e.g., "What do you expect from a service provider?" "Where do your expectations come from?" "Have your expectations changed over time?"). Discussion in each group centered on customers' expectations and experiences relating to the service in general (e.g., business insurance), as opposed to the specific service of the sponsor firm. The identities of the participating firms were not revealed to the respondents.

ANALYSIS OF FOCUS GROUP INTERVIEWS

An extensive written transcript of each focus group was prepared by one researcher as the interview was being conducted by another. All focus groups were also audiotaped. The written transcripts, supplemented by the audiotapes, formed the basis for the model of expectations developed in this article.

The primary objective of the focus groups was to generate constructs and hypotheses that would serve as building blocks for the model. As such, the approach for conducting and analyzing the interviews incorporated several recommended guidelines for theory construction through qualitative research (Belk, Sherry, and Wallendorf 1988; Thompson, Locander, and Pollio 1989).

First, at the conclusion of each focus group interview the researchers informally discussed their impressions about the interview to identify emerging themes for verification in subsequent groups and for potential use in the model. This procedure is similar to what Belk, Sherry, and Wallendorf (1988) term *memoing:* "Memoing involves sporadic oral or written briefings of other team members regarding one's emerging interpretations of data or sense of project progress" (p. 454). To maximize the benefits of this memoing-type process, and to verify that members of our research team (consisting of three researchers) were interpreting the focus group interviews consistently, all three researchers took part in the first 5 of the 16 focus group interviews (two as observers/note-takers and one as moderator). Two of the three researchers took part in each of the remaining focus group interviews.

Second, consistent themes identified from initial focus groups through the memoing process were informally verified in subsequent interviews. In most instances the themes emerged on their own during the discussion and reinforced the preliminary insights. In other instances the moderator introduced the themes to check whether they were consistent with the respondents' experiences.

Third, each researcher independently reviewed the written transcripts and developed a list of constructs and hypotheses after all 16 focus groups were completed. The researchers then shared their inferences with one another and discussed them in several lengthy meetings to achieve "triangulation across researchers" (Belk, Sherry, and Wallendorf 1988) and identify key components of the model. Thus the constructs and relationships embedded in the model are based on insights that reflect researcher consensus and are supported by consistent patterns of responses obtained from multiple focus groups.

THE MODEL

Common themes emerging from the focus group interviews and insights from previous research led to the development of the conceptual model of customer service expectations shown in Figure 1. Although differences were anticipated across the comparison pairs described above, the nature and sources of expectations were similar across the groups. Expectations of end- and business-customer groups, of experienced and inexperienced customers, and of customers of pure and product-related services had fundamentally the same nature and antecedents.

The generic model of customer expectations is divided into four main sections: (1) the expected service component, (2) antecedents of desired service, (3) antecedents of adequate service, and (4) antecedents of both predicted and desired service. These four sections will be discussed along with propositions about the nature and relationships of the components of the model.

THE EXPECTED SERVICE COMPONENT

Previous research on service quality (Sasser, Olsen, and Wyckoff 1978; Gronroos 1982; Lehtinen and Lehtinen 1982; Parasuraman, Zeithaml, and Berry 1985, 1988; Brown and Swartz 1989) supports the notion that perceived service quality stems from customers' comparisons of what they wish to receive from firms and what they perceive actual service performance to be. In other words, perceived service quality is viewed as the degree and direction of discrepancy between customers' perceptions and desires (Parasuraman, Zeithaml, and Berry 1985, 1988).

The focus group interviews supported the normative standard as the appropriate comparison frame. Based on the interviews and past literature, we are terming this standard of expectation *desired service,* which is defined as the level of service the customer hopes to receive. Desired serviced is a blend of what the customer believes "can be" and "should be." Desired service is similar to what Liechty and Churchill (1979) view as the level of performance the customer ought to receive, or deserves, given a perceived set of costs.

Although customers hope to realize their service desires, they recognize that this is not always possible. Thus, they hold another, lower level expectation for the threshold of acceptable service. We define this lower level expectation as *adequate service,* the level of service the customer will accept. This level of expectation is comparable to Miller's (1977) minimum tolerable expectation, the bottom level of performance acceptable

FIGURE 1   Nature and Determinants of Customer Expectations of Service

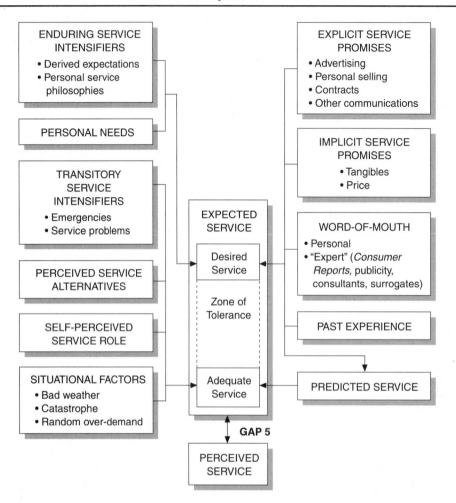

to the customer, as well as Woodruff, Cadotte, and Jenkins' (1987) experience-based norms. The focus groups consistently showed that customers' view of what a service "should be" exists at two levels: a desired level and an adequate level. A participant in one of the focus groups articulated the difference between these two types of expectations: "Expectation and tolerance differ—your expectations don't change but your tolerance changes—what you'll accept changes." This leads to our first proposition:

> **P1:** Customers assess service performance based on two standards: what they desire and what they deem acceptable.

Services are heterogeneous in that performance may vary across providers, across employees from the same provider, and even within the same service employee (Zeithaml, Parasuraman, and Berry 1985). The extent to which customers recognize and are willing to accept heterogeneity we call the *zone of tolerance*. This zone, representing the difference between desired service and the level of service considered adequate, can expand and contract. In other words, customers' service expectations are characterized by a range of levels (bounded by desired and adequate service) rather than a single level. A focus group participant expressed the existence of this range: "There is a certain level of service you expect . . . as long as the service is within a certain 'window' of that level you don't complain." This leads to our second proposition:

> **P2:** A zone of tolerance separates desired service from adequate service.

We found considerable variation in customers' tolerance zones. Some customers had a narrow zone of tolerance, requiring a consistent level of service from providers, whereas other customers tolerated a greater range of service. We also found that an individual customer's zone of tolerance increases or decreases depending on a number of factors, including company-controlled factors such as price. A business insurance customer commented, "Price increases don't really drive up expectations. But my tolerance level will become more stringent/less flexible with an increase." A business equipment repair customer claimed, "My expectations are higher when I've paid for a maintenance agreement, because I've paid money up front."

The customer's zone of tolerance may also vary for different service attributes. Parasuraman, Zeithaml, and Berry (1988) found that customer evaluation of service quality occurs along five dimensions: reliability, responsiveness, assurance, empathy, and tangibles. Our focus group interviews suggest that customers might have narrower zones of tolerance for some dimensions than for others. In particular, respondents seemed less tolerant about unreliable service (broken promises, service errors) than other service breakdowns. In fact, for service attributes that certain customers may assess in categorical terms (i.e., either the service provider possesses the attribute or it does not), the zone of tolerance could be zero (i.e., adequate and desired service will be at the same level).

The fluctuation in the individual customer's zone of tolerance is more a function of changes in the adequate service level, which moves readily up and down due to contextual circumstances, than a function of changes in the desired service level, which tends to move more incrementally and do so in an upward direction due to the accumulation of experiences. Desired service is relatively idiosyncratic and stable as these comments from two business insurance customers illustrate:

☐ My expectations about certain basics, for example, good faith, haven't changed.

☐ Expectations won't change when the market is tight but you become more tolerant.

Fluctuation in the zone of tolerance can be likened to an accordion's movement, but with most of the gyration coming from one side (the adequate service level) rather than the other (the desired service level). These conclusions can be summarized by means of three propositions:

P3: The zone of tolerance varies across customers.

P4: The zone of tolerance expands or contracts within the same customer.

P5: The desired service level is less subject to change than the adequate service level.

ANTECEDENTS OF DESIRED SERVICE

Davidow and Uttal (1989) acknowledge the myriad of customer-related factors that influence the expectation formation process.

[Service] expectations are formed by many uncontrollable factors, from the experience of customers with other companies and their advertising to a customer's psychological state at the time of service delivery. Strictly speaking, what customers expect is as diverse as their education, values, and experience. The same advertisement that shouts 'personal service' to one person tells another that the advertiser has promised more than it possibly can deliver (p. 85).

Delineation of these multiple influences was one of the objectives of this research. Patterns of responses in the focus group interviews indicated that the level of desired service depends on six antecedents, two of which are discussed in this section: (1) enduring service intensifiers and (2) personal needs. The four remaining antecedents, which also influence predicted service, another type of expectation, are discussed in a subsequent section.

Enduring service intensifiers are individual, stable factors that lead the customer to a heightened sensitivity to service. One of those factors is derived service expectations, where the customer's expectations are driven by another party. An example of this is when service employees depend on others to serve their own customers. An equipment repair customer, for example, stated, "I'm analyzing blood. We're under a lot of pressure (from the doctors). It's important that when repair people come in (to repair blood analysis equipment) they be well equipped." In this case, the doctors' expectations for timely blood test results elevated the equipment repair customer's expectations for timely repair service

Employees may also derive their expectations from their managers and supervisors. Asked when their own expectations were highest, several respondents commented that, "The needs of upper administration can change your expectations" or, "When top management expects more of me."

Another enduring service intensifier is personal service philosophy—the customer's underlying generic attitude about the meaning of service and the proper conduct of service providers. Customers who are themselves in service businesses or have worked for them in the past seem to have especially strong philosophies: "You expect to be treated the way you treat other people" was one respondent's comment. A business insurance customer claimed, "Your own basic philosophies and attitudes about how to do business carries over into what you expect from insurance companies." To the extent that customers have personal philosophies about service provision, their expectations of most service providers will likely be intensified. We therefore propose that:

P6: Enduring service intensifiers elevate the level of desired service.

Personal needs, states or conditions essential to the physical or psychological well-being of the customer are a second factor that shape desired service. Personal needs can fall into many sub-categories, including physical, social, and psychological. A customer with high social and dependency needs, for example, may have relatively high expectations for a hotel's ancillary services—hoping, for example, that the hotel has a bar with live music and dancing. The impact of personal needs on desired service is illustrated by the different expectations held by two business insurance customers:

☐ Most of my expectations pertain to brokers. I expect the broker to do a great deal of my work because I don't have the staff. . . . I expect the broker to know a great deal about my business and communicate that knowledge to the underwriter.

☐ My expectations are different . . . I do have a staff to do our certificates, etc., and use the broker minimally.

Given these observations, we propose that:

P7: A positive relationship exists between the level of personal needs and the level of desired service.

ANTECEDENTS OF ADEQUATE SERVICE

The customer's level of adequate service is influenced by five factors: (1) transitory service intensifiers, (2) perceived service alternatives, (3) customer self-perceived service roles, (4) situational factors, and (5) predicted service.

Transitory service intensifiers are temporary, usually short-term, individual factors that lead the customer to a heightened sensitivity to service. Personal emergency situations where the customer strongly needs service and perceives that the company ought to be able to respond (such as automobile insurance service in an accident) raise the level of adequate service, particularly the level of responsiveness considered acceptable. Comments by two focus group participants illustrate the impact of transitory service intensifiers:

☐ An automobile insurance customer: "The nature of my problem influences my expectations, for example, a broken window versus a DWI accident requiring

brain surgery."

☐ A business equipment repair customer: "I had calibration problems with the X-ray equipment. They should have come out and fixed it in a matter of hours because of the urgency."

Problems with the initial service can also lead to heightened expectations. As one auto repair customer put it: "I am willing to be understanding the first time but would expect much more and be more impatient the second time around." Therefore, we propose that:

P8: In the presence of transitory service intensifiers, the level of adequate service will increase and the zone of tolerance will narrow.

Perceived service alternatives are customers' perceptions of the degree to which they can obtain better service through providers other than the focal company. If customers have several service providers to choose from, or if they can provide the services for themselves (such as lawn care or bookkeeping), their levels of adequate service may be higher than those of customers who believe it is not possible to get sufficiently better service elsewhere. The influence of this factor was clearly articulated by a business insurance customer who said, "Sometimes you just don't have many options . . . so you have to effectively settle for less." This leads to our ninth proposition:

P9: The customer's perception that service alternatives exist raises the level of adequate service and narrows the zone of tolerance.

A third factor affecting the level of adequate service is the customer's *self-perceived service role*. We define this as customers' perceptions of the degree to which they themselves influence the level of service they receive. The importance of this factor, which relates to customer involvement with the service, has been stressed in previous research (e.g., Bowen 1989).

When the provision of the service depends critically on customers' participation, their expectations are partly shaped by how well they believe they are performing their own roles. An automobile insurance customer acknowledged his responsibility in service provision: "You can't blame it all on the insurance agent. You need to be responsible too and let the agent know what exactly you want." A truck leasing customer recognized her role by stating, "There are a lot of variables that can influence how you get treated, including how you deal with them."

Customers' zones of tolerance seem to expand when they sense they are not fulfilling their roles. When, on the other hand, customers believe they are doing their part in delivery, their expectations of adequate service are heightened. The comment of an automobile repair customer illustrates: "Service writers are not competent. I prepare my own itemized list of problems, take it to the service writer and tell him or her: 'Fix these.'" This leads us to propose that:

P10: The higher the level of a customer's self-perceived service role, the higher the level of adequate service.

The focus group interviews indicated that levels of adequate service were also influenced by *situational factors,* defined as service-performance contingencies that customers perceive are beyond the control of the service provider. For example, whereas personal emergencies such as serious automobile accidents would likely intensify customer service expectations of insurance companies (proposition 8), catastrophes that affect a large number of people at one time (earthquakes or hurricanes) would likely lower service expectations since customers recognize that insurers are inundated with demand for their services. Customers appear to recognize that these contingencies are not the fault of the service company and accept lower levels of adequate service given the context. We therefore propose that:

P11: Situational factors temporarily lower the level of adequate service, widening the zone of tolerance.

The final variable hypothesized to influence adequate service is *predicted service,* the level of service customers believe they are likely to get. This variable is synonymous with the definition of expectations in the dominant paradigm in the CS/D literature (Oliver 1980a,b; Olson and Dover 1979).

Figure 2 illustrates the critical differences between customer satisfaction and perceived service quality assessments that result from the different standards of comparison used by customers in forming these assessments. As conceptualized in the CS/D literature, assessments of customer satisfaction result from a comparison between predicted service and perceived service. As conceptualized in the services marketing literature, assessments of service quality result from a comparison of desired service and perceived service. Parasuraman, Zeithaml, and Berry (1985) refer to this comparison as Gap 5 in their model of service quality.

Based on the present research, Gap 5—the gap between customer expectations and perceptions—can be conceptualized to reflect two comparison standards: desired and adequate service. The comparison between desired service and perceived service, which we call perceived service quality (PSQ) Gap 5A, is the *perceived ser-*

FIGURE 2 Comparison between Customer Evaluation of Perceived Quality and Satisfaction

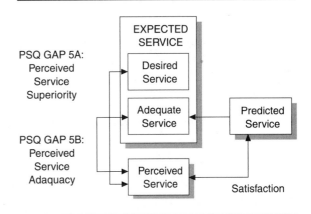

vice superiority gap; and the comparison between adequate service and perceived service, which we call PSQ Gap 5B, is the *perceived service adequacy gap.* The smaller the gap between desired service and perceived service, the higher the perceived service superiority of the firm. The smaller the gap between adequate service and perceived service, the higher the perceived service adequacy of the firm. These two service quality assessments (of perceived service superiority and perceived service adequacy) therefore replace the single Gap 5 in the Gaps Model. For these reasons, we propose that:

P12: Two types of service quality assessments are made by consumers: perceived service superiority, which results from a comparison between desired service and perceived service; and perceived service adequacy, which results from a comparison between adequate service and perceived service.

Customer satisfaction is distinct from service quality assessments in that satisfaction results from a comparison between predicted service and perceived service. While the focus groups did not specifically address the way in which predicted service influences satisfaction, the literature on satisfaction suggests that it plays a direct role (Figure 2). While predicted service plays a direct role in satisfaction assessment, it only indirectly affects service quality assessment (Gap 5B) by influencing adequate service. If customers predict good service, for example, their levels of adequate service are likely to be higher than if they predict poor service. A business insurance customer illustrates: "When the market is soft you can expect and get great service." An auto repair customer reflected: "The dealer is supposed to be an expert. I'm paying more for a dealer's service. Therefore, I should expect the dealer to do it right the first time."

If customers predict that service levels will be low, their levels of adequate service decrease and their zones of tolerance widen. Therefore:

P13: The higher the level of predicted service, the higher the level of adequate service and the narrower the zone of tolerance.

ANTECEDENTS OF BOTH DESIRED AND PREDICTED SERVICE

Beales et al. (1981) describe two general categories of search for information about product quality: external search and internal search. External search includes product information acquired through outside sources; the information can be acquired actively, such as calling a store, or passively, such as watching television. Three factors that can be categorized as external affect both desired service and predicted service: (1) explicit service promises, (2) implicit service promises, and (3) word-of-mouth communications. One internal search factor, past experience, also influences both desired and predicted service.

Explicit service promises are personal and nonpersonal statements about the service made to customers by the organization. These promises take different forms, among them advertising, personal selling, contracts, and communications from service or repair departments. All have a direct impact on desired service as well as predicted service. The nature of the effects of explicit promises, while not heavily researched, may vary depending on the difficulty consumers have in evaluating product or service quality. Deighton (1984) and others (Hoch and Ha 1986, Ha and Hoch 1989), for example, suggest that advertising affects the way customers interpret objective and ambiguous evidence about quality. The more ambiguous the available evidence about quality, the larger and more dramatic the effects of advertising; this effect is believed to be due to advertising-induced hypothesis testing and search.

A hotel customer describes the impact of these promises on his expectations: "They get you real pumped up with the beautiful ad. When you go in you expect the bells and whistles to go off. Usually they don't." A business equipment repair customer states: "When you buy a piece of equipment you expect to get a competitive advantage from it. Service is promised with the sale of the equipment." We therefore propose that:

P14: The higher the level of explicit service promises, the higher the levels of desired service and predicted service.

Implicit service promises are service-related cues other than explicit promises that lead to inferences about what the service should and will be like. These quality cues include price and the tangibles associated with the service. Research has shown that customers often use price and tangibles as surrogates of quality (Zeithaml 1988). Consider a customer who shops for insurance, finding two firms charging radically different prices. The customer may make the inference that the firm with the higher prices should and will provide higher quality service. Similarly, a customer who stays at a posh hotel is likely to desire and predict a higher standard of service from it as compared to a hotel with lower rates and less impressive facilities.

Focus group participants repeatedly emphasized the importance of implicit promises, particularly price, in shaping their expectations. One hotel customer said, "What will a hotel provide? That depends on what you will pay." Another said, "You expect the service to be better in a nice-looking hotel." This leads to our next proposition:

P15: Implicit service promises elevate the levels of desired service and predicted service.

The importance of *word-of-mouth communication* in shaping expectations of service is well documented (Davis, Guiltinan, and Jones 1979; George and Berry 1981; Donnelly 1980; Zeithaml, Parasuraman, and Berry 1985). These personal and sometimes nonpersonal statements made by parties other than the organization convey to customers what the service will be like (i.e., what they can expect). Word of mouth about service performance carries particular weight as an information source because it is perceived as unbiased. Word of mouth tends to be quite important in services because services are difficult for customers to evaluate prior to purchasing and directly experiencing them. Experts (including *Consumer Reports,* friends, and family) are all sources that affect the levels of desired service and predicted service. In the words of one focus group participant, "What you hear from others about higher service levels in their companies can influence my expectation levels . . . I will check around to see why my company isn't providing the same level of service." We therefore propose that:

P16: Positive word-of-mouth communication elevates the levels of desired and predicted service.

Past experience, the customer's previous exposure to service that is relevant to the focal service, is another force in shaping predictions and desires (Scott and Yalch

1980; Smith and Swinyard 1983). The service experiences relevant for prediction can involve previous exposure to the focal firm's service (e.g., the XYZ Hotel), to other firms in the industry (other hotel chains), or exposure to any service firm (e.g., department stores or banks). In the CS/D literature, Cadotte, Woodruff, and Jenkins (1987) provide evidence of the use of different experience norms leading to customer satisfaction. Possible norms include experience with the focal brand, typical performance of a particular brand (favorite brand, last-purchased brand, top-selling brand) or average performance a customer believes represents a group of similar brands. Sample quotes from the focus groups include:

> My expectations are definitely influenced by my past experience . . . my expectations are more realistic because of the knowledge I've gained.

> The more years you spend in this business the more you expect because the more you learn and know.

This leads to our final proposition:

P17: A positive relationship exists between levels of past experience with a service and the levels of desired service and predicted service.

RESEARCH IMPLICATIONS

The model presented in this paper provides a comprehensive framework of service expectations and their potential antecedents. The model offers a more precise foundation for measuring customer expectations of service than that which existed previously. The model also clarifies the distinction between customer satisfaction and service quality assessment within a single framework by specifying three different levels of customer expectations: (1) desired service, which reflects what customers want; (2) adequate service, the standard that customers are willing to accept; and (3) predicted service, the level of service customers believe is likely to occur.

The constructs and propositions embedded in the model augment the extant literature on customer expectations. In addition, they raise a number of intriguing questions and methodological challenges for future research.

First, empirical testing of the propositions advanced would require developing psychometrically sound measurers of the model's constructs, particularly the focal constructs of desired, adequate, and predicted service. While the domain of customers' service expectations (i.e., the general dimensions and criteria customers use in evaluating services) has been well established

(Parasuraman, Zeithaml, and Berry 1985, 1988), more work is needed to operationalize those domains in the context of the three types of expectations—desired, adequate, and predicted service. A noteworthy challenge in undertaking such research is to ensure that the wording of the instructions and/or scale items is sufficiently distinct for the three types of expectations to establish high discriminant validity among them (especially between desired and adequate service).

Second, since desired service is likely to be more stable than adequate service and therefore less subject to change (P5), research focusing on strategies to manage adequate service level expectations, and the relative effectiveness of those strategies, would be especially helpful to service companies. The posited difference between the stability of desired and adequate service also implies a need for research focusing on measurement of these two constructs. For example, should a service firm measure adequate service more frequently than desired service? Should measures of adequate service be more situation-specific than those of desired service?

Third, the possible role of predicted service in influencing how customers evaluate the gap between perceived and expected service (i.e., the service quality gap) is worthy of investigation. The proposed framework clearly distinguishes between service quality assessment and satisfaction assessment by implying that predicted service is directly relevant only for the latter. The influence of predicted service on service quality assessment is only indirect through its positive correlation with adequate service (P12). However, an intriguing possibility is that the predicted service level may moderate how a customer interprets Gap 5, the service quality assessment gap. For instance, suppose the level of service perceived by a customer falls at the midpoint of his/her tolerance zone. Would this customer's interpretation of this performance level (and hence assessment of service quality) vary depending on whether the predicted service level was above or below the adequate service level? Relatedly, can the predicted service level ever exceed the adequate service level? These and other research questions would provide important insights into customer evaluation of service quality.

Fourth, researching ways service firms could use the zone of tolerance concept to formulate effective marketing strategies would be beneficial. Intuitively, it would seem that managers would want their customers to have wide tolerance zones for service. On the other hand, if customers have relatively wide zones of tolerance for service, does this make it more difficult for firms with superior service to earn customer loyalty? Would superior service firms be better off to attempt to narrow customers' tolerance zones to reduce the competitive appeal of mediocre providers?

The zone of tolerance is an intriguing new construct but the nature and degree of its managerial relevance requires much additional investigation. For instance, can customers be meaningfully segmented into groups according to their zones of tolerance with different marketing strategies developed for each of them? What is the impact of strategies such as relationship marketing and service guarantees on the zone of tolerance?

A related research issue involves measurement of the zone of tolerance. One approach is to operationalize the zone as the difference between measures of the desired and adequate service constructs. However, such an approach may be problematic in view of the proposed difference in the stability of the two measures (as previously discussed) and potential problems with operationalizing constructs as difference scores in models involving multiple constructs (see, e.g., Johns 1981; Prakash 1984). A need and a challenge exist for developing direct measures of the zone of tolerance, perhaps by having customers specify the range of expectations that they possess for service.

Fifth, since the propositions developed in this paper are based on exploratory focus group research, there is a clear need for testing them through empirical, confirmatory research. Such research will help identify the antecedent constructs that have significant effects on the different types of expectations. In addition, from a managerial standpoint, it is useful to determine the relative importance of the significant antecedent constructs. For instance, what is the relative weight of word of mouth, explicit service promises, and implicit service promises in shaping desired service and predicted service? What is the relative impact of self-perceived service role, enduring service intensifiers, and transitory service intensifiers on adequate service levels? Empirically based answers to these questions are essential for establishing the relative efficiency of various expectation–management strategies implied by our conceptual model.

ACKNOWLEDGMENT

The authors gratefully acknowledge the financial support and cooperation provided by the Marketing Science Institute and eight of its corporate sponsors.

REFERENCES

Beales, Howard, Michael B. Mazis, Steven C. Salop, and Richard Staelin, 1981, "Consumer Research and Public Policy," *Journal of Consumer Research* 8 (June): 11–22.

Belk, Russell W., John F. Sherry, Jr., and Melanie Wallendorf, 1988, "A Naturalistic Inquiry into Buyer and Seller Behavior at a Swap Meet," *Journal of Consumer Research* 14 (March): 449–470.

Bellenger, Danny N., Kenneth L. Bernhardt, and Jac L. Goldstucker, 1976, *Qualitative Research in Marketing* Chicago: American Marketing Association.

Bowen, David, 1989, "Leadership Aspects and Reward Systems of Customer Satisfaction," Speech given at CTM Customer Satisfaction Conference, Los Angeles, CA, March 17, 1989.

Brown, Stephen W. and Teresa A. Swartz, 1989, "A Dyadic Evaluation of the Professional Services Encounter," *Journal of Marketing* 53 (April): 92–98.

Cadotte, Ernest R., Robert B. Woodruff, and Roger L. Jenkins, 1987, "Expectations and Norms in Models of Consumer Satisfaction," *Journal of Marketing Research* 24 (August): 305–314.

Calder, Bobby J., 1977, "Focus Groups and the Nature of Qualitative Marketing Research," *Journal of Marketing Research* 14 (August): 353–364.

Davidow, William H. and Bro Uttal, 1989, "Service Companies: Focus or Falter," *Harvard Business Review* 67 (July–August): 77.

Davis, Duane L., Joseph G. Guiltinan, and Wesley H. Jones, 1979, "Service Characteristics, Consumer Research and the Classification of Retail Services," *Journal of Retailing* 55 (Fall): 3–21.

Deighton, John, 1984, "The Interaction of Advertising and Evidence," *Journal of Consumer Research* 11 (December): 763–770.

Deshpande, Rohit, 1983, "Paradigms Lost: On Theory and Method in Research in Marketing," *Journal of Marketing* 47 (Fall): 101–110.

Donnelly, James H., Jr., 1980, "Service Delivery Strategies in the 1980s—Academic Perspectives," in *Financial Institution Marketing Strategies in the 1980s,* Eds. Leonard L. Berry and James H. Donnelly, Jr. Washington, D.C.: Consumer Bankers Association, 143–150.

Forbes, J. D., David K. Tse, and Shirley Taylor, 1986, "Toward a Model of Consumer Post-Choice Response Behavior," in *Advances in Consumer Research* Vol. 13. Ed. Richard L. Lutz. Ann Arbor, MI: Association for Consumer Research, 658–661.

George, William R. and Leonard L. Berry, 1981, "Guidelines for the Advertising of Services," *Business Horizons* 24 (May–June): 52–56.

Gilly, Mary C., 1979, "Complaining Consumers: Their Satisfaction with Organizational Response," in *New Dimensions of Consumer Satisfaction and Complaining Behavior.* Eds. Ralph L. Day and H. Keith Hunt. Bloomington: School of Business, Indiana University, 99–107.

Gilly, Mary C., William L. Cron, and Thomas E. Barry, 1983, "The Expectation-Performance Comparison Process: An Investigation of Expectation Types," in *International Fare in Consumer Satisfaction and Complaining Behavior.* Eds. Ralph L. Day and H. Keith Hunt. Bloomington: School of Business, Indiana University, 10–16.

Gronroos, Christian, 1982, *Strategic Management and Marketing in the Service Sector.* Helsingfors: Swedish School of Economics and Business Administration.

Ha, Young-Won and Stephen J. Hoch, 1989, "Ambiguity, Processing Strategy, and Advertising Evidence Interactions," *Journal of Consumer Research* 16 (September): 354–360.

Hoch, Stephen J. and Young-Won Ha, 1986, "Consumer Learning: Advertising and the Ambiguity of Product Experience," *Journal of Consumer Research* 13 (September): 221–233.

Johns, Gary, 1981, "Difference Score Measures of Organizational Behavior Variables: A Critique," *Organizational Behavior and Human Performance* 27 (June): 443–463.

Kahneman, Daniel and Dale T. Miller, 1986, "Norm Theory: Comparing Reality to Its Alternatives," *Psychological Review* 93 (April): 136–153.

Lehtinen, Uolevi and Jarmo R. Lehtinen, 1982, "Service Quality: A Study of Quality Dimensions," Unpublished working paper. Helsinki, Finland. OY: Service Management Institute.

Liechty, Margaret and Gilbert A. Churchill, Jr., 1979, "Conceptual Insights into Consumer Satisfaction with Services," in *Educator's Conference Proceedings,* Series 94. Eds., Neil Beckwith, et al. Chicago: American Marketing Association: 509–515.

Lovelock, Christopher H., 1983, "Classifying Services to Gain Strategic Marketing Insights," *Journal of Marketing* 47 (Summer): 9–20.

Miller, John A., 1977, "Studying Satisfaction, Modifying Models, Eliciting Expectations, Posing Problems, and Making Meaningful Measurements," in *Conceptualization and Measurement of Consumer Satisfaction and Dissatisfaction.* Ed., H. Keith Hunt. Bloomington: School of Business, Indiana University, 72–91.

Oliver, Richard L., 1980a, "A Cognitive Model of the Antecedents and Consequences of Satisfaction Decisions," *Journal of Marketing Research* 17 (November): 460–469.

————. 1980b, "Conceptualization and Measurement of Disconfirmation Perceptions in the Prediction of Consumer Satisfaction," in Refining Concepts and Measures of Consumer Satisfaction and Complaining Behavior. Eds., H. Keith Hunt and Ralph L. Day. Bloomington: School of Business, Indiana University, 2–6.

————. 1981a, "What Is Customer Satisfaction?" *The Wharton Magazine* 5 (Spring): 36–41.

————. 1981b, "Measurement and Evaluation of Satisfaction Processes in Retail Settings," *Journal of Retailing* 57 (Fall): 25–48.

————. 1985, "An Extended Perspective on Post-Purchase Phenomena: Is Satisfaction a Red Herring?" Unpublished paper presented at 1985 Annual Conference of the Association for Consumer Research, Las Vegas (October).

Olson, Jerry C. and Philip Dover, 1979, "Disconfirmation of Consumer Expectations through Product Trial," *Journal of Applied Psychology* 64 (April): 179–189.

Parasuraman, A., Valarie Zeithaml, and Leonard Berry, 1985, "A Conceptual Model of Service Quality and Its Implications for Future Research," *Journal of Marketing* 49 (Fall): 41–50.

Parasuraman, A., Valarie Zeithaml, and Leonard Berry, 1988, "SERV-QUAL: A Multiple-Item Scale for Measuring Consumer Perceptions of Service Quality," *Journal of Retailing* 64 (Spring): 12–40.

Peter, J. Paul and Jerry Olson, 1983, "Is Science Marketing?" *Journal of Marketing* 47 (Fall): 111–125.

Prakash, Ved, 1984, "Validity and Reliability of the Confirmation of Expectations Paradigm as a Determinant of Consumer Satisfaction," *Journal of the Academy of Marketing Science* 12 (Fall): 63–76.

Sasser, W. Earl, Jr., R. Paul Olsen, and D. Daryl Wyckoff, 1978, *Management of Service Operations: Text and Cases.* Boston: Allyn & Bacon.

Scott, Carol A. and Richard F. Yalch, 1980, "Consumer Response to Initial Product Trial: A Bayesian Analysis," *Journal of Consumer Research* 7 (June): 34–41.

Sirgy, M. Joseph, 1984, "A Social Cognition Model of Consumer Satisfaction/Dissatisfaction: An Experiment," *Psychology and Marketing* 1 (Summer): 27–44.

Smith, Robert E. and William R. Swinyard, 1983, "Attitude-Behavior Consistency: The Impact of Product Trial versus Advertising," *Journal of Marketing Research* 20 (August): 257–267.

Swan, John E. and I. Frederick Trawik, 1980, "Satisfaction Related to Predictive vs. Desired Expectations," in *Refining Concepts and Measures of Consumer Satisfaction and Complaining Behavior.* Eds., H. Keith Hunt and Ralph L. Day. Bloomington: School of Business, Indiana University, 7–12.

Tse, David K. and Peter C. Wilton, 1988, "Models of Consumer Satisfaction Formation: An Extension," *Journal of Marketing Research* 25 (May): 204–212.

Thompson, Craig J., William B. Locander, and Howard R. Pollio, 1989, "Putting Consumer Experience Back into Consumer Research: The Philosophy and Method of Existential Phenomenology," *Journal of Consumer Research* 16 (September): 133–146.

Westbrook, Robert A. and Michael D. Reilly, 1983, "Value-Precept Disparity: An Alternative to the Disconfirmation of Expectations Theory of Consumer Satisfaction," in *Advances in Consumer Research,* Vol. 10. Eds., Richard P. Bagozzi and Alice M. Tybout. Ann Arbor, MI: Association for Consumer Research, 256–261.

Wilton, Peter and Franco M. Nicosia, 1986, "Emerging Paradigms for the Study of Consumer Satisfaction," *European Research* 14 (January): 4–11.

Winer, Russell S., 1985, "Formation of Consumer Expectations," Working paper. Owen Graduate School of Management, Vanderbilt University.

Woodruff, Robert B., Ernest R. Cadotte, and Roger L. Jenkins, 1983, "Modeling Consumer Satisfaction Processes Using Experience-Based Norms," *Journal of Marketing Research* 20 (August): 296–304.

Woodruff, Robert B., Ernest R. Cadotte, and Roger L. Jenkins, 1987, "Expectations and Norms in Models of Consumer Satisfaction," *Journal of Marketing Research* 24 (August): 305–314.

Zaltman, Gerald, Karen LeMasters, and Michael Heffring, 1982, *Theory Construction in Marketing: Some Thoughts on Thinking.* New York: John Wiley & Sons, Inc.

Zeithaml, Valarie A., 1988, "Consumer Perceptions of Price, Quality, and Value: A Means-End Model and Synthesis of Evidence," *Journal of Marketing* 52 (July): 2–22.

Zeithaml, Valarie A., Leonard L. Berry, and A. Parasuraman, 1985, "Problems and Strategies in Services Marketing," *Journal of Marketing* 49 (Spring): 33–46.

Zeithaml, Valarie A., Leonard L. Berry, and A. Parasuraman, 1988, "Communication and Control Processes in the Delivery of Service Quality," *Journal of Marketing* 52 (April): 35–48.

ABOUT THE AUTHORS

Valarie A. Zeithaml (Doctor of Business Administration, University of Maryland) is Partner in Schmalensee Zeithaml Consulting and was previously on the faculty at Duke University and Texas A&M University. Her research interests include services marketing and consumer perceptions of price and quality. Her articles have appeared in the *Journal of Consumer Research, Journal of Marketing, Journal of Marketing Research, Journal of Consumer Affairs, Journal of Retailing,* and *Management Accounting.* She is co-author (with Len Berry and Parsu Parasuraman) of *Delivering Quality Service: Balancing Customer Perceptions and Expectations* (The Free Press, 1990).

Leonard L. Berry (Ph.D., Arizona State University) holds the J. C. Penney Chair of Retailing Studies, is Professor of Marketing, and is director of the Center for Retailing Studies at Texas A&M University. He is a former national president of the American Marketing Association. His research interests are services marketing, service quality, and retailing strategy. He is the author of numerous journal articles and books, including *Marketing Services: Competing through Quality* (The Free Press, 1991), which he wrote with A. Parasuraman.

A. Parasuraman (D.B.A., Indiana University) is Foley's/Federated Professor of Retailing and Marketing Studies at Texas A & M University. His research interests include services marketing, sales management, and marketing strategy. He has written numerous articles in journals such as the *Journal of Marketing, Journal of Marketing Research, Journal of Business Research, Sloan Management Review,* and *Business Horizons.* He is the author of *Marketing Research* (Addison-Wesley, 1991) and coauthor (with Leonard L. Berry and Valarie A. Zeithaml) of *Delivering Quality Service: Balancing Customer Perceptions and Expectations* (The Free Press, 1990).

PERCEIVED CONTROL AND THE SERVICE ENCOUNTER

John E. G. Bateson

The concept of personal control has received a great deal of attention from psychologists. A number of psychologists have, for instance, suggested that the primary cause of stress in everyday life is lack of control (Sells 1970). This chapter suggests that the concept of personal control could usefully be applied in the understanding of the service encounter—the face-to-face interaction between customer and service personnel.

The first section of the chapter reviews the concept of perceived control as it has been used by psychologists, social psychologists, researchers in behavioral medicine, and psychopathologists. In the second and third sections these concepts are placed into the context of the service encounter and the limited literature that relates directly to this area is reviewed. The fourth section deals with some of the managerial implications of this control model of the encounter. The final section deals with the advantages and disadvantages of the perceived-control approach as a research paradigm.

THE THEORY OF PERCEIVED CONTROL

The idea of control, perceived or actual, is deeply rooted in the various fields of study that are concerned with the way people manage their environments. The control concepts have been well developed in psychology, particularly the social and environmental branches. However, studies have also been done on control in medicine and health care. As a result of its origins, personal control is not a simple psychological variable, but is a complex composite of different concepts linked only by the basic idea.

CONTROL IN EXPERIMENTAL PSYCHOLOGY

Averill (1973) reviewed the state of the art of the experimental laboratory approach to control. He suggests that there are three forms of control: behavioral, cognitive, and decisional.

Behavioral control is the "availability of a response which may directly influence or modify the objective characteristics of a threatening event" (Averill 1973, 286). Averill notes that studies have used a number of different ways of operationalizing behavioral control. Some studies have been concerned with allowing subjects real or perceived control over how, when, and by whom the stimulus is administered. Others have given subjects the opportunity to modify the nature of the stimuli.

There are numerous studies investigating the impact of control on respondents' reactions to aversive stimuli. These are laboratory studies involving the administration of electric shocks, hurtful noises, or even pictures of dead bodies. The impact of these stimuli on the respondent, often a student, is then measured. The measurement is often physiological—palm sweating, for example—or in terms of some stated measure of stress. Other studies measure the impact of these stimuli on respondents' ability to perform tasks such as sorting cards. Control is varied in these kinds of studies by giving respondents a switch with which they can turn off the stimuli (for example, see Straub, Tursky, and Schwartz 1971).

Cognitive control refers to the way a potentially harmful event is interpreted and Averill defines it as "the processing of potentially threatening information in such a manner as to reduce the net long-term stress" (1973, 293). He defines cognitive control in two elements: information gain and appraisal. *Information gain*

Source: Reprinted with permission of Lexington Books, an imprint of Macmillan, Inc., from "Perceived Control and the Service Encounter," by John E. G. Bateson, which appeared in *The Service Encounter*, edited by John A. Czepiel, Michael R. Solomon, and Carol F. Surprenant, 1985, 67–82. Copyright © 1985 by Lexington Books.

refs to the predictability of the event and to its antici-pation. *Appraisal,* by comparison, has an evaluative component and involves the evaluation of the events.

In his review, Averill points out that information, per se, does not ameliorate stress. A number of studies have shown that the presence of information alone may increase rather than decrease stress. The Cromwell et al. (1977) study described in the next section clearly demonstrates this point.

Decisional control is defined by Averill (1973, p. 289) as "choice in the selection of outcomes or goals." Initially, it appears to be the same as behavioral control. However, the distinction rests on the idea that the avail-ability of alternative goals in complex situations need not be related to the aversive stimulus. Thus by chang-ing or having the option of changing the focus of achievement in a particularly stressful situation, the individual may be able to achieve a sense of control even though no behavioral control over the aversive stimulus is available.

Averill stresses that these modes of control do not operate alone but that often interactions occur. Langer and Saegert (1977) in their discussion of control models suggest that behavioral and cognitive control may oper-ate in a hierarchical way. If behavioral control is unavail-able, individuals may reduce the aversiveness by first believing that they have control (perceived control), then by reappraising the threatening event, and finally by having information about what will happen to them as a result of the stimulus.

THE CONTROL CONCEPT AND REAL-LIFE SITUATIONS

This broader concept of perceived control is one that has generally found application in real-world studies. Studies using the concept have been performed within a number of institutional frameworks. The basic idea being pursued is that stressful life events and crises will have less of a negative impact on health to the extent that they are perceived to be predictable and/or control-lable. Typical of this kind of study are those performed in hospitals and homes for the aged.

A number of studies have been performed on car-diac-rehabilitation patients. Hospitalization constitutes a stressful event in its own right for most people. There have been a number of medical studies that have focused on the impact of the medical procedures themselves on the health of patients. Many procedures regarded as rou-tine by medical staff are perceived by the patient as extremely stressful and may indeed have a detrimental effect on health (Cromwell et al. 1977).

In studying the effects of institutionalization on the elderly, considerable success has been achieved using the perceived-control approach. Krantz and Schultz (1980) in a recent review of the relocation literature suggested that an individual's response to relocation can be under-stood in terms of: (1) the perceived controllability and predictability of events surrounding a move; and (2) dif-ferences in environmental controllability between pre- and post-relocation environments.

Studies such as these suggest that the broader con-cept of perceived control can have considerable benefits in these particularly stressful situations. As will be dis-cussed later, there are obvious analogies to the typical service encounter. However, it is important to note that these effects were measured under extreme changes of control and high levels of stress.

PERCEIVED CONTROL AND THE SERVICE ENCOUNTER

Assuming the validity of the perceived-control concept or concepts, this section discusses the implications for the service encounter and describes perceived-control studies more directly relevant to the service encounter.

PERCEIVED CONTROL AND THE SERVICE CUSTOMER

Two studies have been done that support the idea of a positive impact of perceived control in the context of a service firm rather than the more institutional situations discussed so far. In one study, Langeard et al. (1981) investigated the consumer's decision-making process for services. In particular, they were concerned with the choice between a do-it-yourself option and a more tra-ditional approach to receiving a service. The initial part of their study was qualitative. One of the outputs of this stage was a series of dimensions along which intervie-wees appeared to be appraising services. (See Bateson [1983] for a detailed description of this part of the study.) These dimensions were:

1. The amount of time involved.
2. The individual's control of the situation.
3. The efficiency of the process.
4. The amount of human contact involved.
5. The risk involved.
6. The amount of effort involved.
7. The individual's need to depend on others.

In trying to separate those consumers who were prepared to do it themselves from those who were not,

Langeard et al. discovered that two dimensions were crucially important: time and control. Those consumers prepared to do it themselves saw clear differences between the two options in the dimension of "individual's control of the situation." They saw the more traditional method of receiving the service as offering less control. This was a crucial factor since the respondents who were prepared to do it themselves also rated this dimension as the most important one to them in choosing between the options. This effect was observed across all of the six services studied, ranging from banks to gas stations to hotels and airlines. It should be stressed that this study was performed in ignorance of the perceived-control literature described previously, and is independent verification of the relevance of this concept to the service encounter.

In the second study, Langer and Saegert (1977) showed the impact of cognitive control in a real-life situation and used it to ameliorate the impact of crowding. A considerable body of knowledge exists showing that crowding can have a negative impact on individuals (for example, see Sundstrom 1975; Griffith and Veitch 1971). Langer and Saegert hypothesized that this negative impact would be lessened if respondents were given information about the likely effects of crowding before being exposed to it. They conceptualized this information giving in terms of increasing cognitive control.

A two-by-two factorial design was employed in a real-life setting—a supermarket—where respondents were subject to variation in crowding and cognitive control. Respondents were given a long shopping list and told to choose the most economical product for each item from amongst the various package sizes and brands. They were allowed thirty minutes for the task. The items were not to be purchased but merely noted as choices. Respondents were also given a supermarket survey after completing the task.

The results showed that crowded respondents attempted to find significantly fewer items on the list than uncrowded respondents; and of those items attempted, significantly fewer were the correct choices. Across the rest of the items in the supermarket survey, crowded respondents scored significantly lower than uncrowded subjects. Contrary to expectations, the impact of the information was independent of crowding. Those respondents who were able to exercise cognitive control in this way attempted more items on the test and answered more correctly. More important, they were significantly more positive on all items in the questionnaire. This is contrary to the hypothesis that this information effect would occur only in those respondents suffering crowding.

Both of these studies support the idea that perceived control is an important variable in the behavior of the customer in the service encounter. They illustrate that the perception of control is seen as important by consumers, and is a dimension along which consumers appraise services. In addition, the Langer and Saegert study suggests that control can significantly influence consumer satisfaction with a service and their perception of attributes that are usually regarded as objective.

PERCEIVED CONTROL AND THE SERVER

The discussion so far has focused on the role of perceived control in understanding the attitudes and behavior of the customer. Schneider, Partington, and Buxton (1980) have performed a number of studies that view the service firm as an "open system" and the server as a boundary-role person. Their framework indicates that the server as well as the customer experiences the physical environment and procedures of the firm. Under such assumptions it seems reasonable to suppose that the servers' behavior will be influenced by their desire for perceived control of the service encounter.

One very early study (Whyte 1949) clearly illustrates this need for control on the part of the server. Adopting a sociological perspective, Whyte studied the operation of a large restaurant. He was particularly concerned with the ability of the waitresses to cope with the stress of the situation. One of his more interesting insights is gained from a study of waitresses who broke down and cried. He studied this group closely and attempted to identify what made them different.

His initial finding was that whether a waitress cried or not depended on her length of service. Longer-serving waitresses were definitely less likely to cry. One of the reasons for this was that waitresses moved by seniority to more desirable locations where the steady customers came. These senior waitresses were able to operate in a different way; as Whyte expresses it (1949, 135): "Actually, it appeared that the waitress who maintains her own emotional equilibrium plays a very active leadership role with the customer. She does not simply respond to the customer but takes the initiative to control his behavior."

Whyte also documents the concrete actions that the waitress used to take control, with the implicit or explicit agreement of the regular customer. These include the giving of menus and then leaving the customer, and the suggestion of dishes she could easily get from the kitchen.

When control is withdrawn from the server, the outcomes can be negative. Saunders (1981, 34) in a study in the United Kingdom focused on those occupations within the service sector that are stigmatized. These include kitchen porter, janitor, car-park attendant, and hospital porter. Working in each of these jobs carries with it a stigma irrespective of how well the job is performed. Saunders was concerned with the factors within the job that caused stigmatization of the role. It is interesting to note that the apparent lack of control (among other factors) was a crucial determinant of whether a job was stigmatized or not.

These studies suggest that individuals desire to have perceived control of the service encounter irrespective of whether they are the customer or the contact person working for the service firm. This idea is the basis of the next section, which attempts to integrate this idea with other emerging perspectives on the service encounter.

THE SERVICE ENCOUNTER: A THREE-CORNERED FIGHT?

I propose that the service encounter can be considered as a compromise between partially conflicting parties: the customer, the server, and the service firm as embodied in the environment and rules and procedures it creates for the service encounter.

One of the characteristics that makes services unique is that the customer has a production role as well as a consumption role in the service encounter. This idea has been suggested by writers in many fields of study. In the marketing field, the early work of Langeard et al. (1981) proposes that the service encounter be viewed as a "servuction system." They use this term to distinguish the service encounter from more traditional views of production, delivery, and consumption. Within the servuction system, production and consumption take place simultaneously and the customer is an integral part of the process.

Lovelock and Young (1979) suggest that productivity within the service firm may be increased by getting the customer to do more work. I followed up this idea by attempting to identify the characteristics of individuals who were prepared to do more work for the firm by using do-it-yourself options (Bateson and Langeard 1982), and whether the propensity to participate transcends a particular service (Bateson 1983).

In the organizational-behavior field, Schneider (1980) has suggested an open-systems approach in which the customer is regarded as part of the service organization. Mills (1983) and Mills and Moberg (1982) have suggested that the customer be regarded as a "partial employee." They go so far as to list the kinds of activities that the customer must perform if the service is to be delivered correctly.

In other areas, Gartner and Reissman (1974) have suggested that the participation of the customer should be recognized by measuring "consumer intensity" in the service sector as well as the more usual capital and labor intensity. In the field of operations management, Chase (1978; 1981) and Chase and Tansik (1982) have suggested that for the efficient operation of the service firm, the customer-contact part of the process must be isolated from the back office. They suggest that operations efficiency is inversely related to the amount of customer contact. Their proposition is based on their assumption that in the customer-impinging part of the operation the customer becomes an integral part of the process, with a consequent loss of efficiency.

The customer must, therefore, be viewed as an integral part of the process and is required to perform certain tasks. There is a mutual interdependence between three parties: the customer, the contact personnel, and the firm as embodied in the operating procedures and the environment.

At one level these three have much to gain by working together. The customer, by working with the service personnel within the framework imposed by the firm, hopes to gain satisfaction and value for money. The contact person, by serving the customer in the way specified by the firm, hopes for job satisfaction, customer satisfaction, and remuneration. The firm can only make money in the long run by satisfying staff and customers in a way that makes economic sense from an operations perspective.

At a completely different level these three parties are in conflict with each other. This is best illustrated by considering three service encounters in which each of the parties, in turn, is hypothetically totally dominant and focusing solely on behavioral control.

THE ENCOUNTER DOMINATED BY OPERATING PROCEDURES AND ENVIRONMENT

This type of encounter will be operationally efficient. The major driving force for operating procedures is efficiency through standardization. In certain sectors such as banking, it has also to do with security. A service encounter dominated by the procedures and environment must be viewed merely as a step in a production line. (See Langeard et al. [1981] for a discussion of operations-dominated firms.) The price paid for such efficiency may be high in terms of the perceived behavioral control of both customer and server.

As individuals, both the server and the served desire control over what can become an aversive situation. From the contact person's viewpoint, all autonomy has been withdrawn and everything must be done "by the book." Schneider (1980) describes such an organizational climate as "bureaucratic," as opposed to his other category of "enthusiast." In his study of bank branches, a bureaucratic atmosphere might be typified by the need to request two forms of identification before cashing a check irrespective of who the customer is. Under such a regime the contact personnel see themselves as having little behavioral control over what happens. This may be especially problematic since Schneider's work suggests that contact personnel are aware of the quality of service they are providing to the customer. The sensitive bank teller may therefore know the customer will be upset when asked for identification but can do nothing about it.

THE CUSTOMER-DOMINATED ENCOUNTER

In this form of encounter, the customer will have high perceived behavioral control over the situation. The service firms' procedures and environment will be organized to generate the maximum flexibility to serve the customer. This will have a negative effect on efficiency so, for example, excess staff will have to be available in case they are needed by the unpredictable and unconstrained customer. The service firm can still be profitable provided the customer is prepared to pay for the inefficiency that results.

From the contact personnel's point of view they will have little control over this type of service encounter. Unlike the waitress described by Whyte, they will be there to satisfy the customer's orders and will have no justification for taking control away from the customer.

THE ENCOUNTER DOMINATED BY CONTACT PERSONNEL

In this case the contact personnel are placed in an autonomous position and will perceive themselves to have high control over the situation. The customer will have little control and will be ordered about by the server, and as a result will probably be unhappy. Schneider (1980) suggests that the servers perceiving this unhappiness would be motivated to change their behavior, but in this hypothetical case we assume that this does not happen. An encounter dominated by the server puts tremendous strains on the back office and the operating procedures of the firm. Each contact person will operate on an independent system and the back office will have to sort out the resultant mess.

All of these potential conflicts are summarized in Figure 1. Despite the fact that the customer, server and firm are mutually interdependent and have many common goals, it seems that the need for control can lead to potential conflicts. The next section suggests how the processes may be adjusted to achieve an appropriate balance of control.

ACHIEVING A BALANCED SERVICE ENCOUNTER

The ideal service encounter should balance the need for control of both the customer and the contact personnel against the efficiency demands of the operations. Is this feasible? If we take the simple behavioral model of control then it is impossible for both the server and the served to do what they want and for the procedures to be followed. However as Averill (1973) has pointed out, the concept of control is far richer than mere behavioral control.

If the cognitive-control idea is included within the perceived-control construct, it becomes easier to envisage a situation in which all parties can be satisfied. Perhaps the easiest way to think of this compromise is in terms of the relation of the service encounter to role and script theory.

Role theory views any social encounter as a set of interrelated roles that must be played by the participants in that encounter. Solomon et al. (1984) have reviewed the role-theory model as it applies to the service encounter. They suggest that many of the concepts of role theory can usefully be applied to the service encounter if the customer is conceived of as having a formal role to play.

FIGURE 1   The Perceived Behavioral Control Conflicts in the Service Encounter

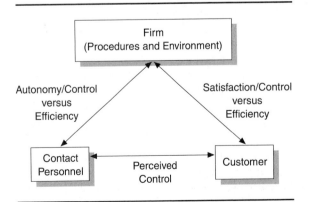

SOURCE: John E. G. Bateson, "Perceived Control and the Service Encounter," in John A. Czepiel, Michael R. Solomon, and Carol F. Suprenant, eds., *The Service Encounter*, Lexington, MA: Heath, 1985.

Smith and Houston (1983) use the related concept of a *script* in their work on service satisfaction. The cognitive-script theory assumes that any repetitive social encounter will become stereotyped in the form of a script. A script may therefore be described as a predetermined, stereotyped sequence of actions that defines a well-known situation. Using the theatrical analogy, the script tells the customer what his role is as an actor, what the sequence of events will be, and what other people will do. Smith and Houston argue that most service experiences that occur reasonably often will become stereotyped and that consumer satisfaction will depend on the service received conforming to the script.

The idea of a service encounter conforming to a script is very close to the cognitive-control concept described earlier. If the encounter follows the script, then at the very least it will be predictable. That predictability can offer cognitive control to both the server and the served. Although both parties may have little direct control over what is happening, the very predictability may give them a sense of control.

If we accept such an argument, then it becomes crucially important for the customer to be aware of his role or script. Mills (1983) approached this same issue from an organizational-behavior outlook. He viewed the customer as a partial employee. Within organizational behavior there is a considerable body of knowledge about the socialization of employees. Socialization is generally perceived as teaching new employees their required behavior. Mills expanded this to encompass the "partial employee"—the customer. The obvious analogy to the control concept is that such socialization is concerned with increasing the perceived control of the customer by increasing his cognitive control.

The same problem could be approached from a marketing perspective. Here it would be viewed as a communications problem with the objective of ensuring that the customer knew what had to be done.

An alternative way of thinking about achieving the desired compromise is to return to the idea of *perceived* versus *actual* control. In balancing the three parties, it may be possible to offer customers options so that they believe they have behavioral control even if they do not. The concept of job enrichment for the employee is often a mixture of real and apparent control.

An assumption throughout this discussion has been that the need for control is highly motivating. However, there may be some flexibility in the minds of the consumer and contact personnel toward the need for control. The idea that control is intrinsically motivating comes from Averill's 1973 review where he suggests that the exercise of control is imbued into young children as part of the socialization process, and as a result may be a deep-seated and motivating factor.

Averill implies that the need for control may be independent of the stimulus considered. Other authors have, however, argued that control carries with it responsibility. They argue that an individual who perceives himself to have control, especially behavioral control, will also take on a sense of responsibility for the outcome. The need to take control may therefore depend upon the situation.

PERCEIVED CONTROL AS A MANAGERIAL TOOL

Whatever else happens in a service encounter, the customer must give up some control. The service firm or servuction system cannot operate without the customer's input. To make that input the customer must give up some control and obey the procedures and the service personnel. If we accept the premise that the loss of control may be viewed negatively by the customer, then we can view the service encounter as a transaction in which the customer exchanges money and control for the benefits obtained. From the manager's point of view, the following questions arise:

☐ Can we increase the perceived control of the customer and thereby increase the perceived value of money for the transaction?

☐ How does the customer view our encounter in terms of perceived control and more importantly how is it viewed relative to our competitors' encounters?

☐ Can we educate the customer so that the encounter is at least predictable—that is, use information to increase cognitive control?

☐ Can we disassemble the components of the encounter and understand how each one influences the perceived control of the customer? Can we build perceived control into our encounters?

In the vast majority of cases the service encounter will also include an employee—the contact person. Schneider (1980) has shown that contact personnel are aware of the needs of the customer but are often inhibited from satisfying those needs by their lack of control over the situation. Equally, I have suggested here that the loss of control by the contact personnel will have a negative effect on their motivation. If we accept both of these propositions, then a second set of managerial questions emerges:

□ Can we give more control to the contact personnel to allow them to serve the customer better?

□ Can we give more real or apparent control to the contact personnel to satisfy their need for control?

□ How do the contact personnel currently see their perceived control?

□ What factors in our environment and procedures do they see as limiting their control?

□ How can we balance giving such control to the contact personnel against operational efficiency? Is personnel and marketing effectiveness worth more than operational efficiency?

Schneider (1980) describes an enthusiast organizational climate in which the focus is on the customer and the procedures and attitudes of the immediate superiors encourage flexibility to meet customer needs. His work shows that bank branches with such climates have customers who have higher levels of satisfaction than those with bureaucratic climates.

PERCEIVED CONTROL AS A RESEARCH PARADIGM

The perceived-control approach as a research paradigm for the study of the service encounter has both advantages and disadvantages. On the positive side, it is a concept that can be clearly understood by managers. Leaving aside the complexities built into the basic idea by later workers, the underlying idea is one that is intuitively attractive. This must not be underestimated as an advantage since, if the ultimate aim of research is to aid those managers in the design of the service encounter, an easily understood concept is a major point.

From a research perspective the approach has the advantage of its roots in social psychology. Research work in the service-management field can therefore be based on the foundations that have already been laid. Within social psychology there are unresolved issues: managerial research could contribute to the underlying discipline. The existence of refined concepts, methodological approaches, and a richness of ideas should lead to early results in service marketing.

On the negative side, these very same psychological underpinnings present problems in the context of the service encounter. The first is, of course, the artificiality of much of the work. The controlled administration of electric shocks to psychology students is not directly transferable to services.

In the real-world applications of the concept in social psychology, another kind of problem arises. Many of the studies have been performed under what, by service-encounter standards, are extreme situations. Both hospitals and homes for the aged are institutions in which a great deal of control has been wrested from the inmates. By comparison the control withdrawn in the typical service encounter is far less. It may well be that the changes involved may be too small for the same kinds of phenomenon to occur. The work of Langeard et al. (1981), Bateson (1983), Bateson and Langeard (1982), and Langer and Saegert (1977) suggests that this may not be the case, but the work is by no means conclusive.

Another major problem with the existing work is that the control variable has generally been treated as an independent variable that is manipulated by the experimenter. In most cases the high and low conditions are taken as givens. By comparison, in the study of the service encounter, perceived control must be measured.

As with other approaches, one of the first questions that may arise is just how much these phenomena are determined by individual characteristics. Hiroto (1974) looked at *locus of control* as a potential predictor of the impact of changes in control. Locus of control is a personality construct developed by Rotter (1966). The internal–external locus-of-control scale was developed in social psychology to measure the degree to which individuals believe events are under their control of independent of it. Hiroto selected two groups of experimental subjects based on this scale. He found that the external control group was much more sensitive to an uncontrollable stimulus—inescapable noise—than the internal control group.

Although there are many potential problems with the perceived-control approach to the study of the service encounter, it appears that its advantages do outweigh these problems and that it could be a fruitful avenue to pursue.

REFERENCES

Averill, J. R. (1973), "Personal Control over Aversive Stimuli and Its Relationship to Stress," *Psychological Bulletin* 80, no. 4, 286–303.

Bateson, J. E. G. (1983), "The Self-Service Consumer— Empirical Findings," in *Marketing of Services,* eds. L. Berry, L. Shostack, and G. Upah. Chicago: American Marketing Association.

Bateson, J. E. G. and E. Langeard (1982), "Consumers' Uses of Common Dimensions in the Appraisal of Services," in *Advances in Consumer Research,* vol. 9, ed. A. Mitchell. Chicago: American Marketing Association.

Chase, R. B. (1978), "Where Does the Customer Fit in the Service Operation?" *Harvard Business Review* 56: 137–142.

Chase, R. B. (1981), "The Customer Contact Approach to Services: Theoretical Bases and Practical Extensions," *Operations Research* 29, no. 4 (July–August): 698–706.

Chase, R. B. and David A. Tansik (1982), "The Customer Contact Model for Organizational Design," *Management Science* 29, no. 9: 1037–1050.

Cromwell, R. L., E. C. Butterfield, F. M. Brayfield, and J. J. Curry (1971), *Acute Myocardial Infarction: Reaction and Recovery*. St. Louis, MO: C. V. Mosby.

Gartner, A. and F. Reissman (1974), *The Service Sector and the Consumer Vanguard,* New York: Harper and Row.

Griffith, W. and R. Veitch (1971), "Hot and Crowded: Influences of Population Density and Temperature on Interpersonal Affective Behavior," *Journal of Personality and Social Psychology* 17: 92–98.

Hiroto, D. S. (1974), "Learned Helplessness and Locus of Control," *Journal of Experimental Psychology* 102: 187–193.

Krantz, D. S. and R. Schultz (1980), "A Model of Life Crisis, Control, and Health Outcomes: Cardiac Rehabilitation and Relocation of the Elderly," in *Advances in Consumer Psychology*, vol. 2, ed. A. Baum and J. E. Singer. Hillsdale, NJ: Lawrence Erlbaum Assoc., Inc.

Langeard, E., J. E. G. Bateson, C. H. Lovelock, and P. Eiglier (1981), *Marketing of Services: New Insights from Consumers and Managers,* Cambridge, MA: Marketing Science Institute, Report No. 81–104.

Langer, E. J. and S. Saegert (1977), "Crowding and Cognitive Control," *Journal of Personality and Social Psychology* 35: 175–182.

Lovelock, C. H. and R. Young (1979), "Look to Consumers to Increase Productivity," *Harvard Business Review* (May–June): 168–179.

Mills, P. K. (1983), "The Socialization of Clients as Partial Employees of Service Organizations," working paper, University of Santa Clara.

Mills, P. K., and D. J. Moberg (1982), "Perspectives on the Technology of Service Operations," *Academy of Management Review* 7, no. 3: 467–478.

Rotter, J. B. (1966), "Generalized Expectancies for Internal versus External Control of Reinforcement," *Psychological Monographs* 80 (Whole no. 609).

Saunders, C. (1981), *Social Stigma of Occupations,* Farnborough, England: Gower Publishing Company.

Scneider, B. J. (1980), "The Service Organization: Climate Is Crucial," *Organizational Dynamics* (Autumn): 52–65.

Schneider, B. J., J. J. Partington, and V. M. Buxton (1980), "Employee and Customer Perceptions of Service in Banks," *Administrative Science Quarterly* 25: 252–267.

Sells, S. B. (1970), "On the Nature of Stress," in *Social and Psychological Factors in Stress,* ed. J. E. McGrath. New York: Holt, Rinehart, and Winston.

Smith, R., and M. Houston (1983), "Script-Based Evaluation of Satisfaction with Services," in *Marketing of Services,* eds. L. Berry, L. Shostack, and G. Upah. Chicago: American Marketing Association.

Solomon, M. R., C. Surprenant, J. A. Czepiel, and E. G. Gutman (1984), "Service Encounters as Dyadic Interaction: A Role Theory Perspective," *Journal of Marketing* (Autumn).

Straub, E., B. B. Tursky, and G. E. Schwartz (1971), "Self-Control and Predictability: Their Effects on Reactions to Aversive Stimulation," *Journal of Personality and Social Psychology* 18: 157–162.

Sundstrom, E. (1975), "An Experimental Study of Crowding Effects of Room Size, Intrusion and Goal Blocking on Nonverbal Behavior, Self-Disclosure and Self-Reported Stress," *Journal of Personality and Social Psychology* 32: 645–655.

Whyte, W. Foote (1949), *Men at Work,* Irwin-Dorsey Series in Behavioral Sciences. Homewood, IL: The Dorsey Press and Richard Irwin.

A ROLE THEORY PERSPECTIVE ON DYADIC INTERACTIONS: THE SERVICE ENCOUNTER

Michael R. Solomon

Carol Surprenant

John A. Czepiel

Evelyn G. Gutman

———————◆———————

This article proposes that the dyadic interaction between a service provider and a customer is an important determinant of the customer's global satisfaction with the service. Based on role theory, a theoretical framework is presented which abstracts some of the critical components of service encounters across industries.

Researchers interested in service marketing are beginning to understand *what* they are studying, but they are not yet clear *how* to study it. As Bateson (1977) said, "The service marketing literature generally has been concerned with listing the differences between services and products. There has been little attempt to point out the implications for marketers in service companies and even less of an attempt to propose new concepts or approaches" (p. 14).

Service marketing refers to the marketing of activities and processes (health care, entertainment, air travel) rather than objects (soap powder, cars). Rathmell (1966) made a similar, fundamental distinction in defining goods as objects and services as deeds or efforts. There are still considerable differences of opinion within the marketing discipline as to whether products and services are fundamentally distinct (Bateson 1977; Judd 1964; Lovelock 1980; Uhl and Upah 1983; Wyckham, Fitzroy, and Mandry 1975). Most attempts to differentiate the two on one or more dimensions ultimately arrive at a continuum (Bell 1981; Liechty and Churchill 1979; Rathmell 1966); products are arrayed at one end, services at another, and there is considerable overlap between the two. This would seem to indicate that while services marketing may not be unique, a focus on the marketing problems predominantly present in this sector may enable us to broaden our horizons and, in fact, contribute to improved marketing concepts applicable to both goods *and* services.

One of the consequences of the recent interest in service marketing is the increased recognition of the importance of the person-to-person encounter between buyer and seller—client and provider—to the overall success of the marketing effort. Many service situations, especially those termed "pure" services, are characterized by a high degree of person-to-person interaction: consulting services, hairdressing, and medical services, to name a few. Recognition of the importance of the encounter is especially relevant in those situations where the service component of the total offering is a major element of that offering. This is so regardless of whether the core element of the offering is a material good or a service.

SOURCE: Michael R. Soloman, Carol Surprenant, John A. Czepiel, and Evelyn G. Gutman, "A Role Theory Perspective on Dyadic Interactions: The Service Encounter," reprinted with permission from the *Journal of Marketing* Winter 1985, Vol. 49, pp 99–111. Published by the American Marketing Association, Chicago, IL, 60606.

In mixed produce/service offerings, the importance of the encounter—the person-to-person interaction between buyer and seller—is often overshadowed by a focus on the more tangible product attributes, and the customer's more enduring interaction with the product itself. In pure service situations where no tangible object is exchanged, and the service quality itself is difficult to measure (financial planning, health care), customer satisfaction and repeat patronage *may* be determined solely by the quality of the personal encounter. That is not to say that the encounter between an industrial salesperson and industrial purchaser is not similar to personal service encounters; it is. To the extent that the interaction with the salesperson is an element in the total offering, the encounter is important and, in fact, constitutes a *service* encounter.

However, it is primarily in the service sector that the dyadic encounter[1] has generated a great deal of managerial concern. The ideas presented are particularly relevant for people-based services (legal and other professional services), rather than equipment-based services (automatic teller machines, direct mail, insurance). It can, of course, be generalized to any marketing situation in which personal interaction is an important element of the total offering. For our purposes, *service encounter* will be used to indicate face-to-face interactions between a buyer and a seller in a service setting.

Two quotations by service marketing managers reported in *Advertising Age* (Knisely 1979) highlight the managerial importance of service encounters this way:

In a service business, you're dealing with something that is primarily delivered by people—to people. Your people are as much of your product in the consumer's mind as any other attribute of that service. People's performance day in and day out fluctuates up and down. Therefore, the level of consistency that you can count on and try to communicate to the consumer is not a certain thing.

The real intangible is the human element which, with the best will in the world, most of us cannot control to anywhere near the same degree that a product manager controls the formulation of a beauty soap, for example (pp. 47–51).

Thus, the service encounter itself occupies a central place in much of service marketing. It impacts on service differentiation, quality control, delivery systems, and customer satisfaction. The centrality of this service component warrants a substantial theoretical focus.

To an extent, all service personnel involved in customer contact are marketers. Each individual represents the firm, defines the product, and promotes it directly to the consumer (Shostack 1977). Given its centrality to the service offering and its variable nature, the service encounter is a worthy if difficult topic to study. This paper presents a conceptual framework by which person-to-person service encounters, whether delivered in conjunction with a tangible product or not, can be understood and analyzed.

The conceptual framework presented is adapted from a social psychological perspective on human interaction. The service encounter is approached as a special case of the more general class of goal-oriented dyadic interactions. Any encounter is assumed to contain learned and consistent behavior patterns; each participant should enact certain behaviors in order for the transaction to proceed smoothly. It will be argued that the degree of congruence with this learned pattern or "script" by *both* the service provider and customer is an important determinant of satisfaction with the encounter. Thus, the focus is on the *interdependence* of both individuals. Each depends upon the other to make the interaction run smoothly (cf. Kelley and Thibaut 1978).

RELEVANT PERSPECTIVES

SERVICE ENCOUNTERS ARE DYADIC

The transaction or exchange is a cornerstone of any marketing activity, yet few researchers have adopted it as the basic unit of analysis. As noted by Pennington (1968), one party to the transaction tends to be studied in isolation. The traditional approach to the salesperson–customer exchange, for example, is to view sales success as determined by the seller's job satisfaction (Cotham 1968), motivation (Oliver 1974), or ability (Ghiselli 1978). Some workers in this area have questioned the simplistic nature of a model based on only one participant, and have recognized the dyadic quality of personal selling (Sheth 1975; Webster 1968; Weitz 1981). This belated recognition was presaged 20 years ago by Evans, who maintained that "The sale is a social situation involving two persons. The interaction of the two persons, in turn, depends upon the economic, social, and personal characteristics of each of them. To understand the process, however, it is necessary to look at both parts of the sale as a dyad, not individually" (Evans 1963, p. 76).

The interactional emphasis employed here highlights the overlooked importance of the service

---

[1]Not all service encounters are simple dyadic relationships. Some may involve a series of dyadic interactions, while others are still more complex and involve a number of different actors.

encounter as a psychological phenomenon that exerts a major impact upon outcomes. This is consistent with the approach of Lutz and Kakkar (1976), who have recognized the importance of the psychological situation and the adoption of a process model to understand behavior. They propose a model incorporating situation, decision processes, and social exchange. Similarly, we propose that the fusion of two people in a service setting is greater than the sum of its parts. Given such a conceptual framework, it will be possible to design research by which the elements of satisfying and nonsatisfying encounters can be identified. It is proposed that these elements will overlap with dimensions of human social interaction that have been shown to exert influence in other classes of goal-oriented behavior.

This approach is influenced by work on the dynamics of both face-to-face encounters and group activity. It stresses the mutuality of behaviors (cf. Thibaut and Kelley 1959) and acknowledges that a service encounter is a form of social exchange in which participants normally seek to maximize the rewards and minimize the costs of the transaction (cf. Homans 1961). It is also assumed that it is at some point feasible and desirable to measure units of behavior, and to assess their contributions to the quality of eventual outcomes (cf. Bales 1950).

The study of the service encounter is also influenced by prior theoretical developments on dyadic interactions in the marketplace. These perspectives have usually centered upon the personal selling process (Evans 1963, Sheth 1975, Willett and Pennington 1966, Wilson 1977). For example, Sheth makes a relevant distinction between two interaction dimensions: the *content* versus the *style* of communication. The latter dimension recognizes the centrality of ritualistic behavior patterns in shaping the outcome of the buyer/seller interaction.

The ability to identify mutually satisfying factors in encounters will be helpful in the design of services, in the setting of service level standards, in the design of service environments, in the selection, training, and motivation of service providers, and in guiding customer behaviors. This approach suggests that the manager look to find ways to channel both provider and customer behavior if satisfaction with the encounter is to be maximized.

SERVICE ENCOUNTERS ARE HUMAN INTERACTIONS

At a superficial level the acts of ordering a meal, obtaining a car loan, making plane reservations, or picking up a suit at the dry cleaners appear to have little in common. At a social or psychological level, however, all of these incidents are conceptually similar: Each act is a purposive transaction whose outcome is dependent on the coordinated actions of both participants. As is the case in many types of dyadic interactions, one cannot predict the quality of outcomes with knowledge of only one actor's behavior. Instead, much of social behavior consists of joint activity—a major task for the interacting person is the *mutual coordination* of appropriate behavior vis-à-vis the other person (Thibaut and Kelley 1959).

Communication between a service provider and a customer is interactive; it is a reciprocal process rather than a linear one. The service experience which distinguishes one service organization from another is a result of the unique interaction between the experiencer and the contact person (Booms and Nyquist 1981). Since the success of a particular service vendor rests on the quality of the subjective experience, the nature of this experience is the critical determinant of long run market success. Facilities may be spotless and the service delivered on time as ordered—but if the customer leaves with a negative impression from the attitude of an employee, other efforts may be overlooked.

Although providers often behave as if they act *on* a static consumer, it is imperative to understand the consumer's participatory role in assigning meaning to marketing stimuli (Booms and Nyquist 1981). Indeed, it is more accurate to think of the service provider as acting *with* the customer. While marketers often emphasize short run indices of seller effectiveness, this perspective may be especially myopic in the service sector (Czepiel 1980, Schneider 1980). Schneider cites three examples of this myopia: Bank tellers' evaluations depend more on how they "prove out" at the end of the day than on the courtesy they display, airline reservation clerks are judged more on paperwork errors than on the goodwill they generate, and the short-term dollar volume generated by insurance salespeople is weighed more heavily than is success in establishing long-term interpersonal relationships. While indices such as accuracy and sales are clearly important, the point here is that other criteria relating to personal service should also be included in evaluating service personnel. To reiterate, the quality of the subjective product—the service experience—is the true outcome of a service interaction. This product is manufactured by *both* parties and must be approached as such. To paraphrase an old Zen saying, we know the sound of two hands clapping; what is the sound of one hand clapping?

SERVICE ENCOUNTERS ARE ROLE PERFORMANCES

A distinguishing feature of service encounters as a class of human interaction is the purposive, task-oriented nature of the interaction. Specific short-term goals are clearly defined and agreed upon by society (procuring airline tickets, depositing a check). Due to this consensus, ritualized behavior patterns evolve which govern the course of the encounter. Each party to the transaction has learned (albeit with differing degrees of facility) a set of behaviors that are appropriate for the situation and will increase the probability of goal attainment. Each participant has a role to play; the script from which he/she reads is often strictly defined.

This socially defined structure renders provider/client interchanges especially amenable to a role theoretical analysis of the service encounter. Role theory, of course, is not new to marketing. Constructs adapted from role theory have been used to explain consumer behavior, especially with regard to expectation formation (Sheth 1967). The major areas in which the theory has been applied are in personal selling, role portrayals in advertising, and husband/wife decision making (see Wilson and Bozinoff 1980 for a comprehensive review of role theory in marketing).

A role theoretic approach emphasizes the nature of people as social actors who learn behaviors appropriate to the positions they occupy in society. Although the "actors" in a service setting may be very different individuals in their leisure time, they must adopt a relatively standardized set of behaviors (i.e., read from a common script) when they come to work or enter the marketplace. In fact, people are often defined by the service roles they play. when an individual is labeled nurse, clerk, or cab driver, one is able to generate a profile of this person based on the characteristics which are believed to covary with this title. The pervasive tendency to "fill out" one's knowledge of a person, given observation of religious, political, or occupational characteristics, is well-documented in the literature on person perception and "implicit personality theory" (cf. Tagiuri 1969).

This implicit structure is not confined to the service provider. The recipient of the service also plays a role. The customer/client role is composed of a set of learned behaviors, a repertoire of roles; the particular script which is read depends upon the demands of the specific service environment and other situational cues (Lutz and Kakkar 1976). The customer role in an elegant restaurant involves very different actions than an appropriate role in a fast-food setting. It will be argued at a later point that the root cause of many provider/client interface problems is the failure of participants to read from a common script. First, it is necessary to briefly introduce some of the basic concepts of role theory as they are relevant to an analysis of the dyadic service encounter.

AN OVERVIEW OF ROLE THEORY

Role theory is based on a dramaturgical metaphor. The study of a role—a cluster of social cues that guide and direct an individual's behavior in a given setting—is the study of the conduct associated with certain socially defined positions rather than of the particular individuals who occupy these positions. It is the study of the degree to which a particular part is acted appropriately (role enactment) as determined by the reactions of fellow actors and observers (the audience). Since one aim in the intangible service environment is to provide consistent service at an acceptable level across individual service providers, this perspective seems particularly fitting (Grove and Fisk 1983).

Each role that one plays is learned. One's confidence that one is doing the right thing leads to satisfaction with a performance (termed role validation) and success in interacting with others who are, of course, also playing their respective roles. One's role specific self-concept is formed by the reactions of others to the quality of one's role enactment. Some roles are more central to the individual than others (e.g., *Lover* versus *Golfer*). The self also can be thought of as a system of identities to which one is more or less committed (Jackson 1981), where commitment to a role implies a concern that one's role enactment be convincing (Sarbin and Allen 1968). Self-concept related to a role constitutes a role identity (McCall and Simmons 1966).

The concern that one be competent in performing a role is applicable in a service setting. If the service provider's occupational role is relatively salient in the self-concept, commitment to the effective performance of that role should be strong; giving good service will matter. In addition to the basic motivation to perform competently (White 1959), desire to perform a service role well should also be a function of group (i.e., company) cohesiveness. Service personnel are members of an organization; group membership brings with it a responsibility to act in accord with prescriptions that define one's position in the group (McCall and Simmons 1966), especially when this position is valued by the group member. For both of these reasons, the issue of morale as it impacts upon service can be viewed as a question of commitment to a role identity.

For both provider and consumer, the successful enactment of even the most basic service scenario involves the mastery of a wide range of behaviors. On the provider side, this learning process is often explicit. It may take the form of a training program or perhaps an apprenticeship to an accomplished role player. On the other hand, the consumer's burden is at times explicit (e.g., the elaborate directions for filling out forms and reporting to various offices when dealing with bureaucracies such as the Department of Motor Vehicles), but it is more typically implicit. Regardless, there are always behaviors which may come automatically to a veteran but which demand great cognitive activity by the novice. Anyone who recalls the adolescent apprehension over "doing the right things" on one's first solo outing to an expensive restaurant can attest to this (how to talk to the waiter, what to order when the menu is written in another language, how much to tip). The heuristic value of this approach is probably maximized in situations involving the execution of well-learned behaviors that possess a high degree of social consensus as to appropriate and expected actions. Many routine service transactions fall in this category.

In the case of a person's encounter with either a novel situation or one perceived as warranting active problem solving (i.e., a high involvement situation), this perspective may still be useful. Though its explanatory power at the molecular level of behavior may be diminished, role theory can still be employed to specify *molar* orientations. It seems likely that the occupant of a novel role who has not yet developed a script specific to that role (promotion to a new job, one's first experience in dealing with an interior decorator or a lawyer) will attempt to employ an existing script similarly structured. Alternatively, he/she will use an idealized script that has been internalized through vicarious socialization. Thus, one may assign the role of *Lawyer* to the larger category of *Authority Figure,* and act deferentially—much as one would act with other known representatives of this category, such as *Physician* or *Teacher.* Or one might approximate behavior based upon expectations derived from TV, movies, or books regarding how lawyers and their clients are supposed to act.

While the gaps in a novel script are filled in by accumulated experience, reference to an idealized script at early stages delimits behavioral options by establishing the parameters of possible activity, a subset is created from one's total behavioral repertoire. Vague role knowledge may not provide specific guidance for appropriate role behavior, but it may go a long way in advising one what *not* to do or say. For example, a person may not know exactly what to talk about with a member of the clergy, but one is probably aware of some subjects which should *not* be discussed.

ROLE EXPECTATIONS

Role expectations are comprised of the privileges, duties, and obligations of any occupant of a social position (Sarbin and Allen 1968). These expected behaviors must always be defined in relation to those occupying the other positions in the social structure. It is important to remember that a role player's behavior is interdependent with the behavior of those in complementary positions. One's role conduct must take into account the role behavior of others. The totality of complementary roles—to a bank teller, for example, there may be customers, co-workers, head teller, and branch manager—is a role set (Merton 1957).

One important result of proper role socialization is the acquired ability to predict the behavior of other role players. In role theory terms, this is known as "taking the role of the other" (Mead 1935). This empathic process whereby the actor anticipates the other's expected role behavior allows the actor to gauge his/her own behavior to the predicted behavior of others (Rose 1962). Research in personal selling has demonstrated that the salesperson whose behavior is contingent upon the behavior of the customer is more effective than one who does not adjust behavior to meet the customer's specific needs (Weitz 1981).

These predictions are based on expectations for behavior implied in common meanings. For example, a customer who walks into a clothing store is communicating consideration of buying a transaction or at least wants to browse. This behavior allows the salesperson to initiate the actions which correspond to a sales role. The salesperson's approach would not have the same meaning outside the store as inside, though in both cases a stranger is initiating conversation and perhaps asking questions of a somewhat personal nature. Once the shopper enters the store, he/she adopts the role of customer and a role-defined dyadic interaction familiar to both parties may begin.

While consumers and providers have common expectations about appropriate role behaviors, these expectations differ among encounters and are moderated by provider/consumer characteristics and perceptions, and by production realities (Czepiel et al. 1982). Provider/consumer characteristics and perceptions about the encounter dictate which behaviors comprise a satisfactory interaction and can serve to differentiate offerings of the same type of service. For example, within a class of service encounters (e.g., buying clothing) the behaviors of the role players will differ as a function of the learned expectations within that specific setting; different behaviors are expected in J. C. Penney stores compared to Brooks Brothers stores. Production realities refer to the set of dimensions associated with production characteristics such as time factors, technology, location, content, and complexity, that constrain the encounter and help determine which role behaviors are appropriate.

The expectations held by each role player about appropriate behaviors are multidimensional. The concept of "bridging the gap . . . between the producers and the consumers with respect to values, perceptions, possession, time, and place dimensions of exchange" [transaction] (Sheth 1982) is relevant here. If the salient dimensions of the encounter are clear, appropriate role behaviors can be identified and evaluated (Czepiel et al. 1982).

ROLE EXPECTATIONS
AFFECT PERFORMANCE

The concept of expectations is not new to marketing. The consumer satisfaction literature defines product satisfaction as a function of consumer expectations and perceived performances. The greater the negative discrepancy between expectations and performance, the greater the corresponding dissatisfaction (Churchill and Surprenant 1982; Czepiel, Rosenberg, and Akerele 1975; Swan and Coombs 1976). The view adopted here is similar: Satisfaction with a service encounter is seen as a function of the congruence between perceived behavior and the behavior expected by role players.

It should be noted that this relationship has received empirical support in some studies on personal selling. In a study of differences between sold and unsold prospects for insurance, Riordan, Oliver, and Donnelly (1977) found that role congruence—the absolute difference between a customer's perceptions of actual and ideal insurance agents—emerged as a parsimonious discriminator between those who purchased a policy and those who did not. An earlier study which used a somewhat similar population found that successful agents fulfilled expectations concerning similarity, expertise, friendliness, and personal interest (Evans 1963). In addition, a study of interactions between wholesale drug salespeople and retail pharmacists showed that the degree to which seller behavior differed from buyers' role expectations of a drug salesperson was related to degree of supplier loyalty (Tosi 1966).

A consideration of role congruence in a service setting is actually a two-dimensional issue of intra-role and inter-role congruence. Intra-role congruence reflects the degree to which the service provider's conception of his/her own role is concordant with the organization's conception of that role.[2] Inter-role congruence is the degree to which provider and client share a common definition of service roles.

INTRA-ROLE CONGRUENCE   The first part of the issue has been addressed by some workers in the area of personal selling. In this domain it comes under the rubric of role ambiguity. A lack of role clarity has been shown to be a major source of job tension, dissatisfaction, and reduced innovativeness as workers are unsure of the exact nature of role expectations (cf. Kahn et al. 1964). This factor has been demonstrated to mediate satisfaction for industrial salespeople (Ford, Walker, and Churchill 1976), managerial personnel (Oliver and Brief, 1977–78), and retail salespeople (Dubinsky and Mattson 1979), as well as committee members (Bible and Brown 1963) and teachers (Bible and McComas 1963).

Role congruence is partly determined by dispositional characteristics (i.e., some people are just not suited to certain roles) and by past experience and amount of interaction in that role (Sarbin and Allen 1968). This may explain why there is less incongruence found in friend roles than in occupational roles (Block 1952).[3]

The amount of overt communication about role expectations is obviously an important mediator (e.g., feedback from sales managers to floor personnel regarding criteria for advancement, or the formulation of explicit criteria in academe for promotion and tenure). Since such communication flows are facilitated in cohesive groups, it is not surprising that greater role consensus is found in small organizations (Thomas 1959). Schneider (1980) has proposed that incongruence

---

[2]An additional variant of this issue centers on the problems that arise when the role conceptions of co-workers do not overlap with those of management. For example, the informal peer group may be highly cohesive yet devote the bulk of its attention to social interaction rather than goal performance (Davis 1969). This situation is exemplified by piece-work operations where overzealous workers who exceed the quota are branded as rate-busters and ostracized by peers. While such disparities in role concepts possess important implications for productivity and morale issues, further delineation of what constitutes the organization's conception of a role is a complex matter and beyond the scope of this article. For our purposes management's role-definition is assumed to be dominant.

[3]The amount of experience in playing friendship roles which leads to greater role congruity may be confounded by the large degree of self-selection exerted in such roles relative to other roles.

between the service orientation of employees who are probably self-selected to be "service enthusiasts," and the perceived orientation of management as "service bureaucrats" who care only about maintaining the system, engenders role ambiguity and conflict. This process in turn translates into dissatisfaction, frustration, and intentions to quit.

INTER-ROLE CONGRUENCE The second type of role congruence is equally crucial: the degree of agreement between both parties involved in the service transaction regarding the appropriate roles to be played. A lack of clarity is likely to influence the efficacy of group or dyadic performance. At the least, the necessity of expending effort to predict an individual's behavior (which is obviated by congruent role enactment) decreases the time available to expend on task activities. Early group dynamics studies demonstrated this quite clearly. For example, the existence of an unclear group structure was shown to impede the ability to survive of Air Force crews under stress (Torrance 1954). In another study, confederates under instructions to remain silent in a group problem solving session decreased productivity, as other members were hampered by ambiguous role expectations. These detrimental effects were eliminated if the confederate was identified as a listener at the outset of the session (Smith 1957). In other words, group effectiveness depends upon each member understanding the role expectations of the other members so that each is clear about his/her *own* role expectations.

It seems likely that accurate mutual comprehension of role expectations is a prerequisite for a satisfying service experience. This joint assignation of roles probably occurs during the initial encounter and persists throughout subsequent encounters in the service environment. As in everyday person perception, the first impression is a pervasive one. The service customer seeks to reduce risk by looking for tangible signs of capability to deliver the service. As a result, the first time customer will be especially vigilant as he/she assimilates such environmental clues as the appearance and demeanor of the service provider (Booms and Nyquist 1981).

This initial labeling process can be thought of as role assignment or "altercasting" (Weinstein and Deutschberger 1963). The outcome of this process drastically affects the subsequent tone and content of the interaction. As one partner identifies a salient role (e.g., a friend prefaces advice with "as your lawyer . . ."), the complementary role of the other partner is simultaneously defined. A pompous suit salesperson calls forth a different customer role than the obsequious haberdash-

er who is eager to please. For instance, it seems likely that the customer will be more assertive about any idiosyncratic preferences in style or tailoring in the second case than in the first, where he/she may be more intimidated and/or submissive. It is important to note that the long-term effectiveness of each type depends upon the customer's expectations. To paraphrase a hotel chain's motto, there will be no surprises.

ROLE DISCREPANCIES Problems arise when there is a discrepancy somewhere in the system. This inconsistency with expectations may be exhibited in one of two ways: (1) the employee's perception of job duties or qualifications differs from the customer's expectations of those duties, or (2) the customer's conception of the customer role differs from the employee's notion of that role.

This proposition can be illustrated by considering either of two extant taxonomies of marketing interactions. Both McMurry's (1961) classic continuum of personal selling and the breakdown in terms of employees' communication functions by Booms and Nyquist (1981) seem to share the recognition that the role requirements of employees can range from those of virtual automaton to those of an equal partner vis-à-vis the customer.[4]

Consider the situation where the employee's role concept is at odds with that projected by the customer. An independent clothes shopper may resent the intrusion caused by the unwanted advice of a clothing salesperson who is regarded as a mere order taker. A counter clerk at McDonald's may not be prepared to make menu recommendations, or a waiter may brush off a patron with "not my station." A patient may resent an overly familiar manner in a doctor, and a doctor in turn may bristle at the patient who performs self-diagnosis.

In these examples it is clear that the role players are not reading from the same script. If the structure of service scripts is better understood, the transaction can be engineered for congruency, and there is a greater probability that a climate for service (Schneider 1980) will prevail.

THE SERVICE SCRIPT

A more precise analysis of the service script can perhaps be aided by recent developments in cognitive psycholo-

---

[4]McMurry's work is centered on personal selling, while Booms and Nyquist work in the area of service marketing. Though beyond the scope of this paper, it is interesting to speculate on where one area ends and the other begins. As an illustration, both approaches begin with order takers and end with positions involving the creative selling of intangibles (insurance salesperson).

gy. Although this area is in some ways far removed from the theoretical sociology of role theory, some cognitive psychologists also (perhaps coincidentally) rely on the heuristic value of the dramaturgical metaphor. Investigations of schematic information processing contain the assumption that much of social interaction is governed by learned assumptions regarding the course the interaction should take. The interface of psychology and artificial intelligence research has produced work on *a priori* plans or scripts. Abelson (1976) defines a script in this context as "a coherent sequence of events expected by the individual, involving him either as a participant or as an observer" (p. 33). Despite the differences in intellectual origin, this definition is quite compatible with the above discussion of role expectations.

If a script is thought of as a learned sequence of causal chains (cf. Schank 1980), it seems plausible to make the leap to service scripts (Smith and Houston 1983). This script would contain information about the role set—one's own expected behavior—plus the expected complementary behavior of others, and would reflect the individual's learned (or imagined) conception of the prototypical service experience. Information about a service encounter would be stored in different levels of memory[5] as a function of its degree of abstraction (Schank 1980). An illustration is provided by Schank's example of a "dentist script." Remembrances of specific visits to a dentist would be stored in Event Memory. Unless some truly unique event occurred ("I got a date with the receptionist"), this recollection would gradually be incorporated into Generalized Event Memory, a collection of events whose common features have been abstracted. Knowledge like "going to a health professional's office," which is information about specific situations in general, would be stored in Situational Memory. Finally, a goal-based information—a major component of a service encounter—would be stored in Intention Memory. This encoding process is depicted schematically in Table 1. It should be kept in mind that the dentist *also* possesses scripts corresponding to patient types (new patient, anxious patient).

Consumers can be thought of as possessing cognitive scripts for a wide variety of service encounters. Although a high degree of consensus can be expected across people regarding script components, a process-oriented approach must acknowledge the fluid nature of such a construct. A variety of variables will mediate the idiographic content of scripts. Most cultural expectations are for ranges of behavior rather than for specific microbehaviors. Some mandate variation rather than conformity, as with scientists or designers (Rose 1962). Expectations may change over time as a script becomes redefined, though acceptance of a new service script is probably facilitated by integration with the old one. As an example, the traditional gas station script included having one's car windows wiped. The revised version frequently no longer includes this act but retains other elements. A related example is consumer resistance to such new forms of transactions as the Universal Product Code, bank machines, and self-service gas stations (Lovelock and Young 1979). These changes involve the sudden learning of radical script changes.

SERVICE TRANSACTION—MINDLESS BEHAVIOR?
For the most part, routine service encounters take place in an almost automatic style with a minimum of cognitive activity. As an illustration, it seems likely that most people cannot accurately recall details of all the service interactions they experience in the course of a day (what a salesperson looked like, what happened when one bought a pack of gum). Like actors in a long running play, people in familiar situations often interact by rote with little conscious attention at the time and even less recall later. This tendency has been termed *mindlessness;* a person interacts with the environment in a passive fashion with a minimum of cognitive activity (Langer 1978). Research supports the idea that adults tend to spend a significant portion of time in a mindless state unless they are provoked into mindfulness (Langer, Blank, and Chanowitz 1978; Langer and Imber 1979). This provocation usually takes the form of an unfamiliar situation or perhaps embarrassment, a jolt back to reality. As long as the structure of a communication is familiar, regardless of its content, mindlessness appears to be the norm.

As long as the structure of a service script is followed, it may be deduced that the encounter is characterized by mindlessness. Any experience in a repetitive job, where one seems to lose time perspective and operate in a partial trance, will serve to illustrate this proposition. It can be argued that it is only when the experience somehow deviates from the service script that the participants are individuated and the situation takes on an affective valence. Suddenly, one must expend cognitive effort to orient behavior as the predictability of the role enactment is diminished. The result of this devia-

---

[5]The notion of different levels of memory is no longer considered accurate. More properly, one would speak of differences in activation. However, as Bettman (1979) notes, a liberal interpretation of Craik and Lockhart (1972) can encompass an activation model and, using the terminology already in place, avoids the problem of defining new terms at length.

TABLE 1   An Artificial Intelligence Approach to the Structure of a Dentist Script[a]

Intention Memory	HEALTH PROBLEM
	FIND PROFESSIONAL + MAKE CONTACT + PROF OFFICE VISIT
Situational Memory	GO TO OFFICE + WAITING ROOM + ENTER OFFICE + HELP + LEAVE + BILL SENT
Generalized Event Memory	Dentist visits include:
	—getting teeth cleaned—dentist puts funny tooth paste on teeth, turns on machine, etc.
	—getting teeth drilled—D does x-ray, D gives shot of Novocaine, D drills, etc.
	Also: Dentists fill the health-care professional role in HEALTH(CARE)VISIT.
Event Memory	The time I went to the dentist last week:
	—I drove to the dentist.
	—I read *Newsweek*. There were holes in all the pictures.
	—I entered.
	—He/she cleaned my teeth.
	—He/she poked me in the eye with the drill.
	—I yelled.
	—The dentist didn't charge me.

[a] Adapted from Schank 1980, p. 263.

tion may be either positive or negative. It is proposed that the jolt from mindlessness puts the customer in an evaluative set. Without this, evaluation may not occur at all. Swan and Trawick (1978) found that for low involvement, frequently purchased goods, more than 50 percent of respondents did not recall forming any opinion at all about the product. There was no deviation from expectations, thus no reason to engage in the cognitive effort necessary to form an evaluation. When some deviation occurs, the customer attempts to discover the reason for the deviation. Sometimes the customer is pleasantly surprised (a bus driver may be unexpectedly courteous). Other events may be experienced negatively ("that woman didn't have to snarl at me when I asked her to wrap my package"). In general, it is proposed that extremes in evaluation (whether positive or negative) will only be experienced when some departure from expected role behavior is encountered and the abrupt cessation of mindless behavior necessitates active processing.

PREDICTABILITY AND PERSONALIZATION OF SERVICE

Service marketers often find themselves on the horns of a dilemma: How to provide efficient, standardized service at some acceptable quality level, while treating each customer as a unique person? Paradoxically it may be argued that the customer often faces a similar conflict. There is a trade-off between the gain in personalization when one is treated as an individual and the loss in predictability as the guidance provided by role expectations dissolves. The circumstances which may give rise to both instances will now be briefly considered.

NEGATIVE DISCREPANCIES

Under what conditions will a disruption of scripted behavior result in a subjectively negative experience? An answer may be found when a key dimension of role behavior is considered—level of involvement. Sarbin and Allen (1968) identify eight levels of role involvement along a continuum of self-role differentiation. At the low end is noninvolvement (a lapsed club membership) and casual role enactment (a customer in a supermarket). The level of ritual acting follows. This is a stage of relatively mechanical behavior, where the need to maintain behavioral consistency requires some involvement of the self. Examples include the waitress who puts on a big smile and the bank teller who inquires, "Is it hot enough today for you?" Engrossed ("heated") acting is the next level. The continuum ascends all the way to ecstasy and bewitchment, which might characterize situations where a consumer becomes totally engrossed in a product. Such extreme involvement may be found during the consumption of aesthetic experiences imparted by art, music, etc. (cf. Holbrook 1980; Levy, Czepiel, and Rook 1980). It seems likely, however, that most (though certainly not all) service encounters are rooted in the lower regions of involvement.

At the low end, minimal visceral participation is involved. It seems likely that a high premium will be placed upon efficiency and predictability. As anyone who has ever been frustrated by the blundering of an inexperienced fast-food employee knows, disruption of the routine, leading to slower service, usually results in a negative experience. Other workers have noted the tendency of clients to become aggressive toward a contact person when dissatisfied (Eiglier and Langeard 1977).

During low end service encounters, the treatment of customers as individuals and not as role occupants will probably not pay. Despite occasional promises to "have it your way," consistency and speed are the scripted attributes which are important and desired by the customer.

POSITIVE DISCREPANCIES

In contrast, the personal touch is desirable in other service situations. The assembly line nature of some medical clinics is seen as a major drawback, and one would certainly hope that a hair stylist would not use a prepackaged mold to cut one's hair. These represent situations of higher ego involvement; their greater centrality to the self results in the high intensity role enactment described as engrossment (Goffman 1961). In such situations we hope that the service provider treats us as a person instead of a number.

MORE ISN'T ALWAYS BETTER

It may be postulated that satisfaction is positively related to predictability for low involvement services, and positively related to flexibility/personalization in the case of high involvement services. The point here is that greater personalization of services does not necessarily result in a more positive service experience. Instead the subjective outcome depends upon the unique demands of the situation. This differential also functions within a class of services. While we expect attentive service at a high priced department store, such attention would seem incongruous in a bargain basement. In a similar vein, an early study of the waitress–diner dyad showed that the optimal relationship varied with the standing of the restaurant (Whyte 1948). In better eating places, the

waitresses suppressed the desire to talk back to customers, and the formality of their behavior was positively related to the perceived status of the diner. On the other hand, in lower standard restaurants it was the norm for a waitress to put customers in their place. Waitresses who conformed to this norm actually received larger tips than those waitresses who acted a middle-class script and were respectful to their customers. Apparently conformity to the role expectations of the consumer is rewarding, even if following the script results in objectively less desirable treatment. The crucial element for improving routinized service transactions may be to give the customer what he/she expects, with no surprises.

IMPLICATIONS FOR SERVICE MARKETING

Viewing service transactions from a role theory perspective has a number of advantages. Role theory compels us to adopt an interactive approach since roles are defined in a social context. Furthermore, appropriate role enactment is determined by the reactions of others. The quasi-ritualized nature of role behavior makes it possible to examine the structure and content of interacting roles apart from the specific individuals occupying the roles. Thus individual difference variables are seen as moderating factors rather than as determinants of behavior.

The concept of role expectations and predictability is an especially powerful one for understanding the nature of the service transaction. These expectations form the basis for service scripts. Using these concepts, deviations from scripted behavior can be examined for both positive and negative consequences. Deviations may occur because one of the parties to the interaction steps out of role, the participants do not share common role definitions, or because the actors are not reading from a common script. Whatever the reason, behavior that is unexpected reduces mindlessness and mandates increased cognitive activity, which results in a closer scrutiny of the service situation—for better or for worse.

PROPOSITIONS

Using the concepts developed above, it is possible to derive a set of propositions which can be used to examine service encounters.

P1: *Service encounters can be characterized as role performances.* The structure of the encounter is socially defined with associated meanings that guide and direct the behavior of the interactants.

P2:   *Role behavior is ritualized, learned behavior.*

   a.   *The content of roles is relatively consistent across actors.* This implies that a high degree of consensus should exist, across individuals, regarding the content of the roles. It should be possible then to discover the content of service provider roles, i.e., role definitions, and to extract the key elements.

   b.   *Facility in role performance is a function of experience and communication.* From this proposition we would expect that novices in a service encounter would expend more cognitive effort than experienced role players. From an organizational point of view, we would also expect communication about role expectations to facilitate the learning of role behaviors and to mediate experience.

   c.   *Service scripts, containing information about the role set, are learned by both service providers and customers.* Experienced role players should have more elaborate scripts than novices. Radical changes in the service script should encounter greater resistance from experienced role performers, since this involves discarding a reasonably efficient, well-developed script and learning a new one.

P3:   *Role similarity is a potential basis for classifying services.* If the key elements of service provider roles are extracted, it should be possible to categorize services in terms of role similarity rather than industry similarity. For example, a bank teller's role may have more in common with an airline reservation clerk's role than with that of a bank loan officer. Such a classification scheme would facilitate the development of general service principles underlying encounters.

P4:   *Role behaviors are interdependent. The appropriateness of behavior is determined by others.* For a service provider in a service setting, *others* include management, co-workers, and customers. Thus, the role player will adjust to the feedback received from all members of the audience. When these groups are not in agreement, we would expect role ambiguity to be high. Because role behaviors are interdependent, each player attempts to identify the other's role early in the interaction to facilitate prediction and also to adjust personal behavior accordingly. Thus, role assignment takes place early in the encounter and influences subsequent interaction.

We would expect that the early stages of the encounter are more important to the ultimate success of the interchange than are the later stages.

P5:   *Congruent role expectations facilitate social interaction.*

   a.   *When customers and service providers read from a common script (high inter-role congruence), the encounter is more satisfying.*

   b.   *When service employees and the organization share common role expectations, role clarity and job satisfaction increase.*

        Both of these propositions reflect the importance of the *shared* nature of the experience. Congruent role expectations enhance predictability and, hence, decrease the amount of effort which must be expended to complete the transaction. Predictability is most desired in services with low involvement. However, even for high involvement services, such as education and therapy, role expectations exist and form a basis for prediction. The script for a visit to a therapist, for example, may include a great deal of variation and the therapist's behavior may not be totally predictable. This is because the role of therapist includes variability rather than conformity. If the patient's script calls for a supportive, nondirective type of behavior and the therapist presents "canned" solutions, inter-role congruence will be low and dissatisfaction is likely to be high. The degree of predictability needed will vary across service encounters, not the need for predictability. The subpropositions above imply that management must be wary of communicating inconsistent or contradictory expectations to employees on the one hand and customers on the other, regarding service levels, image, customer base, etc.

P6:   *Discrepant role expectations decrease efficiency.* When role expectations are discrepant from actual behavior, communication will be inhibited and productivity reduced. When role players read from different scripts, considerable confusion is likely to result and the encounter no longer follows a predictable sequence. This should result in increased dissatisfaction.

FUTURE DIRECTIONS

These propositions represent only some of the more fundamental relationships that can be derived from a role playing perspective. Many others could be generated and tested.

In addition to empirically validating these propositions, the discussion of role theory and service encounters gives rise to numerous other questions. A brief description may indicate some issues for future investigation.

At the beginning of this article it was necessary to delimit service encounters, considering only face-to-face interactions between a buyer and seller. To what extent do role theory concepts hold when we relax our definition of a service encounter? For example, do role expectations operate similarly when the interaction takes place over the telephone? Another interesting question concerns man/machine interactions. Most automatic teller machines appear to be programmed to simulate the role of a bank teller. Some even call the customer by name. Can we talk about a man/machine dyad? An ATM role? To what extent is a theoretical structure like role theory applicable in this situation?

Another direction for future investigation might well include polyadic interactions, those interactions which include multiple service personnel. One might hypothesize that interacting with several service providers (a maitre d'hotel, wine steward, waiter, and bus boy) could be studied as a series of dyadic interactions. An interesting question here would be how the customer integrates the experience. One possibility would be to use an averaging process. An alternative might be a lowest common denominator or weakest link model. Of course it is possible that the dyadic model is not appropriate for analyzing polyadic interactions at all. A group dynamic approach may be more suitable, particularly when the customer interacts with service providers as a group.

These examples illustrate only a few of the many areas in which the concepts presented could be extended. Other researchers could easily expand this list. Regardless of the particular route chosen, it is hoped that the concepts developed in this paper will stimulate further research.

CONCLUSION

Role theory and the related concepts developed here make it possible to consider both customer–service provider interactions as well as service provider–organization interactions. The emphasis is on the joint behaviors of the actors. The setting the organization provides, together with the implicit and explicit cues it gives service employees, helps to determine the content of the employee role which, in turn, has an impact on and is affected by the customer role.

Using a mid-range theoretical structure such as role theory to examine service encounters permits us to develop general principles applicable in a range of service settings across individual role performers. It minimizes the need to treat each service encounter as a unique experience. Furthermore, the theoretical structure permits marketing researchers to integrate findings from other social science disciplines and to apply them in a service setting. Since control of the service encounter is a crucial area of managerial concern and a difficult task to accomplish, the perspective gained is important.

REFERENCES

Abelson, Robert F. (1976), "Script Processing in Attitude Formation and Decision Making," in *Cognition and Social Behavior,* John S. Carroll and John S. Payne, eds., Hillsdale, NJ: Erlbaum.

Bales, Robert F. (1950), *Interaction Process Analysis: A Method for the Study of Small Groups,* Reading, MA: Addison-Wesley.

Bateson, John (1977), "Do We Need Service Marketing?" in *Marketing Consumer Services: New Insights,* P. Eiglier, et al., eds., Cambridge, MA: Marketing Science Institute, report no. 77–115, 1–30.

Bell, Martin (1981), "A Matrix Approach to the Classification of Marketing Goods and Services," in *Marketing of Services,* J. H. Donnelly and W. R. George, eds., Chicago: American Marketing.

Bettman, James (1979), "Memory Factors in Consumer Choice: A Review," *Journal of Marketing,* 43 (Spring), 37–53.

Bible, B. L., and E. J. Brown (1963), "Role Consensus and Satisfaction of Extension Advisory Committee Members," *Rural Sociology,* 28, 81–90.

———, and J. D. McComas (1963), "Role Consensus and Teacher Effectiveness," *Social Forces,* 42, 225–233.

Block, J. (1952), "The Assessment of Communication Role Variations as a Function of Interactional Context," *Journal of Personality,* 21, 272–286.

Booms, Bernard H., and Jody Nyquist (1981), "Analyzing the Customer/Firm Communication Component of the Services Marketing Mix," in *Marketing of Services,* James Donnelly and William George, eds., Chicago: American Marketing.

Churchill, G. A., and C. F. Surprenant (1982), "An Investigation into the Determinants of Customer Satisfaction," *Journal of Marketing Research,* 20 (November), 491–504.

Cotham, James C., III (1968), "Job Attitudes and Sales Performance of Major Appliance Salesmen," *Journal of Marketing Research,* 5 (November), 370–375.

Craik, Fergus, and Robert S. Lockhart (1972), "Levels of Processing: A Framework for Memory Research," *Journal of Verbal Learning and Verbal Behavior,* 11, 671–684.

Czepiel, John A. (1980), *Managing Customer Satisfaction in Consumer Service Businesses,* Cambridge, MA: Marketing Science Institute.

———, E. Gutman, M. Soloman, and C. F. Surprenant (1982), "A Contingency Approach to Understanding Service Encounters: Theoretical Inputs for Management Action," paper presented at the Workshop on Research into the Management of Service Businesses, London Business School.

———, L. Rosenberg, and A. Akerele (1975), "Perspectives on Consumer Satisfaction," *Proceedings,* Chicago: American Marketing, 119–123.

Davis, J. H. (1969), *Group Performance,* Reading, MA: Addison-Wesley.

Dubinsky, Alan J., and Bruce E. Mattson (1979), "Consequences of Role Conflict and Ambiguity Experienced by Retail Salespeople," *Journal of Retailing,* 55 (Winter), 70–86.

Eiglier, Pierre, and Eric Langeard (1977), "A New Approach to Service Marketing," in *Marketing Consumer Services: New Insights,* P. Eiglier, et al., eds., Cambridge, MA: Marketing Science Institute, report no. 77–115.

Evans, Franklin (1963), "Selling as a Dyadic Relationship—A New Approach," *American Behavioral Scientist,* 6 (May), 76.

Ford, N. M., O. C. Walker, and G. A. Churchill, Jr. (1976), "The Psychological Consequences of Role Conflict and Ambiguity in the Industrial Sales Force," in *Marketing: 1776–1976 and Beyond,* K. L. Bernhardt, ed., Chicago: American Marketing.

Ghiselli, Edwin E. (1978), "The Validity of Aptitude Tests in Personnel Selection," *Personnel Psychology,* 26 (Winter), 461–477.

Goffman, Erving (1961), *Encounters: Two Studies in the Sociology of Interaction,* Indianapolis: Bobbs-Merrill.

Grove, Stephen J., and Raymond P. Fisk (1983), "The Dramaturgy of Services Exchange: An Analytical Framework for Services Marketing," in *Emerging Perspectives in Services Marketing,* Leonard L. Berry, G. Lynn Shostack, and Gregory D. Upah, eds., Chicago: American Marketing.

Holbrook, Morris B. (1980), "Introduction: The Esthetic Imperative in Consumer Research," in *Symbolic Consumer Behavior,* Elizabeth C. Hirschman and Morris B. Holbrook, eds., Ann Arbor: Association for Consumer Research.

Homans, George C. (1961), *Social Behavior: Its Elementary Forms,* New York: Harcourt.

Jackson, Susan E. (1981), "Measurement of Commitment to Role Identities," *Journal of Personality and Social Psychology,* 40, 138–146.

Judd, Robert C. (1964), "The Case for Redefining Services," *Journal of Marketing,* 28 (January), 58–59.

Kahn, Robert L., Donald M. Wolfe, Robert P. Quinn, J. Diedrick Snoek, and R. A. Rosenthal (1964), *Organizational Stress: Studies in Role Conflict and Ambiguity,* New York: Wiley.

Kelley, Harold H., and John W. Thibaut (1978), *Interpersonal Relations: A Theory of Interdependence,* New York: Wiley-Interscience.

Knisely, G. (1979), "Greater Marketing Emphasis by Holiday Inns Breaks Mold," *Advertising Age* (January 15), 47–51.

Langer, E. (1978), "Rethinking the Role of Thought in Social Interaction," in *New Directions in Attribution Research,* J. Harvey, W. Ickes, and R. Kidd, eds., Hillsdale, NJ: Erlbaum.

———, A. Blank, and B. Chanowitz (1978), "The Mindlessness of Ostensibly Thoughtful Action: The Role of Placebic Information in Interpersonal Interaction," *Journal of Personality and Social Psychology,* 36, 635–642.

———, and L. Imber (1979), "When Practice Makes Imperfect: Debilitating Effects of Overlearning," *Journal of Personality and Social Psychology,* 37, 2014–2024.

Levy, S. J., J. A. Czepiel, and D. W. Rook (1980), "Social Division and Aesthetic Specialization: The Middle Class and Musical Events," in *Symbolic Consumer Behavior,* E. C. Hirschman and M. Holbrook, eds., Ann Arbor: Association for Consumer Research.

Liechty, M., and G. A. Churchill, Jr. (1979), "Conceptual Insights into Consumer Satisfaction with Services," in *Proceedings,* Chicago: American Marketing.

Lovelock, Christopher H. (1980), "Toward a Classification of Services," in *Theoretical Developments in Marketing,* C. W. Lamb and P. M. Dunne, eds., Chicago: American Marketing, 72–78.

———, and Robert F. Young (1979), "Look to Consumers to Increase Productivity," *Harvard Business Review,* 57 (May–June), 168–178.

Lutz, R. J., and P. Kakkar (1976), "Situational Influence in Interpersonal Persuasion," in B. B. Anderson, ed., *Advances in Consumer Research,* V. 3, Cincinnati: Association for Consumer Research, 370–378.

McCall, G. J., and J. L. Simmons (1966), *Identities and Interactions,* New York: Free Press.

McMurry, Robert (1961), "The Mystique of Supersalesmanship," *Harvard Business Review,* 39 (March–April), 114.

Mead, George H. (1935), "Mind, Self, and Society," in *Works of Mead,* Charles W. Morris, ed., Chicago: University of Chicago Press.

Merton, Robert K. (1957), "The Role Set," *British Journal of Sociology,* 8, 106–120.

Oliver, Richard L. (1974), "Expectancy Theory Predictions of Salesmen's Performance," *Journal of Marketing Research,* 11 (August), 243–253.

———, and A. P. Brief (1977–1978), "Determinants and Consequences of Role Conflict and Ambiguity among Retail Sales Managers," *Journal of Retailing,* 53 (Winter), 47–58.

Pennington, Allan L. (1968), "Customer–Salesman Bargaining Behavior in Retail Transactions," *Journal of Marketing Research,* 5 (August), 255–262.

Rathmell, John M. (1966), "What Is Meant by Services?" *Journal of Marketing,* 30 (October), 32–36.

Riordan, Edward A., Richard L. Oliver, and James H. Donnelly, Jr. (1977), "The Unsold Prospect: Dyadic and Attitudinal Determinants," *Journal of Marketing Research,* 14 (November), 530–537.

Rose, Arnold M. (1962), "A Systematic Summary of Symbolic Interaction Theory," in *Human Behavior and Social Processes: An Interactionist Approach,* Arnold M. Rose, ed., Boston: Houghton Mifflin.

Sarbin, Theodore R. and Vernon L. Allen (1968), "Role Theory," in *The Handbook of Social Psychology,* 2d ed., V. I. Gardner Lindzey and Elliott Aronson, eds., Reading, MA: Addison-Wesley.

Schank, Roger C. (1980), "Language and Memory," *Cognitive Science,* 4, 243–284.

Schneider, Benjamin (1980), "The Service Organization: Climate is Crucial," *Organizational Dynamics,* 9 (Autumn), 52–65.

Sheth, J. N. (1967), "A Review of Buyer Behavior," *Management Science,* 13, 8718–8756.

——— (1975), "Buyer–Seller Interaction: A Conceptual Framework," *Proceedings,* Sixth Annual Conference, Association for Consumer Research, 382–386.

——— (1982), "Toward an Integrated Theory of Marketing," presentation given at the AMA Doctoral Consortium, University of Minnesota.

Shostack, G. Lynn (1977), "Human Evidence: A New Part of the Marketing Mix," *Bank Marketing* (March), 32–34.

Smith, E. E. (1957), "The Effects of Clear and Unclear Role Expectations on Group Productivity and Defensiveness," *Journal of Abnormal Sociology and Psychology,* 55, (no. 4), 213–217.

Smith, Ruth A., and Michael J. Houston (1983), "Script-Based Evaluations of Satisfaction with Services," in *Emerging Perspectives in Services Marketing,* Leonard L. Berry, G. Lynn Shostack, and Gregory D. Upah, eds., Chicago: American Marketing.

Swan, John, and Linda Coombs (1976), "Product Performance and Consumer Satisfaction: A New Concept," *Journal of Marketing Research,* 13 (April), 25–33.

———, and I. Fredrick Trawick (1978), "Testing an Extended Concept of Consumer Satisfaction," in *New Dimensions of Consumer Satisfaction and Complaining Behavior,* Ralph L. Day and H. Keith Hunt, eds., Bloomington: Indiana University Press, 56–61.

Tagiuri, Renato (1969), "Person Perception," in *The Handbook of Social Psychology,* 2d ed., V. 3, Gardner Lindzey and Elliott Aronson, eds., Reading, MA: Addison-Wesley.

Thibaut, John W., and Harold H. Kelley (1959), *The Social Psychology of Groups,* New York: Wiley.

Thomas, E. J. (1959), "Role Conceptions and Organizational Size," *American Sociological Review,* 24, 30–37.

Torrance, E. P. (1954), "The Behavior of Small Groups under the Stress of Conditions of 'Survival,'" *American Sociological Review,* 19, 751–755.

Tosi, Henry L. (1966), "The Effects of Expectation Levels and Role Consensus on the Buyer–Seller Dyad," *Journal of Business,* 39 (October), 516–529.

Uhl, K. P. and G. D. Upah (1983), "The Marketing of Services: Why and How Is It Different?" in *Research in Marketing,* V. 6, J. N. Sheth, ed., New York: Elsevier.

Webster, Frederick E. (1968), "Interpersonal Communication and Selling Effectiveness," *Journal of Marketing,* 32 (July), 7–13.

Weinstein, E. A. and P. Deutschberger (1963), "Some Dimensions of Altercasting," *Sociometry,* 26, 454–466.

Weitz, Barton A. (1981), "Effectiveness in Sales Interactions: A Contingency Framework," *Journal of Marketing,* 45 (Winter), 85–103.

White, R. W. (1959), "Motivation Reconsidered: The Concept of Competence," *Psychological Review,* 66, 297–333.

Whyte, William F. C. (1948), *Human Relations in the Restaurant Industry,* New York: McGraw-Hill.

Willett, Ronald P. and Allan L. Pennington (1966), "Customer and Salesman: The Anatomy of Choice and Influence in a Retail Setting," in *Science, Technology and Marketing,* R. M. Haas, ed., Chicago: American Marketing.

Wilson, David T. (1977), "Dyadic Interactions," in *Consumer and Industrial Buying Behavior,* Arch Woodside, Jagdish Sheth, and Peter Bennett, eds., New York: North-Holland, 355–365.

———, and Lorne Bozinoff (1980), "Role Theory and Buying–Selling Negotiations: A Critical Overview," in *Marketing in the '80s,* Richard Bagozzi, ed., Chicago: American Marketing, 118–121.

Wyckham, R. G., P. T. Fitzroy, and G. D. Mandry (1975), "Marketing of Services: An Evaluation of the Theory," *European Journal of Marketing,* 9, 59–67.

CHAPTER 3

UNDERSTANDING THE SERVICE OPERATION

CHAPTER OVERVIEW

*One way of viewing the marketing task is to conceptualize it as the marrying of consumers'
needs with the technology and manufacturing capabilities of the firm. Such a marriage
obviously will involve compromises since consumers' needs seldom can be met completely
and economically. Within a goods firm, this marriage requires marketing's understanding
of the capabilities of manufacturing and of research and development. The task of marketing is made somewhat easier because the different functions can be separated by means
of inventory.*

*In a service firm, this problem is magnified. Significant aspects of the operation are
the product, since it is these aspects that create the interactive experience that delivers the
benefit to the customer. A successful compromise between operations efficiency and marketing effectiveness is therefore that much more difficult to achieve. Success in services
marketing demands a much greater understanding of the constraints and opportunities
posed by operations.*

*To introduce these complexities, in this chapter we first adopt the perspective of an
operations manager and ask, "What would be the ideal way to run the system from the
operations perspective?" The impact on marketing and the opportunities for marketing to
assist in the creation of this ideal then are developed. The major topics discussed are: The
prerequisite for manufacturing efficiency and alternative strategies for achieving it, the
application of this model to services, potential solutions to service operations problems, and
marketing and operations interdependence. Many of these topics are discussed from different perspectives in later chapters. They are introduced here to show their relationship to
the operational demands of services.*

As pointed out in Chapter 1, the key distinctive characteristic of services is that the
produce is an experience. That experience is created by the operating system of the
firm interacting with the customer. Thus the operating system of the firm, in all its
complexity, is the product. For a marketing manager, this fact imposes constraints on
the strategies that can be employed, but it also presents new and challenging opportunities for improving the profitability of the firm.

Chapter 2 provided one base on which to build an understanding of the prod-
uct-design problem for services. An understanding of consumer behavior always has
been a necessary condition for successful marketing. One way of viewing the pro-
duce-design process is to think of it as the process of combining such an understanding with the technological and manufacturing skills of the organization. A
knowledge of consumer behavior is not sufficient in itself to produce economically
successful products.

As pointed out in Chapter 1, in a goods firm it is possible to separate the problems of manufacturing and marketing by the use of inventory. Even so, there are
many areas of potential conflict.[1] These problems are summarized in Table 3.1.
Although the issues have been characterized as conflicts, they can be reconceptual-
ized as opportunities. In each area, it is clear that a better integration of marketing
and manufacturing plans could yield a more efficient and profitable organization.
For example, the determination of the extent of the product line should be seen as a
compromise between the heterogeneous demands of the market and the manufacturing demand for homogeneity. Too large a marketing bias will mean many products and an inefficient operation. As long as this is compensated for by higher prices,
then a successful strategy can ensue. Too large a manufacturing bias will mean a sin-

TABLE 3.1   Marketing/Manufacturing Areas of Necessary Cooperation but Potential Conflict

Problem Area	Typical Marketing Comment	Typical Manufacturing Comment
Capacity planning and long-range sales forecasting	"Why don't we have enough capacity?"	"Why didn't we have accurate sales forecasts?
Production scheduling and short-range sales forecasting	"We need faster response. Our lead times are ridiculous."	"We need realistic customer commitments and sales forecasts that don't change like wind direction."
Delivery and physical distribution	"Why don't we ever have the right merchandise in inventory?"	"We can't keep everything in inventory."
Quality assurance	"Why can't we have reasonable quality at reasonable cost?"	"Why must we always offer options that are too hard to manufacture and that offer little customer utility?"
Breadth of product line	"Our customers demand variety."	"The product line is too broad—all we get are short, uneconomical runs."
Cost control	"Our costs are so high that we are not competitive in the marketplace."	"We can't provide fast delivery, broad variety, rapid response to change, and high quality at low cost."
New-product introduction	"New products are our lifeblood."	"Unnecessary design changes are prohibitively expensive."
Adjunct services, such as spare parts inventory support, installation, and repair	"Field service costs are too high."	"Products are being used in ways for which they weren't designed."

SOURCE: Reprinted by permission of the *Harvard Business Review*. An exhibit from "Can Marketing and Manufacturing Coexist?" by Benson P. Shapiro (September/October 1977), 105. Copyright © 1977 by the President and Fellows of Harvard College; all rights reserved.

gle product, which may be less attractive to the market. As long as this is compensated for by lower costs and hence lower prices, a successful strategy can emerge.

The purpose of this chapter is to extend to services the logic of this type of compromise. In the service sector, the possible areas of conflict or compromise are much broader because the operation itself is the product. Again, there are no single solutions since operational efficiency and marketing effectiveness may push in opposite directions. By its very nature, this chapter is operations oriented rather than marketing oriented. To polarize the issues, the perspective adopted in this chapter is that of the operations manager, just as in Chapter 2 the consumer's position was taken. The focus is on the requirements for operational efficiency and the ways that marketing can help to achieve those requirements. It should be stressed that, in the drive for competitive advantage in the marketplace, marketing demand may in the end mean less operational efficiency.

THE PREREQUISITES FOR MANUFACTURING EFFICIENCY

The starting point for this discussion is the work of J. D. Thompson.[2] Thompson, who started from an organizational perspective, introduced the idea of a "technical core," that is, the technical heart of the organization. He specified that, to operate efficiently, the firm must be able to operate "as if the market will absorb the single kind of product at a continuous rate and as if the inputs flowed continuously at a steady rate and with specified quality." At the center of his argument was the idea that uncertainty creates inefficiency. In the ideal situation envisaged by Thompson, the technical core is able to operate without uncertainty on both the input and output side, thereby creating many advantages for management.

The absence of uncertainty means that decisions within the core can become programmed and individual discretion can be replaced by rules; the removal of individual discretion means that jobs are deskilled and lower-quality labor is used. Alternatively, the rules can be programmed into machines and labor can be replaced with capital. Since output and input are fixed, it is very easy to plan capacity and to run at the high levels of utilization needed to generate the most efficient operations performance.

A system without uncertainty is very easy to control and manage. Performance can be measured using objective standards. Since the system is not subject to disturbances from outside, it is also very easy to diagnose the causes of any problems.

Clearly, such an ideal world is virtually impossible to create, and, even in goods companies, the demands of procurement and marketing management have to be traded off against the ideal operations demands. Within goods manufacturing, Skinner has operationalized this concept with his idea of the focused factory.[3] He argues for focusing a factory on a particular job; once this is achieved, the factory does a better job because repetition and concentration in one area allow the work force and managers to become effective and experienced in the task required for success. He broadens Thompson's concept in that he argues that focus generates effectiveness as well as efficiency. In other words, the focused factory can meet the demands of the market better whether the demand is low cost through efficiency, or quality, or any other criterion.

ALTERNATIVE STRATEGIES FOR ACHIEVING MANUFACTURING EFFICIENCY

Skinner extends the idea of the focused factory in another direction with his concept of a "plant within a plant" (PWP). Since there are advantages to having production capability at a single site, Skinner introduces the concept of breaking up large, unfocused plants into smaller units buffered from each other so that they each can be focused separately.

In goods manufacturing, the concept of buffering is a very powerful one. Thompson expressed the idea as decoupling: "Organizations seek to buffer environmental influences by surrounding their technical core with input and output components."[4] A PWP thus can be operated close to Thompson's ideal if buffer inventories are created on the input and output sides. On the input side, the components needed within a plant can be inventoried and quality controlled before they are needed; in this way, it can appear to the PWP that "inputs flow continuously at a steady rate and with specified quality." In a similar way, the PWP can be separated from downstream plants or from the market by creating finished goods inventories.

The alternatives to buffering proposed by Thompson were smoothing, anticipating, and rationing. Smoothing and anticipating focus on the uncertainty introduced into the system by the flow of work; smoothing involves managing the environment to reduce fluctuations in supply and/or demand, and anticipating mitigates the worst effects of those fluctuations by anticipating them. Finally, rationing involves resorting to triage when the demands placed on the system by the environment exceed its ability to handle them.

APPLYING THE EFFICIENCY MODEL TO SERVICES

We saw in Chapters 1 and 2 that the application of operations concepts to services is fraught with difficulty. The problem can be understood easily by thinking about the servuction system model discussed in Chapter 1 and illustrated in Figure 1.2. From an operations point of view, the key characteristics of the model are that the customer is an integral part of the process and that the system operates in real time. Because the system is interactive, it can be (and often is) used to customize the service for each individual.

It is clear from this simplified model that services, by their very nature, do not meet the requirements of the Thompson model. The closest the servuction model comes to the Thompson ideal is that part of the system is invisible to the customer. Even here, however, the customization taking place may introduce uncertainty into the system. Providing that all customization can take place within the servuction system itself, then the part invisible to the customer can be run separately. It often can be located in a place different from the customer contact system.[5] However, when the customization cannot be done within the servuction system, it can introduce uncertainty into the back office.

The servuction system itself is an operations nightmare, since it is impossible to use inventories and impossible to decouple the system from the market. Instead of measuring demand "at a continuous rate," the system is linked directly to a market that frequently varies dramatically from day to day, hour to hour, and even minute to minute. This creates massive problems in capacity planning and utilization.

Instead of "the single kind of product" specified by Thompson, the system can be called upon to make a different "product" for each customer. Indeed, it could be argued that, since each customer is different, each customer is an integral part of the process, and each experience or product is unique, this creates massive task uncertainty.

Thompson specifies inputs that flow continuously and at a steady rate with specified quality. Consider the inputs to the servuction system: the physical environment, the contact personnel, the other customers, and the individual customer. The environment may stay constant, but the other three inputs are totally variable, not only in their quality but also in their rate of arrival in the process.

Contact personnel are individuals, not inanimate objects. They have emotions and feelings, and, like all other people, are affected by what is happening in their lives outside work. If they arrive at work in a bad mood, this can influence their performance throughout the day. And that bad mood directly affects the customer, since the service worker is part of the experience being purchased. This problem is discussed again in Chapter 4, which is concerned with the service provider.

Customers also can be subject to moods that can affect their behavior toward the service firm and toward each other. Some moods are predictable, like that caused when a home team wins and the crowds hit the local bars. Other moods are individual, specific, and totally unpredictable until after the customer is already part of the servuction system.

Customers arrive at the service firm at unpredictable rates, making smoothing and anticipation very difficult. One minute a restaurant can be empty, and in the next few minutes it can be full. Analysis often can show predictable peaks that can be planned for; but even this precaution introduces inefficiency, since the firm ideally would prefer that customers arrive in a steady stream. Worse still are the unpredictable peaks. Planning for these peaks produces large amounts of excess capacity at

SERVICES IN ACTION 3.1

ARBY'S

Armed with a slew of high-tech innovations, Arby's is starting to look like a fast-food joint straight out of *The Jetsons*. The roast beef sandwich chain is testing automated systems for food selection and payment and has some revolutionary plans for its kitchens. All the changes are the result of consumer demand, said George Nadvit, executive vice president of operations for Arby's Inc., Atlanta.

As menus at fast-food restaurants have increased in size, service has slowed down, and consumers don't like that. Technology can help speed things up and cut labor needs.

"The predicted labor crisis of the '90s occupies the mind of every fast-food operator," says Nadvit. "Arby's is developing automated systems as potential cost-effective solutions to provide faster service and thus allow personnel to focus on providing hospitality."

Technology can do all the mundane and repetitive tasks, such as slicing roast beef, while employees help customers at the counter or in the dining room. Arby's is not alone. Many fast-food chains are taking a closer look at technology. Some are having more success than others, he says, but they have to stick with it. If not, they'll be in big trouble. "They have to continue to look at better and new ways of doing business, or they aren't going to be around in a few years," he stresses.

Arby's is testing Touch 2000, a computerized system that allows customers to order food from a touch-sensitive display screen. As the food selection is touched on the screen, it is processed through an IBM PS/2 Model 30 computer and displayed on IBM monitors in the food-preparation area. The machine's screen automatically indicates the selections made and keeps a running tab of the order. Some of the restaurants in Southwestern markets are using bilingual machines, allowing customers to order in English or Spanish.

Touch 2000 saves labor and food costs, Nadvit claims, providing faster service and allowing personnel to focus on the consumer. "We don't want to lose the human touch in fast food. We just want to provide the best service possible. Touch 2000 allows us to have the best of both worlds."

Arby's has found that Touch 2000 helps to increase sales by proposing the purchase of other items. If a customer doesn't order dessert, for example, the system will suggest a little something. Nadvit said the average check increased four percent on chains using the system.

Although Arby's thought it would be the younger customers using the machines, the chain is finding that use runs across the board and even includes some senior citizens. A recent study by Arby's found that 77 percent of its customers prefer ordering through Touch 2000. Ninety percent said the system was easy to use, and 54 percent said using the computer was faster than the traditional means. But some customers prefer the old-fashioned way. They give their orders to a cashier who then enters the data through a similar device behind the counter.

The system is used in more than 30 locations, and because 90 percent of the 2,300 Arby's restaurants are franchised, Nadvit said he expects the innovative franchisees to help move the customer-activated system forward.

Arby's also announced its plans to integrate its credit-card program into the Touch 2000 system. The chain is accepting payment by Visa and MasterCard credit cards at its company-owned restaurants in Cleveland and Phoenix, and has been testing acceptance of the Discover card in 50 company and franchised locations in Pittsburgh and Youngstown, Ohio. Accepting credit also stimulates add-on purchases, Nadvit said. The average cash purchase in Arby's restaurants is about $2.80, he said, but the credit-card average has been between $5 and $6.

In Phoenix, Arby's recently expanded its credit-card program with a new satellite broadcasting system that lets restaurants obtain credit-card authorization in less than three seconds. Nadvit said the chain is using that same satellite technology for other communications between the point-of-sale and regional and corporate offices. Arby's can move financial information as well as audio and visual information. Videos, for example, can be sent from corporate headquarters to individual restaurants.

Even the kitchens at Arby's restaurants will be going high-tech. "Customers will be seeing more extensive use of 'smart kitchens,' which control the cooking process based on analysis of sales volume," said Nadvit. "These systems will cook according to projected demand and continuously track food stocks to prevent shortages."

Arby's is working on a really nifty slicer for its roast beef. Linked to the point of sale, the machine turns on and delivers the current number of portions to the assembling area according to orders. Arby's wants to resolve some safety considerations and make the unit self-heating so the beef can be kept at the proper temperature.

The chain also plans to make some changes in the actual cooking process, so that the meat is cooked more evenly and doesn't have to be watched so closely. Arby's is testing ovens that feature temperatures that can be preset and monitored throughout the cooking process to see how long the meat took to cook and how much weight was lost. All the employee has to do is put the beef in, and the oven's probing system will send a signal when it's done.

The chain also is looking at a prototype of a product that would toast sandwich buns in one-third less time than its current model. And the Arby's self-service beverage area will be getting a make over, he said, opting for a new long-profile look so "there's not as much ugly equipment showing."

SOURCE: *Marketing Week,* vol. 24, no. 23 (November 12, 1990).

most times. They strain the entire system, undermining the experience for the customer and the contact personnel alike.

POTENTIAL SOLUTIONS TO SERVICE OPERATIONS PROBLEMS

Within the operations management literature of the past decade, there is a growing body of ideas about how to overcome some of the problems of service operations. These ideas can be classified into four broad areas: isolating the technical core; minimizing the servuction system; production-lining the whole system, including the servuction system; and creating flexible capacity. Other solutions, such as moving the time of demand and increasing customer participation, have been suggested in the marketing literature.

These solutions are not operations solutions alone. To make any of them work requires a marketing input, and to ignore that marketing input is to risk increasing efficiency at the expense of the effectiveness of the system in the mind of the customer. It is this characteristic that differentiates services marketing from any other type of marketing. We shall discuss each solution from an operations perspective and then from a marketing viewpoint.

ISOLATING THE TECHNICAL CORE AND MINIMIZING THE SERVUCTION SYSTEM

THE OPERATIONS PERSPECTIVE Isolating the technical core and minimizing the servuction system have been combined because they are closely related from an operations point of view and their marketing implications are similar. Both of these approaches have been suggested by Richard B. Chase, who, in Article 3.1, introduces his "customer contact model." Following Thompson, he advocates the clear separation of the servuction system from the back office. Once this is achieved, he argues, completely different management philosophies should be adopted for each entity.

In the servuction system, Chase argues against the use of traditional production-lining approaches, focusing instead on optimizing the experience for the customer. Conversely, once the technical core has been isolated, it should be subjected to all of these procedures. This is precisely the approach that has been adopted in some areas of banking.[6] Thus, large-scale banking networks have been consolidated, and the traditional administrative tasks associated with a branch have been brought together in one location. This frees up the branch itself to focus on customer service. The resulting "paper factory" offers all of the same characteristics as any other factory and can be subject to the same kind of logic.

Chase maintains that high-contact systems should sacrifice efficiency in the interest of the customer but that low-contact systems need not do so. His position is summarized in Exhibit 2 in Article 3.1. Later, Chase extends his ideas,[7] arguing for the minimization of the customer contact component; he expresses this argument in the form of an equation:

$$\text{Potential operating efficiency} = \int \left(1 - \frac{\text{Customer contact time}}{\text{Service creation time}} \right)$$

Operating efficiency thus is reduced by the uncertainty introduced into the system by the customer. Another author has similarly argued that "clients . . . pose problems for organizations . . . by disrupting their routines, ignoring their offers for service, failing to comply with their procedures, making exaggerated demands, and so forth."[8] This latter problem is illustrated well by two empirical studies that show that one of the key causes of service failure is the unrealistic expectations of the customers.[9]

Chase suggests a number of ways of decoupling the technical core. For example, only exceptions should be handled on a face-to-face basis, with routine transactions being handled as much as possible by telephone or, even better, by mail. Mail transactions have the great advantage of being able to be inventoried.[10]

Chase's final refining of the concept was done with a number of colleagues.[11] Together, they suggest that the degree of customer contact should be matched to customer requirements, and that the extent of high-contact service offered should be the minimum acceptable to the customer. This approach is summarized in Table 3.2, below. Operational efficiency always favors low-contact systems, but effectiveness from the customer's point of view favors the correct matching.

Each cell in the table shows the extent to which marketing *effectiveness* has been met and the extent to which operational *efficiency* has been achieved. Offering high-

TABLE 3.2   Matching Customer and Firm

Firm Provision	Customer Requirement	
	High Contact	Low Contact
High Contact	Inefficient	Inefficient
	Effective	Ineffective
Low Contact	Efficient	Efficient
	Ineffective	Effective

contact services to customers who demand low contact is both inefficient and ineffective, and is clearly the least-desirable quadrant. Low-contact requirement and delivery offers the opportunity to be both efficient and effective. The other two quadrants represent the classic marketing/operations compromise and the choice would be determined best by the competitive environment.

THE MARKETING PERSPECTIVE   At this point, the need for a marketing involvement in this approach becomes clear, as a decision about the extent of customer contact favored by the customer is clearly a marketing issue. In some cases, a high degree of customer contact can be used to differentiate the service from its competitors; in these cases, the operational costs have to be traded against the competitive benefits.

Conversely, in some situations the segment of the firm that the operations group views as the back office is not actually invisible to the customer. For example, in some financial services, the teller operation takes place in the administrative offices. Operationally, this means that staff members can leave their paperwork to serve customers only when needed. Unfortunately, customers frequently view this operationally efficient system very negatively. A customer waiting to be served can see a closed teller window or service point and observe staff who apparently do not care because they sit at their desks and do not serve. In fact, they are extremely busy, but the nature of administrative work is such that this may not be the impression given.

Even if it is decided that part of the system can be decoupled, marketing has a major role in evaluating and implementing alternative approaches. Any change in the way in which the servuction system works implies a change in the behavior of the customer. A switch from a personal service to a combined mail and telephone system clearly requires a massive change in the way the customer behaves in the system. Marketing always has been the function that understands and modifies consumer behavior, and this must be the case here.

Perhaps the easiest way to understand this problem is in terms of script theory, which was described in Chapter 2. If this perspective is accepted, then clearly any change in the operations of a service business that impacts on the customer requires a change in the script. If the change of script is not managed, then it will be perceived by the customer as a breakdown compared to expectations. It is marketing's task to ensure the correct education of the customer to the new script.

PRODUCTION-LINING THE WHOLE SYSTEM

Theodore Levitt advocates a "production-line approach,"[12] which involves the application of hard and soft techniques to both the "front" and the "back" of the house. In his examples of McDonald's, he draws from both the servuction system

SERVICES IN ACTION 3.2

THE CHUBB GROUP OF INSURANCE COMPANIES

The Chubb Group is one of the larger financial service organizations in the United States. About two-thirds of its turnover is handled by 11 wholly owned subsidiary insurance companies in the United States and Canada, all of which are diversified operations, handling insurance for a variety of large industrial concerns as well as for personal and homeowner insurance.

The regulations surrounding the insurance industry require, on the whole, a considerable amount of attention to operational detail. A customer cannot simply walk into an office, purchase an insurance product, consume it, and walk out again. In addition to offering different policies, companies frequently offer different premiums on the same policy to different customers, e.g., nonsmokers pay lower life insurance premiums than smokers. All of this means that insurance companies must collect and process a great deal of data from their customers.

For the Chubb Group, with its highly diversified insurance-industry and customer base, making the collection of data more efficient became a major goal. The aim was to develop a data-collection system that would allow brokers and agents to spend less time filling in forms and filing them. As well as saving operational time, such a process also would save on the amount of training necessary for staff. At the same time, it was felt that a simpler, more user-friendly method of collecting data would reduce perceived risk and would attract customers.

In the personal insurance sector, the Chubb Group's answer to the problem was a new personal insurance package called Masterpiece. The goal of Masterpiece was to reduce the amount of data needed to complete a policy from over 300 questions to the number that would fit on a single sheet of paper. Through the use of computers, the layout and type of questions on the sheet could by customized, depending on the customer and the nature of the policy. Each form contains only the premium amount and other information relevant to that particular policy. The form was designed to apply to all personal insurance policies, including automobile, home, personal liability, and valuables.

To back up this system, Chubb also instituted a centralized toll-free telephone service to deal with any alterations, such as changes of address, thereby relieving agents and customers of the necessity of filling out new forms. The goal was to reduce the amount of paperwork and thus to create operational efficiency and a service attractive to consumers at the same time.

---

and the back of house. This kind of solution is relatively rare and, indeed, the fast-food firms provide a classic example, together with dry cleaners and some auto-maintenance firms. Their rarity stems largely from the marketing demands imposed on such systems. Those demands mean minimal customization, large-volume throughput, and high levels of customer participation. Even Burger King, with its "Have It Your Way" approach, still has minimal customization.

The generation of any kind of operational efficiency in such a servuction system implies a very limited product line; in this case, the menu. Moreover, customization must be kept to a minimum, since the whole operating system is linked straight through to the customer. A number of authors have discussed precisely this problem of how to provide efficient, standardized service at some acceptable level of quality, while simultaneously treating each customer as a unique person.[13] Their conclusions show the complexity of the problem, since attempts at a routine personalization—the "have a nice day syndrome"—have positive effects on perceived friendliness, but have negative effects on perceived competence. Thus, an apparently simple operations decision can have complex effects on customer perceptions.

The servuction system of a restaurant also depends for its success on large volumes of customers available to take the food that is produced. Since the invisible component is not decoupled and food cannot be prepared to order, the operating system has to run independently of individual demand and assume that, in the end, aggregate demand will absorb the food produced.

Such a servuction system is also extremely demanding of its customers. They must preselect what they want to eat. They are expected to have their order ready when they reach the order point. They must leave the order point quickly and carry their food to the table. Finally, they are expected to bus their own table.

CREATING FLEXIBLE CAPACITY

THE OPERATIONS PERSPECTIVE   As pointed out earlier, the servuction system creates major capacity-planning problems. Rather than tackle the cause directly, Sasser[14] suggests alternative strategies for matching supply and demand, one of which is the creation of flexible capacity. To meet the fluctuating demand, he advocates the use of:

☐ part-time employees

☐ a strategy that focuses on customer-serving jobs during peak demand

☐ shared capacity with other firms

In the first strategy, part-time employees can be used to provide extra capacity at peak times without increasing the costs at off-peak times. The second strategy suggests that, during peak demand, personnel focus only on those parts of the operation needed to serve customers. Chase, in a similar way, advocates the use of roving greeters to channel away from service employees purely informational tasks and hence to keep the main operation performing at maximum capacity.[15] Finally, Sasser suggests the sharing of capacity with other firms—firms that have different peak demands and can share facilities.

THE MARKETING PERSPECTIVE   Part-time employees appear to be a useful strategy from an operations point of view. There are, however, a number of marketing implications inherent in this approach that Sasser does not discuss. Part-time employees may deliver a lower-quality service than full-time workers; their dedication to quality may be less, as probably will be their training. They are used at times when the operation is at its worst, and this may be reflected in their attitude. As Schneider has shown, such attitudes can be very visible to the customer and are likely to influence negatively the perceptions they have of the service.[16]

In a similar way, the two other approaches suggested by Sasser have major marketing implications. Focusing on customer-serving jobs during peak demand presupposes that it is possible to identify the key part of the service from the customer's point of view. From a marketing perspective, the dangers with sharing capacity are numerous. Confusion may be produced in the customer's mind over exactly what the service facility is doing, and this could be particularly acute during change-over times when customers from two different firms are in the same facility, each group with different priorities and different scripts.

INCREASING CUSTOMER PARTICIPATION

Increasing customer participation has been discussed by a number of marketing researchers, among them Lovelock and Young.[17] The essence of the idea is to replace the work done by the employees of the firm with work done by the customer. Unlike the other strategies discussed, this approach is not necessarily an efficiency argument, but rather a cost-based argument. It moves the operation no closer to the ideal suggested by Thompson,[18] but it reduces the costs, no matter what the state of the operation.

Following the script-theory analogy, it is clear that such an approach demands a major change in the script. Moreover, the customers are called upon to take a greater responsibility for the service they receive. For example, the automatic teller machine (ATM) is seen by many operations personnel as a way of saving labor. The substitution of capital for labor is a classic operations approach, and the ATM can be viewed in that light. From the customer's point of view, such ATMs provide added convenience in terms of the hours during which the bank is accessible. However, it has been shown that, for some customers, this represents increased risk, less control of the situation, and a loss of human contact.[19]

Such a switching of activities to the customer clearly has major marketing implications, since the whole nature of the product received is changing. Such changes in the customer's script therefore require much customer research and detailed planning.

MOVING THE TIME OF DEMAND TO FIT CAPACITY

To overcome the capacity-utilization problem outlined earlier, Sasser suggests that marketing should be used to smooth the peaks in demand. Perhaps the classic example of this problem is the mass transit system that needs to create capacity to deal with the rush hour and, as a consequence, has much of its fleet and labor idle during the nonrush hours. A number of authorities have tried to reduce the severity of the problem by inducing passengers to travel in nonrush periods. Unfortunately, since much travel is a derived demand and is based on work hours, little success can be expected.

PUTTING IT ALL TOGETHER

Given the complexity of the interface between the service organization and the customer, it would seem to be the logical place to look for a framework.[20] Variations in complexity should drive the choice of operations. Larsson and Bowen (Article 3.2)[21] start from a simple matrix aligning diversity of demand versus customer disposition to participate to understand the uncertainty of input into the service operation. Diversity of demand refers to the uniqueness of customer demands, and a high score reflects a greater amount of specific information possessed by the organization before the actual service encounter.

Customer disposition to participate refers to the extent to which the customer tends to play an active role in simplifying labor or information input. Table 3.3 shows typical examples for each quadrant and highlights the key players for firms in a quadrant. The latter is broken down according to the servuction model: back office, front office, and customer.

Following operations-management logic, firms then are able to take each quadrant and design the optimal systems linkages using all of the tools described earlier.

SERVICES IN ACTION 3.3

CITICORP

Between 1975 and 1985, the major American bank Citicorp completely overhauled its consumer banking services. Prior to that time, Citicorp's personal-banking services had been very much operations oriented. The bank had strict but traditional measures of good performance. Unfortunately, these measures of good performance did not match what the bank's customers perceived to be good service, with the result that the personal-banking arm of the company was losing money.

Money is the same no matter what bank it comes from, and banks can only market themselves on the basis of the services they offer. For Citicorp, the challenge became one of finding a marketing perspective. At the same time, the company could not afford to give service at any expense or it would lose still more money. There was thus a second challenge—of matching a marketing perspective to the operations perspective and making the two work together.

Personal-banking customers, it was found, wanted services delivered efficiently and quickly, without having to wait in long lines. One possible solution was the automated teller machine (ATM). The advantages of the machine were several: It could be open when the bank itself was closed; it could be set up to operate quickly; and it could be configured to perform a variety of functions, depending on consumer needs. Later, Citicorp ATMs included multilingual versions and had keyboards that allowed customers to issue more complex instructions.

ATMs thus could satisfy both marketing and operations requirements by increasing capacity, production, and profitability while also extending the available range of services and extending capacity to meet demand over a greater range of time. However, such an innovation was easy to copy and Citicorp's widespread introduction of ATMs quickly was imitated by other banks.

Nationally, all bank customers use ATMs for just under one-half of their transactions: in the New York area, where Citicorp has over 1,000 "banking centers," Citicorp's customers use ATMs for over 80 percent of all transactions. It is also worth noting that Citicorp's personal-banking arm made a profit of $548 million in 1987. However, rival banks offering the same types of services were unlikely to let Citicorp retain this position without a struggle. The next challenge was to improve the ATM and the service it offered while continuing to keep both the marketing and operations perspectives.

The result is shown in Table 3.4. The state-of-the-art logic is to tie together the earliest work of Chase with emerging ideas in both marketing and operations.

SUMMARY: THE MARKETING/ OPERATIONS INTERDEPENDENCE

The purpose of this discussion has been to highlight the fact that operations-management problems in services often cannot be solved by the operations function alone. The search for operations efficiency can be crucial to long-run competitiveness. Unfortunately, efficiency has to be balanced against the effectiveness of the system from the customer's point of view, as will be discussed in the next chapter.

TABLE 3.3 A Typology of Service Interdependence Pattern Matching Input Uncertainty

		Customer Disposition to Participate	
		Low	High
	High	Sequential customized design	Reciprocal service design
		Examples: 　Appliance and car repair 　Cleaning	Examples: 　Psychotherapy 　Medical care 　Higher education
Diversity of Demand		Key Player: 　Front office–back office 　Employee interactive	Key Player: 　Customized customer 　Employee interactive
	Low	Pooled-service design	Sequential standard design
		Examples: 　Banks 　Theaters 　Fast-food restaurants	Examples: 　Laundromats 　Supermarkets
		Key Player: 　Standardized back-office 　Dominated	Key Player: 　Customer

Frequently, it is too easy to view the customer as a constraint: "If we could just get rid of these customers, we could run a good service!" Such a negative perspective ignores a golden opportunity. Customers in a service operation can be used to help service operations. Such a positive view, however, does require that operations personnel recognize the importance of their marketing counterparts.

More importantly, such a view also requires that marketing personnel have an intimate knowledge of the operating system and its problems. It is not enough to propose new products that can be delivered through the system. The impact of such products on the whole system needs to be considered.

CHAPTER 3 READINGS

The readings in this chapter focus on the operation problems faced by service firms. In Article 3.1, Chase argues for a clearer understanding of the different roles played by the parts of the organization that do and do not interface with the customer. He argues that the parts of the organization that interface should focus on effectiveness, if necessary at the expense of efficiency. Article 3.2 is relatively theoretical, but draws together the latest themes in service-operations management. Moreover, it provides a powerful integrating framework.

QUESTIONS

1. Using the framework in this chapter, categorize the various ways Arby's has tried to industrialize its service.

2. Describe a recent example familiar to you in which operational demands have necessitated a change in script for the consumer. How was that change managed?

3. A local bank is considering the introduction of a single-line queuing system to replace its current multiline system. Advise the bank's management from both

TABLE 3.4 Portfolios of Coordination Mechanisms for Alternative Designs of Service Interdependence Patterns

Design of service	Interdependence patterns	Area of Coordination		
		Front-office coordination of service interaction	Front/back-office coordination of service support	Back-office coordination of support processing
Sequential standardized service design	Customer dominated	Customer self-adjustment to presupply Large, tightly specified scripts	Routines for presupply	Logistic Planning Decoupling
Reciprocal service design	Customized customer/employee interactive	Customer/employee mutual adjustment Large, loosely specified scripts	Communication Limited decoupling	Programming
Sequential customized service design	Front/back-office employee interactive	Communication and agreement Limited, loosely specified scripts	Adjusting customer orders and input to agreed performances	Planning
Pooled service design	Standardized back-office dominated	Standardization Limited, tightly specified scripts	Information systems Decoupling	Standardized pooling

operations and marketing perspectives, discussing the advantages and disadvantages of change.

4. Choose one of the operations-based strategies discussed in this chapter and discuss its impact on the service providers—the contact staff members.

NOTES

1. Benson P. Shapiro, "Can Marketing and Manufacturing Coexist?" *Harvard Business Review* (September–October 1977): 107–117.

2. J. D. Thompson, *Organizations in Action* (New York: McGraw-Hill, 1967).

3. W. Skinner, "The Focused Factory," *Harvard Business Review* 52, no. 3 (May–June 1974): 113–121.

4. Thompson, *Organizations in Action,* 69.

5. For the application of this idea to banking, see R. J. Matteis, "The New Back Office Focuses on Customer Service," *Harvard Business Review* 57, no. 3 (May–June 1979): 146–159.

6. *Ibid.*

7. These extensions of the customer contact model are developed in Richard B. Chase, "The Customer Contact Approach to Services: Theoretical Base and Practical Extensions," *Operations Research* 29, no. 4 (July–August, 1981): 698–706; and Richard B. Chase and David A. Tansik, "The Customer Contact Model for Organization Design," *Management Service* 29, no. 9 (1983): 1037–1050.

8. B. Danet, "Client–Organization Interfaces," in *Handbook of Organization Design,* vol. 2, eds. P. C. Nystrom and W. N. Starbuck (New York: Oxford University Press, 1981), 384.

9. These studies employed the critical incident technique to look at service encounters that fail. They are described in Mary J. Bitner, Jody D. Nyquist, and Bernard H. Booms, "The Critical Incident Technique for Analyzing the Service Encounter," in *Service Marketing in a Changing Environment,* eds. Thomas M. Block, Gregory D. Upah, and Valarie A. Zeithaml

(Chicago: American Marketing Association, 1985), 48–51; and Jody D. Nyquist, Mary J. Bitner, and Bernard Booms, "Identifying Communications Difficulties in the Service Encounter: A Critical Incident Approach," in *The Service Encounter,* eds. J. Czepiel, M. Solomon, and Carol Surprenant (Lexington, MA: Heath, 1984).

10. Chase, "The Customer Contact Approach to Services," 698–706.

11. For detailed descriptions, see Richard B. Chase and Gerrit Wolf, "Shaping a Strategy for Savings and Loan Branches," Working Paper, Department of Management, College of Business and Public Administration, University of Arizona, 1982; and Richard B. Chase, Gerrit Wolf, and Gregory B. Northcroft, "Designing High Contact Service Systems: Applications to Branches of Savings and Loans," Working Paper, Department of Management, College of Business and Public Administration, University of Arizona, 1983.

12. T. Levitt, "Production-Line Approach to Services," *Harvard Business Review* 50, no. 5 (September–October 1972): 41–52.

13. Carol F. Surprenant and Michael Solomon, "Predictability and Personalization in the Service Encounter," *Journal of Marketing* 51 (April 1987): 86–96.

14. W. Earl Sasser, "Match Supply and Demand in Service Industries," *Harvard Business Review* 54, no. 5 (November–December 1976): 61–65.

15. Chase, "The Customer Contact Approach to Services," 698–706.

16. Benjamin Schneider, "The Service Organization: Climate Is Crucial," *Organizational Dynamics* (Autumn 1980): 52–65.

17. Christopher M. Lovelock and Robert F. Young, "Look to Consumers to Increase Productivity," *Harvard Business Review* (May 1979): 168–178. See also J. E. G. Bateson, "Self-Service Consumer: An Exploratory Study," *Journal of Retailing* 61, no. 3 (Fall 1986): 49–74.

18. Thompson, *Organizations in Action,* 69.

19. Bateson, "Self-Service Consumer," 49–74.

20. See Article 3.3.

21. *Ibid.*

WHERE DOES THE CUSTOMER FIT IN A SERVICE OPERATION?

Richard B. Chase

What do you have to give up in order to let the customer "have it his way"?

While management skills can improve service systems, a manager is better off if he or she first has a clear understanding of the operating characteristics that set one service system apart from another. This author offers one view of services, which, if followed, results in a "rational approach to the rationalization" of services. His view, quite simply, is that the less direct contact the customer has with the service system, the greater the potential of the system to operate at peak efficiency. And, conversely, where the direct customer contact is high, the less the potential that exists to achieve high levels of efficiency. This distinction between high- and low-contact systems provides a basis for classifying service production systems and can enable the manager to develop a more effective service operation.

With the recently legislated increase in the minimum wage law in the United States and the current economic downswing in Europe, service system managers in Western economies can look forward to continued pressure to run their operations more efficiently. While most managers are aware of the success stories of companies in a few industries (notably fast foods), there is little in the way of theory to help them decide how far they should go in altering their products, technologies, work forces, and work methods in attempting to achieve the nebulous goal of an efficient production system for services.

To appreciate the nature of the problem, consider the following stereotypical comment from the operations vice president of a finance company:

"I just don't understand it—the branch managers of our company never seem to run their offices in an efficient fashion. They rarely have the right match between lending personnel and clients demanding their services; they need more typists and clerks to do essentially the same amount of clerical duties that we perform in the home office. In my opinion, what we need is more work out of our methods department to get these branches as efficient as my home office operations. After all, we are in the same company providing the same general service to our customers."

Much has been written about improving service company operations, and many useful distinctions have been drawn among different kinds of service operations. In this article, I wish to propose still another way of looking at service organizations, a method of analysis that can be very helpful to managers. The essential features of this method are a classification scheme for service systems and a list of leading questions to be used in developing a production policy for the service system at hand.

EXTENT OF CONTACT

Service systems are generally classified according to the service they provide, as delineated in the Standard Industrial Classification (SIC) code. This classification, though useful in presenting aggregate economic data for comparative purposes, does not deal with the production of activities through which the service is carried out. What the manager needs, it would seem, is a service classification system that indicates with greater precision

SOURCE: Reprinted by permission of the *Harvard Business Review.* "Where Does the Customer Fit in a Service Operation?" by Richard B. Chase (November–December 1978), pp. 137–142. Copyright © 1978 by the President and Fellows of Harvard College; all rights reserved.

the nature of the demands on his or her particular service system in terms of its operating requirements. In manufacturing, by contrast, there are fairly evocative terms to classify production activities (e.g., unit, batch, and mass production), which, when applied to a manufacturing setting, readily convey the essence of the process.

It is possible, of course, to describe certain service systems using manufacturing terms, but such terms, as in the case of the SIC code, are insufficient for diagnosing and thinking about how to improve the systems without one additional item of information. That item—which I believe operationally distinguishes one service system from another in terms of what they can and cannot achieve in the way of efficiency—is the extent of customer contact in the creation of the service.

To elaborate, *customer contact* refers to the physical presence of the customer in the system, and *creation of the service* refers to the work process that is entailed in providing the service itself. *Extent* of contact here may be roughly defined as the percentage of time the customer must be in the system relative to the total time it takes to serve him. Obviously, the greater the percentage of contact time between the service system and the customer, the greater the degree of interaction between the two during the production process.

From this conceptualization, it follows that service systems with high customer contact are more difficult to control and more difficult to rationalize than those with low customer contact. In high-contact systems, such as those listed in *Exhibit 1,* the customer can affect the time of demand, the exact nature of the service, and the quality of service since he tends to become involved in the process itself. In low-contact systems, by definition, customer interaction with the system is infrequent or of short duration and hence has little impact on the system during the production process.

TECHNICAL CORE

One way to conceive of high- versus low-contact business is that the low-contact system has the capability of decoupling operations and sealing off the "technical core" from the environment, while the high-contact system does not. As one researcher has pointed out, "The technical core must be able to operate as if the market will absorb the single kind of product at a continuous rate, and as if inputs flowed continuously at a steady rate with specified quality."[1] Indeed, decoupling production from outside influences (for example, via inventory

buffers) is a common objective in designing manufacturing systems.

Several industries provide examples of shifts in customer contact through two or more of the stages given in *Exhibit 1:*

☐ Automatic banking tellers, with their 24-hour availability and their location for easy access, illustrate pure service; branch offices, with their provision of drive-in tellers, coordinated waiting lines, and often visible back offices, illustrate mixed service; and home offices, designed for efficient receipt, processing, and shipping of bank paper, illustrate quasimanufacturing.

☐ Airlines exhibit mixed-service characteristics at their terminals (high-contact ticket counters and low-contact baggage handling), pure service characteristics within the planes, and quasimanufacturing characteristics in their billing and airplane maintenance operations.

☐ Blood collection stations provide an obvious example of pure service—they are (or should be) operated with the psychological and physiological needs of the donor in mind and, in fact, often take the "service" to the donor by using bloodmobiles. The blood itself is processed at specialized facilities (bloodbanks) following "manufacturing" procedures common to batch processing.

☐ Many consulting firms switch back and forth between pure service and quasimanufacturing. Pure service takes place when data are gathered at the client's facility, while quasimanufacturing takes place when data are analyzed and reports are prepared at the firm's home offices. Other firms, of course, have facilities designed for mixed service operations; their client waiting areas are planned in detail to convey a particular image, and back offices are arranged for efficient noncontact work.

EFFECT ON OPERATIONS

Of course, the reason it is important to determine how much customer contact is required to provide a service is that is has an effect on every decision that production managers must make. *Exhibit 2* is a list of some of the more interesting decisions relating to system design. The points made in this exhibit lead to four generalizations about the two classes of service systems.

First, high-contact systems have more uncertainty about their day-to-day operations since the customer can always make an input to (or cause a disruption in) the production process. Even in those high-contact systems that have relatively highly specified products and

---

[1]James D. Thompson, *Organizations in Action* (New York: McGraw-Hill, 1967), 20.

EXHIBIT 1   Classification of Service Systems by Extent of Required Customer Contact in Creation of the Service

High contact	*Pure service:*	**Increasing freedom in designing efficient production procedures**
	Health centers	
	Hotels	
	Public transportation	
	Restaurants	
	Schools	
	Personal services	
	Mixed service:	
	Branch offices of:	
	Banks	
	Computer companies	
	Real estate	
	Post offices	
	Funeral homes	
	Quasimanufacturing:	
	Home offices of:	
	Banks	
	Computer companies	
	Government administration	
	Wholesale houses	
	Post offices	
	Manufacturing:	
	Factories producing durable goods	
	Food processors	
	Mining companies	
Low contact	Chemical plants	

processes, the customer can "have it his way." Burger King will fill special orders, TWA will (on occasion) delay a takeoff for a late arrival, a hospital operating room schedule will be disrupted for emergency surgery, and so on.

Second, unless the system operates on an appointments-only basis, it is only by happenstance that the capacity of a high-contact system will match the demand on that system at any given time.[2] The manager of a supermarket, branch bank, or entertainment facility can predict only statistically the number of people that will be in line demanding service at, say, two o'clock on Tuesday afternoon. Hence employing the correct number of servers (neither too many nor too few) must also depend on probability.

Low-contact systems, on the other hand, have the potential to exactly match supply and demand for their services since the work to be done (e.g., forms to be completed, credit ratings analyzed, or household goods shipped) can be carried out following a resource-oriented schedule permitting a direct equivalency between producer and product.

Third, by definition, the required skills of the work force in high-contact systems are characterized by a significant public relations component. Any interaction with the customer makes the direct worker in fact part of the product and therefore his attitude can affect the customer's view of the service provided.

Finally, high-contact systems are at the mercy of time far more than low-contact systems. Batching of orders for purposes of efficient production scheduling is rarely possible in high-contact operations since a few minutes' delay or a violation of the law of the queue (first come, first served) has an immediate effect on the customer. Indeed, "unfair" preferential treatment in a

[2]For a detailed discussion of capacity planning in services, see W. Earl Sasser, "Match Supply and Demand in Service Industries," *Harvard Business Review* (November–December 1976): 132.

EXHIBIT 2   Major Design Considerations in High- and Low-Contact Systems

Decision	High-Contact System	Low-Contact System
Facility location	Operations must be near the customer.	Operations may be placed near supply, transportation, or labor.
Facility layout	Facility should accommodate the customer's physical and psychological needs and expectations.	Facility should enhance production.
Product design	Environment as well as the physical product define the nature of the service.	Customer is not in the service environment, so the product can be defined by fewer attributes.
Process design	Stages of production process have a direct immediate effect on the customer.	Customer is not involved in the majority of processing steps.
Scheduling	Customer is in the production schedule and must be accommodated.	Customer is concerned mainly with completion dates.
Production planning	Orders cannot be stored, so smoothing production flow will result in loss of business.	Both backlogging and production smoothing are possible.
Worker skills	Direct work force comprises a major part of the service product and so must be able to interact well with the public.	Direct work force need only have technical skills.
Quality control	Quality standards are often in the eye of the beholder and hence variable.	Quality standards are generally measurable and hence fixed.
Time standards	Service time depends on customer needs, and therefore time standards are inherently loose.	Work is performed on customer surrogates (e.g., forms), and time standards can be tight.
Wage payment	Variable output requires time-based wage systems.	"Fixable" outputs permit output-based wage systems.
Capacity planning	To avoid lost sales, capacity must be set to match peak demand.	Storable output permits setting capacity at some average demand level.
Forecasting	Forecasts are short term, time-oriented.	Forecasts are long term, output-oriented.

line at a box office often gives rise to some of the darker human emotions, which are rarely evoked by the same unfair preferential treatment that is employed by a distant ticket agency whose machinations go unobserved by the customer.

IMPLICATIONS FOR MANAGEMENT

Several implications may be drawn from the foregoing discussion of differences between high-contact and low-contact systems.

To start with, rationalizing the operations of a high-contact system can be carried only so far. While technological devices can be substituted for some jobs performed by direct-contact workers, the worker's attitude, the environment of the facility, and the attitude of the customer will determine the ultimate quality of the service experience.

Another point to keep in mind is that the often-drawn distinction between for-profit and not-for-profit services has little, if any, meaning from a production

management standpoint. A not-for-profit home office can be operated as efficiently as a for-profit home office, and conversely, a high-contact for-profit branch is subject to the same inherent limitations on its efficiency as its not-for-profit counterpart.

Clearly, wherever possible, a distinction should be made between the high-contact and low-contact elements of a service system. This can be done by a separation of functions: all high-contact activities should be performed by one group of people, all low-contact activities by another. Such an adjustment minimizes the influence of the customer on the production process and provides opportunities to achieve efficiency where it is actually possible to do so.

Finally, it follows that separation of functions enhances the development of two contrasting classes of worker skills and orientations—public relations and interpersonal attributes for high-contact purposes and technical and analytical attributes for low-contact purposes. While some writers have urged mixing of duties under the general rubric of job enrichment, a careful analysis before doing so seems warranted when one recognizes the considerable differences in the skills required between high- and low-contact systems.

POLICY DEVELOPMENT

Applying the foregoing concepts for developing a production policy for services entails answering several questions:

What kind of operating system do you have?

Is it a pure service, mixed service, or quasimanufacturing? What percentage of your business activity in terms of labor hours is devoted to direct customer contact?

A good indication of where a production system falls along the contact continuum can be obtained by using the industrial engineering technique of work sampling. This approach involves taking a statistically determined random sample of work activities to find out how much time is being spent in customer-contact work. The Pacific Finance Company has regularly used this method to determine if a branch office is properly staffed and if some of its paperwork activities should be shifted to the home office. Another industrial engineering technique, process charting, has been used successfully to help specify the proper balance between front-office and back-office capacity in the mixed services operations of the Arizona Auto Licensing Bureau.

Are your operating procedures geared to your present structure?

Specifically, have you matched your compensation system to the nature of the service system—for example, high-contact systems based on time and low-contact systems on output? Are you appropriately allocating contact and no-contact tasks? Are you using cost or profit centers where these two measures are subject to control by the on-site manager?

Obviously, paying service workers according to the number of customers served tends to speed up service in the high-contact system. However, with the exception of extremely simple standardized operations, such as toll booths, mailing a package from a post office, and supermarket checkouts, speed of processing is not the most important element of service to the customer. Indeed, if the customer feels rushed in a hospital, bank, or restaurant, he is likely to be dissatisfied with the organization.

Further, it makes little sense for a seller of any service that can be at all customized to measure system effectiveness in terms of total number of customers served when in fact one should be giving more leisurely attention to a similar number of "big spenders." (The reader may verify this point by comparing the attention accorded the casino bettor at the $2 blackjack table with the amenities observed at the $25 table.)

Can you realign your operations to reduce unnecessary direct customer service?

Can tasks performed in the presence of the customer be shifted to the back office? Can you divide your labor force into high-contact and no-contact areas? Can you set up plants within plants to permit development of unique organizational structures for a narrower set of tasks for each subunit of the service organization?[3]

The idea of shifting operations to the back office has recently become popular among tax preparation companies that now take a client's tax records and prepare a computer-processed return in his absence. Likewise, word-processing centers prepare documents in the absence of the customer, who provides original copy.

Managers have long recognized the desirability of having "attractive" personnel greet the public in such job classifications as receptionist, restaurant hostess, and stewardess, while being more concerned with technical skills on the part of those individuals removed from customer contact, such as typists, cooks, and those in maintenance positions. Plants-within-plants are typical in hospitals (e.g., labs, food service, and laundry), in insurance companies (e.g., underwriters, pool typists, and records), and in restaurants (e.g., cooking, table service, and bar).

Can you take advantage of the efficiencies offered by low-contact operations?

In particular, can you apply the production management concepts of batch scheduling, forecasting, inventory control, work measurement, and simplification to back-office operations? Can you now use the latest technologies in assembling, packaging, cooking, testing, and so on, to support front-office operations?

The production management literature offers numerous applications of the foregoing concepts to low-contact systems. One interesting example concerns the improvement of the forecasting procedure used to determine manpower requirements at the Chemical Bank of New York.[4] Daily volume of transit checks (checks drawn on other banks and cashed at Chemical Bank)

---

[3]See Wickham Skinner, "The Focused Factory," *Harvard Business Review* (May–June 1974): 113.

[4]Kevin Boyd and Vincent A. Mabert, "Two-Stage Forecasting Approach at Chemical Bank of New York for Check Processing," *Journal of Bank Research* (Summer 1977): 101.

averages $2 billion a day, often with a $1 billion variation from day to day. The new forecasting method employs a two-stage approach using multiple regression followed by exponential smoothing to forecast daily loads in pounds of checks per day. This approach yields significant improvement in forecast accuracy over the previous intuitive methods and thereby provides a basis for effective production planning.

Can you enhance the customer contact you do provide?

With all nonessential customer-contact duties shifted, can you speed up operations, by adding part-time, more narrowly skilled workers at peak hours, keep longer business hours, or add personal touches to the contacts you do have?

The key to employing this step lies in recognizing the implications of Sasser's and Pettway's observation: "Although bank tellers, chambermaids, and short-order cooks may have little in common, they are all at the forefront of their employer's public images."[5] If the low-contact portion of a worker's job can be shifted to a different work force, then the opportunity exists to focus that worker's efforts on critical interpersonal relations aspects.

For example, store sales personnel are frequently called on to engage in stock clerk activities which often must take precedence over waiting on customers. However, since the salesperson's central function is as a company representative within the store, it may be better to hire more stock clerks and free the salesperson to fulfill that personal function.

Can you relocate parts of your service operations to lower your facility costs?

Can you shift back-room operations to lower rent districts, limit your contact facilities to small drop-off

facilities (à la Fotomat), or get out of the contact facilities business entirely through the use of jobbers or vending machines?

Unless it is an essential feature of the service package, or an absolute necessity for coordination purposes, managers should carefully scrutinize back-office operations before appending them to customer-contact facilities. As advocated throughout this article, high- and low-contact operations are inherently different and should be located and staffed to maximize their individual as well as joint contribution to the organization. The notion of decentralizing service depots as indicated by my examples is, of course, a well-understood marketing strategy, but it deserves additional consideration as an alternative use of service "production" capacity.

APPLYING THE CONCEPT

Going through the process of answering these policy questions should trigger other questions about the service organization's operation and mission. In particular, it should lead management to question whether its strength lies in high contact or low contact, and it should encourage reflection on what constitutes an optimal balance between the two types of operations relative to resource allocation and market emphasis.

Also, the process should lead to an analysis of the organization structure that is required to effectively administer the individual departments as well as the overall organization of the service business. For example, it is quite probable that separate managements and internally differentiated structures will be in order if tight coordination between high-contact and low-contact units is not necessary. Where tight coordination is necessary, particular attention must be paid to boundary-spanning activities of both labor and management to assure a smooth exchange of material and information among departments.

---

[5]W. Earl Sasser and Samuel H. Pettway, "Case of Big Mac's Pay Plans," *Harvard Business Review* (July–August 1974): 30.

ORGANIZATION AND CUSTOMER: MANAGING DESIGN AND COORDINATION OF SERVICES

Rikard Larsson

University of Southern California and University of Lund, Sweden

David E. Bowen

University of Southern California

Customer participation in the operations of service organizations can be a major source of input uncertainty. A framework for analyzing service organizations is presented in which different conditions of input uncertainty are matched with the design of different interdependence patterns which, in turn, are matched to different portfolios of coordination mechanisms. The composition of portfolios drawn on both the conventional organizational literature and recent work on control mechanisms at the client/service firm interface.

The organization–customer interface deserves to be an important focus of analysis within organizational theory, particularly given the shift from a manufacturing-oriented economy to one that is more service dominated (Davis, 1983). The production and delivery of services typically involves considerable contact between the organization and customers; customers frequently participate in service production tasks performed at the organization–customer interface (Bowen & Schneider, 1988; Lovelock, 1984; Mills, 1986). Nevertheless, the tendency remains for authors to depict customers as being buffered from the core technology and to treat them only as consumers, not as producers.

This paper examines how varying forms of co-production by employees and customers affect the design and coordination of service systems. First, we review alternative perspectives on the service organization–customer interface. Then we develop a framework for coordinating service interdependencies that integrates orga-

nizational contingency theory (e.g., Lawrence & Lorsch, 1967; Thompson, 1967) and the emergent services literature (e.g., Czepiel, Solomon, & Surprenant, 1985). This is done with some support from the areas of marketing and economics. Our framework treats customer participation in service production and delivery as a source of input uncertainty (Argote, 1982), a concept that we elaborate on relative to prior treatments of the uncertainty concept (e.g., Brass, 1985; Galbraith, 1973; Slocum & Sims, 1980; Thompson, 1967). Next, we present a typology of four service interdependence patterns that matches alternative designs of the service system to alternative conditions of input uncertainty. Finally, we match these alternative interdependence patterns of the typology to appropriate portfolios of coordination mechanisms (cf. McCann & Galbraith, 1981), which have been drawn from the conventional *intra*organizational coordination literature and the service literature's

SOURCE: © *Academy of Management Review* vol. 14, no. 2 (1989): 213–233.

Rikard Larsson is a doctoral candidate of the University of Lund, Sweden, and the School of Business, University of Southern California.

David E. Bowen (Ph.D., Michigan State University) is Assistant Professor of Management and Organization in the School of Business, University of Southern California, Los Angeles. Correspondence regarding this paper can be sent to him at the MOR Department, School of Business, University of Southern California, Los Angeles, CA 90089-1421.

This research has in part been funded by Tore Browaldh's Research Foundation, Sweden. We thank Gareth R. Jones, Peter W. Kreiner, and Bjorn Bjerke for comments on an earlier draft.

description of the control mechanisms at the organization–customer interface. We conclude with research propositions that are indicated by the framework and implications for strategic management and marketing.

THE SERVICE ORGANIZATION—CUSTOMER INTERFACE: AN OVERVIEW OF DIFFERENT PERSPECTIVES

Organization–customer relationships have been conceptualized from diverse perspectives. In economics they are viewed in terms of aggregated meetings of supply and demand coordinated by the invisible hand of the price mechanism (Smith, 1937; cf. Scherer, 1980). In organization theory an open systems perspective is applied in which organizations adapt to conditions of the environment of which customers are components (Lawrence & Lorsch, 1967; Scott, 1981; Thompson, 1967). In marketing, an organization reactively adapts to customers through the marketing concept, and actively influences customers through product, place, promotion, and price variables (Borden, 1964; Houston, 1986; Kotler, 1980).

Many works in the literature on services claim that these established perspectives include a bias toward manufacturing that limits their applicability to service organizations, given the differences between goods and services (Berry, 1980; Mills & Margulies, 1980; Sasser, 1976; Shostack, 1977; Thomas, 1978; Zeithaml, Parasuraman, & Berry, 1985). Indeed, the phenomenon of customers participating in the production of services (more so than goods) is not easily addressed through established perspectives. For example, in economics the focus is on the market coordination of organizational supply of output and the customer demand for it. However, in services, customers are not simply a source of demand, they also are a source of production inputs in the form of information, their bodies, or their labor (Fuchs, 1968; Hill, 1977; Lovelock, 1983; Mills, 1986). Thus, in order to be effective, the price mechanism would require complete contracting of not only organizational supply of output but also customer supply of inputs and the coordination of co-production (i.e., joint production by service employees and customers). However, customer supply of inputs introduces substantial uncertainty in service production that prohibits complete contracting and restricts the utility of a market governance mechanism (cf. Arrow, 1974; Mills, 1986; Williamson, 1975, 1979). Organization theory is limited given the noted tendency to view production as internal conversion processes by employees who are sealed off/buffered from environmental uncertainty, for example, customers (Mills & Moberg, 1982; Thompson, 1967). With respect to marketing, traditionally, its functions are viewed as separate from production. However, service co-production tends to merge the two (Gronroos, 1982; Gummesson, 1979; Northcraft & Chase, 1985).

Recognizing these limitations, a number of researchers in the services literature have explicitly addressed the service organization–customer interface, yet their works also have limitations, which are understandable because these were initial attempts to explain a relatively ignored issue. The customer-contact model (Chase, 1978, 1981; Chase & Tansik, 1983) differentiated between high- and low-customer-contact services and suggested some of the possible organizational design implications of each. However, the model has limitations because it is based on only one dimension, customer contact, and this dimension also fails to differentiate between active versus passive customer presence (Schmenner, 1986). Several two-dimensional typologies have been developed that, at least implicitly, extended Chase's customer-contact model. For example, the two dimensions, extent of customer contact and extent of customization, were used by Lovelock (1983) and Maister and Lovelock (1982); the two dimensions, degree of interaction and degree of customization, were used by Schmenner (1986).

The most visible service organization typology, however, is found in Mills' work (Mills, 1986; Mills & Margulies, 1980; Mills & Morris, 1986), which presents three types of service organizations that are classified based on various low-, medium-, or high-level combinations of seven service organization–customer interface variables (e.g., information exchange at the interface, time spent interfacing). Although this framework offers a more finely grained treatment of the interface, it also is burdened with how the resulting complexity compromises the typology. For example, the typology is not exhaustive because the three types do not cover all possible combinations of the seven interface variables, and it is not mutually exclusive (as noted by Snyder, Cox, & Jesse, 1982) because any service organization could include characteristics of more than one of the three alternative types of organizations.

Another limitation of most service organization typologies is that they are developed as definitional classifications of alternative designs that are outside of a contingency framework. That is, the characteristics of the interface are themselves the characteristics used to type organizations—the interface characteristics are *not* treated as contingencies faced by the organization which, in turn, suggest a separate set of design characteristics which then become the basis for labeling alternative types of service organizations. An analogous approach to the one used in such typologies would have been if Burns and Stalker (1961) specified the characteristics of organic and mechanistic organizational designs without stating that they are most appropriate in turbulent and stable environments, as described by a different set of characteristics.

Mills (1986), who mixed both environmental and organizational characteristics in his typology, may be viewed as an exception to this non-contingency rule in service frameworks. A clear exception is the transaction cost analysis of service organization–customer exchange offered by Bowen and Jones (1986), which presented four different types of service organizations that were based on matching the use of different governance mechanisms at the organization–customer interface to varying conditions of performance ambiguity and goal congruence faced by the organization.

Another limitation of these prior service perspectives is that they were focused primarily on coordination issues at the service organization–customer interface without researchers developing the implications of this unique interface for the overall coordination of the service system. Although the customer-contact model (Chase, 1978, 1981; Chase & Tansik, 1983) stresses the importance of coordinating back-office and front-office operations, it offers little guidance on how to do so. Even though the works of Lovelock (1983), Maister and Lovelock (1982), and Schmenner (1986) raise management issues relevant to each of their types, they generally ignore coordination concerns and totally ignore a systematic, theoretical development of the issues. Clearly, Mills' typology (Mills, 1986; Mills & Margulies, 1980; Mills & Morris, 1986) is based on characteristics of the service organization–customer interface, and only recently does some empirical work begin to address the relationship between that interface and organizational technology and structure (Mills & Turk, 1986).

Although there are individual exceptions to each of the above cited limitations of previous service typologies, very few efforts handle most of them and no single typology appears to overcome them all. In what follows, we address these limitations by offering a contingency framework for examining the total system design and coordination implications of the service organization–customer interface. The focus is on how the relationship between the service organization and customers influences the management of differentiation and inte-

gration across the entire system (cf. Lawrence & Lorsch, 1967). We attempt to integrate the explanatory power of established frameworks, particularly organizational contingency theory, with the more recent frameworks of the services literature, rather than contributing to the apparent development of allegedly separate traditional manufacturing and service theories. The starting point is the development of the concept of input uncertainty.

A FRAMEWORK FOR THE DESIGN AND COORDINATION OF SERVICE INTERDEPENDENCIES

Figure 1 offers a model to guide the design and coordination of service operations in which differing conditions of input uncertainty are matched with alternative interdependence patterns which, in turn, are matched to different coordination mechanisms, consistent with the contingency framework of the organizational literature on coordination.

INPUT UNCERTAINTY IN SERVICE OPERATIONS

In general, uncertainty is conceptualized as incomplete information about varying foci, including tasks (e.g., the use of different technologies), the environment (e.g., customer demands), and inputs to production (e.g., raw material quality). For instance, Galbraith (1973, p. 5) defined *uncertainty* as "the difference between the amount of information required to perform the task and the amount of information already possessed by the organization." The task, as with any instrumental action, can be seen as rooted in desired outcomes and beliefs of cause/effect relationships (Thompson, 1967). Thus, organizations can have incomplete information about what outcomes are desired and how to accomplish the tasks that produce them.

Slocum and Sims (1980) further specified the uncertainty concept by identifying two sources: task uncertainty, which is incomplete information about how to accomplish tasks, and workflow uncertainty, which is incomplete information about when input will arrive to be processed. Brass (1985) identified three sources: input uncertainty, conversion uncertainty, and output uncertainty. Brass's input uncertainty resembles Slocum and Sims's (1980) workflow uncertainty, and conversion uncertainty resembles task uncertainty. Brass's output uncertainty resembles the desired outcome uncertainty at least implied by Thompson (1967). However, Brass's output uncertainty is restricted to knowledge of when and where outputs will be distributed and not what outputs to distribute.

FIGURE 1   A Framework for the Design and Coordination of Service Interdependencies

Input Uncertainty		Interdependence Patterns		Portfolios of Coordination Mechanisms

Contingent upon:
—Diversity of demand
—Customer disposition to participate
	First Match	—Division of work:
		  Front-office employees
		  Back-office employees
		  Customers
		—Customized vs. standardized inter-dependencies
			Second Match	—Different mechanisms
				—Main locus of portfolio

The relationship among these various sources of uncertainty is depicted in Table 1, which also indicates how they can be extended to a service setting. Extending Slocum and Sims's (1980) and Brass's (1985) conceptions of uncertainty to a service setting is complicated because they did not distinguish whether their sources of uncertainty stem directly from the environment or from within the organization. Yet this distinction is crucial to how organizations approach different sources of uncertainty (cf. Thompson's, 1967, environmental contingencies versus internal interdependence). Furthermore, their separation of the input and conversion subsystems is more relevant to manufacturing than to service industries due to customer input of labor and information during the service operation.

Argote's (1982) concept of input uncertainty offered researchers a means by which to integrate these sources of uncertainty relative to the service organization–customer interface. She suggested a movement "from diffuse characterizations of an organization's environment or task to more precise descriptions of the uncertainty characterizing a particular element of an organization's task environment" (1982, p. 422). Thus, in her study of hospital emergency units, Argote presented patient inputs as the principle source of uncertainty and developed the concept of input uncertainty differently from Brass (1985) in that it "bridges the somewhat artificial distinction between environmental and task-related uncertainty. Input uncertainty stems from the external environment with which the various units are in continuous contact, yet it has an immediate impact on the tasks that the units perform" (1982, p. 422).

We suggest that Argote's view of input uncertainty generally is a useful conceptualization for service operations. Bridging environmental and task uncertainty is

the essence of boundary operations in service production (cf. Rousseau, 1979). Customer inputs can be (a) his/her specification of desired outcomes; (b) his/her body, mind, and/or goods to be serviced; and (c) his/her actions participating in the service production. These inputs, controlled by the customers, are relatively unknown to the service organization before the specific service performance (Thompson, 1962). Thus, customer inputs are environmental sources of incomplete information for the service organization's performance of specific service tasks, at least until the actual service encounter. There are, of course, internal sources of uncertainty, for example, incomplete employee knowledge of how to perform a specific task, given high task difficulty. However, we can expect an organization to have more complete knowledge about the tasks it offers with supposed expertise than about what customer input it will face because in this latter case it has far less authority (Thompson, 1962).

Building on these prior treatments, we offer the following definition: *Customer-induced input uncertainty is the organization's incomplete information about what, where, when, and how customer input is going to be processed to produce desired outcomes.* This includes the full set of uncertainty sources in Table 1. Overall, this concept of input uncertainty is different from conventional concepts of environmental uncertainty, which can be buffered from the technical core, and task uncertainty, which includes internal sources of uncertainty under hierarchical control of the organization. Although buffering and hierarchical control are present to some extent, these options, which are readily available in manufacturing operations, are limited in services by the predominance of customer input and boundary operations.

TABLE 1   General and Service Sources of Uncertainty

Sources of Uncertainty	General Concepts			Service Concepts
Incomplete information about:	Slocum and Sims, 1980	Brass, 1985	Thompson, 1967	Input uncertainty stemming from the customer(/environment building on Argote, 1982)
what to process, where to process it,	} Input uncertainty			Customer's supply (of object) Customer's supply (place)
when to process it,	Workflow uncertainty			Customer's supply (time)
how to process it,	Task uncertainty	Conversion	Cause–effect uncertainty	Customer's supply (of labor) relationships
into what, distributed where,	} Output uncertainty		} Desired outcomes	Customer's desired (object) outcome Customer's desired (place) outcome
distributed when.				Customer's desired (time) outcome

CONDITIONS OF INPUT UNCERTAINTY

We can expect the input uncertainty that the customer poses for service operations to vary with two environmental variables: the diversity of customer demand and the tendency of customers to participate in the performance of the service (Bowen & Jones, 1986). Customers present the service organization with incomplete information regarding either what (customer mind, body, and/or goods) is to be serviced toward which desired outcomes or what actions they will contribute in service co-production. Thus, these two sources can be used for a two-dimensional framework of different conditions of input uncertainty in service production.

Diversity of demand refers to the uniqueness of customers' demands. This includes both the uniqueness of the customer's supply of goods and/or self that is to be serviced and the uniqueness of the desired outcome. It corresponds to how wide a range of patient conditions/inputs the emergency units faced in Argote's (1982) study. The wider the range of unique customer demands, the greater the specific information not possessed by the organization before the actual service encounter and, thereby, the higher the input uncertainty faced by the organization. Also, high diversity refers to qualitative differences in demand, for example, different car problems; demand of the same service in different quantities is viewed as low diversity, for example, different amounts of deposits in similar bank accounts. Thus, the dimension is related to the customization-standardization distinction found in the literature on service organizations (Berry, 1980; Levitt, 1976; Matteis, 1979), but it represents environmental condi

tions *facing* organizations to which they can respond with more or less customized service designs. Therefore, customization-standardization can be seen as the designed diversity of service supply that can be matched to the diversity of demand.

Customer disposition to participate refers to the extent the customer tends to play an active role in supplying labor or information inputs to the service production process. The more actions the customers tend to contribute, the higher the input uncertainty because the organization has incomplete information about what the customer actually will do before the service encounter (Thompson, 1962). This dimension stresses the degree of active customer participation as opposed to Chase's (1978, 1981) high versus low contact dimension, which depends only on the customer's presence.

The disposition to participate is driven primarily by customer motivation, which, in turn, stems from at least two sources: (a) Customers find doing it for themselves intrinsically attractive (Bateson, 1983), which means customers prefer to be involved in serving themselves even without a price reduction, and (b) customers may feel that their active involvement is necessary to guarantee quality. This is in line with the agency theory rationale for the customer principal to monitor the service agent's fulfillment of the service contract (Mills, 1986). It also includes the possibility of unique customer competencies, such as information about the financial, legal, psychological, or physical situations that the customer may need to supply, firsthand, during service production.

Customer disposition to participate can be constrained by insufficient ability (in terms of knowledge, physical strength and skills, and time) or role clarity (in terms of understanding their role in the service co-production). In other words, customers may lack the competence and role readiness necessary to participate (Mills & Morris, 1986). Thus, this dimension represents how willing the customers are to actively participate, given that they are capable of handling what the role entails and are clear about it (Bowen, 1986; cf. Vroom, 1964).

In sum, customers are a source of input uncertainty relative to the diversity of their demands and their disposition to participate. These variables are customer characteristics external to the organization, constituting constraints and contingencies to which the design of the organization must adapt (Thompson, 1967). This adaptation can be both anticipatory in start-up designs and reactive as the service operations evolve over time. It should be observed that the service organization can also actively influence these environmental variables. Advertising can increase customer awareness of, and positive attitudes toward, product differences, thereby raising diversity of demand (e.g., Kotler, 1980). Also, lowering prices can induce customers to sacrifice more expensive customized product differentiation and/or motivate customers to provide some of the service labor themselves. For instance, banks can impose service charges for transactions using bank tellers but not for transactions using automatic teller machines. For the sake of clarity, first, we will present the reactive contingency framework, and, second, we will address how to influence these environmental contingencies in the discussion.

INTERDEPENDENCE PATTERNS

The design of service operations can be viewed in terms of different interdependence patterns consisting of (a) division of service work between employees and customers and (b) customization versus standardization of service actions and interdependencies. The design of service production includes the division of work not only among employees but also between employees and customers. Traditionally, organizational theorists have focused on the division of work among employees (which is natural from a manufacturing standpoint). Yet in service organizations, Chase's (1978, 1981) two-fold division of labor between front and back offices can be elaborated on to more fully identify the customer's place in the division of service work. According to Chase, front-office work is performed by service employees in contact with customers and/or it is performed by the customers themselves; back-office employees perform functions separate from customers. Whereas Chase's

work addressed the implications of only front- versus back-office activity, the present discussion develops the implications of service work divided among three parties: back-office (low-contact) employees, front-office (high-contact) employees, and customers.

This division of work creates interdependencies among the actions of the three parties. The character of these interdependencies can be more or less customized or standardized. The more customized the service, the more unique (highly differentiated) the interdependencies between the actions of the divided service work. (Differentiation, here, refers to providing unique products to meet customer needs [Porter, 1985]. It should not be confused with structural differentiation in relation to division of work and decoupling.) Correspondingly, the more standardized the service, the more repetitive and the less differentiated the actions and the interdependencies.

MATCHING INPUT UNCERTAINTY AND INTERDEPENDENCE PATTERNS

Dichotomizing the two customer input dimensions yields four basic conditions of input uncertainty facing the service organization. The contingency logic of the first match in Figure 1 is that organizations attempt to adapt the design of service interdependence patterns to the conditions they face. This design determines the input uncertainty *allowed* in the service production. Conceivably, a service organization that faces both high demand diversity and high customer disposition to participate could design a highly standardized and nonparticipative service system. This would reduce customer-induced uncertainty in the production. However, we suggest that this would be counterproductive because it can be expected to frustrate customer demands. Thus, the underlying rationale of the proposed contingency relationship is that of the marketing concept: to achieve organizational goals by adapting the organization to satisfy target customer desires (Houston, 1986; Keith, 1960; Kotler, 1980). Also, it would be unnecessarily costly to allow for more diversity and/or participation than the service organization typically faces (cf. Chase, 1978, 1981; Levitt, 1972, 1976).

Different conditions of input uncertainty can be matched with different designs of service interdependence patterns. First, customization follows the logic that the higher the demand diversity, the greater the need for customization rather than standardization, and vice versa. If customers want uniqueness, they are willing to pay a premium price for differentiated services (Porter, 1985). This conclusion is consistent with the economic notion of product differentiation in which the seller can raise prices without sacrificing the entire sales volume, as opposed to the case of product homogeneity (Scherer, 1980). If this customization is less important to the customer, then "speed, consistency, and price savings [through standardized mass production] may be more important to many customers than customized service" (Lovelock, 1984, p. 57).

Regarding the match to division of work, the less customer disposition to participate, the more work can be shifted from customers to service employees. Further, the lower the customer disposition to participate, the greater the amount of work that can be shifted to the more efficient operations of the back office decoupled from the more disruptive front office (Chase, 1978, 1981; Danet, 1981; Levitt, 1976). Conversely, the more the customer disposition to participate, the greater the amount of work that can be shifted to the customer. This is in line with suggestions to utilize customers as partial employees in order to take advantage of customer motivation, competencies, and labor (Bowen, 1986; Eiglier & Langeard, 1977; Lovelock & Young, 1979; Mills & Morris, 1986). It seems more appropriate to decouple front- and back-office operations when the service design is standardized because customization requires more coupling/interaction between customer/front office and back office to ensure accurate performance of unique demand (cf. Chase & Tansik, 1983). Therefore, decoupled divisions can be expected to accompany standardized service designs matching low demand diversity. These decoupled divisions allow either the customers or back-office employees to do most of the service work. Conversely, coupled divisions between two of the three parties that work more interactively are likely to accompany customized service designs matching high demand diversity.

Figure 2 shows how the two contingencies governing input uncertainty—diversity of demand and customer disposition to participate—create four distinct conditions of input uncertainty. Combining the matching logic above gives rise to four different service design configurations (cf. Mintzberg, 1979) with distinct interdependence patterns that match these four conditions. The interdependence patterns are symbolized in the figure in terms of the three parties of the service work division (Back- and Front-office employees and Customers) and the main locus of interdependencies. The latter is centered around the dominant party(ies) of the division of service work (i.e., where the most interdependencies are located). The labels of the interdependence patterns are discussed in the next section.

FOUR ALTERNATIVE SERVICE INTERDEPENDENCE PATTERNS

Quadrant I. In situations of high customer disposition to participate and low diversity of demand, the bulk of the workload can be placed on customers if they have adequate ability and are clear about their roles. Here, customers are expected to be more sensitive to prices since they forgo customization and provide most of the labor themselves. By standardizing the supply of goods, facilities, and so forth, organizations can mass-produce inexpensive services. (If not, these may be services that customers will perform for themselves.) This also means that employees' work is held to a minimum to keep costs down, while the organization utilizes customer disposition to participate. Some customers may simply enjoy serving themselves. It is unlikely that their participation will be motivated by a need to monitor service quality, given the clarity of standardized options (Mills, 1986). Furthermore, standardization allows extensive decoupling between front and back office for efficient delivery of service. Typical examples of this design include laundromats, car rentals, and self-service retails stores, that is, businesses that have relatively standardized options.

Quadrant II. If customers have complex and unique problems (i.e., high demand diversity), then it can be expected that they will be less price sensitive and will want expertise for customized solutions to their problems. The customer's self, rather than his or her goods, is often the focus of these complex services. This can be a strong source of motivation for them to actively participate in order either to obtain intrinsic rewards or to monitor the quality of the service. The high disposition to participate also can stem from the need for the customer to provide information for adequate problem solving throughout service production. This leads to interactive service production between mainly customer and front-office employees that is typically found in professional services such as psychotherapy, medical care, legal advice, and higher education (cf. Sasser, Olsen, & Wyckoff, 1978).

Quadrant III. High diversity of demand also can be accompanied by low customer disposition to participate. Many unique services are purchased for mere convenience when customers prefer to have others perform the services for them (without necessarily lacking the expertise as in the case of professional services). This could be because of the lack of time (cf. Fuchs, 1968) or the customer's low intrinsic motivation to participate in menial services. Here, the bulk of the workload is placed on service employees. Front-office employees take in the customer's specifications of the service, and it is per-

FIGURE 2   A Typology of Service Interdependence Patterns Matching Input Uncertainty

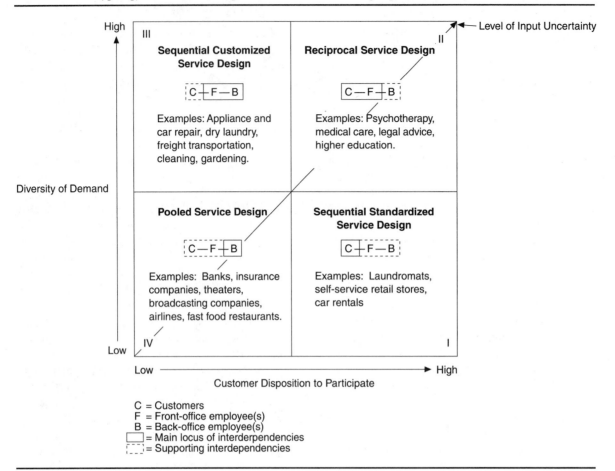

C = Customers
F = Front-office employee(s)
B = Back-office employee(s)
☐ = Main locus of interderpendencies
⌐⌐⌐ = Supporting interdependencies

formed by back-office employees. Examples include tailoring of clothes and repair services. The separation of high- and low-contact functions allows for the specialization of interpersonal versus technical skills of front- and back-office employees, respectively (Chase, 1978, 1981; Chase & Tansik, 1983). However, this service design requires coupling between front- and back-office employees because front-office employees have received the customer's unique specifications. In many services of this design, this coupling is achieved by front- and back-office functions being performed by the same employees, particularly when the service is performed at the customer's location (e.g., gardening and cleaning).

Quadrant IV. This last quadrant represents low demand diversity and low customer disposition to participate in the service production. Low disposition of customers to participate can stem, for example, from their low need to monitor standardized services or their inability to perform large-scale services (e.g., handling insurance needs). This allows for allocating most of the work to efficient back-office operations composed of standardized interdependencies and decoupling from most front-office disturbances (Chase, 1981). Here, division of work between back-office employees can result in advantages of specialization because the repetitiveness of standardized operations creates a higher tolerance for interdependencies (March & Simon, 1958). Standardization also can utilize economies of scale in the form of low-cost, mass-service production for relatively price-sensitive customers with low demand diversity. Examples of this are mass-services with quantitative rather than qualitative differences in demand such as banks, insurance companies, mass-passenger transportation, theaters, broadcasting companies, and fast-food restaurants.

These four interdependence patterns represent different combinations of the customization and customer participation allowed in different service designs. Thus, these two design parameters constitute the defining dimensions of our typology of service interdependence patterns. Dichotomization of the design dimensions into high or low allowed customization and participation creates a two-by-two service design framework. It is proposed to correspond to the faced conditions of the input uncertainty matrix in Figure 2, thereby giving the framework its contingency basis. Furthermore, it covers all possible combinations of different degrees of customization and participation with one of the four specific service designs. Therefore, it overcomes the limitation of not being mutually exhaustive and exclusive that compromises some other service typologies. The interdependence patterns could be labeled with their respective combinations of high or low customization and participation, but this would be awkward and repetitive. Instead, we will next identify/label four alternative service designs that can both add to the description of the interdependence patterns and relate them to the literature on coordination.

A SERVICE DESIGN TYPOLOGY OF INTERDEPENDENCE PATTERNS

Consistent with how the coordination literature prescribes coordination mechanisms based on degree of input and task uncertainty (e.g., Argote, 1982; Galbraith, 1973), typing the four interdependence patterns relative to their level of input uncertainty can guide researchers in selecting the appropriate coordination mechanisms developed in the second match in Figure 1. This typology can be created through using a diagonal in the matrix in a manner analogous to Perrow's (1967) use of a diagonal to represent routineness in his technology matrix. The highest level of input uncertainty is Quadrant II, in the upper right-hand corner (high demand diversity, high customer disposition to participate), and vice versa. Similar to Perrow's schema, the two off-diagonal quadrants represent viable, distinct cases of intermediate levels of input uncertainty in service operations: Quadrant III has high demand diversity and low customer disposition to participate, and Quadrant I low demand diversity and high customer disposition to participate.

Furthermore, Thompson's (1967) interdependence typology can be aligned in order of complexity (pooled → sequential → reciprocal) along the same diagonal. This further connects our framework to the coordination literature, especially since significant similarities can be seen between Thompson's typology and the service interdependence patterns. The customized interactive service design between customers and front-office employees in Quadrant II seems to correspond to his reciprocal type of interdependence "referring to the situation in which the output of each becomes the input for the others" (1967, p. 55). Also, the standardized, decoupled, and back-office-dominated service design in Quadrant III is similar to his pooled type of interdependence in which "each part renders a discrete contribution to the whole and each is supported by the whole" (1967, p. 54), in the sense that each customer does not extensively interact with service employees (or fellow customers being served simultaneously) while, at the same time, engaging in the sharing of resources that makes the mass-service possible. This pooling allows large-scale operations to provide low-cost, standardized services such as linking customers who indirectly want to be interdependent (e.g., depositors and borrowers, insurance pooling of risks, and sharing costs of air transportation and broadcasting).

Basically, the different off-diagonal interdependence patterns have sequential characteristics corresponding to Thompson's intermediate type of interdependence as well as intermediate levels of input uncertainty. The self-service character of the decoupled customer-dominated design in Quadrant I is mainly sequential in the sense that customers serve themselves *after* service employees have provided the goods and facilities needed for the self-service. The opposite seriality is found in the customized front- and back-office interactive design in Quadrant III. Here, customer specification of the demanded services *precedes* employee performance of the service.

Thus, we label the diagonal patterns *reciprocal service design* (II) and *pooled service design* (IV). The different off-diagonal patterns are labeled *sequential customized service design* (III) and *sequential standardized service design* (I). It should be emphasized that this is a typology of service interdependence patterns, not a typology of service organizations per se. Consequently, the examples of different service businesses offered in Figure 2 are only illustrations of services that typically apply the service design indicated.

It should also be emphasized that this application of Thompson's interdependence types refers only to the main type of interdependence characterizing each service interdependence pattern. It can be expected that the other types will be found to some extent in the patterns. This is, in a sense, represented by the alignment of Thompson's three types along the diagonal, with the intermediate sequential types being placed in the center, thereby making it to some extent relevant to all four designs. The Guttman scale character of Thompson's typology further supports the notion of one interdependence pattern also containing interdependencies of lower complexity (i.e., reciprocal service design also contains sequential and pooled while sequential designs also include pooled). Indeed, this coexistence of more than one interdependence type in a pattern is necessary because our concept of interdependence *patterns* goes beyond Thompson's simple classification of *single* types of interdependence between two parts (indirect, one-way, or two-way). We address the whole configuration of a number of interdependencies between three or more parts of the service production, and the labels indicate the dominant type of interdependence within a pattern. Thus, one interdependence pattern consists of many single interdependencies, but the patterns themselves are distinct from one another (due primarily to their underlying differences in either high or low allowed customization and participation).

MATCHING SERVICE INTERDEPENDENCE PATTERNS AND COORDINATION PORTFOLIOS

The second match in Figure 1 can now be developed, consistent with the logic that specific types of interdependence can be matched by specific coordination mechanisms to achieve concerted action (Thompson, 1967). Since no mechanism can coordinate all the interdependencies of an organization (Galbraith, 1973; Lawrence & Lorsch, 1967), a *portfolio* of coordination mechanisms, or what McCann and Galbraith (1981) call a portfolio of control and coordination strategies, is required. McCann and Galbraith emphasized "the importance of organizations using multiple strategies [i.e., coordination mechanisms], selected in an explicit, conscious manner. These strategies should not interfere with each other too much, but, instead, complement each other as much as possible" (p. 79). Their call for more research on the selection process of these coordination portfolios has been left mainly unheeded.

The framework presented here develops this selection process by relating different configurations of mechanisms in terms of coordination portfolios that match different interdependence patterns. This perspective extends conventional coordination frameworks that match individual coordination mechanisms to specific interdependencies and that ignore the mechanisms necessary for coordinating customer activities.

A description of the portfolios of coordination mechanisms that match alternative patterns of service interdependencies requires the resolution of two issues: (a) determining the mechanisms to be included and (b) identifying the emphasis of the portfolio.

ALTERNATIVE COORDINATION MECHANISMS

The organizational literature on coordination provides numerous lists of possibilities, building largely on classic works by March and Simon (1958) and Thompson (1967). Thompson's seminal work proposed that pooled interdependence was coordinated through standardization, sequential interdependence through planning, and reciprocal interdependence through mutual adjustment. More recently researchers have developed comprehensive and sophisticated lists of coordination mechanisms, including lateral relations, the design of work, and different human resource management practices (e.g., Galbraith, 1973; McCann & Galbraith, 1981; Mintzberg, 1979; Van de Ven, Delbecq, & Koenig, 1976).

The present focus is only to note two summary characteristics of this literature, not to fully review it. First, this literature has an internal focus that does not address the role of customers in operations. Second, most coordination mechanisms rest on the assumption of hierarchical control, which applies only to customers in exceptional circumstances (e.g., prisons and monopolies without substitute products). Relative to both these points, it is worth repeating that price, in the absence of complete contracting, cannot coordinate the actual coproduction of services (cf. Arrow, 1974).

Service organizations, then, have a need to coordinate the inputs of participating customers that cannot be filled by the conventional coordination literature. Here, the emerging service literature is helpful. A particularly promising contribution is the application of the dramaturgical metaphor to *script* the service encounter (Solomon, Surprenant, Czepiel, & Gutman, 1985; Smith & Houston, 1983). Abelson (1976, p. 33) defined a script as "a coherent sequence of events expected by the individual, involving him either as a participant or an observer." Relative to services, customers can be thought of as possessing cognitive scripts for a wide variety of service encounters that reflect the individuals' learned (or imagined) conception of the prototypical service experience.

The importance of customer scripts is that they represent customers' knowledge of what to do for effective participation in the service production. Missing or inadequate knowledge of what to do leaves customers with two options: either they must successfully invent what to do or they must be told what to do in order to participate in a well-coordinated manner. But relying on customers' creativity or complete acceptance of employee instructions seems risky for both the customers and the service organization.

Service organizations need to influence the scripts customers follow as a mechanism for coordinating customer participation. Given that customers can retain a variety of potentially relevant scripts in memory, the organization needs to offer cues to the customer to indicate which script fits the given setting. For example, McDonald's presents the customer with an overall restaurant staging, but it also uses highly visible tray racks and garbage cans to inform the customer of what particular script to follow (i.e., one busses one's table after eating).

The notion of shaping customer scripts in use is similar to the concept of socializing customers as partial employees of the service organization (Mills, 1986; Mills & Morris, 1986). This socialization can reduce uncertainty in service operations through developing conformity to role requirements. Customers also can be selected on the basis of the organizations' suppositions about what scripts customers would be likely to follow. It may even be possible to provide customers with a realistic service preview of the behaviors expected of them during service production (Mills & Morris, 1986). In a similar vein, Bowen (1986) described how to manage customers as human resources in service organizations. A central focus here is ensuring that customers clearly understand their roles so they can perform them effectively.

In this discussion, we suggest that how suitable different customer scripts are is contingent upon the characteristics of the service design. Thus, service organizations can be expected to foster and cue different types of customer scripts for different interdependence patterns of service operations. These scripts can be expected to differ on two dimensions that are best described in the language of the dramaturgical metaphor (Goffman, 1961; Grove & Fisk, 1983; Solomon et al., 1985). The first dimension is the size of the role, or part, that the organization wants the customer to play in the service production. The script can offer either a large or limited role. The second dimension is the flexibility, or freedom to ad-lib, afforded the customer in how to play the role. This dimension is the same as the degree to which the terms of the service encounter are loosely or tightly specified (Chase & Bowen, in press). It is also similar to the concept of the customer engaging in some role making, rather than simply role taking (Mills & Morris, 1986). Overall, organizations need to cue large roles when confronted with high customer motivation to participate; also, organizations cue loose scripts for conditions of high diversity of demand.

MAIN LOCUS OF PORTFOLIO

The main locus of the portfolio can be considered in the context of which of the three areas of coordination arising from the division of work poses the most critical coordination requirements: (a) front-office coordination of service interaction between front-office employees and customers, (b) front- and back-office coordination of the service support between front- and back-office employees, and (c) back-office coordination of the processing of service support by back-office employees.

Thompson (1967) suggested that coordination costs can be minimized by giving first priority to the more complex interdependencies in order to localize the more difficult and costly coordination mechanisms. In line with this, we suggest that the main locus of the coordination portfolio (i.e., the area with most critical/frequent mechanisms) needs to center around the most complex area of coordination. This area is the most complex part(s) of the interdependence pattern (i.e., most numerous exchanges), and it is identified as the main locus of interdependencies in Figure 2. In this way, coordinative efforts become focused where they are most needed, rather than on less complex interdependencies.

PORTFOLIOS OF COORDINATION MECHANISMS

Table 2 displays the portfolios of coordination mechanisms that match each of the four designs of interdependence patterns. Specifically, a portfolio for a given design is composed of the *row* of mechanisms, with the main locus indicated by the highlighted cell.

In the *sequential standardized service design* the main locus is the front office. Coordination mechanisms include, foremostly, customer *self*-adjustment of his or her service-producing actions to presupplied facilities and goods. The presupply provides the customer with different standardized options that are supported by employee maintenance of service facilities and storage of goods. This back-office processing (i.e., decoupled from the customers) can be coordinated by traditional mechanisms such as logistic planning (Chase, 1981) routines for maintenance, refilling shelves with goods, and so forth. Customer scripts for this self-service-oriented design must be tightly specified. Customers need a clear definition of their central role in producing and delivering the service, within the limits of the preadjusted routines for delivering a set of standardized services. The dominant self-serving role of customers casts them in a large role in service performance. This allows customers

TABLE 2   Portfolios of Coordination Mechanisms for Alternative Designs of Service Interdependence Patterns

Design of Service Interdependence Patterns	Area of Coordination		
	Front-office coordination of service interaction	Front/back-office coordination of service support	Back-office coordination of support processing
Sequential Standardized Service Design (Customer dominated)	**Customer self-adjustment to presupply** **Large, tightly specified scripts**	Routines for presupply Decoupling	Logistic planning
Reciprocal Service Design (Customized customer/ employee interactive)	**Customer/employee mutual adjustment** **Large, loosely specified scripts**	Communication Limited decoupling	Programming
Sequential Customized Service Design (Front/back-office employee interactive)	Communication and agreement Limited, loosely specified scripts	**Adjusting customer orders and input to agreed performance**	Planning
Pooled Service Design (Standardized back-office dominated)	Standardization Limited, tightly specified scripts	Information systems Decoupling	**Standardized pooling**

some role-making discretion for innovative and spontaneous behavior (Mills & Morris, 1986).

In *reciprocal service design,* the main locus of interdependencies is also in the front office. However, *mutual* adjustment is the primary mechanism of coordination between front-office employee and customer (Thompson, 1967). This mutual adjustment cannot be preadjusted because it involves the continuous transmission of new information or feedback (March & Simon, 1958); it is impossible to specify *a priori* the full range of idiosyncratic demands that could arise in this type of service encounter (Mills, Chase, & Margulies, 1983); nonprogrammed coordination mechanisms are appropriate (Argote, 1982). The mutual adjustment of the service production is generally led by the professional expertise of the front-office employee in relation to the often unique and complex problem input from the customer.

Here the script guiding the service encounter customers can be only loosely specified *a priori.* Still, the customer plays a large part in helping the service employee to diagnose the problem. Thus, the script must emphasize the customer's assisting role (cf. Mills, Hall, Leidecker, & Margulies, 1983) in terms of acceptance of instructions for how to participate effectively in the problem solving. Although this acceptance cannot be based on hierarchical authority over the customer, it can rest on (a) the legitimacy afforded professionals based on expertise or tradition (Weber, 1947) and (b) the customer's dependence on the professional (McCallum & Harrison, 1985). Indeed, it will be likely that the customer's need for the service provider's exper-

tise brought them together (Lefton & Rosengren, 1966).

Relative to the employees' role in mutual adjustment, professional service employees are similar to customers because their behavior is also difficult to control through hierarchical mechanisms. Research indicates that professional service employees exercise self-management involves employees taking responsibility for the management (Mills & Posner, 1982); self-management of their task-related activities rather than having their task activities closely monitored by a supervisor (Mills, 1986). Also, these professionals may rely on substitutes for leadership (Kerr & Jermier, 1977), such as professional norms and cohesive work groups.

Lastly, even though most of the work in this service design is done in the front office, activities, such as the processing of tests, can be decoupled and delegated to the back office. Again, the back-office processing of the service support can be coordinated with conventional mechanisms such as programming (Argote, 1982). Both delegation and decoupling are limited by the unique nature of interdependencies. Customization requires communicating the particularities of each customer problem in the coordination of the service support between front and back offices.

In *sequential customized service design,* the main locus is between the front and back offices. The main coordination task is to adjust unique customer requests communicated to front-office employees to the performance of back-office employees. One means for making this adjustment is to have the same employees assume both front- and back-office roles. The front-office activities of receiving the customer orders and input are mainly coordinated through communication and agreement of specific service performance. Loosely specified customer scripts geared to giving relevant performance instructions to the service employees are expected to adequately allow for demand diversity and clear communication for correct customization. Given low disposition to participate, the customer plays a limited part in the service performance for his/her convenience.

The actual transformation of the customer input is done primarily through back-office activities coordinated by planning of tools and personnel and other internal mechanisms. Even if these front- and back-office activities can be physically separated, such decoupling leads to risks of wrong service performances due to miscommunication between decoupled front and back offices.

Finally, *pooled service design* of interdependence patterns have the back office as the main locus of interdependencies and coordination. The pooled mass-service-oriented design is mainly coordinated by standardization of both front and back offices (Thompson, 1967). The customer contact is standardized through the use of preadjusted options (e.g., bank accounts and insurance policies), forms, programs, routines, and so forth. This allows for decoupling of the back office for efficient operations (Chase, 1978, 1981) and using preadjusted information systems (Galbraith, 1973) as links between the front and back office. The back office coordinates its operations through standardized pooling of customer input for mediating and large-scale purposes. Here, it is likely that tightly specified customer scripts will be useful because they provide narrowly specified action sequences corresponding to the standardized options. Limited customer scripts accommodate both low motivation to participate and large-scale specialization by back-office employees. Furthermore, the mass character of this service design will benefit from imitative customer role behavior in order to standardize customer conduct and to utilize interacting customers as role models (Mills, 1986).

IMPLICATIONS

This contingency framework for service production can be summarized in terms of a set of research propositions that focus on the various proposed matches. This provides a coherent, relatively parsimonious framework integrating some hypotheses similar to propositions found scattered throughout the organizational and services literatures with some hypotheses unique to the present proposed typology. First, the overall *design* proposition is that service organizations tend more to use, and to be more effective when using, service designs that match the demand diversity and customer disposition to participate they face. Specifically, the design of service production matches input uncertainty as follows:

> *Proposition 1A: The higher the demand diversity, the higher the degree of customization.*
>
> *Proposition 1B: The higher the customer disposition to participate, the greater the amount of service work shifted to the customer; the lower the customer disposition to participate, the greater the amount of service work shifted to back-office employees.*
>
> *Proposition 1C: The higher the demand diversity, the greater the amount of service work shifted to front-office employees in interaction with either the customer or back-office employees, depending on the customer disposition to participate (as in Proposition 1B).*
>
> *Proposition 1D: The lower demand diversity is, the more decoupled are service designs between the front and back office.*

Proposition 1 breaks down the service design into hypothesized main effects. But the design of the overall service interdependence patterns is likely to also include interaction effects between the two input uncertainty variables. For instance, on the one hand, the mere question of *who* does the main part of the service work is proposed to depend on the simultaneous main effects of Propositions 1B and 1C. On the other hand, the overall question of *how* the service production is designed also includes the possibly changing nature of service work itself. For example, moving from Quadrant I to Quadrant II in Figure 2 does not simply add front-office employees to the customer as dominating parties of the division of service work. It can also be expected to change the nature of the service work to be divided due to the interactive design between these parties (as compared with customer self-service in Quadrant I or front- and back-office employee interaction in Quadrant III). Thus, viewing service work as a dynamic rather than static set of activities can provide a rationale for hypothesizing interaction effects, but their specification needs further research.

> *Proposition 2: Service organizations are more effective if they design their service production according to Proposition 1 than those service organizations that do not, all other things being constant.*

Turning to the second matching process between interdependence patterns and *coordination* portfolios, we propose that the selection of service organizations' portfolios of coordination mechanisms depends on the following:

> *Proposition 3A: The more complex the interdependence pattern (i.e., the closer to the upper right-hand corner in Figure 2), the more nonprogrammed mechanisms are utilized, and vice versa.*

> *Proposition 3B: The more standardized the service design, the more decoupled the coordination between front and back offices, and vice versa.*

> *Proposition 3C: Back-office activities are primarily coordinated by programmed mechanisms, whereas front-office activities are more coordinated by nonprogrammed mechanisms.*

> *Proposition 3D: The emphasis of the coordination portfolio (i.e., main coordinative effort) follows the main locus of interdependencies of the service design (indicated in Figure 2).*

> *Proposition 4: Service organizations that match their interdependence patterns with their coordination portfolios according to Proposition 3 are more effective than those that do not, all other things being constant.*

Finally, the overall matching of these two design and coordination matching processes is addressed as follows:

> *Proposition 5: Service organizations match both their design of interdependence patterns to faced conditions of input uncertainty and their selection of coordination portfolios according to Propositions 1 and 3 (illustrated by Figure 1).*

> *Proposition 6: Service organizations with the overall match between design and coordination according to Proposition 5 are more effective than those without, all other things being constant.*

This set of propositions expresses the often intertwined prescriptive and descriptive statements of contingency relationships. The matching rationales *prescribe* certain fits between designs and situations as being more effective than misfits. At the same time, these fits are likely to *describe* most organizations because a given organization "may be driven toward configuration in order to achieve consistency in its internal characteristics, synergy (or mutual complementarity) in its processes, and fit with its situation" (Miller & Mintzberg, 1983, p. 69). This can occur through both strategic adaptation and environmental selection (cf. Child, 1972; Hannan & Freeman, 1977; Hrebreniak & Joyce, 1985). The testing of both the frequency and the effectiveness of these fits can empirically disentangle descriptive and prescriptive aspects of the contingency framework, and this can have potentially interesting implications. For instance, findings of proposed fits being more effective but not more frequent than misfits would suggest either a lack of competitive pressure (cf. Pfeffer & Leblebici, 1973; Rushing, 1976) or a lack of rationality and/or knowledge on the part of organization designers (Argote, 1982; cf. Thompson, 1967). Alternatively, the effectiveness measure may be inappropriate (Argote, 1982); for example, it may not include external assessment criteria as legitimacy needed for success in institutionalized environments (Meyer & Rowan, 1977).

Finally, additional specification to the basics of the framework may be needed before its effectiveness is fully realized in research or practice. For example, researchers in this area should address how to coordinate the different mechanisms that constitute a portfolio. That is, what strategies and mechanisms can be used to coordinate the interdependence that exists *across* the three cells in the row of a portfolio? Compatibility of strategies is required within a portfolio because one mechanism can nullify or reinforce another (McCann & Galbraith, 1981). The portfolio selection process can be viewed partly as coordination of interdependent coordination mechanisms. This leads us to Ashby's (1960) concept of *amplification* in the context of how the overall coordination capacity of an organization can be amplified through coordination of interdependent coordination mechanisms. For example, in pooled service design, it is necessary to coordinate the standardized forms, routines, and so forth, of the front-office interaction; the information system between front and back office; and the main coordination effort of standardized back-office processing of the customer pool. Propositions should be developed that will help us to understand this amplification process.

STRATEGIC MANAGEMENT AND MARKETING IMPLICATIONS

A second area for future analysis involves the strategic and marketing implications of the presented framework. One strategic concern involves the service organization's distinctive coordination competencies. For instance, if an organization has great back-office strength in dealing with large-scale standardized operations, then a pooled service design may be appropriate not only for conditions of low input uncertainty but also for conditions of intermediate uncertainty, assuming the organization is weak in implementing sequential designs. In a broader context, the organization's coordination competence may provide a rationale for not pursuing reactive adaptation to environmental conditions emphasized in the framework and, instead, actively influencing the demand diversity and customer disposition to participate it faces. For example, an organization that has distinctive programming capability could utilize price reductions and advertising in order to emphasize product homogeneity, thereby decreasing demand diversity so that there would be a match with standardized service offerings. Another example would be that front-office strengths can be capitalized upon by inducing customers to participate more actively through price reductions, intrinsic rewards, and/or customer socialization toward role readiness and requisite ability.

Another strategic and marketing implication is that the framework can guide the market segmentation of customers and the provision to these segments of suitable service designs. This is possible because a service organization can use several different service designs simultaneously, especially if it faces different uncertainty conditions. For instance, a bank that has a predominantly pooled service design can incorporate a sequential standardized service design via automatic teller machines that fit a market segment of customers who are disposed to participate and who have low demand diversity. The bank also could use a reciprocal service design by offering a broader range of professionalized financial services to fit a segment of customers who have diverse demands and a disposition to participate. In all, the reactive marketing concept rationale for the contingency framework, together with these active marketing influences on the customer/environmental variables, provides a conceptual vehicle for jointly optimizing the organization and marketing of services.

CONCLUSION

We have offered a framework for analyzing design and coordination issues at the service organization–customer interface. The attention this interface should receive in organizational theory is clearly indicated by the growth of the service sector. Yet the importance of service operations to manufacturing firms is also a growing concern (Bowen, Siehl, & Schneider, 1989). There is a need, then, to better understand the management of service interdependencies in the economy as a whole—a need that we hope this framework begins to address.

REFERENCES

Abelson, R. P. (1976) Script processing in attitude formation and decision making. In J. S. Carroll & J. W. Payne (Eds.), *Cognition and social behavior* (pp. 33–46). Hillsdale, NJ: Erlbaum.

Argote, L. (1982) Input uncertainty and organizational coordination in hospital emergency units. *Administrative Science Quarterly*, 27, 420–434.

Arrow, K. J. (1974) *The limits of organization.* New York: Norton.

Ashby, W. R. (1960) *Design for a brain.* London: Chapman and Hall.

Bateson, J. E. G. (1983) The self service customer: Empirical findings. In L. Berry, L. Shostack, & G. Upah (Eds.), *Emerging perspectives in services marketing* (pp. 50–53). Chicago: American Marketing Association.

Berry, L. L. (1980, May–June) Services marketing is different. *Business,* pp. 24–29.

Borden, N. J. (1964, June) The concept of marketing mix. *Journal of Advertising Research,* 4, 2–7.

Bowen, D. E. (1986) Managing customers as human resources in service organizations. *Human Resource Management,* 25, 371–383.

Bowen, D. E., & Jones, G. R. (1986) A transaction cost analysis of service organization–customer exchange. *Academy of Management Review,* 11, 428–441.

Bowen, D. E., & Schneider, B. (1988) Services marketing and management: Implications for organizational behavior. In B. M. Staw & L. L. Cummings (Eds.), *Research in Organizational Behavior* (Vol. 10, pp. 43–80). Greenwich, CT: JAI Press.

Bowen, D. E., Siehl, C., & Schneider, B. (1989) A framework for analyzing customer service orientations in manufacturing. *Academy of Management Review,* 14, 75–95.

Brass, D. J. (1985) Technology and the structuring of jobs: Employee satisfaction, performance, and influence. *Organizational Behavior and Human Decision Processes,* 35, 216–240.

Burns, T., & Stalker, G. M. (1961) *The management of innovation.* London: Tavistock.

Chase, R. B. (1978) Where does the customer fit in the service operation? *Harvard Business Review,* 56(6), 137–142.

Chase, R. B. (1981) The customer contact approach to services: Theoretical bases and practical extensions. *Operations Research,* 29, 698–706.

Chase, R. B., & Bowen, D. E. (in press) Integrating operations and human resource management in the service sector. In C. C. Snow (Ed.), *Strategy, organization design, and human resource management.* Greenwich, CT: JAI Press.

Chase, R. B., & Tansik, D. A. (1983) The customer contact model for organizational design. *Management Science,* 29, 1037–1050.

Child, J. (1972) Organization structure, environment, and performance: The role of strategic choice. *Sociology,* 6, 1–22.

Czepiel, J. A., Solomon, M. R., & Surprenant, C. F. (1985) *The service encounter.* Lexington, MA: Heath.

Danet, B. (1981) Client-organizational relationships. In P. C. Nystrom & W. H. Starbuck (Eds.), *Handbook of organizational design* (pp. 382–428). New York: Oxford University Press.

Davis, S. (1983, Spring) Management models for the future. *New Management,* pp. 12–15.

Eiglier, P., & Langeard, E. (1977) A new approach to service marketing. In E. E. Langeard, C. Lovelock, J. Bateson, & R. Young (Eds.), *Marketing consumer services: New insights* (Report 77-115)(pp. 37–41). Boston: Marketing Science Institute.

Fuchs, V. R. (1968) *The service economy.* New York: Columbia University Press.

Galbraith, J. (1973) *Designing complex organizations.* Reading, MA: Addison-Wesley.

Goffman, E. (1961) *Encounters: Two studies in the sociology of interaction.* Indianapolis: Bobbs-Merrill.

Grove, S. J., & Fisk, R. P. (1983) The dramaturgy of services exchange: An analytical framework for services marketing. In L. L. Berry, G. L. Shostack, & G. Upah (Eds.), *Emerging perspectives in services marketing* (pp. 45–49). Chicago: American Marketing Association.

Gronroos, C. (1982) An applied service marketing theory. *European Journal of Marketing,* 16(7), 30–41.

Gummesson, E. (1979) The marketing of professional services: An organizational dilemma. *European Journal of Marketing,* 13(5), 308–318.

Hannan, M. T., & Freeman, J. (1977) The population ecology of organizations. *American Journal of Sociology,* 82, 929–964.

Hill, T. P. (1977) On goods and services. *Review of Income and Wealth,* 23, 315–338.

Houston, F. S. (1986) The marketing concept: What it is and what it is not. *Journal of Marketing,* 50(2), 81–87.

Hrebiniak, L. G., & Joyce, W. F. (1985) Organizational adaptation: Strategic choice and environmental determinism. *Administrative Science Quarterly,* 30, 336–349.

Keith, R. J. (1960, January) The marketing revolution. *Journal of Marketing,* 24, 35–38.

Kerr, S., & Jernier, J. (1977) Substitutes for leadership: Their meaning and measurement. *Organizational Behavior and Human Performance,* 22, 375–403.

Kotler, P. (1980) *Marketing management: Analysis, planning and control* (4th ed.). Englewood Cliffs, NJ: Prentice-Hall.

Lawrence, P. R., & Lorsch, J. W. (1967) *Organization and environment: Managing differentiation and integration.* Boston: Harvard University Press.

Lefton, M., & Rosengren, W. R. (1966) Organizations and clients: Lateral and longitudinal dimensions. *American Sociological Review,* 31, 802–810.

Levitt, T. (1972) Production-line approach to service. *Harvard Business Review,* 54(5), 63–74.

Levitt, T. (1976) The industrialization of service. *Harvard Business Review,* 54(5) 41–52.

Lovelock, C. H. (1984) *Services marketing.* Englewood Cliffs, NJ: Prentice-Hall.

Lovelock, C. H., & Young, R. F. (1979) Look to customers to increase productivity. *Harvard Business Review,* 57(3), 168–178.

Maister, D. H., & Lovelock, C. H. (1982) Managing facilitator services. *Sloan Management Review,* 23(2), 19–32.

March, J. G., & Simon, H. A. (1958) *Organizations.* New York: Wiley.

Matteis, R. J. (1979) The new back office focuses on customer service. *Harvard Business Review,* 57(2), 146–159.

McCallum, J. R., & Harrison, W. (1985) Interdependence in the service encounter. In J. A. Czepiel, M. R. Solomon, & C. F. Surprenant (Eds.), *The service encounter* (pp. 35–48). Lexington, MA: Heath.

McCann, J., & Galbraith, J. R. (1981) Interdepartmental relations. In P. C. Nystrom & W. H. Starbuck (Eds.), *Handbook of organizational design* (Vol. 2, pp. 60–84). New York: Oxford University Press.

Meyer, J. W., & Rowan, B. (1977) Institutionalized organizations: Formal structure as myth and ceremony. *American Journal of Sociology,* 83, 340–363.

Miller, D., & Mintzberg, H. (1983) The case for configuration. In G. Morgan (Ed.), *Beyond method: Strategies for social research* (pp. 57–73). Beverly Hills, CA: Sage.

Mills, P. K. (1986) *Managing service industries: Organizational practices in a postindustrial economy.* Cambridge, MA: Ballinger.

Mills, P. K., Chase, R. B., & Margulies, N. (1983) Motivating the client/employee system as a production strategy. *Academy of Management Review,* 8, 301–310.

Mills, P. K., Hall, J. L., Leidecker, J. K., & Margulies, N. (1983) Flexiform: A model for professional service organizations. *Academy of Management Review,* 8, 118–131.

Mills, P. K., & Margulies, N. (1980) Toward a core typology of service organizations. *Academy of Management Review,* 5, 255–265.

Mills, P. K., & Moberg, D. J. (1982) Perspectives on the technology of service operations. *Academy of Management Review,* 7, 467–478.

Mills, P. K., & Morris, J. H. (1986) Clients as "partial" employees of service organizations: Role development in client participation. *Academy of Management Review,* 11, 726–735.

Mills, P. K., & Posner, B. Z. (1982) The relationships among self-supervision, structure, and technology in professional organizations. *Academy of Management Journal,* 25, 437–441.

Mills, P. K., & Turk, T. (1986) A preliminary investigation into the influence of customer–firm interface on information processing and task activities in service organizations. *Journal of Management,* 12(1), 91–104.

Mintzberg, H. (1979) *The structuring of organizations.* Englewood Cliffs, NJ: Prentice-Hall.

Northcraft, G. B., & Chase, R. B. (1985) Managing service demand at the point of delivery. *Academy of Management Review,* 10, 66–75.

Perrow, C. (1967) A framework for the comparative analysis of organizations. *American Sociological Review,* 32, 194–208.

Pfeffer, J., & Leblebici, H. (1973) The effect of competition on some dimensions of organizational structure. *Social Forces,* 52, 268–279.

Porter, M. E. (1985) *Competitive advantage: Creating and sustaining superior performance.* New York: Free Press.

Rousseau, D. M. (1979) Assessment of technology in organizations: Closed versus open systems approaches. *Academy of Management Review,* 4, 531–542.

Rushing, W. A. (1976) Profit and nonprofit orientations and the differentiation-coordination hypothesis for organizations: A study of small general hospitals. *American Sociological Review,* 41, 676–691.

Sasser, W. E. (1976) Match supply and demand in service industries. *Harvard Business Review,* 54(6), 133–140.

Sasser, W. E., Olsen, R. P., & Wyckoff, D. D. (1978) *Management of service operations.* Boston: Allyn & Bacon.

Scherer, F. M. (1980) *Industrial market structure and economic performance.* Chicago: Rand McNally.

Schmenner, R. W. (1986) How can service businesses survive and prosper? *Sloan Management Review,*(3), 21–32.

Scott, W. R. (1981) *Organizations: Rational, natural, and open systems.* Englewood Cliffs, NJ: Prentice-Hall.

Shostack, G. L. (1977) Breaking free from product marketing. *Journal of Marketing,* 41(2), 73–80.

Slocum, J. W., & Sims, H. (1980) A typology for integrating technology, organization, and job design. *Human Relations,* 33, 193–212.

Smith, A. (1937) *An inquiry into the nature and causes of the wealth of nations.* New York: The Modern Library. (Original work published 1776).

Smith, R., A., & Houston, M. J. (1983) Script-based evaluations of satisfaction with services. In L. L. Berry, G. L. Shostack, & G. Upah (Eds.), *Emerging perspectives in services marketing* (pp. 59–62). Chicago: American Marketing Association.

Snyder, C. A., Cox, J. F., & Jesse, R. R. (1982) A dependent demand approach to service organization planning and control. *Academy of Management Review,* 7, 455–466.

Solomon, M. R., Surprenant, C., Czepiel, J. A., & Gutman, E. G. (1985) A role theory of dyadic interactions: The Service Encounter. *Journal of Marketing,* 49(1), 99–111.

Thomas, D. R. E. (1978) Strategy is different in service businesses. *Harvard Business Review,* 56(4), 158–165.

Thompson, J. D. (1962) Organizations and output transactions. *American Journal of Sociology,* 68, 309–324.

Thompson, J. D. (1967) *Organizations in action.* New York: McGraw-Hill.

Van de Ven, A. H., Delbecq, A. L., & Koenig, R., Jr. (1976) Determinants of coordination modes within organizations. *American Sociological Review,* 41, 322–338.

Vroom, V. (1964) *Work and motivation.* New York: Wiley.

Weber, M. (1947) *The theory of social and economic organization.* New York: Free Press.

Williamson, O. E. (1975) *Markets and hierarchies: Analysis and antitrust implications.* New York: Free Press.

Williamson, O. E. (1979) Transaction-cost economics: the governance of contractual relations. *Journal of Law and Economics,* 22, 233–262.

Zeithaml, V. A., Parasuraman, A., & Berry, L. L. (1985) Problems and strategies in services marketing. *Journal of Marketing,* 49(2), 33–45.

CHAPTER 4

UNDERSTANDING THE SERVICE WORKER

THE CUSTOMERS FROM HELL

THE CROWN OF CREATION

Call him *Egocentric Edgar.* This is the guy Carly Simon had in mind when she sang, "You're so vain, you probably think this song is about you." Stand in line? Him? My dear, his time is much too valuable. "Excuse me, I'm in a hurry here! Coming through!"

It turns out, of course, that Edgar's big emergency involves buying a plane ticket—for a flight next month. Or a sudden need to cash 97 savings bonds—except he doesn't have them signed and his checking account is in another bank and there is only one teller on duty. "You *do* advertise that you believe in service to the customer, *n'est-ce pas?*" Then again, he may simply be in urgent need of directions to the nearest hot comb.

Edgar *will* speak to the owner, the president, the chairman, "the man in charge," as he will never fail to put it. Actually, he doesn't care if the individual in charge is male, female, or a Swiss mountain goat as long as there is a chance it's someone he can intimidate through some judicious name-dropping. And he'll delight in walking over a front line person to get there.

Edgar is the one who loudly demands that your organization stop the hurricane, quell the civil insurrection, or create the replacement part out of thin air so his flight can leave on time. "Don't tell me this airplane can't be moved! I want it moved!" Me first, me last, me only—that's his creed. You? You're just a bit player, an extra, an extraneous piece of scenery in his grandest of all productions. "Edgar: The Greatest Story Ever Told."

THE BREATH OF SPRING

Bad-Mouth Betty: Her mother would be proud. Such an extensive vocabulary! It takes timing, talent, and a total lack of shame to walk into a department store or a bank lobby and cuss like a drunken stevedore, but Betty makes it look easy.

You: "Good morning, Ms. Coupon Clipper."

Betty: "Don't good morning me, you ————! I know what you ————s are doing. You're holding on to my ————ing money so you can get rich on the ————ing float!"

You: "But Ms. Clipper, the payment isn't due until the first of the month and this is only the 25th."

Betty: "———— you, you little ————! I know your game, you ————ing lousy, two-bit ————. You were two days late last ————ing month. Let it happen again and I'll have your ————s in court, you ————ing ————s!"

If she can't be right, she'll be caustic, crude, cruel, and as foul as a pig-pen in July.

THE AIR RAID SIREN

Hysterical Harold is a screamer. The Harolds of the world blow their corks higher and faster than an agitated bottle of cheap champagne—and come down a lot slower. The second Harold senses a possible deviation from the plan—his plan—he goes off at 10,000 decibels.

Allen Funt would love this guy: he's so animated and photogenic. Harold is likely to turn vein-popping purple and jump up and down on the hood of his own car when the service manager tells him a part is out of stock and has to be emergency ordered—for the next day. Naturally, Harold expects the dents he inflicted to be fixed at the dealership's expense, during the same visit.

And wouldn't you know it, Harold is *always* the guy who gets the banana split without any banana in it. All of his friends think this is hilarious. Harold does his rabid-dog impersonation while everyone else is doubled over laughing.

If it's true that there is a child in all of us yearning to break free; Harold demonstrates the dark side of that happy thought. He is the classic tantrum-thrower, the adult embodiment of the terrible twos. Only louder. Much louder.

THE PRIDE OF THE REICH

"Und you *vill* follow orders, und you *vill* do it my vay! *Macht schnell!*" That's *Dictatorial Dick*. Any wonder that this guy gets dose after dose of malicious obedience? People follow his mandates to the letter, even those that make no sense.

Suspected to being Edgar's even-eviler twin, Dick often shows up with written marching orders: a copy for the service person, a copy for the service person's manager, a copy for himself. The original will have been dated, time-stamped, and sent to his lawyer by registered letter.

By a happy coincidence, Dick "used to be in this business" and knows all the little tricks of the trade that you, you sneaky peon, were planning to pull on him. As soon as you hear his plan for how the impending transaction is going to work, you realize whey he isn't in the business any more.

Dick issues ultimatums, sets arbitrary deadlines, and tells everyone exactly how to do their jobs. And when his plan doesn't work? It's your company's fault, of course. Better still, it's *your* fault. Obviously, you were incompetent. Either that or you were trying to sabotage his brilliant plan.

THE SOUL OF CHARITY

A material girl in a material world, *Freeloading Freda* wants her dollar's worth—and yours, and mine, and anyone else's she can get. If the deal is "Buy one, get one free," she wants two for nothing. If the offer is buy the Jumbo Stuperific size and get a small for free, she wants a regular. She orders the small drink, complains that it's too small, and demands a large. She orders the wild boar stew, inhales nine of the ten ounces in the bowl, then calls the waitress over and pronounces it too gamy: "Take it back and bring me a hamburger instead." If asked to pay for either the stew or the burger, she carries on like the victim of a stock swindle.

If it wears out, breaks, or begins to bore her, Freda takes it back. Her kid dribbles the portable TV down the basement stairs, she takes it back. She buys a fancy dressing gown, wears it to the company Christmas party (where she rolls in the punch bowl), and takes it back. There is not a store in town she hasn't hit up for a cash refund for that cuckoo clock Aunt Sarah sent from France in 1955. But don't you dare accuse her of taking advantage. She will scream lawsuit, slander, Eyewitness News, and Better Business Bureau at the top of her lungs.

SOURCE: Ron Zemke and Kristin Anderson, "Customers from Hell," *Training*, 26 (February 1990): 25–31.

CHAPTER OVERVIEW

The public faces of the service firm are the contact personnel, the service workers in day-to-day contact with the customers from hell described in this chapter. Part factory workers, part administrators, part servants, theirs is a complex and difficult job. Despite this, they are often the lowest-status people in the organization, and often in society.

This chapter highlights the importance of the contact personnel to the firm and their particular role in creating customer satisfaction. It goes on to explain the pressures and tensions on the service workers as they try to play a boundary-spanning *role. They are the permeable surface of the organization, interfacing outward with the environment and inward with the organization itself. They thus have a complex role to play, and the impact of the resulting stress on the people occupying these roles has been explored extensively in the literature of organizational behavior. To alleviate that stress, several alternative strategies are open to boundary spanners. Unfortunately, many of these strategies have negative consequences for customers.*

THE IMPORTANCE OF CONTACT PERSONNEL

Strategically, contact personnel can be the source of product differentiation. One way to consider the problem of product differentiation is to break the service firm into three parts: the benefit concept, the servuction system, and the service level. The benefit concept is the bundle of benefits received by the customer, and it can be measured only in the mind of that customer. The basis of the service-level idea is that the operating system itself should be separated from the way it operates. This rather arbitrary separation allows for the separation of systems design from the operating performance of that design.

It is often impossible for a service organization to differentiate itself from other similar organizations in regard to the benefit bundle it offers or its delivery servuction system. For example, one extreme view is that many airlines offer similar bundles of benefits and fly the same planes from the same airports. Their only hope of a competitive advantage is therefore from the same service level—the way things are done. Some of this differentiation can come from staffing levels or the physical systems designed to support the staff. Often, however, the deciding factor that distinguishes one airline from another is the attitude of the service providers.[1]

Article 4.1 describes an interesting analysis of the sources of satisfaction and dissatisfaction for service consumers. The approached used is the critical incident procedure, which is a powerful tool for gaining insights into complex phenomena. Respondents were asked to recall a time when, as a customer, they had a particularly satisfying or dissatisfying interaction with an employee of an airline, hotel, or restaurant and then were asked a series of questions:

☐ When did the incident happen?

☐ What specific circumstances led to this situation?

☐ Exactly what did the employee say or do?

☐ What was the result?

☐ Do you feel the interaction was satisfying or dissatisfying?

The result was 699 descriptions of specific incidents (347 satisfactory and 352 unsatisfactory) from customers who had interacted with airlines, restaurants, and hotels. Through a process of classification, the incidents were sorted according to the source

TABLE 4.1   Classification of Type of Incident and Outcome

	Outcome	
	Percent Satisfactory	**Percent Dissatisfactory**
Group 1: Employee Responses to Service Delivery Failure		
Response to unavailable service	7	8
Response to unreasonably slow service	5	15
Response to other core service failure	11	20
Subtotal	23	43
Group 2: Employee Responses to Customer Needs and Requests		
Response to "special needs" customers	10	2
Response to customer preferences	15	11
Response to admitted customer error	6	2
Response to potentially disruptive others	2	1
Subtotal	33	16
Group 3: Unprompted and Unsolicited Employee Actions		
Attention paid to customer	14	13
Truly out-of-the-ordinary employee behavior	6	12
Employee behaviors in the context of cultural norms	5	12
Gestalt evaluation	16	4
Performance under adverse circumstances	3	—
Subtotal	44	41

of satisfaction and dissatisfaction and a simplified version of the results is shown in Table 4.1.

A number of things become immediately apparent from this table. The first is that service failures, such as unavailable service or slow service, do not automatically lead to dissatisfied customers. If handled correctly by contact personnel, they can lead to satisfaction—as they did with 23 percent of the incidents.

Customers do not always obey the rules. Their personal preferences, behavior, and mistakes can place demands on contact personnel that fall outside the scope of standard procedures and practices. Again, the way the employee responds to these needs and requests can influence the satisfaction level of the customer dramatically.

Finally, and most importantly, nearly half of satisfied and dissatisfied customers described incidents in which the primary action was an unprompted employee action. These ranged from positive actions: "The bus boy ran after us to return a $50 bill my boyfriend had dropped under the table," to negative actions: "I needed a few more minutes to decide on a dinner. The waitress said, 'If you would read the menu and not the road map, you would know what you wanted to order.'"

All of these actions are outside the scope of normal operating procedures. Each represents an independent positive or negative action by a contact person. Part of designing a service is to understand what it is that influences people to behave as they do.

THE BOUNDARY-SPANNING ROLE

The boundary-spanning role has been defined as one that links an organization with the environment within which it operates.[2] Participants in such a role create these links for the organization by interacting with nonmembers. Persons in such roles have two purposes: information transfer and representation.[3] Boundary spanners collect information from the environment and feed it back into the organization, and they communicate with the environment on behalf of the organization. They are also the organization's personal representatives. Such roles often carry high status and are filled by highly trained people; salespeople are a classic example.

In Article 4.3, Boas Shamir suggests that there are two types of roles in service firms—subordinate service roles and service roles based on professional expertise. In reality, there is not a dichotomy of roles but a spectrum. At one extreme are the "subordinate service roles" existing at the bottom of the organization. People in these roles work for service firms where the customers' purchase decision is entirely discretionary. They are subordinate to the organization and to the customer. These are the waiters, porters, drivers, and the like who operate at the very base of the organization and yet are the organization's contact personnel with the outside world.

At the other extreme are the professionals. They, too, are boundary-spanners, and yet their status is very different. Because of their "professional" qualifications, they have a status that is independent of their place in the organization. Customers, or (as they more often are called) clients, are not superior to them because they acknowledge the professional's expertise on which they wish to draw.

ROLE STRESS IN BOUNDARY-SPANNING ROLES

Article 4.4 provides a detailed observational study of one such contact role, the supermarket cashier. This qualitative study highlights the sources of stress faced by the cashier as well as the paradoxes of the role. Customers have the major influence on cashiers since their influence is instantaneous, continuous, and simultaneous with the performance of the job. The manager, by comparison, who holds the legitimate influence, only can create the environment and set the stage for employee performance. It is the customers who directly create the stress in this role.

Rafaeli suggests that there are four main sources of stress:

☐ An inability of contact personnel to develop a strong social network amongst co-workers because of a discipline imposed by the customers who do not want the staff to be too "chatty" while they are working. This is obviously an idiosyncrasy of the supermarket situation, but occurs to a greater or lesser extent in other settings as well.

☐ The constrained nature of the customer–cashier relationship means that cashiers often are denied the freedom to engage in normal social interaction with customers. This, combined with the inability to socialize with other staff, makes this particular contact role a lonely one.

☐ Role conflict and ambiguity.

☐ The fight for control.

The latter two sources of stress are addressed by other authors, notably Shamir (Article 4.3) and Bateson (Article 2.2).

SERVICES IN ACTION 4.1

HOLDING IT FOR EIGHT HOURS I

The following conversations with waitresses in London illustrate how the boundary-spanning role creates stress.

ANNA HAMILTON:

Silly things happen—you know, you have to pretend as if everything they do is OK. If drunk people come along, particularly when they start eating off the flowers and throwing glasses on the floor. "It's quite all right sir; don't worry about it," you know, and you have to pretend that everything they do is fine.

ANNE LEVER:

I was approaching this woman and she was there, calmly reading her Listener, I think it was, I just plonked the whole thing on her dress (laughs), you know, and it just completely fell and, you know, did a nice neat turnover, you know, so no savory, I mean no dough side—it had to be all the toppings . . . weeeraaarghhh.

SHEILA COLE:

The difficulty is to keep smiling of course. I always remember at the end of a long shift someone saying to me "Smile!" You know, why don't you smile, and you just feel like saying no *you* smile—now hold it for eight hours.

EVA MILENSKA:

If you really wish something bad to happen to your friend, just wish her to be a waitress! (laughs)

SHEILA:

I play sort of little games sometimes. I suppose to relieve the boredom of the monotony of the job, but I go to a table and I'll be really really you know over the top or really, um, jolly and witty and whatever and then other times I'll be sort of slightly different. You know, it's just a sort of interesting how people react to you and you also look at the people you're going to serve and I think that has a lot to do with how you are as well. Um, sometimes I'm overwhelmed by peoples' shyness. You know that sometimes I feel that I'm very overpowering and I haven't meant to be. You realize that from the way they've reacted to you that you're coming across as very different to how you really are or you've been misinterpreted somehow.

BERNADETTE GEIFER:

Sometimes, I'd prefer challenging customers if the challenge is all right. There was a woman who came in who wasn't happy with anything at all and she didn't like anything on the menu, and your first response was to just slam down things down and be very snippy towards her. But, in the end, I felt no, she was looking to find something wrong with the place and with me and I thought no, I'm not going to give her the satisfaction. And I was so brilliant towards her and so polite; in the end she, you know, she was brilliant, hugged me when I left, and all that.

ANNE KOVAL:

I find that because alot of the customers are young and, um, they are involved in jobs where they're making lots of money and they bring their friends around to the wine bar, er, they tend to, um, use you—the waitress—as a servant. It's the closest I've ever become to being a servant, um, for someone. It's quite disturbing at times when they treat you, in front of their friends, as a non-human being in a lot of ways. I went up to a table and a group of gentlemen and, um, I think

(continued)

(continued from previous page)

they were probably estate agents or something of that genre, and, um, one of the gentlemen had, um, one of those portable telephones and it rang while he was talking to me or doing some ordering, and, um, he was talking on the telephone and the other gentlemen didn't take up the initiative and finish the order, so they expected me to wait around. It was very busy at that moment, so I walked away and was waiting for him to complete his phone call, and then I'd return to the table and when I did return to the table he, um, he was quite put out—the fact that I hadn't waited around until he'd finished his conversation on his portable telephone.

SHEILA:

People can be incredibly rude, unbelievably rude. We had an instance a few weeks ago that happened here; a waitress, who's since left the profession, and she was dealing with a man who was just outrageous and she just couldn't stand any more, come to her wits' end, and he said the classic one-liner, "This food isn't fit for a pig!"—which had only one retort which was "I'll get you some that is, sir," and I think when you get to that, you're on your way out. That's it and you know you won't keep going unless you keep up the performance. In a way, waitressing is a kind of performing thing where you're putting on an act in a way. So I think that's why you find so many people within the arts involved in waitressing, partly because of the hours, but partly because they can put on different roles and no one's going to know whether it's them or not them.

BERNADETTE:

I write fiction, mostly short stories, and, I mean, obviously, I would like to do that full time for a living if I could make enough money at it, but it's one of those things where you obviously can't make enough money in the beginning, you know. So you try and get a few stories out to publications, and, while you're waiting to hear from them, or, you know, you write three hours a day or four hours a day, you know you obviously need to be doing something else as well. I do find that I like meeting people, um, I just like talking to people. I'll basically talk to anyone and, in some ways, that's quite a good . . . I never think about writing stories about the people I meet, but some of the things they say to me make me stop and think, and some of the things that happen, um, would make a humorous story. So that's one of the aspects that I like about that is that it keeps me in contact with more than just, you know, a bunch of office people that I know every day. I mean, I'm constantly meeting people I've never met before.

SOURCE: BBC Radio, "Holding It for Eight Hours," September 8, 1988.

SOURCES OF CONFLICT IN BOUNDARY-SPANNING ROLES

Shamir develops a long list of potential conflicts imposed on subordinate personnel because they have boundary-spanning roles. This list can be applied to a greater or lesser extent to professionally oriented roles as well.

PERSON/ROLE CONFLICTS Conflicts between the individual and his or her assigned role can be related to the role theory and script theory perspectives discussed in Chapter 2. For services to operate successfully, both customer and contact personnel must conform to a script or role. Each must play his or her part. A person/role conflict indicates that playing such a role may be inconsistent with an individual's self-perception. Some customers may wish boundary-spanners to be servile, a role that the boundary-spanner normally would not play; especially with that type of customer. Boundary-spanning personnel (BSPs) often are called on to subordinate personal feelings to their role, to smile and be helpful while feeling miserable and aggressive; this is particularly the case for low-level staff.[4] Professionals are much more likely to be able to operate within their own self-image and to feel less obligated to maintain a "bedside manner."

ORGANIZATION/CLIENT CONFLICTS Conflicts between the demands of the organization and those of the client are the most commonly discussed issues in boundary-spanning literature. Put simply, a conflict arises when the client or customer requests services that violate the rules of the organization. Such a violation can be as simple as a request for a second bread roll in a restaurant and as complex as a request that a bus driver leave the established route to drop off a passenger at home.[5]

Such conflicts are exacerbated if the BSP agrees with the customer. Benjamin Schneider, in Article 4.2, adds an interesting insight into this type of conflict. He approaches the boundary-spanning role problem from a different perspective, that of organizational climate. One of his findings is that contact personnel in a subordinate role do know whether they are giving good or bad service; moreover, they are well aware when the rules and procedures prevent them from delivering good service. This is precisely the organization/client conflict suggested by Shamir. Often, it is aggravated by the BSP's siding with the customer.

For subordinate service personnel, this kind of conflict is very stressful, since they have no status with the customer or the organization and no power to alter the situation. They cannot change the rule or procedure, and often they cannot tell the customer the reason for the rule or procedure. Professionals, with their higher status, are more able to control what happens.

INTERCLIENT CONFLICTS Conflicts between clients arise because many servuction systems have within them a number of clients, some of whom may be operating with conflicting standards. In a sense, these individuals have completely different scripts for themselves, the contact personnel, and the other customers. When customers come into conflict, it is usually the BSP who is called upon to resolve it. For example, it is the airline cabin attendant who generally is summoned to ask one's neighbor not to smoke in a nonsmoking section. Moreover, any attempt to satisfy all of the clients involved can escalate the conflict or bring the BSP into the battle. A restaurant customer requesting speedy service and receiving it can cause complaints from other tables about the unevenness of the service. Once again, those in subordinate roles start from the weakest position since they have low status with the clients. Professionals may face the same problems; for example, consider the patient in the hospital waiting room demanding preferential treatment. In this case, however, the professional can invoke his or her status and expertise to resolve the situation.

THE FIGHT FOR CONTROL

John Bateson, in Article 2.2, suggests that the service encounter can be viewed as a fight for control. This model, which applies equally to customers and to contact personnel, suggests that individuals like to feel in control of what happens to them. Therefore, there is a fight between these two parties for control of the encounter. An early study of restaurants, for example, found that waitresses coped with the pressures of their jobs by managing their customers. They were able to wrest control away from the customer by suggesting menu items and telling customers how long they would have to wait.[6] This is precisely the strategy employed by many professionals who use their status, and the fact that the client is not in a position to leave, to take control.

This is not simply a two-cornered fight, however; the organization itself also wishes to establish control of the encounter. The procedures and systems established by the organization are not always created for sheer bureaucratic pleasure, as implied by Schneider. Often the procedures and systems are the heart of the economics of the organization. Deviation can jeopardize profitability.

THE IMPLICATIONS OF ROLE STRESS FOR BOUNDARY-SPANNING PERSONNEL

The consequences of role conflict and stress have been investigated extensively. Generally, such stress produces dissatisfaction, frustration, and turnover intention in personnel. Schneider, in Article 4.2, shows that organization/client conflict in service organizations can lead to such outcomes. He shows that contact personnel, who are more service enthusiastic than their management, find the rules and procedures frustrating and have higher intentions of quitting.

When faced with such role stress in their jobs, people do not accept it passively but rather attempt to ameliorate the stress. The simplest way of avoiding conflict is to avoid the customer. This is exemplified by the waiter who refuses to notice a customer who wishes to place an order. This strategy also allows the waiter to increase his sense of control over the encounter. An alternative strategy is to move into "people-processing mode,"[7] where customers are treated as inanimate objects to be processed rather than as individuals. This reduces the requirement for the BSP to associate or empathize with the individual.

Many strategies are employed by the BSP to maintain a sense of control of the encounter. Physical symbols and furniture are often used to boost the BSP's status and, hence, his or her control.[8] In the extreme case, the BSP overacts the role and forces the customer into the subservient role, as is the case with many waiters and waitresses.

An alternative strategy used by BSPs to reduce organization/client conflict is to side completely with the customer. When forced to obey a rule with which they disagree, BSPs will proceed to list for the customer all of the other things about the organization with which they disagree. In this way, they attempt to reduce stress by seeking sympathy from the customer.

MANAGING THE CUSTOMER–CONTACT PERSONNEL INTERFACE

Chapter 6 deals with the problem of how to design the human-resources policies of the organization to maximize the likelihood of success in the service encounter. However, Article 4.4 is included here to highlight the need to truly understand the employee if such initiatives are to be successful.

The study describes an analysis of the results of an in-store initiative in a chain of convenience stores. The stores had used a variety of local and corporate-wide practices to reward clerks who acted in a friendly fashion during transactions with customers, including mystery shoppers and in competitions. To assess the results of the

SERVICES IN ACTION 4.2

HOLDING IT FOR EIGHT HOURS II

The following conversations with waitresses in London further illustrates how the boundary-spanning role creates stress.

SHEILA:

Of course it's great having regular customers, but sometimes it can be a bit difficult. I remember one chap used to come in an awful lot, every week, you know, sometimes twice a week, and he would always come in with a different woman every time. I mean, it was phenomenal, but he used to start off by kissing them across the table and it would get more and more involved until he was practically making love in quite an offensive way. I mean, people around would be quite put off until, in the end, we had to, you know, say I'm sorry, but we can't have this any more, and he was asked to leave, which is awful for him, but we haven't seen him since.

BERNADETTE:

Arguments are very difficult—when a couple's having an argument—because you inevitably go up at the very wrong time and say, you know, would you like to see a dessert menu or something stupid. And, you know, you're trying to wait for a point to break in, and you can't do it very easily and you can see them fuming and, er, some of that gets very difficult. Because once there was a friend of mine—instead of saying "Would you like to see a dessert menu?" he said, "Would you like to see a divorce menu?" and they went . . . !

SHEILA:

Oh yes, yes, there's been a few divorces over, um, dinner, um, yes, and people, um, flirting with each other. Er, it's very very amusing. I mean, obviously, you don't mean to listen, but you know some man shooting off about how brilliant he is all night—you know, every time you go up it's I, I, I, and the girl's sort of slowly . . . or some woman who's talking so much, I mean, you can see the nervousness of people, you know, and when they've blown it or when they haven't.

BERNADETTE:

Oh, you smell when you come out alot of times. You go out after work—if it's an afternoon shift—you go out for an evening and you bring your clothes in, but you want to hide them somewhere—because any time you leave your good clothes somewhere they always smell—and you want to hide them in the office, and you want to put them in bags and, er, so that you don't smell like the restaurant when you go out. Or you want to bring lots of perfume or something to make you get away from that smell, whatever smell that is. I mean, certain restaurants smell worse or different than others, but it's, just, it's one of those feelings where you wish that you could go in to a job, you know, clean and come out still smelling of perfume and still smelling clean and you can't.

SHEILA:

There's no doubt about it—you just feel so grimy all the time. I just find it really unromantic, you know. Especially—it's all right if you go out with someone you work with and you *both* go home together or whatever, and you go out and you're *both* smelly. It's sort of, you don't notice, but if you, um, if you go out with someone who doesn't work in a restaurant, it's, er, you know, if they meet you for tea . . . I always remember one story I, um, an old boyfriend of mine, we went back for tea at his mother's. He'd met me after lunch time, after I'd been working lunch time, 'cause we had to go for tea. And, um, we were sitting down,

(continued)

(continued from previous page)

and she said, "What is that smell?" And we were all sort of, I didn't think it was me to start with, you know, I didn't know what it was. Anyway, it came down to it that it was my hair, because the oil, it was sometimes the oil. I don't know what it is, but it gets . . . I suppose if it's near the end when it just needs changing it gets much a bit smellier, like more oniony or something, and my hair absolutely stunk of this oily . . . And it was the most embarrassing thing. I thought after that I never go out after work. I mean, I won't go out after work like to a club or anything unless I can change and wash and I won't go out straight from work in the afternoon. I'll have to go home and wash before and change.

BERNADETTE:

My back aches, my arms ache, um, you just feel drained. I mean, it's not mentally drained, but in a way it is, if you've been dealing with, you know, with sort of horrendous customers all day, you're just exhausted—completely exhausted physically as well as mentally. Though, because you are dealing with people and having to understand how they're feeling and what sort of mood they're in and what they want and what they don't want, um, but it's the sort of thing where, when you've finished, you can't very easily go home and go straight to bed. You can't just collapse somewhere, because you're still buzzing—whether it's from a really good night—say you've made, you know, brilliant tips and it's a brilliant night, or it's been a very bad night and, you know, you're very upset about things that happened or customers that you've had. You're still buzzing. You can't just collapse and fall asleep, you have to unwind. It's one of those things where you just you need at least an hour before you go to bed to, sort of, become normal again.

SHEILA:

I've always had lots and lots of energy, physical energy. And you have to almost have that nervous energy, you know, you have to have an element of that. Everyone who does it has to be highly energetic and very healthy; obviously, you can't do it if you've got a bad back or whatever. I feel, when it gets to about twelve o'clock in the evening, especially if it's been a busy night, I just feel like I could go to sleep there and then on the table.

ANNE KOVAL:

But when you climb in to your bed at the end of a long night, um, your bones ache and it always helps to have a, um, a hot bath. Er, I usually find that it's very difficult to wind down, um, it's a bit like any sort of job which requires a lot of energy. At the end of it, you just, you keep, you know, even when you're sleeping, you're still going. And I, when I'm waitressing a lot, I find that I have a lot of waitress dreams which are sort of notorious, um, dreams where you're constantly going crazy serving people and somehow your orders are always getting confused. And, um, it's, you know, sort of a typical nightmare, which is a waitress's dream. And I always know when I get those dreams too much that I'm obviously working too hard!

SHEILA:

When I get in the cab at the end of a long shift, I mean, I'm on my feet for eight hours and I just, I think what I'm going to be doing tomorrow. And all my friends, we all think the same. We're all doing our acting or our designing or our painting and it's like another little world, and you have to shut out what you've just been doing, and the danger is, of course, that you lose sight of what you should be doing because you work so much. And you're at the restaurant more than you're at the recording studio and, in the end, you know, you don't become that dancer or singer or actress any more. You're just left with being a waitress.

SOURCE: BBC Radio, "Holding It for Eight Hours," September 8, 1988.

initiative, a sample of 576 stores were observed in order to look at the behavior of the staff. In each store, 20 transactions were coded for four features: greeting ("Hello," "How are you today?"), thanking, smiling, and eye contact.

The subsequent analysis attempts to relate the behaviors of the staff to total sales. Given the variations to be found between stores, control variables were introduced to allow for customer gender compensation, store ownership, store supervision cost, etc. The surprising finding was a negative and significant relationship between store sales and the positive display of emotion by staff.

Only after detailed qualitative analysis was it possible to understand the complexity of the relationship. Qualitative comparisons of stores during slow and busy times suggest that pace of business is a cue for norms of expressed emotions. The norm or script for a busy time is that both customers and staff expect customers to be processed rapidly. Any attempt to display emotions during the service period is seen as a waste of time. Busy times are stressful times, and expressing irritation toward people who hamper efficiency was found to be especially legitimate during busy times.

During normal or non-busy times, customer processing can be a source of entertainment. Staff are more likely to display emotions, and customers are more likely to be friendly as the script is now different. Thus, the pace of the store, reflected in levels of store sales, fixes the norms of behavior. High pace and, hence, high sales are associated with a non-friendly processing model.

SUMMARY: PEOPLE AS THE PRODUCT

Much has been written about the fact that, for many service firms, personnel constitutes the bulk of their product. It is thus important that the place of the personnel within the organization be understood.

Marketing theory is ill-equipped to provide insights into the problem of where contact personnel fit into the hierarchy of the service firm. Organizational behavior, by comparison, is a field focused on this and similar problems. By drawing on the concepts of organizational behavior and, in particular, on the concept of a boundary-spanning role, this chapter has provided a solid framework on which to develop the marketing implications of people as the product. This approach has served to stress the increased levels of interdependence among the various functions within a service firm.

CHAPTER 4 READINGS

Article 4.1 views the role of the contact personnel from the perspective of the customer. It highlights the key role of the employee and the potential to turn a service failure into a satisfying experience. This is the whole concept of service recovery, discussed in Chapter 11. Article 4.2, by comparison, takes an internal perspective and focuses on the climate in the organization. As such, it could as easily have been included in Chapter 6, but it does, however, highlight the openness of service organizations to their customers and the potential sources of role conflict and ambiguity for service personnel. Article 4.3 develops in detail the boundary-spanning perspective. It also stresses the distinction between the boundary-spanning roles of professionals and non-professionals, and demonstrates that personnel at the lowest level often have the most important role to play in delivering service. Article 4.4 provides a detailed probe into a single-service encounter, that of the supermarket cashier with the supermarket customer. Within that single encounter are captured the essence of the problems described in this chapter. Finally, Article 4.5 shows an attempt to relate "friendliness" programs to sales and the understanding of the service employee needed to really understand what happens.

QUESTIONS

1. In designing a new restaurant, management must decide whether to add a service charge to the bill or encourage patrons to tip the staff directly. What are the implications of tipping for the role conflict of the subordinate service personnel?

2. Provide examples of marketing programs that you believe have served to increase the role stress for service providers. Why do you believe that these programs have increased the stress?

3. Describe an instance in which you have received particularly good or bad service from a service provider. Using the boundary-spanning concept, analyze the interaction and the role played by yourself and the provider.

4. Give examples of the organization/client role conflict you have witnessed or experienced. Could that conflict have been removed for the service provider? How? Why do you think the organization has not taken the steps you describe?

5. What is the role of the uniforms worn by many service providers? What is their impact on the relationship between the provider and the customer? As a service provider, would you rather be in uniform or not in uniform when interacting with customers?

NOTES

1. This idea was originally suggested in a slightly different form in W. Earl Sasser, P. Olsen, and D. Daryl Wyckoff, *Management of Service Operations: Text, Cases, and Readings* (Boston: Allyn and Bacon, 1978).

2. J. D. Thompson, "Organization and Output Transactions," *American Journal of Sociology* 68 (1967): 309–324.

3. See U. Aldrich and D. Huber, "Boundary-Spanning Roles and Organization Structure," *Academy of Management Review* 2 (1977): 217–230, which discusses the role of boundary spanners as information processors and filters; and J. D. Thompson, *Organizations in Action* (New York: McGraw-Hill, 1967), which discusses the representation aspect of the boundary-spanning role.

4. See Arlie Hochschild, *The Managed Heart* (Berkeley, CA: University of California Press, 1983).

5. For examples of these kinds of conflicts and of a research methodology to assess them, see Mary Jo Bitner, Jody D. Nyquist, and Bernard H. Booms, "The Critical Incident Technique for Analyzing the Service Encounter," in Thomas M. Block, Gregory D. Upah, and Valarie A. Zeithaml, eds., *Service Marketing in a Changing Environment* (Chicago: American Marketing Association, 1985); and Jody D. Nyquist, Mary Jo Bitner, and Bernard Booms, "Identifying Communications Difficulties in the Service Encounter: A Critical Incident Approach," in John Czepiel, Michael R. Solomon, and Carol F. Surprenant, eds., *The Service Encounter* (Lexington, MA: Heath, 1984).

6. See W. Foote Whyte, *Men at Work,* Dorsey Series in Behavioral Sciences (Homewood, IL: Dorsey Press and Irwin, 1949).

7. Peter Klaus, "The Quality Epiphenomenon," in John Czepiel, Michael R. Solomon, and Carol F. Surprenant, eds., *The Service Encounter* (Lexington, MA: Heath, 1983), 15.

8. Charles T. Goodsell, "Bureaucratic Manipulation of Physical Symbols: An Empirical Investigation," *American Journal of Political Science* XXI (February 1977): 79–91.

THE SERVICE ENCOUNTER

DIAGNOSING FAVORABLE AND UNFAVORABLE INCIDENTS

Mary Jo Bitner
Arizona State University

Bernard H. Booms
Washington State University

Mary Stanfield Tetreault
George Mason University

The service encounter frequently is the service from the customer's point of view. Using the critical incident method, the authors collected 700 incidents from customers of airlines, hotels, and restaurants. The incidents were categorized to isolate the particular events and related behaviors of contact employees that cause customers to distinguish very satisfactory service encounters from very dissatisfactory ones. Key implications for managers and researchers are highlighted.

Service industries continue to grow in importance to the U.S. economy while at the same time service quality is generally perceived to be declining (Koepp 1987). For the customer, the observable symptom is decreasing quality in what has been termed the "service encounter," or the moment of interaction between the customer and the firm (Czepiel, Solomon, and Surprenant 1985; Lovelock 1988; Shostack 1985; Solomon et al. 1985; Surprenant and Solomon 1987). Many times that interaction *is* the service from the customer's point of view, yet front-line employees are not trained to understand customers and do not have the freedom and discretion needed to relate to customers in ways that ensure effective service. The fact that customer contact employees often are underpaid and undertrained results in low levels of motivation, job dissatisfaction, high turnover, and ultimately dissatisfied customers.

Some service firms have avoided this downward spiral through practices that reflect their understanding of the service encounter and recognition of the marketing role of all front-line personnel (Albrecht and Zemke 1985). These exemplary firms understand that managing the service encounter involves more than training employees to say "have a nice day" or to answer the phone on or before the third ring. Effective management of the service encounter involves understanding the often complex behaviors of employees that can distinguish a highly satisfactory service encounter from a dissatisfactory one, and then training, motivating, and rewarding employees to exhibit those behaviors.

We conducted a study of critical service encounters in three service industries to gain understanding of the particular events and related behaviors of contact employees that cause customers to distinguish very satisfactory services from very dissatisfactory ones. Through the research, 700 incidents (approximately half satisfac-

SOURCE: Mary Jo Bitner, Bernard H. Booms, and Mary Stanfield Tetreault, "The Service Encounter: Diagnosing Favorable and Unfavorable Incidents," reprinted with permission from the *Journal of Marketing,* January 1990, Vol. 54, pp. 71–84, published by the American Marketing Association, Chicago, IL, 60606.

Mary Jo Bitner is Assistant Professor of Marketing, Arizona State University. Bernard H. Booms is Professor, College of Business and Economics, Seattle Center for Hotel & Restaurant Administration, Washington State University. Mary Stanfield Tetreault is Assistant Professor of Marketing, George Mason University. The authors express special thanks to Michael Hutt and also thank Christopher Lovelock, Lawrence Crosby, and Leonard Berry for their helpful comments on the manuscript. The useful and considered suggestions of three anonymous *JM* reviewers are acknowledged.

tory and half dissatisfactory) were collected from customers of airlines, hotels, and restaurants to answer the following questions:

□ What specific events lead to *satisfying* service encounters from the customer's point of view? What do contact employees do that causes these events to be remembered favorably?

□ What specific events lead to *dissatisfying* service encounters from the customer's point of view? What do contact employees do that causes these events to be remembered with distaste?

□ Are the underlying events and behaviors that lead to satisfactory and dissatisfactory encounters similar? That is, are these events and behaviors opposites or mirror images of each other?

□ Are there "generic" events and behaviors, cutting across service industries, that could be considered the underlying causes of satisfactory and dissatisfactory encounters?

To address these questions, we use the critical incident method originally developed for industry use by Flanagan (1954). The method has been used extensively in diverse disciplines including management (e.g., White and Locke 1981), human resources (e.g., Hough 1984; Latham and Saari 1984; Latham et al. 1980; Pursell, Campion, and Gaylord 1980), and education (e.g., Copas 1984; Cotterell 1982). Here, in a marketing context, the method is adapted to identify the sources of both satisfactory and dissatisfactory service encounters from the customer's point of view. The resulting categories are based on specific events and behaviors and hence are amenable to direct management application. Before discussing the method, procedure, and results of the study, we review previous research on the service encounter and service satisfaction and quality.

THE PROBLEM SETTING

THE SERVICE ENCOUNTER

The term "service encounter" has attained widespread use in marketing speeches, articles, and research in a few short years. Surprenant and Solomon (1987) define the service encounter as "the dyadic interaction between a customer and service provider." This definition draws on their earlier work suggesting that "service encounters are role performances" (Solomon et al. 1985) in which both customers and service providers have roles to enact. This use of the term "service encounter" focuses on the interpersonal element of service firm performance. Shostack

(1985) defines the service encounter somewhat more broadly as "a period of time during which a consumer directly interacts with a *service*." Her definition encompasses all aspects of the service firm with which the consumer may interact, including its personnel, its physical facilities, and other visible elements. Shostack's definition does not limit the encounter to the interpersonal interactions between the customer and the firm, and in fact suggests that service encounters can occur without *any* human interaction element. We focus on the personal interactions between customers and employees in service encounters, while recognizing that the service encounter encompasses more as Shostack suggests.

SERVICE QUALITY AND SERVICE SATISFACTION

Empirical research in both service quality and service satisfaction affirms the importance of the quality of customer/employee interactions in the assessment of overall quality and/or satisfaction with services. Parasuraman, Zeithaml, and Berry (1985, 1988) define service quality as the overall evaluation of a specific service firm that results from comparing that firm's performance with the customer's general expectations of how firms in that industry *should* perform. Through focus group interviews, they initially identified 10 dimensions of service quality (1985). Through empirical validation and rigorous scale development procedures, they later reduced these dimensions to five independent dimensions of service quality (1988); tangibles, reliability, responsiveness, assurance, and empathy. Close examination of the scale items for each dimension reveals that a majority of all the items relate directly to the human interaction element of service delivery.

Several service-based studies of service satisfaction also suggest that the human interaction component of service delivery is essential to the determination of satisfaction/dissatisfaction. A study of relationship marketing in the life insurance industry found clients' satisfaction with their contact person (or agent) to be a significant predictor of overall satisfaction with the service (Crosby and Stephens 1987). Other researchers have found the human interaction component to be of importance in evaluating professional services (Day and Bodur 1978; Quelch and Ash 1981), medical services (Brown and Swartz 1989), and retail outlets (Westbrook 1981). Similarly, experimental studies of service satisfaction also have uncovered the importance of particular contact employee behaviors (Bitner 1990; Surprenant and Solomon 1987).

By demonstrating the importance of the human interaction component of the service encounter to service quality and satisfaction, these empirical studies provide a valuable contribution. However, the results are either intentionally general and do not specify particular *behaviors* associated with good and poor service, or the behaviors reported are applicable to one specific industry. Unlike previous research, our study identifies *specific events and behaviors* rather than general dimensions and explores the causes of both satisfactory and unsatisfactory service encounters. The behaviors identified cut across several industries rather than being related to one industry only.

METHOD AND PROCEDURE

CRITICAL INCIDENT TECHNIQUE

After considering several research methods (Bitner, Nyquist, and Booms 1985), we selected the critical incident technique (CIT) as most appropriate for discovering the underlying sources of satisfaction and dissatisfaction in service encounters (Nyquist and Booms 1987). CIT consists of a set of specifically defined procedures for collecting observations of human behavior and classifying them in such a way as to make them useful in addressing practical problems (Flanagan 1954). The CIT as a method of classification can be categorized with other inductive grouping procedures such as factor analysis, cluster analysis, and multidimensional scaling (Hunt 1983, p. 354). Such methods determine categories based on analysis of a specific set of data and are particularly useful when there is little documentation of the properties that are likely to be important for classifying. Unlike the other grouping procedures, however, CIT uses Content analysis of stories, rather than quantitative solutions, in the data analysis stage of the procedure. Content analysis "takes the communications that people have produced and asks questions of the communications" (Kerlinger 1973, p. 525). Similarly, CIT takes the stories that people have told and asks questions of the stories in order to classify each one within the scheme.

Through interviews or observation, the CIT records events and behaviors that have been observed to lead to success or failure in accomplishing a specific task (Ronan and Latham 1974). The specific descriptions of events and behaviors are identified as critical incidents. An *incident* is defined as an observable human activity that is complete enough in itself to permit inferences and predictions to be made about the person performing the act. A *critical* incident is one that contributes to

or detracts from the general aim of the activity in a significant way. We define critical incidents as specific interactions between customers and service firm employees that are especially satisfying or especially dissatisfying. Hence, not *all* service incidents were classified, only those that customers found memorable because they were particularly satisfying or dissatisfying. Examining such memorable critical incidents is likely to afford insight into the fundamentally *necessary* factors leading to customers' dis/satisfactory evaluations. An incident was required to meet the four criteria of (1) involving employee–customer interaction, (2) being very satisfying or dissatisfying from the *customers'* point of view, (3) being a discrete episode, and (4) having sufficient detail to be visualized by the interviewer. Research conducted by Andersson and Nilsson (1964) on the general reliability and validity aspects of the CIT led them to conclude that the information collected by this technique is both reliable and valid; Ronan and Latham (1974) and White and Lock (1981) reached similar conclusions.

METHODOLOGICAL CONSIDERATIONS

The CIT is essentially a classification technique employing content analysis of stories or "critical incidents" as data. Content analysis of a variety of forms of communication has a long history in political science, journalism, education, social psychology, and communication research and recently has been applied in marketing to analyze the content of advertising (Pollay 1985) and comics (Belk 1987; Kassarjian 1984; Spiggle 1986), as well as retail store image (Zimmer and Golden 1988). As a research method, CIT shares the advantages and disadvantages generally attributed to content analysis (Kassarjian 1977; Viney 1983; Weber 1985). The primary advantage is "its capacity to provide accurate and consistent interpretations of people's accounts of events without depriving these accounts of their power or eloquence" (Viney 1983, p. 560). Another advantage is that CIT and content analysis utilize both qualitative and quantitative examination of communications (combining "rigor and vigor"), usually thought to be antithetical forms of analysis (Viney 1983). Criticism of content analysis typically centers on issues of reliability and validity of the categories. Reliability and validity problems may arise as a result of the ambiguity of word meanings, category labels, and coding rules in a particular study (Weber 1985). Though use of computerized content analysis programs may reduce reliability problems to some extent, computerization introduces other potential problems, such as the possibility of "mindless content analysis" (Weber 1985, p. 69). As an explanatory method, CIT also shares the advantages and disadvantages of other exploratory inductive methods. However, when the purpose of the research is to increase knowledge of a phenomenon about which relatively little has been documented and/or to describe a real-world phenomenon based on thorough understanding, an approach such as CIT seems particularly well suited to the task.

DATA COLLECTION

Three industries—hotels, restaurants, and airlines—were selected as representative of high-contact services in which contact employees' communication skills are particularly important (Chase 1978). The incidents were collected by 75 students who interviewed a convenience sample of customers of airlines, hotels, and restaurants over a period of three weeks. Each student was asked to recruit and interview five people to collect a total of 10 incidents—half satisfactory and half dissatisfactory. They were instructed to recruit people who traveled relatively frequently (for business or pleasure) and who ate regularly in restaurants. They were specifically instructed *not* to recruit fellow students. The principal investigators gave the interviewers detailed training and written instructions for the interviews: the interviewers practiced the procedure by role-playing. The following questions were asked of all respondents and answers were recorded on standardized questionnaires.

☐ Think of a time when, as a customer, you had a particularly *satisfying (dissatisfying)* interaction with an employee of an airline, hotel, or restaurant.

☐ When did the incident happen?

☐ What specific circumstances led up to this situation?

☐ Exactly what did the employee say or do?

☐ What resulted that made you feel the interaction was *satisfying (dissatisfying)?*

Note that respondents were not asked to identify the underlying causes of dis/satisfaction, but rather to describe a specific instance in which good or poor service interaction occurred. Reporting events or stories in this way is something most people do very easily. It is the researcher who takes responsibility for abstraction and inference, not the respondent. The interviewers collected a total of 719 incidents. Twenty incidents failed to meet at least one of the four critical incident criteria and were eliminated from further analysis, leaving a sample

of 699 incidents (347 satisfactory and 352 dissatisfactory). Of the 347 satisfactory incidents, 86 were from airlines, 165 from restaurants, and 96 from hotels. Of the 352 dissatisfactory incidents, 77 were from airlines, 191 from restaurants, and 84 from hotels. The firms from which incidents were reported represented a full range of airlines, hotels, and restaurants in terms of size and level of service offered. The customer interviewees also represented a cross section of the population. Fifty-three percent of the respondents were men and 47% were women. The median age of the respondents was 36.5 years, with a range from 16 to 82.

CLASSIFICATION OF INCIDENTS

Once the data were collected, the incident classification system of the CIT was used to categorize the incidents with the goal of making the data useful for answering the research questions while sacrificing as little detail and comprehensiveness as possible. This analytic induction process consists of repeated, careful readings and sorting of the incidents into groups and categories according to similarities in the reported experiences. After the researcher has read many incidents, similarities among incidents begin to become apparent. Next comes the process of articulating or identifying the exact nature of the similarity, which forms the basis for the labeling of each category of incidents. Over and over the incidents are sorted, combined, and resorted until all incidents in a category are more similar to each other than they are to those in any other category.

In our study, the first stage of the incident analysis was the inductive delineation of major groupings that collectively could account for all of the incidents and begin to answer in a general way the basic research question: What are the events and behaviors leading to satisfying and dissatisfying service encounters from the customer's perspective? Two successive clustering processes conducted by two researchers resulted in the emergence of three major groups. After consensus on the major groups, the process of delineating categories within the groups was initiated. Using an iterative process, two researchers read, sorted, reread, and recombined the incidents until consensus was achieved on category labels and the assignment of each incident to one of 12 resulting categories. All incidents then were sorted by a third researcher who was given the 12 categories but had not participated in the initial categorization tasks. Interjudge agreement (based on the third researcher's sorting of the incidents) on assignment of the incidents to the 12 categories was 88 and 92% for satisfactory and dissatisfactory incidents, respectively.

RESULTS AND DISCUSSION

The primary results of studies using the CIT are the groups and categories that emerge through the classification procedure. In this section we describe the groups and categories. The proportions shown in both Tables 1 and 2 are analyzed and discussed subsequently to provide insights into the original research questions. Figure 1 is a tree diagram of the final sorting process that evolved through the inductive analysis of the incidents.

INCIDENT CLASSIFICATION SYSTEM—MAJOR GROUPS

The initial sorting of the incidents resulted in three major groups of employee behaviors that could account for all satisfactory and dissatisfactory incidents, as shown in Table 1 and Figure 1.

GROUP 1. EMPLOYEE RESPONSE TO SERVICE DELIVERY SYSTEM FAILURES When the service delivery system fails, contact employees are required to respond to consumer complaints or disappointments. The content or form of the employee response determines the customer's perceived satisfaction or dissatisfaction. All group 1 incidents are related directly to failures in the *core service* (the hotel room, the restaurant meal service, the airplane flight) and inevitable system failures that occur for even the best of firms. The ability and/or willingness of the contact employee to respond and handle such failures can result in the incident being remembered as very satisfactory or very dissatisfactory.

GROUP 2. EMPLOYEE RESPONSE TO CUSTOMER NEEDS AND REQUESTS When a customer requires the contact employee to adapt the service delivery system to suit his or her unique needs, the contact employee's response determines the customer's dis/satisfaction. To be classified in group 2, incidents were required to contain either an explicit or inferred request for customized service. "Customized" was interpreted from the customer's point of view because much of what customers perceive as "special needs/requests" may actually be routine (or even legally required) from the firm or contact employee's point of view. What is important is whether or not the customer perceives that his or her "special" requests or needs have been accommodated.

TABLE 1   Group and Category Classification by Type of Incident Outcome

| | Type of Incident Outcome | | | | Row Total | |
| | Satisfactory | | Dissatisfactory | | | |
Group and Category	No.	%	No.	%	No.	%
Group 1. Employee Response to Service Delivery System Failures						
A: Response to unavailable service	24	6.9	29	8.2	53	7.6
B: Response to unreasonably slow service	17	4.9	53	15.1	70	10.0
C: Response to other core service failures	40	11.5	69	19.6	109	15.6
Subtotal, group 1	81	23.3	151	42.9	232	33.2
Group 2. Employee Response to Customer Needs and Requests						
A: Response to "special needs" customers	36	10.4	6	1.7	42	6.0
B: Response to customer preferences	51	14.7	37	10.5	88	12.6
C: Response to admitted customer error	20	5.8	8	2.3	28	4.0
D: Response to potentially disruptive others	7	2.0	4	1.1	11	1.6
Subtotal, group 2	114	32.9	55	15.6	169	24.2
Group 3. Unprompted and Unsolicited Employee Actions						
A: Attention paid to customer	48	13.8	48	13.6	96	13.7
B: Truly out-of-the-ordinary employee behavior	22	6.3	41	11.6	63	9.0
C: Employee behaviors in the context of cultural norms	16	4.6	42	11.9	58	8.3
D: Gestalt evaluation	55	15.9	15	4.3	70	10.0
E: Performance under adverse circumstances	11	3.2	—	—	11	1.6
Subtotal, group 3	152	43.8	146	41.5	298	42.6
Column Total	347	49.6	352	50.4	699	100.0

FIGURE 1   Incident Sorting Process

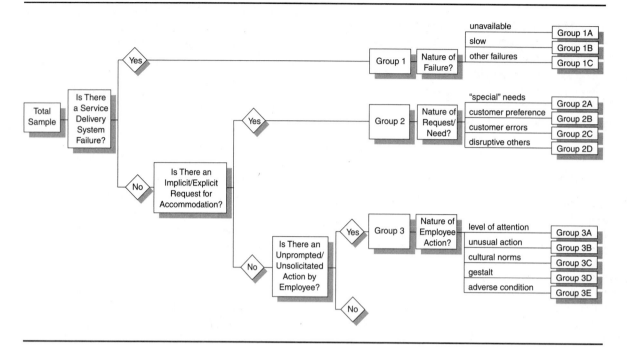

TABLE 2   Incident Classification by Type of Industry

	Type of Service Industry							
	Airline		Restaurant		Hotel		Row Total	
Groups	No.	%	No.	%	No.	%	No.	%
Satisfactory Incidents								
Group 1[a]	21	24.4	39	23.6	21	21.9	81	23.3
Group 2[b]	39	45.3	40	24.2	35	36.5	114	32.9
Group 3[c]	26	30.2	86	52.1	40	41.7	152	43.8
Column total	86	24.8	165	47.6	96	27.7	347	100.0
Dissatisfactory Incidents								
Group 1	35	45.5	76	39.8	40	47.6	151	42.9
Group 2	21	27.3	19	9.9	15	17.9	55	15.6
Group 3	21	27.3	96	50.3	29	34.5	146	41.5
Column total	77	21.9	191	54.3	84	23.9	352	100.0

[a]Employee response to service delivery system failures.
[b]Employee response to curstomer needs and requests.
[c]Unprompted and unsolicited employee actions.

GROUP 3. UNPROMPTED AND UNSOLICITED EMPLOYEE ACTIONS Events and employee behaviors that are truly unexpected from the customer's point of view are included in group 3. Satisfactory incidents represent very pleasant surprises (special attention, being treated like royalty, something nice but unrequested) whereas dissatisfactory incidents comprise negative and unacceptable employee behaviors (rudeness, stealing, discrimination, ignoring the customer). To be included in group 3 the employee behavior could not be triggered by a failure in the delivery of the core service, nor could there by any evidence (explicit or inferred) of the customer having a special need or making a special request. Hence these incidents represent truly unexpected and unrequested employee behaviors that either enhance or detract from the delivery of the core service.

INCIDENT CLASSIFICATION SYSTEM—CATEGORIES WITHIN GROUPS

Within the three major groups, a total of 12 categories emerged. Table 1 gives the frequency of occurrence of satisfactory and dissatisfactory incidents in each category. Tables 3, 4, and 5 list sample incidents for each of the 12 categories.

1A. RESPONSE TO UNAVAILABLE SERVICE Services normally available are lacking or absent: the hotel room is not available because of a "lost" reservation, the airplane is overbooked, or the reserved window table is occupied. The way in which unavailability is handled

influences the customer's perception of the service. The customer actually may remember the encounter as very satisfactory if, for example, he or she is upgraded to a better room, compensated by a free ticket, or offered a free meal or drink. Even acknowledging the problem, explaining why the service is unavailable, and assisting the customer in solving the problem by suggesting possible options can be enough to cause the customer to remember the event favorably. In contrast, failure to apologize, offer to compensate, or give an explanation can result in an unavailability incident being remembered as very dissatisfactory. Making the customer feel the failure is somehow his or her fault and implying that "you're on your own" to find alternative arrangements are other behaviors that infuriate customers who are victims of unavailable service.

1B. RESPONSE TO UNREASONABLY SLOW SERVICE This category reflects incidents in which services or employee performances are perceived as inordinately slow. Employee reaction to such delays determines the customer's satisfaction level. Acknowledging the delay, explaining the cause of the delay, and offering to compensate can alleviate dissatisfaction and even cause the customer to remember the event favorably. In contrast, acting as though nothing is wrong, not explaining the delay, and leaving customers to figure out what to do on their own are ways to aggravate the customer.

1C. RESPONSE TO OTHER CORE SERVICE FAILURES Because unavailability (1A) and slowness (1B) were

TABLE 3 Group 1 Sample Incidents: Employee Response to Service Delivery Failures

	Incident	
	Satisfactory	**Dissatisfactory**
A. Response to Unavailable Service	They lost my room reservation but the manager gave me the V.P. suite for the same price.	We had made advance reservations at the hotel. When we arrived we found we had no room—no explanation, no apologies, and no assistance in finding another hotel.
B. Response to Unreasonably Slow Service	Even though I didn't make any complaint about the hour and a half wait, the waitress kept apologizing and said that the bill was on the house.	The airline employees continually gave us erroneous information; a one-hour delay turned into a six-hour wait.
C. Response to Other Core Service Failures	My shrimp cocktail was half frozen. The waitress apologized, and didn't charge me for any of my dinner.	One of my suitcases was all dented and looked as though it had been dropped from 30,000 feet. When I tried to make a claim for my damaged luggage, the employee insinuated that I was lying and trying to rip them off.

TABLE 4   Group 2 Sample Incidents: Employee Response to Customer Needs and Requests

	Incident	
	Satisfactory	**Dissatisfactory**
A. Response to "Special Needs" Customers	The flight attendant helped me calm and care for my airsick child.	My young son, flying alone, was to be assisted by the stewardess from start to finish. At the Albany airport she left him alone in the airport with no one to escort him to his connecting flight.
B. Response to Customer Preferences	The front desk clerk called around and found me tickets to the Mariners' opening game.	The waitress refused to move me from a window table on a hot day, because here was nothing left in *her* section.
	It was snowing outside—car broke down. I checked 10 hotels and there were no rooms. Finally, one understood my situation and offered to rent me a bed and set it up in one of their small banquet rooms.	The airline wouldn't let me bring my scuba gear on board coming back from Hawaii even though I brought it over as carry-on luggage.
C. Response to Admitted Customer Error	I lost my glasses on the plane; the stewardess found them and they were delivered to my hotel free of charge.	We missed our flight because of car trouble. The service clerk wouldn't help us find a flight on an alternative airline.
D. Response to Potentially Disruptive Others	The manager kept his eye on an obnoxious guy at the bar, to make sure that he didn't bother us.	The hotel staff wouldn't deal with the noisy people partying in the hall at 3 A.M.

dominating causes of core service failure, separate categories were established for each. Category 1C encompasses incidents in which *other* aspects of the core service do not meet basic performance standards for the industry (e.g., the hotel room is not clean, the restaurant meal is cold, or the baggage arrives damaged). How the employee responds to these failures determines the customer's perceptions of the encounter. Again, as in the case of unavailable and unreasonably slow services, the keys to success are to acknowledge the problem, apologize when appropriate, explain what happened, and offer to compensate. In poorly managed organizations, customers may be left to fend for themselves or the employee may even imply that the customer is somehow to blame.

2A. RESPONSE TO "SPECIAL NEEDS" CUSTOMERS This category involves customers who have special medical, dietary, psychological, language, or sociological difficulties. Some of the incidents in this category were medical emergencies as well as needs to accommodate the elderly, children, and persons with language difficulties. Failure to recognize the seriousness of the customer's need and/or inappropriate or inadequate treatment of the problem can result in a very dissatisfactory incident. In contrast, acknowledgment of and success in accommodating the needs of these special customers

often will be remembered as very satisfying from the customer's perspective.

2B. RESPONSE TO CUSTOMER PREFERENCES This category includes incidents when, from the customer's perspective, "special" requests are made. These requests reflect personal preferences unrelated to the customer's sociological, physical, or demographic characteristics (2A). Requests in this category *may* be within industry/firm policy and norms, but nevertheless require the employee to adapt the system in some way. This category also includes incidents in which the customer requests a level of service customization clearly beyond the scope of or in violation of firm/industry policies or norms. In the case of satisfying incidents, the employee acknowledges the request, exhibits an accommodating attitude, and at least attempts to adapt to the customer's preferences. Frequently only a minor adjustment of the system is necessary. Sometimes the employee even shows initiative in anticipating a request or actually "bends the rules" to fit the customer's need. However, customers can be very dissatisfied when their preferences are not accommodated, especially if the employee shows no interest and exerts no effort to be responsive, is unwilling to consider "bending the rules," or promises to do something and then fails to follow through.

TABLE 5   Group 3 Sample Incidents: Unprompted and Unsolicited Employee Actions

	Incident	
	Satisfactory	**Dissatisfactory**
A. Attention Paid to Customer	The waiter treated me like royalty. He really showed he cared about me.	The lady at the front desk acted as if we were bothering her. She was watching TV and paying more attention to the TV than the hotel guests.
B. Truly Out-of-the-Ordinary Employee Behavior	We always travel with our teddy bears. When we got back to our room at the hotel we saw that the maid had arranged our bears very comfortably in a chair. The bears were holding hands.	I needed a few more minutes to decide on a dinner. The waitress said, "If you would read the menu and not the road map, you would know what you want to order."
C. Employee Behaviors in the Context of Cultural Norms	The busboy ran after us to return a $50 bill my boyfriend had dropped under the table.	The waiter at this expensive restaurant treated us like dirt because we were only high school kids on a prom date.
D. Gestalt Evaluation	The whole experience was so pleasant . . . everything went smoothly and perfectly.	The flight was a nightmare. A one-hour layover went to 3 1/2 hours. The air conditioning didn't work. The pilots and stewardesses were fighting because of an impending flight attendant strike. The landing was extremely rough. To top it all off, when the plane stopped, the pilots and stewardesses were the first ones off.
E. Performance under Adverse Circumstances	The counter agent was obviously under stress, but kept his cool and acted very professionally.	

2C. RESPONSE TO ADMITTED CUSTOMER ERROR In this category the triggering event is a customer error that strains the service encounter (e.g., lost tickets, incorrect order, missed reservations). Highly satisfactory encounters result when the employee acknowledges the customer's problem, takes responsibility, and assists the customer in solving the dilemma without embarrassing the customer in the process. To do so often requires considerable effort on the part of the employee (personally escorting a passenger without a visa through customs; calling around to find an alternative flight/room when a reservation is missed). Dissatisfactory employee responses include laughing at and embarrassing the customer for his or her mistake, avoiding any responsibility, and demonstrating an unwillingness to assist the customer in solving the problem.

2D. RESPONSE TO POTENTIALLY DISRUPTIVE OTHERS Within the environment of the service encounter, other customers' behaviors can strain the encounter (e.g., intoxication, rudeness, social deviance). The contact employee or firm either does or does not cope with the disruptive person(s) to the satisfaction of other customers present.

3A. ATTENTION PAID TO CUSTOMER This category includes incidents in which the level of attention paid the customer is viewed very favorably or very negatively. Satisfactory encounters result when contact employees make the customer feel "unique" or "pampered" by taking extra time, being attentive and anticipating needs without interfering, showing an interest in the customer's comfort, or providing extra information to the customer. Dissatisfactory encounters occur when contact employees demonstrate poor attitudes toward the customer, ignore the customer, or treat the customer impersonally as evidenced by such behaviors as being impatient, not anticipating needs, not caring about the customer's comfort, and failing to provide information.

3B. TRULY OUT-OF-THE-ORDINARY EMPLOYEE BEHAVIOR In this category are incidents in which the employee does some small thing that for the customer translates into a highly satisfactory or dissatisfactory encounter. For satisfactory service encounters, out-of-the-ordinary behavior consists of extraordinary actions or expressions of courtesy or thoughtfulness, such as unrequested acknowledgment of an occasion with a special song or gift or giving a hotel guest a vase of flowers he had admired. In the case of dissatisfactory encounters, extraordinary employee behavior may consist of profanity, yelling, inappropriate touching, or rudeness.

3C. EMPLOYEE BEHAVIORS IN THE CONTEXT OF CULTURAL NORMS Incidents in this category reflect employee behaviors relating to cultural norms such as equality, honesty, and fairness. Satisfactory encounters are associated with customers' pleasant surprise that an ideal cultural norm is upheld by an employee (tourists are not "ripped off," women and children customers are treated respectfully or "equally," a waiter returns a large tip left in error). Dissatisfactory encounters are associated with employee behaviors that clearly violate cultural norms (discrimination against female/black/young customers; employee theft, bribery, or lying).

3D. GESTALT EVALUATION For both satisfactory and dissatisfactory incidents in this category, customers are unable to attribute dis/satisfaction to any single feature of the service encounter. Instead, the service encounter is evaluated holistically, either "everything went right" or "everything went wrong." Each incident in this category reflects a number of employee behaviors and it is not possible to categorize the incident within one of the other, more specific categories. Satisfactory incidents in this group are reported by a combination of such words and phrases as "a sincere and professional team effort," "accommodating," "polite, but not pushy," "warm atmosphere," "courteous, efficient, and professional," "no waiting," "best service I ever received," "everything was perfect." Reports of dissatisfactory incidents, in contrast, refer to a combination of the following types of behaviors: inefficient, unprepared, slow, not accommodating or attentive, no assistance, unprofessional, bad decor/atmosphere. Also included in this category are cases in which customers remember favorably or unfavorably a series of encounters they have had with one provider.

3E. EXEMPLARY PERFORMANCE UNDER ADVERSE CIRCUMSTANCES This category includes incidents in which the customer is particularly impressed/displeased with the way a contact employee handles a stressful situation. This category emerged only for satisfactory encounters. Apparently, customers' empathy for contact employees and admiration for their "grace under pressure" leaves a significantly delible impression to countervail customer discomfort with crowds, shorthandedness, or "acts of God."

INSIGHTS INTO RESEARCH QUESTIONS

What conclusions about the initial research questions can we draw by examining the classification of the incidents and the frequencies and proportions reported in Tables 1 and 2? The classification schema itself as well as contingency table analyses (Fineberg 1980; Freeman 1987) of Tables 1 and 2 provide insights. The results of the contingency table analyses, based on hierarchical model tests, illuminate statistically significant relationships among classification variables in both tables. For Table 1, significant relationships are found between (1) type of outcome and categories (Δ L.R. χ^2 = 117.28; p. < .000) and (2) type of outcome and group (Δ L.R. χ^2 = 42.58; p < .000). The analysis of Table 2 reveals significant interactions between (1) type of outcome and group (Δ L.R. χ^2 = 42.58; p < .000) and (2) industry and group (Δ L.R. χ^2 = 34.63; p < .000). Neither the three-way interaction in Table 2 nor the interaction between type of outcome and industry is significant. The significant interactions are highlighted and explained in the following discussion, which is structured around the four research questions posed at the beginning of the article.

SOURCES OF SATISFACTION IN SERVICE ENCOUNTERS The three broad groups and 12 categories capture the types of events and behaviors that lead to very satisfactory encounters. Examination of the frequencies and proportions reported in Table 1 provides further insights. Note that 23.3% of the memorable satisfactory encounters are in group 1. Incidents in this group relate to *the way employees respond* to difficulties attributable to failures in core service delivery. Thus, when an employee compensates a customer for his or her long wait in a restaurant by offering a free drink, or when a hotel guest is upgraded to a better room when the originally requested room is not available, the customer frequently remembers such incidents as *very satisfying* even though the incident began with a failure of the system. From a management perspective, this finding is striking. It suggests that even service delivery system *failures* can be remembered as highly satisfactory encounters if they are handled properly.

Another substantial proportion (32.9%) of satisfying encounters are classified within group 2. Group 2 represents all of the incidents in which employees are able to accommodate customer needs for customized service. The data show that these incidents range from minor "special requests" such as a vegetarian asking for a special meal to "extraordinary requests" such as a hotel guest asking the room service employee to wear a blindfold because the guest and his companion are in bed naked.

Finally, observe from Table 1 that 43.8% of satisfactory encounters are a result of customer delight with unprompted and/or unsolicited employee actions (group 3). These exemplary attitudes and behaviors are truly unexpected by the customer. In these cases the core service (meal, hotel room, airplane flight) appears adequate, but the employee's attitude (i.e., "treating me like royalty") or unusual exemplary behavior (i.e., the maid "arranged our teddy bears so they were holding hands") transforms the encounter into a highly satisfactory incident. Thus, independent of core service requirements, and even when customers have no special need or request, customers remember with considerable frequency those occasions when they receive special treatment by the service employee.

SOURCES OF DISSATISFACTION IN SERVICE ENCOUNTERS The classification system also details the major groups and categories of behaviors associated with dissatisfactory encounters. Examination of Table 1 reveals that a large proportion of dissatisfactory encounters (42.9%) were related to employee's inability or unwillingness to respond in service failure situations (group 1). Interestingly, repeated, careful reading of the incidents indicates that it is not the initial failure to deliver the core service alone that causes dissatisfaction, but rather the *employee's response* to the failure. The importance of the employee's response comes out very vividly in the respondents' answers to the question, "What resulted that made you feel the interaction was dissatisfying?" In all group 1 dissatisfactory incidents, the employee failed to handle the situation in a way that could have satisfied the customer. Perceived inappropriate and/or inadequate response to failures in the service delivery system may represent a "double deviation" from role expectations that consumers hold for providers, resulting in magnification of the negative evaluation.

Group 2 has the lowest proportion (15.6%) of dissatisfying service encounters. These incidents reflect the employee's response to customer needs and requests for customized service. Perhaps the service industries studied do a good job handling customer requests for customized service so that the proportion of failures in this

group is, in reality, relatively small. Many of the incidents in group 2 reflect customer *perceptions* of the need for customized service. Possibly, from the employee's point of view, most of these requests are routine and the ability to respond is well practiced. Thus, failures to accommodate the need for customized service are *relatively* infrequent in comparison with other sources of dissatisfaction.

Finally, Table 1 reveals that a substantial proportion of dissatisfactory service encounters (41.5%) are related to customers' negative reactions to unprompted and unsolicited employee behaviors (group 3). In all of these group 3 incidents, it is *not* the quality of the core service or failure to address a special need or request that causes dissatisfaction, but rather the assessed character or attitude of the service employee as inferred from particular behaviors, both verbal and nonverbal.

UNDERLYING SIMILARITIES BETWEEN SATISFACTION AND DISSATISFACTION The third exploratory question is whether relationships are present among the underlying causes of satisfactory and dissatisfactory service encounters. In other words, are the underlying causes of satisfaction and dissatisfaction mirror images of behaviors along particular dimensions? Examination of Table 1 reveals that, though the underlying causes appear to be the same, the frequency of occurrence differs when satisfactory and dissatisfactory incidents are compared. This observation is supported by the contingency table analysis that shows statistically significant interactions between (1) type of outcome and group (Δ L.R. χ^2 = 42.58; p. < .000) and (2) type of outcome and category (Δ L.R. χ^2 = 117.28; p. < .000).

First, a considerably larger proportion of dissatisfactory incidents (42.9%) than satisfactory incidents (23.3%) is found in group 1. This finding is hardly surprising; nobody likes a failure in service delivery. However, it is how employees respond to such failures that determines how the incident is remembered. The details reported in the incidents suggest that offering sincere apologies, compensatory actions, and explanations can dissipate anger and dissatisfaction. One might expect that dissatisfaction could be mitigated in failure situations if employees are trained to respond, but the fact that such incidents can be remembered as very satisfactory is somewhat surprising.

From Table 1 note the large difference between satisfactory and dissatisfactory incident proportions for group 2. The relationship is the reverse of that in group 1, however, with group 2 having twice as many satisfactory as dissatisfactory incidents. A relatively small proportion (15.6%) of all dissatisfactory incidents occur because needs or requests are not met, whereas twice as many (32.9%) satisfactory incidents are memorable because employees are willing and able to accommodate needs for customization. The results suggest that, across the three industries studied, employees are doing a good job of accommodating the explicit needs and requests of their customers and that customers frequently remember such accommodations as very satisfying.

Finally, the large proportion of *both* satisfactory (43.8%) and dissatisfactory (41.5%) encounters attributed to unprompted and unsolicited employee actions (group 3) warrants mention. These memorable incidents result from unprompted exhibition of truly exemplary or egregious service demeanor. The fact that there are so many satisfactory *and* dissatisfactory incidents in this group suggests two conclusions. First, the importance of spontaneous interactive quality in service delivery cannot be overemphasized. With more than 40% of all incidents reported being the direct result of unexpected treatment by an employee, the importance of the "how" in service delivery is clearly substantiated. Second, the large proportion of both satisfactory and dissatisfactory incidents in group 3 may indicate a high degree of variability in interactive quality.

GENERALIZABILITY ACROSS INDUSTRIES The objective of the final exploratory research question is to examine whether there are "generic behaviors" across all three service industries that could be associated with satisfactory and dissatisfactory service encounters. A general answer to the question is "yes." All satisfactory and dissatisfactory incidents for each of the industries can be classified within the schema. Thus, the classification system appears to work equally well for hotels, restaurants, and airlines. Contingency table analysis reveals a significant industry by group interaction (Δ L.R. $\chi^2 = 34.63$; $p < .000$), however, suggesting that the proportion of satisfactory and dissatisfactory incidents in each group does vary across the three industries. Examination of the frequencies shows that all three industries have similar proportions of their total incidents in group 1 (airline 34.3%, restaurants 32.3%, hotels 33.9%). The significant industry by group interaction is therefore attributable to the differences in proportions within groups 2 and 3. The restaurant industry has significantly fewer incidents in group 2 (16.6% overall) and significantly more incidents in group 3 (51.5% overall) than the other two industries. The reverse relationship holds for the airline industry, which has significantly more incidents in group 2 (36.8% overall) and fewer in group 3 (28.9%).

CONCLUSIONS
MANAGERIAL IMPLICATIONS

For service firm managers seeking to improve customer satisfaction in service encounters, the study has implications related to (1) the usefulness of the method and (2) the generalizability of the classification system and the insights based on the group and category frequencies.

First, the critical incident method appears to be a useful tool for assessing customer dis/satisfaction in service encounters. Use of the method uncovers specific events and behaviors that underlie service encounter dis/satisfaction, which then can be used as a base for developing customer satisfaction monitoring programs, designing service procedures and policies, and training contact personnel. The method enables the researcher to get behind such general concepts as "friendly, efficient, professional" to the actual contact employee behaviors that are linked to those concepts. The results of CIT studies provide much greater detail and depth of understanding than do typical customer satisfaction surveys.

Second, the classification system that emerged from the data can be used by managers of the industries studied and may be applicable to other high-contact transaction-based service industries as well. The classification system is abstract enough to generalize across several industries, but is sufficiently detailed to suggest an overall management approach to improving customer satisfaction in service encounters. For example, with the proper employee response, dissatisfactory encounters due to failure of the delivery system can be transformed into satisfactory encounters (group 1). Likewise, the proper response to customer needs and requests can lead to customer satisfaction (group 2). The data from our study suggest that the ability of an employee to make a proper response is largely a function of the employee's knowledge and control. The CIT enables managers to identify what knowledge is needed and what control is required as well as providing a basis for determining which is more important for a given type of encounter.

→ Knowledge of the service concept, the service delivery system and its operation, and the system standards enables employees to inform customers about what happened, what can be done, and why their needs or requests can or cannot be accommodated. The incidents show that often a customer's need is for knowledge. Frequently, information alone creates satisfaction or mitigates dissatisfaction. However, for many encounters, action of some kind is needed to create satisfaction. Having control enables employees to take appropriate action. Though standardized responses or actions can be used for some types of incidents, in most cases the response must be tailored to the specifics of the incident. Giving employees control empowers them to act and enables them to fix problems and respond to requests in effective ways.

Managers have the ability to influence the level of customer contact employees' knowledge and control. The CIT can identify what employees need to know by making clear what general information *customers* consider important in different encounters. It is crucial that employees not only be taught scripts, but also be given appropriate knowledge. Training programs should be designed to develop a broad repertoire of responses (range of knowledge) and to allow for practice in selecting from the repertoire.

The CIT also can assist managers in isolating situations in which employees need control rather than rules, determining the range of control to grant employees, and specifying a repertoire of action alternatives. Again, employees must be empowered (given discretion and latitude) to take whatever action is proper in a specific situation. Many companies appear to believe that a management philosophy of endorsing action will empower employees. Broad endorsements, encouragements, and guidelines such as "the customer is always right" or "we put service first" are not enough. As all customer contact employees soon find out, not all customers are right, and some are even abusive and out of control. Further, such open-ended criteria leave the employee in the very ambiguous position of not knowing what action is possible or how any action taken will by judged by managers.

The CIT can be used by managers to define a range of action alternatives that employees can exercise. These alternatives can be focused on groups of incidents that emerge from a CIT analysis. Various types of service failures can be addressed by spelling out specific action steps and authorization levels that can be used to fix problems. A set of "Plan B" actions can be developed jointly with managers and line employees and then incorporated as "failsafes" in the service system. Employees would have discretion, but they would be supported by efforts to build a repertoire, classroom practice in selecting from that repertoire, and guidelines about what actions are permissible with and without authorization.

Unprompted and unsolicited employee actions (group 3), whether pleasing or unpleasing to the customer, are less subject to management control. Even the best employees have bad days. However, recruitment and selection procedures can be used to hire employees with a strong service orientation (Hogan, Hogan, and Busch 1984; Schneider and Schecter 1988). A strong service culture, effective supervision and monitoring, and quick feedback to employees also will control to some extent the seemingly random occurrence of group 3 behaviors.

IMPLICATIONS FOR RESEARCH

Our study deepens general knowledge and understanding of service encounter satisfaction and service quality. Unlike previous research that has identified general, abstract dimensions of service quality, our study isolates specific events and behaviors that result in dis/satisfaction. The classification system identifies sources of dis/satisfaction that are generalizable across the three industries studied, and possibly others, giving the results broader applicability than previous findings in service satisfaction. In addition, the study supports the appropriateness of the CIT for marketing applications. The critical incident method employed in the study is well used in other fields. Our results suggest that the CIT is also an appropriate and useful method for studying marketing questions and for assessing customer perceptions. Other marketing uses of the technique might include the study of salesperson interactions with customers or incidents in the provision of professional and business-to-business services. In addition, the data analysis procedure prescribed by CIT could be modified to test predetermined classification schemes based on theory or previous empirical evidence.

The results are theoretically fruitful in suggesting hypotheses that could be tested in future research. For example, the research should be replicated across industries differing in characteristics such as those identified by Lovelock (1983). Given that specificity of events and behaviors is the desired outcome of such studies, the generalizability of the classification system may well be limited to transaction-based service industries in which communication between employees and customers is relatively routine. Different groups and categories are likely to result for industries such as professional services in which communication patterns are complex and long-term and customer problems are more involved. In such cases, the events and behaviors that determine the favorableness of an encounter may depend on the phase of the buyer–seller relationship (Dwyer, Schurr, and Oh 1987).

Another direction for future research involves comparing manager, customer, and contact employee perceptions of critical incidents in service encounters and the specific role expectations of all parties. Service quality theory suggests that to achieve customer satisfaction in service encounters, agreement between the firm's managers, contact employees, and customers as to what constitutes dis/satisfactory service is important (Parasuraman, Zeithaml, and Berry 1985). Though some previous work suggests that customers and employees share common perceptions of quality of service provided (Schneider and Bowen 1985), other research suggests that customers and employees may disagree about the causes of dis/satisfaction (Folkes and Kotsos 1986; Nyquist, Bitner, and Booms 1985). A comparison of manager, employee, and customer perceptions of critical service encounters, combined with the assessment of customer and employee role performance scripts (Leigh and Rethans 1984), would begin to address the interactive complexities of service encounters. In addition, whereas our study and others focus on interpersonal factors, future research should consider also the role of nonhuman elements (e.g., equipment, facilitating goods, atmospherics) in service encounter dis/satisfaction.

REFERENCES

Albrecht, Karl and Ron Zemke (1985), *Service America.* Homewood, IL: Dow Jones-Irwin.

Andersson, Bengt-Erik and Stig Goran Nilsson (1964), "Studies in the Reliability and Validity of the Critical Incident Technique," *Journal of Applied Psychology,* 48 (6), 398-403.

Belk, Russell W. (1987), "Material Values in the Comics: A Content Analysis of Comic Books Featuring Themes of Wealth," *Journal of Consumer Research,* 14 (June), 26–42.

Bitner, Mary Jo (1990), "Evaluating Service Encounters: The Effects of Physical Surroundings and Employee Responses," *Journal of Marketing,* forthcoming.

———, Jody D. Nyquist, and Bernard H. Booms (1985), "The Critical Incident as a Technique for Analyzing the Service Encounter," in *Services Marketing in a Changing Environment,* T. M. Bloch, G. D. Upah, and V. A. Zeithaml, eds. Chicago: American Marketing Association, 48–51.

Brown, Stephen W. and Teresa A. Swartz (1989), "Gap Analysis of Professional Service Quality," *Journal of Marketing,* 53 (April), 92–98.

Chase, Richard B. (1978), "Where Does the Customer Fit in a Service Operation?" *Harvard Business Review,* 56 (November/December), 137–142.

Copas, Ernestine M. (1984) "Critical Requirements for Cooperating Teachers," *Journal of Teacher Education,* 35 (6), 49–54.

Cotterell, John L. (1982) "Student Experiences Following Entry into Secondary School," *Educational Research,* 24 (4), 296–302.

Crosby, Lawrence A. and Nancy J. Stephens (1987), "Effects of Relationship Marketing on Satisfaction, Retention and Prices in the Life Insurance Industry," *Journal of Marketing Research,* 24 (November), 404–411.

Czepiel, John, Michael R. Solomon, and Carol F. Surprenant (1985), *The Service Encounter.* New York: Lexington Books.

Day, Ralph L. and Muzaffer Bodur (1978), "Consumer Response to Dissatisfaction with Services and Intangibles," in *Advances in Consumer Research,* Vol. 5, H. Keith Hunt, ed. Ann Arbor, MI: Association for Consumer Research, 263–272.

Dwyer, F. Robert, Paul H. Schurr, and Sejo Oh (1987), "Developing Buyer–Seller Relationships," *Journal of Marketing,* 51 (April), 11–27.

Feinberg, S. E. (1980), *The Analysis of Cross-Classified Categorical Data,* 2nd ed. Cambridge, MA: MIT Press.

Flanagan, John C. (1954), "The Critical Incident Technique," *Psychological Bulletin,* 51 (July), 327–357.

Folkes, Valerie S. and Barbara Kotsos (1986), "Buyers' and Sellers' Explanations for Product Failure: Who Done It?" *Journal of Marketing,* 50 (April), 74–80.

Freeman, Daniel H., Jr. (1987), *Applied Categorical Data Analysis.* New York: Marcel Dekker, Inc.

Hogan, Joyce, Robert Hogan, and Catherine M. Busch (1984), "How to Measure Service Orientation," *Journal of Applied Psychology,* 69 (1), 167–173.

Hough, Leatta M. (1984), "Development and Evaluation of the 'Accomplishment Record' Method of Selecting and Promoting Professionals," *Journal of Applied Psychology,* 69 (1), 135–146.

Hunt, S. D. (1983), *Marketing Theory: The Philosophy of Marketing Science.* Homewood, IL: Richard D. Irwin, Inc.

Kassarjian, Harold H. (1977), "Content Analysis in Consumer Research," *Journal of Consumer Research,* 4 (June), 8–18.

——— (1984), "Males and Females in the Funnies: A Content Analysis," in *Personal Values and Consumer Psychology,* Robert E. Pitts, Jr. and Arch G. Woodside, eds. Lexington, MA: Lexington Books.

Kerlinger, Fred N. (1973), *Foundations of Behavioral Research,* 2nd ed. New York: Holt, Rinehart and Winston, Inc.

Koepp, Stephen (1987), "Pul-eeze! Will Somebody Help Me?" *Time* (February 2), 28–34.

Latham, Gary and Lise M. Saari (1984), "Do People Do What They Say? Further Studies on the Situational Interview," *Journal of Applied Psychology,* 69 (4), 569–573.

———, ———, Elliott D. Pursell, and Michael A. Campion (1980), "The Situational Interview," *Journal of Applied Psychology,* 65 (4), 422–427.

Leigh, Thomas W. and Arno J. Rethans (1984), "A Script-Theoretic Analysis of Industrial Purchasing Behavior, *Journal of Marketing,* 48 (Fall), 22–32.

Lovelock, Christopher H. (1983), "Classifying Services to Gain Strategic Marketing Insights," *Journal of Marketing,* 47 (Summer), 9–20.

——— (1988), *Managing Services: Marketing, Operations and Human Resources.* Englewood Cliffs, NJ: Prentice-Hall, Inc.

Nyquist, Jody D., Mary Jo Bitner, and Bernard H. Booms (1985), "Identifying Communications Difficulties in the Service Encounter: A Critical Incidents Approach," in *The Service Encounter,* John Czepiel, Michael Solomon, and

Carol Surprenant, eds. Lexington, MA: Lexington Books, 195–212.

——— and Bernard H. Booms (1987), "Measuring Services Value from the Consumer Perspective," in *Add Value to Your Service,* Carol Surprenant, ed. Chicago: American Marketing Association, 13–16.

Parasuraman, A., Valarie A. Zeithaml, and Leonard L. Berry (1985), "A Conceptual Model of Service Quality and Its Implications for Further Research," *Journal of Marketing,* 49 (Fall), 41–50.

———, ———, and ——— (1988), "SERVQUAL: A Multiple-Item Scale for Measuring Consumer Perceptions of Service Quality," *Journal of Retailing,* 64 (1), 12–40.

Pollay, Richard W. (1985), "The Subsiding Sizzle: A Descriptive History of Print Advertising 1900–1980," *Journal of Marketing,* 49 (Summer), 24–37.

Pursell, Elliott D., Michael A. Campion, and Sarah A. Gaylord (1980), "Structured Interviewing: Avoiding Selection Problems," *Personnel Journal* (November), 907–912.

Quelch, John A. and Stephen B. Ash (1981), "Consumer Satisfaction with Professional Services," in *Marketing of Services,* James H. Donnelly and William R. George, eds. Chicago: American Marketing Association, 82–85.

Ronan, William W. and Gary P. Lathan (1974), "The Reliability and Validity of the Critical Incident Technique: A Closer Look," *Studies in Personnel Psychology* 6 (1), 53–64.

Schneider, Benjamin and David E. Bowen (1985), "Employee and Customer Perceptions of Services in Banks: Replication and Extension," *Journal of Applied Psychology,* 70 (3), 423-433.

——— and Daniel Schecter (1988), "The Development of a Personnel System for Service Jobs," presented at Symposium on Quality in Services, University of Karlstad, Karlstad, Sweden; in *Quality in Services,* Stephen W. Brown and Evert Gummesson, eds. Lexington, MA: Lexington Books (forthcoming).

Shostack, G. Lynn (1985), "Planning the Service Encounter," in *The Service Encounter,* John A. Czepiel, Michael R. Solomon, and Carol F. Surprenant, eds. Lexington, MA: Lexington Books, 243–254.

Solomon, Michael R., Carol Suprenant, John A. Czepiel, and Evelyn G. Gutman (1985), "A Role Theory of Perspective on Dyadic Interactions: The Service Encounter," *Journal of Marketing,* 49 (Winter), 99–111.

Spiggle, Susan (1986), "Measuring Social Values: A Content Analysis of Sunday Comics and Underground Comix," *Journal of Consumer Research,* 13 (June), 100–113.

Surprenant, Carol F. and Michael R. Solomon (1987), "Predictability and Personalization in the Service Encounter," *Journal of Marketing,* 51 (April), 73–80.

Viney, Linda L. (1983), "The Assessment of Psychological States through Content Analysis of Verbal Communications," *Psychological Bulletin,* 94 (3), 542–563.

Weber, Robert Philip (1985), *Basic Content Analysis,* Sage University Paper Series on Quantitative Applications in the Social Sciences, 07-049. Beverly Hills and London: Sage Publications, Inc.

Westbrook, Robert A. (1981), "Sources of Consumer Satisfaction with Retail Outlets," *Journal of Retailing,* 57 (Fall) 68–85.

White, Frank M. and Edwin A. Locke (1981), "Perceived Determinants of High and Low Productivity in Three Occupational Groups: A Critical Incident Study," *Journal of Management Studies,* 18 (4), 375–387.

Zimmer, Mary R. and Linda L. Golden (1988), "Impressions of Retail Stores: A Content Analysis of Consumer Images," *Journal of Retailing,* 64 (Fall), 265–294.

THE SERVICE ORGANIZATION
CLIMATE IS CRUCIAL

Benjamin Schneider

———— • ————

Management concentration on easily countable, relatively short-run indices of human effectiveness may be shortsighted in the manufacturing sector; in the service sector, it's positively myopic.

Behavioral science studies of work have generally concentrated on those outcomes of worker participation in the organization that can be easily counted—for example, days absent—particularly in manufacturing when production levels, absenteeism, and turnover are the "bottom line" in evaluating the usefulness of the behavioral sciences.

I think this emphasis on the "bottom line" is based on the fact that our theories and models about organizational dynamics come from the manufacturing sector. Thus, because the score is kept by accountants, organizations tend to monitor the easily identifiable cost. It has not been noticed that this focus on "easily countables," gives a short-run perspective and cuts down, or even eliminates, attention paid to organizational constituencies that aren't directly involved with financial matters. Accountants, economists, and financial analysts provide the data on which decision makers base their decisions so the only constituencies that influence decisions are stockholders and banks; customers, suppliers, employees, or the families of employees are given scant attention.

The emphasis on easily countable, relatively short-run indices of human effectiveness may be short-sighted in the manufacturing sector; in the service sector, it is myopic. Yet service organizations tend to adopt a straight accounting-oriented, productivity frame of reference when they evaluate employee performance and determine organizational effectiveness. In banks, for example, tellers are evaluated on how they "prove out" at the end of each day, rather than on how courteous they are to the bank's customers; the competence of airline

reservation clerks is judged on the number of paperwork errors they make when they book passengers, rather than on the goodwill they generate when they handle a transaction to the satisfaction of the customer; and life insurance managers monitor salespersons' dollar volume rather than their "bedside manner" as a basis for rewards. The primary measure turns out to be a short-run concern for easily countable performance standards that are relevant to short-run financial concerns.

It would be useful if the definition of "productivity"—especially in service industries—was broadened to include at least courtesy and style of performance—particularly because the long-term effectiveness of the organization depends on service. Because the performance of employees in service organizations is directed at animate (human) objects rather than the nonfeeling, nonresponsive raw materials handled in the manufacturing world, the appropriate judges of performance should be those who are served.

The underlying thesis of this article is that in service organizations, organizational dynamics have a direct impact on the people the organization serves, as well as on employee performance and attitudes. This article focuses on the nature of employees who work in service organizations, how management's orientation to service affects employees, how management's orientation to service affects customers, and the relationship

SOURCE: Benjamin Schneider, "The Service Organization: Climate Is Crucial," *Organizational Dynamics,* Autumn 1980, 52–65, published by AMACOM, a division of American Management Association. Permission to reprint was provided by Benjamin Schneider.

between employee and customer views of the service orientation of the organization. The project that illustrates these concerns was conducted in 23 branches of an East Coast commercial bank.

WORKING FRAMEWORK

The working framework is based on research from two viewpoints—the employee's and the customer's. Let's look at the research background from each of these vantages.

RESEARCH BACKGROUND: THE EMPLOYEE SIDE

As I've already noted, our models of organizational dynamics have been developed in, and concentrate on, manufacturing organizations—that is, organizations that transform raw materials into consumable products. Employees' efforts in such organizations are aimed at essentially nonreactive targets. In contrast, service organization employees have face-to-face contact with customers; their work involves much greater interpersonal interaction than manufacturing work. This type of work seems to result in increased stress and strain because employees try to meet conflicting demands from management and customers. Management ought to try and reduce this stress. But how? To answer this question, we must identify the types of people likely to be employed in customer contact jobs in service organizations.

We assumed that an individual's choice of occupation or organization wasn't a random process and that people *choose* the kinds of jobs they have and the kinds of organizations in which they work. Research literature on occupational and organizational choice suggests that people who choose service jobs in for-profit organizations probably have strong desires to give good service, to work with people in face-to-face relationships, and, interestingly, they are probably concerned with organizational success. Therefore, management can potentially manage employee stress by establishing a climate in which employees' desires to give good service are made easier and encouraged; a climate in which service, as

proved by management word and deed, is an organizational imperative.

When managers in service organizations establish policies and procedures, and otherwise engage in behaviors that show concern for the organization's clients, they are service *enthusiasts*. Service *enthusiasts* engage in activities designed to satisfy the organization's customers. Service *bureaucrats,* on the other hand, are interested in system maintenance, routine, and adherence to uniform operating guidelines and procedures. The most important difference between these orientations is the service enthusiast's emphasis on the importance of interpersonal relationships at work, concern for the customer, and flexible application of rules as opposed to the bureaucrat's avoidance of interpersonal issues and stress on rules, procedures, and system maintenance. When employee opinions about how their organization should function are not congruent with what they perceive the organization is actually emphasizing, role stress and strain—that is, role ambiguity and role conflict—usually result. Employees' role stress and strain would also manifest itself in other negative outcomes such as dissatisfaction, frustration, and plans to leave the organization. This framework is shown in Figure 1.

RESEARCH BACKGROUND: CUSTOMER SIDE

Consumers who make decisions about the goods or services offered by an organization are the ultimate judges of the quality of those goods and services in the American free-market system. What is surprising is that (1) researchers and businessmen have concentrated far more on how to attract consumers to products and services than on how to retain those customers, (2) there is almost no published research on the retention of service consumers, and (3) consumer evaluation of products or services has rarely been used as a criterion or index of organizational effectiveness. The study of organizational behavior has left relatively unexplored the questions of why consumers continue to utilize the services of a bank, an airline, a hospital, a university, an insurance agency, and so on, and of how the dynamics or processes of these

FIGURE 1   How Employee–Management Incongruence Leads to Employee's Negative Feelings

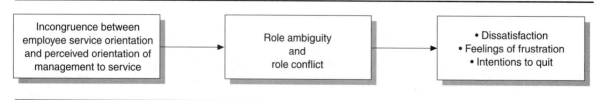

organizations are related to consumer evaluation of the services they receive.

In an earlier study, I hypothesized that service consumers are responsive to the same kinds of organizational practices and procedures that affect employees. I suggested that consumers would be better served if service organizations were structured to meet and satisfy the needs of their employees. The logic for the hypothesis is quite simple: Employees in service organizations desire to give good service and when those desires are made easier by management's support, both employees and consumers are likely to react positively—that is, employees should have feelings of satisfaction, not frustration, and so on; customers should feel good about the quality of the service they receive.

It is important to note that positive outcomes for both customer and employee are a direct function of the same set of organizational dynamics—namely, the extent to which the organization, through its practices and procedures, demonstrates a "climate for service." Of course, positive employee outcomes are in a totally different realm from customer outcomes; the former involve the largest chunk of daytime hours (employees' total work experiences); the latter involve only a fleeting or transient relationship (a three- or four-minute visit every now and then to a bank, for example). However, these two groups share an experience with the same organizational behavior; this suggests that the way *customers* perceive their treatment when they use the organization's services should be positively related to what *employees* say about the organization's service practices and procedures. These ideas are portrayed schematically in Figure 2.

Note also that these thoughts about the impact on *customers* of managerial orientation to *employees* represent, in fact, a "boundary-spanning" or "spill-over" concept. This suggests that human resources processes and procedures established for customer-contact employees in service organizations have unintentional consequences because they cannot be hidden from the consumer; there is no room for "quality control" between the employees' behavior and the customer's "purchase." The climate for service "shows" to those who are served.

It could be no different. Service organizations are established to attract and retain customers through service; their reason for being is (or should be) the customer. In fact, this logic indicates that when employees feel their service organization is *not* customer-oriented, both employees and customers should report the customer has less positive experiences. Conversely, in organizations where employees report that management displays characteristics of the service enthusiast and establishes customer-oriented policies and procedures, *customers* should report higher levels of quality of service and they should be more likely to keep their service accounts with the organization.

THE RESEARCH PROCESS

Data for this project were collected in three distinct phases: preparation of the organization for the data

FIGURE 2   Antecedents and Consequences of "Climate for Service" in Banks

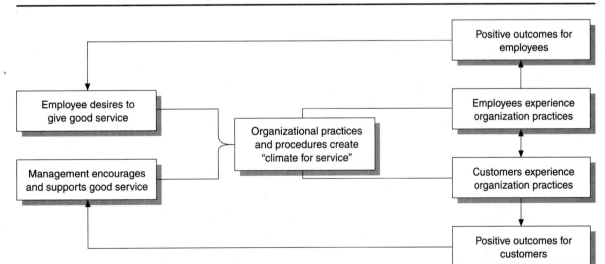

collection process, interviews with bank branch employees and customers, and survey development and administration to employees and customers.

PREPARATION OF THE ORGANIZATION

It took the researcher five years to find a bank in which to test these hypotheses because banks, like most service organizations, separate their employee "attitude" research from their customer "opinion" research; this thwarted any opportunity to examine relationships between employees and customers. Fortunately, the management of the bank that eventually cooperated (financially as well as psychologically) realized that while customer opinions about quality were an index of branch effectiveness, actual attempts to change branch practices and procedures would be nonproductive unless techniques were available for measuring how higher-quality differed from lower-quality branches. My research framework provided a technique for identifying the relationships, if any, between customer opinions about service and employee descriptions of branch practices and procedures. Because these descriptions referred specifically to actual branch routine and the research provided diagnostic data that were useful for organizational change, the bank finally agreed to participate.

Both parties to the project took on specific responsibilities. The bank was expected to:

☐ *Arrange a meeting with branch managers to solicit their cooperation.* This gave those branch managers who would participate in the study an opportunity to meet and observe the research team and to ask questions about their roles.

☐ *Arrange corporate newspaper announcements describing the research and research team.* This alerted the whole organization to the research effort and helped allay false rumors.

☐ *Arrange for all customer and employee interviews and conduct the customer interviews after the research team trained the interviewers.* The idea of using bank employees to conduct the customer interviews was to get nonbranch people (especially marketing types) to speak to actual customers.

☐ *Appoint a liaison team to work with the research team.* The liaison team acquainted researchers with some of the language of the organization (every organization has its own language) and specified "obvious" ways to conduct the research. This team was used as a sounding board and critic and was particularly valuable in critiquing the proposed surveys.

☐ *Print and mail surveys to all sampled customers and employees, and select the customer samples (all employees in the relevant branches were asked to respond).*

The research team had the duty to:

☐ *Explain the research effort to participating bank employees*—on a face-to-face basis with bank branch managers and in writing to other branch employees.

☐ *Interview branch employees.*

☐ *Develop the survey drafts for both customers and employees, and check them with the liaison team.*

☐ *Analyze data and write reports.*

☐ *Feed data back to branch managers and employees.*

MANAGER AND EMPLOYEE INTERVIEWS

As preparation for the employee survey, the branch manager, one nonteller, and one teller were interviewed from each branch. Some interviews were "one-on-one," while others were conducted in groups. Groups were always composed of employees holding jobs at the same level—all managers or all tellers, for example. These interviews were tape-recorded and concentrated on the following issues:

☐ What happened to and around them on a typical day that made them feel particularly good or particularly bad about their work.

☐ What came to mind when they thought about customer service and the bank.

☐ What they thought giving good service involved; what are the components of good service.

☐ How they felt when they weren't giving good service; what prevented them from providing good customer service.

CUSTOMER INTERVIEWS

Customers were interviewed from each of the branches by randomly selecting three account holders from mailing lists, telephoning them, and asking them to participate in an interview for which they would be paid $15. Interviews were conducted at a branch convenient to the customer and were conducted "one-on-one." Customers were asked the following questions:

☐ In a few words, how would you describe the service you generally receive at the branch where you do most of your banking?

☐ Can you tell me about a time you went to your branch and received service you thought was particularly good? Please tell me what happened, who was involved, how you felt, and why you think you were treated well.

☐ Now tell me about a time when service was particularly bad.

SURVEY DEVELOPMENT AND ADMINISTRATION

Based on an informal analysis of the interviews, one survey was designed for employees and one for customers. The surveys differed from the interviews in the level of detail of the questions and, very importantly, in the number of people from whom we were able to collect data. The latter difference permitted more systematic, quantitatively based exploration of the hypotheses.

In all, survey responses came from 263 employees and 1,657 customers from 23 branches of the bank; about 70 customers and about 11 employees per branch.

RESULTS OF EMPLOYEE INTERVIEWS

The employee interviews suggested a complex set of issues in the service orientation of branches. At a more general level, as expected, employees responded to our questions with the themes of both enthusiasts and bureaucrats. The issues that reflected an enthusiastic orientation referred to the branch's philosophy of a flexible and interpersonally open form of involvement with the branch's customers and the community in the delivery of service. In the survey, the enthusiastic orientation was measured by these items, for example: keeping a sense of "family" among branch employees, having the branch involved in community affairs, and giving customer service in new and creative ways. In contrast, the bureaucratic orientation was measured by constraints on giving good service—for example, stress on rules, procedures, and system maintenance that, we were told, often diverted energy away from providing good customer service. Other measures of the bureaucratic theme included strict adherence to rules and procedures, routine performance of one's job, and the use of only established methods for solving customers' problems.

On an everyday activity level, employees said that the activities that represented good service included the degree to which the branch manager assumed the traditional managerial functions of giving good service (planning, coordinating, goal setting, establishing routine), the extent to which extra effort in serving customers was rewarded and appreciated, and the degree to which there was an active attempt to retain customers in the branch.

Employees also told us about some primarily central bank-controlled (as compared with predominantly branch-controlled) support systems that would help them give better or poorer customer service. Four apparently independent and identifiable support systems were noted:

☐ *Personnel support* ("The employees sent by Personnel are not able to do their jobs well.")

☐ *Central processing support* ("Having all customer records in a central location makes it easier on the branch.")

☐ *Marketing support* ("We are well-prepared by Marketing for the introduction of new products and services.")

☐ *Equipment/supply support* ("Equipment and machinery in the branch are well-serviced and rarely break down.")

The managerial functions scale is presented in Figure 3 as an illustration of the kinds of items in a complete scale from the employee survey.

Parenthetically, it is worth noting that the three interviewers were remarkably unanimous in their agreement about the very strong desire of the employees in this system to give customers good service. Indeed, a central theme coming out of the interviews was a sense of *frustration*—that is, the feeling that "the system" set up obstacles that frustrated their desire to provide the best possible customer service.

RESULTS OF CUSTOMER INTERVIEWS

In response to the open-ended questions about service, customers identified ten issues associated with the climate for service at their branch. These ten, with an example of the kind of statements used in the customer survey, are:

1. *Teller courtesy* ("Tellers care about customers as people in my branch.")

2. *Officer courtesy* ("Some officers in the branch know me by name.")

3. *Teller competence* ("Tellers in the branch seem to be well-trained and knowledgeable.")

4. *Adequate staff* ("My branch seems to have enough employees to handle its customers.")

5. *Branch administration* ("It sometimes seems to me that tellers have to walk all over the place to get things done.")

6. *Handling services* ("Deposits are promptly credited to my account(s).")

7. *Convenience* ("I like the fact that the bank has a large number of branches.")

FIGURE 3   Items Composing the Managerial Function Scale from the Employee Survey

Item Number	Item
4	My branch manager supports employees when they come up with new ideas on customer service.
7	My branch manager sets definite quality standards of good customer service.
9	My branch manager meets regularly with employees to discuss work performance goals.
13	My branch manager accepts the responsibilities of his/her job.
20	My branch manager gets the people in different jobs to work together in serving branch customers.
21	My branch manager works at keeping an orderly routine going in the branch.
29	My branch manager takes time to help new employees learn about the branch and its customers.

8. *Employee turnover* ("There seems to be a high turnover of employees in my branch.")

9. *Selling* ("Officers of the bank have tried to get me to open new accounts.")

10. *Employee attitudes* ("My impression is that the branch employees really try to give the customers good service.")

Statements from the branch administration scale from the customer survey are presented in Figure 4.

SURVEY FINDINGS

Results of the survey will be presented in two parts: (1) data on employee desires to give good service, and what happens when the stress of customer vs. management demands is encountered, and (2) data on the relationships between the way employees and customers experience service.

EMPLOYEE DESIRES TO GIVE GOOD SERVICE

To explore employee desires to give good service, we took a two-pronged approach: First, we asked employees to tell us how essential both the enthusiastic approach

and the bureaucratic approach were to good service. Then we asked the same employees to tell us how essential they felt *management* thinks both the enthusiastic and the bureaucratic approaches are to giving good service.

Ascertaining employees' perceptions of management's perspective, as well as their own, permitted the examination of two interesting questions: First, do service employees generally see themselves emphasizing different approaches to service than they believe management wants? As shown in Figure 5, the answer is "Yes"; employees see themselves more as enthusiasts and less as bureaucrats than they believe management is. The second question is considerably more subtle: it asked for the consequences of a discrepancy between the way employees believe service should be given and the way they think management wants service provided.

Answers to the second question provided information that enabled us to calculate, for each employee, the *discrepancy* between employee emphases and perceived management emphases and then to relate that discrepancy to employee reports of role stress—that is, of role conflict and ambiguity, job dissatisfaction, frustration

FIGURE 4   Items Involved in the Branch Administration Scale from the Customer Survey

Item Number	Item
3	An officer (or someone else) takes charge of things when the bank becomes overcrowded.
– 4	It sometimes seems to me that tellers have to walk all over the place to get things done.
– 12	When I've opened new accounts or had to change old ones, something usually got messed up.
34	My branch has an adequate supply of deposit and withdrawal tickets.
– 36	I sometimes feel lost in the branch, no knowing where to go for a certain transaction.
– 39	It is difficult to know who to call or where to write when I need specific kinds of bank-related information.

Note: A minus sign before the item number indicates that the item was reverse-scored.

FIGURE 5   Employee Views on Own and Management's Service Orientation

Approach to Service	Average Employees' Own Views	Average Employees' Views of Management
Bureaucrat	1.92	2.33
Enthusiast	2.48	2.35

Note: All responses were made on a three-point scale. The differences between employees' own views and employees' views of management are both statistically significant.

over being unable to give good service, and intentions to change jobs. Following the logic presented earlier, it was assumed that the larger the discrepancy, the more negative feelings employees would experience. In fact, as shown in Figure 6, this was the case. This means that a host of negative consequences follow when employees think customer service should be handled in ways that differ from the way they believe management wants service given.

Additional analyses, not shown here, revealed that the service orientation discrepancy *first* creates role conflict and ambiguity, and then the other negative outcomes. Thus incongruence between employee desires and the perceived orientation of management *first* seems to lead to role stress; it is this stress that *then* seems to result in frustration, dissatisfaction, and intentions to quit.

RELATIONSHIP BETWEEN CUSTOMER AND EMPLOYEE VIEWS OF SERVICE

It is one thing to be aware that employees may suffer feelings of conflict or frustration when they disagree with management's orientation to service, but it is another thing to find out that management's orientation to service is related to other indices of organizational success. The present study defines organizational success in terms of customer evaluations of the level or quality of service rendered by their bank branch.

At this point our frame of reference switched from how individual employees experience their work world to the ways in which employees and customers, as groups, experience their bank branches. Thus, the reference is not to individuals but to organizations—that is, bank branches. Therefore, the focus shifts from the 263 branch employees to the 23 branches. This change was necessary because organizations are really aggregates of people and, in evaluating organizational effectiveness, meaningful aggregates constitute the appropriate frames of reference.

Customer data combined with employee data provided the answer to the question: Are employees' descriptions of customer service in their branch related to what *customers* have to say about the service they receive? Once again, the answer was yes.

For example, Figure 7 shows how customer views of service are related to employee views of service in the 23 branches. The dots in the figure each represent a branch.

The data for employees were based on their responses to the question: "How do you think the customers of your branch view the general quality of the service they receive in your branch?" Customers were asked to: "Describe the general quality of the service you

FIGURE 6   Correlations between Service-Orientation Discrepancy and Employee Outcomes

Employees' Negative Feelings	Correlation
Role conflict	.45
Role ambiguity	.20
Dissatisfaction	.42
Frustration	.33
Turnover intentions	.32

Note: A large discrepancy means less agreement; all correlations are significantly different from zero.

FIGURE 7   Relationship between Customer and Employee Perceptions of Customer Service

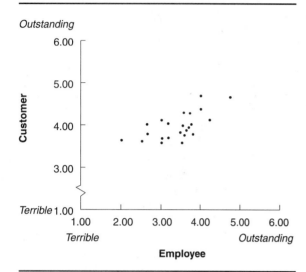

receive in your branch." Both groups graded service on the following six-point scale: outstanding, excellent, good, not so good, bad, terrible. The analysis showed that customers report better service in branches when employess report that:

☐ There's a more enthusiastic service emphasis.

☐ The branch manager emphasizes service as he or she carries out the role of the branch manager.

☐ There's an active attempt to retain all customer account holders, not only large accounts.

☐ The personnel departtmnet provides a sufficient number of well-trained tellers.

☐ Equipment is well-maintained and supplies are plentiful.

In fact, the correlation of the data from the analyses of employee nad customer responses was so consistently strong that it was possible to isolate a few customer perceptions that warrant particular note—that is, it was possible to identify which facets of service from the *customer's* view were most strongly related to selected facets of service as described by *employees*.

For example, when employees describe their branch as one in which the manager emphasizes customer service as he or she carries out the traditional managerial role, customers report no only generally superior service but, nore specifically, that:

☐ The tellers are courteous.

☐ The tellers are competent.

☐The staffing level is adequate.

☐ The brach is administered well.

☐ Teller turnover is low.

☐ The staff has positive work attitudes.

Similar findings were observed when branches were described by employees as having more of an enthusiast approach and also when employees reported they worked in a branch that actively tries to retain all categories of account holders.

SUMMARY

The results may be summarized as follow. When branch employees perceive a strong service orientation in their branch, the customers of those branches report not only that they receive generallly superior service, but that specific facets of service are handled in a superior manner. In addition, employees *thenselves* experience less negative consequences at work when their branch has more of an enthusiastic orientation to service. Thus, employees are *less* dissatisfied and frustrated, *more* likely to plan to remain in their branch, and they experience less role conflict and role ambiguity when the branch is more like the employees feel it should be—that is, more enthusiastic in its approach to service.

A major conclusion from this study: Employees and customers of service organizations will each experience positive outcomes when the organization operates with a customer service orientation. This orientation seems to result in superior service practices and procedures that are observable by customers and that seem to fit employee views of the appropriate style for dealing with customers. More specifically, this research supposrt the following assumptions:

☐ Employees perceive themselves to be more enthusiastic and management to be more bureaucratic in service orientation. This suggests gaps between the goals of employees vis-a-vis service and the management goals of that emplkoyees perceive. It is important for organizations to be aware of *where* these differences exist so they can take steps to remedy them. Figure 8 pinpointed these differences for the branch employees in this study, and, thus, where the bank needed to change to be more congruent with the employees' more enthusiastic, less bureaucratic orientation to service.

☐ Employees who work in settings that are more congruent with their own service orientation experience less role ambiguity and role conflict and, as a result, are generally more satisfied, experience less frustration in theri efforts to give good service, and are more

FIGURE 8   Discrepancies between Employee and Management Perceptions of Service Facets

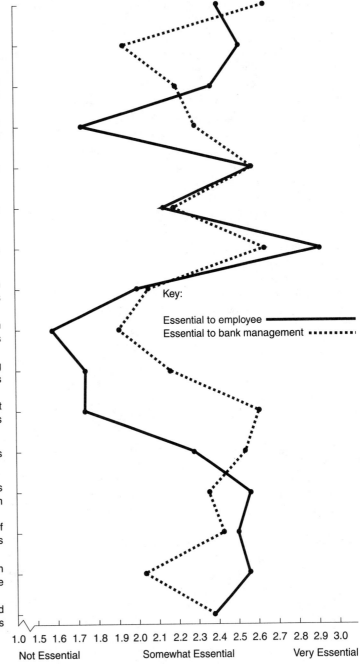

likely to report they intend to keep working for the organization. This assumption was clearly supported; it also sugests that what management frequently perceives as employee disinterest or lack of motivation is really employees' lack of enthusiasm for carrying out policies that are incongruent with their own desires. In fact, employees in this study seemed very interested in meeting *customer* service needs, but less interested in satisfying management's bureaucratic needs.

☐ Even though they view service from a different perspective, employee and customer perceptions of organizational effectiveness are positively related. Support for this assumption was quite strong; that is, when employees report that their branch emphasized service by word and deed, customers report superior banking experiences. These data, and my earlier work with bank customers also show that customers who report a more positive service climate are less likely to switch their accounts to other banks. These findings clearly indicate that management emphasis in a service organization cannot be hidden from those who are served: climate shows in service organizations.

This idea of an organization's climate being apparent to customers goes to the heart of issues presented in the introduction about the determination of organizational effectiveness. A finance-oriented conspiracy seems to promote a short-run productivity orientation rather than a more long-term, wholistic perspective to determine organizational effectiveness. A more succinct way of summarizing this issue is through the concept of "good will."

An organization accrues good will over long periods of time by varied behaviors. Good will is reflected in the way people who have direct (that is, employees), indirect (that is, employees' families), and in-between (that is, customers, suppliers) contact with an organization think and speak about it; good will is the organization's reputation—that is, the way it is viewed by the multiple constituencies it affects and by which it is affected.

While the present study concentrated on the goodwill perceptions of customers, there probably would have been similar results from research concentrated on other branch constituencies. Thus suppliers to the branches could have been asked for their opinions about the branch, and branch employees could have been asked about how suppliers are treated. Or employees' families could have reported their opinions about the way the bank affects their spouse/parent and so on, and employees might have reported on the general quality of consideration given them as employees. Perhaps more interestingly, *potential* branch employees could have

been surveyed about what they think it would be like to work in a particular branch, and those perceptions could have been related to what *incumbents* report it is like to work there.

In each of these hypothetical research efforts, the interesting issue would be the way in which climates created in the branch are "picked up" by the various groups important to the long-term survival of the organization. I suspect these questions are infrequently asked, and rarely if ever pursued systematically. Yet, organizations need the good will of families when an employee is making turnover decisions; they need to have a positive reputation as a place to work in order to attract good employees; and, especially in a time of strife (for example, in a situation like that of the Chrysler Corporation), they need the good will of suppliers.

A very general conclusion, then, culled from this research effort: It is just as important for an organization to be interested in its relationships with the many groups that affect its long-term viability as it is for it to be concerned with the short-run financial considerations affecting stockholders and creditors, and so on.

SELECTED BIBLIOGRAPHY

For a more technical treatment of the research reported here, see "Employee and Customer Perceptions of Service in Banks," by Benjamin Schneider, John J. Parkington, and Virginia M. Buxton, in *Administrative Science Quarterly,* June 1980; "Some Correlates of Experienced Job Stress: A Boundary Role Study," by John J. Parkington and Benjamin Schneider, in *Academy of Management Journal,* June 1979; and "The Perception of Organizational Climate: The Customer's View," by Benjamin Schneider, in *Journal of Applied Psychology,* June 1973.

For conflicting views on the role of service organizations in a consumer society, the industrialization of service is promoted by Theodore Levitt in *The Harvard Business Review,* September–October 1972 and 1976; the consumer's view is promoted by Alan Gartner and Frank Riessman in *The Service Society and the New Consumer Vanguard* (Harper & Row, 1974).

For further discussion of the multiple constituency view of organizational effectiveness, see "Toward a Workable Framework," by Johannes M. Pennings and Paul S. Goodman in their book *New Perspectives on Organizational Effectiveness* (Jossey-Bass, 1977).

For a general treatment of the organizational climate construct, see "Organizational Climates: An Essay," by Benjamin Schneider, in *Personnel Psychology,* Winter 1975, and (the less biased treatment) "Climates in Organizations," by William F. Joyce and John W. Slocum in Steven Kerr's (ed.) *Organizational Behaviors* (Grid, 1979).

The nature of boundary roles in organizations and the stress experienced by employees who occupy those roles is well described in "Interorganizational Processes and Organization Boundary Activities," by J. Stacy Adams in the book *Research in Organizational Behavior, Volume 2,* edited by Barry M. Staw and Larry L. Cummings (JAI Press, 1980).

BETWEEN SERVICE AND SERVILITY

ROLE CONFLICT IN SUBORDINATE SERVICE ROLES[1]

Boas Shamir

Hebrew University of Jerusalem,
The Work and Welfare Research Institute

The concept Subordinate Service Roles (SSRs) is introduced to denote organizational boundary roles in which an organization member performs direct service to a nonmember whose status is higher than that of the service giver. The relative inattention of Industrial/Organizational Psychology and Organizational Sociology to such roles is pointed out. Various types of role conflict in SSRs are discussed. Some factors affecting the level of conflict in SSRs are proposed, and typical responses of SSRs occupants to role conflict are presented and illustrated. The discussion is based on a review of the literature and on critical incidents of service collected from service givers and clients in two areas: hotels and public transport in Israel.

INTRODUCTION

Recent theoretical and research literature in the fields of Organizational/Industrial Psychology and Organizational Sociology has given considerable attention to the subject of organizational role stress. It is commonly believed that job-related stress could interfere with the physical and psychological functioning of the individual and lead to undesirable organizational consequences (for recent reviews of the literature, see: Cooper & Marshall, 1976; Beehr & Newman, 1978). It is also generally accepted that certain organizational conditions tend to bring about a particularly high level of role stress. One of these organizational conditions which has received increased attention is role conflict, defined as the simultaneous occurrence of two or more incompatible sets of pressures regarding the role occupant's expected behavior (Kahn, Wolfe, Quinn, Snoek, & Rosenthal, 1964; Rizzo, House, and Lirzman, 1970).

It has been shown that certain roles in organizations are more exposed than others to situations of role conflict, particularly boundary roles (referred to sometimes as output roles or boundary-spanning roles). Boundary roles were defined by Thompson (1962) as those roles that link the organization with its environment through interaction between an organization member and a nonmember. In the case of such roles, conflict is created by expectations and pressures directed to the role occupant (focal person) not only from intraorganization sources but also from extraorganization sources. This puts the role occupant in a particularly difficult situation both because in the typical case there is a conflict of interests between intraorganization sources and extraorganization sources, and because his ability to control and manipulate expectations and pressures that come from sources outside the organization is in many cases more limited than his ability to control, manipulate, and influence intraorganizational expectations and pressures (Adams, 1976). Since the classic study by Kahn et al. (1964) several studies have supported this argument, but most of them concentrated on specific occupational categories, mainly on managers and organizational leaders (French & Caplan, 1972; Rogers & Molnar, 1976; Whetten, 1978), though some studies dealt with professional level employees (Miles & Perreault, 1976) and people in bar-

[1]The research on which this paper is based was supported by a grant from the Vocational Training Bureau of the Israeli Ministry of Labour and Welfare.

SOURCE: Boas Shamir, "Between Service and Servility: Role Conflict in Subordinate Service Roles," *Human Relations,* Vol. 33, No. 10, 741–756. Reprinted with permission of Plenum Publishing Corporation and Professor Boas Shamir.

gaining situations (Organ, 1971; Adams, 1976, 1175–1199).

There are, however, other boundary roles that could be expected to suffer from high levels of role conflict. I refer here to subordinate service roles: the waiter, the receptionist, the taxi driver, the bus driver, the bank teller, the salesperson in a store, the hairdresser and the like. The service organizations in which these roles are carried out have two main characteristics: first of all, unlike human processing organizations such as hospitals or schools, they have no "mission" and no intention to change or mold the behavior of their clients. The employees of such organizations are commonly not considered professionals or "experts." Secondly, clients' participation in the activities of the organization is voluntary, they do not have to use the service, but have to be motivated to do so. As a result of these two characteristics, the status of the service role occupant in such organizations is subordinate relative to that of the client, contrary to the situation in professional service organizations (Parsons, 1970, 1–16). That is why we shall refer to such roles as subordinate service roles (SSRs).

There are good reasons for expecting the level of conflict in subordinate service roles to be even higher than the level of conflict in organizational leadership roles. Some of these reasons will hopefully become explicit later in this article. In general, they are related to four characteristics of SSRs: (1) their relatively high boundary relevance—operationally defined as the number or frequency of contacts with individuals outside the focal person's organization; (2) their high degree of exposure to role senders outside the organization; (3) their lower status relative to role senders outside the organization; and (4) their low status relative to role senders inside the organization. In comparison, managers and professional-level boundary-role occupants tend to have less contacts with outsiders, to be less exposed in these contacts, to have contacts with outsiders whose status level is similar to theirs, and to have more control over expectations and pressures directed at them from intraorganizational resources.

The importance of discussing SSRs, however, extends beyond their obvious relevance to role stress models. It derives from a gap that exists in the theoretical and research literature on work and organizations. Most of the literature refers either to managers and professional-level workers or to operative-level workers in industry. Relatively little attention has been paid to nonprofessional service workers, in spite of the fact that they constitute very large occupational categories in Western societies and the number of organizations which rely on

such workers for performing their tasks seems to be growing.

It is the purpose of the present article to make a small contribution to the filling of the above-mentioned gap. The article is based mainly on two types of sources. First, a review of the sparse literature on subordinate service roles, and second, a collection of critical incidents of "good" and "bad" service, collected for training purposes from service givers and clients in two types of organizations: hotels (waiters, waitresses, reception clerks, and customers) and public transport (bus drivers, bus passengers, taxi drivers, and taxi passengers) in Jerusalem. (On the critical incident method, see Flanagan, 1954). Some illustrations will also be taken from other sources, such as occasional personal contacts and Terkel's book *Working* (1972), which is a collection of journalistic interviews with American workers. Relying on such sources and attempting to generalize beyond specific situations and occupational groups is, of course, highly speculative and open to criticism. The justification for such an approach is based on the belief that there is a "service ideal" which extends beyond specific situations and creates certain general conditions in subordinate service roles, and on the hope that this article can advance theoretical propositions for operationalization and empirical testing in a variety of specific situations.

Limitations of space require that the article will be limited to person-role conflicts and intersender conflicts. There is no particular rationale for this selection of conflict types other than their clear salience in the literature and in the material we have collected. The analysis will be followed by a presentation of typical responses to role conflict of individuals in subordinate service roles.

PERSON-ROLE CONFLICTS IN SUBORDINATE SERVICE ROLES

Person-role conflicts exist when role expectations are incongruent with orientations, internal standards, or values of the role occupant (House & Rizzo, 1972). There are several typical person-role conflicts in subordinate service roles.

INEQUALITY DILEMMAS

It has already been emphasized that in SSRs, contrary to professional service situations in the "quinary" sector (Parson, 1970, 1–16; Gersuny & Rosengren, 1973) there is an asymmetry of status and power in favor of the client. Not only that, in many SSRs there are expectations both from clients and from superiors that the role occupant will emphasize his subordinate status in his behavior. It is commonly assumed in service organizations that the client wishes to feel important, and the service worker is expected to "build up the client's ego." This expectation is more explicit in hotels where training literature refers to customers as Mr. King and Mrs. Queen, and in lower status service roles, such as washroom attendant (Terkel, 1972, p. 154), but exists in other SSRs as well. The motto "the customer is always right—even when he's wrong" is an expected norm in stores, banks and other service organizations. An air stewardess interviewed by Terkel says: "it's always the passenger is right. When a passenger says something mean, we're supposed to smile and say: I understand" (1972, p. 78). Another significant expression of the emphasis put on the SSR's subordinate position can be found in the mutual address forms used in service situations. While the client is addressed as "Sir" or "Madam," the service giver is addressed by his first name, by a nickname or by the name of his job (Butler & Snizek, 1976). Thus there is a conflict between service-role requirements and values of equality that exist in society outside the service organization. In certain respects, SSRs conserve norms of interpersonal behavior that no longer exist in other social institutions.

Moreover, there is a conflict between role requirements and the self-image or self-esteem of the role occupant. In Israel, for instance, most buses are operated by one man, the driver, who is responsible for selling tickets. No trays are installed in buses for the transferring of bus fare from passenger to driver, and the money is transferred directly. Bus drivers often complain about the humiliating experience of having to stretch out their hands like beggars in order to collect the fare. Another typical case in Israeli buses is when money changes hands and a coin falls down accidentally onto the bus floor. The question, who will bend down to lift the coin, the driver or the passenger, clearly reflects the driver's role conflict. It often happens that both sides freeze in their places expecting the other side to pick up the money, and the quiet conflict sometimes escalates to an open and loud argument between the parties.

Illustrations of similar conflict -laden situations and of the stress they create for SSR occupants could be brought from many other service areas. Suffice here to cite just one more incident told by a waiter. "There was a guest from _____, one of those who think they are kings of the world. I brought him a fried egg. He said: 'without a tip you are not doing anything,' and threw twenty Agora[2] at me. So I said to him: 'here I give you

honor, if you have honor, come outside with me.'" This last sentence expresses the waiter's wish to step outside his subordinate service role in order to regain his self-respect. No wonder we can find in training literature of hotels and department stores chapters titled "Service Is an Honorable Profession" and "Is Selling Respectable?"

The sociopsychological literature claims that the higher the status of the role-sender relative to that of the focal person, the higher the level of role conflict (French & Caplan, 1972; Miles & Perreault, 1976). This claim may hold for other types of role conflict, but does not seem to hold for the type of person-role conflict we have been discussing in this section. The washroom attendant interviewed by Terkel says: "I don't enjoy waiting on my peers. I feel that if I am to occupy a position that's menial, let it be to someone perhaps a cut above me" (1972, p. 154). Whyte, in his classic study of restaurants (1948), explains that European waiters create fewer problems than American waiters because the former are more accustomed to class differences and low social mobility and are therefore less resentful toward social distinctions. The explanation is in terms of lower level of felt person-role conflict. Some behavioral support for an argument of this type was found in a comparative study of American and Costa Rican postal clerks (Goodsell, 1976).

Based on such arguments we can put forward the hypothesis that in subordinate service roles, the level of person-role conflict will be inversely correlated with the status difference between the client and the role occupant—the more equal the status of the two parties, the higher the level of person-role conflict.

FEELINGS VS. BEHAVIOR

"You've got as much privacy as a goldfish," "you're constantly on display." These are typical remarks from people who occupy subordinate service roles. The difficulties in impression management and "maintaining a face" have been extensively discussed by Goffman (1959) who brings some illustrations from SSRs and need not be repeated here. Only a number of points characteristic of person-role conflict in SSR should be mentioned.

The first point is the expectation from the role occupant to create the impression that he enjoys performing his role. The most salient expression of this expectation is the requirement to smile. "I begin at eight in the morning. I have to have a smile on my face. Some mornings that's a little difficult" (Terkel, 1972, p. 332). "She must smile when it is time to smile ... When a customer approaches she immediately assumes her hard, forced smile" (Mills, 1956, p. 272).

[2]Less than a penny.

Another aspect of the conflict between requirements of SSRs and personal attitudes and feelings of the role occupant has to do with the service workers' appearance. Instruction manuals to new employees, in banks, hotels, department stores, etc. are full of explicit instructions regarding employees' clothes, hair length, hair style, jewelry, makeup, nails, shaving, and even more intimate and more difficult to control aspects of appearance such as body weight and body odors. Training courses for service workers also devote much time to the subject of appearance—airline stewardesses training is an obvious example.

Subordinate service role requirements extend to other aspects of interpersonal behavior. One focus of conflict is the initiation and termination of an interaction. Contrary to most interpersonal relationships where both sides have some rights and ability to control their entrance into interaction and exit from interaction, in SSRs, due to the subordinate position of the role occupant and his or her exposure, the right to determine the beginning and the end of the interaction is mainly at the hands of the client. Thus an important aspect of the role is outside the role occupant's control, but moreover, the nature of the relationship and the degree of intimacy can also be determined in many cases by the client, ignoring the wishes, tendencies, attractions and repulsions of the service giver. Clients have the prerogative of high status parties to increase and decrease the degree of intimacy (Mehrabian, 1971), a prerogative which is often used in cases where the client is male and the service worker a female: ". . . like he's rubbing your body somewhere, you're supposed to just put his hand down and not say anything and smile at him" (an airline stewardess interviewed by Terkel, 1972, p. 79).

THE CONFLICT OVER TERRITORY

The human species is considered in a certain sense a territorial species. There are many indications of the fact that humans derive from territories clear psychological advantages such as a sense of identity and added power and energy (Ardrey, 1967; Scheflen, 1976). Human territoriality is expressed in many areas including the area of work. Workers tend to acquire a sense of ownership regarding their workplace, to mark the borders of their work territory by locks and by certain personal items, to feel secure within these borders and to fear trespassing.

If we accept the assumption of human territoriality and of the territorial relationship between a person and his workplace, together with the added assumption that being in another person's territory causes stress, and another person's being in your territory also causes stress,

then we have a potential area of conflict in subordinate service roles. Other boundary-role occupants also have to deal with people outside their own territories and to accept strangers in their own territories, but in other boundary roles the definition of territorial ownership is usually clear. In many subordinate service roles, however, there is a conflict-producing situation of *territorial ambiguity*—both service giver and client have claims over the territory in which the interaction takes place. Waiters, chambermaids, taxi drivers, and other SSR occupants regard their workplace as their territory which gives them the above-mentioned psychological advantages, but the clients who order a room, a table, or a taxi also regard the same territory as their own temporary territory (Argyle, 1975) and they too need this sense of ownership to feel relaxed and secure.

Service organizations sometimes try to clarify territorial borders between workers and clients, by giving customers "do not disturb" signs or installing partitions between bus drivers or taxi drivers and their passengers, but such means are not sufficient to reduce ambiguity and conflict. Richman tells about a problem facing British bus drivers and conductors: "Some crews like to eat their snacks in a given part of the bus. So, in order to prevent passengers sitting opposite them and treating them as non-persons, they will circumscribe their personal territory with their equipment" (1969, p. 244). Marking the borders of your territory in order to feed in peace is one of the most significant expressions of territorial behavior.

Perhaps one of the most extreme expressions of the territorial conflict was related by an ex-stewardess: "Before flight one of us used to stand at the plane's door, and when she saw the passengers coming from the terminal or debusing, she would warn the other members of the crew by shouting: 'Hey, guys, the enemy is coming!'"

INTERSENDER CONFLICTS IN SUBORDINATE SERVICE ROLES

Intersender conflict is defined as a situation in which role expectations from one source (role-sender) oppose those from other sources. Such a conflict can be created by incompatible policies, conflicting requests from others and incompatible standards for evaluation (Rizzo et al., 1970).

THE ORGANIZATION VS. THE CLIENT: THE TWO BOSSES DILEMMA

Probably the most salient type of conflict in service roles and the one which has received relatively much theoretical and research treatment is the conflict between the requirements directed at the role occupant from his employing organization in the form of policies, rules, regulations, or verbal instructions from supervisors and the requirements directed at him from clients. Several studies of bureaucracies (Blau & Scott, 1963; Bar-Yosef & Schild, 1966; Katz & Danet, 1973) have pointed out that organizations normally require universal and specific treatment of clients—i.e., they expect the service role occupant to treat all clients equally and the interaction between service worker and client to be limited to those things which are officially defined as relevant—while the client expects the service-giver to consider his special case and to treat him as a whole person. This type of conflict is particularly severe in subordinate service roles where the status of the client is typically higher than that of the role occupant, who finds himself in a situation of having to comply with conflicting expectations from two different bosses.

Illustrations of conflicts of this type are numerous; only one shall suffice here. After collecting critical incidents of service from bus passengers in Jerusalem, we were amazed to find that in the majority of incidents of "good service" reported by passengers a driver had broken a rule or a regulation in order to accommodate the passenger's special circumstances. In other words, passengers' internal standards for evaluating bus drivers' performance, their ideal of bus driver service, included an expectation that he would stop between bus stops to collect a passenger or let a passenger off the bus, that he would deviate from the official route to bring a passenger closer to his destination, that he would allow a passenger to ride the bus if he forgot his money and could not pay the fare, and similar behavior, all of which is in clear opposition to state and company regulations. Whether the passengers are aware of this conflict is doubtful, but drivers are very aware of it and find it distressing.

There are certain situations in which the conflict between organization or management demands on one hand, and clients' demands on the other hand, is intensified. One category of such situations are circumstances when the SSR occupant finds himself identifying with the clients' demands, particularly when he has to enforce certain organizational regulations and management instructions which are "against" the clients. The Jerusalem hotel clerk who has to move customers from their rooms to inferior rooms or to other hotels due to the unexpected arrival of the American Secretary of State, the airline clerk who has to tell a passenger he is not going to board a flight in spite of his early reservation due to overbooking policies of the airline—in these

and similar cases a person-role conflict is mixed with the intersender conflict to make things worse for the SSR occupant.

Intersender conflicts between organization and client become even more problematic in cases where the client has direct or indirect means of control over the service giver. One of the commonest means of control of SSR occupants is the tip. In roles where it is normal to receive a tip and where the tip constitutes a major part of the service giver's earnings like waiters, taxi drivers, and hairdressers, the SSR occupant has to comply with the conflicting demands of two bosses, both of whom can directly reward him or withhold their rewards. No wonder that a survey of hotel and restaurant managers reports a feeling among these managers that they lose control over their workers due to tipping (NEDO, no date). To some extent this type of situation also exists when customers' control is indirect and operates through the organization. Salespersons and booking clerks whose pay depends on a commission relative to the volume of their sales may also face a relatively severe intersender conflict. Therefore we can hypothesize that intersender conflict in SSRs will be directly related to the extent that the client has control over rewarding and sanctioning of the role occupants' behavior.

This hypothesis can be extended and stated in a somewhat more abstract form. Above-mentioned literature referred to the relative status of the focal person and his role senders as a variable affecting the degree of role conflict. We can add to that now that the level of intersender conflict is also related to the status (and power) of role senders *relative to each other*. The more equal is the status of the role senders the higher is the expected level of intersender conflict.

INTERCLIENT CONFLICTS

A type of intersender conflict which is not mentioned in the literature is the conflict between incompatible expectations and requirements of different clients. Such a conflict is prevalent in situations where the SSR occupant has to give simultaneous service to more than one customer or when service to one client is given in the presence of other clients. A common situation of this kind exists in taxis giving intercity shuttle service in Israel. Arguments between passengers regarding smoking or radio listening are very common. One passenger wants to smoke or listen to the radio and another passenger is disturbed. Usually they expect the driver to arbitrate *between* them, an expectation which drivers try to avoid precisely because they are bound to lose whichever way they arbitrate. Another typical situation is the queue in banks or in front of reception desks. In this situation pressures are not expressed as open arguments but they nevertheless exist, as reflected in a story told by a hotel reception clerk: "I was talking to a couple of guests and a man came who was in a hurry and wanted something. I asked him to wait so that I could finish with that couple, and he became angry—you could see it on his face. So I asked the couple I was serving to let me see what was his request. At the same time I was worried that the couple might also feel annoyed. It was really unpleasant."

Conflicts resulting from incongruent expectations of different clients have other dimensions, which extend beyond specific situations, due to differences among clients and their image of "good service." Two such dimensions are particularly relevant. First of all, the pace dimension. Some clients in restaurants, banks, stores, etc., are interested in the quickest possible service, others would like to be served at a more leisurely pace. The need to adapt your performance to the pace which each customer dictates and to change pace from customer to customer is a problem frequently mentioned by SSR occupants. Another dimension is specificity. This dimension of conflict has been mentioned in reference to conflict between clients' and organization's expectations, but it also exists on the level of inter-client conflict. Some clients prefer a correct, specific service limited to the official business. Others prefer personal recognition and a degree of familiarity and intimacy. Having to serve a client in the presence of others who have different conceptions of service puts the SSR occupant in a situation of conflict.

It follows from the literature and from our discussion that the level of role conflicts which involve clients as role senders will be affected by certain characteristics of the clients and certain characteristics of the service given to them. Several more specific hypotheses can be proposed to illustrate this point. First, we can expect the level of conflict to be directly related to the level of variance in clients' characteristics—the more varied the clientele in terms of age, sex, education, and needs, the higher the level of interclient conflicts. Secondly, we can expect the level of conflict to be inversely related to the permanence of clientele, since in the case of permanent clients, a process of mutual adjustment between client and service giver is supposed to take place. Thirdly, we can expect the level of conflict to be directly related to the degree of sensitiveness of the service. Certain service roles bring the SSR occupant in contact with intimate aspects of the client (see Miller & Rice, 1967, for discussion of services that are "primary group surrogates"). Other services, like an airline flight involve a degree of risk. In such situations clients' level of stress is high and their anxiety is expected to intensify SSR conflict.

INDIVIDUAL RESPONSES TO STRESS IN SUBORDINATE ROLES

We shall not discuss here organizational responses to stress-producing service situations (Menzies, 1960; Bar-Yosef & Schild, 1966; Katz & Danet, 1973; Shamir, 1978). We shall only present some typical behavior of individuals in subordinate service roles, that are performed in order to avoid or reduce role conflict.

AVOIDANCE OF CONFLICT

One way to reduce role conflicts is simply to avoid or defer contacts with clients. The waiter who serves some tables and does not "see" other tables and the bank teller or reception clerk who is so immersed in paper work that his eyes are not lifted even once to notice waiting clients are trying to keep away or block pressures. Once they let the customer catch their eye, they are committed to continuing the interaction, so they try not to enter into it. In a recent laboratory of human relations training, a group of Jerusalem bus drivers was asked to imagine the "ideal" passenger. Surprisingly, the first answer, accepted immediately by the whole group was "the Arab who boards the bus at Nablus gate" (a place in East Jerusalem). What are the characteristics of this passenger which make him so ideal? The first, which was not explicated by the drivers is his obvious lower status relative to the driver. The second, which was openly stated by the drivers, is the fact that he boards the bus, does not look into the driver's eyes, pays his fare without a word and quickly moves to the rear of the bus. In other words, he is the passenger with the least required contact.[3]

PSYCHOLOGICAL WITHDRAWAL AND AUTOMATIC BEHAVIOR

One way to deal with SSR conflicts, in particular with person-role conflict, is to become alienated from the role. It is important to note that one typical expression of alienation in nonservice occupations—daydreaming or "thinking about other things"—is much more restricted in subordinate service roles for obvious reasons. This form of psychological withdrawal and escapism is not readily available to them. Nevertheless, bus drivers in Israel are known to turn on their radios in

---

[3]It should be explained that Jerusalem buses, particularly those that stop at East Jerusalem, have often been targets of bombing. The Arab who boards such a bus is therefore regarded with suspicion by Jewish drivers and passengers.

such a volume that they operate as an audial barrier between them and their passengers, and allow them to concentrate on other things. A more typical expression of alienation is to perform the role in an automatic manner. To some extent this seems necessary in order to cope with service role requirements, however, if carried too far it becomes dangerous. Mills refers to this phenomenon as "self-estrangement," and has a few things to say about its dangers (1956, pp. 183–184, 272).

OVERACTING

Goffman (1961) has discussed overacting in a role as a form of maintaining "role distance" and reducing person-role conflict. However, overacting in service roles is not always done with the purpose of maintaining role distance. On the contrary, it is sometimes done with the purpose of reaching a high level of identification with role requirements and reducing person-role conflict through this identification. The waitress who moves like a ballerina (Terkel, 1972) is an example of an attempt to reduce person-role conflict through emphasizing role embracement rather than role distance. This is an essentially opposite strategy to the one of the automatic behavior described above.

CONTROLLING THE INTERACTION

The most frequently discussed form of reacting to potential conflict and stress in subordinate service roles, and the one which has received considerable attention in the literature, is gaining control over the interaction with clients. Various methods of control have been mentioned:

PHYSICAL CONTROL Air crews, for example, are known to keep the signs "fasten your seatbelt" on longer than needed in order to keep passengers in their seats.

CONTROL THROUGH LEADERSHIP Whyte (1948) refers to taking the initiative or "getting the jump" as a way for gaining control, leading the interaction, and avoiding pressures. This is done through certain physical acts (cleaning the table), through tone of voice or through showing expertise.

CONTROL THROUGH ANTICIPATION Most writers who described behavior in SSRs have mentioned that role occupants have typologies for customers that help them anticipate their needs and requirements. This has been found in the case of taxi drivers (Davis, 1959; Henslin, 1973, 338–356), bus drivers (Richman, 1969), and salespersons (Lombard, 1955; Mills, 1956; Woodward, 1960).

CONTROLLING REWARDS It has been demonstrated that SSR occupants can control their rewards either by ingratiating, "buttering up" and "cultivating" clients, or through more direct techniques of increasing sales. These techniques have been discussed in relation to the role of milkman by Bigus (1972) and in relation to the role of waitresses by Butler and Snizek (1976).

EDUCATING THE CLIENT

Reducing intersender conflict by teaching clients the rules of the organization has been discussed in the past with reference to Israeli bus drivers (Katz & Eisenstadt, 1960). There are, however, other forms of teaching or even punishing clients, for instance strict adherence to rules to the detriment of customers. Richman relates a story of bus crews who used to make 10 minutes on a long track for a tea break at the terminus, which pleased crew and customers alike. Once customers complained in a brisk manner about the bus being five minutes late at one of the stops. The crew punished passengers by reaching their destination for the rest of the week at the schedule time. "The crew missed their brew but enjoyed the subjection and humiliation suffered by their passengers" (1969, p. 299).

CONCLUDING REMARKS

The main purpose of this article was to draw attention to subordinate service roles as a special occupational category and a special case of organizational boundary roles. It has attempted to do so by presenting and discussing typical role conflicts in SSRs and typical individual responses to such conflicts which are not common to other organizational roles, not even in other boundary roles. The discussion has been limited to two types of role conflict—person-role and intersender conflicts—though other types of conflict and stress could be used to characterize SSRs. Thus it could be claimed, for instance, that role overload and role ambiguity have special meanings for SSR incumbents due to what has been called "the reactive nature of clients" (Katz & Kahn, 1966).

Several hypotheses about the determinants of role conflict in SSRs were put forward in the discussion to indicate the directions further theorizing and research could take. Future theorizing and research should, no doubt, extend beyond the simple, two-variable hypotheses presented in this paper, and deal with more complex, interactive relationships. In the meantime, however, there seems to be enough support for our speculative suggestions to warrant some practical implications.

Organizations could look for better ways to defend their employees from some of the conflicts mentioned in this article and to train them how to deal with these conflicts. Measures of job satisfaction, job motivation and role stress should attempt to incorporate relationships with clients in addition to the more conventional aspects and factors measured.

Some researchers (Rizzo et al., 1970; Abdel-Halim, 1978) report difficulties in trying to distinguish empirically between the various types of role conflict suggested by theory. Such difficulties may lead to abandoning the various types and treating role conflict as a unidimensional concept. This trend may be risky and unjustified since certain organizations and personal factors could have different relationships with various conflict types, as exemplified in this article by the relationships between role-sender's status and different types of conflict. Only more sensitive measures of role conflict than the one standardly used will enable us to verify the existence of conflict types and differentially to identify their antecedents, determinants, and consequences.

Finally, the present article concentrated on conflict and stress, but in no way did the author want to imply that contact with clients in SSRs has only negative aspects. Every student of such roles knows that contact with clients could also be a major source of satisfaction. Indeed, "meeting people" or "meeting the public" may be the major attraction of such roles for many of their occupants. In addition to that, SSRs have some advantages. They allow the service giver to "borrow prestige" from his client (Mills, 1956). Being exposed to the public is not only a source of stress, but an avenue of self-expression for many service-role occupants, who like to be on display, and to "make a show" in front of others. Subordinate service roles also have an advantage that many industrial and clerical jobs lack, and which is therefore a major element in job-enrichment programs for industrial and clerical employees. They get immediate feedback on their performance through smiles, nods, gestures, words, tips, curses, and various other means, allowing them to feel immediately how well they are doing, at least in the eyes of the client. Not only that, but boredom and monotony, which are frequent complaints among job holders in industry and offices, are much less frequent among service givers due to contacts with different people and to the immediate feedback. Many service roles are in general more enriched than production and clerical jobs. The role of clients in determining job-related strain, job satisfaction, work motivation, and performance deserves more attention than it has received so far by students of organizational behavior.

REFERENCES

Abdel-Halim, A. A. Employee affective responses to organizational stress: Moderating effects of job characteristics. *Personnel Psychology,* 1978, *31,* 561–579.

Adams, J. S. The structure and dynamics of behavior in organizational boundary roles. In M. D. Dunnette (Ed.). *Handbook of industrial and organizational psychology.* Chicago: Rand-McNally, 1976.

Ardrey, R. *The territorial imperative.* New York: Atheneum, 1967.

Argyle, M. *Bodily communication.* London: Methuen, 1975.

Bar-Yosef, R. W., & Schild, E. O. Pressures and defenses in bureaucratic roles. *American Journal of Sociology,* 1966, *71,* 665–673.

Beehr, T. A., & Newman, E. O. Job stress, employee health, and organizational effectiveness: A facet analysis model and literature review. *Personnel Psychology,* 1978, *31,* 665–699.

Bigus, O. The milkman and his customer: A cultivated relationship. *Urban Life and Culture.* 1972, *1,* 131–165.

Blau, P. M., & Scott, W. R. *Formal organizations.* London: Routledge & Kegan Paul, 1963.

Butler, S. R., & Snizek, W. E. The waitress–diner relationship: A multivariate approach to the study of subordinate influences. *Sociology of Work and Occupations,* 1976, *3,* 207–222.

Cooper, C. L., & Marshall, J. Occupational sources of stress. *The Journal of Occupational Psychology,* 1976, *49,* 11–28.

Davis, F. The cab driver and his fare. *American Journal of Sociology,* 1950, *45,* 158–165.

Flanagan, J. C. The critical incident technique. *Psychological Bulletin,* 1954, *51,* 327–358.

French, J. R. P., & Caplan, R. D. Organizational stress and individual strain. In A. J. Marrow (Ed.). *The failure of success.* New York: AMACOM, 1972.

Gersuny, C., & Rosengren, W. R. *The service society.* Cambridge, MA: Shenkman, 1973.

Goffman, E. *The presentation of self in everyday life.* Garden City, NY: Doubleday, 1959.

Goffman, E. *Encounters.* Indianapolis: Bobbs, Merrill Co., 1961.

Goodsell, C. T. Cross-cultural comparisons of behavior of postal clerks towards clients. *Administrative Science Quarterly,* 1976, *21,* 140–150.

Henslin, J. M. Trust and the cabdriver. In E. Katz & B. Danet (eds.). *Bureaucracy and the public.* New York: Basic Books, 1973.

House, R. J., & Rizzo, J. R. Role conflict and ambiguity as critical variables in the model of organizational behavior. *Organizational Behavior and Human Performance,* 1972, *7,* 467–505.

Kahn, R. L., Wolfe, P. M., Quinn, R. P., Snoek, D., & Rosenthal, R. A. *Organizational stress: Studies in role conflict and ambiguity.* New York: Wiley, 1964.

Katz, D., & Kahn, R. L. *The social psychology or organizations.* New York: Wiley, 1966.

Katz, E., & Danet, B. (Eds.). *Bureaucracy and the public.* New York: Basic Books, 1973.

Katz, E., & Eisenstadt, S. N. Some sociological observations on the response of Israeli organizations to new immigrants. *Administrative Science Quarterly,* 1960, *5,* 113–133.

Lombard, G. F. F. *Behavior in a selling group.* Cambridge, MA: Harvard University Press, 1955.

Mehrabian, A. *Silent messages.* Belmont, CA: Wadsworth, 1971.

Menzies, I. E. P. A case study in the functioning of social systems as a defense against anxiety. *Human Relations,* 1960, *13,* 95–131.

Miles, R. H., & Perreault, W. D. Organizational role conflict: Its antecedents and consequences. *Organizational Behavior and Human Performance,* 1976, *17,* 19–44.

Miller, E. J., & Rice, A. K. *Systems of organization.* London: Tavistock Publications, 1967.

Mills, C. W. *White collar.* New York: Oxford University Press, 1956.

Nedo, (National Economic Development Office), Economic Development Committee for Hotels and Catering. *Why tipping?* London: HMSO, no date.

Newman, J. E., & Beehr, J. A. Personal and organizational strategies for handling job stress: A review of research and opinion. *Personnel Psychology,* 1979, *1,* 1–44.

Organ, D. W. Some variables affecting boundary role behavior. *Sociometry,* 1971, *34,* 524–537.

Parsons, T. How are clients integrated into service organizations? In W. R. Rosengren & M. Lefton, (Eds.). *Organizations and clients: Essays in the sociology of service.* Columbus, OH: C. Merril & Co., 1970.

Richman, J. Busmen vs. the public. *New Society,* 1969, *14,* 243–245.

Rizzo, J. R., House, R. J., & Lirzman, S. R. Role conflict and ambiguity in complex organizations. *Administrative Science Quarterly,* 1970, *15,* 150–163.

Rogers, D. R., & Molnar, J. Organizational antecedents of role conflict and ambiguity in top level administration. *Administrative Science Quarterly,* 1976, *21,* 528–610.

Shamir, B. Between bureaucracy and hospitality: Some organizational characteristics of hotels. *Journal of Management Studies,* 1978, *15,* 285–307.

Scheflen, A. E. *Human territories.* Englewood Cliffs, NJ: Prentice-Hall, 1976.

Terkel, S. *Working.* New York: Aron Books, 1972.

Thompson, J. D. Organizations and output transactions. *American Journal of Sociology,* 1962, *60,* 309–324.

Whetten, D. A. Coping with incompatible expectations: An integrated view of role conflict. *Administrative Science Quarterly,* 1978, *23,* 254–271.

Whyte, W. F. *Human relations in the restaurant industry.* New York: McGraw-Hill, 1948.

Woodward, J. *The Saleswoman.* London: Pitman and Sons, 1960.

WHEN CASHIERS MEET CUSTOMERS

AN ANALYSIS OF THE ROLE OF SUPERMARKET CASHIERS

Anat Rafaeli

Hebrew University of Jerusalem

———◆———

The customer is paying for the merchandise. But he is not paying my salary. Why does he think he can tell me what to do?

—a supermarket cashier

In a qualitative investigation of the role of supermarket cashiers, the influence of management, co-workers, and customers over cashiers was analyzed. Customers had immediate influence over cashiers at the time of job performance; management influence was more legitimate but more remote. The analysis further revealed that cashiers and customers held different views on who had the right to control service encounters and that cashiers employed various strategies to maintain their control of those encounters.

Service organizations and "service encounters" (Czepiel, Solomon, & Surprenant, 1985) are an inevitable part of modern life. We can hardly get through a day without engaging in a service transaction—with a bank, a grocery store, or the phone company. In view of this social trend, management theoreticians and practitioners are also trying to understand, and improve, the context of service (Albrecht & Zemke, 1985; Czepiel et al., 1985; Desatnick, 1987; Hochschild, 1983).

Key participants in any service transaction are service employees. It is they whom customers meet on entering a department store or boarding an aircraft. Thus, a single employee may tint a customer's image of a service enterprise. Indeed, research has documented that service employees can be important to promoting organizational goals. Schneider, Parkington, and Buxton (1980), for example, reported that bank employees' perceptions of the organization they work for are closely related to customers' perceptions of the quality of service that the organization provides. Moreover, Sutton and

Rafaeli (1988) found a complex relationship between the behavior of clerks in convenience stores and organizational sales.

Some evidence has also suggested that organizational strategies can manipulate the external facade that service employees convey. In particular, Hochschild (1983) reported that the gracious behavior of flight attendants and the aggressiveness of bill collectors is largely attributable to the mandates of their management. Rafaeli and Sutton (1987) extended Hochschild's (1983) work and illustrated how service organizations attempt to shape their organizational image by monitoring and controlling the emotions that their employees convey.

Nonetheless, a host of issues about service contexts and service employees remain unexamined. There is a consensus that service is bad (Russel, 1987), but there isn't much agreement about how it can be improved.

One critical question concerns the relationship between employee–customer dynamics and the attainment of organizational goals. Marketing experts have long acknowledged the influence of this relationship over consumer behavior and resultant organizational

SOURCE © *Academy of Management Journal,* 1989, vol. 32, No. 2, 245–273.

I would like to thank two anonymous reviewers for their detailed and thoughtful comments that significantly improved this paper. I would also like to thank Bob Sutton, Eyal Ben-Arie, and Boaz Shamir for their comments on earlier versions of the paper. The study was supported by a grant to the author from the Mutual Fund of the Hebrew University of Jerusalem.

profits. In *Personal Selling,* for example, Jacoby and Craig addressed the question, "How can the salesperson influence the customer to buy?" (1984:1). Jacoby and Craig discussed strategies that salespeople use for persuasion and influence and contended that interpersonal attraction affects selling effectiveness.

There is also initial evidence that, because service occupations are boundary spanning (Adams, 1976; Bowen & Schneider, 1985), interactions with customers hold special qualities for service employees. Lombard (1955) reported how salespeople took a customer's rejection of merchandise as a personal rejection of themselves. Similarly, Whyte (1948) related the personal aggravation, sometimes to the point of crying, that waitresses felt when customers did not leave a tip.

Whyte (1948) and later Mars and Nicod (1984) argued that the relationship between waiters or waitresses and their customers is especially complex because of the conflict between servers' interest in controlling service encounters and their desire that customers feel good about the service and leave large tips. In his famous restaurant survey, Whyte referred to the waitresses' struggle to "get the jump" on the customers (1948: 132–133). Butler and Snizek (1976) documented how this struggle can affect a waitress's tip. Mars and Nicod later generalized the notion to a discussion of "the politics of service" (1984: 65).

Whyte (1948), Butler and Snizek (1976), and Mars and Nicod (1984) examined only restaurant employees. Nonetheless, their reasoning suggests that other service organizations may benefit from considering the special complexities of transactions with customers. The present study extended that notion. My goal was to place another stone on the path toward improved service by offering a close examination of the role of service employees and their interaction with customers. Understanding the role of service employees should promote the development of knowledge and theory about service operations.

The initial goal of the study was to understand the relationship between service employees and various members of their organizations.[1] For the sake of simplicity, I chose a very mundane service context—that of supermarket checkout clerks. Relationships between cashiers and customers were initially perceived as one part of a web of relationships involving various other parties, including management and co-workers. As the study evolved, however, customers emerged as having a unique role in shaping cashiers' "role set" (Biddle, 1979; Katz & Kahn, 1978: 188–192; Merton, 1957). Customers were found to have a great degree of immediate influence while cashiers are on the job; management's influence on the other hand, was legitimate, but remote. The work of Marks and Mirvis (1981) and Trist (1977) would suggest that customers constitute the transactional environment of supermarket employees and therefore affect behavior at the time of task execution. In contrast, management authority only sets the general tone of the environment and affects extreme behaviors of service employees, notably those governed by rules.

Unraveling the reasons for the immediate cashier–customer relationship was therefore an objective. Observations of the cashiers studied suggested that the immediacy of the clerk–customer relationship creates a certain tautness. Closer scrutiny revealed a tension about who was in control. Thus, as in the findings of Whyte (1948) and of Mars and Nicod (1984), the struggle for control between cashiers and customers seemed to strain the checkout process. Cashiers and customers had very different perceptions of who had the right to control this process. And cashiers, who considered the checkout process a part of their job, were observed to develop strategies to maintain control of their encounters with customers.

The study described was inductive (Glaser & Strauss, 1967). My goal was to conduct an in-depth investigation of a set of people employed in a service job, in the interest of advancing the development of theory on the service encounter. Because of the logic of inductive research (Glaser & Strauss, 1967), the methodology employed is first described; the insights and theory that emerged from the analysis of the data then follow.

METHODS

A qualitative study was conducted in a chain of supermarkets in Jerusalem, Israel, during the winter and spring of 1986. The individuals studied were cashiers and customers in six stores that were randomly selected from all the chain's stores in Jerusalem.

THE RESEARCH CONTEXT: SUPERMARKETS IN ISRAEL

Supermarket technology in Israel is similar to that in the United States: a multibrand product assortment of foods and nonfoods, a large physical scale, a large sales volume, and self-service are typical features of supermarkets

---

[1]Several authors have recently referred to customers as "partial employees" (cf. Mills & Morris, 1986: 726). The term is used to suggest that customers are actually temporary members or participants of service organizations because their participation is crucial to service production.

(Goldman, 1981; Rachman, 1975). After loading their carts with desired items, customers wait in line until a cashier processes the purchases and accepts payment. Cash registers are automated; cashiers type in the code of an item and the register rings up the price. Electronic scanners are still rare in Israel; only one of the stores included in the study had them. Pay for cashiers is low, usually around the minimum wage.

Four distinct attributes of Israeli supermarkets should be noted. First, Israeli customers pack their own purchases. Customers are expected to bring their own shopping bags and to pack each item right after a cashier has processed it as counters by the cash registers are usually small. Second, Israeli supermarkets offer a home delivery service, usually for a nominal fee. When this service is requested, it is the cashier's responsibility to pack the merchandise in a large plastic crate. Third, in Israel, going to a farmers' market is the prevalent alternative to supermarket shopping; such shopping is considered cheaper but less convenient. Fourth, consumer rights and the concept of service are not as developed in Israel as they are elsewhere in the West. Cashiers and other service employees are often argumentative, and rudeness is common.

Jerusalem is a large, cosmopolitan city. Most supermarket shoppers are permanent residents, although there are also tourists and students. The city has rich and poor neighborhoods, but the diversity is not extreme. Supermarkets and shoppers in Jerusalem are representative of Israel as a whole.

All the observed supermarkets employed a store manager, a head cashier, and 8–15 cashiers. All the store managers studied were men and all the head cashiers and cashiers were women.[2] Personnel files indicated that this was representative of the organization. Store managers were the official supervisors of all store employees and were also responsible for other aspects of store performance, including ordering merchandise and dealing with vendors. Thus, managers were the top authority for cashiers. Managers did, on occasion, order cashiers back to their registers or discuss work schedules with them; such monitoring was, however, the direct responsibility of head cashiers.

Head cashiers, the direct supervisors of line cashiers, were usually senior cashiers who had been promoted. Head cashiers were also responsible for collecting and counting the money from the various registers.

Head cashiers usually sat in the manager's office, answered the phone, went over work schedules, and did other administrative chores; only rarely (once or twice during the day) would a head cashier walk "down" to the registers.[3]

DATA COLLECTION AND ANALYSIS

Data collection included unstructured observations of cashiers and customers, participant observation as a cashier, interviews with cashiers, and interviews with customers. I conducted the observations and interviews in Hebrew but took notes and developed thoughts and theory throughout the study in English. Research notes did not name individuals; when it was necessary—where repeated references to a particular cashier were desired—specific cashiers were coded by a letter or a set of letters to ensure confidentiality of the data.

I did most of the data collection and analysis, employing research assistants as needed in various portions of the study. One assistant made unstructured observations. Two other assistants helped in the process of data analysis by working with me on categorizing incidents and phenomena and participating in brainstorming sessions.

Unstructured observations were conducted in all six stores. Observation times were predetermined to ensure appropriate time sampling. Store hours in Israel are 7:30 a.m.–1:00 p.m. and 3:30 p.m.–7:00 p.m.; observations were planned so that each store was visited once during early morning, once during late morning, once during early afternoon, and once during late afternoon. Additional visits were conducted, one in each store, after the initial round of observations was completed. These visits were randomly spaced throughout the day.

Observations were conducted in a nonobtrusive manner, and each lasted 30–45 minutes; the exact duration of an observation could not be predetermined because the observers did not want to evoke suspicion. After entering the store, an observer usually walked around the aisles for a few minutes and then stopped at the magazine rack or the chocolate rack as if searching for an item; these racks are usually close to the checkout area and offer a good vantage point for observation of cashiers and customers. After selecting an item, the observer stood in one of the lines and continued to

---

[2]Since all the cashiers observed and interviewed in the study were women, I use the feminine pronoun hereafter in reference to cashiers for the sake of convenience.

[3]Employees use the term "down" in all of the stores included in the study when referring to the register area; cashiers referred to the office as "up there" and to the cash register area as "down." The usage may reflect the physical structure of these stores, since the office is usually situated a few steps higher than the registers. It may also reflect the hierarchical relations in the stores.

observe the cashier and the customers. If the lines were short, the observer acted as if she had forgotten to buy something and walked out of the line and back into the store.[4] After a few minutes she again began to stand in line. After her order had been processed, the observer stood behind the cash register area, as if waiting for someone. Because of the size of the stores and the heavy influx of customers, this process did not seem to evoke suspicion.

The management of the corporation was advised that such observations would possibly be conducted; store managers, however, were not informed about specific store visits. Considering the public nature of the behaviors observed, it does not seem that there is an ethical question about such observations (Mintzberg, 1979; Salancik, 1979; Webb, Campbell, Schwartz, Sechrest, & Grove, 1981).

A second form of data collection involved *participant observation*. I went through the process of applying, training, and working as a cashier.[5] The participant observation consisted of three months of part-time employment for about 18 hours a week. My part-time, short-term status was not unusual; about 60 percent of the cashiers in this chain are employed part-time, and turnover among cashiers is high, up to 50 percent a year. Detailed field notes, in English, were taken after each shift of participant observation.

Semistructured interviews with cashiers were the third means of data collection. I conducted interviews with a random sample of 30 cashiers employed in stores other than the one in which the participant observation was conducted. The sample was stratified by age and tenure. The interview included general questions about the work as well as questions probing perceptions of customers and customer behavior. The interview also asked about two critical incidents (Flanagan, 1954) involving customer attempts to influence cashiers. Cashiers were asked how they would react to the following two incidents that had been observed during the unstructured observation phase of the data collection: 1) A customer said to a cashier, "How can you wear three earrings on one ear? That is ridiculous." 2) A customers said to a cashier, "Will you stop talking and start working! You're

wasting everyone's time." The Appendix gives the complete interview schedule.

Interviews, which were conducted on store premises during the employee's shift hours, each lasted 45–90 minutes; the motivation and participation levels of the interviewee determined the exact length. All interviews were conducted in one session, in Hebrew, and were tape-recorded. I summarized notes from these interviews in English. I also interviewed store managers and head cashiers, using an adapted version of the cashier's interview schedule.

Semistructured interviews with customers were also conducted. I interviewed 30 men and women who had shopped in one of the stores, 5 from each store. I approached customers after they had finished their shopping and asked them if they were willing to participate in the study, telling them that they would be asked to discuss their shopping experience. Customers who agreed to be interviewed (about 60 percent of those who were approached) were invited for a cup of coffee at a nearby coffee shop. Of the customers interviewed, 21 (70%) were women. The interviewees' ages ranged from 32 to 65. The Appendix also presents the schedule for the interviews with customers.

Data analysis began with unstructured brainstorming sessions among members of the research team and proceeded following Miles's proposals for qualitative data analysis (Miles, 1983; Miles & Huberman, 1984). Miles did not offer a structured sequence of steps to guide such analyses. Rather, he suggested continuous conceptual development throughout projects. Specifically, he discussed a process of "intertwining of analysis and data collection, in an attempt to formulate classes of phenomena, and to identify themes in the data" (1983: 126). Three specific rules of thumb proposed by Miles guided the present analysis: examining whether any particular generalization held true for different people or occasions, testing all possible implications of any one proposition, and examining closely any extreme-bias cases (Miles, 1983: 127).

The analysis started with a rough working framework: understanding the relationship between the observed service employees (cashiers) and various members of their role set. We went back and forth between the emerging theory and the data and mostly attempted to let ideas stimulated by the sites and the data revise and reshape the general framework. This process revealed the set of relations that a cashier encounters.

An attempt to understand the qualitative difference between customers, managers, and co-workers followed. This phase included repeated references to the notes

---

[4] All the research assistants who acted as observers were women.

[5] The corporate personnel manager chose the site of my participant observation according to store needs for a cashier. Senior management and the store manager were aware that I was conducting a study about supermarket cashiers. I informally told individual cashiers about the study whenever they asked or whenever it seemed appropriate. At the end of the study, all the cashiers were briefed about the study.

from the various data sources. I followed an iterative process of systematically going back and forth between theoretical insights and data. The goal of the process, which followed the recommendations of Glaser and Strauss (1967), was to verify support of theoretical developments and search for inconsistencies between new insights and the data.

This iterative process suggested that, compared to their relationships with their managers and co-workers, cashiers spent more time with customers, were physically closer to customers, and got more feedback and information from customers. Cashiers also viewed customers as more crucial than managers or co-workers. In short, customers appeared to have immediate influence over cashiers, and management's influence, although perceived as legitimate, was remote.

During the iterative process, the importance of control for both cashiers and customers began to emerge. In light of previous writings on the importance of control, which I encountered in a preliminary literature review, I pursued a closer focus on the dynamics of control over the observed service encounters. This focus suggested interesting and important differences between cashiers' and customers' perceptions of the right to control the encounters. Thus, another round of data-scanning was necessary to search for support and inconsistencies between theoretical insights on the struggle for control and the data. During the process of refining the theoretical implications of the data, I also drew on feedback from colleagues and organizational contacts.

To familiarize the reader with the socialization of supermarket cashiers, a brief overview of the process of becoming a cashier follows. Next, the set of relations a cashier encounters on the job is presented. The differences between the influence role of customers and that of management, and cashiers' and customers' perceptions of control of service encounters are then examined. Finally, I present a typology of strategies employed by cashiers to gain control of interactions with customers.

FINDINGS

THE PROCESS OF BECOMING A CASHIER

Learning how to be a cashier was, in my experience, an extremely informal process. Table 1 summarizes the various stages of the socialization process through the end of my first day of participant observation. As can be seen, I spent less than a half hour with the various members of the organizational hierarchy, other than peers or customers.

The formal socialization began with a brief meeting with the personnel manager of the corporation about two weeks before the participant observation started. The meeting consisted of a few personal questions and assignment to a store. After the meeting a secretary asked me to take a short screening test, which mostly concerned knowledge of arithmetic, and had me sign a form labeled "Basic Rules of Cashier Behavior." This form included ten rules of behavior; I later learned that, among cashiers, the form is nicknamed the "Ten Commandments." The Appendix displays these rules.

The encounter with the formal organization also included a two-minute meeting with the store manager who basically said "See the head cashier," and a five minute talk with the head cashier, who gave me a general introduction to the store including information on store hours, instructions on how to punch the time clock, and about where to put my coat and purse, and a very brief and informal introduction to my "trainer," an older woman with 16 years of experience on the job. The shortness of my interaction with members of the formal hierarchy contrasted sharply with three and three-quarter hours I spent with customers on the very first day. These hours were spent standing behind the cashier who had been designated as my trainer. She explained that she was often selected as a trainer for new cashiers because she "enjoyed it and also knew the work really well." Nonetheless, it was quite quickly evident that she had little structured, formal training to offer. After a few minutes of "This is the register," "See, there are special keys for produce, drinks, meats," and "You need to learn the codes for the various items," she said "OK, now you can watch me work"; she then went on to "pass customers through,"[6] expecting me to continue watching.

During the training period, the trainer occasionally reentered her training role. For instance, pulling a large notebook from her drawer, she said "Here are all the codes for the different items. Take it home and you can learn the codes in the evening." Yet structured training was a rare event, for me and for other trainees who were observed throughout the study; most of the time trainers passed customers through while trainees sat or stood behind them and watched.

---

[6]The term used by the cashiers to describe a transaction was "pass through." Thus, a cashier might say, "I passed [the customer] through and then went to get change," or "Let me just pass her through and then I'll help you." This terminology is especially interesting because in reality it is merchandise that is being passed through, not customers.

TABLE 1   Cashier Socialization Process up to the End of the First Day of the Participant Observation

Stage	Approximate Duration
Telephone call to head office	2 minutes
Meeting with personnel manager	13 minutes
Meeting with store manager	2 minutes
Waiting	7 minutes
Meeting with head cashier	5 minutes
Session with training cashier and customers	3 3/4 hours
Time spent with other cashiers and employees	20 minutes

In short, in the process of becoming a cashier, there was little structured, formal interaction with the trainer or with management. Because of the store's open-space design, however, there was a lot of unmediated exposure and close physical proximity to customers. Such exposure is an integral part of a cashier's job from the very beginning. It was also the first clue to the differences between the various role senders, that is, the various holders of expectations about the cashiers' role (Katz & Kahn, 1978: 190).

THE SET OF RELATIONS THAT CASHIERS ENCOUNTER

Figure 1 summarizes several aspects of the relationship of customers, co-workers, and management to cashiers. Cashiers were placed outside the figure because the intent is to summarize the relationships of the various other parties to cashiers. Furthermore, the figure displays *only* relations to cashiers. The solid arrows in Figure 1 imply direct influence. Thus, customers have direct influence over cashiers, as do co-workers and management. The broken lines in Figure 1 indicate influence; customers also have indirect influence over cashiers through other employees and through management.

Figure 1 includes two axes that facilitate the understanding of cashiers' role set. The horizontal axis refers to legitimate influence. The person with formal authority over a cashier—her manager—has the strongest legitimate right to influence the cashier's behavior. The vertical axis in Figure 1 suggests the dimension of immediate influence. The results of this study suggest that customers hold more immediate influence at the time of job performance than either co-workers or management. The immediacy of customer influence is due to the physical proximity between cashiers and customers, the extent of time they spend together, customers' opportunity for supplying direct feedback and other information

tion, and the immediate importance that cashiers attribute to customers.

MANAGEMENT POWER. The horizontal axis of Figure 1 refers to legitimate influence. In the cashiers' formal organization (Katz & Kahn, 1978), management holds the greatest amount of legitimate influence because it represents the employing organization and has the power to reward (French & Raven, 1960).

Legitimate power belongs to management by definition, and cashiers are well aware of this. Cashiers usually accentuated behavior according to the rules (the Ten Commandments) whenever the manager or assistant manager walked around the register area. Similarly, during my training I was explicitly told, "Sure you can keep a cup at the register. Just be sure he [the manager] doesn't see it." Moreover, implied consent of the manager or the head cashier allowed the breaking of organizational rules. To illustrate, when a cashier wanted to get a pastry from the bakery across the street, she usually asked the manager or the head cashier if he or she would also like something (PO).[7] Because of insurance liability, cashiers were not allowed to leave the store during work hours (PO). But the unwritten rule seemed to be that if a member of management was a party to such activity, "It was OK to do it." (PO).

Management's legitimate influence (Figure 1) is also due to the store manager's apparent control over formal rewards; the manager handed out monthly pay checks and holiday bonuses (PO). Management's reward power is not as strong as it could be since wages in the chain are centrally determined and are not linked to performance. Moreover, the store managers have very little

---

[7]For the sake of simplicity, where it is not evident from the text the following codes are used to denote the source of quotations: I = an interview with a cashier, UO = unstructured observation, PO = participant observation, and CI = an interview with a customer.

FIGURE 1   Parties and Dynamics Driving Cashers; Behavior: Customer, Co-worker, and Management Influence

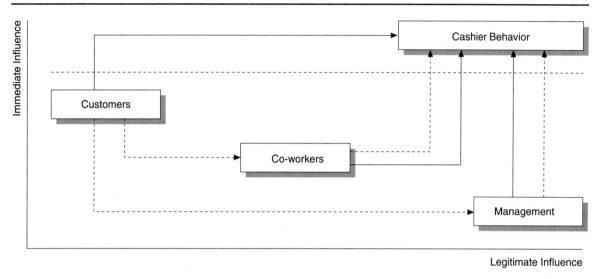

leverage when it comes to personnel policies. However, a manager can fire a cashier, especially if she is caught disobeying rules, and can have an effect on promotions. Thus, cashiers refused to be tape-recorded when they talked about eating or smoking at the register because the Ten Commandments prohibited such activities. As one cashier said, "They could immediately fire me if they knew" (I). Similarly, when one cashier was called to the manager because a customer had reported that she pocketed some money, the other cashiers immediately began to sympathize: "Poor D., now he will fire her" (PO).

As Figure 1 further indicates, customers have no legitimate influence. Co-workers—other cashiers—were, however, occasionally observed to exert a moderate amount of legitimate power. This was rare, but it occurred, for example, when as a newly hired cashier, I felt that my trainer was an authority. Trainers had the authority to decide how well a trainee was doing and when she could begin working alone (PO, I). I also heard a senior cashier urge a younger co-worker to "work more quickly, stop talking to your friends, can't you see that there is a long line waiting?" (PO). The younger cashier clearly reacted to this comment by focusing more directly on her register and discontinuing her conversation with her friend; she also said to her friend (casually, but in a very soft voice), "She [the more senior cashier] is almost like the manager around here" (UO).

Occasionally, customers might also attempt to influence cashiers' rewards. But such attempts have to operate through co-workers or management, as implied by the broken arrows in Figure 1. In order to punish a

cashier who pocketed money, a customer had to report the incident to the manager (PO); the cashier in this event was ultimately fired. Similarly, when customers wanted to reward cashiers for desirable behavior, they commented about it to the manager or to other cashiers. To illustrate, several customers said to me while I was in training: "You really have a very good trainer; she is the best one around." This was always said when my trainer was around, and in a loud enough voice so that she could hear. Thus, it was a form of indirectly complementing the trainer. Along similar lines, one customer was heard saying to a manager who happened to be standing by a cash register, "You should really do something for her; give her a bonus or something; she does such a good job" (UO).

CUSTOMER POWER. The vertical axis of Figure 1 suggests that customers, and therefore customer influence, are much more immediate than management and management influence. Co-workers, in turn, have more immediate influence over cashiers than management, but less than customers. Five factors cause this immediacy: physical proximity, the amount of time customers and cashiers spend together, the amount of feedback customers give, the amount of information they provide, and the crucial role cashiers attribute to customers. The following examines each of these factors in detail.

Cashiers are physically much closer to their customers than to anyone else. About 25 inches separate a cashier and her customer, as opposed to the 80 inches or more separating two cashiers. Management is very remote, usually many yards away. The physical structure of supermarkets means that cashiers have little opportunity to interact with each other or with management without an audience of customers.

Moreover, cashiers usually view other cashiers either from the back (during training) or from the side. They view management from below (see footnote 3), or from far away. In contrast, there is constant frontal contact with customers. To gain the physical proximity that people enjoy, a cashier has to leave her work station and walk over to whomever she wishes to meet. That is, she must stop her work. Customers resent such breaks, as does management (I, CI). Thus, because of the physical structure of the supermarkets, cashiers can easily and continuously get verbal and nonverbal messages from customers. Communication with co-workers and with management is more difficult than it is with customers, and it is much less intimate since it is usually in front of an audience.

In short, the physical layout of supermarket work constrains interpersonal relationships among cashiers and makes customers the most immediate source of communication. Throughout the study I observed that the physical layout makes for little informal interaction among cashiers and that the informal network of relations among cashiers was very weak. To illustrate, approximately two hours of my first participant observation shift had passed before any of the other cashiers asked my name. By the end of the participant observation, I had not managed to collect much information about the other cashiers. I barely knew the names of all the other cashiers. I knew little about their personal lives. Likewise, they knew very little about me.

Several cashiers specifically mentioned that the physical distance between cashiers, combined with the noise and hustle in the store, usually do not allow interaction among cashiers or between cashiers and management (PO, I). Indeed, during the participant observation, it was often impossible to talk to cashiers while they were working. One cashier said,

> You need to talk to someone. And the only one you can talk to is customers. But if you talk to them too much you can make mistakes (I).

A second reason for the greater immediacy of customer influence is the amount of time cashiers spend with customers, compared to the amount of time they spend with any of the other members of their role set. This was first evident from the extremely brief formal socialization procedure encountered in the process of becoming a cashier (see Table 1).

Observations of cashiers during their routine work revealed a pattern similar to that encountered on my first day and reported in Table 1. Approximately 78 percent of cashiers' time was spent interacting with customers; only 13 percent of their time was spent interacting with management, including task-related interactions, such as verifying a price or getting change. The constant interaction with others was an attractive job attribute for many cashiers:

> I looked for a job where I would be with people. I couldn't see myself in an office job (I).

> I liked the fact that there would be a lot of people around me. Otherwise I would get bored (I).

Nonetheless, once she has started working, a cashier may find it burdensome that the customers are constantly there.

Cashiers spend most of their time with customers because that is the way their work is structured. They are instructed to work independently; what one cashier does is usually relevant only to customers, and a cashier is expected to be equipped to deal with most customer needs. Certain events do require a cashier to interact with management or co-workers (e.g., verifying a price, getting check approval, asking for a break), but walking over to a fellow employee for a friendly chat is clearly a waste of time that interferes with the work.

Events that include interacting with co-workers or with management require time. Such use of time is often unpleasant to the cashiers because customers view it as a waste of time (UO, CI). One cashier summarized this feeling well: "What do I care how I pass my eight hours, but the customers get really angry when things move really slowly or if I have to leave the register" (UO). Thus, cashiers try to avoid "wasting" their time dealing with management or other store employees. To illustrate, cashiers expressed annoyance when customers changed their mind about purchases, and the head cashier had to be called for a cancellation (PO, UO). Many cashiers were aggravated when their registers seemed stuck for some reason and they had to call for help (UO, PO). Likewise, upon encountering an unmarked item, many cashiers relied on the price that the customer reported, rather than asking a co-worker or the manager (UO). Several cashiers specifically mentioned that they encouraged customers to pay cash to avoid spending the time to get checks approved:

> For checks I have to get approval and it wastes time; but I can get in trouble if I don't get approval. So I like cash, only cash (I).

A third reason for the greater immediacy of customer influence is the amount and immediacy of the feedback that customers provide. The physical proximity between cashiers and customers increases the degree of verbal and nonverbal communication between them. The great amount of time that cashiers spend with customers also increases the probability of such communication. Thus, customers have the opportunity to provide cashiers with immediate positive or negative feedback.

Comments like "Oh, that is really nice of you" (PO) and "You work so fast" (UO) constitute positive feedback; "Your check-out is slower than all the other ones, you know" (UO) and "Why can't you be more polite?" (PO) are examples of immediate negative feedback from customers. In contrast, management gives inconsistent, delayed, partial feedback that previous research has shown to have less powerful effects than immediate feedback (Hilgard & Bowers, 1975).

Customers' attempts to discourage cashiers from interacting with other cashiers or with management are another form of feedback. Customers make such attempts because they resent the "time wasted" (UO, I). They often try to persuade cashiers that it is unnecessary to take this time, saying "It is OK, the check is OK, you don't have to waste time getting approval" (UO) or "Why do you have to keep running back and forth to the office? It is such a waste of time" (UO).

Customers may also offer information that a cashier wants but cannot get elsewhere on her job. Since cashiers attend to customers in order to get this information, the stage is set for immediate customer influence. Customers offer three types of information: work-related information, general knowledge, and information about their status that may help cashiers elevate their self-attributed status.

First, customers may offer information that helps a cashier continue her work, such as information about the price or code of an item. Although such information is available elsewhere, obtaining it through the manager or through a co-worker would cause an unwelcome delay.

Second, customers may offer general knowledge that is not work-related. To illustrate, a cashier asked a regular customer[8] who was the owner of a local furniture store how much a rocking chair cost, explaining that she wanted to buy someone a rocking chair as a present (PO).

Along similar lines, a cashier asked a customer, "What do you do with this? Do you boil it?" (UO). One cashier presented the opportunity to obtain such information as a positive attribute of the job. She tried to encourage me to feel that the job was not as boring as it seemed:

> After a while, after you learn how to work the cash register, it gets to be fun. You can talk to the customers and you can learn from them how to cook different things. You'll see (PO).

Third, customers may offer information that helps cashiers elevate their self-perceived status. Goodsell (1976) documented that service employees clearly observe customer status cues. There were several indications here that cashiers derived status from the status of their customers. The head cashier's introduction to the store in which I conducted the participant observation was very brief (see Table 1), but it included the comment "You know, this is an important store, and very important people shop here, including people from [the local] TV [network]" (PO). Similarly, an interviewed cashier said, "We have some really famous customers here, and some of them buy on credit, without even paying, like the prime minister's house and the president's house."

Moreover, when asked "Who are your favorite customers?" several cashiers responded by referring to a high-status person: "this professor who shops here with his wife" (I) or "the president's house" (I). Another cashier gave a more general response:

> . . . people that have style. Some people just look classy. You know, they are dressed well and they know how to behave. I like them. It is respectable to work with them (I).

It is as if the status of the client raises the status of the clerk.

Finally, the immediacy of customer influence is enhanced because cashiers view customers as crucial. Cashiers summarized this notion:

> We should always try to keep the customers happy. Sometimes I even sing to them. And if I see a customer leave a full cart by my register and prepare to leave the store I call him and try to convince him to stay. Because if the customers leave us, where will we be? They make the store. They make my salary (I).

> Without the customers the store would never exist. Without the cashiers it might be hard. Without the manager—we get along, and you can always find a replacement for cashiers or managers. But not without the customers. They make the money (I).

In sum, although management's legitimate influence allows it to have a certain degree of remote control

---

[8]Cashiers frequently referred to "regular " or "permanent" customers. These were customers who shopped in the store regularly. Such customers often selected a favorite cashier, and cashiers frequently knew the names and addresses of these customers from taking checks or delivery orders.

over cashiers, several factors set the customers apart as having the potential for immediate influence over cashiers. Management plans and rules may set the stage for the interaction between a cashier and her customer, but because of their physical proximity, the amount of time spent together, the flow of feedback and information, and the crucial role cashiers attribute to customers, it is the cashier and the customer who determine how this interaction unfolds.

THE STRUGGLE FOR CONTROL BETWEEN CASHIERS AND CUSTOMERS

As mentioned above, the interaction with customers was an attractive job for many cashiers. The constant exposure to customers, however, may be more than was bargained for. Specifically, customers' perspective on the interaction with cashiers appears to be qualitatively different from cashiers' perceptions of the same interaction. As one cashier said, "He is one of the customers and I have to pass him through and take money from him" (I). In contrast, customers said "I am paying, so I should get service" (CI) and "Since it is my time, don't I have a right to try and avoid wasting it?" (CI). What emerges is a struggle for control of the interaction.

SERVICE ENCOUNTERS: CUSTOMERS' PERSPECTIVE The data suggested two key resources that guide customers' perceptions of service encounters in the supermarket: money and time. Customers who have given or are about to give money expect to get something in return. Customers may enjoy spending time selecting merchandise, but they resent time spent waiting for a cashier.

As far as customers are concerned, they are paying not only for merchandise but also for service:

> When I go to the market all I want is good, cheap stuff. But a supermarket is supposed to offer something more. You pay more. So you should at least get a pleasant shopping experience (CI).

> Why can't you be more polite? I am paying! And *you* are serving *me* you know! (UO).

Moreover, customers often view cashiers as liaisons between the retail organization and themselves: "She works for the organization, doesn't she?" (CI) and "She's the only one from the store that I get to talk to" (CI). Since they pay the organization, customers expect to have some say about how it functions. Thus, customers may comment to a cashier about things that are obviously not part of her job: "Why are shopping bags so expensive here?" (PO) or "Why don't they get those

imported sardines anymore?" (UO). This is the only opportunity that customers see to influence the organization. Since customers are paying, they believe that the organization and its representatives—the cashiers—should deliver (CI).

From a customer's point of view, cashiers also determine how much money the customer must part with. Because money is very important, customers see themselves as having a right to monitor and control its expenditure. Customers were often suspicious that they were being cheated, as these comments from my interviews with them show:

> Cashiers always steal.

> You always have to watch over them carefully.

> It's real easy for them to overcharge. You never have time to watch when they type the stuff. And every time I check the slip I find some error.

I also observed customers saying:

> Please slow down. Last time they cheated me so I want to see what you type (PO).

> Can't you wait so I can watch what you do? (UO).

It was hard, if not impossible, to assess the extent to which cashiers actually engaged in cheating (Mars, 1984). Over 80 percent of the incidents noted in the present study in which customers asked to check a price or a sales slip indicated no fault on the cashier's part. Nonetheless, the point is that since the customers are paying, they feel they have a right to monitor and control how much is paid, which implies monitoring and controlling the cashiers' behavior.

As with money, the desire to save time also drives customers to monitor the cashiers. The checking out process often causes bottlenecks in the store. Customers are forced to stand, wait, and do nothing while a cashier processes orders. Such waiting is a nuisance (Maister, 1985). Indeed, customers waiting in line were often annoyed, angry, and helpless; the aggressive reactions mentioned in Seligman's (1975) discussion of helplessness were frequently evident. To illustrate:

> I can't stand it. Why can't they open another register? [very aggressive tone of voice] (UO).

> I don't believe it [to a cashier who didn't know a code]. You sit here all day and you don't know the code for potatoes? As if this is something unusual! (UO).

Exhibiting behavior that is consistent with Maister's (1985) observations on the psychology of waiting in line, customers seek means to shorten their objective or subjective waits. They may do this by suggesting to cashiers various mechanisms for saving time. They also try to do things instead of letting the cashiers do them. I saw customers packing delivery crates (the cashiers' job), going to the shelves to check a price or a code, placing fruit and vegetables on the scale to be weighed, or placing items so the codes were easily visible (UO, PO). One customer tried to create group support, saying to other people waiting in line "Come on, let's help her, if we help her maybe things will move along a little bit more quickly" (UO). The following incident, which occurred during the participant observation, is also illustrative:

> One customer could not find her checkbook, and seemed to be "wasting everybody's time" looking for it. Customers waiting in line put pressure on the cashier to start processing their orders; they glared at the cashier and glared at the customer. They offered suggestions about where the checkbook might be or suggested that maybe she could pay with a credit card. Then they began requesting that the cashier process the next customer's order while this woman was looking for her checkbook. One customer attempted to explain to the cashier that such a move would be logical. He said, "Since she is paying with a check, when she finds her checkbook you can take it from her."

In sum, because of the time and money involved, customers seek, and see themselves as having a right, to control their encounter with a cashier.

SERVICE ENCOUNTERS: CASHIERS' PERSPECTIVE Customers' intense involvement in the service encounters studied creates resistance and resentment among cashiers. As suggested by the quote at the beginning of this article, cashiers realize that customers want to control them, but they are not willing to relinquish control of the encounters. Cashiers seek control of service encounters because they feel they need and have a right to this control in order to do their job.

Cashiers perceive their main responsibilities to be to "pass customers through" (I) and "take money and give change" (I), functions requiring a fair amount of concentration. A cashier needs to recall the codes or prices of many unmarked items, to verify that she has entered the correct information into the register, to count the money she receives, and to count the change she gives out. At the same time, she needs to keep track of which items she has entered and to guard against customer theft. These tasks entail a responsibility, and errors may be personally costly to the cashier since cash differences can be deducted from her salary. Cashiers seek to maintain control over the checkout process in order to avoid errors.

Customers' attempts to control an encounter can also be offensive to cashiers. The consensus among cashiers is that they know best how to do the job, even though customers sometimes try to tell them otherwise:

> It is my job. I know best how to do it (I).

> He thinks that because he shops here he can run things. But I am here every day. It's my job. I know how to do it. And it drives me nuts when he tells me what to do (I).

Thus, when customers attempt to monitor cashiers' behavior and to tell them what to do, cashiers seek ways to establish who is in control.

There is also a strong theoretical rationale behind cashiers' struggle for control. Extensive research has discussed the psychological importance of personal control (Langer, 1983; Seligman, 1975; Sutton & Kahn, 1986). Goffman (1959) argued that control over an individual's immediate environment is especially important, explaining that "we seek control over the people in our environment with whom we interact, particularly individuals who are likely to react to us" (1959:3). Since cashiers constantly interact with customers, it is clear why they struggle to control them. What is intriguing is the way in which this struggle is conducted.

STRATEGIES IN CASHIERS' STRUGGLE FOR CONTROL The existing literature on service employee's fight for control (Bigus, 1972; Butler & Snizek, 1976; Mars & Nicod, 1984; Whyte, 1948) was used as a point of departure for developing a typology of the strategies employed by cashiers for reclaiming control of service encounters. The data suggested four such strategies: ignoring customers, rejecting customers' right to control, reacting to customers' attempt at control, and engaging customers so that they don't try to seek control. Table 2 presents examples of the use of each of these strategies. The strategies presented in Table 2 can be viewed as a continuum of actions by cashiers ranging from passive, through reactive, to proactive. Ignoring a customer means taking no action. Rejecting is somewhat more active; it reflects some active thought on the cashier's part about why the customer does not have a right of control. Reacting entails an overt response to a customer's behavior, a response that makes the customer aware that the cashier is annoyed. Finally, engaging is a proactive strategy in which a customer is occupied and thus too busy to demand control.

Ignoring is the most passive strategy. Cashiers can ignore a customer, and frequently do so, by avoiding eye contact. Less than half the cashiers observed during

TABLE 1   Cashiers' Strategies in the Struggle for Control

Strategies	Source of Data		
	Unstructured Observations	**Participant Observation**	**Interviews**
Ignoring	Cashiers focus their eyes on the cash register, avoid eye contact with customers if they can.	Trainer told observer: "Sometimes they say really nasty things about how you should do your work. I think you should ignore them because there is no end to such comments."	"When they tell me what to do, like how many earrings to wear, and I don't want to do it, I simply ignore them and don't listen."
Rejecting	No evidence noted.	Cashiers label customers who request continuous monitoring of prices entered as "pests" and "naggers."	"He is paying for the merchandise. He is not paying my salary. Why does he think he can tell me what to do?"
Reacting	Customer was angry that cashier had to "waste" time looking for a code, started yelling. Cashier tried to calm him down by saying, "Why do you have to yell? Why do you have to talk like that?"	A customer said, "In America, all the cashiers smile." Cashier replied: "So go to America. What do you want from me?"	"After a customer has rushed me through his purchases I love to sit back, cross my arms, watch him, and let everyone see how *he* is wasting everyone's time now."
Engaging	Cashier to customer: "Now if you smile, everything will be OK." Cashiers ask customers to put produce on scale.	Cashier keeps customers busy by telling them what to do: "You can take the bread, now pack the oranges, I typed the coffee."	"If I see that they are upset I might sing. I don't sing that well but it makes them laugh and forget they were angry."

the unstructured observation phase made some form of eye contact with customers. In another study, which included structured observations, 61 percent of the cashiers observed made no eye contact with customers, and an additional 32.8 percent made eye contact only once, for less than one minute (Rafaeli, 1989).

Cashiers may also ignore customers' comments or their attempts to take charge. To illustrate, when customers commented that a cashier should "speed things up" (UO) or "stop talking to your friend" (UO), many cashiers simply continued what they were doing and ignored the comment.

The terminology that cashiers have developed to refer to their interaction with customers is in itself a form of ignoring. As noted earlier, cashiers refer to "passing customers through," an impersonal term that does not acknowledge any individual differences among customers and suggests that a customer is another item to be processed. In actuality, it is the merchandise that cashiers "pass through"; considering a customer as one of the items that is being passed through allows ignoring the customer as a social partner and promotes perceived control of the encounter.

Ignoring is sometimes a necessary strategy for survival; it enables cashiers to concentrate on their work:

I feel really stressed at the register, because I don't really know all the codes yet. And then customers come and tell me what to do and I get into even more stress. The only way I can keep going is by ignoring them and going my own way (I).

Cashiers who ignore customers may justify this behavior to themselves by being slightly more active and rejecting the customers' right of control. This strategy entails the internal justification that "the customers has no business telling me what to do" (I). The transition from ignoring to rejecting is not always obvious and may be known only to the cashier herself. Conceptually, the difference is important, however, both because cashiers make the distinction (e.g., "Before I ignore her, I make sure I am right" [I]) and because rejecting implies a more active and involved employee.

Reacting is a yet more active strategy; a cashier not only thinks that a customer has no right of control but also finds a way to convey that to the customer. The reaction may be verbal but emphasized with blatant nonverbal gestures.

A reaction may simply convey rejection; that was the strategy adopted by the following cashier:

You need to let the customer know that this is how you work and if he doesn't like it he has a problem.

If he complains about how I work I don't even bother replying to what he asks. I just say "My name is _____ and you can tell the manager if you don't like me or my work" (I).

It might be noted that this cashier provided legitimacy for her reaction by implying that management will support her behavior.

A reaction may also attempt to convince customers that they are wrong or to dissuade them from an attempt at control. When a customer got upset and started scolding a cashier about not knowing the code for a certain item, she replied,

Why do you have to yell? Why do you have to talk like that? You think I do it on purpose? You think it will help that you yell? It only slows things down and makes them worse! (UO).

Furthermore, a reply may attempt to calm the customer by expressing agreement. To illustrate, during the participant observation one customer got annoyed that the codes on several items were wrong. The cashier replied,

Ok. Yes, you are right. They put codes on the items and don't bother to check. But why are you yelling at me? I didn't put the codes on. I am just trying to help you (PO).

Nonverbal components of a reaction may include sitting with folded arms, glaring, and purposefully dropping merchandise. The first was a favorite strategy of a young and very efficient cashier. When asked how she dealt with difficult customers she replied,

What I love is to finish my work, announce out lout his total, then twiddle my thumbs. It can really embarrass him because everyone can see who is waiting for whom (I).

Reactions may get extreme and may entail raised voices:

I can't stand the customers who bullshit. It must be something about me, maybe because I have all these personal problems and I got divorced. Maybe it is my personality. But I like working fast. And when they move slowly and they try to slow me down it drives me nuts. And I let them know it in the way I do things, like packing their stuff or giving them change. One time I even yelled at a customer.

Engaging is the most proactive strategy a cashier can adopt. It entails keeping customers busy so that they don't bother her. A cashier may engage customers by telling jokes, making small talk, or asking them to do certain things, such as put their vegetables on the scale to be weighed. Engaging the customers requires extensive experience because a cashier needs to do it while she continues with her routine tasks. Engaging is therefore more frequently evident among senior cashiers, as was apparent from observing and talking to both new and experienced cashiers:

My mother is also a cashier, so I am lucky. I learned from her how to handle the job and how to handle customers. But still, I feel I need more experience to really know what to do (cashier with four months tenure, PO).

I always keep the customer busy, it helps me with my work and they are happy. I have been on the job for 16 years. I know it really well (I).

One cashier developed an engaging strategy that appeared very sophisticated. She focused her eyes on the register and only glanced at the strip with the items on it, calling out the items she had entered on the register. She constantly told the customer which items to pack while she worked the register. Her communication with the customer mostly included comments such as "You can take the bread" and "OK, I got the coffee." Occasionally, however, she would remind the customer that she was in control by saying "No wait, I haven't entered the ice cream yet" (PO). The last statement reinforced her control because it verified that she was monitoring the customer's behavior; that is, she was the one in charge.

DISCUSSION

The goal of this study was to examine closely the role of service employees. This close examination called for a qualitative, in-depth investigation of one group of employees. Previous research has revealed that organizations invest in efforts to monitor the image set by such employees (Hochschild, 1983; Rafaeli & Sutton, 1987), that organizational sales bear a complex relationship to the behavior of these employees (Sutton & Rafaeli, 1988), and that such employees hold a special relationship to their customers (Adams, 1976; McCallum & Harrison, 1985; Mars & Nicod, 1984; Whyte, 1948). The present study placed in focus a central component of the work of service employees—service encounters (Czepiel et al., 1985).

The study suggests four notions relevant to the research and management of service employees. First, the tight interdependence between cashiers and customers suggests that it is important to focus additional research effort on their encounters, rather than on the participants—clerks or customers—singly. Second, the complexity of the role-sending process that cashiers face suggests that a high degree of tension and strain accompany their service encounters. Third, the contrast between the data collected and other research findings on service suggests several paradoxes about service encounters. And fourth, the dynamics that customers inspire in service encounters suggest several threats to service employees and to service organizations.

Customer influence was instantaneous, continuous, and simultaneous with job performance. Moreover, customer influence stimulates cashiers to react in certain ways. Thus, customers form the transactional environment of these service employees (Marks & Mirvis, 1981; Trist, 1977). In contrast, management, which holds legitimate influence, creates the organizational environment and sets the stage for employee's performance. Management is ultimately responsible for setting up service encounters and also bears responsibility for extreme behaviors. For example, management must get involved if rules are broken or money is stolen. But routine service transactions are affected most by an interplay between service employees and their customers. Their interdependence implies the impropriety of studying service employees independently of their customers.

Other authors have written about interdependence in service encounters (McCallum & Harrison, 1984). What emerged here, however, was that such encounters cannot be understood without a full view of both participants and an emphasis on the interaction between them. Thus, the encounters themselves are important units of analysis in the study of service. Most previous writings have emphasized either employees (cf. Hochschild, 1984) or customers (Desatnick, 1987; Peters & Waterman, 1982).

The findings about interdependence suggest a new research question: How much interpersonal interaction is beneficial and motivating? Job design theoreticians (e.g., Sims, Szilagyi, & Keller, 1976) have argued that the opportunity for interacting with others is a positive job attribute. Indeed, employees may enjoy constant exposure to, and interaction with, clients. As discussed above, however, constant exposure can also be a burden. It is unclear to what extent dealing with others is desirable when the others pose a threat and introduce strain. Too much interaction may not be highly positive and may be a source of frustration.

A second question raised by the findings on interdependence is how customers fit into organizational theory. Customers' role as active participants reinforces the notion that there is room to study the management of customers (Bowen, 1988) because they are actually "partial employees" (Mills & Morris, 1986: 726). Bowen (1988:2) suggested applying Vroom's (1964) model of employee performance to the assessment of customer performance and noted some questions that such an application raises: Do customers understand how they are expected to perform? Are they able to perform as expected? And are there valued rewards for performing as expected?

The present study also suggests various constraints that introduce tension into service encounters and put a strain on service employees. Four such constraints come to mind: employee's inability to develop a strong social network with co-workers, the limited and constrained nature of relations with customers, the role conflict and ambiguity resulting from a multiply defined role, and the constant struggle for control with customers.

Social frustration was not the focus of the present study. Nonetheless, customers were observed to hinder the development of an informal network among cashiers. Thus, it is likely that cashier's social needs remain frustrated because it is difficult to imagine that the weak set of interpersonal relations evident among the cashiers studied could fulfill social needs.

A second source of strain is the constrained nature of interactions with customers. Cashiers themselves may desire interaction with customers to experience some form of social interaction. (Recall the cashier who said "The only one you can talk to is the customer.") In this case, however, strain may arise as the result of the very short, superficial interactions with a long line of only vaguely familiar people, circumstances that hardly constitute a social network.

Informal interactions between cashiers and customers can create a stressful service encounter if they detract from the cashiers' ability to concentrate on the monetary components of the job, and cause errors. Perhaps the customers' suspiciousness about theft is attributable to such swaying of the cashiers' attention. Furthermore, informal interaction with customers may also generate customers' resistance if they view it as a waste of time (Sutton & Rafaeli, 1988).

Service employees may also suffer strain because of the role ambiguity and role conflict associated with multiple role senders (Kahn, Wolfe, Quinn, & Snoek, 1981; Miles & Perreault, 1976; Parkington, 1979; Shamir, 1980). Customer expectations and comments were sometimes found to run counter to management rules (e.g., there is no need to get a check approved), setting the stage for role conflict. Similarly, there is a fair extent of ambiguity about customer service. The Ten Commandments, the organization's rules for cashiers, did not mention good-quality service, yet customers felt they were paying for good service and conveyed to cashiers that they expected it. The difference in the quality of management's and customers' influence likely exacerbates the strain of the conflict between role senders. It is as if a cashier needs to choose between the immediate, current demands of customers and the formal, but remote, influence of management.

The disagreement about control is also a source of tension in the service encounters observed at the supermarkets. Customers feel they have a right to control these encounters, but cashiers view the encounters as part of their job and engage in a struggle to destroy customer control. In short, the presence of customers constrains the cashiers' interaction with other people and is itself accompanied by a struggle, all of which provides fertile ground for tension and strain.

The tight interdependence between cashiers and customers and the tension inherent in the observed service encounters also suggest several paradoxes about the concept of service. First, it is paradoxical that service employees, who face customer demands all day, actually have very little autonomy to deal with those demands. Second, from the customers' point of view it is paradoxical that the only representative of the organization with whom they interact has so little leeway; the cashiers take the customers' money but can do little more than take money.

Third, from the cashiers' perspective, it is paradoxical that their interpersonal relations at work are so weak and superficial, in spite of their constant exposure to, and interaction with, other people. Of course, the fact that the constant interaction consists of many short interactions with hurried customers who do not view themselves as cashiers' social partners accounts for the paradox; nonetheless, it sheds light on the complexities of service encounters.

Fourth, the strategies developed by cashiers to establish their control of service encounters also pose a paradox. Many of the cashiers observed reinforced a consensus that exists among career counselors, that people who go into service occupations seek and enjoy interpersonal interactions (cf. Osipow, 1973). At the same time, this group of service employees was busy developing strategies to unnerve the people with whom they interacted.

Finally, it is paradoxical that although popular authors concerned with organizational management recommend that organizations, and in particular, service employees, keep "close to the customer" (Peters & Waterman, 1982: 156), in reality, employees often must tune out customer communication in order to pay close attention to the financial details of their work. Worse

yet, some service employees intentionally engage their customers in behavior that conforms with their own needs rather than customer needs

Customers may actually pose a threat to service employees and organizations. Errors and losses may occur when customers divert attention from a cash register or when they try to sway cashiers from complying with organizational rules. Furthermore, cashiers may perceive customers as a threat because they claim to have the right to control the cashiers' work and sometimes use indirect channels to punish cashiers (recall the cashier who was fired because a customer reported that she put money in her purse).

Organizations may also incur indirect costs because of the struggle for control. Obviously, cashiers ignoring customers or reacting unpleasantly to customer demands in order to establish who is in control may have a negative influence on customer satisfaction and on the likelihood that they will return, that is, on "encore gains" (Rafaeli & Sutton, 1987: 32). Similarly, the strains cashiers endure may result in mental and physical health costs to an organization (Beehr & Newman, 1978; Kasl, 1978) as well as turnover and absenteeism costs. It is not unlikely, for example, that the high turnover rate reported in this study is related to the strain that the employees have to endure.

In closing, it is important to note the limitations of the present study. The encounters examined may differ from other service encounters. Supermarket service encounters are relatively short; they do not require the customers' active involvement (customers have to tell waiters what food to bring and cab drivers where to go); they usually do not involve direct monetary payment to a cashier from the customer (no tips); and they aren't that important to the customer.

Moreover, some of the special attributes of supermarket shopping in Israel may have tinted the results. Since customers in Israel usually bag their own groceries, customer involvement may be more active and their influence more immediate than is true in other countries. The lenient attitude in Israel about rudeness, and the poorly developed service concept, may allow cashiers greater freedom in their struggle for control than might be evident elsewhere. Nonetheless, the present study offers a point of departure for further research and theory development on service employees and service encounters.

Finally, the qualitative nature of the present study offers a rich and deep picture of thenature of interactions between clerks and customers in one setting. Such investigations are useful for theory building (Glaser & Strauss, 1967; Mintzberg, 1979). However, more qualitative and quantitative data on supermarkets and on other service settings are essential before researchers will really understand service encounters.

REFERENCES

Adams, J. S. 1976. The structure and dynamics of behavior in organization boundary roles. In M. D. Dunnette (Ed.), *Handbook of industrial and organization psychology.* 1175–1200. Chicago: Rand McNally College Publishing.

Albrecht, K., & Zemke, R. 1985. *Service America! Doing business in the new economy.* Homewood, IL: Dow Jones-Irwin.

Beehr, T. A., & Newman, J. E. 1978. Job stress, employee health, and organizational effectiveness: A facet analysis, model, and literature review. *Personnel Psychology,* 31: 665–699.

Biddle, B. J. 1979. *Role theory: Expectations, identities, and behaviors.* New York: Academic Press.

Bigus, O. E. 1972. The milkman and his customer: A cultivated relationship. *Urban Life and Culture,* 1: 131–165.

Bowen, D. E. 1988. *Managing the on-site customer in service organizations: A human resource management perspective.* Paper presented at the annual meeting of the Academy of Management, Anaheim, CA.

Bowen, D., & Schneider, B. 1985. Boundary-spanning-role employees and the service encounter: Some guidelines for management and research. In J. A. Czepiel, M. R. Solomon, & C. E. Surprenant (Eds.), *The service encounter:* 127–148. Lexington, MA: Lexington Books.

Butler, S. R., & Snizek, W. E. 1976. The waitress–diner relationship: A multimethod approach to the study of subordinate influence. *Sociology of Work and Occupations,* 3: 2209–2223.

Czepiel, J. A., Solomon, M. R., & Surprenant, C. F. 1985. *The service encounter.* Lexington, MA: Lexington Books.

Desatnick, R. L. 1987. *Managing to keep the customer.* San Francisco: Jossey-Bass.

Flanagan, J. C. 1954. The critical incident technique. *Psychological Bulletin,* 51: 327–358.

French, J. R. P., & Raven, B. H. 1960. The bases of social power. In D. Cartwright & A. Zander (Eds.), *Group dynamics:* 607–623. New York: Harper & Row.

Glaser, B., & Strauss, A. 1967. *The discovery of grounded theory: Strategies for qualitative research.* London: Widenfeld & Nicholson.

Goffman, E. 1959. *The presentation of self in everyday life.* Garden City, NY: Doubleday.

Goldman, A. 1981. Transfer of a retailing technology into the less developed countries: The supermarket case. *Journal of Retailing,* 57(2): 5–29.

Goodsell, C. T. 1976. Cross-cultural comparisons of behavior of postal clerks toward clients. *Administrative Science Quarterly,* 21: 140–150.

Hilgard, E. R., & Bowers, G. H. 1975. *Theories of learning.* Englewood Cliffs, NJ: Prentice-Hall.

Hochschild, A. R. 1983. *The managed heart.* Berkeley: University of California Press.

Jacoby, J., & Craig, C. S. 1984. *Personal selling.* Lexington, MA: Lexington Books.

Kahn, R. L., Wolfe, D. M., Quinn, R. P., & Snoek, J. D. 1981. *Organizational stress: Studies in role conflict and ambiguity.* Malabar, FL: Krieger Publishing.

Kasl, S. V. 1978. Epidemiological contributions to the study of work stress. In C. L. Cooper & P. Payne (Eds.), *Stress at work:* 3–48. New York: Wiley.

Katz, D., & Kahn, R. L. 1978. *The social psychology of organizing.* New York: Wiley.

Langer, E. J. 1983. *The psychology of control.* Beverly Hills: Sage Publications.

Lombard, G. F. 1955. *Behavior in a selling group.* Boston: Harvard University Press.

McCallum, J. R., & Harrison, W. 1985. Interdependence in the service encounter. In J. A. Czepiel, M. R. Solomon, & C. E. Surprenant (Eds.), *The service encounter:* 35–48. Lexington, MA: Lexington Books.

Marks, M., & Mirvis, P. 1981. Environmental influences on the performance of a professional baseball team. *Human Organization,* 40: 355–360.

Maister, D. H. 1985. The psychology of waiting lines. In J. A. Czepiel, M. P. Solomon, & C. F. Surprenant (Eds.), *The service encounter:* 113–124. Lexington, MA: Lexington Books.

Mars, G. 1984. *Cheats at work: An anthropology of workplace crime.* Winchester, MA: Allen & Unwin Inc.

Mars, G., & Nicod, M. 1984. *The world of waiters.* Boston: George Allen.

Merton, R. K. 1957. *Social theory and social structure.* New York: Free Press.

Miles, M. B. 1983. Qualitative data as an attractive nuisance. In J. Van Maanen (Ed.), *Qualitative methodology:* 117–134. Beverly Hills: Sage Publications.

Miles, M. B., & Huberman, A. M. 1984. *Qualitative data analysis.* Beverly Hills: Sage Publications.

Miles, R. H., & Perreault, W. O. D. 1976. Organizational role conflict: Its antecedents and consequences. *Organizational Behavior and Human Performance,* 17: 19–44.

Mills, P. K., & Morris, J. H. 1986. Clients as partial employees of service organizations: Role development in client participation. *Academy of Management Review,* 11: 726–736.

Mintzberg, H. 1979. An emerging strategy of "direct" research. *Administrative Science Quarterly,* 24: 580–589.

Osipow, S. H. 1973. *Theories of career development.* Englewood Cliffs, NJ: Prentice-Hall.

Parkington, J. J. 1979. Some correlates of experienced job stress: A boundary role study. *Academy of Management Journal,* 22: 270–281.

Peters, T. J., & Waterman, R. H., Jr. 1982. *In search of excellence.* San Francisco: Harper & Row.

Rachman, D. J. 1975. *Retail strategy and structure.* Englewood Cliffs, NJ: Prentice-Hall.

Rafaeli, A. 1989. *Service employees' emotional behavior: Cause or effect?* Paper in progress, Hebrew University of Jerusalem, Israel.

Rafaeli, A., & Sutton, R. I. 1987. The expression of emotion as part of the work role. *Academy of Management Review,* 12: 23–37.

Russel, G. 1987. Pul-eeze! Will somebody help me? *Time,* February 2: 28–34.

Salancik, G. R. 1979. Field stimulations for organizational behavior research. *Administrative Science Quarterly,* 24: 638–649.

Schneider, B., Parkington, J. J., & Buxton, V. M. 1980. Employee and customer perceptions of service in banks. *Administrative Science Quarterly,* 25: 252–267.

Seligman, M. E. P. 1975. *Helplessness: On depression, development and death.* San Francisco: Freeman.

Shamir, B. 1980. Between service and servility: Role conflict in subordinate service roles. *Human Relations,* 33: 741–756.

Sims, H. P., Szilagyi, A. D., & Keller, R. T. 1976. The measurement of job characteristics. *Academy of Management Journal,* 19: 195–212.

Sutton, R. I., & Kahn, B. 1986. Prediction, understanding, and control as antidotes to occupational stress. In J. Lorsch (Ed.), *Handbook of organizational behavior:* 272–285. Englewood Cliffs, NJ: Prentice-Hall.

Sutton, R. I., & Rafaeli, A. 1988. Untangling the relationship between displayed emotions and organizational sales: The case of convenience stores. *Academy of Management Journal,* 31: 461–487.

Trist, E. 1977. Collaboration in work settings: A personal perspective. *Journal of Applied Behavioral Science,* 13: 268–278.

Vroom, V. H. 1964. *Work and motivation.* New York: Wiley.

Webb, E. J., Campbell, D. T., Schwartz, D. S., Sechrest, L., & Grove, G. B. 1981. *Nonreactive measures in social sciences.* Boston: Houghton Mifflin Co.

Whyte, W. 1948. *Human relations in the restaurant industry.* New York: McGraw-Hill Book Co.

APPENDIX

Semistructured Interview with Cashiers

How long have you been working as a cashier? At this store?

How did you get to be a cashier?

Who do you talk to while at work? About what? Why?

Do you know the other cashiers who work with you? What can you tell me about them?

Do you meet other cashiers or other employees after work? Why?

Which customers do you like most? Why? How do you deal with them?

Which customers do you like least? Why? How do you deal with them?

Can you describe to me an interaction with an "especially good customer"?

Can you describe to me an interaction with an "especially bad customer"?

How did you learn how to do your job? How to deal with customers?

How would you react to the following situations?

1. Customer who said to cashier: "How can you wear three earrings on one ear? That is ridiculous."

2. Customer who said to cashier: "Will you stop talking and start working! You're wasting everyone's time."

What else do you have to tell me about the job? About your manager? About the other cashiers? About customers? About anything else?

Semistructured Interview with Customers

How long have you been shopping at this store?

Why do you shop here? Do you enjoy it? Why?

Do you feel you know any of the cashiers? Do you like them?

What are your perceptions of the cashiers? What do you think about the way they work?

What would you like to see different in the way they work?

Can you recall specific examples where you felt especially *content* about a cashier's work?

Can you recall specific examples where you were especially *annoyed* with a cashier?

Would you like to tell me anything else about cashiers or about the store?

How old are you?

Basic Rules of Cashier Behavior ("The Ten Commandments")[a,b]

1. Each cashier should wear a smock and a name tag while at work.

---

[a]In translating this set of instructions from Hebrew to English, I kept the style as close to the original as possible. Thus, problems of clarity or style reflect the originally convoluted presentation of the various rules.

[b]As Hebrew is a gender-specific language, these rules are all phrased as addressing only woman cashiers.

2. It is forbidden while at work to hold by the cash register and/or on the body—money, a wallet, or a personal handbag.

3. It is forbidden to have merchandise in the area of the cash registers and/or to eat and/or drink and/or to smoke and/or to chew gum while on the job.

4. Upon receiving money from a customer, and after giving out change, it is mandatory to immediately put the money or the checks that were received into the register drawer. It is forbidden to receive money from a client before the price of the merchandise has been entered into the register. IT IS DEFINITELY PROHIBITED to work while the register drawer is open.

5. It is mandatory to ask every person and an employee while he is a customer to display the merchandise he purchased on the table for payment.

6. It is forbidden to let a relative pay for merchandise that he purchased at the register that you are working. Family members will pay for their purchases at a register where the cashier is not a relative.

7. In the case of an error or a return you write a PAY OUT slip (withdraw from the register). The merchandise and the sales slip on which the returned sum appears should be immediately shown to the head cashier and/or the assistant manager and/or the manager in order to get their signed approval.

At the registers where the VOID operates the note should be attached to the PAY OUT slip.

8. PERSONAL SHOPPING IS DONE ONLY AFTER YOU HAVE FINISHED WORKING.

9. It is strictly forbidden for the cashiers to enter their own merchandise.

10. (a) Keeping the area clean is the cashier's responsibility.

(b) Also, when leaving the register for a break or at the end of your work you should remove the key from the register and lock the path (to your register) with a chain.

Anat Rafaeli earned her Ph.D. degree in industrial and organizational psychology at the Ohio State University. She is an assistant professor in organizational behavior at the Graduate School of Business Administration in the Hebrew University of Jerusalem. Her research interests include the unique dynamics of customer service roles and the expression of emotion as part of work roles.

ARTICLE 4.5

UNTANGLING THE RELATIONSHIP BETWEEN DISPLAYED EMOTIONS AND ORGANIZATIONAL SALES

THE CASE OF CONVENIENCE STORES

Robert I. Sutton
Stanford University

Anat Rafaeli
Hebrew University of Jerusalem

People want to be happy! Be happy and they
will be glad they came to your store.

Loyal, regular customers are a source of steady sales for
your store. Smile!! Service with a smile and a friendly attitude
will keep them loyal and keep them coming back!

—From "Effective Customer Service Increases Sales," a training program used by
a chain of convenience stores

It has been proposed that the emotions expressed by role occupants influence the behavior of others. We hypothesized a positive relationship between employees' display of pleasant emotions to customers and sales in retail stores and tested that relationship in a sample of 576 convenience stores. An unexpected negative relationship was observed. A subsequent qualitative study suggested that sales is an indicator of a store's pace, or the amount of time pressure on clerks and customers, and that pace leads to displayed emotions, with norms in busy settings supporting neutral displays and norms in slow settings supporting positive displays. Reanalysis of the quantitative data confirmed that clerks in rapidly paced stores with high sales and long lines were less likely to display positive feelings than clerks in slow-paced stores.

Much theory and research has focused on the role of emotion in organizational life. Emotions are typically viewed as intrapsychic states caused by factors such as job characteristics (Hackman & Oldham, 1980), stress (Kahn, 1981), relationships with supervisors (Bass, 1982), or compensation (Lawler, 1981). Such studies most frequently have examined the determinants of job satisfaction, which Locke defined as "a pleasurable or positive emotional state" (1976: 1300).

Recent theoretical work, however, has emphasized that employees' emotions are displayed as well as felt (Hochschild, 1979, 1983; Rafaeli & Sutton, 1987, 1989). A variety of forces may explain variation in

SOURCE © *Academy of Management Journal*, 1988, Vol. 31, No. 3, 461–487.

We wish to thank Mary Kay Benson, David Bowen, Larry Ford, Connie Gersick, James Jucker, Benjamin Schneider, Caren Siehl, Barry Staw, Lorna Weisenger, Tim Whitten, and John Van Maanen for their help with this article. We thank the Department of Industrial Engineering and Engineering Management at Stanford and the Mutual Fund of the Hebrew University of Jerusalem for supporting this research. Portions of this paper were prepared while Robert Sutton was a fellow at the Center for Advanced Study in the Behavioral Sciences. He is grateful for financial support provided by the Carnegie Corporation of New York and the William and Flora Hewlett Foundation.

organizational members' displayed emotions. Internal feelings certainly influence such behavior: satisfied employees may display genuine broad smiles and laughter during interactions with co-workers and customers; dissatisfied or tense employees may frown and groan during such transactions.

Yet there is an imperfect match between the emotions people feel and emotions they express on the job because employees are often expected to display emotions that are unrelated, or even in conflict, with their true feelings. Many organizations use practices, including recruitment and selection, socialization, and rewards and punishments, to assure that their members will conform to normative expectations, or "display rules" (Ekman, 1980: 87–88), that specify which emotions should be expressed and which should be hidden.

Organizations can support display rules by recruiting and selecting employees who are predisposed to express required emotions. Hochschild (1983) reported, for example, that Delta Airlines tries to select new flight attendants who will display good cheer to passengers and who have the emotional stamina to endure long, crowded flights without abandoning their smiles. Organizations may use socialization practices to teach display rules to newcomers. For example, a woman who supervises bill collectors reported that her subordinates learn—through both formal and informal means—to be pleasant to clients who are a month or two late on their Visa and Mastercard payments, to express firm disapproval to clients who are three or four months late, and to use nasty insults (e.g, "Why do you keep lying to me?") when speaking with clients who are five or six months late (Rafaeli & Sutton, 1989).

Organizations may also use reward and punishment systems to maintain display rules once socialization has been completed. Many service organizations like airlines, telephone companies, department stores, and grocery stores monitor their employees to assure that they are conveying correct emotions to customers (Hochschild, 1983; Rafaeli & Sutton, 1987). Employees who display the wrong emotions may be punished, and those who convey the right emotions may be rewarded. Management may even invite customers to help enforce display rules. For example, a store in Hayward, California, offers customers a five-dollar reward if a clerk does not offer them a "friendly greeting" and a "cheerful smile."

A primary reason that organizations develop and enforce display rules is that displayed emotions are thought to operate as "control moves." Goffman (1969: 12) defined control moves as an individual's strategic

manipulation of expressions, including emotional expressions, to influence the behavior of others. Along those lines, the emotions displayed by employees in organizational settings can function as control moves that influence the behavior of clients and fellow organizational members (Rafaeli & Sutton, 1987).

A modest body of evidence confirms that expressed negative, neutral, and positive emotions can serve as control moves for individuals. Police interrogators convey negative and esteem-degrading emotions to suspects in an effort to gain confessions (Arther & Caputo, 1959). In the same vein, the incomes of professional poker players depend heavily on their ability to display neutral emotion, regardless of their internal feelings (Hayano, 1982). Furthermore, field stimulations (Salancik, 1979) have suggested that smiling cocktail waitresses receive larger tips than unsmiling ones (Tidd & Lockhard, 1978) and that smiling nuns garner larger donations than glum nuns (Bradshaw, 1980).

Our contention is that displayed emotions are not only descriptors of individual employees; conveyed emotions can also be attributes of organizations. Specifically, we proposed that displayed pleasant emotions can act as control moves at the organizational level of analysis.

DISPLAYED EMOTIONS AS ORGANIZATIONAL ATTRIBUTES

Customers of service organizations often interact with only one or two boundary-spanning employees during a given visit (Bowen & Schneider, 1985; Shamir, 1980). Furthermore, the emotions encountered by customers are displayed by individual employees. Yet customers typically develop an overall image of the emotions that members of a given organization will display. Such overall images arise because stimuli generalization occurs. Indeed, stimuli generalization enables authors of guidebooks to publish overall judgments about the level of courtesy that can be expected at hotels and restaurants (e.g., Birnbaum, 1987; Unterman & Sesser, 1984). After patronizing a service organization, customers may develop opinions about the *emotional front* they expect to encounter.

Those opinions—whether based on slight or extensive experience with an organization—reflect a characteristic of the organization because customers do not usually expect to be served by the same employee during each visit. Customers may also discern differences in emotional fronts because organizations differ in norms about displayed emotions (Hochschild, 1983; Rafaeli & Sutton, 1987). Norms are attributes of social systems rather than of individuals (Katz & Kahn, 1978).

Writings intended for managerial audiences also imply that the emotional front is a meaningful organizational attribute. Indeed, some recent managerial folklore suggests that employees who display good cheer to customers can enhance sales and customer loyalty (Ash, 1984; Hochschild, 1983; Peters & Austin, 1985; Peters & Waterman, 1982; Richman, 1984). The emerging literature on customer service (Czepiel, Solomon, & Surprenant, 1985; Parasuraman, Zeithaml, & Berry, 1985) also implies that belief. Those writings suggest that, when all other factors are held equal, the display of positive emotions by employees can, in the aggregate, act as control moves that bring about gains for an organization. The implication is that to the extent each potential customer associates a positive emotional front with a given organization, a larger proportion of the potential population will patronize that organization.

Theories of learning may explain why displaying warm feelings to customers can promote sales. Encountering employees who display warm, socially desirable feelings may be reinforcing for most people. Initial encounters with friendly employees may mark the start of an operant conditioning cycle (Skinner, 1953) in which the emotions displayed by employees are the reinforcers and patronizing the organization is the reinforced behavior. The probability that a given customer will visit an organization a second time is increased by employees' display of positive emotions. The organization's emotional front may also reinforce customer behavior indirectly through vicarious learning (Bandura, 1977). A customer may watch other customers encounter positive emotions or may visit a service organization after reading that its employees are nice, friendly, or polite.

Empirical support for this conceptual perspective was sought through study of a sample of 576 convenience stores. Specifically, we hypothesized that store sales would be greater to the extent that clerks displayed positive emotions during transactions with customers.

QUANTITATIVE AND DEDUCTIVE STUDY: METHODS

RESEARCH CONTEXT

These data were collected as part of an evaluation of employee courtesy in a large national chain of convenience stores. The corporation's human resources staff conducted this research as part of a chain-wide effort to enhance employee courtesy; top executives had decided that they could gain an advantage over their competitors by improving customer service in their stores. A prima-

ry reason that executives made this decision was that they had read *In Search of Excellence* and were swayed by Peters and Waterman's arguments that staying "close to the customer" (1982: 156) and having a "service obsession" (1982: 157) are characteristics of excellent firms.

During the year before these data were collected, the human resources staff had changed employee handbooks and the classroom training provided to new employees so that—rather than vaguely encouraging clerks to be friendly to customers—the training clerks received instructed them to greet, smile at, establish eye contact with, and say "thank you" to every customer. In addition, a variety of local and corporation-wide training programs were developed to teach store managers about how they could improve courtesy among their clerks. For example, the introduction to this article quotes a program entitled "Effective Customer Service Increases Sales" that included lectures, readings, role-plays, and group discussions to help managers improve the level of courtesy in their stores.

A variety of local and corporate-wide practices were used, both before and after the collection of the data, to reward clerks who acted friendly during transactions with customers. Clerks in most regions were informed that "mystery shoppers" would be used to observe levels of employee courtesy. In some regions, clerks who were caught displaying the required good cheer to customers received a $25 bonus. In other regions, clerks who were observed greeting, smiling, establishing eye contact, and saying "thank you" could win a new automobile instantly.

The corporation held a contest, costing over $10 million, in which the owners of franchised stores and the managers of corporation-owned stores could qualify to enter a drawing for a million dollars if their clerks consistently offered good cheer to customers. The corporation also awarded large bonuses (over 25 percent of base salary) to regional managers when a high percentage of sales clerks in the stores they managed were observed greeting, smiling at, establishing eye contact with, and saying "thank you" to customers.

We had no influence over the design and implementation of this data gathering. The firm gave us the data because one of us had attended graduate school with the firm's director of field research. Other corporate executives were also interested in our findings because most of them believed that employee courtesy led to increased sales. They were curious to discover if quantitative evidence would support their beliefs. Small but significant relationships between displayed emotions and store sales could mean millions of dollars of sales for this national chain. For example, 2 percent increase in sales would increase corporate revenues by over $100 million.

SAMPLE

The sample comprised 576 of the convenience stores in this national chain. There are over 7,000 stores in the United States and Canada, 36 percent of which are franchised. The corporation owns the remainder. The typical store has 8 to 10 employees, with a range of 6 to 20 employees. The stores sell a wide range of items, including food, drinks, cigarettes, and magazines. The corporation uses a variety of rules and inducements to assure that there will be similarity in the products sold in each of these stores, but there is variation because people who manage the corporation's stores and people who own franchised stores have some authority to decide what products will be sold. The stores with greater sales tend to carry larger inventories. Yet, compared to supermarkets, these stores all carry tiny inventories because they have little storage space. Thus, they must be replenished frequently by suppliers.

A random sample of 576 urban stores was selected for the study. The stores selected were from all 18 divisions in the United States and Canada. The corporation defines divisions, which include between 300 and 600 stores, by geographical boundaries. The firm chose the four most heavily populated urban districts (35–40 stores) from each division for the research, for a total of 72 districts. Rural districts were excluded to reduce travel costs. Eight stores were randomly selected from each district, for a total of 576 stores. Thus, the sample is representative of the urban stores in this national chain.

The extent to which employees display positive emotions to customers can be considered a store, or organization, attribute, as we suggested earlier. Yet this attribute can only be observed in the behaviors of individual employees. Thus, displayed emotions were measured by observers who coded clerks' behavior during transactions with customers. These observations were made during three months in 1984. Observers visited each of the 576 stores twice: once during the day shift and once during the swing shift. They visited 25 percent of the stores (144 stores) a third time during the night shift (11:00 p.m.–7:00 a.m.). A store visit could occur at any juncture in each eight-hour shift since observers also worked shifts that were approximately eight hours. The most efficient route of travel usually determined the order in which selected stores were visited.

Observers coded as many as 20 transactions between customers and clerks during each store visit, for a total of up to 60 transactions per store. The number of transactions coded during a visit ranged from 1 to 20 and was determined primarily by the number of customers in the store during the visit. The modal number of transactions coded at each visit was 8 and the mean was 9. The final sample included 11,805 clerk–customer transactions. A total of 1,319 clerks were observed; 44 percent were men, and about 75 percent of the customers were men.

PROCEDURES

Observers acted as incognito participant observers (Webb, Campbell, Schwartz, Sechrest, & Grove, 1981: 200). They were participant observers since they acted like typical customers. The firm notified store managers that mystery shoppers might be visiting their stores during the spring or summer of 1984 to observe employee courtesy, but managers received no specific information about the timing of the visits.

The firm's marketing information indicated that typical customers were working class men and, less often, women, 18 to 34 years old. Observers were selected accordingly and instructed how to dress. The firm did not hire observers especially for this task. Rather, members of the corporate staff, particularly of the human resources staff, who fit the profile of a typical customer were asked to spend one to four weeks working as observers. The people who gathered the data held a wide range of jobs in the corporation, including those of organizational development specialist, executive development specialist, director of field research, secretary, and marketing manager.

The corporation's director of field research trained the other corporate employees who volunteered to help gather the data. Before visiting stores included in the study, each volunteer observer visited some pretest stores with the director of field research. They coded clerks' behaviors and compared observations after each visit. The volunteers and the director discussed and clarified differences in coding until they agreed consistently.

Observers visited each store in pairs. They acted independently and did not communicate with each other while inside the store. Observations were noted on preformatted three-by-five-inch cards. Only one clerk, the operator of the primary cash register, was observed during each visit, even if more than one register was operating. Observers walked around the store for a few minutes and noted how well the store was stocked with merchandise. They also noted whether the clerk was wearing a name tag and a smock and whether the smock was clean. Typically, the observers then walked to the magazine rack or coffee pots, which were usually close to the primary cash register. Observers usually coded clerks' behaviors toward customers from those vantage points. The observers then selected a small item like a candy bar and stood in line. They continued to note employees' behaviors toward customers while standing in line. Observers left the store after paying for their purchases.

The amount of time in each store varied from 4 to 12 minutes; the amount of time could not be predetermined because observers were instructed to stay in each store as long as possible. But they also had to avoid evoking suspicion. The visit was kept short if there were few customers in the store to prevent the clerk's becoming suspicious. Observers also noted if they felt that a clerk suspected that they were not ordinary customers. Clerks were thought suspicious in less than 3 percent of the observations; we excluded these observations from the analyses.

The firm's director of field research, an experienced organizational researcher who had responsibility for designing and implementing this study, established the interobserver reliability of this method. The director visited a sample of 274 stores and observed a clerk at each store. During each of those visits, one of seven other members of the data-gathering team accompanied the director. Interobserver reliability was assessed by comparing the research director's coding of clerks' emotional displays with the coding of the seven second observers. The correlations between the research director's coding and the second observer's ranged from .94 to .67. The mean correlation was .82 and the median correlation was .85.

PREDICTOR VARIABLE: DISPLAY OF POSITIVE EMOTION

The concept of displayed positive emotions is related to employee courtesy, an idea mentioned often in the literature on service organizations (Czepiel et al., 1985; Schneider, Parkington, & Buxton, 1980). The concept of courtesy, however, is broader than displayed positive emotion, since courtesy may also include working quickly, dressing neatly (Parasuraman et al., 1985), and doing favors for customers (Shamir, 1980). The display of positive emotion refers specifically to presenting a warm outward demeanor during transactions with customers.

The corporate researchers gathered evidence about two social amenities, greeting and thanking, and two forms of nonverbal behavior, smiling and establishing eye contact, that reflected the presentation of a warm outward demeanor. These four aspects of clerks' displayed positive emotion were observed at the transaction level of analysis and were operationally defined as follows. (1) Greeting: only "Hello," "how are you today," or another polite phrase at the outset of a transaction was considered to be a greeting. "Is that all for you?" and "Anything else?" were not coded as greetings. (2) Thanking: the word thank or a derivative had to be used. (3) Smiling: a smile was considered a noticeable uptwist of the lips (Tidd & Lockhard, 1978). (4) Eye contact: a direct gaze by a clerk was coded as a sincere attempt at eye contact, regardless of whether a customer reciprocated.

The observers assigned a value of 1 if a behavior was displayed and a value of 0 if it was not displayed. Thus, each transaction was coded as to whether the clerk smiled at, greeted, thanked, and maintained eye contact with the customer. The data were aggregated to the store level of analysis to form an index of display of positive emotion as a store attribute.

For each store, a score was computed for each of the four emotional expressions by calculating the proportion of transactions in which the behaviors were displayed over the total number of transactions coded. For each store, the variable measuring the display of positive emotion was an index composed of the mean level of greeting, thanking, smiling, and eye contact observed in that store (α = .76).

The aggregation of transaction-level data to an organizational level can be justified if the ratio of between-group variance to within-group variance is statistically significant. A significant ratio suggests that the aggregated variable is measuring an organizational-level construct (Rousseau, 1985). We performed an ANOVA with display of positive emotion as the dependent variable and store identifiers as the independent variable. The between-store variance was significantly greater than the within-store variance (ms = .82 and .06, respectively; $F_{576, 11,804}$ = 14.311; p < .01).

CONTROL VARIABLES

This study sought to document the effects of a store's emotional front above and beyond the effects of other factors. Thus, it was important to control for the effects of other store attributes on store sales. Observers gathered data for five control variables: clerks' gender composition, customers' gender composition, clerks' image, store's stock level, and length of line. Data for three other control variables were obtained from company records: store ownership, supervision costs, and geographical region. We operationally defined those variables as follows. (1) Clerks' gender composition was defined as the proportion of a store's clerks who were women. Observers noted the gender of the clerk during each visit. In order to aggregate to the store level of analysis, we computed the proportion of women over the total number of clerks observed across all visits as an index of the store's gender composition. We used this measure to control for variation in displayed emotion due to gender (Deaux, 1985; Putnam & McCallister, 1980). (2) Customers' gender composition referred to the proportion of customers who were women. The observers noted the gender of the customer in each transaction. We aggregated those observations to the organizational level by computing the proportion of woman customers in each store over all the customers present during all observations in the store. This variable was introduced to help account for the different buying patterns of men and women (Engel, Blackwell, & Miniard, 1986). (3) Clerks' image was the degree to which clerks in a store maintained the dress code specified by corporate guidelines. This variable had three items: whether clerks wore a smock, whether their smock was clean, and whether they wore a name tag. Ratings were on a 2-point scale with 1 = no and 2 = yes (α = .74). This variable was used to help control for compliance with other corporate norms. (4) For store's stock level, three items were used to rate how well each store was stocked with merchandise. Observers used 5-point Likert scales to rate the extent to which the shelves, snack stands, and refrigerators were fully stocked (α = .81). We controlled for this variable because high stock levels may promote strong sales regardless of displayed emotions. (5) For average line length, observers recorded the largest number of customers in line at the primary cash register during each store visit. Average line length reflects the mean number of people standing in line across all visits to a store. We controlled for this variable because stores with longer lines may sell more than others, regardless of displayed emotions. (6) Store ownership captured whether a store was franchised (coded 1) or corporation-owned (coded 0). The firm's executives have the authority to enforce policies about employee courtesy in corporate stores but can only encourage such practices in franchised stores. (7) Store supervision costs was the amount of money spent by the corporation on salaries, benefits, and training costs for the field supervisors who dealt directly with each store manager. This corporation provided us with standardized data about the number of dollars spent on each store for such supervision. A field supervisor typically oversees the operation of eight to ten stores, but such supervision costs varied considerably across stores in the sample. Variation

occurred because regional, district, and division managers have some autonomy over how many stores each supervisor oversees, the amount such supervisors are paid, and how much training they receive. This variable was used to help control for the influence of quality of supervision on store sales. (8) Region reflected the corporation's grouping of stores into four geographical regions, each under the authority of a regional vice-president; the northeastern region was coded 1; the western, 2; the midwestern, 3; and the southern, 4. We used this variable to control for variability in administrative practices and for differences in regional norms about displayed emotion. The variable was dummy-coded so that it could be used in multiple regression analysis.

CRITERION VARIABLE: TOTAL STORE SALES

The criterion variable used in this study was total store sales during the same year that the observational data were gathered. Total store sales was the dollar value of sales for each store from all products sold during the 1984 calendar year, including grocery items, cigarettes, dispensed drinks, hot food, video games, oil, and gasoline. This measure was obtained from company records and was standardized among the stores included in the sample. We received standardized rather than raw data because executives preferred not to release that sensitive financial information. Standardization was accomplished by transforming total store sales into a new variable by assigning a value of 0 to the mean of each variable and a value of 1 to the standard deviation. The value for each store was the number of standard deviations that the store's sales deviated from the mean.

RESULTS OF THE QUANTITATIVE AND DEDUCTIVE STUDY

Table 1 presents the means, standard deviations, and intercorrelations of study variables. We performed multiple regression analyses to determine the relationship between the display of positive emotion and total store sales following a hierarchical procedure. The eight control variables were entered simultaneously into the first equation, which yielded a multiple R of .28 and an adjusted R-square of .06. The second regression equation included the eight control variables along with the index of displayed positive emotion. Total store sales was the criterion variable in both equations.

Table 2 reports results for the complete model. The control variables significantly related to total sales were store supervision costs, customers' gender composition,

TABLE 1   Means, Standard Deviations, and Intercorrelations of Quantitative Variables[a]

	Variables[b]	Means	Standard Deviations	1	2	3	4	5	6	7	8
1.	Display of positive emotion	0.51	0.23								
2.	Store ownership	0.36	0.48	−.06							
3.	Stock level	3.26	0.59	.26	.23						
4.	Customers' gender composition	0.19	0.13	−.04	.07	.08					
5.	Clerks' gender composition	0.56	0.37	.13	−.11	−.07	−.08				
6.	Clerks' image	0.74	0.34	.13	−.67	−.04	−.05	.10			
7.	Supervision costs	0.00	1.00	−.01	.16	.00	.00	.08	−.13		
8.	Average line length	2.88	1.16	−.18	.04	.10	.28	.00	−.02	.06	
9.	Total sales	0.00	1.00	−.06	.00	.09	.10	.09	−.02	.13	.18

[a]$n = 576$.

[b]Store ownership was coded 0 for corporation-owned stores and 1 for franchised stores. Customers' gender composition is the proportion of woman customers. Clerks' gender composition is the proportion of woman clerks. Supervision costs and total sales were standardized for all stores included in the sample; thus, the mean is 0.00, and the standard deviation is 1.00.

clerks' gender composition, and average line length. The second equation yielded a significant beta for the display of positive emotion, an R of .30, and an adjusted R-square of .07.

The statistically significant beta weight of the variable measuring display of positive emotion indicates a significant increment in R-square. That is, compared to the variance explained by the first equation, which included only control variables, the new variable included in the second equation contributed significantly to the variance explained (Cohen & Cohen, 1975). But the direction of the observed relationship contradicted our hypothesis: higher levels of displayed positive emotion were associated with lower levels of store sales. This finding was unexpected and confusing; it was also thought-provoking.

The modest positive relationship between line length and total store sales, along with the modest negative relationship between line length and the display of positive emotions (see Table 1), gave us a hint that by thinking about the differences between slow and busy settings we might be able to untangle the relationship between displayed emotion and store sales. As a result, we gathered evidence about the differences between slow and busy settings as part of the qualitative research conducted to help understand why the quantitative evidence contradicted our central hypothesis.

THE QUALITATIVE AND INDUCTIVE STUDY

Scholarly knowledge is developed through alternating phases of induction and deduction. When empirical observations do not confirm a theory, investigators should embark on a new phase of theory building so that they can revise or reject the inadequate framework and replace it with a new framework (Merton, 1957; Wallace, 1971). As a result, our paper does not end with the usual discussion of quantitative findings. Instead, we conducted a qualitative and inductive study to help explain the unexpected negative relationship between the expression of positive emotion and store sales. The qualitative data provided rich information that helped us to view the convenience stores in a different light and to develop new predictions that could be tested in a reanalysis of the quantitative data.

QUALITATIVE METHODS

The qualitative phase included case studies, a day spent working as a clerk. conversations with manager, a customer service workshop, and about 40 visits to different stores.

Case studies of four stores in Northern California were conducted. We used data on employee courtesy and store sales collected by the corporation to select

TABLE 2   Beta Weights of Store Emotional Display and Control Variables as Predictors of Total Store Sales[a]

Variables[b]	Total Sales
Store ownership	−.10
Supervision costs	.13[**]
Stock level	.06
Customers' gender composition	.07[c]
Clerks' gender composition	.11[**]
Clerks' image	−.07
Average line length	.14[**]
Region 1	−.07
Region 2	.11
Region 3	.08
Display of positive emotion	−.10[*]
Multiple R	.30
Adjusted R-square	.07[**]

[a]$n = 576$

[b]Store ownership was coded 0 for corporation-owned stores and 1 for franchised stores. Customers' gender composition is the proportion of woman customers. Clerks' gender composition is the proportion of woman sales clerks. Region 1, region 2, and region 3 are dummy codes representing the four regions.

[c]$p < .10$, two-tailed test.

[*]$p < .05$, two-tailed test.

[**]$p < .01$, two-tailed test.

cases that fit each of following four categories: (1) high sales and clerks who typically displayed positive emotions to customers, (2) high sales and clerks who typically did not display positive emotions, (3) low sales and clerks who typically displayed positive emotions, and (4) low sales and clerks who typically did not display positive emotions.

A pair of one-hour observations of transactions between clerks and customers were conducted in each of the four stores, one during a busy time and one during a slow time. Clerks working during each observation consented to participate in the study. An observer stood or sat near the cash register and took notes on predetermined topics, including customer demographics, line length, the number of customers in the store, customer behavior, and pressure from other tasks (e.g., stocking, cleaning, and dealing with vendors). The observers also had informal conversations with clerks about customer service.

A semistructured interview was conducted with the manager of each store. The interview contained 17 open-ended questions about the manager's prior experience; the selection, socialization, and reward systems used in the store; employee courtesy; and its influence on store sales. These questions appear in the Appendix. Interviews lasted between 30 and 60 minutes.

The qualitative study included a brief but instructive experience in which one of the authors spent a day working as a clerk in a store. About 30 minutes of training was provided, which included viewing a film on employee courtesy. This store had previously been rated as having low sales and frequent display of positive emotions.

We also had extensive in-person and telephone conversations with managers about the expression of emotion by store employees. At least 150 hours of conversations took place with corporate executives, customer service representatives, field supervisors, and store managers. These informal conversations focused on employee courtesy, especially the negative relationship we had observed between displayed positive emotion and sales. We also discussed interventions that could be used to enhance courtesy.

One of the authors attended a customer service workshop designed for franchisees and store managers. The two-hour program focused on methods for coaching and rewarding clerks in order to enhance their courtesy and satisfaction. It also provided an opportunity to hear managers discuss the role that expressed emotions play in the stores. Finally, the qualitative phase included approximately 40 visits to different stores located in three geographical regions. We made small purchases during those visits in order to observe clerks' displayed emotions.

The method of qualitative analysis used here draws on descriptions of how to generate theory by Glaser and Strauss (1967) and Miles and Huberman (1984). This juncture in the research was primarily inductive since facts were gathered to help us generate new theory. Nonetheless, as Miles and Huberman suggested, the data gathering and the interpretations attached to the data were guided by our explicit prior assumptions. Specifically, since the quantitative results suggested the importance of a store's average line length, we gathered qualitative data about store pace. We also made initial conceptual speculations about the differences between slow and busy stores.

We had frequent conversations during and after the collection of the qualitative data to discuss how we should modify the theory in light of the evidence. We traveled back and forth between the qualitative evidence and our conceptual explanations about why a negative relationship had emerged between displayed positive emotions and sales. Collecting and analyzing the five new sources of data led us to refine our understanding of differences between busy and slow settings and the implications of store pace for displayed emotions.

THE REVISED PERSPECTIVE: BUSY AND SLOW TIMES AS CUES FOR EXPRESSED EMOTIONS

Customer: Can I please have a plastic bag for my merchandise?

Sales Clerk: Lady, we don't have time for your please and thank you. Can't you see how busy we are? Just say what you want.

—A transaction between one of the authors and a clerk in a very busy store.

The qualitative evidence led us to conclude that the expression of positive emotion by clerks may not be a control move that influences the buying behavior of customers who visit these stores. The "service ideal"—the aspects of service that customers should expect to receive when they patronize an organization—portrayed in advertising and promotions for this national chain had historically emphasized speedy service and name-brand products rather than good cheer. Our conversations with executives also indicated that encounters with friendly clerks had only recently been included as part of the corporate marketing strategy.

Store managers throughout the corporation had received literature emphasizing the importance of offering smiles, greetings, eye contact, and thanks to customers only a few months before the quantitative data were gathered. Training programs for new employees had also recently been changed to include segments encouraging those behaviors. Further, some regional managers had implemented new customer service training programs like the one quoted at the outset of this article.

Yet the qualitative evidence that we encountered led us to question whether this new service ideal had been accepted. Managers and clerks typically believed that outright rudeness drove away customers. But they often contend that friendliness and warmth were unnecessary because "our customers just want to get in and out quickly" and "our customers don't care if the clerk is perky."

Nonetheless, the qualitative evidence did help us untangle the relationship between expressed emotion and store sales. The data led us to propose that store sales reflect store pace, or the amount of time pressure on clerks and customers. It also led us to propose that store pace is a cause, rather than an effect, of expressive behavior in the convenience stores studied.

Qualitative comparisons of stores during slow and busy times suggested that store pace is a cue for norms about expressed emotions. We followed Bettenhausen and Murnighan's (1985) view that norms are implicit agreements among members of a social system concerning which scripts they should and should not use to guide the behavior. Scripts are cognitive structures that specify "basic actions that can be executed in a range of possible manners and contexts" (Nisbett & Ross, 1980: 34). Scripts help people decide how to act in given situations.

Novel situations require participants to engage in considerable trial and error before they reach tacit agreement, or develop norms, about which scripts should guide actions (Bettenhausen & Murnighan, 1985). But the settings examined in this research were not novel. The membership of these stores is in constant flux as customers come and go, but both customers and clerks have well-developed scripts because of their extensive experience with such settings. Corporate records indicate that the average clerk serves hundreds of customers each day. Customers also have extensive experience with such stores; the average customer visits three times a week. Moreover, customers have much related experience with other businesses designed for convenience, such as fast-food restaurants. As a result, the scripts that guide behavior in these transactions are enacted quickly and frequently.

Indeed, there is usually instant, tacit agreement between clerks and customers about which norms of emotional expression should guide their behavior in such stores. Store pace is a primary cue that determines which norms apply at a given moment. During busy times, both clerks and customers tacitly agree that the expression of pleasant emotions is not essential. Conversely, both clerks and customers tacitly expect that pleasant emotions should be expressed during slow times.

NORMS DURING BUSY TIMES: CUSTOMERS AS OBJECTS FOR RAPID PROCESSING

Data from the five sources summarized in Table 3 led us to conclude that a set of tacitly agreed upon, but well-defined, norms exist during busy times that encourage clerks in convenience stores to view customers as inputs for rapid processing. We also propose that those norms are reflected in differences at the store level of analysis because busy stores have a higher proportion of times during which clerks view customers—and customers view themselves—as inputs for rapid processing.

Isenberg (1981) reported a pilot study in which he found that people under time pressure expected themselves to be more task-oriented and less friendly. The pattern observed in the qualitative data was consistent with Isenberg's findings. When there were many customers in a store and lines were long, both clerks and customers usually tried to move as quickly as possible to speed transactions. We heard clerks apologize for moving slowly during busy times. We also heard customers apologize for making large purchases when a long line of customers was waiting behind them. Such apologies by clerks and customers were heard even if only two or three people were standing in line because these stores are so strongly oriented towards convenience.

Consistent with Isenberg's findings, data from the case studies indicated that both clerks and customers in the busiest of the four stores were the least likely to display positive emotions; this store had the highest proportion of busy times. Moreover, visits to all four stores during busy times revealed that employees were less likely to offer greetings, eye contact, smiles, and thanks to customers than they were during slow times. Indeed, as Table 3 reveals, all five data sources suggested that positive emotions were less likely to be expressed during busy times.

Two reasons may explain why such norms are in place during busy times. First, such norms help maintain efficiency. Katz and Kahn (1978) and Feldman (1984) proposed that norms are enforced when they express core values of an organization or group and clarify what is distinctive about a social system. Efficiency is a core value for these convenience stores. Advertisements for the chain emphasize how quickly customers can get in and out of the stores. Indeed, speed of service is perhaps the primary reason that customers visit these stores.

Greeting, smiling at, thanking, and establishing eye contact with customers take only a small amount of extra time. But displaying those simple behaviors can encourage customers to prolong a transaction. One experienced clerk who worked in a store that was often busy told us that he learned not to smile or establish eye contact with customers because "being friendly" often caused customers to start prolonged conversations that he did not have time to finish. We also observed that people waiting in line are less likely to become irritated at "no nonsense" clerks who focus only on moving customers along quickly. Courteous clerks may be able to process customers just as quickly as clerks who do not interact with customers, but they appear to be slower. In short, customers and clerks are not likely to exchange good cheer during busy times because such acts hamper objective and perceived efficiency.

Second, a busy pace can create stress. Several of the clerks we spoke with reported feeling tense when lines were long. Table 3 also quotes a store manager who reported that customers feel tense when lines are long. Over-loaded clerks who are displaying their inner feelings—rather than trying to follow corporate display rules—are not likely to be smiling. Even the display of anger or irritation may be acceptable during busy times; it is clearly more acceptable than it is during slow times. Expressing irritation toward people who hampered efficiency was found to be especially legitimate during busy times.

Indeed, we encountered some evidence that sanctions are applied to both clerks and customers who hamper efficiency during busy times. The following incident occurred during the day that one of us worked as a clerk: A customer initially requested only a hot dog and a soft drink. In the middle of his purchase, however, he decided to "grab a few things" including two Bic lighters, two toothbrushes, Ex-Lax, and aspirin; the three people waiting in line started glaring at this customer. To make things worse, the clerk did not have the skill to process this complicated order rapidly; he was also sanctioned.

TABLE 3   Qualitative Evidence About the Influence of Store Pace on Displayed Emotions

Sources of Data	Evidence About Displayed Emotions in Stores During Busy Times	Evidence About Displayed Emotions in Stores During Slow Times
Four case studies	One store manager reported that clerks were less likely to be friendly during busy times. Customers are "more stressed and tense," as another store manager put it. Observers also noted that clerks tended to become less friendly during busy times. In both stores that were low on expressed positive emotion, there was a tendency to wait longer to open a second register than in the two stores that were high on the expression of positive emotion. Thus, during busy times, lines tended to be longer in the two "unfriendly" stores than in the two "friendly" stores.	The store managers reported that clerks were likely to be friendly during slow times; the observers noted that clerks tended to become more friendly during slow times. The observers also noted that extended conversations took place between clerks and regular customers during slow times, especially in the two "friendly" stores.
Day spent working as a clerk	The field notes reveal the following: (when the line of customers got long) "I never looked up at the customers. I never established eye contact. I never said thank you. I was breaking the rules, and I knew it. But I couldn't help it."	The field notes reveal the following: (during slow times) "There were regular customers. And my coworkers and I would often engage in brief, friendly banter, and sometimes even extended conversations, with these folks."
Conversations with managers	The negative relationship between positive emotion and performance was attributed to the "Manhattan effect," the notion that New Yorkers are less polite than people in other parts of the country because they are under greater time pressure.	There was widespread agreement that lack of courtesy should not be tolerated when it was slow because there are no excuses for such behavior.
Customer service workshop	A store manager remarked, "Customers who are in a long line don't care if we smile or not. They just want us to run like hell."	There was a general discussion about slow and busy stores. All agreed that it was easy to smile, greet, establish eye contact, and thank customers when it was slow, but being courteous was thought to be a challenge when it was busy.
Store visits	We noticed that clerks and customers tried to move as fast as possible when the store was busy. Everyone was less friendly. We also found that our own irritation from waiting in long lines was sometimes expressed to clerks.	We noticed that clerks tended to be more friendly when there were fewer customers in the store; customers and we ourselves also tended to be more friendly during slow times.

One impatient customer commented pointedly that "it is hard to get good help these days."

Along similar lines, a customer service manager told us about a time when—even though there was a line of seven customers at the primary cash register—the second clerk continued an animated conversation with his friend rather than open a second cash register. Both the clerk operating the cash register and a regular customer who was in line reacted by taunting the chatty clerk.

NORMS DURING SLOW TIMES: CUSTOMERS AS ENTERTAINMENT

Norms during slow times contrast strongly with those during busy times. As with busy times, a set of tacitly agreed upon, but well-defined, behavioral expectations can be identified for slow times. Isenberg's (1981) previously cited laboratory research suggests that people under low time pressure expect themselves to be less task-oriented and more friendly than those under high time pressure. Findings from the five sources of qualitative evidence summarized in Table 3 are consistent with those findings. Clerks were more likely to greet, smile at, establish eye contact with, and say "thank you" to customers during slow times. Customers were also more likely to be friendly. Moreover, the norms for expressive behavior during slow times are also reflected at the store level because slow stores have a high proportion of slow times.

We identified three primary reasons why norms in slow stores support the expression of positive emotion. First, pressure on clerks for speed and efficiency is low during slow times. Clerks can take the time to greet customers, establish eye contact, smile, and say "thanks" without suffering the negative consequences that occur during busy times. Indeed, as Table 3 indicates, managers believe that lack of courtesy should not be tolerated during slow times because there is no excuse for such behavior.

Second, our observations suggested that customers who enter stores during slow times have different expectations about what constitutes correct behavior. In contrast to scripts for busy times, scripts for slow times have more "scenes" (Nisbett & Ross, 1980: 34) that emphasize interpersonal exchanges and the display of positive and esteem-enhancing emotions. Customers who entered stores that had few other customers were more likely to offer greetings and smiles to clerks. We also noticed this pattern in our own behavior when we visited stores.

Third, and perhaps more important, clerks in slow stores were often genuinely happy to see customers enter the store. They were most enthusiastic about seeing regular customers, but they acted happy even if it was someone they had never met. Recalling Roy's (1959) classic discussion of "banana time," our data indicated that informal social interaction with customers was an important means for introducing variety into a boring job. Clerks are especially friendly during slow times because they view customers as entertainment. Thus, the expression of positive emotions during slow times—and, in the aggregate, in stores that are usually slow—may be influenced more strongly by true feelings than by corporate display rules.

Field notes from the day one of us spent working as a clerk illustrate that point:

> There weren't a lot of customers. I was bored with the jobs they were giving me. When no customers were around, I'd spend my time putting prices on things, putting cans on shelves, and doing thrilling jobs such as cleaning the nacho machine. I'd get excited when a customer walked into the store because talking to customers was the only vaguely interesting thing to do.

In short, norms for slow times encourage the expression of positive and esteem-enhancing emotions. But such expectations do not appear to stem from efforts by the formal organization to increase sales.

REANALYSIS OF THE QUANTITATIVE DATA: TESTING THE REVISED THEORETICAL PERSPECTIVE

The revised theoretical perspective presented above provided considerable guidance for reanalysis of the quantitative data. A comparison of busy and slow times facilitated interpretation of the qualitative data. It appeared that stores with a high proportion of busy times were less likely to have a set of clerks who displayed positive emotions to customers and that stores with a low proportion of busy times were more likely to have a set of clerks who did display good cheer to customers. Stores could be placed on a continuum from rapidly to slowly paced. Thus, we proposed that clerks working in a store that was usually busy would be guided less frequently by norms supporting the display of positive emotions. We came to view store pace—time pressure placed on clerks and customers—as cause of displayed emotion. Thus, although the display of positive emotion was a predictor variable in the initial analysis of the quantitative data, our revised perspective suggested that it be used as the criterion variable.

The revised perspective also suggested that we use two indicators of store pace—store sales and line length—as the predictor variables. Compared to stores with low sales, stores with high sales have more customers, more vendors coming and going, more telephone calls, and more people playing video games. Thus, stores with high sales have a high proportion of busy times. Furthermore, busy stores usually have longer lines than slow stores. Thus, average line length, one of the control variables used in the initial analysis, also indicates how much objective and subjective time pressure is usually placed on clerks and customers in a store.

Table 1 presents a modest positive relationship between sales and line length. But the small magnitude of that correlation, along with findings based on our observations of the stores, suggested that line length is a distinct indicator of store pace. High store sales may reflect large purchases rather than long lines. Moreover, stores with high sales place other demands on clerks that line length does not reflect, such as more frequent visits by vendors and more pressure to restock shelves.

In short, we proposed that stores with a high proportion of busy times would be less likely to have clerks who greeted, smiled at, established eye contact with, and said "thank you" to customers. Specifically, we expected that (1) store sales would be negatively related to the expression of positive emotion and (2) a store's average line length would be negatively related to the expression of positive emotion.

These expectations were tested in the same data set used for the first quantitative analyses; multiple regression analyses were again used in the sample of 576 stores. A hierarchical procedure similar to that used in the first quantitative analysis was employed. The first equation included seven control variables—ownership, supervision costs, stock level, customers' gender composition, clerks' gender composition, clerks' image, and region—as predictors of the display of positive emotion. This analysis yielded a multiple R of .40 and an adjusted R-square of .15 ($p < .001$). In the second equation, we added the predictor variables of line length and total store sales to the seven control variables used in the first equation. Table 4 presents the results of this equation; a multiple R of .44 and an adjusted R-square of .18 were obtained. Table 4 indicates that both store sales and average line length were significantly and negatively related to the display of positive emotion. The significant beta weights for both total store sales and average line length indicate that these variables make a significant contribution to the variance explained by the model. That is, the increment in R-square is statistically significant. These results support our revised perspective.[1]

Several control variables were also significantly related to the display of positive emotion: store ownership, stock level, clerks' gender composition, and region. Clerks in corporation-owned stores presented positive emotions more often than clerks in franchised stores. This finding may occur because executives can enforce policies about emotional expression in corporate stores but can only encourage such behavior in franchised stores. Stock level was positively related to pleasant displays; both maintaining well-stocked shelves and displaying good cheer may reflect general adherence to corporate guidelines. The positive relationship between clerks' gender composition and expressed positive emotions is consistent with prior findings that women are more likely to smile and display warmth than men (Deaux, 1985). Finally, as Table 4 shows, two of the three dummy-coded region variables had significant beta weights. A comparison of means (Pedhauzer, 1982: 289) for the regions indicated that clerks in the West were the most likely to express positive emotions and clerks in the Northeast were the least likely to do so. The negative relationship shown in Table 4 between the two indicators of store pace and the expression of positive

emotion are consistent with our revised perspective. A key underlying assertion of this perspective is that clerks are less likely to display positive emotions during busy times than during slow times.

Further evidence for this assertion was obtained by comparing clerks' behavior during busy and slow times. The line-length variable, which was gathered at the clerk level of analysis, is an indicator of store pace at a given time. If norms about expressed emotions were linked to pace in the convenience stores studied, we expected that, across the 1,319 clerks who were observed for this study, there would be a negative relationship between the length of the line a clerk faced and his or her display of positive emotions.

A hierarchical multiple regression procedure at the individual level of analysis confirmed that expectation. We introduced the relevant control variables into the first equation: clerks' gender composition, proportion of woman customers, clerks' image, and store's stock level during the observation. This analysis yielded an R of .27 and an adjusted R-square of .07. In the second equation, we added average line length as an additional predictor. Line length was significantly and negatively related to the display of positive emotion by clerks (beta = –.14, $p < .001$, $n = 1,319$). The complete model yielded an R of .32 and an adjusted R-square of .10.

These analyses did not, however, address the question of whether constant exposure to busy or slow times influences all transactions in a store regardless of whether a particular time happens to be slow or busy. If recurring pace does influence store norms about expressive behavior, the relationship between line length and the display of positive emotion is likely to be different in typically busy stores than in typically slow stores.

The qualitative evidence led us to expect that clerks in stores that are usually busy will be less sensitive to the number of customers standing in line than clerks in stores that are usually slow. During slow times in typically busy stores, clerks may be indifferent or even unhappy about seeing customers because they must use slow times to cope with other demands such as stocking shelves, dealing with vendors, and answering phone calls. But such distracting demands are lower in stores that are typically slow. During slow times in stores that are usually slow, clerks are more likely to offer good cheer because they are bored and need the entertainment provided by customers.

In addition, we proposed that clerks in stores that are usually slow are less likely to offer pleasant emotions during busy times than clerks in stores that are usually busy. Clerks in stores that are usually slow have less

---

[1] We also conducted additional analyses to rule out nonlinear relationships between total store sales and displayed emotion and between line length and displayed emotion. An argument based on activation theory (Scott, 1966) suggested that, if store pace was a stressor and decrement in displayed positive emotion was a form of on-the-job performance, there would be an inverted U-shaped relationship between store pace and the display of positive emotion. We used multiple regression analyses with quadratic (X^2) terms of store sales and line length to explore that hypothesis (Cohen & Cohen, 1975). The squared variable did not bear a significant relationship to displayed emotion ($p < .10$) in either of the analyses. Thus, we found no support for a U-shaped or an inverted-U-shaped relationship between sales and displayed emotion or between line length and displayed emotion.

TABLE 4   Results of Regression Analysis of Store Pace as a Predictor of Display of Positive Emotion[a]

Variables[b]	Betas
Control variables	
Store ownership	−.14[c]
Supervision costs	.01
Stock level	.23**
Customers' gender composition	.04
Clerks' gender composition	.15**
Clerks' image	.06
Region 1	−.03
Region 2	.25*
Region 3	.12**
Store pace	
Total store sales	−.09*
Average line length	−.20**
Multiple R = .44	
Adjusted R-square = .18**	

[a]n = 576.

[b]Store ownership was coded 0 for corporation-owned stores and 1 for franchised stores. Customers' gender composition is the proportion of woman customers. Clerks' gender composition is the proportion of woman sales clerks. Region 1, region 2, and region 3 are dummy codes representing the four regions.

[c]$p < .10$, two tailed test.

*$p < .05$, two-tailed test.

**$p < .01$, two-tailed test.

experience in coping with the pressure of busy times. Thus, clerks in stores that are usually slow may be more likely to feel and thus express neutral, or even negative, feelings when lines do get long.

Thus, we expected a stronger negative relationship between the line lengths faced by individual clerks and their display of positive emotion in stores that are usually slow than in stores that are usually busy. Store sales is an indicator of whether a store is typically busy or slow. The expected relationship implies a significant interaction effect at the individual level of analysis between the length of a line that clerks face and the level of total sales of the store in which they work. We expected that interaction to have a significant effect on the display of positive emotion by clerks. Thus, an additional regression equation was examined. In this equation, the interaction term (line length × total sales) was included, in addition to the individual-level control variables—clerks' gender composition, customers' gender composition, clerks'

image, and store's stock level during the observation

As expected, the interaction term bore a significant relationship to displayed positive emotion (beta = −.07, $p < .001$), and the equation yielded a multiple R of .29 and an adjusted R-square of .08, compared to a multiple R of .27 and an adjusted R-square of .07 obtained with the model including only the control variables.

Subgroup analyses were conducted in order to understand the pattern of this interaction. Specifically, we split the sample of 576 stores at the mean of store sales, classifying 326 stores as slow and 250 stores as busy. We then conducted multiple regression analyses within each subsample on the relationship between line length and the expression of positive emotion by individual clerks.

As with the other multiple regressions at the clerk level of analysis, we first introduced clerks' gender, customers' gender, clerks' image, and store's stock level as control variables. Line length was then introduced as the predictor variable. The display of positive emotion by clerks was the criterion variable. In slow stores, the relationship between line length and the display of positive emotions was negative and significant (beta = −.19, $p <$ .001, $n = 708$ clerks). In busy stores, that relationship was not nearly as strong and was only marginally significant (beta = −.06, $p < .10$, $n = 611$ clerks). Those results affirm that there is a stronger negative relationship between line length and the display of positive emotion by individual clerks in typically slow stores than in typically busy stores. We repeated this analysis with the sample split at the median of store sales and observed the same pattern of results.

DISCUSSION

Our initial conceptual perspective focused on expressed positive emotions as control moves that influence the shopping behavior of customers. We hypothesized that stores in which employees were more likely to offer positive emotions to customers would have greater sales. But a quantitative study of 576 convenience stores revealed a negative relationship between displayed positive emotions and store sales.

Our revised perspective emphasized that store sales reflect store pace and that store pace is a cause, rather than an effect, of expressed emotions. We found some empirical support for the revised perspective. But our sample included only one variety of convenience stores; the service ideal associated with these stores has not traditionally included friendly service. Emotions expressed in organizations in which a different service ideal is present may act as control moves that influence sales. That is, a warm emotional front may promote sales when customers expect that it should and will be a central part of a firm's service. Examples of organizations where customers expect to receive good cheer from employees include Nordstrom's (Peters & Austin, 1985), Disneyworld (Tyler & Nathan, 1985), and Delta Airlines (Hochschild, 1983). Furthermore, expectations of fast service need not exclude warmth and friendliness; McDonald's is an example of a national chain in which the service ideal includes both rapid and friendly service.

The convenience stores studied are settings in which transactions between employees and customers are very brief. Expressed emotions may also be more powerful control moves during long transactions between employees and customers. When waiters serve customers in restaurants, for example, the interaction may last anywhere from 30 minutes to one and a half hours (Mars & Nicod, 1984), far longer than the 2 or 3 minutes that a typical customer spends in the stores we studied. There is more time during a long transaction for the customer to notice and react to the emotional behavior of an employee; thus, the operant conditioning cycle we discussed earlier is more likely to become established.

Our initial conceptual perspective had a far different focus than our revised perspective. The initial perspective emphasized control moves and corporate display rules. The revised perspective emphasized store pace, widely held norms for convenience settings, and employees' inner feelings. Nonetheless, some integration of those two perspectives on the expression of emotion in organizational life may have benefits for both organizational theory and managerial practice.

First, the qualitative evidence suggested that the concept of control moves might still be useful for understanding the convenience stores we studied but that future research might benefit from considering how expressed emotions influence variables other than sales volume. Evidence about busy times suggested that an emotionally neutral demeanor discouraged customers from initiating extended conversations. Presenting a neutral demeanor can act as a control move because it helps clerks influence the behavior of their customers and thus helps clerks provide fast service. Further, evidence about slow times suggested that pleasant displays can encourage customers to engage in conversations that are an important source of variety in a boring job. Thus, the display of good cheer during slow times may be a control move that promotes individual rather than organizational goals.

Second, organizational theorists have not extensively studied the emotions displayed by organizational members (Hochschild, 1983; Rafaeli & Sutton, 1987). One central question for this emerging area is the extent to which leaders can prescribe employees' expressive behavior. Our initial perspective emphasized emotions expressed on the job as the outcome of corporate practices. But our revised perspective emphasizes that, although corporate display rules do constrain displayed emotions, store norms and inner feelings can sometimes be a more powerful influence over such behavior.

One combination of the initial and revised perspectives has direct implications for managers who want to design jobs so that subordinates who work in busy settings will be pleasant towards customers. Organizational norms specifying the display of good cheer to customers may be easier to enforce if managers take steps to reduce the objective and subjective stress placed on employees and customers. For example, the introduction of a single line for multiple clerks may reduce the perceived pressure on both employees and customers in busy environments. The physical distance between clerks and customers waiting in line may act as a buffer; clerks can offer polite and friendly service to the customer they are serving without risking sanctions from other customers. The single-line system with multiple clerks also reduces customer anxiety about having chosen the fastest clerk and discourages customers from focusing anger and irritation on any single clerk.

In closing, we would like to return to the methods used in this study. The observational methods used here are not widely employed in organizational research. Thus, questions may arise about whether it is ethical to secretly observe employees. Procedures used in the present research were, however, consistent with ethical guidelines on the conduct of nonreactive research and contrived observations (Salancik, 1979; Sechrest & Phillips, 1979; Webb et al., 1981). The American Psychological Association discourages "covert investigations in private places" (American Psychological Association, 1973: 13). The convenience stores used in the present research are, however, public places. Moreover, the corporation's use of incognito observers and our own use of that method during the qualitative phase were only partly covert. Although specific, informed consent was not obtained from each clerk observed, all clerks had been informed that encounters with mystery shoppers were part of the job: the corporate training program explained the use of mystery shoppers and the expected expressive behaviors. Furthermore, the names of individual clerks were not recorded in either the quantitative research conducted by the corporation or in our own qualitative research. Thus, in terms of a harms-benefit analysis, such data were not, and could not , but be used to harm any individual clerk.

Finally, we learned much about the role of expressed emotion in organizational life from this research because it entailed two complete cycles of induction and deduction. Unfortunately, however, it is not normative in the organizational studies literature, nor in other scholarly areas, to report unsuccessful efforts at induction or deduction. Studies that find no significant relationships are usually not published. Moreover, we occasionally hear of studies in which the findings contradict initial hypotheses but that are written as if the unexpected results were predicted at the outset of the investigation. The tendency to report only successful predictions persists even though failed predictions offer important lessons about the research process and about organizational life (Mirvis & Berg, 1977). We hope that, in some small way, this research is a step toward changing those norms.

REFERENCES

American Psychological Association, 1973. *Code of ethics of the American Psychological Association.* Washington, D.C.: American Psychological Association.

Arther, R. O., & Caputo, R. R. 1959. *Interrogation for investigators.* New York: William C. Copp and Associates.

Ash, M. K. 1984. *Mary Kay on people management.* New York: Warner Books.

Bandura, A. 1977. *Social learning theory.* Englewood Cliffs, NJ: Prentice-Hall.

Bass, B. M. 1982. *Stogdill's handbook of leadership.* New York: Free Press.

Bettenhausen, K., & Murnighan, J. K. 1985. The emergence of norms in competitive decision-making groups. *Administrative Science Quarterly,* 30: 350–372.

Birnbaum, S. 1987. *Birnbaum's Italy.* Boston: Houghton-Mifflin.

Bowen, D. E., & Schneider, B. 1985. Boundary-spanning-role employees and the service encounter: Some guidelines for management and research. In J. A. Czepiel, M. R. Solomon, & C. F. Surprenant (Eds.), *The service encounter:* 3–15. Lexington, MA: Lexington Books.

Bradshaw, D. 1980. Sister can you spare a smile? *New York,* 13(8): 7.

Cohen, J., & Cohen, P. 1975. *Applied multiple regression/correlation analysis for the behavioral sciences.* New York: Wiley.

Czepiel, J. A., Solomon, M. R., & Surprenant, C. F. (Eds.). 1985. *The service encounter.* Lexington, MA: Lexington Books.

Deaux, K. 1985. Sex differences. *Annual Review of Psychology,* 36: 49–82.

Ekman, P. 1980. Biological and cultural contributions to body and facial movement in the expression of emotion. In A. O. Rorty (Ed.), *Explaining emotions:* 73–102. Berkeley, CA: California Press.

Engel, J. F., Blackwell, R. D., & Miniard, P. W. 1986. *Consumer behavior.* New York: Dryden Press.

Feldman, D. C. 1984. The development and enforcement of group norms. *Academy of Management Review,* 9: 47–53.

Glaser, B., & Strauss, A. 1967. *The discovery of grounded theory: Strategies for qualitative research.* London: Wiedenfeld and Nicholson.

Goffman, E. 1969. *Strategic interaction.* Philadelphia: University of Pennsylvania Press.

Hackman, J. R., & Oldham, G. R. 1980. *Work redesign.* Reading, MA: Addison-Wesley.

Hayano, D. M. 1982. *Poker faces.* Berkeley, CA: University of California Press.

Hochschild, A. R. 1979. Emotion work, feeling rules, and social structure. *American Journal of Sociology,* 85: 551–575.

Hochschild, A. R. 1983. *The managed heart.* Berkeley, CA: University of California Press.

Isenberg, D. J. 1981. Some effects of time pressure on vertical structure and decision making accuracy in small groups. *Organizational Behavior and Human Performance, 27:* 119–134.

Kahn, R. L. 1981. *Work and health.* New York: Wiley.

Katz, D., & Kahn, R. L. 1978. *The social psychology of organizations* (2d ed.). New York: John Wiley & Sons.

Lawler, E. E. III. 1981. *Pay and organization development.* Reading, MA: Addison-Wesley.

Locke, E. A. 1976. The nature and causes of job satisfaction. In M. D. Dunnette (Ed.), *Handbook of industrial and organizational psychology:* 1297–1349. Chicago: Rand McNally & Co.

Mars, G., & Nicod, M. 1984. *The world of waiters.* London: George Allen & Unwin.

Merton, R. 1957. *Social theory and social structure.* Glencoe, IL: Free Press.

Miles, M. B., & Huberman, A. M. 1984. *Qualitative data analysis.* Beverly Hills, CA: Sage Publications.

Mirvis, P., & Berg, P. 1977. *Failures in organizational development.* New York: Wiley.

Nisbett, R., & Ross, L. 1980. *Human inference: Strategies and shortcomings of social judgment.* Englewood Cliffs, NJ: Prentice-Hall.

Parasuraman, A., Zeithaml, V. A., & Berry, L. L. 1985. A conceptual model of service quality and its implications for future research. *Journal of Marketing,* 49 (4): 41–50.

Pedhauzer, E. J. 1982. *Multiple regression in behavioral research: Explanation and prediction.* New York: Holt, Rinehart & Winston.

Peters, T. J., & Austin, N. 1985. *A passion for excellence.* New York: Random House.

Peters, T. J., & Waterman, R. H., Jr. 1982. *In search of excellence.* New York: Harper & Row Publisher.

Putnam, L., & McCallister, L. 1980. Situational effects of task and gender on nonverbal display. In D. Nimmo (Ed.), *Communications yearbook,* vol. 4: 679–697.

Rafaeli, A., & Sutton, R. I. 1989. The expression of emotion as part of the work role. *Academy of Management Review,* 12: 23–37.

Rafaeli, A., & Sutton, R. I. 1987. The expression of emotion in organizational life. In L. L. Cummings & B. M. Staw, (Eds.), *Research in organization behavior,* vol. 11: Forthcoming. Greenwich, CT: JAI Press.

Richman, T. 1984. A tale of two companies. *Inc.,* 6(7): 38–43.

Rousseau, D. M. 1985. Issues of level in organizational research: Multi-level and cross-level perspectives. In L. L. Cummings & M. Staw (Eds.), *Research in organization behavior,* vol. 7: 1–37. Greenwich, CT: JAI Press.

Roy, D. F. 1959. "Banana time": Job satisfaction and informal interaction. *Human organization,* 18 (4): 158–168.

Salancik, G. R. 1979. Field stimulations for organizational behavior research. *Administrative Science Quarterly,* 24: 638–649.

Schneider, B., Parkington, J. J., & Buxton, V. M. 1980. Employee and customer perceptions of service in banks. *Administrative Science Quarterly,* 25: 252–260.

Scott, W. E. 1966. Activation theory and task design. *Organizational Behavior and Human Performance,* 1: 3–30.

Shamir, B. 1980. Between service and servility: Role conflict in subordinate service roles. *Human Relations,* 33: 741–756.

Skinner, B. F. 1953. *Science and human behavior.* New York: Macmillan Book Publishing Co.

Tidd, K. L., & Lockhard, J. S. 1978. Monetary significance of the affiliative smile. *Bulletin of the Psychonomic Society,* 11: 344–346.

Tyler, S., & Nathan, J. 1985. *In search of excellence* (film). New York: Public Broadcast System.

Unterman, P., & Sesser, S. 1984. *Restaurants of San Francisco.* San Francisco: Chronicle Books.

Wallace, W. 1971. *The logic of science in sociology.* New York: Aldine Publishing.

Webb, E. J., Campbell, D. T., Schwartz, D. S., Sechrest, L., & Grove, G. B. 1981. *Nonreactive measures in the social sciences.* Boston: Houghton-Mifflin.

APPENDIX

Guide for Semistructured Interviews with Store Managers

1. How long have you been the manager of this store?

2. Why did you become a store manager?

3. Have you worked at the cash register in this store? (Prompts: How frequently? In another store?)

4. What qualities do you look for in selecting employees?

5. What sort of training do employees get? (Prompts: From the store? From the corporation?)

6. How are employees rewarded? (Prompts: How much pay? Anything other than pay? From the corporation? From the store?)

7. Do employees act differently when the store is busy? When the store is not busy?

8. Do customers act differently when the store is busy? When the store is not busy?

9. What do difficult customers do to make the clerk's work difficult? Tell me about a time when a really difficult customer entered the store. What are examples of good management of such customers? What are examples of bad management of such customers?

10. Is there anything special you tell employees about handling difficult customers?

11. Do you think there is a relationship between sales and courtesy?

12. What do you think of the corporation's push for courtesy?

13. What things do you do as a store manager to affect employee courtesy?

14. Is there any special employee training that emphasizes courtesy?

15. What do you think influences how courteous employees are?

16. Have you ever fired anyone for being rude to a customer?

17. In closing, are there any other important issues that we should have mentioned, but have not?

Robert I. Sutton received his Ph.D. degree in organizational psychology from the University of Michigan in 1984. He is an assistant professor of organizational behavior in the Department of Industrial Engineering and Engineering Management at Stanford University. His primary research interests are organizational decline and death, the expression of emotion in organizational life, and job stress. His other interests include impression management, cognition, organizational effectiveness, and organizational factors in prevention of international conflict.

Anat Rafaeli received her Ph. D. degree in industrial and organizational psychology from the Ohio State University in 1984. She is an assistant professor at the School of Business Administration at the Hebrew University of Jerusalem. Her primary research interests are the expression of emotion in organizational life, the special dynamics of service occupations, and the use of handwriting analysis for personnel selection. Her other interests include attitudes towards working with computers, job stress, and quality circles.

PART TWO

MANAGING THE
SERVICE EXPERIENCE

MANAGING THE
SERVICE EXPERIENCE I
CONFIGURING THE OPERATION
AND THE ENVIRONMENT

—————◆—————

CHAPTER OVERVIEW

Chapters 2, 3, and 4 have provided the foundation for an understanding of the problem of designing a service experience. Chapter 2 discussed alternative models of consumer behavior, and Chapter 3 addressed the demands and constraints imposed on the service marketer by the operations component of the service product. Chapter 4 added the necessary understanding of the role of contact people in the service experience.

In this chapter and Chapter 6, we shall be looking at the design problems of the service product. The servuction system model, introduced in Chapter 1, views the service product as an experience. That experience is an interactive process involving the consumer, the physical environment created by the service firm, and the service employees. This chapter focuses on the design of the interactive process and the environment. The role played by the service provider and the problems encountered in designing that role are discussed in Chapter 6.

In one sense, the interactive process can be viewed as a production process similar to any other production process. As such, it should be amenable to the flowcharting procedures commonly used in manufacturing. In this chapter, we shall see how a flowchart can be used to understand and design the interactive process that is the heart of the service product. We shall also learn how a physical environment should be created to contain that process. That discussion draws heavily on the field of environmental psychology, which is concerned specifically with the impact of the environment on individuals.

DESIGNING THE INTERACTIVE PROCESS

The heart of the service product is the experience of the consumer, which takes place in real time. This interaction can take place in a building or in an environment created by the service firm, but it need not necessarily do so. It is the interactive process itself that creates the benefits desired by the consumer. Designing that process therefore becomes key to the product design for a service firm.

The interactive process visible to the consumer constitutes the product. However, as the servuction model, discussed in Chapter 1, demonstrates, the visible part of the operations process with which the consumer interacts has to be supported by an invisible process.

One of the most commonly used operations-management techniques is flowcharting. It is used to analyze and manage complex production processes since it involves the identification of flows, stocks, costs, and bottlenecks. The flowcharting of service operations can also serve a number of purposes, not only for operations management but also for marketing management. This concept has been renamed "blueprinting" by G. Lynn Shostack, who has written a number of papers advocating its use.

As pointed out in Chapter 3, because services are delivered by an interactive process involving the consumer, a marketing manager in a service firm must have a detailed knowledge of the operation. Flowcharting provides a useful analytical way of acquiring that knowledge. Flowcharting also allows the manager to understand which parts of the operating system are visible to the consumer and hence are part of the servuction process.

The search for operational efficiency is not unique to services, but it does pose interesting problems in this field. A shift in the underlying process may be more efficient, for example, but it may also change the nature of the interaction with the consumer. A detailed flowchart provides communication between operations and marketing that can highlight the potential problems that were discussed in Chapter 3.

Figure 5.1 shows a simple process in which, for now, it is assumed that the entire system is visible to the customer. It covers the stages involved in getting a meal in a cafeteria-style restaurant. The diagram illustrates the various components in the process. In this example, each task is represented by a box. The "raw material" flowing through the process are the customers. There are no inventories in the process, but clearly there would be an inventory of people in the form of a line in front of each stage. A restaurant run in such a fashion would be a single long chain of counters with customers progressing along the chain and emerging after paying. In Figure 5.1, the cost figure by each stage represents the cost of providing personnel to service each counter; the service cost per meal is computed by dividing the total cost of the personnel per hour by the maximum number of people that can be served per hour.

THE SERVICE OPERATIONS MANAGER'S PERSPECTIVE

The first thing that the flowchart does is provide a check on the logical flow of the whole process. Clearly, a flowchart makes it immediately apparent if a task is being performed out of sequence. In this case, we shall further assume that only the cashier stage is fixed (because paying the cashier has to be the last stage) and that the other tasks can be performed at other times.

Once the different steps have been identified, it is relatively easy to identify the potential capacity bottlenecks. The hot-food counter stage is an obvious bottleneck since it represents the longest process time, that is, the longest time to process one individual through that stage. A balanced production line is one in which the process

FIGURE 5.1 A Simple Process Flowchart of a Cafeteria-Style Restaurant

	Stations	Activity Time	Process Time	Maximum Output/Hour
Appetizer Counter	1	15 secs.	15 secs.	240
$3.00/hour				
Salad Counter	1	30 secs.	30 secs.	120
$3.00/hour				
Hot-Food Counter	1	60 secs.	60 secs.	60*
$3.00/hour				
Dessert Counter	1	40 secs.	40 secs.	90
$3.00/hour				
Drinks Counter	1	20 secs.	20 secs.	180
$3.00/hour				
Cashier	1	30 secs.	30 secs.	120
$6.00/hour				

*Capacity Bottleneck

$$\text{Service cost per meal} = \frac{\$21.00}{60} = \$0.35$$

times of all steps are the same. The process time is calculated by dividing the activity time (the time required to perform the activity) by the number of stations or locations performing the activity. In Figure 5.1, the process and activity times are the same since there is only one station for each activity.

To solve this particular bottleneck problem, we could consider adding one extra station, in this case an extra counter, to the hot-food stage. The process time would drop to 30 seconds (60 seconds divided by 2). The bottleneck would then become the dessert counter, which has a process time of 40 seconds and a maximum capacity of 90 persons per hour. Costs would go up by $3.00 per hour for the extra counter, but since the number of customers served would go up to 90 persons per hour, the service cost per meal would go down to $0.27 per meal.

The creative use of additional staff may produce a model such as that shown in Figure 5.2, which combines certain activities and uses multiple stations. This process is capable of handling 120 customers per hour compared to 60 in the process shown in Figure 5.1. Although costs rise, the service cost per meal falls because of this increase in capacity.

THE SERVICE MARKETING MANAGER'S PERSPECTIVE

A marketing manager dealing with the process illustrated in Figure 5.1 has some of the same problems as her operations colleague. The process as defined is designed to operate at certain production levels, and these are the service standards that customers should perceive. But, if the process is capable of processing only 60 customers per hour, there may be a problem. Also, it is clear that the bottleneck at the hot-food counter will produce queues within the line.

The marketing manager should recognize the capacity benefits immediately. However, what the chart also shows is the change in consumer behavior required for

FIGURE 5.2   Reducing the Cost Per Meal Still Further

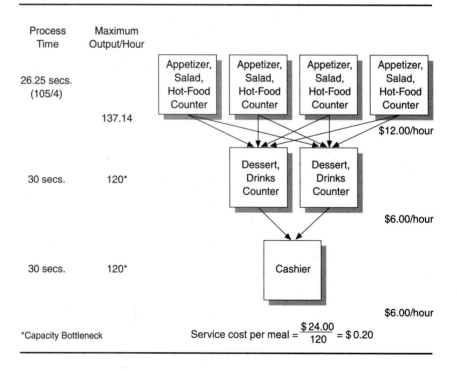

SERVICES IN ACTION 5.1

LANDS' END

Lands' End is a catalog retail company operating nationally from a base in Wisconsin. The company sells mainly clothing, along with accessories and luggage, to a mostly young, affluent, well-educated, and quality-oriented customer base. The Lands' End catalog, which offers around 600 distinct items with a total option range of over 10,000, provides customers with information about products. Some customers order by mail, but about 75 percent use the Lands' End toll-free telephone number to place their orders by phone. This telephone line is open 24 hours a day every day except Christmas.

Operations management for catalog retailers involves, first, having stock on hand to meet demand, and, second, managing a system where orders are filled and processed quickly to avoid delays to the customers. Service management depends on being able to meet each customer's inquiry individually and, since customers cannot actually see or try on garments over the telephone, offer as much guidance as possible. Success overall entails the resolving of the contradiction between personal service and assembly-line production.

The focus of this effort is on the customer sales representatives who answer the telephones. In the case of Lands' End, these representatives are well trained and are able to give full descriptions of all items in the catalog to supplement the information given in print. The customer sales representatives are further supported by a team of "specialty shoppers" who can give even more detailed information and advice, and who can attempt to provide more service than the customer expects.

The front-line operation then needs systems back-up to provide the second half of the service—the fast dispatch of goods. This is accomplished at Lands' End by providing customer service representatives with links to the computer mainframe so that they can check stock, look up credit ratings, and place delivery orders while the customer is still on the phone. Automation, particularly in the distribution center, has served to decrease order processing time to less than 24 hours for most orders.

Lands' End so far has succeeded by remaining relatively small and keeping all systems simple and free from bureaucracy. In 1987, when executives began thinking about expanding the company, one of the prime considerations was how to increase volume and at the same time maintain service quality.

the system to operate. In Figure 5.1, the consumer goes from counter to counter, has only one choice at each counter, and probably will queue at each station but will wait for a longer time at the hot-food counter. Moreover, the wait at each stage almost certainly will far exceed the time spent in each activity. In the process proposed in Figure 5.2, the consumer visits fewer stations, but frequently is faced with a choice between different stations. Clearly, the script to be followed by consumers will be different; indeed, the restaurant will look completely different. This obviously will impose different marketing demands.

The use of the flowcharting approach allows the marketing and operations personnel to analyze in detail the process that they are jointly trying to create and manage. Flowcharting can easily highlight the kind of conflict discussed in Chapter 3 and can provide a common language for their discussion and for the resolution of their problems.

USING FLOWCHARTS TO IDENTIFY THE SERVUCTION PROCESS

Flowcharts also may be used for a different purpose. Consider Figure 5.3, which shows a much more detailed flowchart for the production of a discount brokerage service. This chart is designed to identify the points of contact between the service firm and the customer. The points above the line are visible to the consumer, and those below are invisible. In assessing the quality of service received, according to the servuction model, the customer refers to the points of contact.

To illustrate, let us consider the customers as being proactive rather than reactive. Consider them as worried individuals looking for clues that they have made the right decision rather than as inanimate objects to which things are done. The points of contact are the clues. In a recent article, Levitt talks about "tangible clues" and argues that the intangible nature of services makes it important to manage the tangible clues provided to the customer.[1] These tangible clues constitute the servuction process.

Besides demonstrating a more complicated process, the chart in Figure 5.3 has a number of added features. First, each of the main features is linked to a target time. In the top right-hand corner, for example, the time to mail a statement is targeted as five days after month end. In designing a service, these target times initially should be set by marketing, and they should be based on consumers' expected levels of service. If the service is to be offered in a competitive marketplace, then it may be necessary to set standards higher than those of services currently available. Once the standards have been set, however, the probability of achieving them must be assessed. If the firm is prepared to invest enough time and money, it may be feasible to meet all of the standards set by marketing; doing so, however, would affect the costs and therefore the price of the service. Hence, the process should be an interactive one.

The chart also highlights potential fail points "F." These key points have two characteristics: The potential for operations malfunction is high, and the result of a malfunction becomes visible. Such points also should represent stages where a malfunction would be regarded by consumers as particularly significant.

A MARKETING OR AN OPERATIONS FLOWCHART?

Although the idea of a flowchart is attractive to both marketing and operations, it may well be that a marketing flowchart should be prepared in a different way. The charts we have used in this chapter have an internal focus: Although they identify clearly the tangible points of contact with the client, they start from within the organization and look outward.

An alternative way to develop a flowchart would be to start from consumer protocol. Respondents, individually or in groups, can be asked to describe the process or the script they follow in using the service. Clearly, such an approach cannot cover the invisible part of the service firm, but it can provide a much better understanding of the points of contact. The process, as described by the consumer, may well differ greatly from that perceived by the firm.

Respondents asked to describe a flight on United Airlines, for example, might start with their experience with the travel agent. They then might proceed to describe the process of getting to the airport, parking, and entering the terminal. If the signs for United and the entrance to its specific terminal are confusing, this will reflect on the airline. A parking lot that is filthy, poorly lit, and inhabited by vagrants also will deter customers. Although the airline may not have direct control over these

FIGURE 5.3 Flowchart of a Discount Brokerage Service

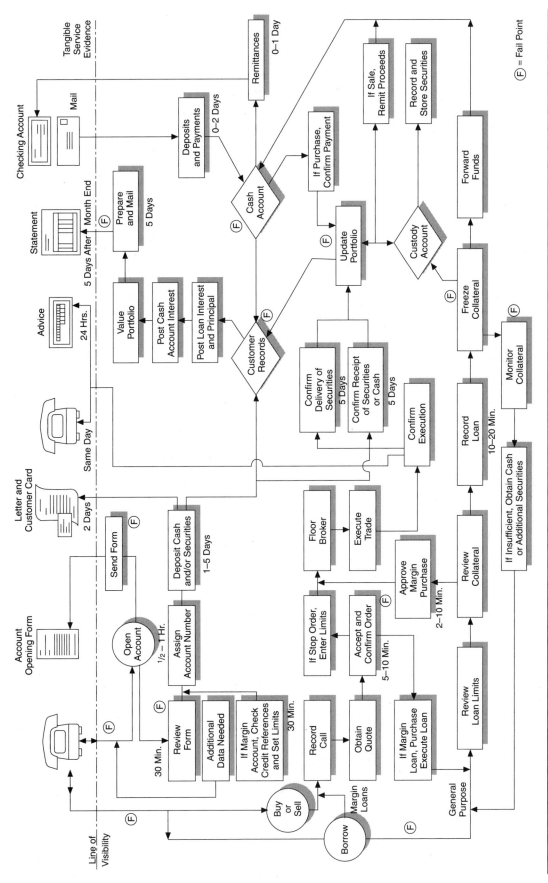

SOURCE: G. Lynn Shostack, "Service Design in the Operating Environment," in William R. George and Claudia Marshall, eds., *Developing New Services* (Chicago, IL: American Marketing Association, 1984): 27–43. Reprinted with permission.

points of contact, it could be a wise investment to use its own staff to improve the parking lot. McDonald's long ago learned the value of removing litter not only from its own property but also from the adjoining roadways.

FLOWCHARTING FOR NEW-PRODUCT DEVELOPMENT

Flowcharts also may be used in new-product development. Once the process has been documented, choices can be made that will produce "new" products. Although the processes in Figures 5.1 and 5.2 are for the same task, from the consumer's point of view, they are very different. The charts define alternatives that are operationally feasible; the choice between them is one for marketing.

Strategically, the decision may be made to move the line separating visibility and invisibility. Operationally, arguments have been made for the minimization of the visible component. From a marketing point of view, however, more visibility may create more differentiation in the mind of the consumer. For example, a restaurant can make its kitchen into a feature of the dining experience by making it visible to the diners. This poses constraints on the operational personnel, but it may add value in the mind of the consumer.

G. Lynn Shostack suggests an alternative view of using flowcharts by introducing the concepts of complexity and divergence as a means of classifying the charts.[2] Complexity is a measure of the number and intricacy of the steps and sequences that constitute the process—the more steps, the more complex the process. Divergence is defined as the executional latitude, or variability, of those steps and sequences. As examples, Shostack develops, for two alternative florists, flowcharts that differ dramatically in their complexity and divergence. Although they perform equivalent tasks operationally, they can be very different from a marketing viewpoint and hence constitute separate products.

Figure 5.4 and Figure 5.5 show two florists, both capable of delivering a bouquet of flowers. For the first—and more traditional—florist, the process is linear and

FIGURE 5.4 Park Avenue Florist

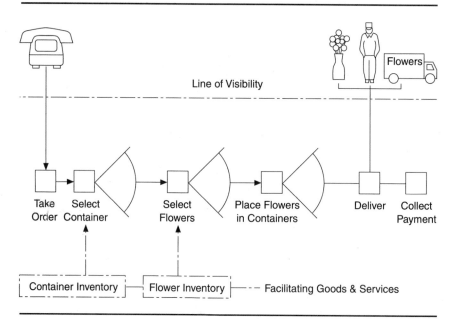

involves a limited number of steps. It has low complexity. However, the generation of bouquets under such a system calls for considerable discretion to be allowed for the florist at each stage—in the choice of vase, flowers, and display—and produces a heterogeneous output. The system therefore has high divergence. Interestingly, the flowchart tells us little about the interactive part of the process.

For the second florist in Figure 5.5, the process can be viewed as an attempt to "production-line the system," as discussed in Chapter 3. Because the objective is to de-skill the job, the system is designed to generate a limited number of standardized bouquets. The divergence of the system therefore is reduced, but, to achieve this, the complexity of the process is increased significantly.

Shostack argues that in developing products in the service sector, manipulation of complexity and divergence are two of the key choices. Reducing divergence creates uniformity, which can reduce costs, but it does so at the expense of increasing conformity and inflexibility in the system. On the other hand, increasing divergence creates flexibility in tailoring the experience to each customer, but it does so at increased expense. Reducing complexity is a specialization strategy often involving the unbundling of the different services offered.

PROCESS RE-ENGINEERING AND SERVICE BUSINESSES

Process re-engineering has become one of the hottest topics in consulting in the past three years. Firms are encouraged to re-engineer all their processes in order to improve efficiency and effectiveness. For service businesses, process re-engineering can be just as effective, providing the uniqueness of the service provider is understood.

Process re-engineering starts with a simple inconsistency in modern organizations. In order to preserve functional excellence, organizations are structured around

FIGURE 5.5   Florist Services: Alternative Design

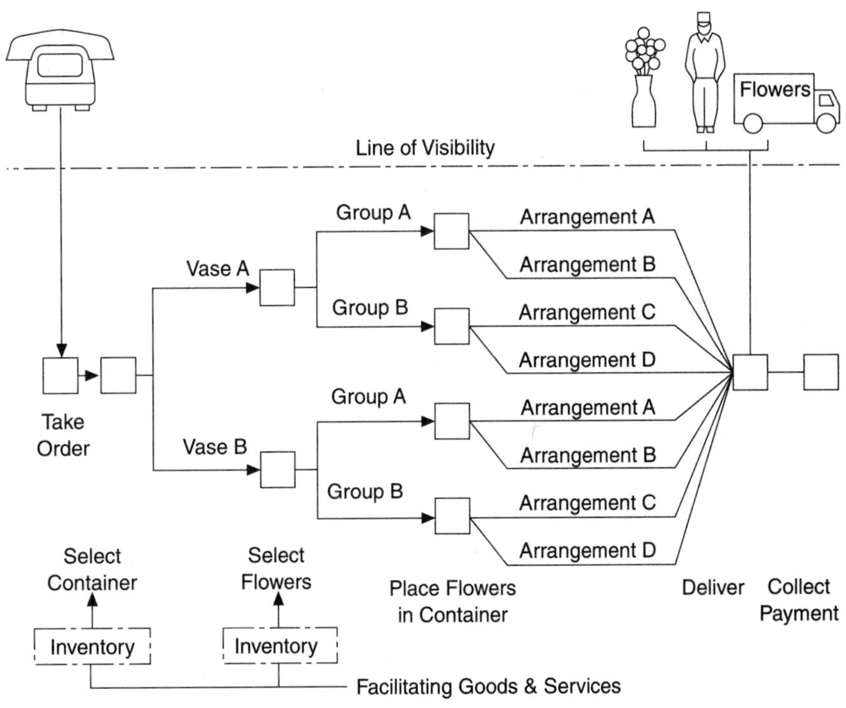

departments, and yet the organization actually runs on cross-functional processes. The new-product development process crosses the functional boundaries of research and development, marketing, manufacturing, logistics, and sales. Even the simple order-fulfillment process needs to coordinate sales, logistics, and manufacturing. It is a sad fact that, as a result, most processes are not designed, but just "happened." "We've always done it this way" is often the epitaph on the gravestone of a sinking process.

Re-engineering is a conceptually simple process, but is extremely difficult to implement. The existing processes, first of all, are defined as they actually happen, not as they are supposed to happen. This involves everyone in the organization helping to create a huge diagram of the processes, often called a "brown paper" because of the huge sheets of brown paper sometimes used. Once this has been done, teams highlight wasted steps and inefficiencies, and design new processes. The skill of the consultant is in creating the change climate necessary to get from the old model to the new one.

Such a process is analogous to many of the things already described in this chapter. Clearly, service processes are more difficult to re-design, as they involve or, at least, influence the consumer. If processes are "visible," then both marketing and operations must be involved in any re-design.

DESIGNING THE PHYSICAL ENVIRONMENT

Many services are delivered in physical environments, or sites, created by the services firm. The design of these environments therefore becomes part of the product design. As with everything else in services, there are two alternative perspectives: that of operations and that of marketing. The operations perspective asks what is needed by way of physical plant to house the operations process. The marketing perspective asks what will be the impact of the environment on the consumer.

THE OPERATIONS PERSPECTIVE

The translation of an operations flowchart into a physical design is relatively straightforward. For example, flowcharts like those in Figures 5.1 and 5.2 can be used to forecast the lines expected at various stations. The lengths of the lines and the physical equipment needed by each station then can be used to work out the square footage required. To a large extent, the logical sequencing of the stages defines the physical layout. All of this, of course, is constrained by the size and shape of the building available.

Following the chapter, Article 5.3 draws heavily on the total quality management tradition of fail-safe systems, but applies this to the service environment and systems. The authors suggest that many common failures caused by contact personnel and staff can be avoided by restructuring the physical environment. Failures on the part of the staff to deliver the basic service can be solved by creating physical aids. Cash drawer keys can be color-coded and change trays provided on the tops of the drawers to improve both the speed and accuracy of taking cash from a customer. The ways in which staff interact with customers also can be built into the systems and facilities. A mirror facing a telephone operator will produce a smiling voice; a request for bank tellers to record the color of their customers' eyes will result in eye contact. Finally, the facilities themselves can be made fail-safe. Uncomfortable chairs stop staff from sleeping and mirrors in strategic points remind staff to check their appearance.

Intriguingly, the same logic can be applied to making customers' behavior fail-safe. Checklists sent to customers can ensure that they are prepared before calling in

SERVICES IN ACTION 5.2

EMBASSY SUITES

Embassy Suites is a chain of about 100 hotels located across the United States. A subsidiary of the Holiday Corporation, which also owns Holiday Inns (among other chains), Embassy Suites was established in 1984 to take advantage of a perceived gap in the market.

Standard hotel rooms are configured with short-term, often one-night guests in mind. The basic service provided by the room is a place to sleep, and the assumption is that travelers will use their rooms only to go to bed.

It became clear that some travelers, business travelers in particular, required other facilities. For example, companies with nationwide links often had salespeople and executives traveling for extended periods and utilizing hotels for long stays. Hotels were being used for meetings, business dinners and lunches, banquets, displays and presentations, and full-scale conventions and trade fairs.

In these circumstances, businesspeople needed the combined facilities of boardroom, office, and temporary home. The basic bedroom could not provide these facilities. One possible answer was for the hotel to provide more extensive dining and conference facilities in its public areas, and many hotels did begin to develop large conference facilities. However, this modification was equally unsuitable when the group meeting consisted of perhaps two dozen or fewer people.

Another option was the development of the suite, an enlarged guest facility that included both the conventional bedroom and other rooms, such as a living room and a work area. Cooking and bar facilities also could be added. Each suite could be utilized for meeting or presentation space and still give the guest privacy.

At the outset of its operations in 1984, Embassy purchased the Phoenix-based Granada Royale Hometel chain of 24 hotels, all of which were all-suite hotels. Embassy then began developing itself as an all-suite chain, catering to business and other long-stay travelers. Configuring itself in this fashion, Embassy presented to both the customer and the employee an environment considerably different from that of the standard hotel.

---

for a service request. Door locks on airline lavatories that turn on lights ensure doors are locked and occupied signs are illuminated. In fast-food restaurants, strategically located tray return stands and trash receptacles remind customers to return their trays.

THE MARKETING PERSPECTIVE

The physical environment encompasses more than the housing for the operations process. The configuration of the room, the decor, the lighting—are all part of the "tangible clues" discussed previously. Many of these physical characteristics are seen by the consumer and therefore must be viewed as part of the product.

The study of how environments influence people provides the rationale for the field of environmental psychology. It is impossible, of course, to consider, within the context of this chapter, the whole of the literature on environmental psychology. In general, however, it can be summarized in a grossly simplified model:

SERVICES IN ACTION 5.3

CLUB MED

The average vacationer requires a number of various services in the course of his or her vacation. Everyone needs sleeping arrangements of some sort: be it a room, suite, or detached cottage. Everyone needs eating facilities and transportation, and individuals have various needs and wants for recreation and exercise facilities. Independent travelers are responsible for finding all of these services separately for themselves, and many enjoy doing so. Others, however, bent on having an enjoyable holiday with a minimum of effort, prefer having these services provided for them.

One way to satisfy the demands of this type of customer is to provide a considerable variety of services together in a package, using the concept of bundling. Club Med, the French-based resort chain, offers vacation packages where all facilities, accommodations, food, and recreation are combined over a specific period for a fixed price.

The vehicle for bundling holiday services is the Club Med holiday village. The basic format of the village is the same throughout Club Med's 100-plus sites: lodging, dining area, sports facilities, and activity areas are all grouped within easy walking distance, obviating the need for transport unless the customer wishes to go sightseeing. In this case, excursions are often arranged, also as part of the basic price.

Managing the environment of each Club Med village depends on the larger environment in which each village is located. While some facilities, such as swimming pools, may be nearly identical from one Club Med to another, other villages may find they have unique services to offer. Vacationers who come to Club Med in the Swiss Alps may be particularly interested in skiing, while those who go to seaside villages will be looking for beaches and water sports. Customers who choose villages in the Caribbean will have different expectations for their holiday from those who choose the Far East.

All of these different expectations can be met by designing the environment of each village in such a way that it reflects the likely demands of customers who come to that village. At the same time, the basic service bundle must be provid-

---

The physical characteristics of the environment generally are hypothesized to create or influence some internal state of the consumer, which in turn influences behavior within the setting or the behavioral intention toward it.

One of the most important intervening variables is orientation, or "way-finding." The physical characteristics of an operating environment provide consumers with the information they need to find their way, in the most general sense, around the environment. Consumers draw meaning from their setting; environmental design sends clear signals and can affect behavior radically, as recent studies of jail environments have shown. Jails with high levels of violence are able to reduce violence by manipulating the physical environment. Bright wall colors, such as orange, were replaced by pastels. Mirrors on sharp corners reduced congestion and barging.

Disorientation occurs when consumers no longer are able to derive clear signals from their environment. Complex operations can increase consumer fears about "getting lost," and poor legibility can lead to incomprehension or uncertainty about how a system actually works. These problems can be partially offset by consumer experience, but, for new customers, they are likely to lead to delays, anger, and frustration.[3]

Much way-finding literature focuses on the concept of control as the intervening variable. This is the concept, discussed in Chapter 2, suggesting that individuals wish to feel in control of the situations in which they find themselves. Clearly, the sense of "knowing where you are" is closely related to the idea of control and to the physical characteristics of the environment.

There is considerable variation in the nature of the hypothesized intervening variable and in the way in which the physical characteristics are conceptualized. One of the most commonly used theories in environmental psychology, the Mehrabian–Russell model proposes that three basic emotional states mediate behavior in environmental situations: pleasure/displeasure, arousal/nonarousal, and, to a lesser extent, dominance/submissiveness. In the researchers' development, the dominance dimension has been dropped to give a framework for environments, as shown in Figure 5.6.

Recent developments suggest that the dominance dimension is in some way a cognitive rather than an affective dimension. As such, it should be viewed as a precursor to the other dimensions, thereby influencing the extent to which it can explain behavioral intention.

Mehrabian and Russell conceptualize physical characteristics at a relatively abstract level, and they conceptualize the environment in terms of the load on the individual. They argue that load of the environment can be thought of in terms of its novelty, complexity, and spaciousness.

Some authors provide models that have no intervening emotional state. Others have directly related the presence and tempo of background music, for example, to the pace of shopping in the store and the amount of money spent by consumers. The results of the study are fascinating, in that they show that slow-tempo music can decelerate the pace at which people shop, slowing it from the level at which they shop without music and certainly slowing it from the level at which they shop with fast-tempo music. The amount of time spent shopping, in turn, is related to the amount of money spent. Slow-tempo music stores average $16,470 per hour, compared with $12,112 per hour for those with fast-tempo music.

FIGURE 5.6   The Mehrabian–Russell Model

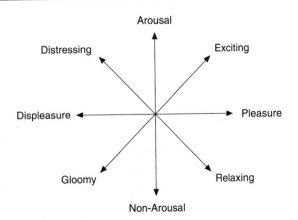

Perhaps most strikingly, the study measured whether consumers noticed the difference in music tempo. The results showed that there was no difference in the degree to which the music was noticed in the fast-tempo versus the slow-tempo manipulations and in the presence or absence of music manipulation. Thus, music, like many other environmental stimuli, can influence behavior without being noticed directly.

CHAPTER 5 READINGS

Article 5.1 shows how the physical environment can be used to influence consumers' perception of waiting time. The introduction of an electric newsboard into a bank lobby distracts customers from the waiting experience. Similarly, an electronic system can warn customers of the likely wait and hence influence their expectations. Article 5.2, by comparison, develops an integrative framework in which to understand the importance of physical surroundings on customers and employees. It takes the perspective that the physical environment must facilitate the achievement of organizational as well as marketing goals. Article 5.3 adapts the idea of poka-yoke, or fail-safe, methods from manufacturing to services in order to prevent human errors from becoming defects. They suggest that the actors in the system, the server and the customer, can be made to be fail-safe.

QUESTIONS

1. From the perspective of the consumer, prepare a flowchart for a service with which you are familiar. How do you think this flowchart would relate to a flowchart prepared by an operations manager in the same service?

2. How does the concept of blueprinting relate to script theory, which was described in Chapter 2?

3. How does blueprinting relate to the idea of isolating the technical core that was developed in Chapter 3? How could blueprints be used to improve efficiency in this way?

4. Using the classification scheme based on the Mehrabian–Russell model (exciting, relaxing, gloomy, distressing), classify a selection of familiar services. Explain why you think that the environment creates those states for each cell of the model.

5. Provide an example or examples of service firms that have moved the "line of visibility" to make part of the back office visible to the consumer and hence part of the servuction process.

6. Flowchart the consumer's experience with an air carrier service, such as Federal Express. What are the indicators of quality?

NOTES

[1]Theodore Levitt, "Marketing Intangible Products and Product Intangibles," *Harvard Business Review* (May–June, 1981): 94–102.

[2]G. Lynn Shostack, "Services Positioning through Structural Change," *Journal of Marketing* Vol. 51 (January 1987): 34–43.

[3]Richard E. Wener, "The Environmental Psychology of Service Encounters," in John A. Czepiel, Michael R. Solomon, and Carol F. Surprenant, eds., *The Service Encounter* (Lexington, MA: Lexington Books, an imprint of Macmillan, Inc., 1985), 101–112.

PRESCRIPTION FOR THE WAITING-IN-LINE BLUES
ENTERTAIN, ENLIGHTEN, AND ENGAGE

Karen L. Katz
Index Group Inc

Blaire M. Larson
Index Group Inc

Richard C. Larson
Massachusetts Institute of Technology

As consumers experience a greater squeeze on their time, even short waits seem longer than ever before. If firms can improve customers' perceptions of the time they spend waiting to be served, then customers will experience less frustration and may feel more satisfied with the service encounter. This paper examines customer perceptions of waiting in line and investigates methods for making waiting more tolerable.

Historically, service businesses interested in customer satisfaction have focused on hiring and training knowledgeable, pleasant servers. Today this approach is insufficient. Consumers not only demand quality, they also demand speed. They do not tolerate waiting in line for long periods of time. Firms must respond to this change if they wish to remain competitive. In this paper, we argue that improving customers' *perceptions* of the waiting experience can be as effective as reducing the actual length of the wait, and we focus on methods for managing perceptions.

WHY IS SPEED IMPORTANT TO CONSUMERS?

Americans today work longer, more varied hours than they have since World War II. The past decade has seen stagnating wages and drastic unemployment shifts. Consequently, many Americans have been forced to work overtime or hold second jobs in order to maintain middle-class lifestyles. The average work week has risen from 40.6 hours in 1973 to 47 hours a week in 1988.[1] During the same period, U.S. leisure time has declined from 26.2 hours to 16.6 hours a week.[2] Furthermore, as the service sector expands, the structure of the traditional forty-hour work week erodes. Today, weekends are workdays for many people, and twenty-four-hour service operations are commonplace. These changes have shifted consumer values. Since workers have fewer nonworking hours, they place a greater value on their free time—witness the increase in time-buying and time-saving services,[3] and the concept of "quality time."

As consumers experience a greater squeeze on their time, short waits seem longer and more wasteful to them than ever before. The lesson for managers, then, is that transactions should seem brief. There are two basic ways to approach that goal: through operations management and through perceptions management.

Source: Reprinted from "Prescription for the Waiting-in-Line Blues: Entertain, Enlighten, and Engage," by Karen L. Katz, Blaire M. Larson, and Richard C. Larson, *Sloan Management Review* (Winter 1991): 44–53, by permission of the publisher. Copyright 1991 by the Sloan Management Review Association. All rights reserved. Karen L. Katz and Blaire M. Larson are consultants at Index Group, Inc., Cambridge, Massachusetts. Richard C. Larson is Professor of Electrical Engineering and Computer Science at the Massachusetts Institute of Technology. This article is based on an MIT Sloan School of Management master's thesis written by Ms. Katz and Ms. Larson; Professor Larson was their advisor.

The logic behind perceptions management—the focus of this research—is that when it comes to customer satisfaction perception is reality. If customers think that they are satisfied, then they are satisfied. Similarly, if customers think that their wait was short enough, then it was short enough, regardless of how long it actually was. A major benefit of perceptions management is that it is often very inexpensive to implement.

PREVIOUS WORK IN QUEUE PSYCHOLOGY

Empirical research into the psychology of waiting dates back to at least 1955, when I. J. Hirsch et al. studied the effects of auditory and visual backgrounds on perceptions of duration. They asked subjects to replicate a tone heard in either a quiet or a noisy environment. Short durations tended to be overestimated, while long durations tended to be underestimated. In addition, subjects thought they heard the tone for a longer time in a quiet environment than in a noisy environment.[4]

A more recent study focused on the perceptions of commuters waiting for and traveling on a train in the Boston subway system. Arnold Barnett and Anthony Saponaro found that, while recent construction had not disturbed the trains' operations, it had disturbed perceptions. The authors concluded that riders experienced an asymmetry in perceptions: although they were quick to sense a decline in service quality, they were far slower to recognize when the problem had been corrected.[5]

David Maister has developed a theory of queue psychology that focuses on a combination of perceptions and expectations management.[6] In particular, he has defined a concept he calls the "First Law of Service":

$$Satisfaction = Perception - Expectation$$

According to Maister,

> If you expect a certain level of service, and perceive the service received to be higher, you will be a satisfied customer. . . . There are two main directions in which customer satisfaction with waits (and all other aspects of service) can be influenced: by working on what the customer expects and what the customer perceives.

Maister proposes eight principles that organizations can use to influence customers' satisfaction with waiting times:

□ Unoccupied time feels longer than occupied time.

□ Preprocess waits feel longer than in-process waits.

□ Anxiety makes waits seem longer.

□ Uncertain waits are longer than known, finite waits.

□ Unexplained waits are longer than explained waits.

□ Unfair waits are longer than equitable waits.

□ The more valuable the service, the longer people will wait.

□ Solo waiting feels longer than group waiting.

Richard Larson has observed that a key determinant in waiting satisfaction is the degree of "social justice." Even when waiting times are very short, customers may become infuriated if the system violates the first in, first out principle.[7] Larson's research has also uncovered instances where perceptions of queuing have influenced satisfaction. For example, for fast food customers, satisfaction in a single-queue system (such as Wendy's) may be higher than in a multi-queue chain (such as McDonald's)—even though customers wait longer in a single-queue system.[8]

Two of the world's foremost test sites for queuing psychology experiments are Disneyland and Disney World. Disney management realizes that "there's a real art to line management," and does its utmost to make the waiting experience less psychologically wearing.[9] Lines at Disney theme parks are always kept moving, even if only to dump customers into one of a series of preride waiting areas. A *Newsweek* reporter observed that, to influence customer expectations,

> the waiting times posted by each attraction are generously overestimated, so that one comes away mysteriously *grateful* for having hung around 20 minutes for a 58-second twirl in the Alice in Wonderland teacups.

Their effort appears to have paid off: even though Disney's theme park lines get longer each year, customer satisfaction, as measured by exit polls, continues to rise.

THE STUDY

In November 1988, the Bank of Boston was contemplating installing two different technologies intended to influence customers' waiting line experiences. The first, by a firm called SilentRadio, is an electronic newsboard. One of these had been installed at an off-premise ATM site, and managers considered it a great success. They were interested in determining if customers waiting for human tellers would respond well to a similar installation. The second, by Camtron Corporation, utilizes "electric eyes" at the entrance and exit of the queue channel to estimate line waits and provide statistics for improving staffing and service levels.

The bank's managers had many questions they wished to answer before investing further. They wondered if the equipment worked accurately, how employees would adapt to the equipment, and, most important, how customers would perceive the improvements. Our own interests focused primarily on the psychology of queuing. We believed that if we could improve customer satisfaction by managing perceptions in a real-world setting, then altering perceived waiting times would be further legitimized as a management tool.

The purpose of the study was to measure customer perceptions of waiting under different conditions. We tested the following hypotheses:

☐ As the perception of waiting time increases, customer satisfaction decreases.

☐ Increased distractions reduce the perception of waiting time, increase customer interest level, and may improve customer satisfaction.

☐ A wait where the length is known in advance is less stressful than an open-ended wait; such knowledge may improve customer satisfaction.

In addition, we explored differences between customers' perceptions of waiting and their actual waiting times, as well as what customers considered a "reasonable" waiting time.

METHODOLOGY

Our study site was the Bank of Boston's 60 State Street branch in downtown Boston. We gathered data on Wednesdays, Thursdays, and Fridays, when the branch had the heaviest traffic. In two of the three phases, our data-gathering days included the first or the fifteenth of the month, which are the most common paydays.

Two video cameras filmed customers as they entered the queue and as they left the queue to see a teller; the cameras recorded the time as they filmed. We and our research assistants then interviewed approximately one-third of the customers after they finished their transactions, and asked them about perceived waiting times. Later, when we identified each interviewed customer on the videotape, we were able to compare individual customers' perceptions with how long they actually waited. (To our knowledge, no earlier studies have matched individual perceptions to reality in this way. Most compare individuals' perceptions with *average* waiting periods.)

We also asked customers to rate their wait on three attributes: duration, boredom, and stress level. We asked an open-ended question of what a "reasonable" wait would be. We measured general satisfaction by asking customers to rate the branch's service overall, and on that day in particular.

The study took place in three phases. The first phase served as a control. In the second and third phases, we introduced variables that we hypothesized would alter the perceived waiting times and customer satisfaction levels. The second-phase variable was Silent-Radio—implemented as a large, black electronic board that displayed two lines of bright red print in "Times Square" fashion. Everyone waiting in line could see the board, which transmitted fifteen minutes of up-to-date news and information, interspersed with Bank of Boston ads. During phase three, we removed SilentRadio and introduced Camtron's digital clock feature. The clock, positioned at the entrance to the line, gave an estimate of how long the customer's wait would be.

During the newsboard and clock phases, we asked customers whether they had noticed the new installations and, if so, whether they had read them.

Altogether we conducted 324 personal interviews, which were distributed fairly evenly over the three phases. In analyzing them, we omitted responses from 14 newsboard-phase respondents who had not noticed the installation and from 33 electronic-clock phase respondents who had not noticed the time indicated.

RESULTS

Table 1 provides summary statistics for the 277 questionnaires included in our analysis.

ACTUAL WAITING TIMES

We determined actual waiting times by analyzing videotapes of customers entering and leaving the teller line. Figure 1 shows the distribution of actual waiting times for the 277 customers we interviewed. Nearly 60 percent of the customers we interviewed waited less than four minutes to be served, and only 3 percent waited over twelve minutes. On average, survey respondents waited in line 4.2 minutes before seeing a teller. Actual average waiting time for all customers was somewhat shorter because we did not interview customers who did not have to wait before being served.

PERCEIVED WAITING TIMES

We asked subjects, "How long do you think you waited in line today (in minutes)?" Figure 2 shows the distribution of perceived waiting times for the 277 customers we interviewed. On average, respondents thought they waited 5.1 minutes to see a teller. Twenty-five percent of respondents believed they had waited five minutes. In general, we observed perceptual "anchor points" at five-minute intervals.

TABLE 1   Summary Statistics for All Respondents

	Phase I (Control)	Phase II* (Board)	Phase III** (Clock)	Total
# Responses	116	89	72	277
Actual Wait				
0–4 minutes	75%	40%	56%	59%
4–12 minutes	19%	60%	44%	38%
> 12 minutes	6%	0%	0%	3%
Average actual wait (In minutes)	3.6	4.8	4.3	4.2
Perceived Wait				
Average perceived wait (In minutes)	4.7	6.0	4.6	5.1
Average overestimate (In minutes)	1.1	1.2	0.2	0.9
Average % overestimate	78%	43%	22%	52%
Reasonable Wait				
Average reasonable wait (In minutes)	5.8	5.9	6.1	5.9
Description of Time in Line (Averages on 1 to 10 scales):				
Short/long	2.9	3.4	3.3	3.2
Boring/interesting	3.9	5.4	3.8	4.3
Stressful/relaxing	6.9	6.6	6.8	6.7
Overall Satisfaction (Averages on 1 to 10 scales):				
Today	9.1	9.2	9.0	9.1
Usually	8.1	8.1	8.0	8.1

*Respondents who noticed the newsboard.

**Respondents who noticed the time on the clock.

As we had expected, people tended to overestimate the amount of time they spent waiting in line. Figure 3 shows the distribution of differences between perceived and actual waiting times. Differences between perceived and actual waiting times were approximately normally distributed, with a mean overestimation of just under one minute and a standard deviation of 2.5 minutes. Waits of less than one minute typically were not perceived to be waits at all.

REASONABLE WAITING TIMES

Customers had very different notions of how long a reasonable wait is. Many said that their concept of "reasonable" varied based on when they came into the bank; for example, they were willing to wait longest during lunchtime or on payday. Figure 4 shows the distribution of responses to the question about reasonable waiting times. On average, customers thought that 5.9 minutes was a reasonable amount of time to wait. However, as with perceived waiting time responses, descriptions of what constitutes a reasonable waiting time tended to anchor around five-minute intervals. More than 40 percent of respondents specified exactly five minutes.

DESCRIPTIONS OF TIME SPENT IN LINE

Subjects tended to fall into one of three groups, which we called "watchers," "impatients," and "neutrals." "Watchers" enjoyed observing people and events at the bank. "Impatients," on the other hand, could think of nothing more boring than waiting in line. "Neutrals," as their name indicates, fell somewhere in the middle.

INTEREST LEVEL When customers were asked to describe how interesting their wait was, on a 10-point scale, with 1 being the least interesting, the three most frequent responses were 1 (26%), 5 (22%), and 10 (11%). Figure 5 provides the distribution of responses to this question.

LENGTH OF TIME IN LINE When asked to describe the length of the wait on a 10-point scale (1 = short, 10 = long), most respondents described their waits as rela-

FIGURE 1   Distribution of Actual Waiting Times

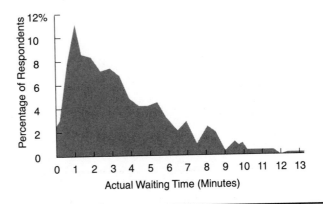

FIGURE 2   Distribution of Perceived Waiting Times

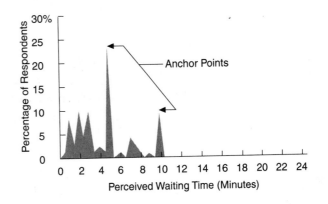

FIGURE 3   Perceived vs. Actual Waits

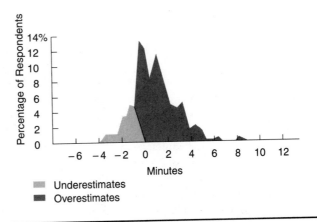

FIGURE 4   Distribution of Reasonable Waiting Times

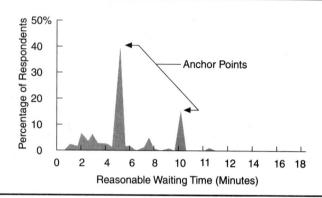

FIGURE 5   Overall Customer Interest Level

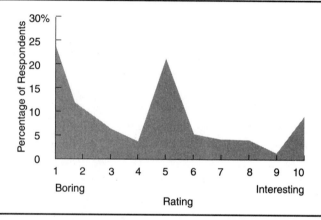

tively short. On average, customers rated the length of their wait as a 3.2 out of 10. Eighty-five percent rated the wait as 5 or lower.

ANXIETY LEVEL We asked customers to describe the waiting experience on a 10-point scale (1 = stressful, 10 = relaxing). The majority of respondents did not find waiting in line stressful. The average response to this question was 6.7, and 83 percent of subjects responded with a 5 or greater.

OVERALL CUSTOMER SATISFACTION

In general, we found that customers were very satisfied with the bank. Overall satisfaction "today" received a rating of 9.1, with 64 percent of respondents indicating their satisfaction was at 10. Overall satisfaction with the bank's usual service received a rating of 8.1, with 41 percent rating it at 10. As a result, it became difficult to detect effects of the installation of the electronic newsboard and clock on customer satisfaction; there simply was not much room for improvement.

CORRELATIONS

Correlations between the variables were as expected. Changes in actual waiting time tended to influence customer perceptions: as actual waiting times increased, overall customer satisfaction tended to decrease and stress levels tended to increase. In addition, as actual waiting times increased, both perceived waiting times and "reasonable" waiting times increased. Thus, customers recognized that they were waiting longer, but also indicated that they were *willing* to wait longer. This correlation suggests that customers' definitions of a reasonable wait may be based on the length of the current service encounter.

Similarly, increases in perceived waiting times were associated with decreases in satisfaction and with increases in stress levels and definitions of a reasonable wait.

Overall satisfaction with the service received on the day of the survey was correlated with descriptions of what constitutes a reasonable wait and with usual satisfaction. Customers who had a longer definition of a reasonable wait tended to be more satisfied than customers with a shorter definition. In addition, customers who were usually satisfied were more likely to be satisfied with the service on the survey date. Customers may have used their survey date satisfaction as a reference point for rating their usual satisfaction.

High interest levels and low stress levels were associated with high levels of customer satisfaction, both in general and on the survey date.

Customer satisfaction appeared to depend on how closely reality matched expectations. During the study, several customers commented that the teller lines were much shorter than usual, and thus that they were very satisfied.

COMPARISONS BETWEEN THE THREE PHASES

In order for us to make comparisons between the survey phases, actual waiting times needed to be equivalent across the three phases. We controlled for this by looking at two subgroups with comparable mean waiting times: those who waited less than four minutes, and those who waited between four and twelve minutes.

This division may have some operational significance. Since customers typically said they were willing to wait around five minutes, but tended to overestimate their waits by around one minute, they may actually be willing to wait only four minutes before the wait becomes "unreasonable."

IMPACT OF THE ELECTRONIC NEWSBOARD
Newsboard installation did not significantly affect perceived waiting times nor the amount by which respon-

dents overestimated their waits. Nor did it affect how customers rated the length of the wait on a 10-point scale.

However, the newsboard did make the time spent in line more palatable. Interest level, measured on a 10-point scale, increased from 3.9 to 5.0 for customers who waited less than four minutes, and from 3.8 to 5.6 for customers who waited four to twelve minutes. Figure 6 shows the effects of the electronic newsboard on customer interest levels.

When asked to describe the wait in line on the boring-to-interesting scale, many respondents said that the line was usually very boring, but having the newsboard to watch made it much more interesting. After the newsboard had been removed, many customers noticed it was gone and said they wished the bank would reinstall it. Respondents who spent a greater percentage of their time in line watching the newsboard were more interested and relaxed than other customers and tended to overestimate the length of their wait by a smaller amount.

In addition, overall satisfaction with the service received from the bank on the survey data increased from 9.3 to 9.5 for customers who waited less than four minutes and from 8.5 to 9.0 for customers who waited from four to twelve minutes when the newsboard was present. While the increase was not statistically significant, the trend was clearly in the hypothesized direction.

The newsboard had a noticeable physical effect on the line, as well. Normally, customers face the back of the person in front of them. This formation can have the symbolic effect of crowding, which is often linked to stress.[10] In order to view the electronic newsboard, customers had to either twist their heads or turn their

FIGURE 6   Effect of Newsboard on Customer Interest

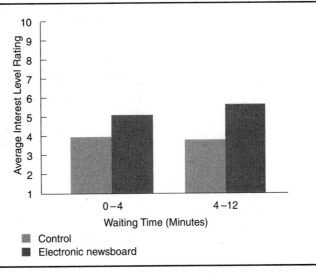

bodies so they stood shoulder to shoulder. In so doing, customers may have subconsciously felt less crowded.

In addition, customers tended to stand completely still with their arms at their sides while watching the newsboard. During other phases of the study, subjects were extremely fidgety; they constantly moved around and touched their faces and hair. We believe that a relaxed customer will have a more positive experience that a tense one.

IMPACT OF THE ELECTRONIC CLOCK Installation of the electronic clock appeared to influence perceived waiting times and overestimation of waiting times. Specifically, perceived waiting times were lower for clock-phase respondents than for control-phase respondents. Clock-phase respondents also tended to overestimate their wait by less than control-phase respondents. While these differences are on the borderline in terms of statistical significance, they are clearly in the hypothesized direction (see Figure 7).

There are two reasons why the clock may have improved the accuracy of perceived waiting times. Customers may have believed what the clock told them about their waiting time and thus adjusted their perceptions. Alternatively, the clock may have made the customers more aware of time, and thus more aware than usual of exactly how much time they spent in line.

We had hypothesized that a wait where the length is known in advance would be less stressful than an open-ended wait, so we hoped to find that the clock reduced stress levels. However, control-phase and clock-phase respondents did not rate their stress levels differently.

Nor did the clock improve customers' overall satisfaction with the service they received. This may be because the clock made respondents more aware of the time wasted standing in line.

We observed that customers liked to play "beat the clock" and felt as if they were "winning" if they spent less time in line than the clock had indicated that they would. Since the lock tended to overestimate waiting times by about one minute, most respondents did beat the clock; however, some customers became annoyed when their wait turned out to be longer than estimated. In addition, the balking rate appeared to increase during the electronic-clock phase: more people looked into the bank, saw the clock, and left (presumably because the wait was too long) than did so when the clock was not there.

FURTHER OBSERVATIONS

Throughout the electronic newsboard and clock phases, customers commented that service had improved dramatically over the last few weeks and that lines were much shorter than they had been in the past. Some even commented that they thought the improvements were due to the addition of new staff members (even though there were no additional staff at the time they made the comments!). These observations may have surfaced because the installation of the Camtron system affected teller productivity or because February was a slow month at the bank. Or these perceptions may have occurred simply because customers were being entertained and interviewed, and they felt that the bank cared about their concerns.

FIGURE 7   Effect of Clock on Time Perception

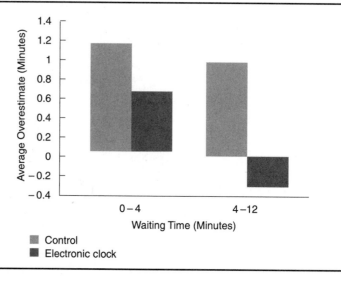

Control
Electronic clock

SUMMARY OF FINDINGS

In general, our findings supported our preliminary hypotheses. However, there were a couple of surprises. The major findings were as follows:

☐ In this setting, the average overestimate is about one minute, and waits of five minutes or less are considered reasonable.

☐ As perceptions of waiting time increase, customer satisfaction tends to decrease.

☐ Increased distractions make the waiting experience more interesting and tend to increase customer satisfaction.

☐ However, information on expected time in queue tends to improve the accuracy of customer perceptions of waiting but does not influence customer satisfaction.

MANAGEMENT IMPLICATIONS

Every line is different. Therefore, when attempting to manage customer perceptions of waiting, managers should consider the experience from the customer's point of view. Important issues include the following:

☐ **Fairness.** Can newcomers cut in front of customers who arrived before them, or is the line first come, first served?

☐ **Interest Level.** Are interesting things happening that the customer can watch?

☐ **Customer Attitudes.** What time pressures do customers face?

☐ **Environment.** Is waiting comfortable? Does the customer have to freeze in the cold or bake in the sun?

☐ **Value of Service.** How important is the result of the transaction to the customer? Could it easily be obtained elsewhere? Can the customer come back another time, or is the transaction urgent?

SUGGESTIONS

We have formulated ten suggestions for managers. Some are direct applications of our research results, while others are based on qualitative observations and previous work in the field of queue psychology.

1. **Do not overlook the effects of perceptions management: consumer concern about waiting is growing.** There is no limit to the frustration that waiting can cause. Cities are becoming more crowded, the work week is expanding, the economy is worsening, and people need more free time to deal with their frustrations. Now, more than ever, excel-

lent service is the key to success. Using perceptions management to improve customer satisfaction is only a tool, but it's a good tool.

2. **Determine the acceptable waiting time for your customers.** One minute of waiting in a bank will probably go unnoticed, whereas a minute on hold on the telephone can be infuriating. Determining an acceptable waiting period will help managers set operational objectives and, if those are met, will improve customer satisfaction.

3. **Install distractions that entertain and physically involve the customer. Keep the content light-hearted.** Piped-in music or live piano players may create a more pleasant atmosphere, but they do not effectively rope the customer into the activity. If the content of the distraction is light, fresh, and engaging, customers remain interested and entertained for many visits. Customers at the bank preferred horoscopes and tabloid headlines to more informative headline news.

The SilentRadio used in our study managed perceptions effectively. It was inexpensive, easy to operate, and did not disrupt normal operations. In addition, since most customers had to stand still to read the screen, they became physically involved with the distraction and did not mind waiting as much. Screen placement forced customers to turn slightly in order to read it; thus they stood shoulder to shoulder rather than front to back.

4. **Get customers out of line.** Whenever customers can be served without having to stand in line, both company and customer can benefit. For example, queues can be avoided by advance reservations, by mail or telephone service, or by better auto mation.

In banking, there are many ways to conduct transactions without using a teller—for example, direct deposit, ATMs, automatic loan payments, and check-cashing machines. The challenge is to increase customer awareness and use of these tools.

5. **Only make people conscious of time if they grossly overestimate waiting times.** There is a tradeoff between the accuracy of waiting time perceptions and the awareness of time. In the bank, perceptions were fairly close to reality, perhaps because customers had previous experience with the branch, or because the lines were short. For whatever reason, informing customers of their expected waiting time backfired. The clock made people more aware of the waiting time. It also appeared to increase balking rates.

However, there may be numerous instances in which information on expected waiting times is helpful. Airline passengers, for example, have no way of knowing when a plane sitting on the runway will take off unless they're told. In such cases, Maister's principle that an informed wait is better than an uninformed wait may still hold.

6. **Modify customer arrival behavior.** customers are often aware of peak times before they arrive at a service location, but they show up then anyway. If some customers could be convinced to arrive at other times, everyone would be better off. To achieve this, signs that list off-peak hours could be posted in stores and banks. Servers could also mention off-peak hours to customers who have waited an inordinate amount of time. In addition, incentives could be used to encourage off-peak arrivals.

7. **Keep resources not serving customers out of sight.** Several customers commented that they do not mind waiting so long as the tellers seem to be working as hard as they can. Customers tend to become annoyed if they see several unstaffed teller windows or if tellers are present but not serving customers. To address this perception, managers can adopt several policies:

   □ Keep idle employees out of view.

   □ Conduct activities that do not involve customer interactions out of the customer's sight.

   □ Staff stations closest to the exit point of the queue first. This practice creates a better first impression for the customer.

   □ Keep unused physical capacity out of view (e.g., portable cash registers for the Christmas season).

8. **Segment customers by personality types.** The three types of customers we observed—watchers, impatients, and neutrals—want different types of service from the bank. Watchers find the bustle of the bank entertaining and prefer a friendly teller with a smile to a shorter line. The impatient group is more apt to emphasize the length of the queue in their definition of overall satisfaction.

   The needs of the "impatients" can be met through innovative products, services, and educational programs that either avoid or reduce the waiting experience. The airline and hotel industries, for example, have developed club memberships that provide express check-in and check-out policies. Some retailers satisfy convenience-seeking consumers by creating express check-out cashier lines.

The emergence of convenience-oriented businesses proves that people are willing to pay more for services that save them time.[11]

9. **Adopt a long-term perspective.** In our research, respondents rated their overall satisfaction significantly lower on a historical basis than on the survey date itself. And, although daily satisfaction improved as the study progressed, historical satisfaction did not. It evidently takes a tremendous number of "good days" before customers' historical opinions change. Managers must take a long-term approach when attempting to improve perceptions.

10. **Never underestimate the power of a friendly server.** Although waiting is an issue worth addressing, managers should not lose perspective. Servers should continually be trained and rewarded for good service, since their efforts can overcome many negative effects of waiting.

REFERENCES

This work was supported in part by the National Science Foundation, Grant No. SES 8709811.

1. "More Time Spent Winning Bread, Less Enjoying It," *Boston Globe*, 16 January 1989, p. 1.

2. J. Richard, "Out of Time," *New York Times*, 28 November 1988, Sec. L., p. A25.

3. C. L. Anderson, "Selling Time: Emerging Trends in the Consumer Service Industries" (Cambridge, Massachusetts: MIT Sloan School of Management, Master's Thesis, May 1988).

4. I. J. Hirsch et al., "The Effects of Auditory and Visual Background on Apparent Duration," *American Journal of Psychology* 69 (December 1956): 561–574.

5. A. Barnett and A. Saponaro, "The Parable of the Red Line," *Interfaces* 15 (March–April 1985): 33–39.

6. D. H. Maister, "The Psychology of Waiting in Lines" (Boston: Harvard Business School Note 9–684–064, Rev. May 1984), pp. 2–3.

7. R. C. Larson, "Perspectives on Queues: Social Justice and the Psychology of Queuing," *Operations Research* 35 (November–December 1987): 895–905.

8. Several studies have examined the concept of the "time budget": How do consumers choose among numerous activities, given the constraint of limited available time? An excellent review of this literature is provided by M. Venkatesan and B. B. Anderson, "Time Budgets and Consumer Services," in *Service Marketing in a Changing Environment*, ed. T. M. Block et al. (Chicago: Proceedings Series, 1985), pp. 52–55.

9. C. Leerhsen, "How Disney Does It," *Newsweek*, 3 April 1989, p. 52.

10. B. Schwartz, *Queuing and Waiting* (Chicago, Illinois: University of Chicago Press, 1975), pp. 177–178.

11. Anderson (May 1988).

ARTICLE 5.2

SERVICESCAPES

THE IMPACT OF PHYSICAL SURROUNDINGS ON CUSTOMERS AND EMPLOYEES

Mary Jo Bitner

Arizona State University

A typology of service organizations is presented and a conceptual framework is advanced for exploring the impact of physical surroundings on the behaviors of both customers and employees. The ability of the physical surroundings to facilitate achievement of organizational as well as marketing goals is explored. Literature from diverse disciplines provides theoretical grounding for the framework, which serves as a base for focused propositions. By examining the multiple strategic roles that physical surroundings can exert in service organizations, the author highlights key managerial and research implications.

The effect of atmospherics, or physical design and decor elements, on consumers and workers is recognized by managers and mentioned in virtually all marketing, retailing, and organizational behavior texts. Yet, particularly in marketing, there is a surprising lack of empirical research or theoretically based frameworks addressing the role of physical surroundings in consumption settings. Managers continually plan, build, change, and control an organization's physical surroundings, but frequently the impact of a specific design or design change on ultimate users of the facility is not fully understood.

The ability of the physical environment to influence behaviors and to create an image is particularly apparent for service businesses such as hotels, restaurants, professional offices, banks, retail stores, and hospitals (Baker 1987; Bitner 1986; Booms and Bitner 1982; Kotler 1973; Shostack 1977; Upah and Fulton 1985; Zeithaml, Parasuraman, and Berry 1985). Because the service generally is produced and consumed simultaneously, the consumer is "in the factory," often experiencing the total service within the firm's physical facility. The factory (or the place where the service is produced) cannot be hidden and may in fact have a strong impact on customers' perceptions of the service experience. Even before purchase, consumers commonly look for cues about the firm's capabilities and quality (Berry and Clark 1986; Shostack 1977). The physical environment is rich in such cues (Rapoport 1982) and may be very influential in communicating the firm's image and purpose to its customers. Research suggests that the physical setting may also influence the customer's ultimate satisfaction with the service (Bitner 1990; Harrell, Hutt, and Anderson 1980).

Interestingly, in service organizations the same physical setting that communicates with and influences customers may affect employees of the firm (Baker, Berry, and Parasuraman 1988). Research in organizational behavior suggests that the physical setting can influence employee satisfaction, productivity, and motivation (e.g., Becker 1981; Davis 1984; Steele 1986; Sundstrom and Altman 1989; Sundstrom and Sundstrom 1986; Wineman 1986). The customer is left out of that research stream, however, just as the employee typically is ignored in the limited atmospherics research in market-

SOURCE: Mary Jo Bitner, "Service scapes: The Impact of Physical Surroundings on Customers and Employees," *Journal of Marketing*, Vol. 56 (April 1992): 57–71. By permision of the American Marketing Association.

Mary Jo Bitner is Assistant Professor of Marketing, Arizona State University. The author acknowledges the support of the First Interstate Center for Services Marketing, Arizona State University, in conducting the research. The extensive assistance of Michael Hutt and the comments of Lawrence Crosby, Stephen Brown, Beth Walker, and Susan Kleine are gratefully acknowledged, as are the helpful suggestions of three anonymous *JM* reviewers.

ing (e.g., Donovan and Rossiter 1982; Kotler 1973; Milliman 1982, 1986). For example, in the Milliman experiments, music tempo was varied and the effect on a variety of consumer behaviors was measured; however, the effects on employee satisfaction and productivity were not explored. Because services generally are purchased and consumed simultaneously, and typically require direct human contact, customers and employees interact with each other within the organization's physical facility. Ideally, therefore, the organization's environment should support the needs and preferences of both service employees and customers simultaneously.

The purpose of this article is to take a first step toward integrating theories and empirical findings from diverse disciplines into a framework that describes how the built environment (i.e., the manmade, physical surroundings as opposed to the natural or social environment), or what is referred to here as the "servicescape," affects *both* consumers and employees in service organizations. First, a typology of service organizations is presented that illuminates important variations in form and usage of the servicescape. Next, a conceptual framework is offered for explaining environment–user relationships in service organizations, and specific research propositions are advanced. The framework is anchored in the environmental psychology research tradition and also draws together relevant literature in marketing, organizational behavior, human factors/ergonomics, and architecture. Finally, the linkages between the service organization typology and the framework are examined, and key managerial and research implications are discussed.

A TYPOLOGY OF SERVICESCAPES

"The way the physical setting is created in organizations has barely been tapped as a tangible organizational resource" (Becker 1981, p. 130). Management of the physical setting typically is viewed as tangential in comparison with other organizational variables that can motivate employees, such as pay scales, promotions, benefits, and supervisory relationships. Similarly, on the consumer side, variables such as pricing, advertising, added features, and special promotions are given much more attention than the physical setting as ways in which customers can be attracted to and/or satisfied by a firm's services. A clear implication of the model presented here is that the physical setting can aid or hinder the accomplishment of both internal organizational goals and external marketing goals.

As is true of any organizational or marketing variable, the importance of physical setting depends on the nature of the job and the nature of the consumption experience. The position advanced here is that the phys-

ical surroundings are, *in general,* more important in service settings because customers as well as employees often experience the firm's facility. However, not all service firms and industries are alike (Lovelock 1983; Schmenner 1986), nor do they face the same strategic issues in planning and designing their servicescapes. Figure 1 is a typology categorizing service organizations on two dimensions that capture important differences in the management of the servicescape. Firms that share a cell within the matrix face similar issues related to the design of their physical spaces.

The vertical dimension relates to *who* is performing actions within the servicescape—the customer, or the employee, or both. One extreme is represented by the "self-service" organization in which few if any employees are present and the level of customer activity is high. At the other extreme is the "remote service" where there is little or no customer involvement in the servicescape and sometimes even little employee involvement, such as in fully automated voice-messaging services. Note from Figure 1 that "interpersonal services" are positioned between the two extremes. In those organizations, both customers and employees are present and performing actions within the servicescape. The relative level of involvement of customers and employees determines whose needs should be consulted in the design of the environment. In interpersonal servicescapes, special consideration must be given to the effects of the physical environment on the nature and quality of the social interaction *between and among* customers and employees.

Whether customers, employees, or both are present within the servicescape also determines the types of objectives a firm might expect to accomplish through use of its physical environment. In self-service settings, the creative use of physical design could support particular positioning and segmentation strategies and enhance specific marketing objectives, such as customer satisfaction, and attraction. At the other extreme, for remote services, organizational objectives such as employee satisfaction, motivation, and operational efficiency could be the primary goals in physical setting design, because few customers would ever see or experience the firm's physical setting. For interpersonal services, both organizational and marketing objectives could potentially be targeted through careful design of the servicescape. Even marketing goals such as relationship building (Crosby, Evans, and Cowles 1990) could be influenced by the design of the physical setting.

The horizontal dimension of Figure 1 captures the complexity of the servicescape. Some service environments are very simple, with few elements, few spaces, and few forms. They are termed "lean" environments.

Ticketron outlets and Federal Express dropoff kiosks would qualify as lean environments, as both provide service from one simple structure. For lean servicescapes, design decisions are relatively straightforward, especially in self-service or remote service situations in which there is no interaction between customers and employees. Other servicescapes are very complicated, with many elements and many forms. They are termed "elaborate" environments. An example is a hospital with its many floors, rooms, sophisticated equipment, and complex variability in functions performed within the physical facility. In such an elaborate environment, the full range of marketing and organizational objectives theoretically can be approached through careful management of the servicescape. For example, a patient's hospital room can be designed to enhance patient comfort and satisfaction while simultaneously facilitating employee productivity. Figure 1 suggests that firms such as hospitals that are positioned in the elaborate interpersonal service cell face the most complex servicescape decisions.

CONCEPTUAL FRAMEWORK

Though the typology in Figure 1 highlights the relative complexity of environmental decisions across different types of service organizations, it does not explain what behaviors are influenced, or *why*, or how one would go about planning and designing an environment to achieve particular objectives. Figure 2 is a rich framework for addressing those questions and for exploring the role of physical environment in service organiza-

tions. The framework suggests that a variety of objective environmental factors are perceived by *both* customers and employees and that both groups may respond cognitively, emotionally, and physiologically to the environment. Those internal responses to the environment influence the behavior of individual customers and employees in the servicescape and affect social interactions between and among customers and employees. Though the model shares similarities with other models (e.g., Mehrabian and Russell 1974), it is unique in its breadth of synthesis (for example, Mehrabian and Russell focus on emotional responses only), the incorporation of *both* customers and employees and their interactions, and its application to commercial settings. In the following sections, each of the components of the framework is defined and developed. Attention centers first on the behaviors that may be influenced by the servicescape and then on the internal responses and the controllable dimensions that constitute the servicescape. Propositions based on the framework are highlighted, and implications for firms within specific cells of the service typology are discussed.

BEHAVIORS IN THE SERVICESCAPE

That human behavior is influenced by the physical setting in which it occurs is essentially a truism. Interestingly, however, until the 1960s psychologists largely ignored the effects of physical setting in their attempts to predict and explain behavior. Since that time, a large and steadily growing body of literature

FIGURE 1   Typology of Service Organizations Based on Variations in Form and Usage of the Servicescape

Types of Service Organizations Based on Who Performs Actions within the Servicescape	Physical Complexity of the Servicescape	
	Elaborate	Lean
Self-service (customer only)	Golf Land Surf 'n Splash	ATM Ticketron Post office kiosk Movie theater Express mail dropoff
Interpersonal services (both customer and employee)	Hotels Restaurants Health clinic Hospital Bank Airline School	Dry cleaner Hot dog stand Hair salon
Remote service (employee only)	Telephone company Insurance company Utility	Telephone mail order desk Automated voice-messaging-based services Many professional services

FIGURE 2   Framework for Understanding the Environment-User Relationships in Service Organizations

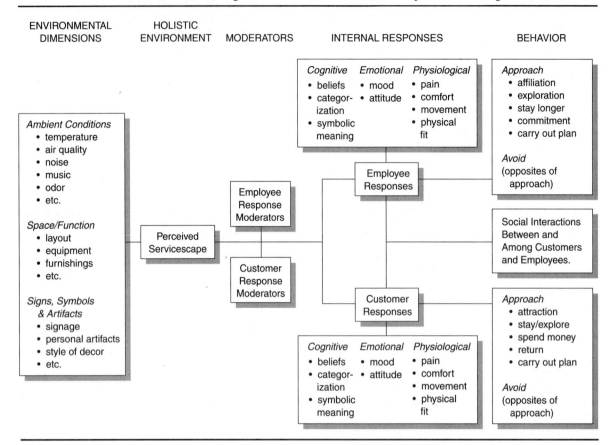

within the field of environmental psychology has addressed the relationships between human beings and their built environments (for reviews of environmental psychology, see Darley and Gilbert 1985; Holahan 1986; Russell and War 1982; Stokols and Altman 1987).[1] Here it is *assumed* that dimensions of the organization's physical surroundings influence important customer and employee behaviors. The types of behaviors that are influenced are identified and discussed next.

INDIVIDUAL BEHAVIORS

Environmental psychologists suggest that individuals react to places with two general, and opposite, forms of behavior: approach and avoidance (Mehrabian and

Russell 1974). Approach behaviors include all positive behaviors that might be directed at a particular place, such as desire to stay, explore, work, and affiliate (Mehrabian and Russell 1974). Avoidance behaviors reflect the opposite, in other words, a desire *not* to stay, explore; work, and affiliate. In a study of consumers in retail environments, Donovan and Rossiter (1982) found that approach behaviors in that setting (including shopping enjoyment, returning, attraction and friendliness toward others, spending money, time spent browsing, and exploration of the store) were influenced by perceptions of the environment. Milliman (1982, 1986) found that the tempo of background music can affect traffic flow and gross receipts in both supermarket and restaurant settings. In actual service settings, examples of environmental cues being used to change behavior are abundant. At one 7-11 store, the owners played "elevator music" to drive away a youthful market segment that was detracting from the store's image. Cinnamon roll bakeries commonly pump the wonderful fragrance of their freshly baked products out into mall traffic areas to entice customers into the store.

[1]Research on the built environment is only one aspect of environmental psychology. The field also encompasses the study of human beings and their relationships with the natural and social environment. What distinguishes environmental psychology from other areas of inquiry is its concern "with the reciprocal and interactive influences that take place between the thinking and behavior of an organism and the environment surrounding that organism" (Darley and Gilbert 1985, p. 949).

In addition to attracting or deterring entry, the servicescape can actually influence the degree of success consumers experience in executing their plans once inside (Darley and Gilbert 1985; Russell and Snodgrass 1987). Each individual comes to a particular service organization with a goal or purpose that may be aided or hindered by the setting. For example, assume that a traveler enters an airport and (1) is confused because he or she cannot find signage giving directions to the assigned gate and (2) is emotionally distressed because of crowds, poor acoustics, and high temperature. The traveler is unable to carry out the purpose for entering the environment, at least not very easily. Here the servicescape directly inhibits the accomplishment of the customer's goal. Similarly, physical surroundings and conditions could constrain an employee's ability to do his or her work and thereby detract from the purpose for being in the servicescape.

Clearly, firms want to encourage approach behaviors and the ability of customers and employees to carry out their plans while at the same time discouraging avoidance behaviors. As Figure 2 shows, the approach/avoidance behaviors of employees and customers are determined largely by individual internal responses (cognitive, emotional, and physiological) to the environment. The three types of internal responses are discussed in greater detail subsequently. The basic assumption is that positive (negative) internal responses lead to approach (avoidance) behaviors.

P$_1$: Positive (negative) internal responses to the servicescape lead to approach (avoidance) behaviors.

   a. For employees, approach includes such behaviors as affiliation, exploration, staying longer, expressions of commitment, and carrying out the purpose for being in the organization. Avoidance is represented by the opposite behaviors.

   b. For customers, approach includes such behaviors as coming in, staying, spending money, loyalty, and carrying out the purpose for being in the organization. Avoidance is represented by the opposite behaviors.

SOCIAL INTERACTIONS

In addition to its effects on their individual behaviors, the servicescape influences the nature and quality of customer and employee interactions, most directly in interpersonal services. Bennett and Bennett (1970) state that "all social interaction is affected by the physical container in which it occurs." They go on to suggest that the physical container affects the nature of social interaction in terms of the duration of interaction and the actual progression of events. In many service situations, a firm may want to ensure a particular progression of events (i.e., a "standard script") and limit the duration of the service. Forgas (1979) suggests that environmental variables such as propinquity, seating arrangements, size, and flexibility can define the possibilities and limits of social episodes, such as those between and among customers and employees. He also suggests that physical environments represent a subset of social rules, conventions, and expectations in force in a given behavior setting, serving to define the nature of social interaction. In developing the concept of behavior settings, Barker (1968) implies that recurring social behavior patterns are associated with particular physical settings and that when people encounter typical settings, their social behaviors can be predicted.

Empirical studies confirm the impact of physical setting on the nature of social interaction. Behaviors such as small group interaction, friendship formation, participation, aggression, withdrawal, and helping have all been shown to be influenced by environmental conditions (Holahan 1982). Similarly, in studies of workplace design, researchers have found that communication patterns, group cohesion, and the formation of friendships and small groups can be influenced by the physical setting (Sundstrom and Sundstrom 1986, Part III). By implication, those findings suggest that the servicescape influences the nature of social interactions between and among customers and employees.

Examples are again abundant in actual service settings. Even casual observation of a Club Med facility confirms that the highly complex setting is designed to encourage social interaction among and between guests and employees. Seating arrangements and the food preparation process at Benihana restaurants similarly encourage interactions among total strangers, as well as contact between patrons and the Japanese chef who prepares their meals in full view. In most airports, in contrast, research suggests that the arrangement of seating typically *discourages* comfortable conversation among travelers and their companions (Sommer 1974).

One of the challenges in designing environments to enhance individual approach behaviors and encourage the appropriate social interactions is that optimal design for one person or group may not be the optimal design for others. Research in a bank setting suggests, for example, that employees and customers have different needs and desires for their physical surroundings (Baker, Berry, and Parasuraman 1988). Similarly, an environment that is conducive to an employee's individual work needs may not enhance the employee's ability to converse and interact interpersonally with customers.

P₂: For interpersonal services, positive (negative) internal responses to the servicescape enhance (detract from) the nature and quality of social interactions between and among customers and employees.

P₃: Optimal design for encouraging employee (customer) approach behavior may be incompatible with the design required to meet customer (employee) needs and/or facilitate positive employee–customer interactions.

SERVICE TYPOLOGY AND BEHAVIOR

The research tradition in environmental psychology strongly suggests that the physical environment can influence behaviors in several ways. Therefore the first step in the purposeful design of the servicescape is to identify desirable customer and/or employee behaviors and the strategic goals that the organization hopes to advance through its physical facility. For example, in designing their corporate headquarters offices, Scandinavian Airline Systems first identified particular goals that it wanted to achieve, among them teamwork and open and frequent communication among managers. The employee behaviors associated with those goals were identified and architects were commissioned to propose designs that would be conducive to the behaviors and ultimately support the strategic goals.

The typology (Figure 1) provides a structure for isolating the relevant behavioral issues. Self-service firms will be most interested in predicting and understanding *customer* behaviors (e.g., coming in, exploration, staying) in the physical setting and the potential achievement of marketing objectives such as customer attraction, satisfaction, and retention. In contrast, firms that operate remote services will focus on *employee* behaviors (e.g., productivity, affiliation with coworkers) and the achievement of organizational goals such as teamwork, productivity, and innovation. Organizations that are positioned in the interpersonal service cell will be concerned with both customer and employee behaviors, as well as the effects of physical setting on the *interactions* between and among customers and employees. There the strategist must understand the plans and goals of all participants and anticipate compatibility dilemmas in designing the servicescape. Once behaviors most likely to be influenced by the servicescape are identified, challenging questions emerge: What internal responses (e.g., feelings, beliefs) will lead to the desired behaviors and

how should the environment be configured to bring about such responses? The next two sections address those questions.

INTERNAL RESPONSES TO THE SERVICESCAPE

One can infer from the environmental psychology literature that employees and customers in service firms respond to dimensions of their physical surroundings cognitively, emotionally, and physiologically, and that those responses are what influence their behaviors in the environment. Hence the perceived servicescape does not directly *cause* people to behave in certain ways. As Figure 2 shows, perceptions of the servicescape lead to certain emotions, beliefs, and physiological sensations which in turn influence behaviors. Behaviors are thus mediated by a person's internal responses to the place. Though the internal responses (cognitive, emotional, and physiological) are discussed independently here, they are clearly interdependent. For example, a person's beliefs about a place, a cognitive response, may well influence emotional response to the place and vice versa.

ENVIRONMENT AND COGNITION

As shown in Figure 2, the perceived servicescape may elicit cognitive responses (Golledge 1987; Kaplan and Kaplan 1982; Rapoport 1982), influencing people's beliefs about a place and their beliefs about the people and products found in that place. In that sense, the environment can be viewed as a form of nonverbal communication (Broadbent, Bunt, and Jencks 1980; Rapoport 1982), imparting meaning through what Ruesch and Kees (1956) called "object language." For example, particular environmental cues such as the type of office furniture and decor and the apparel worn by a lawyer may influence a potential client's beliefs about whether the lawyer is successful or not successful, expensive or not expensive, and trustworthy or not trustworthy. In a consumer study, variations in verbal descriptions of store atmospherics were found to alter beliefs about a product (perfume) sold in a store (Gardner and Siomkos 1986). Another study showed that a travel agent's office decor affected customer attributions for the travel agent's behavior (Bitner 1990). Variations in environmental cues may also affect *employee's* beliefs. For example, office size and type of furnishings may affect an employee's beliefs about the importance of his or her function within the firm in relation to other employees. In all of those cases, perceptions of the servicescape influence beliefs about the environment itself, but also appear to affect beliefs about other, seemingly unrelated, service attributes.

In other cases, perceptions of the servicescape may simply help people to distinguish a firm by influencing how it is categorized. Categorization is the process by which people assign a label to an object; when people see a feathered animal flying through the air, they categorize it as a "bird" and not a "fish" (Loken and Ward 1990; Mervis and Rosch 1981). Similarly, the overall perception of the servicescape enables the consumer or employee to categorize the firm mentally. For example, research shows that in the restaurant industry a particular configuration of environmental cues suggests "fast food" whereas another configuration suggests "elegant sit-down restaurant" (Ward, Bitner, and Barnes 1992). In such situations, environmental cues serve as a mnemonic or shortcut device enabling customers to categorize and distinguish among types of restaurants.

Because services are relatively intangible in comparison with most manufactured goods (Shostack 1977) and because many services are high in experience and credence attributes (Zeithaml 1981), they generally afford fewer intrinsic cues on which to form beliefs about service quality, particularly in initial purchase situations. Hence, in such situations consumers and employees tend to use extrinsic cues (such as the physical surroundings) to infer quality (Zeithaml 1988). In other words, people may use their beliefs about the servicescape as surrogate indicators in forming beliefs about service quality and other attributes of the service and/or the people who work in the organization.

> P$_4$: Perceptions of the servicescape and associated positive (negative) cognitions can lead to positive (negative) beliefs and attributions associated with the organization, its people, and its products.
>
> P$_5$: Perceptions of the servicescape influence how people categorize the organization; thus, the environment serves as a mnemonic in differentiating among firms.
>
> P$_6$: The servicescape's influence on beliefs, attributions, and categorization of the organization is stronger for inexperienced customers or new employees, and when few intrinsic cues are available on which to categorize or base beliefs.

ENVIRONMENT AND EMOTION

In addition to influencing cognitions, the perceived servicescape may elicit emotional responses that in turn influence behaviors. In a long stream of research, Mehrabian and Russell and their colleagues have pro-grammatically explored emotional responses to environments (e.g., Mehrabian and Russell 1974; Russell and Lanius 1984; Russell and Pratt 1980; Russell and Snodgrass 1987). Through their research they have concluded that the emotion-eliciting qualities of environments are captured by two dimensions: pleasure–displeasure and degree of arousal (i.e., amount of stimulation or excitement). In other words, any environment, whether natural or manmade, can be located in a two-dimensional space reflecting peoples' emotional response to the place. Research shows that emotional response measured on those dimensions can predict behaviors with respect to the environment. For example, environments that elicit feelings of pleasure are likely to be ones where people want to spend time and money (Donovan and Rossiter 1982; Mehrabian and Russell 1974), whereas unpleasant environments are avoided. Similarly, arousing environments are viewed positively unless the excitement is combined with unpleasantness (Mehrabian and Russell 1974). That is, unpleasant environments that are also high in arousal (lots of stimulation, noise, confusion) are particularly avoided. Hui and Bateson (1991) found that in the context of environmental crowding, increased perceptions of personal control are related positively to increased pleasure. Other environmental dimensions (e.g., clear signage, good ventilation, adequate space) may also increase perceptions of personal control.

Research also suggests that emotional responses to the environment may be transferred to people and/or objects within the environment (Maslow and Mintz 1956; Mintz 1956; Obermiller and Bitner 1984). In the Obermiller and Bitner study, respondents who viewed retail products in an emotionally pleasing environment evaluated the products more positively than did subjects who viewed the same products in an unpleasing environment. Hence, perceptions of the servicescape appear to have influenced seemingly unrelated feelings about the products.

Other researchers also have emphasized the emotion-eliciting or affective qualities of environments, suggesting that environments can be viewed as aesthetic stimuli capable of eliciting affect (Wohlwill 1976). In his work aimed at explaining the affective assessment of outdoor environments, Kaplan (1987) concluded that preference for or liking of a particular environment can be predicted by three environmental dimensions: complexity, mystery, and coherence. Complexity (visual richness, ornamentation, information rate) has been found consistently to increase emotional arousal, whereas coherence (order, clarity, unity) has been found to enhance positive evaluation (Nasar 1989). In addition, compatibility has been found to influence perceptions of order, and preference has been found to increase with compatibility (Nasar 1987). Compatibility in natural settings refers to how well a place blends in with its surroundings and is related inversely to contrasts (in color, texture, size, and shape) with the natural background; in urban settings compatibility results from replication of features such as materials, style, and overall shapes (Nasar 1989). Other research has shown that people respond positively to nature and prefer natural to man-made elements (Kaplan and Kaplan 1982), whereas the presence of what Nasar (1989) terms environmental "nuisances" has been found to reduce preference and perceptions of quality in urban settings. In urban settings such things as poles, wires, signs, and dilapidated buildings and vehicles are classified as nuisances. Research is needed to define the cues that would determine compatibility and the objects that would be classified as nuisances in service settings.

P$_7$: Customer and employee emotional responses to the servicescape can be captured by two dimensions, pleasure and arousal.

    a. Pleasure increases approach behaviors.

    b. Arousal, except when combined with unpleasantness, increases approach behaviors.

P$_8$: Perceptions of greater personal control in the servicescape increase pleasure.

P$_9$: Complexity in the servicescape increases emotional arousal.

P$_{10}$: Compatibility, the presence of natural elements, and the absence of environmental "nuisances" in the servicescape enhance pleasure.

P$_{11}$: Perceptions of the servicescape and associated positive (negative) emotions can lead to positive (negative) feelings associated with the organization, its people, and its products.

ENVIRONMENT AND PHYSIOLOGY

The perceived servicescape may also affect people in purely physiological ways. Noise that is too loud may cause physical discomfort, the temperature of a room may cause people to shiver or perspire, the air quality may make it difficult to breathe, and the glare of lighting may decrease ability to see and cause physical pain. All of those physical responses may in turn directly influence whether or not people stay in and enjoy a particular environment. For example, it is well known that the relative comfort of seating in a restaurant influences how long people stay. When they become uncomfort-

able (subconsciously or consciously) sitting on a hard surface in a fast food restaurant, most people leave within a predictable period of time. Similarly, environmental design and related physiological responses affect whether a person can perform his or her job function (e.g., Riley and Cochran 1984).

A vast amount of research in engineering and design has addressed human physiological responses to ambient conditions as well as physiological responses to equipment design (Bennett 1977; Oborne 1987; Sanders and McCormick 1987). Such research fits under the rubric of human factors design or ergonomics. Human factors research systematically applies relevant information about human capabilities and limitations to the design of things and procedures people use. The primary focus and application of the research has been within the military, in space programs, and in the design of computers, automobiles, and employee work stations. Such research has great potential for application in the design of commercial environments, taking into account the effects of design on both customers and employees who coexist and interact in the environment.

In addition to directly affecting behavior, physiological responses may influence seemingly unrelated beliefs and feelings about the place and the people there. Research has shown that when people are physically uncomfortable because of ambient temperature, their affective response to strangers is less positive than when they are physically comfortable (Griffitt 1970). Mehrabian and Russell (1974, ch. 4) review numerous studies of emotional reactions to sensory stimuli such as color, thermal conditions, light intensity, sound, and odors.

P$_{12}$: Positive (negative) physiological responses to the servicescape can result in positive (negative) beliefs and feelings associated with the organization, its people, and its products.

SERVICE TYPOLOGY AND INTERNAL RESPONSES

Combining the typology of servicescapes (Figure 1) with the conceptual understanding of the internal responses of customers and employees leads to insights for designing and managing the servicescape. For example, a self-service firm that wants to enhance customer approach behaviors such as attraction and staying longer can assess the environmental dimensions or cues that may elicit particular cognitive, emotional, or physiological responses. Attraction would most likely be facilitated by positive cognitive and emotional responses to the firm's exterior, whereas staying would depend more on positive emotional and physiological responses to the organization's interior space. In measuring the emotion-eliciting qualities of a particular servicescape, attention might be given to emotional dimensions identified by Mehrabian and Russell (pleasure–displeasure and degree of arousal) as well as to perceptions of control (Hui and Bateson 1991).

For interpersonal services, an effective servicescape design anticipates the likely responses of employees and customers to environmental conditions and creates the proper setting for the service encounter. In such cases, several goals and behaviors will be identified for both customers and employees as well as for their interactions. The desired behaviors then can be linked directly to their internal response counterparts. For example, what type of emotional response on the part of customers will be needed to encourage them to interact comfortably with each other as in the case of a Club Med? Or, in the case of a hospital, what beliefs, emotions, and physiological responses will encourage patients to get up and walk around the facility if that is a desired behavior for their recovery?

Because elaborate services (e.g., banks, hospitals, restaurants) consist of many forms and spaces, planning for compatibility and coherence is a particularly challenging task. In lean environments, coherence would be easier to achieve and measure and nuisances easier to identify and eliminate. Similarly, enhancing personal control is more straightforward in remote and self-service firms than in interpersonal service firms, where giving a sense of control to both employees and customers simultaneously may be difficult.

RESPONSE MODERATORS

In general, people respond to environments in the ways described here—cognitively, emotionally, physiologically—and their responses influence how they behave in the environment. As with all behavioral relationships, however, the strength and direction of the relation between variables is moderated by personal and situational factors. Here, and in Figure 2, those factors are referred to as "response moderators."

Studies have shown that individual personality traits can influence a person's reaction to his or her physical surroundings (Mehrabian and Russell 1974; Russell and Snodgrass 1987). Arousal-seeking is one such trait. Arousal-seekers enjoy and look for high levels of stimulation, whereas arousal-avoiders prefer lower levels of stimulation. Thus, an arousal-avoider who found him- or herself in a loud, bright disco with flashing neon might show strong dislike for the environment whereas an arousal-seeker would be very happy. In a related vein, Mehrabian (1977) proposed that some people are better screeners of environmental stimuli than others. Screeners of stimuli would be able to experience high levels of stimulation, but not be affected by it. In other words, they can ignore external environmental stimulation. Nonscreeners would be highly affected and might exhibit extreme responses even to low levels of stimulation.

An individual's response to an environment often depends on situational factors as well, such as his or her plan or purpose for being in the environment (Russell and Snodgrass 1987; Snodgrass, Russell, and Ward 1988). Though the individual differences in personality traits are *relatively* stable, plans and purposes for being in or seeking out a particular environment may vary from day to day or hour to hour. What the individual notices and remembers about the environment, as well as how he or she feels about it, is influenced by the purpose for being there. In a laboratory study, subjects' knowledge of environmental details and affective response to a place were found to be influenced by what they had planned to do while there—wait, explore, spy, or redecorate (Ward et al. 1988).

In addition to the plan or purpose, each individual enters an environment in a particular mood state (e.g., happy, depressed, lonely, anxious, excited, impatient). Such mood states are likely to affect as well as be differentially affected by variations in physical surroundings (see Gardner 1985). A person who is feeling anxious and fatigued after a frustrating day at work is likely to be affected differently by a highly arousing restaurant environment than he or she would be after a relaxing three-day weekend. Similarly, Harrell and Hutt (1976) suggest that people who are impatient or very time sensitive on entering a retail store are more affected by crowding than those who are patient and not sensitive to time factors.

What an individual expects to find in an environment also affects how the individual responds to the place. In general, when expectations are negatively disconfirmed, the person is likely to dislike the place. The opposite occurs when expectations are met or when the environment exceeds expectations. Expectations vary across individuals on the basis of their past experiences in the environment or in similar environments, as well as what they have heard or read about the place.

P_{13}: Personality traits (such as arousal-seeking tendencies and ability to screen environmental stimuli) moderate the relationship between the perceived servicescape and internal responses.

P[14]: Situational factors (such as expectations, momentary mood, plans and purposes for being in the servicescape) moderate the relationship between the perceived servicescape and internal responses.

DIMENSIONS OF THE SERVICESCAPE

A complex mix of environmental features constitute the servicescape and influence internal responses and behaviors. Specifically, the dimensions of the physical surroundings include all of the objective physical factors that can be controlled by the firm to enhance (or constrain) employee and customer actions. Those factors include an endless list of possibilities, such as lighting, color, signage, textures, quality of materials, style of furnishings, layout, wall decor, temperature, and so on. On the basis of a review of diverse literatures, three composite dimensions were identified as being particularly relevant to the present analysis: ambient conditions, spatial layout and functionality, and signs, symbols, and artifacts (see Figure 2). Because the base of research findings is context-specific and therefore not easily generalized, the effect of a single dimension on customers and employees is difficult to forecast. However, relevant dimensions of the servicescape can be isolated and general patterns can be explored.

Environmental psychologists contend that people respond to their environments holistically. That is, though individuals perceive discrete stimuli, it is the total configuration of stimuli that determines their responses to the environment (Bell, Fisher, and Loomis 1978; Holahan 1982; Ittelson et al. 1974). Hence, though the dimensions of the environment are defined independently here, it is important to recognize that they are perceived by employees and customers as a holistic pattern of interdependent stimuli. Note in Figure 2 that the holistic pattern is reflected in the perceived servicescape construct.

P[15]: Customers and employees perceive the environment holistically, as a composite of three dimensions: ambient conditions; spatial layout and functionality; signs, symbols, and artifacts. Each dimension may affect the overall perception independently and/or through its interactions with the other dimensions.

AMBIENT CONDITIONS

Several authors have identified ambient conditions as a factor that affects perceptions of and human responses to the environment (Baker 1987; Baker, Berry, and Parasuraman 1988; Becker 1981; Darley and Gilbert 1985; Russell and Snodgrass 1987; Sundstrom and Sundstrom 1986; Wineman 1982). Ambient conditions include background characteristics of the environment such as temperature, lighting, noise, music, and scent. As a general rule, ambient conditions affect the five senses. However, sometimes such dimensions may be totally imperceptible (gases, chemicals, infrasound), yet may have profound effects (Russell and Snodgrass 1987), particularly on employees who spend long hours in the environment.

A very limited number of empirical studies in consumer research confirm that ambient factors may influence customer responses. For example, in studies of restaurants and supermarkets, it has been illustrated that music tempo can affect pace of shopping, length of stay, and amount of money spent (Milliman 1982, 1986). In another study, familiarity of music played in a department store setting was found to affect shopper's perceptions of how long they spent shopping; when the music was unfamiliar to subjects, they believed they had spent more time shopping (Yalch and Spangenberg 1988). Hundreds of studies of the workplace spanning many decades have shown that lighting, temperature, noise, music, and color can all influence employee performance and job satisfaction (see Sundstrom and Sundstrom 1986, Part II, for a review).

P[16]: The effects of ambient conditions on the overall, holistic perception of the servicescape are especially noticeable when they are extreme (e.g., loud music, high temperature), when the customer or employee spends considerable time in the servicescape (e.g., hospital stay vs. visit to dry cleaner), and when they conflict with expectations (e.g., loud music in a law office).

SPATIAL LAYOUT AND FUNCTIONALITY

Because service encounter environments are purposeful environments (i.e., they exist to fulfill specific needs of consumers, often through the successful completion of employee actions), spatial layout and functionality of the physical surroundings are particularly important. Spatial layout refers to the ways in which machinery, equipment, and furnishings are arranged, the size and shape of those items, and the spatial relationships among them. Functionality refers to the ability of the same items to facilitate performance and the accomplishment of goals. Much of the empirical research in organizational behavior and psychology has illustrated effects of the spatial layout and functionality dimension, always from the employee's point of view (for reviews, see Davis 1984; Sundstrom and Sundstrom 1986; Wineman

1982, 1986). With the exception of some research on retail store layout, crowding (Harrell and Hutt 1976; Harrell, Hutt, and Anderson 1980; Hui and Bateson 1990, 1991), and use of orientation aids (e.g., Levine, Marchon, and Hanley 1984; Seidel 1983; Wener 1985), surprisingly little has been published about the effects of spatial layout and functionality on *customers* in commercial service settings. Logic suggests that spatial layout and functionality of the environment are highly salient to customers in self-service environments where they must perform on their own and cannot rely on employees to assist them. Similarly, if the tasks to be performed are very complex, efficiency of layout and functionality will be more important than when the tasks are mundane or simple. When either the employees or customers are under time pressure, they will also be highly conscious of the relative ease with which they can perform their tasks in the environment.

> P_{17}: The effects of spatial layout and functionality are particularly salient in self-service settings, when the tasks to be performed are complex, and when either the employee or customer is under time pressure.

SIGNS, SYMBOLS, AND ARTIFACTS

Many items in the physical environment serve as explicit or implicit signals that communicate about the place to its users (Becker 1977, 1981; Davis 1984; Wener 1985; Wineman 1982). Signs displayed on the exterior and interior of a structure are examples of explicit communicators. They can be used as labels (e.g., name of company, name of department), for directional purposes (e.g., entrances, exits), and to communicate rules of behavior (e.g., no smoking, children must be accompanied by an adult). Signage can play an important part in communicating firm image. Signs have even been found to reduce perceived crowding and stress in a jail lobby setting (Wener and Kaminoff 1982).

Other environmental objects may communicate less directly than signs, giving implicit cues to users about the meaning of the place and norms and expectations for behavior in the place. Quality of materials used in construction, artwork, presence of certificates and photographs on walls, floor coverings, and personal objects displayed in the environment can all communicate symbolic meaning and create an overall aesthetic impression. Restaurant managers, for example, know that white table cloths and subdued lighting symbolically convey full service and relatively high prices, whereas counter service, plastic furnishings, and bright lighting symbolize the opposite. In office environments, certain cues such as desk size and placement symbolize status and may be used to reinforce professional image (Davis 1984; McCaskey 1979; Peters 1978; Pfeffer 1981; Sundstrom and Sundstrom 1986). Studies of faculty office design indicate that desk placement, presence of diplomas on the wall, and tidiness of the office can influence students' beliefs about the person occupying the office (Campbell 1979; Morrow and McElroy 1981). In another study of faculty offices, certain environmental cues were found to be symbolically associated with personality traits of the faculty member believed to occupy the office (Ward, Bitner, and Gossett 1989). Such symbolic and aesthetic communication is extremely complex—it may be intentionally conveyed or it may be accidental, it may be subject to multiple interpretations, and it may have intended and unintended consequences (Becker 1977; Davis 1984).

> P_{18}: Signs, symbols, and artifacts are particularly important in forming first impressions, for communicating new service concepts, for repositioning a service, and in highly competitive industries where customers are looking for cues to differentiate the organization.

SERVICE TYPOLOGY AND ENVIRONMENTAL DIMENSIONS

In a classic study, Whyte (1980) observed human activity in public spaces and found that even subtle changes in design (e.g., adding plants and flowers, providing comfortable perches) led to a rather dramatic increase in activity and utilization. Similar results might be achieved by examining the direction and flow of activities in a particular servicescape. For example, changes in the layout and furnishings of the service facility can be made to speed the flow of transactions, encourage particular forms of interaction between and among customers and employees, or provide opportunities for customers to linger.

The importance of particular environmental dimensions is likely to vary across the typology of service organizations (Figure 1). For example, for self-service situations such as Ticketron facilities, ATMs, or Golf Land, the spatial layout and functionality dimension of the servicescape is extremely important. Clear directions and simple layout aid the customer in completing the transaction. At the other extreme, for remote services, ambient conditions assume more importance because employees tend to spend extended periods of time in the servicescape. Their physical comfort (temperature level, lighting) and responses to noise level and/or music affect productivity and overall satisfaction. Ambient conditions are similarly important to employee productivity in many interpersonal service businesses such as banks, hospitals, and hotels, but in those cases employee preferences must be balanced against customer needs. These are just a few of many possible examples.

Rather than a single element, it is ultimately the total configuration of environmental dimensions that defines the servicescape.

MANAGERIAL IMPLICATIONS

By isolating the impact of the servicescape on both customers and employees, the theoretical framework raises several challenging managerial implications. The overall conclusion is that through careful and creative management of the servicescape, firms may be able to contribute to the achievement of both external marketing goals and internal organizational goals. Many specific implications are discussed in preceding sections; some general strategic observations are offered here.

The typology of service organizations combined with the theoretical framework suggests that the physical environment may assume a variety of strategic roles in services marketing and management. First, the servicescape provides a visual metaphor for an organization's total offering. In other words, the dimensions of the servicescape act as a package, similar to a product's package, by conveying a total image and suggesting the potential usage and relative quality of the service (Solomon 1985). Yet, the care given to product package design is commonly lacking in service "package" design. Second, the servicescape can assume a facilitator role by either aiding or hindering the ability of customers and employees to carry out their respective activities. The floor plan, layout of equipment, and equipment design can have a major impact on the ability of users to complete their tasks and achieve their service goals. As a facilitator, the servicescape can also encourage and nurture particular forms of social interaction among and between employees and customers. Finally, the physical environment can serve as a differentiator in signaling the intended market segment, positioning the organization, and conveying distinctiveness from competitors. Each of the roles can be shaped to a significant degree to support important services marketing and management objectives of the organization.

The typology of service organizations (Figure 1) and the theoretical framework (Figure 2) help to direct managers to relevant issues and questions that should be asked in forming servicescape strategy around the basic roles. In addition, service organizations can gain strategic insights by examining how the servicescape is designed and managed in other industries that occupy the same cell in the typology and thus share similar characteristics.

To secure strategy advantages from the servicescape, the needs of ultimate users and the requirements of various functional units must be incorporated into environmental design decisions. The services marketing manager must be a strong advocate for using the servicescape as an element of the organization's strategy. Yet, in most organizations, environmental management is a separate function performed by persons with titles such as "environmental space manager," "facility planner," and "facility manager" (Becker 1981; Davis and Szigeti 1982). In many organizations, environmental decisions are made routinely without much attention to the impact on employee (or consumer) behavior (Becker 1981, p. 5).

A clear implication of the conceptual framework (Figure 2) is the need for cross-functional cooperation in decision making about service environments. "Facility planning and management . . . is a problem-solving activity that lies on the boundaries between architecture, interior-space planning and product design, organizational [and consumer] behavior, planning and environmental psychology" (Becker 1981, p. 7). As such, decisions about the physical facility can have an impact on human resource goals (e.g., worker retention, worker productivity), operations goals (e.g., efficiency, cost reduction), and marketing goals (e.g., consumer attraction, consumer satisfaction). Ideally, therefore, major changes in physical design or the planning of new environments should benefit from input from managers in all three areas, grounded in direct input from actual users—that is, employees and customers.

RESEARCH IMPLICATIONS

The conceptual framework and the servicescape typology suggest a wide range of research possibilities. Given the scarcity of research reported in the consumer behavior and marketing literature, there is a tremendous opportunity for theory building, empirical testing, development of better measures and methods, and application/replication of findings from other fields. Figure 2 and the preceding specific propositions provide numerous starting points for research. The propositions are purposefully general. Each one could be explored and expanded through empirical research. For example, given a specific commercial environment, how does a consumer's (or employee's) purpose for being there affect the person's response to the place? That question addresses the moderating effects of situational factors in determining environmental responses. Alternatively, one could start with a particular social interaction behavior such as teamwork among employees and work back through the framework to discover the types of internal responses and relevant environmental dimensions that would encourage such behavior. In addition to the basic research suggested by the framework and propositions, there is a need for research that will illuminate the differential importance and differential effects of physical surroundings across types of service industries such as those identified in Figure 1. Research opportunities also are available in exploring the ability of the physical environment to achieve particular objectives of the firm, and at what cost.

In many cases, extensive work in environmental psychology and organizational behavior (e.g., the stream of research by Russell and his colleagues and the review of workplace research by Sundstrom and Sundstrom 1986) can be applied and extended into the consumer service setting. In other cases, as in the effects of the environment on social interactions among customers and employees, the fact that there is relatively little empirical work in any field to draw on allows for true pioneering research to be done.

Given the complexity of environment/behavior relationships, a variety of methods will be appropriate (see Bechtel, Marans, and Michelson 1987). Direct observation of environmental conditions and customer and employee behaviors may be most appropriate in some cases—for example, in research on the effect of facility layout options on customer/employee interaction patterns. The application of direct observation methods has just recently gained acceptance in the marketing literature (e.g., Belk, Sherry, and Wallendorf 1988; Belk, Wallendorf, and Sherry 1989), but has not yet been applied to the observation of consumption environments (for an exception, see Sherry and McGrath 1989). Using observation methods, trained observers could make detailed accounts of current environmental conditions (i.e., environmental dimensions in Figure 2) and the actual behaviors of the occupants. Such observations could be extremely detailed and useful in an applied sense in redesigning a facility or in comparing environments. For theory development, direct observation could be the source of additional propositions.

Experimental methods and surveys also would be appropriate for assessing the impact of design dimensions on consumers and employees. Because of the expense involved in constructing actual environments,

some form of simulated environment (verbal descriptions, photos/slides, scale models, videos) could be used in experimental studies (see Bechtel, Marans, and Michelson 1987, ch. 5). The environmental psychology tradition has shown that simulated environments work well in achieving generalizable results (Nasar 1989). In designing experiments, the researcher should recall that people perceive environments holistically. It may be necessary to vary several environmental dimensions (e.g., artifacts, layout, color, tidiness) simultaneously to achieve an overall perception of the surroundings that will significantly influence behavior. User surveys are likely to be most appropriate in assessing basic customer/employee needs and preferences prior to the design of experimental simulations, and later for postdesign evaluation.

For both experiments and surveys, applicable response measures are needed. If one uses Figure 2 as a guide, appropriate measures of cognitive, emotional, and physiological response to environments are needed, as well as measures of relevant individual differences. Though several standardized measures already are available (e.g., Lemke et al. 1979; McKechnie 1974; Mehrabian 1977; Russell and Snodgrass 1987), most have not been applied to consumers in commercial settings, thus opening an opportunity for replication and assessment of generalizability. Other, more novel approaches to measuring customer and employee responses to environments also could be considered. For example, Ward, Bitner, and Gossett (1989) suggest an approach to measuring the symbolic meaning of service environments that adapts and extends ideas from research on object meaning (Kleine and Kernan 1988; Szalay and Deese 1978).

The typology, framework, and propositions provide direction for research on a topic that is incredibly rich, and invite application of the full range of consumer and organizational methods and theories to gain a better understanding of its impact.

REFERENCES

Baker, Julie (1987), "The Role of the Environment in Marketing Services: The Consumer Perspective," in *The Services Challenge: Integrating for Competitive Advantage*, John A. Czepiel, Carole A. Congram, and James Shanahan, eds. Chicago: American Marketing Association, 79–84.

———, Leonard L. Berry, and A. Parasuraman (1988), "The Marketing Impact of Branch Facility Design," *Journal of Retail Banking*, 10 (2), 33–42.

Barker, Roger G. (1968), *Ecological Psychology*. Stanford, CA: Stanford University Press.

Bechtel, Robert B., Robert W. Marans, and William Michelson (1987), *Methods in Environmental and Behavioral Research.* New York: Van Nostrand Reinhold Company, Inc.

Becker, Franklin D. (1977), *Housing Messages.* Stroudsburg, PA: Dowden, Hutchinson & Ross, Inc.

———— (1981), *Workspace.* New York: Praeger Publishers.

Belk, Russell W., John F. Sherry, Jr., and Melanie Wallendorf (1988), "A Naturalistic Inquiry into Buyer and Seller Behavior at a Swap Meet," *Journal of Consumer Research,* 14 (March), 449–470.

————, Melanie Wallendorf, and John F. Sherry, Jr. (1989), "The Sacred and the Profane in Consumer Behavior: Theodicy on the Odyssey," *Journal of Consumer Research,* 16 (June), 1–38.

Bell, Paul, J. D. Fisher, and R. J. Loomis (1978), *Environmental Psychology.* Philadelphia: W. B. Saunders Co.

Bennett, Corwin (1977), *Spaces for People, Human Factors in Design.* Englewood Cliffs, NJ: Prentice-Hall, Inc.

Bennett, David J. and Judith D. Bennett (1970), "Making the Scene," in *Social Psychology through Symbolic Interactionism,* G. Stone and H. Farberman, eds. Waltham, MA: Ginn-Blaisdell, 190–196.

Berry, Leonard L. and Terry Clark (1986), "Four Ways to Make Services More Tangible," *Business* (October–December), 53–54.

Bitner, Mary Jo (1986), "Consumer Responses to the Physical Environmental in Service Settings," in *Creativity in Services Marketing,* M. Venkatesan, Diane M. Schmalensee, and Claudia Marshall, eds. Chicago: American Marketing Association, 89–93.

———— (1990), "Evaluating Service Encounters: The Effects of Physical Surroundings and Employee Responses," *Journal of Marketing,* 54 (April), 69–82.

Booms, Bernard H. and Mary J. Bitner (1982), "Marketing Services by Managing the Environment," *Cornell Hotel and Restaurant Administration Quarterly,* 23 (May), 35–39.

Broadbent, Geoffrey, Richard Bunt, and Charles Jencks (1980), *Signs, Symbols and Architecture.* New York: John Wiley & Sons, Inc.

Campbell, David E. (1979), "Interior Office Design and Visitor Response," *Journal of Applied Psychology,* 64 (6), 648–653.

Crosby, Lawrence A., Kenneth R. Evans, and Deborah Cowles (1990), "Relationship Quality in Services Selling: An Interpersonal Influence Perspective," *Journal of Marketing,* 54 (July), 68–81.

Darley, John M. and Daniel T. Gilbert (1985), "Social Psychological Aspects of Environmental Psychology," in *Handbook of Social Psychology,* 3rd ed., Vol. II, Gardner Lindzey and Elliot Aronson, eds. New York: Random House, Inc., 949–991.

Davis, Gerald and Francoise Szigeti (1982), "Planning and Programming Offices: Determining User Requirements," *Environment and Behavior,* 14 (3), 302–304, 306–315.

Davis, Tim R. V. (1984), "The Influence of the Physical Environment in Offices," *Academy of Management Review,* 9 (2), 271–283.

Donovan, Robert and John Rossiter (1982), "Store Atmosphere: An Environmental Psychology Approach," *Journal of Retailing,* 58 (Spring), 34–57.

Forgas, Joseph P. (1979), *Social Episodes.* London: Academic Press, Inc.

Gardner, Meryl P. (1985), "Mood States and Consumer Behavior: A Critical Review," *Journal of Consumer Research,* 12 (December), 281–300.

———— and George J. Siomkos (1986), "Toward a Methodology for Assessing Effects of In-Store Atmospherics," *Advances in Consumer Research,* Vol. 13, Richard J. Lutz, ed. Ann Arbor, MI: Association for Consumer Research, 27–31.

Golledge, Reginald G. (1987), "Environmental Cognition," in *Handbook of Environmental Psychology,* Vol. I, Daniel Stokols and Irwin Altman, eds. New York: John Wiley & Sons, Inc., 131–174.

Griffitt, William (1970), "Environmental Effects on Interpersonal Affective Behavior: Ambient Effective Temperature and Attraction," *Journal of Personality and Social Psychology,* 15 (3), 240–244.

Harrell, Gilbert D. and Michael D. Hutt (1976), "Crowding in Retail Stores," *MSU Business Topics* (Winter), 33–39.

————, ————, and James C. Anderson (1980), "Path Analysis of Buyer Behavior under Conditions of Crowding," *Journal of Marketing Research,* 17 (February), 45–51.

Holahan, Charles J. (1982), *Environmental Psychology.* New York: Random House, Inc.

———— (1986), "Environmental Psychology," *Annual Review of Psychology,* 381–407.

Hui, Michael K. M. and John E. G. Bateson (1990), "Testing a Theory of Crowding in the Service Environment," *Advances in Consumer Research,* Vol. 17, Marvin E. Goldberg, Gerald Gorn, and Richard W. Pollay, eds. Ann Arbor, MI: Association for Consumer Research, 866–873.

———— and ———— (1991), "Perceived Control and the Effects of Crowding and Consumer Choice on the Service Experience," *Journal of Consumer Research,* 18 (2), 174–184.

Ittelson, William H., Harold M. Proshansky, Leanne G. Rivlin, and Gary H. Winkel (1974), *An Introduction to Environmental Psychology.* New York: Holt, Rinehart and Winston, Inc.

Kaplan, Stephen (1987), "Aesthetics, Affect, and Cognition," *Environment and Behavior,* 19 (January), 3–32.

Kleine, Robert E. and Jerome B. Kernan (1988), "Measuring the Meaning of Consumption Objects: An Empirical Investigation," *Advances in Consumer Research,* Vol. 15, Michael J. Houston, ed. Provo, UT: Association for Consumer Research, 498–504.

Kotler, Phillip (1973), "Atmospherics as a Marketing Tool," *Journal of Retailing,* 49 (4), 48–64.

Lemke, S., R. Moos, B. Mehren, and M. Ganvain (1979), *Multiphasic Environment Assessment Procedure (MEAP): Handbook for Users.* Palo Alto, CA: Social Ecology Laboratory.

Levine, Marvin, Iris Marchon, and Gerard Hanley (1984), "The Placement and Misplacement of You-Are-Here-Maps," *Environment and Behavior,* 16 (March), 139–157.

Loken, Barbara and James Ward (1990), "Alternative Approaches to Understanding the Determinants of Typicality," *Journal of Consumer Research,* 17 (September), 111–126.

Lovelock, Christopher H. (1983), "Classifying Services to Gain Strategic Insights," *Journal of Marketing,* 47 (Summer), 9–20.

Maslow, A. L. and N. L. Mintz (1956), "Effects of Esthetic Surroundings," *Journal of Psychology,* 1 (41), 247–254.

McCaskey, Michael B. (1979), "The Hidden Messages Managers Send," *Harvard Business Review,* 57 (November–December), 135–148.

McKechnie, G. E. (1974), *Manual for the Environmental Response Inventory.* Palo Alto, CA: Consulting Psychologists Press.

Mehrabian, Albert (1977), "Individual Differences in Stimulus Screening and Arousability," *Journal of Personality,* 45 (2), 237–250.

—— and James A. Russell (1974), *An Approach to Environmental Psychology.* Cambridge, MA: Massachusetts Institute of Technology.

Mervis, C. and E. Rosch (1981), "Categorization of Natural Objects," *Annual Review of Psychology,* M. R. Rosensweig and L. W. Porter, eds. Palo Alto, CA: Annual Reviews, Inc. 32, 89–115.

Milliman, Ronald (1982), "Using Background Music to Affect the Behavior of Supermarket Shoppers," *Journal of Marketing,* 46 (Summer), 86–91.

—— (1986), "The Influence of Background Music on the Behavior of Restaurant Patrons," *Journal of Consumer Research,* 13 (September), 286–289.

Mintz, Norbett L. (1956), "Effects of Esthetic Surroundings II: Prolonged and Repeated Experience in a 'Beautiful' and an 'Ugly' Room," *Journal of Psychology,* 41, 459–466.

Morrow, Paula C. and James C. McElroy (1981), "Interior Office Design and Visitor Response: A Constructive Replication," *Journal of Applied Psychology,* 66 (5), 646–650.

Nasar, Jack L. (1987), "Effect of Sign Complexity and Coherence on the Perceived Quality of Retail Scenes," *Journal of the American Planning Association,* 53 (4), 499–509.

—— (1989), "Perception, Cognition, and Evaluation of Urban Places," in *Public Places and Spaces,* Irwin Altman and Ervin H. Zube, eds. New York: Plenum Press, 31–56.

Obermiller, Carl and Mary Jo Bitner (1984), "Store Atmosphere: A Peripheral Cue for Product Evaluation," in *American Psychological Association Annual Conference Proceedings, Consumer Psychology Division,* David

C. Stewart, ed. American Psychological Association, 52–53.

Oborne, David J. (1987), *Ergonomics at Work,* 2nd ed. New York: John Wiley & Sons, Inc.

Peters, Thomas J. (1978), "Symbols, Patterns, and Settings: An Optimistic Case for Getting Things Done," *Organizational Dynamics,* 7 (Autumn), 3–23.

Pfeffer, Jeffrey (1981), "Management as Symbolic Action: The Creation and Maintenance of Organizational Paradigms," *Research in Organizational Behavior,* 3, 1–52.

Rapoport, Amos (1982), *The Meaning of the Built Environment.* Beverly Hills, CA: Sage Publications, Inc.

Riley, M. W. and D. J. Cochran (1984), "Dexterity Performance and Reduced Ambient Temperature," *Human Factors,* 26 (2), 207–214.

Ruesch, Jurgen and Weldon Kees (1956), *Nonverbal Communication.* Berkeley and Los Angeles: University of California Press.

Russell, James A. and U. F. Lanius (1984), "Adaptation Level and the Affective Appraisal of Environments," *Journal of Environmental Psychology,* 4 (2), 119–135.

—— and Geraldine Pratt (1980), "A Description of the Affective Quality Attributed to Environments," *Journal of Personality and Social Psychology,* 38 (2), 311–322.

—— and Jacalyn Snodgrass (1987), "Emotion and the Environment," in *Handbook of Environmental Psychology,* Vol. 1, Daniel Stokols and Irwin Altman, eds. New York: John Wiley & Sons, Inc., 245–281.

—— and Lawrence M. Ward (1982), "Environmental Psychology," *Annual Review of Psychology,* 651–688.

Sanders, Mark S. and Ernest J. McCormick (1987), *Human Factors in Engineering and Design.* New York: McGraw-Hill Book Company.

Schmenner, Roger W. (1986), "How Can Service Businesses Survive and Prosper?" *Sloan Management Review,* 27 (Spring), 21–32.

Seidel, A. (1983), "Way Finding in Public Space: The Dallas-Ft. Worth, U.S.A. Airport," in *Proceedings of the Fourteenth International Conference of the Environmental Design Research Association,* D. Anmeseo, J. Griffen, and J. Potter, eds. Lincoln, NB: Environmental Design Research Association.

Sherry, John F., Jr. and Mary Ann McGrath (1989), "Unpacking the Holiday Presence: A Comparative Ethnography of Two Gift Stores," in *Interpretive Consumer Behavior,* Elizabeth C. Hirschman, ed. Provo, UT: Association for Consumer Research, 148–167.

Shostack, G. Lynn (1977), "Breaking Free from Product Marketing," *Journal of Marketing,* 41 (April), 73–80.

Snodgrass, Jacalyn, James A. Russell, and Lawrence M. Ward (1988), "Planning, Mood and Place-Liking," in *Journal of Environmental Psychology,* 8 (3), 209–222.

Solomon, Michael R. (1985), "Packaging the Service Provider," *Services Industries Journal,* 5 (July), 64–71.

Sommer, R. (1974), *Tight Spaces: Hard Architecture and How to Humanize It.* Englewood Cliffs, NJ: Prentice-Hall, Inc.

Steele, Fritz (1986), *Making and Managing High-Quality Workplaces,* New York: Teachers College Press.

Stokols, Daniel and Irwin Altman (1987), *Handbook of Environmental Psychology.* New York: John Wiley & Sons, Inc.

Sundstrom, Eric and Irwin Altman (1989), "Physical Environments and Work-Group Effectiveness," *Research in Organizational Behavior,* 11, 175–209.

―――― and Mary Graehl-Sundstrom (1986), *Work Places.* Cambridge, UK: Cambridge University Press.

Szalay, Lorand B. and James Deese (1978), *Subjective Meaning and Culture: An Assessment through Word Associations.* Hillsdale, NJ: Lawrence Erlbaum Associates.

Upah, Gregory D. and James N. Fulton (1985), "Situation Creation in Services Marketing," in *The Service Encounter,* John Czepiel, Michael Solomon, and Carol Surprenant, eds. Lexington, MA: Lexington Books, 255–264.

Ward, James C., Mary Jo Bitner, and John Barnes (1992), "Measuring the Prototypicality and Meaning of Retail Environments," *Journal of Retailing,* forthcoming.

――――, ――――, and Dan Gossett (1989), "SEEM: Measuring the Meaning of Service Environments," in *Designing a Winning Service Strategy*, Mary Jo Bitner and Lawrence A. Crosby, eds. Chicago: American Marketing Association, 34–39.

Ward, Lawrence M., Jacalyn Snodgrass, Barry Chew, and James A. Russell (1988), "The Role of Plans in Cognitive and Affective Responses to Places," *Journal of Environmental Psychology,* 8 (1), 1–8.

Wener, Richard E. (1985), "The Environmental Psychology of Service Encounters," in *The Service Encounter,* John Czepiel, Michael Solomon, and Carol Surprenant, eds. Lexington, MA: Lexington Books, 101–112.

―――― and Robert Kaminoff (1982), "Improving Environmental Information: Effects of Signs on Perceived Crowding and Behavior," *Environment and Behavior,* 14 (6), 671–694.

Whyte, William H. (1980), *The Social Life of Small Urban Spaces.* Washington, DC: The Conservation Foundation.

Wineman, Jean D. (1982), "Office Design and Evaluation," *Environment and Behavior,* 14 (3), 271–298.

―――― (1986), Behavioral Issues in Office Design. New York: Van Nostrand Reinhold Co.

Wohlwill, Joachim F. (1976), "Environmental Aesthetics: The Environment as a Source of Affect," in *Human Behavior and Environment,* Vol. 1, Irwin Altman and Joachim F. Wohlwill, eds. New York: Plenum Press.

Yalch, Richard F. and Eric Spangenberg (1988), "An Environmental Psychological Study of Foreground and Background Music as Retail Atmospheric Factors," in *Efficiency and Effectiveness in Marketing, 1988 AMA Educators' Proceedings,* Gary Frazier et al., eds. Chicago: American Marketing Association, 106–110.

Zeithaml, Valarie (1981), "How Consumer Evaluation Processes Differ between Goods and Services," in *Marketing of Services,* James H. Donnelly and William R. George, eds. Chicago: American Marketing Association, 186–190.

―――― (1988), "Consumer Perceptions of Price, Quality, and Value: A Means–End Model and Synthesis of Evidence," *Journal of Marketing,* 52 (July), 2–22.

――――, A. Parasuraman, and Leonard L. Berry (1985), "Problems and Strategies in Services Marketing," *Journal of Marketing,* 49 (Spring), 33–46.

MAKE YOUR SERVICE FAIL-SAFE

Richard B. Chase
University of Southern California

Douglas M. Stewart

One of the most useful concepts of the TQM movement in manufacturing is the application of poka-yoke, or fail-safe, methods to prevent human errors from becoming defects in the end product. Here the authors argue that these methods apply equally well to services and provide a framework for systematically applying poka-yokes to service encounters. They suggest that actions of the system, the server, and the customer can be fail-safed, and provide numerous examples to stimulate service managers to think in fail-safe terms.

Total quality management (TQM) has become accepted practice in services. Concepts from TQM in manufacturing, such as benchmarking, diagnostic tools (fishbone diagrams, Pareto charts, and so on), and customer-driven design (through quality function deployment), have joined with such concepts as service guarantees and service recovery planning to drive the quality philosophies of many service firms. Nevertheless, there remains the monumental challenge of quality assurance when the goal is to achieve zero defects in the day-to-day provision of services. Our objective here is to suggest how another concept with proven success in manufacturing, fail-safing, can and should be applied systematically to services to achieve this goal.[1]

THE NATURE OF FAIL-SAFING

The idea of fail-safing is to prevent the inevitable mistake from turning into a defect. The late Shigeo Shingo (known as "Mr. Improvement" in Japan) articulated this basic concept. In his writings, Shingo gave examples of how manufacturing companies have set up their equipment and manual processes to prevent errors in parts counts, sequence of work performance, and product configurations. Shingo's concepts are seen as particular-

ly appropriate where full-scale automation is too costly or is otherwise impractical. According to Hall, "Simple fail-safe methods are the low-cost route to parts-per-million error rates."[2]

The objective of fail-safing is similar to what Taguchi methods have attempted in creating robust products and processes—that is, ensuring that they can withstand the effects of factors beyond the producer's control. We see two main differences between fail-safing and these methods. The first is the relative complexity of Taguchi methods compared to fail-safing: Taguchi methods rely heavily on sophisticated statistical techniques to set optimal product and process parameters. Fail-safing, by contrast, does not require that a specific value be put on process parameters. It requires only the ability to discriminate good from bad. As such, it is easier to apply to intangible service processes.

The second difference is more subtle, concerning the strategy taken by each approach in controlling the process. As mentioned, Taguchi methods strive to make the product or process resistant to factors beyond its control. Fail-safing, instead, governs factors *within* the producer's control and then strives to extend the scope of the control to outside factors.

POKA-YOKES AS MISTAKE-PROOFING

Central to Shingo's approach are inspection and poka-yokes (automatic devices or methods). Shingo defines

SOURCE: Richard B. Chase and Douglas M. Stewart, "Make Your Service Fail-Safe," *Sloan Management Review* (Spring 1994): 35–44.

Richard B. Chase is the Justin Dart Professor of Operations Management and Douglas M. Stewart is a doctoral candidate in operations management at the School of Business Administration, University of Southern California.

three categories of inspection, all of which should be done at the 100 percent level. In *successive checks*, the person in the next stage immediately feeds back information to the supplying operator to stop production and fix the error. In *self-inspection*, the operator inspects his or her own work. In *source inspection*, the operator inspects for mistakes that have not yet caused an error. These inspection practices shorten the feedback loop between when a mistake occurs and its detection and subsequent correction. Immediate feedback is essential for effective process control.

To facilitate the 100 percent inspection process, Shingo uses poka-yoke devices or procedures. Poka-yokes are either *warnings* that signal the existence of a problem or *controls* that stop production until the problem is resolved. The distinction between the two is that warning poka-yokes indicate only that a mistake has been made, while control poka-yokes will force the operator to correct the mistake before proceeding. For example, limit switches are commonly used to indicate when parts are improperly positioned on machines. A warning poka-yoke would be the lights connected to such switches to alert the worker to a misalignment. A control poka-yoke would be the direct connection of the switch to the machine's power source to shut down the machine automatically. (Control poka-yokes have the obvious advantage of being impossible to overlook or ignore.) Although many poka-yokes are equipment based, involving locking clamps, pressure sensors, part jigs, and switches, they can also be procedures, such as assembling kits of parts to ensure that the right number are used or checking lists to ensure that all design steps are followed.

Shingo further classifies his poka-yokes by three different methods of detecting errors. *Contact* methods rely on the part's physical dimensions to indicate improper dimensions, orientation, or placement. *Fixed value* methods signal that some known quantity of components is not available or has not been used. Finally, *motion step* methods require that some error-prone step in the process must be completed before an obvious step, such as removing the part from the machine, is performed. All of these detection methods can occur as either control or warning methods.[3]

Poka-yoke approaches differ from complex automated inspection systems in that they are designed to be very inexpensive, within the process, and used to stop one particular error each. Additional poka-yokes are added for each additional inspection. (Shingo notes that Toyota Motor's machines are equipped with an average of twelve poka-yokes each.[4])

FAIL-SAFING SERVICES

While Shingo's work was primarily production- and product-oriented, involving the manipulation of physical items, service fail-safing is an application of these same techniques (at least at the fundamental level) to service operations. There are two obvious differences between manufacturing and service operations that must be addressed in this new application. First, service fail-safing must account for the customer's activities as well as those of the producer. Customer errors can directly affect the service outcome and must be fail-safed if the service is to be defect-free. In fail-safing the production of a manufactured item, only the actions of the producer (or supplier) are controlled. Fail-safing a customer's actions takes into account only what happens after the customer takes possession of or leaves with the product and is often done for liability reasons, such as the "dead man's" levers on power mowers, which disengage power on the cutting blade of the operator releases the push handle.

Second, many services evolve through multiple forms of interaction between the service company and its customers, which often occur at different locations. Thus, fail-safe methods must be set up for interactions conducted directly or by phone, mail, or through standalone technology like an ATM. Of course, manufacturers confront the same issues in the service side of their business, but their deliverable is a physical product.

These differences lead us to focus on applying fail-safe principles to the front-office activities of service organizations. Of course, great improvements can be made by fail-safing the back-office activities as well (and we provide several examples). But we believe the really critical area is where the customer and the system interact. Here we find amazingly little in the way of design principles to make even the most basic encounters error-free. The back-office problem is much simpler—the customer isn't there—and hence it lends itself to the application of established fail-safe approaches from manufacturing.

CLASSIFYING SERVICE POKA-YOKES

There are already numerous examples of service poka-yokes that either have been suggested or are in use. Theodore Levitt, an early pioneer, suggested applying manufacturing approaches to services. Citing examples from the highly successful McDonald's of the 1960s, Levitt proposed using machinery and clever devices, akin to Shingo's poka-yokes, to create consistency in service delivery. He also hinted that the organization might even be able to exhibit some control over customer actions.[5]

What is missing from Levitt's work and the literature on services in general is a fail-safing framework that can be used to guide systematic poka-yoke development across a wide range of services. Hence, we propose that service poka-yokes be classified instead by the type of error they are designed to prevent.

Errors in services can be divided first into *server errors* and *customer errors*. Server errors can be further classified as errors in the task, the treatment, or the tangible aspects of service, while customer errors can be classified as errors in the preparation for the encounter, the encounter, or the resolution of the encounter (see Figure 1).

The "three T" breakdown is critical to our approach for fail-safing the server because it explicitly relates fail-safing actions to specific dimensions of service. A limitation of previous efforts to "engineer" services has been the failure to recognize that each of these facets can be addressed separately for improvement purposes. A widely used instrument (SERVQUAL) for measuring service quality identifies five critical dimensions of service: reliability, responsiveness, assurance, empathy, and tangibles.[6] Though valuable for marketing analysis, the definitions of the SERVQUAL dimensions tend to confound attitude and action and, hence, are of limited value in analyzing operations.[7]

While "the customer is always right," he or she is also frequently error-prone. In fact, research done by TARP, a service research firm, indicates that one-third of all customer complaints are related to problems caused by the customers themselves.[8] We do not present this finding as a way for management to justify poor service but, rather, to indicate that companies need to develop processes that eliminate the foul-ups leading to complaints. We need to find tools to help the customer do things right.

Unlike the server, the customer generally does not view the service as a continuous stream of encounters in which all necessary materials and knowledge are kept close at hand. For customers, there is preparation for the encounter, the encounter, and a resolution to the encounter. Nevertheless, because of the customers' integral role in the service, their actions should be fail-safed at each stage to ensure that the service works as designed.

Perhaps the best way to gain an understanding of what service poka-yokes are, and how they are used as process control, is through examples. Here we provide examples of each poka-yoke category. The common fea-

FIGURE 1   Poka-Yoke Classification

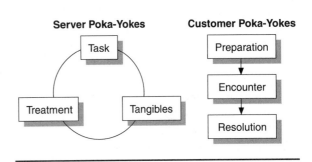

ture of each example is a built-in inspection process to either warn or prevent mistakes from becoming defects.

FAIL-SAFING THE SERVER

TASK POKA-YOKES Task errors are those in the service functions such as the repair shop not repairing the car properly or promptly. These include doing work:

☐ Incorrectly.

☐ Not requested.

☐ In the wrong order.

☐ Too slowly.

The many examples of poka-yoke devices to detect and avoid task errors include computer prompts to aid in technical discussions, strategically placed microphones to ensure that server's and customer's voices are audible, color-coded cash register keys, a change tray on top of the cash register, appropriate measuring and weighing tools (such as McDonald's French-fry scoop), and signaling devices. Sewell Cadillac and other similar facilities use color-coded tags or icons on car roofs to identify the customer's service adviser and order of arrival. The adviser can look out across the sea of cars and find the next car he or she should deal with.[9]

Due to the extreme cost of their errors, hospitals are heavy users of poka-yokes in their direct medical processes (though they seem less widely used in activities surrounding patient care, such as scheduling and billing). Trays for surgical instruments have indentations for each instrument, and all of the instruments for a given operation are nested in the tray so it is clear if the surgeon has not removed all instruments from the patient before closing the incision. Similarly, all gauze used during the operation is contained in a fixed number of small packages to facilitate counting the packages before closing. All material needed to insert a catheter is included in a kit, itself a poka-yoke because any unused item remaining in it, such as the syringe for inflating the catheter, signals an improper procedure or installation. On the medication cart, each patient's medication is prepackaged in the correct dosage before it is placed on the cart. If the nurse, after making rounds, has any remaining medication, a doctor must rectify the situation.

TREATMENT POKA-YOKES Treatment errors occur in the contact between the server and the customer, such as lack of courteous, professional behavior. Specific examples of this type include the failure to:

☐ Acknowledge the customer.

☐ Listen to the customer.

☐ React appropriately to the customer.

Standard treatment poka-yokes in particular contexts are signals, such as eye contact, to acknowledge a customer's presence in a restaurant, candy distributed before a plane takes off, and a bell on the shop door. A major hotel chain uses a novel poka-yoke to fail-safe acknowledging a guest's repeat business. When the bellman greets an arriving guest to bring in his or her luggage, he asks if this is a first visit. If the guest says he or she has been there before, the bellman will discreetly tug on his ear, so the clerk at the front desk will then greet the guest with a hearty "Welcome back!"

A bank ensures eye contact by requiring tellers to record the customer's eye color on a checklist as they start the transaction. Similarly, some companies place mirrors next to customer service reps' phones to fail-safe a "smiling voice" to their unseen customers. A Korean theme park uses a more controlling poka-yoke: it sews the pockets of its new employees' trousers closed to ensure that they maintain a formal decorum (i.e., no hands in their pockets).

Many service companies train their personnel to read customers' negative nonverbal cues early in the encounter. This inspection helps the employee to prevent miscommunication from escalating into a full-blown service failure. For some day-to-day service situations, behavioral-management-based standards and rewards can be used to specify the actions that aid in mistake-proof treatment. For example, a fast-food restaurant listed "friendliness" as one aspect of front-line employee behavior that it wished to fail-safe. Rather than mandating that employees "smile all the time," the trainers provided four specific cues for when to smile: when greeting the customer, when taking the order, when telling the customer about the dessert special, and when giving the customer change. The restaurant

encouraged employees to observe whether the customers smiled back—a natural reinforcer for smiling. Employees also learned opening lines, ranging from information about food to inquiries about customer preferences. Incidentally, Luthans and Davis advocate applying the approach only to those 20 percent of behaviors that affect 80 percent of the quantity and quality of service.[10] It is tempting to disparage such behavioral management as simply Skinnerian manipulation, but when properly executed, the approach has led to positive results for both the server and the served. Luthans and Davis document success with the approach in such services as banking, real estate sales, and drug and department stores.

TANGIBLE POKA-YOKES Tangible errors are those in the physical elements of the service, such as dirty waiting rooms, incorrect or unclear bills, and so on. Such errors are caused by failure to:

☐ Clean facilities.

☐ Provide clean uniforms.

☐ Control noise, odors, light, and temperature.

☐ Proofread documents for content and presentation.

There are many examples of poka-yokes to prevent tangible errors. A mirror placed where a worker can automatically check his or her appearance before greeting a customer fosters a neat appearance. To prevent people from sleeping in their facilities, bus and train stations, airports, and similar facilities install chairs with fixed armrests to make it impossible to lie down. Hotels can wrap paper strips around towels to help the housekeeping staff identify the clean linen and show which towels should be replaced. For proofing, most software programs have built-in checks for spelling and arithmetic errors. W. M. Mercer, a consulting firm specializing in benefits and health care, uses peer review—systematic auditing by pairs of its associates—of all reports. Motorola's legal department performs similar double-checking with its "two lawyer rule." A second lawyer reviews all aspects of the legal work, memorandums, oral presentations, contract drafts, and so on.[11]

FAIL-SAFING THE CUSTOMER

PREPARATION POKA-YOKES Customer errors can occur before the encounter, both inside and outside the service facility. Specific examples of this type of error include failure to:

☐ Bring necessary materials to the encounter.

☐ Understand and anticipate their role in the service transaction.

☐ Engage the correct service.

During the encounter, marketing can use poka-yokes for shaping prior expectations and informing the customer on how to access the service. For example, Digital Equipment marketers put a poka-yoke in a flier sent to DEC customers to prevent preparation errors. The flier uses a simple flowchart to specify how to place a service call. By guiding them through three "yes or no" questions, it ensures that customers have the necessary information (e.g., their equipment model) and that they contact the appropriate provider to obtain service.

Other preparation poka-yokes are dress code requests on invitations, reminders about dental appointments, and bracelets inscribed with the wearer's special medical condition.

ENCOUNTER POKA-YOKES Customer errors during an encounter can be due to inattention, misunderstanding, or simply a memory lapse. Such errors include failure to:

☐ Remember steps in the service process.

☐ Follow system flow.

☐ Specify desires sufficiently.

☐ Follow instructions.

Some poka-yoke devices and procedures that warn and control customer actions are chains to configure waiting lines, locks on airline lavatory doors that must be turned to switch on lights (and, at the same time, activate the "occupied" sign), height bars at amusement rides to ensure that riders do not exceed size limitations, turnstiles, frames at airport check-in counters so passengers can gauge the allowable size of their carry-on luggage, beepers that signal customers to remove their cards from the ATM, and so on. Even symbols employees wear can be warnings. Trainee buttons, badges, and gold braid are standard signals that shape expectations about service before the employees take any actions.

An example of a low-cost technology for fail-safing is the use of pagers at the three-hundred-seat Cove Restaurant in Deerfield Beach, Florida. Since there is often a forty-five minute wait for a table, the mâitre d' provides customers with small pagers that vibrate when activated from the master seating control board at the host stand. This allows guests to roam outside without missing their table call. The system cost about $5,000.[12]

In another example, a dentist, whose office is in a mall, loans parents a similar pager so that they can shop while their child is being treated. And for customers who don't want to stroll around, a bar across the street from the Denver Department of Motor Vehicles has an inexpensive electronic display board showing the queue numbers for waiting motorists. Drivers can play pool, shoot darts, and have a soft drink while waiting for their licenses. A retailers uses an electronically preset cash register that can be adjusted to reduce the number of keystrokes necessary when it sells a limited variety of items during a sale. The device keeps the line moving and avoids congestion at checkout. A simple poka-yoke can help customers who pay with credit cards and take the wrong copy of the receipt. Some cashiers fold the top edge of the receipt back, holding together the restaurant's copies while revealing the customer's copy. Another restaurant poka-yoke is using a circular coaster to indicate which diner gets decaffeinated coffee.

Many service encounters occur on the phone. The most common mistake cable TV companies face in their telephone troubleshooting happens when customers report a supposed reception problem when, in fact, they have inadvertently changed the channel setting on their TV. However, if a service representative asks the customer if his or her TV is "on the correct channel," the customer will often feel embarrassed and automatically say "yes." One company uses a multi-step fail-safing process to instruct the customer to "turn the channel selector from channel 3 (the correct setting) to channel 5, and then back to 3." This ensures that the customer performs the check, while preventing him or her from feeling inept.[13]

RESOLUTION POKA-YOKES Customers may also make errors at the resolution stage of the service encounter. Following the encounter, the customer typically evaluates the experience, modifies expectations for subsequent encounters, and, ideally, provides feedback to the service provider. A range of errors can occur in this process, including failure to:

☐ Signal service failures.

☐ Learn from experience.

☐ Adjust expectations appropriately.

☐ Execute appropriate post-encounter actions.

For example, hotel management may include a comment card plus a certificate for a small gift in its bill envelope to encourage the guest to spend the time to provide feedback. Child-care centers use toy outlines on walls and floors to show where toys should be placed after use. (In fact, a child-care consultant advocates placing photographs by the door to show children what a "clean" room looks like.) At the University of Pennsylvania, the food service director encourages students to register complaints using "bitch boards" posted at all food service facilities. In fast-food restaurants, strategically located tray-return stands and trash receptacles remind customers to return their trays.

The bathrooms at L'Hotel Louis XIV in Quebec provide an example of a clever poka-yoke. Because the bathrooms were shared by two rooms, problems arose when a guest forgot to unlock the door leading to the other room. The hotel installed a poka-yoke to replace the locks on the bathroom doors. Since the doors, on opposite sides of the bathroom, opened out into the guest rooms, it connected a leather strap to the handles on each door. A guest in the bathroom was to hook the straps together, thus holding both doors shut. It was impossible for the guest to leave the bathroom without unhooking the strap and thus unlocking both doors.[14]

GENERAL STEPS IN THE FAIL-SAFING PROCESS

The first step in fail-safing is to review each stage of the service process and identify where and when failures occur. In practice, there are two places where problems are most likely. One, obviously, is during the provision of one-on-one service; the other is when the customer is handed off to another person or stage of the service process. For any service, a blueprint can trace the processing steps and the information flow between the customer and the server.[15] The information flow should include such items as the directions the customer receives, the customer's service request, and the nature of customer feedback. Separating the front- and back-office environments is the line of visibility. This line indicates those process steps where customers can see defects. The handoffs between the customer and the server occur across a line of interaction. Similarly, lines of internal iteration indicate handoffs between various servers in the back office. Generally, a "fresh pair of eyes" can detect the mistakes during handoffs.

Once a mistake is detected, the next step is to trace through the process to find its source. One could conceivably cross several lines (visibility and interaction) many times before locating the source.

The final step is to set up a fail-safe system to block each mistake from turning into a defect. Juran calls this step "error cause removal." This may call for source inspection, self-inspection, or sequential checks as defined earlier, or it may call for what we term "joint

inspection," involving both customer and server. For example, the server could repeat an order back to a customer to ensure that the correct information was accessed, exchanged, and understood.

FAIL-SAFING A TYPICAL AUTOMOTIVE SERVICE OPERATION

Now let us look at how to fail-safe an existing service operation. Figure 2 shows a simplified version of standard service at a car dealership, starting when the customer calls for a service appointment and ending when the customer leaves the facility. The complete blueprint for this operation is much more complex, including capacity and time control activities, warranty claims processing, customer credit approval, and the possibility of additional mechanical work, but this simplified version is suitable for illustration. We have indicated four stages, each including various failpoints and suggestions for preventing errors.

STAGE ONE The first stage consists of scheduling the appointment and all of the preliminary activities such as greeting the customer and obtaining the vehicle information. A potential failure arises if the customer forgets the appointment. To preclude this, a fail-safe procedure is to call the customer the day before the intended service.

After arrival at the facility, the customer may be unable to locate the service department. Clear, informative signs will prevent the customer from getting lost. The next failure can occur if the service adviser fails to notice the customer's arrival. This is a particular problem during the slow periods when the service advisers may be performing other duties, such as checking on the progress of other cars. A drive-over signal, such as the bell chains found in old full-service gas stations, will ensure that the customer receives attention.

If this is a large service facility with many service teams, the dealer can overlook customers and serve them out of turn, particularly in the morning rush. Numbered color-coded tags, such as those Sewell Cadillac uses, can be placed on the cars, identifying the service team and order of arrival.[16]

Errors also occur in recording the vehicle information for the work order. Most people who come to an automobile service facility are repeat customers, so their vehicle information (with the exception of mileage) remains the same each time. By maintaining a customer database, the dealer can preprint forms with this background information, decreasing errors and the work load.

STAGE TWO At the problem diagnosis stage, one of the first errors is incorrect diagnosis due to poor communication between the customer and service adviser. A good fail-safe method for overcoming this is joint inspection, in which the service adviser repeats his or her understanding of the problem for the customer to confirm or elaborate on.

Even with a good understanding of the problem, the service adviser can still err in diagnosing its cause. A fail-safe system can be a high-tech checklist such as an expert system to guide the adviser's referral of repairs or problems to a mechanic for exploratory diagnosis. Expert systems and computer-assisted diagnostic equipment can also support the mechanic's decisions.

Once the adviser diagnoses the problem, he or she must complete a cost and time estimate. A checklist, possibly computerized, that itemizes the costs by common repair types or procedures (such as dashboard removal) will prevent errors in this step.

The last step in this stage is the customer's approval of the required work. If customers do not understand the service and why it is necessary, they may think they are being taken advantage of and may refuse the service, which can result in severe damage to the vehicle or injury to the customer. To prevent errors in understanding and decision making, the service adviser can provide preprinted material for most services, detailing the work, the reasons for the work, and possibly a graphic representation. (This is in addition to a careful explanation.)

If the customer has left the facility, he or she needs to be located after the cause of the problem has been determined, to approve the needed service. Many customers leave a telephone number where they can be reached; however, some customers, such as sales and service representatives, students, and those just running errands, may not know where they will be during the day or cannot be phoned during working hours. Giving a beeper to these customers as they leave the facility is a good poka-yoke to ensure that they can always be contacted directly and allows them to call back when they can get to a phone.

STAGE THREE During the work stage, the customer and the vehicle take different paths. The customer proceeds to the waiting room or takes a service shuttle to home or work, while the vehicle goes to the service bays (the back office). As the car moves into the back office, out of the customer's sight, the work becomes production, rather than service, oriented. Although poka-yokes are able to provide great benefits in the back office, their application is very similar to those in Shingo's manufac-

turing environments. One example from manufacturing, which can be used in the stockroom, ensures that miscellaneous parts are not out of stock. Dealerships can use computerized inventory control systems that track most of the parts in the service area and indicate when the parts department manager should reorder or even reorder automatically. Some miscellaneous parts are commonly used in a large variety of repairs, but, for various reasons, are not worth tracking individually in the inventory system. If the parts manager fails to notice when the stock level of these parts is low, running out can seriously disrupt operations. A poka-yoke to prevent this error involves limit switches in the part bins, placed so that a signal lamp lights up to prompt reordering when the level falls below a certain point.[17]

Meanwhile, the customer has found that the service shuttle schedule is overbooked or inconvenient (e.g., going uptown when he or she needs to go downtown). When the dealership traces the problem back through the process to find the source of the error, it finds that the customer was scheduled for an appointment at the wrong time (i.e., when too many other shuttle riders, or riders who were heading uptown, were scheduled). A poka-yoke can include the shuttle's schedule in the appointment log. When a customer makes an appointment, the service adviser can quickly check the availability of seats in the shuttle and its direction of travel and reserve a place for the customer.

STAGE FOUR The final stage in the service delivery process involves billing and reuniting the customer and vehicle. If customers have left the facility, they must be located, perhaps using the beeper system discussed earlier. When the customer arrives at the cashier, he or she may find the invoice illegible, and, if it is a carbonless copy, it may grow increasingly more so over time. A simple fail-safe is to either provide the top sheet for the customer or, now quite common, use plain-paper invoices printed on a laser printer.

To ensure that the car arrives promptly after the customer has paid the bill, a dealer can use a motion step poka-yoke. At Sewell Cadillac, when the customer arrives at the cashier, the cashier electronically notifies a lot lizard (vehicle retrieval specialist) in the holding lot when entering the customer's name into the billing computer. The lot lizard then retrieves the car while the customer is paying.[18]

Before returning the vehicle to the customer, the lot lizard can use an itemized checklist to ensure that it has been properly cleaned by the car wash crew. If the vehicle is not up to standard (e.g., fingerprints on the hood

FIGURE 2   Fail-Safing a Typical Automotive Service Operation

Failure: Customer forgets the need for service.
Poka-Yoke: Send automatic reminders with a 5 percent discount.

Failure: Customer cannot find service area or does not follow proper flow.
Poka-Yoke: Clear and informative signs directing customers.

Failure: Customer has difficulty communicating problem.
Poka-Yoke: Joint inspection— service adviser repeats his/her understanding of the problem for confirmation or elaboration by the customer.

Failure: Customer does not understand the necessary service.
Poka-Yoke: Preprinted material for most services, detailing work, reasons, and possibly a graphic representation.

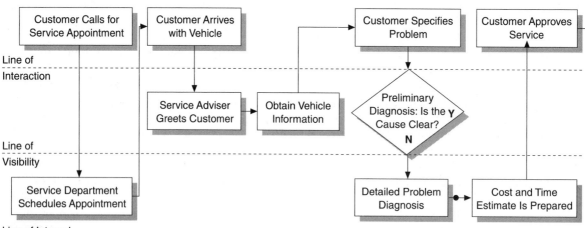

Failure: Customer arrival unnoticed.
Poka-Yoke: Bell chain to signal arrivals (service adviser acknowledges the customer).

Failure: Customers not served in order of arrival.
Poka-Yoke: Place numbered markers on cars as they arrive.
Failure: Vehicle information incorrect and process is time consuming.
Poka-Yoke: Maintain customer database and print forms with historical information.

Failure: Incorrect diagnosis of problem.
Poka-Yoke: High-tech checklists such as expert systems and diagnostic equipment.

Failure: Incorrect estimate.
Poka-Yoke: Checklists itemizing costs by common repair types.

or door that did not come off when washed, or spots from an unfriendly bird who discovered the car), it is returned for a quick touch-up. If the dealership has an automatic carwash, the car can go through the wash as it goes from the holding lot to the customer. As an extra fail-safe, the lot lizard can remove the protective floormat and plastic seat cover in the customer's presence to communicate that the mechanics took proper precautions to ensure cleanliness. In essence, the server facilitates the customer's inspection process and makes service quality visible.

The final step in any service is to obtain performance feedback. One way of ensuring this is to provide a postage-paid questionnaire along with the keys to the vehicle. Sewell Cadillac uses a very short questionnaire (three questions with space for comments) for customers to complete while waiting for the billing and payment to be processed.[19]

All these fail-safe devices and procedures can drastically reduce or eliminate the errors they were designed to detect. In addition, a dealership can quickly introduce almost all of them at little or no cost. That most of the

FIGURE 2   *(continued)*

Failure: Customer not located.
Poka-Yoke: Issue beepers to customers who wish to leave facility.

Failure: Bill is illegible.
Poka-Yoke: Top copy to customer, or plain paper bill.

Failure: Feedback not obtained.
Poka-Yoke: Customer satisfaction postcard given to customer with keys to vehicle.

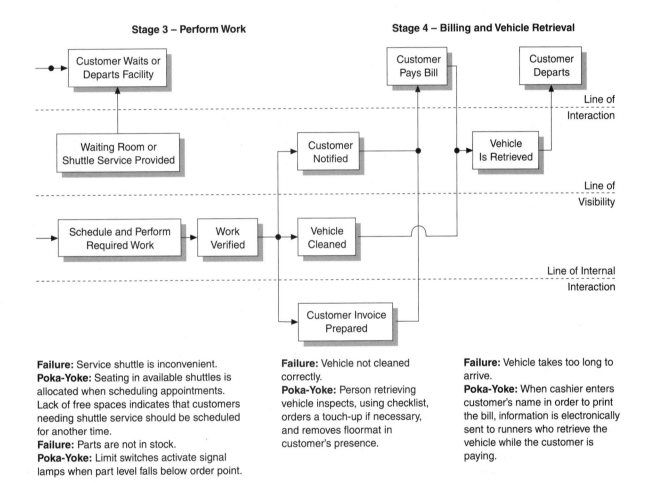

Failure: Service shuttle is inconvenient.
Poka-Yoke: Seating in available shuttles is allocated when scheduling appointments. Lack of free spaces indicates that customers needing shuttle service should be scheduled for another time.
Failure: Parts are not in stock.
Poka-Yoke: Limit switches activate signal lamps when part level falls below order point.

Failure: Vehicle not cleaned correctly.
Poka-Yoke: Person retrieving vehicle inspects, using checklist, orders a touch-up if necessary, and removes floormat in customer's presence.

Failure: Vehicle takes too long to arrive.
Poka-Yoke: When cashier enters customer's name in order to print the bill, information is electronically sent to runners who retrieve the vehicle while the customer is paying.

procedures seem trivial is actually the beauty of fail-safing. It does not require highly trained quality practitioners; indeed, given a basic understanding of the fail-safing process, any employee can contribute to fail-safing the service delivery system.

CONCLUSION

Managers need to think about specific actions to take for achieving the first principle of quality—doing it right the first time. All books on quality advocate this in chapter one, but no book or article provides any detailed theory and examples on how to do this for services. While we are in favor of creating quality cultures, continuous improvement processes, quality training in statistics, and the like, we think managers are missing a good bet by not starting to fail-safe in parallel with these traditional quality initiatives. Current TQM theory, as practiced in manufacturing, usually places fail-safing downstream, lumped in with the other activities that quality improvement teams pursue. But in services, fail-safing is a product design decision. Thus, it must be included up front—at the start of any quality improvement effort. Moreover, even reengineering efforts that are information-technology-driven can benefit from poka-yokes, because defects in order entry, for example, can disrupt a vast computer network in no time.

Designing poka-yokes is part art and part science. Our framework to systematize their development is a modest, practical approach to making immediate improvements in service delivery. The success of fail-safing in manufacturing, coupled with examples from services, suggests that service managers should consider it seriously.[20]

REFERENCES

1. We believe that fail-safing has decided advantages over the other logical choice for service process control, statistical process control (SPC). This is due to the humanistic nature of services, which makes them particularly prone to human error. As a statistical method, SPC is designed to ignore random variation and signal statistically significant events. Human error is, however, a random event and thus will be ignored by SPC. (In SPC terminology, human error will become part of the common cause variation.) Therefore, if SPC cannot detect human error, then it will not be able to control its effect on the service process.

2. R. Hall, *Attaining Manufacturing Excellence* (Homewood, IL: Dow Jones-Irwin, 1987).

3. S. Shingo, *Zero Quality Control: Source Inspection and the Poka-yoke System,* trans. A. P. Dillon (Cambridge, MA: Productivity Press, 1986).

4. A. G. Robinson and D. M. Schroeder, "The Limited Role of Statistical Quality Control in a Zero Defect Environment," *Production and Inventory Management Journal* 31 (1990): 60–65.

5. T. Levitt, "Production-line Approach to Service," *Harvard Business Review,* September–October 1972, pp. 41–52. Levitt reveals how, to keep its surrounding property clean, McDonald's placed numerous conspicuously colored trash cans throughout the parking lots. The assumption was that customers would not litter while looking at an obvious trash can only steps away.

6. A. Parasuraman, V. Zeithaml, and L. Berry, "SERVQUAL: A Multiple-Item Scale for Measuring Customer Perceptions of Service Quality," *Journal of Retailing,* Spring 1988, pp. 12–40.

7. SERVQUAL is primarily a measurement tool, and, although its dimensions represent important aspects of the service in the eyes of the customer, they do not directly relate to the activities of the server. This is because the SERVQUAL dimensions were obtained by disaggregating a perceptual construct, service quality, into factors that best explained different perceived levels of quality, rather than by grouping the fundamental observed components of the service delivery system into larger more homogenous categories.

8. K. Anderson and R. Zemke, *Delivering Knock Your Socks Off Services* (New York: AMACOM, 1991).

9. C. Sewell and P. B. Brown, *Customers for Life* (New York: Doubleday, 1990).

10. F. Luthans and T. Davis, "Applying Behavioral Management Techniques in Service Organizations." *Service Management Effectiveness,* ed. D. Bowen et al. (San Francisco: Jossey-Bass, 1990), pp. 177–209.

11. R. E. Yates, "Lawyers Not Exempt from Quality Crusade," *Recrafting America* (Chicago: Chiago Tribune Company, 1991).

12. J. Edelson, "The Food Service Industry: Examples of Products and Services" (Los Angeles: University of Southern California. Failsafe Project Report, June 1989).

13. Anderson and Zemke (1991).

14. R. Caplan, *Why There Are No Locks on the Bathroom Doors in Hotel Louis XIV and Other Object Lessons* (New York: McGraw-Hill, 1984).

15. J. Kingman-Brundage, "The ABCs of Service System Blueprinting," *Designing a Winning Service Strategy,* ed. M. J. Bitner and L. A. Crosby (Chicago: American Marketing Association, 1989).

16. Sewell and Brown (1990).

17. Nikkan Kogyo Shimbun/Factory Magazine, ed., *Poka-Yoke: Improving Product Quality by Preventing Defects* (Cambridge, MA: Productivity Press, 1988), p. 100.

18. Sewell and Brown (1990).

19. Ibid.

20. Services could benefit from a compendium of poka-yoke examples similar to those compiled for manufacturing in: *Nikkan Kogyo Shimbun/Factory Magazine* (1988).

CHAPTER 6

MANAGING THE SERVICE EXPERIENCE II
MANAGING THE SERVICE EMPLOYEES

CHAPTER OVERVIEW

More than 45 million people (or roughly 42 percent of the U.S. work force) are employed in serving food; selling merchandise in retail stores; performing clerical work in service industries; cleaning hospitals, schools, and offices; or providing some other form of personal service. These are the occupations that accounted for most of the U.S. job growth in the 1980s, a pattern that will continue at least until the turn of the century. Yet, for the most part, these jobs are poorly paid, lead nowhere, and provide little, if anything, in the way of health, pension, and other benefits.[1]

The service providers are the human face of the organization and are required to provide excellent service. They are caught between the organization and the customer, and are expected to cope with all the ensuing conflicts of their role (see Chapter 4). In return for achieving this miracle, they are paid virtually nothing and have no career prospects.

It is little wonder, therefore, that service jobs often have extremely high levels of staff turnover. In 1989, 119,000 sales jobs turned over within the retail network of the Sears Merchandise Group. The cost of hiring and training each new sales assistant was $900, or more than $110 million in total, a sum that represented 17 percent of Sears' 1989 income.[2] Even this figure does not represent the true cost of employee turnover. In a 1990 study, Philips highlighted the additional costs of disruptions to work relationships from high turnover.[3] He quoted the Merck Corporation, which had calculated that combining disruption costs with more traditional transaction costs meant that getting employees on and off the payroll cost an average of 1.5 times an employee's salary, and that eliminating turnover, therefore, had a pay-back period of less than one year.

The purpose of this chapter is to talk about the management of contact personnel. Human resources policies can be shown to have a direct relationship with the outcomes experienced by customers and to have an indirect relationship on the climate created within the organization. Despite this, many firms still are stuck in a model of human resources management based on old manufacturing models of cost minimization. Current thinking is looking for ways to break out of this mindset and, in particular, how to use empowerment or enfranchisement to break the mold. Such approaches can be very powerful, but only in certain settings.

HUMAN RESOURCES POLICIES AND THE CUSTOMER

Schneider (Article 4.2) argued that service organizations are open systems and that the policies and practices of the organizations, as well as the climate or culture those policies created, would be visible to the consumer. Article 6.1, by the same author, provides even more conclusive proof of this proposition. It relates empirically a range of internal variables to the experience of the consumer. The key relationships are highlighted in Table 6.1.

The data in Table 6.1 relates employees' perception of the organization in terms of both its climate and its procedures to outcomes perceived by customers of that organization. The customer experience indicators are relatively straightforward, but some of the employee perception indicators warrant further explanation. The *managerial behavior* factor listed under service climate includes items relating to branch managerial behavior concerning planning, organizing, and managing service. *Customer attention* assesses the behaviors in the branch demonstrating the importance of customers to the branch.

The human resources management (HRM) practices are relatively straightforward. *Work facilitation* measures organizational and job attributes that facilitate and

TABLE 6.1 Statistical Significant Correlations between Employee and Customer Perception Data

Employee Perceptions	Customer Experiences					
	Overall Quality	Courtesy/ Competency	Utility/ Security	Adequate Staff	Employee Morale	Branch Admin.
Service Climate						
Managerial Behavior	•				•	•
Systems Support	•				•	•
Customer Attention	•				•	•
Logistics Support	•			•		
Human Resources Management Practices						
Work Facilitation	•	•		•	•	•
Supervision	•				•	•
Organization Career Facilitation						
Organizational Status	•				•	•
New-Employee Socialization	•				•	
Overall Quality	•	•	•	•	•	•

inhibit task performance. *Organizational career facilitation* uses factors that assess the organization's practices concerning employee career growth; and *organizational status* includes the image employees believe the organization has in the eyes of outsiders.

The table highlights the crucial role that both climate and HRM practices have in determining customers' perception of quality and employee morale. Moreover, customers' assessment of the administration of the organization is related directly to administrative practices and to the staff's perception of these practices. For these branches, at least, the organization is an "open system."

HUMAN RESOURCES POLICIES AND CLIMATE OR CULTURE

Article 6.1 builds on Article 4.2 to stress the importance of the climate created within the organization and its importance in supporting or inhibiting good service. *Climate* is conceptualized as employee perceptions of one or more strategic imperatives. A passion for service within the organization therefore would lead to a climate that sets service as the key strategic imperative.[4]

In previous studies, such a climate has been shown to be associated strongly with positive outcome variables for customers. But what are the signals within the organization that can trigger such a perception for service contact personnel?

When service commitment is high, the service unit reveals a passion for doing things directly related to the provision of service. Employees speak often and favorably about the service-delivery process and the product offered to consumers, as well as about the concern for and/or responsiveness of the unit to customer opinions.

HRM issues also feature strongly in creating a passion for service within the organization. When this passion is strong, employees speak favorably about performance feedback, internal equity of compensation, training, and staff quality. Even the physical design of the setting can have an influence, with service passion being associated with excellent office conditions and facilities and automation systems.

CREATING THE RIGHT TYPE OF ORGANIZATION

Hotel: not idiot-proof — They do care about personnel.

Human resources management practices are the key levers available to senior management for creating a type of organization that can be a source of sustainable competitive advantage. Often, however, front-line customer contact jobs are designed to be as simple and narrow as possible so that they can be filled by anyone; in other words, idiot-proof jobs. Employers place few demands on employees, selection criteria are minimal, and wages are low.

The result is the classic cycle of failure.[5] Fewer and less-knowledgeable contact people are available and hence the customer gets less and lower-quality help. The customers vent their feelings of impatience and dissatisfaction on the staff, which, in turn, de-motivates the employees, especially the most conscientious ones, since they already are aware of the poor service they are being forced to give. The best staff leave and are replaced with poorly trained recruits—and the cycle continues.

What prevents service firms from breaking out of this cycle? One answer seems to be that they are locked into the old manufacturing logic, which argues that, all things being equal, it is better to rely on machines, systems, and technology than on people.[6] Machines, it is believed, are more efficient and productive and cost less to run. More importantly, they are easier to manage than people, since they do not need to be recruited, supervised, trained, and motivated. This is, of course, the ideal logic for operations (as laid out in Chapter 3), and is applied here to the role of the contact person.

However, it is possible to break out of the old thinking and, hence, escape from the classic cycle of failure. To do this, the organization must build a new model that:[7]

☐ values investments in people as much as (or more than) investments in machines;

☐ uses technology to support the efforts of employees on the front line, not just to monitor or replace them;

☐ makes recruitment and training as crucial for the sales clerks and housekeepers as for managers and senior managers; and

☐ links compensation to performance for employees at every level, not just for those at the top.

Thus the organization must use the full battery of HRM policies to break out of this cycle.

Hotel: sees training as a way of keeping staff active and not as comp. perf adv.

Successful companies that use these policies strategically[8] see training, for example, as a means to greater competitive performance. In addition to educating and motivating employees, training sessions typically provide the context in which employees commit themselves to the company and its service expectation. Once committed, employees remain loyal but also provide a source of new employees by referring their friends. Such referrals reduce recruiting costs but also dramatically increase the quality of the applicants.

Good for hotel

EMPOWERMENT AND ENFRANCHISEMENT

Perhaps one of the most powerful tools to break out of the old logic is the whole area of empowerment and enfranchisement of employees. *Empowerment* means giving discretion to contact employees to "turn the front line loose"[9] or, as so powerfully expressed by Jan Carlson of Scandinavian Airlines, "To free someone from vigorous control by instructions, policies, and orders, and to give that person freedom to take

SERVICES IN ACTION 6.1

PRE-OPENING TRAINING AT THE SHERATON PALACE HOTEL

The Sheraton Palace Hotel had been closed for a two-year, $150 million refurbishment, and now faced the task of training some 300 staff to ensure a successful opening. Sheraton's management knew that, after re-opening, they would need to increase room rates to recoup their investment. Higher room rates, in turn, would lead to higher service expectations on the part of customers. Sheraton set about trying to meet those expectations.

With the assistance of a professional training consultancy company, Sheraton began working with its department managers and supervisors two and a half months before the re-opening. The first step was to develop generic service manuals for some 50 hotel jobs. Next, the trainers began customizing job guidelines based on how each department manager believed the job would work. This meant that managers had to think through the process of staff training *before* staff were hired or even interviewed. The plan was to use bi-level training, so that managers would train staff to the standards they themselves had helped develop.

Every job description, from host to front-desk person, was divided up and analyzed in detail. Step-by-step procedures were developed for each procedure that each employee would carry out. Once standards were in place, department managers learned how to walk their staff members through each procedure in "train the trainer" seminars conducted by the training consultants and the hotel's own training director.

Before the hotel finally opened, management arranged a three-day simulated opening with half the managers playing the role of guests and half the staff performing their specified jobs. The management team "guests" received the full range of the hotel's services, including checking in, using room service and the hotel restaurant, using laundry services, and calling an engineer to examine the room thermostat. Each "guest" acted according to a scenario worked out in advance by the human resources department and the trainers. Internal procedures, such as cashiering and accounting, also were tested.

The result was that, by the time the hotel's doors opened for real, all systems had been tested and the bugs had been worked out. Staff knew their roles explicitly and were fully prepared to offer the kind of service that would meet or exceed customer expectations.

SOURCE: Based on Jennifer J. Laabs, "Sheraton Remodels a Hotel and a Service Plan," *Personnel Journal* (August 1991): 35.

responsibility for his ideas, decisions, and actions is to release hidden resources that would otherwise remain inaccessible to both the individual and the organization."[10] *Enfranchisement* carries this logic even further by first empowering the individual and then coupling this with a compensation method that pays people for their performance. The most significant and successful enfranchisement programs have occurred in the field of retailing. Here, advocates argue that it can improve sales and earnings dramatically while, at the same time, require less supervision from corporate management. Perhaps the most commonly used example is Nordstrom, which pays salespeople a commission not only on what they sell, but on the extent to which they exceed their superiors' projected sales forecasts. At the same time,

SERVICES IN ACTION 6.2

TACO BELL RECRUITMENT AND EMPOWERMENT

Taco Bell's new recruitment model is based on a very simple premise: customers value the food, the service, and the physical appearance of a restaurant, and that is all. Everything that helps the company deliver value to the customers along these lines deserves reinforcement and management support. Everything else is non-value-adding overhead.

At the outset, Taco Bell management realized that the company could not execute the new strategy as long as its old, seven-layer organization remained in place. To compete on service and maintain low prices, the stores had to be staffed with talented, motivated people.

The management's view was that front-of-house jobs required staff who could take responsibility, manage themselves, and respond well to pressure from customers. Management further assumed that service workers, just like customers, come into the work place with a wide variety of attitudes, assumptions, and expectations. Some have the potential to reach the goals set by management and to fulfill customer expectations, and some do not. The important task is to differentiate between them.

To do so, Taco Bell uses a selection process that aims to elicit prospective employees' values and attitudes toward responsibility, teamwork, and other values that have been shown to correlate with successful service. One important side effect is that the selection process has been able to identify high-potential candidates regardless of race, gender, or age.

Taco Bell complements these selective hiring policies with detailed training efforts. Revised job descriptions for the company's restaurant managers require them to spend more than half their day, or twice the time they formerly spent, on human resource matters. They now also receive training and communications support, learning about team building, performance management, coaching, and empowerment. They pass these skills on to front-line employees.

Changes in job design and supervisory style have stimulated marked improvements in employee morale. In a recent companywide survey, 62 percent of respondents said they felt more empowered and accountable; 55 percent felt they had more freedom to act independently; 66 percent felt they had the authority they needed to act; and 60 percent felt a strong sense of accountability.

SOURCE: Based on Leonard Schlesinger and James L. Heskett, "The Service-Driven Service Company," *Harvard Business Review* (September–October 1991): 71–81.

Nordstrom's management frees salespeople of normal constraints and publicly celebrates "associates'" outstanding service accomplishments.

Empowerment encompasses a broad range of discretion that can be given to the contact personnel. *Routine discretion* is typified by employees who are given a list of alternative actions from which to choose. The employees' list may be based on training or previous experience. Article 6.2 provides an example of such procedural discretion—in this case, how to deal with angry customers. *Creative discretion,* by comparison, requires the employee to develop the list of alternatives as well as to choose between them.

MAKING EMPOWERMENT WORK

Article 6.3 discusses the various factors that can actively discourage or encourage empowerment or discretion, as shown in Figure 6.1. In each case, it identifies which factors are more likely to generate creative discretion rather than routine discretion. For example, the article points out that organizational socialization (teaching someone a role), which focuses on novel strategies and tactics to achieve certain ends, is more likely to produce empowered behavior than focusing on routines, role playing, and structure. This clearly has large implications for training.

Control systems, clearly, are very different in empowered and non-empowered organizations—as is the role of the middle manager. Empowerment control systems are outcome- rather than behavior-oriented. There is a much lower level of monitoring of activities and much less managerial directions. Performance is measured on objective outcomes, not on subjective assessment by the manager. All of this moves the role of the manager from that of controller to that of coach.

Finding managers who can behave as a coach is by no means easy. Because many unit and middle managers are promoted from the front line, it is difficult for them to resist the inclination to continue to participate actively in the jobs under their supervision. Instead, they must focus on encouraging the winners and helping the losers become winners (or at least to make their exit from the firm seem like a win). Not only must they identify problems now, but they must be the facilitator who makes the necessary resources available to the front line.

If empowerment changes the role of unit and middle managers, it has an even bigger impact on service management. Instead of being "super-supervisors," managers must become more strategic and create the direction for the firm and the framework in which empowerment can work.

MAKING ENFRANCHISEMENT WORK

Enfranchisement gives discretion over earnings to the employee as well as discretion over work. It has been shown to be very powerful in retail settings for salespeople. If empowerment changes organizational relationships, then enfranchisement polarizes

FIGURE 6.1 Antecedents of Empowerment

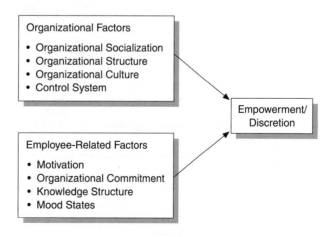

SERVICES IN ACTION 6.3

DISNEY WORLD

One of the keys of Disney World's success has been the consistently high quality of service provided by the theme park's many employees. Disney World places a high priority on attracting good people to work for it, training and preparing them thoroughly before they start their jobs, and motivating them to want to do well.

Disney World is an entertainment business, and management have adopted show-business terminology. The personnel department is the "casting" department, employees are "cast members;" those who work in contact with the public are "on stage," and those who work out of sight of the public are "backstage." No difference is made between on-stage and backstage employees; management emphasizes that the skills of both are needed to "put on the show."

Combined with this showbiz metaphor, there is an emphasis on hosting, rather than serving or controlling. All employees in the theme park have the word *host* in their job title; waiters are referred to as "food and beverage hosts," and street cleaners as "custodial hosts." Customers always are referred to as "guests."

When new cast members are hired, they are provided with written information about their training program, telling them when and where to report, what is expected in terms of personal appearance, and the length of each training phase. Every new employee, from junior staff to senior management, must attend the company's training school, Disney University. The first part of the curriculum is called Traditions 1, where new employees learn the Disney philosophy of business, the company's history, and how the various theme-park divisions, such as operations, food and beverage, and entertainment, work together to "put on the show."

Each group attending Traditions 1 has a photograph taken, which is printed on the front page of the weekly employee newspaper, *Eyes and Ears*. The newspaper provides news about employee activities, educational and training offerings, and special benefits, along with a classified section. There are numerous pictures of employees.

Disney also has a policy of using first names only; everyone, regardless of rank or job description is known by his or her first name, and employee name tags show only first names. To further ensure that management and staff mix and work together, each executive-level manager takes part in an annual one-week "cross-utilization" program, in which he or she works in the theme park doing basic service tasks, such as selling tickets or loading and unloading rides. This program is meant to give managers greater insight into the role of both staff and guests.

Disney World hires many part-time employees for the busy summer season. When the season is over, each of these employees completes an anonymous questionnaire on subjects such as hiring practices, the orientation program, training, communications, wages, and fairness of treatment. This data helps Disney World enhance and improve its personnel management policies still further. The result is an organization that, as one observer has commented, owes its success to the ways in which it looks upon people.

SOURCE: Based on N. W. Pope, "Mickey Mouse Marketing," *American Banker,* July 25, 1979, 16; N. W. Pope, "More Mickey Mouse Marketing," *American Banker,* September 12, 1979, 18.

them even further. All of the job role changes described in the previous section become even more polarized with enfranchisement. To this must be added two other key factors: equity and inadequate conditioning.

Clearly, under enfranchisement, issues such as assignment take on major equity dimensions. A particular assignment within a store or hotel can dramatically influence the income of the individual concerned. To the extent that participants feel that the enfranchisement program is being managed unfairly, the program is wide open for criticism.

Enfranchisement may seem instantly obvious to management, but it involves large amounts of perceived risk for participants. It violates many of the normal roles within the organization and changes the risk/reward relationship. Introducing such a program therefore requires a great deal of communication and pre-conditioning to ensure that everyone in the organization knows what the new roles are to be.

WHEN TO EMPOWER AND ENFRANCHISE

Is there a single solution to managing contact personnel? Do empowerment and enfranchisement always win out against the manufacturing-based models? Consider the examples of Federal Express and UPS given in Article 6.4.

> In 1990, Federal Express became the first service organization to win the Malcolm Baldrige National Quality Award. . . . Behind its blue, white, and red planes and uniforms are self-managed work teams, gainsharing plans, and empowered employees seemingly concerned with providing flexible and creative service to customers with varying needs.

> At UPS . . . we find turned-on people and profits. But we do not find empowerment. Instead we find controls, rules, a detailed union contract, and carefully studied work methods. How do we find a promise to do all things for customers? . . . In fact, rigid operational guidelines help guarantee the customer reliable, low-cost service.[11]

Empowerment clearly brings benefits. Empowered employees are more customer-focused and will be much quicker in responding to customer needs. They will customize the product or remix it in real time.[12] Empowered employees are more likely to respond positively to service failures and to engage in service recovery (see Chapter 11). Fixing something after doing it wrong the first time can turn a dissatisfied customer into a satisfied, even loyal, customer.

Employees who are empowered tend to feel better about their jobs and themselves. This is reflected automatically in the way they interact with customers. They will be genuinely warmer and friendlier. Empowerment therefore not only can reduce costs, but also can improve the quality of the product.

Being close to the front line, an empowered employee continuously is seeing the good and the bad things about the service operation. This employee can be the key to new service ideas and often can be a cheaper source of market research than going to the customers directly.

Unfortunately, empowerment and enfranchisement do carry costs. The balance between benefits and costs determines the appropriateness of the approach. Empowerment increases the costs of the organization. A greater investment is needed in remuneration and recruitment to assure that the right people are empowered. A low-cost model using cheap labor and part-time labor cannot cope with empowerment, so the basic labor costs of the organization will be higher.

If costs are higher, then there are also marketing implications. By definition, an empowered employee will "customize" the product. This means that the service

SERVICES IN ACTION 6.4

ENFRANCHISEMENT AT FAIRFIELD INNS

Fairfield Inns is a division of the Marriott Corporation with a chain of 135-room inns, the first of which opened in 1987. Rooms are priced economically, often as low as $39 per night. Fairfield's management policy is to "impress" its customers (i.e., deliver service that exceeds expectations). To do so, it carefully selects staff who have what the company considers to be appropriate attitudes and the capability to deliver two things: the friendliest atmosphere and the cleanest rooms.

The company's human resource strategies include excellent systems for selection, performance management, and incentives for employees. The focal point of these strategies is the Scorecard computer-assisted measurement system, which uses guest feedback to assess service quality. Measurement is frequent, and staff rewards and bonuses are based on performance.

Empowerment is an important feature of employment and management practices. Housekeepers, known as guest-room attendants, or GRAs, at Fairfield, are assigned to clean 14 rooms in an eight-hour work day. If the rooms can be cleaned faster, a full day's wage still is paid. On busy days, GRAs can ask for additional rooms to clean, and are paid an additional half hour's wages for each room cleaned; this "overtime" is paid in cash at the end of each shift. This policy has two benefits: Fairfield is able to maintain a relatively small core of regular housekeepers, and it has staff who are motivated to increase their work load at peak times.

Housekeepers are also empowered to manage their own schedules over the longer term. They earn paid leave through regular attendance on the job, but they can maintain their attendance record on days they do not work; each housekeeper has the option of finding a trained replacement who can substitute for them.

Each inn in the chain has two discretionary budgets of $150 for each 28-day period. The first is an employee-relations budget that is spent at the discretion of the inn's managers as seen fit. The second, however, is a guest-relations budget, which is managed and spent by the employees themselves. Employees frequently show great creativity in managing customer relations; many keep records of customer preferences for return customers, and will go out of their way to see those preferences are met.

Independent surveys of Fairfield Inns suggest that the company has achieved high product quality, high customer loyalty, and high occupancy rates, while maintaining a cost structure that compares favorably with its competitors. Employee turnover is 60 to 70 percent of that of competing firms. Enfranchisement programs are actually reducing recruitment costs. Fairfield further reduces costs by reducing some forms of traditional supervision; housekeeping supervisors, for example, have been eliminated. Operations costs are thus lessened and unit managers are free to spend time on more positive tasks, such as selecting and motivating employees.

SOURCE: Based on Leonard A. Schlesinger and James L. Heskett, "Enfranchisement of Service Workers," *California Management Review* (Summer 1991): 44.

received will be inconsistent, varying with the employee. It is also likely to be a slower service since it is customized.

The balance of empowerment and enfranchisement therefore comes down to the benefit concept of the organization. A branded organization that guarantees consistency of product and service dare not empower for fear of the inconsistency it would produce. What would be the implications on McDonald's of empowerment?

An organization that competes on the basis of value driven by a low cost base cannot afford to empower because of the costs involved. Equally, a high-cost service organization using a non-routine and complex technology almost certainly has to empower because the ability to use a "manufacturing" approach is severely limited.

THE IMPLICATIONS FOR MARKETING

Although the focus of this chapter has been on human resource policy, the servuction system implies that decisions made within one function will have implications within others. The decisions made about the way contact personnel are to be managed impact marketing at three levels: strategy, mix, and tactics.

Strategically, the role of marketing is to be involved actively when making the decision on the benefit concept to be offered to consumers. That decision will determine the feasibility of empowerment or enfranchisement. Therefore, the debate is a two-way one since the benefit concept may have to adapt to management style preference.

An empowered organization has major implications for the marketing mix, especially for the "product." Empowerment implies high levels of customization—so where is the product designed? Clearly, the marketing group itself takes on the role of coach to the front-line staff, where the product is continually being "remixed."[13] New-product development cannot be done without the active and complete involvement of the front line (see Article 6.6). These contact people know the customer and the system, and provide a unique resource. More importantly, they have to be involved in order to maintain a sense of equity.

REDUCING ROLE STRESS WITH MARKETING

Traditionally, marketing can cause or reduce the role stress, discussed in Chapter 4, merely by the way it implements its tactics. Marketing can, without making major strategic changes, help to reduce service employee stress levels. It is in the best interests of the marketing department to do so. Clearly, unhappy, frustrated, and disagreeing contact personnel are visible to the customer, and Schneider has shown that such employees will deleteriously affect customers' perceptions of a service's quality.[14]

The contact personnel's use of any of the stress-reducing strategies described in Chapter 4 also will influence customers' perceptions of the quality of the service. Customers obviously do not like being ignored by waiters or treated as if they were inanimate objects. If contact personnel maintain their sense of control over their encounters, there is every likelihood that they will be at the expense of the sense of control felt by customers. Finally, although we may sympathize with service providers who tell us how the organization stops them from giving good service, such a narration will reflect negatively on our perception of the organization.

PERSON/ROLE CONFLICTS Conflicts between the individual and the assigned role often can be reduced simply by being sensitive to the issue. A promotional gimmick dreamed up at the head office may look great on paper. A medieval-theme day in the hotel almost certainly will have great public relations value. But how will the staff feel when called upon to wear strange costumes? How will it affect their relationship with the hotel guests?

To improve the quality of service, a change in operating procedure may be needed. However, it is important to ensure that service providers are well trained in the new script. Should they not be, they may well be extremely embarrassed in the presence of customers. This situation can be aggravated if the new service is advertised so that the customers are more aware of the new script than the staff.

ORGANIZATION/CLIENT CONFLICTS Similarly, marketing can help to reduce conflicts between the organization and its clients. It is crucial, for example, that customer expectations should be consistent with the capabilities of the service system. Customers should not ask for services the system cannot perform. Advertising is one of the main sources of inflated expectations, as the temptation is to exaggerate claims in advertising in order to maximize the impact. Consider, for example, the airline that portrayed in its advertising a stewardess reading a story to a child passenger. The ad was designed to demonstrate the friendliness of the airline. Unfortunately, in subsequent weeks, a number of passengers took the advertisement literally, either because they believed it or could not resist the temptation, and called upon the stewardess to read stories (see also Chapter 7).

INTERCLIENT CONFLICTS Conflicts between clients can be avoided if the clients are relatively homogenous in their expectations. In Chapter 7, we shall discuss the importance of segmentation for the success of a service—a concept based on other customers forming part of the service. In this case, however, it is the impact of two disparate groups of customers on the service providers that is crucial. As long as all clients share the same script and expect the same standard of service, the chances of interclient conflict are much reduced.

CHAPTER 6 READINGS

Article 6.1 lays out the basic logic that a service organization is an open system with the customers as part of the organization, and thus describes the organizational-behavior equivalent of the servuction model. Human resources policies are shown to influence customers both directly and through the climate these policies create. Articles 6.2 and 6.3 focus on the area of the discretion given to employees. Routine discretion is based on a fixed range of alternatives, usually produced by procedures manuals and/or training. Article 6.3 provides a good example of routine discretion and on routinized responses to angry customers. However, full empowerment implies creative discretion where the list of alternatives is not prescribed. Articles 6.4 and 6.5 deal with the key issues of when empowerment and enfranchisement are appropriate, their benefits, and their costs. Finally, Article 6.6 takes an organizational-behavior perspective on new-product development, to argue for the involvement of contact personnel in new-product development because of their unique understanding of both the customer and the systems.

QUESTIONS

1. Suggest how empowerment could be introduced at McDonald's and describe the implications for the customer.

2. Under what situations would you suggest that a service business, other than a

retailer, move to enfranchisement? Why?

3. For a service business with which you are familiar, describe the human resource policies. How do these policies influence the organizational climate?

4. Based on Table 1 in Article 6.4, decide whether you would recommend empowerment in the following organizations: a repair garage and an HMO.

NOTES

1. Leonard A. Schlesinger and James L. Heskett, "The Service-Driven Service Company," *Harvard Business Review* (September–October 1991).

2. Dave Ulrich, et al., "Employee and Customer Attachment: Synergies for Competitive Advantage," *Human Resource Planning,* vol. 14, no. 3 (1991).

3. J. Douglas Philips, "The Price Tag of Turnover," *Personnel Journal* (December 1990).

4. Benjamin Schneider, Jill K. Wheeler, and Jonathan F. Cox, "A Passion for Service: Using Content Analysis to Explicate Service Climate Themes," *Journal of Applied Psychology,* vol. 77, no. 5 (1992): 705–716.

5. Schlesinger and Heskett, "The Service-Driver Service Company," 71–81.

6. *Ibid.*

7. *Ibid.*

8. Ron Zemke and Dick Schaaf, *The Service Edge: 101 Companies that Profit from Customer Care* (New York: NAL Books, 1989), 148.

9. *Ibid.,* 170.

10. J. Carlson, *Moment of Truth* (New York: Balligen, 1987), ch. 1.

11. David E. Bowen and Edward E. Lawler, III, "The Empowerment of Service Workers: What, Why, How, and When," *Sloan Management Review* (Spring 1992): 31–39.

12. Martin L. Bell, "Tactical Services Marketing and the Process of Remixing," in *Marketing of Services,* W. R. George and J. M. Donnelly, eds. (Chicago, IL: American Marketing Association, 1986): 162–165.

13. *Ibid.*

14. Schneider, Wheeler, and Fox, "A Passion for Service," 705–716.

THE SERVICE ORGANIZATION
HUMAN RESOURCES MANAGEMENT IS CRITICAL

Benjamin Schneider
University of Maryland

David E. Bowen
Arizona State University West

———— • ————

Let's take a close look at what appears to be an intuitively obvious proposition:

☐ When employees see their organization as having a strong service orientation, customers report more positive service experiences.

This correlation emerged from a study of the banking industry, conducted a decade ago and published in an article entitled, "The Service Organization: *Climate Is Crucial.*" Service climate was defined as employees' perceptions that (a) practices and procedures were in place to facilitate the delivery of excellent service, and (b) management rewarded, supported, and expected excellent service.

We need to examine this finding, not because the correlation is invalid (the relationship, in fact, has been validated repeatedly since the seminal study), but because further probing may yield useful information.

Why does this happen? Why would service employees' perceptions of their organization's service climate correlate with customers' perceptions of the quality of service?

Part of the answer is that the internal organizational climate visible to employees "spills over" on external customers, a consequence of the psychological and physical closeness that exists between employees and customers in service encounters. Services are frequently exchanged face-to-face, with the service being produced and consumed simultaneously. A bank teller, for example, produces a deposit for a waiting customer, who walks away with a deposit slip. Moreover, the customer actually helps to co-produce the service by filling out a portion of the deposit slip before approaching the teller, thus reinforcing the closeness.

It is inherent in many services, then, for customers to have some exposure to the organization's climate. But why does this strongly influence their perceptions of service quality? We reason that because services like banking are experiences, it is the *way, style,* or *manner* with which a service is delivered that contributes to customers' overall impression of service quality. Being served (versus purchasing a product) is not only a consumptive act but a personal and psychological experience. Many services, then, are judged for quality based on *seemingly* tangential cues experienced during the delivery process. The service climate is the source of many of these cues.

The results of the earlier bank study (and how we made sense of it) have deepened our conviction that the customers' *experience* is the key issue in understanding service quality. This reflects the very nature of services— they are intangible and customers are "close" to the organization. In turn, the key to managing the customer's experience of service quality is to manage employees' experiences within their own organization. And when it comes to managing employee experiences at work, *human resources management is crucial.*

SOURCE: Benjamin Schneider and David E. Bowen, "The Service Organization: Human Resources Management Is Crucial," *Organizational Dynamics* (Spring 1993): 39–52.

In what follows, we describe recent research (our own, as well as others') that *documents* the importance of HRM practices in the delivery of superior customer service quality. We stress *document* for an important reason. It is common these days for service gurus to advocate certain HRM practices based on no evidence, soft evidence, or isolated case anecdotes. Typically, these sages offer nothing to substantiate the strength of association between a myriad of HRM practices (pay, hiring, training, etc.) and specific dimensions of service quality (speed, adequacy of staff, etc.).

Thus, we miss the most valuable correlations: Service managers need to know *which* HRM investments yield the largest returns on *different* dimensions of service quality. We close with a discussion of four key rules to follow in managing human resources in service firms.

THE HRM-SERVICE QUALITY CONNECTION

Our belief in the HRM-service quality connection reflects two conclusions we have reached about service:

☐ Service organizations, unlike typical manufacturing organizations, have only a flimsy and permeable boundary between themselves and their customers.

This is the point about psychological and physical closeness made earlier. Because employees and consumers frequently work together, observe each other, and interact, what employees experience in their work gets transmitted to consumers.

☐ The firm's climate or culture must stress service quality throughout the *entire* organization, not just for those employees in physical contact with customers.

Since services are produced and consumed simultaneously, it is not possible to do a quality control check after production to ensure quality. The *total* environment of the work place needs to literally breed service quality. A *total* emphasis on quality would involve not only a focus on customers but a focus on service quality-oriented HRM throughout the organization.

These two points have led us to conduct a series of studies on relationships between employees' total experiences at work and customer perceptions of service quality. In addition to our own work, a dozen or more studies yielding similar results have been published. And we know of many more proprietary (unpublished) studies that report supporting evidence. In brief, all of these studies show a positive relationship between what employees report about their experiences as employees and what customers report about their experiences as service consumers. We summarize our own research first.

HRM PRACTICES, SERVICE CLIMATE, AND CUSTOMER PERCEPTIONS OF SERVICE QUALITY: A QUANTITATIVE STUDY

This study had two purposes. First, we wanted to replicate the results obtained in the prior study. That is, we wanted to confirm the relationships between employee perceptions of service-related practices of the branch (the climate for service) and customer perceptions of service quality. Second, we wanted to examine the hypothesized relationship between employee perceptions of HRM practices and customer perceptions of service quality. Again, the belief was that if employees rated their organization's HRM practices favorably, they would behave toward customers in ways that would yield positive service experiences. In other words, a positive work experience for employees should be reflected in a positive service experience for customers.

With regard to this new effort, we used both an employee survey and a customer survey. All of the employees in each of the 28 branches completed a survey that contained a set of 36 items assessing five facets of HRM (see Exhibit 1); a set of 28 items assessing four facets of Service Climate (see Exhibit 2); and a single overall rating of what they thought customers' attitudes were about the quality of service, using a six-point scale (outstanding, excellent, good, not-so-good, bad, terrible).

Customers completed the same survey used in the first study. This survey assesses five facets of the service experience customers have when visiting the branch (see Exhibit 3). Customers also indicated the overall quality of service they actually received using the same scale (outstanding to terrible).

To collect the customer data, we mailed surveys to a sample of customers asking for their input. About 25 percent responded. For each branch, then, we had a pool of employee surveys and a pool of customer surveys. We aggregated the employee data to get one set of scores for each branch, and we did the same for customer responses for each branch. We then correlated the two sets of responses. These correlations reveal the degree to which employee perceptions of service climate, HRM practices, and service quality are associated with *customer* perceptions of service quality. The results are shown in Table 1.

A number of conclusions can be drawn from the statistical correlations shown in this table:

EXHIBIT 1   HRM Dimensions

☐ **Work Facilitation**—organizational and job attributes that facilitate or inhibit task performance (e.g., "Conditions on my job do not permit people to reach their work goals").

☐ **Supervision**—supervisory behaviors such as providing feedback, establishing reward contingencies, and sharing information (e.g., "Supervisors I work with use the rewards they have [praise, performance appraisals] to let people know when they've done a fine job").

☐ **Organizational Career Facilitation**—organizational practices concerning employee career growth and development (e.g., "[The organization] provides information and counseling about my career").

☐ **Organizational Status**—the status and image employees believe the organization has in the eyes of outsiders (e.g., "People outside [the organization] think the people who work here are high-caliber people").

☐ **New Employee Socialization**—organizational practices regarding the orientation/training/socialization of newcomers (e.g., "People coming on the job get special training that helps them get started").

1. Knowing how employees experience their work world provides a statistically significant prediction of customer experiences of overall service quality. Every facet of employee experience for both the service climate issues and the HRM issues yields important information about what customers say about service quality. Of special interest is the overall correlation (.63) shown for the relationship between customer experiences of quality and employee beliefs about customer quality attitudes. In short, employees in the branches were able to accurately predict how customers of their branches rated service quality.

2. Customer experiences of *Employee Morale* and *Branch Administration* are especially strongly correlated with all employee experiences. This is shown by reading down the columns in the table labeled *Employee Morale* and *Branch Administration* and noting that almost every statistical correlation in these two columns has an asterisk.

3. The degree to which employees believe their work is facilitated yields the most consistent information

EXHIBIT 2   Service Climate Dimensions

☐ **Managerial Behavior**—branch manager behaviors concerning planning, organizing, and managing service (e.g., "The branch manager sets definite quality standards of good customer service").

☐ **Systems Support**—marketing, personnel, and operations/systems support of service (e.g., "Bank management makes sure each branch is adequately staffed").

☐ **Customer Attention/Retention**—behaviors in the branch demonstrating the importance of customers to the branch (e.g., "When customers try to close their accounts no one really tries to keep them" [reverse scored]).

☐ **Logistics Support**—the availability of necessary tools/equipment/supplies to deliver service (e.g., "Equipment and machinery in the branch are well-serviced and rarely break down").

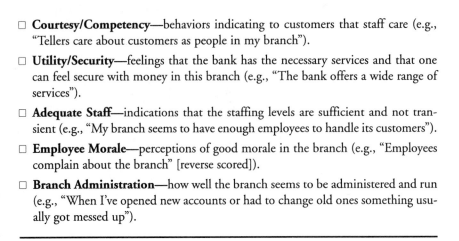

EXHIBIT 3   Service Experience Dimensions

☐ **Courtesy/Competency**—behaviors indicating to customers that staff care (e.g., "Tellers care about customers as people in my branch").

☐ **Utility/Security**—feelings that the bank has the necessary services and that one can feel secure with money in this branch (e.g., "The bank offers a wide range of services").

☐ **Adequate Staff**—indications that the staffing levels are sufficient and not transient (e.g., "My branch seems to have enough employees to handle its customers").

☐ **Employee Morale**—perceptions of good morale in the branch (e.g., "Employees complain about the branch" [reverse scored]).

☐ **Branch Administration**—how well the branch seems to be administered and run (e.g., "When I've opened new accounts or had to change old ones something usually got messed up").

about customer experiences. This is shown by reading the row in the table labeled *Work Facilitation.* Note that almost all customer experiences are statistically significantly related to employee reports of work facilitation.

In summary, the results show that employee perceptions about both service climate and HRM experiences within their organizations get reflected in how their customers experience service. This supports our contention that when an organization promotes a quality atmosphere for service *and* for its employees, these efforts will be reflected in positive customer experiences also. In other words, when service is promoted through practices and procedures like those assessed here, *and* when HRM is more positive on the kinds of issues assessed here, *then* customers are likely to report they receive positive service experiences.

This research points out that managers, in their pursuit of service quality, need to create *two* related, but different, climates: a climate for *service* and a climate for *employee well-being.* The first requires practices such as systems and logistics support—anything that creates an organization setting in which customers feel their needs are being met. The second focuses on meeting the needs of *employees* through quality HRM practices.

Our research indicates that a climate for employee well-being serves as a foundation for a climate for service. Employees need to feel that their own needs have been met within the organization before they can become enthusiastic about meeting the needs of customers. And although the climates are related, one set of

organizational practices will not fully satisfy both employees and customers. The service climate dimensions (e.g., systems support, customer attention/retention) are only *moderately* correlated with the employee well-being dimensions (e.g., supervision, socialization). Thus, we conclude that our questions on service climate and HRM climate are tapping related, but still different, organizational dynamics.

ADDITIONAL EVIDENCE

The results of our research are supported by numerous studies accomplished by others. The following studies all addressed the question, "What is the statistical correlation between employees' work attitudes and customers' satisfaction with service?" The most useful way to summarize this research is by referring to the variety of companies in which the work was done:

Sears Stores. Research at Sears has shown that customer satisfaction with service is related to employee turnover rates (an index of employee dissatisfaction). For example, in stores with the highest customer satisfaction, service employee turnover was 54 percent; in stores with the lowest customer satisfaction, turnover was 83 percent (the data are from 771 stores).

NCR. Over several years, NCR has monitored employee perceptions as a correlate of the quality of the products they produce and the extent to which those products meet customer desires. In these efforts, there is a clear indication that in plants where employees perceive that management emphasizes quality and customers, job security, good management, cooperation,

TABLE 1   Statistical Correlation Coefficients between Employee and Customer Data for Data Collected in 28 Branch Banks

Employee Perceptions	Customer Experiences					
	Overall Quality	Courtesy/ Competency	Utility/ Security	Adequate Staff	Employee Morale	Branch Admin.
Service Climate:						
Managerial Behavior	.53*	.14	−.24	.17	.40*	.40*
Systems Support	.58*	.25	−.28	.16	.61*	.52*
Customer Attention/Retention	.37*	.14	−.16	.09	.58*	.48*
Logistics Support	.36*	.11	−.19	.36*	.28	.23
HRM Practices:						
Work Facilitation	.42*	.31*	.06	.31*	.41*	.42*
Supervision	.51*	.16	.24	.07	.38*	.37*
Organizational Career Facilitation	.35*	.15	.07	.24	.35*	.36*
Organizational Status	.56*	.21	.26	.24	.54*	.46*
New Employee Socialization	.30*	.18	.05	.01	.32*	.23
Overall Quality	.63*	.34*	.41*	.33*	.67*	.58*

Interpretation Guidelines:
The higher the correlation (i.e., the closer it is to 1.00), the stronger the relationship.

$p \leq .05$ (i.e., the relationship would occur by chance only 5 times in 100).

and the setting of goals and objectives, customers receive higher quality products.

Ryder Truck has been conducting an ongoing effort to examine the relationship between employees' attachment to Ryder and customers' attachment to the company. The work has proceeded under the hypothesis that Ryder's management practices have an effect on employees' reactions, and these, in turn, have an effect on customer reactions. In particular, the model focuses on management's HRM practices. Ryder has demonstrated that when management puts *negative* pressure on pay advancement, equipment, supervision, and communication, the employee reaction is low motivation, dissatisfaction, and tension. Ultimately, this results in poorer quality service and negative customer reactions.

In addition to studies in which the names of the companies have been made public, similar results have been obtained in the following kinds of industries:

Banking. A study of 30 banks (not branches, but banks) in the Midwest showed some support for the employee–customer hypothesis. (Some data, however, were not in line with the basic hypothesis. We will return to these findings later.)

Retailing. A study of over 200 retail outlets of a large chain of stores showed quite strong relationships between employee attitudes and customer satisfaction. Of interest in this particular project was the availability of store profitability data. Interestingly, customer satisfaction was *not* related to store profitability; indeed, sometimes the relationships were *negative*. (Again, we will return to this finding later.)

In sum, these studies as well as our results present quite dramatic proof that much of what happens inside a service organization cannot be hidden from the consumers with whom the organization's employees interact. In a real sense, the results support a conception of service organizations as open systems, i.e., systems open to the larger environment in which they function. A systems perspective also emphasizes that the various subsystems (e.g., departments) of the organization are interdependent and reciprocally interacting.

These conclusions heightened our curiosity about the full set of organizational ingredients that employees and customers identified as keys to providing service quality. That is, what were the individual elements of organizational climate, or culture, that added up to a shared passion for customer service? Finding answers to this question required more than survey research.

ELEMENTS OF A PASSION FOR SERVICE: A QUALITATIVE STUDY

We began this phase of our research by identifying a broad range of facets of organizational activity. We then explored which of those facets correlated, at a statistically significant level, with what we called *service passion.*

Service passion was defined as an index that summarized employee comments about the service orientation of their organizations. It was measured by coding employee responses during open-ended interviews in terms of both the amount of time they spent talking about service and the favorability with which they discussed service. Interviews in which employees spoke both *a lot* and *favorably* about service were said to represent a positive service passion. Interviews in which employees spoke at length about service, but in unfavorable terms, were said to have a negative passion for service.

We spoke with 97 groups of employees from three different financial services companies to collect thedata used for this study. The groups typically consisted of three or four people. They were asked only one question:

□ Would you describe the climate or culture of your organization and the role of service in it?

Employees were always curious as to what we meant by climate or culture. Rather than provide a definition, we let them tell *us* what they thought *we* meant. Often, participants responded with words like "comfortable," "ambitious," "cheap," "aggressive," or "caring" as *global* descriptors of the climate. Next, the interviewer asked employees to give the basis (or bases) of their global impressions. These responses provided information on the kinds of practices and procedures that characterize the organization, as well as the kinds of behaviors employees see as being rewarded, supported, and expected. We call the policies, practices, and procedures the *routines* of organizations. We label the behaviors that get rewarded, supported, and expected as the *behaviors* of organizations. Routines and behaviors define for us the psychology of an organization—the organization's climate.

During the interview sessions, note-takers recorded all the information that emerged from the group about the climate of the organization and the role of service in it. Employees talked about everything under the sun—equipment, co-worker relationships, supervisory behavior, and so forth. In our subsequent coding and analyses, we identified thirty-three different themes. The thirty-three themes were representative of six meta-themes (see Exhibit 4).

The question of interest to us in analyzing these themes was the following: When employees have a positive passion for service, what are the other kinds of themes for which they have a passion? The data we used to answer this question came from coding each interview for passion on the thirty-three themes and then looking for correlations with the service passion theme (the emphasis given to service in the unit). A summary of these results is presented in Table 2. This table shows the statistical correlation between the service passion theme and all of the other themes. It can be seen that:

EXHIBIT 4   Organizational Climate Dimensions

□ Environmental themes—two themes having to do with the larger environment, or with the organization and the larger company of which each of the three organizations was a part.

□ Coordination themes—five themes referring to planning, the rules and guidelines governing work, and all kinds of communication (within the work group, between units and levels, and between internal and external entities).

□ Interpersonal relationship themes—three themes dealing with supervisor–subordinate relationships as well as co-workers and interdepartmental relationships.

□ Service themes—five themes concerning service process, service excellence, solicitation and responsiveness to customer opinion, and emphases on service within the location and within the larger corporation.

□ Human resources themes—thirteen themes dealing with all manner of HRM issues (quality of new staff, training, staffing levels, equity of rewards, turnover of employees, career development, job security, performance appraisal policies and practices, feedback, and so forth).

□ Other resource themes—five themes addressing other kinds of resources like equipment, office conditions and facilities, automation, supplies, and budget.

1. When service passion is high, the unit reveals a passion for doing the things directly tied to service. Employees speak a lot, and favorably, about the service delivery process (.47) and the product offered consumers (.28), as well as about the solicitation and/or responsiveness of the unit to customer opinions. The latter issue is especially critical, as shown by the very strong statistical correlation of .72.

2. When service passion is high, the employees in the unit also speak favorably (and a lot) about various HRM issues like performance feedback (.46), internal equity of compensation (.43), training (.40), and staff quality (.34). Especially critical for a passion for service are favorable and lengthy discussions about hiring procedures, i.e., *who* gets hired and *how* the hiring gets done. This is shown by the very strong statistical correlation of .64 between hiring procedures passion and service passion.

3. When service passion is high, then some other resources are also high. For example, there is stronger service passion when office conditions and facilities (.36) and automation systems (.27) receive a lot of positive passion, as well.

4. Knowing the level of service passion employees in a unit feel, however, tells us nothing (at least nothing that is statistically reliable) about a whole host of issues, including such HRM concerns as staffing levels, career development opportunities, job security, or the performance appraisal process. Thus, in Table 2, it is important to examine what is *not* related to service passion. If service passion is the goal, the place to put emphasis in an organization change effort concerns those issues that *are* strongly related to this passion. In brief, these concerns are those statistical correlations with an asterisk (*) in Table 2.

In summary, this project showed us that employees speak about many things when asked to describe the climate or culture of their work unit and the role of service in it. We identified thirty-three different themes that emerged from these group sessions. It turns out that many of the issues about which they spoke are related to a tendency to also speak a lot about the service emphasis in their unit. Table 2 shows that the key issues related to service passion concern elements of each of the meta-themes we identified.

We conclude from these results that organizations desiring to create a service passion among their employees need to focus attention on *many* facets of the work environment. As in the study described earlier (summarized in Table 1), it appears to be true that a focus on only service issues, *per se,* will be insufficient to generate a true service passion. More specifically, Table 2 shows that the two strongest statistical correlates of service passion are solicitation and responsiveness to customer opinion and staffing procedures—one a service issue and the other an HRM issue.

Where do all these various studies leave us on the issue of the crucial role of HRM in service? It is well-proven that some facets of HRM (as seen in the eyes of employees) are related to customers' satisfaction with the service they receive. Our problem is that the research evidence we have produced and the research evidence others produce fails to tell us *precisely* which facets of HRM are critical. In some of our own work, employee reports about staffing procedures are critical. In some of our other projects, however, employee descriptions of work facilitation are critical. Still other studies show that supervision is the key. From the customers' vantage point, our own research shows that HRM practices are related to customer perceptions of overall service quality, employee morale, and how well the service facility is administered. But the HRM practices (except for work facilitation) are statistically unrelated to customer perceptions of employee courtesy or whether the facility has adequate staff. Research from other sources shows that sometimes service quality as perceived by employees is unrelated to bottom line profitability!

What's going on here?

MANAGING HRM IN SERVICE ORGANIZATIONS

We cannot provide a general, simple, and accurate answer to the question just asked. But we can provide four key ground rules—guidelines that point toward answers. If service managers follow these leads, they will find the HRM answers that best fit their own organization.

MANAGE HUMAN RESOURCES *STRATEGICALLY*

The data are clear: There is a relationship, overall, between how employees feel about their organization's HRM practices and how customers feel about the service they receive from the organization. HRM *is* crucial.

Service managers need to take more seriously the HRM–service quality connection. We find that service managers tend to view their HRM function from one of two perspectives. One camp sees HRM as simply providing a basis on which to compete. In other words,

TABLE 2   Means and Standard Deviations for Frequency and Passion; Correlations of Passion for Service (Theme 13) with All Other Themes

Themes	r with service passion
Environmental	
1. Organizational characteristics	.34*
2. Environmental characteristics	.07
Coordination	
3. Organizational Planning	.38*
4. Rules, guidelines, & procedures	.31*
5. Task-related interactions within the work group	.16
6. Task-related interactions between functional units or levels of management	.39*
7. Task-related interactions between branch and other locations	.23*
Interpersonal Relationships	
8. Supervisor–subordinate relationships	—
9. Co-worker relationships	—
10. Group-level relationships	—
Service	
11. Service process	.47*
12. Product offered	.28*
13. Emphasis on service at location	—
14. Emphasis on service outside location	.38*
15. Solicitation/responsiveness to customer opinions	.72*
Human Resources	
16. Psychological outcomes	.22*
17. Overall job attitudes	.34*
18. Staff quality	.34*
19. Hiring procedures	.64*
20. Staffing levels	.17
21. Turnover	.32*
22. Training	.40*
23. Career development opportunities	.11
24. Job security	.19
25. Performance appraisal process	.34a
26. Performance feedback	.46*
27. Internal equity of compensation	.43*
28. External equity of compensation	.16
Other Resources	
29. Office conditions and facilities	.36*
30. Equipment	.09
31. Automation systems	.27*
32. Supplies	—
33. Budget	—

Correlations based on fewer than 20 groups are not presented.

[a]Although as large as some other correlations that are statistically significant, this correlation has no asterisk because it is based on fewer groups; as the number of groups studied goes down, a correlation must be stronger to reach statistical significance.

*$p \leq .05$

putting people in place is "a production factor"—a way to get the work done. You have to do it in order to "play the game." In this perspective, HRM is nothing more than filling a personnel requirement (e.g., finding another warm body) or a legal or clerical requirement (e.g., complying with EEOC guidelines). This HRM focus is purely tactical and operational.

The second camp sees HRM as a source of competitive advantage—a means available for differentiating your firm from others in the industry. It's how you gain the sustainable edge necessary to not just play the game—but to "win" it. Firms like SouthWest Airlines, Four Seasons Hotels, and Nordstroms manage their human resources in ways that put them above their less-successful competitors. They recognize the need to manage their human resources strategically, viewing them as their competitive edge in the marketplace. And they realize that effective human resources management requires the careful and possibly even expensive design of service-oriented selection, training, and compensation practices. It cannot be done by intuition or by an undeveloped, understaffed personnel department.

We agree with others that the "type of organization" a firm is—its people, design, culture, and so on—is becoming the "new" basis of sustainable competitive advantage in the marketplace. This replaces, or gains preeminence over, historical bases such as superiority in product or process technology, marketing or advertising, or capitalization. A key reason why "type of organization" or "culture" is the most sustainable source of competitive advantage is that things like the mix of people and values are far more difficult for competitors to imitate than the prior alternatives. Other retailers, for example, can copy Nordstroms by introducing a similar product line, setting a piano in the lobby, or installing similar merchandise-return policies. But they do not seem able to imitate the more ephemeral "type of organization" Nordstroms is.

Human resources management practices like selection, training, and compensation are the key levers available to senior management for creating a "type of organization" that can be the basis of sustainable competitive advantage. The service role models recognize this and appear to follow Len Berry's advice to "compete for talent market share" (not just sales market share). So Marriott Corporation has adopted as a key business strategy becoming the "preferred employer of choice" through offering superior benefits programs; McDonald's attracts elderly talent through its McMaster's program; and Fidelity hires college graduates to handle its telephones—and its customers.

These strategic approaches to HRM make particular sense in light of two critical trends in the business environment for services. One is the shrinking pool of available talent in the job market. Len Schlesinger and Jim Heskett have described how the demographics for the important younger age group typically hired by service organizations reveal a scarcity of people to draw from. This throws the competitive edge to the Marriotts and McDonald's, firms that are creative in their recruitment and selection practices.

A second trend is that a slow economy, coupled with increasing competition in domestic markets, may make holding on to one's customers, more so than attracting new ones, the competitive focus. "Relationship management" with customers is the key in such an environment. And the firm's human resources are the relationship managers. To support this relationship, organizations need to *manage their relationships with their employees* via well-thought-out HRM practices.

MANAGE HUMAN RESOURCES *CONTINGENTLY*

Exactly *how* HRM practices must be designed to fill their crucial role should depend on the organization and the market it faces. Generic, boiler-plate HRM practices designed to achieve generically excellent service will not get the job done. We have concluded that some well-intentioned service managers may be placing too much emphasis on selecting, training, and rewarding employees to provide TLC-service to their customers—even when tender loving care may not be what their customers want the most! For example, in convenience stores and fast-food restaurants, customers often value speed and efficiency over anything else. HRM practices should be designed contingent upon this *particular* customer definition of good service. In other words, selection, training, and reward systems should aim at producing employees who are quick.

A company may not even want to empower all service employees (contrary to advice from service gurus). Some businesses function in markets where strict procedure-driven employee behavior is the key to delivering what customers want. In such businesses, employees who are free to exercise personal discretion in service encounters can actually be disruptive, or at least very slow.

The point is that different facets of service can be differentially relevant for customers, and service facilities must be organized so that they emphasize the appropriate facets. This can be done by recruiting and selecting appropriate people (i.e., appropriate for the market and market segment), training them to deliver against the market segment, and rewarding them in ways that are meaningful for the demands placed on them.

The evidence for the need to manage human resources contingently comes from two pieces of research we reviewed earlier. We reported on two studies, one of banks and one of retail establishments, where the relationship between customer satisfaction and profits were *negative* even when the relationship between employee perceptions of HR practices and customer satisfaction were *positive*. We believe this kind of situation can occur when HR practices emphasize issues like warmth and courtesy while customer satisfaction measurement also focuses on these dimensions. Suppose, for a moment, that the really critical issue for these customers is speed of service. Unless customers are asked about their satisfaction with speed, the measurements will be misleading.

For example, a service business that competes in a market where speed of service is a key element in the service strategy must train human resources to be quickly and reliably responsive as well as warm and courteous. Because pricing, advertising, the nature of the physical facilities of the service establishment, and so forth, will be designed around a quick service strategy, employees must deliver speed for the firm to be profitable. Delivering only courtesy and warmth can, indeed, be inappropriate when civility and speed are required in a particular market niche. The motto is to manage human resources *contingently*—to manage human resources in ways that promote competitiveness in a particular market niche.

MANAGE HUMAN RESOURCES *SCIENTIFICALLY*

Organizations should not just guess or go with their hunches about what customers want and what HRM practices will help deliver it to them. The customers' definition of good service (e.g., TLC, convenience, speed, or whatever) must come from asking customers via surveys, focus groups, and so on. The burgeoning TQM movement has helped serve notice that quality comes from quality data, particularly concerning customer expectations and satisfaction levels.

Relatedly, HRM practices like hiring and compensation should be validated against customer criteria like their perceptions of service quality. This is what we have done repeatedly in our research. Companies should assess the effectiveness of their HRM practices against both employee outcomes (like job satisfaction and turnover) and also against whether these practices contribute to delighted customers. These are likely the

repeat buyers, people who spread a good word about the company to other potential customers. And only after analyzing the relationships between HRM practices and customers' reactions can service managers conclude (with confidence) which HRM practices have the highest leverage on service quality.

MANAGE RESOURCES *CROSS-FUNCTIONALLY*

The research reported here has emphasized that, although HRM is crucial, the organization must manage many other non-HRM practices and themes to create a passion for service. There must be highly integrated and coordinated climates for employee well-being and service. The evidence seems clear: Focusing *only* on service quality or focusing *only* on employee well-being is inappropriate. The resources (systems, logistics, facilities) required to deliver service, combined with the human resources management practices that facilitate delivery (staffing, equity of compensation) must work in concert.

CONCLUSION

At this point, readers could be wondering if we haven't succeeded in making the HRM–service link overly complicated. Why not just keep it simple and stick with the point we first made—treat your employees well, and they'll deliver superior service?

Based on our research, we have to say that this isn't a *bad* point. It's just incomplete. Let's face it—McDonald's hires, trains, and pays their workers differently than does Jean Louis in Washington, D.C. Our point is that HRM practices need to fit the market niche the business occupies or would like to occupy. *And within that niche, superior HRM practices can provide one key to competitive advantage.*

The second key is the focus on customer service. The data that emerged from our quantitative and qualitative studies show that managerial practices that emphasize service delivery are basic requirements. These practices include soliciting and being responsive to customer input, having the necessary logistics and systems support, and so forth.

This two-pronged strategy for service excellence is based on the fundamental notion that service is an *experience*. Businesses must ask themselves: "How can I create a positive experience for my customers?" Our work shows that HRM and a focus on service *per se* are crucial.

SELECTED BIBLIOGRAPHY

Schneider and his colleagues have published three empirical studies of service climate issues that are referred to in this article: Benjamin Schneider, John Parkington, and Virginia Buxton, "Employee and Customer Perceptions of Service in Banks," *Administrative Service Quarterly,* 1980, Vol. 25, pp. 252–267; Benjamin Schneider and David Bowen, "Employee and Customer Perceptions of Service in Banks: Replication and Extension," *Journal of Applied Psychology,* 1985, Vol. 70, pp. 423–433; and Benjamin Schneider, Jill Wheeler, and Jonathan Cox, "A Passion for Service: Using Content Analysis to Explicate Service Climate Themes," *Journal of Applied Psychology,* 1992, Vol. 77, pp. 705–716. Also, some of the data from the 1980 study were published by Benjamin Schneider in "The Service Organization: Climate Is Crucial," *Organizational Dynamics,* Autumn 1980, pp. 52–65.

The studies referred to conducted in particular organizations (Sears, Ryder) can be found in *Human Resource Planning,* 1991, Vol. 14 (whole issue No. 2).

The idea that "organizational type" can be a key source of competitive advantage, and that HRM plays a crucial role, is summarized well by Edward Lawler III, *The Ultimate Advantage* (San Francisco: Jossey-Bass, 1991).

The importance of competing for "talent market share" is described by Leonard Berry, Valarie Zeithaml, and A. Parasuraman, "Five Imperatives for Improving Service Quality," *Sloan Management Review,* Summer 1990, pp. 29–38.

Changes in labor force demographics, and how they affect service, are presented by Leonard Schlesinger and James Heskett, "De-Industrializing the Service Sector: A New Model for Service Firms," in T. Swartz, D. Bowen, and S. Brown (eds.), *Advances in Services Marketing and Management* (Greenwich, CT: JAI Press, 1992).

Contingency-based HRM practices in the service sector are discussed in David Bowen and Edward Lawler III, "The Empowerment of Service Workers: What, Why, How, and When," *Sloan Management Review,* Spring 1992, pp. 31–39) and Ben Schneider, "Service Quality and Profits: Can You Have Your Cake and Eat It, Too?" *Human Resource*

WINNING BACK ANGRY CUSTOMERS

Madhav N. Sinha

———•———

No business has 100% happy customers. Companies that claim they do are only fooling themselves. At some point, all businesses have to deal with dissatisfied customers. Such customers, however, can range from those who are simply unhappy or inconvenienced, to gripers and grumblers, to those who are enraged, developing life-long grudges, seeking punitive action in court, or, worst of all, considering life-threatening revenge.

What can a company do after the quality of its products or services has made customers angry, hurt their feelings, ruined their plans, or destroyed their confidence in the company? When a business sells its product or service, it's too late to change the blueprint, fix process capabilities, or announce a new inspection procedure. Trying to forget daily happenings at the customer service counter is not the answer. Companies have tried many solutions, from toll-free 800 telephone numbers and liberal refund policies to fresh roses and booths where irate customers can vent their anger on videotape.[1] Still, according to research, more than 60% of dissatisfied customers are so sick and tired of poor service that they think it's futile to complain any more.[2] Whatever efforts are being made by companies, nothing seems appropriate or even enough. Customers see these efforts as nothing more than novel varieties of service or new, improved tactics for diversion and delay.[3]

The answer? Implement a quality improvement program for the angry customer. It is a gold mine of opportunity for a company's priceless stock: its reputation and image.

CUSTOMERS' FEELINGS AS QUALITY PROBLEMS

Consider the following:

"I can't stand around here talking to you all day."

"I thought my phone call to the manager last week would accomplish something."

"I have been waiting almost an hour for the person in charge to come back from coffee break."

"Your promised my car would be ready by lunchtime. It's 8 P.M."

"Why me? Why does it have to happen to me?"

"I am fed up. It's a hopeless situation. I don't know what to do."

These are the voices of customers. They raise many vital questions about the missing ingredient in the total quality improvement program: the human factor. Because of what customers are saying, organizations must ask themselves two important questions:

☐ What does the company do to stay in touch with customers' feelings? Possible answers include market research, having a vice president of public relations, or committing to an array of ceremonial activities such as hosting events at trade gatherings where company representatives can meet with customers. Such approaches can require significant investment, but they are not the best way if customers are receiving a shoddy product or service and shoddy treatment on top of that.

☐ How does the company manage customers' feelings? Dealing with internal and external customers' total dissatisfaction, including their emotions and perceptions, can be accomplished by making the handling of anger and dissatisfaction a part of the total quality improvement program.

SOURCE: Madhav N. Sinha, "Winning Back Angry Customers," *Quality Progress* (November 1993): 53–56. © 1993 American Society for Quality Control. Reprinted with permission.

Madhav N. Sinha is a technical development officer with the Manitoba Department of Labor, Winnipeg, Manitoba, Canada. He holds a doctorate in material science and engineering from the University of Manitoba in Winnipeg. Sinha is an ASQC Fellow and certified quality auditor.

HUMANIZE THE QUALITY PROGRAM

The changing perception of quality is such that customers now buy expectations, not just products or services. Consider the following statistical data on customers' attitudes, feelings, and loyalty:

☐ An average customer who has a complaint tells nine or 10 people about it; on the other hand, customers who have complaints resolved satisfactorily tell only five other people.[4]

☐ For every complaint a corporate headquarters receives, there are 19 other dissatisfied customers who did not take time to complain to headquarters.[5]

☐ It costs five to 10 times more in resources to replace a customer than it does to retain one.[6]

☐ A customer must have 12 positive experiences to overcome one negative experience.[7]

☐ Most companies spend 95% of service time redressing problems and only 5% trying to figure out what went wrong to make the customer angry in the first place.[8]

☐ For those companies that try to do something about the customer's anger, more than half of all efforts responding to customer complaints actually reinforce negative reactions, making the customer more frustrated.[9]

Thus, there is more at stake than simply buying and selling products or services in plain dollar value. In terms of actual dollars lost, customer dissatisfaction and loss of reputation are considered examples of indirect cost. No thorough calculations of these costs have been done, so they are unknown and might be unknowable. Matsushita Electric of Japan, however, offers one glimpse with its estimate that the indirect cost is approximately 100 times greater than the direct cost.[10] Another view offered by Harvard Business School research shows that companies can boost profits by almost 100% by retaining just 5% more of their customers.[11]

DESIGNING A QUALITY PROGRAM FOR ANGRY CUSTOMERS

Whether they're on the telephone, sending letters, or in the lobby, angry customers want two things: someone to listen to them and their problems solved instantly with no "ifs" or "buts."

At this point, the mistake has been made and the question is how to best satisfy the customer. The company's revised quality manual, procedures, or up-to-date complaint handling system are the last things in which a customer is interested. Customers judge the quality of a company and its management by judging the responsiveness of the first person they come in contact with in their attempt to complain about poor quality. The emphasis on frontline responsibility is not incidental. It is known to enhance an intangible asset of the company, commonly known as goodwill, which translates into hard assets when customers return.

Training people in the skills needed to handle angry customers must therefore be emphasized and given a place in the overall company's quality policy, in quality training sessions, and in quality manuals. How can angry customers be properly handled? The answer is a three-step process that involves recognition, listening, and taking action.

RECOGNIZE ANGRY CUSTOMERS

A customer's anger must be recognized and dealt with before any listening skills are applied and the customer's actual problem is solved. If the anger is not dealt with first and the customer is still angry, he or she won't hear what is being said.

Of the two types of anger, aggressive anger is easily recognized from the tone or volume of the customer's voice or by visible signs such as a tight face, clenched jaw, glaring or piercing eyes, waving hands, nervous gestures, pointing fingers, shaking body, pacing, hands on the hips, or door slamming.

Passive anger is more difficult to recognize because the customer outwardly appears calm but is really seething underneath. Here, the customer first needs help bringing the anger into the open. This is normally achieved by acknowledging the anger with a statement such as "I am sorry, sir (or madam), that you're really upset about this." Figure 1 gives some tips on how employees can handle their own anger while handling the anger of customers.

Human behavior, however, is never a neatly wrapped package. Patterns change quickly and can escalate into uncontrollable or violent behavior. The only thing to do is to try to defuse or de-escalate the crisis. Anger is always less costly if prevented at the start. The dos and don'ts for four recognized levels of anger are described in Figure 2.

LISTEN TO ANGRY CUSTOMERS

There are four key elements of listening:

LISTEN EMPATHETICALLY A dictionary describes empathy as "mentally entering into the feeling and spir-

FIGURE 1   Handling the Anger

Handling your own anger	The first step toward improvement is recognizing that anger is not the worst thing in the world. Anger doesn't disappear if we refuse to deal with it. Self-awareness always helps. Dealing with the effects of anger gives clues (the cause) to the accompanying discomfort and unpleasantness.
Handling the customer's anger	Diagnose the anger levels, note the differences in seriousness, opinions, styles, upbringing, etc.
	Share the customer's perception. Use neutral words, not fight-starting words ("I" and "we" against "you"). Avoid giving orders. Take responsibility. Avoid causing defensiveness. Use verbal cushions when needed.
	Weigh the reaction and responses. Anger is never an off or on state; it varies from mild to intense. Respond only after weighing the customer's reaction.
	Forgiveness. Forgiving and forgetting cleans the slate.

it of a person." It means that the company's representative ought to be listening to the customer from the point of view that the company is totally responsible for what has happened. The employee should be open-minded, nonjudgmental, and unbiased. He or she must not be blocked by his or her own preconceptions or personal values and must never compel the customer to end the conversation.

INTERPRET THE MESSAGE The employee must suspend his or her personal judgment and assumptions and try to understand the customer's situation and viewpoint. After listening empathetically and getting the customer's feedback, the employee should ask the customer a few questions to better understand the situation. This will not only clarify any misunderstandings but will assure the customer that the employee is really listening.

EVALUATE THE MESSAGE The employee must not only hear the customer's words but also the urgency, pain, or anger in them. Once again, the employee must listen without bias and give empathetic feedback throughout the conversation. By doing so, the employee will show the customer that he or she really cares and wants to resolve the problem.

Remember that the customer and the employee both:

☐ Have the right to be treated respectfully.

☐ Have the right to express ideas, opinions, and feelings.

☐ Have the responsibility to let others know what can and can't be done.

☐ Have the responsibility to say "no" at some point, rather than say "yes" and not be able to deliver.

FIGURE 2   Recognizing the Anger Levels

Customer's anger level	Responses that affect customer's anger level	
	Positive response	**Negative response**
Anxiety level	Be supportive. Remain empathetic. Listen actively. Hear the real feelings. Don't judge. Keep an open mind.	Rushing to get to the bottom of the problem. Being verbal and defensive. Not letting customer's anger dissipate.
Defensive level	Remain professional and rational. Be prepared for the worst. Be alert for abuse. Don't get hooked. Be ready to get physical help just in case.	Raising voice over customer. Giving an ultimatum, threats, not giving any choice.
Acting out level	Never touch customer. Don't lose control. Don't take it personally, realize it's the release of pent-up energy.	Responding to match tit for tat. Telling about company's good qualities.
Cooling off level	Avoid fight-starting words. Recognize the emotional strain. Listen to responses.	Continuing to show off as winner in the argument and not responding as a reasonable person.

☐ Have the right to make mistakes and the responsibility to learn how to not repeat them.

RESPOND TO THE MESSAGE First, the employee should verbally summarize what the customer has said to ensure a mutual understanding. The customer will then feel that he or she is speaking to someone who is genuinely interested, cares, and is willing to help. By this time, the customer's anger will be subsiding.

DEAL WITH CUSTOMER'S PROBLEMS

Anger cannot be eliminated by listening. What customers want, of course, is to have their problems solved instantly without having to go through some grueling test. The steps necessary to handle a customer's problem are:

☐ Find out what the customer wants.

☐ If the customer can't be given exactly what he or she wants, suggest alternatives.

☐ With the customer, determine the acceptability of the solution.

☐ Agree on a solution.

☐ Follow-up or act quickly.

If followed, these steps close a loop and make customers a part of the company's extended quality control program. If not followed, the chances remain that satisfied customers will once again become angry and dissatisfied.

THE QUALITY IMPROVEMENT PLAN

Revitalizing a company's reputation and winning back upset or angry customers involves a five-step quality improvement process:

Step one is planning to deal with customers' anger. Top management must fully support and concur with the plan to recover customers. The plan should include provisions for fast decision making, problem classification and prioritization, compensating customers for the cost of inconveniences, and, when necessary, criteria for breaking these rules when they don't go far enough.

If a company is going to promise the moon, it must be ready to deliver it. Remember that all complaints or dissatisfaction are about a lack of fulfillment of customers' quality expectations.

Step two is setting standards. Determine where the company stands on after-the-sale service quality and where it wants to go in terms of fulfilling promises. Focus the service strategy. Set performance standards on how to listen to angry customers (Figure 3), especially

---

FIGURE 3   Standards of Effective Listening

1. Learn to want to listen.

2. Be mentally present, don't daydream.

3. Prepare for full-body listening. Use eyes, ears, and feelings.

4. Be self-aware. Control your emotions.

5. Control surrounding distractions.

6. Listen now, repeat later.

7. Take notes while listening.

8. Have an open mind. Expect excellence.

A good listener takes the responsibility for understanding, clarifies to ensure the understanding, and assures the customer that he or she has been heard.

---

for frontline employees, and incorporate them into the company's quality policy and procedures. Communicate with all employees about this new addition to the company's total quality program.

Step three is training. Anger management must be institutionalized, but in the process, it must be humanized. Conduct training sessions for all staff in what anger is all about and how to deal with both external and internal customers' anger.

Step four is implementing the program. The program implementation should be carried out in four stages: planning and controlling the start-up of the designed and approved program; motivating, informing, and directing people, initiating the complaint handling system; and compiling, processing, and using data from complaints and horror stories to improve products and services.

Step five is auditing to continually improve the program's effectiveness. This will allow management to make future decisions on the basis of damages done to targeted individual customers or groups so that the weaknesses in the quality program can be targeted for improvement.

IMPLEMENTING THE PROGRAM

Winning back the dissatisfied or angry customer is a new management philosophy. Its return on investment is enormous provided that traditional quality control mind-sets are broadened and emphasis is placed on human values. Customers' happiness must be built into the company's long-term business plan.

Clearly the idea now is to implement the plan that deals specifically with methods and strategies of handling unhappy customers. After the business plan for reclaiming customers is in place, the standards on anger and the customer's behavior have been defined, and the gains-losses factor has been estimated, the training part is ready for implementation.

The implementation of a complete plan would involve various phases, and a phased-in approach would be most effective. A detailed plan should be developed to include items such as:

☐ Statement of corporate policy regarding calming and reclaiming customers.

☐ Organizational and operational systems.

☐ Goals, according to severity of customer's rejection.

☐ Action plan, impact measures, and feedback system.

☐ Training and education.

☐ Prioritization according to product or service type, customer segments, etc.

☐ Timetable for implementation.

COMPANIES NEED THOSE ANGRY CUSTOMERS

Dealing with customers' anger is more than a service department responsibility and involves more than installing a toll-free telephone number. Don't try to bypass or short circuit customers' anger in total quality management programs. The effective use of the skills available to deal with customers' anger can work to heal the wound that a shoddy product or service often inflicts.

REFERENCES

1. Patricia Sellers, "How to Handle Customers' Gripes," *Fortune*, Oct. 24, 1988, p. 90.

2. Technical Assistance Research Project, *Consumer Complaint Handling in America, An Update Study, Part 2,* (Washington, D.C.: U.S. Office of Consumer Affairs, 1986).

3. Christopher W. L. Hart, James L. Heskett, and W. Earl Sasser, Jr., "The Profitable Art of Service Recovery," *Harvard Business Review*, July–August 1990, p. 148.

4. Technical Assistance Research Project, *Measuring the Grapevine, Consumer Response, and Word of Mouth* (Atlanta, GA: Coca-Cola USA, 1981).

5. Technical Assistance Research Project, *Consumer Complaint Handling in America, An Update Study, Part 2.*

6. Technical Assistance Research Project, unpublished, industry-specific research gathered from 1990–1993.

7. *Ibid.*

8. John Goodman, "The Nature of Customer Satisfaction," *Quality Progress*, February 1989, pp. 37–40.

9. Christopher W. L. Hart, James L. Heskett, and W. Earl Sasser, Jr., "The Profitable Art of Service Recovery."

10. Milton Chen, "Phase-In Implementation of Total Quality Management," *1990 ASQC AQC Transactions*, pp. 913–918.

11. Frederick F. Reichheld and W. Earl Sasser, Jr., "Zero Defections: Quality Comes to Services," *Harvard Business Review*, September–October 1990.

DISCRETION AND THE SERVICE EMPLOYEE

Scott W. Kelley

College of Business and Economics
University of Kentucky
Lexington, Kentucky

Services marketing managers have begun to recognize that services can be enhanced by allowing employees to exercise discretion during service delivery. A conceptual framework is presented which considers the discretion of employees and its antecedents. Two groups of antecedents are included: organizational factors and employee-related factors. The framework introduces a set of variables to the services marketing literature which take into account some of the unique aspects of service delivery.

T he issue of managerial control is one of the major challenges faced by service marketing managers (Bowen and Schneider 1988). Managerial control proves challenging for service managers because the resources contributed by employees during the service encounter are intangible and cannot be controlled in the same fashion as tangible resources (Zeithaml, Berry, and Parasuraman 1988). Customer participation in the service delivery process also inhibits managerial control, as participation is a source of uncertainty faced by managers during service delivery (Argote 1982; Larsson and Bowen 1989).

The difficulty in implementing managerial controls for many service jobs often makes it necessary to empower the employee when designing service tasks. Empowerment involves the "process of enhancing feelings of self-efficacy among organizational members" in order to enable them to accomplish assigned tasks (Conger and Kanungo 1988). When employees are empowered they have greater opportunities to exercise *discretion* during service provision. Recently, service managers have begun to realize that empowering employees and encouraging them to exercise discretion can have a positive impact on customer satisfaction and

service quality (Phillips et al. 1990). However, the empowerment of employees does not ensure that discretion will actually be exercised.

The purpose of this paper is to increase our understanding of the discretion exercised by service personnel. To achieve this, three distinct types of discretion are identified. A conceptual framework which classifies several determinants of discretion is presented, and propositions are offered in conjunction with the framework. Finally, managerial and research implications pertaining to discretion are discussed.

TYPES OF DISCRETION

The concept of discretion was initially considered by organization theory researchers over 30 years ago (March and Simon 1958). Subsequently, little attempt has been made to define and clarify the concept of discretion. Early discretion research focused on different ways individuals exercise discretion to achieve desired ends. Discretion was associated with (1) the *selection,* and (2) the *development* of alternative means for performing a task (March and Simon 1958).

The selection of means for performing a task may occur in several ways (March and Simon 1958). First, means may be selected through training-based knowledge or prior experience. Second, means may be selected

SOURCE: Scott W. Kelley, "Discretion and the Service Employee," *Journal of Retailing,* vol. 69, no. 1 (Spring 1993): 104–126.

This research was supported by a Summer Research Grant from the College of Business and Economics of the University of Kentucky. The grant was made possible by a donation of funds to the College by Ashland Oil, Inc.

through external search activities (e.g., consulting other employees or manuals). Third, the selection of means may occur through the application of a strategy prescribed by the organization for specific circumstances. On the other hand, the development of means for performing a task occurs through problem-solving and learning processes (March and Simon 1958). Discretion is subsequently classified based on the extent to which means for accomplishing tasks are available to the employee (March and Simon 1958; Thompson 1967).

ROUTINE DISCRETION

During the *selection* of means for performing a task, the exercise of discretion tends to be highly routinized and does not involve a great deal of active consideration (March and Simon 1958). This type of discretion is exercised when an employee selects an alternative from a "list" of possible actions. The employee's list may be based on training or previous experience, external search activities, or strategies prescribed by the organization (March and Simon 1958).

For example, the tasks associated with the job of an investment counselor are often routinized by the individual or the organization. Investment counselors generally have a list of investment opportunities that they recommend to their clients. The list of recommended investments might be based on either previous experience, financial reports (external search), a list of recommended investments provided to them by the organization, or some combination of the three. Discretion is then exercised when investment recommendations are made to individual clients based on the counselor's list of recommended investments.

When the potential means for performing service tasks are available to service personnel and they select an appropriate means of task performance, *routine discretion* is being exercised. Employees exercise routine discretion when selecting a course of action from a set of possible means for accomplishing a task. The behaviors associated with routine discretion are expected, and essentially required, by the service organization. The exercise of routine discretion involves the enactment of role-prescribed behaviors, which are behaviors specified by the organization as a formal part of the employee's role (Brief and Motowidlo 1986; Katz 1964).

CREATIVE DISCRETION

Discretion is also necessary during the *development* of alternative means for performing a task (March and Simon 1958). The creative development of means for accomplishing a task is often necessary during service provision. When employees must develop the means for accomplishing a task they are exercising *creative discretion*. For example, legal services and consulting services often require creative discretion. The development of a means for accomplishing a task is judged to be creative if it is both novel and appropriate and is heuristic rather than algorithmic (Amabile 1983a). In the case of creative discretion, the service employee is provided with a goal or end; however, the means associated with the accomplishment of the goal are developed by the employee.

Creative discretion involves behaviors that are not formally specified, yet are still viewed positively by the organization. As such, creative discretion involves extra-role behaviors, which are acts that are not formally specified as role requirements by the organization (Brief and Motowidlo 1986).

DEVIANT DISCRETION

Thus far the exercise of discretion has been conceptualized as a desirable activity on the part of the service employee. However, there are situations in which the exercise of discretion may be viewed as undesirable by the organization (Staw and Boettger 1990; Thompson 1967). Therefore, a third type of discretion—*deviant discretion* is considered (Thompson 1967). Deviant discretion involves the performance of counter-role behaviors. Counter-role behaviors include behaviors that are not part of the employee's formal job description, and are not included in management's role expectations for the ideal employee (Staw and Boettger 1990).

Deviant discretion involves the exercise of discretion by individuals that have not been empowered to do so by the organization, or the employment of criteria in exercising discretion that are unacceptable to the organization (Thompson 1967). Deviant discretion can occur while exercising either routine or creative discretion, as it may arise during either the selection or development of means for performing tasks.

It is important to emphasize that in situations where routine or creative discretion are exercised, the determination as to whether the discretionary behavior is in the realm of acceptable job performance or involves deviant discretion is made by the organization. Additionally, it should be noted that there are instances where discretionary activities may be judged as deviant by the organization, but at the same time may lead to high levels of customer satisfaction and favorable perceptions of service quality. For example, the retail salesperson that offers a customer a refund on returned merchandise counter to company policy is exercising deviant discretion based on the judgment of the organization. However, this service encounter will in all likelihood result in a high level of customer satisfaction, favorable perceptions of service quality, and increased customer loyalty.

ANTECEDENTS OF DISCRETION

A conceptual framework based on literature pertaining to antecedents of discretion is presented in Figure 1. Two groups of antecedents are included in the framework: (1) organizational factors, and (2) employee-related factors.

ORGANIZATIONAL FACTORS

The organizational factors considered in the framework are organizational socialization, organizational structure, organizational culture, and the control system used by the organization.

ORGANIZATIONAL SOCIALIZATION Organizational socialization is a process that leads to individuals understanding the values, abilities, expected behaviors, and social knowledge necessary for performing organizational roles (Louis 1980). The process of organizational socialization has been recognized previously as a viable control mechanism for service organizations (Kelley, Donnelly, and Skinner 1990).

Organizational roles are often viewed as consisting of a bundle of tasks (Hughes 1964; Van Maanen and Schein 1979). These organizational roles, which are created and transmitted through organizational socialization, include *content characteristics* and *process characteristics* (Van Maanen and Schein 1979). Content characteristics provide the employee with the possible means for performing tasks regularly encountered on the job. Process characteristics provide the employee with the ground rules for selecting appropriate means for performing tasks. In the service organization that has effectively socialized its employees, a clear understanding of the content and process characteristics associated with the employee's role will facilitate the exercise of routine discretion.

Employee responses to organizational socialization with respect to the bundle of tasks associated with an organizational role can be broadly classified as *custodial* and *innovative* (Van Maanen and Schein 1979). When employees respond to socialization efforts with custodial behavior, the substantive requirements of the job are learned (content characteristics) and the customary strategies for meeting those requirements are enacted (process characteristics). Tasks that employees develop

FIGURE 1   Conceptual Framework

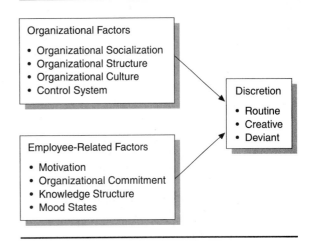

custodial orientations toward are more likely to be performed through the exercise of routine discretion.

When an employee develops innovative responses to the socialization process, novel strategies and tactical alternatives regarding the means to certain ends are sought out or developed by the employee (Van Maanen and Schein 1979). Innovative role orientations are developed when applicable content and process characteristics are not available relevant to a specific task, when the employee deems the content and process characteristics available to them as inadequate, or when a novel task is introduced into the employee's role. Employees are more likely to exercise creative discretion in these situations.

The exercise of deviant discretion is also influenced by the socialization process. As an individual is effectively socialized into an organizational role, role perceptions and definitions within the organization become clearer (Dubinsky et al. 1986; Feldman 1976). As a result, the effective implementation of organizational socialization programs decreases the likelihood of deviant discretion being exercised by the service employee.

P1a: The content and process characteristics of roles facilitate the exercise of routine discretion.

P1b: Custodial role orientations increase the likelihood of the exercise of routine discretion.

P1c: Innovative role orientations increase the likelihood of the exercise of creative discretion.

P1d: Effective organizational socialization decreases the likelihood of the exercise of deviant discretion.

ORGANIZATIONAL STRUCTURE. Researchers have considered organizational structure through the assessment of formalization, centralization, and complexity. Each of these aspects of organizational structure is examined with regard to the exercise of discretion.

a. formalization Formalization is the extent to which an organization relies on written rules and standard operating procedures to predetermine the actions of employees (Ruekert and Walker 1987). In cases of high organizational formalization, employees will be provided with the means for accomplishing tasks, in which case the opportunity for the employee to exercise discretion will be restricted to routine discretion. When employees do exercise creative discretion in organizations with highly formalized structures, it will tend to be viewed as deviant discretion by the organization.

P2a: Formalization increases the likelihood of the exercise of routine discretion.

P2b: Formalization increases the likelihood of the exercise of creative discretion being viewed as deviant discretion by the organization.

b. centralization Centralization considers the hierarchical level of the organization that is allocated decision-making authority (Ferrell and Skinner 1988). As an organization becomes more decentralized and decision-making authority is delegated to lower levels of the organization, the behavior of customer-contact employees will be less restricted. The greater decision-making authority allocated to personnel in decentralized organizations allows greater opportunities for the exercise of discretion. Employees in decentralized organizations are more likely to exercise discretion, and the exercise of discretion is less likely to be viewed as deviant discretion by the organization.

P3a: Decentralization increases the likelihood of the exercise of routine and creative discretion.

P3b: Decentralization decreases the likelihood of the exercise of discretion being viewed as deviant discretion by the organization.

c. complexity Complexity considers the number of units within an organization and the scope of the activities assigned to each unit (Gibson, Ivancevich, and Donnelly 1991). In general, greater organizational complexity is characterized by greater specialization of labor, narrower spans of control, and lengthier chains of command (Gibson, Ivancevich, and Donnelly 1991). Based on these relationships, in the context of employee discretion greater complexity increases the likelihood of routine discretion being exercised, and decreases the likelihood of creative discretion occurring. In addition, in complex organizations employees undertaking discretionary tasks outside the realm of their organizational unit will be viewed as exercising deviant discretion by the organization.

P4a: Greater complexity increases the likelihood of the exercise of routine discretion and decreases the likelihood of the exercise of creative discretion.

P4b: Greater complexity increases the likelihood of discretion being viewed as deviant discretion by the organization when tasks outside the employee's organization unit are undertaken.

ORGANIZATIONAL CULTURE The third organizational factor considered in the framework is organizational culture. The culture of an organization, the shared set of assumptions about the functioning of the organization (Deshpande and Webster 1989), provides service managers with an ad hoc means of conveying expected service delivery behaviors to employees while still allowing employees control of their tasks. Managers can use the culture as a method for supplying employees with appropriate means of task performance. Thus, organizational culture can be used to encourage the exercise of routine discretion. When it is impossible to specify the potential means for accomplishing tasks to employees, the culture of the organization can be used to provide broad guidelines that employees can use in the development of means for accomplishing tasks during the exercise of creative discretion.

The culture of the organization can also be used as a mechanism for controlling deviant discretion. When an organization has a strong culture the goal incongruence between the organization and its employees will be low. Low levels of goal incongruence will decrease the likelihood of deviant discretion being exercised.

P5a: Organizational culture increases the likelihood of the exercise of routine discretion.

P5b: Organizational culture can be used to provide employees with broad guidelines for the exercise of creative discretion.

P5c: Organizational culture decreases the likelihood of the exercise of deviant discretion.

CONTROL SYSTEM The control system of an organization is designed to monitor, direct, evaluate, and compensate employees in the performance of their job-related tasks (Anderson and Oliver 1987). Control systems can be categorized as behavior-based or outcome-based. Behavior-based control systems are characterized by high levels of activity monitoring, a great deal of managerial discretion, and subjective evaluation of activities. Outcome-based control systems are characterized by low levels of monitoring, little managerial direction, and objective measures of the outcomes achieved by individuals (Anderson and Oliver 1987).

In service organizations, behavior-based control systems focus on task performance during the process of service delivery. The high levels of activity monitoring and managerial direction associated with behavior-based control systems increase the likelihood of the exercise of routine discretion, and decrease the likelihood of the exercise of deviant discretion. In addition, previous research suggests that the subjective evaluation of activities associated with behavior-based control systems will tend to hamper creative discretion (Amabile 1983a).

Outcome-based control systems are less direct in providing employees with guidance as to the appropriateness of specific activities (Anderson and Oliver 1987). The characteristics of outcome-based control systems suggest they will result in greater creative discretion (Amabile 1983a), and are less effective in controlling deviant discretion.

P6a: Behavior-based control systems increase the likelihood of the exercise of routine discretion, and decrease the likelihood of the exercise of creative and deviant discretion.

P6b: Outcome-based control systems increase the likelihood of the exercise of creative discretion.

P6c: Outcome-based control systems are less effective than behavior-based control systems in controlling deviant discretion.

EMPLOYEE-RELATED FACTORS

The exercise of discretion is a decision which is ultimately made by the employee. Several employee-related factors contributing to the level of discretion exercised are included in the framework: (1) motivation, (2) organizational commitment, (3) knowledge structure, and (4) mood states.

MOTIVATION Motivation has three aspects—intensity, persistence, and choice (Weitz, Sujan, and Sujan 1986). A great deal of motivation research has focused on effort-related issues pertaining to intensity and persistence, while research pertaining to the choice component of motivation has been limited (Staw 1984). Other researchers have offered a dichotomized view of motivation, suggesting that motivational effort (intensity and persistence) and motivational direction (choice) contribute uniquely to performance (Katerberg and Blau

1983; Sujan 1986). Motivational effort involves the amount of effort exerted (Weitz, Sujan, and Sujan 1986), while motivational direction can be defined as the appropriateness of the effort exerted by an individual (Katerberg and Blau 1983).

Service personnel with high levels of motivational effort are more likely to exercise creative discretion, as the level of effort required during the development of means for accomplishing a task coincides with a high degree of motivational effort. Further, when employees are granted latitude in determining their work activities, motivational direction may be more important than motivational effort (intensity or persistence) (Katerberg and Blau 1983; Naylor, Pritchard, and Ilgen 1980; Terborg and Miller 1978; Weitz, Sujan, and Sujan 1986). When employees with high levels of motivational direction do exercise either routine or creative discretion it is more likely to be viewed as appropriate by the organization, and hence is less likely to be considered deviant discretion.

P7a: Motivational effort increases the likelihood of the exercise of creative discretion.

P7b: Motivational direction decreases the likelihood of the exercise of discretion being considered deviant discretion by the organization.

ORGANIZATIONAL COMMITMENT. Organizational commitment can be defined as the strength of an individual's involvement and identification with an organization (Steers 1977). Several researchers have proposed that the organizational commitment of employees has an impact on performance (Hunt, Chonko, and Wood 1985; Steers 1977; Weiner 1982). Other researchers have empirically demonstrated a positive relationship between organizational commitment and performance (Mowday, Porter, and Dubin 1974; Van Maanen 1975).

Researchers have not investigated the relationship between organizational commitment and discretion. However, organizational commitment is generally believed to result in the acceptance of organizational goals and values (Porter et al. 1974; Steers 1977). As service employees become more committed to an organization, resulting in greater acceptance of organizational goals and values, it is possible for managers to allow them greater latitude regarding the means for performing tasks.

The committed employee will be willing to put forth greater effort for the organization (Porter et al. 1974; Steers 1977), suggesting the likelihood of creative discretion being exercised may be enhanced. In addition, discretion is less likely to be viewed as deviant in the case of the committed employee as a result of the goal and value congruence between the employee and organization.

P8a: Organizational commitment increases the likelihood of the exercise of creative discretion.

P8b: Organizational commitment decreases the likelihood of the exercise of discretion being considered deviant discretion by the organization.

KNOWLEDGE STRUCTURE Research in marketing has focused on two types of knowledge structures—declarative and procedural (Leigh and McGraw 1989; Sujan, Sujan, and Bettman 1988; Szymanski 1988; Szymanski and Churchill 1990; Weitz, Sujan, and Sujan 1986). Declarative knowledge concerns the set of facts associated with a knowledge category. For example, the characteristics used by the service employee to describe a customer or service encounter constitute declarative knowledge. Procedural knowledge is made up of action sequences associated with a knowledge category (Leigh and Rethans 1984; Weitz, Sujan, and Sujan 1986).

Previous research on declarative and procedural knowledge suggests the exercise of discretion is a two-step process (Szymanski 1988). When confronted with a service encounter in which the exercise of discretion is required, service employees will first utilize declarative knowledge in order to classify the customer and service encounter. After classifying the customer and encounter, service employees will select the appropriate means for accomplishing the service task based on procedural knowledge. As the employee develops more elaborate declarative and procedural knowledge structures a wider range of actions is possible.

Knowledge structures apply to routine discretion, because in this case the appropriate means for performing the task is stored in the employee's knowledge structures. If either the declarative or procedural knowledge structures of the employee are inadequate for the service encounter, then creative discretion will be exercised as the employee must develop the means for performing the service task. This is consistent with previous work on creativity which suggests that the extent to which efforts of an individual can be considered creative depends on the individual's task-related knowledge. In situations where an individual does not have previous knowledge of potential means for performing a task, the development of a means for completing the task is considered a creative effort (Amabile 1983b). Finally, in situations where declarative and procedural knowledge structures are poorly developed, deviant discretion is more likely to occur.

P9a: Declarative and procedural knowledge structures are used during the exercise of routine discretion.

P9b: If appropriate declarative and procedural knowledge structures are unavailable, the likelihood of the exercise of creative discretion increases.

P9c: If appropriate declarative and procedural knowledge structures are poorly developed, the likelihood of the exercise of discretion being considered deviant discretion by the organization increases.

EMPLOYEE MOODS Moods are feelings, generally viewed as ranging from positive to negative (Hill and Ward 1989). While research consistently suggests that positive mood states result in positive outcomes (Twible and Frank 1992), research findings concerning negative mood states have been inconsistent (Isen 1984). For instance, previous research has indicated that negative mood states lead to behaviors associated with both negative (e.g., Gouaux 1971; Griffitt 1970; Veitch and Griffitt 1976) and positive outcomes (e.g., Cialdini and Kenrick 1976; Forest et al. 1979). Because of the lack of consensus regarding the impact of negative mood states, the conceptual framework focuses on positive employee mood states as an antecedent to discretion.

It is possible to consider both the mood state and mood trait of individuals. Mood state concerns a person's feelings at a specific point in time. Mood trait involves the mood *generally* experienced by an individual (George 1991; Watson and Pennebaker 1989). Previous research suggests mood states have an impact on individuals' behavior, judgment, and recall; and their effects may be greater for situations characterized by ambiguity and subjectivity, such as the service encounter (Gardner 1985). Research considering the impact of mood state on employees' work behavior indicates that mood state is significantly related to employee behavior (George 1991), while studies considering mood trait have found the trait–employee behavior relationship to be nonsignificant (George 1991; Organ and Konovsky 1989).

The mood state experienced by an individual while performing job-related tasks is influenced by the employee's mood trait (George 1989), situational factors (Gardner 1985; George 1991; Peterson and Sauber 1983), and the interaction between situational factors and the employee's personality (George 1991). Although the organization may have little impact on employee mood trait and personality, many of the situational factors that impact employee mood state can be managed by the organization.

Previous research and the nature of the service encounter suggest employee mood state is an important antecedent of discretion. For example, individuals in positive mood states tend to be risk prone when significant losses are unlikely; and risk averse when significant losses are likely to occur (Arkes, Herren, and Isen 1988; Isen and Geva 1987; Isen and Patrick 1983). This suggests that in organizations with harsh penalties for inappropriate behavior, service personnel in positive mood states will be more likely to exercise routine discretion, as this type of discretion may be viewed as less risky. Furthermore, these employees will be less likely to exercise creative discretion, as it may be viewed as being inherently more risky because during the exercise of creative discretion the means for accomplishing tasks have not been supplied by the organization but must be developed by the service employee. On the other hand, employees in positive mood states in organizations with less severe penalties for inappropriate behavior will be more likely to exercise creative discretion.

P10a: In service organizations with harsh penalties for inappropriate behavior, positive employee mood states will increase the likelihood of the exercise of routine discretion and decrease the likelihood of the exercise of creative discretion.

P10b: In service organizations with less severe penalties for inappropriate behavior, positive employee mood states will increase the likelihood of the exercise of creative discretion.

STRATEGIC IMPLICATIONS OF DISCRETION

The empowerment of front-line service personnel is a strategic decision that must be made by service managers based on the goals and service objectives of the organization. This is not to say that all service organizations should empower their front-line personnel in an effort to encourage the exercise of discretion. Some service organizations have been very successful implementing production-line or industrialized approaches to service delivery (Levitt 1972, 1976). These types of approaches provide personnel with little or no empowerment and as a result do not lead to the exercise of discretion. When discretion is exercised in these situations it is generally considered deviant discretion by the organization.

Although the heightened control offered by industrialized approaches to service delivery may be appealing, the reliance on industrial management techniques may reduce customer orientation which is vital during the service encounter (Mills and Moberg 1982). In situations where the exercise of discretion is a desired strate-

gic aspect of employee performance, the proposed conceptual framework may offer service managers a number of strategic implications for service delivery that extend beyond the issue of simply empowering their employees.

RECRUITMENT AND SELECTION

The proposed conceptual framework provides several managerial implications for the recruitment and selection of service personnel. For example, organizations may want to screen candidates for personal characteristics expected to increase the likelihood of the exercise of appropriate forms of discretion. Specifically, during the recruitment and selection process organizations may want to evaluate the mood trait of potential employees. The evaluation of mood trait could be conducted informally during the course of job interviews or formally through psychological testing. Although the mood trait of an individual has not been found to be directly related to behavior (George 1991; Organ and Konovsky 1989), its relationship with mood state makes it important in the context of employee discretionary behaviors.

Along similar lines, if creative discretion is an expected aspect of job performance, organizations may wish to assess the creative abilities of potential employees during the recruitment and selection process. Creativity tests designed to assess the creative abilities of an individual could be administered during the recruitment and selection process. For example, personality inventories, biographical inventories, and behavioral tests might all prove to be viable means for assessing the creative abilities of prospective employees (Amabile 1983a).

ORGANIZATIONAL SOCIALIZATION

The proposed conceptual framework explicitly recognizes the importance of the process of organizational socialization in service organizations requiring employees to exercise discretion. The socialization program enacted by the organization must convey the expected behaviors of the organization to front-line service personnel. The implementation of an effective organizational socialization program will have an impact on discretion in a variety of ways.

First, an effective socialization program provides the employee with more accurate role perceptions (Dubinsky et al. 1986; Feldman 1976, 1981) and greater motivational direction (Porter and Lawler 1968; Terborg 1977). As employees are socialized and develop higher degrees of motivational direction they should be empowered and expected to exercise discretion while performing tasks for the organization.

The values and expected behaviors expressed through the socialization process will also have an impact on the culture of the organization. As employee values and expected behaviors become more consistent through organizational socialization, the organizational culture becomes stronger and provides a more viable control mechanism for the service manager resulting in the increased likelihood of the exercise of appropriate forms of discretion.

The process of organizational socialization also enhances the organizational commitment of individual employees (e.g., Hunt, Chonko, and Wood 1985). As noted previously, commitment to the organization is expected to increase the likelihood of the exercise of appropriate forms of discretion and decrease the likelihood of the exercise of deviant discretion by employees.

TRAINING

The proposed conceptual framework also has implications for the training of employees. Organizations expecting their employees to exercise routine discretion should emphasize the development of knowledge structures during employee training through modeling, role playing, social reinforcement, and transfer of training (Szymanski 1988). These training programs should be designed to teach service personnel to categorize customers and service encounters in a functional way that makes use of common service delivery strategies across categories (Sujan, Sujan, and Bettman 1988). The enhanced knowledge structures of the trainees will provide them with a larger number of alternatives to select from during the course of service delivery and will reduce the likelihood of the exercise of deviant discretion.

Organizations desiring the exercise of creative discretion by their service personnel should consider implementing a creativity training program. Although there are many creativity training programs available, some of the more popular programs involve brainstorming, synectics, and creative problem solving (Amabile 1983a). The implementation of a creativity training program should facilitate the development of potential means for performing a task resulting in the effective exercise of creative discretion.

PERFORMANCE ASSESSMENT

The conceptualization of discretion presented here also provides managers with a perspective for performance evaluation. Traditionally, financial performance measures have been used to assess performance. However, the short-term thinking that is perpetuated by financial performance measures has been sharply criticized (Eccles 1991). In addition, the accounting standards borrowed from the industrial sector to assess service productivity have been deemed inadequate (Roach 1991). "Services need an accounting framework that can identify which activities add the most value, enabling organizations to distinguish between routine and creative tasks" (Roach 1991). The first step toward such an accounting framework would seem to be the development of a perspective explicitly recognizing the exercise of routine and creative discretion. Once the effect of discretionary activities on performance has been assessed, organizations in the service sector may be able to more readily determine their level of productivity.

DISCRETION AND SERVICE DELIVERY OUTCOMES

The exercise of discretion may result in several desirable service delivery outcomes. First, the exercise of discretion during service delivery enables service personnel to provide more customer-oriented service, which results in greater customer satisfaction (Saxe and Weitz 1982). As customer satisfaction with individual service experiences is enhanced through customer-oriented discretionary behaviors, perceptions of service quality will also become more favorable (Parasuraman, Zeithaml, and Berry 1988). Ultimately, as customer satisfaction increases and perceptions of service quality become more favorable, customer loyalty to the organization will also be enhanced.

RESEARCH IMPLICATIONS

The concept of discretion deserves further consideration from services researchers. Conceptual definitions for three types of discretion and a discussion pertaining to antecedents of discretion have been presented. The conceptualization of discretion and the framework presented here offer implications for the development of a systematic program of research investigating these and related issues through several different research methods.

QUALITATIVE RESEARCH METHODS

Qualitative research is a particularly viable research method in situations where the phenomenon of interest is difficult to study outside of its natural context and does not readily lend itself to quantification (Bonoma 1985). Several of the antecedents of discretion in the proposed framework seem to meet these criteria. For example, organizational socialization and organizational culture can be effectively studied through qualitative research methods (Deshpande and Webster 1989). In addition, aspects of organizational structure and the control systems employed by service organizations (e.g., monitoring and managerial direction) and their relationships with discretion might also be investigated through qualitative research methods.

MEASUREMENT ISSUES

The development of a quantitatively-oriented research program focusing on discretion will initially require the various types of discretion to be operationalized. Several options exist for the operationalization of discretion. First, it may be possible to adapt procedures from behavior-expectation scaling to assess discretion. Behavior-expectation scaling has been used extensively for the development of performance appraisal scales (Bernardin and Smith 1981). In order to operationalize discretion using a behavior-expectation scaling methodology it will be necessary to collect critical incidents potentially leading to the exercise of different types of discretion. Behaviorally-anchored rating scales providing discretion-based responses to each of the critical incidents would be provided, allowing for the assessment of discretion.

A second possible means for assessing discretion is based on previous creativity research (e.g., Amabile, Hennessey, and Grossman 1986). The level of creativity associated with task performance could be rated through the consensual assessment technique. This technique requires the evaluation of the level of creativity associated with the task by multiple expert judges and has been demonstrated to have a high degree of reliability across judges (Amabile, Hennessey, and Grossman 1986).

In adapting this methodology to the assessment of discretion, it might be possible to provide service personnel with a task potentially requiring some form of discretion. Upon completion of the task, multiple expert judges (possibly service managers, fellow employees, or customers) would rate the performance of the task with regard to the creativity involved (creative discretion vs. routine discretion) and its appropriateness (deviant discretion). Staw and Boettger (1990) utilized a similar methodology to assess task revision, a type of extra-role behavior, in an experimental setting. They provided subjects with a written task that they were asked to revise. Task revision was assessed by judges based on the extent of the revision completed by the subject.

It also might be possible to operationalize discretion in a more general fashion. Instead of assessing employee responses to specific critical incidents or task assignments, it may be possible to develop a multiple-item scale assessing general levels of discretionary responses. Other types of extra-role behaviors have been operationalized previously in a similar manner. For example, Smith, Organ, and Near (1983) operationalized organizational citizenship behavior through a sixteen item self-administered scale. This instrument was designed to be administered to managers as a means of performance evaluation. A similar methodology utilizing service managers as respondents might be used to assess the discretion of service personnel.

SURVEY RESEARCH

After confronting issues focusing on the operationalization of discretion, survey research may be useful for the investigation of some of the relationships discussed. For example, there are measures of organizational structure (e.g., John 1984), organizational commitment (O'Reilly and Chatman 1986; Porter et al. 1974), motivational effort and direction (Katerberg and Blau 1983), and mood states (Watson, Clark, and Tellegen 1988) that might be used to test some of the relationships proposed in the framework. In some cases, it may be possible to use these scales as they were originally developed, while in other cases it may be necessary to revise some scale items to meet the needs of a particular research setting.

The knowledge structures of service personnel might be investigated with regard to discretion through the free elicitation procedure (Szymanski 1988; Szymanski and Churchill 1990). This procedure could be used to assess both declarative and procedural knowledge. First, in order to assess the declarative knowledge of service personnel, employees might be asked to provide a list of the cues they use in evaluating service customers or situations. Each of these possible responses would then be assigned an importance weight by the respondent. The relationship between declarative knowledge structures and discretion could then be assessed in a fashion similar to that employed by Szymanski and Churchill (1990) for the evaluation of knowledge structures and sales performance.

The procedural knowledge of service personnel might be assessed in a similar fashion. Specifically, it might be possible to provide respondents with a set of service delivery situations potentially requiring discretion. Respondents could then be asked to provide a list of possible responses to the service delivery situation that they would consider during the course of service delivery. The respondent could then evaluate each response provided with regard to its likelihood of being exercised.

EXPERIMENTAL RESEARCH

Experimental research utilizing scenarios might be conducted to investigate some of the relationships proposed in the framework. The scenario methodology has been used by researchers in a variety of circumstances (e.g., Bellizzi and Hite 1989; Staw and Boettger 1990; Surprenant and Solomon 1987). For example, scenarios could be developed in which aspects of the control system are manipulated. After the respondents are exposed to the experimental manipulation, their anticipated discretionary responses to the scenarios could be assessed through one of the means of measuring discretion described above.

In addition, research by Amabile, Hennessey, and Grossman (1986) considering the relationship between rewards and creativity might provide a useful experimental methodology for the investigation of the control system-discretion relationship. Their research used a laboratory setting to investigate the reward-creativity relationship. It may be possible to refine the methodology used by Amabile, Hennessey, and Grossman (1986) and use it to investigate the control system–discretion relationship. Specifically, control systems might be experimentally manipulated through scenarios as described above with participants providing their responses to the situations regarding the exercise of discretion. The nature of these discretionary responses could then be evaluated through the consensual assessment technique.

Finally, propositions focusing on the mood state–discretion relationship could be tested through experimental methods similar to those previously employed by psychologists investigating the mood construct (e.g., Arkes, Herren, and Isen 1988; Isen and Geva 1987; Isen and Patrick 1983). It might be possible to manipulate the moods of respondents experimentally and then assess discretionary behaviors through the assessment of behavioral intentions.

CONCLUSION

The empowerment of service personnel has become a key issue among service managers. However, empowerment is only the first step toward the exercise of discretion by service personnel in that it provides the employee with the opportunity to exercise discretion. The proposed conceptual framework suggests potential organizational and employee-related antecedents to the actual exercise of discretion. The conceptualization of discretion and the framework presented here will hopefully provide the impetus for services marketing researchers to consider these types of issues.

REFERENCES

Amabile, Teresa M. (1983a), *The Social Psychology of Creativity*, New York, NY: Springer-Verlag.

——— (1983b), "The Social Psychology of Creativity: A Componential Conceptualization," *Journal of Personality and Social Psychology*, 45 (2), 357–376.

———, Beth Ann Hennessey, and Barbara S. Grossman (1986), "Social Influences on Creativity: The Effects of Contracted-for Reward," *Journal of Personality and Social Psychology*, 50 (1), 14–23.

Anderson, Erin, and Richard L. Oliver (1987), "Perspectives on Behavior-Based versus Outcome-Based Salesforce Control Systems," *Journal of Marketing*, 51 (October), 76–88.

Argote, Linda (1982), "Input Uncertainty and Organizational Coordination in Hospital Emergency Units," *Administrative Science Quarterly*, 27 (September), 420–434.

Arkes, Hal R., Lisa Tandy Herren, and Alice M. Isen (1988), "The Role of Potential Loss in the Influence of Affect on Risk-Taking Behavior," *Organizational Behavior and Human Decision Processes*, 42 (October), 181–193.

Bellizzi, A. Joseph and Robert E. Hite (1989), "Supervising Unethical Salesforce Behavior," *Journal of Marketing*, 53 (April), 36–47.

Bernardin, H. John, and Patricia Cain Smith (1981), "A Clarification of Some Issues Regarding the Development and Use of Behaviorally Anchored Rating Scales," *Journal of Applied Psychology*, 66 (August), 458–463.

Bonoma, Thomas V. (1985), "Case Research in Marketing: Opportunities, Problems, and a Process," *Journal of Marketing Research*, 22 (May), 199–208.

Bowen, David E., and Benjamin Schneider (1988), "Services Marketing and Management: Implications for Organizational Behavior," in *Research in Organizational Behavior*, 10, 43–80.

Brief, Arthur P., and Stephan J. Motowidlo (1986), "Prosocial Organizational Behaviors," *Academy of Management Review*, 11 (4), 710–725.

Cialdini, Robert B., and Douglas T. Kenrick (1976), "Altruism and Hedonism: A Social Development Perspective on the Relationship of Negative Mood State and Helping," *Journal of Personality and Social Psychology*, 34, 907–914.

Conger, Jay A., and Rabindra N. Kanungo (1988), "The Empowerment Process: Integrating Theory and Practice," *Academy of Management Review*, 13 (3), 471–482.

Deshpande, Rohit, and Frederick E. Webster, Jr. (1989), "Organizational Culture and Marketing: Defining the Research Agenda," *Journal of Marketing*, 53 (January), 3–15.

Dubinsky, Alan J., Roy D. Howell, Thomas N. Ingram, and Danny N. Bellenger (1986), "Sales Force Socialization," *Journal of Marketing*, 50 (October), 192–207.

Eccles, Robert G. (1991), "The Performance Measurement Manifesto," *Harvard Business Review*, 69 (January–February), 131–137.

Feldman, Daniel Charles (1976), "A Contingency Theory of Socialization," *Administrative Science Quarterly*, 21 (September), 433–450.

——— (1981), "The Multiple Socialization of Organization Members," *Academy of Management Review*, 6 (2), 309–318.

Ferrell, O. C., and Steven J. Skinner (1988), "Ethical Behavior and Bureaucratic Structure in Marketing Research Organizations," *Journal of Marketing Research*, 25 (February), 103–109.

Forest, Duncan, Margaret S. Clark, Judson Mills, and Alice M. Isen (1979), "Helping as a Function of Feeling State and Nature of the Helping Behavior," *Motivation and Emotion*, 3 (June), 161–169.

Gardner, Meryl Paula (1985), "Mood States and Consumer Behavior: A Critical Review," *Journal of Consumer Research*, 12 (December), 281–300.

George, Jennifer M. (1989), "Mood and Absence," *Journal of Applied Psychology*, 74 (April), 317–324.

——— (1991), "State or Trait: Effects of Positive Mood on Prosocial Behaviors at Work," *Journal of Applied Psychology*, 76 (2), 299–307.

Gibson, James L., John M. Ivancevich, and James H. Donnelly, Jr. (1991), *Organizations: Behavior, Structure, Processes*, seventh edition, Homewood, IL: Richard D. Irwin, Inc.

Gouaux, Charles (1971), "Induced Affective States and Interpersonal Attraction," *Journal of Personality and Social Psychology*, 20 (1), 37–43.

Griffitt, William (1970), "Environmental Effects on Interpersonal Affective Behavior: Ambient Effective Temperature and Attraction," *Journal of Personality and Social Psychology*, 15 (July), 240–244.

Hill, Ronald Paul, and James C. Ward (1989), "Mood Manipulation in Marketing Research: An Examination of Potential Confounding Effects," *Journal of Marketing Research*, 26 (February), 97–104.

Hughes, Everett Cherrington (1964), *Men and Their Work*, Glencoe, IL: The Free Press.

Hunt, Shelby, D., Lawrence B. Chonko, and Van R. Wood (1985), "Organizational Commitment and Marketing," *Journal of Marketing*, 49 (Winter), 112–126.

Isen, Alice M. (1984), "Toward Understanding the Role of Affect in Cognition," in Robert S. Wyer and Thomas K. Srull (eds.), *Handbook of Social Cognition, Volume III*, Hillsdale, NJ: Lawrence Erlbaum Associates.

———, and Nehemia Geva (1987), "The Influence of Positive Affect on Acceptable Level of Risk: The Person with a Large Canoe Has a Large Worry," *Organizational Behavior and Human Decision Processes*, 39 (April), 145–154.

———, and Robert Patrick (1983), "The Effect of Positive Feelings on Risk Taking: When the Chips Are Down," *Organizational Behavior and Human Performance*, 31 (April), 194–202.

John, George (1984), "An Empirical Investigation of Some Antecedents of Opportunism in a Marketing Channel," *Journal of Marketing Research*, 21 (August), 278–289.

Katerberg, Ralph, and Gary J. Blau (1983), "An Examination of Level and Direction of Effort and Job Performance," *Academy of Management Journal*, 26 (2), 249–257.

Katz, Daniel (1964), "The Motivational Bias of Organizational Behavior," *Behavioral Science*, 9 (April), 131–146.

Kelley, Scott W., James H. Donnelly, Jr., and Steven J. Skinner (1990), "Customer Participation in Service Production and Delivery," *Journal of Retailing*, 66 (3), 315–335.

Larsson, Rikard, and David E. Bowen (1989), "Organization and Customer: Managing Design and Coordination of Services," *Academy of Management Review*, 14 (2), 213–233.

Leigh, Thomas W., and Patrick F. McGraw (1989), "Mapping Procedural Knowledge of Industrial Sales Personnel: A Script-Theoretic Investigation," *Journal of Marketing*, 53 (January), 16–34.

———, and Arno J. Rethans (1984), "A Script-theoretic Analysis of Industrial Purchasing Behavior," *Journal of Marketing*, 48 (Fall), 22–32.

Levitt, Theodore (1972), "Production-Line Approach to Service," *Harvard Business Review*, 50 (September–October), 41–52.

——— (1976), "The Industrialization of Service," *Harvard Business Review*, 54 (September–October), 63–74.

Louis, Meryl Reis (1980), "Surprise and Sense-Making: What Newcomers Experience in Entering Unfamiliar Organizational Settings," *Administrative Science Quarterly*, 25 (June) 226–251.

March, James G., and Herbert A. Simon (1958), *Organizations*, New York, NY: John Wiley & Sons, Inc.

Mills, Peter K., and Dennis J. Moberg (1982), "Perspectives on the Technology of Service Operations," *Academy of Management Review*, 7 (3), 467–478.

Mowday, Richard T., Lyman W. Porter, and R. Dubin (1974) "Unit Performance, Situational Factors, and Employee Attitudes in Spatially Separated Work Units," *Organizational Behavior and Human Performance*, 12 (October), 231–248.

Naylor, James C., Richard D. Pritchard, and Daniel Ilgen (1980), *A Theory of Behavior in Organizations*, New York, NY: Academic Press, Inc.

O'Reilly, Charles III, and Jennifer Chatman (1986), "Organizational Commitment and Psychological Attachment: The Effects of Compliance, Identification, and Internalization on Prosocial Behavior," *Journal of Applied Psychology*, 71 (3), 492–499.

Organ, Dennis W., and Mary Konovsky (1989), "Cognitive versus Affective Determinants of Organizational Citizenship Behavior," *Journal of Applied Psychology*, 74 (1), 157–164.

Parasuraman, A., Valarie A. Zeithaml, and Leonard L. Berry (1988), "SERVQUAL: A Multiple-Item Scale for Measuring Consumer Perceptions of Service Quality," *Journal of Retailing*, 64 (Spring), 12–40.

Peterson, Robert, and Matthew Sauber (1983), "A Mood Scale for Survey Research," in Patrick Murphy et al. (eds.), *1983 Educators' Proceedings*, Chicago, IL: American Marketing Association.

Phillips, Steven, Amy Dunkin, James B. Treece, and Keith H. Hammonds (1990), "King Customer," *Businessweek,* (March 12), 88–94.

Porter, Lyman W., and Edward E. Lawler, III (1968), *Managerial Attitudes and Performance,* Homewood, IL: Richard D. Irwin, Inc.

————, Richard M. Steers, Richard T. Mowday, and Paul V. Boulian (1974), "Organizational Commitment, Job Satisfaction, and Turnover among Psychiatric Technicians," *Journal of Applied Psychology,* 59 (5), 603–609.

Roach, Stephen S. (1991), "Services under Siege—The Restructuring Imperative," *Harvard Business Review,* 69 (September–October), 82–91.

Ruekert, Robert W., and Orville C. Walker, Jr. (1987), "Marketing's Interaction with Other Functional Units: A Conceptual Framework and Empirical Evidence," *Journal of Marketing,* 51 (January), 1–19.

Saxe, Robert, and Barton A. Weitz (1982), "The SOCO Scale: A Measure of the Customer Orientation of Salespeople," *Journal of Marketing Research,* 19 (August), 343–351.

Smith, C. Ann, Dennis W. Organ, and Janet P. Near (1983), "Organizational Citizenship Behavior: Its Nature and Antecedents," *Journal of Applied Psychology,* 68 (4), 653–663.

Staw, Barry M. (1984), "Organizational Behavior, A Review and Reformulation of the Field's Outcome Variables," in *Annual Review of Psychology,* 35, 627–666.

————, and Richard D. Boettger (1990), "Task Revision: A Neglected Form of Work Performance," *Academy of Management Journal,* 33 (3), 534–559.

Steers, Richard M. (1977), "Antecedents and Outcomes of Organizational Commitment," *Administrative Science Quarterly,* 22 (March), 46–56.

Sujan, Harish (1986), "Smarter versus Harder: An Exploratory Attributional Analysis of Salespeople's Motivation," *Journal of Marketing Research,* 23 (February), 41–49.

————, Mita Sujan, and James R. Bettman (1988), "Knowledge Structure Differences between More Effective and Less Effective Salespeople," *Journal of Marketing Research,* 25 (February), 81–86.

Surprenant, Carol F., and Michael R. Solomon (1987), "Predictability and Personalization in the Service Encounter," *Journal of Marketing,* 51 (April), 86–96.

Szymanski, David M. (1988), "Determinants of Selling Effectiveness: The Importance of Declarative Knowledge to the Personal Selling Concept," *Journal of Marketing,* 52 (January), 64–77.

————, and Gilbert A. Churchill, Jr. (1990), "Client Evaluation Cues: A Comparison of Successful and Unsuccessful Salespeople," *Journal of Marketing Research,* 27 (May), 163–174.

Terborg, James R. (1977), "Validation and Extension of an Individual Differences Model of Work Performance, 18 (February), 188–216.

————, and Howard E. Miller (1978), "Motivation, Behavior, and Performance: A Closer Examination of Goal Setting and Monetary Incentives," *Journal of Applied Psychology,* 63 (1), 29–39.

Thompson, James D. (1967), *Organizations in Action,* New York, NY: McGraw-Hill Book Company.

Twible, Jacquelyn L., and Stacey B. Frank (1992), "The Construct Validity of Mood: An Assessment of Convergent and Discriminant Dimensions," in Chris T. Allen et al. (eds.), *Marketing Theory and Applications: 1992 Winter Educators' Conference Proceedings,* Chicago, IL: American Marketing Association.

Van Maanen, John (1975), "Police Socialization: A Longitudinal Examination of Job Attitudes in an Urban Police Department," *Administrative Science Quarterly,* 20 (2), 207–228.

————, and Edgar H. Schein (1979), "Toward a Theory of Organizational Socialization," in Barry M. Staw (ed.), *Research in Organizational Behavior,* Vol. 1, Greenwich, CT: JAI Press, Inc.

Veitch, Russell, and William Griffitt (1976), "Good News–Bad News: Affective and Interpersonal Effects," *Journal of Applied Social Psychology,* 6 (January–March), 69–75.

Watson, David, and J. W. Pennebaker (1989), "Health Complaints, Stress, and Distress: Exploring the Central Role of Negative Affectivity," *Psychological Review,* 96 (April), 234–254.

————, Lee Anna Clark, and Auke Tellegen (1988), "Development and Validation of Brief Measures of Positive and Negative Affect: The PANAS Scales," *Journal of Personality and Social Psychology,* 54 (6), 1063–1070.

Weiner, Yoash (1982), "Commitment in the Organization: A Normative View," *Academy of Management Review,* 7 (3), 418–428.

Weitz, Barton, A., Harish Sujan, and Mita Sujan (1986), "Knowledge, Motivation, and Adaptive Behavior: A Framework for Improving Selling Effectiveness," *Journal of Marketing,* 50 (October), 174–191.

Zeithaml, Valarie A., Leonard L. Berry, and A. Parasuraman (1988), "Communication and Control Processes in the Delivery of Service Quality," *Journal of Marketing,* 52 (April), 35–48.

THE EMPOWERMENT OF SERVICE WORKERS

WHAT, WHY, HOW, AND WHEN

David E. Bowen
Arizona State University

Edward E. Lawler III
University of Southern California

In recent years, businesses have rushed to adopt an empowerment approach to service delivery in which employees face customers "free of rulebooks," encouraged to do whatever is necessary to satisfy them. But that approach may not be right for everyone. Bowen and Lawler look at the benefits and costs of empowering employees, the range of management practices that empower employees to varying degrees, and key business characteristics that affect the choice of approaches. Managers need to make sure that there is a good fit between their organizational needs and their approach to frontline employees.

Empowering service workers has acquired almost a "born again" religious fervor. Tom Peters calls it "purposeful chaos." Robert Waterman dubs it "directed autonomy." It has also been called the "art of improvisation."

Yet in the mid-1970s, the production-line approach to service was the darling child of service gurus. They advocated facing the customer with standardized, procedurally driven operations. Should we now abandon this approach in favor of empowerment?

Unfortunately, there is no simple, clear-cut answer. In this article we try to help managers think about the question of whether to empower by clarifying its advantages and disadvantages, describing three forms that empower employees to different degrees, and presenting five contingencies that managers can use to determine which approach best fits their situation. We do not intend to debunk empowerment, rather we hope to clarify why to empower (there are costs, as well as benefits), how to empower (there are alternatives), and when to empower (it really does depend on the situation).

THE PRODUCTION-LINE APPROACH

In two classic articles, the "Production-Line Approach to Service" and the "Industrialization of Service," Theodore Levitt described how service operations can be made more efficient by applying manufacturing logic and tactics.[1] He argued:

> Manufacturing thinks technocratically, and that explains its success. . . . By contrast, service looks for solutions in the performer of the task. This is the paralyzing legacy of our inherited attitudes: the solution to improved service is viewed as being dependent on improvements in the skills and attitudes of the performers of that service.
>
> While it may pain and offend us to say so, thinking in humanistic rather than technocratic terms ensures that the service sector will be forever inefficient and that our satisfactions will be forever marginal.[2]

He recommended (1) simplification of tasks, (2) clear division of labor, (3) substitution of equipment

Source: David E. Bowen and Edward E. Lawler III, "The Empowerment of Service Workers: What, Why, How, and When," *Sloan Management Review*, (Spring 1992): 31–39.

David E. Bowen is associate professor of management, business programs, Arizona State University, West. Edward E. Lawler III is director of the Center for Effective Organizations, Graduate School of Business Administration, University of Southern California.

and systems for employees, and (4) little decision-making discretion afforded to employees. In short, management designs the system, and employees execute it.

McDonald's is a good example. Workers are taught how to greet customers and ask for their order, including a script for suggesting additional items. They learn a set procedure for assembling the order (for example, cold drinks first, then hot ones), placing items on the tray, and placing the tray where customers need not reach for it. There is a script and a procedure for collecting money and giving change. Finally, there is a script for saying thank you and asking the customer to come again.[3] This production-line approach makes customer-service interactions uniform and gives the organization control over them. It is easily learned; workers can be quickly trained and put to work.

What are the gains from a production-line approach? Efficient, low-cost, high-volume service operations, with satisfied customers.

THE EMPOWERMENT APPROACH

Ron Zemke and Dick Schaaf, in *The Service Edge: 101 Companies That Profit from Customer Care,* note that empowerment is a common theme running through many, even most, of their excellent service businesses, such as American Airlines, Marriott, American Express, and Federal Express. To Zemke and Schaaf, empowerment means "turning the front line loose," encouraging and rewarding employees to exercise initiative and imagination: "Empowerment in many ways is the reverse of doing things by the book."[4]

The humanistic flavor of empowerment pervades the words of advocates such as Tom Peters:

> It is necessary to "dehumiliate" work by eliminating the policies and procedures (almost always tiny) of the organization that demean and belittle human dignity. It is impossible to get people's best efforts, involvement, and caring concern for things you believe important to your customers and the long-term interests of your organization when we write policies and procedures that treat them like thieves and bandits.[5]

And from Jan Carlzon, CEO of Scandinavian Airlines Systems (SAS):

> To free someone from rigorous control by instructions, policies, and orders, and to give that person freedom to take responsibility for his ideas, decisions, and actions is to release hidden resources that would otherwise remain inaccessible to both the individual and the organization.[6]

In contrast to the industrialization of service, empowerment very much looks to the "performer of the tasks" for solutions to service problems. Workers are asked to suggest new services and products and to solve problems creatively and effectively.

What, then, does it really mean—beyond the catchy slogans—to empower employees? We define empowerment as sharing with frontline employees four organizational ingredients: (1) information about the organization's performance, (2) rewards based on the organization's performance, (3) knowledge that enables employees to understand and contribute to organizational performance, and (4) power to make decisions that influence organizational direction and performance. We will say more about these features later. For now, we can say that with a production-line approach, these features tend to be concentrated in the hands of senior management; with an empowerment approach, they tend to be moved downward to frontline employees.

WHICH APPROACH IS BETTER?

In 1990, Federal Express became the first service organization to win the Malcolm Baldrige National Quality Award. The company's motto is "people, service, and profits." Behind its blue, white, and red planes and uniforms are self-managing work teams, gainsharing plans, and empowered employees seemingly consumed with providing flexible and creative service to customers with varying needs.

At UPS, referred to as "Big Brown" by its employees, the philosophy was stated by founder Jim Casey: "Best service at low rates." Here, too, we find turned-on people and profits. But we do not find empowerment. Instead we find controls, rules, a detailed union contract, and carefully studied work methods. Nor do we find a promise to do all things for customers, such as handling off-schedule pickups and packages that don't fit size and weight limitations. In fact, rigid operational guidelines help guarantee the customer reliable, low-cost service.

Federal Express and UPS present two different faces to the customer, and behind these faces are different management philosophies and organizational cultures. Federal Express is a high-involvement, horizontally coordinated organization that encourages employees to use their judgment above and beyond the rulebook. UPS is a top-down, traditionally controlled organization, in which employees are directed by policies and procedures based on industrial engineering studies of how all service delivery aspects should be carried out and how long they should take.

Similarly, at Disney theme parks, ride operators are thoroughly scripted on what to say to "guests," including a list of preapproved "ad libs!" At Club Med, however, CEO Jacques Giraud fervently believes that guests must experience *real* magic, and the resorts' GOs, (*gentils organisateurs,* "congenial hosts") are set free to spontaneously create this feeling for their guests. Which is the better approach? Federal Express or UPS? Club Med or Disney?

At a recent executive education seminar on customer service, one of us asked, "Who thinks that it is important for their business to empower their service personnel as a tool for improving customer service?" All twenty-seven participants enthusiastically raised their hands. Although they represented diverse services—banking, travel, utilities, airlines, and shipping—and they disagreed on most points, they all agreed that empowerment is key to customer satisfaction. But is it?

EMPOWERING SERVICE EMPLOYEES: WHY, HOW, AND WHEN

WHY TO EMPOWER: THE BENEFITS

What gains are possible from empowering service employees?

☐ **Quicker On-Line Responses to Customer Needs during Service Delivery.** Check-in time at the hotel begins at 2 p.m., but a guest asks the desk clerk if she can check in at 1:30 p.m. An airline passenger arrives at the gate at 7:30 a.m., Friday, for a 7:45 a.m. departure and wants to board the plane with a travel coupon good Monday through Thursday, and there are empty seats on the plane. The waitress is taking an order in a modestly priced family restaurant; the menu says no substitutions, but the customer requests one anyway.

The customer wants a quick response. And the employee would often like to be able to respond with something other than "No, it is against our rules," or "I will have to check with my supervisor." Empowering employees in these situations can lead to the sort of spontaneous, creative rule-breaking that can turn a potentially frustrated or angry customer into a satisfied one. This is particularly valuable when there is little time to refer to a higher authority, as when the plane is leaving in fifteen minutes. Even before greeting customers, empowered employees are confident that they have all the necessary resources at their command to provide customers with what they need.

☐ **Quicker On-Line Responses to Dissatisfied Custo-mers during Service Recovery.** Customer service involves both delivering the service, such as checking a guest into a hotel room, and recovering from poor service, such as relocating him from a smoking floor to the nonsmoking room he originally requested. Although delivering good service may mean different things to different customers, all customers feel that service businesses ought to fix things when service is delivered improperly. Figure 1 depicts the relationships among service delivery, recovery, and customer satisfaction.

Fixing something after doing it wrong the first time can turn a dissatisfied customer into a satisfied, even loyal, customer. But service businesses frequently fail in the act of recovery because service employees are not empowered to make the necessary amends with customers. Instead, customers hear employees saying, "Gee, I wish there was something I could do, but I can't," "It's not my fault," or "I could check with my boss, but she's not here today." These employees lack the power and knowledge to recover, and customers remain dissatisfied.

☐ **Employees Feel Better about Their Jobs and Themselves.** Earlier we mentioned Tom Peters' thinking on how strict rules can belittle human dignity. Letting employees call the shots allows them to feel "ownership" of the job; they feel responsible for it and find the work meaningful. Think of how you treat your car as opposed to a rented one. Have you ever washed a rental car? Decades of job design research show that when employees have a sense of control and of doing meaningful work they are more satisfied. This leads to lower turnover, less absenteeism, and fewer union organizing drives.

☐ **Employees Will Interact with Customers with More Warmth and Enthusiasm.** Research now supports our long-standing intuition that customers' per-

FIGURE 1   Possible Outcomes during Service Delivery and Recovery

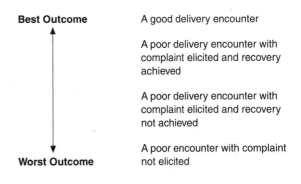

Best Outcome

A good delivery encounter

A poor delivery encounter with complaint elicited and recovery achieved

A poor delivery encounter with complaint elicited and recovery not achieved

Worst Outcome

A poor encounter with complaint not elicited

ceptions of service quality are shaped by the courtesy, empathy, and responsiveness of service employees.[7] Customers want employees to appear concerned about their needs. Can empowerment help create this? One of us has done customer service research in branch banks that showed that when the tellers reported feeling good about how they were supervised, trained, and rewarded, customers thought more highly of the service they received.[8] In short, when employees felt that management was looking after their needs, they took better care of the customer.

In service encounters, employees' feelings about their jobs will spill over to affect how customers feel about the service they get. This is particularly important when employee attitudes are a key part of the service package. In banking, where the customer receives no tangible benefits in the exchange other than a savings deposit slip, a sour teller can really blemish a customer's feelings about the encounter.

☐ **Empowered Employees Can Be a Great Source of Service Ideas.** Giving frontline employees a voice in "how we do things around here" can lead to improved service delivery and ideas for new services. The bank study showed that the tellers could accurately report how customers viewed overall service quality and how they saw the branches' service climate (e.g., adequacy of staff and appearance of facilities).[9]

Frontline employees are often ready and willing to offer their opinion. When it comes to market research, imagine the difference in response rates from surveying your employees and surveying your customers.

☐ **Great Word-of-Mouth Advertising and Customer Retention.** Nordstrom's advertising budget is 1.5 percent of sales, whereas the industry average is 5 percent. Why? Their satisfied-no-matter-what customers spread the word about their service and become repeat customers.

THE COSTS

What are the costs of empowerment?

☐ **A Greater Dollar Investment in Selection and Training.** You cannot hire effective, creative problem solvers on the basis of chance or mere intuition. Too bad, because the systematic methods necessary to screen out those who are not good candidates for empowerment are expensive. For example, Federal Express selects customer agents and couriers on the basis of well-researched profiles of successful performers in those jobs.

Training is an even greater cost. The production-line approach trains workers easily and puts them right to work. In contrast, new hires at SAS are formally assigned a mentor to help them learn the ropes: Nordstrom department managers take responsibility for orienting and training new members of the sales team; customer service representatives at Lands' End and L. L. Bean spend a week in training before handling their first call. They receive far more information and knowledge about their company and its products that is the norm.

The more labor intensive the service, the higher these costs. Retail banking, department stores, and convenience stores are labor intensive, and their training and selection costs can run high. Utilities and airlines are far less labor intensive.

☐ **Higher Labor Costs.** Many consumer service organizations, such as department stores, convenience stores, restaurants, and banks, rely on large numbers of part-time and seasonal workers to meet their highly variable staffing needs. These employees typically work for short periods of time at low wages. To empower these workers, a company would have to invest heavily in training to try to quickly inculcate the organization's culture and values. This training would probably be unsuccessful, and the employees wouldn't be around long enough to provide a return on the investment. Alternatively, the organization could pay higher wages to full-time, permanent employees, but they would be idle when business was slow.

☐ **Slower or Inconsistent Service Delivery.** Remember the hotel guest wanting to check in early and the airline passenger requesting special treatment at the gate? True, there is a benefit to empowering the employee to bend the rules, but only for the person at the front of the line! Customers at the back of the line are grumbling and checking their watches. They may have the satisfaction of knowing that they too may receive creative problem solving when and if they reach the counter, but it is small consolation if the plane has already left.

Based on our experiences as both researchers and customers, we believe that customers will increasingly value speed in service delivery. Purposeful chaos may work against this. We also believe that many customers value "no surprises" in service delivery. They like to know what to expect when they revisit a service business or patronize different outlets of a franchise. When service delivery is left to employee discretion, it may be inconsistent.

The research data show that customers perceive reliability—"doing it right the first time"—as the most important dimension of service quality. It matters more than employees' responsiveness, courtesy, or competency, or the attractiveness of the service setting.[10] Unfortunately, in the same research, a sample of large, well-known firms was more deficient on reliability than on these other dimensions. Much of the touted appeal of the production-line approach was that procedurally and technocratically driven operations could deliver service more reliably and consistently than service operations heavily dependent upon the skills and attitudes of employees. The production-line approach was intended to routinize service so that customers would receive the "best outcome" possible from their service encounters—service delivery with no glitches in the first place.

We feel that service managers need to guard against being seduced into too great a focus on recovery, at the expense of service delivery reliability. We say "seduced" because it is possible to confuse good service with inspiring stories about empowered employees excelling at the art of recovery. Recovery has more sex appeal than the nitty-gritty detail of building quality into every seemingly mundane aspect of the service delivery system, but an organization that relies on recovery may end up losing out to firms that do it right the first time.

□ **Violations of "Fair Play."** A recent study of how service businesses handle customer complaints revealed that customers associate sticking to procedures with being treated fairly.[11] Customers may be more likely to return to a business if they believe that their complaint was handled effectively because of company policies rather than because they were lucky enough to get a particular employee. In other words, customers may prefer procedurally driven acts of recovery. We suspect that customers' notions of fairness may be violated when they see employees cutting special deals with other customers.

□ **Giveaways and Bad Decisions.** Managers are often re-luctant to empower their employees for fear they will give too much away to the customer. Perhaps they have heard the story of Willie, the doorman at a Four Seasons Hotel, who left work and took a flight to return a briefcase left behind by a guest. Or they have heard of too many giveaways by empowered Nordstrom employees. For some services, the costs of giveaways are far outweighed by enhanced customer loyalty, but not for others.

Sometimes creative rule breaking can cause a major problem for an organization. There may be a good reason why no substitutions are allowed or why a coupon cannot be used on a certain day (e.g., an international airfare agreement). If so, having an empowered employ-ee break a rule may cause the organization serious problems, of which the employee may not even be aware.

These are some of the costs and benefits of empowerment. We hope this discussion will help service businesses use empowerment knowledgeably, not just because it is a fad. But we must add one more caveat: There is still precious little research on the consequences of empowerment. We have used anecdotal evidence, related research (e.g., in job design), and our work on service. More systematic research must assess whether this array of costs and benefits fully captures the "whys" (and "why nots") of empowerment.

HOW TO EMPOWER: THREE OPTIONS

Empowering service employees is less understood than industrializing service delivery. This is largely because the production-line approach is an example of the well-developed control model of organization design and management, whereas empowerment is part of the still evolving "commitment" or "involvement" model. The latter assumes that most employees can make good decisions if they are properly socialized, trained, and informed. They can be internally motivated to perform effectively, and they are capable of self-control and self-direction. This approach also assumes that most employees can produce good ideas for operating the business.[12]

The control and involvement models differ in that four key features are concentrated at the top of the organization in the former and pushed down in the organization in the latter. As we have discussed above, these features are the following: (1) information about organizational performance (e.g., operating results and competitor performance); (2) rewards based on organizational performance (e.g., profit sharing and stock ownership); (3) knowledge that enables employees to understand and contribute to organizational performance (e.g., problem-solving skills); and (4) power to make decisions that influence work procedures and organizational direction (e.g., through quality circles and self-managing teams).

Three approaches to empowering employees can be identified (see Figure 2).[13] They represent increasing degrees of empowerment as additional knowledge, information, power, and rewards are pushed down to the front line. Empowerment, then, is not an either/or alternative, but rather a choice of three options:

1. **Suggestion Involvement** represents a small shift away from the control model. Employees are encouraged to contribute ideas through formal suggestion programs or quality circles, but their day-to-day work

FIGURE 2   Levels of Empowerment

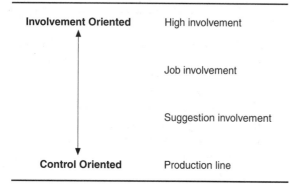

activities do not really change. Also, they are only empowered to recommend; management typically retains the power to decide whether or not to implement.

Suggestion involvement can produce some empowerment without altering the basic production-line approach. McDonald's, for example, listens closely to the front line. The Big Mac, Egg McMuffin, and McDLT all were invented by employees, as was the system of wrapping burgers that avoids leaving a thumbprint in the bun. As another example, Florida Power and Light, which won the Deming quality award, defines empowerment in suggestion involvement terms.

2. **Job Involvement** represents a significant departure from the control model because of its dramatic "opening up" of job content. Jobs are redesigned so that employees use a variety of skills. Employees believe their tasks are significant, they have considerable freedom in deciding how to do the work, they get more feedback, and they handle a whole, identifiable piece of work. Research shows that many employees find enriched work more motivating and satisfying, and they do higher-quality work.[14]

Often job involvement is accomplished through extensive use of teams. Teams are often appropriate in complex service organizations such as hospitals and airlines because individuals cannot offer a whole service or handle a customer from beginning to end of service delivery. Teams can empower back-office workers in banks and insurance companies as well.

Employees in this environment require training to deal with the added complexity. Supervisors, who now have fewer shots to call, need to be reoriented toward supporting the front line, rather than directing it. Despite the heightened level of empowerment it brings, the job involvement approach does not change higher-level strategic decisions concerning organization struc-

ture, power, and the allocation of rewards. These remain the responsibility of senior management.

3. **High-Involvement** organizations give their lowest-level employees a sense of involvement not just in how they do their jobs or how effectively their group performs, but in the total organization's performance. Virtually every aspect of the organization is different from that of a control-oriented organization. Business performance information is shared. Employees develop skills in teamwork, problem solving, and business operations. They participate in word-unit management decisions. There is profit sharing and employee ownership.

High-involvement designs may be expensive to implement. Perhaps most troublesome is that these management techniques are relatively undeveloped and untested. People Express tried to operate a high-involvement airline, and the ongoing struggle to learn and develop this new organizational design contributed to its operating problems.

Today, America West is trying to make the high-involvement design work. New hires spend 25 percent of their first year's salary on company stock. All employees receive annual stock options. Flight attendants and pilots develop their own work procedures and schedules. Employees are extensively cross-trained to work where they are needed. Only time will tell if America West can make high-involvement work as it struggles with its financial crisis stemming from high fuel costs and rapid growth.

Federal Express displays many high-involvement features. A couple of years ago, it began a companywide push to convert to teams, including the back office. It organized its 1,000 clerical workers in Memphis into superteams of five to ten people and gave them the authority and training to manage themselves. These teams helped the company cut customer service problems, such as incorrect bills and lost packages, by 13 percent in 1989.

WHEN TO EMPOWER: A CONTINGENCY APPROACH

Management thought and practice frequently have been seduced by the search for the "one best way to manage." Unfortunately, business does not lend itself to universal truths, only to "contingency theories" of management. For example, early job enrichment efforts in the 1960s assumed that all employees would prefer more challenging work and more autonomy. By the 1970s it was clear that only those employees who felt the need to grow at work responded positively to job enrichment.[15] As the research on it is still thin, it is at least possible that empowerment is a universal truth, but historical evidence weighs against its being the best way to manage in all situations.

We believe that both the empowerment and production-line approaches have their advantages, and that each fits certain situations. The key is to choose the management approach that best meets the needs of both employees and customers.

Table 1 presents five contingencies that determine which approach to adopt. Each contingency can be rated on a scale of 1 to 5 to diagnose the quality of fit between the overall situation and the alternative approaches. The following propositions suggest how to match situations and approaches. Matching is not an exact science, but the propositions suggest reasonable rules of thumb.

Proposition 1: The higher the rating of each contingency (5 being the highest), the better the fit with an empowerment approach; the lower the rating (1 being the lowest), the better the fit with a production-line approach.

Proposition 2: The higher the total score from all five contingencies, the better the fit with an empowerment approach; the lower the total score, the better the fit with a production-line approach. A production-line approach is a good fit with situations that score in the range of 5 to 10. For empowerment approaches, suggestion involvement is a good fit with situations that score in the range of 11 to 15, job involvement with scores that range from 16 to 20, and high involvement with scores that range from 21 to 25.

Proposition 3: The higher the total score, the more the benefits of increasing empowerment will outweigh the costs.

In what follows, we describe each contingency's implications for a production-line or empowerment approach.

BASIC BUSINESS STRATEGY A production-line approach makes the most sense if your core mission is to offer high-volume service at the lowest cost. "Industrializing" service certainly leverages volume. The question is: what is the value-added from spending the additional dollars on employee selection, training, and retention necessary for empowerment? This question is especially compelling in labor-intensive services (e.g., fast food, grocery stores, and convenience stores) and those that require part-time or temporary employees.

The answer depends on what customers want from the service firm, and what they are willing to pay for. Certain customer segments are just looking for cheap, quick, reliable service. They do want quality—a warm hamburger rather than a cold one. But they are not necessarily expecting tender loving care. Even if they wanted it, they wouldn't pay for it.

These customers prefer a production-line approach. A recent study of convenience stores actually found a negative relationship between store sales and clerks being friendly with customers.[16] Customers wanted speed, and friendly clerks slowed things down. The point is that customers themselves may prefer to be served by a nonempowered employee.

At Taco Bell, counter attendants are expected to be civil, but they are not expected or encouraged to be creative problem solvers. Taco Bell wants to serve customers who want low-cost, good quality, fast food. Interestingly, the company believes that as more chains move to customized, service-oriented operations, it has more opportunities in the fast, low-price market niche.

The production-line approach does not rule out suggestion involvement. As mentioned earlier, employees often have ideas even when much of their work is routinized. Quality circles and other approaches can capture and develop them.

An empowerment approach works best with a market segment that wants the tender loving care dimension

TABLE 1   The Contingencies of Empowerment

Contingency	Production-Line Approach		Empowerment
Basic business strategy	Low cost, high volume	1 2 3 4 5	Differentiation, customized, personalized
Tie to customer	Transaction, short time period	1 2 3 4 5	Relationship, long time period
Technology	Routine, simple	1 2 3 4 5	Nonroutine, complex
Business environment	Predictable, few surprises	1 2 3 4 5	Unpredictable, many surprises
Types of people	Theory X managers, employees with low growth needs, low social needs, and weak interpersonal skills	1 2 3 4 5	Theory Y managers, employees with high growth needs, high social needs, and strong interpersonal skills

more than speed and cost. For example, SAS targets frequent business travellers (who do not pay their own way). The SAS strategy was to differentiate itself from other airlines on the basis of personalized service. Consequently, the company looked at every ingredient of its service package to see if it fit this segment's definition of service quality, and, if so, whether or not customers would pay for it.

TIE TO THE CUSTOMER Empowerment is the best approach when service delivery involves managing a relationship, as opposed to simply performing a transaction. The service firm may want to establish relationships with customers to build loyalty or to get ideas for improving the service delivery system or offering new services. A flexible, customized approach can help establish the relationship and get the ideas flowing.

The returns on empowerment and relationship-building are higher with more sophisticated services and delivery systems. An employee in the international air freight industry is more likely to learn from a customer relationship than is a gasoline station attendant.

The relationship itself can be the principle valued commodity that is delivered in many services. When no tangibles are delivered, as in estate planning or management consulting, the service provider often is the service to the customer, and empowerment allows the employee to customize the service to fit the customer's needs.

The more enduring the relationship, and the more important it is in the service package, the stronger the case for empowerment. Remember the earlier comparison between Disney, which tightly scripts its ride operators, and Club Med, which encourages its GOs to be spontaneous? Giraud, Club Med's CEO, explains that Disney employees relate to their guests in thousands of brief encounters; GOs have week-long close relationships with a limited number of guests. The valuable service they sell is "time."

TECHNOLOGY It is very difficult to build challenge, feedback, and autonomy into a telephone operator's job, given the way the delivery technology has been designed. The same is true of many fast-food operations. In these situations, the technology limits empowerment to only suggestion involvement and ultimately may almost completely remove individuals from the service delivery process, as has happened with ATMs.

When technology constrains empowerment, service managers can still support frontline employees in ways that enhance their satisfaction and the service quality they provide. For example, managers can show employees how much their jobs matter to the organization's success and express more appreciation for the work they do. In other words, managers can do a better job of making the old management model work!

Routine work can be engaging if employees are convinced that it matters. Volunteers will spend hours licking envelopes in a fundraising campaign for their favorite charity. Disney theme park employees do an admirable job of performing repetitive work, partly because they believe in the values, mission, and show business magic of Disney.

BUSINESS ENVIRONMENT Businesses that operate in unpredictable environments benefit from empowerment. Airlines face many challenges to their operations: bad weather, mechanical breakdowns, and competitors' actions. They serve passengers who make a wide variety of special requests. It is simply impossible to anticipate many of the situations that will arise and to "program" employees to respond to them. Employees trained in purposeful chaos are appropriate for unpredictable environments.

Fast-food restaurants, however, operate in stable environments. Operations are fairly fail-safe; customer expectations are simple and predictable. In this environment, the service business can use a production-line approach. The stability allows, even encourages, management with policies and procedures, because managers can predict most events and identify the best responses.

TYPES OF PEOPLE Empowerment and production-line approaches demand different types of managers and employees. For empowerment to work, particularly in the high-involvement form, the company needs to have Theory Y managers who believe that their employees can act independently to benefit both the organization and its customers. If the management ranks are filled with Theory X types who believe that employees only do their best work when closely supervised, then the production-line approach may be the only feasible option unless the organization changes its managers. Good service can still be the outcome. For example, most industry observers would agree that Delta and American Airlines are managed with a control orientation rather than a strong empowerment approach.

Employees will respond positively to empowerment only if they have strong needs to grow and to deepen and test their abilities—at work. Again, a checkered history of job enrichment efforts has taught us not to assume that everyone wants more autonomy, challenge, and responsibility at work. Some employees simply prefer a production-line approach.

Lastly, empowerment that involves teamwork requires employees who are interested in meeting their social and affiliative needs at work. It also requires that employees have good interpersonal and group process skills.

THE FUTURE OF SERVICE WORK

How likely is it that more and more service businesses will choose to face the customer with empowered employees? We would guess that far more service organizations operate at the production-line end of our continuum than their business situations call for. A recent survey of companies in the "Fortune 1000" offers some support for this view.[17] This survey revealed that manufacturing firms tend to use significantly more employee-involvement practices than do service firms. Manufacturing firms use quality circles, participation groups, and self-managing work teams far more than service firms.

Why is this so? We think that the intense pressure on the manufacturing sector from global competition has created more dissatisfaction with the old control-oriented way of doing things. Also, it can be easier to see the payoffs from different management practices in manufacturing than in service. Objective measures of productivity can more clearly show profitability than can measures of customer perceptions of service quality. However, these differences are now blurring as service competition increases and service companies become more sophisticated in tracking the benefits of customer service quality.

As service businesses consider empowerment, they can look at high-involvement manufacturing organizations as labs in which the various empowerment approaches have been tested and developed. Many lessons have been learned in manufacturing about how to best use quality circles, enriched jobs, and so on. And the added good news is that many service businesses are ideally suited to applying and refining these lessons. Multisite, relatively autonomous service operations afford their managers an opportunity to customize empowerment programs and then evaluate them.

In summary, the newest approaches to managing the production line can serve as role models for many service businesses, but perhaps not all. Before service organizations rush into empowerment programs, they need to determine whether and how empowerment fits their situation.

REFERENCES

1. T. Levitt, "Production-Line Approach to Services," *Harvard Business Review*, September–October 1972, pp. 41–52; and T. Levitt, "Industrialization of Service," *Harvard Business Review,* September–October 1976, pp. 63–74.

2. Levitt (1972).

3. D. Tansik, "Managing Human Resource Issues for High-Contact Service Personnel," in *Service Management Effectiveness*, eds. D. Bowen, R. Chase, and T. Cummings (San Francisco: Jossey-Bass, 1990).

4. R. Zemke and D. Schaaf, *The Service Edge: 101 Companies That Profit from Customer Care* (New York: New American Library, 1989), p. 68.

5. As quoted in Zemke and Schaaf (1989), p. 68.

6. J. Carlzon, *Moments of Truth* (New York: Ballinger, 1987).

7. V. Zeithaml, A. Parasuraman, and L. L. Berry, *Delivering Quality Service: Balancing Customer Perceptions and Expectations* (New York: The Free Press, 1990). See also: B. Schneider and D. Bowen, "Employee and Customer Perceptions of Service in Banks: Replication and Extension," *Journal of Applied Psychology* 70 (1985): 423–433.

8. Schneider and Bowen (1985).

9. *Ibid.*

10. Zeithaml, Parasuraman, and Berry (1990).

11. C. Goodwin and I. Ross, "Consumer Evaluations of Responses to Complaints: What's Fair and Why," *Journal of Services Marketing* 4 (1990): 53–61.

12. See E. E. Lawler III, *High-Involvement Management* (San Francisco: Jossey-Bass, 1986).

13. See E. E. Lawler III, "Choosing an Involvement Strategy," *Academy of Management Executive* 2 (1988): 197–204.

14. See for example J. R. Hackman and G. R. Oldham, *Work Redesign* (Reading, MA: Addison-Wesley, 1980).

15. Ibid.

16. R. J. Sutton and A. Rafaeli, "Untangling the Relationship between Displayed Emotions and Organizational Sales: The Case of Convenience Stores," *Academy of Management Journal* 31 (1988): 461–487.

17. E. E. Lawler III, G. E. Ledford, Jr., and S. A. Mohrman, *Employee Involvement in America: A Study of Contemporary Practice* (Houston: American Productivity & Quality Center, 1989).

ENFRANCHISEMENT OF SERVICE WORKERS

Leonard A. Schlesinger

James L. Heskett

The customer pointed out to the Nordstrom salesperson that she had bought a pair of shoes at Bloomingdales (a competitor) that were too small for her. She liked the style, but Bloomingdales didn't have her size. After being fitted with the same shoe of the proper size, the customer started to pay for the shoes. The salesperson instead suggested that she merely take the too-small shoes in exchange for the new purchase. When the customer reminded the salesperson that she hadn't bought the first pair at Nordstrom, the salesperson said to her, "If I take these shoes for you, you won't have any reason to return to Bloomingdales."[1]

This typifies the kinds of stories told by customers of Nordstrom, the well-known fashion department store chain. Such results are possible only when an organization gives its employees latitude to satisfy customers and rewards the employees for their efforts. It is what we refer to as "enfranchisement."

Enfranchisement is a way of granting freedom and responsibility to an employee within a franchise without requiring a monetary investment or ownership on the part of the employee. It is achieved through a combination of what has come to be known as "empowerment"[2] coupled with compensation methods that pay people for their performance.[3] It has the potential for producing extraordinarily responsive service, extra employee effort, and unusually high rewards to those who are enfranchised. The efforts of service organizations to enfranchise their employees address several major concerns.

☐ A major source of frustration for employees is that management may publicly proclaim that it wants to serve its customers but will actually impede its employees, or fail to provide them with the necessary resources, or will even penalize them for attempting to do so.[4]

☐ The time "window" for recovery from many service errors is small. If a service error is not corrected quickly, especially for high-cost services, it becomes nearly impossible to regain the level of customer satisfaction that would have been achieved had the service been performed correctly the first time.[5]

☐ In many services, there is greater risk in not empowering employees than in giving them too much latitude. As Jan Carlzon, CEO of Scandinavian Airlines System, noted:

> What's the danger of giving away too much? Are you worried about having an oversatisfied customer? That's not much of a worry. You can forget about an oversatisfied customer, but an unsatisfied customer is one of the most expensive problems you can have . . . the danger is not that employees will give away too much. It's that they won't give away anything—because they don't dare.[6]

Employees often need to be encouraged—through performance-based programs—to use the discretionary latitude which they are given.

ACHIEVEMENTS TO DATE

The most significant and successful enfranchisement programs have occurred in the field of retailing. Retail

SOURCE: Leonard A. Schlesinger and James L. Heskett, "Enfranchisement of Service Workers," *California Management Review* (Summer 1991): 83–100. Copyright © 1991 by The Regents of the University of California. Reprinted from the *California Management Review*, vol 33, no. 4. By permission of The Regents.

organizations, both large and small, have turned to a combination of empowerment and pay-for-performance to fuel rapid internal growth and to increase sales productivity. Advocates of enfranchisement argue that it can dramatically improve sales and earnings, while at the same time require less direct supervision from corporate management and provide increased employee earnings, job satisfaction, and retention. Employee retention is of particular importance in retailing because it can have a positive impact on customer retention, which in turn has been found to be an important determinant of profit in many companies.[7]

Exhibit 1 provides evidence from two retail chains, Ito Yokado in Japan and Nordstrom in the United States, that demonstrates the positive effects of enfranchisement. Furthermore, the efforts of the two companies have become a matter of intense curiosity (if not an actual model) for their competitors and other retailers.

ITO YOKADO'S REFORM PROGRAM

The Ito Yokado Group is a Japanese chain of department stores, convenience stores, and other retail shops and restaurants.[8] It is one of several large, non-traditional Japanese retailing organizations that got their start during Japan's retailing boom of the late 1950s by offering a wider range of utilitarian goods to a broader spectrum of the Japanese public than more traditional department stores. In 1988, its sales were approximately $16 billion.

Faced with the prospect of slower growth, and unable to distinguish its profit performance from that of its major competitors, the Group's founder initiated the "Reform Program" in 1982. The Program is centered on understanding customers' needs, concentrating inventory management decisions to achieve ample in-stock inventory positions, and redesigning and merchandising stores to reflect this new emphasis on providing value to customers.

The Reform Program was designed to be consistent with Ito Yokado's emphasis on seniority and job flexibility (rather than a particular job as a symbol of status), the heavy use of part-time employees, and a culture that supports the delegation of decision making to a large number of people. Given its mission to improve asset management, the Reform Program focuses on the buying function. It was implemented by selecting large numbers of full- and part-time employees to be buyers of small portions of the total product line; supplying them with the best computerized decision tools and complete current information; fully training them in the use of these resources; giving them full responsibility for decision making; and rewarding them at above-market

rates and, in part, on the basis of the organization's overall performance.[9]

Six years after its initiation, the Reform Program enabled Ito Yokado to achieve a return on sales that was more than double and a return on assets that was nearly double that of its four major competitors. At the same time, it grew at a significantly faster rate than these same competitors (see Exhibit 1).

NORDSTROM'S "OBSESSION" WITH CUSTOMER SATISFACTION

Expanding from a chain of shoe stores in 1963, Nordstrom has grown into a chain of 61 fashion department stores operating largely on the West Coast of the United States and realizing sales at an annual rate of roughly $2.7 billion.[10] Members of the family (of which most of senior management is composed) attribute their rapid growth and success in apparel to their application of the principles of the shoe business: offer an unusually wide selection of merchandise in attractive stores with a high level of service and competitive prices.

Nordstrom's store personnel have been told for years that their single responsibility is to satisfy customers. While this broad statement allows for a wide range of interpretation, it is brief, clear, and well-understood by the entire organization. Furthermore, it is indicative of the wide latitude given managers and associates at all levels in the organization.

Nordstrom is the generally recognized leader in paying its salespeople a commission not only on what they sell, but on the extent to which they exceed their superiors' projected sales forecasts. Nordstrom's practice of discarding the term "employee" in favor of "associate" has been emulated throughout U.S. retailing. The philosophy of enfranchisement is exemplified by its public display of the results achieved by all personnel and by the frequent celebration of associates' accomplishments. Some of the extraordinary services performed on behalf of Nordstrom's customers include such things as warming up customers' automobiles in cold weather, delivering products to their offices or homes, or taking them to the airport in emergencies.

The contractual arrangement between sales associates and Nordstrom assumes that associates will do what they deem necessary to enhance sales per hour during the time they are "clocked in" on the job. This may include spending time "off the clock" writing thank-you notes or reminders to customers or running errands for them. All of this is intended to enhance associates' sales per hour for officially recorded selling hours. This is the basis for the guaranteed base hourly wages established

EXHIBIT 1   Comparative Data for Ito Yokado and Nordstrom

	Ito Yokado[a]	Nordstrom[b]
Annual Sales Volume	$14.9 billion	$2.7 billion
Annual Growth Rate, Past Five Years:		
Subject Company	8.0%	24.2%
Major Competitors	5.1%	8.3%
Return on Sales:		
Subject Company	2.8%	4.5%
Major Competitors	1.1%	2.1%
Return on Assets:		
Subject Company	3.4%	8.4%
Major Competitors	1.9%	3.5%
Degree of Empowerment	Extensive	Extensive
Amount of Incentive, as % of total compensation	Up to 33%	Up to 100%
Nature of Incentive	Group	Individual
Levels Enfranchised	Managers and Employees	Managers and Employees
Employees Included	All full-time and 1/3 of part-time	All full-time
Primary Concentration	Buying, Inventory Control	Sales
Role of Management	"Teachers and advisors"	"Satisfying customers"
Results:	Fewer stockouts, lower inventory levels, less inventory loss, higher merchandise quality, employee commitment	Sales per sales hour and sales per square foot of selling space roughly double industry averages, low recruiting and advertising costs, average costs for sales labor and real estate in relation to sales, high employee and customer loyalty

[a]Operating data are for 1983–1988 and exclude franchised operations
[b]Operating data are for 1983–1988

periodically between Nordstrom's management and its sales associates as well as for the commission that is paid in addition to the base wage (usually about 6.75% of sales).[11]

The combination of excellent locations, store ambiance, and complete merchandise selection along with a focus on customer satisfaction, the heavy use of commissions and other incentives, and efforts to build an intense loyalty among associates at Nordstrom and its mission has produced remarkable results. They include sales per square foot that are more than twice industry averages, with an attendant high return on assets. Sales associates have been compensated at rates ranging from two to four times industry averages. Customers readily profess unusually high levels of loyalty to Nordstrom, its people, and its service. And the profits generated by the enfranchisement concept have fueled unusually high internal growth.

PRODUCTIVITY

Noting Nordstrom's success, managements of other retailing organizations have adopted aspects of its enfranchisement strategy to help solve other problems, including low space productivity and rising labor costs. Two of the more recent and notable companies are Younkers and Dayton Hudson. Efforts are being made to implement such concepts in consumer services other than retailing, as illustrated by the Fairfield Inn hotel experience.

YOUNKERS' SATISFACTION PLUS

Younkers, a 37-store chain of department stores in the Midwest, implemented its "Satisfaction Plus" program on April 1, 1988.[12] It was part of an effort to inject new life into a 100-year-old, traditionally managed chain that had enjoyed unusually high market share for much of its history and whose sales and profits had stagnated.

Satisfaction Plus involves careful selection of personnel, with heavy reliance on referrals from associates and on training and recognition. It has been integrated with long-standing methods of recognition such as the Company's Hall of Fame, which now bases its admission decisions on the sales per hour measure used for Satisfaction Plus. Unlike Nordstrom, Younkers does not pay a commission on sales, but wage rates are adjusted every six months based on a trailing twelve-month sales-per-hour basis. A percentage of sales factor is used to determine a negotiated sales-per-hour rate on which compensation will be based. Failure to meet the agreed sales level may trigger a downward adjustment of the base wage, additional training, or eventual dismissal.

Quality of customer service is encouraged through an effort called "30/30 STAR," which refers to the desire to have sales associates acknowledge customers within 30 seconds of their arrival in a department at a distance of no more than 30 feet. In addition, through a "mystery shopping program" (the evaluation of service quality conducted by a cadre of professionally trained shoppers), evaluations of associates' efforts are based on Smile, Time spent with the customer, Attention to the customer's needs, and Respect shown the customer. One unsatisfactory mystery shopping experience produces a warning, two eliminates a person from consideration for the Hall of Fame for a given year, and three is grounds for dismissal. However, unsatisfactory mystery shops are accompanied by increased training activities to help associates improve.[13]

The results of Younker's program (as shown in Exhibit 2) have been quite remarkable, especially in view of the fact that for most of the period during which Satisfaction Plus has been in effect, the company has been publicly offered for sale. In spite of the uncertainty and reduced morale created by the imminent sale, Younker's sales productivity, compensation levels, and quality of service have all increased significantly. At the same time, the turnover of sales associates has been cut in half. While the cost of labor relative to sales has risen, this has been offset, in part, by the lower costs of recruitment.

DAYTON HUDSON'S PERFORMANCE PLUS

Dayton Hudson, a chain of 34 upscale full-line department stores and three home stores, was created from a merger of the Dayton and the Hudson department store chains.[14] Dayton Hudson stores located in the Detroit area retain the name "Hudson's" and stores in the Minneapolis area operate under the name "Dayton's." The company achieved sales of $1.7 billion in 1989.

Building on its history of excellence in customer service, the company initiated its Performance Plus program in 1987. This program focuses on selection, training, and incentives aimed at providing superior customer service performed by sales "consultants" (comparable to Nordstrom's and Younkers' "associates") who "go the extra mile" for the customer.

Initially, the company implemented the program in two departments across the entire company. After further consideration, management decided to switch to a store-by-store implementation. By the end of 1988, four stores had fully implemented the program and another seven were added in 1989.

The company encourages its sales consultants to be creative in serving customers. This is emphasized in its training and reinforced by recognition and rewards on the selling floor. While on the sales floor, consultants are encouraged to take customers into different departments when needed and to develop a repeat clientele by sending thank you notes and informing customers of sales or new merchandise. Sales consultants are rewarded on a pay-for-performance basis similar to Nordstrom's.

The company believes that selection plays an important role as well. Interviewers look for candidates hoping to make retail sales a career. After being hired, new employees go through a two-day "Celebration Training" in which the underlying theme is "it's my company."

Even though Performance Plus is in early stages of implementation, results to date, when comparing Performance Plus with non-Performance Plus stores, suggest that per hour sales have increased substantially along with average earnings per sales consultant (as shown in Exhibit 2). The rate of salesperson turnover in stores one year after implementation has increased 22%; this is attributed by management to the self-selection still taking place among its sales consultants, and is typical of other firms in our study. However, reduced turnover is still a long-term objective of the program. A combination of increased compensation and greater opportunity for personal development has given stores operating under Performance Plus greater access to college graduates. As a result, the proportion of selling managers who are promoted from sales consultants in those stores has risen by roughly 150%, according to management estimates. Just as important, increases in customer service levels (based on the company's "Extra Mile" measures that are obtained from customer interviews) are 56% greater in Performance Plus stores than

EXHIBIT 2   Results Achieved by Recent Enfranchisement Programs at Two U.S. Department Store Chains

	Younkers[a]	Dayton Hudson[b]
Number of Stores	34[c]	34
Total Sales, 1989	$0.3 billion	$1.7 billion
Average per Hour Sales	+20%	+25%
Average per Hour Compensation	+24%	+17%
Percentage of New Hires from Associates' Recommendations	Doubled to 60%	Not measured
Quality of Service	+18%[d]	+5%
Employee Morale	"Dramatically improved"	Not available[e]
Turnover of Sales Personnel (one year after initiation of the process)	−50%	+22%
Cost of Sales Labor to Sales	+10%	+33%
Cost of Recruiting and Personnel Development	Lower	Lower

[a]Measurements are for all stores for a period beginning in March 1988, and ending in July 1990.
[b]Based on information from four stores implementing the concept in 1987 and 1988.
[c]Since the initiation of Satisfaction Plus, Younkers has closed three of its stores.
[d]This represents the increase in the proportion of acceptable or higher mystery shops.
[e]In the process of being measured.

in the stores that have yet to implement it. Overall service quality measures also have risen faster in Performance Plus than in other Dayton Hudson stores.

QUALITY

High quality and its favorable long-term impact on profit is at the heart of several other efforts being made to implement enfranchisement.

FAIRFIELD INN

Fairfield Inn, a division of Marriott Corporation, seeks to impress (not just satisfy) guests with rooms often priced as low as $39 per night.[15] To staff its 135-room economy priced inns, Fairfield Inn carefully selects only those people who have the appropriate attitudes and capabilities to deliver two things: the friendliest atmosphere and the cleanest rooms. Whether they are hired as managers, desk clerks, or housekeepers, they must be the kind of people who respond favorably to frequent measurement and rewards based on performance, even though the incentive offered represents only a 10% premium over prevailing wages.

Fairfield Inn has developed a method of selection, performance measurement, and incentives that incorpo-

rates a guest-driven, computer-assisted Scorecard measurement system as the focal point of its human resource and control strategies. Even though Fairfield Inn opened its first economy inn only as recently as 1987, when confronted with particularly competitive labor markets, its management has been able to alter its template to set itself apart from other employers.

Consider, for example, Fairfield Inn's approach to the employment and management practices for the job category of housekeepers, known as "GRAs" (guest room attendants) at Fairfield Inn. Empowerment of GRAs occurs through the assignment of 14 rooms to clean as the equivalent of an 8-hour work day. If the rooms can be cleaned faster, a full day's compensation is paid. Further, on particularly busy days GRAs can "bid" on additional rooms for which they are paid an additional half-hour in wages for each additional room cleaned. ("Overtime" is paid in cash at the end of the shift, reflecting the typical short-term needs for compensation that often motivate GRAs to clean additional rooms on a given day.) This allows Fairfield Inn to maintain a relatively small core of regular housekeepers who are given incentives to expand their work at busy times. Housekeepers earn paid leave through regular attendance on the job. But they have the option of maintaining their regular attendance by taking responsibility for finding an already-trained replacement on days when they are not able to appear for work.

Finally, each inn establishes two discretionary budgets of $150 each for each 28-day period. The first is an employee relations budget which is spent at the discretion of the inn's manager for anything ranging from "employee of the month" awards to morale-building events. The second is a guest relations budget which frequently is managed by employees. In the words of a recent Fairfield Inn general manager, the budgets are managed with great care and spent with considerable creativity:

> One of our properties in Kansas is not unusual. Here, a guest service representative keeps a careful log of the preferences of frequent customers, those regional business travelers by auto who may log 40 to 50 nights per year at our inns and who return to the same places quite frequently. Preferences are collected by all staff members. The list of incoming guests is checked in advance. If a particularly frequent guest likes a certain kind of cookie, a GSR or GRA will go to the store for them. It is handled entirely by the hourly employees; managers don't have time to do it. This is so important to us that managers are cautioned to make sure the budgets are spent, regardless of short-term preferences.[16]

Indices of performance for Fairfield Inn in the third year of its existence are shown in Exhibit 3. These include comparisons with other economy lodging chains obtained through an independent survey. They suggest that Fairfield Inn has in a short time achieved higher "product" quality, higher customer loyalty, a significantly higher occupancy rate, and a comparable cost structure. Its employee turnover rate is 60–70% of that of its competitors. Further, in a recent poll, 92% of employees indicated that the scorecard measurement and reward system should be maintained. Also, as with several of the examples of enfranchisement programs cited earlier, one major benefit is the need for less traditional supervision. Housekeeping supervisors are being eliminated at some Fairfield Inns. This not only allows for a reduction in an important cost of operation, but also represents a reallocation of a unit manager's time to more positive activities of selecting and motivating employees.

CONDITIONS FOR EFFECTIVE ENFRANCHISEMENT

These successful efforts to enfranchise employees reveal the conditions under which the concept works best.[17] They include:

☐ Each effort reflects the culture of the organization or individual department in which it is being implemented. In particular, employees have to be comfortable with a pay-for-performance-oriented atmosphere. Beyond this, an important question is whether rewards should be based on individual or group performance. Nearly every U.S. retailing executive with whom we have spoken argues that rewards based on individual performance are most appropriate, particularly for sales-related jobs. On the other hand, rewards at Ito Yokado are based on the company's performance, with loyalty to the company emphasized as a major motivating force.

☐ Enfranchisement is only one part, albeit sometimes the most visible, of a process that begins with recruitment and selection of people and continues through to training, development, assignment, and recognition.[18]

☐ Each of the programs we have described grants employees varying degrees of control over both operating decisions and compensation.

☐ All of the programs involve efforts to encourage communication from lower to higher ranks of the organization.

☐ All of the efforts are accompanied by controls covering what is thought to be the critical core of the organization's activities. At Nordstrom, for example, the critical core is defined as customer satisfaction. At Younkers, it is embodied in the quality control effort.[19]

☐ Employee turnover is largely management-initiated. Non-performers are dismissed so that those remaining feel they are associated with a high-performance organization. While voluntary turnover is dramatically lowered, the involuntary turnover is roughly comparable to that of competitors who have not enfranchised their employees (or those who have not taken the trouble to replace non-performing employees).

☐ A large proportion of new people are hired on the basis of referrals from existing employees. This is a result of the excellent compensation and working conditions provided by companies that emphasize employee enfranchisement. It is critical to the creation of a self-selected work force whose values and expectations are consistent with those of the organization.

☐ An array of resources is made available to the enfranchised employees to help them succeed. At Ito Yokado, these resources include current information

EXHIBIT 3   Early Results of Fairfield Inn's Effort to Enfranchise Employees

	Fairfield Inn	Other Economy Lodging Chains
Index of Compensation Rates, Hourly Employees:[1]		
Wage	1.00	1.00
Incentives	1.10	1.00
Employee Turnover (annual)		
1990:	100–120%	167%
1989:	120–140%	167%[2]
Occupancy Rates Percentage of Rooms Filled on Average[3]		
1989–1990:	70–75%	60%
Average Number of Trips per Year among Economy Business Travellers[4]	50–70	30–40
Management Salary Index[5] (Unit Level)	1.05	1.00
Nonmanagement Labor Costs as a Percentage of Revenue (Unit Level)[6]	18–20%	16–19%
Indices of Customer Satisfaction[4]		
Overall Cleanliness of Hotel	80–90	55–85
Overall Value for Money	70–80	55–65
Overall Maintenance and Upkeep of Hotel	80–90	45–80
Hotel Service Overall	80–90	50–70
Speed and Efficiency of Check-In and Check-Out	70–80	40–70
Friendliness of Hotel Personnel	70–80	50–60

[1]Based on competitive wage surveys in various markets. Hourly incentives include bonus and bonus leave.

[2]1989 Gallup Survey.

[3]Average of competitors based on Smith Travel Research Data. Fairfield Inn numbers exclude inns open less than one year. Competitor chains are believed to average 55–75%.

[4]Based on Economy Business Transient Tracting Study, 1990, commissioned by FFI.

[5]This is an average. Index for a particular FFI manager can be much higher due to bonus potential.

[6]Range based on various competitor operating statements.

and computerized inventory management decision tools. At Nordstrom they include excellent store locations and ambiance and great depth of merchandise selection, which is especially important for fashion retailing to an affluent market segment. At Younkers, the resources range from an exchange of information about selling skills and ideas to a greater effort to focus merchandising efforts on a particular market target. (For example, when Younkers faced a recent recession and loss of customers in the markets it serves, it encouraged sales associates to increase average sales per customer. It did this by making available carefully-selected "Satisfaction Plus" add-on items, displaying them prominently, and training its sales associates to suggest these items to customers to achieve more add-on sales.) At Dayton Hudson, implementation of Performance Plus is accompanied by a review of merchandise "content," intended to provide better or a greater depth of goods for sales associates to sell. At Fairfield Inn, employees are provided with good working conditions, clear-cut objectives, and a measurement and reward system that appeals to them.

Would these conditions produce superior performance without enfranchisement? We are doubtful. Enfranchisement not only makes the value of these changes visible, but provides improved performance that helps defray their cost.

A more important question is how much of what we have observed in these examples is the result of the so-called Hawthorne Effect: improved morale and performance resulting from increased attention of any kind paid to a long-neglected group of workers?[20] Undoubtedly, some portion of early results that we have reported can be attributed to this phenomenon. However, what we have observed are much more basic changes concerning selection as well as job design, compensation, and the development of supporting devices, all of which are intended to "lock in" significant improvements in performance over time.

Longer-term tracking of results from sites such as these should provide evidence of the sustainability of these incentives and results. Similar studies in both manufacturing and service-producing settings have yielded mixed results, although each of the programs observed differed in substantial ways from those we have reported here.[21] Already, the efforts we have observed have produced changes in output and quality far in excess of those observed in other experiments.[22] We have no reason to believe that they are not sustainable, although early experience suggests that there are major challenges to be encountered in implementing such programs.

MAJOR CHALLENGES TO IMPLEMENTATION

Enfranchisement can be highly satisfying and rewarding during times of success, at least for those who share in that success. Even then, of course, the concept may not be appropriate for all employees. However, a negative environment producing disappointing sales results can challenge the fortitude of even the most avid believer in the concept. Major challenges include:

☐ Unit managers with the human and technical skills to interpret policies associated with enfranchisement and to make them work may be in short supply. Because decisions are often pushed down into an organization under these kinds of programs, fewer managers with operating knowledge may be needed at the corporate level. But the wider latitude of decision making involved at the unit level will require managers with good business insight and particularly strong human resource skills to "stroke" winners,

work to help losers develop into winners, and make losers feel like winners as they leave the firm. It is this shortage of managers that proponents of the concept discuss most frequently.

☐ Middle management may be unwilling to support enfranchisement. Under this kind of program, the role of middle managers shifts from operating the firm to coaching and advising unit managers. Middle managers go beyond the mere identification of problems in their units, making sure that unit managers have the resources to solve them. Because many middle managers in service organizations are promoted from the unit management ranks, it is difficult for them to resist the inclination to continue to participate in the actual management of units under their supervision. Furthermore, it is difficult for them to see their unit managers making what appear to be poor decisions without stepping in to assume command.

☐ Senior managers may not be able to allow enfranchisement to work. In enfranchisement programs, the role of senior management shifts from an operational to a strategic orientation. Supervisory roles are replaced by planning, policy setting, and negotiating of major contractual arrangements. Experience suggests that senior management may accept these role shifts as long as performance is good. However, when either growth in sales or profitability level off—often for reasons totally unrelated to internal efforts—there is a natural tendency for senior management to begin to "tinker" with apparently sound enfranchisement policies. Senior managers often are encouraged in this practice by disenchanted operating managers who may see their compensation declining for reasons beyond their control and who wish to abrogate their "contracts."

☐ Managers may be perceived as being unfair by associates. Under most enfranchisement programs, assignments influence rewards. At Nordstrom, Dayton Hudson, and Younkers, the hours assigned to sales associates determine in some measure the amount of merchandise they may be able to sell. Similarly, the number of salespeople assigned to a given department will influence the amount that any one of them may be able to sell. A Fairfield Inn with an unusually high occupancy rate may be one at which higher or even acceptable customer satisfaction ratings—on which compensation is based—may be particularly difficult to achieve. This produces an anomaly where the employees of the most profitable units are personally penalized. To the extent that participants feel that the enfranchisement program is being managed unfairly, the program will be a target for criticism within the organization.

☐ Participants' expectations may be inadequately conditioned. There is a natural tendency for parties to enfranchisement programs to assume that a positive result will be achieved that will benefit both parties. Too little emphasis may be placed on spelling out in advance the expected behavior by both parties if such results are not continually achieved. In effect, enfranchisement gives employees a kind of contractor status. This can be a problem, especially if employees don't see themselves as contractors, particularly when adverse conditions arise.

It is impossible to place too much emphasis on the conditioning of expectations. Enfranchisement is not a benign program. It rewards winners and punishes losers. It asks participants to accept the bad with the good. When the worst does happen, individuals are often psychologically unprepared and disappointed.

☐ Programs may be improperly designed and implemented. The design of an enfranchisement effort must fit the culture of the organization. A major concern is the extent to which individuals should have a choice regarding their participation. In most of the enfranchisement efforts in the U.S. to date, participants indicate the compensation level they wish to achieve, which in turn influences the sales goal set for them. While actual compensation for sales above the goal may be on a commission basis, it is a negotiated commission level. Such design features have been intended in part to reduce the appearance of arbitrariness.

When implementing enfranchisement, one of the first concerns is whether to implement it in all operating units simultaneously or to install it progressively on a unit-by-unit basis. Younkers' managers introduced its "Satisfaction Plus" program in all 36 of its department stores simultaneously to avoid what management termed the "grapevine effect"—communication from employees at stores with the program to those in stores yet to implement it. Their assumption was that negative responses often travel more rapidly and tend to be more exaggerated or distorted than positive ones. By contrast, Dayton Hudson opted for a store-by-store implementation, beginning with stores where reactions might be the most positive. These decisions

are extremely critical, because improperly designed or implemented programs will not only disrupt the status quo, they may be seen as grounds for grievances, union organizing drives, or even government intervention.

☐ Organized labor may be uncomfortable with the concept of individual employees as contractors. Union organizations generally have seen one of their roles as being contractors for groups of employees. Enfranchisement, to the extent that it is seen as regarding employees as contractors, may run counter to the role model assumed by union leadership. Further, given the difficulty of separating nonperforming employees from potentially lucrative jobs (especially those employees who may have achieved substantial seniority), efforts to enfranchise employees can be targets for disgruntled employees. For example, employees at one store where Dayton-Hudson's Performance Plus program has yet to be implemented have voted to accept unionization.[23]

In perhaps the most-publicized case of this occurrence, a union representing a small proportion of Nordstrom employees in the state of Washington has had a complaint upheld by the Washington State Labor and Industries Department. It was charged that the company did not pay sales associates for time spent performing non-selling activities such as home deliveries, company meetings, and preparation of personal correspondence with customers. It ruled that Nordstrom had to compensate associates retroactively for time spent in such activities even though they were being paid on the basis of a commission. Now the union has filed a suit to require Nordstrom to make similar restitution in every state in which it operates in the United States.[24]

These events have triggered several reactions. They have somewhat divided employees in Nordstrom's stores involved in the complaint, with one group loyal to the company actively seeking to have the union decertified so that it no longer represents them. The events have also influenced Nordstrom's emulators to take a more cautious approach to the implementation of similar programs in their companies. This situation has fueled a great deal of speculation as to the possible reasons for the dispute at Nordstrom, with cited causes including: senior management's sincere belief that all activities, whether selling or not, are recognized in a commission-base compensation system; too much empowerment for managers who might have allowed practices that abused the spirit of the program; inadequate corporate control over human resource management practices in the store; disgruntled associates unable to succeed under a pay-for-performance program; and inadequate conditioning of associates' expectations regarding the workings of the concept. The common theme running through much of this speculation is whether or not adverse reactions in this and other cases could have been avoided with more effective ongoing communication between senior management, associates, and union representatives.

CONCLUSION

Our data reflect results obtained from what most researchers would term extreme examples or experiments. They were selected for that reason in order to illustrate what is possible.

An important unanswered question, however, is whether or not these results are sustainable. Although only time will tell, the Nordstrom experience suggests that under conditions in which both empowerment and pay-for-performance are important elements of a basic, long-term business strategy, substantial positive long-term benefits from enfranchisement are achievable.

Theoretically, enfranchisement should be a win–win concept, the cornerstone of truly outstanding performance. Not only are there rewards for both managers and associates, but customers benefit as well from the improved service that enfranchisement provides. The customers develop such strong loyalty to companies practicing it that their favorable word-of-mouth recommendations to others often replace some part of the advertising budget for a company. In most cases, companies practicing enfranchisement have become preferred employers—a particularly important advantage at a time of tight labor markets.

Why then isn't enfranchisement more widely accepted and practiced? One of the biggest reasons is the demands it places on people to manage two highly volatile concepts, empowerment and pay-for-performance. When combined, these concepts can become explosive, especially in the hands of one or more empowered, but misguided managers. Once it reaches that stage, it becomes an understandably appropriate matter of interest for other parties, including associates, unions, and state and federal agencies.

As attractive as it seems, enfranchisement will continue to encounter a number of challenges, including: an unsupportive culture of the organization itself; a shortage of unit managers with the requisite technical and human skills, of middle managers willing to support the program, and of senior managers who are able to let

it work; the inability to condition participants' expectations; the improper design and implementation of the concept; and the perceived threat that it may represent to labor union organizations.

Such challenges can be overcome with effective communication between all levels of management and employees with the objective being to establish realistic expectations on everyone's part in advance. Labor organizations should not be excluded from the process, but it will require that their leadership reassess the kind of representation that the enfranchised require. It will involve greater emphasis on working conditions and benefits and less on compensation per se. More important, it will inevitably alter evaluations of what is "fair treatment" and strike to the very heart of the employee grievance procedure itself. Further, it may challenge union notions of individuals' loyalty to the labor movement just as it does those of employees' loyalty to the company.

Enfranchisement can be a potent long-term competitive force, but only when it is part of an organizational culture and strategy that is built on careful selection and development of people to whom the concept appeals and for whom it functions well. By itself, it will not produce the relatively spectacular results shown here. Nor is it for everyone.

The concept, so seemingly universal in its appeal, will continue to be controversial. To the extent that it requires a sharing of both rewards and risks in good times and bad, long-term adherence to the concept will require an unusual level of management dedication. Given the special qualities of supporting behavior and restraint that it requires of managers, not all of who adopt it will be able to make enfranchisement work. Nevertheless, for those who can make it work, enfranchisement is a potent competitive strategy.

REFERENCES

1. James L. Heskett, W. Earl Sasser, Jr., and Christopher W. L. Hart, *Service Breakthroughs* (New York, NY: The Free Press, 1990), pp. 13–14.

2. Empowerment is perhaps an overworked and underdefined term. We use it here as the rough equivalent of what industrial psychologists and political economists alike term "participation" in decision making. See, for example, David I. Levine and Laura D'Andrea Tyson, "Participation, Productivity, and the Firm's Environment," in Alan S. Blinder, ed., *Paying for Productivity* (Washington, D.C.: The Brookings Institute, 1990), pp. 183–243.

3. Edward E. Lawler III addresses pay-for-performance issues in *Strategic Pay* (San Francisco, CA: Jossey-Bass Publishers, 1990), especially pp. 55–131.

4. For evidence concerning this kind of stress, see the work of J. J. Parkington and Benjamin Schneider, "Some Correlates of Experienced Job Stress: A Boundary Role Study," *Academy of Management Journal,* 22 (1979): 270–281. Also see Warren Bennis, "Beyond Bureaucracy," in Warren Bennis, ed., *American Bureaucracy* (Chicago, IL: Aldine, 1970), pp. 3–17; and Peter M. Blau, *On the Nature of Organizations* (New York, NY: John Wiley and Sons, 1974), pp. 80–84.

5. In our service management classes we require students to write and mail letters of complaint (as well as commendation) about services they have experienced recently. In more than half the cases in which service providers respond, often with substantial offers of restitution, students tell us that they feel no more positively about poorly performed services after getting their responses than before. This suggests the difficulty of correcting a service poorly performed or delivered long after the time of the error.

6. "The Art of Loving," *Inc.* (May 1989), p. 36.

7. Frederick F. Reichheld and W. Earl Sasser, "Zero Defections: Quality Comes to Service," *Harvard Business Review* (September/October 1990), pp. 105–111.

8. Information in this section is drawn from Ito Yokado, Case No. 9-589-116 (Boston, MA: Publishing Division, Harvard Business School, 1989).

9. *Ibid.*

10. Information in this section is drawn from Nordstrom, Case No. 9-579-218 (Boston, MA: Publishing Division, Harvard Business School, 1979) and Francine Schwadel, "Nordstrom's Push East Will Test Its Renown for the Best in Service," *The Wall Street Journal,* August 1, 1989, pp. A1 and A4.

11. The actual process involves establishing a guaranteed base wage and dividing it by the commission rate (6.75% of sales in most cases) to obtain a targeted sales per hour. Overtime (for more than 40 hours per week) is paid at the rate of 1.5 times the guaranteed base wage. If commissions (6.75% of total sales) exceed the guaranteed base wage plus overtime, they are paid. If salary exceeds commissions, it is paid. However, salaries regularly exceeding commissions result in renegotiation of the guaranteed base wage.

12. Information in this section is based on interviews with company executives, August 1990.

13. The positive relationship between courteous salespeople and store productivity has been supported by Robert I. Sutton and Anat Rafeli, "Untangling the Relationship between Displayed Emotions and Organizational Sales: The Case of Convenience Stores," *Academy of Management Journal,* 31/3 (1988): 461–487.

14. Information in this section is based on interviews with company executives conducted during February and March of 1990.

15. Certain information in this section is based on material in the case Fairfield Inn, Case No. 9-689-092 (Boston, MA: Publishing Division, Harvard Business School,

1989), and interviews with company executives in March and October 1990.

16. Interview with Michael Ruffer, General Manager, Courtyard Hotels, and former General Manager of Fairfield Inn, October 1990.

17. For an analysis of the impact of multi-level hierarchies on the extent of control over employee behavior, see William G. Ouchi, "The Relationship between Organizational Structure and Organizational Control," *Administrative Science Quarterly,* 22 (1977): 95–113.

18. For a similar conclusion, based on extensive exploration of the "informing" impact of technology (particularly in the ability to have an impact on learning and on the power imparted to operatives), see Shoshana Zuboff, *In the Age of the Smart Machine* (New York, NY: Basic Books, Inc., 1988), pp. 413–414. This view is reflected in an examination of various studies of the effects of pay on performance, reported by Thomas A. Mahoney, "Multiple Pay Contingencies: Strategic Design of Compensation," *Human Resource Management* (Fall 1989), pp. 337–347.

19. Appropriate bounds on acceptable behavior under empowerment initiatives should be clearly drawn and universally understood. While not the primary thrust of our work, it is addressed explicitly in a much broader context by Robert L. Simons, "Beliefs and Boundaries," a paper presented at the 1990 Strategic Management Society Annual Meeting, Stockholm, September 24–27, 1990.

20. The effect gets its name from research designed to identify determinants of employee productivity, satisfaction, and motivation carried out at the Hawthorne plant of The Western Electric Company from 1924 to 1927. For a description, see F. J. Roethlisberger in George F. F. Lombard, ed., *The Elusive Phenomena* (Boston, MA: Division of Research, Graduate School of Business Administration, Harvard University, 1977), pp. 45–48.

21. For example, in contrast to other studies, two of our cases involve companies which either have practiced enfranchisement for many years (Nordstrom) or for which a business strategy was literally constructed with the concept as a major element (Fairfield Inn).

22. See, for example, the summary conclusions of the work of others by Alan S. Blinder, op. cit., pp. 1–13, that participation (empowerment), if it is to improve productivity for more than short periods of time, must be bolstered in the long run by pay schemes that reward individual or group performance. But even under these conditions, only small positive long-term effects on productivity are usually observed.

23. Francine Schwadel, "Chain Finds Incentives a Hard Sell," *The Wall Street Journal,* July 26, 1990, pp. B1 and B4.

24. For more complete descriptions of recent events, see "Nordstrom: Dissension in the Ranks," Case No. 9-191-002 (Boston, MA: Publishing Division, Harvard Business School, 1990); and Charlene Mermer Soloman, "Nightmare at Nordstrom," *Personnel Journal* (September 1990), pp. 76–83.

NEW SERVICES DESIGN, DEVELOPMENT AND IMPLEMENTATION AND THE EMPLOYEE

Benjamin Schneider
University of Maryland, College Park

David E. Bowen
University of Southern California, Los Angeles

ABSTRACT

Three critical ways in which products/manufacturing organizations differ from services/service organizations are presented as a basis for designing the "service cube." These differences (intangibility, simultaneous production and consumption, customer participation in production) are used as a framework against which six propositions about employee involvement in the design, development and implementation (ddi) of new services are presented. The propositions specify the benefits that accrue to organizations when employee participation is high, specific facets of new service ddi to which employees are likely to make contributions, and the role of customers as "partial employees" in new services ddi.

The major purpose of the present paper is to explore the role of employees in the design, development and implementation (ddi) of new services. Originally, the focus was to be new service development exclusively, but as that topic was pursued it became clear that design is the first step in the process of bringing new services on line and implementation perhaps the most critical. As will become clear, it appears as if employees in that part of the service sector characterized by high contact with the consumer may be more useful in the development and implementation of services than in their initial design.

It is important to underscore at the outset that this consideration of the employee's role in ddi is framed in a particular context—the service sector, and from a particular vantage point—the literature of organizational behavior. Since the reader of this paper is likely to be

more familiar with the marketing and consumer behavior literature on the service sector a brief introduction to the role of the service sector, in contemporary organizational behavior (OB) is presented first. Then a definition of service is presented that keys on three characteristics of service and the nature of service organizations. These three characteristics yield the "service cube" which provides a useful way to identify the service employees who are the focus of ddi. Some propositions are then offered regarding the importance of the employee in new service ddi in the service sector.

INTRODUCTION: OB, AND SERVICE

The organizational dynamics of the rapidly growing service sector have received considerable attention in the organizational behavior literature recently. This attention has typically focused on relatively macro issues with a particular emphasis on the overall organizational design of the service system. Examples include a typology of service organizations (Mills & Margulies 1980), perspectives on the technology of service operations (Mills & Moberg 1982), the application of a dependent demand approach to service operation planning and control (Snyder, Cox, & Jesse 1982), and the design of professional service organizations (Mills, Hall, Leidecker, & Margulies 1983). Additionally, Chase

Source: Benjamin Schneider and David E. Bowen, "New Services Design, Development and Implementation and the Employee," reprinted with permission from *Developing New Services*, William R. George and Claudia Marshall, eds., 1984, pp. 82–101, published by the American Marketing Association, Chicago, IL 60606.

(1978) has dealt with ways of buffering core technology of the service system to enhance efficiency and Levitt (1972; 1976) has argued for the "industrialization of service" in service system designs to achieve the same end. These works have helped reverse the tendency to view the principles of organization and management that emerged from the study of manufacturing organizations as central, typical, and applicable to all organizations (Miller and Rice 1967; Shamir 1978).

A number of unique characteristics have been attributed to services and service organizations (SO) by different writers. While their lists may vary somewhat, most would agree to the presence and importance of the following three characteristics (Bowen, 1983):

1. *The output of service organizations is intangible.* Services are intangible or much less tangible than physical goods/products (Levitt 1980). The typical unavailability of physical evidence for judging the quality of service leads customers to rely upon factors associated with the delivery of the service (employees' dress, manner of speaking, behaving, etc.) in forming their service quality views. Shostack (1977a) notes that because of this intangibility, more than one version of "reality" may be found in a service market. In her words, ". . . the reality of a service varies according to the mind of the beholder . . ." (1977b; p. 42). In a similar vein, Swan and Comb (1976) speak of services as having "expressive performance" (compared to "instrumental performance") and Gronroos (1982) refers to "functional quality" (compared to "technical quality"). What they mean is that in the relative absence of tangibility, the process by which the intangible is delivered becomes the focus for what the service is. In fact, Schneider and his colleagues (Schneider, Parkington, & Buxton 1980; Schneider & Bowen 1983) have shown that employee descriptions of how they deliver service is strongly reflected in customer descriptions of the quality of service they receive.

2. *Services are produced and consumed simultaneously.* Whereas with goods there is typically a delay between production and consumption, with many services production and consumption occur simultaneously. In services, there typically are no middlemen or intermediate distribution linkages between production and consumption. Consequently, the production function cannot be divorced from the marketing function (Fitzsimmons & Sullivan 1982) and the sales force and production team are

sometimes one and the same—particularly in professional service firms (Lovelock 1981). This characteristics of services yields some unique management problems, especially the coordination of supply and demand (Sasser 1976; Snyder et al. 1982) due to the impossibility of inventorying services on the intangible or high customer contact extreme (Chase 1978).

3. *Customers often participate in producing services.* In many SOs, productivity is in part dependent upon the knowledge, experience, motivation, behavior, and cooperation of the customer (Gersuny & Rosengren 1973; Lovelock 1981). For example, the reliability of a doctor's diagnosis may depend upon the patient's ability and willingness to describe his/her illness. Additionally, SOs having any element of self-service (e.g., automatic teller machines) require considerable self-discipline and autonomous action from customers (Eiglier & Langeard 1977). The SO's ability to manage customer behavior will, therefore, be a determinant of organizational effectiveness. In other words, managers in SOs can be thought of as simultaneously managing organizational and consumer behavior (Bowen 1983).

Especially as the service becomes more high contact and intangible, SOs are increasingly faced with the management of the behavior of both employees and consumers. This is true because, at the boundary of high-contact SOs, employees and consumers are not only physically close but close psychologically as well. They are psychologically close for three reasons: (1) employees of SOs tend to choose service sector jobs rather than jobs in other sectors because they are service-oriented and empathize with the consumer (Schneider 1980; Schneider & Bowen 1983); (2) consumers complain to employees at the boundary about service quality; and, (3) service sector employees tend to be consumers of the same kinds of services they deliver.

A convenient way to think about the nature of services and the organizations that deliver them is shown in Figure 1, the "service cube." The service cube summarizes the three attributes outlined above (intangibility, simultaneous production and consumption, and customer participation in the production of service). In what follows, the word service will refer to attributes more toward the bottom right-hand portion of the cube while goods will refer more to the top left-hand portion of the cube. In addition, we will restrict our comments to that portion of the service sector called consumer service organizations rather than to those known as profes-

FIGURE 1   The Service Cube

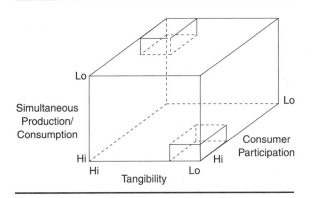

sional service organizations (Fitzsimmons & Sullivan 1982; Sasser, Olsen, & Wyckoff 1978). Professional service organizations have large numbers of highly educated, highly skilled, and highly paid individuals working as doctors, dentists, and lawyers. Our focus is more on the fast-food, retailing and banking lower level employees who have high contact with consumers to whom they deliver a relatively intangible service.

While these service employees work in organizations that provide services more tangible than those typically offered by a lawyer or doctor, the fact that they work with people rather than inanimate raw materials makes their job unique from the manufacturing sector. In this context, a most interesting summary of how SOs generally differ from their manufacturing counterparts can be found in two metaphors from Bell's (1973) book on post-industrial society. Bell described work in the post-industrial world as primarily a "game between persons." In contrast, Bell described work in an industrial society as a ". . . game against fabricated nature, in which men become dwarfed by machines as they turn out goods and things" (1973: pp. XVI, XVII). In what follows, the emphasis is clearly on the game between persons.

EMPLOYEES AND NEW SERVICES

The organizational behavior literature on employee participation in workplace decisions indicates that participative decision making is superior to authoritarian decision making (i.e., management alone making the decisions) when employees possess important information that management does not (Vroom & Yetton 1973). Also, employee participation in workplace decisions increases their understanding and acceptance of the decision which, in turn, facilitates implementation of those decisions (Locke & Schweiger 1979; Maier 1983). Since service organizations management may under-

stand customer needs less well than employees do and since customers often equate services with the manner in which employees render them, the following proposition is offered:

Proposition 1: The more employees are involved in service as defined by the service cube, the more important it is to involve them in the ddi of new services.

In a recent study by Langeard, Bateson, Lovelock, and Eiglier (1982), field managers from two large banking institutions were unable to accurately assess the needs customers, themselves, claimed they had. This example of management being out of "sync" with customers is probably not unique. Proposition 1 follows from a view of service employees as "boundary spanners" with empathy both for the employing organization and the consumers being served. As stated earlier, these employees are both physically and psychologically close to their customers. Because of this, service employees at the boundary of the organization are a source of valuable information about customer needs. In a sense, then, when these boundary employees participate in ddi, customers, too, are represented in the ddi process. Thus, particularly in settings of high customer–employee contact, employees are more likely to be aware of the kinds of new services likely to meet customer needs. Perhaps more importantly they are likely to be a source of valuable ideas for how to implement the new service so that customers will respond favorably to change. In this latter perspective on employees, i.e., that they are a source of valuable information to facilitate change, management would involve employees not only to gain their acceptance and commitment but because they are a source of valuable ideas.

Capoor (1981), in reporting on Touche Ross' approach to understanding service businesses, clearly promotes this vantage point. He notes that a cycle of people providing service in partnership with customers generates the success that rewards people, and so on. This cycle obviously treats employees (people) as an integral component of service success, especially through their interventions with customers.

A second reason for this proposition builds on the ideas of Swan and Comb (1976) and Gronroos (1982) regarding the principle that as the service becomes more intangible, how the service is delivered is what the service is to the consumer. Gronroos (1982, pp. 5–6) put it thus: In service businesses, "the consumer is not only interested in what he receives as an outcome of the production process, but in the process itself. *How* he gets the technical outcome—or technical quality—functionally, is also important to him and to his view of the service he has received." Schneider (1980), from a similar vantage point, has proposed that the climate for service created in an organization, including how service is delivered, is critical for service unit effectiveness. In fact he has shown that (a) customers can sense the climate for service in different establishments (indeed, how customers viewed employee morale in these establishments was related to how they viewed service quality) and (b) when consumers feel the service climate is "warm and friendly" their perceptions of service quality are more positive and loyalty to the service unit is enhanced (Schneider 1973).

In sum, if how employees deliver a service shapes the customer's definition of the service reality, then using participative decision making to make service employees accepting and understanding providers of the new service seems advisable. Thus, while models for employee participation in the manufacturing sector are quite compelling, in the service sector participation would seem to be a requirement. Specification of some of the more subtle ways employee involvement in ddi can facilitate customer acceptance of new services is the foundation of proposition two.

> *Proposition 2:* Employee involvement in ddi of new services should focus not only on the service, per se, but on the organizational or contextual issues required for supporting delivery of the service to customers.

Given new services are intangible, involve customers, and are simultaneously produced and consumed, it is likely the customers will rely heavily on the *act* by which the service is delivered in determining their satisfaction with the service, itself. An important question becomes: What organizational conditions facilitate the act of providing services?

Organizational behaviorists have produced considerable evidence to support the following elements as being important components of work effectiveness:

☐ Employees must have sufficient aptitudes and attitudes to meet the major demands of their job and/or to learn their new job.

☐ Reward systems in organizations must be tied to behaviors that are important for organizational effectiveness and which fit the needs of employees.

☐ The behaviors desired from employees must be made clear through the establishment of goals, through providing necessary training, and through the design of appropriate reward systems.

While the management of organizations know at some abstract level that these factors are important, they seem to lack a clear understanding of how to implement them and thus they are rarely put into practice. This is particularly true of management in the still lightly-studied service sector. We suggest that in the service sector managers turn to those individuals who may be most knowledgeable of these components of work effectiveness—the employees themselves.

For example, some recent experience the authors have had when involving employees in new services ddi has yielded the following suggestions for insuring the infrastructure necessary for a new service's success:

☐ The marketing department (the source of ideas for new services in this organization) should work with personnel and computer operations to be sure that the new requirements on people and machinery can be met by the time the new service is rolled out; selection, training, software, and so forth.

☐ The advertising program for the new service should be developed with employee input because employees are familiar with the day-to-day needs and concerns of customers. This familiarity allows employees to provide input on the ways various kinds of customers are likely to respond to an advertising campaign. Parenthetically it is interesting to note that services advertising campaigns are frequently tested on a small sample of customers whereas testing them on a small sample of employees would (a) provide data from a large sample of customers (because each employee interacts with numerous customers) and (b) gain the acceptance and commitment of employees.

☐ The performance evaluation system should emphasize the kinds of behaviors on the part of employees the new service requires, and employees need to be reinforced for displaying them. Employees meant by this behaviors such as ensuring customer understanding, revealing interest in customer desires, and so forth, rather than easily countable issues like balancing out at the end of the day.

In summary, the principle behind proposition 2 is that employees know the infrastructure details that have to be attended to in ddi of new services so that the new service has a chance for success.

> *Proposition 3:* Involvement of employees in new service ddi should focus more on development and implementation than on design.

This proposition follows from the principle mentioned earlier that participation should capitalize on the expertise of participants. In the case of lower level employees in consumer service organizations it can be assumed that, generally speaking, they will be relatively unaware of the financial and market forces requiring or dictating the essential design of new services. However, once the nature of a new service has been specified, employees can be valuable as aids in development and implementation. That is, given their psychological closeness to customers, employees can be trusted to provide relatively accurate impressions about how customers are likely to respond to different forms of a new service, and they are particularly likely to be valuable in specifying what is needed in order to make the roll-out of a new service a success.

In the latter case, as noted above, employees are able to specify the training needs of employees so the new service can be delivered, the possible reaction of customers to planned advertisements of the new service, ways of adapting computer routines for efficiency in delivering the new service, and possible sequencing of the introduction of the new service to make it acceptable to consumers. A way to summarize the importance of this proposition is to refer to the style and pace of new services: Because employees are the providers, they are likely to be aware of the style of delivery most useful to consumers and the pace of the introduction of the new service.

Much of what has been presented so far has focused on style of service delivery but pace is equally important because it connotes change and change is something people typically resist. People resist change when their perception of the status quo is that it is "ok." When people think their needs are being gratified to an acceptable level, they will resist change.

What management typically fails to consider in introducing change, however, is that its current consumers are relatively satisfied; if they were not they would have taken their business elsewhere. Given this situation, management is taking a risk by introducing a new service because the new procedure is likely to be resisted. In Levitt's (1980, p. 100) words: "The most important thing to know about intangible products is that the *customers usually don't know what they're getting until they don't get it.*"

What Levitt is saying with respect to the issue of change is that customers will become aware of what used to happen only after it no longer happens! The caution is obvious: Any change is a risk in terms of consumer reaction. Fortunately employees are available as a source of input on a pace for implementation that might prove less disruptive and cause less recognition of what was.

Perhaps the best reason for consulting with employees is because it operationalizes a procedure for showing concern for customers. Lovelock and Young (1979), for example, mention seven steps to avoid insensitivity to customers, five of which are relevant here:

1. Develop customer trust

2. Understand customer habits

3. Pretest new procedures and equipment

4. Understand determinants of consumer behavior

5. Teach consumers how to use service innovations

From what has been presented earlier, it becomes clear here that employee involvement in ddi can help make these all happen, i.e., employees can provide management with important information on each of these points.

> *Proposition 4:* Involvement of employees in new service ddi will help insure that new services will reflect an "ethic of service" as well as an "ethic of efficiency."

Most new services in organizations are introduced for reasons of efficiency. In other words, the changes are desired by management to facilitate productivity through more efficient (less costly) service delivery. This is the logic behind articles like Levitt's (1972, 1976) classic pieces on the industrialization of service.

Similarly, some writers have recommended sealing employees off from customers so that they will be more efficient (Chase 1978; Levitt 1976) or so they are not co-opted by customers (Aldrich & Herker 1977). For example, Chase and Tansik (forthcoming) agree with Danet (1981) that customers are problems for organizations because they disrupt routines, fail to do what they are supposed to do, make unwarranted or exaggerated demands, and so on.

These above positions are contrary to two other principles that appear critical to new service ddi: First, it is important to view service organizations against an "ethic of service" rather than solely against an "ethic of efficiency" (Lefton & Rosengren 1966). To adhere exclusively to an efficiency ethic in new service ddi is to pursue a course more appropriate to manufacturing organizations than to service organizations. It also may be an unacceptable course to customers who frequently rely on how warm and friendly the service atmosphere is as a basis for their attraction to the service (Schneider 1973).

Secondly, sealing employees off from customers would deny the service organization an opportunity to learn how customers judge the services they receive against their ethic of service. Simply put, the more the needs and capabilities of customers are addressed during new service ddi, the more likely it is that customers will be attracted to take advantage of what the new service has to offer. The more employees both have contact with customers and are involved in new service ddi, the more likely it is that efficiency goals will not overwhelm the service needs of customers. When the latter happens, efficiency becomes a moot issue.

At Citibank, Matteis (1979, p. 150) reports how this happened:

> In taking our cue from the production management disciplines of manufacturing enterprises—a necessary first step, to be sure—we had tended to blur the difference in what a customer expects from a manufactured product as distinct from a service delivered. In gaining the control needed to achieve production efficiency, we had perforce homogenized the service that we processed. By imposing a kind of product uniformity on our processing, we had sacrificed what is the very essence of a financial transaction service: its uniqueness.

The message in Matteis's report of Citibank's industrialization of service is that for each customer the service s/he receives is a unique experience regardless of how many times the organization must deliver the "same" service to others.

In sum, employee involvement in ddi may protect customer service needs from the productivity and efficiency concerns of the organization. The necessity of achieving this balance is underscored by the following observation by Lovelock & Young (1979, p. 169): "In our experience, attempts to improve productivity in service industries all too often demonstrate lack of sensitivity to consumer needs and concerns."

Proposition 5: In the ddi of new services, organizations should treat their employees as if they were highly valued customers.

Levitt (1980, p. 102) said that:

> . . . a customer is an asset usually more precious than the tangible assets on the balance sheet. Balance sheet assets can generally be bought. There are lots of willing sellers. Customers cannot so easily be bought. Lots of eager sellers are offering them many choices. Moreover, a customer is a double asset. First, the customer is the direct source of cash from the sale and, second, the existence of a solid customer can be used to raise cash from bankers and investors—cash that can be converted into tangible assets.

If customers are so valuable to organizations why do organizations spend so little on retaining them but so much on attracting them? By assuming a perspective that integrates organizational behavior and consumer behavior it becomes clear that the vehicle for retaining customers in the service sector is by focusing on the employees who provide customer services. This perspective suggests the principle that when employees feel they are trusted, understood, and deemed important by the organization, they will want to treat customers in the same way. By wanting to treat customers appropriately, when asked to participate in ddi of new services, they will.

This proposition has some similarity to a recent insightful proposal by Mills, Chase, and Margulies (1983). They suggested, because of the close relationship between employees and customers in service systems, that management of such systems view productivity as a problem in motivating not only employees but motivating customers as well. Indeed, they suggested that motivating customers to participate in the production of their own services should be part of an employee's job. *Why* employees might want to do this and *how* the service system could foster such employee behavior were not specified by Mills et al. (1983); Proposition 5 constitutes that specification.

In a broad sense, Proposition 5 might be thought of as the Quality of Work Life (QWL) proposition. This is true because QWL programs are introduced by organizations in an attempt to enhance the esteem and personal worth employees experience in their work role. It seems fairly clear that QWL programs have little direct effect on short-term productivity but that they have some substantial indirect long-term impact on unit effectiveness. The difference between the short-term productivity and long-term indirect impact on unit effectiveness concerns the difference between, for example, number of sales per hour and absenteeism or turnover; QWL programs affect the latter but not the former (Schneider, forthcoming). Organizations are not the only ones concerned about turnover. In Schneider's (1980; Schneider et al. 1980) research he has found that customers of banks are concerned about employee turnover. In fact, he found that in some bank branches' customers would switch their accounts to branches that employees moved to! This is not an uncommon phenomenon in some service organizations, e.g., hairdressers, retail sales of higher priced clothes, auto mechanics, and so on, but to find it in bank branches was a surprise.

Schneider and Bowen (1983) have recently demonstrated statistically that (a) employee reports on organizational human relations practices are correlated with customer reports of the service quality they receive, and (b) employee reports of their own turnover intentions are correlated with the turnover intentions of the customers they serve. These kinds of data clearly lend support to the idea that when organizations treat their employees as if they are valuable customers, employees will treat their customers in a similar fashion. At least one organization, Marriott, has publicly expressed (in the *HBR*) its decision to build service quality through the retention of quality employees. Furthermore, it has established human resources policies and procedures to achieve that goal (Hostage 1975). Numerous other organizations with similar philosophies are cited in Peters and Waterman's (1983) recent book on organizational excellence.

A closing thought on the relationship between high quality treatment of employees and new service ddi can be offered. Improved treatment by management of the lower-level employees in contact with customers may, in and of itself, transform an "old" service into a "new" one. That is, improved treatment of employees may result in employees improving their treatment of customers. This would likely be perceived by customers as an entirely new service! Indeed, differentiation in its treatment of employees may be a vehicle by which service management can differentiate its service from comparable services offered by competitors.

Proposition 6: New service ddi can be facilitated by thinking of customers as "partial employees."

This proposition is the converse of Proposition 5 and builds on the notion that increasing the customer's involvement in the service production process (Lovelock & Young 1979) can be one general approach to new service ddi. For example, when customers use an automated teller machine they are acting as both a consumer and a producer. In their role as service producers, customers can be thought of as "partial employees" of the service organization (Bowen 1983; Mills et al. 1983). The service organization then becomes dependent upon the performance of these partial employees (more so than their own employees) for the successful implementation of the new service.

An interesting issue for service management then becomes how to manage the performance of customers as partial employees. Unfortunately, there is little prior research that deals with how customer inclinations to participate in producing their own service can be influenced (an exception is the Langeard et al. 1981 study that will be reviewed below). However, a theoretical guide to managing customers is the insight by Mills et al. (1983) and Bowen (1983) that customer performance might be usefully viewed as being dependent on the same issues that affect employee performance: abilities and traits, role perceptions, and motivation. That is, if management can impact these ingredients within customers, they may be better able to shape how well customers perform in the implementation of new services.

Bowen (1983) discussed some management strategies for shaping customer performance. For example, the recent study by Langeard, et al. (1981), identified the traits of customers who were more willing to participate in the service creation process. Participatively-inclined customers were more likely to be younger, male, and more educated, to be impatient, to dislike waiting in line, and to like to play with machines. Thus, organizations may be able to select certain customers who are willing to produce their own service.

It was also noted that if the organization wants customers to act as partial employees, i.e., participate in creating their own service, it must make it clear to customers that it indeed wants them to play that role. For example, McDonald's expects its customers to fill the role of "busser," cleaning their own tables after eating. They make this expectation known with numerous highly visible trash cans and tray racks. Other service organizations, if they are designing and developing new self-service alternatives, must consider how the service setting makes clear to the customer the kind of participation required. If this is not done, customers as partial employees will likely perform poorly in implementing the new service.

Finally, service organizations must manage customers' motivation to be attracted to new services. As service organization management approaches the issue of customer motivation, it should be careful not to repeat the errors made in understanding worker motivation. Management theorists initially assumed that employees were motivated solely by economic needs. Over time, it became clear that employees' work behavior was also directed to other needs, e.g., affiliation and self-actualization. The lesson to be learned is that if new services are being planned that involve customers as partial employees then the new services should attempt to appeal to customer needs other than their economic needs. That is, customers may be motivated to participate in new services that are not only less costly, but also new services that are more challenging, fun, etc.

The summary point is that customers represent a unique pool of partial employees when one considers the topic, "New services design, development and implementation and the employee." Indeed, when the new service is a form of automation, e.g., automated bank tellers, the customer as partial employee becomes the central figure in new service implementation.

SUMMARY

The service sector is now the lead sector in the United States economy. Given this, new service development becomes the very cutting edge of economic growth. The effective management of employees in new service ddi is a critical factor in how sharp this cutting edge can be.

Unfortunately, most of what we know about managing employees has been learned from studies conducted in industrial organizations. In effect, management models have been relatively unidimensional, developed for organizations whose dynamics center on the production of goods, rather than services.

In this paper, the "service cube" was offered to capture the dimensions along which services and service organizations differ from manufacturing organizations. These dimensions (intangibility, simultaneous production and consumption, and customer participation in the production of the service) frame how service employees should be managed, generally, and what their role should be in new service ddi more specifically.

A number of propositions involving new services ddi and the employee were offered that can be summarized as follows:

☐ Employee involvement in new services ddi is important for at least two general reasons: (1) Employees, because they are psychologically and physically close to customers, can identify customer needs as new service ddi proceeds. They can guide management's choice of: the kinds of new services offered, the procedures that will facilitate the act of providing these services, and the pace at which new services are introduced. (2) Employee involvement in ddi increases the likelihood that employees will behave knowledgeably and willingly in the implementation of the new service. This is critical, since customers may evaluate the new services on the basis of how employees act in rendering them.

☐ Employee involvement in new service ddi helps guarantee that the process will not allow the efficiency needs/desires of the organization to overwhelm the service needs of the customer. It appears that an "ethic of efficiency" is often the overly-dominant driving force behind new service ddi.

☐ Treating employees as highly valued customers may encourage employees to, in turn, treat customers bet-

ter and actively represent their needs in new services ddi. This proposition is built upon an integration of organizational and consumer behavior—a common set of organizational human resources practices can be reflected in the attitudes and behavior of both employees and customers.

☐ Customers can be viewed as "partial employees" in the ddi of new services. When new services require self-service of customers, service organizations must try to manage how these partial employees implement the new service. This can be done by managing the traits, role perceptions, and motivation of customers.

These propositions present a picture of the employee involved in new service ddi in partnership with both management and customers. This partnership is a natural outgrowth of the unique characteristics of service organizations. Hopefully, research and practice guided by these propositions will generate creative new service alternatives. More fundamentally, attention to these propositions can further our understanding of how services marketing differs from product marketing, as well as how principles of consumer and organizational behavior developed in the manufacturing sector may need to be amended when applied to various locations in the service cube.

REFERENCES

Aldrich, H. E., and D. Herker (1977), "Boundary-Spanning Roles and Organizational Structure," *Academy of Management Review,* 2 (April) 217–230.

Bell, D. (1973), *The Coming of Post-Industrial Society: A Venture in Social Forecasting,* New York: Basic Books.

Bowen, D. E. (1983), "Managing Employees and Customers in Service Organizations: Some Lessons from Organizational Behavior and Consumer Behavior," unpublished manuscript, University of Southern California.

Capoor, R. (1981), "Strategic Planning—Part II," *Restaurant Business* (June), 154–166.

Chase, R. B. (1978), "Where Does the Customer Fit in a Service Operation?" *Harvard Business Review,* 55 (November–December), 137–142.

———— and D. A. Tansik (1983), "The Customer Contact Model for Organizational Design," *Management Science,* 29, 1037–1050.

Danet, B. (1981), "Client-Organization Interfaces," in *Handbook of Organization Design, Vol. 2,* P. C. Nystrom and W. H. Starbuck, eds., New York: Oxford University Press.

Eiglier, P. and E. Langeard (1977), "A New Approach to Service Marketing," in *Marketing Consumer Services: New Insights, Report 77–115,* Boston: Marketing Sciences Institute.

Fitzsimmons, J. A. and T. S. Sullivan (1982), *Service Operations Management,* New York: McGraw-Hill.

Gersuny, C. and W. R. Rosengren (1973), *The Service Society,* Cambridge, MA: Shenkman.

Gronroos, C. (1982), "A Service Quality Model and Its Management Implications," unpublished paper, Swedish School of Economics and Business Administration.

Hostage, G. M. (1975), "Quality Control in a Service Business," *Harvard Business Review,* 53 (July–August), 98–106.

Langeard, E., J. E. G. Bateson, C. H. Lovelock, and P. Eiglier (1981), *Services Marketing: New Insights from Consumers and Managers, Report 81–104.* Cambridge, MA: Marketing Sciences Institute.

Lefton, M. and W. R. Rosengren (1966), "Organizations and Clients: Lateral and Longitudinal Dimensions," *American Sociological Review,* 31 (December), 802–810.

Levitt, T. (1972), "Production Line Approach to Services," *Harvard Business Review,* 50 (September–October), 802–810.

——— (1976), "The Industrialization of Service," *Harvard Business Review,* 54 (September–October), 63–74.

——— (1980), "Marketing Success through Differentiation-of Anything," *Harvard Business Review,* 58 (January–February), 83–91.

Locke, E. A. and D. M. Schweiger (1979), "Participation in Decision-Making: One More Look," in *Research in Organizational Behavior, Vol. 1,* B. M. Staw, ed., Greenwich, CT: JAI Press.

Lovelock, C. H. (1981), "Why Marketing Management Needs to Be Different for Services," in *Marketing of Services,* J. H. Donnelly and W. R. George, eds., Chicago: American Marketing Association.

——— and R. F. Young (1979), "Look to Consumers to Increase Productivity," *Harvard Business Review,* 57 (May–June), 168–178.

Maier, N. R. F. (1983), "Assets and Liabilities in Group Problem Solving: The Need for an Integrative Function," in *Perspectives on Behavior in Organizations,* J. R. Hackman, E. E. Lawler, III, and L. W. Porter, eds., New York: McGraw-Hill.

Matteis, R. J. (1979), "The New Back Office Focuses on Customer Service," *Harvard Business Review,* 57 (March–April), 146–159.

Miller, E. J. and A. K. Rice (1967), *System of Organizations,* London: Tavistock.

Mills, P. K., R. B. Chase, and N. Margulies (1983), "Motivating the Client/Employee System as a Service Production Strategy," *Academy of Management Review,* 8 (April), 301–310.

———, J. L. Hall, J. K. Leidecker, and N. Margulies (1983), "Flexiform: A Model for Professional Service Organizations," *Academy of Management Review,* 8 (April), 301–310.

——— and N. Margulies (1980), "Toward a Core Typology of Service Organizations," *Academy of Management Review,* 5 (April), 255–266.

——— and D. Moberg (1982), "Perspectives on the Technology of Service Operations," *Academy of Management Review,* 7 (July), 467–478.

Peters, T. J. and R. Waterman (1982), *In Search of Excellence: Lessons from America's Best Run Companies,* New York: Harper and Row.

Sasser, W. (1976), "Match Supply and Demand in Service Industries," *Harvard Business Review,* 56 (November–December), 133–148.

———, R. P. Olsen, and D. D. Wyckoff (1978), *Management of Service Operations,* Boston: Allyn & Bacon.

Schneider, B. (1973), "The Perception of Organizational Climate: The Customer's View," *Journal of Applied Psychology,* 57 (April), 248–256.

——— (1980), "The Service Organization: Climate Is Crucial," *Organizational Dynamics,* 9 (Autumn), 52–65.

——— (forthcoming), "Industrial–Organizational Psychology Perspective," in *Research on Productivity,* A. P. Brief, ed., New York: Praeger.

——— and D. E. Bowen (1983), "Employee and Customer Perceptions of Service in Banks: Replication and Extension with Implications for Integrating Consumer and Organizational Behavior." Unpublished paper, University of Maryland.

———, J. J. Parkington, and V. M. Buxton (1980), "Employee and Customer Perceptions of Service in Banks," *Administrative Science Quarterly,* 25 (June), 252–267.

Shostack, G. L. (1977a), "Breaking Free from Product Marketing," *Journal of Marketing,* 41 (April), 73–80.

——— (1977b), "Banks Sell Services—Not Things," *Bankers Magazine,* 32 (January), 40–45.

Snyder, C. A., J. R. Cox, and J. Jesse (1982), "Dependent Demand Approach to Service Organization Planning and Control," *Academy of Management Review,* 7 (July), 455–466.

Swan, J. E. and L. J. Comb (1976), "Product Performance and Consumer Satisfaction: A New Concept," *Journal of Marketing,* 40 (April), 17–30.

Shamir, B. (1978), "Between Bureaucracy and Hospitality—Some Organizational Characteristics of Hotels," *Journal of Management Studies,* 15 (August), 285–307.

Vroom, V. R. and P. W. Yetton (1973), *Leadership and Decision-Making,* Pittsburgh: University of Pittsburgh Press.

COMMUNICATIONS STRATEGY

CHAPTER OVERVIEW

Communications can have a profound effect upon the service experience. They can be used in the pre-consumption choice process to attract new customers, but, if used wrongly in this way, they can fill a service setting with incompatible segments of customers, each with different expectations, and can induce operational inefficiency and customer dissatisfaction. Communications can be used to teach the consumer the service-consumption script. Communications can educate the consumer to use the service more effectively (particularly if the script is being changed). Finally, communications have a major impact on post-consumption evaluation, since they can influence the expectation against which perceptions are compared. Such expectations can be set by broad-ranging mass media or personal contact.

This chapter uses a single communications strategy framework to highlight the constraints and opportunities of the service experience for this key element of the marketing mix.

SETTING COMMUNICATIONS STRATEGY FOR SERVICES

The setting of a communications strategy follows a common pattern irrespective of whether the firm is producing goods or services (see Figure 7.1). The first step is to define a target audience and a clear objective for the complete communications mix. The term *communications mix* sometimes is used to describe the array of communications tools available to marketers. Just as marketers need to combine the elements of the marketing mix (including communications) to produce a marketing program, so they also need to select the most appropriate ingredients for the communications program.

The traditional elements of the communications mix fall into four broad categories: personal selling, media advertising, publicity and public relations, and promotional or information activities at the point of sale. Only personal selling is normally a two-way process. The remainder are one-way communications, from the marketer to the customer only. With services, however, the service providers at the point of communication also can have an important two-way communications role.

In addition to a target audience and a clear objective it is also important at this stage to determine the likely total communications budget. After this has been established, the target audience or audiences, objectives, and budgets are divided among the different areas of the mix. Each area does not have to have the same task or audience, so long as, together, they meet the overall objective. Once this has been done, information delivery can be planned and executed and the results monitored.

DEFINING THE TARGET AUDIENCE FOR SERVICE COMMUNICATION

The target audience should flow from the overall marketing plan and from a sound understanding of consumer behavior. The target audience for the service needs to be decided early in the process lest the whole service formula becomes malformed. Defining the target customer for the service is thus the foundation of the service formula (see Chapter 9). Unlike goods, however, the target audience has to be much more precisely defined.

Although segmentation is applied in both goods and service companies, the consequences of reaching an inappropriate segment with a part of the advertising are far less serious for goods companies than for services. If the wrong group of con-

FIGURE 7.1   The Communications Strategy Process

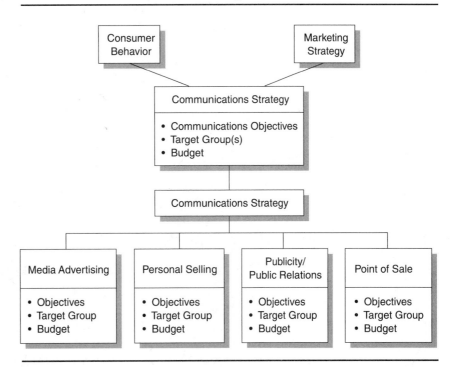

sumers buys a particular brand of detergent, for example, it does not really affect the company making the detergent; sales still are being generated. A product may have been developed for the youth market, but through some quirk of the advertising execution or the media plan, it has attracted some senior citizens. This group visits the supermarket, buys the product, and uses it in their homes. The negative consequences to the company are few.

Suppose, however, that some of the wrong segment decides to buy a restaurant service. An up-market concept has been developed, but to launch it, the restaurant management has a price promotion and the advertising agency develops inappropriate advertising. Or, through poor management, publicity activity is unfocused and produces feature articles in the wrong media. The result is that the restaurant gets two types of customers: middle-aged couples and groups of students. The former were the original target, the latter were attracted by inappropriate marketing tactics. Unfortunately for the restaurant, and for many other services, the other customers are part of the product. The result is that neither segment enjoys the experience because of the presence of the other, and neither type of customer returns.

ADVERTISING TO EMPLOYEES

The staff of service firms frequently forms a secondary audience for any advertising campaign.[1] This is distinct from developing communications strategies directed at staff as advocated in "internal marketing."[2] In this case, the target group is clearly the customers. The media are not selective enough to screen out the staff, who indeed may be customers when off duty.

Clearly, advertising seen by the staff, if it empathizes with them, can be highly motivating. However, if the advertising is developed without a firm understanding of operational problems, it can intimate service performance levels that are technically or bureaucratically impossible; that is, it can set expectation levels unrealistically high. This has a doubly damning effect on the staff since it: (1) shows that the people who developed the advertising (the marketing department) did not understand the business, and (2) raises the prospect that customers actually will expect the service to operate that way and it will be the staff that will have to tell them that reality differs from the advertisement. In both cases, the impact will be a negative influence on staff motivation, which will, in turn, negatively influence customer satisfaction.

SETTING COMMUNICATIONS OBJECTIVES FOR SERVICES

Communications can be used to influence any stage in the choice, consumption, and evaluation processes. Although communication objectives traditionally try to motivate choice (getting more consumers to choose a brand), it is a unique characteristic of services that communications can be used to impact all three phases.

THE PRE-CONSUMPTION CHOICE PHASE

Setting objectives in this phase can be thought of as using either the role-taking model of consumer choice or the rational mathematician model (see Chapter 2). Consumers will try to minimize the risk taken in the purchase phase. Since risk is some combination of consequences and uncertainty, these are the two dimensions along which communication can operate. In each case, the objective must be to ensure that the company's service is the one perceived to be the least-risky alternative.

Communications obviously can offer information that is a key factor in reducing the uncertainty component of all risky decisions. It also can seek to offer reassurance. As for consequences, these generally are thought of as being of three basic types: financial, performance, and social. Financial consequences can be reduced by communications that ensure that consumers correctly understand the likely financial consequences of a purchase, particularly if a money-back guarantee is offered. Social consequences can be reduced by highlighting the fact that other people are using the service and that it would not be embarrassing for them to use the service. Performance consequences need to be made explicit and must be clearly communicated to ensure that consumers clearly understand what would happen if the performance was not 100 percent successful. Clearly, most services are perceived as more risky on the performance and social dimensions, and communications have a key role to play in reassuring consumers.

The rational mathematician model assumes consumers are rational decision makers using a choice matrix of attributes, brand or company scores, and importance weights. Services in the evoked set are scored using the matrix and the one with the highest score is chosen. Clearly, communications could be used to try to influence the choice process in the following ways:

☐ To ensure that the firm's service offering is in the evoked set . If the company is not in the evoked set, to build enough awareness of the offering to arouse inclusion.

☐ To alter the weights attached to different attributes by consumers to favor those on which the company is strong.

☐ To alter the score on a given attribute for the company, particularly if there is a gap between performance and consumers' perceptions.

SERVICES IN ACTION 7.1

INFLUENCING THE PRECONSUMPTION CHOICE
PROCESS: NASDAQ INTERNATIONAL

Nasdaq International is a London-based financial services company providing a market for European companies wishing to enter the U.S. capital market. Using several high-tech electronics systems, Nasdaq aims to put European companies into these U.S. markets as efficiently as possible, allowing them access to new sources of capital and new shareholder bases. The following advertisement was placed by Nasdaq in *Business Week* (January 21, 1991).

(continued)

(continued from previous page)

Targeting communications in this market requires the company to take into account several factors relating to the customer. First, the market, like all capital markets, is uncertain and efficient flows of information are vital. Second, because of the scale of investment, risk levels are likely to be high. The company must understand what customer perceptions of such a service are likely to be and should aim its advertising toward reassuring customers on all counts.

☐ To alter the score on a given attribute given to a competitor, again particularly if there is a gap between performance and consumers' perceptions.

It is important to stress that there are differences between *tangible* performance and *perceived* performance. If actual performance exceeds perceived performance, then communications may be more effective than if the reverse is the case. Alternatively, advertising can be used to maintain a situation that is favorable to the firm. Consumers need reminding that a firm does well on particular attributes and those attributes should be regarded as important by the consumer.

THE CONSUMPTION PHASE

During this phase, the services consumer is a more or less active participant in the production process. It is important that consumers perform that production role successfully. From the firm's point of view, successful performance will improve the efficiency of the operation and the satisfaction of other customers. From the consumer's point of view, successful performance will ensure a high level of perceived control and, in all probability, a high level of satisfaction in the post-consumption phase.

Communications, in the broadest sense, can be used to ensure successful performance by giving the consumer a clear script. The nature of this script depends on the nature of the service operation, and on such factors as the levels of technology employed and whether the operation has high or low levels of customer contact. The script for a single point-of-contact operation, such as an insurance company, where most business is done over the telephone with an agent, will vary greatly from that of an airline, where the customer is in contact with several different employees over an extended period of time during booking, check-in, flight, and landing. Technology is also important; the script for using a bank ATM is different from that used when seeing a teller face to face over a counter. Service operations need to take these factors into account when designing the script and communicating with the customer.

In times of operational change, management of the consumers' script takes on even more importance. An example can be seen in a bank that is changing from multiple-line queuing to single-line queuing. No longer may customers wait in front of an individual teller window. Instead, they must form a single line and go to the first free window available to them when they are at the head of the line. Operationally, this can be shown to offer shorter and more predictable waiting times. No matter which model of consumer behavior choice we adopt, these achievements should be valued by the customer.

However, such a shift requires a change of script. Arriving at the bank without prior warning of the change, the consumer finds a new experience that no longer conforms to the existing script. It is not immediately obvious how the new system works, and the customer may feel a loss of control. The queue seems to be extremely long, and worse still, it is no longer possible to choose a specific, favorite teller to provide service. Clearly, the script needs to be modified.

It is fairly obvious how the various elements of the communications mix can be used to achieve modification. Media advertising or leaflets can be used to describe the new process. "Salespeople" positioned outside the bank can explain the new system to customers before they enter. Public relations can be used to generate editorial comment about the benefits of the new system. Inside the branch, the layout and signage must clearly signal the desired customer behavior. Finally, service providers can reassure customers personally and reinforce the new script.

THE POST-CONSUMPTION EVALUATION PHASE

Chapter 2 introduced the disconfirmation model of consumer satisfaction. This model hypothesizes that consumers judge satisfaction by comparing their prior expectations of performance with perceived actual performance.

Consumer expectations come from a number of sources, some within the control of the service firm and some outside its control. Expectations arise either from previous experience with the firm and/or its competitors, or from some form of communication. The latter can encompass all aspects of the communications mix. Advertising, designed to influence pre-purchase choice behavior, can set expectations in the customer's mind about the quality of service that will be received. Indeed, setting such an expectation may be a key aspect of a firm's advertising strategy.

Further, and often most importantly, expectations can be set by service providers. These are real-time expectations created during the service experience itself. They may reinforce pre-existing ideas or they may dramatically alter them. They can be set by something as explicit as a promise ("Your food will be ready in five minutes") or as implicit as a behavior pattern that sets a tone. Often, such expectations are created unwittingly, as when a server promises to "be right back." Such a statement can be viewed as both a binding contract by a customer and a farewell salutation by the server.

Perceived service also has many sources. "Technical service quality" is an objective level of performance produced by the operating system of the firm. It is measurable with a stop watch, temperature gauge, or other measuring instrument. Unfortunately, this is not the level of performance perceived by the consumer. Perception acts as a filter that moves the perceived service level up or down.

Perception is itself influenced by the same factors that dictate expectations. For example, advertising can create warm feelings toward the organization that has raised perceived service levels. Inappropriately dressed and ill-behaving staff can deliver high-quality service, but be poorly perceived by the consumer, which will downgrade the perceived service level.

COMMUNICATIONS TO INFLUENCE
CHOICE OR EVALUATIONS?

It is clear that many of the sources of expectations are under the direct control of a firm. Only past experience and competitor activity cannot be influenced directly. Given such control over expectations, the firm then must determine what should be the objectives of the communications mix.

SERVICES IN ACTION 7.2

TEACHING THE CONSUMER THE SCRIPT: WENDY'S HAMBURGERS

Wendy's, with McDonald's and Burger King, is one of the big three international hamburger restaurant chains. One Wendy's strategy was to attempt to differentiate itself from the market leader, McDonald's, by providing made-to-order burgers rather than the standard product range featured by its competitor.

To do so, Wendy's first had to explain to customers what was required of them. The leaflet, reproduced here, was an attempt to tell customers about the servuction system at Wendy's. It presented a new and, to customers won over from McDonald's, possibly unfamiliar script. In making this script change, Wendy's cast both order-takers and customers in different roles.

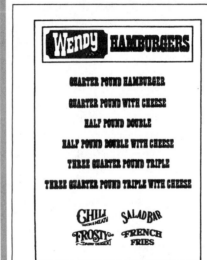

WENDY HAMBURGERS

QUARTER POUND HAMBURGER

QUARTER POUND WITH CHEESE

HALF POUND DOUBLE

HALF POUND DOUBLE WITH CHEESE

THREE QUARTER POUND TRIPLE

THREE QUARTER POUND TRIPLE WITH CHEESE

CHILI WITH REAL MEAT   SALAD BAR

FROSTY DAIRY DESSERT   FRENCH FRIES

Your recipe for a great Hamburger.

At Wendy Restaurants we don't tell you how to have your hamburger. You tell us.

The order-taker will want to know what size hamburger you'd like. A glance at the menu will help you to make up your mind. With cheese or without?

Then you've a choice of what goes on top. Mayonnaise, Ketchup, Pickle, Fresh Onion, Juicy Tomato, Crisp Lettuce, Mustard. Choose as many as you like - or have the lot - all at no extra charge.

The rest is up to us. In no time at all you'll have a pure beef hamburger that's hot, fresh and juicy - and made just the way you like it.

In the absence of competition, reduced expectations will result in higher satisfaction levels, provided levels of perceived service are maintained. One strategy therefore would be to reduce expectations as much as possible. Irrespective of the service actually delivered, the customer would be satisfied.

Unfortunately, communications must also be called upon to play their more traditional role of stimulating demand. It is inconceivable to think of achieving this by promising bad service, even if this might minimize customers' expectations (for the few customers who use the service!). In competitive terms, firms wish to make promises and build expectations that will differentiate them in the marketplace and will cause customers to choose them and not their competitors. As mentioned earlier, the temptation, therefore, is to over-promise and to raise expectations to a level that is not realistic and cannot be met. It is perhaps fortunate that the variability of services is well known to consumers and that they normally discount many such promises. When they do not, however, the result is often dissatisfied customers.

It is probably more effective to attempt to match customers' expectations to the performance characteristics of the servuction system. It is under such circumstances that the match between expectations and perceptions is most likely to be made. In such a scenario, the behavior of the customer is also most likely to conform to the script required by the operating system. There is little point, for example, in encouraging McDonald's customers to specify how well they want their hamburgers done. Not only will they be disappointed, but any attempt to meet their demands could destroy the operating system.

DIVIDING THE COMMUNICATIONS OBJECTIVES AND TARGET AUDIENCES AMONG THE CHANNELS

Once the overall objectives and target audiences for the whole communications mix are set, it is necessary to divide the tasks amongst advertising, selling, publicity and public relations, and point-of-sale messages. This is a process of matching tasks to the capabilities of the different communications channels, and to the ways consumers use those channels and the different objectives.

CAPABILITIES OF DIFFERENT CHANNELS

One way of assigning tasks across the array of communications channels is to consider the degree to which the message can be targeted at specific audiences. Media advertising itself varies along this dimension. At the broadest, "shotgun," level, TV advertising can reach very broad audiences, but is not very selective (except in the variation in audiences across channels and by time of day). National print media, such as newspapers and magazines, offer more selective focus as they themselves tend to be targeted at more specific segments of consumers. Trade magazines are even more specific in their readership. Direct mail offers the most focused of the impersonal media. The choice amongst these media must be made based on the cost per thousand members of the target audience and the risk and cost of reaching the wrong segments. As mentioned at the start of the chapter, the latter is particularly important for services.

Where there is a broadly defined audience and little cost of targeting the wrong segments, TV advertising may work out to be the cheapest vehicle. However, it is unlikely to be efficient for a specialist service with a tightly defined target audience and a high cost of attracting the wrong segment.

Public relations and publicity can be broad or highly focused, depending on how they are used. Editorial comment can be solicited in broad or narrow media through distribution of press releases. Public relations carries with it the advantages and disadvantages of not being paid advertising. On the positive side, it is given more credence by the consumer; on the negative side, it is much more difficult to control. The content may not be designed, or the coverage may be limited.

Both media advertising and public relations and publicity are one-way communications. They cannot respond to consumers inquiries or tailor the message to the characteristics of the receiver. Personal or telephone selling is far more expensive per member of the target audience, but does offer that personal touch. If the message is difficult to communicate or a great deal of persuasion is needed, personal communication may be most appropriate: a sales force can be highly trained to make complex arguments interactively, responding to the inputs of customers during the process.

Users can be reached through all the channels just discussed, and can be further reached by communications through the service provider and the point-of-sale environment.

UNDERSTANDING CONSUMER INFORMATION ACQUISITION

Article 7.1 provides an empirical test of the key differences in information usage between goods and services. These differences are crucial to understanding how to divide the communications objectives, target audiences, and budgets between the different channels.

Consumers of services are less likely to purchase without information than those buying goods. This relates to the increased perceived risk associated with services and the need for the consumer to reduce that risk by collecting information before purchasing.[3]

Consumers of services will prefer personal over impersonal sources of information. Because services are experiential, it is extremely difficult to describe or specify the "product" before purchase. It might be possible to use TV advertising to convey the experience, but it is clear that consumers prefer to obtain their information from individuals who have experienced the service directly or indirectly. This is a form of vicarious learning.[4]

Even among personal services, the high levels of risk inherent in the process mean that *consumers will give greater credibility to independent sources of information* rather than those perceived to be controlled by the firm. All of this implies that word-of-mouth communication from peers is far more likely than mass advertising to be used by consumers as a source of information.

However, it is possible to use advertising and other forms of promotion to leverage word-of-mouth communication.[5] Such an approach might use advertising and promotional tools to persuade satisfied customers to tell other consumers about their satisfactory service experience. Many firms, American Express for example, have created programs to reward customers who introduce their friends and colleagues to the company. Others create material for customers to give to non-customers. Finally, word-of-mouth communication can be used directly in media advertising, in the form of testimonials from satisfied customers.

Consumer information sources can be classified broadly into internal or external sources. Both types can be used to help consumers cope with perceived risk. Internal sources are fundamentally linked to memory scan.[6]The study in Article 7.1 clearly shows that *consumers who have had prior experience with a service are more likely to turn to their memories first before collecting new external information.*

PUTTING THE COMMUNICATIONS MIX TOGETHER

If the objective is to reach non-users of the service at the pre-consumption phase, then the choice of communications channels is limited. Media advertising can be used, whether directly or as a way to harness or create word-of-mouth communication in the marketplace. If the number of target customers is limited, it might be possible to use other means, such as a personal sales force or direct marketing, to reach them. The decision would depend on the cost effectiveness of the different channels and the complexity of the message to be conveyed.

By the time consumers reach the consumption and post-consumption phases, they are already part of the servuction process. On a cost-per-audience-member basis, it would seem more logical to use the point-of-sale environment or the service provider to handle the communication.

Using the service provider as a communications channel can be very cost-effective, but there are implications for operational efficiency and for levels of stress experienced by the providers themselves. An apparently simple decision, for example, to have a bank teller sell services, can have profound negative consequences. Following the logic of Chapter 4, it could well be that the decision produces role conflict for tellers. There may be role versus self conflict caused by the tellers wanting to see themselves not as salespersons but as bankers, or vice versa. There may be direct conflict between the two roles when the operations role demands fast service and a minimization of time spent with each customer, and the selling role demands the opposite.

As demonstrated in Chapter 2 and 6, there may be a breakdown in the script for both the service provider and the customer as the teller tries to do something new. The customer may be expecting a brisk, business-like transaction, and suddenly the teller wants to build a rapport (before starting to sell) by talking about the weather.

Potentially, such a decision also can diminish operational efficiency as the transaction time per customer rises. This problem is well illustrated by the problems experienced by Federal Express before it centralized its telephone customer-contact system. In times of peak demand, especially if these times were unpredicted, everyone in the Federal Express depots answered telephones, including the field salespersons who were based at the depots. The result, as salespeople tried to sell instead of deliver service, was that calls took much longer than usual, and the telephone bottleneck consequently worsened.

CHAPTER 7 READING

Article 7.1 looks at some of the ways in which consumers use information sources to evaluate services. The author evaluates the role of perceived risk in determining which information sources are used, and notes how the value of different information sources changes as perceived risk levels increase. He establishes six hypotheses concerning the pre-purchase use of information by consumers and describes the research that tested these hypotheses. He concludes by suggesting consumers need not just use general information to help them evaluate risk, but information from particular highly specific sources.

QUESTIONS

1. Collect a series of magazine advertisements for a number of firms within a service industry. What differential advantage is each firm claiming? What service-level expectations is each firm setting?

2. From your own experience, choose an advertisement that you believe creates too high an expectation level. Explain why.

3. Identify advertisements that you believe would have a negative effect on the service providers within the particular service firm.

4. Identify a physical environment created by a service firm that you believe communicates the wrong script to consumers. Explain.

5. Is the concept of "branding through advertising" applicable to services? Why and how?

6. Identify an advertisement that runs the risk of attracting mixed segments to a service business. Explain why this may happen and state what negative consequences, if any, there are likely to be.

NOTES

1.   William B. Locander and Peter W. Herman, "The Effects of Self-Confidence and Anxiety on Information Seeking in Consumer Risk Reduction," *Journal of Marketing Research,* 16 (May 1979), 268–274.

2.   See Leonard L. Berry, "The Employee as Customer," *Journal of Retail Banking*, vol. 11, no. 1 (1981): 33–40.

3.   See P. Nelson, "Advertising as Information," *Journal of Political Economy* 81 (July–August 1974): 729–754.

4.   William R. George and Leonard L. Berry, "Guidelines for the Advertising of Services," *Business Horizons,* vol. 24, no. 4 (July–August 1981): 52–56.

5.   See J. Bettman, *An Information Processing Theory of Consumer Choice* (Reading, MA: Addison-Wesley, 1979).

6.   See George and Berry, "Guidelines for Advertising of Services," 52–56.

A TEST OF SERVICES MARKETING THEORY
CONSUMER INFORMATION ACQUISITION ACTIVITIES

Keith B. Murray

Northeastern University

The author explores the information needs of service consumers. In the purchase decision process, search behavior is motivated in part by perceived risk and the consumer's ability to acquire relevant information with which purchase uncertainty can be addressed. Marketing theory suggests that consumers use information sources in a distinctive way to reduce the uncertainty associated with services. Hence, six hypotheses are developed to test the information acquisition of service buyers. An experimental approach is employed to compare, in a pre-purchase context, the information sources used by consumers of services and those used by consumers of goods. The resulting data support the predictions offered and extend marketing theory.

Thought the marketing discipline has directed attention to the field of services marketing in recent years, much of the work in that area has centered on the development of conceptual models with an emphasis on managerial paradigms. Considerably less attention has been given to understanding the behavior of the service consumer, though efforts to examine consumer activity (e.g., Surprenant and Solomon 1987; Vredenburg and Wee 1986) are noteworthy and highlight the linkage between service consumer behavior and the management task. An area of particular importance to managers is an understanding of the prepurchase information acquisition process used by service customers. Knowledge of information acquisition strategies is vital to both marketing managers and scholars because information search is an early influential stage in the purchase decision process.

In general, the greater the degree of perceived risk in a prepurchase context, the greater the consumer propensity to seek information about the product. The role of risk in the consumption of services has been addressed both conceptually (e.g., Eiglier and Langeard 1977; Zeithaml 1981) and empirically (e.g., Brown and Fern 1981; Davis, Guiltinan, and Jones 1979; George, Weinberger, and Kelly 1985; Guseman 1981; Murray and Schlacter 1990), with theory and evidence suggesting that services are perceived to be riskier than goods. Comparatively little attention, however, has been directed to understanding the impact of the riskier nature of services on the purchase process and the information "needs" of services consumers.

The research reported here explores the use of information sources by service consumers. The aim of this article is to present a theoretical, empirical, and managerial perspective on consumer preferences for information in the consumption decision process involving services. In particular, the study examines the information acquisition of consumers in light of heightened perceived risk associated with service products. First, relevant consumer information acquisition literature is reviewed. Then six hypotheses are offered on information sources and consumer behavior related to services in

SOURCE: Keith B. Murray, "A Test of Services Marketing Theory: Consumer Information Acquisition Activities," reprinted with permission from the *Journal of Marketing,* January 1991, vol. 55, pp. 10–25, published by the American Marketing Association, Chicago, IL 60606.

Keith B. Murray is Assistant Professor of Marketing, College of Business Administration, Northeastern University. The author thanks four colleagues at Arizona State University, Stephen W. Brown, Lawrence Crosby, Michael Hutt, and John L. Schlacter, for their detailed comments on drafts of the article and the three anonymous *JM* reviewers for their helpful suggestions. A previous version of the article was part of the First Interstate Center for Services Marketing working paper series.

comparison with goods. The method and experimental procedures used to test these predictions are described and the study results are reported. Finally, the findings and their implications are discussed.

OVERVIEW OF PERCEIVED RISK AND INFORMATION ACQUISITION

Despite difficulties in precisely defining what a service is, marketing literature reflects broad agreement in terms of both conceptual description and empirical substantiation as to what characterizes services (e.g., Zeithaml, Parasuraman, and Berry 1985). Generalizations that have widespread acceptance among scholars and practitioners in the field as being characteristic of services include intangibility, simultaneity of production and consumption, and nonstandardization. In both theory and practice, marketers have recognized that the fundamental, qualitative differences between goods and services, in addition to requiring special management paradigms, may elicit distinctive behavior on the part of consumers. That services are not directly perceptible, are frequently experimental, and typically are unpredictable in their outcomes for the buyer implies that they would influence purchasing behavior of consumers. Though varying degrees of perceived risk characterize all consumer purchases, evidence suggests that by their fundamental nature services may be perceived to be particularly risky (Guseman 1981; Murray and Schlacter 1990). Furthermore, because of the transitory and varied nature of services, product evaluation may occur primarily *after* purchase and consumption (Young 1981), heightening prepurchase uncertainty.

The concept of risk implies that most individuals make purchase decisions under some degree of uncertainty about a particular product and/or brand. Conceptualized as the likelihood of negative consequences (i.e., danger, loss, etc.), perceived risk represents consumer uncertainty about loss or gain in a particular transaction and has six components (e.g., Brooker 1984; Jacoby and Kaplan 1972; Roselius 1971): financial, performance, social, psychological, safety, and time/convenience loss. Overall perceived risk represents the aggregate impact of these various factors. Given the level of aggregation for goods and services, this study focuses on inherent risk (Bettman 1972, 1973), the latent risk a generic product category holds for a consumer.

Marketing theorists long have argued that consumers seek information from a variety of sources when faced with risk or uncertainty (e.g., Cox 1967). Because services appear to create particularly uncertain and risky purchase situations, it is logical to expect that consumers acquire information as a strategy of risk reduction in the face of this specific uncertainty. Zeithaml (1981) argues that services are more difficult to evaluate than goods and that, as a consequence, consumers may be forced to rely on different cues and processes when evaluating services. Indeed, service marketing scholars suggest that consumers evaluate information about services in a more complex and distinctive way (e.g., Bateson 1977; Booms and Nyquist 1981; Davis, Guiltinan, and Jones 1979) and often demand increased information for predominantly service-type products (Deshpande and Krishnan 1977). The following discussion briefly identifies a simple typology of information sources and reviews the relevant literature on risk and information sources.

SOURCES OF INFORMATION

Consumer information sources can be classified into two broad types, internal and external; both types are used by consumers to gather information and cope with perceived risk. Internal search is fundamentally linked to memory scan (Bettman 1979a, b; Leigh and Rethans 1984; Lynch and Srull 1982), though understanding of internal search dynamics is largely speculative (Hansen 1972). When faced with a purchase decision, the consumer first examines information in memory about past purchase experience, including experiences in a product class and previous learning about the environment. Experience creates knowledge, which in turn leads to internal search in subsequent decision situations (Jacoby, Chestnut, and Silberman 1977; van Raaij 1977). Hence, internal search can be viewed as an important source of information available to the consumer.

The marketing literature is replete with evidence suggesting that external information search represents a motivated and conscious decision by the consumer to seek new information from the environment (e.g., Berning and Jacoby 1974; Furse, Punj, and Stewart 1984; Moore and Lehmann 1980; Winter 1975). Though sources of external information can be classified in terms of whether the source is marketer-dominated or whether information comes from personal or impersonal communication (e.g., Engel, Blackwell, and Miniard 1986), other typologies encompass a wider range of information sources that are amenable to empirical operationalization and classification (Andreasen 1968; Lutz and Reilly 1973), including forms of personal, impersonal, and direct experience information sources.

ROLE OF PERCEIVED RISK

Depending on the level of risk perception, several risk-handling strategies may be adopted by the consumer, one of which is the search for further information and evaluation of alternatives. Other risk-handling strategies include risk adoption and reduction of aspiration levels, but here the focus is solely on information sources as they may be associated with a risk-reduction strategy by consumers. Cox (1967, p. 604) argues that the "amount and nature of perceived risk will define consumers' information needs, and consumers will seek out sources, types, and amounts of information that seem most likely to satisfy their particular information needs." Evidence supports this position in relation to depth of search, types of sources, types of risk, and personality factors (e.g., Capon and Burke 1977; Locander and Hermann 1979; Lutz and Reilly 1973), but none of the studies examined risk associated with services *per se* or risk reduction specifically by service consumers.

Several findings point to the use of specific strategies by the consumer to diminish prepurchase uncertainty. First, as total risk of the purchase situation increases, an individual's direct observation and experience become a preferred information source (Lutz and Reilly 1973), suggesting that as risk increases, the search pattern for information expands and the tendency simply to buy without prepurchase deliberation decreases (Locander and Hermann 1979). Second, consumers appear to use information or personal channels primarily in situations in which perceived risk and uncertainty have not been reduced sufficiently by formal information sources and in which uncertainty and involvement are high enough to justify seeking information through informal channels (Cox 1963a). Perry and Hamm (1969) show that the greater the perceived risk of purchase decision, the greater the importance of personal influence. These findings support those of several studies (e.g., Arndt 1967; Lutz and Reilly 1973) showing that word-of-mouth is the most important source of risk-reducing information and has a greater impact on consumers than mass media communications because of clarification and feedback opportunities. Midgley (1983) notes that both the nature and degree of risk distinguish between different sources of interpersonal information, suggesting that for products dominant in social aspects, information from other individuals rather than from objective or impersonal sources is likely to be preferred by consumers. These conclusions are supported by the findings of Price and Feick (1984) that point to interpersonal influence as an important component

of information acquisition. Hence, evidence suggests that types of information used by consumers to reduce prepurchase uncertainty vary across levels of perceived risk and that as perceived risk increases, personal sources are the most preferred *external* source of information, second only to direct observation and product trial (Locander and Hermann 1979; Lutz and Reilly 1973).

Third, Lutz and Reilly (1973) note that consumers use more sources of information when faced with increasing levels of perceived performance risk and that consumers' relative preference for various information sources shifts dramatically, depending on performance risk factors. Over a wide range of products that are low or moderate in performance risk, the most frequently used method of information acquisition is simply to *buy* the product, conceivably on a "trial" basis. However, as performance risk increases, trial purchase becomes less preferred. Furthermore, Lutz and Reilly (1973) observe that direct observation and/or experience with a product is generally preferred to any secondary source of product information. Of various information sources external to the individual, word-of-mouth is particularly useful and independent impersonal sources may be preferred under conditions of high performance risk.

In short, consumers use various amounts and types of information sources to reduce perceived risk, depending on the amount and type of risk. Though consumer decision models identify information search as a prominent aspect of the purchase decision process, the literature has a critical gap in terms of examining risk specifically associated with services and concomitant types of information sources. In the following discussion, extant services marketing and risk theory is used, as well as information acquisition knowledge, to develop research hypotheses for subsequent verification.

RESEARCH HYPOTHESES

Several predications can be made about acquisition of prepurchase information on services. The following hypotheses seek to test and extend service marketing and information acquisition theory by examining the differences in search behavior and information source usage by consumers contemplating the purchase of goods and services.

INTERNAL SOURCES AND PREPURCHASE INFORMATION ACQUISITION

As services are associated, *ceteris paribus,* with greater perceived risk, it follows that service consumers would use more information sources as a risk-coping strategy than would consumers of less risky products. This rationale suggests an extended information acquisition process, which may mean that consumers are more likely to defer a service purchase because the information search is more time-consuming. One approach to conceptualizing this phenomenon is to examine the proclivity of service consumers to make an outright purchase as a way to learn more about the product. Hence,

> H_1: The incidence of outright purchase as a consumer information strategy is lower for services than for goods.

TYPES OF EXTERNAL INFORMATION SOURCES AND RISK REDUCTION

Services are conceptualized as *experiential* (e.g., Booms and Bitner 1981; Lovelock 1981; Young 1981; Zeithaml 1981) and as such are difficult to specify or evaluate precisely in advance of the purchase event. Consequently, consumers wanting to reduce prechoice uncertainty may be compelled to seek information from other individuals who have experienced the service directly or indirectly. Information from individuals with previous product experience is subjective and evaluative. It logically reduces the prospective consumer's uncertainty by means of vicarious learning and approximates direct experience with the product. Consistent with Nelson's (1974) theory of information and consumer behavior and Urbany and Weilbaker's (1987) prediction that personal sources are more important for consumers in the purchase of experience-type products, the second hypothesis is:

> H_2: Consumers choose more personal sources of information for services than for goods.

EFFECTIVENESS OF INFORMATION SOURCES USED BY SERVICE CONSUMERS

In view of the distinguishing characteristics of services (i.e., intangibility, nonstandardization, and inseparability), Zeithaml (1981) argues that services are more difficult to evaluate prior to initial purchase than goods. Hence, service prospects may simply engage fewer *prepurchase* information sources than consumers contemplating goods, consistent with an attribution-dissonance model (Ray 1973) positing that nonmarketing communication sources precipitate consumer purchase choice, subsequently followed by attitude change and learning. The absolute number of information sources an individual uses, however, may not be the most useful measure of the extent of information acquisition. Source *effec-*

tiveness is more relevant to understanding source usage (e.g., Engel and Blackwell 1982; May 1965), reflecting the *decisive* influence of a source and its importance in relation to exposure. Decisiveness implies that some types of sources are more instrumental than others in providing meaningful information to an individual (e.g., Davis, Guiltinan, and Jones 1979; Houston 1979).

For many services, physical and point-of-purchase cues typically associated with tangible products are not available. Indeed, Young (1981) argues that consumers acquire only limited evaluative information prior to the initial service purchase, suggesting that service consumption is highly personal and difficult to comprehend until directly experienced. Even if prior information exists for services, mass media are not expected to be particularly conducive to effective communication of service attributes (Shostack 1977). Instead, non-marketer-dominated information sources are expected to play a particularly important role in the consumer decision process for services. Consistent with primary research reported by Engel, Blackwell, and Miniard (1986), the expectation is that service consumers would prefer the opinions and experiences of other comparable individuals in making service purchase decisions. Hence,

> H_3: Personal independent sources of information are more effective for services than for goods.

THE EFFECT OF SUBJECTIVE INFORMATION ABOUT SERVICES

That consumers' use of information sources is related to confidence in the source has long been established. Cox (1963b), for example, supports the notion that source trustworthiness and expertise are important and appear to influence source usage. Though virtually any type of information can provide some degree of instrumental utility to the consumer in terms of risk reduction, particular *types* of information sources are known to be sought by consumers for specific utilities (Hansen 1972; Houston 1979). The ephemeral nature of services, coupled with the absence of an objective and uniform product, suggests that experiential and subjective data are likely to be more relevant and offer greater prepurchase evaluative utility than other types of informational data.

Objective and technical product specifications may be feasible for a service (e.g., dentist A is licensed to perform root canals and can do so tomorrow at 3:30 p.m. for less than $300), but information of an interpretive, subjective, and affective nature may address key customer information needs more directly (e.g., dentist A is a very competent professional and also does not want his patients to suffer a lot of pain), allaying expected prepurchase apprehensions. Bateson (1989) suggests, for example, that a static, multiattribute model is insufficient in assisting the consumer to understand services. Instead, he argues that such models afford a static perspective on an experience that consists essentially of a series of dynamic interactions. This observation leads to the prediction that personal sources engender relatively greater levels of consumer confidence for service products than for nonservice products.

H₄: Consumers have greater confidence in personal sources of information for services than for goods.

TRIALABILITY AS A SOURCE OF INFORMATION FOR SERVICE CONSUMERS

As perceived risk of a purchase increases, consumers engage in risk-reduction by means of direct observation and product trial (Locander and Hermann 1979; Lutz and Reilly 1973). However, that strategy may not work for services because of their experiential nature (e.g., Booms and Bitner 1981; Young 1981; Zeithaml 1981). In addition to the limited opportunities for direct experience or product observation, "trialability" of the service is problematic. For example, consumers can visit a retail location and examine a nonservice product directly for fit, styling, structural integrity, package information, and/or expressed warranties; occasionally, consumers alter the perceived uncertainty of some nonservice purchases by buying a small quantity or a popular brand. Such prepurchase strategies, however, are rarely possible in the case of services because they are typically ephemeral and intangible. It is reasonable to argue that service consumers will make a service purchase decision on some basis other than observation or trial. Therefore,

H₅: Service consumers use direct observation and/or trial as a source of prepurchase information less often than consumers of goods.

PRIOR EXPERIENCE AND INFORMATION ACQUISITION OF SERVICE CONSUMERS

Service consumers' prepurchase information search activities can be analyzed in terms of costs and benefits (Moore and Lehmann 1980). Though consumers may perceive services to be inherently more risky and otherwise may be inclined to acquire more prepurchase information, accessing information sources may not be feasible or accomplished without considerable effort. Indeed, impersonal information for services may not be easily organized by brand or attribute, implying decreased

search processes (Olander 1975). Furthermore, personal sources are inconvenient to acquire, thus increasing the costs of information search and decreasing the number and types of sources used (Staelin and Payne 1976). Marketing literature suggests that because less information is available for services (Booms and Bitner 1981; Lovelock 1981; Young 1981; Zeithaml 1981), the cost of an extended search will be elevated and, as the cost of acquiring information increases, less information will be sought and acquired (e.g., Jacoby, Speller, and Berning 1974). Consequently, the internal information search made possible by prior learning from past purchase experiences in a product class and/or previous learning about the environment is particularly instrumental in providing useful product information in the case of services.

H₆: Consumers with prior experience have a greater preference for internal sources of information for evaluating services than for evaluating goods.

The hypotheses were examined empirically in terms of the experimental framework and procedures described in the following section.

METHOD

To test the hypotheses, an experimental context was developed to examine the information needs of service consumers. The research objective was to assess the effect of varying levels of perceived service attributes on consumer behavior in terms of information sources used in a prepurchase context. In this section, the pre-experimental procedures, methodological choice considerations, research design, procedures, dependent measures, statistical approach, and sample are described.

To operationalize the independent variable (i.e., the service construct) more precisely, an extensive pretest process was followed to establish control over key aspects of the experimental treatment, specifically in relation to "serviceness," expected cost, and respondent familiarity. Briefly, 146 subjects, drawn from the population of interest for the study, used a 7-point interval scale to evaluate a sample of 235 products in terms of product familiarity, expected cost, and perceived characterization as a service, good, or some combination of the two. The pretest ratings by this separate and independent group of subjects were used to eliminate products with which respondents were unfamiliar and to array products hierarchically on the basis of expected cost and relative perceived service attributes. In view of the association between expected financial cost and overall risk (Jacoby and Kaplan 1972), selection of products was limited to those within the expected cost range of $20 to $50. Consistent with Park's (1976) work, only those products with which respondents expressed at least moderate familiarity were included in the final sample. Products within this specified familiarity and monetary value range were arrayed along a goods–service continuum on the basis of mean scores, from those relatively high in service attributes (i.e., "pure" services) to those relatively low in service attributes (i.e., goods), with products of a "mixed" nature being at midpoint on the continuum (i.e., those sharing both service *and* goods qualities). The relative product attribute rating values derived from this pre-experimental procedure were used to choose a sample of five products from those that were rated extremely high, midlevel, and extremely low in service content. These three samples, consisting of five products each and drawn from three disparate points along the product continuum, constituted the manipulations of the independent variable (i.e., the degree of service attributes characterizing a product). This empirical approach to operationalizing the service construct is consistent with the call by Shostack (1977) to use consumer judgments to define the "image" of products and is described in greater detail by Murray and Schlacter (1990). The use of multiple product stimuli in the study was intended to contribute to generalizability of the findings beyond any single product class (see Richins 1983).

METHODOLOGICAL CHOICE CONSIDERATIONS

Several methods for examining the information needs and source usage of consumers were considered before a purchase scenario approach was selected. Retrospective questioning of subjects is a nonexperimental approach and thus implies little capacity to control key factors, either theoretical or extraneous. Similarly, techniques involving observation of purchase behavior and/or eye movement analysis were deemed deficient. Two other approaches were considered—protocol analysis and information display board (IDB) technique. In view of problems associated with protocol analysis (see Bettman 1977; Bettman and Zins 1977), IDB initially seemed to hold considerable promise by way of analytic precision and quantitative rigor, rivaling the purchase scenario approach. However, in the context of this particular study, specific shortcomings of artificiality and demand effects were evident with the use of an IDB technique (see Lehmann and Moore 1980). Though IDB research to date has involved subjects in the *actual selection* of products in the experimental setting (thus comparing

favorably with other approaches in achieving "mundane realism"), products typically have been limited to *inexpensive goods within a single product class* (e.g., Bettman and Jacoby 1976; Hofacker 1984; Hoyer and Jacoby 1983; Jacoby, Chestnut, and Fisher 1978; Lehmann and Moore 1980). Given the study's focus on nontrivial products, however, the absence of actual purchase behavior by subjects in the experimental setting implied forfeiture of a major appeal of the IDB paradigm. Also, with a conventional IDB brand-by-attribute format, services potentially represent a range of products for which directly comparable *brands* typically do not exist, further diminishing the direct applicability of the method. In terms of demand effects, an IDB imposed an unrealistic task environment for examining perceptions and use of information sources for services, which are expected to be relatively low in "search" qualities and high in "experience" qualities (see Zeithaml 1981). Consequently, an IDB technique for services implied the provision of information that, in an actual purchase setting, may be either nonexistent or accessible to buyers only at great relative difficulty.

Hence, though a projective scenario approach was potentially subject to similar drawbacks, the limitations associated with IDB—given the research objectives—were sufficiently compelling to justify use of a hypothetical purchase task technique. To the degree that reactivity and demand properties were feasible with a projective method, however, two observations are relevant. First, the study represents a controlled, comparative analysis of sources in terms of their perceived utility, consumers' preferences, and relative efficacy to address the implicit information needs of consumers in a service purchase context. Inferences about a precise delineation of information search, *per se,* simply go beyond the method and the data. Instead, the research seeks to examine what, in a relative sense, consumers' information needs are and which sources (and types of sources) address those needs in the context of services. Second, to the degree that the experimental conditions do promote reactivity, it would be expected to be distributed across both types of sources and types of products; given the experimental design and nature of the study, one could reasonably assume that reactivity would influence all treatment levels and dependent measures uniformly.

RESEARCH DESIGN

The specific experimental layout used in the study was a completely balanced block, repeated-measure design with nested factors in a hierarchical arrangement, whereby all respondents were presented one factor (of five possible) from each of three levels of the independent variable, ranging from pure good to pure service. Because information seeking is, in part, a function of individual factors (Moore and Lehmann 1980), this design was selected to control for between-subject error variance and to obtain a more precise estimate of treatment effects, thereby obtaining a more powerful test of a false null hypothesis (Kirk 1982). The decision to operationalize the independent variable in the context of a purchase scenario was predicated on the increasing number of studies that use scenarios to manipulate variables and contexts that cannot be easily replicated in a real-life setting (e.g., Jackson, Keith, and Burdick 1984; Puto, Patton, and King 1985). The specific merits of this approach are not discussed here, but have been identified by Eroglu (1987).

The experimental treatments consisted of three levels of the independent variable—high, moderate, and low service attribute products. Five product stimuli were associated with each treatment level, resulting in a total sample of 15 hypothetical purchase decision situations. As noted previously, all treatments were controlled for respondent familiarity and economic risk and were identical (as indicated by manipulation checks) except for the product to be "purchased."

Subject reactivity to the experimental procedures and the data collection method was assessed. Specifically, subjects were tested for order effects of the independent variable administration as well as order effects of the questionnaire items (constituting the dependent measures). Dependent measures under contrasting conditions for each potential reactivity factor were analyzed statistically. No statistical differences in the dependent measures were found for either order effects in terms of administration of the independent variable or for the sequence of items constituting the data collection instrument. These findings suggest that experimental reactivity attributable to treatment order of the independent variable or dependent measures was not significant. Figure 1 shows the research design.

PROCEDURES

Consistent with established experimental practices involving scenarios (e.g., Jackson, Keith, and Burdick 1984; Mowen et al. 1985; Puto, Patton, and King 1985), the procedures consisted of presenting to subjects a randomly preassigned sequence of three hypothetical purchase scenarios. Each scenario described the purchase of a specific product and constituted the administration of one level of the independent variable. Subjects were encouraged to read each hypothetical scenario twice.

After exposure, each scenario was removed from view. Subjects were asked to respond to a questionnaire in the presence of the experimenter. They were queried about three types of dependent variable: type of preferred prechoice information source and confidence in and importance of each respective information source. In addition, covariate measures of respondent age, sex, and experience with the product were taken. Manipulation checks of perceived service attributes, risk, and respondent familiarity with the product also were employed. (See Appendix A for the scenario stimulus and specific product stimuli varied by levels of perceived service attributes.)

This approach to examining information sources for products that are varied in service attributes was viewed to be most desirable in terms of several critical research factors. Specifically, the administration of a projective purchase task allowed experimental control of key elements of interest, namely the purchase context and the prior selection of subjects. This approach had the advantage of incorporating extant operationalizations and accepted measures (as well as an assessment of the validity and reliability of such dependent measures) within the context of a within-subjects design. A within-subjects design, in turn, maximizes the degree of experimental and statistical control over a wide range of important consumer purchase determinants not previously found in the literature on this topic.

The hypothetical purchase scenario was adapted from previous contributions in the field (Locander and Hermann 1979; Lutz and Reilly 1973), reflecting Bettman's (1972) concept of inherent risk for products having varied service attributes. As purchase decisions reflecting emergency circumstances may involve atypical information-seeking processes by consumers (Wright 1974), the decision context of the purchase scenario was a nonemergency one. The scenarios across all levels of the independent variable (the degree of perceived service attributes of the product being purchased) were identical except for the mention of the specific product embedded in the stimulus.

DEPENDENT MEASURES, ITEM RELIABILITY ESTIMATES, AND MANIPULATION CHECKS

INFORMATION SOURCES A 25-item rating scale derived from Andreasen (1968) served to operationalize the following seven sources of consumer information: impersonal advocate, impersonal independent, personal independent, personal advocate, direct observation, personal experience, and outright purchase. This typology

FIGURE 1 Layout of the Balanced Complete Block Design with Repeated Measures

Product Characteristics

Exposure to One of Five Randomly Selected, High Service Attribute Products:	Exposure to One of Five Randomly Selected, Moderate Service Attribute Products:	Exposure to One of Five Randomly Selected, Low Service Attribute Products:
• Teeth cleaning	• Auto upholstery (instld)	• Windbreaker jacket
• Tax advice and prep	• Smoke/fire protection	• Tennis racket
• Wheel alignment	• Furniture rental, sofa	• Barbeque grill
• Interior design advice	• Auto muffler (instld)	• Electric vacuum cleaner
• Eye examination	• Fine restaurant meal	• Pocket camera

Products	1	2	3	4	5	6	7	8	9	10	11	12	13	14	15	
Respondents																
1–48	•					•					•					48
49–96		•					•					•				48
97–144			•					•					•			48
145–192				•					•					•		48
193–240					•					•					•	48
Overall N:																= 240
Replications:	48	48	48	48	48	48	48	48	48	48	48	48	48	48	48	= 720

NOTE: Five product stimuli were selected from three disparate portions of a goods-services continuum composed of 235 products, each rated by a comparable consumer sample for their relative service attribute level. Products represent empirically determined stimuli which operationalize the independent variable. Subjects were exposed to one product stimulus from each sample of five for each of three levels of the experimental variable.

is similar to that advocated by Kotler (1980) and Anderson and Engledow (1981) and included response items that did not "force" respondents to consult external sources of information in a purchase situation. In effect, these items gave subjects response alternatives that sought to tap internal search predispositions and consumer inclinations *not* to engage in extended external search behaviors. All dependent measures for information acquisition had multiple items. This 25-item set was employed to collect data on sources accessed, source effectiveness, and source confidence. (See Appendix B for information sources used in the study.)

MEASURE OF INFORMATION EFFECTIVENESS AND CONFIDENCE Source effectiveness is a function of the importance of an information source in relation to the exposure value of that source (Engel and Blackwell 1982). In this study, source importance was measured on a 7-point importance scale ranging from "most important" to "not important at all" for each source examined in the study. Variable scores for importance were obtained by summing across each type of information source (e.g., personal advocate, impersonal independent, etc.). Effectiveness was determined by a ratio value of the summated importance scores for a particular source type to the subjects' reported exposure scores for that information source (e.g., Engel and Blackwell 1982). The confidence variable was operationalized by a 7-point interval scale ranging from "extreme confidence" to "extreme lack of confidence" across 7- and 9-item measures of personal and impersonal sources of information, respectively. Dependent variable data were computed as the net positive difference between confidence in personal sources and confidence in impersonal sources of information.

Other data collected included multiple-item scales to measure confidence in specific information sources, a covariate addressing extent of respondent product experience, and respondent age and gender.

ESTIMATES OF ITEM RELIABILITY The reliability of each type of dependent variable measurement scale was assessed, consistent with the assumptions of domain sampling theory (Churchill 1979) and the coefficient alpha calculations of Peter (1979). All dependent measures had acceptable correlations with true scores, consistent with Nunnally's (1967) suggested reliability estimates for this type of research.

ANALYSIS OF THE EXPERIMENTAL CONDITIONS AND MANIPULATIONS Though extensive pretesting led to the isolation of independent variable factors with considerable face validity, a manipulation check of the independent variable was recorded by respondents for each experimental factor. On a 7-point scale, the ratings of perceived service attributes across all factors were 6.32, 3.77, and 1.75 for high, moderate, and low levels of the independent variable, respectively. The MANOVA F-value for significant difference among the three levels of the manipulation check of the independent variable was statistically significant (F = 254.00, p < .000). Bonferroni multiple comparison t-test statistics for contrasts among the three means were all significant at the α < .001 level. These data suggest that the levels of the independent variable were manipulated successfully in terms of service attributes to test the proposed hypotheses adequately.

Consistent with previous marketing literature, an underlying assumption of the research is that services are characterized by higher levels of perceived risk. To minimize the opportunity for any potentially significant research findings to be attributed to other factors, a manipulation check was incorporated in the data collection instrument to verify that the factors of the independent variable (i.e., product stimuli varied in service attributes) were significant in terms of expected risk differences. Specifically, respondents were asked to rate each product stimulus on a 6-item, 7-point scale as "not risky at all" to "extremely risky," consistent with the six types of perceived risk (e.g., Jacoby and Kaplan 1972; Peter and Tarpey 1975; Roselius 1971) previously noted. Perceived risk measures were summated to reflect an overall measure of perceived risk. Across all factors of the independent variable, the MANOVA F-value for differences among the three levels of the independent variable in terms of perceived risk was statistically significant (F = 15.449, p < .000). Bonferroni multiple comparison t-test statistics for contrasts among the three means for perceived risks were significant for contrasts between the low and high and between the moderate and high operationalizations of the independent variable at the α < .001 level. These findings suggest that perceived risk associated with levels of the independent variable was in the expected direction as predicted by the literature.

Though expected cost of each experimental operationalization (i.e., each product stimulus) was not examined specifically in the experimental setting because of questionnaire length and subject fatigue considerations, pretest data indicated that the mean perceived cost for products high, moderate, and low in service attributes was $34.66, $34.16, and $35.00, respectively. However, tests for economic risk and familiarity in relation to the product factors were conducted during the experimental procedures. Perceived financial risk was analyzed statistically for significant differences across all levels of the independent variable. The results were not statistically significant at conventional levels (F = 2.106; p < .124), indicating that financial risk was held constant across all levels of the independent variable. Mean product familiarity scores were analyzed for evidence of respondent unfamiliarity with experimental stimuli. On the basis of a 7-point interval measure, mean familiarity values for low, moderate, and high service product levels were 4.85, 4.44, and 4.42, indicating greater than average familiarity across all respondents for products used in the study. These data provide evidence that economic risk and familiarity across all factors associated with the levels of the independent variable were sufficiently controlled to minimize their contamination of the study results.

STATISTICAL PROCEDURES

Respondent questionnaire ratings on the dependent measures were analyzed within the framework of a repeated-measures design in which dependent measures were within-factor and product service attributes between-factor elements. The research design was a 1 x 3 factor design. Subjects' responses to questionnaire items were analyzed by the SPSS^X multivariate analysis of variance (MANOVA) procedure for repeated measures.

SUBJECTS

A total of 273 experimental forms were administered to university students at a large, urban university in the southwestern United States. However, 17 questionnaire sets were incomplete, leaving 256 acceptable response sets for tabulation and analysis. Of the sample, 120 subjects were men (46.9%) and 136 were women (53.1%). The average age of the respondent population was 23.8 years, with a standard deviation of 3.4 years.

RESULTS

The data collected in the experimental setting were analyzed statistically and are described here in terms of the stated hypotheses.

Consistent with marketing evidence showing services to be more risky than goods, H_1 proposes that respondents would indicate a relative preference to defer an outright purchase of a service. This variable was operationalized by a 3-item measure assessing respondent preferences for making a product purchase without engaging information sources. The MANOVA F-statistic for the variable is significant at the α < .05 level (F = 10.465, p < .000), with the mean values of the independent variable in support of the predicted hypothesis. In a planned Bonferroni t-test ($\alpha < .05$) of mean differences, significant differences are found between moderate and high (t = 4.080, p < .000) and between low and high (t = 3.700, p < .000) levels of the independent variable. These results support the stated hypothesis, suggesting that consumers engage in comparatively less outright purchase of products high in service attributes and implying that extended information acquisition may be preferred for services.

H_2 states that personal sources of information are more preferred by service consumers than by goods consumers. Preference for personal and impersonal sources of information was measured by 7- and 9-item measures, respectively. Dependent variable data were computed as the net difference in the preference for personal sources over impersonal sources of information at each level of the independent variable. MANOVA procedures yield significant findings (F = 5.897, p < .003) in the expected direction for the effect of service attributes on the preference for personal sources of information. Bonferroni t-tests ($\alpha < .05$) for differences among the means are significant for differences between high and low factors of the independent variable (t = 3.315, p < .000). The data support the prediction that respondents have a greater prepurchase preference for personal sources of information for services than for goods.

H_3 predicts that personal, independent sources of information are more effective to service consumers than to goods consumers. Computation of information effectiveness values from respondent data was consistent with Engel and Blackwell's (1982) approach, whereby source effectiveness is "controlled for" by exposure and use. The information sources range from ineffective to decisively effective. When this index is less than 1.0, the exposure to a source exceeds importance of that source; when the index is greater than 1.0, importance exceeds exposure and the effectiveness of that source in consumer decision-making processes increases (Katz and Lazarsfeld 1955). MANOVA procedures were run to test for differences in effectiveness for all external sources of information at different levels of the independent variable. Only personal independent sources show significant differences in effectiveness (F = 4.275, p < .008), with mean effectiveness scores in the predicted direction. In a Bonferroni t-test ($\alpha < .05$) of differences between treatment levels, statistically significant differences were found between low and moderate levels and low and high levels of the independent variable.

H_4 predicts that respondents would indicate a greater confidence in personal sources of information for services. MANOVA F-procedures yield significant findings (F = 14.226, p < .000) in support of the predicted outcome. Bonferroni t-tests for planned comparisons ($\alpha < .05$) among the means are significant for contrasts between low and high levels (t = 4.593, p < .000) and moderate and high levels (t = 5.039, p < .000) of the independent variable. Thus, the findings are consistent with the prediction that respondents have greater confidence in personal sources of information for services and corroborate Cox's (1963b) finding that source trustworthiness and expertise are important and that consumer confidence influences types of sources used. The confirmation of H_2, H_3, and H_4 substantiates the predictions of services marketing theory and suggests a need for promotional strategies for services that stimulate and/or simulate personal sources of information.

Consumer behavior theory suggests that as perceived risk of a purchase increases, consumers will engage in risk-reduction behavior by means of direct observation and trial. However, the relative lack of tangible cues may preclude this alternative for consumers. H_5 predicts that direct product observation and/or product trial will be preferred to a greater extent for goods than for services. This hypothesis is confirmed by the data. The variable was composed of a 3-item measure that addressed direct product inspection and/or limited product involvement prior to purchase. The MANOVA F-value for these data is significant (F = 14.823, p < .000), with mean scores in the predicted direction. Bonferroni t-test statistics ($\alpha < .05$) for planned contrasts among the means are significant for mean differences between low and moderate (t = 3.176, p < .000) and low and high (t = 5.364, p < .000) levels of the independent variable. Thus, the data support the prediction that respondents indicate less preference for the use of direct observation and/or trial for services than they do for goods.

H_6 states that consumers with product experience have greater preference for internal sources of information for evaluating services than for evaluating goods. This variable was operationalized by employing a 3-item measure tapping respondents' preference for using previous knowledge and information in a prepurchase situation. MANOVA procedures are significant (F = 3.805, p < .027). Thus, the data support the prediction that experience is a more preferred source of information for consumers in the purchase of services than in the purchase of goods. Bonferroni t-tests of differences ($\alpha < .05$) between the levels of the independent variable are statistically significant between low and moderate and low and high treatment levels. Descriptive statistics pertaining to the six hypotheses are summarized in Table 1.

DISCUSSION

This article identifies an area of relevance and interest to both marketing scholars and practitioners. The fundamental thesis of the research is that because services are higher in perceived risk, they may create distinctive information needs in consumers. The service construct is operationalized and employed in the context of a controlled experiment examining important consumer decision-making phenomena. In this section, the limitations as well as the contributions and implications of the study are discussed.

CONTRIBUTIONS AND LIMITATIONS OF THE RESEARCH

This study contributes to marketing and information acquisition literature by specifically addressing the information needs of service consumers. Service scholars have proposed that prior evaluation is more difficult for services than for goods (Zeithaml 1981) and that consumers may evaluate them differently than they do goods (Young 1981). Several findings of the study converge to support this prediction. First, the data provide evidence of consumers' inclination to deter making an outright purchase of services. This finding is consistent with the prediction of risk theory that in the face of greater uncertainty and loss, consumers engage in an extended decision process. Second, the role of personal sources of information is noteworthy. The data show that for services, personal sources are preferred over impersonal sources of information, more so than for goods. Similarly, consumers indicate greater confidence in personal sources when contemplating a service purchase. Further, personal independent sources are more effective for services than for goods. These findings provide indirect support for the notion that products with service attributes are largely subjective and experiential. Third, the data suggest that internal sources, in contrast to external ones, are particularly relevant to service consumers.

TABLE 1   Statistical Results for Effects of Service Attributes on Consumer Information Acquisition Behavior

Hypothesis	Level of Service Content	n	Mean	F Score	Prob-ability	r2	Con-trast	t Score	Prob-ability	Empirical Conclusions
In comparison with purchasers of goods, consumers contemplating the purchase of services:										
—show a decreased preference for outright purchase (H₁)	Low		5.431				L-M	0.190	.500	
	Moderate	252	5.429	10.47	.000	.04	M-H	4.080	.000	Confirmed
	High		5.772				L-H	3.700	.000	
—prefer personal over impersonal sources (H₂)	Low		.044				L-M	1.753	.039	
	Moderate	231	.159	5.90	.003	.03	M-H	2.028	.023	Confirmed
	High		.299				L-H	3.315	.000	
—find personal independent sources more effective (H₃)	Low		1.027				L-M	2.610	.005	
	Moderate	242	1.095	4.28	0.15	.02	M-H	0.180	>.250	Confirmed
	High		1.105				L-H	2.860	.002	
—have more confidence in personal sources (H₄)	Low		.127				L-M	0.176	>.250	
	Moderate	241	.118	14.23	.000	.06	M-H	5.039	.000	Confirmed
	High		.375				L-H	4.593	.000	
—depend less on observation and/or trial (H₅)	Low		3.035				L-M	3.176	.000	
	Moderate	253	3.414	14.82	.000	.05	M-H	2.117	.020	Confirmed
	High		3.685				L-H	5.364	.000	
—prefer internal sources over all others when they have experience in the product category (H₆)	Low		1.922				L-M	2.642	.005	
	Moderate	68	1.931	3.81	.027	.06	M-H	1.137	>.100	Confirmed
	High		1.627				L-H	2.491	.010	

These data point to a distinctive information acquisition pattern for service consumers. Specifically, the findings suggest a greater need for risk-reducing information and an extended consumer decision process for services. However, in view of the intangible, ephemeral, and experimental nature of services, there may be less opportunity to diminish uncertainty by direct observation and/or trial for services, suggesting a prolonged consumer adoption process and, ultimately, a more lengthy diffusion process for services. The conclusions from this research have important implications for a better understanding of consumer behavior and marketing management.

Because of such factors as intangibility, variability, and consumer–provider interaction, service phenomenology is not conducive to controlled empirical operationalizations. Indeed, despite the continued interest in the services marketing area, the number of experimental studies involving services has been limited. The research reported here sought to test theory-derived hypotheses by controlling the experimental setting, randomly assigning subjects, and collecting data on service phenomenology in a context advocated by Calder, Phillips, and Tybout (1981). This research was an exploratory effort to understand better the information needs of service consumers and their use of sources. To put the findings into proper perspective, however, limitations of the study must be noted. Given the degree of experimental control sought, the findings are necessarily subject to the criticism that a real-world context is lacking in the experimental setting. Further, demand effects may have exerted some influence on the dependent measures. For example, the scenario instructions may have biased the subsequent behavior of subjects. Though steps were taken to minimize and subsequently identify (via debriefing procedures) these effects, the degree to which they occurred in this specific study is not definitely known. In general, however, a projective purchase task poses several threats, including spurious effects stemming from instructions to subjects, setting artificiality, occurrence of novel behavior, and the desire of subjects to accommodate the experimenter. Clearly, these factors may have affected the dependent measures.

On balance, we have ample reason to believe that there is some *a priori* validity to a role-playing technique as a research procedure in that numerous real-life purchase situations are, implicitly, role-playing situations for consumers. To the extent that role-playing behavior tracks behavioral intention, indications in the literature suggest that behavior intention does predict actual behavior of consumers (e.g., Bonfield 1974; Vinokur-

Kaplan 1978), with positive correlation having been shown to be present (e.g., Ryan and Bonfield 1980). In any event, information acquisition can be viewed as probabilistic. Though it is feasible that the task characteristics may have influenced the absolute level of intention to acquire information, the consistent confirmation of theoretical predictions in a relational, comparative sense (of services vs. goods) generally supports the decision to employ this particular approach. When asked to indicate their likely response to the hypothetical purchase scenarios, subjects had no prior knowledge of the experimental intent or predictions, and debriefing did not reveal any awareness of those factors. Hence they had limited opportunity to please the experimenter.

Nonetheless, the robustness of the results across different environments can only be determined empirically. In view of this demonstration of replicable laboratory behavior, other approaches, including information process monitoring, protocol, and script-based methods, should be explored to provide convergent and complementary evidence in marketing strategy development and theory for services. Confirmatory research, based on theoretical underpinnings but characterized by greater external validity, should be conducted to facilitate further conceptual development in services. Furthermore, it is entirely fitting and necessary now to field test the hypotheses in more complex environments. The present study is hoped to prompt such research on consumer information needs and behavior.

RESEARCH IMPLICATIONS

The study highlights the need to explore more fully the decision-making process associated with the purchase of services. The testing of hypotheses grounded in extant theory affords empirical evidence that consumers use information sources distinctively in evaluating services. Further study should be conducted to address issues raised here. First, the research data imply that service consumers are inclined to seek additional prepurchase information. For services, this finding appears to contradict the expectation that as information sources become more scarce, difficult to access, and "costly" in terms of consumer expenditures of time and effort, consumer preference for seeking additional information decreases. What heuristics affect the service prepurchase situation is not readily apparent and warrants further research attention.

The study results also appear to contradict previous findings suggesting that as perceived risk of a purchase increases, individuals seek to reduce risk by means of direct observation and trial. Two considerations must be noted, however. First, risk and information acquisition theory has been based exclusively on empirical research involving tangible goods and characterized by an objective reality. Risk and information acquisition for services may not necessarily conform to previous research conclusions based exclusively on nonservice products. Second, given the fundamental nature of services, the opportunity for consumer observation and trial is logically limited and findings divergent from the ones in this study would be difficult to explicate fully. Though the unique nature of services is precisely what might heighten risk perceptions, it also appears to prevent the consumer from carrying out the same information strategies they employ for goods. More research is needed to identify how prospective service consumers make observations from visible cues and service trial.

The hypothesis that consumers with direct prior knowledge would have greater preference for internal sources of information when evaluating services than when evaluating goods is consistent with that proposed in Young's (1981) hierarchy of effects model for service promotion and is supported by the study data. In view of the limitations associated with the direct application of an IDB brand-by-attribute analytic framework to many services, subsequent research might examine how prior experience is organized.

MANAGERIAL IMPLICATIONS

The research results suggest that the consumer's increased information need is for information from *particular types of sources.* Beyond consumers' general proclivity for personal sources of information, those sources are even more preferred and appear to have an even greater degree of consumer confidence than impersonal sources in the context of service purchases than in purchase contexts involving goods. Personal independent sources are particularly more effective for services than for goods. Influence exerted by those sources appears to confirm service marketing theory, which suggests that consumers desire subjective and experiential information. Consequently, the study conclusions point to a prominent role for opinion leaders and reference group members who may be early service adopters. These types of sources, however, have been viewed by managers as largely beyond the direct control of the marketing function. Nonetheless, the prominence of word-of-mouth (WOM) generally and for services in particular has received renewed attention and interest (e.g., Midgley 1983; Reingen and Kernan 1986). There is reason to believe that WOM may be particularly relevant to services (e.g., Brown and Reingen

1987), and cost to a firm that neglects negative WOM has been noted (Richins 1983). Consequently, several approaches may be possible that specifically address prospective service consumers' need for word-of-mouth information.

First, the study findings show that managers should not only train and equip service employees to carry out their service functions *per se,* but also ensure their knowledgeability and understanding of the service product and process. Managers' ability to influence contact employees' knowledge and understanding of the service encounter—and hence their ability and willingness to communicate that to customers—may directly enhance customer satisfaction or mitigate dissatisfaction. These positive effects are achieved by service providers who are prepared and able to offer WOM information to customers, depending on the demands of different encounters. Early evidence from other research supports this view (Bitner, Booms, and Tetreault 1990). Second, service providers should equip customers with information (from both personal and impersonal sources) about the service, thereby making them more informed and potentially more likely and effective transmitters of information to other prospects. Third, WOM between service customers and prospective service customers could be motivated by the provision of incentives for referral of new customers to the firm.

In terms of marketing strategy development, during the service's introductory stage a decision to encourage early service adoption by likely service prospects implies that increased numbers of service personnel may be necessary at the service or purchase site to address consumer information needs. Throughout the life cycle of the service, the firm should take measures to provide specially trained service personnel who can respond to the heightened information needs of the first-time service customer. The findings suggest that for customers with product experience, internal sources play a key role in providing information. Thus, it is particularly important that early service encounters be informative and satisfactory ones because of the role experience in addressing the information needs of service consumers.

Finally, the provider of services may be able to engage in marketing activities beyond word-of-mouth communication to encourage the adoption process. The preference of consumers for personal information suggests that persuasive communication strategies should stress experiential rather than technical or objective dimensions of the offering. Similarly, WOM simulation may be an effective promotional approach, particularly when spokespersons and endorsers are selected carefully for their perceived similarity to the service customer prospect. Incentives to induce trial are likely to motivate prospects to acquire relevant experience and "information" that would provide the basis for continued service usage. The banking industry's use of contests to encourage consumer use of ATMs is an example of how incentives can promote patronage of a particular service. Finally, the data underscore the need for the firm to "tangibilize the offer" by providing visible or explanatory cues that prospective service consumers can use to evaluate the ultimate benefits and quality of the product. This notion has been noted in the literature (e.g., Levitt 1981) as a useful heuristic, and the present research provides some empirical basis for its particular relevance.

In summary, the study findings suggest that the information needs of service consumers warrant special attention from both marketing scholars and practitioners. The data suggest that the information requirements of prospective service buyers result in unique information acquisition strategies by consumers and point to special marketing and communication strategies on the part of marketers. The theoretical and managerial implications should be tested further to provide confirmation of the study data.

APPENDIX A.
FORM OF THE HYPOTHETICAL PURCHASE SCENARIO

_____ Purchase Situation

You plan to purchase _____. However, when you consider all possible alternatives of _____ with which you are familiar, none are available. In fact, the only alternatives are ones which you are not familiar with.

Assume that you plan to purchase _____ and will make a choice in the near future.

For you to make a decision without any information about the options available would be virtually the same as making a selection at random. Therefore, you are asked to indicate what your strategy would be before making a final selection . . .

THE SPECIFIC PRODUCT STIMULI ASSOCIATED WITH THE THREE LEVELS OF THE INDEPENDENT VARIABLE AND INCORPORATED INTO PURCHASE SCENARIOS

High Service Attribute Products	Moderate Service Attribute Products	Low Service Attribute Products
Teeth cleaning by a dentist or hygienist	Auto reupholstery (including installation)	Windbreaker jacket
Income tax advice and preparation	Smoke detector/alarm protection	Tennis racket
Auto wheel alignment	Furniture rental, sofa	Barbecue grill
Professional interior decoration advice	Auto muffler (including installation)	Small electric vacuum cleaner
Eye exam	Fine restaurant meal	Pocket camera

APPENDIX B
SOURCE ITEMS USED IN THE STUDY:
25 ITEMS TAPPING INFORMATION SOURCES
USED IN A PURCHASE SITUATION

Circle the number below that best describes your reaction when considering the purchase of a

definitely would
| generally would
| | would be inclined to
| | | may or may not
| | | | would not be inclined to
| | | | | generally would not
| | | | | | definitely would not

I...	1	2	3	4	5	6	7	...ask for a demonstration of the product or service.
I...	1	2	3	4	5	6	7	...think about my previous involvement with this type of product or service.
I...	1	2	3	4	5	6	7	...try to remember what alternative my friends use.
I...	1	2	3	4	5	6	7	...ask the opinion of the salesperson.
I...	1	2	3	4	5	6	7	...pay attention to magazine ads about the product before buying.
I...	1	2	3	4	5	6	7	...ask member of my family or a relative for their opinion.
I...	1	2	3	4	5	6	7	...pay attention to radio commercials for the product or service.
I...	1	2	3	4	5	6	7	...check some type of printed consumer information source for objective product ratings, i.e., *Consumer Reports,* etc.
I...	1	2	3	4	5	6	7	...rely on past personal experience.
I...	1	2	3	4	5	6	7	...consider what a magazine article may say about the product.
I...	1	2	3	4	5	6	7	...pay attention to newspaper ads about the product before buying.
I...	1	2	3	4	5	6	7	...simply go ahead and make a selection of the product or service without additional information or further pre-purchase deliberation.
I...	1	2	3	4	5	6	7	...ask the opinion of a friend or someone I know.
I...	1	2	3	4	5	6	7	...try to recall relevant events which I can associate with this product or service.
I...	1	2	3	4	5	6	7	...ask to try to sample the product before purchasing.
I...	1	2	3	4	5	6	7	...pay attention to TV commercials about the product before buying.
I...	1	2	3	4	5	6	7	...buy the first purchase alternative I found.
I...	1	2	3	4	5	6	7	...ask the opinion of the owner or manager of the store, office, or retail outlet.
I...	1	2	3	4	5	6	7	...try to experience first-hand all I could about the product or service.
I...	1	2	3	4	5	6	7	...see a written description of the product or service or study a detailed descriptive analysis of the product or service.
I...	1	2	3	4	5	6	7	...read available information such as printed brochure, pamphlet, point-of-purchase display, or other information provided by the seller.
I...	1	2	3	4	5	6	7	...ask the opinion of an employee of the firm offering the product such as a receptionist, delivery person, etc.
I...	1	2	3	4	5	6	7	...be ready to make a purchase selection and not worry about acquiring more information prior to buying.
I...	1	2	3	4	5	6	7	...read a report written by a knowledgeable third party, such as a critic, authority in the field, or product specialist.
I...	1	2	3	4	5	6	7	...pay attention to what previous customers had to say about the product or service.

REFERENCES

Anderson, Ronald D., and Jack L. Engledow (1981), "Perceived Importance of Selected Product Information Sources in Two Time Periods by United States and West German Consumers," *Journal of Business Research*, 9 (December), 339–351.

Andreasen, A. R. (1968), "Attitudes and Customer Behavior: A Decision Model," in *Perspectives in Consumer Behavior*, H. H. Kassarjian and T. S. Robertson, eds. Glenview, IL: Scott, Foresman and Company, 498–510.

Arndt, Johan (1967), "Word of Mouth Advertising and Information Communication," in *Risk-Taking and Information Handling in Consumer Behavior*, D. F. Cox, ed. Boston: Harvard University Press, 188–239, 289–316.

Bateson, John E. G. (1977), "Do We Need Service Marketing?" in *Marketing Consumer Services: New Insights*, Pierre Eiglier et al., eds. Cambridge, MA: Marketing Science Institute, 1–30.

———— (1989), *Managing Services Marketing*, Hinsdale, IL: Dryden Press.

Berning, Carol, A. Kohn, and Jacob Jacoby (1974), "Patterns of Information Acquisition in New Product Purchases," *Journal of Consumer Research*, 1 (September), 18–22.

Bettman, James R. (1972), "Perceived Risk: A Measurement Methodology and Preliminary Findings," in *Proceedings, Third Annual Conference of the Association for Consumer Research*, M. Venkatesan, ed. College Park, MD: Association for Consumer Research, 394–403.

———— (1973), "Perceived Risk and Its Components: A Model and Empirical Test," *Journal of Marketing*, 10 (May), 184–189.

———— (1977), "Data-Collection and Analysis Approaches for Studying Consumer Information Processing," in *Advances in Consumer Research*, Vol. 4, William D. Perreault, Jr., ed. Chicago: Association for Consumer Research, 342–348.

———— (1979a), *An Information Processing Theory of Consumer Choice*. Reading, MA: Addison-Wesley Publishing Company.

———— (1979b), "Memory Factors in Consumer Choice: A Review," *Journal of Marketing*, 43 (Spring), 37–53.

———— and Jacob Jacoby (1976), "Patterns of Processing in Consumer Information Acquisition," in *Advances in Consumer Research*, Vol. 3, B. B. Anderson, ed. Urbana, IL: Association for Consumer Research, 315–320.

———— and Michael A. Zins (1977), "Constructive Processes in Consumer Choice," *Journal of Consumer Research*, 3 (September), 75–85.

Bitner, Mary Jo, Bernard M. Booms, and Mary Stanfield Tetreault (1990), "The Service Encounter: Diagnosing Favorable and Unfavorable Incidents," *Journal of Marketing*, 54 (January), 71–84.

Bonfield, E. H. (1974), "Attitude, Social Influence, Personal Norms, and Intention Interactions as Related to Branch Purchase Behavior," *Journal of Marketing Research*, 11 (November), 379–389.

Booms, Bernard H., and Mary J. Bitner (1981), "Marketing Strategies and Organization Structures for Service Firms," in *Marketing of Services*, James H. Donnelly and William

R. George, eds. Chicago: American Marketing Association, 47–51.

———— and Jody L. Nyquist (1981), "Analyzing the Customer/Firm Communication Component of the Services Marketing Mix," in *Marketing of Services*, James H. Donnelly and William R. George, eds. Chicago: American Marketing Association, 172–177.

Brooker, George (1984), "An Assessment of an Expanded Measure of Perceived Risk," in *Advances in Consumer Research*, Vol. 11, Thomas C. Kinnear, ed. Urbana, IL: Association for Consumer Research, 439–441.

Brown, Jacqueline Johnson, and Peter H. Reingen (1987), "Social Ties and Word-of-Mouth Referral Behavior," *Journal of Consumer Research*, 14 (December), 350–362.

Brown, James R., and Edward F. Fern (1981), "Goods vs. Services Marketing: A Divergent Perspective," in *Conceptual and Theoretical Developments in Marketing*, O. C. Ferrell, S. W. Brown, and C. W. Lamb, Jr., eds. Chicago: American Marketing Association, 205–207.

Calder, Bobby J., Lynn W. Phillips, and Alice M. Tybout (1981), "Designing Research for Application," *Journal of Consumer Research*, 8 (September), 197–207.

Capon, Donald, and Marian Burke (1977), "Information Seeking Behavior in Consumer Durable Purchases," in *Contemporary Marketing Thought, 1977 Educators' Proceedings*, Barnett A. Greenberg and Danny N. Bellenger, eds. Chicago: American Marketing Association, 110–115.

Churchill, Gilbert A., Jr. (1979), *Marketing Research*. Hinsdale, IL: Dryden Press.

Cox, Donald F. (1963a), "The Audience as Communicators," in Toward Scientific Marketing, *Proceedings of the Winter Conference of the American Marketing Association*, Stephen A. Greyser, ed. Chicago: American Marketing Association, 58–72.

———— (1963b), "The Measurement of Information Value: A Study in Consumer Decision-Making," in *Emerging Concepts in Marketing*, W. S. Decker, ed. Chicago: American Marketing Association, 413–421.

———— (1967), *Risk-Taking and Information Handling in Consumer Behavior*. Boston: Harvard University.

Davis, Duane L., Joseph P. Guiltinan, and Wesley H. Jones (1979), "Service Characteristics, Consumer Search, and the Classification of Retail Services," *Journal of Retailing*, 3 (Fall), 3–23.

Deshpande, Rohit, and S. Krishnan (1977), "A Consumer-Based Approach for Establishing Priorities in Consumer Information Programs: Implications for Public Policy," in *Contemporary Marketing Thought, 1977 Educators' Proceedings*, Barnett A. Greenberg and Danny N. Bellenger, eds. Chicago: American Marketing Association, 338–343.

Eiglier, Pierre, and Eric Langeard (1977), "A New Approach to Service Marketing," in *Marketing Consumer Services: New Insights*, Pierre Eiglier et al., eds. Cambridge, MA: Marketing Science Institute, 33–58.

Engel, James F., and Roger D. Blackwell (1982), *Consumer Behavior*. New York: Dryden Press.

Eroglu, Sevgin (1987), "The Scenario Method: A Theoretical, Not Theoretical, Approach," in *AMA Educators' Conference*

Proceedings, Susan P. Douglas et al., eds. Chicago: American Marketing Association, 220.

Furse, David H., Girish N. Punj, and David W. Stewart (1984), "A Typology of Individual Search Strategies among Purchasers of New Automobiles," *Journal of Consumer Research,* 10 (March), 417–431.

George, William R., Marc G. Weinberger, and J. Patrick Kelly (1985), "Consumer Risk Perceptions: Managerial Tool for the Service Encounter," in T*he Service Encounter: Managing Employee/Customer Interaction in Service Businesses,* John A. Czepiel, Michael R. Solomon, and Carol F. Surprenant, eds. Lexington, MA: Lexington Books, 83–100.

Guseman, Dennis S. (1981), "Risk Perception and Risk Reduction in Consumer Services," in *Marketing of Services,* John H. Donnelly and William R. George, eds. Chicago: American Marketing Association, 200–204.

Hansen, Flemming (1972), *Consumer Choice Behavior.* New York: The Free Press.

Hofacker, Thomas (1984), "Identifying Consumer Information Processing Strategies: New Methodologies of Analyzing Information Display Board Data," in *Advances in Consumer Research,* Vol. 11, Thomas C. Kinnear, ed. Provo, UT: Association for Consumer Research, 579–584.

Houston, Michael J. (1979), "Consumer Evaluations and Product Information Sources," in *Current Issues & Research in Advertising,* 1979, James H. Leigh and Claude R. Martin, Jr., eds. Ann Arbor, MI: University of Michigan, 135–144.

Hoyer, Wayne D., and Jacob Jacoby (1983), "Three Dimensional Information Acquisition: An Application to Contraceptive Decision Making," in *Advances in Consumer Research,* Vol. 10, Richard P. Baggozi and Alice M. Tybout, eds. Ann Arbor, MI: Association for Consumer Research, 618–623.

Jackson, Donald W., Jr., Janet E. Keith, and Richard K. Burdick (1984), "Purchasing Agents' Perceptions of Industrial Buying Center Influence: A Situational Approach," *Journal of Marketing,* 48 (Fall), 75–83.

Jacoby, Jacob, Robert W. Chestnut, and William Fisher (1978), "A Behavioral Process Approach to Information Acquisition in Nondurable Purchasing," *Journal of Marketing Research,* 15 (November), 532–544.

———, ———, and William Silberman (1977), "Consumer Use and Comprehension of Nutrition Information," *Journal of Consumer Research,* 4 (September), 119–128.

——— and Leon B. Kaplan (1972), "The Components of Perceived Risk," in *Proceedings, Third Annual Conference of the Association for Consumer Research,* M. Venkatesan, ed. College Park, MD: Association for Consumer Research, 382–393.

———, Donald E. Speller, and Carol Kohn Berning (1974), "Brand Choice Behavior as a Function of Information Load: Replication and Extension," *Journal of Consumer Research,* 1 (June), 33–42.

Katz, Elihu, and Raul F. Lazarsfeld (1955), *Personal Influences.* New York: The Free Press.

Kirk, Roger E. (1982), *Experimental Design: Procedures for the Behavioral Sciences.* Belmont, CA: Brooks/Cole Publishing.

Kotler, Philip (1980), *Marketing Management.* Englewood Cliffs, NJ: Prentice-Hall, Inc.

Lehmann, Donald R., and William L. Moore (1980), "Validity of Information Display Boards: An Assessment Using Longitudinal Data," *Journal of Marketing Research,* 17 (November), 450–459.

Leigh, Thomas W., and Arno J. Rethans (1984), "A Script-Theoretic Analysis of Industrial Purchasing Behavior," *Journal of Marketing,* 48 (Fall), 22–32.

Levitt, Theodore (1981), "Marketing Intangible Products and Product Intangibles," *Harvard Business Review,* 59 (May–June), 94–102.

Locander, William B., and Peter W. Hermann (1979), "The Effects of Self-Confidence and Anxiety on Information Seeking in Consumer Risk Reduction," *Journal of Marketing Research,* 16 (May), 268–274.

Lovelock, Christopher L. (1981), "Why Marketing Management Needs to Be Different for Services," in *Marketing of Services,* James H. Donnelly and William R. George, eds. Chicago: American Marketing Association, 5–9.

Lutz, Richard J., and Patrick J. Reilly (1973), "An Exploration of the Effects of Perceived Social and Performance Risk on Consumer Information Acquisition," in *Advances in Consumer Research,* Vol. 1, Scott Ward and Peter Wright, eds. Urbana, IL: Association for Consumer Research, 393–405.

Lynch, John G., Jr. and Thomas K. Srull (1982), "Memory and Attentional Factors in Consumer Choice: Concepts and Research Methods," *Journal of Consumer Research,* 9 (June), 18–37.

May, Fredrick C. (1965), "An Appraisal of Buying Behavior Research," in *Marketing and Economic Development,* Peter D. Bennett, ed. Chicago: American Marketing Association, 392.

Midgley, David F. (1983), "Patterns of Interpersonal Information Seeking for the Purchase of a Symbolic Product," *Journal of Marketing Research,* 20 (February), 74–83.

Moore, William L., and Donald R. Lehmann (1980), "Individual Differences in Search Behavior for a Nondurable," *Journal of Consumer Research,* 7 (December), 296–307.

Mowen, John C., Janel E. Keith, Stephen W. Brown, and Donald W. Jackson, Jr. (1985), "Utilizing Effort and Task Difficulty Information in Evaluating Salespeople," *Journal of Marketing Research,* 22(May), 185–191.

Murray, Keith B., and John L. Schlacter (1990), "The Impact of Services versus Goods on Consumers' Assessment of Perceived Risk and Variability," *Journal of the Academy of Marketing Science,* 18 (1), 51–65.

Nelson, P. (1974), "Advertising as Information," *Journal of Political Economy,* 81 (July/August), 729–754.

Nunnally, Jum C. (1967), *Psychometric Theory.* New York: McGraw-Hill Book Company.

Olander, Folke (1975), "Search Behavior in Non-Simultaneous Choice Situations: Satisficing or Maximizing," in *Utility, Probability and Human Decision Making,* D. Wendt and C. A. J. Ulek, eds. Dordrecht, Holland: D. Reidel.

Park, C. Whan (1976), "The Effect of Individual and Situation-Related Factors on Consumer Selection of Judgmental Models," *Journal of Marketing Research*, 13(May), 144–151.

Perry, Michael, and B. Curtis Hamm (1969), "Canonical Analysis of Relations between Socioeconomic Risk and Personal Influence in Purchase Decisions," *Journal of Marketing Research*, 6 (February), 351–354.

Peter, John Paul (1979), "Reliability: A Review of Psychometric Basics and Recent Marketing Practices," *Journal of Marketing Research*, 16 (February), 6–17.

——— (1981), "Construct Validity: A Review of Basic Issues and Marketing Practices," *Journal of Marketing*, 18 (May), 133–145.

——— and Lawrence X. Tarpey (1975), "A Comparative Analysis of Three Consumer Decision Strategies," *Journal of Consumer Research*, 2 (June), 29–37.

Price, Linda L., and Lawrence F. Feick (1984), "The Role of Interpersonal Sources in External Search: An Informational Perspective," in *Advances in Consumer Research*, Vol. 11, Thomas C. Kinnear, ed. Provo, UT: Association for Consumer Research, 250–255.

Puto, Christopher P., Wesley E. Patton III, and Ronald H. King (1985), "Risk-Handling Strategies in Industrial Vendor Selection Decisions," *Journal of Marketing*, 49 (Winter), 89–98.

Ray, Michael L. (1973), "Marketing Communications and Hierarchy of Effects," in *New Models for Mass Communication Research*, Peter Clarke, ed. Beverly Hills, CA: Sage Publications, Inc., 147–176.

Reingen, Peter H., and Jerome B. Kernan (1986), "Analysis of Referral Networks in Marketing: Methods and Illustration," *Journal of Marketing Research*, 23 (November), 370–378.

Richins, Marsha L. (1983), "Negative Word-of-Mouth by Dissatisfied Consumers: A Pilot Study," *Journal of Marketing*, 47 (Winter), 68–78.

Roselius, Ted (1971), "Consumer Rankings of Risk Reduction Methods," *Journal of Marketing*, 35 (January), 56–61.

Ryan, Michael J., and E. H. Bonfield (1980), "Fishbein's Intention Model: A Test of External Pragmatic Validity," *Journal of Marketing*, 44 (Spring), 82–95.

Shostack, G. Lynn (1977), "Breaking Free from Product Marketing," *Journal of Marketing*, 41 (April), 73–80.

Staelin, Richard, and John W. Payne (1976), "Studies of the Information Seeking Behavior of Consumers," in *Cognition of Social Behavior*, J. Carroll and J. W. Payne, eds. New York: Lawrence Erlbaum Associates, 185–202.

Surprenant, Carol F. and Michael R. Solomon (1987), "Prediction and Personalization in the Service Encounter," *Journal of Marketing*, 51 (April), 86–96.

Urbany, Joel E., and Dan C. Weilbaker (1987), "A Critical Examination of Nelson's Theory of Information and Consumer Behavior," in *AMA Educators' Conference Proceedings*, Susan P. Douglas et al., eds. Chicago: American Marketing Association, 220.

van Raaij, W. Fred (1977), "Consumer Information Processing for Different Structures and Formats," in *Advances in Consumer Research*, Vol. 10, William D. Perreault, ed. Atlanta: Association for Consumer Research, 176–184.

Vinokur-Kaplan, Diane (1978), "To Have—Or Not to Have—Another Child: Family Planning Attitudes, Intention, and Behavior," *Journal of Applied Social Psychology*, 8 (January–March), 29–46.

Vredenburg, Harrie, and Chow-Hou Wee (1986), "The Role of Customer Service in Determining Customer Satisfaction," *Journal of the Academy of Marketing Science*, 14 (Summer), 17–26.

Winter, Fredrick W. (1975), "Laboratory Measurement of Response to Consumer Information," *Journal of Marketing Research*, 12 (November), 390–401.

Wright, P. (1974), "The Harassed Decision Maker: Time Pressures, Distractions, and the Use of Evidence," *Journal of Applied Psychology*, 59 (October), 55–61.

Young, Robert F. (1981), "The Advertising of Consumer Services and the Hierarchy of Effects," in *Marketing of Services*, James H. Donnelly and William R. George, eds. Chicago: American Marketing Association, 196–199.

Zeithaml, Valarie A. (1981), "How Consumer Evaluation Processes Differ between Goods and Services," in *Marketing of Services*, James H. Donnelly and William R. George, eds. Chicago: American Marketing Association, 186–190.

———, A. Parasuraman, and Leonard L. Berry (1985), "Problems and Strategies in Services Marketing," *Journal of Marketing*, 49 (Spring), 33–46.

CHAPTER 8

SERVICE PRICING POLICY

CHAPTER OVERVIEW

A group of passengers traveling from London to New York are delayed, and to entertain themselves, decide to compare the price they have paid for their tickets. To their surprise, they discover many different prices. Apart from an expected differential between first, business, and economy class, they find many variations within each class. Some booked early and paid less, others didn't book and went stand-by and also paid less. Some are staying for the weekend and paid less, others bought the airfare and hotel as a package to bundle and have a different price. Some remember paying a different price when making an identical trip, but at a different time of the year.

A group of train travelers discover that they too have paid very different prices for their tickets. Their pricing analysis is complicated further by the fact that some have bought season tickets allowing for unlimited travel for a period of time.

In certain parts of the world, a full-service gas station will charge more for a gallon of gasoline than a self-service station, even though the gasoline and the stations are identical.

The purpose of this chapter is to show how the need to manage the service experience, combined with its time dependency and the nature of service costs, makes the various examples of service prices described above not only logical, but profitable.

TIME-DEPENDENT CAPACITY AND ITS IMPACT ON PRICING

The idea that services cannot be inventoried was introduced in Chapter 1, and the operations-management problems of services were explained in some detail in Chapter 3. The interaction that creates the service experience, which is what the consumer buys, takes place in real time. It is possible to create an inventory of the physical components of the service experience, but not of the experience itself.

Since consumers, in most cases, must come to the service setting to be part of the experience, this means that capacity utilization depends on when they arrive. For most services, consumers tend to arrive unevenly and unpredictably. The result is often periods of low utilization of capacity, since it is impossible to match capacity to demand.

Capacity, in turn, represents the bulk of the costs for a service. The restaurant has to be open, staffed, and stocked, even at times when it has no customers. As Dearden points out, the result is a very low level of variable costs for services and a high value attributable to incremental customers even at discount prices.[1] As a result, pricing is called upon to try to smooth demand in two ways:

☐ creating new demand in off-peak, low-capacity utilization periods, and

☐ flattening peaks by moving existing customers from peaks to less-busy times.

Price discrimination is essential, however, if a cheap "off-peak" airfare used to shift demand is not to be available to full-fare-paying passengers. If such an exchange is possible, the result will be an overall reduction in revenue and none of the desired movement to off-peak periods will take place.

The use of time-based price discrimination, therefore, conveys a double benefit. As well as minimizing consumer surplus and maximizing the number of customers, it also maximizes capacity utilization.

The Mass Transit Authority (MTA) in Boston attempted to reduce rush-hour crowding through pricing. The alternative would have been to invest in more capacity, which would stand idle outside the peak periods. The MTA offered a 60 percent fare discount between 10 A.M. and 2 P.M. Although the strategy did generate extra riders, those riders did not come from the peak periods and were new to the system. The reason is fairly obvious: Most rush-hour travelers have little discretion over their time of travel, since this is dictated by their work. No matter how much they want to save money by traveling at other times, they have to be at work before 9 A.M. The program, therefore, solved one problem by helping to fill low capacity, but it did nothing to solve the underlying peak period problem.

The MTA attempted to alleviate the rush-hour problem by tackling the underlying cause. Working together with the city government and major companies, it created a staggered working-day program. By varying the start and finish of the working day, the MTA was able to smooth demand at key stations. This had economic benefits for the MTA as well as offering the commuters a more pleasant ride to work.

This is the basic argument that will be developed in this chapter and that can explain much of the proliferation of service prices. To complete the argument, the idea of consumer surplus needs to be extended to include the costs of both participation in service production and the cost of ticket acquisition. Each one of the building blocks in the argument now will be elaborated: the low level of variable costs in services, the high level of shared costs, price discrimination, and the ability to price by time of usage or reservation.

THE NATURE OF SERVICE COSTS

When deciding on a pricing policy, the seller must be aware that the range of pricing options open to him is limited. Demand considerations provide a ceiling to the price that may be charged, while cost considerations create a price floor. The difference between what buyers are willing to pay and what sellers can afford to charge creates a vital price discretion.

This price discretion is narrowed at both ends. Sellers must consider corporate objectives, as well as costs, when setting the price floor. Merely covering costs is insufficient, since the firm needs to meet its financial objectives and generate a profit. At the other end, competitive factors usually reduce the price ceiling and often can prevent the firm from charging the full value as it is perceived by the customer.

Calculating the cost of a product raises two problems, according to Dearden:

☐ identifying which of the company's costs are relevant when calculating the profitability of a particular product, and

☐ creating methods to assign relevant costs to that product.[2]

Dearden argues that, for services, the best answer to the relevance question is to consider "uniquely attributable costs." These are costs that can be uniquely attributed to the production and sale of a particular service. One way of approaching this concept is to realize that these are costs that disappear if the service is not produced.

The concept of uniquely attributable costs differs from the traditional cost-accounting distinction between variable and fixed costs. Variable costs are those costs that change with volume, assuming that the company continues to produce and market the service. The unique-cost concept assumes that no amount of the product would be produced. At zero volume, many costs can be eliminated that would have to be incurred at higher levels. Revenues minus uniquely attributable costs constitute the total profit contribution of a service for a specific period.

The uniquely attributable cost concept is necessary because of the characteristics of services. Variable costs for goods consist of such things as direct labor, material, and energy costs, and some indirect labor and maintenance costs. All of these vary directly and proportionately with volume. As a consequence, variable costs tend to range between 60 percent and 90 percent of total manufacturing costs.

By contrast, many service organizations have little or no direct material or labor costs and limited variable overhead costs. As a result, variable costs for these businesses represent a very small proportion of total costs. Because variable costs are so low, the financial impact of most factors affecting the volume of sales in the short run can be estimated by simply calculating the revenue impact. Variable costs, therefore, have little use in setting a pricing floor. Following the uniquely attributable cost idea, however, it is possible for a product's price to exceed its variable cost and the sale of a service to result in a loss of net worth.

Unique-cost analysis is a hierarchical process that starts with the most aggregated definition of the product and breaks this down by stages as the definition of the product is narrowed. Starting with the most aggregate definition—the business unit—the traditional profit and loss statement provides an accurate indication of costs.

The next step is to calculate the profitability of the various product lines. For this figure, it is necessary to separate the total costs into those that can be attributed to specific products and those that are joint costs. The attributable costs are determined by calculating which costs would *not* have been incurred had Service A (e.g., NOW accounts in a bank) not been produced. The difference, then, between total unique costs and total costs are the joint costs. Such a process should be sequential, starting with the business unit, then proceeding to each product group, and then breaking down each product or service into the next divisible unit until it is no longer possible to divide the product or service. It is evident that, as we move down the hierarchy, more costs become joint and, consequently, fewer costs are unique.

Although a uniquely attributable cost is likely to be higher than a simple variable cost, it is still clear that the price floor for many services can be very low. An extra customer usually will generate a large incremental profit. This is logical at an intuitive level if one considers the time-dependent nature of service capacity. However, it should not be surprising that many service firms offering an undifferentiated product can end up in deadly price wars.

Incremental customers are only valuable if the service operation has the capacity to service them. That capacity often is dictated by the quality of the experience that can be provided. There is a steep deterioration in the quality of the experience as the system reaches capacity and queries and crowds become a problem.

The problem for the service firm is that, at times of peak demand, it wants both to charge as much as possible and to be as close to the consumers' reservation prices (the maximum amounts buyers are willing to pay) as possible. Consumers exchange their money, time, and effort for the bundle of benefits offered by the service provider. Economic theory suggests that consumers will have a reservation price that captures the value they place on these benefits. As long as the total cost to the consumer is less than the reservation price, consumers will be prepared to buy. If they can purchase the service for less than their reservation price, there will be a consumer's surplus. However, in non-peak times, there is a large opportunity to reduce price and return surplus to the consumer, but still make a profit because of the low uniquely attributable costs and the high fixed or shared costs. Such a strategy is only possible if it is possible to price discriminate the element.

THE NATURE OF SERVICE DEMAND

PRICE DISCRIMINATION AND TIME-BASED PRICING

The reservation price idea suggests that consumers determine a price that captures the benefits they perceive in a service. The consumer's surplus is then the difference between this price and the reservation price. Such an idea is at the heart of price discrimination and time-based pricing.

Up to this point, we have assumed implicitly that a reservation price is fixed and homogeneous across the market. Segmentation theory would argue that it is more likely that the market will be heterogeneous and that different groups of consumers will put different valuations or reservation prices on a service. For example, when considering the reservation price for an airline shuttle ticket between Boston and New York City, the value placed on that ticket can vary even with the same individual. One reservation price applies to business travel, but, when the traveler is paying for the ticket out of his or her own pocket, there will be a different valuation. For the airline, on the other hand, the cost of operating a particular flight will not vary because of who its passengers are. Where different groups of customers are willing to pay different prices, price discrimination can be employed to set differing prices that do not reflect a proportional difference in marginal cost.

To successfully price discriminate and hence minimize aggregate consumer surplus, the following criteria must be met:

1. Different groups of consumers must have different responses to price, i.e., they must value the service differently.

2. The different segments must be identifiable, and a mechanism must exist to price them differently.

3. There should be no opportunity for individuals in one segment who have paid a low price to sell their tickets to other segments.

4. The segment should be large enough to make the exercise worthwhile.

5. The cost of running the price-discrimination strategy should not exceed the incremental revenues obtained. This is partly a function of item 4 above.

6. The customers should not become confused by the use of different prices.

It is an interesting characteristic of services that these criteria frequently can be met through the time-based nature of demand. Discrimination can be practiced by time of usage of the service or by time of reservation or ticket purchase.

DISCRIMINATION BY TIME OF USAGE

There are a number of obvious examples of price discrimination by time of usage. To return to the airline ticket example, it is clearly impossible to identify the business and leisure travelers separately as they approach the ticket counter. Even if they were identifiable, it would be impossible to then offer them differential prices at the same time. The fact that a Hawaiian shirt guaranteed a low ticket price would soon produce a rash of such shirts. Clearly, criterion 2 above would have been violated.

There is, however, a good surrogate for travel occasion in the *time* of travel. Business travelers are unlikely to want to travel at awkward hours (the time costs of the transaction are too high), but leisure travelers may be willing to do so. Hence,

SERVICES IN ACTION 8.1

SEALINK CROSS-CHANNEL FERRIES

Sealink Ferries is one of four companies that compete in offering ferry services on several major routes across the English Channel. Sealink also operates ferry services from southern England to Brittany and to Ireland. The busiest routes are those across the narrowest point of the channel from Dover, England, to Calais, France—a distance of about 35 miles. Ferries on this route are large roll-on, roll-off vessels capable of carrying several hundred cars and up to a thousand passengers.

As with its competitors, Sealink fine-tunes its fare structure, raising fares during peak periods, such as legal and school holidays, and lowering them in midweek and in midwinter. The accompanying exhibits show (1) the fare structure used and (2) the times at which various fares are in operation.

By adjusting its fare schedules day by day and sailing by sailing, Sealink attempts to fill both car and passenger berths that otherwise might remain empty. During peak periods, such as summer, the service is used to capacity, but in winter, and especially on the late-night sailings, demand is relatively low. The intention is to try to stimulate demand during the off-peak periods, when fewer people take holidays and the only steady travelers are people going between France and England on business. These travelers obviously prefer to travel during the day.

Sealink, again in line with its major competitors, currently is facing a major challenger. Prior to this time, the only alternatives to cross-channel ferries have been airlines, which are expensive, and water-borne services such as hovercraft and jetfoils, which are at the mercy of rough weather. However, the Channel Tunnel will soon connect England and France by rail, with uninterrupted service that feasibly can be operated around the clock and with greater frequency than the ferries. The railway link also will be considerably faster than the two-hour ferry journey. Sealink's pricing strategy now must take into account this new competition and the variation in demand patterns that it inevitably will bring.

PRICES FOR DOVER-CALAIS AND FOLKESTONE-BOULOGNE.

ALL CAR PRICES NOW INCLUDE DRIVER

	STANDARD SINGLE FARE & FARESAVER 2½ DAY RETURN				FARESAVER 5 DAY RETURN			
	E	D	C	B	E	D	C	B
	£	£	£	£	£	£	£	£
CAR / MOTORISED CARAVAN / MINIBUS INCLUDING DRIVER	FARES INCLUDE DRIVER				FARES INCLUDE DRIVER			
Up to 6.00 metres in length	46.00	71.00	95.00	106.00	88.00	107.00	143.00	162.00
Over 6.00 metres, each additional metre or part metre	7.00	7.00	9.00	11.00	11.00	11.00	14.00	17.00
TOWED TRAILER / CARAVAN								
Up to 3.00 metres in length	10.00	10.00	13.00	15.00	15.00	15.00	19.00	23.00
Up to 6.00 metres in length	20.00	20.00	26.00	35.00	30.00	30.00	39.00	53.00
Over 6.00 metres, each additional metre or part metre	1300	13.00	13.00	15.00	20.00	20.00	20.00	23.00
ADDITIONAL MOTORIST PASSENGERS								
Adult	8.00	13.00	13.00	13.00	16.00	20.00	20.00	20.00
Child (4 but under 14 years)	8.00	8.00	8.00	8.00	12.00	12.00	12.00	12.00
Infant (under 4 years)	FREE	FREE	FREE	FREE	FREE	FREE	FREE	FREE
MOTORCYCLE / SCOOTER AND RIDER	30.00	35.00	40.00	43.00	45.00	52.00	60.00	65.00
BICYCLE / TANDEM (rider charged as foot passengers)	FREE	FREE	FREE	FREE	FREE	FREE	FREE	FREE
FOOT PASSENGERS								
Adult	21.00	21.00	21.00	21.00	31.00	31.00	31.00	31.00
Student	17.00	17.00	-	-	25.00	25.00	-	-
Child (4 but under 14 years)	10.00	10.00	10.00	10.00	15.00	15.00	15.00	15.00
Infant (under 4 years)	FREE	FREE	FREE	FREE	FREE	FREE	FREE	FREE
FAMILY SAVER RETURN -NEW								
Car and up to 2 adults and 2 children	124.00	184.00	232.00	-	-	-	-	-

NOTES

1. FARESAVERS:
2½ DAY AND 5 DAY RETURNS
Both are return fares. The price is determined by the date, time and route of the outward sailing. The return journey may be made on any sailing departing up to a maximum of 2½ days (60 hours) or 5 days as appropriate from the time of arrival in France. (Additional charges become payable if the ticket validity is exceeded).

2. FAMILY SAVER
The price is determined by the tariff band which applies to the date and time of outward travel. The fare shown is for up to 2 adults and 2 children travelling in the same car. Additional adults and children pay the "Additional Motorist Passengers" fare. The special offer is not valid on B tariff sailings in either direction.

(continued)

(continued from previous page)

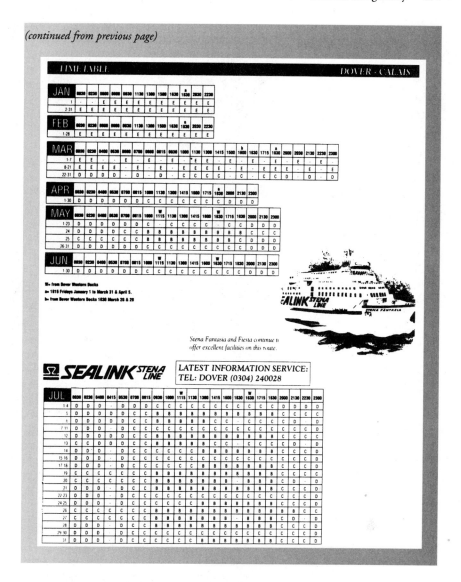

Stena Fantasia and Fiesta continue to
offer excellent facilities on this route.

LATEST INFORMATION SERVICE:
TEL: DOVER (0304) 240028

airlines can offer inexpensive late-night flights to attract leisure demand without risking price dilution.

DISCRIMINATION BY TIME OF RESERVATION OR TICKET PURCHASE

Price discrimination by time of reservation or ticket purchase has long been employed by the hotel industry. Conference or group bookings offer the hotel the advantage of guaranteed demand but usually require cheaper prices. The lone traveler arriving at 6 P.M. without a reservation has, by comparison, little bargaining power and will quite happily pay the full rate. Profitable hotel management therefore depends on a balancing act between capacity utilization and yield. Filling the hotel with low-rate guests who have booked six months in advance precludes higher-priced, same-day sales. On the other hand, reserving capacity runs the risk that capacity will be unused.

SERVICES IN ACTION 8.2

THE PARKER HOUSE

The Parker House in Boston is the oldest continuously operating hotel in the United States, having first opened its doors in 1855. The Parker House had experienced hard times, but after Dunfey Hotels bought the building, it was completely refurbished between 1973 and 1975, and, for a time, it was the undisputed king of the Boston hotel market. The Parker House philosophy was that customers were part of the hotel's ambiance, i.e., part of the product, and great attention was paid to choosing clientele to match the hotel's mission. Management defined the hotel's market very narrowly, looking ideally for professionals and executive travelers either as individuals or companies.

Room-pricing policies were aimed at this segment. Although, because of its nineteenth-century design, the hotel did have a number of small single rooms that were low-priced, usually on a contract basis to government employees, the bulk of the rooms were relatively luxurious. The Parker House aimed to keep its prices in the top ten percent of the local room-rate price spread, in order to get the right kind of customer rather than simply fill the hotel. This policy was matched closely by a strong sales effort aimed at the executive market.

Matching demand to price involved examination of the room sales efficiency (RSE) rate. Most hotels use some form of discounting in order to fill rooms. The RSE represents the total occupancy rate at a given time multiplied by the average percentage of the full room rate, after discounting, being paid by all guests (i.e., if occupancy is 90 percent and guests are paying an average of 90 percent of the full rate, the RSE is then 81 percent). This measure, unlike the more generally used occupancy measure, includes both occupancy and yield.

In markets where demand is high, there is a wide spread of potential customers in many different segments. RSE thus also tends to be high, as there is little need for discounting. Strategically, the hotel then tries to move the "bottom up," squeezing out the lower-priced segments by increasing room rates. Dunfey Hotels' strategic principle was that any hotel with an RSE of 85 percent or more needed a rate increase in order to move further up in the market.

In 1979, the Parker House was faced with a major challenge. Three new hotels were about to open within a few miles of the hotel, all, like the Parker House, positioned in the top ten percent price range and almost certainly planning to aim at the same market segments. The challenge facing the Parker House was how to use a combination of physical facilities and price to meet this new competition.

The airline industry uses time of reservation to tap into the leisure and business segments. Few business travelers can risk booking flights weeks in advance and often need to book tickets on the day of departure. Leisure travelers, by comparison, plan their trips in advance and are willing to buy tickets in advance. Discrimination is therefore possible, and low prices can be offered for early booking with little dilution of the business-traveler yield.

Both airlines and hotels have an advantage in that tickets are not interchangeable, so that cross-selling of tickets by different segments is impossible. Confusion in the consumer's mind is avoided because the strategies follow an economic logic, which is consistent with the nature of service costs.

The complexity of airline pricing becomes apparent when it is realized that airlines use both of the above forms of discrimination simultaneously. Fares between a single pair of cities vary both by time of day and time of booking. Airline pricing schedules have been made even more complex by the introduction of the stand-by flight. This idea taps into yet another market segment by providing very low prices without any guarantee of a seat. As in many other service businesses, these types of strategies are driven by the nature of costs as well as by demand considerations.

MULTIPLE SERVICES AND PRICE BUNDLING

Most service organizations provide more than one service. In recent years, the practice of bundling services has become more prevalent. *Bundling*, broadly defined, is the practice of marketing two or more products and/or services in a single package. Common examples include hotels putting together weekend packages that include meals, and sometimes entertainment, as well as lodging at an inclusive rate. Airlines routinely price vacation packages that include air travel, car rental, and hotel accommodations.

Such price bundling follows logically from both the nature of service costs and the nature of service demand. Individual services have low uniquely attributable costs and high joint costs, making the incremental cost of adding a service to a bundle very low.

On the demand side, there is interdependence as well. This stems partly from the search theory perspective on demand. Search theory provides a paradigm for examining the elasticity of demand. It argues that price sensitivity depends on the number of alternatives considered for the purchase. The fewer the number of alternatives considered, the more inelastic the demand curve will be. The number of alternatives, however, can be said to depend on the number of alternatives about which the consumer is knowledgeable.

It has been argued that the consumer's ability to obtain knowledge of alternatives depends on the nature of the attributes of the service. Three types of attributes have been defined: search attributes, experience attributes, and credence attributes.

Search attributes are characteristics that can be evaluated before purchase of a service by asking questions or looking up information, such as airline flight durations or the location of a particular restaurant. *Experience attributes* are characteristics that can be evaluated only after purchase; they include such things as the quality of a meal or the quality and speed of photo-processing services. *Credence attributes* often cannot be evaluated until some time after receiving the service and are thus experienced over time; they are particularly common in professional services such as health care or in technical consultancies.

Demand is likely to be most elastic for services that can be evaluated on the basis of search attributes. Consumers will be aware of more alternatives since such information is easier to collect. On the other hand, if service personnel themselves dictate the quality or nature of the service, and if the service can be customized, consumers will be less able to evaluate the service and thus less sensitive to price differences between alternatives.

Using this framework, consider a financial institution that can create a range of services that could meet different needs for the same individual. If the services are bundled together, the time and effort needed for consumers to find information is reduced. At the same time, the data on several attributes will not be collected and experience and credence attributes from other services may be pooled. The result is that demand is likely to be inelastic and interdependent.

Generally, services are concerned with mixed bundling, which allows consumers either to buy Service A and Service B together or purchase one service separately. The simplest argument for bundling is based on the idea of consumer surplus. Bundling makes it possible to shift the consumer surplus from one service to another service that otherwise would have a negative surplus (i.e., would not be purchased). Thus, the combined value of the two services is less than the combined price, even though, separately, only one service would be purchased.

This argument is made more complex if a competitive marketplace is assumed, and if the reservation price, or value, of the combined bundle is not assumed to be merely the sum of its parts. Assuming a competitive market means that the objectives of price bundling can be broadened. The combination of Services A and B can be targeted at purchasers of A or B but not both, at A and B separately and concurrently, or at nonpurchasers of either A or B. Each target demands a different perspective.

Relaxing the reservation price additivity assumption is worth further exploration. Three reasons have been suggested for why the sum of the parts would have less value than the whole. First, information theory would argue that there is value to the consumer in easy access to information. Consumers of one financial service from an institution have a lower information cost when buying another service from the same institution than when buying that service from a different institution. A second case argues that the bundling of Service B with Service A can enhance a consumer's satisfaction with Service A. Guiltinan, in Article 8.1, uses the example of a ski resort that offers a ski-rental and lessons package. The reservation price for the lessons is likely to be the same whether or not the skis are rented because the value of the lessons depends on the skills and needs of the skier. However, the reservation price of the ski rental will be enhanced, at least for novices, by lessons. The final argument is that the addition of Service B to Service A can enhance the total image of the firm. A financial-planning service offering both investment advice and tax advice enhances its credibility in both services.

The extent to which there is more incremental value in a bundle than in the parts determines the price that can be charged. Ideally, the reservation prices of the separate services and of the bundle should be measured separately. A number of researchers have argued that it is possible to measure reservation prices directly by asking what is the most that consumers are willing to pay.

Alternative approaches are the utility estimation approaches, such as conjoint analysis. Although these do not attempt to measure reservation prices directly, they do measure utilities for various price/attribute combinations.

Clearly, reservation prices will vary because of institutional factors. Segmentation by occasion will be important since the reservation price of a service will depend on the use to which it is put. An airline ticket will have a different reservation price for the same individual depending on whether it is purchased for a business trip or a leisure trip.

INTRODUCING NONMONETARY COSTS INTO THE ANALYSIS

Thus far in this chapter, monetary and information costs have been included in the analysis. Economic theory itself has included the information costs through search theory. One of the key characteristics of services is that they may demand an effort cost from the consumer in the form of effort made during the process and during the purchase as well.

THE SELF-SERVICE CONSUMER—EFFORT DURING THE PROCESS It has been argued throughout this book that the consumer is, to a greater or lesser extent, part of the servuction process. In addition to providing information as a minimum input to the system, the consumer often, and increasingly, is called upon to provide physical effort to aid the process.

The rationale for including the consumer in the servuction system is discussed in Chapter 3. Essentially, it is possible to reduce costs by having the consumer do part of the work. The issue then arises as to whether it is necessary to change the price to reflect the added cost of that effort to the consumer. Is it necessary for self-service gas stations to be cheaper than full-service stations?

At first sight, it would appear that a price cut is necessary in order to balance the consumer's value equation. However, this assumes that the consumer attaches the same benefit or value to the service delivered in two different ways. There is considerable evidence to suggest that this may not be the case.

Research suggests that consumers' response to such do-it-yourself offerings is variable. One segment of consumers would prefer to "do it themselves" even if no price incentive is offered. Conversely, there is another segment that would not use these kinds of service even for large price discounts. This segmentation is consistent with the consumer behavior discussed in Chapter 2.

The do-it-yourself consumers attach a high value to perceived control and time. They perceive that increasing their participation increases their value through a greater sense of control over the situation and lower time costs. Members of the second group of consumers see these services as equal to full-service options on control and time but lacking in "human content." The value of these services is reduced for them because of the lack of contact with service personnel.

THE EFFORT COST OF PURCHASING Services, like goods, require effort from the consumer in order to acquire the right to use them. Discussions about goods focus on convenience and ensuring that goods will be "conveniently available." In a similar way, there is a transaction cost for the purchase of services. This cost is compounded in the case of frequently used services, such as transportation, where the cumulative effort can become very large. In these situations, consumers may be prepared to buy bulk access to save such costs, particularly if a bulk purchase-price discount is offered. The key components of pricing then become how, when, where, and to whom the price should be paid.

The "who, when, where, and how" of price collection is perhaps best illustrated by certain prepayment programs. These programs, frequently used by services such as transportation, minimize the nonmonetary cost for the consumer and offer bulk

TABLE 8.1   Fare Prepayment Schemes

		Maximum Number of Uses	
		Fixed	**Unlimited**
Duration of Instrument	**Unlimited**	Trip Pass: "Good for 10 Trips" (e.g., Punch Card, Ticket Book)	Nonexpiring Pass —Employees —Senior Citizens Credit Card
	Fixed	Timed Trip Pass: "10 Trips This Week"	Fixed Duration Pass Daily/Monthly Pass

TABLE 8.2   Increasing and Maintaining Program Usage

	Current Regular User	Current Irregular User	Nonuser
Increasing Usage	*Objective:* Get a regular user to travel off-peak more often	*Objective:* Get an irregular user to increase frequency	*Objective:* Generate usage
	Typical program: Unlimited use, fixed time	*Typical program:* Stress discount component of bulk purchase	*Typical program:* Stress reduced monetary and effort costs
Maintaining Usage	*Objective:* Avoid losing a regular user because of a system failure	*Objective:* Stop an irregular user from drifting away	
	Typical program: Fixed use or long fixed duration, unlimited usage	*Typical program:* Bulk discount, ensure fixed duration or use in order to penalize nonuse	Not applicable

discounts, although they also are used to achieve service-related objectives. A simple classification of fare prepayment schemes is shown in Table 8.1. As technology has developed, it has become increasingly possible to use such systems as automatic passes. These passes offer major cost savings in fare collection in that they can be used to operate automatic turnstiles or other entry machines.

In general, the pass program must be designed to minimize the nonmonetary cost to the consumer. However, pass programs also can be used to meet other objectives. Programs can be set up to increase usage or to maintain it. They can be targeted at current regular users, current irregular users, or nonusers. A typical set of objectives is shown in Table 8.2.

CHAPTER 8 READING

Article 8.1 is one of the very few published articles to look at the pricing of services. In particular, it looks at the appropriateness of bundling certain services together and the nature of the bundling. It draws a distinction between pure and mixed bundling. In the former, the services are only available together; in the latter, the services can be bought separately, but a special price is created for the combination. The objective of the article is to identify the conditions under which the different forms of mixed bundling are most likely to be effective.

QUESTIONS

1. How many different airfares would you expect to find for the Los Angeles–New York routes? Consult a price guide and document the range of fares and restrictions. Explain the logic of this fare structure.

2. A hotel will offer discounts from the basic rate for advanced, group, and weekend bookings. Why?

3. Discuss the use of pricing mechanisms to encourage the use of self-service options for consumers. Give examples.

NOTES

1. John Dearden, "Cost Accounting Comes to Service Industries," *Harvard Business Review,* 56 (September–October, 1978): 132–140.

2. *Ibid.*

THE PRICE BUNDLING OF SERVICES
A NORMATIVE FRAMEWORK

Joseph P. Guiltinan

As product lines have broadened in many industries (particularly service industries), the use of mixed price bundling has increased. In mixed price bundling, a firm offers its customers the choice of buying one or more products/services individually or of buying a "bundle" of two or more products or services at a special discount. The author presents a normative framework for selecting appropriate types of services for different mixed-bundling discount forms. The framework extends the economic theory of bundling (which historically has been applied to tie-in sales) to permit explicit consideration of different types of complementarity relationships and strategic marketing objectives.

Broadly defined, *bundling* is the practice of marketing two or more products and/or services in a single "package" for a special price. Certainly this practice is not new to the field of marketing. For years, firms in a number of industries have used such tactics as the block-booking of a set of movies and the sale of maintenance contracts with computer hardware. Economists have been examining the issue of tie-in sales for several decades, primarily to assess the implications of this practice for competition, antitrust law, and consumer welfare (cf. Burstein 1960; Dansby and Conrad 1984; Stigler 1968; Telser 1979). However, the use of bundling appears to have been expanding in recent years, especially for consumer services. For example:

☐ Some banks offer special programs in which customers with large certificates of deposit can obtain credit cards at no annual fee, free traveler's checks, and other services.

☐ Hotels are offering weekend packages that combine lodging and some meals at special rates.

☐ Some health clubs offer access to individual programs (such as aerobics classes, racquetball courts, weight room) and access to packages combining two or more of these activities.

☐ Some car wash operators offer a simple car wash or a car wash with a set of cleaning packages.

☐ Physicians bundle diagnostic tests into their physical examinations.

☐ Airlines routinely bundle vacation packages combining air travel with car rentals and lodging.

From a managerial perspective, the rationale for bundling is based on two realities. First, the cost structure of most service businesses is characterized by a high ratio of fixed to variable costs and by a high degree of cost sharing (such that the same facilities, equipment, and personnel are used to provide multiple services) (Dearden 1978). For example, once an individual establishes a relationship with a financial institution on one product (such as a checking account), the *marginal* cost associated with marketing (e.g., teller sales costs, statement stuffers) or operations (e.g., computer time, teller processing) from selling additional services (such as certificates of deposit) to this individual are generally low in comparison to the firm's total costs.

Second, the services offered by most service businesses are generally interdependent in terms of demand. That is, financial services are designed to meet related consumer needs so that customers often are potential

SOURCE: Joseph P. Guiltinan, "The Price Bundling of Services: A Normative Framework," reprinted with permission from the *Journal of Marketing*, vol. 51 (April 1987): 74–85, published by the American Marketing Association, Chicago, IL 60606.

buyers of a range of services from the same service business. Because of these relationships, service marketers have increasingly accepted the notion that "relationship management" and "systems selling" (efforts to broaden a firm's relationship with its customers) are keys to marketing effectiveness in the service sector.

The effectiveness of price bundling, then, appears to be a function of the degree to which it stimulates demand in a way that achieves cost economies. The broad purpose of this article is to identify the demand conditions under which price bundling can be an effective marketing tool. First, however, because there are several forms of bundling, we must distinguish among the various approaches that can be taken in developing bundles.

APPROACHES TO BUNDLING

One major choice available to decision makers (at least in theory) is whether to employ *pure* or *mixed* bundling. In the former case, the services are available only in bundled form—they cannot be purchased separately. For example, some physicians may insist that a patient seeking a physical exam purchase diagnostic blood and urine testing as well as the traditional personal inspection. Mixed bundling, in contrast, enables the consumer either to purchase one or more of the services individually or to purchase the bundle. (Typically, there is some price incentive for purchasing the bundle.) In other situations, bundling may simply take the form of add-on services. The customer may purchase a single core service (e.g., a car wash) or may select additional amenities (e.g., vacuuming) that are sold only with the core service at a single "bundled" price.

Managers can elect either of two forms of mixed bundling. In *mixed-leader* bundling, the price of one of the two products is discounted when the other product is purchased at the regular price. That is, given P_A and P_B, customers can buy A at P_A^*, (where $P_A > P_A^*$) if B is purchased at P_B. In the *mixed-joint* form, a single price P_{A+B} is set when the two products are purchased jointly (where $P_{A+B} < P_A + P_B$).

OBJECTIVE

The objective of this article is to identify the conditions under which each form of *mixed bundling* is most likely to be effective in pricing services. We are not concerned with tie-in sales (pure bundling) because they have been treated extensively elsewhere and are applicable only in the relatively rare case in which a firm holds monopoly power over one of the components of the bundle.

Our emphasis on services is not meant to suggest that the framework we offer cannot be extended to products. Usually, however, products are the components of a bundle only in the case of *add-on* bundling. As discussed subsequently, add-on bundling is really just a special case of the mixed bundling problem.

Specifically, a framework is provided to determine which combination of services managers should select in forming bundles and whether mixed-leader or mixed-joint bundling is most appropriate for a given combina-

TABLE 1   Economics of Bundling under Independent Demand

| Customer | Reservation Prices ($) | | | Consumer Surplus ($) | |
	RP_A	RP_B	RP_{A+B}	$RP_A - P_A$	$RP_B - P_B$
1	8	1	9	1	—
2[a]	3	6	9	—	2
3	8	7	15	1	3
4	5	2	7	—	—

If P_A = \$7, P_B = \$4, then:

1 buys only A

1 buys only B

3 buys both A and B

4 buys neither A nor B

If P_{A+B} is set at \$9:

1 buys bundle

2 buys bundle[a]

3 buys bundle

4 does not buy

[a]Under independent demand, $RP_{A+B} = RP_A + RP_B$. Thus, customer 2 will buy the bundle even though P_A exceeds RP_A by \$4. The gap $RP_A - P_A$ has been closed; the bundled price (P_{A+B}) provides a discount of \$2 in comparison with the sum of $P_A + P_B$ because customer 2 has a consumer surplus of \$2 from the purchase of B ($RP_B - P_B$ = \$2). In effect, the consumer surplus from B has been transferred to A.

tion. The framework explicitly considers the demand considerations required for the success of a given mixed-bundling program, and recognizes the different strategic purposes for which bundling can be employed. From a managerial perspective, these elements are necessary *extensions* of the basic economic principles of bundling.

ECONOMIC PRINCIPLES OF BUNDLING

Economists began examining bundling as applied to tie-in sales during the 1960s. More recently, Telser (1979) and Schmalensee (1984) examined the rationale for pure and mixed bundling given certain assumptions. As Schmalensee explains (1984, p. 227):

> The advantage of pure bundling is its ability to reduce effective buyer heterogeneity, while the advantage of unbundled sales is its ability to collect a high price for each good from some buyers who care very little for the other. Mixed bundling can make use of both of these advantages by selling the bundle to a group of buyers with accordingly reduced effective heterogeneity, while charging high markups to those on the fringes of the taste distribution who are mainly interested in only one of the two goods.

Consider, for example, a case in which we have two products or services and can estimate the distributions of *reservation prices* (the maximum amounts buyers are willing to pay) for each product. By bundling the products together, we essentially obtain a new product. If the two products are independent in demand, some customers who would buy only one of the products if they were priced individually will now buy both products. The reason is that the value these customers place on one product is so much higher than its price that the combined value of the two products exceeds the bundled price. In economic terminology, the *consumer surplus* (the amount by which the individual's reservation price exceeds the actual price paid) from the highly valued product is transferred to the less valued product.

For example, consider the reservation prices of four customers for product A and product B in Table 1. (Let P_A, P_B, and P_{A+B} represent the prices of A, B, and A and B bundled together in the mixed-joint form.) If bundling is not available, only customer 3 will buy both products because at $P_A = \$7$ and $P_B = \$4$ only customer 3 has a reservation price greater than or equal to both of these prices. However, if customers' reservation prices for the bundle are equal to the sum of the individual reservation prices, then at $P_{A+B} = \$9$ customers 1 and 2 will also purchase the bundle. As shown in Table 1, cus-

tomer 2 has a \$2 consumer surplus on B. When customer 2 is confronted with the chance to buy both A and B at the bundled price, this surplus plus the discount $P_{A+B} - (P_A + P_B)$ provides the motivation to buy the bundle.[1]

EXTENDING THE ECONOMIC RATIONALE

The basic economic rationale for the success of bundling centers on the transfer of consumer surplus. However, because economists have examined bundling primarily in terms of tie-in sales, their analyses traditionally assume that

☐ the seller holds monopoly power at least over one of the elements of the bundle and

☐ the products/services being bundled are independent in demand—an assumption that requires the reservation price for the bundle to equal the sum of reservation prices for the individual products.[2]

In practice, these assumptions do not hold for the typical service firm. The framework presented here therefore differs from the traditional economic rationale in some important respects.

First, we assume the firm is operating in a competitive market. The traditional economic perspective emphasizes the *cross-selling* gains from bundling, and assumes these gains come from customers whose only alternative is to forgo purchase of the second product or service. Our framework explicitly recognizes that bundling can be used to *attract new customers from competitors* and demonstrates how differences in demand elasticity will influence the success of a given service bundle.

Second, we assume that the two services may have a complementary relationship. As demonstrated in Table 2, complementarity implies that the reservation price for one product or service is increased if the other is pur-

---

[1]Schmalensee (1984) examined the relationships among some of the key bundling parameters in detail and concluded that the profitability of bundling is enhanced when the individual reservation price distributions are uncorrelated and symmetric and when the mean reservation price is high in relation to unit cost.

[2]Burstein (1960) does argue that, under pure bundling, tying in sales of a second product will be easier if complementarity is present. However, his analysis is based on the assumption that the seller holds a monopoly position. Given that assumption, he shows that complementarity is desirable but not necessary. Warhit (1980) does examine the problem of choosing between pure bundling and unbundled sales under complementarity. However, because the analysis assumes that there is monopoly power over the tying good (hence the option of pure bundling) and that the tied good has no value except when used with the tying good, it is *not* applicable to the *mixed-bundling* problem.

TABLE 2   Economics of Bundling under Complementary Demand

Customer	Reservation Prices ($)				
	RP_A	RP_B	$RP_{A/B}$	$RP_{B/A}$	RP_{A+B}[a]
1	8	1	8	4	12
2	3	6	3	8	11
3	8	7	8	8	16
4	5	2	5	4	9

In this case, A apparently enhances the value of B and thus B is worth more if A is purchased. At P_{A+B} = $9, economic theory would predict that all four customers purchase the bundle.

[a] $RP_{A+B} = RP_{A/B} + RP_{B/A}$.

chased. That is, the reservation price of B/A (B given A) may exceed the reservation price of B. Therefore the reservation price for the bundle (RP_{A+B}) may *exceed* the sum of the reservation prices for the individual services ($RP_A + RP_B$).[3]

From a managerial viewpoint, this relaxation of the additivity assumption is extremely important. Strict additivity would imply that the *only* mechanism by which bundling can succeed is the transfer of consumer surplus. However, among potential customers who buy neither A nor B, some may have no consumer surplus and for others the amount of the consumer surplus may be very low. By relaxing the additivity assumption, therefore, our framework provides a rationale for bundling that applies to a broader range of situations than would be permitted by the traditional economic rationale.[4]

In sum, for any framework to be managerially useful, it must extend the economic theory of bundling to account fully for the impact of complementarity among services and to facilitate the development of bundling decisions that fit alternative managerial objectives. In the next sections we present the basic elements of such a framework. These elements might be conceptualized as

the following series of steps to be taken in developing price bundles.

1. For a given pair of services under consideration for bundling, define the segment structure and select the *strategic objective.*

2. Given the strategic objective, (a) determine the *demand conditions* required for success (under mixed-leader bundling and under mixed-joint bundling) and (b) determine whether the services under consideration are of the type likely to ensure that the demand conditions will be met.

3. Examine the profitability considerations (including cost factors and displaced sales effects).

SELECTING A STRATEGIC OBJECTIVE

Assume a firm is considering developing a bundle of services A and B. (A and/or B may be new or available services, but we illustrate the case for available services as it is the most comprehensive in terms of the analyses required). Figure 1 shows the possible consequences of mixed bundling in terms of potential revenue changes. There are four basic segments (sources of customers) for the bundle, each of which is characterized by a different set of reservation price distributions.

☐ Segment 1: customers who buy A but not B

☐ Segment 2: customers who buy B but not A

☐ Segment 3: customers who already buy B and A

☐ Segment 4: noncustomers

Strategically, our hypothetical firm could attempt to draw customers to the bundle from all four potential segments. If our strategic objective were *cross-selling*, we would target our effort toward either segment 1 or seg-

[3]Indeed, the assumption of demand independence calls into question the transferability of consumer surplus. that is, given services A and B, unless these services are complements there seems no compelling reason to assume that any current consumer surplus on A would be transferred to B rather than to some other product C. If A and B are complements, such a transfer is more likely.

[4]Kinberg and Sudit (1979) and Dansby and Conrad (1984) show that the utility of a bundle also can be less than the sum of the individual components' reservation prices when certain restrictions are imposed on the use of the bundle. For example, special airfare and hotel bundles may be available only with certain restrictions on the timing of travel.

FIGURE 1   Possible Customer Flows Resulting from
Mixed Bundling of A and B

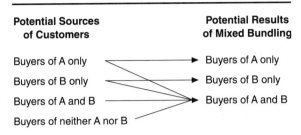

ment 2, or toward both segments. If our objective were the *acquisition of new customers,* we would focus on segment 4, seeking new customers for A and B simultaneously. Finally, in certain situations bundling can be used to achieve a *retention* objective and segment 3 would be the target. Usually, however, segment 3 is only important because bundles targeted to the first two segments or to the fourth segment may also be available to and accepted by customers who already purchase both services, resulting in reduced profits from this segment.

To understand how these objectives can be achieved, we begin by examining what the segments mean and what changes must occur to achieve the objectives. Table 3 gives a basic economic explanation for each segment. In effect, it provides an explanation of the demand schedules for Services A and B at the prevailing prices offered by our firm (P_A and P_B) and by our competition (P_C and P_D).

Specifically, there are two important elements to Table 3. First, managers may not yet know what the full distributions of reservation prices for A and B look like. However, they *do* know or usually can estimate the *demand levels* (in the absence of bundling) within each segment during a specific period of time. This information is important (as discussed in the next section) to the selection of a mixed-bundling *form.*

Second, the explanations of each segment enable us to decipher the *demand responses* required to change behavior. Consider, for example, the A-only buyers. To convert these buyers we know (from Table 3) that we must somehow close the gap between P_B and $RP_{B/A}$ in the case where the customer is not buying a service competing with B. Similarly, in the case where a customer buys A from us but buys service D from a competitor (a pattern common among consumers of financial services), we need to make our service more attractive relative to its price than our competitor does, so that $(RP_{B/A} - P_B) > (RP_D - P_D)$. Combined with the information on demand levels, an understanding of the

required demand response indicates the specific demand conditions necessary for success for a given strategic objective (as the following sections demonstrate).

Our primary focus from this point on is the mixed bundling of services when the strategic objective is either to *cross-sell* current customers who buy one (but not both) services or to *acquire new customers* from the set of potential buyers not purchasing either service. For simplicity and to avoid confusing bundling effects with quantity discount effects, we assume that buyers purchase only one "unit" of a service on each purchase occasion. Thus, demand effects are limited to changes in the number of buyers for each service or bundle. Further, we assume that the services are either frequently purchased or purchased under continuing repurchase arrangements (e.g., checking accounts).[5]

DEMAND CONDITIONS FOR CROSS-SELLING

DEMAND LEVELS

Cross-selling is the primary objective of bundling when the strategic focus is customers who purchase A or B but not both.

Let

UQ_{A+B} = quantity sold of both A and B with unbundled sales

UQ_A = quantity sold of A only with unbundled sales

UQ_B = quantity sold of B only with unbundled sales

BQ_{A+B} = quantity of bundles sold

BQ_A = quantity sold of A only with mixed bundling

BQ_B = quantity sold of B only with mixed bundling

$RP_{A/B}$ = conditional reservation price of A given B

$RP_{B/A}$ = conditional reservation price of B given A

In examining cross-selling opportunities, an important consideration is the relative unbundled demand levels for A and B. That is, if UQ_A is substantially greater than UQ_B, then under *mixed-leader* bundling A normally will be the best leader: a reduced price for A is tied to the purchase of B. For example, if a bank has 10,000 credit card accounts and only 1000 accounts with $5000 or more in certificates of deposit, the credit card

[5]The analysis presented here is directly extendable to nondurable goods. Extensions to durable goods would require explicit consideration of an additional factor: the potential of bundling to reduce the time between the sales of a main durable and add-on products and services.

TABLE 3   Explanations of Segments under Unbundled Sales

Buyers of A only

$P_A \leq RP_A$ and

$P_B > RP_{B/A}$ or $0 \leq (RP_{B/A} - P_B) < (RP_D - P_D)$

Buyers of B only

$P_B \leq RP_B$ and

$P_A > RP_{A/B}$ or $0 \leq (RP_{A/B} - P_A) < (RP_C - P_C)$

Buyers of A and B

$P_A \leq RP_{A/B}$ and

$P_B \leq RP_{B/A}$

Buyers of Neither A nor B

$P_A > RP_A$ and $P_B > RP_B$

or

$(RP_B - P_B) < 0 \leq (RP_A - P_A) < (RP_C - P_C)$

or

$(RP_A - P_A) < 0 \leq (RP_B - P_B) < (RP_D - P_D)$

or

$0 \leq (RP_{A/B} + RP_{B/A} - P_A - P_B) < (RP_{C/D} + RP_{D/C} - P_C - P_D)$

where C, D are competing services—C competing with A and D competing with B

---

generally will be the better leader. In this case, the bank would have many *more* opportunities to develop certificate of deposit accounts among credit card customers than to develop new credit card customers among the deposit certificate clientele.

When UQ_A and UQ_B are approximately equal, the volume gains from bundling can be approximately equal in either direction. However, the greater potential gain comes if A-only buyers buy B *and* B-only buyers buy A. Whereas mixed-leader bundling generally encourages one-directional gains, *mixed-joint* bundling seems more appropriate when such bidirectional gains are needed. For example, a health club may have a number of customers who only purchase aerobic classes and an equal number who only purchase use of the weight room. A bundling scheme that provides a discount on the *total* cost of the two services (i.e., mixed-joint bundling) would maximize the number of cross-selling opportunities.

DEMAND RESPONSE AND COMPLEMENTARITY

When a cross-selling objective is being pursued, the key to effective demand response to bundling is the degree and type of complementarity among services. As discussed before, when the services in a bundle are complements, the likelihood that any current consumer surplus on one service will be transferred to the other service is enhanced and strict additivity of reservation prices is not necessary.

The issue of complementarity has received scant direct attention in marketing. However, the selection of services to be bundled and the selection of a bundling form (mixed-leader vs. mixed-joint) require some assessment of the type as well as the extent of complementarity. Oxenfeldt (1966) identified eight possible sources of complementary demand and categorized them into three types of complementarity relationships.

☐ Products/services that are complements because of economies in time and effort from purchasing them together.

☐ Products/services that enhance customers' levels of satisfaction with other products.

☐ Products/services that enhance the overall image of the seller so that all products are valued more highly.

Oxenfeldt's propositions have not been subject to empirical testing. However, this typology has direct implications for bundling.

SEARCH ECONOMIES When complementarity is due to search economies, the real cost to the consumer is reduced. For example, most motorists will appreciate the convenience of having an oil change performed by the same service station or dealer they select to perform an engine tune-up. Consequently, the motorist may be willing to pay slightly more for the oil change or for the tune-up once the decision to purchase *one* of these services from a specific firm has been made. Thus, $(RP_{B/A} > RP_B)$ and/or $(RP_{A/B} > RP_A)$.

ENHANCED CUSTOMER SATISFACTION When one service enhances customer satisfaction with another, the complementarity is one-way. That is, if B enhances A but not vice versa, $RP_{A/B} > RP_A$ but $RP_{B/A} = RP_B$. This relation implies that $RP_{A+B} > RP_A + RP_B$, but only because of the enhancement generated by B. Thus B can be tied to the leader A but not vice versa, and mixed-leader bundling can work if A is the leader (i.e., P_A is reduced). Consider, for instance, a ski resort that offers a ski rental and lessons package. The reservation price for the lessons (RP_B) is likely to be the same whether or not skis are rented because their value depends on the skills and the needs of the skier. However, the reservation price of the ski rental will be enhanced (so that $RP_{A/B} > RP_A$), at least for persons with no skiing experience, if lessons can be acquired.

IMPROVED TOTAL IMAGE Services that provide an improved total image for the firm as the basis for complementarity can be viewed as bidirectional in their effects. Inherent in this statement is the suggestion that synergies are present among such services so that $RP_{B/A} > RP_B$ and $RP_{A/B} > RP_A$. Thus, a financial consultant who offers both investment advice and tax preparation services enhances his or her credibility in both services. Similarly, a firm offering lawn care services and shrub care services is likely to find that each service complements the other.

Given the unbundled demand levels for A and B and given the complementarity typology developed by Oxenfeldt, the specific demand conditions for cross-selling can be presented.

CROSS-SELLING/MIXED-LEADER CASE

Equation 1 in Table 4 represents the demand conditions required for the success of cross-selling/mixed-leader bundling. If we assume that A is already regularly or continuously purchased by a number of customers of a service firm, and that $UQ_A > UQ_B$, then A is the leader. The managerial issue in the cross-selling/mixed-leader case is how to close the gap $(P_B - RP_{B/A})$. Among customers who buy competing service D instead of B, the gap is $(RP_D - P_D) + (P_B - RP_{B/A})$. Theoretically, the gap can be closed in one of four ways:

1. Direct transfer of any current consumer surplus $(RP_A - P_A)$ from service A to service B.
2. A price reduction on the leader $(P_A - P_A^*)$ that increases the consumer surplus on A.
3. Selection of B so as to enhance the utility of A (so that $RP_{A/B} > RP_A$).
4. Selection of B so as to create search economies when it is purchased with A, reducing the real cost of B and thus reducing $(P_B - RP_{B/A})$.

As discussed before, one-directional complementarity is desirable for cross-selling because it would enhance the likelihood that the current consumer surplus or any surplus created by a price reduction on the leader would be transferred to the second service. Additionally, if B enhances the utility (reservation price) of A, the chances of buying the bundle increase.

Recall the example of the ski rentals and lessons. A price reduction on the rentals would increase the consumer surplus available on this service. However, the odds of gaining widespread purchases of lessons in return for a lower rental fee are increased because the consumer surplus on rentals is very likely to be transferable to lessons and because lessons enhance the utility of rentals.

CROSS-SELLING/MIXED-JOINT CASE

Equation 2A or 2B in Table 4 represents the demand conditions for this case, depending on whether A or B is already purchased. If A is already purchased, equation 2A applies. Here the customers' decision is whether to continue buying only A and receiving the current consumer surplus $(RP_A - P_A)$ or to buy the bundle. If these customers are to add B, the current gap $(RP_D - P_D) + (P_B - RP_{B/A})$ must be closed, which is possible only if B enhances A and/or if the price of A + B is sufficiently reduced. As suggested before, the mixed-joint approach is more appropriate when UQ_A and UQ_B are about equal, so that *bidirectional* gains are desired. Such gains are clearly more likely to occur to the extent that bidirectional complementarity is present between the two services.

Recall the example of the health club with a large number of members who purchase only an aerobics membership and a comparable number who purchase only a weight room membership. With no obvious

TABLE 4   Demand Conditions Required for Purchase of Bundles

Cross-Selling/Mixed-Leader

(1) $(RP_{A/B} - RP_A) + (RP_A - P_A) + (P_A - P_A^*) \geq (RP_D - P_D) + (P_B - RP_{B/A})$

Cross-Selling/Mixed-Joint

(2A) $(RP_{A/B} - RP_A) + (RP_A - P_A) + (P_A + P_B - P_{A+B}) \geq (RP_D - P_D) + (P_B - RP_{B/A})$

or

(2B) $(RP_{B/A} - RP_B) + (RP_B - P_B) + (P_A + P_B - P_{A+B}) \geq (RP_C - P_C) + (P_A - RP_{A/B})$

Customer Acquisition/Mixed-Leader

(3) $(RP_{A/B} - RP_A) + (RP_{B/A} - RP_B) + (P_A - P_A^*) \geq (RP_{C/D} + RP_{D/C} - P_C - P_D) + (P_A - RP_A) + (P_B - RP_B)$

Customer Acquisition/Mixed-Joint

(4) $(RP_{A/B} - RP_A) + (RP_{B/A} - RP_B) + (P_A + P_B - P_{A+B}) \geq (RP_{C/D} + RP_{D/C} - P_{C+D}) + (P_A - RP_A) + (P_B - RP_B)$

If C is not purchased, $(RP_C - P_C) = (RP_{C/D} - P_C) = 0$

If D is not purchased, $(RP_D - P_D) = (RP_{D/C} - P_D) = 0$

leader, the club must develop a combination membership for both aerobics and the weight room in the hope of simultaneously cross-selling both groups. Though some increase in sales of the two services usually can be anticipated if a sizable discount is offered, the magnitude of the increase will depend on the degree to which the two services are viewed as mutually reinforcing so that $RP_{A/B} > RP_A$ and $RP_{B/A} > RP_B$.

DEMAND CONDITIONS FOR CUSTOMER ACQUISITION

Customer acquisition is the primary bundling objective when the strategic focus is potential new customers—those buying neither A nor B. The following conditions distinguish these potential customers.

1.   Within the target segment, $UQ_A = UQ_B = 0$, so there is no way to define a "leader" on the basis of unbundled sales levels.

2.   Because customers currently buy neither A nor B, conditional reservation prices $(RP_{A/B}, RP_{B/A})$ are not likely to be strongly established.

3.   Noncustomers include those for whom $P_A > RP_A$ and $P_B > RP_B$ (in which case there is no current consumer surplus) as well as those for whom $RP_A \geq P_A$ and/or $RP_B \geq P_B$ but who purchase competing services C or D (see Table 3).

Given these conditions, managers attempting to select bundles to achieve a customer acquisition objective must rely more heavily on the price discount ele-

ment of bundling than they would if cross-selling were the objective. That is, the role of price bundling in this case is to create a consumer surplus where none is present or to provide a consumer surplus that rivals the surplus obtainable from competing providers. Accordingly, managers must examine the price elasticity of demand of potential candidates for bundling.

ELASTICITY

Economics of information theory (or search theory) provides a paradigm for examining elasticity of demand. Essentially, this theory recognizes that price sensitivity depends on the number of alternatives about which the customer is knowledgeable. The more costly it is to acquire information (relative to the expected gains of information), the fewer the number of alternatives about which consumers inform themselves and the more inelastic the demand curve (cf. Goldman and Johansson 1978; Nelson 1970). Work by Nelson (1970), Darby and Karni (1973), and Wilde (1980) indicates that the number of alternatives about which a consumer is knowledgeable depends on whether the benefits can be conveyed by search, experience, or credence attributes where:

☐ search attributes (characteristics) are those that can be evaluated before purchase (such as savings account interest, air travel time, or seat location at a play).

☐ experience attributes are those that cannot be evaluated until after a service has been received (e.g., a haircut, the effectiveness of a rug cleaning service, or the music at an opera), and

☐ credence attributes are those that cannot be evaluated confidently immediately after receipt (e.g., legal advice, a physical examination, or an education).

The implication of being able to type a service or a bundle of services into these categories is that demand is more likely to be elastic for services in which the salient attributes are search attributes. Moreover, the cost of switching from one service provider to another will be lower relative to the gains from switching for search-based attributes than for experience/credence-based attributes.

Two important distinctions among types of services seem to be of use in determining whether the salient attributes are search-oriented. First, Rathmell (1969) and Thomas (1979) have suggested that equipment-based services differ from human-based services. Similarly, Lovelock (1983) distinguished services in terms of the "degree to which contact personnel exercise judgment" in providing the service. A second distinction discussed by Lovelock is the degree of customization of the service.

Lovelock did not explicitly link these distinctions to any pricing implications. Nevertheless, it is argued that the salient service attributes are more likely to be search-oriented if services are not customized and if the personnel involved in delivery need not exercise judgment. Conversely, higher degrees of customization and personal judgment increase the difficulty of evaluating alternatives and, thus, imply that the salient attributes are experience/credence-oriented.

These distinctions have direct implications for selecting services for bundles. Specifically, the *direct price effects* of bundling will be more effective in the following situations.

1. *Customer acquisition/mixed leader.* Here, the "lead" service must be demand elastic and therefore should have salient attributes that are search-based.

2. *Customer acquisition/mixed-joint.* Because target consumers own neither product, they must evaluate P_{A+B} against the total utility of the bundle. Hence, the greater the degree to which the total bundle is composed of search attributes, the greater the impact of a lower price on the success of a bundling strategy.

By combining the elasticity considerations with the complementarity typology discussed before, we can articulate the conditions for success of each form of bundling for the strategic objective of acquiring new customers.

CUSTOMER ACQUISITION/ MIXED-LEADER CASE

Equation 3 in Table 4 identifies the relevant evaluation. Because there is no consumer surplus, the gap created by current reservation prices and the prices charged for A, B, C, and D must be overcome by a combination of the price effect (which will be greater if demand for the chosen "leader" is elastic) and the complementarity effect. Specifically, because A is the leader, the primary complementarity effect of concern is $RP_{A/B} - RP_A$. That is, A must be worth more if B also is purchased from the same source than A would be worth if purchased alone. (Recall that the customer must also purchase B to get the discount $P_A - P_A^*$ in mixed-leader bundling).

In the selection of candidates for bundling in this situation, if A is the leader, A should be price elastic (composed primarily of search attributes) and B must complement A. If A is composed primarily of search attributes, those attributes are not likely to be enhanced easily by bundling A with a credence/experience-based product or service. Thus, complementarity probably must derive from the degree to which B enhances the search attributes of A, or from search economies between B and A. For example, many credit unions offer free traveler's checks (and often other services) to members who set up share draft (checking) accounts. Because both of these services are essentially composed of search attributes, demand for the leader (traveler's checks) can be assumed to be somewhat elastic and there are search economies from having both services available in the same location.

CUSTOMER ACQUISITION/ MIXED-JOINT CASE

The demand conditions required for success in this case are represented in equation 4 of Table 4. Because the customer must evaluate the total package (A + B), the gap between prices and reservation prices can be overcome only if the price discount for the bundle generates a large gain in bundled sales or if the products have strong complementary relationships so that the reservation price for the bundle exceeds the sum of the individual reservation prices. (The latter situation is more likely if bidirectional complementarity is present so that $RP_{A/B} > RP_A$ and $RP_{B/A} > RP_B$.) Thus, this policy may be effective for two types of bundles:

☐ where both products are composed of search attributes, so demand tends to be elastic and search cost economies create complements (e.g., air travel/car rental packages), and

□ where bidirectional complementary relationships are strong but have not been established previously in the customers' minds. By implication, bidirectional complementarity based on enhanced total image will be present if the two products/services are composed primarily of experience-based or credence-based attributes (e.g., financial counseling and tax preparation services).

PROFITABILITY CONSIDERATIONS

Table 5 summarizes the basic profit equations for bundled and unbundled sales. If we assume most bundling offers will be accessible to current customers, the profit effects of bundling will depend largely on the extent of cannibalization due to

□ reduced profit margins among customers already buying both A and B and

□ reduced numbers (though at the same margins) of A-only and/or B-only buyers.[6]

Any reduction in the number of A-only and B-only buyers presumably occurs because these buyers now purchase the bundle. However, it is important to recognize that if $P_A - C_A$ and $P_B - C_B$ are unequal, the profit consequences of bundling may be decidedly different depending on whether the bundle results in larger sales gains in the segment now buying A only or in the segment now buying B only. That is, within these two segments, the profitability of a bundle is enhanced if the *larger increase* in bundled sales comes from the segment that previously bought only the *lower margin* product.

Accordingly, the selection of services for the bundle should be based on the following criteria.

1. Select A and B where UQ_{A+B} (the quantity of A and B sold without bundling) is small to minimize cannibalization effects.

2. Even if cross-selling is the primary objective, selecting products that also generate new customers for

both A and B will help offset cannibalization effects.[7]

3. In *mixed-leader* bundling, the leader should be the lower margin product. That is, if A is the leader, $(P_A^* - C_A)$ should be less than $(P_B - C_B)$. The logic here is that displacement effects of cannibalization are more likely to occur on A, assuming A is the leader, because UQ_A is greater than UQ_B.

4. Mixed-joint bundling will be more attractive when the margins of the two services are about equal and when the unbundled sales volumes (UQ_A and UQ_B) are about equal. Under these conditions, there is no profitability imperative for emphasizing a single direction for gains in sales of the bundle.

To contrast the situations in criteria 3 and 4, assume that a financial institution is looking for a service to bundle with its trust service. Normally, trust accounts are highly profitable but are fewer in number than most other types of accounts offered by banks or savings institutions. For example, a bank is likely to have more safe deposit box customers and to earn much less on each safe deposit box account. Consequently, if trust services and safe deposit boxes were offered in a bundle, *mixed-leader* bundling should be used with safe deposit boxes as the leader. In contrast, *mixed-joint* bundling will be more appropriate if trust services are to be bundled with other services (such as very large denomination certificates of deposit) for which the number of accounts and average account profitability are comparable to those of trust services.

These profitability calculations and criteria apply basically to the cross-selling situation. However, criterion 3 should be interpreted with care, depending on the strategic objective for which mixed-leader bundling is used. Frequently, managers will select a "tied" product (B) that they believe is very likely to be purchased in order to obtain savings on the leader (A) because the value of B is very low in relation to the value of A, yet B complements A. (Indeed, Burstein 1960, pp. 72–73, argues that this is a characteristic of the *ideal* tied good under pure bundling.) However, if the price of A greatly exceeds the price of B, the absolute size of the profit margin on A is likely to exceed that of B. If this is true, and if cross-selling is the object (so $UQ_A > UQ_B$), the

---

[6]Specifically, the profitability of each *form* of bundling can be assessed as follows. Under *mixed-leader* bundling the expected gain is

$$(P_A^* + P_B - C_A - C_B)(BQ_{A+B} - UQ_{A+B})$$

and the expected loss is

$$(P_A - C_A)(UQ_A - BQ_A) + (P_B - C_B)(UQ_B - BQ_B)$$
$$+ (P_A - P_A^*)UQ_{A+B}$$

Under mixed-joint bundling the expected gain is

$$(P_{A+B} - C_A - C_B)(BQ_{A+B} - UQ_{A+B})$$

and the expected loss is

$$(P_A - C_A)(UQ_A - BQ_A) + (P_B - C_B)(UQ_B - BQ_B)$$
$$+ (P_A + P_B - P_{A+B})UQ_{A+B}$$

[7]In examining profitability, managers should recognize that sometimes the effect of bundling may be simply to speed up cross-selling that would have occurred anyway at some future period. There also may be important future gains on sales of other products and services not in the bundle resulting from the acquisition of new products.

TABLE 5   Calculating Short-Run Profit Effects of Bundling

ZB = total profit with mixed bundling

ZU = total profit with unbundled sales

$UQ_{A + B}$ = quantity sold of both A and B with unbundled sales

UQ_A = quantity sold of A only with unbundled sales

UQ_B = quantity sold of B only with unbundled sales

$BQ_{A + B}$ = quantity of bundle sold

BQ_A = quantity sold of A only with mixed bundling

BQ_B = quantity sold of B only with mixed bundling

P_A = price of A

P_B = price of B

$P_{A + B}$ = price of bundle

C_A = cost of A per unit

C_B = cost of B per unit

$C_{A + B}$ = cost of bundle per unit

Then:

(1) $ZB = (P_{A + B} - C_{A + B})BQ_{A + B} + (P_A - C_A)BQ_A + (P_B - C_B)BQ_B$

(2) $ZU = (P_A - C_A)(UQ_A + UQ_{A + B}) + (P_B - C_B)(UQ_B + UQ_{A + B})$

resulting gain in bundled sales may well be unprofitable because

$$(UQ_A - BQ_A)(P_A - P_A^\star)$$
$$> (BQ_{A + B} + BQ_B - UQ_{A + B} - UQ_B)(P_B - C_B).$$

That is, the displaced profit from the reduced price of A will exceed the increased profit accruing from added sales of B—at least within the A-only segment. As an extreme example, it generally would not pay a financial institution to reduce the price of trust services or loans to *current* accounts in order to tie in the purchase of traveler's checks. Even a modest reduction in the rate charged for those services would more than offset any potential profit gains from new traveler's check sales for the typical customer.

However, when the objective of mixed-leader bundling is to *acquire new customers* and the bundling offer can be restricted to noncustomers, no sales are displaced. Thus, the rather commonplace practice of bundling add-ons and other minor services to a main product or service generally is justified more easily in the customer acquisition/mixed-leader case than in the cross-selling/mixed-leader case.

SELECTING A BUNDLING FORM

We have summarized the basic demand conditions that must be met if a bundling program is to change the purchase behavior of a customer in the desired direction

(cross-selling vs. new customer acquisition) for each mixed-bundling form (mixed-leader vs. mixed-joint). The strategic task involved in bundling is to identify pairs of services/products that are most likely to meet these conditions. As we have attempted to demonstrate, the likelihood of simultaneously meeting the demand conditions and limiting the effects of displaced sales depends on

☐ sales volume in the absence of a bundling program (UQ_A, UQ_B, $UQ_{A + B}$),

☐ relative profitability ($P_A - C_A$, $P_B - C_B$),

☐ demand elasticities for A, B, and A + B, and

☐ the extent and nature of the complementarity between A and B.

Table 6 summarizes the specific conditions under which each type of bundling program is most likely to be successful. In addition to these specific conditions, a general condition is that $UQ_{A + B}$ be small in order to minimize displacement effects. Though a relatively high level of $UQ_{A + B}$ would seem to indicate a strong natural complementarity, in such a case the need for a bundling program may not be great and the profit gains realized may be minor.

ADD-ON BUNDLING

Add-on bundling is not strictly a mixed-bundling option because, by definition, an add-on service is one

TABLE 6   Conditions Leading to Success of Bundling Programs

Cross-Selling/Mixed-Leader

$UQ_A > UQ_B$

$(P_A - C_A) < (P_B - C_B)$

Large consumer surplus on A

B enhances value of A and/or search economies reduce the real cost of B

Cross-Selling/Mixed-Joint

$UQ_A = UQ_B$

$(P_A - C_AA) = (P_B - C_B)$

Each customer has large consumer surplus on A or on B

Bidirectional complementarity between A and B due either to enhanced image of seller or to joint search economies

Customer Acquisition/Mixed-Leader

If A is leader, demand for A elastic

B and A complements because of search economies or enhanced value

A valued much more highly than B

Customer Acquisition/Mixed-Joint

Demand for A + B elastic (both A and B composed primarily of search attributes)

Strong bidirectional complementarity (or it can be established) between A and B

that will not be purchased unless the lead service is purchased. In other words, if A is the lead service (e.g., a car wash) and B is an add-on service (e.g., extra wax), the customer's options are limited to purchasing A only or A + B. Moreover, add-on bundling implies that A and B are purchased contemporaneously at a special price. Thus, add-on bundling *excludes* those bundling situations in which B has a distinct utility, even in the absence of A. (For example, if A is a car wash and B is vacuuming, one can acquire B separately, in both spatial and temporal terms, from A. This case would be an example of mixed bundling.) Add-on bundling, then, has the following key features.

1.   Because the customer must choose between A and A + B (i.e., buying B only is not an option), $P_B = 0$ and the *mixed-joint* form is the only feasible bundling approach.

2.   Because B has no value independent of A, $RP_B = 0$. Moreover, $RP_{B/A} = RP_B$ because complementarity must be unidirectional in the add-on case.

3.   Most add-on services will be so intertwined with the lead service that split relationships among service providers are not feasible. Thus (from Table 4), D can be purchased only with C, and B only with A.

Given the foregoing features, the demand conditions for add-on bundling can be derived from those presented for mixed-joint bundling in Table 4. Specifically, equations 2A and 4 provide the basic demand conditions applicable to add-on bundling. (Recall that only the mixed-joint form is applicable.) However, given the features of add-on bundling, these equations can be reduced.

$$RP_{A/B} \geq P_{A+B} \qquad (2A)$$
$$RP_{A/B} \geq P_{A+B} + (RP_{C/D} + RP_{D/C} - P_{C+D}) \quad (4)$$

METHODOLOGICAL CONSIDERATIONS

Operationally, a firm ultimately must decide on a specific price discount. A knowledge of specific costs, elasticity and cross-elasticity (where data permit), and reservation price distributions (including conditional reservation price distributions) would be desirable.

Gabor and Granger (1965) and others before them have argued that direct responses to the question, "What is the most you would be willing to pay?", provide useful and generally reliable information on reservation prices. Alternatively, various tradeoff techniques have been used to determine the differences in imputed value between products or bundles of products providing different combinations of benefits or characteristics (cf. Goldberg, Green, and Wind 1984 and previous research in this area by Green and other coauthors). The latter approach does not attempt to measure reservation prices directly, but rather attempts to measure preferences for various levels of price/characteristic combinations. Because of these different objectives, one might use both measures—with reservation price estimates helping define the specific price levels selected for a preference study.

When managers attempt to measure reservation prices or to use tradeoff procedures for bundling, they should recognize several key factors. First, as mentioned before, the range of prices that a consumer will find acceptable is not independent of the consumer's awareness of the prices currently available for products or services of comparable value (Monroe 1973). For infrequently purchased products and services, a consumer's price awareness is usually lower and, in the absence of any reference price information, the reservation price may be understated (Gabor and Granger 1965). Consequently, direct estimates of reservation prices may be less reliable when (1) products or services are new and/or infrequently purchased and/or (2) the product or bundle is so unique that consumers have difficulty in determining reference prices.

Second, the results of direct response questions on reservation prices and of tradeoff analyses can be confounded easily by individual and/or situational factors. Reservation prices and elasticities of demand can vary among socioeconomic groups and the effects of situational factors are well documented (Dickson 1982). Because procedures for addressing these confounding effects are available (cf. Gabor and Granger 1965; Green and DeSarbo 1979), they do not present insurmountable problems if recognized prior to measurement.

Finally, the most problematic issue is likely to derive from the nature of services. Particularly when experience- or credence-based services are involved, it is not a simple matter to define levels of salient characteristics for use in tradeoff analyses.[8] Further, responses to direct questions about reservation prices would be more reliable if one could be assured that all customers have a common perception of the levels of benefits (characteristics) that might be available from services such as investment counseling or preventive health care pro-

grams. To our knowledge, this issue has not been addressed directly by pricing researchers.

CONCLUSION

Pricing decisions long have been dominated by cost-based and "follow-the-leader" considerations, even when marketing managers have a key role in the decision making process. (Zeithaml, Parasuraman, and Berry 1985 found that cost was reported as the dominant basis for pricing in their study of service firms. However, the pervasiveness of competitor-oriented pricing in services is obvious in many industries, including airline travel, movie theaters, and banking.) To the extent that firms (particularly those in financial, health care, hospitality, and other service industries) expand their product lines, these simplistic approaches will be less effective for two reasons. First, as the number of products and services offered increases, the opportunities for differentiation are enhanced and the utility of follow-the-leader approaches is reduced. Second, the high ratio of fixed to variable costs that characterizes service businesses makes average costing increasingly arbitrary, because indirect cost allocations will change as the product mix changes.

The framework developed here provides some guidance for the potential use of price bundling by a firm with a broad line of complementary products. In effect, the framework can serve as a screening model for selecting potential bundles. Additionally, it gives managers criteria to use in developing any concept tests or market tests that may be feasible. The framework stresses the importance of developing price bundles within the context of clear strategic marketing objectives and with some analysis of the demand requirements of the specific bundling program. It is hoped that the framework will encourage greater consideration of these factors in other types of pricing decisions.

REFERENCES

Adams, W. J., and J. L. Yellen (1976), "Commodity Bundling and the Burden of Monopoly," *Quarterly Journal of Economics,* 90 (August), 475–498.

Burstein, M. L. (1960), "The Economics of Tie-In Sales," *Review of Economics and Statistics,* 42 (February), 68–73.

Dansby, Robert E., and Cecilia Conrad (1984), "Commodity Bundling," *American Economic Review,* 74 (May), 377–381.

Darby, Michael R., and Edi Karni (1973), "Free Competition and the Optimal Amount of Fraud," *Journal of Law and Economics,* 16 (April), 67–88.

Dearden, John (1978), "Cost Accounting Comes to Service Industries," *Harvard Business Review,* 56 (September–October), 132–140.

---

[8]Essentially, this is a problem of defining "service quality." For an expanded discussion, see Parasuraman, Zeithaml, and Berry (1985).

Dickson, Peter (1982), "Person-Situation: Segmentation's Missing Link," *Journal of Marketing*, 56 (Fall), 56–64.

Gabor, Andre, and C. W. J. Granger (1965) "The Pricing of New Products," *Scientific Business,* 10 (August), 141–150.

Goldberg, Stephen, Paul E. Green, and Yoram Wind (1984), "Conjoint Analysis of Price Premiums for Hotel Amenities," *Journal of Business,* 57 (January), 111–132.

Goldman, Arieh, and Johnny K. Johansson (1978), "Determinants of Search for Lower Prices: An Empirical Assessment of the Economics of Information," *Journal of Consumer Research,* 4 (December), 176–186.

Green, Paul, and Wayne S. DeSarbo (1979), "Componential Segmentation in the Analysis of Consumer Trade-offs," *Journal of Marketing,* 43 (Fall) 43, 83–91.

Kinberg, Yoram, and Ephraim F. Sudit (1979), "Country/Service Bundling in International Tourism: Criteria for the Selection of an Efficient Bundle Mix and Allocation of Joint Revenues," *Journal of International Business Studies,* 10 (Fall), 51–63.

Lovelock, Christopher (1983), "Classifying Services to Gain Strategic Marketing Insights," *Journal of Marketing,* 47 (Summer), 9–20.

Monroe, Kent (1973), "Buyer's Subjective Perceptions of Price," *Journal of Marketing Research,* 10 (February), 70–80.

———, and A. A. Zoltners (1979), "Pricing the Product Line During Periods of Scarcity," *Journal of Marketing,* 43 (Summer), 49–59.

Nelson, Philip (1970), "Information and Consumer Behavior," *Journal of Political Economy,* 78 (March–April), 311–329.

Oxenfeldt, Alfred (1966), "Product Line Pricing," *Harvard Business Review,* 44 (July–August), 135–143.

Parasuraman, A., Valarie A. Zeithaml, and Leonard L. Berry (1985), "A Conceptual Model of Service Quality and Its Implications for Future Research," *Journal of Marketing,* 49 (Fall), 41–50.

Rathmell, John (1974), *Marketing in the Service Sector.* Cambridge, MA: Winthrop Publishing.

Schmalensee, Richard (1984), "Gaussian Demand and Commodity Bundling," *Journal of Business,* 57 (January), 211–230.

Stigler, G. J. (1968), "A Note on Block Booking," in *The Organization of Industry.* Homewood, IL: Richard D. Irwin, Inc.

Telser, L. G. (1979), "A Theory of Monopoly of Complementary Goods," *Journal of Business,* 52 (April), 211–230.

Thomas, Dan R. E. (1979), "Strategy Is Different in Service Businesses," *Harvard Business Review,* 57 (July–August), 158–165.

Warhit, Ellen (1980), "The Economics of Tie-in Sales," *Atlantic Economic Journal,* 8 (December), 81–88.

Wilde, Louis (1980), "The Economics of Consumer Information Acquisition," *Journal of Business,* 53 (July), S143–S158.

Zeithaml, Valarie, A. Parasuraman, and Leonard L. Berry (1985), "Problems and Strategies in Services Marketing," *Journal of Marketing,* 49 (Spring), 33–46.

PART THREE

MARKETING IMPLEMENTATION

COMPETING AS A SERVICE FIRM I
GENERIC COMPETITIVE STRATEGIES

CHAPTER OVERVIEW

This chapter provides the framework for the whole of this section of the book, which deals with competition. It suggests that, when competing in the marketplace, a service firm has a broad range of alternatives available to it. Fundamentally, however, it first must create an economically viable service formula on which to build.

Once the formula exists, depending on the restrictions imposed by the nature of the service, the firm can employ any of the following strategies separately or together. Competing for share can take place in one or many markets at the same time and can involve expansion of both the services offered and the segments served. It also requires consideration of the other strategies described in this section; service firms must compete to retain customers (Chapter 10), to recover from service failures and capitalize on them (Chapter 11), to create the highest levels of service quality (Chapter 12), and to become customer focused (Chapter 13).

Competing for reach is the major thrust for those firms that succeed by attracting customers to travel to their fixed sites. Hotels and tourist attractions compete by their reach into as many markets as possible.

Competing for geography is based on the twin premises that service formulas are often easy to copy and that being second to enter into a market is a disadvantage. Success, therefore, comes from rapid geographic expansion using multiple sites.

The major constraint on the use of multiple sites is the potential loss of focus. Complexity increases as the number of sites, segments, services, and countries increases. Unless carefully managed, this increase means that the firm becomes uncompetitive in each area.

COMPETING FOR A BASIC FORMULA

A successful service firm should operate on the KISS principle—*Keep It Simple, Stupid!* It should have a highly focused strategy built on a tightly defined target segment, a clearly defined benefit concept, a highly focused servuction system, and a clear service image (see Figure 9.1).[1]

From the arguments developed in the rest of this book, it is clear why such a strategy might be appropriate. The whole concept of segmentation takes on a different meaning within different services. Mixing segments in the same servuction system means that two groups will influence each other's experience and also can be the cause of role stress for service providers. A tightly defined target segment, therefore, can lead to many service benefits.

The benefit concept is the encapsulation in the consumer's mind of the bundle of benefits received from the service firm. A clearly defined benefit concept allows the correct amount of focus to be directed to the servuction system. The complexity of that servuction system means that the more clearly objectives can be established for its design, the simpler and more elegant that design will be. Simplicity is likely to lead to efficiency.

The complexity of the product purchased by consumers means that a clearly defined image can be difficult to achieve. That image comes not only from advertising and communications, but also from the whole part of the organization that is visible to the consumer.

A clearly defined formula also can simplify the nature of the task for the service providers. If they know what the organization is supposed to be delivering, to whom it is to be delivered, and what image is to be defined, then the possibility of role conflict is reduced. If a firm possesses a "strategic service vision," that vision will guide the behavior of both the service provider and the consumers.[2]

FIGURE 9.1 The Basic Formula for Success

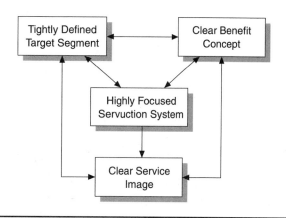

Finding a successful formula is, by definition, the first level of competition for service firms. One of the characteristics of service firms that is seldom discussed is the lack of patent protection. The formula for a particular brand of detergent or drug can be patented and will provide a competitive advantage for as long as the patent protection lasts. Unfortunately, not only is this not possible for a service formula, but the formula itself is often totally transparent to competition. The United States recently witnessed office-supply wars, with established firms, such as Office Depot and Staples, competing with start-ups all over the country. Once the first operation was operating successfully, many people visited it and immediately tried to copy it. Indeed, start-ups and competition are one of the key sources of new formulas for any service organization.

THE BASIC COMPETITIVE CHOICES

Once a successful formula has been created, the firm is faced with an array of alternative competitive strategies that it can choose to implement individually or in combination. Although the alternatives are generic, there are basic choices that have to be made. These can best be explained by considering the matrix shown in Figure 9.2, which was first formulated by Riddle when discussing international services.[3] Firms in different cells of the matrix have greater or less degrees of freedom in developing competitive strategies.

The inseparability of customers from the servuction process means that it is relevant to consider the mobility of both the customers and the rest of the servuction system. Cell A consists of two basic types of services. The first types are those that have made a strategic choice to remain in one geographic location, and to serve one geographic market. They only can *compete for market share*. The second type in this cell are firms whose servuction system is based on the telephone and/or the mail system. They are truly place-independent firms, such as the telecommunications network, the global commodity-trading businesses, many non-retail banking firms, and mail-order businesses, such as L. L. Bean. These, too, only can *compete for market share*, but often do so in a global market.

A firm can decide to remain in one geographic location, but can serve many geographic markets. To do this, it requires the customers to be mobile (cell B). Firms in this category include all those based on tourism or travel. Such firms *compete for*

FIGURE 9.2   The Competitive Choice Matrix

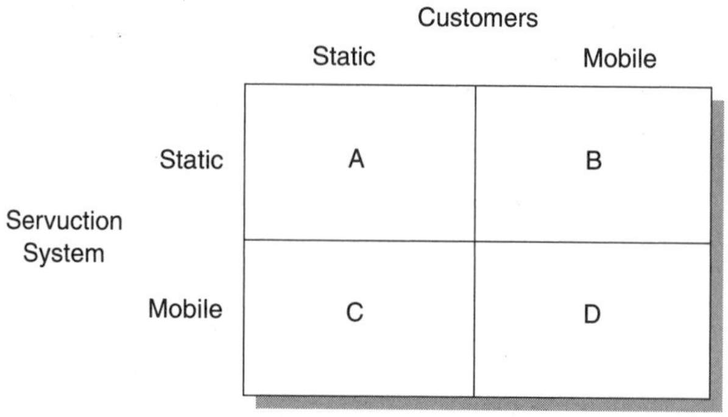

Customers

	Static	Mobile
Static	A	B
Mobile	C	D

Servuction
System

reach. For instance, hotel chains will create competitive programs to market their services throughout the globe. They also can compete for market share of the local market.

If customers are to remain in their geographic location, but the servuction system is mobile, then they must *compete for geography* (cell C). This is the area of the multi-site firms who spread "factories in the field" across geography and countries. In the absence of patent protection, preemptively occupying geography is one of the few competitive barriers that can be built. To be the second supplier into the market can be economically impossible since the volume of customers is potentially low and the cost of taking customers from existing suppliers is high. If competition does arrive or the firm is second into the market, then competition clearly will be either for share or to increase the size of the catchment area (reach).

Cell D combines the characteristics of both cell B and cell C. It is perhaps best typified by a Club Méditerranée in, for example, Kuantan, Malaysia. This club has been built on a beautiful beach in the middle of nowhere. It is surrounded by guards and was built by a French company. It is clearly part of competition-for-geography strategy, but, in this case, the site has not been built where the customers were. Instead, the customers themselves are mobile, coming predominantly in this case from France, Australia, and Japan. The ability to handle older, affluent French couples, Australian singles from Perth, and honeymooning Japanese couples in the same servuction system is only part of the competitive advantage. The other part is the ability to attract these groups to the operation in the first place.

COMPETING FOR MARKET SHARE

With a fixed market or catchment area, a service firm still has many strategies it can employ. Without modifying the range of service it offers, or the segments it tries to attract, it still can look to compete based on retention, recovery, quality, or customer focus. Retention marketing, discussed in more detail in Chapter 10, is a strategy based on the logic that existing customers are more profitable than new ones and it is easier to create a marketing program for them. Instead of investing to acquire new customers, firms, therefore, should focus on not losing the old ones.

Part of a retention strategy could well be a recovery strategy. This, again, is discussed in more detail in Chapter 11. This competitive strategy is based on the fact that the complexity of the servuction system means that it is impossible for it to operate successfully 100 percent of the time. A strategy to recover from service failures, therefore, is important. It becomes a major competitive strategy because research has shown that consumers whose service is recovered successfully after a failure are often more satisfied than customers for whom service is right the first time. Hence, failure and successful recovery can be more valuable than initial success.

There are two other interrelated strategies that focus on the service operation. The service quality movement comes from the Total Quality Management tradition and argues not only for "doing things right" but also for "doing the right thing" for the consumer. Chapter 12 provides a detailed overview of this approach. A rival but complementary movement, also imported from goods manufacturing and marketing, is the "market-focused" strategy described in Chapter 13. This theory argues that service firms have a tendency to become too operations-oriented and need to be refocused on the customer in order to stay competitive.

THE MULTI-SERVICE STRATEGY

Service firms also can compete for market share by broadening the range of services that they offer. In this strategy, the service organization capitalizes on its reputation and on its knowledge of its customers in order to sell other services. A good model for this strategy is the professional service firm. Large accounting firms, for example, have broadened the range of services they offer their clients to include tax advice, management consulting, executive recruitment, and compensation consulting. A firm that follows a pure multi-service strategy restricts itself to a single site and to a single segment of customers.

The basic marketing challenge for such an approach is the development of new services. Such development must be rooted not only in a knowledge of the segment, but also in a firm understanding of exactly what the servuction system is capable of delivering (see Chapter 3). Langeard and Eiglier suggest distinguishing between core and peripheral services.[4] The latter are added to the basic formula to increase profitability as, for example, boutiques or a bar in a hotel lobby. Such peripheral services add considerable complexity to an operation. La Quinta Inns, for example, has chosen to avoid this problem and offers a very simple service—a bedroom.[5]

Langeard and Eiglier point out that the complexity can multiply if one of the peripheral services becomes a second core. For example, the restaurant in a hotel can be established as a profit center. At that point, strategy may broaden to multi-service/multi-segment as the manager searches for a profitable business beyond the hotel-guest restriction. Worse still, the bar may lose its focus and guests may find that it is packed in the evening and they are unable to get a drink. This can reflect badly on the hotel.

THE MULTI-SEGMENT STRATEGY

Service firms also can increase their share of the market by broadening the range of segments that they serve. This strategy often emerges from a fixed-cost/spare-capacity argument. Site costs generally are fixed, so if there is spare capacity during operating hours, why not fill it with a different segment? In the mass-transit field, for example, spare daytime capacity outside of commuter hours often is met with a demand to fill the trains and buses with shoppers.

The marketing problem is, of course, to find new consumer segments that want to buy the existing bundle of services. This is almost an anti-marketing argument,

SERVICES IN ACTION 9.1

AMERICAN EXPRESS

American Express Travel-Related Services Company is the arm of the American Express Corporation that manages traveler's checks and card services. The business includes 27 million charge cards of all types in circulation worldwide, and a traveler's checks issue that ran to $20 billion in 1987.

These services are quite basic. Traveler's checks provide a secure substitute for cash, with American Express guaranteeing to replace any checks that are lost or stolen. Unless the customer's checks *are* lost or stolen, however, it is unlikely that the customer ever will see an Amex employee; even the purchase of the checks usually is done through a cooperating bank.

Card services are a little more detailed in that cardholders do receive a monthly statement of their account from the company. Provided they pay their bills, however, and provided their cards are not lost or stolen, the customers, again, have little contact with the company and are unlikely to see a service employee face to face.

These are the basic services. But there are a number of opportunities for American Express to provide further services to its customers and thus enhance its own profitability, either through direct contact or using existing service channels.

These services are most commonly offered to cardholders rather than to traveler's check purchasers, who do not usually receive any additional services. One common service offered to cardholders is travel assistance and travel insurance. Insurance, travel planning, and ticket booking and delivery are offered as additional services to basic cardholders; at upper levels, such as the corporate card, these services are bundled under the Travel Management System at no extra cost to the cardholder.

Another common service is a merchandising feature that accompanies each card statement. American Express does not rent or sell its membership list, preferring to keep control of merchandising to cardholders in its own hands. Books, music, *objets d'art,* and commemoratives frequently are showcased in promotional literature accompanying Amex statements.

Customers use American Express traveler's checks or take out charge cards because they appreciate the security and quality of service that Amex offers. It is possible to capitalize on this appreciation by offering new services that continue to fit customer demand.

---

since, in its purest form, it implies finding customers to fit the service rather than fitting the service to the customers' needs. The temptation always is to deviate from the pure strategy and to drift into a single-site/multi-service/multi-segment approach.

COMPETING FOR REACH

If the service firm is to remain static, and the service requires the physical presence of the customer, then the customer must come to the service. This competition focuses on the size of the catchment area. The firm needs to know how large the area is on which it can draw, and how far customers will travel to use the service. This is clearly a function of the distinctiveness and uniqueness of the firm. Customers will travel from all over the world to shop at Harrods in London because it is a unique experience. They will not travel more than a block to McDonald's because that is how far it is to Burger King. Obviously, this strategy requires distinctiveness and an understanding of the multi-site strategy.

In order to create a large catchment area, the firm must create a "destination." This does not necessarily mean providing beautiful and/or unique characteristics, such as in the Club Méditerranée example above. Large groups of shoppers now travel hundreds of miles to visit Factory Outlet malls in out-of-the-way places all of over the United States. The barrier to entry protecting firms using this strategy is not location, but the cost of marketing to such broad geographic areas. The identical problem is faced by luxury-destination hotels. Consider the Royal Scotsman, a luxury hotel built on a train that cruises through Scotland. With a six-month season each year and capacity for only 28 passengers per trip, occupancy is the key. The major problem is to find an economical way to reach a tiny market segment that is spread worldwide. It is precisely for this reason that the "channel of distribution" represented by travel agencies emerged. Although the physical service never can use channels of distribution, tickets for the use of that service can.

COMPETING FOR GEOGRAPHY

If the service formula cannot be defended with a patent, the only alternative is to spread out geographically and to do so quickly. This is the essence of the multi-site strategy. This strategy involves the replication of the same basic formula in multiple sites. It is perhaps best represented by the fast-food chains and certain large motel chains. A simple formula is established in one or two locations and is perfected (see Article 9.4). It then is replicated in a large number of sites, with everything, other than location, remaining constant. The complexities involved concern only the selection of locations and the management of the ever-increasing infrastructure.

From a marketing perspective, the decisions that need to be made can be divided into capital decisions and tactical decisions. The creation of the successful formula will have involved much research input from marketing (see Article 9.4). Once the formula is fixed, however, the critical marketing decision is the choice of location— the capital decision. The organization needs to answer the question: "Will it work here?" After the facility is built, all that remains are the tactical marketing problems of optimizing the number of customers and their spending. This tactical marketing is very much a street fight in a war among local competitors.

FRANCHISING AND THE COMPETITION FOR GEOGRAPHY

Franchising involves the sale of the basic formula to an outsider who establishes a new site. Such an arrangement can be viewed from the perspective of either the franchisor or the franchisee.

Why would a company with a successful formula wish to sell franchises? There are many reasons cited for such an approach. Franchising provides outside capital to fund growth that might not otherwise be available; and, perhaps more importantly, it provides management in the form of the franchisee. The Domino's Pizza chain, for example, opened over 800 outlets in 1987. To have found suitable management to run those sites would have been extremely difficult without franchising.

There are many negative aspects to franchising, however. Obviously, there is a financial cost since a franchise has to be profitable for the franchisee and that profit is lost to the franchisor. The problem of quality control is also very real. Under a franchising agreement, the franchisee buys the franchise name and the formula.

Failure to maintain the franchising firm's quality standards—operate by the franchise manual—will result in lost image not only for the single site but for the entire chain because of the shared franchise name.

From the franchisee's perspective, it is helpful to view the franchisor as being in a separate service business, that of selling franchises. Using the perspective of this book, the franchisee then must ask, what is the benefit and what is the servuction system for that franchise? The implied benefit is guaranteed profit. Buying a franchise is supposed to be a less-risky way of going into business than setting up on one's own.

The servuction system for the franchising business is complex, however, and the development of the prototype (see Article 9.4) is crucial. A prototype is a demonstration site in which the formula has been perfected and in which the franchisee can see the complete system to be provided. The profit track record of that site and of any existing franchises becomes part of the product offering. So, too, does the equipment layout, and so does the training. Overlaying this is the marketing support that the franchisor provides for the franchisees. Only if all these parts of the servuction system provide an assurance of guaranteed profit will the purchase be made.

INTERNATIONALIZATION

The internationalization of a service firm often develops from the same profit pressures that drive domestic expansion. It is too easy to view such strategies as purely multi-site strategies. The interactive nature of the service experience means that the consumer is an integral part of the process. For internationalization to be viewed as purely a multi-site strategy, it is clear that the consumers must be identical in both domestic markets and in foreign countries. In certain cases, this is feasible—fast-food chains have succeeded to a large extent in finding the same "occasion segment" in many countries. However, a McDonald's in the center of Beijing is unlikely to be drawing on the same segment as one in the heart of New York City.

Multi-site retail chains have had less success. Often, the foreign consumer attracted by the retail formula is different from the one in the domestic market. This raises all the problems of a multi-segment approach. Also, management may not realize that it is actually dealing with a different segment. At the most prosaic level, McDonald's has found it difficult to persuade customers in the United Kingdom to clear their own tables after eating. This simple difference in cultural norms can have major operational impacts.

All of these problems are compounded by the simple logistics of managing multiple sites some distances apart and by managers who may themselves have different cultural backgrounds.

THE DANGERS OF LOSS OF FOCUS

The generic service strategies presented here have been described as the multi-site, multi-service, and multi-segment strategies. Implicitly, we have assumed that a firm will use only one of these approaches. Each carries with it a set of management challenges and requires a unique set of skills. However, many firms adopt multiple strategies at the same time. Whether driven by a competitive threat or a need for growth, the complexity produced by multiple strategies can lead to a loss of focus and control.

The major European retail banks show the operating and marketing complexity of such multiple strategies. With 3,000 branches selling 285 different services,

SERVICES IN ACTION 9.2

VICTORIA STATION

Victoria Station was founded in 1969 as a chain of "railroad theme" restaurants. Capitalizing on a nostalgia for railways, the chain's founders converted unused railway boxcars into restaurants, and used period furnishings intended to evoke an ambiance reminiscent of British Rail in the United Kingdom. The restaurants were decorated with railway memorabilia and souvenirs imported from England. The target market was the family looking for a good meal but unable to afford high prices. A typical Victoria Station could seat about 200 people.

In the beginning, the firm used no paid advertising or publicity, relying solely on word of mouth. There was no marketing manager or director as such, only a relatively junior manager of public relations. As a result, management placed a great deal of emphasis on quality control. Main menu items, such as beef and shrimp, were purchased nationally, dressed, and then shipped to each site. Other produce was bought locally, but from a list of purveyors approved by the head office. All invoices for supplies were paid from the San Francisco head office. Regional managers were required to evaluate the performance of each restaurant on the basis of quality criteria laid down by the head office.

Financial control was also a prominent feature. The company maintained profitability and low prices through a rigorous system of financial control, which included daily inventory checks at all sites. Expenses were carefully controlled to meet targets.

By 1973, the chain had expanded to 17 sites, with five more under construction and ten in the process of design. The company had set considerable expansion targets, and had put in place mechanisms to allow it to grow further. The initial aim was to establish restaurants in every American population center with more than one million inhabitants.

Growth, however, would bring with it problems. Management asked itself if a chain of more than 50 restaurants could continue to operate without any formal marketing department. On the other side of the coin, could a rigorous central operating system continue to maintain existing quality in a much larger organization? Finally, how would the two functions end up working together?

Senior management expressed fears that the company was losing sight of its initial objectives in pursuit of growth. By growing, the company would have to face marketing and organizational issues that had not previously been important.

---

complexity exists at all levels. The services are difficult for service providers to understand, and, indeed, many bank tellers are incapable of selling or delivering even a small percentage of them. It is also difficult for consumers to comprehend the range of banking services, since the banks offer everything from check cashing to sophisticated financial advice, from foreign exchange to will preparation. Often these services are offered to the customer from a single site or branch of the bank.

Each of these banking services can have a different script for the consumer and the service provider to follow. Service providers have a tendency to become bureaucratically oriented simply in order to cope with the range of scripts they have to delivery. Finally, the banks are making matters worse by broadening their target markets to encompass multiple segments. A single branch will attempt to service regular and high-net-worth individuals as well as large and small firms.

MULTI-SERVICE/MULTI-SEGMENT FIRMS

These firms operate on a single site, but offer multiple core and peripheral services to multiple firms. The problems of operating with multiple segments within the same site are compounded if the firm also wishes to provide multiple services and cannot keep the segments separated from one another.

Perhaps the classic example of a multi-service/multi-segment firm is a large luxury hotel. At any one time, the hotel may be serving various segments: the standard-rate hotel guest, the package-tour guest, the conference/seminar guest, the large-banquet guest, the restaurant-only guest, and the bar-only guest. All of these different guests can be using the hotel on business or for pleasure. They may have similar demographic profiles, but they are segmented by occasion and by the benefits they are seeking.

Each of the segments is being offered a benefit concept of varying complexity and involving different mixes of the services provided. The ultimate segment might be the conference guest who is allowed to use all of the hotel's services as part of the package deal set up by the conference sponsor.

The marketing problems in such situations are wide-ranging. The price bundling of different services becomes very complex. Appealing to the different segments selectively without detracting from the overall image of the hotel is very difficult.

The problems of quality maintenance are also profound. Each guest can approach the same servuction system with a different script. The standard-rate guest expects a very different level of service than a conference guest, who can be paying as little as 30 percent of the full rate. Even the perceived restaurant dress code may be different, with standard-rate guests wearing ties and jackets and conference guests arriving in the informal wear customary during conferences.

MULTI-SITE/MULTI-SEGMENT FIRMS

These firms offer a restricted number of services out of any given site, but try to attract multiple segments. In one sense, McDonald's operates this way, although the range of menu items that it offers might preclude the company from this category. Clearly, such firms are forced to mix different groups of segments closely together. Because of the focused nature of each site, it is impossible to segregate different segments into different parts of the room.

The need to attract multiple segments comes from a desire to utilize excess capacity. The segments must be different, otherwise their demands are likely to coincide and they will fail to alleviate the capacity problem. Unfortunately, unless great care is taken, the segments do interfere with one another. Consider the steak-house restaurant chain that wants to attract families in the early evening to soak up spare capacity. To this end, it offers a children's meal. However, unless the project is managed carefully, the children will occupy empty seats that otherwise could have been taken by adults, who offer a greater profit opportunity.

REFOCUSING THE SERVICE FIRM

An emerging phenomenon amongst mature service networks has been the attempt to refocus. If we return to our European bank networks, there is a trend now for fragmentation and specialization. Networks of branches are being broken up, and traditional geographical operating units are being replaced with segmented approaches. Designated "high-net-worth individual" branches are appearing all over the world. These branches have a much-simplified formula because their target segment has been much simplified. Similarly, small-business bank branches now are appearing, and large business accounts are being withdrawn from branches and are becoming "national or multi-national accounts."

On the service side of banking, refocusing also is taking place. Cash shops are being created in branches that only can provide cash either from tellers or machines. Mortgage offices are being created to provide expert advice to customers who are prepared to travel much further to get a mortgage than to get cash. Banking by telephone is moving banks to cell A of Figure 9.2 and is dispensing with the need for multiple branches.

Geographic retrenchment, particularly withdrawing from international operations, also has been forced on the banks by the complexity of maintaining quality standards at great distance from the headquarters. The specialization of outlets implies the removal of customers and services from other branches, reversing the original shared-cost logic. This, in turn, is leading to branch closure programs by banks all over the world.

CHAPTER 9 READINGS

Article 9.1 relates to the competition-for-share portion of this chapter. Competing for customers means that the firm needs to have the most appropriate operational structure and framework in place. Article 9.2 integrates all of the strategies described above in what is called the profit chain and provides an alternative framework to the one presented in this chapter. Article 9.3 discusses internationalization and alternative entry strategies, and Article 9.4 discusses the role of prototypes in developing franchising as part of a multi-site strategy.

QUESTIONS

1. Discuss the management problems that might emerge for large multi-site firms.

2. A chain of barbershops in Arizona is selling tickets for haircuts through indirect channels. These are not coupons, but are actual purchases of the right to a haircut. Discuss the advantages and disadvantages of adopting such an approach.

3. Give an example, other than those in the chapter, of how combining multiple segments within a service business can cause problems for customers and staff.

4. How would you classify a chain of department stores using the various competitive strategies? What problems would you expect these stores to have?

NOTES

1. Eric Langeard and Pierre Eiglier, "Strategic Management of Service Development," in Leonard Berry, G. Lynn Shostack, and Greg Upah, eds., *Emerging Perspectives on Services Marketing,* (1983): 68–72.

2. James M. Carman and Eric Langeard, "Growth Strategies for Service Firms," *Strategic Management Journal,* vol. 1, (1980): 7–22.

3. Dorothy L. Riddle, *Service Led Growth,* (New York: Praeger Publishing, 1986): 196.

4. Langeard and Eigler, "Strategic Management of Service Development," 68–72.

5. "La Quinta Inns Face the Eighties," Harvard Business School case no. 9-581-038. (Boston, MA: HBS Case Services, Harvard Business School, 1981).

BEEFING UP OPERATIONS IN SERVICE FIRMS

Richard B. Chase
University of Southern California

Robert H. Hayes
Harvard University

Many articles exhort service firm managers to empower workers and first-line supervisors, exploit technology, focus on the customer, and, above all, provide outstanding service. This article proposes a framework to help you evaluate your company's competitive standing in each of these areas. It discusses four types of companies on a continuum, from the company that is simply "available for service" to the firm that delivers world class service. The authors focus on operations, the function that controls the service encounter, and apply the manufacturing strategy paradigm to services as a means of implementing change.

A national preoccupation with U.S. international industrial competitiveness, driven by our continuing enormous balance of payments deficit, has tended to focus media and political attention during the 1980s on manufacturing. A torrent of books and articles has inundated business managers, offering guidance on how to improve manufacturing performance. Terms like "world class manufacturing" and "dynamic manufacturing" sprinkle discussions in college classrooms, corporate boardrooms, and the halls of Congress. The concept of "manufacturing strategy," considered somewhat esoteric only a few years ago, gets increasing attention from both top managers and academics.

There is, however, another battlefield of economic competitiveness where operations effectiveness is just as crucial to success as it is on the factory floor. This less visible battlefield is that huge, ill-structured arena called the "service sector," which employees 76 percent of our workforce and accounts for 68 percent of our real GNP. It is also, unfortunately, a sector—comprising activities such as banking, engineering, transportation, commu-

nication, and myriad others—whose trade surplus went negative for the first time in mid-1989 and is now barely in the black.

We have no quarrel with the assertion that the United States needs a strong manufacturing base in order to maintain and improve its standard of living. But we have to get serious about service competitiveness as well. Just as our machine tool and semiconductor industries should have studied the successful attacks of foreign steel, auto, and consumer electronics producers on our domestic market—and prepared themselves for similar onslaughts—so should our service industries study and learn from our manufacturing sector's decline. Those manufacturing firms that have remade themselves or sustained their leadership position have shared a common approach: they have focused attention on their most important markets and then mobilized their operations organization, through a well-planned strategy, to squarely meet those markets' needs.

In this article we will discuss how to make operations in service organizations more competitive. We will examine ideas that have emerged from successful manufacturers and outstanding service firms. Our key conclusions are that service firms, like manufacturing firms, can structure their operations according to a four-stage model of competitiveness and that they can apply the

SOURCE: Richard B. Chase and Robert H. Hayes, "Beefing Up Operations in Service Firms," *Sloan Management Review* (Fall 1991): 15–26.

Richard B. Chase is Justin Dart Professor of Operations Management at the School of Business Administration, University of Southern California. Robert H. Hayes is Philip Caldwell Professor of Business Administration at the Graduate School of Business Administration, Harvard University.

manufacturing strategy concepts of focus and integration as they move from lower to higher stages.

Before developing this perspective, however, it is useful to first review some basic concepts.

SERVICE FIRM MANAGEMENT: THE BASICS

Service firm management, especially of operations, is best understood within the context of three key constructs.

THE STRATEGIC SERVICE VISION The strategic service vision is "the logically organized plan for implementing new businesses and ideas."[1] It consists of four elements: a target market (Who is our intended customer?), a service concept (What are the most important elements of our service from the customer's perspective?), a competitive strategy (How will we differentiate ourselves from our competitors?), and a service delivery system (How will we provide this differentiated service?).[2]

The vision focuses on the customer's perceived value of the service. To remain competitive, a service firm must consistently meet or exceed customers' expectations of value—the price they pay relative to the quality and convenience of the service they receive.

LEVELS OF SERVICE The core service is the essential set of services that the firm must provide just to participate in its market. Peripheral services facilitate the core service or are expected features of the service bundle. Amenities are add-ons that are not essential to the core service but that might sway a customer's buying decision.

An airline's core service, for example, is getting someone from one place to another. Its peripheral services include its reservation and baggage handling systems, while amenities consist of such things as cabin food service and in-flight entertainment. As a general principle, the firm must provide basic competency in core and peripheral services to survive. No amount of add-ons can save a firm that is clearly deficient in these dimensions. Put another way, the core and primary peripheral services define the lower limit of customer expectations about performance.

THE OPERATIONS FUNCTION In service firms, operations consists of two quite different spheres of activity. One sphere is the service encounter or cycle of encounters between the customer and the organization. The medium by which these encounters are carried out (i.e., face-to-face, by phone, or by electromechanical device) constitutes the firm's service delivery system. The other sphere encompasses those activities that take place be-

hind the scenes and constitute the "back office" support system. These involve such tasks as processing paperwork, cooking a restaurant meal, or taking baggage off a plane. These latter activities are analogous to the production processes in the factory—working on things rather than people. The existence of these two spheres of activity and, more important, the emphasis on the encounter as the core output function in most service organizations are what differentiate services from manufacturing.[3] The extent to which value is added in the front office rather than the back office often distinguishes one service business from another and determines structure and staffing of the operations organization itself.

AN OPERATIONS FRAMEWORK

Regardless of a firm's particular competitive strategy, senior management needs some framework for relating operations' activities to the firm's overall service performance. This is so for several reasons. One is to help pinpoint the key elements that must be addressed in the strategy development process itself. Another is to help position the firm's operations relative to competitors. The final and most compelling reason, in our opinion, is to provide a current perspective and future vision that can be communicated to the organization's members. The questions "where are we now?" and "where do we want to be?" are more easily answered if they can be related to even a rough performance classification.

The classification we propose for addressing these issues is the four-stage scheme depicted in Table 1. This scheme distinguishes among service firms according to their general effectiveness in service delivery at different stages of their development. Accompanying each stage are the management practices and attitudes that, based upon our experience, generally indicate how service firms at each stage deal with key operations issues. (An analogous framework, developed by Wheelwright and Hayes, is widely used to analyze the role of operations in strategy development for manufacturing firms.[4])

Before discussing the stages, we must consider two issues. First, the stage attained by a firm at any given time is a composite. Every service delivery system embodies a unique set of choices about such factors as service quality, role of the back office, workforce policies, and the like. A company may fall at a different point along the continuum for each category or have some organizational units that are further or less advanced than others. What determines the firm's stage is the overall balance among these different positions—where, in a sense, the firm's center of gravity lies.[5] In

TABLE 1   Four Stages of Service Firm Competitiveness

Stage	1. Available for Service	2. Journeyman	3. Distinctive Competence Achieved	4. World Class Service Delivery
	Customers patronize service firm for reasons other than performance.	Customers neither seek out nor avoid the firm.	Customers seek out the firm based upon its sustained reputation for meeting customer expectations.	The company's name is synonymous with service excellence. Its service doesn't just satisfy customers, it *delights* them, and thereby expands customer expectations to levels its competitors are unable to fulfill.
	Operations is reactive, at best.	Operations functions in a mediocre, uninspired fashion.	Operations continually excels, reinforced by personnel management and systems that support an intense customer focus.	Operations is a quick learner and fast innovator; it masters every step of the service delivery process and provides capabilities that are superior to competitors'.
Service Quality	Is subsidiary to cost, highly variable.	Meets some customer expectations, consistent on one or two key dimensions.	Exceeds customer expectations, consistent on multiple dimensions.	Raises customer expectations and seeks challenges, improves continuously.
Back Office	Counting Room.	Contributes to service, plays an important role in the total service, is given attention, but is still a separate role.	Is equally valued with front office, plays integral role.	Is proactive, develops its own capabilities, and generates opportunities.
Customer	Unspecified, to be satisfied at minimum cost.	A market segment whose basic needs are understood.	A collection of individuals whose variation in needs is understood.	A source of stimulation, ideas, and opportunity.
Introduction of New Technology	When necessary for survival, under duress.	When justified by cost savings.	When promises to enhance service.	Source of first-mover advantages, creating ability to do things your competitor's can't do.
Workforce	Negative constraint.	Efficient resource, disciplined, follows procedures.	Permitted to select among alternative procedures.	Innovative, creates procedures.
First-Line Management	Controls workers.	Controls the process.	Listens to customers, coaches and facilitates workers.	Is listened to by top management as a source of new ideas. Mentors workers to enhance their career growth.

defining this center of gravity, the model assumes a weighing of each dimension's relative importance. Thus a firm can achieve Stage 3 or possibly Stage 4 status, even if it is not outstanding on all dimensions, providing that it is clearly superior on the critical success fac-

tors for its industry. An example here is UPS, whose mastery of its core service, through its technology and back office capabilities, enables it to "go global" and compete effectively on price. It does not, however, do a particularly good job at tracking overseas shipments, nor does it excel in its service quality practices. Thus, in our view, it averages out to a Stage 3 company.

Second, it is difficult, if not impossible, for a company to skip a stage in its quest for world class status. A company obviously must achieve journeyman performance levels before it achieves distinctive competence, and distinctive competence is a necessary foundation for becoming world class. This does not mean that a company can't pass through a stage in a relatively short time, however. Scandinavian Airlines Systems (SAS) moved from Stage 1 to Stage 3 in about a year and a half. After suffering a huge operating loss in fiscal year 1979–1980, its CEO, Jan Carlzon, instituted a program involving some 120 service improvements designed to help it become the airline of choice for its selected target market, the full-fare business passenger. The improvements focused on achieving exceptional on-time performance and excellent service by all personnel. By January 1982, SAS had the best on-time record in Europe, and in August 1983, *Fortune* named it the best airline for business travelers in the world.[6]

At the same time, companies can very easily slide back a stage. This can come about gradually, typically from losing touch with the market, or overnight as the result of a widely publicized service failure. An example of a gradual decline is that of Sears, whose complacency and bureaucratization have made them play catch-up in everything from pricing to customer service. An example of an overnight downfall is the case of the Los Angeles Police Department, which was nationally recognized as a leader in policing practices prior to the Rodney King incident in the spring of 1991.[7]

Also, while it is appealing in theory for a service firm to move as a single entity through these stages, the sheer size of major companies precludes immediate across-the-board shifts. Even when a company has developed a clearly defined new service delivery system and debugged it on a pilot basis, getting it operational can involve months of retraining, extensive systems work, and so forth. Woolworth takes a couple of years to test its new store concepts; Burger King runs extensive experiments in its R&D lab.

Often, people assume that new technology will put them on the fast track through the four stages. However, we know of no firms that have leapfrogged a stage solely by relying on a new technology. A new fleet of planes, a new telecommunications system, or a new point-of-sale scanning system may be necessary for "upstaging," but innovation can't do the job overnight—or alone. For example, while American Airlines and the American Automobile Association have achieved their dominant

industry positions through aggressive use of information technologies, effective integration required major managerial and procedural refinements over the course of many years. Likewise, implementation of Fidelity Investment's Investors Express package, which allows active traders to initiate security trades from their personal computers, and Mrs. Field's Cookies computerized point-of-sale inventory tracking system worked because appropriate infrastructures were already in place.[8]

With these points in mind, we now consider the stages themselves.

STAGE 1: AVAILABLE FOR SERVICE

Service firms that fall into this category tend to consider their operations organizations "necessary evils." They often see operations' mission as almost totally reactive: to deliver the service that some other person or group in the company has defined and to deliver it in the manner specified. Thus management pays little attention to how other firms, whether direct competitors or not, design and manage similar service delivery systems. It assumes that if operations can do what it is supposed to do, without major disruptions, the firm will be able to make a profit. The major guidance given operations, therefore, is "don't screw up."

In order to keep costs down, operations receives minimal back office support. The company makes little investment in specialized equipment, and it staffs operations with people who have marginal skills—and who are therefore willing to work for relatively low wages. Constantly looking at the bottom line, management designs operations jobs that require little skill or creativity, and it provides almost no training. Few people advance out of operations into another function or into general management, so operations tends to be regarded as a dead end. Thus supervisors must continually monitor and direct frontline staff, and there is a high rate of turnover. Moreover, because operations employees acquire only limited skills in their jobs, they seldom can achieve major advancement by transferring to other companies. Ironically, as in the case of the banking industry, efforts to cut labor costs frequently result in higher total costs because of the need to fix quality problems.

The companies that fit this mold tend to be either relatively young firms that offer a new or unique service or those that serve a niche market (often one based on minimum service at a minimum price).

STAGE 2: JOURNEYMAN

The problem with niches is that one usually outgrows them, or they grow to the point where other companies decide to move in. Therefore, after maintaining a sheltered existence for some time, Stage 1 firms often find themselves coming into direct competition with other companies that offer similar services in the approximate geographic area. No longer can they simply ask operations to get the job done; they must seek feedback from their customers on the relative cost and perceived quality of their service, and ensure that they are not penalizing themselves unduly through idiosyncratic approaches, such as odd business hours or complicated credit procedures.

The goal becomes: "Don't let our competitors gain too much of an advantage over us." And the firm begins to adopt industry practice in its operations. Instead of reacting to internal directives, operations reacts to external practices, particularly in its back office (which usually is trying to minimize cost no matter what service priorities the front office identifies).

Over time, such companies' operations organizations tend to look more and more like those of their competitors. They build similar facilities, use similar equipment and systems (often purchased from the same equipment or software suppliers), purchase materials or ancillary services from the same suppliers, adopt similar management practices, and routinely even hire workers and managers from competing firms. Such people blend into their new environment almost immediately because it is so much like their previous one, and even use many of the same procedures. Line management's role is to ensure that workers faithfully follow the procedures established by top management; improvisation is not encouraged. (Stage 2 companies, like Stage 1 companies, are not big on worker empowerment.)

In effect, companies that have adopted a Stage 2 approach have agreed not to compete against each other in terms of operations effectiveness; they all operate essentially the same way. (Quickly, can you name any difference in service between, say, J. C. Penney and Montgomery Ward?) Instead, they compete, often quite vigorously, along other dimensions: breadth of product line, advertising, and financial incentives. Management still regards operations employees as specialists, and therefore they have limited upward mobility. They do have more mobility between firms, however, and as a result begin to acquire an industry orientation. In fact, their allegiance to their industry profession, often quite narrowly defined, usually surpasses their allegiance to the particular company they happen to work for at any given time.

In summary, the challenge confronting Stage 2 firms is keeping pace with competitors that do just as good a job in the core service and that raise the ante by excelling on service quality or by providing peripheral services that have real value to the customer. This problem faces upscale retail department stores such as Bullocks, Saks, and Robinson's, in the wake of Nordstrom's legendary customer service. An equally effective service system may take months or years to duplicate. It is a fragile structure in which the competitive edge is often the invisible internal capabilities and organizational culture rather than the visible Steinway Grand on the mezzanine.

STAGE 3: DISTINCTIVE COMPETENCE

In a Stage 3 firm, senior management has a clear vision of what creates value in the customer's eyes, and it designs operations carefully to deliver that value. Richard Rosenberg, CEO of Bank of America, saw value as providing one-stop shopping, in this case, one account that bundled checking, savings, and safe deposit privileges at a price that was cheaper than getting them individually. The burden fell on virtually every part of the operations organization to convert this vision into reality, which it did with great success.[9]

The operations organization in a Stage 3 firm also reflects a coherent operations strategy, that is, making consistent choices for each element in Table 1 relative to price, quality, flexibility, and convenience objectives. Operations also provides the tactics and leadership to implement the strategy. Relative to service quality, for example, operations is the typical advocate of a Total Quality Management philosophy, and it assumes the lead role in implementing service guarantees and service enhancing technologies, and fostering worker empowerment. Federal Express is probably the classic example of a company that relies on its operations personnel to push, as well as execute, actions in these three areas.

These innovations are especially practicable because Stage 3 firms have, by definition, mastered their core service. They understand the essential strengths and limitations of their operations and are well aware of the careful analysis that must precede change. First Interstate Bank of California, for example, spent three years shaping up its back office operations and its branch operations before it launched its five-point service guarantee.

The achievement of distinctive competence, however, can bring certain personnel problems. Workers whose responsibilities in Stage 2 companies were limited to following set procedures are now encouraged to take initiative and make choices among alternative procedures. Delta Airlines goes even further. It encourages all of its employees to learn multiple jobs in order to pre-pare themselves for advancement and to appreciate the problems and jobs of the other guy.

The challenge for operations, and for the whole firm at this stage, is to assure that the operations strategy remains supportive of the rest of the company, particularly marketing. At the same time, sales, marketing, and product development must be open to new service initiatives that operations personnel propose.

STAGE 4: WORLD CLASS SERVICE DELIVERY

The ultimate stage represents an apparently natural extension of Stage 3, but a traditionally managed company will probably find this the hardest transition of all. The company must develop the capabilities and credibility of its operations organization to the point where operations becomes proactive, forcing higher performance standards on the whole company, identifying new business opportunities, and helping redefine the firm's competitive strategy. Rather than simply investigating customer needs and attempting to fulfill them, Stage 4 companies (e.g., Disney, Four Seasons Hotels, and Singapore Airlines) seek to create needs, establish expectations, and continually expand those expectations. They define the quality standards by which their competitors are judged.

Customers, in fact, become consultants, sources of ideas as well as revenue, as in the case of CIGNA's Customer Advisory Board. Competitors provide stimulation as well as pressure. The company bases its performance standards not on its own historical achievements, but on the performance achieved by its best competitors around the world, that is, it does competitive benchmarking. It designs controls and rewards to motivate continuous improvements upon those standards, and it gives employees the tools and training to achieve them. NYNEX, for example, offers its employees the Chairman's Award for World Class Service and provides extensive training in process management to help them attain it.

The company's view of technology undergoes a similar transformation. Rather than being simply a means for cutting costs and removing people, it becomes a potential means for developing competitive advantage, making it possible for the organization to do things its competitors can't do. The company worries less about technological risk than about losing the first mover advantage. For example, some leading firms have adopted an "informate and automate" strategy to let the customer know vital information and to facilitate the server's job. Hertz has established business centers at some

airports that are equipped with flight monitors providing the latest information on airline schedules and departure gates, and handouts that provide driving directions in five languages. Faster service is facilitated by personnel using hand-held computers to print receipts in the parking lot so that customers don't have to go to the counter when returning cars.

Workers in Stage 4 companies become "company men and women" in the best sense. They are "Marriott people," "Southwest Airlines types," and "Home Depot folks." Their identity with the company they work for often matches or even exceeds that with their alma mater or hometown team. Like production employees of world class manufacturers (the Millikens, Xeroxes, and Motorolas), operations employees of world class service firms, no matter what their job, know they are working someplace special and doing something valued by the company. Indeed, just as the Honda janitor sweeping the floor is "building cars," the Disney Maintenance Host sweeping the lot is "helping the guests enjoy their day at the Park."

Of course, managers of such companies also have tremendous pride in the organization's service and appreciate the centrality of operations in providing it. Often such firms regard an outstanding service delivery system as so important that operations experience is considered essential to one's upward mobility. In a similar vein, it is common for senior executives who run Stage 4 firms, in order to maintain their feel for operations as well as staying close to the customer, to spend time "in the trenches." Bill Marriott, Sr., often took a turn at the registration desk, and the CEO of Columbus' Riverside Methodist Hospital, a leader in health care service quality, occasionally works as an orderly. The president of Swissair has been seen dispensing boarding passes and has instructed all managers of the airline, regardless of function, to spend one day a month dealing directly with customers.

A world class operations function has two major challenges. One challenge is sustaining superior performance at every point in its service delivery system and throughout its service network, as service firms often are judged more by the performance of their weakest links than by the things they do especially well. To be world class, therefore, all organizational units must meet impeccable standards of service and productivity.

The other major challenge, especially for multisite services, is managing the increasing complexity of personnel recruitment, training and motivation, technological innovation, and communication as the firm grows. Operations' ability to reproduce and manage its proven system in highly diverse cultural settings—McDonald's in Moscow—ultimately determines the firm's permanence, literally, as a world class competitor.

THE MANUFACTURING STRATEGY PARADIGM APPLIED TO SERVICE

The concept of manufacturing strategy has been around for over twenty years, but only in the last decade has it received serious consideration from academics and practitioners. The strategy is based on the widely observed rule that general purpose systems, like general purpose tools, are seldom as effective as those that are designed and managed for a specific purpose.[10] Therefore, a company must begin designing a manufacturing system with a careful, and broadly shared, assessment of how the firm will compete in a particular industry—in what respects will its products and services be distinctive? Once the company establishes its competitive priorities, the paradigm provides an orderly approach for examining the organization's structure (facilities and equipment) and infrastructure (policies and systems) to determine if they are consistent with those priorities. If inconsistencies are detected, the paradigm also provides guidelines for making appropriate alterations. The term "manufacturing strategy" encompasses the whole process: setting competitive priorities, making structural and infrastructural decisions, and establishing a discipline (such as the notion of focused factories and plant charters) for ensuring that the structure and infrastructure remain consistent with the priorities.

We can easily adapt the same framework to service companies, although we must make a few modifications to accommodate the differences between services and manufactured products. For our purposes, the key difference is that, for the service firm, the customer encounter with the system is the focal point of all operations activities.

PLANNING THE TRANSITION

Assuming that the service company is a going concern and knows how it will compete in its industry, management may move around the wheel in Figure 1—baselining operations' performance, setting priorities, focusing operations, achieving coherence, and incorporating learning—with each step linked to customer requirements.

Baselining performance is determining the operating system's success on those things that are important to the customer, both by itself and in comparison with its competitors.

FIGURE 1   The Manufacturing Strategy Paradigm Applied to Service

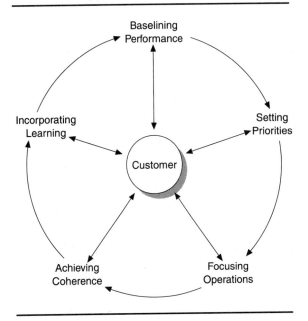

A useful tool for this purpose is performance-importance mapping. This involves gathering information, typically via customer surveys, on each aspect of service delivery and placing it on a grid (see Figure 2).

In this example, we have plotted factors of importance to bank customers. The map shows that customers value short lines and think this bank's lines are too long. Customers do not value extended hours, and the bank apparently does not provide them. Customers believe statement accuracy is very important, and they think the bank performs very well in this area.

The second part of baselining is comparing oneself with the competition. One could plot a similar grid showing on one axis selected competitors' performance relative to the bank and, on the other, importance to customers. When a company performs about the same as the rest of the industry on important elements, strategists call this "qualifying to compete." When it performs better on important elements, strategists call this "order winning." When it performs better than competitors on an unimportant element, we refer to it as an "air ball"—essentially a waste of effort and resources. Performance that is worse than that of the industry on important elements is generally termed "order losing," and obviously requires urgent action.

Setting priorities for manufacturing operations boils down to choosing on which specific delivery attrib-

FIGURE 2   Performance-Importance Map

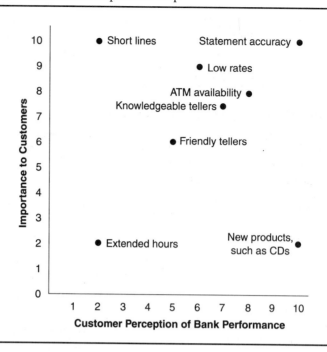

utes to excel: cost-price, flexibility, quality, or dependability. Services have to make similar choices, each of which has direct implications for the service delivery elements shown in Table 1. Here we encounter the notion of trade-offs. The company must choose not only a limited set of things to do well, but it must choose the right set. And it must be precise. As manufacturing strategy pioneer Wickam Skinner observed in 1969, "The variables of cost, time, quality, technological constraints, and customer satisfaction place limits on what management can do, force compromises, and demand an explicit recognition of a multitude of trade-offs and choices. Yet everywhere I find plants that have inadvertently emphasized one yardstick at the expense of another, more important one."[11] This is a key lesson for service executives as well. The priority-setting process must stem from the findings of the performance-importance baseline analyses just described. If short lines have a higher priority to the bank's target customer than extended hours, then labor use must be adjusted accordingly. The trade-off is between flexibility (of access to the service) and speed.

Focusing operations requires aligning the operating system, operations personnel, and facilities with the performance priorities. Lens Crafters' priority is speed, so it targets all of its equipment and procedures toward fast turnaround; H & R Block's priority is low cost, so its

operating system is geared to volume; First Wachovia Bank and Trust of North Carolina emphasizes relationship banking, so its operating system excels at database management; and Andersen Consulting, which prides itself on being able to provide consulting anywhere in the world at the drop of a hat, focuses its operating organization on getting its consulting staff quickly into the field.

In manufacturing, focus calls for organizing factories according to the product's specific processing requirements. The essential issue is whether to design for high volume, standardized products using dedicated machines and specialized workers, or low volume, customized products using flexible equipment and broadly skilled workers. Matching the right equipment to the product is critical for services as well. Kentucky Fried Chicken got into trouble a few years ago by not recognizing this when it introduced spareribs. The problem was that its technology and operating system were designed around frying and pressure cooking, not barbecuing. The result: soggy ribs served by frustrated workers.

Designing focused operating units for service companies presents some unique problems. One problem is that customers don't like to be treated as high-volume products, even when the cost is low. Another is that the typical direct service worker is often ill prepared in skills and policy knowledge to effectively customize a service.

Service companies that lose focus, like their brethren in manufacturing, fail due to one or more of the following reasons:

☐ Corporate management has not clearly spelled out the operation's task; it's excessively general. This results in trying to do everything "a little bit well."

☐ Overly ambitious marketing programs have made promises that operations can't keep. For example, an airline billboard ad several years ago showed flight attendants lavishing personal service on passengers flying coach in a 747.

☐ The priorities are inconsistent. For example, a company tries to provide highly personalized service and high volume, low-priced service in the same facility.

☐ Service products have proliferated out of control. Too many items on the fast food menu, too many services sold by the consultant, and too many products, rates, and terms offered by banks lead to unfocused operations.

Achieving coherence in the operating system means that the individual components are mutually reinforcing, all contributing to the organization's goals. The Benihana Restaurant operating system is a classic example. Everything from the chef pacing the meal by serving directly from the teppenyaki, the hard seats, sherbet desserts that melt quickly (they're placed on the table next to the grill), to communal dining at tables of eight, contributes to the system's throughput objectives. While few service firms can achieve this level of coherence—or to use a manufacturing term, system integration—it is nevertheless a good ideal to strive for. A quick test is to focus on one element of a system and see if changing it adds to or subtracts from the operation's overall performance.

Incorporating learning requires both gathering and disseminating new ideas obtained from analyzing operations. We can distinguish between two types of service organizations, relative to the way they do this: street smart services and systematically smart services. Street smart services learn on an ad hoc basis. Managers and workers pick up ideas through their interactions with customers and general awareness of industry developments. Managing by wandering around, suggestion systems, and some low-key competitive benchmarking constitute the usual approaches. While these may work effectively for smaller service firms, large multisite service organizations must, in our opinion, employ more efficient and scientific ways of finding and implementing operational improvements. We advocate the use of carefully designed experiments at representative branches and development of an information infrastructure to routinely share successful, and unsuccessful, results. Manufacturing product design is generally way ahead of service design in this area. Perhaps the primary reason for this is that factory product designers are accustomed to experimenting with the functioning of each component of a product in minute detail, both individually and as part of the end product.

By way of example, if an HMO chain seeks to improve the atmosphere of its waiting rooms, it can selectively change magazines, provide fresh coffee, or manage other forms of visible "evidence" of service quality. It could administer customer surveys to ferret out the attitudinal effects of these seemingly minor modifications. Similar things could be done in the process side, such as changing greeting "scripts" at reception. Findings from such experiments, both good and bad, could then be conveyed systematically to its other HMO clinics. Some service firms are working along these lines, of course. Banc One has a formalized process for providing the results of operations experiments to its member banks, a practice that CEO John McCoy credits for rapid implementation of its operating improvements. Likewise, Cal Fed Savings uses every other Monday conference calls among its regional managers to share sales and operating techniques that worked and didn't work. The regional managers then share this information with their branch managers.

Another approach is to use home office "pilot plants" to evaluate the layout and appearance of a field unit. The Limited has full-size store interiors next to the president's office in its hangar-like home office, enabling executives to tinker with the design until they get it right.

MAKING THE TRANSITION

Unlike manufacturing, which has often pushed operations to the background, the service sector challenges operations executives to use their inherently central position more effectively. We believe these executives should take the lead in changing their area's relationship to customers, employees, and processes. We propose three broad categories of change.

1. FROM CLOSED SYSTEM TO OPEN SYSTEM In a 1978 article, one of us advocated that many service activities should be shifted to a remote back office in order to maximize efficiency.[12] This, after all, seemed to work well for manufacturers because it kept outside influences, that is, customers, from disturbing the production process. If a technician is assembling a widget,

you don't want the customer asking him what he's doing. Or if a clerk is processing forms, talking to the customer on the phone takes her away from her job. In retrospect, this closed system philosophy overlooked the fact that there are positive benefits to both the customer and the organization by having the customer closely linked to the server, even though the job is traditionally performed in the customer's absence. From an information exchange perspective, the greater the links between consumer and producer, the easier it is to understand and respond to the customer's needs. In manufacturing, the ability to link the producer with the consumer through direct computer linkups driving CAD/CAM systems has provided the technological wherewithal to go "forward to the past" to a craftsman-type organization. That is, it has reintegrated design, production, and even sales into the manufacturing firm's "back office" — its factory.

That this open systems philosophy can be applied to services can be seen in the following practices:

☐ Desk sharing between customer service representatives and operations clerks at the London suburb administrative offices of Citibank. (In the Letter of Credit department, a customer service rep told the customer on the phone that a special request couldn't be processed by operations. The operations clerk, overhearing the conversation, said, "Oh yes, we can.")[13]

☐ Assignment of back office production workers in insurance companies and banks to specific customers so that they can give personalized service.

☐ Production worker outreach programs. For example, Chestnut Hill (Philadelphia) Toyota's mechanics are required to call recent customers to find out how the car they repaired is working.

☐ Bringing traditionally behind-the-scenes production workers on stage to "do their stuff" in front of the customer. Stu Leonard's Norwalk, Connecticut, Dairy Store (of Tom Peters fame) has several such show-off jobs. One involves a meat cutter and a packer slicing rolls of beef into steaks and packaging them in styrofoam. The team works in the center of the store in a glass booth. The cutter puts on a show, performing artistic flourishes with his cleaver, while his helper smoothly flips and wraps the steaks.

2. FROM PROCEDURES FOCUS TO CUSTOMER FOCUS Every service firm executive will aver that his or her organization is customer oriented and service driven. However, if you scratch the surface of the organization, you will encounter an armadillo-like armor of procedures and rules that quickly indicates otherwise. "Bureaucracy, thy name is service firm."

To break out of the procedures trap, ask how you can make the encounter more "user friendly"; each rule you eliminate is value added from the customer's perspective. It is here, by the way, that systems and procedures groups should direct more of their attention, rather than to back office work simplification. In fact, we would go even further and advocate a new position—customer task analyst—to look for ways to simplify the customer's role in the service encounter. Admittedly, many services find ways of easing the customer's job, but rarely do they approach it with the same degree of analysis that they apply to their employees' jobs.

3. FROM ISLANDS OF ACTIVITY TO TOTAL ENTERPRISE INTEGRATION Manufacturing and service firms face a common problem—coordination of activities around a common purpose. Although both have made extensive use of information technology—CAD/CAM and materials management in manufacturing and database management and transaction processing in services—both are still wrestling with the age old problem of getting departments to work together. The common contemporary solution is to cast each operating unit as a service supplier to the next downstream operation unit, that is, establishing an internal "supplier–customer" relationship. American Express, Xerox, and Hewlett-Packard are primary exponents of this philosophy. For many firms, however, this approach is only marginally successful, for the simple reason that many important supplier duties are not explicitly measured, monitored, and most of all, rewarded in performance reviews. Let's face it, no matter how company oriented the manager, helping the other guy will always be a secondary priority, unless it is an important and rewarded priority on the management by objectives sheet. We are not advocating that the downstream customer philosophy be dropped. Far from it. What we do advocate is that internal supplier service duties and actions be clearly acknowledged in the organization's performance measurement and reward system.

CONCLUSION

A company's stage of operations effectiveness reflects directly on its vulnerability to competition. A Stage 1 company, for example, will generally operate successfully as long as it remains protected by location or personal relationships, or if all its competitors are also in Stage 1. Corner groceries, dry cleaners, and hamburger joints are examples. Such companies become vulnerable, however, as soon as their niche is invaded by a company that is more representative of the industry as a whole and has elevated its operating capabilities to Stage 2 status. The corner grocery becomes threatened by a new 7-11 store, and the hamburger joint by a new Burger King. They must then either differentiate themselves from these new competitors, elevate their operations to Stage 2 status, or retreat to a new niche.

Almost by definition, Stage 2 companies can compete with reasonable success within their domestic industry. But if one or more of their competitors elevates its operations capabilities to Stage 3, and can thereby offer superior cost, quality, flexibility-responsiveness, or convenience, they find themselves in trouble. This happens most dramatically after an industry restructuring. A bank, for example, that was able to offer one-stop banking services profitably under regulation may find itself unable to compete against other banks or financial service firms that focus on providing superior service of a more restricted product line. Like those airlines that found themselves after deregulation suddenly vulnerable to competitors that had consciously focused and upgraded their operating capabilities, such companies often end up seeking salvation through merger.

Stage 3 companies are like elephants and whales; they are the kings of their respective environments and have no natural predators, except one. But that one, humanity, is decimating both species. So it is that the only competitor that a Stage 3 company has to fear is a world class Stage 4 company—one that has developed its capabilities and honed its operations to the point that it can compete anywhere in the world. Once it has attained Stage 4, a company can successfully enter a number of national markets, and it often does so with surprising speed and effectiveness. Witness the speed with which Citicorp's $8 billion consumer banking division entered and came to dominate many of its forty foreign markets.

The danger for a Stage 3 company is that, despite its evident success and lack of visible challengers, one or more Stage 4 companies may be gestating out of sight in some foreign environment. When such competitors enter a new country, they usually force a rapid escalation in competitive intensity. This can be seen in the case of airline competition, where seven of the top ten international airlines are foreign competitors, with only American Airlines ranking in the top five (fifth), in a 1989 poll.[14] And there is evidence that additional Stage 4 companies are incubating in many other service industries: DHL (express mail), Japan's Yaohan Department Stores, Hong Kong's Chuo Trust & Banking, and

Thailand's Oriental Hotel. Clearly, the time to prepare one's operations strategy for the eventual battle is now, while those emerging world class service organizations, be they foreign or domestic, are still preparing themselves for the attack.

REFERENCES

1. J. Heskett, *Managing in the Service Economy* (Boston: Harvard Business School Press, 1986), p. 1.

2. Heskett (1986), p. 2.

3. There are, of course, other dimensions by which services differ from manufacturing, particularly at the point of encounter. Services are intangible, perishable (they can't be inventoried), and heterogeneous (no two are exactly alike), and they are produced and consumed simultaneously. See: W. E. Sasser, R. P. Olsen, and D. D. Wyckoff, *Management of Services Operations, Text and Cases* (New York: Allyn & Bacon, 1978), pp. 8–18.

4. S. C. Wheelwright and R. H. Hayes, "Competing through Manufacturing," *Harvard Business Review,* January–February 1985, pp. 99–109.

5. At this point in the model's development, positioning of a firm within it must depend upon managerial judgment rather than a formal scoring methodology.

6. R. Hill, "How the Business Traveler Changed the Economics and the Bottom Line at SAS," *International Management,* February 1985, pp. 61–68.

7. One of the authors of this article had the unique experience of leading a service quality seminar for 103 members of the LAPD, including the chief, in June. The seminar focused on people as customers of police services.

8. See B. Ives and R. O. Mason, "Can Information Technology Revitalize Your Customer Service?" *Academy of Management Executives* 4 (1990): 52–69; and R. E. Walton, *Up and Running, Integrating Information Technology and the Organization* (Boston: Harvard Business School Press, 1989).

9. G. Hector, "It's Banquet Time for Bank of America," *Fortune,* 3 June 1991, pp. 69–78.

10. W. Skinner, "The Focused Factory," *Harvard Business Review,* May–June 1974, pp. 113–121.

11. W. Skinner, "Manufacturing—The Missing Link in Corporate Strategy," *Harvard Business Review,* May–June 1969, p. 141.

12. R. B. Chase, "Where Does the Customer Fit in a Service Operation?" *Harvard Business Review,* November–December 1978, pp. 137–142.

13. Example provided by Dr. John Bateson of the MAC consulting group.

14. The reasons: Attentive customer service and free drinks and movies provided by foreign carriers. While U.S. airlines carp that "foreign service isn't really better, just different from what they usually get," passengers are voting with their seats, resulting in a two percent drop in one year in market share for U.S. carriers in trips between the U.S. and Europe. See: "Patrons Are Defecting to Foreign Carriers," *Wall Street Journal,* 15 May 1990, p. B2.

PUTTING THE SERVICE-PROFIT CHAIN TO WORK

James L. Heskett

Thomas O. Jones

Gary W. Loveman

W. Earl Sasser, Jr.

Leonard A. Schlesinger

*When service companies put employees and customers first,
a radical shift occurs in the way they manage
and measure success.*

Top-level executives of outstanding service organizations spend little time setting profit goals or focusing on market share, the management mantra of the 1970s and 1980s. Instead, they understand that in the new economics of service, frontline workers and customers need to be the center of management concern. Successful service managers pay attention to the factors that drive profitability in this new service paradigm: investment in people, technology that supports frontline workers, revamped recruiting and training practices, and compensation linked to performance for employees at every level. And they express a vision of leadership in terms rarely heard in corporate America: an organization's "patina of spirituality," the "importance of the mundane."

A growing number of companies that includes Banc One, Intuit Corporation, Southwest Airlines, ServiceMaster, USAA, Taco Bell, and MCI know that when they make employees and customers paramount, a radical shift occurs in the way they manage and measure success. The new economics of service requires innovative measurement techniques. These techniques calibrate the impact of employee satisfaction, loyalty, and productivity on the value of products and services delivered so that

managers can build customer satisfaction and loyalty and assess the corresponding impact on profitability and growth. In fact, the lifetime value of a loyal customer can be astronomical, especially when referrals are added to the economics of customer retention and repeat purchases of related products. For example, the lifetime revenue stream from a loyal pizza eater can be $8,000, a Cadillac owner $332,000, and a corporate purchaser of commercial aircraft literally billions of dollars.

The service-profit chain, developed from analyses of successful service organizations, puts "hard" values on "soft" measures. It helps managers target new investments to develop service and satisfaction levels for maximum competitive impact, widening the gap be-tween service leaders and their merely good competitors.

SOURCE: James L. Heskett, Thomas O. Jones, Gary W. Loveman, W. Earl Sasser, Jr., and Leonard A. Schlesinger, "Putting the Service-Profit Chain to Work," *Harvard Business Review*, (March–April 1994): 165–174. Reprinted by permission of *Harvard Business Review*. Copyright © 1994 by the President and Fellows of Harvard College; All rights reserved.

James L. Heskett, Thomas O. Jones, Gary W. Loveman, W. Earl Sasser, Jr., and Leonard A. Schlesinger are members of the Harvard Business School faculty and service-management interest group.

THE SERVICE-PROFIT CHAIN

The service-profit chain establishes relationships between profitability, customer loyalty, and employee satisfaction, loyalty, and productivity. The links in the chain (which should be regarded as propositions) are as follows: Profit and growth are stimulated primarily by customer loyalty. Loyalty is a direct result of customer satisfaction. Satisfaction is largely influenced by the value of services provided to customers. Value is created by satisfied, loyal, and productive employees. Employee satisfaction, in turn, results primarily from high-quality support services and policies that enable employees to deliver results to customers. (See the chart, "The Links in the Service-Profit Chain.")

The service-profit chain is also defined by a special kind of leadership. CEOs of exemplary service companies emphasize the importance of each employee and customer. For these CEOs, the focus on customers and employees is no empty slogan tailored to an annual management meeting. For example, Herbert Kelleher, CEO of Southwest Airlines, can be found aboard airplanes, on tarmacs, and in terminals, interacting with employees and customers. Kelleher believes that hiring employees that have the right attitude is so important that the hiring process takes on a "patina of spirituality." In addition, he believes that "anyone who looks at things solely in terms of factors that can easily be quantified is missing the heart of business, which is people." William

Pollard, the chairman of Service-Master, continually underscores the importance of "teacher-learner" managers, who have what he calls "a servant's heart." And John McCoy, CEO of Banc One, stresses the "uncommon partnership," a system of support that provides maximum latitude to individual bank presidents while supplying information systems and common measurements of customer satisfaction and financial measures.

A closer look at each link reveals how the service-profit chain functions as a whole.

CUSTOMER LOYALTY DRIVES PROFITABILITY AND GROWTH

To maximize profit, managers have pursued the Holy Grail of becoming number-one or -two in their industries for nearly two decades. Recently, however, new measures of service industries like software and banking suggest that customer loyalty is a more important determinant of profit. (See Frederick F. Reichheld and W. Earl Sasser, Jr., "Zero Defections: Quality Comes to Services," *Harvard Business Review* September–October 1990.) Reichheld and Sasser estimate that a 5% increase in customer loyalty can produce profit increases from 25% to 85%. They conclude that *quality* of market share, measured in terms of customer loyalty, deserves as much attention as *quantity* of share.

Banc One, based in Columbus, Ohio, has developed a sophisticated system to track several factors

The Links in the Service-Profit Chain

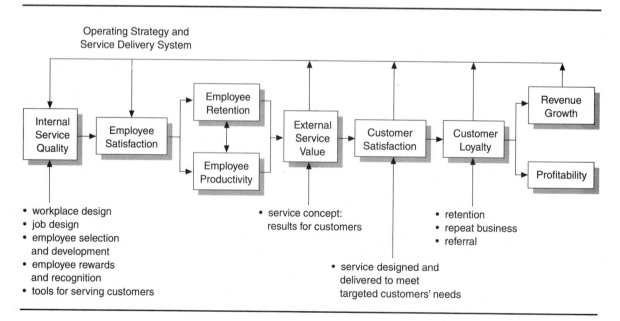

involved in customer loyalty and satisfaction. Once driven strictly by financial measures, Banc One now conducts quarterly measures of customer retention; the number of services used by each customer, or *depth of relationship;* and the level of customer satisfaction. The strategies derived from this information help explain why Banc One has achieved a return on assets more than double that of its competitors in recent years.

CUSTOMER SATISFACTION DRIVES CUSTOMER LOYALTY

Leading service companies are currently trying to quantify customer satisfaction. For example, for several years, Xerox has polled 480,000 customers per year regarding product and service satisfaction using a five-point scale from 5 (high) to 1 (low). Until two years ago, Xerox's goal was to achieve 100% 4s (satisfied) and 5s (very satisfied) by the end of 1993. But in 1991, an analysis of customers who gave Xerox 4s and 5s on satisfaction found that the relationships between the scores and actual loyalty differed greatly depending on whether the customers were very satisfied or satisfied. Customers giving Xerox 5s were six times more likely to repurchase Xerox equipment than those giving 4s.

This analysis led Xerox to extend its efforts to create *apostles*—a term coined by Scott D. Cook, CEO of software producer and distributor, Intuit Corporation, describing customers so satisfied that they convert the uninitiated to a product or service. Xerox's management currently wants to achieve 100% apostles, or 5s, by the end of 1996 by upgrading service levels and guaranteeing customer satisfaction. But just as important for Xerox's profitability is to avoid creating *terrorists:* customers so unhappy that they speak out against a poorly delivered service at every opportunity. Terrorists can reach hundreds of potential customers. In some instances, they can even discourage acquaintances from trying a service or product. (See the graph "A Satisfied Customer Is Loyal.")

VALUE DRIVES CUSTOMER SATISFACTION

Customers today are strongly value oriented. But just what does that mean? Customers tell us that value means the results they receive in relation to the total costs (both the price and other costs to customers incurred in acquiring the service). The insurance company, Progressive Corporation, is creating just this kind of value for its customers by processing and paying claims quickly and with little policyholder effort.

A Satisfied Customer Is Loyal

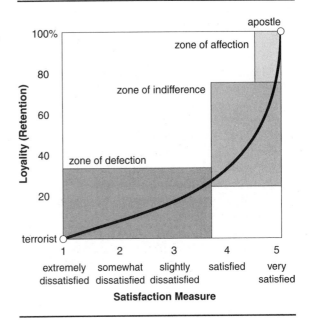

Members of the company's CAT (catastrophe) team fly to the scene of major accidents, providing support services like transportation and housing and handling claims rapidly. By reducing legal costs and actually placing more money in the hands of the injured parties, the CAT team more than makes up for the added expenses the organization incurs by maintaining the team. In addition, the CAT team delivers value to customers, which helps explain why Progressive has one of the highest margins in the property-and-casualty insurance industry.

EMPLOYEE PRODUCTIVITY DRIVES VALUE

At Southwest Airlines, the seventh-largest U.S. domestic carrier, an astonishing story of employee productivity occurs daily. Eighty-six percent of the company's 14,000 employees are unionized. Positions are designed so that employees can perform several jobs if necessary. Schedules, routes, and company practices—such as open seating and the use of simple, color-coded, reusable boarding passes—enable the boarding of three and four times more passengers per day than competing airlines. In fact, Southwest deplanes and reloads two-thirds of its flights in 15 minutes or less. Because of aircraft availability and short-haul routes that don't require long layovers for flight crews, Southwest has roughly 40% more pilot and aircraft utilization than its major competitors: its pilots fly on average 70 hours per month versus 50 hours at other airlines. These factors explain how the company can charge fares from 60% to 70% lower than existing fares in markets it enters.

At Southwest, customer perceptions of value are very high, even though the airlines does not assign seats, offer meals, or integrate its reservation system with other airlines. Customers place high value on South-west's frequent departures, on-time service, friendly employees, and very low fares. Southwest's management knows this because its major marketing research unit—its 14,000 employees—is in daily contact with customers and reports its findings back to management. In addition, the Federal Aviation Administration's performance measures show that Southwest, of all the major airlines, regularly achieves the highest level of on-time arrivals, the lowest number of complaints, and the fewest lost-baggage claims per 1,000 passengers. When combined with Southwest's low fares per seat-mile, these indicators show the higher value delivered by Southwest's employees compared with most domestic competitors. Southwest has been profitable for 21 consecutive years and was the only major airline to realize a profit in 1992. (See the graph "How Southwest Compares with Its Competitors.")

EMPLOYEE LOYALTY DRIVES PRODUCTIVITY

Traditional measures of the losses incurred by employee turnover concentrate only on the cost of recruiting, hir-

ing, and training replacements. In most service jobs, the real cost of turnover is the loss of productivity and decreased customer satisfaction. One recent study of an automobile dealer's sales personnel by Abt Associates concluded that the average monthly cost of replacing a sales representative who had five to eight years of experience with an employee who had less than one year of experience was as much as $36,000 in sales. And the costs of losing a valued broker at a securities firm can be still more dire. Conservatively estimated, it takes nearly five years for a broker to rebuild relationships with customers that can return $1 million per year in commissions to the brokerage house—a cumulative loss of at least $2.5 million in commissions.

EMPLOYEE SATISFACTION DRIVES LOYALTY

In one 1991 proprietary study of a property-and-casualty insurance company's employees, 30% of all dissatisfied employees registered an intention to leave the company, a potential turnover rate three times higher than that for satisfied employees. In this same case, low employee turnover was found to be linked closely to high customer satisfaction. In contrast, Southwest Airlines, recently named one of the country's ten best places to work, experiences the highest rate of employee retention in the airline industry. Satisfaction levels are so high that at some of its operating locations, employee turnover rates are less than 5% per year. USAA, a major provider of insurance and other financial services by

How Southwest Compares with Its Competitors

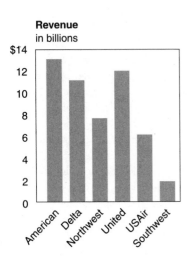

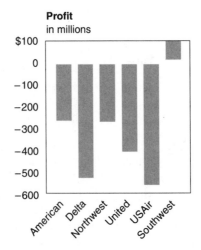

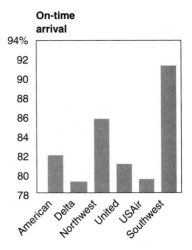

direct mail and phone, also achieves low levels of employee turnover by ensuring that its employees are highly satisfied. But what drives employee satisfaction? Is it compensation, perks, or plush workplaces?

INTERNAL QUALITY DRIVES EMPLOYEE SATISFACTION

What we call the *internal quality* of a working environment contributes most to employee satisfaction. Internal quality is measured by the feelings that employees have toward their jobs, colleagues, and companies. What do service employees value most on the job? Although our data are preliminary at best, they point increasingly to the ability and authority of service workers to achieve results for customers. At USAA, for example, telephone sales and service representatives are backed by a sophisticated information system that puts complete customer information files at their fingertips the instant they receive a customer's call. In addition, state-of-the-art, job-related training is made available to USAA employees. And the curriculum goes still further, with 200 courses in 75 classrooms on a wide range of subjects.

Internal quality is also characterized by the attitudes that people have toward one another and the way people serve each other inside the organization. For example, ServiceMaster, a provider of a range of cleaning and maintenance services, aims to maximize the dignity of the individual service worker. Each year, it analyzes in depth a part of the maintenance process, such as cleaning a floor, in order to reduce the time and effort need-

ed to complete the task. The "importance of the mundane" is stressed repeatedly in ServiceMaster's management training—for example, in the seven-step process devised for cleaning a hospital room: from the first step, greeting the patient, to the last step, asking patients whether or not they need anything else done. Using this process, service workers develop communication skills and learn to interact with patients in ways that add depth and dimension to their jobs.

LEADERSHIP UNDERLIES THE CHAIN'S SUCCESS

Leaders who understand the service-profit chain develop and maintain a corporate culture centered around service to customers and fellow employees. They display a willingness and ability to listen. Successful CEOS like John Martin of Taco Bell, John McCoy of Banc One, Herb Kelleher of Southwest, and Bill Pollard of ServiceMaster spend a great deal of time with customers and employees, experiencing their companies' service processes while listening to employees for suggestions for improvement. They care about their employees and spend a great deal of time selecting, tracking, and recognizing them.

For example, Brigadier General Robert Mc-Dermott, until recently chairman and CEO of USAA, reflected, "Public recognition of outstanding employees flows naturally from our corporate culture. That culture is talked about all the time, and we live it." According to Scott Cook at Intuit, "Most people take culture as a

---

How Southwest Compares with Its Competitors *(continued)*

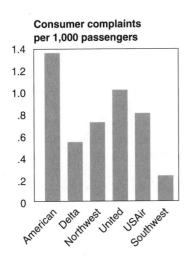
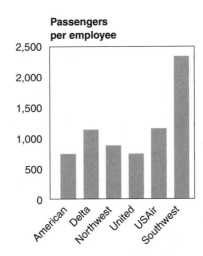
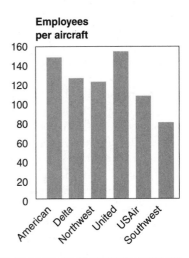

given. It is around you, the thinking goes, and you can't do anything about it. However, when you run a company, you have the opportunity to determine the culture. I find that when you champion the most noble values—including service, analysis, and database decision making—employees rise to the challenge, and you forever change their lives."

RELATING LINKS IN THE CHAIN FOR MANAGEMENT ACTION

While many organizations are beginning to measure relationships between individual links in the service-profit chain, only a few have related the links in meaningful ways—ways that can lead to comprehensive strategies for achieving lasting competitive advantage.

The 1991 proprietary study of a property-and-casualty insurance company, cited earlier, not only identified the links between employee satisfaction and loyalty but also established that a primary source of job satisfaction was the service workers' perceptions of their ability to meet customer needs. Those who felt they did meet customer needs registered job satisfaction levels more than twice as high as those who felt they didn't. But even more important, the same study found that when a service worker left the company, customer satisfaction levels dropped sharply from 75% to 55%. As a result of this analysis, management is trying to reduce turnover among customer-contact employees and to enhance their job skills.

Similarly, in a study of its seven telephone customer service centers, MCI found clear relationships between employees' perceptions of the quality of MCI service and employee satisfaction. The study also linked employee satisfaction directly to customer satisfaction and intentions to continue to use MCI services. Identifying these relationships motivated MCI's management to probe deeper and determine what affected job satisfaction at the service centers. The factors they uncovered, in order of importance, were satisfaction with the job itself, training, pay, advancement fairness, treatment with respect and dignity, teamwork, and the company's interest in employees' well-being. Armed with this information, MCI's management began examining its policies concerning those items valued most by employees at its service centers. MCI has incorporated information about its service capabilities into training and communications efforts and television advertising.

No organization has made a more comprehensive effort to measure relationships in the service-profit chain and fashion a strategy around them than the fast-food company, Taco Bell, a subsidiary of Pepsi-Co. Taco Bell's management tracks profits daily by unit, market manager, zone, and country. By integrating this information with the results of exit interviews that Taco Bell conducts with 800,000 customers annually, management has found that stores in the top quadrant of customer satisfaction ratings outperform the others by all measures. As a result, it has linked no less than 20% of all operations managers' compensation in company-owned stores to customer satisfaction ratings, realizing a subsequent increase in both customer satisfaction ratings and profits.

However, Taco Bell's efforts don't stop there. By examining employee turnover records for individual stores, Taco Bell has discovered that the 20% of the stores with the lowest turnover rates enjoy double the sales and 55% higher profits than the 20% of stores with the highest employee turnover rates. As a result of this self-examination, Taco Bell has instituted financial and other incentives in order to reverse the cycle of failure that is associated with poor employee selection, subpar training, low pay, and high turnover.

In addition, Taco Bell monitors internal quality through a network of 800 numbers created to answer employees' questions, field their complaints, remedy situations, and alert top-level management to potential trouble spots. It also conducts periodic employee roundtable meetings, interviews, as well as a comprehensive companywide survey every two or three years in order to measure satisfaction. As a result of all this work, Taco Bell's employee satisfaction program features a new selection process, improved skill building, increased latitude for decision making on the job, further automation of unpleasant "back room" labor, and, finally, greater opportunities for employee promotion into management positions.

Relating all the links in the service-profit chain may seem to be a tall order. But profitability depends not only on placing hard values on soft measures but also on linking those individual measures together into a comprehensive service picture. Service organizations need to quantify their investments in people—both customers and employees. The service-profit chain provides the framework for this critical task.

SERVICE-PROFIT CHAIN AUDIT

A service-profit chain audit helps companies determine what drives their profit and suggests actions that can lead to long-term profitability. As they review the audit, managers should ask themselves what efforts are under way to obtain answers to the following questions and what those answers reveal about their companies.

PROFIT AND GROWTH

1. *How do we define loyal customers?*

    Customers often become more profitable over time. And loyal customers account for an unusually high proportion of the sales and profit growth of successful service providers. In some organizations, loyalty is measured in terms of whether or not a customer is on the company rolls. But several companies have found that their most loyal customers—the top 20% of total customers—not only provide all the profit but also cover losses incurred in dealing with less loyal customers.

    Because of the link between loyal customers and profit, Banc One measures *depth of relationship*—the number of available related financial services, such as checking, lending, and safe deposit, actually used by customers. Recognizing the same relationship, Taco Bell measures "share of stomach" to assess the company's sales against all other food purchases a customer can potentially make. As a result, the fast-food chain is trying to reach consumers through kiosks, carts, trucks, and the shelves of supermarkets.

2. *Do measurements of customer profitability include profits from referrals?*

    Companies that measure the stream of revenue and profits from loyal customers (retention) and repeat sales often overlook what can be the most important of the three Rs of loyalty: referrals. For example, Intuit provides high-quality, free lifetime service for a personal finance software package that sells for as little as $30. The strategy makes sense when the value of a loyal customer is considered—a revenue stream of several thousands of dollars from software updates, supplies, and new customer referrals. With this strategy in place, Intuit increased its sales to more than $30 million with just two U.S. field sales representatives.

3. *What proportion of business development expenditures and incentives are directed to the retention of existing customers?*

    Too many companies concentrate nearly all their efforts on attracting new customers. But in businesses like life insurance, a new policyholder doesn't become profitable for at least three years. In the credit-card finance business, the break-even point for a new customer is often six or more years because of high-marketing and bad-debt costs in the first year of a relationship with cardholders. These costs must be defrayed by profits from loyal customers, suggesting the need for a careful division of organizational effort between customer retention and development.

4. *Why do our customers defect?*

    It's important to find out not only where defectors go but also why they defect. Was it because of poor service, price, or value? Answers to these questions provide information about whether or not existing strategies are working. In addition, exit interviews of customers can have real sales impact. For example, at one credit-card service organization, a phone call to question cardholders who had stopped using their cards led to the immediate reinstatement of one-third of the defectors.

CUSTOMER SATISFACTION

5. *Are customer satisfaction data gathered in an objective, consistent, and periodic fashion?*

    Currently, the weakest measurements being used by the companies we have studied concern customer satisfaction. At some companies, high levels of reported customer satisfaction are contradicted by continuing declines in sales and profits. Upon closer observation, we discovered that the service providers were "gaming" the data, using manipulative methods for collecting customer satisfaction data. In one extreme case, an automobile dealer sent a questionnaire to recent buyers with the highest marks already filled in, requiring owners to alter the marks only if they disagreed. Companies can, however, obtain more objective results using "third party" interviews; "mystery shopping" by unidentified, paid observers; or technologies like touch-screen television.

    Consistency is at least as important as the actual questions asked of customers. Some of Banc One's operating units formerly conducted their own customer satisfaction surveys. Today the surveys have been centralized, made mandatory, and are administered by mail on a quarterly basis to around 125,000 customers. When combined with periodic measurement, the surveys provide highly relevant trend information that informs the managerial decision-making process. Similarly, Xerox's measures of satisfaction obtained from 10,000 customers per month—a product of an unchanging set of survey questions and very large samples—make possible period-to-period comparisons that are important in measuring and rewarding performance.

6. *Where are the listening posts for obtaining customer feedback in your organization?*

Listening posts are tools for collecting data from customers and systematically translating those data into information in order to improve service and products. Common examples are letters of complaint. Still more important listening posts are reports from field sales and service personnel or the logs of telephone service representatives. Intuit's content analysis of customer service inquiries fielded by service representatives produced over 50 software improvements and 100 software documentation improvements in a single year. USAA has gone one step further by automating the feedback process to enter data online, enabling its analysis and plans departments to develop corrective actions.

7. *How is information concerning customer satisfaction used to solve customer problems?*

In order to handle customer problems, service providers must have the latitude to resolve any situation promptly. In addition, information regarding a customer concern must be transmitted to the service provider quickly. Customers and employees must be encouraged to report rather than suppress concerns. For example, one Boston-area Lexus dealer notified its customers, "If you are experiencing a problem with your car or our service department and you can't answer '100% satisfied' when you receive your survey directly from Lexus, please give us the opportunity to correct the problem before you fill out the survey. Lexus takes its customer surveys very seriously."

EXTERNAL SERVICE VALUE

8. *How do you measure service value?*

Value is a function not only of costs to the customer but also of the results achieved for the customer. Value is always relative because it is based both on perceptions of the way a service is delivered and on initial customer expectations. Typically, a company measures value using the reasons expressed by customers for high or low satisfaction. Because value varies with individual expectations, efforts to improve value inevitably require service

organizations to move all levels of management closer to the customer and give frontline service employees the latitude to customize a standard service to individual needs.

9. *How is information concerning customers' perceptions of value shared with those responsible for designing a product or service?*

Relaying information concerning customer expectations to those responsible for design often requires the formation of teams of people responsible for sales, operations, and service or product design, as well as the frequent assignment of service designers to tasks requiring field contact with customers. Intuit has created this kind of capability in product development teams. And all Intuit employees, including the CEO, must periodically work on the customer service phones. Similarly, at Southwest, those responsible for flight scheduling periodically work shifts in the company's terminals to get a feel for the impact of schedules on customer and employee satisfaction.

10. *To what extent are measures taken of differences between customers' perceptions of quality delivered and their expectations before delivery?*

Ultimately, service quality is a function of the gap between perceptions of the actual service experienced and what a customer expected before receiving that service. Actual service includes both final results and the process through which those results were obtained. Differences between experiences and expectations can be measured in generic dimensions such as the reliability and timeliness of service, the empathy and authority with which the service was delivered, and the extent to which the customer is left with tangible evidence (like a calling card) that the service has been performed.

11. *Do our organization's efforts to improve external service quality emphasize effective recovery from service errors in addition to providing a service right the first time?*

A popular concept of quality in manufacturing is the importance of "doing things right the first time." But customers of service organizations often allow one mistake. Some organizations are very good at delivering service as long as nothing goes wrong. Others organize for and thrive on service emergencies. Outstanding service organizations do both by giving frontline employees the latitude to effect recovery. Southwest Airlines maintains a policy of allowing frontline employees to do whatever they feel comfortable doing in order to satisfy customers. Xerox authorizes frontline service employees to replace up to $250,000 worth of equipment if customers are not getting results.

EMPLOYEE PRODUCTIVITY

12. *How do you measure employee productivity?*
13. *To what extent do measures of productivity identify changes in the quality as well as the quantity of service produced per unit of input?*

In many services, the ultimate measure of quality may be customer satisfaction. That measure should be combined with measures of quantity to determine the total output of the service organization. At ServiceMaster, for example, measures of output in the schools and hospitals cleaned under the company's supervision include both numbers of work orders performed per employee hour and the quality of the work done, as determined by periodic inspections performed by ServiceMaster and client personnel. Similarly, Southwest Airlines delivers relatively high levels of productivity in terms of both quality and quantity. In fact, outstanding service competitors are replacing the typical "either/or" trade-off between quality and quantity with an "and/also" imperative.

EMPLOYEE LOYALTY

14. *How do you create employee loyalty?*

Employee loyalty goes hand in hand with productivity, contradicting the conventional wisdom that successful service providers should be promoted to larger supervisory responsibilities or moved to a similar job in a larger business unit. ServiceMaster and Taco Bell have expanded jobs without promoting good service workers away from their customers. At ServiceMaster, effective single-unit managers are given supervisory responsibilities for custodial, maintenance, or other workers at more than one hospital or school. Taco Bell gives restaurant general managers a "hunting license" to develop new sales sites in the neighborhoods served by their restaurants and rewards them for doing it.

15. *Have we made an effort to determine the right level of employee retention?*

Rarely is the right level of retention 100%. Dynamic service organizations require a certain level of turnover. However, in calibrating desired turnover levels, it is important to take into account the full cost of the loss of key service providers, including those of lost sales and productivity and added recruiting, selection, and training.

EMPLOYEE SATISFACTION

16. *Is employee satisfaction measured in ways that can be linked to similar measures of customer satisfaction with sufficient frequency and consistency to establish trends for management use?*

Taco Bell studies employee satisfaction through surveys, frequent interviews, and roundtable meetings. Customer satisfaction is measured by interviews with customers conducted biannually and includes questions about satisfaction with employee friendliness and hustle. Both the employee and customer satisfaction rankings are comprehensive, store-specific, and conducted frequently. With these data, the company can better understand overall trends and the links between employee and customer satisfaction.

17. *Are employee selection criteria and methods geared to what customers, as well as managers, believe are important?*

At Southwest Airlines, for example, frequent fliers are regularly invited to participate in the auditioning and selection of cabin attendants. And many take time off from work to join Southwest's employee selection team as it carries out its work. As one customer commented, "Why not do it? It's my airline."

18. *To what extent are measures of customer satisfaction, customer loyalty, or the quality and quantity of service output used in recognizing and rewarding employees?*

Employee recognition may often involve little more than informing individual employees or employees as a group about service improvements and individual successes. Banc One goes one step further, including customer satisfaction measures for each banking unit in its periodic report of other performance measures, mostly financial, to all units.

INTERNAL SERVICE QUALITY

19. *Do employees know who their customers are?*

It is particularly difficult for employees to identify their customers when those customers are internal to the company. These employees often do not know what impact their work has on other departments. Identifying internal customers requires mapping and communicating characteristics of work flow, organizing periodic cross-departmental meetings between "customers" and "servers," and recognizing good internal service performance.

In 1990, USAA organized a PRIDE (Professionalism Results in Dedication to Excellence) team of 100 employees and managers to examine and improve on a function-by-function basis all processes associated with property-and-casualty insurance administration, which included analyzing customer needs and expectations. The PRIDE effort was so successful that it led to a cross-functional review of USAA's service processing. Service processing time has been reduced, as have handoffs of customers from one server to another.

20. *Are employees satisfied with the technological and personal support they receive on the job?*

The cornerstone of success at Taco Bell is the provision of the latest in information technology, food service equipment, simple work-scheduling techniques, and effective team training. This practice led to the establishment of self-managing teams of service providers. Also, the quality of work life involves selecting the right workers. Winners like to be associated with winners. Better employees tend to refer people they like and people like themselves. Internal service quality can also be thought of as the quality of work life. It is a visible expression of an organization's culture, one influenced in important ways by leadership.

LEADERSHIP.

21. *To what extent is the company's leadership:*
    a. energetic, creative vs. stately, conservative?

    b. participatory, caring vs. removed, elitist?

    c. listening, coaching, and teaching vs. supervising and managing?

    d. motivating by mission vs. motivating by fear?

    e. leading by means of personally demonstrated values vs. institutionalized policies?

22. *How much time is spent by the organization's leadership personally developing and maintaining a corporate culture centered around service to customers and fellow employees?*

Leaders naturally have individual traits and styles. But the CEOs of companies that are successfully using the service-profit chain possess all or most of a set of traits that separate them from their merely good competitors. Of course, different styles of leadership are appropriate for various stages in an organization's development. But the messages sent by the successful leaders we have observed stress the importance of careful attention to the needs of customers and employees. These leaders create a culture capable of adapting to the needs of both.

RELATING THE MEASURES

23. *What are the most important relationships in your company's service-profit chain?*

24. *To what extent does each measure correlate with profit and growth at the frontline level?*

25. *Is the importance of these relationships reflected in rewards and incentives offered to employees?*

Measures drive action when they are related in ways that provide managers with direction. To enjoy the kind of success that service organizations like Southwest Airlines, ServiceMaster, and Taco Bell have enjoyed, looking at individual measures is not enough. Only if the individual measures are tied together into a comprehensive picture will the service-profit chain provide a foundation for unprecedented profit and growth.

SERVICE FIRMS' INTERNATIONAL ENTRY-MODE CHOICE

A MODIFIED TRANSACTION-COST ANALYSIS APPROACH

M. Krishna Erramilli
University of North Texas

C. P. Rao
University of Arkansas

Some peculiar characteristics of service firms, such as low capital intensity and the inseparability of production and consumption, have necessitated the modification of the traditional transaction-cost framework used to study entry-mode choice. By relaxing some unduly restrictive assumptions of the conventional transaction-cost analysis (TCA) model, the paper argues that firms prefer to start with full-control modes. It postulates that substantial variation in entry-mode choice occurs when firms that are characterized by low asset specificity relinquish control in response to the rising costs of integration or the diminishing ability to integrate. Several hypotheses on the propensity of service firms to employ shared-control entry modes are developed and tested. The results not only provide insights into entry-mode choice by service firms but also indicate how the transaction-cost framework can be broadened to develop a more comprehensive model for understanding entry-mode choice.

After a firm decides to enter a certain foreign market, it must choose a mode of entry, i.e., select an institutional arrangement for organizing and conducting international business transactions, such as contractual transfers, joint ventures, and wholly owned operations (Root 1987).

The choice of the correct entry mode for a particular foreign market is "one of the most critical decisions in international marketing" (Terpstra and Sarathy 1991, p. 361). The chosen mode determines the extent to which the firm gets involved in developing and implementing marketing programs in the foreign market, the amount of control the firm enjoys over its marketing activities, and the degree to which it succeeds in foreign

markets (Anderson and Gatignon 1986; Root 1987; Hill et al. 1990; Terpstra and Sarathy 1991). In fact, Wind and Perlmutter (1977) describe entry-mode choice as a "frontier issue" in international marketing.

As service firms assume greater prominence in international business (U.S. Congress 1986; Cateora 1990, p. 451), researchers are beginning to ask how service firms effect entry into foreign markets and whether they differ from manufacturers in this respect (Carman and Langeard 1980; Cowell 1983; Sharma and Johanson 1987; Erramilli 1990). However, for several reasons the international marketing literature offers few concrete answers to these questions.

First, previous investigations examining entry-mode choice have focused almost exclusively on manufacturing firms (see Agarwal and Ramaswami 1992; Gatignon and Anderson 1988; Kogut and Singh 1988; and Hill et al. 1990 for excellent reviews of this literature). Second, most published studies on the international operations of service firms do not directly address

SOURCE: M. Krishna Erramilli and C. P. Rao, "Service Firms' International Entry-Mode Choice: A Modified Transaction-Cost Analysis Approach," *Journal of Marketing*, Vol. 57 (July 1993): 19–38.

M. Krishna Erramilli is Assistant Professor of Marketing at the University of North Texas. C. P. Rao is University Professor of Marketing and Walton Lecturer in Strategic Marketing at the University of Arkansas. The authors thank Barbara Coe, Subhash Jain, Essam Mahmoud, and Jeffrey Sager for their helpful comments on earlier versions of this paper. They also gratefully acknowledge the suggestions made by William Darden and Tracy Murray on the original research project that resulted in this manuscript. In addition, they are deeply obliged to three anonymous JM reviewers for their contributions.

the question of entry-mode choice (e.g., Bower 1968; Gaedeke 1973; Hackett 1976; Cowell 1983; Palmer 1985; Sharma and Johanson 1987; and Terpstra and Yu 1988). Finally, the few studies that do examine the issue provide limited insights, because entry-mode choice is not the focus of their investigations (Weinstein 1974, 1977; Lo and Yung 1988) or because they are not driven by well-established theory (Erramilli 1990; Erramilli and Rao 1990).

Thus, existing knowledge concerning how firms choose entry modes has emanated almost entirely from the manufacturing sector. However, a growing stream of recent literature suggests that service firms differ from manufacturing firms (Bowen, Siehel, and Schneider 1989; Larsson and Bowen 1989; Berry 1980; Lovelock 1983; Chase and Tansik 1989) and face unique challenges in their foreign-market entry and expansion process (Carman and Langeard 1980). This article will strive to demonstrate some peculiar characteristics of service firms (e.g., low capital intensity) that warrant adaptation of the underlying theory used to investigate entry-mode choice. Moreover, case studies on the internationalization of technical consultancy firms by Sharma and Johanson (1987) suggest that results obtained for manufacturing firms are not necessarily generalizable to service firms. Therefore, there exists a strong need to rigorously examine the process by which service firms choose entry modes.

SCOPE AND PURPOSE

This study focuses on the choice of entry modes in the *service* sector and includes a broad range of service industries, spanning both business and consumer services. It covers choice among wholly owned operations, joint ventures, and contractual transfers but not export modes of entry, because the theory employed, transaction-cost analysis (TCA), is not appropriate for comparing exports with foreign direct investment methods (Hennart 1989).[1] Unlike previous entry-mode investigations, which were generally confined to the activities of large multinational corporations, it includes small and medium-sized firms as well.

As Figure 1 depicts, contractual methods, joint ventures, and wholly owned operations represent increasing degrees of ownership, vertical integration, resource commitment, and risk from the firm's perspective (Root 1987; Kotler 1991, p. 413; Hill et al. 1990). Since wholly owned operations give the firm complete control of foreign production and marketing activities, they are designated *full-control* modes. In all other modes the firm generally has to share control with external entities; therefore, they are labeled *shared-control* modes.

The purpose of this paper is to *investigate how service firms choose between full-control and shared-control entry modes.* There are important reasons for confining the investigation to this binomial choice. When comparing entry modes, the only generalization that could be made with reasonable certainty is that wholly owned operations allow the firm more control than do other arrangements. The differences in control levels between different types of joint ventures and between joint ventures and contractual methods may often be indistinguishable or may be other than expected (Lecraw 1984). More to the point, the theory employed, TCA, has had less success in explaining the more complex multinomial choice among entry modes. For example, Gatignon and Anderson (1988) concluded that, while TCA is well equipped to explain why firms prefer full ownership to partnership, it does not distinguish well between the different *degrees* of partnership. Similarly, in reporting their investigation of integration in export channels, Klein, Frazier, and Roth (1990, p. 204) concede that "attempting to classify across four different options is difficult."

Following this introductory section the transaction-cost theory is described, as is the conceptual framework. The paper will argue why conventional TCA needs adaptation, describe the assumptions and approach, explain transaction-specific assets in the service sector, and develop several hypotheses on how the relationship between asset specificity and entry-mode choice is moderated. Then, separate sections will describe the sample and variables, and the model to be tested, followed by a discussion of the estimation process and results. Finally, the results will be summarized, including an understanding of their managerial and theoretical implications, along with the limitations of the study and suggestions for future research.

TRANSACTION-COST ANALYSIS

Applications of TCA have become fairly common in the general marketing literature (Anderson and Weitz 1986; Anderson and Schmittlein 1984; Dwyer and Oh 1988;

---

[1] It is inappropriate to use transaction costs to compare exports with foreign direct investment (FDI), since these two modes involve production in different locations. The choice between exports and FDI is less of a transaction-cost problem and more of a production-cost problem. This is supported by prevalent thinking on why firms would exploit their ownership-specific advantages using FDI rather than exports: the advantages of host-country production vis-à-vis home country production.

FIGURE 1   Entry Modes in the Service Sector

Basic Modes	Variations	Degree of Ownership/ Integration	Resource Commitment/ Risk	Designation
Contractual Transfer	Licensing, Franchising, Correspondent Banking	None/Little	None/Little	Shared-Control Mode
Joint Venture	Partnership, Consortium, Affiliate	↓	↓	Shared-Control Mode
Wholly Owned Operation	Subsidiary, Office, Branch, Project Office, Representative Office	Full	High	Full-Control Mode

Source: Based partly on Hill et al. (1990), Kotler (1991), and Anderson and Gatignon (1986).

Heide and John 1988, 1992), especially in entry-mode investigations (Anderson and Gatignon 1986; Anderson and Coughlan 1987; Gatignon and Anderson 1988; Klein 1989; Klein, Frazier, and Roth 1990). The theory appears to be especially effective in explaining vertical integration decisions.

A given task could be contracted out to external agents, partners, or suppliers (market-contracting or low-control modes) or it could be internalized and performed by the company's own employees (integration or full-control modes). The particular *governance* structure that is actually utilized in a given situation depends on the comparative transaction costs, that is, the costs of running a system, including the *ex ante* costs of negotiating a contract and the *ex post* costs of monitoring the performance and enforcing the behavior of the parties to the contract (Williamson 1985).

The TCA approach begins with the assumption that markets are competitive—i.e., that there are many potential suppliers—and that market pressures minimize the need for monitoring and enforcing supplier behavior (Hennart 1989). Under these conditions, market-contracting arrangements, or low-control modes, are favored because the threat of replacement dampens opportunism and forces suppliers to perform efficiently (Anderson and Coughlan 1987; Anderson and Gatignon 1986). When markets fail and the range of suppliers available to the firm is restricted (resulting in "small-numbers bargaining"), the supplier's tendency to behave opportunistically is reduced only through stringent negotiation and supervision of contractual relationships (Dwyer and Oh 1988), thereby greatly increasing the transaction costs associated with low-control modes. In such circumstances, the firm can significantly reduce its transaction costs by replacing external suppliers with its own employees, whose behavior it can monitor and

control more effectively (Hennart 1989; Klein 1989). Thus, market failure is the primary antecedent to the firm's decision to integrate and assume greater control.

From the transaction-cost perspective, the most important determinant of market failure is the presence of *transaction-specific assets* (Williamson 1986; Klein et al. 1990). Transaction-specific assets are nonredeployable physical and human investments that are specialized and unique to a task (Williamson 1985, 1986). For example, the production of a certain component may require investment in specialized equipment, the distribution of a certain product may necessitate unique physical facilities, or the delivery of a certain service may be predicated on the existence of an uncommon set of professional know-how and skills.

The *benefits* of integration under market failure (higher control, with attendant reduction of market transaction costs) must, however, be compared with the *costs* of integration. Establishment of an integrated operation entails significant *internal organization* or *bureaucratic* costs, including investments in legal, administrative, and operating infrastructures (Davidson and McFetridge 1985). The high overhead is thought to diminish the firm's ability to dissolve one type of institutional arrangement and move to another, resulting in high switching costs. As such, control is assumed to carry a high price. Anderson and Gatignon (1986) postulate that, in choosing entry modes, firms make trade-offs between *control* (benefit of integration) and *cost of resource commitments* (cost of integration). Transaction-cost theory predicts that firms integrate when asset specificity is high, because the higher costs of vertical integration are more than offset by the benefits flowing from such an arrangement. When specificity is low, firms refrain from integration because the benefits of control fall short of the costs of attaining it.

CONCEPTUAL FRAMEWORK

WHY MODIFY THE TCA MODEL?

Although the TCA framework has become a popular theoretical approach to investigating integration issues, there is a growing realization that "middle-range theoretical extensions . . . are needed to enable TCA to address specific classes of situations not adequately addressed in the global specification" (Heide and John 1988, p. 21). For instance, John and Weitz (1989) augment the transaction-cost framework with motivational variables to better explain sales force compensation. Similarly, Heide and John (1988) extend the model by employing dependence theory to explain how small firms with limited resources safeguard their transaction-specific investments. More recently, Heide and John (1992) have embellished the TCA approach with relational norms to explain buyer control over suppliers.

The authors' application of TCA to the service firm's entry-mode choice has uncovered certain shortcomings which necessitate modification of the basic model. TCA studies usually begin with the assumption that market-contracting or low-control modes represent the default choice for situations characterized by low asset specificity (e.g., Gatignon and Anderson 1988; Klein et al. 1990). For this assumption to be valid, the following two conditions must hold: (1) the only benefits of integration are a reduction of transaction costs in imperfect markets (thus eliminating all incentives for low-specificity[2] firms to integrate) and (2) the costs of integration are always high. Given these stipulations, low-specificity firms, i.e., firms characterized by low asset specificity, would find the cost-benefit analysis to unambiguously favor low-control ventures.

In practice, however, the first condition does not always hold true, as Anderson and Gatignon (1986) acknowledge. The literature is quite clear in emphasizing that, in addition to reducing transaction costs, firms often have numerous non-TCA motives to integrate. For instance, in their study of U.S. multinational corporations, Stopford and Wells (1972) observed a strong, well-entrenched "drive for unambiguous control" (p. 107). This occurs because control facilitates global integration and coordination of strategies in multinational corporations (Kobrin 1988; Hill et al. 1990), extends market power (Teece 1981), obtains a larger share of the foreign enterprise's profits (Anderson and Gatignon 1986), and overcomes the disadvantages inherent in shared-control ventures (conflicts with partners, partners becoming competitors, etc.) (Contractor and Lorange 1988).

Similarly, the second stipulation, concerning the high costs of integration, may not be strictly true in the case of many (although not all) service firms. Unquestionably, ownership of overseas *manufacturing* facilities entails considerable resource commitment, risk, and switching costs for most firms. This may not be true, however, for many service firms, especially in the professional and business services sector (e.g., advertising agencies and management consultants). For these firms, the creation of a wholly owned subsidiary is limited to establishing an office, which frequently involves little fixed overhead. Large-scale investments in plants, machinery, buildings, and other physical assets are not required. Even switching costs may be comparatively small, because the true value-generating assets in these types of service firms are often people, and people are relatively mobile.

Not surprisingly, Sharma and Johanson (1987) observed that Swedish technical consultancy service firms bypassed the incremental establishment chain followed by manufacturing firms, because "resource commitments are of minor significance" for the former. Consequently, the authors believe control can be acquired at comparatively low expense by many service firms. It must be emphasized that there are service firms for which integration entails large-scale investments in physical facilities (hospitals, hotels, airlines, etc.). The authors are merely contesting the general presumption that integration is *always* a high-resource proposition.

It is clear that the assumption that low-specificity firms will automatically resort to shared-control modes is unduly restrictive. If internal organization costs are low enough, such firms can be expected to assume control in order to exploit non-TCA benefits. Therefore, the effect of asset specificity on the firm's choice of integrated versus shared-control modes is contingent on *other factors* that affect the relative costs and benefits of integration. Since the traditional TCA approach does not normally consider this eventuality, there is need to modify it.

ASSUMPTIONS AND APPROACH

The *non*-TCA benefits flowing from integration (such as global integration, market power, and avoidance of conflicts with partners) are available in equal measure to all service firms in this analysis. On the other hand, the

---

[2]For the sake of convenience and brevity, firms characterized by low asset specificity will be hereafter referred to as "low-specificity" and those characterized by high asset specificity as "high-specificity" firms.

magnitude of *TCA-related* benefits (reduction of transaction costs) will vary with the degree of asset specificity, being great for high-specificity firms but approaching zero in the case of low-specificity firms. Because there are strong incentives (both TCA and non-TCA) for firms to assume control, the analysis starts by assuming that service firms prefer maximum control when establishing entry modes. This assumption is not only plausible but actually conforms better to empirical evidence that indicates U.S. multinational companies prefer integration *per se* (Gatignon and Anderson 1988). More importantly, three-fourths of the respondents to the authors' survey agreed with the statement, "If circumstances permit, we would always prefer to use a foreign-market entry method that will enable us to have maximum control." The assumption of full-control modes being the default option is, therefore, realistic. At worst, it is no more deficient than assuming low-control modes are the default choice. Since full-control modes represent the default choice, this *study develops hypotheses predicting circumstances under which firms establish shared-control modes.* This approach is different from traditional TCA studies, which investigate why firms assume greater control.

In keeping with TCA tradition, the assumption is made that the benefits of integration are so immense for high-specificity firms, i.e., firms characterized by high asset specificity, that they will tend to shun shared-control modes in virtually all situations, regardless (within reasonable limits, of course) of costs and other factors. Breaking with tradition, however, the authors assume that low-specificity service firms also have incentives to integrate because of the presence of non-TCA benefits. However, since these firms lack TCA-related motives, they tend to be less fervent than high-specificity firms in retaining control. For instance, to start with, low-specificity firms can be expected to avoid shared-control arrangements with nearly the same intensity as high-specificity firms. But as costs of integration increase, low-specificity firms find shared-control arrangements increasing more attractive compared to full-control modes. Alternatively, these firms can be expected to move to shared-control arrangements when costs remain constant but their ability to integrate diminishes, (for example, because of decreasing firm size). Accordingly, the following two scenarios emerge:

☐ When internal organization costs are high, or their ability to integrate is low, low-specificity firms are more likely to *prefer* shared-control modes than are high-specificity firms, as predicted by conventional TCA/

☐ When internal organization costs are low, or their ability to integrate is high, low-specificity firms are nearly as likely to *avoid* shared-control modes as are high-specificity firms.

According to this argument, the transaction-cost framework loses much of its ability to explain the variation in entry-mode choice when costs are low or when the ability to integrate is high (as in the first scenario). However, *the theory becomes increasingly powerful as costs of control-acquisition mount or as the ability to integrate diminishes and low-specificity firms rush to establish shared-control ventures.* Following this line of logic, it is clear that asset specificity alone may not produce significant variation in entry-mode choice. Rather, its efficacy depends upon other factors which drive low-specificity firms to establish shared-control modes. This represents the basic premise of the current study. In the following sections asset specificity will be described in the context of the service sector, and certain moderating factors that influence the relationship between asset specificity and entry-mode choice will be explained.

ASSET SPECIFICITY IN THE SERVICE SECTOR

The literature provides few insights into the origin of transaction-specific investments in the service sector. Consequently, the circumstances under which the service firm's arm's-length relationship with its supplier deteriorates into bilateral dependence are yet to be understood. Perhaps the answer lies in identifying situations in which potential agents, contractors, partners, or suppliers are required to make significant physical and human investments which cannot be productively employed outside the context of the specific transaction under consideration.

One such situation is the marketing of *idiosyncratic* services. An idiosyncratic service is defined as one which is characterized by "high" levels of professional skills, specialized know-how, and customization.

☐ *Professional skills:* Professional expertise and skills are acquired only through several years of education and training (e.g., accounting or management consulting). Accordingly, services requiring professional skills will be associated with significant physical and, especially, human investments.

☐ *Specialized know-how:* Knowledge that is useful in only a narrow range of applications cannot be easily put to use elsewhere. Consequently, the greater the specialized know-how characterizing a service, the less likely it is that associated investments will be utilized outside the current context (e.g., management consulting for a specific industry, such as health care).

☐ *Customization:* The degree to which the service is customized to one or a few users (e.g., data processing tailored for an individual client company) will also determine the nature and specificity of the investments. Generally speaking, the more customized the service, the greater the attendant transaction-specific assets.

It is proposed that the production and delivery of idiosyncratic services is characterized by high asset specificity, necessitating, as it does, nontrivial, transaction-specific physical and human investments in the value-added chain. A supplier that is asked to provide these services on the firm's behalf will have to make significant investments in acquiring skills, expertise, and know-how that are uncommon and not easily transferable to other situations. Therefore, as the service becomes more idiosyncratic, the asset specificity of transactions increases.

MODERATORS

TCA predicts that the firm's utility for shared-control modes *diminishes* with increasing asset specificity. The *strength* of this inverse relationship is, however, contingent upon the influence of a number of moderating factors. The authors' hypotheses will focus on the effects of these factors and argue that increasing capital intensity, widening cultural distance between home and host countries, escalating host country risk, the inseparability of production and consumption in services (all of which raise the costs of integration), and decreasing firm size (which diminishes the ability to integrate) cause a significant variation in entry-mode choice by encouraging low-specificity firms to employ shared-control modes. All hypotheses are proposed on the assumption that effects not under consideration are being held constant at some "average" level.

CAPITAL INTENSITY[3] Although service firms may be generally less capital-intensive than manufacturing firms, capital intensity varies significantly across service industries (from relatively low levels in consulting firms and advertising agencies to fairly high levels in hospitals, hotels, and airlines). Since the level of capital intensity represents the relative magnitude of fixed investment, increasing capital intensity signifies rising resource com-

mitments and escalating costs of integration.[4] All else being equal, the rising costs make it more difficult to establish wholly owned operations, thereby forcing firms to seek resources of partners and associates in shared-control arrangements. Although previous entry-mode studies have not explicitly considered the effects of capital intensity, Gatignon and Anderson's (1988) finding that the incidence of joint ventures increased with the increasing size of the foreign subsidiary underscores the impact of rising resource commitments on entry-mode choice.

Generally speaking, low-specificity firms are more likely to favor shared-control modes than high-specificity ones. Still, in situations characterized by *low* levels of capital intensity (and hence low costs of integration), low-specificity firms would be reluctant to relinquish control and lose the opportunity to exploit the non-TCA benefits of integration. As capital intensity *increases* (and internal organization costs escalate), however, low-specificity firms find deployment of full-control modes less and less justifiable in relation to the benefits they gain and, consequently, they shift to shared-control modes. High-specificity firms, on the other hand, will insist on integrated modes, regardless of capital intensity, because savings resulting from the reduction of transaction costs will continue to be substantial. The net result is that the differences in entry-mode choice between low- and high-specificity firms become more pronounced with increasing capital intensity. Hence:

> H_1: The inverse relationship between asset specificity and service firms' utility for shared-control modes will become stronger with increasing capital intensity.

INSEPARABILITY Many internationally marketed services are "separable" (Sampson and Snape 1985), i.e., their production and consumption can be decoupled. These services are frequently produced outside the host country and then transferred to it as a document, disk, or in some other tangible form. Examples include software services, engineering design, and architectural services.

However, a large number of services are produced and consumed simultaneously. *Inseparability* is a feature that distinguishes many service firms from manufacturers (Zeithaml et al. 1985). For instance, the competent delivery of services by hospitals, hotels, consulting firms,

---

[3]The authors are grateful to an anonymous JM reviewer for bringing the capital-intensity issue to their attention.

[4]For instance, the fixed investment of the "typical" advertising agency (SIC 7311) is only $36,347, but it increases to $4,694,874 for a "typical" hospital (SIC 8062), according to Dun and Bradstreet's *Industry Norms and Key Business Ratios(1985–86 Edition)*.

and advertising agencies requires the close physical proximity of providers and receivers. Inseparability "forces the buyer into intimate contact with the production process" (Carman and Langeard 1980, p. 8) and necessitates close buyer–seller interactions (Gronroos 1983).

In order to ensure effective delivery of inseparable services, elaborate systems have to be put in place to monitor the performance of employees who deal directly with customers. Inseparable services are conceivably more sensitive to cultural differences and may have to be better adapted to local tastes. Carman and Langeard (1980) also argue that service firms that provide inseparable services face special risks. They have to face customers and produce their services on foreign soil from day one without the benefit of initially exporting to the market and gaining experience.

For all these reasons, inseparability inflicts significant additional costs and risks on service firms which they can either bear themselves or share with their associates. While high-specificity firms find the first option worthwhile, low-specificity firms will more likely opt for the second. Consequently, asset specificity will more effectively distinguish between full- and shared-control choice for inseparable services than for separable ones. Hence:

H₂: The inverse relationship between asset specificity and service firms' propensity for shared-control modes will be stronger for inseparable services than for separable services.

CULTURAL DISTANCE Foreign-market entrants often perceive a significant amount of internal uncertainty caused by the *cultural distance* between the firm's home country and the host country. Numerous empirical studies have concluded that cultural distance encourages deployment of shared-control modes (Davidson and McFetridge 1985; Kogut and Singh 1988; Gatignon and Anderson 1988).

To better understand the effect of cultural distance on entry-mode choice in a transaction-cost context, the costs of acquiring information needed to monitor and evaluate the performance of employees in bureaucracies must be considered (Jones and Hill 1988). Since Kogut and Singh (1988) argue that differences in organizational characteristics increase with increasing cultural distance, such information-acquisition activity will be proportional to the cultural distance of the host country. When management moves to a country that is culturally similar to the home country, it may already possess most of the information to operate in the market; hence, information-acquisition costs will approach zero. However, when management enters an unfamiliar for-

eign culture, it may have great difficulty in imposing subjective judgment to determine how people should behave and in evaluating hard-to-quantify inputs and results (Gatignon and Anderson 1988). As a general rule, information-acquisition costs and, therefore, integration costs, can be expected to increase with the increasing cultural distance of the host country.

When specificity is *high,* firms will insist on integrated modes because control continues to be immensely rewarding, even when the host country's culture is extremely disparate. However, when asset specificity is *low,* expanding cultural distance will diminish the firm's desire for control since rising information costs will outstrip integration benefits. The net result is that low- and high-specificity firms increasingly diverge in their entry-mode choices as the host country becomes culturally less and less familiar to the firm. Hence:

H₃: The inverse relationship between asset specificity and service firms' propensity for shared-control modes will become stronger with increasing cultural distance between the home and host countries.

COUNTRY RISK High volatility in the external environment of the host country, i.e., high country risk, has been demonstrated to promote the use of shared-control arrangements (Goodnow and Hansz 1972; Mascarenhas 1982; Gatignon and Anderson 1988). In high-risk countries, firms must possess the necessary *flexibility* to shift to a different mode of operation should the original mode be rendered inefficient by unpredictable changes in the environment (Anderson and Gatignon 1986). Integrated modes are associated with high switching costs and, as a result, are not generally recommended in these environments. Low-control modes, on the other hand, offer the necessary flexibility and are characterized by low switching costs.

Low-specificity firms find little reason to give up control in low-risk countries. However, as countries become riskier and the need for flexibility becomes more important, low-specificity firms will increasingly seek shared-control arrangements. High-specificity firms, on the other hand, will continue to insist on full-control modes regardless of country risk. In fact, TCA argues that these firms will find control even more desirable in high-risk situations. When specificity is high, the frequent changes in the external environment provide more opportunities for suppliers, irreplaceable as they are, to shirk their obligations and to renegotiate contracts to their advantage (Gatignon and Anderson 1988; Williamson 1987). The resultant costs of haggling and maladaptation will further enhance the attractiveness of full-control modes in volatile environments and reduce the desire to share control. The net result is that entry-mode choice by low- and high-specificity firms can be expected to differ minimally in low-risk countries but substantially in high-risk countries. Hence:

> H_4: The inverse relationship between asset speci-
> ficity and service firms' propensity for shared-
> control modes will become stronger with
> increasing country risk.

FIRM SIZE Frequently, it is the firm's *ability* to integrate that determines its choice of entry modes. The typical argument in the literature is that integration entails significantly higher resource commitments and carries greater risk than shared-control arrangements (see Figure 1). Consequently, larger firms that have a greater ability to expend resources and absorb risks than smaller ones will conceivably be more likely to establish integrated modes. Also, larger firms may have greater bargaining power to negotiate for greater ownership and control in countries with restrictive investment policies (Lecraw 1984). Empirical studies demonstrate that the firm's ability to marshal resources is a potential determinant of entry-mode choice (Gatignon and Anderson 1988; Agarwal and Ramaswami 1992).

Because the benefits flowing from control (both TCA and non-TCA) are immense, high-specificity firms will insist on full-control modes regardless of size. Even when they are small, these firms will scrounge for resources to establish integrated modes. However, low-specificity firms, which do not share the same fervor to preserve control at any cost, will more readily establish shared-control modes when they are small to take advantage of resources pooled by associates. But as they grow larger and their ability to integrate increases, these firms can be expected to become more reluctant to relinquish control. Consequently, the power of asset specificity to distinguish between full- and shared-control modes is greatest when firms are small, but it becomes progressively weaker with increasing firm size. This relationship is hypothesized as follows:

> H_5: The inverse relationship between asset speci-
> ficity and service firms' propensity for shared-
> control modes will become weaker with the
> increasing size of the firm.

Figure 2 depicts the conceptual framework for the study. Asset specificity is shown as inversely influencing the service firm's propensity for shared-control modes. This relationship is strengthened (shown by negative sign) or weakened (positive sign) by the five moderators.

FIGURE 2   Conceptual Framework: Asset Specificity's Influence on Service Firm's Propensity for Shared-Control Modes Moderated by Various Factors

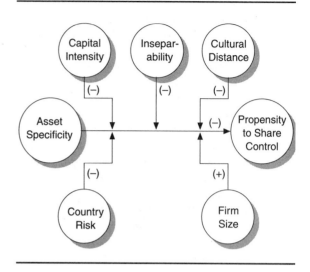

HYPOTHESES ACCORDING TO CONVENTIONAL TCA

Although the impact of the increasing costs of integration or of the diminishing capability to integrate on the influence of asset specificity has not be explicitly discussed in the TCA studies reported in the literature, it is likely that conventional TCA would have predicted increasing capital intensity, widening cultural distance, and inseparability to have minimal effects as moderators. This occurs because low-specificity firms are automatically assumed to favor low-control modes and high-specificity firms are expected to insist on full-control ones, regardless of costs or firm capabilities. So H_1, H_2, and H_3 have no bases.

However, conventional TCA would have proposed the same hypothesis as H_4 but for different reasons. Increasing country risk, while having little impact on low-specificity firms, is expected to further heighten the need for control in high-specificity firms. The net result is that the differences in entry-mode choice among low- and high-specificity firms would grow larger in high-risk countries.

On H_5, conventional TCA might have predicted just the opposite. While low-specificity firms are expected to insist on shared-control modes regardless of size, high-specificity firms may favor full-control modes ever more strongly with increasing size. As such, the differences between low- and high-specificity firms are perceived to grow *stronger* not weaker (as predicted) with increasing firm size.

SAMPLE AND VARIABLES

SAMPLE

The unit of analysis used is an *individual foreign-market entry decision* made by a service firm. Data for this investigation was collected through a mail survey of United States service firms engaged in international operations. Despite much effort, no sampling frame for the study could be obtained from any source: government agencies, trade groups, or commercial vendors. Therefore, a systematic sample of service firms known to be engaged in international operations was drawn from various business directories.[5]

To be included in the study, the firm had to belong primarily to a service sector SIC and also had to be in international business. A total of 463 companies, representing a wide variety of service industries, were included in the mail survey. Questionnaires were mailed to managers who were most likely to be involved in the foreign-market entry decision process in their firms, including vice presidents and directors in charge of international operations, presidents, and CEOs. Each respondent was asked to provide data on up to six foreign-market entry decisions with which he/she was very familiar.[6]

Twenty-five questionnaires were returned undelivered, and forty-three companies wrote back expressing regret at their inability to participate for various reasons, usually because they were no longer in international business. From the remaining pool of 395 potential respondents, usable responses were received from 175. The response rate of 44.3% compares favorably with rates reported in other surveys involving international marketing executives (e.g., Klein 1989) and service firms (e.g., Zeithaml, Parasuraman, and Berry 1985). Respondents did not differ significantly from nonrespondents in industry distribution, mean firm size, or mean sales revenue. Therefore, nonresponse bias, if any, may be negligible.

Of the firms responding, forty-seven reported serving foreign markets only through export operations, and fourteen had insufficient information on some key variables and were dropped from the analysis. The remaining 114 service firms provided data on a total of 381 foreign-market entry decisions, complete in every aspect.[7]

As Table 1 (section A) shows, the number of entries reported by each firm varied considerably. The foreign-market entries included in the sample differ considerably by size of the responding firm (section B, Table 1), when firm size is measured in terms of the *number of employees* as reported in the directories consulted. Also, the observations span several service industries (section C, Table 1), although there is heavier representation from professional and commercial service firms. Furthermore, as section D of Table 1 indicates, nearly two-thirds of the reported entries are into industrialized countries, including Australia, Canada, Japan, New Zealand, and the market economies of Europe. Finally, entries associated with wholly owned modes represent about 60% of the sample; the other 40% involve joint ventures and contractual transfers (section E, Table 1).

VARIABLES

The Appendix contains details of measurement and validity assessment of all the variables. The dependent variable, entry-mode choice, is represented by a dichotomous variable that becomes zero for *full-control* modes—since they represent the default or base option in the study (contrary to conventional TCA operationalizations)—and 1 for *shared-control* modes. *Asset specificity* is a 3-item scale measuring the extent to which the service is characterized by professional skills, specialized know-how, and customization. *Capital intensity* of a particular service industry is measured as the ratio of fixed assets to sales revenue. *Firm size* is measured as the number of company employees. *Inseparability* is a dummy variable (1 = inseparable service; 0 = separable service). *Cultural distance* is a composite index representing the host country's cultural distance from the United States. *Country risk* is a dummy variable (1 = entry into high-risk country; 0 = entry into lower-risk country) representing environmental volatility in the host country. Moderator effects are represented as *interactions* between asset specificity and the corre-

---

[5](a) *Consultants and Consulting Organizations Directory* (1984), Janice McLean, ed. Detroit, MI: Gale Research Company; (b) Dun and Bradstreet's *Million Dollar Directory* (1986), Parsippanny, NJ: Dun & Bradstreet Inc.; (c) *Standard & Poor's Register of Corporations* (1986), New York: Standard & Poor; (d) *Standard Directory of Advertising Agencies* (1985–86), New York: National Register Publishing Co.

[6]Respondents provided detailed data on one decision and some very basic data on five others.

---

[7]The practice of using multiple observations from individual firms is common in entry-mode studies (Gatignon and Anderson 1988; Davidson 1982; Davidson and McFetridge 1985).

TABLE 1   Characteristics of Foreign-Market Entries in Sample

Number of Entries in Sample = 381			
A. Entries per Firm		**B. Distribution by Firm Size**	
Entries/Firm	**No. of Firms**	**Number of Employees**	**Percentage of Entries**
1	34	a. <500	30.4
2	20	b. 500–1000	3.7
3	15	c. 1001–2000	11.0
4	11	d. 2001–4000	17.6
5	10	e. 4001–10,000	17.6
6	28	f. >10,000	19.7

C. Distribution by Industry	
Service Industry	**Percentage of Entries**
Advertising	13.1
Architecture	2.4
Banking	13.4
Computer Software and Data Processing	15.8
Engineering	10.8
Health Care	3.7
Management Consulting	21.5
Research and Development	3.9
Restaurants and Hotels	11.0
Miscellaneous Services (Accounting, Leasing, Maintenance, etc.)	4.4

D. Distribution by Country of Entry		**E. Entry Modes Employed**	
Country of Entry	**Percentage of Entries**	**Entry Mode**	**Percentage of Entries**
1. English-speaking industrialized	26.5	1. Wholly Owned Subsidiary	33.2
2. Non English-speaking industrialized	37.5	2. Other Wholly Owned Operation	27.4
3. Others	36.0	3. Joint Venture	24.4
		4. Contractual Method	15.0

sponding moderating variables. All interaction effects are represented by cross products of the main effects (as recommended by Neter, Wasserman, and Kunter 1983).

THE MODEL

The model examines the impact of asset specificity and its interactions on service firms' propensity to establish shared-control entry modes, as opposed to full-control ones. Logistic regression is utilized for estimation of the effects, because it is recommended when (1) the dependent variable is binary, (2) there are qualitative and quantitative independent variables, and (3) underlying assumptions of multivariate normality cannot be met (Cox 1970; Bali and Tschoegl 1982; Afifi and Clark 1984; Kachigan 1986).

Many recent studies related to entry-mode choice have employed logistic regression models (Davidson and McFetridge 1985; Gatignon and Anderson 1988; Kogut and Singh 1988; Agarwal and Ramaswami 1992; Kim and Hwang 1992). The probability of a service firm choosing a shared control entry mode in preference to a full-control one can be modeled as a function of the main effects and the interaction terms as follows:

Probability of choosing shared-control mode

$$= 1/\{1 + exp^{1-Y}\} \quad\quad\quad (1)$$

where

$$Y = ß_0 + ß_1X_1 + ß_2X_2 + \ldots + ß_pX_p \quad\quad (2)$$

$X_1, X_2, \ldots, X_p$ are explanatory variables (including asset specificity, the moderators, and interactions between asset specificity and moderators), $ß_1, ß_2, \ldots, ß_p$ are the corresponding coefficients, and $ß_0$ is the intercept term.

The parameters are estimated using maximum likelihood, employing the LOGISTIC procedure of the SAS statistical package (SAS Institute 1989). The overall efficacy of the model is assessed using the likelihood ration χ^2, which is twice the difference in log likelihoods for the current model and the intercept-only model. Large χ^2 values and small p values indicate statistical significance. The predictive ability of the model can be gauged by the correct classification rate *in conjunction with* the τ statistic (Klecka 1980), which represents the percentage reduction in classification errors relative to random selection. A statistically significant parameter indicates the extent to which the corresponding variable contributes to the *utility* of a shared-control mode relative to the full-control option. It does not *directly* signify the *probability* of firms using shared-control modes. Once equation (2) is estimated, the probabilities could be computed for a given situation using equation (1).

The estimated model includes all the main effects, including asset specificity and the moderators and the hypothesized interaction effects. Preliminary analysis led the authors to believe that the relationship between *capital intensity* and *entry-mode choice* is not linear over the range of values considered in the analysis, apparently following the pattern portrayed in Figure 3.

As capital intensity increases from "low" to "moderate" levels (i.e., from A to B in Figure 3), the propensity to employ shared-control modes increases, as expected. As it increases further from "moderate" to "high" levels (i.e., from B to C in Figure 3), the propensity to share control *diminishes,* contrary to expectations. The reason why firms avoid shared-control modes at high levels of capital intensity is not clear; perhaps they feel compelled to protect their rather heavy investments by integration. Notwithstanding its origin, this nonlinearity necessitated the inclusion in the model of two quadratic terms, [*capital intensity*]^2 and *asset specificity* X [*capital intensity*]^2.

FIGURE 3   Observed Relationship between Capital Intensity and Desire for Shared-Control Modes

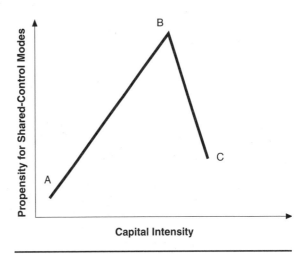

ESTIMATION AND RESULTS

MULTICOLLINEARITY

When such a large number of interaction terms involving one variable are included in the model, the likelihood of serious multicollinearity problems exists. Because some of the correlations among the variables were indeed high, the original the variables were rescaled using procedures recommended by Aiken and West (1991). All continuous variables were "centered" (by subtracting the corresponding variable mean from each value), and dummy variables were recorded using "weighted effects coding" (Darlington 1990).[8] Such rescaling, however, does not affect the substantive interpretation of the coefficients (Aiken and West 1991). An examination of the correlation matrix of the rescaled variables reported in Table 2 indicates that, except for those involving asset specificity and capital intensity, none of the interaction term terms appears to be highly correlated with other variables.

Variance inflation factors for terms included in the model did not indicate serious levels of collinearity.

---

[8]The authors are grateful to Leona Aiken, Arizona State University, for suggesting "weighted effects coding" as a technique to reduce collinearity. In this method the zero in the original dummy variable is replaced by a value calculated as follows (Darlington 1990):

$$\frac{\text{Weight of cell identified by the variable}}{\text{Weight of base cell}}$$

TABLE 2   Correlation Matrix for Independent Variables

	B	C	D	E	F	G	H	I	J	K	L	M
A	−.29	−.23	−.13	.00	.07	−.34	.32	.39	.21	.05	.11	.35
B		.93	.19	−.09	−.09	.28	−.60	−.63	−.21	.06	.04	−.12
C			.20	−.10	−.09	.17	−.58	−.65	−.15	.05	.06	−.04
D				−.03	−.16	.26	−.15	−.14	.07	−.03	.00	−.10
E					.37	−.02	.05	.04	−.03	−.02	.11	.02
F						−.04	.03	.05	.01	.10	.18	.07
G							−.13	−.12	−.14	.03	.11	−.52
H								.93	.35	−.07	−.09	.08
I									.29	−.06	−.11	.05
J										.01	−.16	.34
K											.26	.02
L												.15

A = Asset Specificity
B = Capital Intensity
C = [Capital Intensity]^2
D = Inseparability
E = Country Risk
G = Firm Size
H = Asset Specificity x Capital Intensity
I = Asset Specificity x [Capital Intensity]^2
J = Asset Specificity x Inseparability
K = Asset Specificity x Cultural Distance
L = Asset Specificity x Country Risk
M = Asset Specificity x Firm Size

Nevertheless, to assess the stability of the parameter estimates, the full model was reestimated for sixteen different subsamples of 300 observations each, drawn randomly from the original sample. The parameter estimates for the interaction terms, particularly the coefficients for *asset specificity x capital intensity* and *asset specificity x [capital intensity]^2*, remained remarkably stable over these runs, thereby discounting the possibility of significant multicollinearity problems.

MODEL ESTIMATION AND FIT

Initial runs revealed that the interaction term, *asset specificity x cultural distance,* was insignificant. Therefore, this term was dropped, and the full model was reestimated. Table 3 reports that this reestimated model is statistically significant (likelihood ratio $\chi^2_{(12)}$ = 73.0, p = 0.0001), which suggests that the variables as a group discriminate well between full- and shared control choice. Furthermore, the model correctly classifies 69% of the entry-mode choices which, as the τ statistic suggests, represents an improvement (36% fewer errors) relative to classification based on chance alone. In the light

of these results, the model appears to have reasonable explanatory and predictive abilities.

A comparison of the full model with the main-effects-only model reveals that the interactions terms account for a substantial amount of the variation of entry-mode choice (incremental $\chi^2_{(5)}$ = 52.0, p = 0.0001). This underscores the important role that moderating effects seem to play in entry-mode choice. Finally, as testimony to TCA's efficacy, asset specificity and its interaction effects together account for a very appreciable amount of the explanation (incremental $\chi^2_{(6)}$ = 57.2, p = .0001).

HYPOTHESES TESTING

A hypothesis is supported by the data if the coefficient for the corresponding interaction term is statistically significant and possesses the predicted sign (see Figure 2). Table 3 reports the parameter estimates, standard errors, and asymptotic t statistics. As argued earlier, the service firm's utility for shared-control modes, relative to the full-control option, *decreases* with increasing asset specificity. A minus sign on the coefficient for an interaction

TABLE 3   Results of Logistic Regression

Effect	**Dependent Variable Is *Entry-Mode Choice* (0 = Full-Control; 1 = Shared-Control Mode)**			
	Label	Parameter Estimate	Standard Error	Asymptotic t Statistic
Intercept	b0	−.143	.166	.86
Asset Specificity	b1	−1.999	.485	4.12^d
Capital Intensity	b2	7.645	2.420	3.16^d
[Capital Intensity]^2	b3	11.799	7.532	1.57^b
Inseparability	b4	.150	.096	1.56^b
Cultural Distance	b5	.200	.091	2.20^c
Country Risk	b6	.238	.333	.72
Firm Size	b7	−.024	.011	2.18^c
Asset Specificity × Capital Intensity	b8	−12.836	5.916	2.17^b
Asset Specificity × [Capital Intensity]^2	b9	109.00	34.229	3.18^d
Asset Specificity × Inseparability	b10	−.932	.219	4.25^d
Asset Specificity × Country Risk	b11	−1.072	.661	1.62^a
Asset Specificity × Firm Size	b12	.040	.016	2.50^d

A. Model Statistics

N	381
Model χ^2	73.0 with 12 df (p = .0001)
−2 Log Likelihood	437.8
Correct Classification %	69
τ	.36

B. Contribution of Interaction Terms:

Incremental χ^2	52.0 with 5 df (p = .0001)

C. Contribution of Asset Specificity and Its Interactions:

Incremental χ^2	57.2 with 6 df (p = .0001)

$a = p < .10$ (one-tail)
$b = p < .05$ (one-tail)
$c = p < .01$ (one-tail)
$d = p < .005$ (one-tail)

term suggests that this inverse relationship is *strengthened* with increasing values of the moderator; a plus sign indicates it is *weakened*. Therefore, barring the coefficient for *asset specificity × firm size,* all interaction terms are predicted to be negatively signed.

To gain further insights into the hypothesized relationships, the probability that service firms employ shared-control modes is estimated for low- and high-specificity situations for different levels of each moderating variable whose interaction with asset specificity was significant (holding the other effects constant at their average levels). Following Aiken and West (1991), "low (or small)" was defined as one standard deviation below mean; "medium" as mean; "high (or large)" as one stan-

dard deviation above mean; and "very high (or very large)" as two standard deviations above mean. The probabilities were then estimated with the help of equations (1) and (2), using these values and the parameter estimates from Table 3. For easy interpretation, these probabilities are shown pictorially in Figure 4. For each level of the moderating variable under consideration, lines are drawn connecting the corresponding probability levels for low- and high-specificity firms. These lines merely connect two discrete points and *do not necessarily depict a direct linear relationship* between asset specificity and probability. However, a downward sloping line suggests that low-specificity firms are more likely to employ shared-control modes than are high-specificity

FIGURE 4   Estimated Probability of Employing Shared-Control Modes: AT a Low and High Levels of Asset Specificity for Different Levels of Moderators

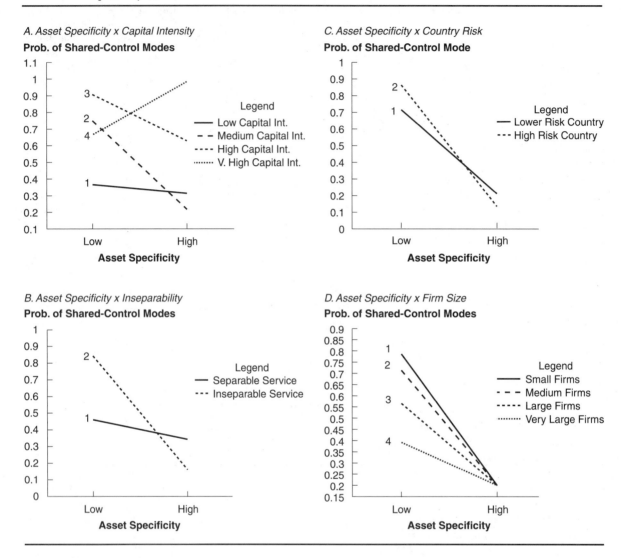

A. Asset Specificity x Capital Intensity

B. Asset Specificity x Inseparability

C. Asset Specificity x Country Risk

D. Asset Specificity x Firm Size

firms; an upward sloping line indicates just the opposite. The steeper the line, the greater the disparity between the two firm types.

HYPOTHESIS 1 Coefficients *b8* and *b9* in Table 3, which represent the interaction between asset specificity and capital intensity, are both statistically significant. The minus sign on *b8* (linear term) suggests that, at lower levels, increasing capital intensity *strengthens* the inverse relationship between *asset specificity* and *entry-mode choice*. However, the plus sign on *b9* (quadratic term) implies that, at higher levels, rising capital intensity *weakens* this relationship. Thus, while H_1 appears to

be supported at lower levels of capital intensity, it is not at higher levels.

To understand this relationship further, Figure 4A could be examined. If H_1 is supported, the line connecting the probability levels for low- and high-specificity firms should be downward-sloping and relatively flat for low levels of capital intensity but should become steeper with increasing capital intensity. This expectation is fulfilled for "low" and "medium" levels of capital intensity (lines 1 and 2). However, as capital intensity increases to "high" levels, the line becomes *flatter* because, although low-specificity firms intensify their preference for control-sharing, high-specificity firms unexpectedly begin to follow the same pattern (line 3). Finally, at "very high" levels, the line reverses its slope as high-specificity firms become *more likely* to employ shared-control modes than low-specificity ones (line 4).

In trying to comprehend this complicated relationship, it is helpful to remember that H_1 assumes increasing capital intensity, raises integration costs, and, consequently, enhances the relative utility of shared-control modes. In other words, it assumes a *positive* relationship between *capital intensity* and *entry-mode choice*. This is the relationship that seems to prevail at lower levels of capital intensity, as depicted by the A–B portion of Figure 3. H_1 appears to hold well for these observations.

However, the hypothesis seems to break down when, at higher levels, *capital intensity* and *entry-mode choice* become *inversely* related (see B–C portion of Figure 3). It is for these observations that the relationship between *asset specificity* and *entry-mode choice* appears to become less negative, or even positive, with rising capital intensity.

It can only be speculated as to why high-specificity firms seem to desire *less*, not more, control than low-specificity firms when capital intensity reaches higher levels. It may be merely a sample-specific aberration, since there are relatively few observations in the sample involving highly capital-intensive firms. But if it is not, a more complex phenomenon may be driving the relationship.

Other sources of asset specificity that are not explicitly included in the model, such as advertising intensity, may be affecting the low-specificity firms characterized by high capital intensity. This is not an unreasonable speculation, since most of these firms appear to be from the consumer services industry. Concurrently, it is possible that, faced with high resource commitments in capital-intensive industries, high-specificity service firms may be designing out specificity from otherwise idiosyncratic services in order to take advantage of resources pooled by partners a possibility consistent with suggestions made by Anderson and Gatignon (1986). Again, this seems plausible because many of the high-specificity firms from capital-intensive industries in the sample appear to be relatively small in size. At any rate, H_1 finds only partial support from the data.

HYPOTHESIS 2 The large negative coefficient for the *asset specificity* x *inseparability* interaction, $b10$ ($p < .005$), is consistent with the hypothesis that the inverse relationship between asset specificity and propensity for shared-control modes is substantially stronger when services are inseparable than when they are separable.

Figure 4B sheds more light on this matter. The relatively flat line for separable services implies that low-specificity firms are not very different from high-specificity firms in their desire for shared-control modes (line 1). The line for inseparable services is, however, noticeably steeper (line 2). Two reasons appear to account for this: (1) as predicted by H_2, low-specificity firms substantially increase the use of shared-control arrangements and (2) for reasons more in tune with conventional TCA, high-specificity firms seem to further reduce their use of shared-control modes. The additional demands of inseparable production and consumption of services may be escalating market transaction costs and making control even more imperative in high-specificity situations.

HYPOTHESIS 3 The hypothesized interaction between *asset specificity* and *cultural distance* did not materialize (result not reported). Apparently, *cultural distance* does not raise costs substantially enough for low-specificity firms to divest control. H_3 is not supported by the data. Although the interaction is not significant, the *main effect* of *cultural distance* is significant and positively signed ($b5$ in Table 3). This result suggests that service firms do not differ from manufacturing firms in favoring shared-control modes over full-control options with increasing cultural distance.

HYPOTHESIS 4 H_4 predicted that increasing country risk will strengthen the inverse relationship between *asset specificity* and *entry-mode choice*. Supporting this prediction, coefficient $b11$ is significant ($p < .10$) and negatively signed (Table 3). An examination of Figure 4C reveals that the line for high-risk countries (line 2) is steeper than that for lower-risk countries (line 1). This seems to arise primarily from low-specificity firms growing keener on employing shared-control modes in riskier environments, as predicted by the modified framework. However, there is also some evidence that high-specificity firms further eschew control-sharing arrangements in high-risk countries, in accordance with conventional TCA arguments.

Given the contention that low-specificity firms tend to avoid shared-control modes when country risk is low, the rather high probability of about .7 is indeed puzzling. Further analysis (not reported), however, showed that this probability drops to .3 when capital intensity is *low* and not "average or medium," as is assumed in all calculations underlying probability estimates reported in Figure 4. This points to a more complex interaction involving asset specificity, country risk, and capital intensity.

HYPOTHESIS 5 The coefficient $b12$ is significant ($p <$ .05 level) and *positively* signed (Table 3). The result suggests a *weakening* of the inverse relationship between specificity and propensity for shared-control modes, thereby supporting H_5. If the hypothesis is to be corroborated, the line connecting the probability levels for low- and high-specificity firms should be steep for small firms and get flatter as firms grow larger, as shown in the pattern evident in Figure 4D.

It is noteworthy that the probability of high-specificity firms engaging shared-control modes is virtually unaffected by firm size. However, the probability for low-specificity firms is highest when they are small, but it declines steadily as they grow larger. This result is consistent with the postulate that low-specificity firms prefer full-control modes to start with but shift to shared-control ventures when their ability to integrate diminishes (because of decreasing size). Therefore, H_5 finds strong support. The modified framework presented here appears to more accurately predict the moderating effect of firm size than conventional TCA, which (as described earlier) would have predicted a negative interaction effect.

SUMMARY OF RESULTS Of the five hypotheses tested, H_3 (host-country cultural distance) does not find any support. H_1 appears to be supported only as capital intensity increases from low to medium levels (the range over which the expected effect of capital intensity on entry-mode choice apparently prevails). Based on the hypotheses that were more fully supported, there is sufficient basis to believe the existence of the following relationships. Service firms generally tend to favor shared-control modes more when asset specificity is low than when it is high. This tendency *intensifies* (1) when services are inseparable (relative to when they are separable), (2) with increasing country risk, and (3) as firms become smaller. In the concluding section of the paper, some implications of these results will be explored, some limitations will be listed, and a few suggestions for future researchers will be made.

CONCLUSION

Traditional entry-mode investigations have tended to concentrate on the behavior of manufacturing multinational corporations. This study focuses on the entry-mode choice by firms from a wide range of service industries and includes very small to very large organizations. Some effects hitherto not empirically investigated in the entry-mode context, such as inseparability and capital intensity, are tested. Furthermore, because of some unduly restrictive assumptions associated with conventional TCA, a framework is developed that extends the TCA model. The conventional TCA approach actually represents a special case of this paradigm, dealing with situations wherein internal organization costs are high *and* non-TCA incentives to integrate are low.

This paper argues that the relationship between asset specificity and entry-mode choice is moderated by numerous factors that either raise the costs of integration or diminish the firm's ability to establish full-control modes. When costs are low or the ability to integrate is high, firms characterized by low asset specificity are nearly as likely as high-specificity firms to establish full-control ventures. But as costs escalate or ability diminishes, low-specificity firms will increasingly seek out shared-control ventures. While not supporting all of the hypotheses, the results do provide a reasonable basis to suggest that substantial variation in entry-mode choice is caused when low-specificity firms are pressed to share control. Some of the principal implications of the results follow.

IMPLICATIONS

MANAGERIAL IMPLICATIONS Managers apparently make cost-control trade-offs in several dimensions in their pursuit of the most efficient mode of entry. It is often claimed that many international marketing decisions are made by managers on a crude, nonsystematic basis (e.g., Aharoni 1966; Goodnow 1985). But the findings of this study and others demonstrate that managers do make choices based on considerations of long-term efficiency. The fact that the authors were able to correctly predict at least some of the behavior of service firms, based on efficiency considerations, suggests that "nonsystematic" does not necessarily mean "inefficient."

Managers in the international service sector can draw useful lessons from the study. When entering a foreign market, they frequently have an array of entry modes from which to choose. TCA provides a framework within which these alternatives can be evaluated. Specifically, this research highlights the usefulness of control as a basis for making an entry-mode choice. All costs and benefits of obtaining and retaining control in a specific situation must be carefully weighed against each other. The most efficient mode is the one with highest benefit-to-cost ratio. In this regard, this research identifies situations in which the benefits of control outweigh the costs of control and vice versa.

ANALYTICAL IMPLICATIONS For researchers, the results underscore the complexity characterizing entry-mode analysis and suggest that a superficial examination of relationships could be dangerously misleading. Effects are often embedded in or intertwined with others, and researchers need to develop strategies to analytically disentangle the underlying relationships. Furthermore, if these results and recent research (Agarwal and Ramaswami 1992) are any indications, researchers should be cautious about interpreting main effects alone, because variables seem to interact with each other in complicated ways. It is necessary to envision how a given variable affects entry-mode choice not only directly but also indirectly.

THEORETICAL IMPLICATIONS From a theory-building standpoint, the results of this study vindicate Bodewyn et al. (1986), who concluded that existing theories could be employed, with suitable adaptations, to investigate issues relating to multinational service enterprises. The transaction-cost framework is useful and universally applicable. However, to be more effective as a general theory of entry-mode choice, it must be extended for several reasons: (1) Firms appear to evaluate alternative institutional arrangements using a wider range of integration costs (e.g., inseparability) than previously recognized. At the same time, these costs do not necessarily need be assumed to be high in all situations. (2) Firms appear to be evaluating the merits of acquiring control based not only on reduction of transaction costs but on other non-TCA related considerations as well. Indeed, non-TCA motives, combined with low integration costs, seem to explain why many service firms establish full-control modes, even in low asset-specificity situations. (3) The firm's ability to integrate should be incorporated in future TCA studies as an important determinant of entry-mode choice.

Furthermore, conventional TCA thinking focuses on factors *promoting,* not *repressing,* integration. Although the results on inseparability and country risk support the conventional model, in the sense that some variation in entry-mode choice appears to result from high-specificity firms demanding greater control, a substantial amount of variation appears to be caused by low-specificity firms switching from full-control to shared-control modes in response to rising costs or diminishing ability to integrate. An examination of the results suggests that, relative to the conventional model, the modified framework appears to have more accurately predicted (1) the strengthening of the relationship between *asset specificity* and *entry-mode choice* with

increasing costs of integration, and (2) the weakening of this relationship with increasing firm size. Therefore, the modified TCA approach appears to have serious merits and deserves further scrutiny.

Although on the surface the research appears to endorse the acquisition of control for control's sake, this is not accurate. The authors are merely arguing that, given all the *TCA* and *non-TCA* incentives to integrate, it is more constructive to view firms as desiring maximum possible control from the start. The relative merits of relinquishing this control, as opposed to maintaining it in a given situation, could then be examined. Finally, although the modified framework was originally developed to accommodate some peculiar characteristics of service firms, it is really broader in its applicability and can be easily extended to entry-mode investigations in the manufacturing sector or even to problems other than entry-mode choice.

LIMITATIONS AND SUGGESTIONS FOR FUTURE RESEARCH

The study suffers from some important limitations. First, the sample is not representative of the general population of service firms in the United States. Non-random sampling became a necessity, however, when the authors were unable to obtain a comprehensive sampling frame. In this connection, they would like to emphasize one major challenge facing researchers investigating entry-mode issues: Since the unit of analysis in entry-mode studies is usually not the firm itself but rather an individual entry decision made by the firm, researchers should sample from the sum total of all entry-mode decisions made by all firms of a given industry or sector to obtain a truly representative sample. Clearly, this is an arduous task.

Second, this study followed previous studies by employing ownership as the determinant of control. This may not always be appropriate. There is increasing recognition that firms may gain control through non-equity, contractual methods (Dunning and McQueen 1982; Dunning 1988; Heide and John 1992). Therefore, it is possible for a service firm to exercise a degree of control that is unrelated to its equity participation. Future researchers must recognize and incorporate contract-based means of acquiring control. Alternately, a degree-of-control construct should be developed and measured independently of the entry mode employed. In this connection, the work of Killing (1983), Klein (1989), and Geringer and Ebert (1989) may offer a strong basis upon which to build.

In the current study, the authors implicitly assumed that the *actual* level of control employed by the service firm (as indicated by the entry mode used) is its *desired* level. However, "foreign government restrictions, the dictates of corporate parents, resource scarcity, and contractual commitments" indicate that there may be a significant difference in the two levels (Klein 1989, p. 258). Discrepancies may occur when firms are *forced to integrate* in countries where market exchange is unfeasible because of lack of indigenous technical capabilities (Contractor 1984), absence of adequate infrastructure and entrepreneurship (Teece 1981), or unavailability of suitable partners (Stopford and Wells 1972; Robinson 1978).

Since theoretical predictions generally focus on the desired level of control, the efficacy of entry-mode models could be greatly improved by measuring the firm's desired level of control *independently* of the actual entry mode employed. This reinforces earlier arguments for the development of an independent measure for control.

As discussed earlier, there may be several benefits and costs associated with integration that have not been explicitly incorporated in previous transaction-cost investigations. Future researchers could give some thought to improving the framework's predictive power by determining how these other costs and benefits could be measured and included in their investigations.

APPENDIX

MEASUREMENT OF VARIABLES

ENTRY-MODE CHOICE   The dependent variable in this study is dichotomous, equaling 1 when the firm employs a shared-control entry mode and 0 when it uses a full-control entry mode. For each entry decision described, the respondent was given a list of possible entry modes (wholly owned subsidiaries, joint ventures, etc.) and asked to indicate which one best described the method his/her company had used to *initially* enter the foreign market under consideration. Responses were appropriately classified into the full- and shared-control categories, as described in Figure 1.

ASSET SPECIFICITY   Represented by the degree of idiosyncrasy that characterizes a service, Asset Specificity is measured using three items that correspond to the three service attributes: (1) *professional skills*, (2) *specialized know-how*, and (3) *customization* (see definition of idiosyncratic services in the text). Customization was reverse-coded and measured as *standardization* (which, pretests revealed, was less ambiguous for respondents to interpret and describe). Respondents indicated the degree to which each attribute (i.e., professional skills, specialized know-how, and standardization) characterized their service on a 5-point scale (where 1 = no extent, and 5 = great extent). Asset specificity represents the mean of responses for the three attributes. Cronbach's alpha for the 3-item scale is .64 and, although modest, compares favorably with the alphas of .69 for the 5-item scale of Anderson and Coughlan (1987) and .65 for the 6-item measure of asset specificity of Klein et al. (1990).

To further examine the validity of the measure, the mean levels of idiosyncrasy associated with services from various industries in the sample were compared. An inspection of the results, presented in Table A-1 (line 1), suggests that consumer services are the least idiosyncratic. However, the across-industry variation, though significant, is not extremely high. Perhaps, this is the result of sample being skewed toward professional and business services. The variation across industries is much more evident when the degree of *customization* characterizing the service as shown in (Table A-1, line 2) is examined. Not surprisingly, consumer services are the least customized (or most standardized) of all services in the sample. The results in Table A-1 appear to be consistent with logic (for example, consumer services are the most standardized) and with information published on the industries (U.S. Congress 1987).

CAPITAL INTENSITY   This is the ratio of fixed assets to sales revenue for the industry to which the service firm belongs. This measure was borrowed from Kim and Lyn (1987), because of contextual similarity (they use it to predict foreign direct investment flows) and data availability. Data for the computation of the ratios are obtained from *Industry Norms and Key Business Ratios (1985–86 edition)* published by Dun and Bradstreet Information Services. The publication reports information for "typical" firms in each SIC. The fixed-assets to sales–revenue ratio computed for the typical firm is taken as representative of the capital intensity of the particular industry. Capital intensity ratios ranged from a low of about .04 for advertising agencies to a high of .76 for hotels.

INSEPARABILITY   In international marketing and trade, the inseparability issue is best seen as a *tradeability* problem (e.g., Sapir 1982; Sampson and Snape 1985; Boddewyn et al. 1986). Separable services are tradeable or exportable; inseparable services are not. Therefore, respondents were asked whether or not it is possible to

TABLE A-1 Across-Industry Variation of Some Independent Effects

	Service Industry						
Effect	Advertising Services [n = 50]	Computer Services [n = 60]	Engineering/ Architecture Services [n = 50]	Management Consulting Services [n = 82]	Consumer Services [n = 58]	Banking Services [n = 51]	Miscellaneous Services [n = 30]
1. Idiosyncracy Mean "Degree of Idiosyncracy" Associated with Industry	4.28[b]	4.28[b]	4.46[ab]	4.57[a]	3.59[c]	4.34[b]	4.34[b]
2. Customization Mean "Degree of Customization" Associated with Industry	3.20[b]	3.33[b]	3.46[b]	4.05[a]	2.03[c]	3.59[ab]	3.70[ab]
3. Client Following Percentage of Entries in Industry Associated with Client Following	46.0	25.0	24.0	26.8	0.0	29.41	26.7
4. Inseparability Percentage of Entries in Industry Associated with Inseparable Services	100.0	51.7	22.0	58.5	100.0	58.8	40.0

NOTES: [a] n = Number of entries reported in each industry.

[b] Idiosyncracy and customization are measured on scales ranging from 1 through 5. Higher means indicate that the characteristic (idiosyncrasy or customization) is more dominant. Means with the same letter are not significantly different (α = .05).

[c] Tests for differences across industries: (1) Idiosyncracy ($F_{(6)}$ = 22.06; $p < .001$), (2) Customization ($F_{(6)}$ = 19.91; $p < .001$), and (3) Client Following (χ^2 = 31.9; $p < .001$), and (4) Inseparability (χ^2 = 110.7; $p < .001$).

export their service ("Is it possible to serve your overseas clients/customers by producing your service here in the U.S. and then 'exporting' the service?"). A positive response suggested a separable service, a negative response an inseparable service. INSEPARABILITY is defined as a dummy variable (0 = separable service; 1 = inseparable service). Table A-1 describes the proportion of inseparable services characterizing each industry. Inseparability appears to dominate advertising and consumer services. On the other hand, engineering and architectural services appear to be most amenable to separation.

CULTURAL DISTANCE This is a measure of the cultural distance between the United States and the host country. Based on information provided by 88,000 respondents from sixty-six countries, Hofstede (1980) developed indices to measure four dimensions of national culture; power distance, uncertainty avoidance, individuality, and masculinity/femininity. Using these indices, Kogut and Singh (1988) computed cultural distances between the United States and other countries as follows:

$$(\text{Cultural distance})_j = [(I_{ij} - I_m)^2/V_i]/4$$

where I_{ij} stands for the index for the ith cultural dimension and jth country, V_i is the variance of the index of the ith dimension, u indicates the United States, and Distance$_j$ is cultural distance of the jth country from the United States. The authors use this index of cultural distance with considerable success to test their hypothesis on the entry-mode choice of foreign firms entering the United States.

COUNTRY RISK This study uses the same measure of country risk that Gatignon and Anderson (1988) had employed in their study. High-risk countries are identified based on the classification system developed by Goodnow and Hansz (1972). In terms of the time frame within which the entry-mode decisions studied here were made, the classification scheme is not greatly outdated. Country risk in this study is represented by a dummy variable that takes on a value of 1 when entry is into high-risk countries and 0 when it is into any other country. As a result, it contrasts entries into high-risk countries with entry into lower-risk ones. High-risk countries include Algeria, Argentina, Bahrain, Bangladesh, Bolivia, Cameroon, Chad, China, Egypt, Gabon, Hungary, India, Indonesia, Iran, Nigeria, Peru, the Philippines, Saudi Arabia, Tanzania, Thailand, Turkey, and the United Arab Emirates.

FIRM SIZE Following Gatignon and Anderson (1988) number of employees was adopted as the measure of firm size. The size of a service firm is measured by its number of employees, as reported in the directories consulted. For firms whose employment figures were unavailable, the median employment estimates (computed from the sample) for other firms in their industries were used.

REFERENCES

Afifi, A. A. and Virginia Clark (1984), *Computer-Aided Multivariate Analysis.* Belmont, CA: Lifetime Learning.

Agarwal, Sanjeev and Sridhar Ramaswami (1992), "Choice of Foreign Market Entry Mode: Impact of Ownership, Location and Internationalization Factors," *Journal of International Business Studies,* 23 (1st Quarter), 1–27.

Aharoni, Yair (1966), *The Foreign Investment Decision Process.* Boston, MA: Harvard Graduate School of Business Administration, Division of Research.

Aiken, Leona S. and Stephen G. West (1991), *Multiple Regression: Testing and Interpreting Interactions.* London: Sage Publications.

Anderson, Erin and David C. Schmittlein (1984), "Integration of the Sales Force: An Empirical Examination," *Rand Journal of Economics,* 15 (Autumn), 385–395.

——— and Hubert Gatignon (1986), "Modes of Entry: A Transactions Cost Analysis and Propositions," *Journal of International Business Studies,* 17 (Fall), 1–26.

——— and Barton A. Weitz (1986), "Make or Buy Decisions: A Framework for Analyzing Vertical Integration Issues in Marketing," *Sloan Management Review,* 27 (Spring), 3–19.

——— and Anne T. Coughlan (1987), "International Market Entry and Expansion via Independent or Integrated Channels of Distribution," *Journal of Marketing,* 51 (January), 71–82.

Ball, Clifford A. and Adrian E. Tschoegl (1982), "The Decision to Establish a Foreign Bank Branch or Subsidiary: An Application of Binary Classification Procedures," *Journal of Financial and Quantitative Analysis,* 17 (September), 411–424.

Berry, Leonard L. (1980), "Service Marketing Is Different," *Business,* 30 (May–June), 24–29.

Boddewyn, Jean J., M. B. Halbrich, and A. C. Perry (1986), "Service Multinationals: Conceptualization, Measurement and Theory," *Journal of International Business Studies,* 17 (Fall), 41–57.

Bowen, D. E., C. Siehel, and B. Schneider (1989), "A Framework for Analyzing Customer Service Orientation in Manufacturing," *Academy of Management Review,* 14(1), 75–95.

Bower, Marvin (1968), "Personal Service Firms Venture Abroad," *Columbia Journal of World Business,* 3 (March–April), 49–58.

Carman, James M. and Eric Langeard (1980), "Growth Strategies of Service Firms," *Strategic Management Journal,* 1 (January–March), 7–22.

Cateora, Philip R. (1990), *International Marketing.* Homewood, IL: Richard D. Irwin, 410–412.

Chase, R. B. and D. A. Tansik (1989), "The Customer Contact Model for Organization Design," *Management Science,* 9, 1037–1050.

Contractor, Farok J. (1984), "Choosing between Direct Investment and Licensing: Theoretical Considerations and Empirical Tests," *Journal of International Business Studies,* 15 (Winter), 167–188.

——— and Peter Lorange (1988), *Cooperative Strategies in International Business.* Lexington, MA: Lexington Books.

Cowell, Donald W. (1983), "International Marketing of Services," *The Service Industries Journal,* 1 (November), 308–328.

Cox, D. R. (1970), *The Analysis of Binary Data.* London: Methuen & Co.

Darlington, R. B. (1990), *Regression and Linear Models.* New York: McGraw-Hill.

Davidson, William H. (1982), *Global Strategic Management.* New York: John Wiley and Sons.

——— and D. G. McFetridge (1985), "Key Characteristics in the Choice of International Technology Transfer Mode," *Journal of International Business Studies,* 16 (Summer), 5–21.

Dunning, John H. (1988), *Explaining International Production.* London: Unwin Hyman.

——— (1989), "The Study of International Business: A Plea for a More Inter-disciplinary Approach," *Journal of International Business Studies,* 20 (Fall), 411–436.

Dunning, John H. and Matthew McQueen (1982), "The Eclectic Theory of the Multi-national Enterprise and the International Hotel Industry," in *New Theories of Multinational Enterprise,* Allen M. Rugman, ed. New York: St. Martin's.

Dwyer, Robert F. and Sejo Oh (1988), "A Transaction Cost Perspective on Vertical Contractual Structure and Interchannel Competitive Strategies," *Journal of Marketing,* 52 (April), 21–34.

Erramilli, M. Krishna (1990), "Entry Mode Choice in Service Industries," *International Marketing Review,* 7(5), 50–62.

——— and C. P. Rao (1990), "Choice of Foreign Market Entry Mode by Service Firms: Role of Market Knowledge," *Management International Review,* 30 (2), 135–150.

Gaedeke, Ralph M. (1973), "Selected U.S. Multinational Service Firms in Perspective," *Journal of International Business Studies,* 4 (Spring), 61–67.

Gatignon, Hubert and Erin Anderson (1988), "The Multinational Corporation's Degree of Control over Foreign Subsidiaries: An Empirical Test of a Transaction Cost Explanation," *Journal of Law, Economics, and Organization,* 4 (Fall), 305–336.

Geringer, Michael J. and Louis Ebert (1989), "Control and Performance of International Joint Ventures," *Journal of International Business Studies,* 20 (Summer), 235–254.

Goodnow, James D. and J. H. Hansz (1972), "Environmental Determinants of Overseas Market Entry Strategies," *Journal of International Business Studies,* 3 (Spring), 33–60.

——— (1985), "Developments in International Mode of Entry Analysis," *International Marketing Review,* 2 (Autumn), 17–30.

Gronroos, Christian (1983), *Strategic Management and Marketing in the Service Sector,* Marketing Science Institute Report, 83–104, May.

Hackett, Donald W. (1976), "The International Expansion of U.S. Franchise Systems: Status and Strategies," *Journal of International Business Studies,* 7 (Spring), 67–75.

Heide, Jan B. and George John (1988), "The Role of Dependence Balancing in Safeguarding Transaction-Specific Assets in Conventional Channels," *Journal of Marketing,* 52 (January), 20–35.

———, and ——— (1992), "Do Norms Matter in Marketing Relationships?" *Journal of Marketing,* 56 (April), 32–44.

Hennart, Jean-Francois (1989), "Can the 'New Forms of Investment' Substitute for the 'Old Forms'? A Transaction Costs Perspective," *Journal of International Business Studies,* 20 (Summer), 211–234.

Hill, Charles W. L., Peter Hwang, and W. Chan Kim (1990), "An Eclectic Theory of the Choice of International Entry Mode," *Strategic Management Journal,* 11 (2), 117–128.

Hofstede, Geert (1980), *Culture's Consequences: International Differences in Work-Related Values,* Beverly Hills, CA: Sage Publications.

John, George and Barton Weitz (1989), "Salesforce Compensations: Compensation: An Empirical Investigation of Factors Related to Use of Salary versus Incentive Compensation," *Journal of Marketing Research,* 26 (February), 1–14.

Jones, Gareth R. and Charles W. L. Hill (1988), "Transaction Cost Analysis of Strategy-Structure Choice," *Strategic Management Journal,* 9 (2), 159–172.

Kachigan, S. K. (1986), *Statistical Analysis: An Interdisciplinary Introduction to Univariate and Multivariate Methods.* New York: Radius Press.

Killing, J. Peter (1983), *Strategies for Joint Venture Success.* New York: Praeger.

Kim, Saeng Wi and Esmaralda O. Lyn (1987), "Foreign Direct Investment Theories, Entry Barriers, and Reverse Investments in U.S. Manufacturing Industries," *Journal of International Business Studies,* 18 (Summer), 53–66.

Kim, W. Chan and Peter Hwang (1992), "Global Strategy and Multinationals' Entry Mode Choice," *Journal of International Business Studies,* 23 (1st Quarter), 29–53.

Klecka, William R. (1980), *Discriminant Analysis.* Beverly Hills, CA: Sage Publications.

Klein, Saul (1989), "A Transaction Cost Explanation of Vertical Control in International Markets," *Journal of the Academy of Marketing Science,* 17 (Summer), 253–260.

———, Gary Frazier, and Victor J. Roth (1990), "A Transaction Cost Analysis Model of Channel Integration in International Markets," *Journal of Marketing Research,* (May), 196–208.

Kobrin, Stephen J. (1988), "Trends in Ownerships of American Manufacturing Subsidiaries in Developing Countries: An Inter-Industry Analysis," *Management International Review,* (Special issue), 73–84.

Kogut, Bruce and Harbir Singh (1988), "The Effect of National Culture on the Choice of Entry Mode," *Journal of International Business Studies,* 19 (Fall), 411–432.

Kotler, Philip (1991), *Marketing Management: Analysis, Planning, Implementation, and Control.* Englewood Cliffs, NJ: Prentice-Hall, 413.

Larsson, R. and D. E. Bowen (1989), "Organization and Customer: Managing Design and Coordination of Services," *Academy of Management Review,* 14 (2), 213–233.

Lecraw, Donald J. (1984), "Bargaining Power, Ownership, and Profitability of Transnational Corporations in Developing Countries," *Journal of International Business Studies,* 15 (Spring/Summer), 27–43.

Lo, T. W. and A. Yung (1988), "Multinational Service Firms in Centrally-Planned Economies: Foreign Advertising Agencies in the PRC," *Management International Review,* 28 (1), 26–32.

Lovelock, Christopher H. (1983), "Classifying Services to Gain Strategic Marketing Insights," *Journal of Marketing,* 47 (Summer), 9–20.

Mascarenhas, Briance (1982), "Coping with Uncertainty in International Business," *Journal of International Business Studies,* 13 (Fall), 87–98.

Neter, John, William Wasserman, and Michael H. Kutner (1983), *Applied Regression Models.* Homewood, IL: Richard D. Irwin, Inc.

Palmer, John D. (1985), "Consumer Service Industry Exports: New Attitudes and Concepts Needed for a Neglected Sector," *Columbia Journal of World Business,* 20 (Spring), 69–74.

Robinson, Richard C. (1978), *International Business Management: A Guide to Decision Making.* Hinsdale, IL: The Dryden Press.

Root, Franklin R. (1987), *Foreign Market Entry Strategies.* New York: AMACOM.

Sampson, G. P. and R. H. Snape (1985), "Identifying the Issues in Trade in Services," *The World Economy,* 171–182.

Sapir, Andre (1982), "Trade in Services: Policy Issues for the Eighties," *Columbia Journal of World Business,* 17 (Fall), 77–83.

SAS Institute (1989), *SAS/STAT User's Guide, Version 6, 4th ed., Vol. 2.* Cary, NC: SAS Institute, Inc.

Sharma, Deo D. and Jan Johanson (1987), "Technical Consultancy in Internationalization," *International Marketing Review,* 4 (Winter), 20–29.

Stopford, John M. and Louis T. Wells, Jr. (1972), *Managing the Multinational Enterprise.* New York: Basic Books.

Teece, David J. (1981), "The Multinational Enterprise: Market Failure and Market Power Considerations," *Sloan Management Review,* 22 (Spring), 3–17.

——— and Chwo-Ming Yu (1988), "Determinants of Foreign Investment of U.S. Advertising Agencies," *Journal of International Business Studies,* 19 (Spring), 33–46.

——— and Ravi Sarathy (1991), *International Marketing,* 5th ed. New York: The Dryden Press.

United States Congress, Office of Technology Assessment (1986), *Trade in Services: Exports and Foreign Revenues-Special Report,* OTA-ITE-316. Washington, D.C.: U.S. Government Printing Office.

——— (1987), *International Competition in Services,* OTA-ITE-328. Washington, D.C.: U.S. Government Printing Office.

Weinstein, Arnold K. (1974), "The International Expansion of U.S. Multinational Advertising Agencies," *MSU Business Topics,* 22 (Summer), 29–35.

——— (1977), "Foreign Investments by Service Firms: The Case of Multinational Advertising Agencies," *Journal of International Business Studies,* 8 (Spring/Summer), 83–91.

Williamson, Oliver E. (1985), *The Economic Institutions of Capitalism.* New York: The Free Press.

——— (1986), *Economic Organization: Firms, Markets and Policy Control.* New York: New York University Press.

——— (1987), "The Economics of Organization: The Transaction Cost Approach," *American Journal of Sociology,* 87 (3), 548–577.

Wind, Yoram and H. V. Perimutter (1977), "On the Identification of the Frontier Issues of International Marketing," *Columbia Journal of World Business,* 12 (Winter), 131.

Zeithaml, Valarie A., A. Parasuraman, and Leonard L. Berry (1985), "Problems and Strategies in Services Marketing," *Journal of Marketing,* 49 (Spring), 33–46.

FRANCHISE PROTOTYPES

A MODIFIED TRANSACTION-COST ANALYSIS APPROACH

Kevin Farrell

When entrepreneurs develop a prototype service operation, they may spend months or years hammering out the details that make the service work well and efficiently. A smoothly running prototype business can often be cloned through franchising, although some adaptation may be needed from one location to another.

Entrepreneurs are discovering the key to building successful big franchises quickly: perfecting the prototype. Investing years, and sometimes millions of dollars, in a pilot unit is profitable for franchisors in virtually every retail business. From ice cream to computers to such brand-new concepts as gift-wrap and packaging franchises, entrepreneurs are learning that if they develop a well-oiled model unit that can be replicated with ease, where the pieces are in place and the bugs eliminated before a single franchise is sold, the world will buy.

The rewards of getting it right the first time can be great. It took three years and $1.6 million for Steven B. Heller, 43, and James J. Edgette, 42, to fashion a model of their retail computer store, Entré Computers. But the work, which involved endless research, paid off handsomely. Barely one year after they began franchising, Entré has sold well over 200 franchises, and is selling them at a rate of 10 a month. "A prototype will enable you to do a tremendously refined job of opening a center," says Edgette. Ron Berger, 35, devoted a year and a half and spent $700,000 to develop a solid prototype for National Video Corp., a Portland, Oregon-based renter of video equipment. Within three years National Video sold 500 franchises. "I would counsel anyone who wants to go into franchising to devote a great deal of time and effort to making absolutely sure the prototype is as efficient as possible before launching into franchise sales," he says. And Ron Strunk, 28, projects he will sell his 200th Phone Source phone store

franchise by 1985, scarcely two years after he opened his prototype store in Omaha. Such success stories are not uncommon today, as franchising continues to pull in nearly one-third of all retail sales. Consumers spent an estimated $436 billion in franchise units in 1983, nearly 13 percent more than 1982.

In its development stage, a prototype becomes a hands-on experiment for the entrepreneur. It is a time to make mistakes, to work out the kinks, and to determine how to sell the franchises. It is not an easy process. It takes months in some industries, years in others, and still a prototype is seldom cast in stone; it is constantly modified as business develops. But the rewards of having a workable prototype are invaluable. In addition to smoothing out an operating system, having a solid model makes it that much easier to sell franchises and impress bankers and backers.

And entrepreneurs are devising their winning formulas in a variety of ways. Not surprisingly, the formulas often seem to have little in common. For some, a prototype unit is basically an opportunity to test design ideas. For others, it is an occasion to draw up training procedures for management and employees, or to create financial goals and a system for realizing them, or to fine-tune distribution and marketing techniques. Clearly, prototypes have different functions for different franchisors, but are in some way or other a proving ground for the entrepreneur's concepts.

Franchisors have always struggled to get the kinks out of their operations. But what today's high-speed franchisors do differently is get a headstart on problems that may surface when, for example, the company has

SOURCE: Kevin Farrell, "Franchise Prototypes," 108–113, reprinted from the January 1984 issue of *Venture* for Entrepreneurial Business Owners & Investors, by special permission. © 1984 Venture Magazine, Inc. 521 Fifth Ave., New York, NY 10175-0028.

dozens of franchises and suddenly discovers its method of inventory control is ineffective, or that poorly trained employees are alienating customers. "We want to make the mistakes, not our franchisees," says Michael J. Coles, 39, chairman of Atlanta-based The Original Great American Chocolate Chip Cookie Inc., a 1977 startup that now has 200 units either open or under construction.

In addition, the prototype affords the entrepreneur an opportunity to discover if, in fact, a business can be cloned through franchising. Says Martin Boehm, a research analyst for the International Franchise Assn., a Washington trade group representing 381 franchisors: "It has to be simple enough to teach someone how to run it, and it has to be profitable enough so the profits can be split."

In some cases, franchisors have been accused of using the prototype as a misleading sales tool to attract franchisees. For instance, in 1978, the original management of Command Performance Hair Salons built a prototype store in a busy San Diego shopping center, and spent relatively large sums of money to advertise and promote the unit, according to Timothy H. Fine, a San Francisco attorney. Fine represents 19 Command Performance Hair Salon franchisees in a suit against the franchisor's former management, charging fraud and misrepresentation in the sale of franchises. The present defendants deny the charges. Fine says franchisees bought Command Performance franchises based on impressive sales records of the prototype. His clients claim that the franchisees could not match the prototype's sales figures on their own because of competition from other nearby Command Performance units which were eventually built, and because the 4 percent-of-sales ad budget required by the franchisor was much less than was spent to promote the prototype.

According to the franchisees' lawsuit, Command Performance heavily promoted its San Diego prototype between November 1978 and August 1979. During that period, they claim, the store sometimes pulled in weekly gross receipts of more than $12,000. The franchisees contend that sales at the prototype declined steadily as the promotion budget dropped, and as competing Command Performance franchises were built. By 1982, they claim, the prototype's weekly receipts dropped to as low as $2,000.

In 1981, the original management of Command Performance left the company and the parent corporation, First National Services Corp., filed for bankruptcy under Chapter XI. The company has since been taken over by some of the owners of Andover, Mass.-based Docktor Pet Centers Inc. and existing Command Performance franchisees. William J. Wright, one of the original Command Performance managers named as defendants, declines to comment on the pending suit.

A former vice-president of Command Performance, Adrian Deacon, says: "It was not a premeditated plan to run the volume of that store up to sell franchises," adding, "we were not pumping any more money into that store than into any others." He says franchisees were only required to spend 2 percent of sales on company advertising campaigns, which he agrees was too small. He adds that it is difficult to judge how many stores will saturate a market. "When you're doing a threshold business, how do you know what's too close?" he says.

A MISLEADING TOOL

"A prototype generally can be a misleading thing," says Fine. "It may have no bearing in real life. It also can be very dangerous. It can be misused by the franchisor to promote sales that are inflated." Adds Edgette of Entré Computers: "A prototype should be something that proves the system works. It should absolutely not be used as a sales tool. That's a dangerous road to follow."

Different entrepreneurs seem to learn different lessons while proving their systems work. Tom Sizer, 42, bought Pac N-Send, an existing 16-unit packaging, gift-wrapping, and shipping business in Florida, from founder Bruce Young in April, 1983, believing he could sell franchises nationally. He changed the name to P.k.g.,'s, hired Young as chairman, and then built a model unit in Orlando. There, he discovered subsequent outlets would need to be strictly uniform in appearance "to avoid looking like a mom-and-pop operation," he says. Also, he learned from his prototype that franchisees should be freed of most operating responsibilities so they could concentrate on selling the service. "The thing we learned was that the store should be a complete turnkey operation, meaning everything down to postage stamps all the way up to cabinetry should be supplied by us. That frees the franchisee to just sell the service," he says. Sizer collects an average 3 1/2 percent royalty from 25 franchises opened in less than a year, and plans to open 150 franchised units by January, 1985.

But others have learned that it won't always work to have a standard operation and standard appearance. Once the Entré Computers prototype in Tysons Corner, Va., was working. "We learned that you can't cookie-cutter the sales process in our industry, it must be tailored for the individual center," says Edgette. "Selling a [computer] system to a farmer in Iowa is different from selling one to a government consulting firm in suburban

Washington," he says. National Pet Care Centers Inc., Newport Beach, Calif., which sells franchises of its pet hospital to existing veterinarians (in much the same way Century 21 sells franchises to realtors), also learned that a prototype can't always be reproduced. "We don't and won't have a prototype unit in terms of design and decor," says co-founder Douglas S. Keane, 37. "But we will have a prototype in terms of the systems we use."

Sometimes the point is that the hard-and-fast rules franchisors are searching for are *not* the answer. For instance, Martin Byrne, 46, who created a concept for John Phillip Tuba ice cream restaurants, realized he should offer a flexible program for franchisees. Depending on how much they plan to spend, franchisees can open either a simple ice cream shop, or a store with ice cream and a take-out menu for food, or a full-service restaurant with an ice cream stand, robotic entertainment, and video games. The startup costs range from $95,000 to $430,000. Byrne has sold 14 franchises since January, and says the flexible plan enables him to penetrate markets relatively quickly.

When entrepreneurs develop a prototype, they may spend months, or even years, hammering out the details that will eventually make it relatively simple to adapt from location to location. In part, it is the gift of time— time to solve a sticky problem. for Strunk, it was a chance to test out design schemes for the Phone Source until he hit upon one that appealed to both men and women. After six months, he settled on a decor based on cedar shelves and cubed glass. For Daniel Rhode, president of King of Prussia, Pa.-based Sparks Tune-Up, it was a chance to establish a one-price auto tune-up. The goal was to offer tune-ups for any car at a price of $44.90. However, after six months of molding a system at the Reading, Pa., prototype—learning how much they could afford to pay mechanics and how many tune-ups a mechanic could do in a day—Rhode realized he could lower the price to $39.90. In two and a half years, he opened 40 franchised units.

A startup franchisor with little or no experience is taken more seriously by financiers if he or she can point to a successful prototype. Byrne had a working prototype of his middle-level John Phillip Tuba franchise—the restaurant with an ice cream stand—when he sought a $200,000 loan from a St. Petersburg, Fla., bank to equip a prototype for his larger franchise, the restaurant with entertainment. "The bank flew five of its officers down to Fort Lauderdale to see our prototype before they would approve the loan," he says. When Strunk wanted an equity partner for franchising the Phone Source, he showed his prototype unit to Gerald Bogard, and Omaha

financial adviser who, after seeing the prototype in operation, invested $30,000 for 50 percent equity interest. Then, Strunk discussed his business plan with a local banker and trotted him through a prototype unit. The banker offered Strunk a $75,000 line of credit.

GAINING FINANCIAL CREDIBILITY

A working model also makes it easier for franchisees to finance their franchise. Explains Berger, founder of National Video: "A young franchisor doesn't have a good record, and when someone wants to buy a franchise, the bank says to a potential franchisee, 'Are you sure this guy's going to be around [very long]?' But a prototype can convince the bank that the franchise is a good investment."

Having a prototype provides the credibility that may be needed to move into a prime location. That's why David Glassman, 32, and Steven Shoeman, 34, cofounders of All American Hero, a hoagie shop franchise, used their prototype to gain acceptance in regional shopping malls, which are virtually impossible to enter without a track record. The prototype was set up in the "food court" of Fort Lauderdale's Hollywood Mall at a cost of $60,000. The unit was treated as an experiment. Food and labor costs were scrutinized and operations continually altered until the founders developed a formula that resulted in operating margins of 24 percent, relatively high for the restaurant industry. At that point, Glassman and Shoeman invited mall developers and managers to view the prototype. "You have to have them on your side to get into their prime locations," says Glassman. All American Hero has expanded to 30 franchise units— most in large shopping malls—each averaging $350,000 in revenues. Glassman has 15 more units under construction, and anticipates the chain will double in units each year the next three years.

Entrepreneurs come upon their winning formulas in a variety of ways. Ray Jacobs, 47, founder and president of America's Number One Software Dealer Inc., never intended to franchise. He spent $7,500 to open a 1,000-sq.-ft. software store in Teaneck, N.J. When he saw "people coming in here from over 50 miles away," he knew the store was "franchisable." He hired a franchise consultant who helped him through the legal maze required to register and sell franchises. And he learned that the stores could locate in "secondary" space, relatively inexpensive strip shopping centers. Since January, he has sold 50 franchises.

Franchisors who create a prototype can use it as a "university" where franchisees can learn the system. As business develops in the model store, training procedures are changed and updated.

But for all the work and worry, the rewards of building a successful prototype can be great. Entré Computers collected $30,000 franchise fees from each of the 55 stores it sold in fiscal year 1983, its second year of operation. Also, it collected royalties of 8 percent on the estimated $39 million total sales of the 59 operating stores. The fees and royalties added up to $3.8 million. In addition, Entré's company-owned prototype earned profits of $750,000 on sales of $4.5 million. In all, the company's profits were $1.7 million. And the profits should continue rolling in, as Entré anticipates opening its 200th unit by the end of fiscal 1984 in August. Together, co-founders Heller and Edgette personally own slightly more than half the company's stock. They filed for an initial public offering last October, and hope to raise at least $20 million for working capital for expansion into foreign markets, and to construct an automated warehouse. If the offering is successful, it would leave Heller and Edgette each with 21.4 percent ownership of a company valued at $140 million.

Even for smaller franchisors, the rewards multiply as units expand. Strunk collected franchise fees of $10,000 from each of the 10 units opened in 1983, and he is raising that fee to $15,000 for the six additional stores he intends to add in 1984. He collected royalties of 3 percent on total franchise sales of $750,000 in 1983, and estimates those sales will increase to $4 million in 1984. He figures his modest profits in 1983 of $10,000 will jump to $120,000 in 1984 as units and sales are added. He owns 50 percent of the company.

Berger, who owns approximately one-third of National Video, expects to see profits of $250,000 on total sales of $4 million from his 190 franchise units for fiscal 1984. But with a $15,900 franchise fee and 3.9 percent royalties from software sales, he estimates his company will earn $12.7 million on sales of $54 million by yearend 1987, when he anticipates having 6,000 stores in operation. And for 1984, the first full year of franchising P.k.g.'s, Sizer expects profits of $350,000 on total franchise sales of $3.5 million. He collected royalties averaging 3 1/2 percent from each of the 25 units for a total of $100,000 in royalties. Also, he collected $7,500 franchise fees from each of the 10 units that were not Pac N-Send franchises he converted. Those rewards should build as the franchise gains momentum. Sizer hopes to have as many as 100 units in place by yearend 1984, and as many as 350 in three to five years. "Having a prototype," says Sizer, "makes all the difference."

EVALUATE THE PROTOTYPE CAREFULLY

An individual looking to buy a franchise still in the prototype stage generally has the advantage of getting in on a good deal, since the prices for franchises typically shoot up after the franchisor achieves success. But early franchisees should be doubly cautious in scrutinizing a prototype. So how can you tell if it can be replicated?

First, find out if the advertising and promotion money being spent on the prototype exceeds the percentage that is called for in the franchise agreement. A franchisor may require a franchisee to spend 4 percent of sales on advertising, for instance, when he or she is spending 10 times that amount to promote a company-owned prototype. The result of the high advertising budget may be much more business in the prototype than you would draw with your relatively low budget, according to Timothy H. Fine, a San Francisco-based attorney who represents franchisees and franchisee trade groups.

Next, try to determine how the franchisor intends to authorize the location of franchises. A prototype may rack up impressive sales, if it is the only unit of its kind within a five-mile radius. Will the franchisor promise not to permit another unit to be built within five miles of your store?

The Federal Trade Commission requires that a franchisor provide you with a Franchise Offering Circular before you buy a franchise. The circular spells out a franchise's investment costs and estimated operating costs. But check the circulars of other franchisors in the industry (they are public documents) and compare their operating costs with the costs of the prototype you are shown. For instance, a franchisor may spend a greater portion of his or her prototype's budget on labor or goods than a competitor spends. In such cases, chances are the franchisor is providing extraordinary services to his prototype that you wouldn't receive as a franchisee, according to Fine.

Also try visiting the prototype when the franchisor is absent from the premises. "If it runs the same way when he isn't there [as it does when he is]," says Craig Slavin, president of Franchise Architects, a Chicago franchise consulting firm, "then it indicates the franchisor has perfected the prototype." Finally, keep in mind that if the prototype is geographically distant from your proposed store, there may be difficulties. "You may have to get the franchisor to your unit immediately if a problem crops up," says Paul J. Stewart, president of Franchise Associates Inc., a Dallas consulting firm, "and he better not be in San Diego if you're in Bangor, Me."

CHAPTER 10

COMPETING AS A SERVICE FIRM II
CUSTOMER RETENTION

———◆———

CHAPTER OVERVIEW

Simply stated, customer retention refers to focusing the firm's marketing efforts toward the existing customer base. In contrast to seeking new customers, firms engaged in customer-retention efforts work to satisfy existing customers and further develop the relationship between the firm and its current customers.

A good example of a firm dedicated to customer-retention efforts is the local Lawn Doctor franchise in Wilmington, North Carolina. The Lawn Doctor is a lawn service that specializes in fertilizing and spraying yards to kill weeds. This particular Lawn Doctor could grow at a much faster rate, but refuses to sacrifice the quality of care provided to the existing customer base in the process. This type of business philosophy facilitates a trusting relationship between the Lawn Doctor and its customers.

As a result, the existing customer base requests additional services, which reaps increased profits for the firm. In addition, due to the positive word-of-mouth advertising generated by the existing customer base, new customers are waiting to purchase the firm's services.

This chapter discusses the nature of retention marketing, relating it to frequency marketing, relationship marketing, and aftermarketing. It goes on to highlight the forces in the marketplace that contribute to the importance of retention marketing.

The second half of the chapter discusses the implementation of retention strategies. It focuses on two key areas: defection management and service guarantees.

WHAT IS RETENTION MARKETING?

Recent interest in customer retention has led to a proliferation of related marketing terms, including *frequency marketing, relationship marketing,* and *aftermarketing.* The brief descriptions that follow illustrate the importance of customer retention within each of these concepts.

FREQUENCY MARKETING

The primary goal of *frequency marketing,* a concept originally developed in the banking industry, is to make existing customers more profitable by broadening the range of services bought by the customer from the bank. Consequently, customer retention is a critical component to frequency-marketing efforts. Optimally, frequency marketing "combines data collection, communications, recognition, and rewards to build lasting relationships."[1]

The first step in implementing a frequency-marketing program is to collect data regarding the firm's best customers and to determine their level of relationship with the firm. The level of relationship is defined narrowly to be the number of different services the customer purchases. For example, bank customers may be involved with their bank through checking accounts, savings accounts, car loans, investments, and a home mortgage.

The next step is to communicate with customers on a personal level. Communications need to be interactive to the point where customers can ask questions and establish a relationship with the firm, and need to be action-oriented in that the firm's communications incite customers to respond.

Personal communications demonstrate to customers that the firm recognizes the importance of the customer to the firm. Moreover, when reward programs are developed that prompt customers to act, the communications become action-oriented.

RELATIONSHIP MARKETING

The marketing term for the 1990s is *relationship marketing*. The relationship-marketing perspective takes place on two levels: macro and micro.[2] At the macro level, firms engaged in relationship marketing recognize that marketing impacts on customer markets, employee markets, supply markets, internal markets, and influencer markets, such as financial and government markets. In contrast, at the micro level, which is the focus here, relationship marketing recognizes that the focus of marketing is to change from making the single transaction and moving on to the next customer to building a relationship with *existing* customers.

Relationship marketing is the union of customer service, quality, and marketing. Relationship marketing emphasizes the importance of customer retention, product benefits, establishing long-term relationships with customers, customer service, increased commitment to the customer, increased levels of customer contact, and a concern for quality that transcends departmental boundaries and is the responsibility of everyone throughout the organization.

AFTERMARKETING

Another marketing concept that is related directly to customer-retention efforts is aftermarketing.[3] *Aftermarketing* refers to the importance of marketing efforts after the initial sale has been made. It is therefore the goods-marketing efforts after the initial sale has been made. It is therefore the goods-marketing analogy to customer retention. Aftermarketing techniques include identifying customers and building a customer database, measuring customer satisfaction, and continuously making improvements based on customer feedback, establishing formal customer communication programs that respond to customer feedback, and creating an aftermarketing culture throughout the organization.

An industry that has made some of the biggest strides in aftermarketing is the automobile industry. Customers frequently are contacted by sales and service personnel after a vehicle has been purchased or after service has been completed on the vehicle. Customers with problems are called back by the general manager or the owner of the dealership to express their sincere interest in the problem and their willingness to resolve any existing problems promptly. Hence, an aftermarketing effort is used to retain an existing customer.

THE GROWING IMPORTANCE OF CUSTOMER RETENTION

Customer retention is important because of five key marketing factors: the market, the cost, the consumer, the operation, and the referral. The market, the consumer, and the referral factors represent things happening outside the firm, while the other two relate to the internal dynamics of the firm.

CHANGES IN THE MARKETPLACE

Many changes in the marketplace[4] are coming together to make it more and more expensive to acquire new customers. It has been estimated that it now costs three to five times less to keep a customer than to get a new one.[5] The first major change within the United States' consumer markets is that they are stagnant. As an example, the U.S. population for the next 50 years is predicted to grow at half the rate of the period spanning from 1965 to 1990. Consequently, there are less new customers to go around.

Concurrent with the decrease in population growth, the gross national product also has slowed substantially to an annual growth rate of less than three percent. In sum, there are not as many new customers as there used to be, and the customers that are around are spending less.

Another reason customer retention has become important to today's marketers is the increase in competition. Factors contributing to increased competition include:

☐ the relative parity and lack of differential advantage of goods and services on the market,

☐ deregulated industries that now must compete for customers in the open market,

☐ and accessible market information that is available to more firms, thereby minimizing informational advantages among competing firms.

As a result of the increase in competition, firms are finding that retaining their current customer base is now more challenging than ever.

A third reason that customer retention is becoming increasingly important can be attributed directly to the rising costs of marketing. In particular, the rising cost of mass marketing, the primary tool of conquest marketers, has increased substantially. For example, the cost of a 30-second television spot in 1965 was $19,700. In contrast, a 1991 30-second spot sold for $106,400.

Coupled with the increased cost of advertising has been the loss of the advertiser's "share of voice." Due to the shorter time period now allotted for individual commercials (the length of commercials has decreased from 60 seconds to 30 seconds to 15 seconds), the sheer number of commercials has increased by approximately 25 percent over the last ten years. Hence, firms are competing for attention in a medium that is constantly expanding. In addition, new forms of advertising have evolved, and consumer markets have become more fragmented, which further dilutes the chances for the advertiser's message reaching its intended target audience.

Interestingly, the growth of direct mail in the 1980s is attributed directly to the high costs of mass marketing and subsequent heightened importance of customer retention efforts. In the last decade, marketers became more selective regarding how and where their advertising dollars were spent. The databases built for direct marketing were used as a means to identify current customers and to track purchases. Subsequently, advertising to current customers became a much more efficient means than mass marketing to reach the firm's target market.

THE CHANGING CONSUMER

The typical consumers in the 1990s, compared to their 1960s and 1970s counterparts, are older, more informed regarding purchasing decisions, command more discretionary income, and are becoming increasingly skeptical about the average firm's concern for the customer's business. Consequently, firms engaged in customer-retention practices are noticed by today's consumers and are rewarded for their efforts via repeat sales.

Chapter 2 highlighted the fact that the purchase of a service carries with it increased consumer risk. One way for the consumer to reduce that risk is to repeat purchase from the same firm. One satisfying experience may be a good predictor of another one. To use the frequency-marketing analogy, if a bank can give satisfaction with a current account, then it may be a lower risk for the consumer to open a deposit account with the same bank than to start again with a new bank. This is particularly the case when the consumer already knows the script for the bank.

PROFITS FROM REFERRALS

Another benefit of customer retention is the positive word-of-mouth advertising generated by satisfied customers. Existing customers are necessary for a firm to develop a reputation that attracts new business. Satisfied customers often refer businesses to their friends and family, which, in turn, reinforces their own decision. As discussed in Chapter 7, personal sources of information are particularly important to consumers of services due to intangibility and the perception of increased risk associated with the purchase. Business attributed to current customer referrals can be dramatic. For example, a leading home builder in the United States has found that 60 percent of its business is based on referrals from past customers.[6]

PROFITS FROM REDUCING FIXED COSTS

In Chapter 8, the cost structure of service firms was discussed in some detail. The very high fixed and semi-fixed costs incurred by these firms means that the cost of the marginal or incremental customer is very small indeed. The profitability of a *retained* customers is therefore very high due to the fact that marketing effort need not be expended on that individual in order to create more sales. It is therefore worth investing considerable amounts of money to retain those customers. This is particularly the case for those services that are increasingly dependent on information technology. The shift in banking from people-based operations to computer-based operations has reduced the cost of each transaction dramatically. It has done so, however, at the cost of a much increased fixed-cost base.

PROFITS FROM REDUCING OPERATING COSTS

Overall, long-term customers tend to have lower maintenance costs. Existing customers become accustomed to the company, employees, and procedures; therefore, they ask fewer questions and have fewer problems. Some unforeseen consequences of the airlines price war that took place in the summer of 1992 demonstrate this theory's relevance. On the one hand, the lower prices did achieve their desired effect: increased sales. However, many of these sales were to passengers who had never flown before and were unfamiliar with ticketing practices, baggage handling, and typical behavior on an airline. Services such as complimentary beverages had to be explained to new passengers who were unfamiliar with the term *complimentary*. In one instance, a flight attendant was requested by a passenger for instructions on how to "roll down her window." The end result of adding new customers to the mix was a stressed-out and overworked flight crew and existing customers who were the recipients of lower-than-average service.

IMPLEMENTING CUSTOMER-RETENTION STRATEGIES

In the same way that the concept of customer retention has been approached by different groups in different ways, such as by examining banking-frequency marketing and goods-companies' aftermarketing, so the *implementation* of customer-retention strategies has been approached in many ways. Two of the most powerful ways are defection management, which emerged from the field of total quality management, and service guarantees.

DEFECTION MANAGEMENT

One important way of looking at increasing customer-retention rates is by reducing customer defections. The concept of defection management has its roots in the total quality management (TQM) movement. *Defection management* is a systematic process that actively attempts to retain customers before they defect. Defection management involves tracking the reasons why customers defect and utilizing this information to improve the service-delivery system continuously—thereby reducing future defections. Cutting defections in half doubles the average company's growth rate. Moreover, reducing the defection rate by five percent can boost profits 25 percent to 85 percent, depending on the industry.[7]

ZERO DEFECTS VERSUS ZERO DEFECTIONS Since the acceptance of total quality management within the manufacturing sector, the guide to follow has been the zero-defects model. Although appropriate within the manufacturing sector, where specifications can be identified well ahead of production, the zero-defects model does not work very well within the service sector.[8]

Service customers carry specifications around in their heads and can only approximate their desires to the service provider. Each consumer has their own set of expectations and corresponding specifications. For example, customers often show hairstylists a picture of another person's hairstyle and request a similar style for their own hair. The picture is an approximation of a desired result. The picture does not specify exact lengths to be cut or specific degree of curve for curls. As one hairstylist bemoaned: "They (some consumers) come in here with two spoonfuls of hair and expect to leave here looking like Diana Ross!" Consequently, specifications that are available within the service sector frequently cannot be standardized for all customers. As a result, the service provider must be able to adapt to each set of expectations on the spot.

Due to the unique properties of the service-delivery system, the traditional zero-defects model held by the manufacturing sector is out of touch with the realities of the service sector. A more appropriate philosophy for service firms is to minimize the amount of defections. In contrast to the defect pile for the manufacturing sector that consists of defective goods, the defect pile for services is customers who will not come back.

THE IMPORTANCE OF DEFECTION MANAGEMENT Businesses commonly lose 15 percent to 20 percent of their customers each year.[9] In some industries, the rate is much higher. For example, the cable television industry loses in excess of 50 percent each year,[10] the cellular phone industry experiences turnover at a rate of 30 percent to 45 percent a year,[11] and customer defections in the pager industry range from 40 percent to 70 percent annually.[12] Reducing customer defections is associated with immediate payoffs for the firm. Within the credit-card industry, a two percent decrease in defections has the same net effect on the bottom line as a ten percent decrease in overhead.[13]

Monitoring customer defections is elusive due to the disturbing fact that customer defection rates may not be associated directly with customer-satisfaction ratings.[14] One would think that satisfied customers would be easily retained. Although intuitively appealing, receiving high satisfaction marks from current customers does not necessarily translate into undying customer loyalty. On average, 65 to 85 percent of consumer defectors say they were satisfied or very satisfied with their former provider.[15] Why, then, do customers defect?

DEFECTOR TYPES Customers defect for a variety of reasons:[16]

☐ *Price defectors* switch to competitors for lower-priced goods and services and are probably the least loyal of any customer type.

☐ *Product defectors* switch to competitors who offer superior quality goods and services.

☐ *Service defectors* defect due to poor customer service.

☐ *Market defectors* exit the market due to relocation or business failure reasons.

☐ *Technological defectors* switch to products outside the industry.

THE DEFECTION MANAGEMENT PROCESS

Although customer defections are frustrating for many firms, defection rates are measurable and manageable.[17] Defections indicate where profits are heading and indicate specific reasons why customers are leaving. Information obtained by analyzing defections can assist firms toward the goal of continuous improvement.

The key to defection management is the creation of a zero-defections culture within the firm. Everyone within the firm must understand that zero defections is a primary goal of the organization. To be established as a primary goal, the first step in the defection-management process is that the firm must communicate to its employees not only the importance of retaining current customers, but also the benefits obtained by reducing defections.

The zero-defections goal communicated to employees must have supporters at all levels, starting at the top of the organization. It is critical that upper management leads by example, and "walks what they talk." Managers that speak of customer service in employee meetings and then bad-mouth customers behind their backs never will successfully implement a zero-defections culture within their firm.

The second step in creating a zero-defections culture is to train employees in defections management. Defections management involves:

1. gathering customer information;
2. providing specific instructions concerning what to do with the information;
3. instructing employees on how to react to the information; and
4. encouraging employees to respond to the information.

Information provided in Chapter 11 regarding identifying service failures and effective recovery strategies provides employees and managers with the specifics of defections management.

The third, and perhaps the most critical, step within the defection-management process is to tie incentives to defection rates. Simply stated, if the firm truly values reducing defections, the reward structure should reinforce customer-retention efforts. Firms such as MBNA, as mentioned in the Services in Action 10.1, are dedicated to customer retention and have developed reward systems that are consistent with their customer-retention efforts. MBNA's employees earn up to 20 percent of their salaries in bonuses associated with customer-retention efforts. As a result of the reward structure and these extra communication efforts with customers, MBNA retains 50 percent of customers who call with the intent to end the relationship.[18] Another example is State Farm Insurance: State Farm agents receive as high a

SERVICES IN ACTION 10.1

THE PROFITABILITY OF CUSTOMER-RETENTION EFFORTS AT MBNA

MBNA America, a Delaware-based credit-card company, recently has improved its industry ranking from 38 to 4, and increased its profits sixteenfold. How did they do it? Profitability in the credit-card industry is linked directly to customer retention.

In general, credit-card companies lose money during the first year of a new account. These companies make money from an individual by collecting fees from the retailer and for each transaction that individual makes. In the first year of the account, the fees obtained from credit-card honoring establishments do not offset the costs of advertising, setting up new accounts, and printing statements. Consequently, retaining customers beyond that first year is critical to the profitability of the credit-card industry.

MBNA reinforces the importance of customer retention to its employees through the company's reward structure. MBNA's employees earn up to 20 percent of their salaries in bonuses associated with customer-retention efforts. MBNA employees talk with every customer that wishes to drop its services and, by doing so, retains 50 percent of these customers.

How do MBNA's customer-retention efforts affect the bottom line? MBNA's customer-retention rate is 95 percent, and MBNA keeps its customers twice as long as industry averages. In addition, MBNA's credit losses due to bad debt are one-third to one-half lower than other companies. Moreover, MBNA customers use their cards more often and maintain higher balances as compared to customers of competing firms.

commission for renewals as they do for getting new customers.[19] As a company, State Farm recognizes the value of customer retention and rewards employees for their customer-retention efforts.

Finally, firms successful in defection management also carefully consider creating "switching barriers" that discourage defections. A customer switching banks is subjected to the time-consuming task of closing one account at the old bank, opening a new account at the new bank, and sometimes paying for new checks to be printed. Likewise, switching to a new dentist may require the cost of new x-rays, and switching to a new physician may translate into completing extensive patient information forms and enduring an extensive physical exam. The key to implementing switching barriers successfully is to develop low entry barriers and nonmanipulative high exit barriers.

Overall, the key to defection management is the realization that customer defections are measurable and manageable. Too often, firms simply write off customers who no longer request their services. Defection management focuses on retaining customers *before* they defect and determining the reasons for defections when defections were not prevented. In sum, defectors are a valuable source of information regarding the firm's operations, its employees, and the firm's future.

SERVICE GUARANTEES

One of the most innovative and intriguing customer-retention strategies to be developed in recent years is the service guarantee. Although guarantees in and of themselves are not particularly new, they are very new with respect to services. Overall, service guarantees appear to facilitate three worthwhile goals: (1) they reinforce customer retention; (2) they build market share; and (3) they force the firm offering the guarantee to improve its overall service quality.

CHARACTERISTICS OF SUCCESSFUL GUARANTEES In general, successful guarantees are unrestrictive, stated in specific and clear terms, meaningful, hassle-free when invoked, and quick to pay out. On the other hand, issues to avoid when constructing a guarantee include: (1) promising something that is trivial and normally expected; (2) specifying an inordinate amount of conditions as part of the guarantee; and (3) making the guarantee so mild that it is never invoked.

In general, there are three types of guarantees: an implicit guarantee, a specific-result guarantee, and an unconditional guarantee. The discussion that follows briefly describes each type of guarantee and the trade-offs associated with each type.

IMPLICIT GUARANTEES An *implicit guarantee* is essentially an unwritten, unspoken guarantee that establishes an understanding between the firm and its customers. An example might be a department store that automatically provides refunds or exchanges goods for dissatisfied customers even though it is under no obligation to do so. Although the guarantee is not specified, customers of firms that offer implicit guarantees are ensured that the firm is dedicated to complete customer satisfaction. Consequently, a partnership spirit is developed between the firm and its customers, based on mutual trust and respect.

The trade-offs associated with an implicit-guarantee strategy are intriguing. On the positive side, since the guarantee is implicit, there are no explicit specifications regarding exactly what the firm will do should the guarantee need to be invoked. Consequently, the service firm can tailor the pay-out of the guarantee to fit the magnitude of the service failure. Hence, an implicit guarantee may not result in an all-or-nothing type of arrangement. Other benefits to the firm associated with the implicit-guarantee strategy include avoiding the appearance of a tacky marketing ploy (as compared to an explicit guarantee) and avoiding stating publicly the possibility that the firm, on occasion, may not fulfill its promises. In sum, an implicit guarantee is thought to be the classy way of pursuing a guarantee strategy.

An implicit guarantee also has its drawbacks. Since an implicit guarantee is unspoken and unwritten, "a firm pursuing an implicit-guarantee strategy has to earn its reputation by repeated acts of goodwill communicated to potential clients via word of mouth, a time-consuming process."[20] Hence, an implicit guarantee does little to differentiate a firm early in its business lifecycle. In addition, since the guarantee is implicit, new customers may be unaware of the firm's stance on customer satisfaction and may not bring problems to the firm's attention.

SPECIFIC-RESULT GUARANTEES Another type of guarantee is a *specific-result guarantee.* This guarantee is considered milder than an explicit unconditional guarantee as "the conditions for triggering the guarantee are narrower and well defined, and the pay-outs are less traumatic."[21] In contrast to an unconditional guarantee, which covers every aspect of the service-delivery process, a specific-result guarantee only applies to specific steps or outputs.

On the positive side, specific-result guarantees are most easily applied to quantitative results. For example, Federal Express guarantees overnight delivery. Moreover, by guaranteeing a specific result as opposed to an overall guarantee, the firm may be able to state its commitment to a particular goal more powerfully. On the negative side, a specific-result guarantee may appear weak compared to an unconditional guarantee, and customers may perceive this as the firm's lack of confidence in its own abilities.

UNCONDITIONAL GUARANTEES An *unconditional guarantee* is the most powerful of the three types of guarantees. The unconditional guarantee "in its pure form, promises complete customer satisfaction, and, at a minimum, a full refund or complete, no-cost problem resolution for the payout."[22] In general, offering unconditional guarantees benefits the firm in two ways. First, the firm benefits from the effect that the guarantee has upon customers. More specifically, customer-directed benefits associated with unconditional guarantees include:

☐ Customers perceive they are getting a better value.

☐ The perceived risk associated with the purchase is lower.

☐ The consumer perceives the firm to be more reliable.

☐ The guarantee helps consumers decide when comparing competing choices; consequently, the guarantee serves as a differential advantage.

☐ The guarantee helps in overcoming customer resistance toward making the purchase.

☐ The guarantee reinforces customer loyalty, increases sales, and builds market share.

☐ A good guarantee can overcome negative word-of-mouth advertising.

☐ The guarantee can lead to brand recognition and differentiation; consequently, a higher price can be commanded.

A necessary condition for a firm to offer an unconditional guarantee is that the firm must first have its own operations in order. If not, the pay-outs associated with an unconditional guarantee eventually will bankrupt the firm. Organization-directed benefits of offering unconditional guarantees include the following:[23]

☐ The guarantee forces the firm to focus on the customer's definition of good service as opposed to the firm's own definition.

☐ In and of itself, the guarantee states a clear performance goal that is communicated to employees and customers.

☐ Guarantees that are invoked provide a measurable means of tracking poor service.

☐ Offering the guarantee forces the firm to examine its entire service-delivery system for failure points.

☐ The guarantee can be a source of pride and provide a motive for team building within the firm.

As with the other types of guarantees, there are a number of risks associated with unconditional guarantees that are worth discussing. First, guarantees may send a negative message to some customers, thereby tarnishing the image of the firm that offers the guarantee. Some customers may ponder why the firm needs to offer the guarantee in the first place. For example, customers may consider whether the guarantee is due to failures in the past, or if the firm is desperate for new business. Another drawback to unconditional guarantees involves the actual pay-out when the guarantee is invoked. Customers may be too embarrassed to invoke the guarantee; consequently, the guarantee actually may motivate customers not to complain. Other potential problems associated with the pay-out involve the amount of documentation the firm requires in order to invoke the guarantee, as well as the time it takes for the actual refund to be completed.

SERVICES IN ACTION 10.2

THE HAMPTON INNS' UNCONDITIONAL SERVICE GUARANTEE

Hampton Inns is a hotel chain based in Memphis, Tennessee, with 240 units across the country. Hampton's rooms are priced in the upper-economy range.

In 1990, Hampton began nationally advertising a "100 Percent Satisfaction Guarantee." This guarantee states that if, for any reason, guests are not entirely satisfied with their stay at a Hampton Inn, they will receive that night's accommodation for free. Hampton is relying on this guarantee to help provide differentiation in the hotel market.

Survey research has found that Hampton's unconditional guarantee of quality has an impact on the perceived value of the hotel by two customer groups: those who were not satisfied with the quality of their stay, and those who were. Further, the guarantee has positively affected employee motivation and attitudes.

Customers who were dissatisfied and who invoked the guarantee pronounced themselves satisfied with the outcome. More than half reported the service at Hampton Inns to be better than that provided by other hotels. When ranking attributes for choosing a hotel, these guests rated the guarantee second among eight possible attributes. Ninety-nine percent of these customers said they would stay at other Hampton Inns, and 90 percent pronounced themselves ready to stay at the same hotel location again. (During the period of the study, nearly 40 percent of these guests actually did use the chain again.)

Customers who were initially satisfied with their stay had less-strong reactions. Fewer found the guarantee to be appealing when making their initial selection of the Hampton Inn, though substantial numbers, particularly leisure travelers, did so. Around two-thirds of these guests felt that the guarantee did differentiate Hampton from its competition and that they received more value for money from the chain than from its competitors. Forty-two percent said the guarantee would make them more likely to stay at a Hampton Inn in the future.

Managers and employees clearly believe in the guarantee, stating that it makes them more motivated and more willing to work hard. Ninety-four percent of employees think the guarantee differentiates Hampton from its competitors. Nearly 70 percent said it has improved employee pride in their company.

For Hampton, the guarantee can provide a unifying role. If motivated employees correctly understand the needs of customers attracted by the guarantee and correctly fill them, the guarantee will not be invoked; customers will be satisfied. On the other hand, it is worth noting that those customers who did invoke the guarantee were almost more satisfied, in the end, than those who did not.

CHAPTER 10 READINGS

Article 10.1 takes up the theme of zero defections, and develops the idea that, for service organizations, zero defections is the equivalent of zero defects to goods organizations. Article 10.2 discusses the concept of guarantees as they apply to service firms. Article 10.3 provides a detailed description of how to develop a customer-retention plan.

QUESTIONS

1. Collect examples of direct-mail campaigns designed to ensure customer retention, such as those by American Express. How are the specific campaigns designed to work?

2. Collect examples of guarantees. Which ones are unconditional? Why?

3. Write an unconditional service guarantee for United Airlines, a local restaurant, and a dentist. Are the guarantees likely to be equally effective? If not , why not?

NOTES

1. Richard Barlow, "Building Customer Loyalty through Frequency Marketing," *The Bankers Magazine,* May/June 1990, 73–76.

2. Martin Christopher, Adrian Payne, and David Ballantyne, *Relationship Marketing* (Oxford: Butterworth-Heinemann, 1991), 268.

3. Terry G. Vavra, *Aftermarketing: How to Keep Customers for Life through Relationship Marketing* (Homewood, IL: Business One Irwin, 1992), 2–6.

4. Vavra, *Aftermarketing,* 1.

5. Barry Farber and Joyce Wycoff, "Customer Service: Evolution and Revolution," *Sales &Marketing Management,* May 1991, 44–51.

6. Frederick F. Reichheld and W. Earl Sasser, Jr., "Zero Defections: Quality Comes to Services," *Harvard Business Review* (September–October 1990): 107.

7. *Ibid.,* 110.

8. Ron Zemke, "The Emerging Art of Service Management," *Training* (January 1992): 37–42.

9. Reichheld and Sasser, Jr., "Zero Defections," 108.

10. "How Five Companies Targeted Their Best Prospects," *Marketing News,* February 18, 1991, 22.

11. *The Cellular Telephone Industry: Personal Communication* (Silver Spring, MD: Herschel Shostack Assoc., 1992): 122.

12. *The Pager Industry,* ProNet Annual Report, 1989.

13. Reichheld and Sasser, Jr., "Zero Defections," 108.

14. Michael W. Lowenstein, "The Voice of the Customer," *Small Business Reports* (December 1993): 57–61.

15. Patricia Sellers, "Keeping the Buyers," *Fortune,* Autumn/Winter 1993, 56–58.

16. Glenn DeSouza, "Designing a Customer-Retention Plan," *The Journal of Business Strategy* (March/April 1992): 24–28.

17. Reichheld and Sasser, Jr., "Zero Defections," 108.

18. Larry Armstrong, "Beyond 'May I Help You?'," *Business Week/Quality,*October 1991, 100–103.

19. Sellers, "Keeping the Buyers," 58.

20. Christopher W. L. Hart, Leonard A. Schlesinger, and Dan Maher, "Guarantees Come to Professional Service Firms," *Sloan Management Review* (Spring 1992): 19–29.

21. *Ibid.,* 28.

22. *Ibid.,* 20.

23. *Ibid.,* 20.

ZERO DEFECTIONS

QUALITY COMES TO SERVICES

Frederick F. Reichheld

W. Earl Sasser, Jr.

To learn how to keep customers, track the ones you lose.

The *real* quality revolution is just now coming to services. In recent years, despite their good intentions, few service company executives have been able to follow through on their commitment to satisfy customers. But service companies are beginning to understand what their manufacturing counterparts learned in the 1980s—that quality doesn't improve unless you measure it. When manufacturers began to unravel the costs and implications of scrap heaps, rework, and jammed machinery, they realized that "quality" was not just an invigorating slogan but the most profitable way to run a business. They made "zero defects" their guiding light, and the quality movement took off.

Service companies have their own kind of scrap heap: customers who will not come back. That scrap heap too has a cost. As service businesses start to measure it, they will see the urgent need to reduce it. They will strive for "zero defections"—keeping every customer the company can profitably serve—and they will mobilize the organization to achieve it.

Customer defections have a surprisingly powerful impact on the bottom line. They can have more to do with a service company's profits than scale, market share, unit costs, and many other factors usually associated with competitive advantage. As a customer's relationship with the company lengthens, profits rise. And not just a little. Companies can boost profits by almost 100% by retaining just 5% more of their customers.

While defection rates are an accurate leading indicator of profit swings, they do more than passively indicate where profits are headed. They also direct managers' attention to the specific things that are causing customers to leave. Since companies do not hold customers captive, the only way they can prevent defections is to outperform the competition continually. By soliciting feedback from defecting customers, companies can ferret out the weaknesses that really matter and strengthen them before profits start to dwindle. Defection analysis is therefore a guide that helps companies manage continuous improvement.

Charles Cawley, president of MBNA America, a Delaware-based credit card company, knows well how customer defections can focus a company's attention on exactly the things customers value. One morning in 1982, frustrated by letters from unhappy customers, he assembled all 300 MBNA employees and announced his determination that the company satisfy and keep each and every customer. The company started gathering

SOURCE: Reprinted by permission of the Harvard Business Review, "Zero Defections: Quality Comes to Services," by Frederick F. Reichheld and W. Earl Sasser, Jr. (September–October 1990), 105–111. Copyright © 1990 by the President and Fellows of Harvard College, all rights reserved.

Frederick F. Reichheld is a vice president in the Boston office of Bain & Company and leader of the firm's customer-retention practice. W. Earl Sasser, Jr., is a professor at the Harvard Business School.

How Much Profit a Customer Generates over Time

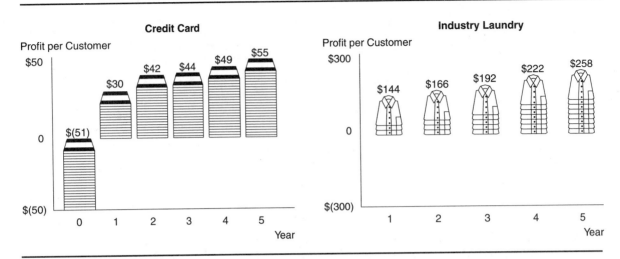

feedback from defecting customers. And it acted on the information, adjusting products and processes regularly.

As quality improved, fewer customers had reason to leave. Eight years later, MBNA's defection rate is one of the lowest in its industry. Some 5% of its customers leave each year—half the average rate for the rest of the industry. That may seem like a small difference, but it translates into huge earnings. Without making any acquisitions, MBNA's industry ranking went from 38 to 4, and profits have increased sixteenfold.

THE COST OF LOSING A CUSTOMER

If companies knew how much it really cost to lose a customer, they would be able to make accurate evaluations of investments designed to retain customers. Unfortunately, today's accounting systems do not capture the value of a loyal customer. Most systems focus on current period costs and revenues and ignore expected cash flows over a customer's lifetime. Served correctly, customers generate increasingly more profits each year they stay with a company. Across a wide range of businesses, the pattern is the same: the longer a company keeps a customer, the more money it stands to make. (See the bar charts depicting "How Much Profit a Customer Generates over Time.") For one auto-service company, the expected profit from a fourth-year customer is more than triple the profit that same customer generates in the first year. When customers defect, they take all that profit-making potential with them.

It may be obvious that acquiring a new customer entails certain one-time costs for advertising, promo-

tions, and the like. In credit cards, for example, companies spend an average of $51 to recruit a customer and set up the new account. But there are many more pieces to the profitability puzzle.

To continue with the credit card example, the newly acquired customers use the card slowly at first and generate a base profit. But if the customers stay a second year, the economics greatly improve. As they become accustomed to using the credit card and are satisfied with the service it provides, customers use it more and balances grow. In the second year—and the years thereafter—they purchase even more, which turns profits up sharply. We found this trend in each of the more than 100 companies in two dozen industries we have analyzed. For one industrial distributor, net sales per account continue to rise into the nineteenth year of the relationship.

As purchases rise, operating costs decline. Checking customers' credit histories and adding them to the corporate database is expensive, but those things need be done only once. Also as the company gains experience with its customers, it can serve them more efficiently. One small financial consulting business that depends on personal relationships with clients has found that costs drop by two-thirds from the first year to the second because customers know what to expect from the consultant and have fewer questions or problems. In addition, the consultants are more efficient because they are familiar with the customer's financial situation and investment preferences.

Also, companies with long-time customers can often charge more for their products or services. Many

How Much Profit a Customer Generates over Time *(continued)*

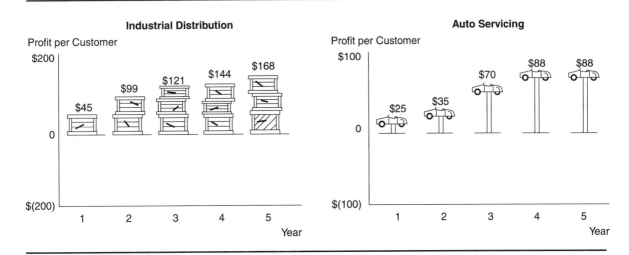

people will pay more to stay in a hotel they know or go to a doctor they trust than to take a chance on a less expensive competitor. The company that has developed such a loyal following can charge a premium for the customer's confidence in the business.

Yet another economic boon from long-time customers is the free advertising they provide. Loyal customers do a lot of talking over the years and drum up a lot of business. One of the leading home builders in the United States, for example, has found that more than 60% of its sales are the result of referrals.

These cost savings and additional revenues combine to produce a steadily increasing stream of profits over the course of the customer's relationship with the company. (See the chart "Why Customers Are More Profitable over Time.") While the relative importance of these effects varies from industry to industry, the end result is that longer term customers generate increasing profits.

To calculate a customer's real worth, a company must take all of these projected profit streams into account. If, for instance, the credit card customer leaves after the first year, the company takes a $21 loss. If the company can keep the customer for four more years, his or her value to the company rises sharply. It is equal to the net present value of the profit streams in the first five years, or about $100.

When a company lowers its defection rate, the average customer relationship lasts longer and profits climb steeply. One way to appreciate just how responsive profits are to changes in defection rates is to draw a defection curve. (See the graph, "A Credit Card Company's Defection Curve.") This shows clearly how small move-

ments in a company's defection rate can produce very large swings in profits.

The curve shows, for example, that as the credit card company cuts its defection rate from 20% to 10%, the average life span of its relationship with a customer doubles from five years to ten and the value of that customer more than doubles—jumping from $134 to $300. As the defection rate drops another 5%, the average life span of a customer relationship doubles again and profits rise 75%—from $300 to $525.

The credit card business is not unique. Although the shape of defection curves varies across industries, in general, profits rise as defection rates fall. Reducing defections by just 5% generated 85% more profits in one bank's branch system, 50% more in an insurance brokerage, and 30% more in an auto-service chain. (See the chart "Reducing Defections 5% Boosts Profits 25% to 85%.") MBNA America has found that a 5% improvement in defection rates increases its average customer value by more than 125%.

Understanding the economics of defections is useful to managers in several ways. For one thing, it shows that continuous improvement in service quality is not a cost but an investment in a customer who generates more profit than the margin on a one-time sale. Executives can therefore justify giving priority to investments in service quality versus things like cost reduction, for which the objectives have been more tangible.

Knowing that defections are closely linked to profits also helps explain why some companies that have relatively high unit costs can still be quite profitable. Companies with loyal, long-time customers can finan-

Why Customers Are More Profitable over Time

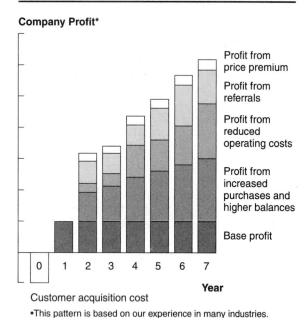

Company Profit*

Profit from price premium

Profit from referrals

Profit from reduced operating costs

Profit from increased purchases and higher balances

Base profit

0 1 2 3 4 5 6 7   **Year**

Customer acquisition cost

•This pattern is based on our experience in many industries.

cially outperform competitors with lower unit costs and high market share but high customer churn. For instance, in the credit card business, a 10% reduction in unit costs is financially equivalent to a 2% decrease in defection rate. Low-defection strategies can overwhelm low-cost strategies.

And understanding the link between defections and profits provides a guide to lucrative growth. It is common for a business to lose 15% to 20% of its customers each year. Simply cutting defections in half will more than double the average company's growth rate. Companies with high retention rates that want to expand through acquisition can create value by acquiring low retention competitors and reducing their defections.

DEFECTIONS MANAGEMENT

Although service companies probably can't—and shouldn't try to—eliminate all defections, they can and must reduce them. But even to approach zero defections, companies must pursue that goal in a coordinated way. The organization should be prepared to spot customers who leave and then to analyze and act on the information they provide.

WATCH THE DOOR

Managing for zero defections requires mechanisms to find customers who have ended their relationship with

the company—or are about to end it. While compiling this kind of customer data almost always involves the use of information technology of some kind, major investments in new systems are unnecessary.

The more critical issue is whether the business regularly gathers information about customers. Some companies already do. Credit card companies, magazine publishers, direct mailers, life insurers, cellular phone companies, and banks, for example, all collect reams of data as a matter of course. They have at their disposal the names and addresses, purchasing histories, and telephone numbers of all their customers. For these businesses, exposing defections is relatively easy. It's just a matter of organizing the data.

Sometimes, defining a "defection" takes some work. In the railroad business, for instance, few customers stop using your service completely, but a customer that shifts 80% of its shipments to trucks should not be considered "retained." The key is to identify the customer behaviors that both drive your economics and gauge customer loyalty.

For some businesses, the task of spotting defectors is challenging even if they are well defined, because customers tend to be faceless and nameless to management. Businesses like retailing will have to find creative ways to "know" their customers. Consider the example of Staples, the Boston-based office products discounter. It has done a superb job of gathering information usually lost at the cashier or sales clerk. From its opening, it had a database to store and analyze customer information. Whenever a customer goes through the checkout line, the cashier offers him or her a membership card. The card entitles the holder to special promotions and certain discounts. The only requirement for the card is that the person fill out an application form, which asks for things like name, job title, and address. All subsequent purchases are automatically logged against the card number. This way, Staples can accumulate detailed information about buying habits, frequency of visits, average dollar value spent, and particular items purchased.

Even restaurants can collect data. A crab house in Maryland, for instance, started entering into its PC information from the reservation list. Managers can now find out how often particular customers return and can contact those who seem to be losing interest in the restaurant.

WHAT ARE DEFECTORS TELLING YOU?

One reason to find customers who are leaving is to try to win them back. MBNA America has a customer-defection "swat" team staffed by some of the company's

A Credit Card Company's Defection Curve

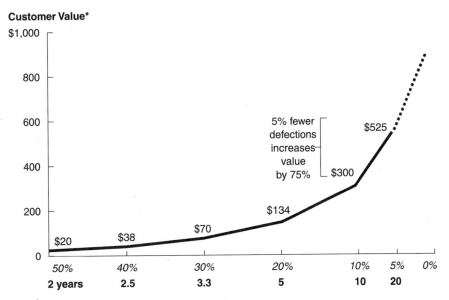

Customer Value*

*The net present value of the profit streams a customer generates over the average customer life. At a 10% defection rate, for example, the average customer life is ten years (1 divided by the defection rate); the customer value is the net present value of the profit streams for ten years.

Key
Defection rate
Average customer life

---

best telemarketers. When customers cancel their credit cards, the swat team tries to convince them to stay. It is successful half of the time.

But the more important motive for finding defectors is for the insight they provide. Customers who leave can provide a view of the business that is unavailable to those on the inside. And whatever caused one individual to defect may cause many others to follow. The idea is to use defections as an early warning signal—to learn from defectors why they left the company and to use that information to improve the business.

Unlike conventional market research, feedback from defecting customers tends to be concrete and specific. It doesn't attempt to measure things like attitudes or satisfaction, which are changeable and subjective, and it doesn't raise hypothetical questions, which may be irrelevant to the respondents. Defections analysis involves specific, relevant questions about why a customer has defected. Customers are usually able to articulate their reasons, and some skillful probing can get at the root cause.

This information is useful in a variety of ways, as the Staples example shows. Staples constantly tracks defections, so when customers stop doing business there

or don't buy certain products, the store notices it immediately and calls to get feedback. It may be a clue that the competition is underpricing Staples on certain goods—a competitive factor management can explore further. If it finds sufficient evidence, Staples may cut prices on those items. This information is highly valued because it pinpoints the uncompetitive products and saves the chain from launching expensive broad-brush promotions pitching everything to everybody.

Staple's telemarketers try to discern which merchandise its customers want and don't want and why. The company uses that information to change its buying stock and to target its catalogs and coupons more precisely. Instead of running coupons in the newspaper, for instance, it can insert them in the catalogs it sends to particular customers or industries that have proved responsive to coupons.

Defections analysis can also help companies decide which service-quality investments will be profitable. Should you invest in computerized cash registers or a new phone system? Which of the two will address the most frequent causes of defection? One bank made a large investment to improve the accuracy of monthly account statements. But when the bank began to study

Reducing Defections 5 Percent Boosts Profits 25 Percent to 85 Percent

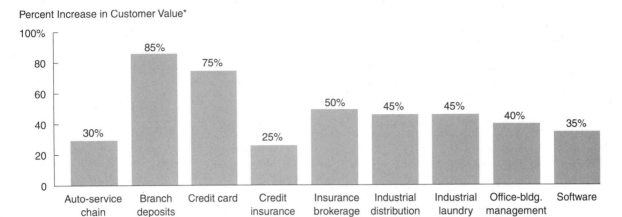

Percent Increase in Customer Value*

*Calculated by comparing the net present values of the profit streams for the average customer life at current defection rates with the net present values of the profit streams for the average customer life at 5% lower defection rates.

defectors, it learned that less than 1% of its customers were leaving because of inaccurate statements.

A company that is losing customers because of long lines can estimate what percentage of defectors it would save by buying new cash registers, and it can use its defection curve to find the dollar value of saving them. Then, using standard investment-analysis techniques, it can compare the cost of the new equipment with the benefit of keeping customers.

Achieving service quality doesn't mean slavishly keeping all customers at any cost. There are some customers the company should not try to serve. If particular types of customers don't stay and become profitable, companies should not invest in attracting them. When a health insurance company realized that certain companies purchase only on the basis of price and switch health insurers every year, for example, it decided not to waste its effort seeking their business. It told its brokers not to write policies for companies that have switched carriers more than twice in the past five years.

Conversely, much of the information used to find defectors can point to common traits among customers who stay longer. The company can use defection rates to clarify the characteristics of the market it wants to pursue and target its advertising and promotions accordingly.

THE ZERO DEFECTIONS CULTURE

Many business leaders have been frustrated by their inability to follow through on their public commitment to service quality. Since defection rates are measurable, they are manageable. Managers can establish meaningful targets and monitor progress. But like any important change, managing for zero defections must have supporters at all organizational levels. Management must develop that support by training the work force and using defections as a primary performance measure.

Everyone in the organization must understand that zero defections is the goal. Mastercare, the auto service subsidiary of Bridgestone/Firestone emphasizes the importance of keeping customers by stating it clearly in its mission statement. The statement says, in part, that the company's goal is "to provide the service-buying public with a superior buying experience that will encourage them to return willingly and to share their experience with others." MBNA America sends its paychecks in envelopes labeled "Brought to you by the customer." It also has a customer advocate who sits in on all major decision-making sessions to make sure customers' interests are represented.

It is important to make all employees understand the lifetime value of a customer. Phil Bressler, the co-owner of five Domino's Pizza stores in Montgomery County, Maryland, calculated that regular customers were worth more than $5,000 over the life of a ten-year franchise contract. He made sure that every order taker, delivery person, and store manager knew that number. For him, telling workers that customers were valuable was not nearly as potent as stating the dollar amount: "It's so much more than they think that it really hits home."

Mastercare has redesigned its employee training to emphasize the importance of keeping customers. For example, many customers who stopped doing business with Mastercare mentioned that they didn't like being pressured into repairs they had not planned on. So Mastercare now trains store managers to identify and solve the customer's problem rather than to maximize sales. Videos and role-playing dramatize these different definitions of good service.

Mastercare's message to employees includes a candid admission that previous, well-intentioned incentives had inadvertently caused employees to run the business the wrong way; now it is asking them to change. And it builds credibility among employees by sharing its strategic goals and customer outreach plans. In the two target markets where this approach has been used, results are good. Employees have responded enthusiastically, and 25% more customers say they intend to return.

Senior executives at MBNA America learn from defecting customers. Each one spends four hours a month in a special "listening room" monitoring routine customer service calls as well as calls from customers who are cancelling their credit cards.

Beyond conveying a sense of urgency, training should teach employees the specifics of defections analysis, like how to gather the information, whom to pass it on to, and what actions to take in response. In one company's branch banking system, retention data is sent monthly to the regional vice presidents and branch managers for review. It allows the regional vice presidents to identify and focus on branches that most need to improve service quality, and it gives branch managers quick feedback on performance.

Employees will be more motivated if incentives are tied to defection rates. MBNA, for example, has determined for each department the one or two things that have the biggest impact on keeping customers. Each department is measured daily on how well performance targets are met. Every morning, the previous day's performance is posted in several places throughout the building. Each day that the company hits 95% of these performance targets, MBNA contributes money to a bonus pool. Managers use the pool to pay yearly bonuses of up to 20% of a person's salary. The president visits departments that fall short of their targets to find out where the problem lies.

Great-West Life Assurance Company of Englewood, Colorado, also uses incentives effectively. It pays a 50% premium to group-health-insurance brokers that hit customer-retention targets. This system gives brokers the incentive to look for customers who will stay with the company for a long time.

Having everyone in the company work toward keeping customers and basing rewards on how well they do creates a positive company atmosphere. Encouraging employees to solve customer problems and eliminate the source of complaints allows them to be "nice," and customers treat them better in return. The overall exchange is more rewarding, and people enjoy their work more. Not just customers but also employees will want to continue their relationship with the business. MBNA is besieged by applicants for job openings, while a competitor a few miles away is moving some of its operations out of the state because it can't find enough employees.

The success of MBNA shows that it is possible to achieve big improvements in both service quality and profits in a reasonably short time. But it also shows that focusing on keeping customers instead of simply having lots of them takes effort. A company can leverage business performance and profits through customer defections only when the notion permeates corporate life and when all organizational levels understand the concept of zero defections and know how to act on it.

Trying to retain all of your profitable customers is elementary. Managing toward zero defections is revolutionary. It requires careful definition of defection, information systems that can measure results over time in comparison with competitors, and a clear understanding of the microeconomics of defection.

Ultimately, defections should be a key performance measure for senior management and a fundamental component of incentive systems. Managers should know the company's defection rate, what happens to profits when the rate moves up or down, and why defections occur. They should make sure the entire organization understands the importance of keeping customers and encourage employees to pursue zero defections by tying incentives, planning, and budgeting to defection targets. Most important, managers should use defections as a vehicle for continuously improving the quality and value of the services they provide to customers.

Just as the quality revolution in manufacturing had a profound impact on the competitiveness of companies, the quality revolution in services will create a new set of winners and losers. The winners will be those who lead the way in managing toward zero defections.

GUARANTEES COME TO PROFESSIONAL SERVICE FIRMS

Christopher W. L. Hart

Leonard A. Schlesinger

Dan Maher

Can lawyers, doctors, investment bankers, accountants, and consultants guarantee their work? Your money back if not absolutely delighted? Some professional service firms are doing exactly that, and they believe they are gaining not only satisfied customers but higher market share and improved service quality. The authors discuss the benefits and risks of unconditional and more limited guarantees. Firms that address this issue proactively now, they argue, will be less likely to rush into poorly considered guarantees later.

Reliability—"the ability to perform the promised service dependably and accurately"—is the "service core," according to Zeithaml et al.[1] They argue that "customers value reliability above all other dimensions."[2] Over the past few years a growing number of service organizations have found that one of the most effective ways to affect customers' perception of reliability is to offer an unconditional guarantee of satisfaction. For many firms, such a guarantee has proven to be a powerful tool for building market share, strengthening customer loyalty, and improving overall service quality.[3] Hampton Inn, a low- to mid-priced hotel chain, promises to waive the cost of the night's stay for dissatisfied customers. Surveys indicate that the vast majority of Hampton Inn customers who invoke the guarantee say they would again stay at a Hampton Inn, and nearly half the customers who don't express dissatisfaction say the guarantee makes them more likely to stay at a Hampton Inn.[4] Thus for the cost of the occasional free room, Hampton Inn seems to be winning a steady stream of loyal customers. In addition, surveys suggest that employees perceive the guarantee as positively affecting their own attitudes and job performance.

Even in the highly risk-averse insurance industry, some firms are using the unconditional guarantee with success. Delta Dental Plan of Massachusetts instituted its Guarantee of Service Excellence[SM] in March 1990 and has documented numerous positive results (see the sidebar).

Although the success of unconditional service guarantees remains hard to quantify, it is not surprising that professional service firms would express interest in them. As competition grows more fierce in the health care, legal, investment banking, advertising, accounting, and other professional service industries, many firms are eager for any means to differentiate themselves from competitors and overcome client concerns about obtaining the highest value for the money. Perhaps in part because of the particularly high cost and hard-to-quantify nature of their work, management consulting firms in particular have been adventurous in exploring the unconditional guarantee.

SOURCE: Christopher W. L. Hart, Leonard A. Schlesinger, and Dan Maher, "Guarantees Come to Professional Service Firms," *Sloan Management Review* (Spring 1992): 19–29.

Christopher W. L. Hart is president of The TQM Group, Ltd., a consulting firm based in Cambridge, Massachusetts, specializing in service guarantee design and implementation and in total quality management. Leonard A. Schlesinger is associate professor of business administration and the Berol Foundation Faculty Research Fellow at the Graduate School of Business, Harvard University. Dan Maher is a principal of The TQM Group, Ltd.

For many professional service firms, an unconditional guarantee may not be a gigantic leap. Some of them have already incorporated the goal of complete customer satisfaction into their corporate philosophies; for them, a customer-satisfaction guarantee may simply be a way of formalizing the concept. Other firms may recognize that, although the costs of improving quality and making the occasional payout will be high, the potential returns in customer loyalty are likely to be far greater.

But such a result is by no means assured, and managers must carefully assess the risks and benefits of unconditional guarantees, some of which are unique to professional service firms. While an unconditional guarantee can indeed provide at least as powerful a competitive edge to these firms as it does to other service companies, the complex nature and unpredictable results of professional services suggest that the rate of payouts could be higher than with other services—and each payout could be a great deal more painful, considering the higher fees and smaller number of clients typical of these firms. Fortunately, these risks can often be managed, but doing so requires great care in the guarantee's design and implementation, as well as in achieving and maintaining exceptionally high service quality.

THE UNCONDITIONAL GUARANTEE

A guarantee is simply a statement explaining what the service customers can expect (the promise) and what the company will do if it fails to deliver (the payout). An unconditional guarantee in its pure form promises complete customer satisfaction, and, at a minimum, a full refund or complete, no-cost problem resolution for the payout. The decision as to whether or not the promise has been kept rests solely with the customer.

The unconditional guarantee is not the only type of guarantee, and other forms are considered below, but it is the most powerful. It says, in effect, "We will meet all of your expectations." An unconditional guarantee makes absolute customer satisfaction the firm's mission. It is the form to which managers appear to be naturally drawn. In one consulting firm, groups of executives were asked to draft proposed guarantees. Although they varied somewhat in wording, the contents of the entries were strikingly similar: All were basically unconditional guarantees.

As powerful as they are, unconditional guarantees are simple to state. One environmental consulting firm places the following sentence in the cover letters it includes with proposals:

The firm unconditionally guarantees customer satisfaction or its fees need not be paid.

Firms operating within such parameters are not only offering to address instances of less than perfect quality, they are confidently bringing the issue to the client's attention.

MARKETING BENEFITS

A professional service firm can derive significant marketing benefits from an unconditional guarantee backed by a strong quality program, particularly in industries where operating standards are not perceived to be uniformly high. By enhancing clients' confidence in its caliber of service, a firm can bring in more business or charge more for its services.

Unconditional guarantees can be especially helpful for firms that depend on referrals and that are vulnerable to negative word-of-mouth. The following conditions associated with professional services make a guarantee especially effective with first-time buyers:

☐ **Prices Are High.** Fees for management consulting, legal, advertising, and many other types of professional service firms often run into six figures. By offering compensation for a service failure, the guarantee reduces perceived risk and creates value for clients.

☐ **The Negative Consequences of Unsolved Problems Are High.** Bad service from a restaurant can ruin someone's evening: bad service from a medical center or law firm can ruin someone's life. The greater the client's expected aggravation, expense, and time lost, the greater the guarantee's power.

☐ **Services Are Highly Customized.** The firm's past performance with other buyers typically does not provide a reliable indication of how the firm will do with a new project, since different customers are often served in entirely different ways. A guarantee can provide a strong indication of a firm's reliability.

☐ **Brand Name Recognition Isn't Easily Achieved through Conventional Means.** Marketing opportunities and differentiating characteristics tend to be restricted for professional service firms. An unconditional guarantee can provide such a differentiator, making the firm stand out in potential clients' minds.

☐ **Buyer Resistance Is High.** Clients tend to purchase professional services very cautiously, which sends the firm on long and often fruitless sales efforts. An unconditional guarantee can effectively overcome resistance and close the sale.

An unconditional guarantee's marketing benefits depend, to a great degree, on how it is presented to potential clients. One manager contended that his executive search firm's guarantee still provides a competitive edge, although guarantees have become more common in his industry. The reason, he says, is that the firm has integrated the guarantee into the heart of its sales pitch, rather than tacking it on in the form of a "by-the-way-in-case-we-fail" statement. As part of the pitch, for example, salespeople ask potential clients to consider the quality improvements *they* would have to make in their own businesses if they offered an unconditional guarantee.

QUALITY BENEFITS

A service guarantee forces internal operational changes. It requires an organization to explicitly define its customer's needs and to understand its service delivery process, including controllable and uncontrollable variables and possible failure points and weaknesses in the system. A service guarantee also requires an organization to establish customer satisfaction measures as key performance indicators and to track and pay for errors, establishing a feedback loop for continual improvement. Finally, a guarantee creates a sense of urgency, forcing an organization to focus all of its resources on satisfying customers.

These efforts are often sorely lacking at professional service firms. The problem is not that managers consciously skimp on quality, but rather that they provide service that meets their own standards of effectiveness instead of aiming for the more elusive service levels associated with complete customer satisfaction. An unconditional guarantee counters this pressure, in large part by providing customers with an incentive to complain, thus making them part of the firm's quality-control team.

The unconditional guarantee also helps guard against the tendency to take on too much work. Manufacturing companies can't deliver half-finished products; they must ask their customers to wait for production to catch up with demand. Professional service firms, however, can be tempted to rush through projects to meet every client's deadline and maximize income. An unconditional guarantee would make that practice exceedingly dangerous.

Unconditional guarantees also reduce the firm's temptation to overpromise during the selling effort, as the firm will be held fully accountable. Guarantees force open and honest dialogue with clients, leading to precise definitions of the client's needs, the firm's capabilities, and joint expectations.

A guarantee motivates a firm to identify its weaknesses. One management consultant considered the quality of his work beyond reproach, until another consultant who unconditionally guaranteed his work joined the firm. The first consultant suddenly found himself reassessing his abilities in light of the fact that he did not have the confidence to offer such a guarantee. After a year of examining and shoring up his potential failure points, he finally felt ready to offer a guarantee himself and did so successfully. In fact, although one of the authors of this paper had been pointing out the benefits of unconditional guarantees to service companies for several years, he went through a difficult weekend of soul searching before he found the courage to sign his firm's first letter providing such a guarantee.

THE RISKS OF UNCONDITIONAL GUARANTEES

Firms hesitate to adopt unconditional guarantees because they are afraid to assume complete responsibility for customer satisfaction. Even when customer dissatisfaction occurs through no fault of the provider—if an air conditioner malfunctions during a consultant's presentation, to provide an extreme example—the firm must provide restitution.

No matter how carefully a firm plans, unanticipated problems will inevitably arise, causing some client dissatisfaction. This will always be the case with services where production and consumption occur simultaneously[1]. Inevitably, the firm will occasionally make payouts that seem unjustified. However, despite their brush with dissatisfaction, clients will feel good about having done business with the firm.

One consultant offering a guarantee was told by a client that he should have provided a full, formal report at the end of a project, although the client had agreed initially to a summary report to hold down costs. The consultant provided a full report at no extra cost. Another client told the same consultant he was surprised to receive a bill for services that he considered part of the consultant's marketing efforts, apparently having forgotten that the consultant had specifically discussed with the client the point at which billing would commence. The consultant waived the fee without argument.

How does the consultant feel about unconditional guarantees now? Completely enthusiastic: the first client has gone on to engage the consultant in several larger projects, and the second client has been a valuable reference and promises to sign on soon for a significant piece of business. Many firms, however, would simply not be able to stomach the idea of making payouts to clients for problems they did not cause, and that may even clearly be the client's fault. Regardless of the long-term benefits of such payouts, these firms do not want to reward a client's unreasonableness.

THE WRONG MESSAGE?

Firms must consider the fact that in some cases unconditional guarantees can hinder marketing efforts. A guarantee can foster skepticism, for example, because customers may wonder why a guarantee needs stating in the first place. Sophisticated buyers usually believe they are entitled to good service and expect it from any firm with which they do business. Emphasizing a guarantee with a specified payout may even irritate clients who assume they already have an implicit agreement with the provider.

A guarantee may conflict with the sophisticated, upscale image that, for example, a consulting firm wants to project. It may also give the impression that a firm is begging for business. Paradoxically, an explicit guarantee can even introduce an element of doubt into customers' minds about the firm's ability to deliver the promised level of service. As one management consultant put it, "Explicit guarantees send out a negative message—that failure is within the realm of possibility."

In some cases, a client may have strong feelings about which factors should drive a project's success and may suspect that a guarantee could undermine those factors. When The TQM Group was preparing to work closely with a client's line managers on a new project, an executive at the client firm expressed concern that the line managers wouldn't pull their weight on the project. He said that the source of his fears was our firm's guarantee: if his managers knew our firm had to take responsibility for fixing anything that went wrong, they simply wouldn't try as hard. In his opinion, the guarantee lowered the probability that the project would fly the first time around.

Some professional service firms have little to gain from an unconditional guarantee. Firms with outstanding reputations and service delivery systems to match, for example, would probably not get much marketing or operational mileage from a stated guarantee. To advertise or promote the obvious would produce few benefits and might actually be perceived as incongruent with a firm's prestigious image. A guarantee is also unlikely to positively differentiate a firm in an industry or industry segment in which operating standards are uniformly high and customers routinely expect excellent service.

GLITCHES IN THE QUALITY PAYOFF

If a firm implements an unconditional guarantee without a commensurate commitment to quality, it has merely employed a potentially costly marketing gimmick. Indeed, improving quality should be regarded as one of the main motivations, if not the main one, for offering a guarantee. Unfortunately, a guarantee doesn't always help achieve quality goals and can occasionally hinder such efforts.

When a money-back guarantee is in force, customers may not invoke the guarantee unless their dissatisfaction is large, commensurate with the payout. For example, clients that are averse to confrontation or that have a strong interest in preserving the relationship with the provider may not invoke the guarantee when they are unhappy with certain aspects of a firm's service, even when they might have done so in the absence of a guarantee. In effect, the guarantee has motivated the client to not complain, which is precisely the opposite of the desired effect. The firm will not obtain valuable information about its flaws that will allow it to improve.

One of The TQM Group's clients, a large company involved in both services and manufacturing, was sending us feedback forms indicating that its managers were not thrilled with our presentations. However, no one at the company would tell us specifically what the problem was, apparently out of concern that doing so would trigger our guarantee. We were so desperate to uncover the source of the problem that we threatened to trigger the guarantee ourselves, but the client wouldn't hear of it and continued to stay mum. Eventually, we discovered in a roundabout fashion that the client had institutionalized a rigid presentation style that conflicted sharply with our own, more spontaneous style. Furthermore, we eventually surmised that the client was more interested in a manufacturing than a services point of view, which we had emphasized. This was invaluable information to us, and we believe the existence of the guarantee made it harder to obtain.

ETHICAL ISSUES

Advertising for professional service firms has sometimes been considered unethical. The U.S. Supreme Court, for example ruling on prohibitions on advertising in the legal profession, stated, "Because the public lacks sophistication concerning legal services, misstatements that might be overlooked or deemed unimportant in other advertising may be found quite inappropriate in legal advertising."[5]

Might guarantees also be considered inappropriate? The Association of Management Consulting Firms

(ACME) hints that this may be the case in its ethical guidelines: "We will present our qualifications for serving a client solely in terms of our competence, experience, and standing, and we will not guarantee any specific result, such as amount of cost reduction or profit increase."[6] While this statement may not apply to unconditional guarantees, it suggests that guarantees in general may be suspect. The widespread use of guarantees in product industries and, to a lesser extent, in nonprofessional services, suggests that guarantees are not intrinsically unethical. However, higher-than-normal ethical standards may apply to professional services, in part because of the services' complex nature.

The main ethical concern about guarantees is whether they mislead potential clients. For example, guarantees may distract clients from evaluating a firm's quality and encourage them to evaluate the service in terms of risk exposure. A guarantee would be unethical if it implied certainty of result or if it suggested that the provider had a greater degree of competence than was actually the case. A physician, for example, wouldn't guarantee the results of a nonroutine surgical procedure nor the outcome of a treatment of a serious disease. Even the offer of a complete refund does not mitigate against the injustice of claiming certainty of result, since such a payout will not cover all of the client's costs—such as lost time, aggravation, or worse—caused by the service failure.

The medical community can offer guarantees if there is reasonable certainty that the stated results will occur. Mission Oaks Hospital in Los Gatos, California, for example, guarantees that if a patient has to wait longer than five minutes for emergency room care, the bill will be reduced by 25 percent. The vast majority of the hospital's emergency care patients do, in fact, receive care within that allotted time. For the same reason, unconditional guarantees in the legal profession would probably first be applied without much controversy for such services as uncontested divorce, uncontested name change, uncontested adoption, the preparation of simple wills and tax returns, probate services, and certain real estate matters.

Another ethical question concerns dignity. Presentations of guarantees that smack of tinny merchandising ("service with a smile or $5 off the bill") or that seek to influence consumers through emotional issues not relevant to professional competence might rightly be considered undignified and thus unethical. Indeed, overt self-promotion of any sort is frowned on (though certainly not absent) in the legal and medical professions, among others. "We're not out there selling cars or underarm deodorant," noted one management consultant. "Firms like ours are perceived to be on some higher plane. We're very sensitive to how a guarantee might be perceived by a potential client, and we'll print it on the back page of the proposal, rather than the front, just to keep it in proper perspective."

Given the increasingly competitive business climate in which professional service firms must operate, it is only natural that ethical standards for marketing their services are loosening. The legal profession has been a microcosm and model for that change. In 1977, the U.S. Supreme Court held that blanket prohibitions against lawyer advertising were unconstitutional infringements of the First Amendment.[7] Subsequent Supreme Court decisions have whittled away most restrictions on advertising except those that prohibit false and misleading claims.

It is likely that any marketing techniques that encourage client confidence without being materially misleading will eventually be accepted to some extent by most professional service communities. By forcing firms to stand behind their work, guarantees may even ultimately be seen as increasing the profession's stature.

MINIMIZING THE RISKS

The decision to offer a guarantee represents a major commitment, philosophically and operationally, and should be made only after assessing every aspect of the business and undertaking a significant measure of cultural change. Service organizations in general must inculcate a vision of customer satisfaction in every employee, from executives down to frontline personnel. Everyone must be empowered to take any necessary steps to satisfy customers, and employee compensation and advancement should be tied directly to measures of customer satisfaction.

For the professional service firm, more than for manufacturers and other types of service providers, an unconditional guarantee exposes it to considerable risk if it does not understand all the quantitative and qualitative results each client seeks, the requirements it must impose on clients to ensure successful service delivery, and the elements of satisfaction that are beyond its control. Obviously, a firm cannot guarantee total satisfaction with any assurance unless it understands all the factors that affect satisfaction. Among the issues an organization must carefully consider:

UNDERSTANDING CLIENT NEEDS Identification of client needs is absolutely essential in any guarantee. The onus is clearly on the service provider to develop as

IMPLEMENTING SERVICE GUARANTEES
THE DELTA DENTAL PLAN STORY

Robert E. Hunter

Thomas Raffio

In March 1990, Delta Dental Plan of Massachusetts began applying Christopher W. L. Hart's service guarantee principles in a program that has already netted significant benefits for the insurance company, its employees, and its customers.

Delta Dental is a managed-care dental insurance company that insures 600,000 people, representing one-fourth of the state's group dental marketplace. As a monoline insurance company competing with big commercial, multiline carriers, Delta Dental relies on its service quality reputation and product differentiation.

INVOLVING EMPLOYEES

When Delta Dental began researching the viability of service guarantees, it was committed to full employee participation. Each employee received a reprint of a Hart article and was asked to read and discuss it during management-facilitated discussion groups.[1] In general, Delta Dental employees were enthusiastic about the concept of service guarantees, primarily as they recognized the quality and value of their own work. Their enthusiasm was tempered, however, by concerns about how such a concept could be implemented within an insurance company. Historically, the only guarantees offered by the industry were related to claims-processing turnaround; Delta Dental was considering far more comprehensive guarantees.

Marketing staff members also expressed misgivings. They were reluctant to use the largely untested service guarantee concept as the underpinning of their advertising and public relations campaigns.

The legal department feared that the program's financial liabilities would more than offset the value of the marketplace information obtained from service failures. Further, the attorneys were not certain that the program could be applied uniformly to all existing corporate accounts, of which there were 1,600, ranging in size from five employees to ten thousand employees. The development of contractual language that could apply equally—without provisos, footnotes, and addenda—presented a major hurdle.

IMPLEMENTING THE PROGRAM

These concerns aside, Delta Dental's employees and managers overwhelmingly endorsed the notion of service guarantees. Therefore, managers and several key employees participated in an off-site brainstorming session facilitated by consultants. Employees then formed several task forces to address fifteen potential services and payouts; these task forces were led by employees, not senior managers, in an effort to promote buy-in from employees at all levels. Other task forces explored the infrastructure requirements of a service guarantee program, researching such matters as companywide training requirements, development of a payout process, analysis of new account requirements, and coordination of the timing of advertising and public relations programs with internal education.

Meanwhile, independent market research sought to prioritize the fifteen potential guarantees via telephone surveys. Delta Dental also commissioned market research to provide additional information from a broader range of companies, which did not necessarily have dental insurance, to determine what they perceived as meaningful insurance guarantees.

Based on the task force recommendations and the research findings, Delta Dental decided on the seven services that it now guarantees. They include such guarantees as "no hassle" customer relations, accurate and quick turnaround of ID cards, and a minimum 10 percent savings on claims paid to its participating dentists. The seven guarantees, all of which have clear refund policies, include cost-containment savings that should lead to price reductions and easy customer relations for existing accounts. They promise total satisfaction—as defined by the customer—with the conversion from the group's current insurer to Delta Dental.

The program was launched following extensive tests as well as a communications campaign focused on all stakeholders, both inside and outside of the organization.

ASSESSING THE RESULTS

Since the formal introduction of the Guarantee of Service Excellence[SM], Delta Dental has made payments of $36,007 to compensate for service failures involving 238 accounts. Delta Dental regards these payouts as an investment in its continuous improvement program, and it expects the process improvements motivated by the payouts to yield economic benefits and to increase the company's internal and external knowledge of the business. Payout feedback has resulted so far in seven process changes.

Employees are armed with a new awareness of past or potential service failures, which makes them more vigilant. When a caller requested a Spanish-speaking customer service representative to explain the details of a form, the employee sought the help of an employee from another department. Together, the employees responded to the caller's need without a callback, symbolizing the total employee acceptance of the team-serving principle.

This awareness has also expressed itself in other ways:

☐ A group of nonmanagement employees formed an independent quality group to provide ongoing feedback to claims-processing operators and analysts with the goal of eliminating rework.

☐ Other employees have developed and implemented internal and external customer satisfaction surveys to provide more data regarding the company's performance and its position in the marketplace.

☐ One employee has volunteered to seek world-class service benchmarks through the Malcolm Baldrige National Quality Award and other quality frameworks.

Delta Dental can also point to other significant wins directly attributable to this program:

☐ The smooth conversion guarantee helped the company sign up seven major accounts in 1990, representing an addition of twenty thousand subscribers to its insured population base in Massachusetts, thereby increasing revenues by 15 percent over plan. In effect, the benefits personnel at these companies felt that the guarantee allowed them to make a risk-free decision.

☐ The company's account-retention rate since the program took effect has been 97.1 percent, compared with 95 percent before the program was initiated.

☐ The program has increased the number of sales leads by 50 percent and the number of quotes by 400 percent.

☐ The close ratio for the period since the program was implemented is 66 percent over target. As a result of the program's success, several other Delta Dental Plans across the country have requested materials pertinent to the development process, and Delta Dental Plan

of Missouri has adopted a similar program.

In summary, the success of Delta Dental's service guarantee program was founded on several factors:

☐ attending to the educational and training needs of the employees, the internal customers;

☐ designing an organization that supports the hassle-free guarantee and embraces the team serving concept;

☐ conducting enough market research to ensure that the services offered would be meaningful to both existing and potential accounts;

☐ testing the service capacity before external rollout; and

☐ communicating the status of the rollout to all stakeholders early and often.

It is true that the size of Delta Dental Plan of Massachusetts (130 full-time-equivalent employees), the flatness of the organization (two layers of management), and a corporate culture already attuned to the principles of total service quality all contributed to the efficient and successful rollout of the program. Nevertheless, the company believes that any organization committed to its customers can achieve the goal of service quality good enough to guarantee.

REFERENCES

1. C. W. L. Hart, "The Power of Unconditional Service Guarantees," *Harvard Business Review*, July–August 1988, pp. 54–62.

Robert E. Hunter, D.M.D., is the president and Thomas Raffio the vice president of operations, Delta Dental Plan of Massachusetts.

comprehensive a list as possible of requirements and objectives and to manage clients' expectations by negotiating clear and concise specifications of the service to be delivered for each project element. One sales training organization, for example, has worked with clients to develop detailed lists of critical success factors for each stage of the training process. For example, the firm and its clients agree ahead of time that "instructor charisma" is critical to success in the classroom and that providing individual feedback to trainees is critical to on-the-job training.

During the needs specification process, the firm should strive to keep expectations reasonable. Performance objectives should be clearly defined, as specific as possible, and measurable with a preestablished objective or subjective yardstick. Objectives should also establish responsibilities, both for the client's and the firm's employees. If the service ultimately meets these objectives, a reasonable client will hesitate before triggering the guarantee even if there is another source of dissatisfaction. In any case, the client is unlikely to feel cheated, misled, or deceived.

This is more easily said than done. Developing a thorough list of terms, obligations, and conditions to cover a complex relationship can be time consuming and still not cover every contingency. Clients, too, can easily tire of the effort required at their end to develop an absolutely thorough definition of objectives, obligations, and feedback mechanisms. Still, firms must be persistent, or the results will be disastrous.

It is worth noting that developing even the most exhaustive set of requirements and specifications may do little good if the people providing the information from the client side are not representative of, or do not see eye-to-eye with, all of the client employees and managers who will be involved in the project. The TQM Group had this experience with a large technology services provider that continued to express dissatisfaction with our efforts no matter how assiduously we worked to meet the agreed-upon specifications. Finally, we discovered that the manager who had brought us in was thoroughly disliked by most other managers at the company, which essentially doomed to failure any efforts made to his specifications. We now make a point of performing the needs evaluation process with a wider group of client representatives.

TRACKING AND MONITORING PERFORMANCE A firm that waits until the end of a project to find out if a client is dissatisfied will not be able to do anything about it. Firms need to develop quality assurance programs to continually monitor their performance and to alert team members to deviations so they can correct them before they get out of control. Firms must establish measurement systems for routine performance checks and create a regular feedback loop with the client and within the firm to facilitate organizational learning.

During each project phase or on a regular basis, the company should obtain written and verbal feedback from those within the client organization charged with evaluating the program's progress. At the provider's urging, the client may want to select a cross section of frontline employees, managers, and project administrators to form a quality assurance committee to assess progress. Control groups may also be required for statistical validation. Formal mechanisms for disseminating error data throughout the firm as the project unfolds will help refine team members' understanding of client needs and ensure that the same mistakes are not committed repeatedly.

LIMITING PAYOUTS An unconditional guarantee need not hang over every piece of work performed for a client. In a long-term project, for example, it may be specified that the payout covers only a particular project phase. The client could still trigger the guarantee out of dissatisfaction with the entire project, but the payout would be limited to the fees or remedial efforts associated with the specified phase. A firm might in some cases also reasonably assert that in the case of a payout it would want to recoup the research and development costs incurred before the project commenced.

In services that involve long-term relationships, the firm and client should agree on how long after project completion the guarantee can still be triggered. A firm may also want to insist that the guarantee not be triggerable until after a certain date or milestone. The quality of legal or business advice, for example, may become apparent only after the recommendations have been implemented and a certain period of time has elapsed.

Provisions that limit payouts should be employed with caution because they can undermine the guarantee's value. The point of guarantee is to cover customers' costs when things go wrong, and limitations on the payout could raise questions about whether these costs will indeed be covered and whether the provider is truly confident about not needing to pay out. In addition, a limited payout may not be stringent enough to force the organization to commit itself to taking every step possible to prevent errors from occurring.

DETERMINING AUTHORIZATION TO TRIGGER THE GUARANTEE Which client manager will measure satisfaction and decide that the conditions of the guarantee have or have not been met? In general, the individual or individuals who authorized project funding might be expected to have the final decision on whether the guarantee has been satisfied. However, operating personnel directly involved with the project will be in a better position to pass judgment fairly on the quality of the service provider. Their input could be essential for a fair performance evaluation.

One information services company authorized only the top-level manager of a client firm to file complaints. This executive was not involved in operations, however, and did not want to take time to evaluate the firm's performance; he never even distributed the firm's complaint forms to operating personnel. The operating personnel were aware of problems with the service but didn't feel they had the authority to complain to the provider and were hesitant to tell their supervisors they were having problems they couldn't solve themselves. Thus the information services company didn't learn about the problems or have an opportunity to correct them. The problems continued to mount until even the oblivious executive couldn't fail to recognize them. By this time the situation was out of control, and the client terminated the provider's contract. In contrast, the sales training organization mentioned above specifies that a cross section of client employees ranging from frontline operators to executive decision makers must agree that there is cause for invoking the guarantee.

OFFERING GUARANTEES SELECTIVELY Guarantees do not have to be offered to every client. In fact, doing so can dull the sense of urgency that a guarantee creates. A firm may opt to target guarantees only at new clients or at clients with whom, for whatever reasons, the marketing benefits seem particularly high or the risks seem particularly low. (While there may appear to be little benefit to offering a guarantee to a client with whom the firm is already in a satisfactory relationship, a guarantee could entice the client into riskier projects on which the client might otherwise have passed and could result in the client becoming a more outspoken and hence useful source of information about quality problems.)

However, offering guarantees to selected clients risks offending those who are uncovered and could send a message to the firm's employees that clients who are not protected by a guarantee are second rate. The challenge for managers is to provide a consistently high level of service to every customer, regardless of the guarantee in force.

SPECIFYING THE TYPE OF PAYOUT A full money-back payout isn't always the best payout. To some

clients, for example, a full payout may seem out of proportion with minor problems, such as a deadline missed by a few days or a personality conflict with one consultant. In such cases a sliding-scale refund based on the severity of the wrong can be instituted; instead of returning all fees, the firm returns a portion of the fees. Lowering the payout in this fashion can make a client more comfortable about triggering the guarantee, thus freeing up a valuable source of quality feedback. When Domino's realized some of its customers felt guilty about demanding a free pizza when delivery was only a few minutes late, the company changed its payout to three dollars, and the number of claims jumped.

There are two alternatives for setting the refund amount. One is to base compensation on a published schedule such as one might find in a death and dismemberment insurance policy. It may, however, be exceedingly time consuming or even impossible to identify and value all possible problems. A more practical option in many cases is to leave the amount of the refund up to the client.

Some clients may feel that refunded fees don't make up for the lost time and aggravation involved in a service failure. To ameliorate this situation, a firm can offer a "money-back-plus-something-extra" payout with an additional sum of money intended to cover customers' hidden failure costs. In the consulting business, one application of this approach is to pay the cost of the client's employee time spent working on the project. Another method is to simply, say, double the money back. However, an offer of a double-money-back payout does not necessarily deliver twice as much positive impact as that of a simple refund; such guarantees are often associated with cheap consumer products of dubious value and might raise red flags with sophisticated buyers.

A money-back payout of any sort may not be appropriate in all circumstances. For one thing, a firm simply may not be able to afford to return all fees in a large project. In addition, the finality of a money-back guarantee may send the wrong signals about a firm's commitment to maintaining a relationship. One alternative to returning money is to state that fees are not due until the assignment is complete (and the client is satisfied).

Another alternative is to offer to work for free after the project is completed to resolve any problems. In addition to obviating the need for a fee refund, this approach can save the client the time, aggravation, and cost of addressing the problems itself or of finding a replacement service firm and can restore the relationship between the firms. As one consultant put it: "It's better to leave behind a legacy of successful projects that a stream of rebates."

The most powerful solution, and possibly the least costly, may be to give clients a choice of the above payouts. If the working relationship has been amicable, there is a high probability that clients will select the least severe option.

FACING UP TO PAYOUTS

Because of the unpredictability of human output, the complexity of client relationships, and the inability to pretest the service, the resources required to make a professional service failure-proof are prohibitive, and efforts to do so would in most cases raise the cost of the service to uncompetitive levels. Besides, an unreasonable or dishonest client may trigger a guarantee anyway. Thus a firm is best off accepting the fact that, in a certain percentage of cases, the guarantee will be invoked. Indeed, that may even be desirable: if a firm never paid out, how would its clients be sure it would make good? On the other hand, if the firm finds itself paying out frequently for no good reason, it has a potential disaster on its hands. Even if the guarantee is helping close deals and raise quality, the pain of payouts may still not be worth it. For start-up or undercapitalized firms in particular the risk may be untenable.

In some industry segments, narrow profit margins and uncontrollable difficulties may make it unfeasible for firms to adopt unconditional guarantees. One firm in the residential construction industry dropped its plans for a guarantee for these reasons, even though it determined that over the long term the guarantee would have significantly raised market share and allowed it to charge a premium for its services. The firm recognized that it never would survive long enough to get to that point.

THE SPECIFIC RESULT GUARANTEE

A firm that can't justify the risks of an unconditional guarantee may want to consider a milder guarantee in which the conditions for triggering are narrower and well defined, and the payouts are less traumatic. Although a "specific result" guarantee tends to have less impact on marketing and quality, it is more predictable and manageable.

Whereas unconditional guarantees cover every element of the service, specific result guarantees apply only to specific steps or outputs of the service process. Specific result guarantees can be targeted to operating areas where customers perceive that a guarantee adds value, forcing a firm to focus on one aspect of the service process and bring it to fruition.

Specific result guarantees are most easily applied to a quantifiable performance attribute, such as delivery time, profitability, or the allocation of a specified number of consultants to a project. Such quantified guarantees create clear expectations. One management consulting firm specializing in just-in-time (JIT) process management guarantees to reduce set-up time—the time it takes to modify a machine to make a different product—by at least 75 percent. Should the firm fail to meet that objective within the agreed upon time frame, it works for free until the 75 percent threshold is reached. Reasonable men and women may disagree about a consultant's attitude, but they should not have as hard a time agreeing on how long it takes to set up a machine.

However, quantitative objectives carry the risk of focusing the firm too closely on short-term results rather than a long-term relationship. In a management consulting assignment, for example, a quantitative specific result guarantee could lead the firm to recommend wholesale layoffs or drastic restructuring to reach a specific cost objective, even though other, less drastic solutions may ultimately create more client satisfaction.

Also, it is often impossible to quantify goals, especially in management consulting and other professional service firms where work varies markedly from client to client, from project to project with a single client, and even within a single project over time. Results are achieved and measured over an extended period of time, and thus the goal of such services should be oriented toward delivering long-term satisfaction rather than making a particular set of numbers.

A specific result guarantee can also be based on achievement of a subjectively evaluated attribute, such as courteous personnel or useful information. One health insurance firm, for example, offered a month's free premium to new customers who encountered difficulties in switching over from their previous insurer. Such a guarantee underscores a firm's commitment to quality and draws attention to its specific promise at relatively small potential cost to the firm. First-time clients unfamiliar with a firm's reputation can perceive the guarantee as a significant risk-reduction tool. Because the guarantee's conditions are so vague, an irate client can trigger the guarantee for dissatisfaction over uncovered elements of the service. Thus in effect the guarantee serves as an unconditional one, focused on a particular element of the service and offering a limited payout.

In fact, if a specific result guarantee promises a full money-back payout in lieu of achievement of a subjective goal, there is little to distinguish it from an unconditional guarantee. But by specifying a result, the firm may be able to state its commitment more powerfully. One management strategy consulting firm offered the following explicit guarantee to a hesitant prospective client: "We guarantee that at the completion of the project you will have the necessary and sufficient information to make the right decision about optimization of your process. If you don't, at your discretion, we will refund your money or work for free until you are satisfied." The client attributed its eventual decision to sign on in part to the guarantee.

The potential drawback to a specific result guarantee is that it may appear weak compared to an unconditional promise, and may even be perceived as reflecting a firm's lack of confidence in its own overall performance. In that case, the guarantee could negatively affect marketing efforts.

THE IMPLICIT GUARANTEE

Some organizations are understood by their customers to be committed to ensuring their complete satisfaction, although no promise is ever specified. These organizations are in the enviable position of being able to offer an implicit guarantee—essentially an unwritten, unspoken, unconditional guarantee. Many outstanding service firms have made the implicit guarantee their operating philosophy.

Implicit guarantees can offer all of the impact of an explicit unconditional guarantee without many of the risks because they do not specify what the firm will do in the event of service failure. The service provider can thus, for example, tailor the punishment to fit the crime, avoiding the risk of paying out $50,000 because it served stale muffins at a coffee break. A firm can also choose to shower a client with a payout that is far more generous than any the client might have asked for, creating feelings of profound satisfaction. Seattle-based Nordstrom, a chain of fashion specialty stores and one of the exemplars of the implicit guarantee strategy, is legendary for this sort of loyalty-capturing largesse.

The implicit guarantee does away with the need for detailed specifications of expectations and deliverables (although these may be advisable for other reasons). Instead, the client–firm relationship is based strictly on mutual trust and good faith, and it is often characterized by a spirit of partnership. Clients simply know that if a problem occurs—any problem—the firm will take care of it.

Yet another benefit to implicit guarantees is the absence of the possible marketing backlash risked with explicit unconditional guarantees. Although customers may infer essentially the same protection, not having to state it explicitly avoids raising suspicions of potential nonperformance and creating the appearance of enlisting tacky marketing techniques. An implicit guarantee is generally perceived as a classier way to impart an image of reliability.

The problem with the implicit guarantee, of course, lies in the difficulty of communicating it. Implicit guarantees can be implied in marketing efforts, but the message is unlikely to be effective unless it is backed up by a solid reputation for high quality work and for applying the guarantee when the customer is not satisfied. A firm pursuing an implicit guarantee strategy has to earn its reputation by repeated acts of goodwill communicated to potential clients via word of mouth, a time-consuming process. Start-up companies or firms with an unimpressive performance history can commit themselves to an implicit guarantee but will probably not win many clients with it. Thus, the offering of an implicit guarantee might best be viewed as part of a latter stage in a firm's quality evolution, a stage that is perhaps best preceded by positive experiences with an explicit unconditional guarantee.

A firm can also ease itself into an implicit guarantee by offering an explicit guarantee that covers a portion of its offerings and employing an implicit guarantee to cover the remainder. The implicit guarantee then acts as a "safety net," catching dissatisfied customers before they leave the system and compensating them to restore their satisfaction. Because customers may not be aware of the implicit guarantee—and therefore may not bring problems to the firm's attention—frontline employees need to be especially vigilant to detect errors and instances of customer dissatisfaction.

It is too soon to say whether unconditional guarantees will become widespread among professional services. If they do, however, many firms will find themselves forced by competitors to rush into guarantees, with predictable results. Some firms will instead wisely choose to approach this difficult territory proactively at their own pace. Even if a firm ultimately determines that the unconditional guarantee and its attendant risks are too intimidating, it may very well discover that the experience of merely considering implementing a guarantee is enough to usefully shake up the organization and address its quality shortcomings.

REFERENCES

1. V. A. Zeithaml, A. Parasuraman, and L. L. Berry, *Delivering Quality Service: Balancing Customer Perceptions and Expectations* (New York: The Free Press, 1990), pp. 20–23.

2. A. Parasuraman, L. L. Berry, and V. A. Zeithaml, "Understanding Customer Expectations of Service," *Sloan Management Review,* Spring 1991, p. 44.

3. C. W. L. Hart, "The Power of Unconditional Service Guarantees," *Harvard Business Review,* July–August 1988, pp. 54–62.

4. C. W. L. Hart, "Hampton Inn's Guests Satisfied with Satisfaction Guaranteed," *Marketing News,* 4 February 1991, pp. 7.

5. 433 U.S. 350, 389.

6. ACME Code of Ethics, article 2.1.

7. 433 U.S. 350.

DESIGNING A CUSTOMER RETENTION PLAN

Glenn DeSouza

———◆———

What is your company's customer retention rate? How many customers are price defectors? Have you identified barriers that prevent customers from switching to a competitor? In this article, the author outlines a game plan to increase customer retention.

Nothing may seem more obvious than the need to keep customers coming back. Yet, customer retention is either overlooked or devalued when it comes to strategy development. Any marketing manager can provide you with a market share estimate, but ask for the customer retention rate and you may well get a blank stare.

Buck Rodgers, who headed worldwide marketing for IBM as the company's sales grew from $10 billion to $50 billion, speaks forcefully about the importance of customer retention in his book, *The IBM Way:* "It seems to me," observes Rodgers, "that most companies are a lot better at prospecting for new customers than maintaining their customer list. As far as I'm concerned, customer maintenance is imperative to doing business. . . . Someone once said I behaved as if every IBM customer were on the verge of leaving and that I'd do anything to keep them from bolting."

It pays to be obsessive about retaining customers. A cost study of service companies by Bain & Co. found that customer retention has a more powerful effect on profits than market share, scale economies, and other variables that are commonly associated with competitive advantage. More specifically, Bain found that companies that reduce customer defections by 5% can boost profits from 25% to 85%.[1]

As customer retention goes up, marketing costs go down. Moreover, loyal customers frequently bring in new business. The role of the customer as salesperson is especially important in the case of complex products. Buying a telecommunications system that will be at the heart of a business is a major risk. Prospects are filled with worries: Will the dealer provide prompt service? Can the system be expanded later? Will the dealer go out of business? To get reliable answers, prospects tend to rely on friends and colleagues rather than on salespersons or brochures.

The true cost of losing a customer is the amount that person could have spent while involved in a business relationship with the company over a lifetime. The bitter and enduring memories created by a bad buying experience are illustrated by the problems currently facing Detroit.

In 1980, according to a J. D. Power and Associates survey, the owners of General Motors, Ford, and Chrysler automobiles recorded three times the number of problems with cars 90 days out of the showroom than did owners of Japanese automobiles. By 1990, U.S. manufacturers had trimmed the quality gap to 25%. Yet, during the same decade, the Japanese market share rose eight points.[2]

A PLAN TO FOIL DEFECTORS

Here are four steps that a company should consider in designing a successful customer retention strategy. These

Source: Glenn DeSouza, "Designing a Customer Retention Plan," *The Journal of Business Strategy* (March/April 1992): 24–28.

Glenn DeSouza is president of Strategic Quality Systems Inc., Belmont, Massachusetts. He is a visiting assistant professor of management at the University of Massachusetts at Boston.

[1] F. F. Reichheld and W. E. Sasser, Jr., "Zero Defections: Quality Comes to Services," *Harvard Business Review* (September–October 1990), p. 106.
[2] "A New Era for Auto Quality," *Business Week* (Oct. 22, 1990), p. 85.

steps integrate concepts from marketing and quality management and apply them to the challenge of keeping customers.

MEASURE CUSTOMER RETENTION

In sports, even in individual events like the long jump, it is essential to keep score. Without measurement, there is no impetus to do better, no records to break. It's the same in business. Nothing is real unless it gets measured.

If customer retention is not measured, it will not be managed. Fortunately, it is easy to calculate measures of customer retention, since only internal file data is required for the calculations.

The crude retention rate measures the absolute percentage of customers that are retained. If the number of customers drops from 500 to 475, the crude rate is 95%. The crude rate treats every customer loss as equivalent. The weighted retention rate resolves this problem by weighting customers by the amount they buy. If the 25 defecting customers had unit purchases that were double the average, the weighted rate is 90%.

If customers source from multiple vendors, high retention rates can mask a problem. For example, when an airline decided to split an order between Boeing 767s and Airbus Industrie A-300s, Boeing retained a customer, but on a shared basis. To reflect multiple sourcing, a customer penetration index must be calculated by evaluating whether sales to retained customers are growing as fast as market-unit sales. The differences reflect changes in customer penetration.

INTERVIEW FORMER CUSTOMERS

Many companies write off customers who are definitely lost; this is a mistake. One can learn a great deal by talking to former customers, either directly or through a consultant. There is no need to guess why customers leave when you can ask them. The information they provide is likely to be more specific and actionable than usual market research.

Customers defect for various reasons, and not all of them are preventable. Some defections result from forces that are external to the business. Other defections can be prevented if corrective actions are taken or new strategies are adopted. Consider these six types of defectors.

☐ Price defectors are customers who switch to a low-priced competitor. For example, low price was the sole attraction of People Express, the discount airline started by Donald Burr in 1981. Passengers could fly between Boston and New York (Newark NJ, actually) for about half the fare charged on the Eastern shuttle. Bargains like this were compellingly attractive to tourists, students, and other discretionary travelers. By 1984, People had become the fastest-growing airline in the history of aviation.

☐ Product defectors are customers who switch to a competitor that offers a superior product. This type of defection can be irreversible. A customer who is lost because of price can be "bought back," but it is almost impossible to get a customer back who has switched to a competitor that is perceived as offering a better product.

☐ Service defectors are customers who leave because of poor service. For example, within a few years, customers of People Express began to leave because of poor service, which included lost bags, scrambled reservations, overbooking, and delayed flights. The exodus accelerated once the major carriers used their computer systems to selectively match People's low prices (e.g., American Airlines offered an Ultimate Saver Fare).

By 1986, the party was over for People Express. Declining load factors and negative cash flows forced a sellout to Continental Airlines. In an ironic footnote, Donald Burr was again working for his old boss, Frank Lorenzo, a man he had called Darth Vader.

☐ Market defectors are customers who are lost, but not to a competitor. The customer may go out of business or move out of the market area. During the early 1980s, for example, companies that sold equipment to oil drillers and explorers lost many of their customers when oil prices dropped sharply and customers filed for bankruptcy.

☐ Technological defectors are customers who convert to a product offered by companies from outside the industry. During the 1980s, Wang Lab's customers converted en masse from dedicated word processors to multipurpose personal computers. Wang could have prevented these defections, but only by embracing the new technology. Wang did eventually introduce a personal computer, but never marketed it with any seriousness. It was too little and too late.

☐ Organizational defectors are customers who are lost because of internal or external political considerations. For example, Being frequently runs into political problems when selling to state-owned airlines in the developing world. Boeing claims that many of these airlines buy Airbus equipment because they are told that the aid they receive from European governments may be contingent on their willingness to buy from Airbus.

ANALYZE COMPLAINT AND SERVICE DATA

It is natural to regard complaints as a nuisance and an irritant—an unpleasant side effect of doing business. However, complaint data can be a gold mine for the analyst who wants to identify problems that cause customer defections. After all, for every customer who complains, there are possibly 10 others who did not voice their complaints. Listening and acting on these grievances can help retain not only the customers who complain, but, more important, those who did not.

The introduction of toll-free complaint lines has increased the amount of complaint data available for analysis. In 1977, Procter & Gamble became the first company to print a toll-free telephone number on all its packages. Doing this did not reduce the volume of mail P&G received, and the net result was an increase in the number of customer contacts. To enable a meaningful statistical analysis, complaints must be classified by problem, product model, product year, and dealer; the product's registration number should also be noted.

Complaint data must be statistically analyzed. The analysis must go beyond the computation of means and variances. Individual elements must be plotted to identify patterns in the data as well as elements that lie outside the normal expected range. Without statistical methods, attempts to improve a process are hit or miss.

As emphasized by W. Edwards Deming, most problems result from systemic factors such as faulty design, poor supervision, and machines out of order. Complaint analysis may reveal that a particular model or factor account for a disproportionate share of complaints. This indicates that the problem is systemic and can be eliminated by management action.

Some systemic problems can be eliminated by product redesign. For example, Polaroid has used complaint information to make its cameras easy to use. On an early model, Polaroid received thousands of calls about torn pictures; customers could not pull the film out without tearing the prints. In the next model, Polaroid built in an automatic ejection feature for the film.

Polaroid also received calls complaining that the camera did not work. When callers were asked if they had checked the battery, most replied that they did not know the camera contained a battery. To handle this problem, Polaroid decided to locate the battery in the film pack so that the battery was changed along with the pack.[3]

---

[3]J. Goodman, *Summary of White House Complaint Handling Study*, Technical Assistance Research Programs (Washington, D.C., 1981), p. 12.

The need for complaint analysis has been recognized by the judges of the Malcolm Baldrige National Quality Award. Baldrige Award judges not only examine whether contestants resolve complaints promptly, but also how they analyze complaints and translate the findings into improvements.

Service data can be helpful in trying to understand why customers defect. In particular, if certain service problems keep recurring, this suggests that the cause is systemic. Some products, such as an automobile, need routine and emergency service if they are to operate at peak efficiency. For other products, service may be as simple as teaching customers how to use the product.

For example, software firms have set up pay-for-service lines where registered customers can receive advice on how to resolve a particular problem or perform a particular application. The callers are often sophisticated users of the software who have a problem that their colleagues are unable to answer. By analyzing the calls, a company can identify attractive new features or insert helpful suggestions into its user manual.

Service data differs from complaint data. The complainer is an aggrieved individual, with a problem that may be trivial or extreme. The person who needs service is a customer with a standard, technical problem that demands and gets actual attention. Because service data differs from complaint data, its analysis may offer new insights into systemic problems.

Complaint and service data is inherently useful; if such data is not being used, this suggests poor statistical analysis or reporting. Few companies use statistics effectively, a point made by Deming in his book *Quality, Productivity, and Competitive Position*. To quote him: "No resource in any company is scarcer than statistical knowledge and ability. No source of knowledge can contribute more to quality, productivity, and competitive position."

In the context of reporting complaint data, the most common mistake made is to prepare a single, multipurpose report. Senior managers will not read a thick report; they will find most of the information irrelevant. A series of reports must be prepared and at least one of them should highlight possible, corrective actions.

IDENTIFY SWITCHING BARRIERS

A company that limits itself to analyzing defections and complaints is backfilling—identifying problems that need to be corrected. But a good retention strategy must move beyond problem resolution. It should identify barriers that will prevent a customer from switching to a competitor, even one who is perceived as offering a better product at a lower price.

Lotus Development Corp., for example, sells against competitors that offer software that is cheaper and in some ways more technically advanced. Yet Lotus still dominates the market. There is a Lotus infrastructure consisting of millions of users, scores of applications and macros, and many special-purpose user groups. Hidden costs associated with a switch from Lotus far exceed the direct savings realized by buying the cheaper software.

To identify switching barriers, look outside your own industry for the best demonstrated practices. If you borrow a practice that is farthest afield from your own industry, your chances of surprising the competition are better. A borrowed practice will, of course, need to be modified to fit your customer's needs.

Electronic data interchange (EDI) is a technological example of a switching barrier. Department stores have traditionally been the most fickle of buyers. In the past, they would readily grant shelf space to a new vendor with a trendy look or a big price discount, but less so today.

Vendors with an EDI link enjoy a protected status. Under EDI, the store and vendor share data. The vendor can look at a terminal, see how many items have sold at the department store, and ship more product. The result is that the department store carries minimal inventory. The reward—a newfound loyalty to the vendor.

Strategic bundling can also create a barrier to defections. A bundle is a group of products or services offered as a single cost-saving and convenient package. A banking bundle, for example, includes checking and savings accounts, a credit card, a preapproved auto loan, and a special cash flow statement. A customer who buys a bundle is less likely to defect if someone offers a better deal on one of the items in the bundle.

Paradoxically, the ultimate barrier to competition may be a new twist on that old standby—account management. Many companies use the Willy Loman approach, where Willy deals with the buyer or some other middle manager. This relationship is placed in jeopardy if Willy moves on to greener pastures or alienates the contact at the account. In the new model, a team approach is used to forge a bond that lasts no matter which person on the sales force is the key contact in the relationship.

The account team may be headed by the CEO.[4] Typically, CEO efforts are limited to talking with fellow CEOs to forge companywide programs. But the involvement can go beyond the ceremonial.

At Xerox, CEO Paul Allaire personally handles six of the copier company's largest accounts. At Bose Corp., founder Amar Bose gets directly involved in opening markets. He visits Japan at least twice a year, which may explain in part why Bose is one of the largest sellers of high-performance loudspeakers in Japan.

Team account management is an all-hands-on proposition. Even the clerical staff should get involved. Nothing can be more frustrating to a customer than a conflict with an anonymous clerk at the billing or shipping department.

I recently surveyed two corporate subsidiaries, both of which were using identical service systems. Yet customers rated one subsidiary higher. The reason was the person who managed customer service at the better subsidiary. She had been with the company for 20 years and was on a first-name basis with customers, many of whom she had met at trade shows.

To companies that are financially strapped, installing a free terminal in a customer's office or sending a clerical supervisor to a trade show may seem like an unwarranted extravagance. However, creating switching barriers requires a willingness to spend, to experiment, and to break with industry tradition. To the extent that customer retention actually improves, the expenditures are a justifiable investment. There are few things that are more closely associated with superior business performance than a high rate of customer retention.

---

[4] See "Chief Executives Are Increasingly Chief Salesmen," *The Wall Street Journal,* August 6, 1991

CHAPTER 11

SERVICE RECOVERY

CHAPTER OVERVIEW

The following are some basic facts about service failures:

☐ *For every complaint a corporate headquarters receives, there are 19 other dissatisfied customers who did not take the time to complain.*[1]

☐ *It costs five to ten times more in resources to replace a customer than it does to retain one.*[2]

☐ *A customer must have 12 positive experiences to overcome one negative one.*[3]

☐ *An average customer who has a complaint tells nine or ten people about it; however, customers whose complaints are resolved satisfactorily tell only five other people about it.*[4]

☐ *Most companies spend 95 percent of service time redressing problems and only five percent of service time trying to figure out what went wrong to make the customers angry in the first place.*[5]

☐ *For those companies that do try to do something about their customers' anger, more than half of all efforts to respond to customer complaints actually reinforce negative reactions, making the customer even more dissatisfied.*[6]

These facts capture the essence of the service-recovery problem. Customers who complain provide the firm with the opportunity to recover from the service failure. Unfortunately, not all customers complain. If they do complain and service recovery is successful, a service-recovery paradox often exists where the customer will rate performance higher if the failure occurs and the contact personnel recover from the failure than if the service had been delivered successfully in the first place.

Unfortunately, service recovery is not always successful, and the consequences are many and disastrous. Customers require many positive experiences to overcome one failure, and often will tell many people about the complaint. Service firms expend huge amounts of energy dealing with the complaints, often with negative results for the consumer and without learning from the failures themselves.

While some companies are great at delivering service until something goes wrong, other companies thrive on recovering from service failures and impressing customers in the process. The purpose of this chapter is first to discuss the reasons why customers complain and the reasons why they do not. It then goes on to explain how the firm can respond once a complaint has been received and how to manage such service-recovery efforts.

SERVICE FAILURES

Despite the firm's best efforts, service failures are inevitable. Planes are late, employees are rude or inattentive, and the maintenance of the tangibles surrounding the service is not always perfect. The very nature of services means that failures are bound to occur.

Consider Table 11.1, adapted from Article 4.1. This is the result of an analysis of 352 dissatisfactory incidents collected from customers in the airline, restaurant, and hotel industries. Each incident was described by a respondent and then classified according to its source. Less than half the failures came from failures in the delivery system, such as unavailable service unreasonably slow service, and other core service failures. Operations management and design and quality system approaches can try to reduce these failures, but perhaps at the expense of the empowerment of the contact personnel, which may be necessary to successfully undertake service recovery.

TABLE 11.1 Dissatisfactory Incidents

	Total	Percent of Total	Airline	Restaurant	Hotel
Employee Responses to Service-Delivery Failures					
Response to unavailable service	29	8.2			
Response to unreasonable service	53	15.1			
Response to other core service failures	69	19.6			
Subtotal	151	42.6	45.5	39.8	47.6
Employee Responses to Customer Needs and Requests					
Response to "special needs" customers	6	1.7			
Response to customer preferences	37	10.5			
Response to admitted customer error	8	2.3			
Response to potentially disruptive others	4	1.1			
Subtotal	55	15.6	37.3	9.9	17.9
Unprompted and Unsolicited Employee Actions					
Attention paid to customer	48	13.6			
Truly out-of-the-ordinary employee behavior	41	11.6			
Employee behaviors in the context of cultural norms	42	11.9			
Gestalt evaluation	15	4.3			
Performance under adverse circumstances	—	—			
Subtotal	146	41.5	27.3	50.3	34.5

Customers themselves can create service failures through their own behaviors. Asking for special treatment because of needs or preferences implies that the contact personnel will have to "break the rules" to tailor the service to the customer. Equally, "customer error" refers to scenarios where the failure is initiated by a customer mistake that the customer admits to making (e.g., lost ticket or hotel key) but that the customer still wants recovered.

Finally, nearly half of incidents of dissatisfaction are caused by the behavior of employees during the process of service delivery. These are the unexpected behaviors not initiated by the customer, but which can influence customer satisfaction dramatically. Article 11.1 describes a detailed methodology for diagnosing service failures.

Customer complaining behavior, however, is not just a result of service failures. Customers consciously choose whether to complain or not when a failure occurs, and often will complain even when a failure has not taken place. The firm must understand complaining behavior if it is to successfully create a recovery strategy.

CUSTOMER COMPLAINING BEHAVIOR

As a striking example regarding the impact of service failures, results from a past study that asked consumers "Have you ever gotten so upset at a store (or manufacturer) that you said 'I'll never go into that store or buy that brand again,' and you haven't?" had to limit respondents to three incidents to keep the interview time reasonable. The oldest incident happened over 25 years ago, and 86 percent of the incidents were more than five years old.

The consequences of service failures can be dramatic. The vast majority of respondents (87 percent) indicated that they were still somewhat or very emotionally upset, and they were more upset about the treatment they received from employees than at the store or at product performance. More than three-quarters of respondents indicated that they had engaged in negative word-of-mouth communications regarding the incident (46 percent claimed they told "lots of people"). Finally, true to form in what is typical consumer-complaint behavior today, only 53 percent voiced their complaint to the store even though 100 percent defected to other firms.[7]

Most companies cringe at the thought of customers that complain, while other companies look at complaints as a necessary evil in conducting business. The truth of the matter is that every company should encourage its customers to complain. Complainers are telling the firm that is has some operational or managerial problems that need to be corrected. Hence, complainers are offering a free gift to the company, that is, they act as consultants and diagnose the firm's problems—at no fee.

Moreover, complainers are providing the firm with the chance to reestablish the customer's satisfaction. Complainers are more likely to do business with the firm again than noncomplainers. Consequently, successful firms view complaints as an opportunity to satisfy unhappy customers and prevent defections and unfavorable word-of-mouth communications.[8]

It's not the complainers the company should worry about, it's the noncomplainers. Customers that do not express their complaints are gone or are ready to defect to the competition at any moment. In fact, 63 percent of dissatisfied customers who do not complain and who have purchased goods or services costing $1.00 to $5.00 will defect to a competitor. Even more disturbing is that, as purchases exceed $100.00, the defection rate approaches 91 percent.[9]

Article 11.2 takes a broader perspective on complaining behavior than that of the service firm, and views this behavior from the context of social interaction. To do so, it looks both at the types of complaints and at the types of outcomes. It also focuses on the decision to complain or not to complain.

TYPES OF COMPLAINTS   Based on past research in consumer psychology, complaints can be instrumental or noninstrumental. *Instrumental complaints* are expressed for the purpose of altering an undesirable state of affairs. For example, complaining to a waiter about an undercooked steak is an instrumental complaint. In this case, the complainer fully expects the waiter to correct the situation. Interestingly, research has indicated that instrumental complaints only make up a very small amount of complaints that are voiced every day.

In contrast, *noninstrumental complaints* are voiced without any expectation that the undesirable state will be altered and are voiced much more often than instrumental complaints. For example, complaints concerning the weather or one's personal physical state, such as: "It's too hot!" or "I'm so ugly!" are voiced without any real expectation that conditions will change. Another case of a noninstrumental complaint is when an instrumental complaint is voiced to a secondary party and not to the offending source. For example, complaining to your friends about your roommate being a slob is a noninstrumental complaint.

Complaints also are categorized as ostensive or reflexive. *Ostensive complaints* are directed to someone or something outside the realm of the complainer. In contrast, *reflexive complaints* are directed to something inside the complainer. Typically, complaints tend to be more ostensive than reflexive for two reasons. First, people generally avoid making negative comments about themselves to avoid reinforcing negative feelings of self-esteem. Secondly, people seldom want to convey negative attributes about themselves to others.

WHY DO CUSTOMERS COMPLAIN? In the case of the instrumental complaint, the answer is pretty clear. The complainer wants the undesirable state to be corrected. However, the answer is not so clear cut with respect to noninstrumental complaints. Experts believe there are several reasons that noninstrumental complaints occur. First, complaining serves the function of a pressure valve and allows the complainer an emotional release from frustration. Hence, the complaint provides the person with the mechanism to "blow off some steam" and "get it off their chest."

Complaining also serves as a mechanism for the complainer to regain some measure of control. (See Chapter 2 for a discussion of the importance of control.) Control is reestablished if the complainer is able to influence other people's evaluation of the source of the complaint. For example, negative word of mouth that is spread by the complainer for the purpose of taking revenge on an offending business provides the complainer with some measure of control through indirect retribution.

A third reason people complain to others is to solicit sympathy and to test for consensus of the complaint, thereby validating the complainer's subjective evaluation of events that led to the complaint. In other words, the complainer wants to know if others would feel the same way under similar circumstances. If so, the complainer then feels justified in voicing the complaint.

Finally, a fourth reason complainers may complain is to create an impression. Strange as it may seem, complainers often are considered more intelligent and discerning than noncomplainers.[10] By complaining, it may be implied that the complainer's standards and expectations are higher than noncomplainers'.

WHY DON'T CUSTOMERS COMPLAIN? A greater percentage of services' problems than goods' problems are not voiced "because potential complainers do not know what to do or think that it wouldn't do any good."[11] This situation can be attributed directly to the intangibility and inseparability characteristics inherent in the provision of services. Due to intangibility, evaluation of the service-delivery process is primarily subjective. Consequently, consumers often lack the security of making an objective observation and may doubt their own evaluation.

Due to inseparability, the customer often provides inputs into the process. Hence, given an undesirable outcome, the customer may shift much of the blame to himself for failing to convey to the service provider a satisfactory description of the level and type of service desired. In addition, the inseparability dimension describes the often face-to-face interaction between the customer and the service provider. The customer may feel uncomfortable about complaining due to the physical presence of the provider.

Finally, many services are technical and specialized. Customers may not feel adequately qualified to voice a complaint for fear that they lack the expertise to evaluate the quality of the service. For example, do you really know when your auto mechanic did everything they billed you for?

COMPLAINING OUTCOMES In general, complaining behavior results in three outcomes: voice, exit, and retaliation.[12] *Voice* refers to the outcome where the consumer verbally communicates his or her dissatisfaction with the store or the product. *High voice* means that the communication is expressed to the manager or someone higher up in the management structure. *Medium voice* occurs when the consumer communicates the problem to the sales clerk. *Low voice* occurs when the consumer does not communicate the problem to anyone associated with the store or product.

Exit means that the consumer stops patronizing the store or using the product. *High exit* occurs when the consumer makes a conscious decision never to purchase from the firm or buy the product again. *Medium exit* reflects the consumer's conscious decision to try not to use the store or product again if at all possible. *Low exit* means that the consumer does not change their purchasing behavior and continues to shop as usual.

The third type of complaint behavior is retaliation. *Retaliation* refers to the situation where the consumer takes action deliberately designed to damage the store or hurt future business. *High retaliation* involves physically damaging the store, or going out of the consumer's way to communicate to others negative aspects concerning the business. *Medium retaliation* is caused by the consumer creating minor inconveniences for the store and only telling a few people about the incident. *Low retaliation* reflects no retaliation against the store at all.

Interestingly, the three complaining-behavior outcomes are not mutually exclusive and can be considered as three dimensions that may occur simultaneously. Consumers experiencing high levels of all three outcomes simultaneously can lead to explosive behavior. For example, "in one high-high-high example, the customer shouted his dissatisfaction at the clerk and the store manager, vowed never to buy at the store again, went out of the store, got in his car, and drove it in the front doors of the store through the checkout counter and between two lines of shelving, destroying everything in its path."[13] In contrast, a consumer that is high voice, low exit, and low retaliation would typify the perpetual complainer who continues to shop at the store.

SERVICE-RECOVERY STRATEGY

If failures are endemic and complaining behavior is limited, it is obvious that three broad building blocks are needed for a recovery strategy:

1. The firm must encourage complaining behavior.
2. The firm must develop the capability to listen to and learn from complaints.
3. The firm must develop recovery strategies throughout the organization and create a culture in which these strategies are used.

ACTIVELY ENCOURAGING COMPLAINTS

Experts explain that actively encouraging complaints is a way to break the silence. Remember that complainers that actually voice their complaint to the source are the exception—most customers don't speak up. This doesn't mean that customers don't complain, the problem is that they complain to friends and family. The average unhappy customer voices her displeasure with the firm to 11 other people.[14] Strategies to encourage complaints include customer surveys, focus groups, and actively monitoring the service-delivery process to ensure customer satisfaction.

LISTENING TO COMPLAINTS

Article 11.3 discusses the whole area of complaint management and potential breaks in the process. Figure 11.1 shows the authors' information-processing model regarding complaint handling. While effective handling of customer complaints is obviously in the consumer's interest, consumer complaints also can offer benefits far beyond the individual complainant. Farrell and Westbrook[15] define *complaint man-*

FIGURE 11.1 Information Flows within Consumer Complaints

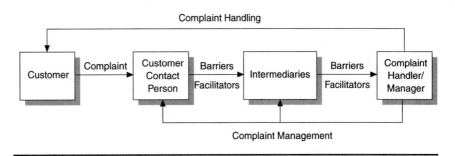

agement as the dissemination of information for the purpose of finding and correcting the causes of consumer dissatisfaction. An organization thus potentially has to respond to a complaint on two levels. The individual incident must be resolved in order to create a satisfied customer. Beyond that, the information about the complaint must reach a level within the organization where steps can be taken to redefine processes and systems in order to eradicate the root cause of the problem.

The barriers and facilitators to information flows identified in Figure 11.2 are related to factors such as the characteristics of individuals, jobs, and the relationship between sender and receiver. Article 11.3 explores these barriers empirically. The article highlights the fact that information flows of this kind must cross organizational boundaries, and that the barriers can be understood in the context of boundary-spanning individuals.

IMPLEMENTING SERVICE-RECOVERY STRATEGIES

Customers expect firms to fail to deliver service on occasion, but they also expect them to be able to recover from those failures. Article 11.4 explores the relationship shown in Figure 11.2. The approach suggested in this article contends that consumers expect higher levels of service recovery from organizations with higher levels of service quality, and from organizations to which they have a higher level of commitment. The latter represents a mutual sharing of roles and expectations between the firm and the individual. In turn, commitment is influenced by customer satisfaction and perceived quality.

A firm wishing to have a high perceived service quality therefore must create recovery strategies. Consumers have high expectations of such strategies and will be doubly dissatisfied if there is a service failure and no recovery strategy in place. Experts in the area of service recovery recommend that, in order to establish service-recovery skills, firms need to consider the following steps in creating such a program.[16]

MEASURE THE COSTS As discussed in the chapter on customer retention, the costs and benefits associated with keeping existing customers as opposed to chasing new customers are substantial. In short, the costs of obtaining new customers are three to five times greater than keeping existing customers; current customers are more receptive to the firm's marketing efforts and therefore are an important source of profit for the firm; existing customers ask less questions, are familiar with the firm's procedures and employees, and are willing to pay more for services.

ANTICIPATE NEEDS FOR RECOVERY As mentioned previously, every service encounter is made up of a series of critical incidents that reflect the points in the

FIGURE 11.2   Antecedents of Customer Expectations for Service Recovery

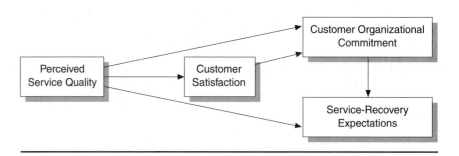

system where the customer and the firm interact. Firms that are effective in service recovery anticipate in advance the areas within the service-delivery process where failures are most likely to occur. Of course, these firms take every step possible to minimize the occurrence of the failure in the first place, but are prepared for recovery if delivery goes awry. Experts believe that firms should pay special attention to areas where employee turnover is high. Many of these positions are low-paying customer-contact positions and employees often lack motivation and/or are inexperienced in effective recovery techniques.

RESPOND QUICKLY   When a service failure does occur, the faster the company responds, the more likely the recovery effort will result in a successful outcome. In fact, past studies have indicated that, if the complaint is handled promptly, the company will retain 95 percent of its unhappy customers. In contrast, if the complaint is not resolved at all, the firm retains just 64 percent of its customers.[17] Time is of the essence. The faster the firm responds to the problem, the better the message the firm sends to customers.

A firm that learned this lesson the hard way is a bank in Spokane, Washington. A customer who had millions of dollars in the bank's checking, investment, and trust accounts was denied getting his parking validated because he only cashed a check, as opposed to making a deposit. The customer was at a branch bank that was not his normal bank. After explaining the situation to the teller who was unimpressed and more loudly voicing his opinion to the branch manager, the customer drove to his usual bank and demanded a response from the bank's upper management by the end of the day or he would close his accounts. As incredible as it may seem, the call never came, and the customer withdrew $1 million first thing in the morning. This action did get the bank's attention, and the bank has been trying to recover ever since.[18]

TRAIN EMPLOYEES   Expecting employees to be naturals at service recovery is unrealistic. Most employees don't know what to do when a failure occurs, and many others find that making decisions on the spot is a difficult task. Employee training in service recovery should take place on two levels. First, the firm must work at creating an awareness of customer concerns within the employee. Placing the employee in the shoes of the customer is often enlightening for employees who are unaware of what it's like to be a customer of the firm. For example, hospitals have placed interns and staff in hospital gowns and have had them rolled around on gurneys to experience some of the hospital's processes first-hand.

The second level of employee training, beyond developing an appreciation for customer needs, is defining management's expectation toward recovery efforts. What is acceptable behavior from management's perspective? Employees really want to know. Effective recovery often means that management has to let go and allow employees to take risks. This transition often leads to empowering front-line employees.

EMPOWERING THE FRONT LINE   Ironically, effective recovery often means the employee has to bend the firm's rules and regulations—the exact type of activity that employees are trained not to do at any cost. Often the rules and regulations of the firm tie the hands of the employee when it comes to effective recovery efforts, particularly in the area of prompt response. In many instances, firms require managerial approval before any effort to compensate the customer is undertaken. However, the manager often is engaged in other duties, which delays the response and adds to the frustration for the customer and the employee.

CHAPTER 11 READINGS

Article 11.1 develops a typology of retail failures and recoveries. Based on an extensive critical-incident survey, the article develops a number of generic types of failures and demonstrates the importance of different recovery strategies. Article 11.2 looks at complaining, which it describes as a pervasive form of social interaction. One of the most important causes of complaint is the behavior of others, a factor with obvious implications for service businesses, where the behavior of the staff is one of the principal sources of customer complaints. Article 11.3 then looks at complaint management, in particular at how information about complaints flows through the organization and also looks at types of responses. Finally, Article 11.4 examines the foundations of recovery strategies, which must relate to original customer expectations and perceptions of service quality. The article argues that recovery strategies need to be based on the customer's original expectations before the service failure occurred. The level of customer and organizational commitment is a key factor in recovery.

QUESTIONS

1. Describe the last time you complained about the service you received. Using it as a "critical incident," classify it in the framework of Table 11.1. Justify your classification.

2. For the incident described in question 1, was your complaint satisfactorily handled? Explain your satisfaction or dissatisfaction using the ideas in this chapter.

NOTES

1.   Technical Assistance Research Project, *Customer Complaint Handling in America: An Update Study,* Part 2. (Atlanta, GA: Coca-Cola USA, 1981).

2.   Technical Assistance Research Project, unpublished, industry-specific research data gathered from 1990 to 1993 by Coca-Cola USA, Atlanta, GA.

3.   *Ibid.*

4.   Technical Assistance Research Project, *Measuring the Grapevine, Consumer Response and Word of Mouth* (Atlanta, GA: Coca-Cola USA, 1981).

5.   John Goodman, "The Nature of Customer Satisfaction," *Quality Progress* (February 1989): 37–40.

6.   Christopher W. L. Hart, James L. Heskett, and W. Earl Sasser, Jr., "The Profitable Act of Service Recovery," *Harvard Business Review* (July–August 1990): 148–156.

7.   N. K. Hunt, N. D. Hunt, and T. C. Hunt, "Consumer Grudgeholding," *Journal of Consumer Satisfaction, Dissatisfaction and Complaining Behavior,* 1 (1988): 116–118.

8. See Article 11.3.

9. Oren Novari, "Thank Heaven for Complainers," *Management Review* (January 1992): 60.

10. T. N. Amabile, "Brilliant But Cruel: Perceptions of Negative Evaluators," *Journal of Experimental Social Psychology,* 19 (1983): 146–156.

11. See Article 11.3.

12. H. Keith Hunt, "Consumer Satisfaction, Dissatisfaction, and Complaining Behavior," *Journal of Social Issues,* vol. 47, no. 1 (1991): 107–117.

13. *Ibid.,* 115.

14. Donna Partow, "Turn Gripes into Gold," *Home Office Computing,* September 1993, 24.

15. Claes Farrell and R. A. Westbrook, "The Relationship between Consumer Complaint Magnitude and Organizational States of Complaint Processing in Large Corporations," in Ralph L. Day and H. Keith Hunt (eds.), *New Dimensions of Consumer Satisfaction and Complaining Behavior* (Bloomington, IL: Bureau of Business Research, 1979), 95–98.

16. Christopher W. L. Hart, Hames L. Heskett, and W. Earl Sasser, Jr., "The Profitable Act of Service Recovery," *Harvard Business Review* (July–August 1990): 148–156.

17. Karl Albrecht and Ron Zemke, *Services America* (Homewood, IL: Down-Jones Irwin, 1985), 129.

18. Christopher W. L. Hart, James L. Heskett, and W. Earl Sasser, Jr., "The Profitable Act of Service Recovery," *Harvard Business Review* (July–August 1990): 150.

A TYPOLOGY OF RETAIL FAILURES AND RECOVERIES

Scott W. Kelley
Associate Professor of Marketing
University of Kentucky
Lexington, Kentucky

K. Douglas Hoffman
Associate Professor of Marketing
Cameron School of Business Administration
University of North Carolina at Wilmington

Mark A. Davis
Assistant Professor of Management
University of Kentucky
Lexington, Kentucky

This study extends previous research by developing a typology of retail failures and recovery strategies. Upon sorting 661 critical incidents pertaining to general merchandise retailers, results revealed fifteen different types of retail failures and twelve unique recovery strategies. In addition, the effectiveness of the recovery strategies are examined and research implications are discussed.

INTRODUCTION

Most retail customers have encountered mistakes and defects during the course of their retail experiences. Furthermore, retail managers and employees spend a great deal of time trying to resolve customer problems. Unfortunately, over one-half of business responses to customer complaints actually strengthen customers' negative feelings toward the business and its representatives (Hart, Heskett, and Sasser 1990). Hence, when a defect or failure does occur, it is imperative for retailers to rectify mistakes through the utilization of effective recovery strategies.

Recovery strategies include the actions retailers take in response to defects or failures (Gronroos 1988). It has been suggested that effective recovery strategies may lead to the paradoxical situation whereby the customer will rate the encounter more favorably after a problem has been corrected than if the transaction had been correctly performed the first time (Etzel and Silverman 1981; McCollough and Bharadwaj 1992). Consequently, in many cases failures represent positive opportunities for retailers to establish long-term customer relationships.

Previous literature has considered what customers do when failures arise by focusing mainly on customer complaints and responses to dissatisfaction (cf. Folkes 1984; Gilly and Gelb 1982; Richins 1983; Singh 1988, 1990). However, a topic of equal importance is what

SOURCE: Scott W. Kelley, K. Douglas Hoffman, and Mark A. Davis, "A Typology of Retail Failures and Recoveries," *Journal of Retailing,* vol. 69, no. 4 (Winter 1993): 429–452.

marketers and retailers are doing about failures and customer dissatisfaction (Etzel and Silverman 1981). In an effort to address this issue, this research investigates customer dissatisfaction and retailer responses through the consideration of retail failures and recoveries.

The objective of this study is to develop classification schemes of retail failures and recovery strategies that are amenable to systematic investigation (Hunt 1991) by both retailers and academicians. In pursuit of this objective, this research utilizes a sample of retail customers and Flanagan's (1954) critical incident technique (CIT) to: (1) identify and classify failures within the retailing sector; (2) identify and classify recovery strategies utilized by retailers to correct failures; (3) measure customer satisfaction with each respective recovery strategy; and (4) assess subsequent shopping behaviors that reflect retailers' customer retention rates. In addition, research implications are discussed.

THE STUDY

CRITICAL INCIDENT TECHNIQUE

Marketing and management researchers have applied the critical incident technique in a wide variety of circumstances (cf. Folkes 1984; Goodman 1979; Machungwa and Schmitt 1983; Stein 1981; White and Locke 1981). In addition, Bitner and various colleagues have specifically utilized the critical incident technique to investigate a variety of service-related issues, such as: communication difficulties (Nyquist, Bitner, and Booms 1985) and favorable and unfavorable incidents in the service encounter (Bitner, Booms, and Tetreault 1990; Gremler and Bitner 1992).

The CIT methodology involves five steps: (1) determine the general aims of the activity, (2) formulate plans and specifications for the collection of critical incidents, (3) collect the data, (4) analyze the data, and (5) interpret the data and report the results (Flanagan 1954). Flanagan (1954), Nyquist, Bitner, and Booms (1985), and Walker and Truly (1992) provide thorough explanations of each step in this research methodology.

DATA COLLECTION

The incidents for this study were collected by 127 students from two different universities. The students were enrolled in either a services marketing course or a retailing course. Prior to data collection, the critical incident technique was explained to the students in class, and examples of research using the CIT were presented to them. Each student was instructed to recruit and conduct personal interviews with three to five participants using convenience sampling methods for the purpose of collecting critical incidents related to retail experiences. Students were given the stipulations that a maximum of one student respondent was to be included in their set of incidents, and that student respondents should not be enrolled in the classes conducting the project. These constraints were imposed in an effort to obtain a sample more representative of the general retail customer population.

Respondents were asked to report a failure they experienced that had resulted in a satisfactory recovery, as well as a failure that had resulted in an unsatisfactory recovery. Half of the respondents were asked to report an incident resulting in a satisfactory recovery first, while the other half of the respondents were asked to report an unsatisfactory recovery first. Of the approximately 900 retail critical incident reports completed for this study, a total of 661 involved general merchandise retailing (i.e., department stores, variety stores, discount stores, and mail order retailers). Critical incident report forms involving services retailing and food retailing (e.g., hotels, restaurants, and grocery stores) were eliminated from the analysis. Of the 661 total responses, 335 (50.7%) of the failures reported resulted in good recoveries and 326 (49.3%) of the failures resulted in poor recoveries.

The questions used to gather the information regarding the failure and recovery incidents are included in the appendix. Each respondent was asked (1) to explain the failure and recovery experienced, (2) to provide his or her attributions as to why the failure occurred, (3) to rate the effectiveness of the recovery, (4) whether they still shop at the retail store in question, and (5) for demographic information including sex, age, and highest level of education attained. Questions 1 through 4 were asked twice of each respondent; once with regard to a failure resulting in a satisfactory recovery, and once with regard to a failure resulting in an unsatisfactory recovery.

The demographic profile of the sample indicated that 206 respondents were female (45.2%) and 250 were male (54.8%). The ages of the respondents were categorized as follows: 37 respondents were less than 21 (8.1%), 133 were between 21 and 25 (29.2%), 112 were between 26 and 35 (24.6%), 67 were between 36 and 45 (14.7%), 80 were between 46 and 55 (17.6%), and 26 were over 55 (5.7%). With regard to education: 4 respondents never graduated from high school (.9%), 63 were high school graduates (13.9%), 183 attended some college (40.3%), 144 were college graduates (31.7%), and 60 had completed some graduate work or had graduate degrees (13.2%).

DATA ANALYSIS

Bitner, Booms, and Tetreault (1990) used the CIT to categorize unfavorable and favorable service encounters in the airline, hotel, and restaurant industries. Their classification scheme resulted in three major groups of behaviors. These three groups included: (1) Employee Response to Service Delivery System Failures; (2) Employee Response to Customer Needs and Requests; and (3) Unprompted and Unsolicited Employee Actions. Subsequent research designed to replicate and extend the initial work of Bitner, Booms, and Tetreault (1990) provides support for the generalizability of these three broad categories across a variety of service industries (Gremler and Bitner 1992).

The work of Bitner and her colleagues (Bitner, Booms, and Tetreault 1990; Gremler and Bitner 1992) served as a starting point for the content analysis of the critical incidents collected for this research. The sorting process for this research was carried out in four steps by the first two authors.

STEP 1: IDENTIFYING THE FAILURE INCIDENT Initially, each critical incident was systematically categorized through a deductive sorting process into one of the three major groups developed by Bitner, Booms, and Tetreault (1990).

STEP 2: IDENTIFYING FAILURE SUBGROUPS WITHIN THE THREE MAJOR GROUPS The second step of the sorting process involved the classification of the failures into subgroups within each of the three broad groups noted above. This inductive process resulted in the identification of 15 unique failure subgroups (nine in Group 1, two in Group 2, and four in Group 3).

STEP 3: CLASSIFYING RECOVERY STRATEGIES The third step in the categorization process involved classifying the recoveries within each failure subgroup. A total of 99 types of recoveries were identified with a great deal of overlap across the 15 failure subgroups. Based on the critical incident forms and respondent recovery ratings, 50 of these recoveries were rated favorably, while 49 resulted in poor recoveries.

STEP 4: COLLAPSING RECOVERY STRATEGIES The final step in the categorization process involved reducing the 99 recovery categories to a more manageable number of recovery strategies applicable to a variety of retail failure situations. This resulted in the reduction of the number of recovery categories from 99 to 12. These 12 recovery strategies represented all 99 of the recovery types identified in step 3.

RELIABILITY

In order to assess the reliability of the 15 failure subgroups and 12 recovery strategies established through the sorting process, an independent judge (the third author) categorized each of the incidents included in the sample. As a starting point, the incident report forms were presorted into the three main categories previously identified by Bitner, Booms, and Tetreault (1990). The independent judge was given the 661 incident report forms and was presented with two sorting tasks in order to assess the reliability of the categories. First, the judge was presented with the 15 previously identified failure subgroups and asked to independently sort each of the failure incidents into one of the 15 categories. This task resulted in agreement rates of 96%, 93%, and 98% for the failure subgroups included in the three main categories identified by Bitner, Booms, and Tetreault (1990). In addition, the index of reliability developed by Perreault and Leigh (1989), I_r, was computed for each of the three groups. This index assesses the reliability of nominal data based on qualitative judgments. The values of I_r for the three groups of failure incidents were .98, .92, and .99, respectively.

After completing this task the independent judge then sorted the recovery incidents based on the twelve categories provided by the researchers. The recovery agreement rate was 97%. The value of I_r was .98. These percentages of agreement and indices of reliability are indicative of a high level of reliability for the categories established in the initial sorting process.

DISCUSSION OF RESULTS

The classification schemes resulting from the CIT process are presented below. Initially, the failure classification scheme is presented (see Table 1), followed by a discussion of the recovery classification scheme (see Table 2).

GROUP 1—EMPLOYEE RESPONSE TO SERVICE DELIVERY SYSTEM/PRODUCT FAILURES

Each of the nine Group 1 failure subgroups described below is directly related to the retailers' core offerings. Ultimately, the manner in which retail personnel responded to each incident contributed to customer satisfaction.

SUBGROUP 1—POLICY FAILURES These failures were the result of store policy, which was perceived by the customer as being inequitable. The majority of the policy failures involved customer returns characterized by extenuating circumstances. For example, incidents

TABLE 1   Retail Failures

Failure Category	Count	%	Recovery Rating[ab]	Approximate Lapsed Time[bc]	Retention %[d]
Group 1. Employee Response to Service Delivery System/Product Failures					
1. Policy Failures	93	14.1%	5.38	11.9	62.4%
			(3.61)	(15.8)	(58/93)
2. Slow/Unavailable Service	27	4.1%	3.96	9.9	66.7%
			(3.20)	(11.0)	(18/27)
3. System Pricing	12	1.8%	7.00	9.6	91.7%
			(3.05)	(7.4)	(11/12)
4. Packaging Errors	21	3.2%	6.71	12.6	71.4%
			(3.44)	(17.2)	(15/21)
5. Out of Stock	16	2.4%	5.94	8.7	75.0%
			(3.94)	(9.0)	(12/16)
6. Product Defect	220	33.3%	6.26	18.5	74.3%
			(3.70)	(30.7)	(162/218)
7. Hold Disasters	15	2.3%	5.93	17.7	100%
			(3.08)	(29.2)	(15/15)
8. Alterations and Repairs	28	4.2%	4.82	9.9	42.9%
			(3.52)	(12.4)	(12/28)
9. Bad Information	34	5.1%	5.18	10.0	64.7%
			(3.70)	(12.7)	(22/34)
Group 1 Total	466	70.5%	5.80	14.7	70.0%
			(3.65)	(24.1)	(325/464)
Group 2. Employee Response to Customer Needs and Requests					
10. Order/Request	43	6.5%	6.12	14.8	69.8%
			(3.72)	(20.7)	(30/43)
11. Admitted Customer Error	10	1.5%	7.70	18.9	100%
			(3.59)	(36.2)	(10/10)
Group 2 Total	53	8.0%	6.42	15.6	75.5%
			(3.72)	(24.0)	(40/53)
Group 3. Unprompted and Unsolicited Employee Actions					
12. Mischarged	89	13.5%	6.53	11.4	83.1%
			(3.30)	(27.2)	(74/89)
13. Accused of Shoplifting	5	.8%	3.60	19.2	40.0%
			(3.71)	(24.4)	(2/5)
14. Embarrassments	29	4.4%	6.00	21.7	72.4%
			(3.82)	(33.5)	(21/29)
15. Attention Failures	19	2.9%	3.53	5.7	36.8%
			(2.97)	(7.6)	(7/19)

(continued)

TABLE 1   Retail Failures *(continued)*

Failure Category	Count	%	Recovery Rating[a][b]	Approximate Lapsed Time[b][c]	Retention %[d]
Group 3 Total	142	21.5%	5.92	13.1	73.2%
			(3.52)	(27.2)	(104/142)
Grand Total	661	100%	5.88	14.4	71.2%
			(3.62)	(24.7)	(469/659)

[a]Recoveries were rated on a scale of 1 (Very Poor) to 10 (Very Good).

[b]Standard deviations are reported in parentheses.

[c]Approximate lapsed time represents the average number of months from the time an incident occurred to the time it was reported.

[d]Retention percentage is the ratio of the number of respondents indicating that they still shop at the retail store involved in the incident to the number of incidents reported.

involved returning merchandise without a receipt, returning merchandise that was subsequently offered on sale, and returning merchandise that was purchased by someone else as a gift. Other policy failures involved a customer purchasing $39.99 worth of cosmetics but being denied the free tote bag offered with purchases of $40.00 or more; and the refusal to cash out-of-state checks. Based on customer attributions, in all of the incidents classified as policy failures, employees were performing their jobs as prescribed by management and were unwilling to make an exception to store policy.

SUBGROUP 2—SLOW OR UNAVAILABLE SERVICE Based on customer attributions, failures due to slow or unavailable service occurred because stores were understaffed, customers were serviced by employees in on-the-job training programs, stores did not service products that they sold, or store employees simply took too long to provide the service requested.

SUBGROUP 3—SYSTEM PRICING FAILURE System pricing failures arose in instances where individual-item pricing was not in agreement with the scanner-based price charged at the register. These pricing failures were not due to errors on the part of contact personnel, but instead arose because of incorrect pricing information contained in the scanner pricing system.

SUBGROUP 4—PACKAGING ERRORS Failures that arose due to packaging errors included situations where packages were labeled incorrectly, the wrong item was included in a package, parts were missing from a package, and clothing sizes were mismatched.

SUBGROUP 5—OUT OF STOCK In all of the critical incidents included in this category, the customer went to the store to purchase a specific item and the item was not in stock. Variations on the out-of-stock scenario included situations where products were not on the shelf, yet were stocked in the backroom; products were advertised, but were not in stock; and a specific location of a multi-site chain store did not have the item in question.

SUBGROUP 6—PRODUCT DEFECT This category was by far the largest failure category included in our classification scheme. One-third of the total responses involved a product defect. Product defect failures frequently reported by respondents included: clothing and shoes that did not last as long as expected, faulty watches and jewelry, electronic products that did not work, poorly constructed merchandise, ad merchandise damaged in transit. Interestingly, while the retailer was not responsible for many of these product defect failures, the attributions of many respondents placed the fault for the failure on the retailer.

SUBGROUP 7—HOLD DISASTERS Hold disasters included situations where: a product on layaway was sold to someone else or lost by the store, customers were told their merchandise was no longer on layaway because they had exceeded the maximum layaway period, the merchandise on layaway was the wrong size or incorrect item when the customer made the final purchase, and pricing complications arose due to the layaway.

TABLE 2   Retail Recoveries

Recovery Category	Count	%	Recovery Rating[a][b]	Good[c]	Poor[c]	Approx. Lapsed Time[b][d]	Retention %[e]
1. Discount	22	3.3%	8.86 (1.70)	18	4	10.4 (10.9)	86.4% (19/22)
2. Correction	81	12.3%	8.81 (1.70)	71	10	8.1 (10.2)	96.3% (78/81)
3. Manager/Employee Intervention	12	1.8%	8.42 (1.44)	11	1	10.4 (12.5)	75.0% (9/12)
4. Correction Plus	21	3.2%	8.24 (2.63)	18	3	13.1 (19.0)	90.5% (19/21)
5. Replacement	173	26.2%	7.91 (2.76)	132	41	14.0 (17.4)	87.8% (151/172)
6. Apology	53	8.0%	6.75 (2.99)	30	23	15.6 (34.6)	77.4% (41/53)
7. Refund	81	12.3%	6.48 (3.43)	43	38	13.7 (21.3)	81.5% (66/81)
8. Customer Initiated Correction	6	.9%	3.83 (2.48)	2	4	4.7 (9.5)	50.0% (3/6)
9. Store Credit	11	1.7%	3.36 (1.50)	0	11	12.5 (9.8)	36.4% (4/11)
10. Unsatisfactory Correction	37	5.6%	2.57 (1.50)	5	32	19.9 (31.0)	62.2% (23/37)
11. Failure Escalation	50	7.6%	2.36 (1.66)	3	47	17.0 (16.3)	42.0% (21/50)
12. Nothing	114	17.2%	1.55 (0.94)	2	112	18.7 (39.8)	31.0% (35/113)
Total	661	100%	5.88 (3.62)	335	326	14.4 (24.7)	71.2% (469/659)

[a]Recoveries were rated on a scale of 1 (Very Poor) to 10 (Very Good).

[b]Standard deviations are reported in parentheses.

[c]Good and Poor represent the number of incidents reported that resulted in good recoveries and poor recoveries, respectively.

[d]Approximate lapsed time represents the average number of months from the time an incident occurred to the time it was reported.

[e]Retention percentage is the ratio of the number of respondents indicating that they still shop at the retail store involved in the incident to the number of incidents reported.

SUBGROUP 8—ALTERATIONS AND REPAIRS This category included failures that arose during the alteration or repair of a product. For example, incidents involving incorrect clothing alterations, product repairs that were done incorrectly, and product repairs with excessive delays were all included in this category.

SUBGROUP 9—BAD INFORMATION In this category, customers were generally provided with incorrect information, which resulted in the purchase of: the wrong size item, items that did not perform as the customer was told they would, and warranties that did not fulfill the customer's needs. In all of these incidents the respondent specifically pointed out that the purchase decision they made was based on incorrect information provided to them by the retailer.

GROUP 2—EMPLOYEE RESPONSE TO CUSTOMER NEEDS AND REQUESTS

The two Group 2 failures described below reflect activities in which consumers perceived that they were making a special request of the retailer. In these incidents, the manner in which the retail personnel responded to the incident dictated the level of customer satisfaction experienced.

SUBGROUP 10—SPECIAL ORDER OR REQUEST Incidents in this group involved merchandise that was not readily available to the customer initially and required delays for preparation or transit from another location. For example, incidents included situations involving special orders that arrived damaged or were incorrect when they arrived, incorrect catalog orders, and orders requiring personalization that were flawed (e.g., engraving).

SUBGROUP 11—ADMITTED CUSTOMER ERROR The defining feature of incidents in this category was that the customer acknowledged his or her own mistake and willingly accepted the blame for the failure that arose. Critical incidents in this category included the purchase of incorrect sizes or items, and the misuse of products after purchase.

GROUP 3—UNPROMPTED AND UNSOLICITED EMPLOYEE ACTIONS

Group 3 failures include incidents that were not prompted by the retail customer. The four failure subgroups discussed below were directly attributed to the actions of retail personnel, and were not attributed to the retailer's core offerings (Group 1) or a customer's special request (Group 2).

SUBGROUP 12—MISCHARGED Failures in this group involved situations where respondents were mischarged for items. The incorrect charges occurred as a result of an employee pricing error; employees giving back incorrect change; and situations where retail salespeople either forgot to honor a sale price or would not give additional discounts on sale items, and gave the customer a hard time when the situation was pointed out. These failures were due to errors made by retail customer contact personnel and did not result from computer scanner error (subgroup 3).

SUBGROUP 13—ACCUSED OF SHOPLIFTING Although the frequency with which this critical incident was cited by respondents was relatively small (5), these incidents merited a category unto themselves because of the severity of the failure in the eyes of the customer. In four of the five incidents the respondent was actually accused of shoplifting, in the other incident the respondent felt discomfort due to excessive surveillance. Interestingly, in all of the cases in which the customer was falsely accused of shoplifting the customer felt it was not possible for the retailer to satisfactorily recover from the failure.

SUBGROUP 14—EMPLOYEE-CREATED EMBARRASSMENTS These critical incidents involved situations in which retail employees were careless or made drastic mistakes in judgment. For example, incidents included situations where retailers failed to remove security tags from garments, customers arrived at home without merchandise they had purchased due to a salesperson's error, customers shopping for clothing were sized too large by the retailer, and customers were accused by retail personnel of being unable to afford merchandise based on their appearance.

SUBGROUP 15—EMPLOYEE ATTENTION FAILURES Critical incidents in this category included situations in which the retail salesperson was overbearing or moody; simply walked away from the customer in order to serve another customer; ignored the customer during the waiting process, resulting in an inequitable wait; or told the customer, "That's not my department."

The critical incidents included in this category differ from those in subgroup 2—slow or unavailable service in that the failures in subgroup 15 were due to employee negligence, while the failures in subgroup 2 were system failures attributable to understaffing.

CLASSIFICATION OF RECOVERIES

After classifying the critical incidents with regard to failures, the next part of the analysis focused on the classification of the recoveries reported by the respondents. The recovery strategies are presented in Table 2 and are discussed below. Table 2 also includes the frequency of occurrence for each recovery strategy, average recovery ratings, the approximate lapsed time since the incident occurred, the number of good and poor recoveries reported, and the self-reported shopping behavior of the respondent following the failure-recovery incident (customer retention).

RECOVERY 1—DISCOUNT The first type of recovery involved the provision of a discount on merchandise as a means of compensating the customer for the problems and inconvenience caused by the failure. The average rating for this type of recovery was 8.86 on a scale of 1 to 10. Customer retention was 86% (19/22).

RECOVERY 2—CORRECTION In a relatively large number of instances, the failures encountered by the customer were simply corrected by the retailer. For example, misplaced merchandise was located, repairs were promptly made, or policies were explained. In all of these instances, the retailer did nothing extra for the customer other than to promptly and courteously correct the mistake that had been made. The average recovery rating for this category was 8.81. Customer retention was 96% (78/81).

RECOVERY 3—MANAGER/EMPLOYEE INTERVENTION A third recovery strategy involved the intervention of either a manager or another employee in order to help resolve the problem. This type of recovery strategy had a mean recovery rating of 8.42, and arose either when the customer was not getting anywhere with the frontline employee and was experiencing frustration, or the employee was apparently not empowered to recover from the failure being encountered. While manager/employee intervention recoveries typically involved another type of recovery (e.g., a discount or correction), the key characteristic of these incidents was judged to be the intervention of a manager or another employee in order to resolve the failure incident. Customer retention for this recovery strategy was 75% (9/12).

RECOVERY 4—CORRECTION PLUS In some instances retailers went beyond a mere correction of the failure and in the process of recovering from the failure not only corrected the mistake, but compensated the customer in some additional way. For example, extra service may have been provided, products may have been upgraded, or the customer may have been offered free merchandise in addition to the correction of the original failure. This form of recovery had a mean rating of 8.24.

The correction plus recovery strategy involved additional compensation beyond the correction of the original failure (see Recovery 2), a defensive marketing strategy suggested previously by Fornell and Wernerfeldt (1987). As such, one might expect this form of recovery to be rated more favorably than others discussed above [e.g., discount (mean recovery rating of 8.86) and correction (mean recovery rating of 8.81)]. However, the effectiveness of the service recovery implemented is largely dependent on the magnitude of the failure (Hart, Heskett, and Sasser 1990). Based on the authors' evalu-

ation, the failure incidents resulting in correction plus recoveries were generally more severe in nature. As a result, the more elaborate correction plus recovery strategy was rated less favorably than the less elaborate discount and correction recovery strategies. Customer retention for the correction plus recovery strategy was 90% (19/21).

RECOVERY 5—REPLACEMENT One of the major forms of retail failure reported was the defective product. As a result, the most frequently occurring recovery strategy involved the replacement of defective merchandise. This type of recovery had a mean rating of 7.91. Customer retention was 88% (151/172).

RECOVERY 6—APOLOGY A sixth recovery strategy involved an apology on the part of the employee. The ratings of the recoveries included in this category were highly dependent on the manner in which the apology was delivered, as well as the magnitude of the failure associated with the apology. The mean rating for this category was 6.75. Customer retention was 77% (41/53).

RECOVERY 7—REFUND Another widely reported recovery strategy that generally resulted from product defect failures was the refund. While the replacement of merchandise was rated more favorably as a recovery strategy, the refund recovery was also seen as acceptable by the customer in many instances (mean rating = 6.48). Customer retention was 81% (66/81).

UNACCEPTABLE RECOVERY STRATEGIES

The remaining attempts at recoveries all had mean recovery ratings below the midpoint of the recovery rating scale. Although the retailer generally attempted to recover from the failure in these instances (with the exception of Recovery 12—Nothing), the attempted recovery was not viewed favorably by the customer.

RECOVERY 8—CUSTOMER INITIATED CORRECTION In order to be included in this category the customer's behavior as an initiator of the recovery was judged to be a key characteristic of the critical incident that was reported. Customers attributed the execution of the recovery they experienced to their pointing the failure out to the retailer. This form of recovery received an average recovery rating of 3.83. Customer retention was 50% (3/6).

RECOVERY 9—STORE CREDIT Many retailers offer their customers a store credit when failures occur rather than refunding the customer's money. This recovery strategy was viewed as decidedly worse than either the refund or the replacement of merchandise recovery strategies. In general, customers encountering this form of recovery resented the fact that they were being forced to shop at a store in which they experienced a failure. The average rating for the store credit recovery was 3.36. Customer retention was 36% (4/11).

RECOVERY 10—UNSATISFACTORY CORRECTION In a number of cases, retailers failed in their recovery efforts in the eyes of the customer. In the case of unsatisfactory corrections, the customer recognized that the retailer did attempt to correct the mistake; however, the recovery did not make amends for the failure. Examples of unsatisfactory corrections included repairs made after much delay and exchanges made after a great deal of hassle. This type of recovery had a mean rating of 2.57. Customer retention was 62% (23/37).

RECOVERY 11—FAILURE ESCALATION Some of the attempts at recovery made matters worse from the customer's perspective. These situations resulted in failure escalation. Examples of failure escalation included repairs which were done incorrectly, blaming the customer for the failure, and providing the customer with incorrect information. The failure escalation recoveries had a mean rating of 2.36. Customer retention was 42% (21/50).

RECOVERY 12—NOTHING In over 17 percent of the "recoveries" recalled, the retailer made no attempt at recovering from the failure that occurred. This nonrecovery strategy arose in a limited number of cases when retailers were unaware of the failure, but in the majority of cases the retailer was aware of the failure and made a conscious decision to do nothing to recover. This form of recovery had a mean rating of 1.55. Customer retention was 31% (35/113).

FAILURES AND CORRESPONDING
RECOVERIES

Table 3 contains cell frequencies for each failure type and corresponding recovery strategy associated with the critical incidents collected. Although many of the cells are either empty or very small, this table does provide some insight into the retail failure-recovery relationship.

For example, when policy failures (subgroup 1) occurred the most common recovery strategies implemented were replacement (recovery 5), refunds (recovery 7), and nothing (recovery 12). System pricing failures (subgroup 3), involving pricing errors due to computer scanner error, were most frequently rectified by simply correcting the mistake (recovery 2). Interestingly, the mischarged failure type (subgroup 12), containing

incidents involving pricing errors attributed to retail contact personnel, resulted in a much more diverse set of recovery strategies. Of the 89 mischarged failures (subgroup 12), 21 were rectified through a correction (recovery 2), 34 through an apology (recovery 6), and 21 of the recoveries resulted in unsatisfactory corrections (recovery 10). So while system pricing failures (subgroup 3) and mischarged failures (subgroup 12) resulted in similar failure outcomes (i.e., an incorrect price for an item), the recovery strategies implemented were decidedly different.

Packaging errors (subgroup 4) and product defects (subgroup 6) were most often corrected by replacing the product (recovery 5). Further, failures associated with alterations and repairs were particularly difficult to recover from, as 17 of the 28 recoveries implemented for these failures resulted in failure escalation (recovery 11). Finally, a variety of recovery strategies were implemented for hold disasters (subgroup 7), bad information (subgroup 9), special orders or requests (subgroup 10), and employee-created embarrassments (subgroup 14).

CORROBORATING EVIDENCE

As noted previously, the three broad groups of incidents developed by Bitner, Booms, and Tetreault (1990) were used as a point of departure for the classificatory process used in the present study. The resulting failure classification scheme included several similarities when compared with the Bitner et al. scheme.

For the most part, the failure categories in our classification scheme that are not accounted for in the Bitner et al. typology (and vice versa) arose due to tangible aspects of the product offerings of general merchandise retailers, or the unique aspects of the services considered by Bitner et al. This was not surprising, as Gremler and Bitner (1992) uncovered similar discrepancies across a variety of service industries in a study investigating the generalizability of the Bitner et al. classification scheme.

In addition to the critical incident study conducted by Bitner, Booms, and Tetreault (1990), other literature also provides corroborating evidence for the failure and recovery classification schemes developed in this study.

RETAIL FAILURES

The present research investigates the specific types of failures occurring in a retail setting. Other research on failures has take a more general approach by considering the nature of failures via variables such as controllability, stability, and locus (cf. Folkes 1984; Folkes, Koletsky, and Graham 1987). Previous research suggests

TABLE 3   Retail Failure Types and Corresponding Recovery Strategies[a]

Failure Type	1	2	3	4	5	6	7	8	9	10	11	12
Group 1. Employee Response to Service Delivery System/Product Failures												
1. Policy Failures		1			26		34		9	4		19
2. Slow/ Unavailable Service	1		5			6					1	14
3. System Pricing		11		1								
4. Packaging Errors	1				19					1		
5. Out of Stock		7		4							1	4
6. Product Defect		12			116		34				24	34
7. Hold Disasters	3	1			3	1	4		2	1		
8. Alterations & Repairs	2	5		4							17	
9. Bad Information	1		4	5	5		5			1	4	9
Group 1 Total	8	37	9	14	169	7	77	0	11	6	48	80
Group 2. Employee Response to Customer Needs and Requests												
10. Order/ Request	10	12		2			1			7		11
11. Admitted Customer Error				1	4		3				2	
Group 2 Total	10	12	0	3	4	0	4	0	0	7	2	11
Group 3. Unprompted and Unsolicited Employee Actions												
12. Mischarged	2	21		2		34				21		9
13. Shoplifting				1		3						1
14. Embarrassments	2	11		1		7				3		5
15. Atten. Failure			3			2		6				8
Group 3 Total	4	33	3	4	0	46	0	6	0	24	0	23

[a]Cell numbers represent the frequency with which a specific failure type was resolved with the pertinent recovery strategy.

[b]Recovery strategies are presented numerically at the head of each column.

that failures perceived by customers as controllable by the organization and/or stable over time (i.e., recurring) are generally judged more harshly by consumers than uncontrollable and/or unstable failures. In the context of the present study, failures concerning policy (subgroup 1), slow or unavailable service (subgroup 2), hold disasters (subgroup 7), failed alterations or repairs (subgroup 8), bad information (subgroup 9), and employee actions (subgroups 12 thru 15) would seem more likely to be viewed by customers as controllable and/or stable, and hence should be judged more harshly and be more difficult to recover from. An examination of the recovery ratings relevant to these failure subgroups confirms the difficulty involved in effectively recovering from failures consumers perceive as controllable and/or stable (see Table 1).

Further, in Folkes' (1984) investigation of locus of failures, she found that in cases where consumers attributed the cause of a failure to themselves they were less likely to expect redress or recovery activities. The minimal recovery expectations associated with customer attributed failures (Folkes 1984) provide a plausible explanation for the high mean recovery rating for admitted customer error failures in our classification scheme (7.70).

In addition, a relatively small number of failure incidents were classified as admitted customer errors in our classification scheme (1.5%). (This was also true of the BBT study (4%) and the Gremler and Bitner study (2.8%).) Psychological theories such as attribution theory, dissonance theory, and equity theory, all suggest that it is a natural tendency for consumers to blame failures on someone or something else (Jacoby and Jaccard 1981). Based on these theories, one might have expected a relatively small number of respondents to report critical incidents in which they perceived themselves to be at fault.

CUSTOMER SATISFACTION/ DISSATISFACTION

When a retail failure does occur, a likely initial response from consumers is dissatisfaction (Day and Landon 1977; Singh 1988). Previous research and our classification scheme suggest that product usage experiences are just one of a number of sources of customer dissatisfaction. Specifically, three different types of consumer dissatisfaction have been identified: (1) shopping system dissatisfaction, (2) buying system dissatisfaction, and (3) consuming system dissatisfaction (Renoux 1973; Westbrook 1981).

Shopping system dissatisfaction concerns evaluations of the availability of products and retail outlets in a market area, and considers a broader level of analysis than is at issue in the present study. Buying system dissatisfaction focuses on the selection, purchase, and receipt of products from retail stores. Consuming system dissatisfaction concerns the usage and consumption of goods and services. The majority of the failure types identified in our classification scheme are associated with buying system dissatisfaction. Only failure subgroups 4—packaging errors and 6—product defect pertain directly to products and/or product usage (i.e., consuming system dissatisfaction). Similarly, Westbrook (1981) found that dissatisfaction with merchandise was only of moderate importance in determining the level of overall customer dissatisfaction with a retailer.

In an investigation of the common retail policy of satisfaction guaranteed, Schmidt and Kernan (1985) found that retailers' perspectives on the satisfaction-guaranteed policy emphasized the shopping experience (i.e., eliminating the potential for buying system dissatisfaction), while consumers felt that redress procedures were the primary mechanism for guaranteeing satisfaction (i.e., resolving buying system dissatisfaction when it occurs). This finding is particularly interesting in light of the fact that the majority of the types of failures included in our classification scheme were concerned with the shopping experience (i.e., buying system dissatisfaction). Apparently, while retailers continually try to provide mistake free shopping experiences in order to ensure customer satisfaction, based on customer expectations they may be better served to focus more strongly on the execution of effective recoveries when failures do occur.

SERVICE QUALITY

Recent research on service quality suggests that customers form two types of expectations—expectations for desired service and expectations for adequate service, with a zone of tolerance separating the two types of expectations. Failures occur when perceptions of service delivery do not meet adequate service expectations. Under these circumstances a paradoxical situation may arise. According to Zeithaml, Berry, and Parasuraman (1993), problems with initial service can lead to heightened adequate service expectations which narrow the zone of tolerance. As the zone of tolerance narrows, it becomes more difficult for retailers to implement effective recoveries

Along similar lines, Solomon et al. (1985) have suggested that customers have tendencies toward mindlessness when involved in service encounters, and that it takes a deviation from the expected script (e.g., a failure) to jar a customer into an evaluative state. The heightened evaluative state resulting from the script deviation is akin to the heightened adequate service expectations noted by Zeithaml, Berry, and Parasuraman (1993).

The work of Zeithaml, Berry, and Parasuraman (1993) and Solomon et al. (1985) provides a plausible explanation for the relatively large number of unsatisfactory correction and failure escalation recovery incidents (13.2%). In these incidents customers may have experienced a narrowing of their zones of tolerance and been jarred into a heightened state of evaluation as a result of the failure precipitating the recovery incident.

RETAIL RECOVERY

Hart, Heskett, and Sasser (1990) discuss procedures for ensuring effective recoveries. These procedures include:

(1) measure the costs, (2) break the silence, (3) anticipate needs for recovery, (4) act fast, (5) train employees, (6) empower the front line, and (7) close the loop. Several of the suggestions they make support the recovery classification scheme developed in this study. For example, recovery incidents that were rated favorably by respondents generally provided compensation consistent with the costs incurred by the customer and were executed promptly by customer contact personnel.

In addition, customers that were satisfied with their recoveries generally were allowed to voice their complaints to receptive retail personnel during the recovery process and received a favorable outcome as well (Goodwin and Ross 1992). Previous research and the incidents collected for this study suggest that the recovery process and outcomes are both key in implementing effective recoveries.

One of the noteworthy aspects of the recovery classification scheme is the large number of unacceptable recoveries (recovery categories 8 thru 12 make up 33 percent of all incidents collected). Further, over 17 percent of the incidents were classified in recovery category 12—nothing. One plausible explanation for the number of nonrecoveries included in our scheme is based on retailer and customer attributions of failures. Research suggests that retailers are more likely than their customers to attribute product failures to the customer (Folkes and Kotsos 1986). When failures are attributed to consumers, retailers may not feel compelled to implement a recovery. However, customers attributing the failure incident to the retailer (rather than themselves) will be dissatisfied with the nonrecovery strategy implemented by the retailer in these instances (Folkes 1984; Folkes and Kotsos 1986).

EVENT MEMORABILITY

Previous research suggests that negative information (i.e., incidents resolved with poor recoveries) has a greater impact on cognitive structure and attitude than positive information (i.e., incidents resolved with favorable recoveries) (Lutz 1975). Within the present study, substantiating evidence pertaining to the issue of event memorability was provided via the approximate lapsed time variable. The approximate time lapse from the occurrence of the failure/recovery to the time of the reporting of the critical incident was nearly 14 and a half months for the entire set of incidents with a range from 7 days to 23 years. Approximate time lapse was approximately 11 months for failures associated with good recoveries, and nearly 18 months for failures associated with poor recoveries.

Approximate lapsed time associated with each of the recovery categories also indicates that less favorable recoveries tend to be more memorable. For example, recovery strategies with mean recovery ratings of less than 3 all had approximate lapsed times equal to or exceeding 17 months. On the other hand, approximate lapsed time was less than eleven months for the three most favorably rated recovery strategies. In addition, the Pearson correlation coefficient between lapsed time and recovery rating was $-.14$ ($p = .00$).

CUSTOMER RETENTION

Perhaps the most interesting finding regarding customers' subsequent self-reported shopping behavior is that a definite pattern does not appear to exist regarding failure types and subsequent shopping behavior. This suggests that it is possible to recover from failures, no matter what type. Retailers encountering a customer that has experienced any type of failure should make an effort to recover from the failure; as it appears that regardless of the type of failure experienced, customers will return—provided that an effective recovery is executed. Overall, customer retention for the incidents considered was over 70%. Even dissatisfied customers experiencing less than acceptable recoveries were still retained at a rate approaching 40%. Previous research offers several insights to the customer retention rates reported in this study.

Recently, Oliva, Oliver, and MacMillan (1992) utilized catastrophe theory to model the complex relationships among consumer satisfaction/dissatisfaction, involvement, and loyalty (i.e., retention). They suggest the customer satisfaction-retention relationship is influenced by the extent of customer involvement or commitment, where highly involved or committed customers are generally more loyal to the retail organization (cf. Beatty, Kahle, and Homer 1988). Even when committed customers are dissatisfied they may still be retained by the retail organization due to customer resistance to belief change under conditions of high involvement or commitment (Laczniak and Muehling 1990).

In an investigation of customer response styles to dissatisfaction, over half the respondents viewed private responses to dissatisfaction [e.g., no longer patronizing a retailer (Singh 1988)] as an unfavorable alternative (Singh 1990). This suggests that a large number of consumers do not consider nonpatronage as a viable alternative when failures occur. Research also suggests that customers experiencing failures that are handled well are likely to experience greater levels of satisfaction than customers who did not experience any problems (Folkes and Kotsos 1986; Gilly and Gelb 1982). Further, Gilly and Gelb (1982) conclude that a customer is more likely to be retained by an organization "if he or she is not greatly dissatisfied with the response to a complaint" (p. 327). Finally, several researchers have suggested that dissatisfied customers (i.e., those experiencing failures) that complain are more likely to be retained even if their complaints are not handled satisfactorily (cf. Richins 1983; Swan and Oliver 1989).

LIMITATIONS AND RESEARCH IMPLICATIONS

LIMITATIONS

Several limitations should be noted regarding this research. First, the data for this study were collected by students. Although these students were well acquainted with the concepts of failure and recovery and an extensive training effort was made regarding the data collection process, some interviewer bias may have occurred. Relatedly, in designing the critical incident report form, relatively simple measures were used for some of the variables (e.g., customer retention) in order to avoid confusion on the part of the student interviewers and their respondents. In addition, the convenience sampling methodology used in this study may have resulted in some bias in the form of selection error. For example, a sample comprised of a more ethnically or socioeconomically diverse group of respondents may have reported a different mix of critical incidents.

RESEARCH IMPLICATIONS

This research used the critical incident methodology to investigate failures and recoveries in the retailing context. In the future, researchers might extend this research in several directions.

First, researchers may want to investigate the occurrence of failures and recoveries in specific sectors of the retailing industry. The present research considered a cross-section of general merchandise retailers; however, customers may hold varying expectations for different types of retailers resulting in differing perceptions of failures and recoveries across retailers.

In the future, researchers investigating failures and recoveries should also consider the magnitude of the failure experienced by the customer. This could be accomplished by asking the respondent to rate the failure incident on a scale of 1 to 10 in a manner similar to the recovery rating method used in the present research. This information would allow a more stringent test of the anecdotal evidence, which suggests that the magni-

tude of the failure should be used to determine an appropriate recovery (Hart, Heskett, and Sasser 1990).

A systematic investigation of the costs associated with failures and recoveries would also expand our knowledge of these phenomena. Researchers might consider a variety of costs incurred by customers and organizations when failures occur and recoveries are enacted. For example, customer incurred costs of interest might include monetary costs, psychological costs, emotional costs, and costs of inconvenience. The effects of these costs on event memorability and the frequency of subsequent store patronage may be of interest to researchers and practitioners. Organizational costs of interest might include monetary costs, the cost of lost customers, the cost of negative word-of-mouth, and costs associated with the recovery itself.

Researchers should also investigate failures and recoveries using different methodologies. The CIT method provides an informative starting point for research in this area; however, future researchers might investigate this phenomenon through survey research methods and experimental methods (e.g., Goodwin and Ross 1992). For example, researchers may wish to consider the relationship between failure and recovery and constructs such as customer satisfaction, service quality, and purchase intentions.

CONCLUSION

Failures are a common occurrence in the retail industry. This research provides an initial investigation of the failures and subsequent recoveries experienced by retail customers using the CIT methodology. Fifteen types of retail failures and 12 types of recovery strategies were identified in this study. This research demonstrates the importance of recovery in the retail industry whenever a retail customer experiences a failure.

APPENDIX
CRITICAL INCIDENT QUESTIONS

FAILURE INCIDENT

1. Think of a time when you had an experience at a retail store where a mistake was made and the retailer tried to correct that mistake, and did a good (bad) job of recovering. Please describe the nature of this service failure.

    Where? (i.e., the name of the retailer and the location)

When? (approximately)

What happened?

Why did it happen? (attributions?)

2. How did the retailer become aware of this mistake or service failure? (i.e., Did you point the failure out to them or did they become aware of the failure on their own?)

RECOVERY AND RECOVERY RATING

3. What did the retailer do to correct this mistake?

4. On a scale of 1 to 10, 1 being VERY POOR and 10 being VERY GOOD, how would you rate the efforts of the retailer regarding the correction of the mistake (i.e., the quality of the service recovery?)

5. If the retailer did not satisfactorily correct the mistake, what could they have done?

6. Did you do anything to correct the mistake or service?

If so, what did you do?

If not, could you have done anything?

SUBSEQUENT SHOPPING BEHAVIOR

7. Do you still shop at this retail store?

REFERENCES

Beatty, Sharon E., Lynn R. Kahle, and Pamela Homer (1988), "The Involvement-Commitment Model: Theory and Implications," *Journal of Business Research* 16 (March), 149–167.

Bitner, Mary Jo, Bernard H. Booms, and Mary Stanfield Tetreault (1990), "The Service Encounter: Diagnosing Favorable and Unfavorable Incidents," *Journal of Marketing,* 54 (January), 71–84.

Day, Ralph L., and E. Laird Landon, Jr. (1977), "Towards a Theory of Consumer Complaining Behavior," in Arch Woodside, Jagdish Sheth, and Peter Bennett (eds.), *Consumer and Industrial Buying Behavior,* Amsterdam: North-Holland Publishing Company.

Etzel, Michael J., and Bernard I. Silverman (1981), "A Managerial Perspective on Directions for Retail Customer Dissatisfaction Research," *Journal of Retailing,* 57 (Fall), 124–136.

Flanagan, John C. (1954), "The Critical Incident Technique," *Psychological Bulletin,* 51 (July), 327–358.

Folkes, Valerie S. (1984), "Consumer Reactions to Product Failures: An Attributional Approach," *Journal of Consumer Research,* 10 (March), 398–409.

———, Susan Koletsky, and John L. Graham (1987), "A Field Study of Causal Inferences and Consumer Reaction: The View from the Airport," *Journal of Consumer Research,* 13 (March), 534–539.

———, and Barbara Kotsos (1986), "Buyers' and Sellers' Explanations for Product Failure: Who Done It," *Journal of Marketing,* 50 (April), 74–80.

Fornell, Claes, and Birger Wernerfeldt (1987), "Defensive Marketing Strategy by Customer Complaint Management: A Theoretical Analysis," *Journal of Marketing Research,* 24 (November), 337–346.

Gilly, Mary C., and Betsy D. Gelb (1982), "Post-Purchase Consumer Processes and the Complaining Consumer," *Journal of Consumer Research,* 9 (December), 323–328.

Goodman, Raymond J., Jr. (1979), "The Use of Critical Incident Methodology Applied to the Development of Waiter-Waitress Training Programs," Ph.D. dissertation, Cornell University.

Goodwin, Cathy, and Ivan Ross (1992), "Consumer Responses to Service Failures: Influence of Procedural and Interactional Fairness Perceptions," *Journal of Business Research,* 25 (September), 149–163.

Gremler, Dwayne, and Mary Jo Bitner (1992), "Classifying Service Encounter Satisfaction across Industries," in Chris T. Allen et al. (eds.), *Marketing Theory and Applications,* Chicago, IL: American Marketing Association.

Gronroos, Christian (1988), "Service Quality: The Six Criteria of Good Perceived Service Quality," *Review of Business,* 9 (Winter), 10–13.

Hart, Christopher W. L., James L. Heskett, and W. Earl Sasser, Jr. (1990), "The Profitable Art of Service Recovery," *Harvard Business Review,* 68 (July–August), 148–156.

Hunt, Shelby D. (1991), *Modern Marketing Theory,* Cincinnati, OH: South-Western Publishing Co.

Jacoby, Jacob, and James J. Jaccard (1981), "The Sources, Meaning, and Validity of Consumer Complaint Behavior: A Psychological Analysis," *Journal of Retailing,* 57 (Fall), 4–24.

Laczniak, Russell N., and Darrel D. Muehling (1990), "Delayed Effects of Advertising Moderated by Involvement," *Journal of Business Research,* 20 (May), 263–277.

Lutz, Richard J. (1975), "Changing Brand Attitudes through Modification of Cognitive Structure," *Journal of Consumer Research,* 1 (March), 49–59.

Machungwa, Peter D., and Neal Schmitt (1983), "Work Motivation in a Developing Country," *Journal of Applied Psychology,* 68 (1), 31–42.

McCollough, Michael A., and Sundar G. Bharadwaj (1992), "The Recovery Paradox: An Examination of Consumer Satisfaction in Relation to Disconfirmation, Service Quality, and Attribution Based Theories," in Chris T. Allen et al. (eds.), *Marketing Theory and Applications,* Chicago, IL: American Marketing Association.

Nyquist, Jody D., Mary J. Bitner, and Bernard H. Booms (1985), "Identifying Communication Difficulties in the Service Encounter: A Critical Incident Approach," in John Czepiel, Michael Solomon, and Carol Surprenant (eds.), *The Service Encounter,* Lexington, MA: Lexington Books.

Oliva, Terence A., Richard L. Oliver, and Ian C. MacMillan (1992), "A Catastrophe Model for Developing Service

Satisfaction and Strategies," *Journal of Marketing,* **56** (July), 83–95.

Perreault, William D., Jr., and Laurence E. Leigh (1989), "Reliability of Nominal Data Based on Qualitative Judgments," *Journal of Marketing Research,* **26** (May), 135–148.

Renoux, Yves (1973), "Consumer Dissatisfaction and Public Policy," in Fred C. Allvine (ed.), *Public Policy and Marketing,* Chicago, IL: American Marketing Association.

Richins, Marsha L. (1983), "Negative Word-of-Mouth by Dissatisfied Consumers: A Pilot Study," *Journal of Marketing,* **47** (Winter), 68–78.

Schmidt, Sandra L., and Jerome B. Kernan (1985), "The Many Meanings (and Implications) of 'Satisfaction Guaranteed'," *Journal of Retailing,* **61** (Winter), 89–108.

Singh, Jagdip (1988), "Consumer Complaint Intentions and Behavior: Definitional and Taxonomical Issues," *Journal of Marketing,* **52** (January), 93–107.

——— (1990), "A Typology of Consumer Dissatisfaction Response Styles," *Journal of Retailing,* **66** (Spring), 57–99.

Solomon, Michael R., Carol Surprenant, John A. Czepiel, and Evelyn G. Gutman (1985), "A Role Theory Perspective on Dyadic Interactions: The Service Encounter," *Journal of Marketing,* **49** (Winter), 99–111.

Stein, David S. (1981), "Designing Performance-Oriented Training Programs," *Training and Development Journal,* **35** (January), 12–16.

Swan, John E., and Richard L. Oliver (1989), "Postpurchase Communications by Consumers," *Journal of Retailing,* **65** (Winter) 516–533.

Walker, Steve, and Elise Truly (1992), "The Critical Incidents Technique: Philosophical Foundations and Methodological Implications," in Chris T. Allen et al. (eds.), *Marketing Theory and Applications,* Chicago, IL: American Marketing Association.

Westbrook, Robert A. (1981), "Sources of Consumer Satisfaction with Retail Outlets," *Journal of Retailing,* **57** (Fall), 68–85.

White, Frank M., and Edwin A. Locke (1981), "Perceived Determinants of High and Low Productivity in Three Occupational Groups: A Critical Incident Study," *Journal of Management Studies,* **18** (4), 375–387.

Zeithaml, Valarie A., Leonard L. Berry, and A. Parasuraman (1993), "The Nature and Determinants of Customer Expectations of Service," *Journal of the Academy of Marketing Science,* **21** (Winter), 1–12.

COMPLAINING BEHAVIOR IN SOCIAL INTERACTION

Mark D. Alicke
Ohio University

James C. Braun

Jeffrey E. Glor
University of Florida

M. L. Klotz
Susquehanna University

Jon Magee
Heather Sederholm
Robin Siegel
University of Florida

Complaining is a pervasive and important form of social communication but one whose social communicative functions have yet to be subject to empirical investigation. The present study was the first to examine the role of complaining in everyday social interactions. College students kept diaries of the complaints they made to other people for 3 consecutive days, twice during the semester. Students recorded the complaint, the reason for expressing it, and the response it elicited. Over 75% of all complaints registered were noninstrumental in nature, in that they were not directed at changing an existing state of affairs but, rather, were expressed for reasons such as to vent frustration or to solicit sympathy. The most frequent complaints involved specific behaviors of another person. The most frequent response to a complaint was to agree with the complainer's statement. The importance of complaining as a form of social communication is discussed, and a number of hypotheses are generated for future research.

Complaining is ubiquitous: Everyone complains sometimes, and some people seem to complain all the time. To date, research on complaining has been con-fined primarily to consumer psychology, which has identified sources of satisfaction and dissatisfaction with consumer products (e.g., Bearden & Teel, 1983; Best & Andreasen, 1973; Gilly & Gelb, 1982; Warland, Helmann, & Willits, 1975). However, complaining behavior potentially has much broader relevance to a number of fundamental issues in person perception and interpersonal behavior. The types of complaints people register, their reasons for complaining, the manner in which complaints are expressed, and the reaction that complaints elicit may all have important consequences for the way complainers are perceived and treated by others. As a first step toward understanding the role of complaining in social life, the present study provides a

SOURCE: Mark D. Alicke, James C. Braun, Jeffrey Glor, M. L. Klotz, Jon Magee, Heather Sederholm, and Robin Siegel, "Complaining Behavior in Social Interaction," *Personality and Social Psychology Bulletin*, vol. 18 no. 3, June 1992, 286–295. © 1992 by the Society for Personality and Social Psychology, Inc.

AUTHORS' NOTE: Requests for reprints should be addressed to Mark D. Alicke, Department of Psychology, Ohio University, Athens OH 45701.

descriptive analysis of the complaints people register in the course of everyday social interaction.

Complaining is defined in *Webster's Third International Dictionary* as "expressing discontent, dissatisfaction, protest, resentment, or regret." Complaining can be distinguished from ordinary criticism in that complaints express a source of dissatisfaction within the complainer, whereas criticism may simply represent an objective and dispassionate observation about an object or event. Coming from a non-baseball fan, for example, the statement "The Yankees are lousy this year" may reflect nothing more than an objective assessment of their won/lost record. However, the same statement uttered by a die-hard Yankee fan is more likely to entail personal suffering over their ineptitude. In this regard, complaints imply or state explicitly that an object, state of affairs, institution, or event falls below the complainer's hopes or expectations.

WHY DO WE COMPLAIN?

Perhaps the image that comes immediately to mind in considering a complaining episode is the demand for redress over inequitable treatment. This is the aspect of complaining that has been studied in the consumer literature, usually involving a demand for repayment or the opportunity to express one's dissatisfaction to an accountable party. However, extensive pilot testing suggested to us that such *instrumental* complaints account for only a minute proportion of the complaints people register in their daily lives. Much more common than direct requests for redress are complaints about personal and environmental physical states ("My head has been hurting all day"; "The weather stinks"), lack of possessions ("I have nothing to wear"), and frustrations in goal attainment ("I'm never going to pass this course"). These complaints are called *noninstrumental* because their expression is not expected to alter the undesirable state of affairs. In fact, even complaints that are potentially instrumental in nature, such as a complaint about a roommate's sloppiness, seem to be expressed infrequently to the offending source.

One function of complaining to a secondary source is to provide an emotional release from frustration—to "get it off one's chest"—thereby assuaging the negative affect associated with the precipitating event. Furthermore, when control is threatened by a person's reluctance or inability to confront directly the source of his or her dissatisfaction, complaining may reclaim some measure of control, if only symbolically, by providing an alternate outlet for expressing displeasure.

In this sense, complaining might serve as a secondary control mechanism (Rothbaum, Weisz, & Snyder, 1982) by which the complainer can exact retribution by influencing other people's evaluation of the source of his or her dissatisfaction.

Complaining may also serve to solicit sympathy and understanding from the listener, as well as to obtain value consensus for his or her subjective interpretation of events. Affirmation by the listener validates the complainer's view of other people, events, and institutions. Complaints may also be expressed strategically to create a specific impression. Research has shown, for example, that negative evaluators are often considered more intelligent and discerning than positive evaluators (Amabile, 1983). In the act of complaining, the complainer may imply that the behavior or policies of others fall below his or her personal standards and expectations.

In keeping with these various possibilities, a major goal of our study was to assess the frequency of instrumental and noninstrumental complaints and to determine the prevalence of noninstrumental reasons for complaining. Instrumental complaints were defined as those that were expressed for the purpose of altering an undesirable state of affairs, whereas noninstrumental complaints served one or more of the social expressive and control-maintaining functions outlined above.

TOPICS OF COMPLAINTS

In assessing categories of complaints, we believed that two dimensions would be important. The first is whether the complaint is expressed ostensively (i.e., pointing to something outside the complainer) or reflexively (i.e., pointing to something within the complainer). Research on self-serving attributional biases (Bradley, 1978; Miller & Ross, 1975; Zuckerman, 1979) suggests that people are reluctant to evaluate themselves negatively. Complaints about one's own undesirable qualities and shortcomings may be infrequent not only because people wish to avoid negative thoughts about themselves but also because they do not wish to convey these thoughts to others. Few attributional studies, however, provide the opportunity to study such phenomena in the context of ongoing social behavior. The present study assesses the relative frequency of ostensive and reflexive complaints as they are expressed during the course of social interaction.

The second dimension of interest is the tendency to express complaints in general or specific terms. Research in attribution suggests that there is a pervasive tendency to explain the behavior of others dispositionally, or in global terms (e.g., Nisbett, Caputo, Legant, & Maracek, 1973). Therefore, we expected to find relatively more complaints stated in general than in specific terms.

At this initial stage of investigation, we were concerned primarily with mapping the terrain of complaining behavior; in the absence of prior theory or research, we opted for a data-driven rather than a theory-driven approach to the development of a reliable coding and classification system for everyday complaints and the responses they elicit. Therefore, our choices of categories of complaints were based on an inventory of complaints made in a pilot study, and subcategories based on the dimensions previously discussed (global/specific and reflexive/ostensive) were used only when such distinctions were supported by the data.

We asked students to keep diaries of all the complaints they registered over a period of 3 consecutive days. The diary method allowed for a continual monitoring of complaining behavior instead of relying on potentially faulty memories of past complaining episodes. Furthermore, this method encouraged literal recording of complaints and the reactions they engendered.

METHOD

PARTICIPANTS

Participants were 47 male and 113 female undergraduate students recruited from undergraduate psychology classes at the University of Florida. Students were offered extra credit toward their final grade for participating. Twelve students failed to keep the diaries properly, and their data were discarded.

PROCEDURE

Participants came to the laboratory in groups of one to six to receive instructions, which provided them with a clear distinction between complaints and other types of negative evaluation and ensured that the instructions for recording complaints and answering the supplementary questions were clear.

Participants were instructed to record each complaint they made over a 3-day period, using language that was as close as possible to a verbatim restatement of the original complaint. They were told not to record any complaint in the presence of the person to whom it was uttered but, rather, to record the complaint as soon as they were alone. The remainder of the diary asked for the time and place where the complaint was made, the response that was made to the complaint, and the reason for the complaint.

The diaries were administered at two different times during the semester (to guard against differential effects of history), for 3 consecutive days on each occasion. If participants missed a day, they simply kept the diary for an extra day.

CODING OF DIARIES

Each diary was coded independently by two of three undergraduate research assistants who had received extensive training with the coding system, and by the second author. In the event of a discrepancy in coding a complaint, the two coders and the first two authors discussed the statement until a unanimous decision about the appropriate category was reached. These ambiguities occurred almost exclusively on subclassifications rather than on the major categories of complaints.

In coding the complaints, every effort was made to avoid making inferences that went beyond the statements recorded. In some circumstances, this was difficult, as with the complaint "I couldn't study." This complaint could be a behavioral complaint if it were interpreted as a statement about the complainer's own attentional abilities, or it could be a physical environment complaint if it referred to external influences on the complainer's attentional capacity. However, in most cases it was possible to disambiguate the complaint by examining the supplemental information about its time, location, and purpose.

CODING SYSTEM

As this was the first study conducted on everyday complaining behavior, we deemed it advisable to develop a system that adhered as closely to the actual data as possible rather than fitting the data to a preconceived conceptual scheme, which might possibly distort the picture of complaining that emerged from this research. The final classification system used in this study was developed over a 2-year period using the data from a large retrospective pilot study (N = 354) in which participants were asked to record every complaint they could remember making during the preceding 3 days. A number of classification schemes were tested until an optimal balance was achieved between including as many categories and subcategories as necessary to describe the data adequately and maintaining a satisfactory degree of reliability. The final categories included in the coding system are described below. The Appendix provides examples of complaints for all subcategories.

MAJOR CATEGORIES   The first two categories represented an attributional distinction between global statements of dispositional qualities and more specific behavioral complaints. The category of *attitude* and *emotional expression* comprised global statements about a person, object, or event, expressions that seemed to ascribe relatively enduring properties to the object.[1] Items placed in the attitude category tended to involve personality characterizations, opinions about events, or dissatisfaction with organizational policies.

Attitude statements were subdivided according to whether they were reflexive (about oneself) or ostensive (about another person, a nonperson or event, a group of others, the work environment, school and school assignments, or organizational policies).

Complaints in the *behavior* category were also classified as reflexive or ostensive (about another person, a group of people, or a nonperson). In addition, behavioral complaints were divided into those that referred to a specific behavioral episode and those that referred to general behavioral tendencies.

Physical state complaints involved dissatisfaction with a physical characteristic of a person (fatigue, weight, pain or discomfort, hunger, appearance other than weight, or sickness) or a state of the environment (immediate surroundings and living environment). Physical states were also classified according to whether they were about oneself or another person.

Falling below achievement expectations referred to a failure to attain desired levels of performance on a task. These complaints represent a concern with what Bandura (1977) has called *self-efficacy*. Complaints in this category included events such as receiving a poor grade on a test or dropping a pass in a football game. This category was subdivided according to whether the complainer was worried about the possibility of falling below expectations or had actually done so. In addition, the targets of the complaints in this category were categorized as self, another person, or a group of people.[2]

Obligations referred to complaints about the means necessary to obtain a desired end. More specifically, the obligation category included complaints about not fulfilling or not wanting to fulfill an implicit or explicit commitment. Examples are not wanting to go to work and a roommate's failure to do the dishes as agreed. For a complaint to be classified in this category rather than the behavior category, the obligatory nature of the behavior had to be evident. For example, if a complaint simply stated that a roommate left the house a mess, it was coded as a behavioral complaint. However, if the complainer made it clear that a previous understanding existed that the room would be cleaned, then the complaint was coded as an obligation. Another guide for

placing complaints in this category was that the behavior was typically one that required willpower to accomplish. Complaints such as "I wish I didn't have to work out today," for example, were included in this category. Obligations were subdivided into ongoing obligations and specific discrete events and were classified as reflexive or ostensive (about another person or a group of people).

The *disappointment* category comprised complaints about service, products, or events falling below the standards the complainer expected. This category corresponded most closely to the type of complaints studied in the consumer literature, as many of the complaints registered in this category pertained to consumer items such as cars, radios, and food items. However, our pilot data indicated that people registered disappointment not only with consumer items but also with events, institutional policies, and facets of their lives. The disappointment category was ultimately subdivided into specific events, service, lack of a product, general dissatisfaction, and the product wearing out or becoming damaged.

Obstacles to goal attainment referred to complaints about frustrations encountered in obtaining a desired object.

The *desire for change* category was differentiated from the others in that it included counterfactual complaints—those that entailed a wish for things to be different from the way they currently were. For example, if a person stated, "I am so ugly," this complaint was coded as physical state; however, if this complaint was phrased "I wish I were more attractive," it was placed in the desire for change category.

RELIABILITY Although all complaints were eventually coded by two research assistants and the second author, who resolved any discrepancies among themselves, we assessed the general reliability of the classification system by selecting 20 diaries at random and calculating the percentage agreement between pairs of coders before they met to resolve discrepancies. Percentage agreement was 91% for classification of complaints into the eight major categories and 70% for classification into all possible categories (45 subcategories plus the two major categories having no subdivisions).

REASONS Subjects' expressed reasons for registering a complaint were divided into 10 categories: to vent frustration, to get attention or sympathy, to shift blame or make an excuse, to solicit advice, to seek information, to coordinate behavior, to change a person's attitude, personality, or behavior, and to convey one's feelings. Percentage agreement between pairs of coders on 20 randomly selected diaries was 79%.

RESPONSES Subjects also recorded the responses made to their complaints. These were coded in six categories: agreement, disagreement, sympathy, attempt to resolve problem, noncommittal, and no response. Percentage agreement between pairs of coders in classifying responses was 94%.

RESULTS

A total of 4,149 complaints were coded in the various categories and subcategories. The average number of complaints recorded per day per individual subject was $M = 4.32$ ($Mdn = 5$).

MAJOR CATEGORIES

Table 1 presents frequencies and percentages of complaints registered in the eight major categories. The largest category was behavioral complaints, accounting for slightly under 25% of all complaints, closely followed by complaints that reflected attitudes toward people, groups, and so forth (21%), complaints about physical states (19%), and complaints about fulfilling obligations (14%). These four categories accounted for almost 80% of the complaints registered. Disappointment with service or products, which could be considered consumer complaints, accounted for only 9% of all complaints.

SUBCLASSIFICATIONS

Also presented in Table 1 are specific subclassifications of the major categories. The most frequent behavioral complaints were specific complaints about another person. In fact, these complaints constituted the largest of all subclassifications. Attitudinal complaints, conversely, were most frequently directed at a nonpersonal entity such as the university, and as is to be expected from the nature of our sample, a sizable proportion of attitudinal complaints were specific to school-related activities and assignments.

The most common physical state complaints referred to one's surroundings, such as the weather and temperature. Complaints about falling below achievement expectations were about equally divided between worry over tasks that were impending and disappointment for tasks that were completed. Complaints about ongoing obligations accounted for a preponderance of the complaints in the obligation category. In the disappointment category, subjects were most frequently disappointed or angered by receiving inadequate service and by a product being insufficient for a desired task.

In addition to the general descriptive analysis of the subclassifications, hypotheses were tested concerning two dimensions that subdivided several of the major categories.

REFLEXIVE VERSUS OSTENSIVE For six of the eight major categories, complaints could be identified as reflexive (directed toward self) or ostensive (directed outward). To test the relative frequency of the two, the proportion of reflexive and ostensive complaints made in each of those six categories was computed, yielding 12 scores per subject. These scores were then analyzed in a 2 (reflexive/ostensive) x 6 (major category) repeated-measures analysis of variance. As expected, subjects registered a significantly smaller proportion of reflexive than ostensive complaints, $F(1,860) = 59.19$, $p < .0001$. This main effect was qualified by a significant interaction with category, $F(5,860) = 130.31$, $p < .0001$. Whereas complaints about attitudes, behavior, obligations, and disappointments were significantly less likely to be made about oneself, complaints about one's own physical state were more numerous than those about the physical state of another. The proportion of reflexive and ostensive complaints about expectations did not differ significantly.

GENERAL VERSUS SPECIFIC In two of the eight major categories, behavior and obligations, subcategories explicitly took into account the specificity of the complaint. The proportions of complaints in those categories coded as general or specific were computed and analyzed in a 2 (Specificity) x 2 (Category) repeated-measures ANOVA. Contrary to prediction, subjects made a significantly larger proportion of specific than general complaints, $F(1,172) = 261.90$, $p < .0001$, for both behaviors ($Ms = 26.4$ and 1.9) and obligations ($Ms = 13.4$ and 1.4). Specificity also interacted with category, $F(1,172) = 45.08$, $p < .0001$: Although subjects recorded significantly more specific behavior than specific obligation complaints, they did not differ in their rate of general complaints in these categories.

PERCEIVED REASONS FOR COMPLAINING

Table 2 presents subjects' reasons for expressing each major category of complaints.[3] The simple desire to vent frustration was by far the most frequently reported reason for complaining and was predominant in all major categories. The most frequent reason with a problem-solving orientation was to solicit advice, followed closely by attempts to influence another person's attitude or behavior. One of the few gender differences we found in complaining behavior was that men and women, though equally likely to seek advice through complaints

TABLE 1   Frequencies and Percentages of Recorded Complaints in All Complaint Categories

Complaint Category	Frequency	Percentage of Major Category	Percentage of Total
Attitude	852		20.5
(M = 5.3, SD = 2.7)[a]			
Self	34	4.0	0.8
Other	188	22.1	4.5
Nonperson	274	32.2	6.6
Group	80	9.4	1.9
Work	19	2.2	0.5
School	202	23.7	4.8
Policy	55	6.5	1.3
Behavior	1,017		24.5
(M = 6.4, SD = 2.3)			
Self (specific)	174	17.1	4.2
Other (specific)	522	51.3	12.6
Group (specific)	197	19.4	4.7
Nonperson	38	3.7	0.9
Self (general)	5	0.5	0.1
Other (general)	67	6.6	1.6
Group (general)	14	1.4	0.3
Physical state	802		19.3
(M = 5.0, SD = 2.8)			
Fatigue	136	17.0	3.3
Fatness	31	3.9	0.7
Pain/discomfort	124	15.5	3.0
Appearance	11	1.4	0.3
Hunger	59	7.4	1.4
Sickness	67	8.4	1.6
Surroundings	246	30.7	5.9
Inanimate	60	7.5	1.4
Miscellaneous	67	8.3	1.6
Expectations	150		3.6
(M = 0.9, SD = 0.6)			
Anticipated			
Self	54	36.0	1.3
Other	8	5.3	0.2
Group	1	0.7	0.0
Actually occurred			
Self	58	38.7	1.4
Other	21	14.0	0.5
Group	8	5.3	0.2
Obligations	580		14.0
(M = 3.6, SD = 1.8)			
Ongoing			
Self (specific)	380	65.5	9.2
Other (specific)	48	8.3	1.2

(continued)

TABLE 1   Frequencies and Percentages of Recorded Complaints in
All Complaint Categories *(continued)*

Complaint Category	Frequency	Percentage of Major Category	Percentage of Total
Group (specific)	20	3.4	0.5
Self (general)	28	4.8	0.7
Group (general)	1	0.2	0.0
Specific event			
Self	80	13.8	1.9
Other	21	3.6	0.5
Group	2	0.3	0.0
Disappointment	373		9.0
(M = 2.3, SD = 1.4)			
Event	10	2.7	0.2
Service	125	33.5	3.
Products			
Insufficient	99	26.5	2.4
Too expensive	29	7.8	0.7
Dissatisfaction	65	17.4	1.6
Wear out/damage	45	12.1	1.1
Obstacles to goal	204		4.9
(M = 1.3, SD = 1.0)			
Desire for change	137		3.3
(M = 0.9, SD = 0.3)			
Miscellaneous	34		0.8
(M = 0.2, SD = 0.9)			
Total	4,149		

[a]M refers to the average number of complaints recorded by an individual subject within each major category; SD refers to the standard deviation of subjects' complaints within each major category.

(Ms = 9.3% and 9.8% of the reasons cited by men and women, respectively), differed in their use of complaining to exert influence over another's attitudes or behavior (Ms = 11.7 and 5.8). Women were also more likely than men to report complaining as a way to seek information (Ms = 2.2 and 4.4 for men and women, respectively) and as an attempt to coordinate behavior (Ms = 2.2 and 4.4).

RESPONSES TO COMPLAINTS

The reactions conveyed in response to the major categories of complaints are reported in Table 3.[3] Overall, the most frequent response was to concur with the complainer's statement, and this response accounted for 34.9% of the codable responses. Sympathetic responses were infrequent, occurring for only 4.2% of the complaints. Attempts to resolve the problem expressed in the complaint were also frequent (23.0%) and occurred most frequently for complaints that involved obstacles to goal attainment, falling below achievement expectations, and physical states.

RESPONSES x REASONS

It seemed likely that the type of response elicited by the complaint would vary with the reason given for complaining, and this was borne out by the data. To make the cross-tabulations more manageable and reduce low-frequency cells, the reasons for complaining were combined into four categories: *direct action* (attempt to change attitude, personality, or behavior of another person); *indirect action* (seek information, coordinate behavior); *emotional* (vent frustration, get attention or sympathy); and *avoid blame* (shift blame or make excuse). Table 4 shows the frequencies of the various types of responses eliciting these categories of reasons.

TABLE 2 Frequencies and Percentages of Reasons for Complaints in Major Categories

Complaint Category	Vent Frustration	No Reason	Change Attitude/Behavior	Seek Advice	Seek Information	Seek Sympathy	Avoid Blame	Coordinate Behavior	Other	Unknown
Attitude	355 (51.6%)	38 (5.5%)	38 (5.5%)	54 (7.9%)	30 (4.4%)	27 (3.9%)	15 (2.2%)	7 (1.0%)	58 (8.4%)	66 (9.6%)
Behavior	446 (50.1%)	21 (2.4%)	124 (13.9%)	84 (9.4%)	38 (4.3%)	29 (3.3%)	12 (1.4%)	53 (6.0%)	54 (6.1%)	30 (3.4%)
Physical state	287 (40.3%)	55 (7.7%)	35 (4.9%)	89 (12.5%)	30 (4.2%)	82 (11.5%)	6 (0.8%)	28 (3.9%)	51 (7.2%)	50 (7.0%)
Expectations	62 (51.2%)	4 (3.3%)	10 (8.3%)	17 (14.1%)	0 (0.0%)	8 (6.6%)	2 (1.7%)	4 (3.3%)	5 (4.1%)	9 (7.4%)
Obligations	284 (57.5%)	33 (6.7%)	19 (3.9%)	33 (6.7%)	5 (1.0%)	30 (6.1%)	8 (1.6%)	20 (4.1%)	38 (7.7%)	24 (4.9%)
Disappointment	141 (47.5%)	15 (5.1%)	18 (6.1%)	45 (15.2%)	17 (5.7%)	12 (4.0%)	1 (0.3%)	8 (2.7%)	22 (7.4%)	17 (5.7%)
Obstacles to goal	108 (61.4%)	10 (5.7%)	6 (3.4%)	6 (3.4%)	10 (5.7%)	16 (9.1%)	4 (2.3%)	4 (2.3%)	6 (3.4%)	6 (3.4%)
Desire for change	74 (60.7%)	1 (0.8%)	4 (3.3%)	10 (8.2%)	2 (1.6%)	9 (7.4%)	0 (0.0%)	8 (6.6%)	3 (2.5%)	11 (9.0%)
Miscellaneous	9 (31.0%)	3 (10.3%)	9 (31.0%)	2 (6.9%)	2 (6.9%)	1 (3.5%)	0 (0.0%)	1 (3.5%)	2 (6.9%)	0 (0.0%)
Total	1,766 (50.0%)	180 (5.1%)	263 (7.5%)	340 (9.6%)	134 (3.8%)	214 (6.1%)	48 (1.4%)	133 (3.8%)	239 (6.8%)	213 (6.0%)

NOTE: In each cell, the frequency of the reason is followed in parentheses by the percentage of complaints within that particular major category that were expressed for that reason. In the Total row, the total number of complaints expressed for the particular reason is followed by the percentage of the total pool of complaints expressed for that reason.

TABLE 3 Frequencies and Percentages of Types of Response to Complaints in Major Categories

Complaint Category	Agree		Disagree		Resolve		Noncommittal		Sympathy		No Response	
	Frequency	Percentage	Frequency	Percentage	Frequency	Percentage	Frequency	Percentage	Frequency	Percentage	Frequency	Percentage
Attitude	263	46.2	32	5.6	88	15.5	39	6.9	15	2.6	132	23.2
Behavior	211	33.1	31	4.9	121	19.0	76	11.9	28	4.4	170	26.7
Physical State	172	29.2	29	4.9	171	29.0	36	6.1	26	4.4	155	26.3
Expectations	17	17.3	10	10.2	33	33.7	9	9.2	5	5.1	24	24.5
Obligations	126	33.5	6	1.6	89	23.7	43	11.4	19	5.1	93	24.7
Disappointment	92	36.9	8	3.2	60	24.1	17	6.8	15	6.0	57	22.9
Obstacles to goal	51	42.9	4	3.4	34	28.6	9	7.6	2	1.7	19	16.0
Desire for change	33	26.2	4	3.2	38	30.2	10	7.9	7	5.6	34	27.0
Miscellaneous	5	29.4	2	11.8	5	29.4	1	5.9	1	5.9	3	17.6

TABLE 4   Frequency of Responses to Complaints by Reasons for Complaints

Response	Reason for Complaint[a]			
	Direct Action	**Indirect Action**	**Emotional**	**Avoid Blame**
Agree	14.2	20.7	27.8	23.4
Disagree	7.4	6.0	2.3	5.0
Try to resolve	12.7	25.4	19.4	8.4
Sympathy	2.2	3.1	4.1	8.4
Noncommittal	6.0	5.3	6.8	11.7
No Response	20.0	6.5	21.8	11.7
Other	37.7	33.2	17.9	31.7
Total[b]	253	262	1,805	45

NOTE: Values are column percentages. Complaints for which data were incomplete were excluded from this analysis.

[a]Direct action = attempt to change attitude, personality, or behavior; indirect action = seek information, coordinate behavior; emotional = vent frustration, get attention or sympathy; avoid blame = shift blame or make excuse.

[b]Total number of complaints for each column.

Although agreement was the response with the highest overall frequency, it was the most commonly cited response only to two classes of complaints: those made to vent frustration or elicit sympathy and those made to shift blame or make excuses. Complaints meant to take direct action were most often met with silence (no response), whereas complaints seeking to effect change through indirect action elicited problem solving and agreement. Disagreement was the least common response across all categories.

DISCUSSION

Our assumption that most complaints would be non-instrumental in nature was strongly confirmed. Most complaints were registered for the express purpose of venting frustration, often stated explicitly as "to get it off my chest." Furthermore, in many cases the subject of the complaint, such as physical states of oneself or the environment, was not something that the person to whom the complaint was registered could change under any circumstances.

Also as expected, subjects were less likely to complain about themselves than about other people, objects, or events. In fact, the only categories for which reflexive complaints outnumbered ostensive were physical states, such as hunger and pain, and falling below achievement expectations. People hardly ever complained about themselves in global attitudinal or dispositional terms. As previous research on self-serving tendencies suggests (Bradley, 1978), people are reluctant to

describe their failures and shortcomings in global, dispositional form. In accordance, self-complaints tended to refer to practical misdoings such as saying the wrong thing to someone or to physical states beyond the complainer's control such as having a headache. Subjects also registered numerous self-complaints regarding duties and obligations. However, although obligations were coded reflexively because they were self-referent (e.g., "*I* hate waking up in the morning"; "(I wish *I* didn't have to work while going to school") they actually pertained to externally imposed states. In registering such complaints, students were not complaining about their inability to wake up so much as about the simple fact of having to do so.

Complaints about appearance and weight were relatively infrequent in our sample. This was surprising because such complaints were among the most numerous in our retrospective pilot study, in which subjects were simply asked to list the kinds of things they complained about most frequently. One implication of this finding is that people may not be highly attuned to the things they actually complain about or may have a poor conception of the frequency with which they complain about specific issues. In particular, people may overestimate the extent to which they disclose sources of dissatisfaction within themselves to others. Specific instances of self-disclosure, when they do occur, may be highly vivid or available and may lead the complainer to miscalculate their general frequency. Our data also indicated that students were hesitant to register complaints that involved threats to their self-esteem, such as being criticized by others, stood up on a date, or outperformed.

Contrary to expectations, students were about three times as likely to express complaints about another person in specific behavioral terms as in global dispositional or attitudinal terms. Subjects preferred linguistic forms such as "He acted so rudely" to "He is rude." One possible explanation for this difference involves expectations of whether the state of affairs mentioned in the complaint is alterable. For example, the complaint "School sucks" may indicate that the complainer has little hope for change. Global complaints may also be indicative of a heightened level of affect. The pervasive tendency for marital partners, for example, to explain each other's undesirable behaviors in dispositional terms (Orvis, Kelley, & Butler, 1976) may be due to the strong level of affect evoked in interpersonal relationships. The majority of complaints expressed during a typical day, in contrast, are likely to be less affectively charged.

Responses to complaints were primarily of two varieties. Most frequent was agreement with the complainer's statement. Agreement satisfies conversational norms by avoiding embarrassing or annoying challenges to the complainer's judgment or veracity (Goffman, 1959). To some extent, agreement is the easiest and safest response to a complaint. Furthermore, the responder usually hears only one side of the story, and hence it is unsurprising that he or she would concur with the statement.

Almost as frequent as agreement, however, were attempts to resolve the issue entailed by the complaint. Attempts at resolution occurred most frequently in response to complaints about failures to attain performance expectations. This orientation with regard to achievement expectations may serve not only to provide objective solutions to a problem but also to convey to the complainer that the listener believes improvement is possible.

Our assumption that complaints constitute an important and prevalent form of social communication was borne out by the finding that, on average, slightly over four complaints were registered per day. Of course, this value could have been inflated by the fact that people were asked to attend to and record their complaints, but it is equally likely that subjects failed to record all the complaints they actually registered because of our instructions to record only complaints, not other negative statements. It would be interesting in future research to determine how much of everyday conversation is dominated by complaining behavior and to trace individual differences in the frequency with which people use complaining as a vehicle for expressing dissatisfaction to others.

APPENDIX
EXAMPLES OF COMPLAINTS IN ALL SUBCATEGORIES

Category	Complaint
Attitude and Emotional Expression	
Self	Sometimes I am such a freak.
Other	The guy next to me on the bus is a dork.
Nonperson	10:00 A.M. is way too early to get up.
Group	Those fraternity brothers are so vain.
Work	I'm sick of my career as a stockboy.
School/class	Nothing is more boring than economics.
Policy/organization	The parking policy on campus is idiotic.
Behavior	
Self (specific)	I ate like a pig at lunch today.
Other (specific)	You forgot to pay the phone bill.
Group (specific)	The Supreme Court's action concerning abortion was pathetic.
Nonperson	The United States has made some dumb international maneuvers lately.
Self (general)	I always spend too much money on the weekend.
Other (general)	You never pitch in around here.
Group (general)	The football team never plays worth a damn in big games.
Physical State	
Fatigue	I just have no energy left after my aerobics class.
Fatness	In my bathing suit, I look like a member of the hippo family.
Pain/discomfort	It hurt so bad when I stubbed my toe.
Appearance	My hair looks as nice as Don King's.
Hunger	If I don't eat soon, I will collapse.
Sickness	This is the worst hangover I've ever experienced.
Surroundings	It is hotter than hell out today.
Inanimate	The shower water is freezing.
Miscellaneous	My eyes won't stop watering.
Falling below Achievement Expectations	
Worried about	
Self	I will probably fail my chemistry class.

| Other | My partner plans on my share of our project being fantastic. |
| Group | I don't think I'll do as well as the other guys on the team expect me to. |

Actually occurred
Self	I can't believe I'm such a bad cook.
Other	My roommate thinks I let him down in the team beer-chugging contest.
Group	Thanks to me, we lost our intra-mural game last night.

Obligations

Ongoing
Self (specific)	I hate this psychology experiment I agreed to do.
Other (specific)	My friend's job duties don't allow us to ever watch football on Sunday.
Group (specific)	The things sorority sisters have to do during this fall's rush are a real pain.
Self (general)	I always hate the jobs I select.
Group (general)	Club members shouldn't have decided to meet with one another so often.

Specific event
Self	I wish I didn't have to pick my sister up after work.
Other	My dad shouldn't have agreed to go to that business meeting over Christmas.
Group	The U.S. diplomats should never have worked out a deal with Iran.

Disappointment

| Event | That party was a real loser. |
| Service | It's taking forever for them to make my McNuggets™. |

Products
Insufficient	The selection in this store is rotten.
Too expensive	A Porsche costs that much!
Dissatisfaction	The food in here makes me want to gag.
Wear out/ damage	My new shirt has three holes in it.

Obstacles to Goal Attainment

I am getting really sick of school.

Desire for Change

I wish I could visit with my friends more.

NOTES

1. A number of complaints in the attitude and emotional expression category were coextensive with those in other categories. For example, the statement "My thighs are so fat," which was placed in the physical state category, could also be considered an attitude statement. In such cases, the item was placed in the more specific category.

2. Again, this category shared some potential overlap with other categories, especially with the behavior category. However, behaviors that also qualified as falling below achievement expectations (such as failing a test) were placed in the more specific category.

3. The total numbers of responses to complaints and reasons for complaints, presented in Tables 2, 3, and 4, do not add up to the total number of complaints listed in Table 1. This is due to instances in which subjects failed to record reasons for or responses to complaints or to cases in which the reasons or responses were uncodable into our major categories.

REFERENCES

Amabile, T. M. (1983). Brilliant but Cruel: Perceptions of Negative Evaluators. *Journal of Experimental Social Psychology*, 19, 146–156.

Bandura, A. (1977). Self-Efficacy: Toward a Unifying Theory of Behavioral Change. *Psychological Review, 84,* 191–215.

Bearden, W. O., & J. E. Teel, (1983). Selected Determinants of Consumer Satisfaction and Complaint Reports. *Journal of Marketing Research*, 20, 21–28.

Best, A., & A. R. Andreasen, (1973). "Consumer Response to Unsatisfactory Purchases: A Survey of Perceiving Defects, Voicing Complaints, and Obtaining Redress." *Law and Society Review*, 11, 701–742.

Bradley, G. W. (1978). Self-Serving Biases in the Attribution Process: A Reexamination of the Fact or Fiction Question. *Journal of Personality and Social Psychology*, 36, 56–71.

Gilly, M. C., & B. D. Gelb, (1982). Post-Purchase Consumer Processes and the Complaining Consumer. *Journal of Consumer Research*, 9, 323–328.

Goffman, E. (1959). *The Presentation of Self in Everyday Life*. Garden City, NY: Doubleday.

Miller, D. T., & M. Ross, (1975). Self-Serving Biases in Attribution of Causality: Fact or Fiction? *Psychological Bulletin*, 82, 213–225.

Nisbett, R. E., C. Caputo, P. Legant, & J. Maracek. (1973). Behavior as Seen by the Actor and as Seen by the Observer. *Journal of Personality and Social Psychology*, 27, 154–164.

Orvis, B. R., H. H Kelley, & B. Butler, (1976). Attributional Conflict in Young Couples. In J. H. Harvey, W. J. Ickes, & R. F. Kidd (Eds.), *New Directions in Attribution Research* (Vol. 1). Hillsdale, NJ: Lawrence Erlbaum.

Rothbaum, F., J. R. Weisz, & S. S. Snyder. (1982). Changing the World and Changing the Self: A Two-Process Model of Perceived Control. *Journal of Personality and Social Psychology*, 42, 5–37.

Warland, R., Helmann, R., & Willits, J. (1975). Dissatisfied Consumers: Who Gets Upset and Who Takes Action. *Journal of Consumer Affairs, 9*, 148–163.

Zuckerman, M. (1979). Attribution of Success and Failure Revisited, or: The Motivational Bias Is Alive and Well in Attribution Theory. *Journal of Personality, 47*, 245–287.

DYNAMICS OF COMPLAINT MANAGEMENT IN THE SERVICE ORGANIZATION

Mary C. Gilly
University of California, Irvine

William B. Stevenson
Boston College

Laura J. Yale
Fort Lewis College

While the consumer affairs and services marketing literatures recognize the importance of input from customers, little is known about how customer feedback systems might operate, particularly in dealing with customer complaints. This paper offers an information processing model of the complaint information flow within the organization and poses hypotheses based on the suggested model. A new field study technique using a type of network analysis is used to empirically test hypotheses and discover barriers and facilitators to the flow of communications. The study provides insight concerning how complaint information flows through the organization after it has been received by a customer contact employee. The results provide support for the thesis that the role of complaint handler and manager in providing the service is at least as important as the role of the customer contact employee.

Most literature on consumer services recognizes the importance of input from customers in producing the service (cf., Solomon *et al.* 1985; Zeithaml, Berry, and Parasuraman 1988); few discuss how input from customers and customer contact personnel is communicated from customer contact personnel at the organizational boundaries to managers who can make decisions regarding policies and procedures. The importance of communication in the delivery of services has been

noted by Zeithaml, Berry, and Parasuraman (1988) who examined the gap between consumer expectations and management *perceptions* of consumer expectations and identified upward communication within the organization as a factor which tends to close this gap.

An important potential input from customer contact personnel to management is consumer complaints. Many researchers and consumer affairs personnel would agree that consumer complaints provide organizations with the opportunity to satisfy unhappy customers and prevent brand switching and unfavorable word-of-mouth communications. While effective handling of customer complaints is obviously in the consumer interest, consumer complaints can also offer benefits far beyond the individual complaint. If the organization disseminates information about complaints to decision

SOURCE: Mary C. Gilly, William B. Stevenson, and Laura J. Yale, "Dynamics of Complaint Managemnt in the Service Organization," *Journal of Consumer Affairs*, vol. 25, no. 2 (Winter 1991): 295–322.

Mary C. Gilly is Associate Professor, Graduate School of Management, University of California, Irvine, CA; William B. Stevenson is Associate Professor, Organizational Studies Department, Boston College, Boston, MA; and Laura J. Yale is Assistant Professor, School of Business Administration, Fort Lewis College, Durango, CO.

This research was supported by grants from the University of California, Irvine Graduate School of Management and Academic Senate Committee on Research. Our appreciation goes to Rob Page for research assistance.

makers who can take steps to eliminate or reduce the cause of the dissatisfaction, consumer interests will also be served.

Dissemination of information for the purpose of finding and correcting the causes of consumer dissatisfaction can be characterized as "complaint management" (Fornell and Westbrook 1979), as opposed to the traditional complaint handling involved in placating unhappy customers. An important component of complaint management is understanding how information from customers flows through the organization to relevant decision makers. This understanding becomes particularly important in some service organizations in which, due to intangibility and simultaneous production and consumption of the service (Bateson 1979), the customer may have repeated contacts with many different employees. Thus, marketers in service organizations have the opportunity to supplement information obtained from marketing research with marketing intelligence provided by customer contact personnel.

In the case of consumer complaints, customer contact personnel may be particularly averse to passing important information up the organizational hierarchy. Fornell and Westbrook (1984) cited research from organizational behavior which "suggests that there may be significant impediments to the intrafirm communication of unfavorable or negatively valued messages" (69). The authors noted that consumer complaints may imply inadequacies of previous marketing policies and may be taken as criticism of policy-makers, thus inhibiting communication. Andreasen (1988) also discussed the aversion managers have to consumer complaints because they do not want to hear about weaknesses.

To understand the dynamics of complaint management, a number of issues must be addressed. Organizational members who facilitate the successful passing of consumer information to those who can take action on complaints must be identified. Second, barriers and facilitators to communication about consumer dissatisfaction need to be determined. Third, it is important to determine who is likely to engage in complaint handling and complaint management. Finally, the type of complaint may have effects on how it is managed in the organization.

As a first step in understanding these issues, a study of complaint management in a hospital was undertaken. Complaints were traced through this service organization from complaint to resolution and beyond, to recommendations for policy or procedural changes that could be enacted to minimize future consumer dissatisfaction.

HANDLING AND MANAGING CONSUMER COMPLAINTS

The focus of the vast majority of research on consumer complaints has been the dissatisfied consumer. Andreasen (1988) contributed an excellent review of the literature on consumer complaints and redress. He concluded that, "consumers experience problems in about 20 percent of their purchases, complain to the seller (rarely to third parties) 40 percent of the time, and perceive that they have received satisfaction from this complaining behavior 60 percent of the time" (675). Andreasen also offered evidence that complaints and outcomes regarding services are different from those regarding goods (although he acknowledged that a great deal of variance exists even within the service category). For example, a greater percentage of services' problems than goods' problems are not voiced "because potential complainers do not know what to do or think that it wouldn't do any good" (708).

A great deal of research has examined who complains and why (Andreasen (1988) estimated over 500 studies related to this topic). A lesser amount of research has looked at what occurs following consumer complaints; that is, how organizations respond to complaints they receive, and how complainants react to these responses. However, even this complaint handling research adopts the consumer's viewpoint in that the focus is on the consumer's reaction to organizational response to complaints (cf., Lewis 1983; Nickels and Zabriskie 1973).

The studies of the consumers' views of organizational responses to complaints do not explicitly tell organizations which complaint responses are better than others. Rather, inferences must be made from these studies about how organizations can improve their complaint handling procedures based on consumer reactions to the complaint responses received. This gap in knowledge about the organization's view of consumer complaints was highlighted by Bryant (1988). He said, "Research in the area must model and investigate empirically firm as well as consumer behavior if we are to be successful in understanding consumer dissatisfaction and complaints" (725).

Research that has focused on the organizational view of consumer complaints has considered this issue in terms of how complaints are handled: what response is given to the complainant (if any), how timely the response is, if a refund is given, etc. For example, Gilly (1987) found that consumer *perceptions* of complaint response were more important than the response itself in determining satisfaction and repurchase. However, for an organization to make full use of the information provided by complaints, the approach called "complaint management" by Fornell and Westbrook (1979) must be adopted. According to these authors, in addition to handling individual consumer complaints, an organization practicing complaint management also deals with consumer dissatisfaction by tracking complaints and taking steps to see that future consumer dissatisfaction is minimized. While not specifically using the "complaint management" term, Landon (1979) also recognized this dual function in his article on consumer affairs departments. He said, "It can be seen that the consumer affairs unit must manage more than the correspondence with the consumer; the unit must also manage the flow of information from the consumer throughout the company" (93).

More recently, Smart and Martin (1989) empirically addressed the complaint management issue by surveying customer relations directors of a number of consumer packaged goods companies. When asked if information about the volume and content of consumer letters is reported to departments other than the consumer affairs department, without exception, all of the surveyed companies reported forwarding this information. Departments receiving this information included quality control, marketing, plant managers, brand managers, and research and development. However, it was beyond the scope of the research to discover if, in fact, complaint information is used by other departments to affect procedures.

Fornell and Westbrook (1984) also surveyed employees of consumer affairs departments in their study of complaint management. They found that the greater the proportion of complaints received by a company (relative to other consumer correspondence), the more isolated the consumer affairs department. Calling this "the vicious circle of consumer complaints," the authors found that isolation from management participation led, in turn, to increased consumer complaints. But again, only consumer affairs personnel were queried, not other employees in the organizations.

Despite the obvious importance of disseminating information about consumer problems to organizational members who can take steps to prevent future dissatisfaction, this aspect of consumer satisfaction/dissatisfaction and complaint behavior has been virtually ignored by consumer affairs and marketing scholars. The failure to research this problem more fully may be due in part to the difficulty in gaining access to all relevant actors within the organization. The studies of complaint handling cited, while perhaps having the cooperation of particular companies, depended on input from consumers, rather than company employees. Regarding the studies of complaint management, Fornell and Westbrook (1984) and Smart and Martin (1989) used data from company employees, but then only consumer affairs employees.

There is a need for examining how organizations deal with consumer complaints internally so that the concept of complaint management can be better understood. By understanding the ramifications of complaint management, service organizations can become more responsive to their customers; first, by satisfying complainants and second, by changing policies/procedures to prevent reoccurrence of problems. Here, a model of complaint management is formulated, and complaints are traced from the initial contact person to other persons throughout the organization to understand the dynamics of complaint management.

INFORMATION PROCESSING MODEL OF CONSUMER COMPLAINTS

Complaint management can be viewed as a problem of information processing within the organization. Information processing models of organizational communication and decision making (e.g., Galbraith 1973, 1977; Nadler and Tushman 1988) proceed from three basic assumptions: (1) the tasks of the organization present uncertainties, (2) these uncertainties can be reduced by increasing the amount of information available, and (3) information can be managed by formal design, that is, by creating formally specified individuals and groups to deal with problems.

Formal design can be used to direct information about problems in several ways. For example, organizational units can be created to focus expertise on specific tasks. However, this approach leads to the creation of barriers between units. Managers have the primary role in crossing these barriers and coordinating across units. Under conditions of interdependence that might overwhelm the usual managerial networks of information flows between units, or when organizational decision makers want to coordinate functions across a particular task, specialized boundary spanners are appointed (Galbraith 1977). Similarly, boundary spanners serve to filter information coming from outside the organization and to disseminate information throughout the organization.

What is not always clear in information processing models, is how the information processing system functions in practice. For example, organizational units are created, but this leads to barriers between units. These barriers have unspecified effects on the daily flow of information about problems, such as consumer complaints, throughout the organization. It is assumed that those in formal positions do a great deal of the coordination across these boundaries. However, what happens when managers and formally designated complaint handlers both are presented with information about a problem? Which of these problem solvers are predominant? Does the type of information, in this case, type of complaint, affect its flow across the organization? These questions are relevant to the study of how consumer complaints enter and flow through the service organization to complaint managers.

Figure 1 presents a model of how information about complaints is processed that draws upon and extends the organizational information processing model. As a first step in the complaint process, a customer expresses a complaint to a boundary spanner, the customer contact person. This is an inherently different process than in consumer packaged goods, where the disgruntled customer complains to the retailer or writes to a distant manufacturer where a specific complaint department would be responsible for disseminating complaints through the organization. Because complaints about consumer goods will potentially affect more than one organization (e.g., manufacturer, retailer), consumer complaints are often handled using formal, established procedures. In the service organization, a large number of people (usually in one organization) may be called upon to act as boundary spanners, making the process less formalized and more unpredictable. For example, in a study by Levy and Surprenant (1982), consumers had a much better sense of the hierarchy of complaint avenues for goods than they did for services.

In the next step of the process, customer contact personnel forward the complaint if they feel they cannot resolve the problem, or if they feel someone else should be informed. The complaint eventually reaches the person who can resolve the problem expressed by the customer, perhaps after being passed by intermediaries. The complaint handler (who may have been the initial contact) then responds in an attempt to satisfy the customer. This response to the customer is what Fornell and Westbrook (1979) termed "complaint handling."

The complaint handler may pass along information about the complaint (and others like it) to a complaint manager, or the complaint handler may act as a complaint manager as well. Complaint managers may then decide that a change in policies and procedures is necessary to prevent future dissatisfaction for all customers, not just the customer(s) who complained. This part of the process is called "complaint management" by Fornell and Westbrook (1979). Change in policies and procedures is communicated to customer contact persons and other affected personnel, and the complaint manager conducts a followup to make sure that the customer's complaint has been resolved.

Barriers and facilitators to information flows may exist among any of the participants in the process. Barriers and facilitators can be related to such factors as the characteristics of individuals, jobs, and relationships between sender and receiver, etc. In addition, the nature of the complaint itself can affect whether information is facilitated or barriers raised.

INFORMATION PROCESSING AND COMPLAINT MANAGEMENT

Feedback to organizational members and the customer is a form of organizational learning that information theorists have begun to address (e.g., Daft and Wieck

FIGURE 1   Information Flows about Consumer Complaints

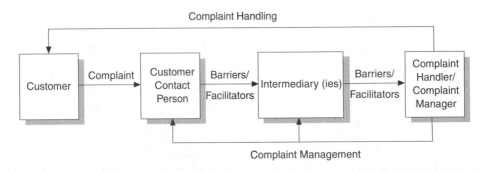

1984). Organizations scan their environments, interpret what is happening, and learn from their actions in the environment (Hedberg 1981).

What has not been addressed in organizational information processing models is how this feedback process may break down. The complaint handling/management process can break down at any of a number of steps. For example, a customer contact person could be unresponsive to dissatisfied customers, or may feel that certain types of complaints are unimportant or unresolvable. Other persons in the chain may feel similarly and fail to forward complaints or take action.

Aside from individual biases against action, the information processing model alerts us to other problems that may inhibit complaint management. A first question to be considered is, what facilitates the flow of information about complaints during complaint processing? Are managers, as coordinators across the organization, effective at passing complaints to resolution, or are specialized complaint handlers more effective for directing the flow of information? Further, the emphasis of traditional information processing models on creation of formal positions neglects the possibility that preexisting pathways between individuals may link members. It may be that having an existing relationship with someone who can handle a complaint is a more effective way to resolve a complaint than creating formal positions to handle complaints.

In addition, this flow of information may be impeded by the barriers that are created between departments and professions within the organization. Thus, complaint handlers may be better at getting problems to someone who can resolve them when passing complaints to someone within their own professional area of expertise.

A second question to be addressed is, who is likely to engage in *complaint management*, i.e., recommending actions within the organization rather than simple complaint handling with the consumer, when confronted with complaints? Daft and Lengel (1984, 1986) have extended the information processing model by suggesting that managerial personnel are key actors in interpreting ambiguous information and formulating policies. However, formally designated problem solvers may have more expertise in the problem area and therefore be more likely than managers to recommend internal action and/or complaint handling action with the consumer.

Finally, type of complaint may have effects on complaint management. Research on communication networks has neglected how the content may alter pathways

that information takes in social groupings (Bernard and Killworth 1978). Type of complaint may affect how important the organizational actors rate the complaint and take action to reduce its reoccurrence.

FACILITATING COMPLAINT PROCESSING

The above questions about how complaint information is processed were formulated as a series of tentative hypotheses based on this information processing model of complaint management. As a first step in exploring this complex issue of complaint management, these hypotheses only test selected portions of the model in Figure 1.

Consider first the question of who is likely to be effective at passing the complaint to someone who can resolve it, regardless of whether those at the next step are complaint handlers or complaint managers. Are managers or formally designated boundary spanners more effective at passing complaints to someone who can resolve them? It would be expected that managers would be more knowledgeable about the organization's structure and other organizational members through their managerial roles such as "linking pins" (Likert 1961) and boundary spanners (Adams 1976; Aldrich and Herker 1977) who coordinate activities across functions. Thus:

> Hypothesis 1A: Managers will be more likely than others to pass complaints to someone who can resolve them.

Similarly, organizations may create formal positions to handle recurring problems and span boundaries (in the case of the hospital studied, each department had a "patient concern" person). This would be an efficient method of channeling information across the organization according to the information processing model (Galbraith 1977). Further, these boundary spanners would be expected to have more specific expertise than someone who was a manager. Therefore:

> Hypothesis 1B: Formally designated complaint handlers will be more likely than others to pass complaints to someone who can resolve them.

Many information processing models assume that those in formal positions of power, such as managers, have a great deal of influence in organizations (Daft and Lengel 1984, 1986; Galbraith 1977). It is noted that those occupying a formal position can be powerless without wide-ranging networks of connections within the organization (Lincoln and Miller 1979). In fact, those in strategic positions in organizational networks may be more effective and influential than their formal positions would imply (Brass 1984). For example, Culnan (1988) studied mail processing in U.S. Senate offices. Her research revealed that structured reports describing the content of incoming letters provided one means of upward communication. But it was also found that "beyond these formal written reports, much of the upward communication on mail is informal" (24). Therefore, one would expect having some sort of personal tie with a problem solver, whether it is a work, social, or advice-giving relationship, would make a complaint handler more effective at forwarding problems to resolution. As a consequence:

> Hypothesis 2: Having a personal tie to someone who can resolve the complaint will make an individual more successful at forwarding complaints to resolution.

Information processing models proceed from the assumption that organizations are designed to account for the limited ability of members to process information (March and Simon 1958; Simon 1947). Interconnected tasks are grouped within organizational units so that members can engage in a specialized division of labor and not be overwhelmed by the complexity of the organization (Thompson 1967). As a consequence, these work groupings can form barriers to interaction across organizational boundaries (Tushman 1979). Therefore, individuals in this division of labor can be expected to be more successful at sending complaints to resolution *within* their area of expertise as compared to passing complaints across professional boundaries. Accordingly:

> Hypothesis 3: Individuals will be more likely to pass complaints to someone who can resolve them within their profession as compared to complaints passed across professions.

COMPLAINT HANDLING AND MANAGEMENT

The next general question considered is who is likely to engage in complaint handling and/or management. Because of their formal positions of authority within the organization, managers can be expected to be more oriented toward taking administrative action than nonmanagers when confronted with a complaint (Mintzberg 1973; Sayles 1989). In addition, managers are more likely to be the interpreters of ambiguous information in organizations (Daft and Lengel 1984, 1986). As a consequence:

> Hypothesis 4A: Managers will be more likely to recommend action (either handling or managing complaints) to be taken in response to complaints compared to others.

Similarly, those formally designated as complaint handlers should be more disposed toward taking action than others. The combination of formal position and specialized knowledge should give the designated complaint handler a great deal of influence concerning complaints. In the hospital studied, all but two of the formally designated complaint handlers were also managers. As a consequence, there should not be differences in influence based on being a manager versus having an advisory position as a complaint handler. Thus:

> Hypothesis 4B: Formally designated complaint handlers will be more likely to recommend action to be taken (either handling or managing of complaints) in response to complaints compared to others.

TYPE OF COMPLAINT

Finally, the effect of type of complaint on complaint management should be considered. Discussing the vividness bias in information processing, Drumwright (1985) stated that informational vividness is created by factors which can be comprehended through the five senses. Thus, consumers may be evaluating the attitude of personnel when, in contrast, personnel are rewarded for quality of service. In this study, a hospital is used as a research site. Persons with medical expertise (e.g., employees of a hospital) can be expected to view quality of care complaints as more important than attitude complaints because their training stresses quality of care. In addition, organizational members often develop a "we versus them" bias toward their fellow employees (Dalton 1959; Homans 1950; Walton and Dutton 1969) in which attitude complaints can be dismissed as, "Anyone can have a bad day." As a consequence:

> Hypothesis 5: Complaints concerned with quality of service will be rated by employees as more important than complaints about attitude of personnel.

It is expected that quality of care complaints will be resolved at lower organizational levels, while attitude complaints must be handled at higher levels as a "personal problem." Employees will tend to feel more comfortable if quality of care problems are resolved (i.e., make sure proper procedures are being followed) rather than dealing with a problem employee's personality. In these cases, managers at higher levels will have to engage in their role of conflict handlers (Mintzberg 1973), and attitude complaints will take longer to resolve as employees pass the problem up the hierarchy. Thus:

> Hypothesis 6: Quality of care complaints will be resolved more quickly than attitude of personnel complaints.

THE STUDY

RESEARCH SETTING

A teaching hospital with approximately 2,000 employees was the service organization chosen for the research site. Consumers of health care (patients) in a hospital frequently come in contact with a variety of personnel, including nurses, doctors, administrators (in admissions, billing, etc.), and ancillary medical personnel (e.g., pharmacists, x-ray technicians). A patient has the opportunity to express dissatisfaction directly to the employee viewed as the source of the problem, or to voice concern about one employee to another (e.g., complain to the nurse about the doctor). These patient contact personnel can be important conduits of information about patient satisfaction.

Organizational responsiveness to patient perceptions of needs has been recognized as important by researchers in the health care field. Carey and Posavac (1982) and Uhlmann, Inui, and Carter (1984) saw both humanistic and practical advantages to obtaining information from patients regarding satisfaction/dissatisfaction and acting upon it. First, health care organizations want patients to be as worry free as possible because this is a healthy state. Finding out patients' perceptions concerning their care is vital to achieving this goal. Weisman and Nathanson (1985) found patient satisfaction to influence compliance behavior. Second, health care administrators want former patients to return when requiring medical care at a future date and to recommend the organization to other potential patients. If patients perceive the health care providers as being responsive to their needs, their evaluation of their experiences will be more positive. Given the growing competitive situation among health care providers, the importance of complaint management (rather than mere complaint handling) is increasing.

RESEARCH DESIGN

To determine factors affecting the flow of information about consumer complaints, a new technique was developed. Rather than surveying employees about past complaint management behavior or attempting to follow actual complaints where little in the way of written records exists, an effort was made to simulate the introduction of consumer complaints to customer contact personnel.

Studies of organizational communication have been done using a variety of methodologies such as: experiments in which information is planted in the organization and traced by questioning organizational members after the dissemination of the information (Albaum 1964); surveys in which people are asked whether they have heard of some incident or rumor (Davis 1953); and relational studies in which information is actually traced through the organization by having each respondent pass the information to others and inform the researchers (Lundberg 1975). A relational approach, having its roots in sociology (Travers and Milgram 1969), was developed to trace information about consumer complaints as it flowed through the organization.

Employees of the hospital were given folders, each of which contained a "scenario" about a patient complaint. (More information is given about the scenarios in the next section.) Folders were sent to a randomly selected sample of four employee groups—doctors, nurses, administrators, and ancillary personnel (e.g., lab, x-ray, pharmacy personnel)—expected to be primarily responsible for health care and somewhat interdependent in delivery of that care. Other, more peripheral personnel such as cafeteria or maintenance workers were excluded from the study. The starter persons were instructed to read the hypothetical scenario and then decide on one of two courses of action.

Action #1: Someone else needs to know about this problem:

☐ This may be someone who has responsibility for the problem.

☐ Or you may not be sure what to do, but you know someone who can handle the problem.

☐ Or you are the person to handle this problem, but you believe someone else should be informed.

In this case, the respondent would (a) put their name on a roster within the folder, (b) decide who should receive the complaint information, (c) tear out a one-page questionnaire asking why they would choose the specific other person to receive the folder, fill out the questionnaire, and send the questionnaire to the investigators, and (d) forward the folder to the people they believe could handle the problem.

Action #2: You do not believe anyone else should be informed:

☐ You can handle this concern and believe nobody else needs to be informed or you do not believe this problem requires any further attention.

In this case, the respondent would (a) write what they would do to respond to the complaint in the folder, and (b) return the folder to the investigators.

During this process, the folders circulated throughout the hospital until the individuals who believed they could handle the complaints were reached. The folders were then returned to the investigators. While the research design is unique, other research has made use of similar network analysis approaches (cf., Hutt, Reingen, and Ronchetto 1988; Reingen *et al.* 1984).

COMPLAINT SCENARIOS

Development of the scenarios involved examining records of past patient complaints received by the hospital, talking with a variety of hospital employees, writing a number of hypothetical scenarios based on past complaints, and then revising them after receiving feedback from a steering committee within the hospital. An effort was made to select patient complaints which were not specifically medical; that is, scenarios were formulated that did not have potential for malpractice litigation. The hospital has a sophisticated quality assurance program to deal with potential malpractice complaints.

While every effort was made to make these scenarios as realistic as possible, respondents were aware they were participating in research, not dealing with an actual consumer complaint. While the use of an experimental design may affect the external validity of results, the participants in a pretest at a university health clinic had indicated upon debriefing that they responded to the hypothetical task in the way that they would for an actual complaint.

Scenarios described problems related to quality of care and attitude of personnel. Distinctions were made between these two types of complaints to see if the complaint process was affected by type of problem. As scenarios were developed, the hospital steering committee was asked to code the complaints as related primarily to quality of care or attitude of personnel. Scenarios were revised until the committee reached 100 percent agreement on the distinction between scenario types.

It was thought that hospital personnel might view quality of care complaints as the more important, while patients might depend heavily on attitude of personnel in assessing their hospital experience because of their inability to evaluate medical care. Drumwright (1985) supported this proposition, ". . . patients at a medical center usually do not have the professional expertise to judge the quality of the medical care they are receiving. However, they do know whether . . . the nursing staff is friendly and courteous" (128). (See also Zeithaml (1981) for a discussion of the credence properties of services and their impact on consumer evaluation processes.) Two scenarios describing problems—one quality of care and one attitude—involving each of the populations of interest (i.e., doctors, nurses, ancillary personnel, and administrators) were used in the study. These eight scenarios appear in Figure 2.

RESULTS

Table 1 shows completion rates for the four professional groups. Overall, 32 percent of the folders were ultimately returned to the researchers by respondents who thought they could resolve the problem. However, if one only considers the folders which were actually begun by the starter people, the completion rate is 67 percent. While there are differences in the overall completion rates for the four professional groups, with doctors having a much lower response rate, once folders were started, completion rates are more similar between groups.

On average, there were three links from the starter person to the individual who thought they could resolve the complaint (counting the starter person as the first "link"). The maximum number of links was six, with 85 percent of chains completed by the fourth link.

FORWARDING OF COMPLAINTS

As stated earlier, consumer affairs professionals must consider barriers to and facilitators of information flows which are created through the formal structure of the organization and informal networks of employees. It was anticipated that managers and patient concern personnel would be more successful than others at passing questionnaires to completion (Hypotheses 1A and B). In addition, having a personal tie to a problem solver should facilitate passing problems to completion (Hypothesis 2), but the presence of organizational boundaries should make completion more difficult across boundaries (Hypothesis 3).

The problem solving sequence studied can be viewed as a chain with a respondent at each point, or node, forwarding the folder until it reaches someone who can handle the problem. To study the characteristics of the respondent that would make him or her a facilitator and to look at conditions that might have presented barriers to forwarding a problem to a problem solver, a logit equation was constructed. The dependent variable was a binary variable indicating whether a respondent forwarded the folder (a) to someone who returned the folder to the researchers as completed, or (b) to someone who could not handle the problem and forwarded the folder to someone else. In the logit model, the independent variables measure the effects of a change in that variable on the probability that a folder

FIGURE 2   Hospital Scenarios

Doctor

Quality: I was in the hospital's Burn Unit for five days, but I only saw my doctor three times. The nurses claimed he came in when I was asleep but I can't be sure he even came in to check on me.

Attitude: I am a Ph.D. candidate in biochemistry at a university so I know a considerable amount about medicine. However, during my stay at the hospital for a colostomy, the surgeons were condescending toward my comments and questions.

Nurse

Quality: When my 9-year-old daughter was in the hospital for an appendectomy, I asked the nurse for her pain medication. She said she would be right back with it but I waited an hour, with my daughter in pain, and I finally had to ask someone else for the medication.

Attitude: Recently, my sister was in the Cardiac Arrhythmia Monitoring Unit for a number of days. While I believe she received good treatment, I don't think her family was well treated. We all felt ignored by the nurses and it was impossible to get any information about my sister's condition from the nurse.

Lab

Quality: My hematology lab results from Pathology were lost and my Oncology Clinic appointment had to be rescheduled, causing me a great deal of inconvenience.

Attitude: I came to the Blood Donor Center right at opening time so I wouldn't have to miss any work, but no one was there. When the staff person arrived twenty minutes later, I didn't get any explanation or apology.

Administration

Quality: I do not want to pay my bill for diagnostic x-rays because the doctors in orthopedic surgery have been unable to diagnose my problem or alleviate the pain.

Attitude: I have moved to Phoenix and when I called long distance to have my medical records sent to my new doctor, I was put on hold for 12 minutes, cut off three times, and told I "would just have to wait."

TABLE 1   Completion Rates for Professional Groups

Professional Group	N	Overall Completion (percent)	From First Link Completion Rate (percent)
Doctor	80	19	75
Nurse	72	36	68
Ancillary Personnel	48	35	65
Administration	72	39	65
Overall	272	32	67

was returned as completed by the next node. For example, a large positive coefficient for the manager variable would indicate that being a manager increased the probability of the folder being returned as completed. (For a more technical discussion of logit analysis, see Aldrich and Nelson 1984.) Independent variables are described in Figure 3.

Data were pooled to include the first respondent passing to the second node, the second node passing to the third node, etc. In some instances, several individuals passed to the same person. This person would be considered the respondent passing to the next node and would appear a number of times as a respondent. To eliminate duplication of respondents, only one occurrence of a respondent passing to the next node is included in this and all subsequent tables. Physical distance

from the respondent to the person who next received the questionnaire (hospital employees were dispersed among several buildings) is added to the equation as a control variable, as distance has been shown to affect the likelihood of interaction between individuals (Barnlund and Harland 1963; Marsden and Campbell 1984).

Results of estimating the logit equations are shown in Table 2. Pooling all respondents who forwarded the questionnaire to the next node indicates that being a manager, having ties to other employees (work, social, or advice), and passing to someone within one's profession did have the expected effects of leading to completion, i.e., the next node returned the questionnaire as completed. Contrary to expectations, being a patient concern person and physical distance were very weak in statistical significance in predicting who would pass a ques-

FIGURE 3   Measurement of Independent Variables

Variable	Operationalization	Data Source
Manager	1 = Managerial job category or	Hospital records
	0 = Non-managerial job category	
Patient Concern Person	1 = Respondent had been assigned the role of "Patient Concern Person" for their department or	Hospital records
	0 = Not Patient Concern Person.	
Tie	Check all the categories that describe your relationship [to the person who will receive the folder]:	Questionnaire
	work tie ___ I used to work with this person.	
	___ I am currently working with this person.	
	advice tie ___ I go to this person for work-related technical advice.	
	social tie ___ I have social (nonwork-related) conversations with this person.	
	___ I see this person socially outside of work.	
	1 = Either a work, social, or advice tie to next link	
	or	
	0 = No tie to next link in chain	
Distance	How close is this person to your work area?	Questionnaire
	1 = We are in the same work area. (Near)	
	2 = We are on the same floor but not the same work area.	
	3 = The person is on a different floor of the same building.	
	4 = The person is in a different building. (Far)	
Same Profession	1 = The respondent and the person to whom they passed the folder were in the same profession (i.e., both doctors, both nurses, both ancillary personnel, or both administrators) or	Questionnaire verified using hospital records
	0 = Next node is not in the same profession as the respondent.	

TABLE 2   Logit Regression Models for Completion of the Patient Complaint by the Next Node

Variable[a]	Coeff.	T-value	Coeff.	T-value	Next Node in Same Profession		Next Node in Different Profession	
					Coeff.	T-value	Coeff.	T-value
Constant	−1.04	1.05	−1.67	2.18**	−3.01	4.18**	−2.16	3.21**
Manager	0.89	1.95**	0.79	1.85*	1.74	2.54**	−0.06	0.10
Patient Concern Person	−0.07	0.12	—	—	—	—	—	—
Tie	0.87	1.80*	0.93	1.95**	0.26	0.40	1.51	2.16**
Distance	−0.18	0.99	—	—	—	—	—	—
Same Profession	−0.66	1.55	−0.59	1.42	—	—	—	—
χ^2	11.72**		10.73**		8.66**		5.59**	
DF	5		3		2		2	
N	171		171		102		69	

[a]Dependent variables: Completed on next node: 0 = not complete, 1 = complete; see Figure 3 for measurement of independent variables.
*p < .10
**p < .05

tionnaire to someone who could complete it. The equation was reestimated with either one or both of these variables deleted, and the drop in the chi-square measure of fit of the model was nonsignificant with either or both variables removed. Accordingly, these variables were dropped from the equation. As shown in Table 2, results of the revised equation are substantially the same.

To determine what the differences in the dynamics of information flow might be when folders are passed within and across professions, the logistic regression was rerun separately for those forwarded to someone within their profession and those who forwarded across professions. As indicated in Table 2, results are somewhat contrary to expectations. Managers, assumed to be facilitators under all conditions, appear to be more effective at forwarding complaints *within* their profession, but *not across* professions. Further, having ties to others, also assumed to facilitate completion, appears to lead to completion across professions but not within professions.

These results imply that professional boundaries had the expected effect of making complaint resolution difficult across boundaries. That is, managers had the local knowledge necessary to successfully forward complaints within professions. However, boundary spanning is more effectively done by having some preexisting tie to a complaint resolver as compared to simply being a manager. Thus, these preexisting ties among individuals are activated to communicate negative information

across boundaries and serve to knit together the diverse professional groupings in the hospital.

RESOLUTION OF COMPLAINTS

Hypothesis 4 concerned the willingness of employees to take action in response to patient complaints rather than forwarding to someone else. As discussed, those who thought that they could resolve a complaint answered questions regarding what action they advocated and mailed the folder back to the researchers. Action was defined both in terms of complaint handling ("What response (if any) would you give to the patient in this situation?" and in terms of complaint management ("What action would you take (if any) within this hospital to prevent this concern from being expressed in the future?"). Figure 4 contains the coding scheme for categorizing the open-ended responses into the categories of advocating taking action or not taking action in response to complaints. The Cohen's kappa interrater reliability of the content coding for distinguishing between the two categories was .84 for the first question and .92 for the second question.

As shown in Table 3, of those recommending action, managers and patient concern personnel were more likely than individuals who were not managers or patient concern people to advocate action be taken in the hospital to prevent reoccurrence of the problem. Interestingly, these individuals did not differ substantially from others

FIGURE 4   Coding Categories for Responses to Open-Ended Question about Resolution of Complaint

Coding categories for response to: What response (if any) would you *give the patient* in this situation?

Take Action:

Ask for additional information.

Explain the medical procedure to the patient.

Offer an apology/excuse why this happened, or reassure the patient that their concern is valid.

No Direct Action Necessary:

The hospital does not need to take action because the procedure was necessary or the complaint was unfounded.

Coding categories for response to: What action would you *take within this hospital* to prevent this concern from being expressed in the future?

Take Action:

Determine what specific employee(s) is responsible and discuss the problem with him/her/them.

Inform the relevant personnel about the problem and inform or remind them of the solution.

No Direct Action Necessary:

Inform the relevant personnel about the problem's occurrence.

No response required (e.g., the problem arises frequently and nothing can be done about it).

in terms of recommending action to aid the patient. This result suggests an unanticipated deviation from the model of complaint handling and management used. Managers and patient concern personnel acted as *limited* complaint *managers* by recommending action for the hospital but were no more likely than others to recommend followup with the patient.

EFFECTS OF TYPE OF COMPLAINT ON RESOLUTION

It is possible that type of complaint could affect differences in the handling and managing of complaints in the hospital. As anticipated in Hypothesis 5, hospital personnel did perceive differences in types of complaints, rating quality of care complaints as more important than attitude complaints. Sixty-eight percent of respondents receiving a quality of care complaint scenario rated its importance a 5 (on a five-point scale varying from "not at all important" to "very important") while only 25 percent of respondents receiving an attitude of personnel complaint scenario rated its importance a 5 ($\chi^2 = 8.79$, p < .032). As expressed in Hypothesis 6, quality of care complaint scenarios also were completed more quickly than attitude. Fifty percent of the quality complaints were completed on the first or second link while only 21 percent of attitude complaints were completed this quickly ($\chi^2 = 10.25$, p < .068).

These results lead to the question of whether attitude complaints were being forwarded up the hierarchy to managers more often than quality complaints. Perhaps attitude complaints, being more difficult for peers to handle, prompted employees to forward the complaint through several links until it reached the appropriate manager. There is some support for this conjecture in the two upper panels of Table 4 which indicates that managers, but not patient concern personnel, were more likely to resolve attitude rather than quality complaints. Furthermore, as shown in the bottom two panels of Table 4, attitude complaints generated more recommendations for hospital actions but not patient actions.

In summary, being a manager and having a personal tie to someone facilitated the passing of problems to someone who could handle the problem. However, the results varied by whether the problem was being passed within a profession or across professions. Managers were effective at passing problems to completion within professions, but having a personal tie, rather than being a manager or patient concern person, was important when passing problems to completion across professional boundaries.

Once the problem was received by a problem solver, managers and patient concern personnel were limited complaint managers who were more likely than others to recommend action be taken in the hospital,

TABLE 3   Recommending Action Be Taken by Managers, Patient Concern Personnel, and Others to Resolve Complaint and to Benefit the Patient or the Hospital

	Manager		Patient Concern Person	
	Yes	No	Yes	No
Patient Action				
N	12	14	7	19
Take Action	50%	50%	43%	53%
No Direct Action	50	50	57	47
	$\chi^2 = 0.00$		$\chi^2 = 0.195$	
Hospital Action				
N	13	12	7	15
Take Action	69%	33%	86%	39%
No Direct Action	31	67	14	61
	$\chi^2 = 3.22^*$		$\chi^2 = 4.43^{**}$	

*$p < .10$
**$p < .05$

but who were no more likely than others to recommend followup with the patient. This result varied by the type of complaint. Managers handled more attitude than quality complaints, and attitude complaints generated more recommendations for hospital action than quality complaints.

Results suggest that managers were handling complaints received after several passes up the chain of command. These complaints were likely to be concerned with attitude of hospital personnel. Furthermore, these managers responded internally to hospital personnel but did not recommend followup with patients.

DISCUSSION

One proposed solution to the problem of managing service organizations is to emphasize the role of the customer contact employee. For example, some researchers have suggested that customer contact employees should participate more in decision making and provide more informational input about the service to the organization (Bowen and Schneider 1988). However, there is more to the management of service organizations than effective handling of the initial contact. Ultimately, this information needs to be transmitted to those who evaluate and alter policy and procedures. This study provides empirical results concerning where this service information goes after it has been initially received by

the employee. The results provide support for the thesis that the role of the complaint handler and manager in providing the service is at least as important as the role of the customer contact employee.

A great deal of this informational flow can be characterized as boundary spanning between the customer and the organization, as well as among units and professions within the organization. Aldrich and Herker (1977) have suggested that organizational units have a tendency to move to an internal state of compatibility with each other, with an attendant isolation from external influence. Thus, Aldrich and Herker argued the organization needs boundary spanning personnel to guarantee that the organization does not seal itself off from the environment and lose touch with its customers. This is an accepted part of the wisdom of how to keep organizations adaptable and innovative (Kanter 1988), but the focus of efforts to maintain organizational responsiveness has been on keeping technical information flowing from the outside. In the hospital studied, for example, the latest technology of health care is rapidly adopted. However, customer input as part of the adaptive system is often neglected.

A difficulty with this emphasis on maintaining the technical information network is that such technical information networks become relied upon to transmit information across the organization. This becomes a

TABLE 4   Category of Personnel Resolving Complaints and Type of Action Recommended by Type of Complaint

	Type of Complaint	
	Quality	Attitude
Manager		
N	17	10
Take Action	35%	70%
No Direct Action	65	30
	$\chi^2 = 3.04^*$	
Patient Concern Person		
N	17	10
Take Action	18%	40%
No Direct Action	82	60
	$\chi^2 = 1.64$	
Patient Action		
N	17	9
Take Action	53%	44%
No Direct Action	47	56
	$\chi^2 = 0.17$	
Hospital Action		
N	17	8
Take Action	41%	75%
No Direct Action	59	25
	$\chi^2 = 2.49$	

$^*p < .10$
$^{**}p < .05$

problem because technical information networks tend to become fragmented, with barriers to interaction around common but nontechnical administrative problems developing among professionals with specialized expertise. This has been shown to be true in this study, with individuals, even managers who had been anticipated to be effective boundary spanners, being more likely to pass complaints to completion when passing to others in their same profession.

In terms of the ultimate destination of complaints in the information processing model of complaint management, managerial personnel were found to be complaint *managers* rather than *handlers,* in that they were likely to recommend actions such as policy changes for the hospital. Interestingly, managers were not likely to recommend followup action for the patient.

Furthermore, there was a division of labor between complaint handlers and managers based on the type of complaint. Ideally, those resolving complaints would recommend policy changes to prevent reoccurrence of the problem and make sure that followup with the customer takes place. However, resolution of complaints in this study depended on type of complaint, with quality of care complaints resolved by nonmanagers rather quickly by responding to the patient, but without a recommendation for action in the hospital. Attitude of personnel complaints presented a more difficult problem that required some passing across the organization until they were received by a manager. The manager then proceeded to recommend hospital action but not followup with the patient.

These results, though tentative given that only one organization was studied, have a variety of implications for managing service encounters in a way that will enhance consumer satisfaction. First, barriers to interaction across professional groupings need to be overcome.

The cultivation of personal ties, which facilitated interaction in this study, should be encouraged. It may be effective to identify those who have a number of contacts across groups and formally designate them as complaint handlers. Further research is needed to determine the characteristics of those who are likely to have contacts that cut across professional groupings, and who can overcome barriers that are often characterized by large disparities in technical expertise, status, and power.

Second, managerial personnel are important links between the initial customer contact employee and feedback to the rest of the organization. In this study, managers were not particularly effective at forwarding problems across professional boundaries. Attempts to improve service to consumers need to focus on procedures for managerial personnel to follow when receiving service information as well as on the procedures for initial customer contact personnel.

Third, as part of service training, managers should be warned about the tendency to forget feedback to the customer. Here, this tendency became particularly acute for complaints that were passed up the chain of command, usually problems involving the attitudes of personnel.

As is true of exploratory studies, results and conclusions are tentative. However, this study has demonstrated the value of considering how information about consumer complaints flows through an organization. Certainly, research is needed to determine if the results found here hold with other types of service organizations. Innovative approaches, such as the network analysis used, are needed to address this complex problem which has implications for both organizational behavior and consumer affairs professionals and researchers.

REFERENCES

Adams, J. Stacy (1976), "The Structure and Dynamics of Behavior in Organizational Boundary Roles," in *The Handbook of Industrial and Organizational Psychology,* Marvin D. Dunnette (ed.), Chicago: Rand McNally.

Albaum, Gerald (1964), "Horizontal Information Flow: An Exploratory Study," *Academy of Management Journal,* 7(March): 21–33.

Aldrich, Howard E. and Diane Herker (1977), "Boundary Spanning Roles and Organizational Structure," *Academy of Management Review,* 2: 217–230.

Aldrich, John H. and Forrest D. Nelson (1984), "Linear Probability, Logit, and Probit Models," Sage University Paper Series on Quantitative Applications in the Social Sciences 07-045, Beverly Hills, CA and London: Sage Publications.

Andreasen, Alan R. (1988), "Consumer Complaints and Redress: What We Know and What We Don't Know," in *The Frontier of Research in the Consumer Interest,* E. Scott Maynes *et al.* (eds.), Columbia, MO: American Council on Consumer Interests: 675–722.

Barnlund, Dean C. and Carroll Harland (1963), "Propinquity and Prestige as Determinants of Communication Networks," *Sociometry,* 26: 467–479.

Bateson, John E. G. (1979), "Why We Need Service Marketing," in *Conceptual and Theoretical Developments in Marketing,* O. C. Ferrell, S. W. Brown, and C. W. Lamb, Jr. (eds.), Chicago: American Marketing Association: 131–146.

Bernard, H. Russell and Peter D. Killworth (1978), "A Review of the Small World Literature," *Connections,* 2: 15–24.

Bowen, David E. and Benjamin Schneider (1988), "Services Marketing and Management: Implications for Organizational Behavior," in *Research in Organizational Behavior,* 10, Barry M. Staw and L. L. Cummings (eds.): 43–80.

Brass, Daniel J. (1984), "Being in the Right Place: A Structural Analysis of Individual Influence in an Organization," *Administrative Science Quarterly,* 29: 518–539.

Bryant, W. Keith (1988), "Consumer Complaints and Redress: Some Directions for Future Research," in *The Frontier of Research in the Consumer Interest,* E. Scott Maynes *et al.* (eds.), Columbia, MO: American Council on Consumer Interests: 723–730.

Carey, Raymond G. and Emil J. Posavac (1982), "Using Patient Information to Identify Areas for Service Improvement," *Health Care Management Review* (Spring): 43–48.

Culnan, Mary J. (1988), "Mail Processing in the U.S. Senate Offices: An Organizational Perspective on Customer Feedback," Working Paper No. 88-15, School of Business Administration, Georgetown University, Washington, D.C.

Daft, Richard L. and Robert H. Lengel (1984), "Information Richness: A New Approach to Managerial Behavior and Organization Design," *Research in Organizational Behavior,* 6: 191–233.

Daft, Richard L. and Robert H. Lengel (1986), "Organizational Information Requirements, Media Richness and Structural Design," *Management Science,* 32: 554–571.

Daft, Richard L. and Karl E. Wieck (1984), "Toward a Model of Organizations as Interpretation Systems," *Academy of Management Review,* 9: 284–295.

Dalton, Melville (1959), *Men Who Manage,* New York: Wiley and Sons.

Davis, Kenneth (1953), "A Method of Studying Communication Patterns in Organizations," *Personnel Psychology,* 6: 301–312.

Drumwright, Minette E. (1985), "Processing Information Regarding Service Industries," in *Services Marketing in a Changing Environment,* Thomas M. Bloch, Gregory D. Upah, and Valarie A. Zeithaml (eds.), Chicago: American Marketing Association: 125–129.

Fornell, Claes and Robert A. Westbrook (1979), "The Relationship between Consumer Complaint Magnitude and Organizational Status of Complaint Processing in Large Corporations," in *New Dimensions of Consumer Satisfaction and Complaining Behavior*, Ralph L. Day and H. Keith Hunt (eds.), Bloomington, IN: Bureau of Business Research: 95–98.

Fornell , Claes and Robert A. Westbrook (1984), "The Vicious Circle of Consumer Complaints," *Journal of Marketing*, 48(2, Summer): 68–78.

Galbraith, Jay R. (1973), "Organizational Design: An Information Processing View," *Interfaces*, 4: 28–36.

Galbraith, Jay R. (1977), *Organization Design*, Reading MA: Addison-Wesley.

Gilley, Mary C. (1987), "Postcomplaint Processes: From Organizational Response to Repurchase Behavior," *The Journal of Consumer Affairs*, 21(2, Winter): 293–313.

Hedberg, Bo (1981), "How Organizations Learn and Unlearn," in *Handbook of Organizational Design*, Volume 1, Paul C. Nystrom and William H. Starbuck (eds.), Cambridge: Oxford University Press: 3–27.

Homans, George C. (1950), *The Human Group*, New York: Harcourt, Brace and Company.

Hutt, Michael D., Peter H. Reingen, and John R. Ronchetto, Jr. (1988), "Tracing Emergent Processes in Marketing Strategy Formation," *Journal of Marketing*, 52(1, January): 4–19.

Kanter, Rosabeth Moss (1988), "When a Thousand Flowers Bloom: Structural, Collective, and Social Conditions for Innovation in Organizations," *Research in Organizational Behavior*, 10: 169–211.

Katz, Daniel and Robert L. Kahn (1966), *The Social Psychology of Organizations*, New York: Wiley and Sons.

Landon, E. Laird (1979), "Responding to Consumer Complaints: Organizational Considerations," in *New Dimensions of Consumer Satisfaction and Complaining Behavior*, Ralph L. Day and H. Keith Hunt (eds.), Bloomington, IN: Bureau of Business Research: 91–94.

Lewis, Robert C. (1983), "Consumers Complain—What Happens When Business Responds?" in *International Fare in Consumer Satisfaction and Complaining*, Ralph L. Day and H. Keith Hunt (eds.), Bloomington, IN: Bureau of Business Research: 88–94.

Levy, Danna and Carol Surprenant (1982), "A Comparison of Responses to Dissatisfaction with Products and Services," in *Conceptual and Empirical Contributions to Consumer Satisfaction and Complaining Behavior*, Ralph L. Day and H. Keith Hunt (eds.), Bloomington, IN: Bureau of Business Research: 43–49.

Likert, Rensis (1961), *New Patterns of Management*, New York: McGraw-Hill.

Lincoln, James R. and John Miller (1979), "Work and Friendship Ties in Organizations: A Comparative Analysis of Relational Networks," *Administrative Science Quarterly*, 24: 181–199.

Lundberg, C. C. (1975), "Patterns of Acquaintanceship in Society and Complex Organizations," *Pacific Sociological Review*, 18(April): 206–222.

March, James G. and Herbert A. Simon (1958), *Organizations*, New York: Wiley and Sons.

Marsden, Peter V. and Karen E. Campbell (1984), "Measuring Tie Strength," *Social Forces*, 63: 482–501.

Mintzberg, Henry (1973), *The Nature of Managerial Work*, New York: Harper and Row.

Nadler, David and Michael Tushman (1988), *Strategic Organization Design: Concepts, Tools and Processes*, Glenview, IL: Scott, Foresman and Company.

Nickels, William G. and Noel B. Zabriskie (1973), "Corporate Responsiveness and the Marketing Correspondence Function," *MSU Business Topics* (Summer): 53–58.

Reingen, Peter H., Brian L. Foster, Jacqueline Johnson Brown, and Stephen B. Seidman (1984), "Brand Congruence in Interpersonal Relations: A Social Network Analysis," *Journal of Consumer Research*, 11(3, December): 771–783.

Sayles, Leonard (1989), *Leadership: Managing in Real Organizations*, 2nd edition, New York: McGraw-Hill.

Simon, Herbert A. (1947), *Administrative Behavior*, New York: MacMillan.

Smart, Denise T. and Charles L. Martin (1989), "Consumer Correspondence: An Exploratory Investigation of Consistency between Business Policy and Practice," *The Journal of Consumer Affairs*, 23 (2, Winter): 364–382.

Solomon, Michael R., Carol Surprenant, John A. Czepiel, and Evelyn G. Gutman (1985), "A Role Theory Perspective on Dyadic Interactions: The Service Encounter," *Journal of Marketing*, 49(Winter): 99–111.

Thompson, James (1967), *Organizations in Action*, New York: McGraw-Hill.

Travers, J. and Stanley Milgram (1969), "An Experimental Study of the Small World Problem," *Sociometry*, 32: 425–443.

Tushman, Michael (1979), "Impacts of Perceived Environmental Variability on Patterns of Work Related Communications," *Academy of Management Journal*, 22: 482–500.

Uhlmann, Richard F., Thomas S. Inui, and William B. Carter (1984), "Patient Requests and Expectations: Definitions and Clinical Applications," *Medical Care*, 22(July): 681–685.

Walton, Richard E. and John M. Dutton (1969), "The Management of Interdepartmental Conflict: A Model and Review," *Administrative Science Quarterly*, 14: 73–84.

Weisman, Carol S. and Constance A. Nathanson (1985), "Professional Satisfaction and Client Outcomes: A Comparative Organizational Analysis," *Medical Care*, 23(October): 1179–1192.

Zeithaml, Valarie A. (1981), "How Consumer Evaluation Processes Differ between Goods and Services," in *Marketing of Services*, J. Donnelly and W. George (eds.), Chicago: American Marketing Association: 186–190.

Zeithaml, Valarie A., Leonard L. Berry, and A. Parasuraman (1988), "Communication and Control Processes in the Delivery of Service Quality," *Journal of Marketing*, 52(April): 35–48.

ANTECEDENTS TO CUSTOMER EXPECTATIONS FOR SERVICE RECOVERY

Scott W. Kelley
University of Kentucky

Mark A. Davis
University of Kentucky

Selected antecedents of customers' service recovery expectations are considered in this study. A conceptual model is proposed in which customer perceptions of service quality, customer satisfaction, and customer organizational commitment function as antecedents to service recovery expectations. The proposed model was tested with covariance structure analysis. The results support the hypothesized relationships, suggesting that service quality and customer organizational commitment have direct effects on customer service recovery expectations and that customer satisfaction has an indirect effect on service recovery expectations.

The focus of many service organizations is the continual improvement of service delivery. However, even the most customer-oriented culture and the strongest quality program will not entirely eliminate mistakes during service delivery. Unfortunately, one negative service encounter can undermine an extraordinary record of superior service, lowering evaluations of service quality and causing customers to search for alternative service providers. Yet service organizations that are prepared to correct mistakes and handle customer concerns may be able to successfully differentiate themselves from competitors by implementing effective service recoveries.

Service recovery refers to the actions a service provider takes in response to service failure (Gronroos 1988). Although recoveries are precipitated by service failures, such episodes can have a positive influence on customer evaluations and behaviors and may actually strengthen the bond between the service customer and organization (Hart, Heskett, and Sasser 1990).

Although practitioners attest to the potency of service recovery efforts, a dearth of empirical research confines any theoretical discussion to anecdotal reports. The apparent significance of recovery efforts warrants more systematic investigation of the concept and related variables. Accordingly, the present study adopts an interdisciplinary approach to examine service recovery expectations.

This study proposes a theoretical model comprising three principal antecedents of service recovery expectations, including perceptions of service quality and customer satisfaction. The third antecedent is an adaptation from the organizational commitment literature. Specifically, the strength of the customer-organization relationship is measured in terms of customer organizational commitment. The commitment and retention of service customers are aspects of the service customer-organization relationship that have received limited attention from researchers (Bowen and Schneider

SOURCE: Scott W. Kelley and Mark A. Davis, "Antecedents to Customer Expectations for Service Recovery," *Journal of the Academy of Marketing Science,* vol. 22, no. 1 (Winter 1994): 52–61. Copyright © 1994 by Academy of Marketing Science.

1985), in spite of the cost and profitability advantages associated with retaining existing customers (Reichheld and Sasser 1990).

CONCEPTUAL BACKGROUND

SERVICE FAILURE AND RECOVERY

Service encounters give rise to different types of service miscues, including episodes of service unavailability, unreasonably slow service, and other core service failures (Bitner, Booms, and Tetreault 1990). In addition, service failures may vary considerably across the dimensions of timing, severity, and frequency. A service failure can occur any time during the customer's relationship with a service organization—from the first encounter to the most recent encounter. A failure occurring early in the customer's relationship with the service organization will weigh more heavily on the customer's overall evaluation of the organization because the customer has fewer successful service experiences to counterbalance the failure (Boulding et al. 1993). Further, some mistakes are more serious than others—serving the wrong soft drink is trivial in comparison to administering the wrong medication. Finally, because of the heterogeneity inherent in services, different customers patronizing the same service organization will experience varied instances of service failure and recovery.

SERVICE DELIVERY AND CUSTOMER EXPECTATIONS

Recent theoretical and empirical studies discriminate between two key standards of service delivery expectations that have been referred to as *will expectations* and *should expectations* (Boulding et al. 1993). Other researchers have used different terminology to make similar distinctions between types of expectations. For example, will and should expectations have been referred to as adequate expectations and desired expectations (Parasuraman, Berry, and Zeithaml 1991), as well as predicted service expectations and desired service expectations (Zeithaml, Berry, and Parasuraman 1993). Zeithaml, Berry, and Parasuraman (1993) also have proposed a third type of expectations, referred to as *adequate service expectations,* which they define as "the level of service the customer will accept" (p. 6).

Will expectations correspond with what customers believe will happen during subsequent contacts with the service delivery system. In contrast, should expectations represent a normative standard that corresponds roughly to "what ought to happen" in subsequent encounters (Boulding et al. 1993).

According to Zeithaml, Berry, and Parasuraman (1993), customer should (or desired service) expectations and will (or predicted service) expectations are based on past experience, word-of-mouth communications, and explicit and implicit service promises made by the organization. Additionally, should (or desired) expectations are also based on enduring service intensifiers and personal needs.

Previous research also suggests that customer perceptions of service quality are multidimensional and include perceptions relating to reliability, responsiveness, tangibles, assurance, and empathy (Parasuraman, Berry, and Zeithaml 1991; Parasuraman, Zeithaml, and Berry 1988), with reliability generally being considered the most important dimension of overall service quality (Boulding et al. 1993). In addition, Boulding et al. (1993) contend that customer will and should expectations are formed in terms of these five dimensions.

Service recovery and the associated expectations are not considered in the dimensions of service quality generally noted by services researchers (e.g., Parasuraman, Berry, and Zeithaml 1991; Parasuraman, Zeithaml, and Berry 1988)—nor should they be. They are separate and distinct from the dimensions of service quality previously noted in the literature. Service recovery involves activities that are performed as a result of customer perceptions of initial service delivery behaviors falling below the customer's zone of tolerance (see Zeithaml, Berry, and Parasuraman 1993).

The present study considers customer predictive expectations for service recovery. These expectations consist of customer predictions of how effectively the service provider will resolve service failures when they arise. As with predictive expectations for the dimensions of service quality (Zeithaml, Berry, and Parasuraman 1993), service recovery expectations are grounded in the customer's prior service experiences (particularly those involving previous recovery efforts), the experiences of others through word-of-mouth communications, and relevant explicit and implicit service promises made by the organization.

The present study focuses on predictive service recovery expectations because prior research demonstrates that will expectations are subject to updating after each service encounter (Boulding et al. 1993). Consequently, service failure experiences should have an impact on the subsequent predictive expectations associated with the corresponding service recovery. In addition, is has been suggested that when problems arise with initial service, will expectations are raised (Parasuraman, Berry, and Zeithaml 1991), and that should expectations change only when they have been exceeded during service delivery (Boulding et al. 1993).

CONCEPTUAL MODEL

SERVICE QUALITY AND RECOVERY EXPECTATIONS

A script theoretic perspective suggests that information related to service delivery is bundled and organized around knowledge structures (e.g., Leigh and McGraw 1989). As a consequence, positive service encounters and effective recoveries (if miscues occurred) should give rise to optimistic scripts or predictive expectations for service delivery, whereas negative experiences and poor recoveries should produce pessimistic scripts or predictive expectations for service delivery (Zeithaml, Berry, and Parasuraman 1993). In turn, when situations (e.g., service failures) activate these knowledge structures, the activated script provides a means of predicting what will happen next. Given that perceptions of service quality provide the basis for the service delivery script, it follows that these perceptions will have a direct influence on the expectations associated with service recovery. Given prior research on predictive expectations and script theory, the following hypothesis is proposed.

> H1: Higher levels of perceived service quality lead to higher expectations for service recovery efforts.

SERVICE QUALITY AND CUSTOMER SATISFACTION

The nature of the perceived service quality-customer satisfaction relationship has been considered previously (e.g., Bitner 1990; Bolton and Drew 1991a, 1991b; Cronin and Taylor 1992), with some discrepancy as to the nature of the relationship. Perceived service quality has consistently been conceptualized as being cumulative in nature (e.g., Cronin and Taylor 1992; Parasuraman, Zeithaml, and Berry 1988). However, conceptualizations of customer satisfaction have varied. In some instances, customer satisfaction has been viewed as transaction-specific in nature and an antecedent of perceived service quality (e.g., Bitner 1990; Bolton and Drew 1991a, 1991b), whereas in other instances it has been viewed as a cumulative evaluation and a consequence of perceived service quality (e.g., Cronin and Taylor 1992). In the present study, both perceived service quality and customer satisfaction are viewed as being cumulative in nature in a fashion consistent with Cronin and Taylor (1992). Based on this research, the following hypothesis is proposed.

> H2: Higher levels of perceived service quality lead to higher levels of customer satisfaction.

CUSTOMER ORGANIZATIONAL COMMITMENT

Organizational commitment reflects an individual's identification with and involvement in an organization (Steers 1977). A committed individual believes in and accepts the goals and values of the organization, expresses genuine interest in its welfare, expends considerable effort on its behalf, and desires to remain a member. Although previous research has focused largely on the commitment of employees, the construct's domain can be extended to the relationship between service provider and customer. The employee commitment-customer commitment analogy is especially relevant when one considers that service customers are often active participants in the service delivery process (Kelley, Donnelly, and Skinner 1990; Mills 1986). From this perspective, just as employees differ in their efforts expended on behalf of the firm, significant variability in customer involvement and willingness to participate in service delivery also exists (Bateson 1985).

SERVICE QUALITY AND CUSTOMER ORGANIZATIONAL COMMITMENT

Several studies in marketing literature have used equity theory as a means of investigating the relationships between customers and organizations or their representatives (e.g., Goodwin and Ross 1992; Huppertz, Arenson, and Evans 1978; Oliver and Swan 1989). Equity theory suggests that exchange relationships are based on an explicit consideration of the outcomes of both parties to an exchange, rather than individual outcomes alone (Oliver and Swan 1989). An equitable relationship is one in which the benefit/cost ratios of each of the exchange partners are equal (West and Wicklund 1980).

Based on equity theory, one would expect that customers receiving superior levels of perceived service quality (i.e., customer benefits) will demonstrate higher levels of commitment to the organization (i.e., organization benefits) in a variety of forms, such as repeat purchases, the exertion of greater effort on behalf of the organization during service delivery, and a greater willingness to become an advocate for the organization. As a result, customers are able to maintain equitable relationships with service organizations. As additional support for this hypothesis, Fornell (1992) and Steenkamp (1989) both suggested that there is a relationship between quality and customer retention, and more recently Boulding et al. (1993) found that favorable perceptions of service quality increased the likelihood of customers' engaging in "behaviors beneficial to the strategic health of the firm" (p. 24).

> H3: Higher levels of perceived service quality lead to higher levels of customer organizational commitment.

CUSTOMER SATISFACTION AND ORGANIZATIONAL COMMITMENT

Conceptual arguments and research with comparable variables provide support for a link between customer satisfaction and customer commitment. For example, in a longitudinal study, LaBarbera and Mazursky (1983) found that consumers' levels of satisfaction were positively related to repeat purchase behavior. Similarly, Crosby and Stephens (1987) indicated that service organizations can increase customer retention through increased customer satisfaction. More recently, Fornell (1992) and Anderson and Sullivan (1993) have demonstrated an empirical relationship between customer satisfaction and customer loyalty. Although these studies do not address the construct of customer organizational commitment explicitly, repeat purchase behavior, customer retention, and customer loyalty can be construed as evidence of commitment. Further support for the satisfaction-commitment link comes from the organizational behavior literature that suggests that employee satisfaction is an important antecedent to organizational commitment (Locke and Latham 1990). Based on evidence from the organizational commitment literature and related research in marketing, the following hypothesis is proposed.

> H4: Higher levels of customer satisfaction lead to higher levels of customer organizational commitment.

CUSTOMER ORGANIZATIONAL COMMITMENT AND SERVICE RECOVERY EXPECTATIONS

As the relationship between a service customer and an organization evolves, role expectations are developed that define the behaviors deemed appropriate in the service customer-organization exchange (Berger, Conner, and Fisek 1974; Berger et al. 1977). These expectations are pertinent to the link between customer organizational commitment and service recovery expectations.

Equity theory research suggests that once an individual becomes committed to an evaluation concerning the equity of an exchange relationship, he or she expects that relationship to be maintained (Lerner and

Simmons 1966; Walster and Prestholdt 1966). Specifically, one can argue that committed customers are likely to expect a favorable response when a service miscue occurs. Thus, although customer commitment encompasses positive outcomes for the service organization (e.g., identification with the organization or retention), it is accompanied by stringent service recovery expectations. In short, committed customers will anticipate impressive responses to service failures as a means of maintaining the equity of the service customer-organization relationship.

> H5: Higher levels of customer organizational commitment lead to higher expectations for service recovery efforts.

PROPOSED MODEL

Collectively, the five hypotheses presented here comprise a model in which perceived service quality has a direct effect on customer satisfaction, customer organizational commitment, and service recovery expectations. In turn, customer satisfaction is posited to bring about higher levels of customer organizational commitment, which also lead to more favorable service recovery expectations. The hypothesized model is presented in Figure 1.

METHOD

SAMPLE

The model was tested with data collected from members of a health club located in a midsized community in the Southeast. Based on Lovelock's (1983) classification schemes, the health club setting provides a service situation in which customers (1) receive services mainly involving tangible actions directed toward people, (2) have a membership relationship with the organization, and (3) are actively participating in the service delivery process.

The health club participating in this study is an upscale full-service health club that is perceived as the market leader in the area. It offers a wide range of services and amenities, including aerobics, aquatics, personal fitness training, body fat analysis, basketball, racquetball, volleyball, an indoor track, exercise equipment (e.g., weight machines, stationary bicycles, rowing machines, and stair climbers), a sauna and steam room, whirlpool, and a children's playroom.

For 12 consecutive days (Monday through the following Friday), self-administered questionnaires were distributed to members entering or departing the health club. To enhance participation, random drawings for club gift certificates were held daily. A total of 296 indi-

FIGURE 1   Structural Model

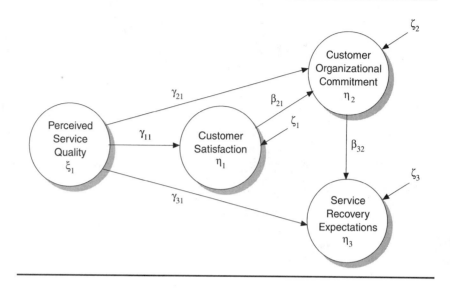

viduals completed the questionnaire. The typical respondent was male (65%) with an average age of 36.7 years (ages ranged from 17 to 83 years). Other selected demographics indicate that the typical respondent had been a member of the health club for approximately three years and worked out an average of three days per week. In addition, the typical visit of the responding health club member lasted one hour and 50 minutes. Approximately one half of the members who regularly used the health club facilities were included in the sample and, based on conversations with the management of the health club, the sample was representative of the core group of regular users.

SCALE DEVELOPMENT

Scale construction for the customer satisfaction and service quality measures began with the generation of item pools for each construct based on constitutive definitions, relevant literature, and the experiences of the researchers as health club members. After the pools of items were generated, the scales were pretested on a sample of 95 undergraduate students with previous health club experience.

Following the pretest, item selection was conducted based on item-to-total correlations. All items with low item-to-total correlations (<.25) were deleted. In addition, three managers from the participating health club inspected the questionnaire for problems with the wording of individual items and their labels in an effort to assure the content validity of the scales.

SERVICE QUALITY The SERVQUAL instrument provided a "skeleton" for the service quality measure used in this study (Parasuraman, Berry, and Zeithaml 1991, 1993). Items included in the SERVQUAL instrument that were pertinent to the health club setting were used, along with other items related specifically to the health club industry. Only a battery of perceptual items was administered in this study. A matching battery of expectations items was not administered because of the measurement problems inherent in the use of difference scores for the assessment of service quality (Brown, Churchill, and Peter 1993; Carman 1990; Peter, Churchill, and Brown 1993). In addition, researchers have found that using only a battery of perception items provides superior measurement properties to the expectations versus perceptions methodology used in SERVQUAL (Brown, Churchill, and Peter 1993; Carman 1990; Cronin and Taylor 1992).

CUSTOMER SATISFACTION The measurement of service customer satisfaction has not been systematically investigated to the extent that service quality has; however, a limited number of studies in the services literature have assessed customer satisfaction. These studies have generally measured service customer satisfaction through single-item measures (e.g., Bitner 1990; Bolton and Drew 1991b; Cronin and Taylor 1992; Crosby and Stephens 1987).

One exception to the single-item measurement of service customer satisfaction is the work of Oliva, Oliver, and MacMillan (1992). They assessed customer satisfaction through an attribute-based, five-item, Likert-type scale. An approach to measuring service customer satisfaction similar to that of Oliva, Oliver, and MacMillan (1992) was taken in the present study. Customer satisfaction/dissatisfaction was treated as a latent construct based on service attributes and was assumed to be unidimensional ranging from *Very Dissatisfied* to *Very Satisfied*. Although many conceptualizations of customer satisfaction are based on the disconfirmation of expectations (e.g., Bolton and Drew 1991a, 1991b), the operationalization of customer satisfaction in the present study incorporated the disconfirmation of expectations in the satisfaction response (Oliva, Oliver, and MacMillan 1992).

CUSTOMER ORGANIZATIONAL COMMITMENT The organizational commitment scale was previously developed by Porter et al. (1974). This scale contained 15 items and followed a 7-point Likert-type format with anchors of *Strongly Agree* and *Strongly Disagree*. This scale was originally developed for the assessment of employee organizational commitment. As a result, minor modifications were necessary for some of the items to match the customer context.

SERVICE RECOVERY EXPECTATIONS Behavioral expectation scaling served as the basis for the service recovery expectations measure. This procedure was originally devised by Smith and Kendall (1963) as a format for employee performance appraisal scales. In an employee appraisal context, behavioral expectation scaling uses the critical incident technique (see Bitner, Booms, and Tetreault 1990) to develop behavioral anchors for job performance rating scales. In the present study, scaled examples derived from actual service encounter incidents served as behavioral anchors representing different levels of service recovery for eight distinct service failure scenarios. The task assigned to respondents was to use the behavioral anchors as a guide in selecting the most likely level of recovery performance.

First, a sample of 60 current and former health club members submitted written critical incidents depicting actual episodes of service failures and recoveries. Second, incidents in the initial pool were rewritten and clarified by the authors as necessary, and duplicate incidents were discarded. This step resulted in a total of eight incidents depicting various health club service failures. In addi-

tion, the authors generated alternative service recovery resolutions for each incident to ensure a full range of service recovery examples (excellent to poor) accompanied each incident.

Finally, a new group of 18 judges familiar with health clubs scaled the service recovery resolutions for each incident using a Likert-type scale ranging from *Excellent Resolution* (7) to *Poor Resolution* (1). Means and standard deviations were calculated for each response. Service recovery resolutions with wide variances in their ratings were discarded (standard deviation of 2.5 or more). Based on their computed mean values, the recovery examples were deployed as anchors on the scale accompanying the appropriate failure incident.

The service recovery expectations scale was pretested on a sample of 95 undergraduate students with previous health club experience. Based on the pretest, none of the recovery scale items were deleted from the final scale, as item-to-total correlations for all items exceeded .25. Finally, three managers from the participating health club inspected the scale for problems with the wording of individual items and their anchors in an effort to assure the content validity of the scale.

MEASUREMENT

The final measurement scales were purified based on item-to-total correlations as recommended by Nunnally (1978). Items with item-to-total correlations of less than .25 were deleted from the analysis. Sample items from each scale are included in the appendix.

It was not necessary to delete any of the items included in the customer satisfaction or service quality scales because all item-to-total correlations exceeded the .25 criterion. Customer satisfaction was measured through an 11-item Likert-type scale with anchors of *Very Dissatisfied* and *Very Satisfied*. The customer satisfaction scale had an alpha coefficient of .95. The service quality scale consisted of 30 items and followed a Likert-type format. Anchors of *One of the Worst (Poor)* and *One of the Best (Excellent)* were used. This scale had an alpha coefficient of .96. Finally, one item was deleted from the organizational commitment scale based on item-to-total correlations, resulting in a 14-item scale with an alpha coefficient of .86.

Eight scenarios were included in the service recovery expectations scale. Respondents were provided with a 7-point scale anchored by three potential responses to each of the eight service failures based on the procedures previously described. The eight-item recovery scale had an alpha coefficient of .78.

ANALYSIS AND RESULTS

LISREL 7 (Jöreskog and Sörbom 1989) was used to further assess the measurement properties of the scales and test the hypothesized relationships.

MEASUREMENT MODEL

Confirmatory factor analysis was used to assess the measurement properties of the scales. Each scale was randomly split into three subscales to provide multiple indicators for each latent variable. Previous consumer and marketing research has used a similar approach by splitting scales into halves (e.g., Bagozzi 1980; Joachimsthaler and Lastovicka 1984; Michaels, Day, and Joachimsthaler 1987). Each scale was split into thirds based on research suggesting that the number of indicators per factor should be at least three whenever feasible (Bagozzi and Yi 1988).

The overall fit of the measurement model was assessed through the fit indices provided by the LISREL 7 program. The values of the overall fit indices were χ^2 = 101.98 with 48 degrees of freedom, goodness of fit (GFI) = .946, adjusted goodness of fit (AGFI) = .912, and root mean square residual = .826. Together, these fit indices provide support for the measurement properties of the confirmatory model.

After considering the overall fit indices for the confirmatory model, individual parameter estimates were evaluated. The individual parameter estimates for all factor loadings (λ_{y11} through λ_{x31}) were statistically significant (see Table 1). The overall fit of the measurement model and the individual parameter estimates indicated that the structural model can be evaluated.

PROPOSED STRUCTURAL MODEL— OVERALL FIT

The overall fit indices provide support for the fit of the proposed structural model. The values of the fit indices were χ^2 = 102.02 with 49 degrees of freedom, GFI = .946, AGFI = .914, and root mean square residual = .825. The coefficient of determination for the structural equations was .583, indicating that more than 58 percent of the variation in the data was explained by the model.

ALTERNATIVE MODELS

Although the fit indices associated with the proposed model indicated that the data fit the model well, it is possible that some alternative models are equally consistent with the data (Breckler 1990). Two plausible alternative models were tested to further assess the appropriateness of the proposed model. In both instances, the overall fit indices of the alternative models indicated that the proposed model provided a better fit with the data, providing further support for the proposed model.

STRUCTURAL MODEL— PARAMETER ESTIMATES

To determine whether the findings were dependent on the subscale split used in the initial analysis, the stability of the parameter estimates was assessed by replicating the statistical analysis using three different scale splits. In all three instances, the direction, magnitude, and significance of all parameter estimates were virtually unchanged. The findings reported in Table 1 are based on the initial set of subscale indicators developed for this analysis.

The perceived service quality of health club members was found to be positively related to service recovery expectations as predicted in Hypothesis 1 (λ_{31} = .368, t = 4.888). This finding suggests that customers who feel that the service organization is delivering a superior level of service quality are likely to hold higher expectations for service recovery when service failures do arise.

Perceptions of service quality were positively related to customer satisfaction as predicted in Hypothesis 2 (γ_{11} .= .699, t = 14.785). This finding supports research conducted by Cronin and Taylor (1992), which indicated that service quality is an antecedent of customer satisfaction.

The path between perceived service quality and customer organizational commitment was statistically significant (γ_{21}.= .342, t = 4.708). This finding supports Hypothesis 3 and suggests that customers receiving higher levels of service quality are more committed to the service organization.

Hypothesis 4 hypothesized that levels of customer satisfaction are positively related to the level of organizational commitment experienced. Hypothesis 4 was supported (β_{21} = .375, t = 5.105), indicating that satisfied health club members were also more committed to the organization.

The final hypothesized relationship (Hypothesis 5) tested in the structural model involving customer organizational commitment and service recovery expectations was also supported (β_{32} = .352, t = 4.488). This finding suggests that as a service customer becomes more committed to a service organization, he or she also

TABLE 1   Parameter Estimates for the Structural Model—
Standardized Solution

Parameter	Standardized Estimate	t Value
β_{21}	.375	5.105
β_{32}	.352	4.488
γ_{11}	.699	14.785
γ_{21}	.342	4.708
γ_{31}	.368	4.888
λ_{y11}	3.470	—[a]
λ_{y21}	3.776	33.722
λ_{y31}	3.184	32.527
λ_{y42}	4.120	—[a]
λ_{y52}	4.287	16.465
λ_{y62}	2.785	12.452
λ_{y73}	1.911	—[a]
λ_{y83}	2.839	10.674
λ_{y93}	1.211	9.961
λ_{x11}	7.703	—[a]
λ_{x21}	7.652	41.001
λ_{x31}	7.696	41.796
φ_{11}	1.000	11.366
ψ_{11}	.511	10.071
ψ_{22}	.562	7.594
ψ_{33}	.583	5.482
$\theta_{\varepsilon11}$	1.663	8.639
$\theta_{\varepsilon22}$	1.324	6.950
$\theta_{\varepsilon33}$	1.154	7.849
$\theta_{\varepsilon44}$	9.368	9.062
$\theta_{\varepsilon55}$	2.866	3.887
$\theta_{\varepsilon66}$	8.467	10.737
$\theta_{\varepsilon77}$	4.918	10.190
$\theta_{\varepsilon88}$	2.717	5.071
$\theta_{\varepsilon99}$	1.382	9.255
$\theta_{\delta11}$	3.245	5.943
$\theta_{\delta22}$	6.073	8.724
$\theta_{\delta33}$	5.743	8.458
χ^2 (49 df)	102.02 ($p = .00$)	
Goodness of fit index	.946	
Adjusted goodness of fit index	.914	
Root mean square residual	.825	

[a]These parameter values were fixed for the purposes of scaling; t values were not computed.

holds higher expectations for recovery efforts when failures occur during service delivery.

MANAGERIAL CONTRIBUTIONS AND IMPLICATIONS

PREDICTIVE SERVICE RECOVERY EXPECTATIONS

Previous contributions to managerial thinking regarding service failures and recoveries have focused on the prevention of failures during the service delivery process and how to recover when failures do occur (e.g., Hart, Heskett, and Sasser 1990). The present study focuses on customer predictive expectations for service recovery and offers a methodology for capturing and scaling these expectations. Understanding what constitutes an effective recovery in the eyes of the customer is important inasmuch as the effective management of customer recovery expectations could have a positive influence on customer perceptions of service subsequent to a failure (Boulding et al. 1993). Further, service recoveries perceived favorably by customers potentially increase the level of customer loyalty more than high-quality original service (Hart, Heskett, and Sasser 1990). The results of the present study suggest that predictive service recovery expectations are directly influenced by two fundamentally different antecedents—customer perceptions of service quality and customer organizational commitment.

PERCEIVED SERVICE QUALITY

Many customers do not have previous failure-recovery experiences at a specific organization on which to directly base their predictive service recovery expectations. As a result, perceptions of service quality become an important antecedent of predictive service recovery expectations. Customers without previous failure-recovery experiences may infer that the firm's response to failures will be similar to performance levels associated with routine service delivery. In effect, customer predictions for service recovery are informed by the day-to-day actions of the firm. However, the firm providing effective service is not necessarily prepared to respond effectively to deviations from the routine service delivery process.

For example, one method often recommended for providing higher levels of perceived service quality is standardization. A standardized service delivery system may result in higher levels of perceived service quality. However, when failures occur in effective standardized service delivery systems, customers may anticipate superior service recoveries. For the manager offering a standardized service, this may be problematic, because in

many instances service recovery procedures are of a non-routine nature. The standardized methods implemented to enhance original service levels may make it difficult to meet customer predictive expectations for recovery, yielding ineffective service recoveries.

CUSTOMER ORGANIZATIONAL COMMITMENT

A second construct included in this study of particular relevance to managers was customer organizational commitment. As operationalized, commitment reflected respondents' expressions of their intentions to stay or leave, their willingness to help the organization, and their views regarding their relationship with the organization.

A BROADENED NOTION OF BRAND LOYALTY Although the customer organizational commitment construct has not been considered previously, the unique character of the commitment construct provides a broader perspective and a better understanding of service customer-organization relationships than was possible with related constructs in the extant literature. For instance, brand loyalty is decidedly more narrow in scope than customer organizational commitment as it was conceptualized in this study. Unlike organizational commitment, notions of brand loyalty do not connote active participation and involvement in service delivery, identification with organizational goals and values, or a sense of personal affiliation with the service organization.

Furthermore, brand loyalty is less relevant for many services than it is for products. Specifically, repeat purchases based on consumer evaluation may not occur as readily for services as they do for products. This is especially true of services that customers are highly involved with or committed to (Oliva, Oliver, and MacMillan 1992). For example, the health club customer is a member of the organization, which results in repeated use of the health club facilities. This membership relationship is common for a wide variety of services (Lovelock 1983), albeit sometimes on a less formal basis. From a managerial perspective, once a customer becomes a "member" of the service organization, the repeat purchases made by that customer may not be based on consumer evaluations alone. Instead, the sense of affiliation with the organization experienced by customers may also contribute to the repeated use of "membership"-type services.

ANTECEDENTS OF COMMITMENT The results of this study indicate that perceived service quality and customer satisfaction are directly related to customer organizational commitment. An extended interpretation of our findings also suggests that customer perceptions of service recoveries may serve as a means of updating customer organizational commitment. For instance, if predictive service recovery expectations are not met after a failure, service recovery efforts will be viewed unfavorably. This will result in lower levels of customer organizational commitment over time, with the eventual possibility of customers leaving the organization (Oliva, Oliver, and MacMillan 1992).

CONSEQUENCES OF COMMITMENT   Committed customers are also likely to hold elevated expectations for recovery. Apparently, these expectations are associated with customer efforts to sustain an equitable exchange relationship between customer and firm. Furthermore, although high service recovery expectations can increase the likelihood of inadequate recovery, recent applications of catastrophe theory suggest that high levels of commitment may also counteract the negative effects of falling below recovery expectations (Oliva, Oliver, and MacMillan 1992). Thus, although increased commitment can elevate service recovery expectations, paradoxically it may also avert the customer losses that accompany unmet recovery expectations.

CONCLUSION AND RESEARCH IMPLICATIONS

The present study provides an initial operationalization of service recovery expectations using a method based on behavior expectation scaling. Research is needed to refine and further develop the measurement method introduced here. In addition, alternative approaches to the assessment of service recovery expectations might be developed.

Future research might compare the service recovery expectations of different customer groups such as new customers, established customers, and former customers. Consideration of these different customer groups would make it possible to evaluate the impact of customer service recovery expectations on behaviors associated with customer defection and loyalty. Further, these issues should be investigated longitudinally by tracing customer expectations and behaviors over time. Service recovery research should also incorporate employee perspectives. For example, it would be interesting to compare and contrast expectations for service recovery from the perspective of customers, frontline service personnel, and service managers.

The present study considered customer organizational commitment in a service organization character-

ized by customer membership and high levels of customer participation in the service delivery process. Several service typologies have been developed that suggest that there are differences in the strategic marketing activities and consumer behavior associated with different types of services (e.g., Bowen 1990; Kelley, Donnelly, and Skinner 1990; Lovelock 1983). Future researchers should consider the relationships investigated in this study in other types of service organizations to assess the generalizability of our findings.

In sum, the domains of service recovery and customer organizational commitment afford researchers several avenues for additional study. Further investigation and development of these constructs will be a useful contribution toward understanding service encounters and the relationship between service customers and organizations.

———— ◆ ————

APPENDIX
SAMPLE SCALE ITEMS

SERVICE QUALITY

How would you rate the quality of your health club with regard to

☐ the personnel/instructors?

☐ the convenience of location?

☐ how well they understand your fitness needs?

CUSTOMER SATISFACTION

How would you rate your satisfaction or dissatisfaction with regard to

☐ the workout/fitness equipment available?

☐ the courtesy of employees?

☐ the attention provided by this health club?

CUSTOMER ORGANIZATIONAL COMMITMENT

I talk up this health club to my friends as a great health club.

I would accept almost any type of service from this health club and still come back.

I am proud to tell others that I am a member of this health club.

SERVICE RECOVERY EXPECTATIONS

You are overcharged for your annual membership fee at the health club. You call the club and notify them of the error.

☐ You receive a full refund within five days along with a personalized letter of apology.

☐ You receive a full refund within two weeks.

☐ You are asked to bring your bill to the club during regular business hours.

You regularly participate in the same aerobics class with the same instructor. Your regular instructor suddenly becomes ill and is unable to lead the class.

☐ Another equally qualified aerobics instructor substitutes for your instructor.

☐ Another less qualified employee substitutes for your instructor.

☐ Your class is canceled.

Upon arriving at the club for your daily swim, you discover that the pool is closed due to a chemical imbalance.

☐ Arrangements are made for pool use at another facility.

☐ After an apology for the inconvenience, a fitness counselor suggests some alternative activities while the pool is closed.

☐ A club employee states that the pool will be closed indefinitely, but does not know why.

ACKNOWLEDGMENT

This research was supported by the Kentucky Small Business Development Center, Janet Holloway, director.

REFERENCES

Anderson, Eugene W., and Mary W. Sullivan, 1993, "The Antecedents and Consequences of Customer Satisfaction for Firms." *Marketing Science* 12 (Spring): 125–143.

Bagozzi, Richard P., 1980, "Performance and Satisfaction in an Industrial Sales Force: An Examination of Their Antecedents and Simultaneity," *Journal of Marketing* 44 (Spring): 65–77.

Bagozzi, Richard P,. and Youjae Yi, 1988, "On the Evaluation of Structural Equation Models," *Journal of the Academy of Marketing Science* 16 (Spring): 74–94.

Bateson, J. E. G., 1985, "Self-Service Customer: An Exploratory Study," *Journal of Retailing* 61 (Fall): 49–76.

Berger, Joseph, Thomas L. Conner, and M. Hamit Fisek, 1974, *Expectation States Theory: A Theoretical Research Program,* Cambridge, MA: Winthrop.

Berger, Joseph M., Hamit Fisek, Robert Z. Norman, and Morris Zelditch, Jr., 1977, *Status Characteristics in Social Interaction: An Expectation States Approach,* New York: Elsevier-North Holland.

Bitner, Mary Jo, 1990, "Evaluating Service Encounters: The Effects of Physical Surroundings and Employee Responses," *Journal of Marketing* 54 (April): 69–82.

Bitner, Mary Jo, Bernard H. Booms, and Mary Stanfield Tetreault, 1990, "The Service Encounter: Diagnosing Favorable and Unfavorable Incidents," *Journal of Marketing* 54 (January): 71–84.

Bolton, Ruth N., and James H. Drew, 1991a, "A Longitudinal Analysis of the Impact of Service Changes on Customer Attitudes," *Journal of Marketing* 55 (January): 1–9.

Bolton, Ruth N., and James H. Drew, 1991b, "A Multistage Model of Customers' Assessments of Service Quality and Value," *Journal of Consumer Research* 17 (March): 375–384.

Boulding, William, Ajay Kalra, Richard Staelin, and Valarie A. Zeithaml, 1993, "A Dynamic Process Model of Service Quality: From Expectations to Behavioral Intentions," *Journal of Marketing Research* 30 (February): 7–27.

Bowen, David E., and Benjamin Schneider, 1985, "Boundary-Spanning-Role Employees and the Service Encounter: Some Guidelines for Management and Research," in *The Service Encounter,* eds. John A. Czepiel, Michael R. Solomon, and Carol F. Surprenant, Lexington, MA: Lexington Books, 127–148.

Bowen, John, 1990, "Development of a Taxonomy of Services to Gain Strategic Marketing Insights," *Journal of the Academy of Marketing Science* 18 (Winter): 43–50.

Breckler, Steven J., 1990, "Applications of Covariance Structure Modeling in Psychology: Causes for Concern," *Psychological Bulletin* 107 (2): 260–273.

Brown, Tom J., Gilbert A. Churchill, Jr., and J. Paul Peter, 1993, "Research Note: Improving the Measurement of Service Quality," *Journal of Retailing* 69 (Spring): 127–139.

Carman, James M., 1990, "Consumer Perceptions of Service Quality: An Assessment of the SERVQUAL Dimensions," *Journal of Retailing* 66 (Spring): 33–55.

Cronin, J. Joseph, Jr., and Steven A. Taylor, 1992, "Measuring Service Quality: A Reexamination and Extension," *Journal of Marketing* 56 (July): 55–68.

Crosby, Lawrence A., and Nancy J. Stephens, 1987, "Effects of Relationship Marketing on Satisfaction, Retention and Prices in the Life Insurance Industry," *Journal of Marketing Research* 24 (November): 404–411.

Fornell, Claes, 1992, "A National Customer Satisfaction Barometer: The Swedish Experience," *Journal of Marketing* 56 (January): 6–21.

Goodwin, Cathy, and Ivan Ross, 1992, "Consumer Responses to Service Failures: Influence of Procedural and International Fairness Perceptions," *Journal of Business Research* 25 (September): 149–163.

Gronroos, Christian, 1988, "Service Quality: The Six Criteria of Good Perceived Service Quality," *Review of Business* 9 (Winter): 10–13.

Hart, Christopher W. L., James L. Heskett, and W. Earl Sasser, Jr., 1990, "The Profitable Art of Service Recovery," *Harvard Business Review* 68 (July–August): 148–156.

Huppertz, John W., Sidney J. Arenson, and Richard H. Evans, 1978, "An Application of Equity Theory to Buyer–Seller Exchange Situations," *Journal of Marketing Research* 15 (May): 250–260.

Joachimsthaler, Erich A., and John L. Lastovicka, 1984, "Optimal Stimulation Level—Exploratory Behavior Models," *Journal of Consumer Research* 11 (December): 830–835.

Jöreskog, Karl C., and Dag Sörbom, 1989, *LISREL 7: A Guide to the Program and Applications,* Second Edition, Chicago: Jöreskog and Sörbom/SPSS.

Kelley, Scott W., James H. Donnelly, Jr., and Steven J. Skinner, 1990, "Customer Participation in Service Production and Delivery," *Journal of Retailing* 66 (Fall): 315–335.

LaBarbera, Priscilla A., and David Mazursky, 1983, "A Longitudinal Assessment of Consumer Satisfaction/Dissatisfaction: The Dynamic Aspect of the Cognitive Process," *Journal of Marketing Research* 20 (November): 393–404.

Leigh, Thomas W., and Patrick F. McGraw, 1989, "Mapping Procedural Knowledge of Industrial Sales Personnel: A Script-theoretic Investigation," *Journal of Marketing* 53 (January): 16–34.

Lerner, Melvin J., and Carolyn H. Simmons, 1966, "Observer's Reaction to the 'Innocent Victim': Compassion or Rejection?" *Journal of Personality and Social Psychology* 4 (August): 203–210.

Locke, Edwin A., and Gary P. Latham, 1990, *A Theory of Goal Setting and Task Performance,* Englewood Cliffs, NJ: Prentice-Hall.

Lovelock, Christopher H., 1983, "Classifying Services to Gain Strategic Marketing Insights," *Journal of Marketing* 47 (Summer): 9–20.

Michaels, Ronald E., Ralph L. Day, and Erich A. Joachimsthaler, 1987, "Role Stress among Industrial Buyers: An Integrative Model," *Journal of Marketing* 51 (April): 28–45.

Mills, Peter K. 1986, *Managing Service Industries,* Cambridge, MA: Ballinger.

Nunnally, Jum C., 1978, *Psychometric Theory,* Second Edition, New York: McGraw-Hill.

Oliva, Terence A., Richard L. Oliver, and Ian C. MacMillan, 1992, "A Catastrophe Model for Developing Service Satisfaction Strategies," *Journal of Marketing* 56 (July): 83–95.

Oliver, Richard L. and John E. Swan, 1989, "Consumer Perceptions of Interpersonal Equity and Satisfaction in Transactions: A Field Survey Approach," *Journal of Marketing* 53 (April): 21–35.

Parasuraman, A., Leonard L. Berry, and Valarie A. Zeithaml, 1991, "Understanding Expectations of Service," *Sloan Management Review* 32 (Spring): 39–48.

Parasuraman, A., Leonard L. Berry, and Valarie A. Zeithaml, 1993, "Research Note: More on Improving Service Quality Measurement," *Journal of Retailing* 69 (Spring): 140–147.

Parasuraman, A., Valarie A. Zeithaml, and Leonard L. Berry, 1988, "SERVQUAL: A Multiple-Item Scale for Measuring Consumer Perceptions of Service Quality," *Journal of Retailing* 64 (Spring): 12–40.

Peter, J. Paul, Gilbert A. Churchill, Jr., and Tom J. Brown, 1993, "Caution in the Use of Difference Scores in Consumer Research," *Journal of Consumer Research* 19 (March): 655–662.

Porter, Lyman W., Richard M. Steers, Richard T. Mowday, and Paul V. Boulian, 1974, "Organizational Commitment, Job Satisfaction, and Turnover among Psychiatric Technicians," *Journal of Applied Psychology* 59 (October): 603–609.

Reichheld, Frederick F., and W. Earl Sasser, Jr., 1990, "Zero Defections: Quality Comes to Services," *Harvard Business Review* 68 (September–October): 105–111.

Smith, Patricia Cain and L. M. Kendall, 1963, "Retranslation of Expectations: An Approach to the Construction of Unambiguous Anchors for Rating Scales," *Journal of Applied Psychology* 47 (April): 149–155.

Steenkamp, Jan-Benedict E. M., 1989, *Product Quality,* Assen/Maastricht, Netherlands: Van Gorcum.

Steers, Richard M., 1977, "Antecedents and Outcomes of Organizational Commitment," *Administrative Science Quarterly* 22 (March): 46–56.

Walster, Elaine, and Perry Prestholdt, 1966, "The Effects of Misjudging Another: Overcompensation of Dissonance Reduction?" *Journal of Experimental Social Psychology* 2 (January): 85–97.

West, Stephen G., and Robert A. Wicklund, 1980, *A Primer of Social Psychological Theories,* Monterey, CA: Brooks/Cole.

Zeithaml, Valarie A., Leonard L. Berry, and A. Parasuraman, 1993, "The Nature and Determinants of Customer Expectations of Service," *Journal of the Academy of Marketing Science* 21 (Winter): 1–12.

ABOUT THE AUTHORS

Scott W. Kelley is Associate Professor of marketing at the University of Kentucky. He received his doctorate in marketing from the University of Kentucky. His research interests include services marketing and ethics. His research has been published in the *Journal of the Academy of Marketing Science, Journal of Retailing,* and the *Journal of Business Research.*

Mark A. Davis is Assistant Professor of management at the University of Kentucky. He received his doctorate in industrial and organizational psychology from Virginia Tech University. His research interests include service quality with a focus on health care settings. His research has been published in the *Journal of Management, Organizational Behavior and Human Decision Processes,* and *Medical Care Review.*

CHAPTER 12

COMPETING AS A SERVICE FIRM III
SERVICE QUALITY

<table>
<tr><td>

CHAPTER OVERVIEW

INTRODUCTION TO SERVICE QUALITY

DIAGNOSING SERVICE QUALITY FAILURES

Consumer Expectations versus Management Perception

Management Perception versus Quality Specifications

Services in Action 12.1: Montgomery County, Ohio

Service Quality Specifications versus Service Delivery

Service Delivery versus External Communication

SETTING AND IMPROVING SERVICE STANDARDS

Creating a Quality Culture

</td><td>

CHAPTER 12 READINGS

Questions

Article 12.1: A Conceptual Model of Service Quality and Its Implications for Future Research

A. Parasuraman, Valarie A. Zeithaml, and Leonard L. Berry

Article 12.2: Communication and Control Processes in the Delivery of Service Quality

Valarie A. Zeithaml, Leonard L. Berry, and A. Parasuraman

Article 12.3: A Longitudinal Analysis of the Impact of Service Changes on Customer Attitudes

Ruth N. Bolton and James H. Drew

Article 12.4: Improving Service Quality in America: Lessons Learned

Leonard L. Berry, A. Parasuraman, and Valarie A. Zeithaml

Article 12.5: Planning Deming Management for Service Organizations

Thomas F. Rienzo

</td></tr>
</table>

CHAPTER OVERVIEW

Service quality rightly deserves its place in the capstone section of this book since it closes many service loops. At the same time, service quality is an elusive and indistinct construct. Researchers, however, do make a distinction between the two constructs of customer satisfaction and service quality. Satisfaction, as discussed in Chapter 2, is the outcome of the evaluation a consumer makes of any specific transaction or experience. Quality is more generally conceptualized as an attitude, the customer's global evaluation of a service offering. Quality is built up from a series of evaluated experiences and, hence, is much less dynamic than satisfaction. More importantly, perhaps, quality is generally viewed as an attribute in consumers' choice processes. Quality closes the loop between evaluation and the choice process.

To deliver a consistent set of satisfying experiences that can build into an evaluation of high quality requires the entire organization to be focused on the task. The needs of the consumer must be understood in detail, as must the operational constraints under which the firm operates. The service providers must be focused on quality, and the system must be designed to support that mission. The system must be controlled correctly and must deliver to its specification. Finally, customers' expectations must be managed through communications and pricing. To achieve all of this, the organization must be consumer-oriented (see Chapter 13). Thus, the delivery of quality requires a deep understanding of all the topics covered in this book.

INTRODUCTION TO SERVICE QUALITY

Service quality offers a way of achieving success among competing services. Particularly where a number of firms that offer nearly identical services are competing within a small area, such as banks, establishing service quality may be the only way of differentiating oneself. Such differentiation can yield a higher proportion of consumers' choices and, hence, mean the difference between financial success and failure.

There is ample evidence to suggest that the provision of quality can deliver repeat purchases as well as new customers. The value of retaining existing customers is amply illustrated in Chapter 10. Repeat customers confer many benefits on the organization. The cost of marketing to them is lower than to new customers. Once customers have become regulars of the service, they know the script and are very efficient users of the servuction system. As they gain trust in the organization, the level of risk for them is reduced and they are more likely to consolidate their business with the firm.

This lesson already has been learned over the past decade by goods manufacturers, many of whom have made goods quality a priority issue. Improving the quality of manufactured goods has become a major strategy for both the establishment of efficient, smoothly running operations and to increase consumer market shares in an atmosphere where customers consistently are demanding higher and higher quality. Goods-quality improvement measures have focused largely on the quality of the product itself, and specifically on eliminating product failure. Initially, these measures relied on rigorous checking of all finished products before they came into contact with the consumer. More recently, quality control has focused on the principal of ensuring quality during the manufacturing process, on "getting it right the first time," and on reducing end-of-production-line failures to zero. The final evolution in goods manufacturing has been to define quality as delivering the appropriate product to the right customer, thus using external as well as internal benchmarks.

However, service quality cannot be understood in quite the same way. The servuction system depends on the customer as a participant in the production process, and normal quality-control measures that depend on eliminating defects in the factory before the consumer sees the product will not suffice. Service quality is not a specific goal or program that can be achieved or completed, but needs to be an ongoing part of all management and service production.

DIAGNOSING SERVICE QUALITY FAILURES

There are obviously many difficulties inherent in evaluating service quality. In the first place, perceptions of quality tend to rely on a repeated comparison of the customer's expectation about a particular service, compared with the actual performance of that service. If a service, no matter how good, fails repeatedly to meet a customer's expectations, then the customer will perceive that service to be of poor quality. Second, unlike goods markets where customers evaluate the finished product alone, in services, the customer evaluates the *process* of the service as well as its outcome. A customer visiting a hairdresser, for example, will evaluate service not only on the basis of whether he or she likes the haircut, but also on whether the hairdresser was friendly, competent, and personally clean.

Article 12.1 describes the service quality process in terms of gaps between expectations and perceptions on the part of management, employees, and customers (as shown in Figure 12.1). The most important gap is between customers' expectations of service and their perception of the service actually delivered. The goal of the service firm must be to close that gap, or at least to narrow it as far as possible. Thus, the model is similar to the disconfirmation-of-expectations satisfaction model. However, it should be remembered that the focus here is on the cumulative attitudes toward the firm, assembled by the consumer from a number of successful or unsuccessful service experiences.

Before the firm can close this gap, however, there are four other gaps that also need to be closed or narrowed.[1] These are:

Gap 1: The difference between what consumers expect of a service and what management *perceives* that consumers expect.

Gap 2: The difference between what management perceives and what consumers expect and the quality specifications set for service delivery.

Gap 3: The difference between the quality specifications set for service delivery and the actual quality of service delivery.

Gap 4: The difference between the actual quality of service delivery and the quality of service delivery described in the firm's external communications.

CONSUMER EXPECTATIONS VERSUS MANAGEMENT PERCEPTION

The most immediate and obvious gap is usually that between what customers want and what managers *think* customers want. Briefly, many managers think they know what their customers want, but are, in fact, mistaken. Banking customers may prefer security to a good rate of interest. Some restaurant customers may prefer quality and taste of food to the arrangement of the tables or the view from the window. A hotel may feel that its customers prefer comfortable rooms, when, in fact, the bulk of them spend little time in their rooms and are more interested in on-site amenities.

FIGURE 12.1   A Conceptual Model of Service Quality

Consumer

Word-of-Mouth Communications

Personal Needs

Past Experience

Expected Service

GAP5

Perceived Service

Marketer

Service Delivery (including pre-/ and post-contacts)

GAP4

External Communications to Consumers

GAP3

GAP1

Translation of Perceptions into Service Quality Specifications

GAP2

Management Perceptions of Consumer Expectations

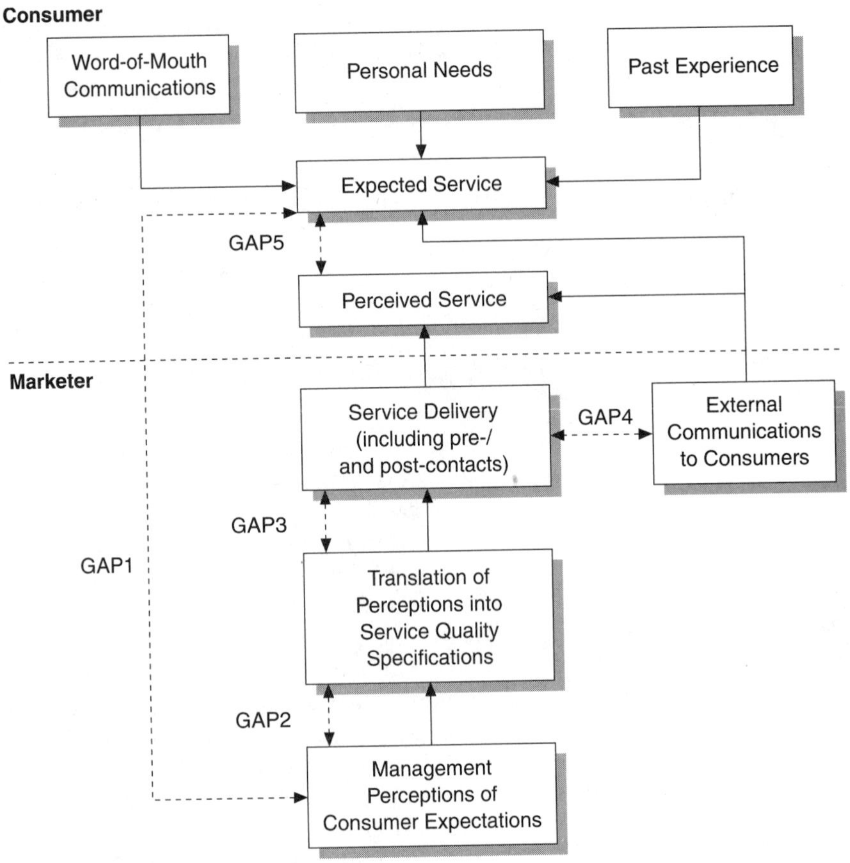

Source: A. Parasuraman, Valarie A. Zeithaml, and Leonard L. Berry, "A Conceptual Model of Service Quality and the Implication for Future Research," reprinted with permission from *Journal of Marketing*, Fall 1985: 141-150. Published by the American Marketing Association, Chicago, IL 60606.

The reasons for this gap are numerous and can be related back to the various issues covered earlier in this book. Chapter 2 suggests that consumer behavior may be extremely difficult to understand. The complexity of the service experience may mean that the simplistic multi-attribute perspective may not be rich enough to capture all of the subtleties.

If such a gap occurs, a variety of other mistakes tend to follow. The wrong facilities may be provided, the wrong staff may be hired, and the wrong training may be given to them. Services may be provided that customers have no use for, while the services they desire remain absent. Closing this gap requires very detailed knowledge of what customers *do* desire and then building a response to that desire into the service operating system.

MANAGEMENT PERCEPTION VERSUS QUALITY SPECIFICATIONS

Even if customer expectations have been accurately determined, another gap then opens between management's perceptions of customer expectations and the actual

SERVICES IN ACTION 12.1

MONTGOMERY COUNTY, OHIO

Montgomery County is in southwestern Ohio, including in its boundaries the city of Dayton. Recently, the area has undergone considerable economic decline. The troubles of the farming economy have been matched by the closure of many small manufacturing plants, formerly the region's chief economic base. As a result, the Montgomery County government has had considerable demands made on it, particularly on its Human Services Department.

As well as Dayton, Montgomery County includes 19 municipalities, 12 rural townships, and 16 school districts, and is also responsible for operating a number of countywide services. These services include a broad spectrum, ranging from managing welfare and schools through providing information and fostering economic development. Although it is not a profit-making business, the county government is, nonetheless, a provider of professional services to a very broad and very diverse group of people. Service quality affects the overall quality of life in the county.

In November 1986, Montgomery County government and its various agencies launched a long-term program to improve services. The first necessary step was customer identification. Each county agency attempted to establish whom it was serving, and customer groups, such as homeowners, parents, patients, and employers, were created. The second step was to study these groups and to learn how the customers perceived the service they were receiving from the county. Where customers deemed services to be of poor quality, the county and its agencies attempted to establish why the service failed to meet customer expectations. Two basic problems were identified: delays in service delivery (long waits for service) and lack of courtesy (service by impersonal bureaucrats). The research also attempted to discover customer needs that were not being met by any existing service, ranging from providing consolidated child-support services to supplying better information about employment vacancies.

Once marketing research determined what customers expected, the next stage was to configure operations in order to provide services to meet customer demands. Each agency had its own distinct client base and, therefore, its own distinct needs. Montgomery County's goal was to meet these needs in a way that showed government was fulfilling its prime purpose and was serving its constituents. The new "Service Excellence" program required changes to operations, redesigning services and service environments, new policies regarding employees, and a new orientation of the county administration and its agencies toward those whom it perceived to be its customers.

specifications set for service delivery. In many cases, management does not believe it can or should meet customer requirements for service. Sometimes there is no commitment on the part of management to the delivery of service quality. Corporate leadership may set other priorities, such as short-term profitability, cutting expenditures necessary to improve service quality. Sometimes there is simply no culture of service quality, and management genuinely fails to understand the issues involved.

In other cases, management may wish to meet customer requirements but feels hampered by insufficient methods of measuring quality or converting those measurements into a specification. The measurement of service quality has been the subject of considerable research. One perspective assumes that, although the exact criteria vary from service type to service type, the elements of service that are evaluated by customers tend to fall into five basic categories.[2]

Tangibles are those factors the customer can see, hear, and touch. In most service firms, tangibles include the physical environment, the facilities, and the appearance of the contact personnel. Tangibles are used when assessing physical quality before the service experience. When approaching a hotel, for example, the customer may make an evaluation based on the cleanliness of the building exterior, its location and proximity to other buildings and services, the amount of traffic noise from a nearby highway, the appearance of the employees, and the decor of the lobby.

Responsiveness is the customer's perception of the willingness and ability of staff to respond to the customer's own needs. Responsiveness is particularly important to customers who have problems or require some service over and above that which is ordinarily provided. Both willingness and ability are important; a waiter of mediocre ability in a restaurant, for example, can create a favorable impression by showing enthusiasm and a desire to be helpful at all times. On the other hand, a highly skilled waiter who ignores customers or keeps them waiting can create an unfavorable impression.

Empathy can be described as "the human touch." As it applies in a business setting, the customers assess whether or not the service personnel are genuinely committed to the customers and the service. One way of assessing empathy is to learn whether or not employees are willing to go beyond the minimum requirements for good service delivery and can deliver something extra (see, for example, the sources of satisfaction described in Article 4.1). Empathy and responsiveness are closely related, but of the two, responsiveness shows willingness to *meet* customer needs while empathy indicates a willingness to *go beyond* customer needs.

Assurance represents the customers' trust and confidence in the service and also the courtesy and competence of service providers. A favorable assessment of assurance will indicate that the customer is satisfied that the staff understood his needs and met them, and that no further problems have been created. A customer who reserves a room at a hotel may be impressed by the competence of the reservation staff, and feel that she has no need to worry about whether or not the room will be available when she arrives. If the reservation staff are vague or rude, however, the customer may feel less assured of the security of her room.

Reliability is the customer's own reflection on the service experience and on how well the service has been or is being performed. In particular, the customer will reflect on the service promise and decide if that promise has been kept. Again, using the hotel example, a customer who reserves a room will have been promised, explicitly or implicitly, the use of that room and the use of certain other facilities within the hotel at an agreed-upon price. If these promises are changed or broken, this will reflect adversely on the customer's perception of the hotel's reliability. Most customers regard reliability as being the most important of the five dimensions of service performance.

These evaluations bring up several points that service providers need to take into account when examining service quality. First, customer perceptions of service are heavily dependent on the attitudes and performance of contact personnel. Of the five dimensions above, responsiveness, empathy, and assurance reflect directly the interaction between customers and staff. Even tangibles depend partly on the appearance, dress, and hygiene of the service staff.

Second, the ways in which customers judge a service depend as much on the service process as on the outcome. How the service is delivered is as important as the frequency of the service and the nature of the service. Customer satisfaction depends on the *production* of services as well as their consumption.

Such a perspective raises considerable difficulties for management when trying to write a service quality specification. A specification can be examined either from the perspective of the consumer or from that of the operating system. The important thing is that the two views of the specification are linked together. Thus, a specification can be written based on consumers' ratings of the responsiveness of the organization. Unfortunately, although this is a tangible measure, it does little to guide the behavior of operations managers and contact personnel. Moreover, such a rating may be influenced in the consumers' minds by factors not readily apparent to managers.

Leaving aside for the moment consumers' idiosyncratic moods and attitudes, a number of studies have shown the diversity of clues used by consumers when rating services. The "Midas touch," described in Chapter 2, shows how a single touch can affect many different evaluations. A recent study shows that, even if a service firm generates a disconfirmation for a consumer, it may not be judged as delivering a poor level of satisfaction. Being part of the process, the consumers may attribute failures to themselves or to factors outside the control of the firm. Such attributions are shown to depend on the physical characteristics of the service firm. A tidy setting leads to negative attributes being directed away from the firm, while an untidy one generates attributes of dissatisfaction directed toward the firm.[3]

Conversely, a flowchart analysis, described in Chapter 5, can be performed in order to identify all points of contact between the firm and its customers. Detailed specifications then can be written for the behavior of the system and contact personnel at each point. Contact personnel, for example, can be instructed to make eye contact and to smile. However, it is then important to understand how such a specification will be assimilated into a quality specification that includes responsiveness and empathy.

Because of the difficulties in measuring quality, as pointed out above, some managers feel that quality measurement is not worth the effort. In still other cases, managers do not believe that customer requirements can be met at all. Some customer expectations are perceived as illogical or impossible, and no attempt is made to meet them. In some cases, especially in financial services, there may be regulatory constraints in the nature of service that are outside the firm's control.

SERVICE QUALITY SPECIFICATIONS VERSUS SERVICE DELIVERY

This gap concerns the actual performance of a service, and can occur even if customer expectations are determined and quality specifications are set correctly. The existence of a service performance gap depends on both the willingness and the ability of employees to provide the service according to specification.

Employees' willingness to provide a service, as noted in Chapter 4, can vary greatly from employee to employee and with the same employee over time. Many employees who start off working at the limit of their potential often become less willing to do this over time because of frustration or dissatisfaction. Furthermore, there is a considerable range between what the employee is actually capable of doing and the minimum the employee must do in order to avoid being dismissed; it is very difficult to keep employees working at full pitch continuously.

Chapter 4 illustrated that satisfying experiences often are generated because employees respond to consumers over and above their expectations and the system design. Moreover, the data clearly illustrates the power that an organization can gain by recovering from a systems failure. A performance in line with expectations generates minimal levels of satisfaction. It is only by exceeding expectations dramatically that the greatest impact is obtained. An excellent time to generate such an impact comes when the system has failed and the consumers' expectations have been lowered dramatically (see Chapter 11).

Other employees, no matter how willing, may not be able to perform a service according to specifications. They may have been hired for jobs which they are not qualified to handle or to which they are temperamentally unsuited, or they may not have been given sufficient training for the roles expected of them. An employee who is not capable of performing a service also, generally, will become less willing to keep trying in that particular role.

One common cause of the service gap, as discussed in Chapter 4, is *role conflict*. Whether or not the gap between management perceptions and customer expectations has been closed, service providers still may feel there is an inconsistency between what the service management expects them to provide and the service their customers want. A waiter who is expected to promote various items on the menu may alienate some customers who prefer to make their choices undisturbed, and this may reflect badly on the waiter if the customers fail to leave a tip. In other cases, the service provider may be expected to do too many different kinds of work, such as simultaneously answering telephones and dealing with customers face to face in a busy office. If this kind of conflict occurs, employees may become frustrated and gradually lose their commitment to providing the best service they can.

Sometimes, rather than perceiving a role conflict, employees may not understand their role at all. *Role ambiguity* results when employees, whether from incompatibility or inadequate training, do not understand the processes of their job or what the job is intended to do. Sometimes, too, they are unfamiliar with the service firm and its goals. Even where there is a clear service quality specification, there still may arise instances where employees fail to comprehend that specification.

A further complication for employees is *dispersion of control*, when control over the nature of the service they provide is removed from their hands. When employees are not allowed to make independent decisions about individual cases without first referring the case to a higher authority, they may feel alienated from the service and less a part of their jobs. When control over certain aspects of service is removed to a different location, such as control over credit being removed from individual bank branches, this alienation may increase. Employees may feel unable to respond to customer requests for help.

Both of the problems above can stem partly from *inadequate support*, when employees do not receive the personal training and/or technological and other resources necessary for them to perform their functions in the best possible manner. Even the best employees can be discouraged if they are forced to work with antiquated or faulty equipment, especially if the employees of competing firms have much superior resources and are able to reach the same level of service with less effort. Failure to properly support employees can lead to wasted effort, poor productivity, and unsatisfied customers.

SERVICE DELIVERY VERSUS EXTERNAL COMMUNICATION

As developed in Chapter 7, the "promises gap" lies between what the firm promises to deliver in its communications and what it actually does deliver to the customer. If advertising or sales pitches promise one kind of service, and the consumer receives a different kind of service, that promise is broken. A diner who sees a bottle of wine on a menu and orders it, only to be told it is out of stock and he will have to make do with one of inferior quality, may feel that the offer held out to him on the menu has not been fulfilled. A customer who is promised delivery in three days and then has to wait for a week will perceive service quality to be lower than expected.

It is worth pointing out that price can, under certain circumstances, become an indicator of quality. In the absence of more tangible clues, consumers will use the price they are paying as a benchmark for the quality of service they expect, through expressions such as: "The restaurant was wonderful and the service superb, but, given the price, it should have been!"

SETTING AND IMPROVING SERVICE STANDARDS

While the model proposed by Parasuraman, Zeithaml, and Berry provides a key diagnostic tool for service quality, in order to be effective, this model needs to be embedded in a service quality process that encompasses the whole firm. Article 12.4 provides a pragmatic list of actions that service organizations can take to improve the quality of the service they deliver. These lessons also capture the key components that need to be built into any service quality system. They include:

Lesson One: *Listening.* Quality is defined by the customer. Conformance to company specifications is not quality; conformance to customers' specifications is. Spending wisely to improve service comes from continuous learning about expectations and perceptions of customers and manufacturers.

Lesson Two: *Reliability.* Reliability is the core of service quality. Little else matters to a customer when the service is unreliable.

Lesson Three: *Basic Service.* American service customers want the basics: they expect fundamentals, not fancies, performance instead of empty promises.

Lesson Four: *Service Design.* Reliably delivering the basic service that customers expect depends, in part, on how well various elements function together in a service system. Design flaws in any part of a service system can reduce the perception of quality.

Lesson Five: *Recovery.* Research shows that companies consistently receive the most unfavorable service-quality scores from customers whose problems were not resolved satisfactorily. In effect, companies that do not respond effectively to customer complaints compound the service failure, and, thus, fail twice.

Lesson Six: *Surprising Customers.* Exceeding customers' expectations requires the element of surprise. If service organizations can not only be reliable in output but also can surprise the customer in the way the service is delivered, then they are truly excellent.

Lesson Seven: *Fair Play.* Customers expect service companies to treat them fairly, and become resentful and mistrustful when they perceive they are being treated otherwise.

Lesson Eight: *Teamwork.* The presence of service "teammates" is an important dynamic in sustaining servers' motivation to serve. Service team building should not be left to chance.

Lesson Nine: *Employee Research.* Employee research is as important to service improvement as customer research.

Lesson Ten: *Servant Leadership.* Delivering excellent service requires a special form of leadership. Leadership must serve the servers, inspiring and enabling them to achieve.

Such lessons alone do not constitute a systematic approach. The traditional quality approach is shown in Figure 12.2. Johnson and Dumas suggest that adopting such a manufacturing-oriented approach is a major source of problems for companies.[4] They argue that most non-manufacturing or service jobs do not have the clear simplified outcomes—the specifications—of manufactured products. Nor do they have the certainty of pre-existing physical measurements that determine whether a product meets those specifications.

In such a situation, starting the improvement cycle with an identified problem often can lead to a wild goose chase since the problem may not be the one that is relevant to the customer. Without specifications of what you have committed to supply the customer, how do you know when it is not being done? A service quality improvement cycle, therefore, must include a step that establishes customer commitments.

A problem or failure identified in a manufacturing process can be removed from the production line and never will reach the customer. Service production takes place in real time and in the presence of the customer. The failure also needs to be rectified in real time. Employees need to be empowered to engage in service recovery and these steps should be built into the service quality cycle. The extended cycle developed by Johnson and Dumas is shown in Figure 12.3.

CREATING A QUALITY CULTURE

Such a mechanistic approach to quality can add value to the perception of a service, but proponents of total quality management will argue that the problem-solving logic must be embedded in the current quality culture if it is to survive. Edward

FIGURE 12.2   The Traditional Quality Approach

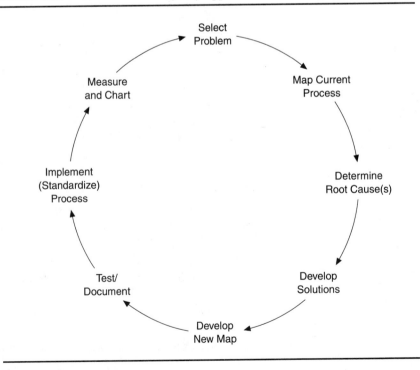

SOURCE: Gary K. Johnson and Roland A. Dumas, "How to Improve Quality If You're Not in Manufacturing," reprinted with permission from *Training*, November 1992, 36.

FIGURE 12.3   Nonmanufacturing Approach

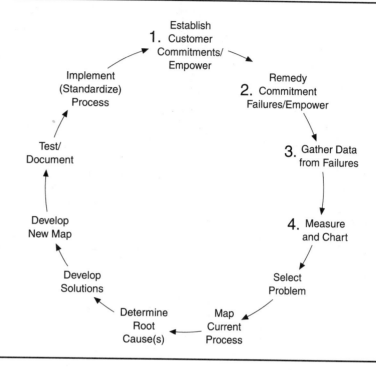

SOURCE: Gary K. Johnson and Roland A. Dumas, "How to Improve Quality If You're Not in Manufacturing," reprinted with permission from *Training*, November 1992, 36.

Deming, the father of modern American and Japanese quality management, argues that a change in management philosophy is necessary. He articulates 14 points in his philosophy, ranging from training to "driving out the fear," all of which relate to the culture and philosophy of the organization rather than to quality per se.

To change organizational culture is a major undertaking and involves building commitment from the top to the bottom of the organization. Article 12.5 articulates the Deming approach and gives examples of its application in a number of service businesses.

CHAPTER 12 READINGS

Articles 12.1 and 12.2 lay out the basic gaps model and use it to identify potential reasons why gaps are not closed in service organizations. Article 12.3 tries to bridge the gap between specific changes in service delivery and assessment of quality. It is all the more powerful because it is empirical and longitudinal. Article 12.4 was discussed earlier in the chapter. It provides a retrospective review of the service quality research and a pragmatic set of action steps. Article 12.5, by comparison, suggests that a new paradigm is not needed and that the Deming approach to quality can be applied to services.

QUESTIONS

1.   Choose an example of a service firm that you believe delivers low quality. Explain your choices using the gaps model.

2. What is the difference between the enthusiast orientation advocated by Schneider in Article 4.2 and a quality orientation?

3. Would you advocate the appointment of a quality vice president for a service firm? Explain your reasoning.

NOTES

1. Valarie A. Ziethaml, Leonard L. Berry, and A. Parasuraman, *Communication and Control Processes in the Delivery of Service Quality,* Marketing Science Institute Working Paper, Report 87-100, 1987. (See Article 12.1.)

2. *Ibid.*

3. Mary Jo Bitner, "Evaluating Service Encounters: The Effects of Physical Surroundings and Employee Responses," *Journal of Marketing* (April 1990), 42–50.

4. Gary K. Johnson and Roland A. Dumas, "How to Improve Quality If You're Not in Manufacturing" *Training* (November 1992): 36.

A CONCEPTUAL MODEL OF SERVICE QUALITY AND ITS IMPLICATIONS FOR FUTURE RESEARCH

A. Parasuraman

Valarie A. Zeithaml

Leonard L. Berry

*People want some wise and perceptive
statement like, "Quality is ballet, not hockey."*

—Philip Crosby (1979)

The attainment of quality in products and services has become a pivotal concern of the 1980s. While quality in tangible goods has been described and measured by marketers, quality in services is largely undefined and unresearched. The authors attempt to rectify this situation by reporting the insights obtained in an extensive exploratory investigation of quality in four service businesses and by developing a model of service quality. Propositions and recommendations to stimulate future research about service quality are offered.

Quality is an elusive and indistinct construct. Often mistaken for imprecise adjectives like "goodness, or luxury, or shininess, or weight" (Crosby 1979), quality and its requirements are not easily articulated by consumers (Takeuchi and Quelch 1983). Explication and measurement of quality also present problems for researchers (Monroe and Krishnan 1983), who often bypass definitions and use unidimensional self-report measures to capture the concept (Jacoby, Olson, and Haddock 1973; McConnell 1968; Shapiro 1972).

While the substance and determinants of quality may be undefined, its importance to firms and consumers is unequivocal. Research has demonstrated the strategic benefits of quality in contributing to market share and return on investment (e.g., Anderson and Zeithaml 1984; Phillips, Chang, and Buzzell 1983) as well as in lowering manufacturing costs and improving productivity (Garvin 1983). The search for quality is arguably the most important consumer trend of the 1980s (Rabin 1983) as consumers are now demanding higher quality in products than ever before (Leonard and Sasser 1982, Takeuchi and Quelch 1983).

Few academic researchers have attempted to define and model quality because of the difficulties involved in delimiting and measuring the construct. Moreover, despite the phenomenal growth of the service sector, only a handful of these researchers have focused on service quality. We attempt to rectify this situation by (1) reviewing the small number of studies that have investigated service quality, (2) reporting the insights obtained in an extensive exploratory investigation of quality in four service businesses, (3) developing a model of service

Source: A. Parasuraman, Valarie A. Zeithaml, and Leonard L. Berry, "A Conceptual Model of Service Quality and Its Implications for Future Research," reprinted with permission from the *Journal of Marketing*, vol. 49 (Fall 1985): 41–50. Published by the American Marketing Association, Chicago, IL 60606.

quality, and (4) offering propositions to stimulate future research about quality.

EXISTING KNOWLEDGE ABOUT SERVICE QUALITY

Efforts in defining and measuring quality have come largely from the goods sector. According to the prevailing Japanese philosophy, quality is "zero defects—doing it right the first time." Crosby (1979) defines quality as "conformance to requirements." Garvin (1983) measures quality by counting the incidence of "internal" failures (those observed before a product leaves the factory) and "external" failures (those incurred in the field after a unit has been installed).

Knowledge about goods quality, however, is insufficient to understand service quality. Three well-documented characteristics of services—*intangibility, heterogeneity,* and *inseparability*—must be acknowledged for a full understanding of service quality.

First, most services are intangible (Bateson 1977, Berry 1980, Lovelock 1981, Shostack 1977). Because they are performances rather than objects, precise manufacturing specifications concerning uniform quality can rarely be set. Most services cannot be counted, measured, inventoried, tested, and verified in advance of sale to assure quality. Because of intangibility, the firm may find it difficult to understand how consumers perceive their services and evaluate service quality (Zeithaml 1981).

Second, services, especially those with a high labor content, are heterogeneous: their performance often varies from producer to producer, from customer to customer, and from day to day. Consistency of behavior from service personnel (i.e., uniform quality) is difficult to assure (Booms and Bitner 1981) because what the firm intends to deliver may be entirely different from what the consumer receives.

Third, production and consumption of many services are inseparable (Carman and Langeard 1980, Gronroos 1978, Regan 1963, Upah 1980). As a consequence, quality in services is not engineered at the manufacturing plant, then delivered intact to the consumer. In labor intensive services, for example, quality occurs during service delivery, usually in an interaction between the client and the contact person from the service firm (Lehtinen and Lehtinen 1982). The service firm may also have less managerial control over quality in services where consumer participation is intense (e.g., haircuts, doctor's visits) because the client affects the process. In these situations, the consumer's input (description of how the haircut should look, description of symptoms) becomes critical to the quality of service performance.

Service quality has been discussed in only a handful of writings (Gronroos 1982; Lehtinen and Lehtinen 1982; Lewis and Booms 1983; Sasser, Olsen, and Wycoff 1978). Examination of these writings and other literature on services suggests three underlying themes:

☐ Service quality is more difficult for the consumer to evaluate than goods quality.

☐ Service quality perceptions result from a comparison of consumer expectations with actual service performance.

☐ Quality evaluations are not made solely on the outcome of a service; they also involve evaluations of the *process* of service delivery.

SERVICE QUALITY MORE DIFFICULT TO EVALUATE

When purchasing goods, the consumer employs many tangible cues to judge quality: style, hardness, color, label, feel, package, fit. When purchasing services, fewer tangible cues exist. In most cases, tangible evidence is limited to the service provider's physical facilities, equipment, and personnel.

In the absence of tangible evidence on which to evaluate quality, consumers must depend on other cues. The nature of these other cues has not been investigated by researchers, although some authors have suggested that price becomes a pivotal quality indicator in situations where other information is not available (McConnell 1968, Olander 1970, Zeithaml 1981). Because of service intangibility, a firm may find it more difficult to understand how consumers perceive services and service quality. "When a service provider knows how [the service] will be evaluated by the consumer, we will be able to suggest how to influence these evaluations in a desired direction" (Gronroos 1982).

QUALITY IS A COMPARISON BETWEEN EXPECTATIONS AND PERFORMANCE

Researchers and managers of service firms concur that service quality involves a comparison of expectations with performance:

> Service quality is a measure of how well the service level delivered matches customer expectations. Delivering quality service means conforming to customer expectations on a consistent basis. (Lewis and Booms 1983)

In line with this thinking, Gronroos (1982) developed a model in which he contends that consumers compare the service they expect with perceptions of the service they receive in evaluating service quality.

Smith and Houston (1982) claimed that satisfaction with services is related to confirmation or disconfirmation of expectations. They based their research on the disconfirmation paradigm, which maintains that satisfaction is related to the size and direction of the disconfirmation experience where disconfirmation is related to the person's initial expectations (Churchill and Surprenant 1982).

QUALITY EVALUATIONS INVOLVE OUTCOMES AND PROCESSES

Sasser, Olsen, and Wyckoff (1978) discussed three different dimensions of service performance: levels of material, facilities, and personnel. Implied in this trichotomy is the notion that service quality involves more than outcome; it also includes the manner in which the service is delivered. This notion surfaces in other research on service quality as well.

Gronroos, for example, postulated that two types of service quality exist: *technical quality*, which involves what the customer is actually receiving from the service, and *functional quality*, which involves the manner in which the service is delivered (Gronroos 1982).

Lehtinen and Lehtinen's (1982) basic premise is that service quality is produced in the interaction between a customer and elements in the service organization. They use three quality dimensions: *physical quality*, which includes the physical aspects of the service (e.g., equipment or building); *corporate quality*, which involves the company's image or profile; and *interactive quality*, which derives from the interaction between contact personnel and customers as well as between some customers and other customers. They further differentiate between the quality associated with the process of service delivery and the quality associated with the outcome of the service.

EXPLORATORY INVESTIGATION

Because the literature on service quality is not yet rich enough to provide a sound conceptual foundation for investigating service quality, an exploratory qualitative study was undertaken to investigate the concept of service quality. Specifically, focus group interviews with consumers and in-depth interviews with executives were conducted to develop a conceptual model of service quality. The approach used is consistent with procedures recommended for marketing theory development by several scholars (Deshpande 1983; Peter and Olson 1983; Zaltman, LeMasters, and Heffring 1982).

In-depth interviews of executives in four nationally recognized service firms and a set of focus group interviews of consumers were conducted to gain insights about the following questions:

☐ What do managers of service firms perceive to be the key attributes of service quality? What problems and tasks are involved in providing high quality service?

☐ What do consumers perceive to be the key attributes of quality in services?

☐ Do discrepancies exist between the perceptions of consumers and service marketers?

☐ Can consumer and marketer perceptions be combined in a general model that explains service quality from the consumer's standpoint?

SERVICE CATEGORIES INVESTIGATED

Four service categories were chosen for investigation: retail banking, credit card, securities brokerage, and product repair and maintenance. While this set of service businesses is not exhaustive, it represents a cross section of industries which vary along key dimensions used to categorize services (Lovelock 1980, 1983). For example, retail banking and securities brokerage services are more "high contact services" than the other two types. The nature and results of the service act are more tangible for product repair and maintenance services than for the other three types. In terms of service delivery, discrete transactions characterize credit card services and product repair and maintenance services to a greater extent than the other two types of services.

EXECUTIVE INTERVIEWS

A nationally recognized company from each of the four service businesses participated in the study. In-depth personal interviews comprised of open-ended questions were conducted with three or four executives in each firm. The executives were selected from marketing, operations, senior management, and customer relations because each of these areas could have an impact on quality in service firms. The respondents held titles such as president, senior vice president, director of customer relations, and manager of consumer market research. Fourteen executives were interviewed about a broad range of service quality issues (e.g., what they perceived to be service quality from the consumer's perspective, what steps they took to control or improve service quality, and what problems they faced in delivering high quality services).

FOCUS GROUP INTERVIEWS

A total of 12 focus group interviews was conducted, three for each of the four selected services. Eight of the focus groups were held in a metropolitan area in the southwest. The remaining four were conducted in the vicinity of the participating companies' headquarters and were therefore spread across the country: one on the West Coast, one in the Midwest, and two in the East.

The focus groups were formed in accordance with guidelines traditionally followed in the marketing research field (Bellenger, Berhardt, and Goldstucker 1976). Respondents were screened to ensure that they were current or recent users of the service in question. To maintain homogeneity and assure maximum participation, respondents were assigned to groups based on age and sex. Six of the twelve groups included only males and six included only females. At least one male group and one female group were interviewed for each of the four services. Consistency in age was maintained within groups; however, age diversity across groups for each service category was established to ascertain the viewpoints of a broad cross section of consumers.

Identities of participating firms were not revealed to focus group participants. Discussion about quality of a given service centered on consumer experiences and perceptions relating to that service *in general,* as opposed to the specific service of the participating firm in that service category. Questions asked by the moderator covered topics such as instances of and reasons for satisfaction and dissatisfaction with the service; descriptions of an ideal service (e.g., ideal bank or ideal credit card); the meaning of service quality; factors important in evaluating service quality; performance expectations concerning the service; and the role of price in service quality.

INSIGHTS FROM EXPLORATORY INVESTIGATION

EXECUTIVE INTERVIEWS

Remarkably consistent patterns emerged from the four sets of executive interviews. While some perceptions about service quality were specific to the industries selected, commonalities among the industries prevailed. The commonalities are encouraging for they suggest that a general model of service quality can be developed.

Perhaps the most important insight obtained from analyzing the executive responses is the following:

> A set of key discrepancies or gaps exists regarding executive perceptions of service quality and the tasks associated with service delivery to consumers. These gaps can be major hurdles in attempting to deliver a service which consumers would perceive as being of high quality.

The gaps revealed by the executive interviews are shown in the lower portion (i.e., the MARKETER side)

of Figure 1. This figure summarizes the key insights gained (through the focus group as well as executive interviews) about the concept of service quality and factors affecting it. The remainder of this section discusses the gaps on the service marketer's side (GAP 1, GAP 2, GAP 3, and GAP 4) and presents propositions implied by those gaps. The consumer's side of the service quality model in Figure 1 is discussed in the next section.

CONSUMER EXPECTATION—MANAGEMENT PERCEPTION GAP (GAP 1) Many of the executive perceptions about what consumers expect in a quality service were congruent with the consumer expectations revealed in the focus groups. However, discrepancies between executive perceptions and consumer expectations existed, as illustrated by the following examples:

☐ Privacy or confidentiality during transactions emerged as a pivotal quality attribute in every banking and securities brokerage focus group. Rarely was this consideration mentioned in the executive interviews.

☐ The physical and security features of credit cards (e.g., the likelihood that unauthorized people could use the cards) generated substantial discussion in the focus group interviews but did not emerge as critical in the executive interviews.

☐ The product repair and maintenance focus groups indicated that a large repair service firm was unlikely to be viewed as a high quality firm. Small independent repair firms were consistently associated with high quality. In contrast, most executive comments indicated that a firm's size would signal strength in a quality context.

In essence, service firm executives may not always understand what features connote high quality to consumers in advance, what features a service must have in order to meet consumer needs, and what levels of performance on those features are needed to deliver high quality service. This insight is consistent with previous research in services, which suggests that service marketers may not always understand what consumers expect in a service (Langeard et al. 1981, Parasuraman and Zeithaml 1982). This lack of understanding may affect quality perceptions of consumers:

> *Proposition 1:* The gap between consumer expectations and management perceptions of those expectations will have an impact on the consumer's evaluation of service quality.

MANAGEMENT PERCEPTION—SERVICE QUALITY SPECIFICATION GAP (GAP 2) A recurring theme in the executive interviews in all four service firms was the

FIGURE 1   Service Quality Model

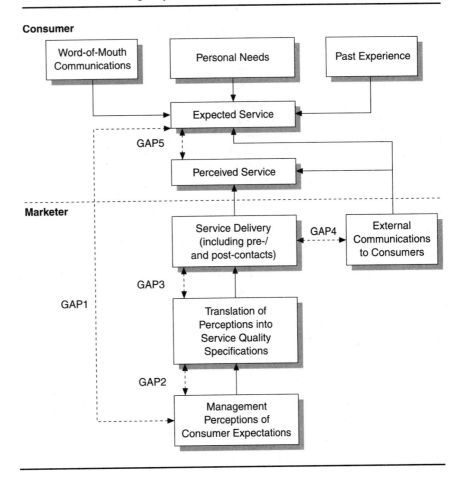

difficulty experienced in attempting to match or exceed consumer expectations. Executives cited constraints which prevent them from delivering what the consumer expects. As an example, executives in the repair service firm were fully aware that consumers view quick response to appliance breakdowns as a vital ingredient of high quality service. However, they find it difficult to establish specifications to deliver quick response consistently because of a lack of trained service personnel and wide fluctuations in demand. As one executive observed, peak demand for repairing air conditioners and lawn-mowers occurs during the summer months, precisely when most service personnel want to go on vacation. In this and numerous other situations, knowledge of consumer expectations exists but the perceived means to deliver to expectations apparently do not.

Apart from resource and market constraints, another reason for the gap between expectations and the actu-

al set of specifications established for a service is the absence of total management commitment to service quality. Although the executive interviews indicated a genuine concern for quality on the part of managers interviewed, this concern may not be generalizable to all service firms. In discussing product quality, Garvin (1983) stated: ". . . the seriousness that management attached to quality problems [varies]. It's one thing to say you believe in defect-free products, but quite another to take time from a busy schedule to act on that belief and stay informed" (p. 68). Garvin's observations are likely to apply to service businesses as well.

In short, a variety of factors—resource constraints, market conditions, and/or management indifference—may result in a discrepancy between management perceptions of consumer expectations and the actual specifications established for a service. This discrepancy is predicted to affect quality perceptions of consumers:

Proposition 2: The gap between management perceptions of consumer expectations and the firm's service quality specifications will affect service quality from the consumer's viewpoint.

SERVICE QUALITY SPECIFICATIONS—SERVICE DELIVERY GAP (GAP 3)

Even when guidelines exist for performing services well and treating consumers correctly, high quality service performance may not be a certainty. Executives recognize that a service firm's employees exert a strong influence on the service quality perceived by consumers and that employee performance cannot always be standardized. When asked what causes service quality problems, executives consistently mentioned the pivotal role of contact personnel. In the repair and maintenance firm, for example, one executive's immediate response to the source of service quality problems was, "Everything involves a person—a repair person. It's so hard to maintain standardized quality."

Each of the four firms had formal standards or specifications for maintaining service quality (e.g., answer at least 90% of phone calls from consumers within 10 seconds; keep error rates in statements below 1%). However, each firm reported difficulty in adhering to these standards because of the variability in employee performance. This problem leads to a third proposition:

Proposition 3: The gap between service quality specifications and actual service delivery will affect service quality from the consumer's standpoint.

SERVICE DELIVERY—EXTERNAL COMMUNICATIONS GAP (GAP 4)

Media advertising and other communications by a firm can affect consumer expectations. If expectations play a major role in consumer perceptions of service quality (as the services literature contends), the firm must be certain not to promise more in communications than it can deliver in reality. Promising more than can be delivered will raise initial expectations but lower perceptions of quality when the promises are not fulfilled.

The executive interviews suggest another perhaps more intriguing way in which external communications could influence service quality perceptions by consumers. This occurs when companies neglect to inform consumers of special efforts to assure quality that are not visible to consumers. Comments of several executives implied that consumers are not always aware of everything done behind the scenes to serve them well.

For instance, a securities brokerage executive mentioned a "48-hour rule" prohibiting employees from buying or selling securities for their personal accounts for the first 48 hours after information is supplied by the firm. The firm did not communicate this information to its customers, perhaps contributing to a perception that "all the good deals are probably made by the brokers for themselves" (a perception which surfaced in the securities brokerage focus groups). One bank executive indicated that consumers were unaware of the bank's behind the counter, on-line teller terminals which would "translate into visible effects on customer service." Making consumers aware of not readily apparent service related standards such as these could improve service quality perceptions. Consumers who are aware that a firm is taking concrete steps to serve their best interests are likely to *perceive* a delivered service in a more favorable way.

In short, external communications can affect not only consumer expectations about a service but also consumer *perceptions* of the delivered service. Alternatively, discrepancies between service delivery and external communications—in the form of exaggerated promises and/or the absence of information about service delivery aspects intended to serve consumers well—can affect consumer perceptions of service quality.

Proposition 4: The gap between actual service delivery and external communications about the service will affect service quality from a consumer's standpoint.

FOCUS GROUP INTERVIEWS

As was true of the executive interviews, the responses of focus group participants about service quality were remarkably consistent across groups and across service businesses. While some service-specific differences were revealed, common themes emerged—themes which offer valuable insights about service quality perceptions of consumers.

EXPECTED SERVICE—PERCEIVED SERVICE GAP (GAP 5)

The focus groups unambiguously supported the notion that the key to ensuring good service quality is meeting or exceeding what consumers expect from the service. One female participant described a situation when a repairman not only fixed her broken appliance but also explained what had gone wrong and how she could fix it herself if a similar problem occurred in the future. She rated the quality of this service excellent because it exceeded her expectations. A male respondent in a banking services focus group described the frustration he felt when his bank would not cash his payroll check from a nationally known employer because it was postdated by one day. When someone else in the group pointed out legal constraints preventing the bank from cashing his check, he responded, "Well, nobody *in the bank* explained that to me!" Not receiving an explanation in the bank, this respondent perceived that the bank was *unwilling* rather than *unable* to cash the check. This in turn resulted in a perception of poor service quality.

Similar experiences, both positive and negative, were described by consumers in every focus group. It appears that judgments of high and low service quality depend on how consumers perceive the actual service performance in the context of what they expected.

> *Proposition 5:* The quality that a consumer perceives in a service is a function of the magnitude and direction of the gap between expected service and perceived service.

A SERVICE QUALITY MODEL

Insights obtained from the executive interviews and the focus groups form the basis of a model summarizing the nature and determinants of service quality as perceived by consumers. The foundation of this model is the set of gaps discussed earlier and shown in Figure 1. Service quality as perceived by a consumer depends on the size and direction of GAP 5 which, in turn, depends on the nature of the gaps associated with the design, marketing, and delivery of services:

> *Proposition 6:* GAP 5 = f(GAP 1, GAP 2, GAP 3, GAP 4)

It is important to note that the gaps on the marketer side of the equation can be favorable or unfavorable from a service quality perspective. That is, the magnitude *and direction* of each gap will have an impact on service quality. For instance, GAP 3 will be favorable when actual service delivery exceeds specifications; it will be unfavorable when service specifications are not met. While proposition 6 suggests a relationship between service quality as perceived by consumers and the gaps occurring on the marketer's side, the functional form of the relationship needs to be investigated. This point is discussed further in the last section dealing with future research directions.

THE PERCEIVED SERVICE QUALITY COMPONENT

The focus groups revealed that, regardless of the type of service, consumers used basically similar criteria in evaluating service quality. These criteria seem to fall into 10 key categories which are labeled "service quality determinants" and described in Table 1. For each determinant, Table 1 provides examples of service specific criteria that emerged in the focus groups. Table 1 is not meant to suggest that the 10 determinants are non-overlapping . Because the research was exploratory, measurement of possible overlap across the 10 criteria (as well as determination of whether some can be combined) must await future empirical investigation.

The consumer's view of service quality is shown in the upper part of Figure 1 and further elaborated in Figure 2. Figure 2 indicates that perceived service quality is the result of the consumer's comparison of expected service with perceived service. It is quite possible that the relative importance of the 10 determinants in molding consumer expectations (prior to service delivery) may differ from their relative importance vis-à-vis consumer perceptions of the delivered service. However, the general comparison of expectations with perceptions was suggested in past research on service quality (Gronroos 1982, Lehtinen and Lehtinen 1982) and supported in the focus group interviews with consumers. The comparison of expected and perceived service is not unlike that performed by consumers when evaluating goods. What differs with services is the *nature* of the characteristics upon which they are evaluated.

One framework for isolating differences in evaluation of quality for goods and services is the classification of properties of goods proposed by Nelson (1974) and Darby and Karni (1973). Nelson distinguished between two categories of properties of consumer goods: *search properties,* attributes which a consumer can determine prior to purchasing a product, and *experience properties,* attributes which can only be discerned after purchase or during consumption. Search properties include attributes such as color, style, price, fit, feel, hardness, and smell, while experience properties include characteristics such as taste, wearability, and dependability.

Darby and Karni (1973) added to Nelson's two-way classification system a third category, *credence properties*—characteristics which the consumer may find impossible to evaluate even after purchase and consumption. Examples of offerings high in credence properties include appendectomies and brake relinings on automobiles. Few consumers possess medical or mechanical skills sufficient to evaluate whether these services are necessary or are performed properly, even after they have been prescribed and produced by the seller.

Consumers in the focus groups mentioned search, experience, and credence properties when asked to describe and define service quality. These aspects of service quality can be categorized into the 10 service quality determinants shown in Table 1 and can be arrayed

TABLE 1   Determinants of Service Quality

Reliability involves consistency of performance and dependability.
　　It means that the firm performs the service right the first time.
　　It also means that the firm honors its promises. Specifically, it involves:
　　　　—accuracy in billing;
　　　　—keeping records correctly;
　　　　—performing the service at the designated time.

Responsiveness concerns the willingness or readiness of employees to provide service. It involves timeliness of service:
　　　　—mailing a transaction slip immediately;
　　　　—calling the customer back quickly;
　　　　—giving prompt service (e.g., setting up appointments quickly).

Competence means possession of the required skills and knowledge to perform the service. It involves:
　　　　—knowledge and skill of the contact personnel;
　　　　—knowledge and skill of operational support personnel;
　　　　—research capability of the organization, e.g., securities brokerage firm.

Access involves approachability and ease of contact. It means:
　　　　—the service is easily accessible by telephone (lines are not busy and they don't put you on hold);
　　　　—waiting time to receive service (e.g., at a bank) is not extensive;
　　　　—convenient hours of operation;
　　　　—convenient location of service facility.

Courtesy involves politeness, respect, consideration, and friendliness of contact personnel (including receptionists, telephone operators, etc.) It includes:
　　　　—consideration for the consumer's property (e.g., no muddy shoes on the carpet);
　　　　—clean and neat appearance of public contact personnel.

Communication means keeping customers informed in language they can understand and listening to them. It may mean that the company has to adjust its language for different consumers—increasing the level of sophistication with a well-educated customer and speaking simply and plainly with a novice. It involves:
　　　　—explaining the service itself;
　　　　—explaining how much the service will cost;
　　　　—explaining the trade-offs between service and cost;
　　　　—assuring the consumer that a problem will be handled.

Credibility involves trustworthiness, believability, honesty. It involves having the customer's best interests at heart.
　　Contributing to credibility are:
　　　　—company name;
　　　　—company reputation;
　　　　—personal characteristics of the contact personnel;
　　　　—the degree of hard sell involved in interactions with the customer.

Security is the freedom from danger, risk, or doubt. It involves:
　　　　—physical safety (Will I get mugged at the automatic teller machine?);
　　　　—financial security (Does the company know where my stock certificate is?);
　　　　—confidentiality (Are my dealings with the company private?).

Understanding/knowing the customer involves making the effort to understand the customer's needs. It involves:
　　　　—learning the customer's specific requirements;
　　　　—providing individual attention;
　　　　—recognizing the regular customer.

Tangibles include the physical evidence of the service:
　　　　—physical facilities;
　　　　—appearance of personnel;
　　　　—tools or equipment used to provide the service;
　　　　—physical representations of the service, such as a plastic card or a bank statement;
　　　　—other customers in the service facility.

FIGURE 2   Determinants of Perceived Service Quality

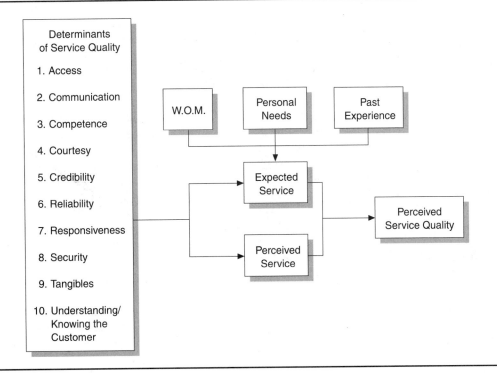

along a continuum ranging from *easy to evaluate* to *difficult to evaluate.*

In general, offerings high in search properties are easiest to evaluate, those high in experience properties more difficult to evaluate, and those high in credence properties hardest to evaluate. Most services contain few search properties and are high in experience and credence properties, making their quality more difficult to evaluate than quality of goods (Zeithaml 1981).

Only two of the ten determinants—tangibles and credibility—can be known in advance of purchase, thereby making the number of search properties few. Most of the dimensions of service quality mentioned by the focus group participants were experience properties: access, courtesy, reliability, responsiveness, understanding/knowing the customer, and communication. Each of these determinants can only be known as the customer is purchasing or consuming the service. While customers may possess some information based on their experience or on other customers' evaluations, they are likely to reevaluate these determinants each time a purchase is made because of the heterogeneity of services.

Two of the determinants that surfaced in the focus group interviews probably fall into the category of cre-

dence properties, those which consumers cannot evaluate even after purchase and consumption. These include competence (the possession of the required skills and knowledge to perform the service) and security (freedom from danger, risk, or doubt). Consumers are probably never certain of these attributes, even after consumption of the service.

Because few search properties exist with services and because credence properties are too difficult to evaluate, the following is proposed:

Proposition 7: Consumers typically rely on experience properties when evaluating service quality.

Based on insights from the present study, perceived service quality is further posited to exist along a continuum ranging from ideal quality to totally unacceptable quality, with some point along the continuum representing satisfactory quality. The position of a consumer's perception of service quality on the continuum depends on the nature of the discrepancy between the expected service (ES) and perceived service (PS):

Proposition 8: (a) When ES > PS, perceived quality is less than satisfactory and will tend toward totally unacceptable quality, with increased discrepancy between ES and PS; (b) when ES = PS, perceived quality is satisfactory; (c) when ES < PS, perceived quality is more than satisfactory and will tend toward ideal quality, with increased discrepancy between ES and PS.

DIRECTIONS FOR FUTURE RESEARCH

The proposed service quality model (Figure 1) provides a conceptual framework in an area where little prior research has been done. It is based on an interpretation of qualitative data generated through a number of in-depth executive interviews and consumer focus groups—an approach consistent with procedures recommended for marketing theory development. The conceptual model and the propositions emerging from it imply a rich agenda for further research.

First, there is a need and an opportunity to develop a standard instrument to measure consumers' service quality perceptions. The authors' exploratory research revealed 10 evaluative dimensions or criteria which transcend a variety of services (Table 1). Research is now needed to generate items or statements to flesh out the 10 dimensions, to devise appropriate rating scales to measure consumers' perceptions with respect to each statement, and to condense the set of statements to produce a reliable and comprehensive but concise instrument. Further, the statements generated should be such that with appropriate changes in wording, the same instrument can be used to measure perceived quality for a variety of services.

Second, the main thesis of the service quality model is that consumers' quality perceptions are influenced by a series of distinct gaps occurring on the marketers' side. A key challenge for researchers is to devise methods to measure these gaps accurately. Reliable and valid measures of these gaps will be necessary for empirically testing the propositions implied by the model.

Third, research is needed to examine the *nature* of the association between service quality as perceived by consumers and its determinants (GAPS 1–4). Specifically, are one or more of these gaps more critical than the others in affecting quality? Can creating one "favorable" gap—e.g., making GAP 4 favorable by employing effective external communications to create realistic consumer expectations and to enhance consumer perceptions—offset service quality problems stemming from other gaps? Are there differences across service industries regarding the relative seriousness of service quality problems and their impact on quality as perceived by consumers? In addition to offering valuable managerial insights, answers to questions like these may suggest refinements to the proposed model.

Fourth, the usefulness of segmenting consumers on the basis of their service quality expectations is worth exploring. Although the focus groups consistently revealed similar criteria for judging service quality, the group participants differed on the *relative importance* of those criteria to them, and their *expectations* along the various quality dimensions. Empirical research aimed at determining whether distinct, identifiable service quality segments exist will be valuable from a service marketer's viewpoint. In this regard, it will be useful to build into the service quality measurement instrument certain statements for ascertaining whether, and in what ways, consumer expectations differ.

Fifth, as shown by Figure 1, expected service—a critical component of perceived service quality—in addition to being influenced by a marketer's communications, is shaped by word-of-mouth communications, personal needs, and past experience. Research focusing on the relative impact of these factors on consumers' service expectations, within as well as across service categories, will have useful managerial implications.

SUMMARY

The exploratory research (focus group and in-depth executive interviews) reported in this article offers several insights and propositions concerning consumers' perceptions of service quality. Specifically, the research revealed 10 dimensions that consumers use in forming expectations about and perceptions of services, dimensions that transcend different types of services. The research also pinpointed four key discrepancies or gaps on the service provider's side that are likely to affect service quality as perceived by consumers. The major insights gained through the research suggest a conceptual service quality model that will hopefully spawn both academic and practitioner interest in service quality and serve as a framework for further empirical research in this important area.

REFERENCES

Anderson, Carl, and Carl P. Zeithaml (1984), "Stage of the Product Life Cycle, Business Strategy, and Business Performance," *Academy of Management Journal*, 27 (March), 5–24.

Bateson, John E. G. (1977), "Do We Need Service Marketing?" in *Marketing Consumer Services: New Insights*, Cambridge, MA: Marketing Science Institute, Report #77-115.

Bellenger, Danny N., Kenneth L. Berhardt, and Jac L. Goldstucker (1976), *Qualitative Research in Marketing,* Chicago: American Marketing Association.

Berry, Leonard L. (1980), "Services Marketing Is Different," *Business,* 30 (May–June), 24–28.

Booms, Bernard H., and Mary J. Bitner (1981), "Marketing Strategies and Organization Structures for Services Firms," in *Marketing of Services,* J. Donnelly and W. George, eds., Chicago: American Marketing Association, 47–51.

Carman, James M., and Eric Langeard (1980), "Growth Strategies of Service Firms," *Strategic Management Journal,* 1 (January–March), 7–22.

Churchill, G. A., Jr., and C. Surprenant (1982), "An Investigation into the Determinants of Customer Satisfaction," *Journal of Marketing Research,* 19 (November), 491–504.

Crosby, Philip B. (1979), *Quality Is Free: The Art of Making Quality Certain,* New York: New American Library.

Darby, M. R., and E. Karni (1973), "Free Competition and the Optimal Amount of Fraud," *Journal of Law and Economics,* 16 (April), 67–86.

Deshpande, Rohit (1983), "'Paradigms Lost': On Theory and Method in Research in Marketing," *Journal of Marketing,* 47 (Fall), 101–110.

Garvin, David A. (1983), "Quality on the Line," *Harvard Business Review,* 61 (September–October), 65–73.

Gronroos, Christian (1978), "A Service-Oriented Approach to Marketing of Services," *European Journal of Marketing,* 12 (no. 8), 588–601.

——— (1982), *Strategic Management and Marketing in the Service Sector,* Helsingfors: Swedish School of Economics and Business Administration.

Jacoby, Jacob, Jerry C. Olson, and Rafael A. Haddock (1973), "Price, Brand Name and Product Composition Characteristics as Determinants of Perceived Quality," *Journal of Applied Psychology,* 55 (no. 6), 570–579.

Langeard, Eric, John E. G. Bateson, Christopher H. Lovelock, and Pierre Eiglier (1981), *Service Marketing: New Insights from Consumers and Managers,* Cambridge, MA: Marketing Science Institute.

Lehtinen, Uolevi, and Jarmo R. Lehtinen (1982), "Service Quality: A Study of Quality Dimensions," unpublished working paper, Helsinki: Service Management Institute, Finland OY.

Leonard, Frank S., and W. Earl Sasser (1982), "The Incline of Quality," *Harvard Business Review,* 60 (September–October), 163–171.

Lewis, Robert C., and Bernard H. Booms (1983), "The Marketing Aspects of Service Quality," in *Emerging Perspectives on Services Marketing,* L. Berry, G. Shostack, and G. Upah, eds., Chicago: American Marketing Association.

Lovelock, Christopher H. (1980), "Towards a Classification of Services," in *Theoretical Developments in Marketing,* C. Lamb and P. Dunne, eds., Chicago: American Marketing Association, 72–76.

——— (1981), "Why Marketing Management Needs to Be Different for Services," in *Marketing of Services,* J. Donnelly and W. George, eds., Chicago: American Marketing Association, 5–9.

——— (1983), "Classifying Services to Gain Strategic Marketing Insights," *Journal of Marketing,* 47 (Summer), 9–20.

McConnell, J. D. (1968), "Effect of Pricing on Perception of Product Quality," *Journal of Applied Psychology,* 52 (August), 300–303.

Monroe, Kent B., and R. Krishnan (1983), "The Effect of Price on Subjective Product Evaluations," Blacksburg: Virginia Polytechnic Institute, working paper.

Nelson, P. (1974), "Advertising as Information," *Journal of Political Economy,* 81 (July/August), 729–854.

Olander, F. (1970), "The Influence of Price on the Consumer's Evaluation of Products," in *Pricing Strategy,* B. Taylor and G. Wills, eds., Princeton, NJ: Brandon/Systems Press.

Parasuraman, A., and Valarie A. Zeithaml (1982), "Differential Perceptions of Suppliers and Clients of Industrial Services," in *Emerging Perspectives on Services Marketing,* L. Berry, G. Shostack, and G. Upah, eds., Chicago: American Marketing Association, 35–39.

Peter, J. Paul, and Jerry C. Olson (1983), "Is Science Marketing?" *Journal of Marketing,* 47 (Fall), 111–125.

Phillips, Lynn W., Dae R. Chang, and Robert D. Buzzell (1983), "Product Quality, Cost Position, and Business Performance: A Test of Some Key Hypotheses," *Journal of Marketing,* 47 (Spring), 26–43.

Rabin, Joseph H. (1983), "Accent Is on Quality in Consumer Services This Decade," *Marketing News,* 17 (March 4), 12.

Regan, William J. (1963), "The Service Revolution," *Journal of Marketing,* 27 (July), 57–62.

Sasser, W. Earl, Jr., R. Paul Olsen, and D. Daryl Wyckoff (1978), *Management of Service Operations: Text and Cases,* Boston: Allyn & Bacon.

Shapiro, Benson (1972), "The Price of Consumer Goods: Theory and Practice," Cambridge, MA: Marketing Science Institute, working paper.

Shostack, G. Lynn (1977), "Breaking Free from Product Marketing," *Journal of Marketing,* 41 (April), 73–80.

Smith, Ruth A., and Michael J. Houston (1982), "Script-Based Evaluations of Satisfaction with Services," in *Emerging Perspectives on Services Marketing,* L. Berry, G. Shostack, and G. Upah, eds., Chicago: American Marketing Association, 59–62.

Takeuchi, Hirotaka, and John A. Quelch (1983), "Quality Is More Than Making a Good Product," *Harvard Business Review,* 61 (July–August), 139–145.

Upah, Gregory D. (1980), "Mass Marketing in Service Retailing: A Review and Synthesis of Major Methods," *Journal of Retailing,* 56 (Fall), 59–76.

Zaltman, Gerald, Karen LeMasters, and Michael Heffring (1982), *Theory Construction in Marketing: Some Thought on Thinking,* New York: Wiley.

Zeithaml, Valarie A. (1981), "How Consumer Evaluation Processes Differ between Goods and Services," in *Marketing of Services,* J. Donnelly and W. George, eds., Chicago: American Marketing Association, 186–190.

COMMUNICATION AND CONTROL PROCESSES IN THE DELIVERY OF SERVICE QUALITY

Valarie A. Zeithaml

Leonard L. Berry

A. Parasuraman

Delivering consistently good service quality is difficult but profitable for service organizations. Understanding why it is so difficult and how it might be facilitated is the purpose of the article. The authors intent is to identify a reasonably exhaustive set of factors potentially affecting the magnitude and direction of four gaps on the marketer's side of their service quality model. Most factors involve (1) communication and control processes implemented in service organizations to manage employees and (2) consequences of these processes, such as role clarity and role conflict of contact personnel. Literature from the marketing and organizational behavior fields on these topics is reviewed and integrated with qualitative data from an exploratory study. Discussion centers on insights that can be obtained from empirical testing of the extended model.

The delivery of quality in goods and services has become a marketing priority of the 1980s (Leonard and Sasser 1982; Rabin 1983). Though marketers of tangible goods have defined and measured quality with increasing levels of precision (Crosby 1979; Garvin 1983), marketers of services experience difficulty in understanding and controlling quality. Because services are performances rather than objects, precise manufacturing specifications for uniform quality rarely can be established and enforced by the firm. Quality in services is not engineered at the manufacturing plant, then delivered intact to the consumer. Most services cannot be counted, measured, inventoried, tested, and verified in advance of sale to ensure quality delivery. Furthermore, the performance of services—especially those with a high labor content—often differs among employees, among customers, and from day to day. In most services, quality occurs during service delivery, usually in an interaction between the customer and contact personnel of the service firm. For this reason, service quality is highly dependent on the performance of employees, an organizational resource that cannot be controlled to the degree that components of tangible goods can be engineered.

Research (Thompson, DeSouza, and Gale 1985) and company experience (Rudie and Wansley 1985) reveal that delivering high service quality produces measurable benefits in profit, cost savings, and market share. Therefore, an understanding of the nature of service quality and how it is achieved in organizations has

SOURCE: Valarie A. Zeithaml, Leonard L. Berry, and A. Parasuraman, "Communication and Control Processes in the Delivery of Service Quality," reprinted with permission from the *Journal of Marketing*, vol. 52 (April 1988): 35–48. Published by the American Marketing Association, Chicago, IL 60606.

Valarie A. Zeithaml is Visiting Associate Professor of Marketing, Fuqua School of Business, Duke University. Leonard L. Berry is Foley's/Federated Professor of Retailing and Marketing Studies and Director of the Center for Retailing Studies, Texas A&M University. A. Parasuraman is Foley's/Federated Professor of Retailing and Marketing Studies, Texas A&M University. The authors thank the Marketing Science Institute and its corporate sponsors for the financial support and cooperation provided for the study.

.come a priority for research. To that end, we previously developed a service quality model (Parasuraman, Zeithaml, and Berry 1985) indicating that consumers' quality perceptions are influenced by a series of four distinct gaps occurring in organizations (see Figure 1). These gaps on the service provider's side, which can impede delivery of services that consumers perceive to be of high quality, are:

☐ Gap 1: Difference between consumer expectations and management perceptions of consumer expectations.

☐ Gap 2: Difference between management perceptions of consumer expectations and service quality specifications.

☐ Gap 3: Difference between service quality specifications and the service actually delivered.

☐ Gap 4: Difference between service delivery and what is communicated about the service to consumers.

Perceived service quality is defined in the model as the difference between consumer expectations and perceptions (gap 5 in Figure 1), which in turn depends on the size and direction of the four gaps associated with the delivery of service quality on the marketer's side.

Delivering consistently good service quality is difficult, as organizations have discovered. Understanding why it is so difficult and how it might be facilitated is the purpose of our article. Our intent is to identify a reasonably exhaustive set of factors potentially affecting the magnitude and direction of the four gaps on the marketer's side. Most of these factors involve communication and control processes implemented in organizations to manage employees. Other factors involve consequences of these processes (e.g., role ambiguity and role conflict) that affect the delivery of service quality. Literature from the marketing and organizational behavior fields on these topics is reviewed and integrated with qualitative data from an exploratory study to help understand the way organizational processes affect service quality.

After describing the exploratory study, we examine gaps 1 through 4 in Figure 1. The theoretical constructs proposed to be responsible for each gap are delineated. In addition, specific organizational variables that can be used to operationalize these constructs in service organizations are itemized and explained. The result is a detailed conceptual explication of the service quality model that can be used as a blueprint for developing measures of the gaps. The steps necessary to develop these measures, and to test the model empirically, are discussed in the final section.

THE EXPLORATORY STUDY

The qualitative technique used to learn about service quality in organizations is what Mintzberg (1979) calls "direct research." Our study was not designed to test hypotheses because the literature on organizational processes involved in service quality delivery is not rich enough to suggest formal relationships among variables. Instead, we sought insights by collecting observations about service quality from managers and employees in actual service organizations. Observations were collected in three research stages. The approach used is consistent with procedures recommended for marketing theory development by several scholars (Deshpande 1983; Peter and Olson 1983; Zaltman, LeMasters, and Heffring 1982).

In the first stage, in-depth personal interviews consisting of open-ended questions were conducted with three or four executives in each of four nationally recognized service organizations (a bank, a brokerage house, a repair and maintenance firm, and a credit card company). The executives were selected from marketing operations, senior management, and customer relations and held titles such as president, senior vice president, director of customer relations, and manager of consumer market research. These executives were interviewed about a broad range of service quality issues (e.g., consumer expectations about service quality, what steps they took to control or improve quality, and what problems they faced in delivering high quality services).

The second state involved a comprehensive case study of a nationally known bank. Three of the bank's regions (each of which had at least 12 branches) were selected. Managers and employees at various levels of the bank were interviewed individually and in focus groups. Top and middle managers responded to open-ended questions about their perceptions of consumer expectations of service quality (gap 1), service quality standards set in the organization to delivery quality (gap 2), and differences between standards set by management and the level of service actually delivered (gap 3). A total of seven focus group interviews with tellers, customer service representatives, lending personnel, and branch managers from within the three regions were held to identify factors contributing to gaps 3 and 4. Finally, managers associated with bank communication with customers (bank marketing, advertising, and consumer affairs executives, as well as the president and creative director of the bank's advertising agency) were interviewed to identify the factors responsible for gap 4.

The third stage of the exploratory study involved a systematic group interview with 11 senior managers of

FIGURE 1   Conceptual Model of Service Quality

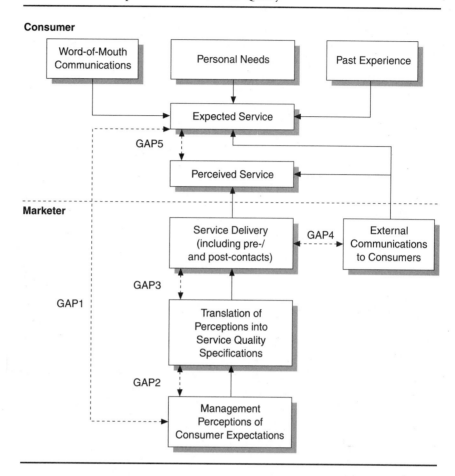

THE FOUR GAPS IN SERVICE QUALITY

GAP 1: DIFFERENCE BETWEEN CONSUMER EXPECTATIONS AND MANAGEMENT PERCEPTIONS OF CONSUMER EXPECTATIONS

six nationally known service firms (two full service banks, two national insurance companies, and two national telephone companies) and was intended to verify and generalize the findings from the two earlier stages. We presented the conceptual framework, explained the four gaps, and questioned managers about the factors responsible for the gaps in their firms. Lists of factors derived from the first two phases were presented and discussed. Managers augmented the lists and evaluated the factors on the basis of experience in their industries and organizations.

In the following discussion, we combine insights from the three exploratory phases with those from relevant literature in marketing and organizational behavior to propose the main theoretical constructs and specific variables associated with the four service quality gaps that can be used to operationalize the constructs.

Service firm executives may not always understand what features connote high quality to consumers, what attributes a service must have in order to meet consumer needs, and what levels of performance on those features are necessary to deliver high quality service (Langeard et al. 1981; Parasuraman and Zeithaml 1983). Because there are few clearly defined and tangible cues for services, the gap between what consumers expect and what managers think they expect may be considerably larger than it is in firms that produce tangible goods

TABLE 1   Service Quality Management Gap 1

Theoretical Constructs	Specific Variables
Marketing research orientation	Amount of Marketing research
	Usage of marketing research
	Degree to which marketing research focuses on service quality issues
	Extent of direct interaction between managers and customers
Upward communication	Extent of employee-to-manager communication
	Extent to which inputs from contact personnel are sought
	Quality of contact between top managers and contact personnel
Levels of management	Number of layers between customer contact personnel and top managers

(Gronroos 1982; Zeithaml 1981). As shown in Table 1, the size of gap 1 in any service firm is proposed to be a function of marketing research orientation, upward communication, and levels of management.

MARKETING RESEARCH ORIENTATION Evidence indicates that service firms lag behind goods firms in their use of marketing research and in other facets of customer orientation (George and Barksdale 1974; Lovelock 1981; Parasuraman, Berry, and Zeithaml 1983). Service organizations also place less emphasis than goods firms on marketing in general (Lovelock 1981), believing that the operations function is more critical. An operations orientation diverts focus from consumers and reduces efforts to understand their needs and expectations. Banks that close their branch lobbies in midafternoon to facilitate balancing the day's transactions and that issue monthly customer statements designed without input from customers exemplify an operations orientation.

Because marketing research is a key vehicle for understanding consumer expectations and perceptions of services, the size of gap 1 should depend greatly on the amount of marketing research conducted. Other research-related variables include the extent to which research data are used (i.e., read, understood, and applied) by managers in the organization and the degree to which the research focuses on service quality issues.

Another factor influencing degree of marketing research orientation is the extent to which top managers interact directly with consumers. In some service firms, especially ones that are small and localized, owners or managers may be in continual contact with consumers, thereby gaining firsthand knowledge of consumer expectations and perceptions. Even in large service organizations, top managers can spend time "on the line," interacting with consumers and experiencing service delivery. Radio Shack, for example, has a program called "Adopt a Store" through which senior managers spend time in stores collecting information and interacting with the staff (Goyne 1985). A major bank in the exploratory study required its managers to interact regularly with customers by telephone. As the degree of contact between top managers and consumers increases, top managers should understand the consumer better and the size of gap 1 should decrease.

UPWARD COMMUNICATION Though top managers may not have a firm grasp of consumer quality expectations, research suggests that customer-contact personnel can accurately predict consumer expectations and perceptions of the service (Schneider and Bowen 1985). Therefore, top managers' understanding of the consumer may depend largely on the extent and types of communication received from customer-contact personnel and from noncompany personnel (e.g., independent insurance agents, retailers) who represent the company and its services. Upward communication typically provides information to upper level managers about activities and performances throughout the organization (Read 1962). Specific types of communication that may be relevant are formal (e.g., reports of problems and exceptions in service delivery, performance reports on contact personnel, and financial and accounting information that would signal inferior or superior performance) and informal (e.g., discussions between contact personnel and upper level managers).

An important facet of upward communication is its quality or effectiveness, which in turn depends on the medium through which it occurs. Face-to-face communication, for example, is more effective than written communication because it uses several communication cues (verbal and visual) simultaneously. Face-to-face communication is preferred when the message is difficult or ambiguous, or when sender and receiver differ in background or opinions (Daft and Lengel 1984). In these situations, media such as written reports do not provide sufficient richness. In service organizations, the types of messages that need to be conveyed are often complex and ambiguous (e.g., problems encountered in service delivery, how employees feel, morale and attitudes within the organization) and top managers often differ considerably in background from contact personnel (Berry, Zeithaml, and Parasuraman 1985). Many successful service organizations (e.g., Marriott, Delta Airlines) pride themselves on using such rich communication channels as management by walking around (Clist 1985; Peters and Waterman 1982) and employee gripe sessions (Rout 1981).

In the focus group interviews conducted in the second stage of the exploratory study, several bank employees clearly illustrated the lack of effective communication.

> *Branch manager:* "I've been in this bank for 27 years and this is the first time I have had a regional VP that has never been in the branch." *Another:* "He never will." *Another:* "I haven't seen the man in a year and a half. That has a lot to do with our attitude. We're getting orders from someone we never see."

> *Customer service representative:* "We have three floors. Our manager, when he first got here, sat on the second floor. Now he's on the third floor in his enclosed office. He told us he doesn't want to be with the public. He needs time for himself. What are his priorities? He doesn't know what's going on on the first floor. I've had lots of customers ask for the manager. I say, 'I'm sorry, he's on a month's vacation.'"

We therefore propose that three specific variables influence the effectiveness of upward communication and hence the size of gap 1: extent of employees-to-managers communication, extent to which inputs from contact personnel are sought, and quality of contact between top managers and contact personnel.

LEVELS OF MANAGEMENT The number of layers of management between customer-contact personnel and top managers is expected to affect the size of gap 1.

Layers of management inhibit communication and understanding because they place barriers between senders and receivers of messages. Therefore, the greater the number of layers between customer-contact personnel and top managers, the larger gap 1 is expected to be.

As shown in Table 1, the gap between consumer expectations and management perceptions of consumer expectations depends on the extent to which a company recognizes the importance of the consumer (marketing research orientation), receives accurate communication about consumers' needs (marketing research orientation, upward communication), and places barriers between contact personnel and top managers (levels of management).

> P_1: The size of gap 1 is related to (a) extent of marketing research orientation ($-$), (b) extent and quality of upward communication ($-$), and (c) levels of management ($+$).

GAP 2: MANAGEMENT PERCEPTION—SERVICE QUALITY SPECIFICATION GAP

Managers of service firms often experience difficulty in attempting to match or exceed customer expectations. A variety of factors—resource constraints, short-term profit orientation, market conditions, management indifference—may account for the discrepancy between managers' perceptions of consumer expectations and the actual specifications established by management for a service. As shown in Table 2, the size of gap 2 in any service firm is proposed to be a function of management commitment to service quality, goal-setting, task standardization, and perception of feasibility.

MANAGEMENT COMMITMENT TO SERVICE QUALITY One explanation for gap 2 is the absence of total management commitment to service quality. Emphasis on other objectives such as cost reduction and short-term profit has outcomes that are more easily measured and tracked and may supersede emphasis on service quality. This tendency to emphasize other objectives is illustrated in the following statement.

> Most U.S. firms suffer significantly from the use of short-term, accounting-driven measures of performance to establish the reward mechanisms for high-level managers, who are mainly responsible for implementing strategic actions (Hax and Majluf 1984, p. 90).

Louis Gerstner, president of American Express, suggests the following reason for lack of management commitment to service quality.

TABLE 2   Service Quality Management Gap 2

Theoretical Constructs	Specific Variables
Management commitment to service quality	Resource commitment to quality
	Existence of internal quality programs
	Management perceptions of recognition for quality commitment
Goal-setting	Existence of a formal process for setting quality of service goals
Task standardization	Use of hard technology to standardize operations
	Use of soft technology to standardize operations
Perception of feasibility	Capabilities/systems for meeting specifications
	Extent to which managers believe consumer expectations can be met

Because of the structure of most companies, the guy who puts in the service operations and bears the expense doesn't get the benefit. It'll show up in marketing, even in new product development. But the benefit never shows up in his own P&L statement (*Business Week* 1984).

Often, service firms take a product-based approach to quality rather than a user-based approach, which results in a de-emphasis on serving the customer (Garvin 1983). In contrast, American Express illustrates a user-based approach to quality.

Overriding all other values is our dedication to quality. We are a market-driven institution, committed to our customers in everything we do. We constantly seek improvement and we encourage the unusual, even the iconoclastic (*Business Week* 1981).

Specific variables related to management commitment to service quality include the proportion of resources committed to service quality (rather than to other goals), the existence of an internal quality program, and the extent to which managers believe their attempts to improve service quality will be recognized and rewarded in the organization.

GOAL-SETTING Research reveals that goal-setting not only improves both organizational performance and individual achievement, but also increases overall control of the organization (Ivancevich and McMahon 1982; Latham and Locke 1979; Locke et al. 1981; Sherwin 1976). Companies that have been successful in delivering high service quality (e.g., American Express, McDonald's, Delta Airlines) are noted for establishing formal goals relating to service quality. Because services are performances, the goals for service delivery usually

are set and measured in terms of human or machine performance. American Express, after analyzing customer complaints, found that timeliness, accuracy, and responsiveness were the important outputs to be achieved. Management then identified 180 goals for different aspects of service quality provided to customers. After the formal goal-setting, they developed monitoring devices to evaluate the speed with which telephones were answered, complaints were handled, bills were mailed, and new applications were approved. The goals established by American Express illustrate many of the characteristics of effective goals (Locke et al. 1987): specific, accepted, cover important job dimensions, reviewed with appropriate feedback, measurable, challenging but realistic, and match individual characteristics.

The development of service goals involves defining service quality in ways that enable providers to understand what management wants to deliver. Existence of a formal quality program that includes identification and measurement of service quality standards is expected to be one variable that reduces the size of gap 2.

TASK STANDARDIZATION The effective translation of managerial perceptions into specific service quality standards depends on the degree to which tasks to be performed can be standardized or routinized. Efforts to conceptualize and measure the standardization of tasks in organizational research have focused on the construct of technology (Perrow 1979; Reeves and Woodward 1970; Woodward 1965). This research suggests that the organization's technology can serve to standardize and regularize employee behavior. If jobs or tasks are routine (such as those needed for opening checking accounts or spraying lawns for pests), specific rules and standards can be established and effectively executed. If services are customized for individual consumers (e.g., investment portfolio management or estate planning), specific standards (such as those relating to time spent with the customer) are difficult to establish. Even in highly customized services, however, some aspects of service provision can be routinized. Physicians and dentists, for example, can standardize recurring and nontechnical aspects of the service such as checking patients in, collecting payment, weighing patients, and taking temperature.

According to Levitt (1976), standardization or (in his terms) industrialization of service can take three forms: (1) substitution of hard technology for personal contact and human effort, (2) improvement in work methods (soft technology), or (3) combinations of these two methods. Hard technology includes automatic teller machines, automatic car washes, and airport X-ray machines, all of which allow standardization of service provision by substituting machines for human effort. Soft technology is illustrated by restaurant salad bars, prepackaged travel tours, and the standardized training given to employees of organizations like McDonald's. Effective combination of these two methods is illustrated by Marshall Field's elimination of "task-interfering duties" for salespeople. The retail store automated check approval, implemented in-store telephone directories, reorganized wrapping stations, and simplified order forms, all of which resulted in faster checkout and more attention to the customer.

We propose that the more managers can standardize tasks for service delivery, the smaller gap 2 will be.

PERCEPTION OF FEASIBILITY The exploratory research revealed the size of gap 2 to be affected by the extent to which managers perceive that meeting customer expectations is feasible. Executives in the repair service firm participating in the exploratory study were fully aware that consumers view quick response to appliance breakdowns as a vital aspect of high quality service. However, they believed that establishing specifications to deliver a quick response consistently was not feasible for two reasons: (1) the time required to provide a specific repair service was difficult to forecast and (2) skilled service technicians were less available in peak season (the summer months) than at any other time. Therefore, the greater the management perception that consumer expectations cannot be fulfilled, the larger gap 2 will be. Variables related to this construct include the organizational capabilities and systems for meeting specifications and the degree to which managers believe expectations can be met economically.

P_2: The size of gap 2 is related to (a) management commitment to service quality (–), (b) setting of goals relating to service quality (–), (c) task standardization (–), and (d) perception of feasibility for meeting customer expectations (–).

GAP 3: SERVICE QUALITY SPECIFICATION— SERVICE DELIVERY GAP

Gap 3 is the discrepancy between the specifications for the service and the actual delivery of the service. It can be referred to as the "service performance gap," that is, the extent to which service providers do not perform at the level expected by management. The service performance gap occurs when employees are unable and/or unwilling to perform the service at the desired level.

As shown in Table 3, the main theoretical constructs proposed to account for the size of gap 3 are teamwork, employee–job fit, technology–job fit, perceived control, supervisory control systems, role conflict, and role ambiguity.

TEAMWORK As revealed in the following statements from the exploratory study, bank employees did not feel they were working together well.

Lending officer: "I worked in the bank 13 years. There is a big difference in when I started and now in terms of how the employees feel about the bank. There used to be so much camaraderie. Now, it's like pulling teeth to get associates to help you."

Customer service representative: "We're *not* working as a family and as a group. We may all come together again but it hasn't happened yet."

Customer service representative: "Our cashier sits there and smokes cigarettes and drinks coffee. She doesn't help with any of our work. She says it isn't in her job description. She's a deadbeat."

The value of teamwork—employees and managers pulling together for a common goal—was emphasized throughout the exploratory interviews. The importance of this construct to achieving organizational goals also has been documented in studies on group cohesiveness (Davis 1969; Shaw 1976) and group commitment (Salancik 1977). In high performing groups , people function as a team and accomplish their goals by allowing group members to participate in decisions and to share in the group's success (Lawler and Cammann 1972).

Teamwork is the focus of service quality programs in several firms known for their outstanding customer service. Merrill Lynch, for example, has involved more than 2500 operations personnel in quality teams of 8 to 15 employees each that work to improve customer service (McMurray 1983). At American Express, employees are involved in setting standards and improving work

TABLE 3   Service Quality Management Gap 3

Theoretical Constructs	Specific Variables
Teamwork	Extent to which employees view other employees as customers
	Extent to which contact personnel feel upper level managers genuinely care for them
	Extent to which contact personnel feel they are cooperating (rather than competing) with others in the organization
	Extent to which employees feel personally involved and committed
Employee–job fit	Ability of employees to perform job
	Importance and effectiveness of selection processes
Technology–job fit	Appropriateness of tools and technology for performing job
Perceived control	Extent to which employees perceive they are in control of their jobs
	Extent to which customer-contact personnel feel they have flexibility in dealing with customers
	Predictability of demand
Supervisory control systems	Extent to which employees are evaluated on what they do (behaviors) rather than solely on output quantity
Role conflict	Perceived conflict between expectations of customers and expectations of organization
	Amount of paperwork needed to complete service transactions
	Number of internal contacts that customer-contact people must make to complete a service transaction or answer customer queries.
	Existence of management policy that conflicts with specifications
Role ambiguity	Perceived clarity of goals and expectations
	Frequency and quality of downward communication
	Extent of constructive feedback given to contact personnel
	Perceived level of competence and confidence
	Product knowledge of contact personnel
	Product-specific training provided to contact personnel
	Training in communication skills provided to contact personnel

procedures so that a sense of teamwork is fostered. Employees in various departments work together to analyze the work of each department, identify opportunities, and seek improvements.

We propose the following aspects as being critical to teamwork: the extent to which employees view other employees as customers, the extent to which employees feel management cares about them, the extent to which employees feel they are cooperating rather than competing with each other, and the extent to which employees feel personally involved and committed.

EMPLOYEE–JOB FIT The exploratory study indicated that service quality problems often occur because contact personnel are not well suited to their positions. Because customer-contact jobs tend to be situated at the lower levels of company organization charts (e.g., car rental agents, telephone operators, and repair technicians), personnel holding these jobs are frequently among the least educated and lowest paid employees in their companies. As a result, they may lack language, interpersonal, or other skills to serve customers effectively. Many service companies have high turnover among contact employees and are inclined to fill openings quickly, even if they must hire persons having background or skill deficiencies. Managers commonly do not give enough attention or devote sufficient resources to hiring and selection processes. We propose that emphasis on matching the employee to the job through selection processes and the consequent ability or skill of employees to perform the job well affect the size of gap 3.

TECHNOLOGY–JOB FIT Provision of high service quality also depends on the appropriateness of the tools or technology the employee uses to perform the job. Technology and equipment, such as bank computers and diagnostic equipment, can enhance the service employee's performance. Appropriate and reliable technology must be provided for high quality service delivery. Equipment failures can interfere with adequate employee performance.

Our exploratory study revealed several instances in which service quality shortfalls resulted from a lack of technology–job fit and/or employee–job fit. For example a product repair executive, in bemoaning the proliferation of new high technology appliances, indicated problems stemming from a lack of both types of fit.

> We may not have all the [technical] specifications needed to train technicians before a new product is marketed [technology–job fit]. Some technicians may never be capable of being trained to service these new "high-tech" products [employee–job fit]. These products are coming too fast.

PERCEIVED CONTROL The notion of perceived control suggests that individual's reactions to stressful situations depend on whether they can control those situations (Geer, Davidson, and Gatchel 1970; Geer and Maisel 1972; Glass and Singer 1972; Straub, Tursky, and Schwartz 1971). Averill (1973) has delineated three forms of control: behavioral, cognitive, and decisional.

Behavioral control is the ability to make responses that influence threatening situations (Averill 1973). Cognitive control is the ability to reduce stress by the way information is processed by an individual (Averill 1973; Cromwell et al. 1971). Decisional control involves a choice in the selection of outcomes or goals (Averill 1973). We propose that when service employees perceive themselves to be in control of situations they encounter in their jobs, they experience less stress. Lower levels of stress, in turn, lead to higher performance. When employees perceive that they can act flexibly rather than by rote in problem situations encountered in providing services, control increases and performance improves.

Perceived control can be a function of the degree to which organizational rules, procedures, and culture limit contact employee flexibility in serving customers. It can also be a consequence of the degree to which an employee's authority to achieve specific outcomes with customers lies elsewhere in the organization. Service companies commonly are organized internally in a way that makes providing fast service to the customer difficult for the service employee. When a contact person must get the approval of other departments in the organization before delivering a certain service, service quality is jeopardized. Though the contact person may be totally committed to serving the consumer, he or she cannot perform well because control over the service has been dispersed among multiple organizational units. Finally, perceived control can be a function of the predictability of demand, which is a major problem in service businesses (Zeithaml, Parasuraman, and Berry 1985).

SUPERVISORY CONTROL SYSTEMS In some organizations, the performance of contact employees is measured by their output (e.g., the number of units produced per hour, the number or amount of sales per week). In these situations, the performance of individuals is monitored and controlled through what are termed "output control systems" (Ouchi 1979; Ouchi and McGuire 1975). Performance is based on written records that measure employee outputs. In many service organizations, however, output control systems may be inappropriate or insufficient for measuring employee performance relating to provision of quality service. For example, most bank customers want bank tellers to be accurate, fast, and friendly. Banks that measure teller performance strictly on output measures, such as end-of-the-day balancing transactions, overlook key aspects of job performance that consumers factor into quality-of-service perceptions.

In these and other service situations, performance also can be monitored through behavioral control systems (Ouchi 1979; Ouchi and McGuire 1975), which consist largely of observations or other reports on the way the employee works or behaves rather than output measurements. The use of behavioral control systems is illustrated by an ongoing "tone-of-service" survey with customers who have recently opened accounts at The Friendly National Bank of Oklahoma City (Berry 1986). Customers answer questions about the way they were treated by the customer service representative opening the account. Friendly also monitors customer service representatives' performance through ongoing "shopper" research (researchers pretending to be customers) and a cross-sales index. Each month, customer service representatives receive tone-of-service and shopper scores (behavioral measures) and a cross-sales score (output measure). The use of these types of behavioral measures encourages employee performance that is consistent with customer expectations of quality service.

ROLE CONFLICT The role attached to any position in an organization represents the set of behaviors and activities to be performed by the person occupying that position (Katz and Kahn 1978). The role is defined through the expectations, demands, and pressures communicated to employees by individuals (e.g., top managers, immediate supervisors, customers) who have a vested interest in how employees perform their jobs (Katz and Kahn 1978). When the expectations of these people are incompatible or too demanding, employees experience role conflict, the perception that they cannot satisfy all the demands of all these individuals (Belasco 1966; Rizzo, House, and Lirtzman 1970; Walker, Churchill, and Ford 1977). Research has shown that perceived role conflict is related positively to feelings of job-related tension and anxiety and negatively to job satisfaction (Greene and Organ 1973; Gross, Mason, and McEachern 1957; Kahn et al. 1964).

Because contact employees are the links between the company and the consumer, they must satisfy the needs of both. Sometimes the expectations of the company and the expectations of the consumer conflict. For example, conflict occurs when an income tax firm expects staff members to process as many consumers as possible in a short time (i.e., limits the time with consumers) and consumers want personal attention from the staff (e.g., to discuss tax avoidance strategies for the future). Role conflict also may occur when employees are expected to cross-sell services to the consumer; the employees may feel they are pushing the services on the consumer and may be torn between the company's expectations and the desire to serve the consumer.

The managers of service organizations can inadvertently create role conflict for employees through excessive paperwork or unnecessary internal roadblocks. For example, new accounts personnel in banks who must complete separate forms for each service they sell to a customer may experience role conflict if other customers are waiting to be served. Does the new accounts employee take the time to cross-sell bank services to the customer at the desk or simply open the requested account and move on to the waiting customer? Complicating the issue is the reality that the new accounts employee may be measured—and rewarded—on the basis of cross-selling achievements.

Perceptions of role conflict are psychologically uncomfortable for the employee (Kahn et al. 1964; Walker, Churchill, and Ford 1977), can have a negative effect on the employee's satisfaction and performance in the organization, and increase absenteeism and turnover. A service organization that recognizes inherent conflicts in the contact person's job will go far in eliminating the distress of role conflict. The result will be better employee performance and hence a reduction of gap 3. Use of performance measurement systems that focus on the consumer in addition to internal efficiency goals is one example of how role conflict can be reduced. Compensation tied to delivery of service quality (by measures of consumer satisfaction, loyalty, etc.) as well as sales is another.

ROLE AMBIGUITY When employees do not have the information necessary to perform their jobs adequately, they experience role ambiguity (Katz and Kahn 1978; Walker, Churchill, and Ford 1977). Role ambiguity may occur because employees are uncertain about what managers or supervisors expect from them and how to satisfy those expectations or because they do not know how their performance will be evaluated and rewarded (Katz and Kahn 1978; Walker, Churchill, and Ford 1977).

Several organizational variables moderate the role ambiguity experienced by service employees. The frequency, quality, and accuracy of downward communication are likely to affect the service employee's role ambiguity. Downward communication involves messages used primarily by managers to direct and influence personnel at lower levels in the organization. It typically pertains to the goals, strategies, and objectives for the organization and its departments, job instruction and rationale, policy and procedures, and assessment and correction of performance (Katz and Kahn 1978). The more frequently managers provide clear and unambiguous communication about these topics, the lower employees' role ambiguity will be.

The training provided by the organization can help employees gain an accurate understanding of what is expected and how they will be evaluated. Training that relates to specific services offered by the firm should help the contact person in dealing with the customer. Training in communication skills, especially in listening to customers and understanding what customers expect, also should give contact personnel greater role clarity. All such organizational training programs should affect the employee's perceived level of confidence or competence, which should result in greater role clarity.

> P$_3$: The size of gap 3 is related to (a) extent of teamwork perceived by employees (−), (b) employee–job fit (−), (c) technology–job fit (−), (d) extent of perceived control experienced by customer-contact personnel (−), (e) extent to which behavioral control systems are used to supplement output control systems (−), (f) extent of role conflict experienced by customer-contact personnel (+), and (g) extent of role ambiguity experienced by customer-contact personnel (+).

GAP 4: DIFFERENCE BETWEEN SERVICE DELIVERY AND EXTERNAL COMMUNICATIONS

Media advertising and other communications by a firm can affect consumer expectations. Discrepancies between service delivery and external communications—in the form of exaggerated promises and/or the absence of information about service delivery aspects intended to serve consumers well—can affect consumer perceptions of service quality. As shown in Table 4, we propose that horizontal communication and propensity to overpromise within an organization affect the size of gap 4.

HORIZONTAL COMMUNICATION Horizontal communications are the lateral information flows that occur both within and between departments of an organization (Daft and Steers 1985). The basic purpose of horizontal communication is to coordinate people and departments so that the overall goals of the organization are achieved. If high service quality is to be perceived by the consumer, horizontal communication among departments is necessary.

One essential form of horizontal communication in service organizations involves the advertising department (and its agency) and contact personnel. When communication occurs between contact personnel and advertising personnel (e.g., the contact personnel provide input to the advertising department about the feasibility of what is being promised in advertising), consumers are led to expect what contact personnel can deliver. If communication is not present and advertising is developed independently, contact personnel may not be able to deliver service that matches the image presented in advertising. Such lack of communication is illustrated by Holiday Inn's unsuccessful "No Surprises" advertising campaign (George and Berry 1981). Holiday Inn's agency used consumer research as the basis for a television campaign promising "no

TABLE 4   Service Quality Management Gap 4

Theoretical Constructs	Specific Variables
Horizontal communication	Extent of input by operations people in advertising planning and execution
	Extent to which contact personnel are aware of external communications to customers before they occur
	Communication between sales and operations people
	Similarity of procedures across departments and branches
Propensity to overpromise	Extent to which firm feels pressure to generate new business
	Extent to which firm perceives that competitors overpromise

surprises" to customers. Top managers accepted the campaign in spite of opposition by operations executives who knew that surprises frequently occur in a complex service organization. When the campaign was aired, it raised consumer expectations, gave dissatisfied customers additional grounds on which to vent frustrations, and had to be discontinued.

In the focus group interviews in our exploratory study, contact personnel expressed the need to be aware of all company communications before they run as a basis for monitoring and responding to the consumer's advertising-induced expectations. They also believed their inputs to the campaign would result in more reasonable consumer expectations.

Service organizations that do not advertise also need horizontal communication, often between the salesforce and the service providers. Frequently salespeople promise more than can be delivered to obtain an order. Consumer expectations are raised and cannot be met by customer-contact personnel, resulting in an increase in the size of gap 4.

An important aspect of horizontal communication is the coordination or integration of departments in an organization to achieve strategic objectives (Anderson 1984). One obvious form of coordination necessary in providing service quality is consistency in policies and procedures across departments and branches. If a service organization operates many outlets under the same name, consumers will expect similar performance across those outlets. If the company allows managers of individual branches significant autonomy in procedures and policies, consumers may not receive the same level of service quality across the branches. In this case, what they expect in a specific branch may be different from what is delivered and the size of gap 4 will increase.

PROPENSITY TO OVERPROMISE Because of the increasing deregulation and intensifying competition in the services sector, an intuitive explanation for gap 4 is that many service firms feel pressured to acquire new business and to meet or beat competition, and therefore tend to overpromise. Specifically, the greater the extent to which a service firm feels pressured to generate new customers, and perceives that the industry norm is to overpromise ("everyone else in our industry overpromises"), the greater is the firm's propensity to overpromise. We further propose that propensity to overpromise is related directly to the size of gap 4.

> P_4: The size of gap 4 is related to (a) extent of horizontal communication (−) and (b) propensity to overpromise (+).

TESTING THE EXTENDED MODEL

The theoretical constructs we have derived from the organizational behavior and marketing literature are germane to an understanding of service quality shortfalls (i.e., gaps 1 through 4 in Figure 1) and in taking corrective action to ensure the delivery of high quality service. Figure 2 is an extended model of service quality, showing the various organizational constructs and their relationships to the service quality gaps. Tables 1 through 4 detail variables that can be used to operationalize and measure the theoretical constructs affecting the four gaps.

We previously developed a multiple-item scale called SERVQUAL (Parasuraman, Zeithaml, and Berry 1986) to measure service quality as perceived by consumers (gap 5 in Figures 1 and 2). The SERVQUAL scale operationalizes and measures service quality along five distinct dimensions: tangibles, reliability, responsiveness, assurance, and empathy. SERVQUAL scores along these dimensions can be viewed as indicators of the construct of perceived service quality. Likewise, measures of the theoretical constructs affecting each gap can be viewed as indicators of that gap. Therefore, it is possible to recast the conceptual service quality model (Figure 1) in the form of a structural equations model wherein perceived service quality (gap 5) is the unobservable dependent variable and the four gaps on the marketer's side (gaps 1–4) are the unobservable independent variables. This model can be tested by collecting data on the indicators of the five gaps through a cross-sectional study of service organizations and analyzing the data with a technique such as LISREL.

In addition to testing the overall soundness of the service quality model, future research must address several specific questions about the model. Let us examine these questions and the research steps necessary to answer them.

Which of the four service quality gaps is (are) most critical in explaining service quality variation? Is one or more of the four managerial gaps more critical than the others in affecting perceived service quality? Can creating one favorable gap (e.g., making gap 4 favorable by employing effective external communications to create realistic consumer expectations and to enhance consumer perceptions) offset service quality problems stemming from other gaps? To answer this questions, measures of each of the four service quality gaps must be developed. Gap 1, the difference between consumer expectations and management perceptions of consumer

FIGURE 2   Extended Model of Service Quality

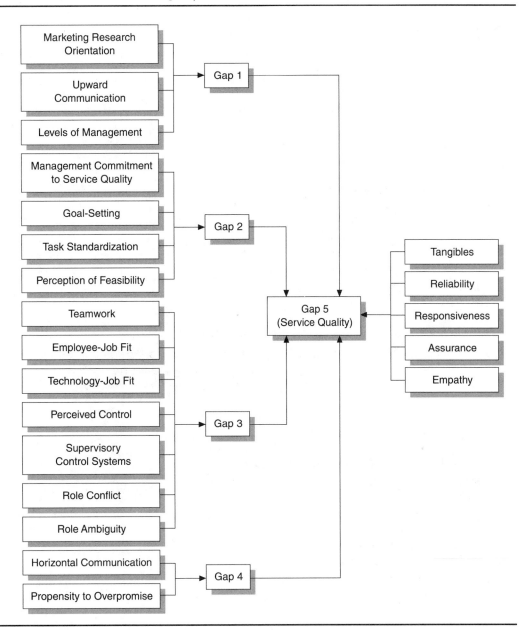

expectations, could be measured by administering the expectations section of the SERVQUAL scale to a set of top managers, then comparing the scores with those obtained from consumers on the same instrument. Gap 2, the difference between management perceptions of consumer expectations and service quality specifications, could be operationalized through questionnaires to top managers that measure the extent to which the organization sets standards to deliver to expectations. Gap 3, the difference between service quality specifications and service delivery, could be gauged through employee questionnaires that address their perceived ability to deliver to established standards. Gap 4, the difference between service delivery and what is communicated about delivery externally to consumers, also would involve employee perceptions of what they deliver in comparison with what external communication promises they will deliver.

As shown in Figure 1, service quality as perceived by consumers depends on the size and direction of an additional gap (gap 5 in Figure 1), which in turn depends on the nature of the gaps associated with the delivery of service quality on the marketer's side. The SERVQUAL scale (or an adaptation of it) could be used to measure gap 5. Then the relative importance of the four managerial gaps could be examined empirically by means of a multiple regression model.

What are the main organizational factors responsible for the size of the four service quality gaps? A key managerial question involves the relative importance of the specific indicators in delivering high quality service to consumers. If a marketer could implement only a few of the many organizational strategies implied by the propositions, which ones should be undertaken? To answer this question, several measures are necessary: (1) overall measures of the four gaps and (2) measures of the organizational strategy variables detailed in Tables 1 through 4. Ways to measure the four gaps are discussed above. Measures of the other factors (e.g., amount of marketing research, extent of face-to-face contact between top managers and customers) must be developed and then can be related statistically (e.g., through regression analysis) to the measures of the four gaps.

SUMMARY

The intent of our study is to identify a reasonably exhaustive set of factors thought to affect the magnitude and direction of four gaps on the marketer's side of a service quality model (Figure 1). These factors, which mainly involve communication and control processes implemented in organizations to manage employees, are reviewed and integrated with qualitative data from an exploratory study. Procedures for testing this extended model of service quality in a cross-sectional study are detailed.

REFERENCES

Anderson, Carl (1984), *Management Skills, Functions, and Organizational Performance,* Dubuque, IA: Wm. C. Brown Publishers.

Averill, J. R. (1973), "Personal Control over Aversive Stimuli and Its Relationship to Stress," *Psychological Bulletin,* 80 (4), 286–303.

Belasco, James A. (1966), "The Salesman's Role Revisited," *Journal of Marketing,* 30 (April), 6–8.

Berry, Leonard L. (1986), "Reconciling and Coordinating Selling and Service," *American Banker* (February 12), 4–5.

————, Valarie A. Zeithaml, and A. Parasuraman (1985), "Quality Counts in Services, Too," *Business Horizons,* 28 (May–June), 44–52.

Business Week (1981), "Boosting Productivity at American Express" (October 5), 62, 66.

———— (1984), "Making Service a Potent Marketing Tool" (June 11), 164–170.

Clist, Todd (1985), "Marriott Philosophies," in *Services Marketing in a Changing Environment,* Thomas Bloch, Gregory Upah, and Valarie Zeithaml, eds. Chicago: American Marketing Association, 13–14.

Cromwell, R. L., E. C. Butterfield, F. M. Brayfield, and J. J. Curry (1971), *Acute Myocardial Infarction: Reaction and Recovery,* St. Louis, MO: The C. V. Mosby Company.

Crosby, Phillip B. (1979), *Quality Is Free,* New York: New American Library.

Daft, Richard L., and Robert H. Lengel (1984), "Information Richness: A New Approach to Managerial Behavior and Organization Design," in *Research in Organizational Behavior,* Vol. 6, Barry Staw and Larry L. Cummings, eds. Greenwich, CT: JAI Press, Inc., 191–233.

———— and Richard Steers (1985), *Organizations: A Micro/Macro Approach,* Glenview, IL: Scott, Foresman and Company.

Davis, J. H. (1969), *Group Performance,* Reading, MA: Addison-Wesley Publishing Company, 78.

Deshpande, Rohit (1983), "Paradigms Lost: On Theory and Method in Research in Marketing," *Journal of Marketing,* 47 (Fall), 101–110.

Ford, Neil M., Orville C. Walker, Jr., and Gilbert A. Churchill, Jr. (1975), "Expectation-Specific Measures of the Intersender Conflict and Role Ambiguity Experienced by Industrial Salesmen," *Journal of Business Research,* 3 (2), 95–111.

Garvin, David A. (1983), "Quality on the Line," *Harvard Business Review,* 61 (September–October), 65–73.

Geer, J. H., G. C. Davidson, and R. J. Gatchel (1970), "Reduction of Stress in Humans through Nonveridical Perceived Control of Aversive Stimulation," *Journal of Personality and Social Psychology,* 16 (4), 731–738.

———— and E. Maisel (1972), "Evaluating the Effects of the Prediction-Control Confound," *Journal of Personality and Social Psychology,* 23 (8), 314–319.

George, William R., and Hiram C. Barksdale (1974), "Marketing Activities in the Services Industries," *Journal of Marketing,* 38 (October), 65–70.

———— and Leonard L. Berry (1981), "Guidelines for the Advertising of Services," *Business Horizons,* 24 (May–June), 52–56.

Glass, D. C., and J. E. Singer (1972), *Urban Stress,* New York: Academic Press, Inc.

Goyne, David (1985), "Customer Service in Retailing," presentation, Center for Retailing Studies Fall Conference (October 11), Houston, TX.

Greene, Charles, and D. W. Organ (1973), "An Evaluation of Causal Models Linking Perceived Role and Job

Satisfaction," *Administrative Science Quarterly*, 18 (March), 95–103.

Gronroos, C. (1982), *Strategic Management and Marketing in the Service Sector*. Helsingfors: Swedish School of Economics and Business Administration.

Gross, Neal, W. S. Mason, and A. W. McEachern (1957), *Expectations in Role Analysis: Studies of the School Superintendency Role*, New York: John Wiley & Sons, Inc.

Hax, Arnoldo and Nicolas S. Majluf (1984), *Strategic Management: An Integrative Perspective*, Englewood Cliffs, NJ: Prentice-Hall, Inc.

Ivancevich, J. M., and J. T. McMahon (1982), "The Effects of Goal Setting, External Feedback, and Self-Generated Feedback on Outcome Variables: A Field Experiment," *Academy of Management Journal*, 25 (2), 359–373.

Kahn, R. L., D. M. Wolfe, R. P. Quinn, J. D. Snock, and R. A. Rosenthal (1964), *Organizational Stress*, New York: John Wiley & Sons, Inc.

Katz, B., and R. Kahn (1978), *The Social Psychology of Organizations*, 2nd ed. New York: John Wiley & Sons, Inc.

Langeard, Eric, John E. G. Bateson, Christopher H. Lovelock, and Pierre Eiglier (1981), *Services Marketing: New Insights from Consumers and Managers*, Cambridge, MA: Marketing Science Institute.

Latham, G. P., and E. A. Locke (1979), "Goal Setting—A Motivational Technique That Works," *Organizational Dynamics*, 8 (Autumn), 68–80.

Lawler, E. E., and C. Cammann (1972), "What Makes a Work Group Successful?" in *The Failure of Success*, A. J. Marrow, ed. New York: AMACOM.

Leonard, Frank S., and W. Earl Sasser (1982), "The Incline of Quality," *Harvard Business Review*, 60 (September–October), 163–171.

Levitt, Ted (1976), "Industrialization of Service," *Harvard Business Review*, 54 (September–October), 63–74.

Locke, E. A., K. N. Shaw, L. M. Saari, and G. P. Latham (1981), "Goal Setting and Task Performance, 1969–1980," *Psychological Bulletin*, 90 (1), 125–152.

Lovelock, Christopher H. (1981), "Why Marketing Management Needs to Be Different for Services," in *Marketing of Services*, J. H. Donnelly and W. R. George, eds., Chicago: American Marketing Association, 5–9.

McMurray, Scott (1983), "Merrill Honors Quality Circles," *American Banker* (August 23), 23.

Mintzberg, H. (1979), "An Emerging Strategy of 'Direct' Research," *Administrative Science Quarterly*, 24 (December), 582–589.

Ouchi, William G. (1979), "A Conceptual Framework for the Design of Organizational Control Mechanisms," *Management Science*, 25 (September), 833–848.

——— and Mary Ann McGuire (1975), "Organizational Control: Two Functions," *Administrative Science Quarterly*, 20 (December), 559–569.

Parasuraman, A., Leonard Berry, and Valarie Zeithaml (1983), "Service Firms Need Marketing Skills," *Business Horizons*, 26 (November), 28–31.

——— and Valarie A. Zeithaml (1983), "Differential Perceptions of Suppliers and Clients of Industrial Services," in *Emerging Perspectives on Services Marketing*, L. Berry, G. L. Shostack, and G. Upah, eds., Chicago: American Marketing Association, 35–39.

———, ———, and Leonard Berry (1985), "A Conceptual Model of Service Quality and Its Implications for Future Research," *Journal of Marketing*, 49 (Fall), 41–50.

———, ———, and ——— (1986), "SERVQUAL: A Multiple-Item Scale for Measuring Customer Perceptions of Service Quality Research," Report No. 86–108, Marketing Science Institute (August).

Perrow, C. (1979), *Complex Organizations: A Critical Essay*, Glenview, IL: Scott, Foresman and Company.

Peter, Paul, and Jerry Olson (1983), "Is Science Marketing?" *Journal of Marketing*, 47 (Fall), 111–125.

Peters, Thomas J. and Robert H. Waterman, Jr. (1982), *In Search of Excellence*, New York: Harper & Row Publishers, Inc.

Rabin, Joseph H. (1983), "Accent Is on Quality in Consumer Services This Decade," *Marketing News*, 17 (March 4), 12.

Read, W. H. (1962), "Upward Communication in Industrial Hierarchies," *Human Relations*, 15 (February), 3–15.

Reeves, T. K., and J. Woodward (1970), "The Study of Managerial Control," in *Industrial Organizations: Behavior and Control*, J. Woodward, ed., London: Oxford University Press.

Rizzo, John, R. J. House, and S. I. Lirtzman (1970), "Role Conflict and Ambiguity in Complex Organizations," *Administrative Science Quarterly*, 15, 150–163.

Rout, Lawrence (1981), "Hyatt Hotel's Gripe Sessions Help Chief Maintain Communication with Workers," *Wall Street Journal* (July 16), 27.

Rudie, Mary J., and H. Brant Wansley (1985), "The Merrill Lynch Quality Program," in *Services Marketing in a Changing Environment*, T. M. Bloch, G. D. Upah, and V. A. Zeithaml, eds., Chicago: American Marketing Association, 7–9.

Salancik, Gerald R. (1977), "Commitment Is Too Easy," *Organizational Dynamics*, 6 (Summer), 62–80.

Schneider, Ben, and David E. Bowen (1985), "Employee and Customer Perceptions of Service in Banks: Replication and Extension," *Journal of Applied Psychology*, 70 (3), 423–433.

Shaw, M. E. (1976), *Group Dynamics: The Psychology of Small Group Behavior*, New York: McGraw-Hill Book Company.

Sherwin, D. S. (1976), "Management of Objectives," *Harvard Business Review*, 54 (May–June), 149–160.

Straub, E., B. Tursky, and G. E. Schartz (1971), "Self-Control and Predictability: Their Effects on Reactions to Aversive Stimulation," *Journal of Personality and Social Psychology*, 18, 157–162.

Thompson, Phillip, Glenn DeSouza, and Bradley T. Gale (1985), *The Strategic Management of Service Quality*, Cambridge, MA: Strategic Planning Institute, PIMSLETTER, No. 33.

Walker, Orville C., Jr., Gilbert A. Churchill, Jr., and Neil M. Ford (1977), "Motivation and Performance in Industrial

Selling: Present Knowledge and Needed Research," *Journal of Marketing Research,* 14 (May), 156–168.

Woodward, Joan (1965), *Industrial Organization: Theory and Practice,* London: Oxford University Press.

Zaltman, Gerald, Karen LeMasters, and Michael Heffring (1982), *Theory Construction in Marketing: Some Thought on Thinking,* New York: John Wiley & Sons, Inc.

Zeithaml, Valarie A. (1981), "How Consumer Evaluation Processes Differ between Goods and Services," in *Marketing of Services,* James Donnelly and William George, eds., Chicago: American Marketing Association, 186–190.

———, A. Parasuraman, and Leonard L. Berry (1985), "Problems and Strategies in Services Marketing," *Journal of Marketing,* 49 (Spring), 33–46.

ARTICLE 12.3

A LONGITUDINAL ANALYSIS OF THE IMPACT OF SERVICE CHANGES ON CUSTOMER ATTITUDES

Ruth N. Bolton

James H. Drew

The authors develop a longitudinal model of the effect of a service change on customer attitudes about service quality. The model is estimated with data from a field experiment with three survey waves. Service changes are found to have a strong influence on customer evaluations of service quality through their effect on customer perceptions of current performance and disconfirmation. The effect of disconfirmation is larger and the effect of prior attitudes is smaller directly after the service change than in a subsequent time period.

In recent years, many large companies have implemented quality measurement programs in an attempt to relate customer evaluations of quality to product/service attributes (Hauser and Clausing 1988). In service industries, companies commonly employ surveys that elicit customer evaluations of the service offering, plus information about customers' recent service experiences (e.g., Andrews et al. 1987). This information is used to identify potential service improvements and predict their effect on customer satisfaction and/or attitudes, as well as to evaluate the organizational units providing the service.

We conducted a study to investigate how customers' evaluations of service quality are influenced by changes in service offerings. We examined such questions as:

☐ How can a company assess the effect of a potential service improvement on customer attitudes?

☐ How do customers' perceptions of changes in current service performance affect their evaluations of service quality?

☐ To what extent do prior customer attitudes carry over during a period of service change?

We addressed these questions with a field experiment in which a significant service change was implemented and a customer panel was surveyed repeatedly.

Unlike previous research, our study focused on temporal changes in individual attitudes. Prior research typically has measured perceived service quality and its underlying dimensions by using cross-sectional data (Parasuraman, Zeithaml, and Berry 1985, 1988). Because the factors that explain differences among customers' attitudes at a given time may not be the same as the factors that cause change in a given customer's attitudes over time, these studies have not explored how perceived service quality is affected by changes in service offerings. On the basis of the customer satisfaction literature (Anderson 1973; Cardozo 1965; Churchill and Surprenant 1982; Oliver 1980a; Olshavsky and Miller

SOURCE: Ruth N. Bolton and James H. Drew, "A Longitudinal Analysis of the Impact of Service Changes on Customer Attitudes," reprinted with permission from the *Journal of Marketing*, vol. 55 (January 1991): 1–9. Published by the American Marketing Association, Chicago, IL 60606.

Ruth N. Bolton is a Senior Member of the Technical Staff and James H. Drew is a Principal Member of the Technical Staff, GTE Laboratories Incorporated.

1972; Swan and Combs 1976), we developed a theoretical model of attitude change for service offerings and operationalized it with panel data from an experiment with three survey waves. We used the results to analyze the effects of a service change on customer attitudes about service quality.

In the following section, we develop the theoretical model of attitude change for services. We then discuss how the model can be formulated as a statistical model, operationalized, and estimated with generalized least squares (GLS). After describing the field experiment and longitudinal survey data, we report the results of our analyses and present our conclusions.

A MODEL OF ATTITUDE CHANGE FOR SERVICES

Researchers distinguish between two constructs, customer satisfaction and attitude. Customer satisfaction refers to a customer's evaluation of a specific transaction. In contrast, a customer's attitude corresponds to a global evaluation of the product/service, rather than to an evaluation of a specific transaction (Holbrook and Corfman 1985; Olshavsky 1985). Consequently, Oliver (1981) argues that satisfaction eventually becomes an input to a less dynamic attitude. However, the distinction between customer satisfaction and attitude becomes rather blurred for frequently or continuously provided services (e.g., utilities services), particularly when changes in the service offering are subtle (Bolton and Drew 1988, 1989). In this section we develop a general model of satisfaction and attitudes toward services, and discuss the appropriate model specification for a continuously provided service, namely local telephone service.

MODELING CUSTOMER SATISFACTION AND ATTITUDE CHANGE

CUSTOMER SATISFACTION Satisfaction is a customer's postpurchase evaluation of a product/service offering (Hunt 1977). A customer is satisfied when an offering performs better than expected and is dissatisfied when expectations exceed performance. Customer satisfaction/dissatisfaction (CS/D) typically is modeled as a function of disconfirmation arising from discrepancies between prior expectations and actual performance (Cardozo 1965; Oliver 1980a; Olshavsky and Miller 1972; Olson and Dover 1979). Hence, a simple model of the antecedents of customer satisfaction with a service offering can be expressed algebraically as

$$CS/D_t = f(DISCONFIRM_t, PERFORM_t, EXPECT_{t-1}). \quad (1)$$

In words, a customer's satisfaction/dissatisfaction with a service offering at time t (CS/D_t) depends on his or her current perceptions of performance ($PERFORM_t$), prior expectations about performance ($EXPECT_{t-1}$), and perceptions of the discrepancy between these two constructs ($DISCONFIRM_t$).

CUSTOMER ATTITUDES Attitude is the customer's global evaluation of a product/service offering. Recent research in services marketing has centered on customers' evaluations of the overall excellence of superiority of a service—that is, evaluations of service quality (Parasuraman, Zeithaml, and Berry, 1985, 1988; Zeithaml 1988)—but there is little research on temporal changes in attitudes toward services. Adaptation level theory provides a useful framework for explaining these changes (Oliver 1980b, 1981). It postulates that prior experience with a phenomenon provides an anchor for subsequent judgments, and that exposure to stimuli above/below the adaptation level modifies those judgments (Helson 1964). Hence, a simple model of a customer's attitude toward a service can be expressed algebraically as

$$ATTITUDE_t = g(CS/D_t, ATTITUDE_{t-1}). \quad (2)$$

In words, a customer's attitude about a service offering at time t ($ATTITUDE_t$) depends on his or her prior attitude ($ATTITUDE_{t-1}$) mediated by his or her satisfaction/dissatisfaction with current service (CS/D_t).

Equation 2 is consistent with the revised Howard and Sheth model (Howard 1974; Howard and Sheth 1969), in which a customer's satisfaction with a brand forms a feedback loop to subsequent attitudes and purchase intentions. For example, in their longitudinal study of consecutive purchase behavior in five product classes, LaBarbera and Mazursky (1983) modeled repeat purchase intentions as a function of prior intentions and customer satisfaction. Equation 2 is also consistent with a Bayesian framework in which the customer makes a posterior probability assessment about service on the basis of current information and a prior attitude.

GENERAL MODEL Substituting equation 1 into equation 2, we have

$$ATTITUDE_t = h(DISCONFIRM_t, PERFORM_t, EXPECT_{t-1}, ATTITUDE_{t-1}). \quad (3)$$

In words, a customer's attitude about a service depends on his or her prior attitude, modified by his or her perceptions of current performance, prior expectations about performance, and the discrepancy between the expectations and subsequent perceptions. A traditional practice is to treat the simple difference in attitude (e.g., $ATTITUDE_2 - ATTITUDE_1$) as the dependent variable (i.e., requiring that the coefficient of $ATTITUDE_{t-1}$ equal one). However, there is no compelling reason for this restriction.

MODELING ATTITUDE CHANGE FOR LOCAL TELEPHONE SERVICE

Recent research demonstrates that disconfirmation, expectations, and actual performance levels have independent effects on customer satisfaction—and the effects are different for different products. For example, Churchill and Surprenant (1982) find that CS/D with a nondurable good is a function of expectations, performance evaluations, and disconfirmation, whereas CS/D with a durable good is a function only of performance evaluations. In his discussion of modes of satisfaction, Oliver (1989) proposes that customer responses for continuously provided services or long-lasting durable goods are characterized by passive expectations, and that disconfirmation will not operate unless service changes occur that are outside the range of experience-based norms. Because telephone service is a continuing service, these notions suggest that customer responses for telephone service should be affected only by performance evaluations. We next discuss whether expectations, performance evaluations, and disconfirmation should have independent , additive effects on customer satisfaction and attitudes about local telephone service quality.

DISCONFIRMATION Local telephone service is different from many other products/services because usually it is regulated; hence prices are not free to fluctuate and the service has no direct competitor in franchised areas. Because it has a long history as a stable, well-established, nearly universal service, most customers have a very clear idea—based on prior experience—of what constitutes traditional telephone service. Customers' evaluations of services that they perceive to have clear and distinct attributes may decrease when an attribute deteriorates. For example, customers' satisfaction with local telephone service may decline when the company drops free telephone repair (as occurred during deregulation) or when the customer moves from one local franchise to another. Consequently, a customer's satisfaction with local telephone service should depend on (favorable or unfavorable) disconfirmation of anticipated performance levels only when a service change occurs that is outside the range of experience-based norms.

PERFORMANCE Because telephone service provision and usage are continuous, a customer can easily form an assessment of performance, and it is readily available for incorporation into an evaluation of satisfaction. Hence, current performance levels should have a direct effect on customer satisfaction, as well as an indirect effect via disconfirmation.

EXPECTATIONS In the CS/D paradigm, expectations typically are defined as anticipated or predicted levels of product/service performance formed by advertising, word-of-mouth, or past experience (e.g., Barbeau 1985; Miller 1977; Swan and Trawick 1980). Exploratory research on customer expectations about telephone service confirmed Oliver's (1989) notion that expectations about a continuing service are not processed actively. Specifically, concurrent verbal protocols collected during in-depth interviews with 50 telephone company customers yielded many speech segments about their perceptions of current performance, but not about their expectations. Perhaps customers do not explicitly conceptualize expectations about service because telephone service is characterized by its stability. Hence, this model postulates that a customer's satisfaction with local telephone service is not affected directly by expectations (but only indirectly through disconfirmation).

TELEPHONE SERVICE MODEL We model customer attitudes about telephone service quality after a change that is outside the range of prior experience. Accordingly, disconfirmation may operate (when the service change is observed), but expectations should be passive (because customers cannot anticipate the change). Hence, a customer's attitude about telephone service is hypothesized to depend on his or her prior attitude, modified by perceptions of current performance and disconfirmation. Excluding expectations from equation 3, we have

$$ATTITUDE_t = k (DISCONFIRM_t, PERFORM_t, ATTITUDE_{t-1}). \quad (4)$$

Equation 4 is a reduced-form model that characterizes attitude change for local telephone service.

AN EXPERIMENTAL MANIPULATION OF SERVICE ATTRIBUTES

Panel data are needed to estimate the attitude change model for local telephone service developed in the preceding section. Furthermore, experimentally generated data are desirable because customer attitudes tend to vary little over time in naturally occurring situations (in which service offerings are stable). Unlike prior longitudinal studies of customer satisfaction, our study uses panel data from a field experiment rather than a laboratory experiment. The field experiment was conducted as part of GTE's customer satisfaction program.

GTE'S CUSTOMER SATISFACTION PROGRAM

GTE, like most franchised suppliers of local telephone service, regularly surveys its customers to identify potential service enhancements, evaluate the effect of enhancements, and meet public utilities commission requirements. In these surveys, the customer's recent telephone experiences are probed, his or her ratings of various service process attributes are reported, and overall service quality and value assessments are obtained. Analyses of these data indicated that voice transmission quality (i.e., lack of noise) was the key determinant of customer satisfaction and attitude. Network monitoring devices showed that crackling static was associated with aged transmission equipment, particularly in rural areas. Hence, company managers systematically implemented a program of network upgrades to decrease telephone line noise and increase customer ratings of local telephone service.

THE FIELD EXPERIMENT

A field experiment was devised to test the effect of a network upgrade program on residential customer's ratings. The program entailed specifying standards for residential loops (between the telephone company's central office and the customer's premises), then making engineering and operational changes (e.g., replacing deficient cable, monitoring systems) to meet those standards. Because customers could not be assigned randomly to treatment groups, a quasi-experimental design was employed. The test took place at four small sites served by the same central office. Two test and two control sites were matched to be similar in their physical plant. The network upgrade program was implemented at the (slightly smaller) test sites, and the control sites were given the usual levels of service.

The network upgrade program involved construction activities that were visible to each household in the two test sites. A flyer was delivered to each household on the day when construction activities began at the residence. Because the experimental program included changes to a physical plant (i.e., construction activities) over a somewhat lengthy implementation period, customers could observe temporary disruptions in service during the change period, as well as long-term improvements in voice transmission quality. Customers at all four sites were surveyed by telephone at three different points in time: approximately six months before the beginning of the network upgrade activities, approximately one month after the end of the network upgrade activities, and six months after that time. For the first wave, the interviewing firm attempted to contact every household. At subsequent waves, the firm attempted to reinterview the same person. Such a design avoids the high interperson variability historically present in this type of survey.

The interviewing firm contacted 216 households during the first wave of interviews. During the second wave, it was able to contact *the same person* in 140 (65%) of the households. During the third wave, it was able to contact *the same person* in 120 (56%) of the 216 households. (If the interviewing firm had not been required to contact the same person for all three waves, the dropout rate between waves would have been much lower.) As one individual refused to complete the interview, the procedure yielded 119 respondents who completed the interview for all three waves. Cooperation rates were roughly equivalent at the control and test sites. The same interview questionnaire was used during each wave.

MODEL OPERATIONALIZATION

In the longitudinal survey, the customer's attitude about service quality was measured by his or her evaluation of the overall quality of *all* services provided by the local telephone company ($QUALITY_t$). Local telephone services include billing, repair, directory and toll assistance, and service order (i.e., service installation or change) processing, as well as the quality of local calls. The question was phrased in the following way: "How would you rate the overall quality of services provided by your local telephone company? Would you say (1) poor, . . ., (5) excellent?"

The customer's overall perception of current performance was measured by the customer's rating of local calls ($LOCAL_t$)—that is, call connection and voice transmission services. Because disconfirmation should be tied closely to customers' prior experiences with local telephone service, it was measured with two questions that elicit comparisons of current and past service: a comparison of the customer's current service with service six months ago ($CHANGE_t$) and the customer's self-report of whether he or she has ever lived in a non-GTE serving area (GTE-ONLY). Perceptions of improved service in comparison with six months ago (i.e., favorable disconfirmation) should be associated with more positive attitudes. Customers who have experienced service from a non-GTE provider may perceive a GTE service to be better, worse, or the same. However, if customers *systematically* perceive that the service provided by GTE is better (or worse) than the service provided in non-GTE areas, their prior experience is an additional source of favorable (or unfavorable) disconfirmation, and it will have an effect on their attitudes about overall telephone service.

Operationalizing equation 4, we obtain the following algebraic expression for the customer's attitude about local telephone service (for t = 2,3).

$$
\begin{aligned}
QUALITY_t = b_0 &+ d_1\, QUALITY_{t-1} \\
&+ b_1 CHANGE_t + b_2\, GTE\text{-}ONLY_t \\
&+ b_3 LOCAL_t + e_{1t}. \quad (5)
\end{aligned}
$$

The $QUALITY_2$ equation describes customers' attitudes directly after the implementation of the network upgrades and associated service disruptions. The $QUALITY_3$ equation describes customers' attitudes under stable "improved service conditions," six months later.

A second equation was specified to establish an explicit linkage between the service change (i.e., the network upgrades to substantially reduce local telephone line noise or $STATIC_t$) and customers' assessments of current performance ($LOCAL_t$) and overall service quality ($QUALITY_t$). In the tradition of multiattribute models, we hypothesized that a customer's rating of local calls would depend on his or her perceptions of the presence/absence of trouble with voice transmission (STATIC), dial tone provision (DIAL), call connection (CONNECT), and call completion (CUTOFF). These constructs were measured by indicator variables that took the value 1 when the customer reported trouble in the past 30 days.

$$
\begin{aligned}
LOCAL_t = c_0 &+ c_1\, STATIC_t + c_2\, DIAL_t \\
&- c_3\, CONNECT_t \\
&+ c_4\, CUTOFF_t + e_{2t}. \quad (6)
\end{aligned}
$$

Equations 5 and 6 do not explicitly include a variable that indicates whether the customer resides in a treated area (i.e., where network upgrades took place). However, $CHANGE_t$ and the determinants of $LOCAL_t$ are a function of the network upgrade activities (i.e., the treatment variable), so an explicit treatment indicator is not necessary.

PRELIMINARY ANALYSES

Seventy-five customers at the control sites and 44 customers at the test sites responded to all three waves of the survey. Descriptive statistics are reported in Table 1. Table 2 is a correlation matrix. Average ratings at the test

sites were relatively stable, but they showed a common pattern across waves. Perceived static ($STATIC_t$) increased in the treated areas from the first to second wave, then decreased from the second to third wave. Performance ratings ($LOCAL_t$) decreased in the treated areas from the first to second wave, then increased from the second to third wave. $QUALITY_t$ ratings almost exactly parallel this movement.

Individual customer ratings varied considerably across waves. Twenty-five to 55% of the respondents changed their ratings from one wave to the next—at both the test *and* control sites. The turnover in customer ratings of $CHANGE_t$ was higher at the test sites than at the control sites. The percentage of respondents noting an improvement at the test sites was 27% for the second wave (i.e., postconstruction) versus 16% for the first wave, whereas the percentages at the control sites were roughly equal (10%) for both waves.

To investigate customers' perceptions of static, we estimated the following model: $STAT_t = a + b\, STAT_{t-1} + c\, TEST$, where TEST is a dummy variable that takes the value 1 when the customer lives at a test site. After controlling for initial static levels, we found that for t = 2, the coefficient c in this equation was positive and statistically significant (p < .15), indicating that the percentage of respondents perceiving static during the second wave significantly *increased* at the test sites in comparison with the control sites. For t = 3 (six months later), the percentage of customers perceiving static *decreased* at both the test and control sites. The decrease in the percentage reporting static was larger at the test site than the control site, but was not statistically significant (p > .15). Hence, customers at the test sites perceived greater increases in static directly after the network upgrades and all customers perceived decreases in static six months later.

In contrast, the average customer ratings of $CHANGE_t$ increased across the three waves—and the magnitude of the increase was larger at the test sites. To investigate customers' perceptions of change, we estimated the following model: $CHANGE_t = a + b\, CHANGE_{t-1} + c\, TEST$. After controlling for initial levels, we found that for t = 2, the $CHANGE_t$ rating *increased* at the test sites in relation to the control sites (p < .10). Again controlling for initial levels, we found that during the third wave, the $CHANGE_t$ rating increased at the test sites in relation to the control sites, but this difference between treatment groups was not statistically significant (p > .15). Hence, more customers at the test sites noticed changes in services after the network upgrades.

TABLE 1   Descriptive Statistics

| | Means | | | Turnover Statistics | |
	Wave 1	Wave 2	Wave 3	Wave 1 to Wave 2	Wave 2 to Wave 3
Control Sites					
QUALITY	3.96	4.03	4.01	.45	.44
LOCAL	3.09	3.08	3.21	.55	.43
CHANGE	3.05	3.13	3.20	.20	.29
STATIC	.40	.36	.31	.25	.29
Test Sites					
QUALITY	3.82	3.98	3.80	.50	.55
LOCAL	3.18	3.00	3.14	.41	.52
CHANGE	3.20	3.41	3.89	.34	.34
STATIC	.43	.50	.36	.34	.32

TABLE 2   Correlation Matrix

	Quality (t = 1)	Change (t = 2)	GTE-Only	Local (t = 2)	Quality (t = 2)	Change (t = 3)	Local (t = 3)	Quality (t = 3)
Quality (t = 1)	+1.00	−.07	.04	+.42[a]	+.52[a]	−.06	+.29	+.42[a]
Change (t = 2)		+1.00	+.07	+.22[b]	+.24[a]	+.45[a]	−.02	+.12
GTE-only			+1.00	−.03	+.03	−.03	−.23[b]	−.21[b]
Local (t = 2)				+1.00	+.65[a]	−.19[b]	+.29[a]	+.35[a]
Quality (t = 2)					+1.00	−.05	+.26[b]	+.41[a]
Change (t = 3)						+1.00	+.17[c]	+.18[b]
Local (t = 3)							+1.00	+.59[a]
Quality (t = 3)								+1.00

[a]Two-tailed test, p < .005.
[b]Two-tailed test, p < .01.
[c]Two-tailed test, p < .05.

In summary, the service change did not simply increase respondents' ratings at the test sites while ratings stayed constant at the control sites. The measures of disconfirmation experiences ($CHANGE_t$) and perceptions of current performance ($LOCAL_t$ and $STATIC_t$) were most sensitive to the effects of the service change. The preliminary analyses indicated that the network upgrades at the test sites affected the percentage of customers reporting static ($STATIC_t$) and the reported levels of disconfirmation ($CHANGE_t$). Hence, one can infer that the experimental manipulation succeeded. Furthermore, GTE's internal monitoring indicated that construction activities affected voice transmission quality.

MODEL ESTIMATION AND RESULTS

To investigate the long-run effect of the service change on customer satisfaction and attitudes, we used the model estimation and results for the 119 customers who responded to all three waves of the survey. The results for equations 5 and 6 at t = 2 and t = 3 are substantively the same when the model estimation and results include customers who did not respond to all three waves.

ESTIMATION

We used four equations: equation 5 for t = 2 and t = 3, and equation 6 for t = 2 and t = 3. The appropriate estimation procedure depends on the error structure of these equations. The measurement error associated with an individual customer's attitudes about service quality seems likely to be correlated across waves. Hence, instrumental variables were formed for the lagged variables, $QUALITY_{t-1}$, in equation 5. Because $QUALITY_t$ and $LOCAL_t$ are measured on different scales, we assume that their measurement errors are uncorrelated for a given time period. However, the results reported here would not change substantively if this assumption were relaxed and an instrumental variable created for $LOCAL_t$ as well. The attitude models for t = 2 and t = 3 (i.e., equation 5) were estimated with GLS and the performance models for t = 2 and t = 3 (i.e., equation 6) were estimated with OLS (Johnston 1972).

The models fit the data reasonably well, and the hypothesis that each vector of coefficients is equal to zero is rejected at p < .005. The estimated coefficients are reported in Table 3. In general, the coefficients are statistically significant (p < .05) and their signs are consistent with prior theory. The hypothesis that the vectors of coefficients for waves 2 and 3 are equal is rejected

(p < .10). This result implies that customers' attitude formation process is affected by the service change.

RESULTS

DISCONFIRMATION In the $QUALITY_2$ equation, the estimated coefficient of $CHANGE_2$ is statistically significant (p < .05). This result supports the hypothesis that a favorable disconfirmation experience (i.e., perceived improvement in telephone service) has a positive effect on customer attitudes. In addition, we hypothesized that there would be systematic differences in attitudes between subscribers who had lived in non-GTE serving areas and those who had not, because of differences in their disconfirmation experiences. However, the estimated coefficient of GTE-ONLY (t = 2) is not significant (p > .15). One possible explanation for this finding is that subscribers who have experienced service from other providers do not have systematically different disconfirmation experiences.

In the $QUALITY_3$ equation, the effects of the two disconfirmation variables ($CHANGE_3$ and GTE-ONLY) on attitude are not statistically significant (p > .15). (Note, however, that the coefficients of $CHANGE_2$ and $CHANGE_3$ are similar in sign and magnitude.) Apparently, the impact of disconfirmation on customer satisfaction and attitude occurred in the time period during which the service changes took place (between the first and second waves) and not subsequently. This result is particularly interesting; it indicates that the effect of disconfirmation (via satisfaction) on attitude diminishes with the passage of time.

PERFORMANCE In both $QUALITY_t$ equations (t = 2,3), the largest coefficient estimates belong to the performance rating item ($LOCAL_t$). Hence, customer perceptions of current performance seem to have the greatest impact on customer satisfaction and attitude. In particular, the effects of current performance are much larger than the effects of disconfirmation. This finding is not surprising because customers' perceptions of current performance are based on their experience with continuously providing local dial service. It is also consistent with Churchill and Surprenant's (1982) finding for a durable good.

In the $LOCAL_t$ equations, customers' perceptions of performance are modeled as a function of their perceptions of service attributes. Both equations (t = 2,3) indicate that customers' perceptions of performance are dominated by their perceptions of noisy voice transmission ($STATIC_t$). Customer perceptions of performance

TABLE 3   Estimates of Model Coefficients

	Wave 2	Wave 3
QUALITY Equation		
$QUALITY_{t-1}$	.2912[a]	.3575[a]
$CHANGE_t$	.1618[c]	.1358
GTE ONLY	.0769	−.1749
$LOCAL_t$	.5555[a]	.5528[a]
Intercept	.6110	.3894
System weighted R^2	.42[a]	
LOCAL Equation		
$STATIC_t$	−.6523[a]	−.6245[a]
$CONNECT_t$	−.2235	−.3348[a]
$DIAL_t$	−.3114	−.1501
$CUTOFF_t$	−.5690[c]	.3134
Intercept	3.4544[a]	3.4871[a]
F-statistic	14.33[a]	13.80[a]
R^2	.33	.32

[a]Two-tailed test, $p < .005$.
[b]Two-tailed test, $p < .01$.
[c]Two-tailed test, $p < .05$.

are influenced also by connection and cutoff problems ($CONNECT_t$ and $CUTOFF_t$), but the effects of these variables are smaller. The virtual elimination of cutoff problems in the treated areas after construction may account for the drop in $CUTOFF_t$ coefficients from $t = 2$ to $t = 3$. Obtaining a dial tone is a very reliable event in U.S. systems, so the small coefficients of $DIAL_t$ are not surprising.

PRIOR ATTITUDES In both $QUALITY_t$ equations ($t = 2,3$), the coefficient estimate for the lagged $QUALITY_t$ variable is significantly different from zero ($p < .005$). This result supports the hypothesis that current attitudes are influenced by prior attitudes. Because the coefficient of the lagged quality variable is less than one, customers seem to be less influenced by the prior attitudes than a simple difference model (that restricts the coefficient of the lagged $QUALITY_t$ variable to be equal to one) would postulate. Consistent with this notion, this coefficient is smaller at $t = 2$ than at $t = 3$, implying that the impact of prior attitudes was smaller during the interval in which the service change took place (between the first and second waves).

CONSTRUCTION ACTIVITIES Customers could observe temporary disruptions in service (i.e., construction activities) during the change period, as well as decreased static and improvements in voice transmission quality (i.e., favorable disconfirmation). The hypothesis that the disruption, as well as the reduction in static, affected customers' attitudes can be tested by adding a dummy variable that represents the treatment (i.e., the network upgrade at the test site) to equation 5 for $t = 2$. The coefficient of this variable represents the effect of the treatment on customer attitude *beyond* the effects of disconfirmation and perceived performance captured by the coefficients of $CHANGE_t$ and $LOCAL_t$. When this model is estimated, the coefficient of the dummy variable is not statistically significant ($p > .15$). This result implies that the construction activities did not directly affect customers' attitudes.

CONCLUSIONS

Prior research has been based on cross-sectional surveys of customers for whom service is very stable. In contrast, our longitudinal model provides useful insights about how customers' perceptions of changes in service performance affect their global evaluations of service quality. These findings should generalize to other continuously provided services (e.g., cable television, utilities, banking, transportation services).

One of the key implications of our findings is that changes over time in *individual* customers' ratings of the *components* of service quality are sensitive to the effects of a service change. In contrast, average ratings of perceived service quality are very stable and change slowly, so the effects of a service change become noticeable only in the long run. At GTE, managers have an increased awareness that customer attitudes have a large carryover component, and that service changes will not result in *immediate* improvements in the customers' global evaluations of service offerings. Consequently, models of the effect of the service change on individual customers' ratings must be used to predict the *long-run* effects of the service change on average ratings of overall quality.

As expected, attitudes are affected strongly by current performance ratings and, to a lesser extent, by disconfirmation. In contrast to prior research, the field experiment indicates that the effect of disconfirmation is relatively transitory. Furthermore, customers' current attitudes depend greatly on their prior attitudes, but the effect of prior attitudes is smaller immediately after the service change than six months later. Hence, attitudes seem to depend more heavily on perceptions of current performance and disconfirmation during the actual service change period than in periods of no change. This surprising finding emphasizes the importance of disentangling short-run and long-run effects of service changes on customer attitudes.

Service changes can be complicated by long implementation periods during which some service disruptions inevitably occur. The longitudinal model suggests that these disruptions affect perceptions and ratings for some time. Because customers' perceptions of current performance and disconfirmation carry over, it is not simple to identify improvements that will unequivocally enhance customer perceptions of service offerings. The experimental implementation of potential service imrovements, followed by a resurveying of the affected customers, forms a straightforward customer-service provider feedback loop that has the potential to foster continuous service improvements. GTE's use of a field experiment within their customer satisfaction program illustrates this notion of a customer feedback loop.

REFERENCES

Anderson, Rolph E. (1973), "Consumer Dissatisfaction: The Effect of Disconfirmed Expectancy on Perceived Product Performance," *Journal of Marketing Research*, 10 (February), 38–44.

Andrews, John F., James H. Drew, Michael J. English, and Melanie Rys (1987), "Service Quality Surveys in a Telecommunications Environment: An Integrating Force," in *The Services Challenge: Integrating for Competitive Advantage*, John A. Czepiel, Carole A. Congram, and James Shanahan, eds. Chicago: American Marketing Association, 27–31.

Barbeau, J. Bradley (1985), "Predictive and Normative Expectations in Consumer Satisfaction: A Utilization of Adaptation and Comparison Levels in a Unified Framework," in *Customer Satisfaction, Dissatisfaction and Complaining Behavior*, H. Keith Hunt and Ralph L. Day, eds. Bloomington: School of Business, Indiana University.

Bolton, Ruth N., and James H. Drew (1988), "A Model of Perceived Service Value," in *Efficiency and Effectiveness in Marketing*, Chicago: American Marketing Association, 213.

———— and ———— (1989), "A Multi-Stage Model of Customers' Assessments of Service Quality and Value," GTE Laboratories Technical Report #0029-03-89-420.

Cardozo, Richard N. (1965), "An Experimental Study of Consumer Effort, Expectation and Satisfaction," *Journal of Marketing Research*, 2 (August), 244.

Churchill, Gilbert A., Jr., and Carol Surprenant (1982), "An Investigation into the Determinants of Customer Satisfaction," *Journal of Marketing Research*, 19 (November), 491–504.

Drew, James H., and Ruth N. Bolton (1987), "Service Value and Its Measurement," in *Add Value to Your Service*, Carol Surprenant, ed. Chicago: American Marketing Association, 49–54.

Hauser, John R., and Don Clausing (1988), "The House of Quality," *Harvard Business Review*, 66 (May–June), 63–73.

Helson, Harry (1964), *Adaptation-Level Theory*, New York: Harper & Row Publishers, Inc.

Holbrook, Morris B., and Kim P. Corfman (1985), "Quality and Value in the Consumption Experience: Phaedrus Rides Again," in *Perceived Quality*, J. Jacoby and J. Olson, eds., Lexington, MA: Lexington Books, 31–57.

Howard, J. A. (1974), "The Structure of Buyer Behavior," in *Consumer Behavior: Theory and Application*, John V. Farley, John A. Howard, and L. Winston Ring, eds. Boston: Allyn and Bacon, Inc. 9–32.

————, and Jagsdish N. Sheth (1969). *The Theory of Buyer Behavior*. New York: John Wiley & Sons, Inc.

Hunt, H. Keith (1977), "CS/D—Overview and Future Research Directions," in *Conceptualization and Measurement of Consumer Satisfaction and Dissatisfaction*, H. Keith Hunt, ed., Cambridge, MA: Marketing Science Institute.

Johnston, J. (1972), *Econometric Methods*, New York: McGraw-Hill Book Company.

LaBarbera, Priscilla A., and David Mazursky (1983), "A Longitudinal Assessment of Consumer Satisfaction/Dissatisfaction: The Dynamic Aspect of the Cognitive Process," *Journal of Marketing Research,* 20 (November), 393–404.

Miller, John A. (1977), "Exploring Satisfaction, Modifying Models, Eliciting Expectations, Posing Problems and Making Meaningful Measurements," in *Conceptualization and Measurement of Consumer Satisfaction and Dissatisfaction,* H. Keith Hunt, ed., Cambridge, MA: Marketing Science Institute, 72–91.

Oliver, Richard L. (1980a), "A Cognitive Model of the Antecedents and Consequences of Satisfaction Decisions," *Journal of Marketing Research,* 17 (November), 460–469.

——— (1980b), "Conceptualization and Measurement of Disconfirmation Perceptions in the Prediction of Customer Satisfaction," in *Proceedings of Fourth Annual Conference on Consumer Satisfaction, Dissatisfaction and Complaining Behavior,* H. K. Hunt and R. L. Day, eds., Bloomington: School of Business, Indiana University.

——— (1981), "Measurement and Evaluation of Satisfaction Processes in Retail Settings," *Journal of Retailing,* 57 (Fall), 25–48.

——— (1989), "Processing of the Satisfaction Response in Consumption: A Suggested Framework and Research Propositions," *Journal of Satisfaction, Dissatisfaction and Complaining Behavior,* 2, 1–16.

Olshavsky, Richard W. (1985), "Perceived Quality in Consumer Decision Making: An Integrated Theoretical Perspective," in *Perceived Quality,* J. Jacoby and J. Olson, eds., Lexington, MA: Lexington Books.

——— and John A. Miller (1972), "Consumer Expectations, Product Performance and Perceived Product Quality," *Journal of Marketing Research,* 9 (February), 19–21.

Olson, Jerry C., and Philip Dover (1979), "Disconfirmation of Consumer Expectations through Product Trial," *Journal of Applied Psychology,* 46 (April), 375–384.

Parasuraman, A., Valarie A. Zeithaml, and Leonard L. Berry (1985), "A Conceptual Model of Service Quality and Its Implications for Future Research," *Journal of Marketing,* 49 (Fall), 41–50.

———, ———, and ——— (1988), "SERVQUAL: A Multiple-Item Scale for Measuring Consumer Perceptions of Service Quality," *Journal of Retailing,* 64 (1), 12–37.

Swan, John E., and Linda J. Combs (1976), "Product Performance and Consumer Satisfaction: A New Concept," *Journal of Marketing,* 40 (April), 25–33.

——— and I. Frederick Trawick (1980), "Inferred and Perceived Disconfirmation in Customer Satisfaction," in *Marketing in the 80's,* Chicago: American Marketing Association, 97–101.

Zeithaml, Valarie A. (1988), "Consumer Perceptions of Price, Quality, and Value: A Means–End Model and Synthesis of Evidence," *Journal of Marketing,* 52 (Summer), 2–22.

IMPROVING SERVICE QUALITY IN AMERICA

LESSONS LEARNED

Leonard L. Berry

A. Parasuraman

Valarie A. Zeithaml

Read !

Delivering excellent service is a winning strategy. Quality service sustains customers' confidence and is essential for a competitive advantage. Yet many companies are struggling to improve service, wasting money on ill-conceived service programs and undermining credibility with management rhetoric not backed up with action. Are there guidelines to help managers chart a service-improvement strategy for their organizations? We think so. In this article ten lessons from an extensive ten-year study of service quality in America are presented—lessons that we believe apply across industries and are essential to the service-improvement journey.

Excellent service is a profit strategy because it results in more new customers, more business with existing customers, fewer lost customers, more insulation from price competition, and fewer mistakes requiring the reperformance of services. Excellent service can also be energizing because it requires the building of an organizational culture in which people are challenged to perform to their potential and are recognized and rewarded when they do.

Service is a key component of value that drives any company's success. To the customer, value is the benefits received for the burdens endured—such as price, an inconvenient location, unfriendly employees, or an unattractive service facility. Quality service helps a company maximize benefits and minimize non-price burdens for its customers.

Over the last ten years, we have been studying service quality in America,[1] focusing primarily on these questions:

- What is service quality?
- How can service quality best be measured?
- What is the nature of customer expectations for service and what are the sources of these expectations?
- What are the principal causes of service-quality deficiencies?
- What can organizations do to improve service quality?

In this article, we focus on the last question, presenting lessons learned that we believe are essential for improving service quality.

LESSON ONE: LISTENING

The downtown Chicago Marriott hotel had been open for fifteen years before its management discovered that sixty-six percent of all guest calls to the housekeeping

SOURCE: Leonard L. Berry, A. Parasuraman, and Valarie A. Zeithaml, "Improving Service Quality in America: Lessons Learned," *Academy of Management Executive*, vol. 8, no. 2 (1994): 32–52. © Academy of Management Executive.

department were requests for irons and/or ironing boards. With this discovery, the hotel manager decided to put irons and ironing boards in all guest rooms—a $20,000 investment. The problem was where to find the $20,000.

The solution was in the following year's capital budget: $22,000 was earmarked to replace black and white television sets with color sets in the bathrooms of concierge-level guest rooms. With no evidence that guests ever requested color television sets for the bathroom, the manager purchased the irons and ironing boards instead.

Although this story has a happy ending, many like it do not. One of the most common service-improvement mistakes that companies make is to spend money in ways that do not improve service. Aside from being wasteful, such spending hurts the credibility of the service-improvement cause. When invested monies do not produce results, there is little incentive to spend more.

Quality is defined by the customer. Conformance to company specifications is not quality; conformance to the customer's specifications is. Spending wisely to improve service comes from continuous learning about the expectations and perceptions of customers and noncustomers. Customer research reveals the strengths and weaknesses of a company's service from the perspective of those who have experienced it. Noncustomer research reveals how competitors perform on service and provides a basis for comparison. Important expectations for the service that competitors fulfill better offer an agenda for action.

Companies need to install an ongoing service research process that provides timely, relevant trend data that managers become accustomed to using in decision making. Companies need to build a service quality information system, not just do a study. Conducting a service quality study is analogous to taking a snapshot. Deeper insight and a sense for the pattern of change come from a continuing series of snapshots taken from many angles.

Table 1 illustrates the concept of ongoing research through a portfolio of research approaches. This table is meant to convey the concept of systematic listening and not to offer definitive guidance on what a service quality information system should entail. The goal is to become a "listening company;" the specifics of how will vary from company to company.

LESSON TWO: RELIABILITY

Our research suggests five broad service dimensions that customers use as criteria to judge service quality. The dimensions are not mutually exclusive, yet they provide a framework helpful in understanding what customers expect from service providers. The five dimensions are:

☐ Reliability (32%): The ability to perform the promised service dependably and accurately.

☐ Responsiveness (22%): The willingness to help customers and provide prompt service.

☐ Assurance (19%): The knowledge and courtesy of employees and their ability to convey trust and confidence.

☐ Empathy (16%): The caring, individualized attention provided to customers.

☐ Tangibles (11%): The appearance of physical facilities, equipment, personnel, and communication materials.

Of these five dimensions of service quality, reliability is the most important. In each of our thirteen customer surveys, respondents rated reliability as the single most important feature in judging service quality. When we asked more than 1900 customers of five large, well-known U.S. companies to allocate a total of 100 points across the five service dimensions, we found thirty-two percent of the points were placed on reliability (see percentages in parentheses for each dimension). Reliability is the core of quality service. Little else matters to customers when a service is unreliable. When a firm makes frequent mistakes in delivery, when it doesn't keep its promises, customers lose confidence in the firm's ability to do what it promises dependably and accurately. Friendliness from the staff and sincere apologies do not compensate for unreliable service. Although most customers appreciate an apology, the apology does not erase the memory of that service. If a pattern of service failure develops, customers conclude the firm cannot be counted on, friendly and apologetic or not.

As Exhibit 1 shows, companies are more deficient on reliability than on any other dimension. Deficiencies are greatest on the service dimension most important to customers. Companies perform the best on the least important dimension of tangibles, suggesting an opportunity for refocusing efforts on improving service reliability.

Some managers believe that it is not practical to try to eliminate mistakes. This attitude is problematic for it does not challenge managers to boldness and creativity in improving the service dimension most important to customers. A company with 100,000 weekly transactions, and with a 98 percent reliability rate, still undermines the confidence of 2,000 customers each week.

TABLE 1   Building a Service Quality Information System

Type of Research	Frequency	Purposes
Customer complaint solicitation	Continuous	Identify dissatisfied customers to attempt recovery; identify most common categories of service failure for remedial action.
Post-transaction surveys	Continuous	Obtain customer feedback while service experience is still fresh; act on feedback quickly if negative patterns develop.
Customer focus group interviews	Monthly	Provide a forum for customers to suggest service-improvement ideas; offer fast, informal customer feedback on service issues.
"Mystery shopping" of service providers	Quarterly	Measure individual employee service behavior for use in coaching, training, performance evaluation, recognition and rewards; identify systemic strengths and weaknesses in customer-contact service.
Employee surveys	Quarterly	Measure internal service quality; identify employee-perceived obstacles to improved service; track employee morale and attitudes.
Total market service quality surveys	Three times per year	Assess company's service performance compared to competitors; identify service-improvement priorities; track service improvement over time.

Hard Rock Cafe, an immensely successful restaurant and retail chain with locations throughout the world, follows religiously the service tenet of "double checking" to minimize errors. The tenet is: *Be careful and don't make a mistake in the first place. If a mistake does occur, correct it before it reaches the customer.* Hard Rock Cafe Orlando implements double checking through two "extra" people in the kitchen. One is stationed inside the kitchen and the other at the kitchen counter. The inside person reviews everything that is going on, looking for signs of undercooked or overcooked meals, wilting lettuce, etc. The counter person, or "expediter," checks each prepared plate against the order ticket before the plate is delivered to the table. While this system is an added expense, it has worked well for this restaurant which on a busy day will serve 6,000 meals to customers who may have waited in line for a table for an hour or more.

Preston Trucking Company, a Maryland-based firm selected in the late 1980s as one of America's ten best companies to work for, nurtures service reliability values in a different way. Preston has each employee sign a service excellence statement. Posted in each Preston facility, the statement reads in part:

> Once I make a commitment to a customer or another associate, I promise to fulfill it on time. I will do what I say when I say I will do it. . . . I understand that one claim or one mistake is one error too many. I promise to do my job right the first time and to continually seek improvement.

LESSON THREE: BASIC SERVICE

Related to the lesson of reliability is the lesson of basic service. America's service customers want the basics—they expect fundamentals, not fanciness; performance, not empty promises. In all of our customer research, we have yet to find any evidence of extravagant customer expectations. Comments from focus group interviews illustrate the lesson of basic service.

> Automobile Repair Customers: Be Competent ("Fix it right the first time"); Explain Things ("Explain why you need the suggested repairs—provide an itemized list"); Be Respectful ("Don't treat me like a dumb female").

> Hotel Customers: Provide a Clean Room ("Don't have a deep-pile carpet that can't be completely cleaned . . . you can literally see germs down there"); Provide a Secure Room ("Good bolts and peephole on door"); Treat Me Like a Guest ("It is almost like they're looking you over to decide whether or not they're going to let you have a room"); Keep Your Promises ("They said the room would be ready, but it wasn't at the promised time").

> Equipment Repair Customers: Share My Sense of Urgency ("Speed of response. One time I had to buy a second piece of equipment because of the huge down time with the first piece"); Be Competent ("Sometimes you are quoting stuff from their instruction manuals to their own people and they don't even know what it means"); Be Prepared ("Have all the parts ready").

EXHIBIT 1   Perceived Service Quality

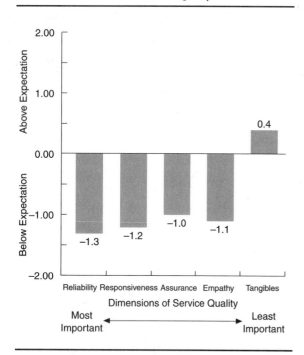

Most Important ←——————→ Least Important

*Based on a five-company study, service quality was determined by measuring customer expectations for the service and customer perceptions of the company against these expectations. If perceptions of the company were below the customer's expectations, the difference was scored negatively. The larger the minus score, the lower the company's service quality.

Automobile Insurance Customers: Keep Me Informed ("I shouldn't have to learn about insurance law changes from the newspaper"); Be on My Side ("I don't want them to treat me like I am a criminal just because I have a claim"); Fair Play ("Don't drop me when something goes wrong"); Protect Me from Catastrophe ("Make sure my estate is covered in the event of a major accident"); Provide Prompt Service ("I want fast settlement of claims").

Clearly, none of these comments would suggest the inflated, unreasonably high expectation levels that some executives attribute to today's customers.

De Mar, a plumbing, heating, air conditioning and refrigeration company in Clovis, California, grew from just over $200,000 annual revenue to $3.3 million in approximately six years by identifying and then responding to customers' most salient expectations. Customers wanted timely service in emergencies and De Mar responded by providing 24-hour-a-day, seven-day-a-week service. De Mar also guarantees same-day service for customers requiring it. Customers wanted accurate cost estimates and De Mar answered by guaranteeing its estimates before the work is done.

The Ritz-Carlton Hotel Company, a 1992 Baldrige Award winner, has captured its essential service strategy in a small plastic card given to all employees. Considered to be part of the uniform, the card contains the company's service credo and its motto: "We are Ladies and Gentlemen Serving Ladies and Gentlemen." It also lists the Ritz-Carlton Basics—twenty prescriptions, such as "Any employee who receives a customer complaint 'owns' the complaint." De Mar and Ritz-Carlton epitomize the lesson of basic service. Both companies have determined the fundamentals of service that are most important to their customers, and are highly focused on delivering these fundamentals well.

LESSON FOUR: SERVICE DESIGN

Reliably delivering the basic service customers expect depends in part on how well various elements function together in a service system. These elements include the people who perform the specific services in the service chain, the equipment that supports these performances, and the physical environment in which the services are performed. Design flaws in any part of a service system can reduce quality. It is tempting to blame poor quality on the people delivering service but frequently the real culprit is poor service system design.

Often, it is in the details that service system designs are flawed: clothing store dressing rooms with only one hook (or sometimes, no hooks) instead of the minimum two hooks required for take-off and try-on clothing; hotel rooms with such poor lighting that guests are discouraged from any night-time activity requiring visual acuity; computer-generated billing statements that are impossible for customers to understand.

Service mapping is one way to improve service system design. A service map is a visual definition of a service system, displaying each subprocess in the system in the sequence in which it appears. In effect, the service map depicts the chronology and pattern of performances that make up a service. If drawn explicitly, it answers the questions: "What is the service?" and "How does it work?"

A service map should not be confused with architectural drawings: an architect works in *space*. A service is a performance and the service system designer orchestrates the service over *time*. By mapping the details of the service system by transforming a series of intangible processes into a tangible picture, the service system becomes more amenable to management control and design improvement.[2]

Two important components of service mapping are "lines of visibility" and "fail points." The line of visibility in a service map separates those processes that are visible to the customer from those that are not. Interconnecting "above-the-line" and "below-the-line" service processes explicates the effect the latter has on the former. Fail points are the processes in the service system most vulnerable to failure. Identifying fail points can lead to system redesign, corrective subprocesses, special staff training, or additional inspection.

Employees from different parts of the service chain can work with a mapping specialist to create a service map. It is slow, laborious, painstaking work. The methodology is to draw increasingly detailed pictures of the service system (what happens first, what happens next, and so on) and then ask: "Is there a better way?" The objective is to redesign the service system to be simpler, more reliable, more efficient, more responsive, or improved in some other way. Customer input is critical in service mapping—first to establish improvement priorities and then to react to proposed new service designs.

A temporary employment company, one of the nation's largest, improved its service system designs by combining service mapping and time and motion studies. It learned that its account representatives spent too little time interacting with customers because of convoluted operating procedures, frequent interruptions, and outdated technology. The company streamlined its procedures and installed more efficient technology.

Delivering quality service is in part a design challenge. The lesson of service design involves developing a holistic view of the service while managing the details of the service. Both perspectives deepen managers' understanding of the service, making it easier to fit it to customers' expectations.

LESSON FIVE: RECOVERY

When a service problem occurs, the customer's confidence in the firm hangs in the balance. The company can make things better with the customer—at least to some extent—or make things worse.

Frequently, service companies make things worse. They do not encourage their customers to resolve their problems and set up roadblocks for those who try to do so. They do not put sufficiently trained personnel, or enough of them, in problem-resolution positions. They do not give employees the authority to solve most problems immediately. They do not invest in the communication and information systems that would support the problem-resolution service.

Three possibilities arise when a customer experiences a service problem: the customer complains and is satisfied with the company's response, the customer complains and is *not* satisfied with the company's response, or the customer does *not* complain to the company and remains dissatisfied.

Our research consistently shows that companies receive the most favorable service quality scores from customers experiencing no recent service problems with them, and, by far, the worst scores from customers whose problems were not resolved satisfactorily. In effect, companies that do not respond effectively to customer complaints *compound* the service failure; they fail the customer twice.

Many dissatisfied customers do not complaint directly to the company—to avoid a confrontation, or because they perceive no convenient way to complain, or do not believe complaining will do much good. Customers' reluctance to complain even when they are faced with serious problems has been well documented.[3] Companies can overcome some of this reluctance and improve recovery service in three ways:

1. *Encourage customers to complain and make it easy for them to do so.* Managers who wish to improve problem-resolution service must overcome the common customer perception that companies don't really care when things go wrong. Many firms rely exclusively on reactive recovery strategies in which customers must initiate contact. Comment cards available in the service facility and toll-free telephone numbers are examples of reactive systems. These approaches are useful but they preclude customers unwilling to take the first step. Thus, proactive strategies, in which the company makes the first contact, should be considered. Customers checking out of the Harvey Hotel in Plano, Texas, may be approached by a "Lobby Lizard," a member of management, who asks: "How can we do better?" This proactive feedback method gives management the opportunity to recover with an unhappy guest and provides ideas for service improvement.

2. *Respond quickly and personally.* Companies often take too long to respond to unhappy customers, and then respond impersonally. By responding quickly, a firm conveys a sense of urgency. Quick response demonstrates that the customer's concern is the company's concern. By responding personally, with a telephone call or a visit, the firm creates an opportunity for dialogue with the customer—an opportunity to listen, ask questions, explain, apologize,

and provide an appropriate remedy. North Carolina's Wachovia Bank has a "sundown rule"—the bank must establish contact with an unhappy customer before sunset on the day the complaint is received.

3. *Develop a problem resolution system.* Service employees need specific training on how to deal with angry customers and how to help customers solve service problems. In some cases, they need access to information systems that will tell them more about the customer, the situation causing the problem, and possible solutions. When American Express card holders telephone the company's toll-free number listed on their monthly statement, they speak to a highly trained customer service representative with the authority to solve eighty-five percent of the problems on the spot.

The lesson of recovery is taking the long view of restoring the customer's confidence in the company. How a company handles recovery service speaks volumes to customers and employees alike about the company's true values.

LESSON SIX: SURPRISING CUSTOMERS

Customers judge the dimensions of responsiveness, assurance, empathy, and tangibles during the service delivery process; hence, these are process dimensions. Reliability, judged following the service, is an outcome dimension. Although reliability is the most important dimension in meeting customers' service expectations, the process dimensions—especially assurance, responsiveness, and empathy—are most important in exceeding them. Companies are supposed to be reliable; they are supposed to provide the service they promise to provide. Thus, it is difficult for firms to exceed customers' expectations by being reliable. The process dimensions of service, however, provide the opportunity to *surprise* customers with uncommon swiftness, grace, courtesy, competence, commitment, or understanding. The opportunity is present to go beyond what is expected. In effect, exceeding customers' expectations requires the element of surprise , and the best opportunity for surprising customers is when service providers and customers interact.

An example of surprising customers comes from Continental Cablevision, a cable television system in St. Paul, Minnesota. Continental has programmed a channel called "TV House Calls" in which a representative demonstrates, live, the solution to a subscriber's problem while that customer is watching. Customer reaction has been extremely positive. A company spokesman says: "People are absolutely astounded. You can almost see jaws dropping at the other end of the phone when they experience this."[4]

Companies must seek excellence on both the outcome and process dimensions of service to develop a reputation for truly outstanding service. Excellent service reliability allows a company to compete. The addition of excellent process service creates a reputation for superior service quality. To reach these heights, companies must capitalize on opportunities to surprise their customers. Managers should consider this question: "What is the 'wow' factor in our service?"

LESSON SEVEN: FAIR PLAY

Customers expect service companies to treat them fairly and become resentful and mistrustful when they perceive otherwise. Fairness underlies all the customers' expectations. Customers expect service companies to keep their promises (reliability), to offer honest communication materials and clean, comfortable facilities (tangibles), to provide prompt service (responsiveness), to be competent and courteous (assurance), and to provide caring, individualized attention (empathy). Fairness is not a separate dimension of service but, rather, touches the very essence of what customers expect.

The intangibility of services heightens customers' sensitivity to fairness issues. Because services are performances rather than objects, they are difficult for customers to evaluate prior to purchase. Customers cannot try on services for fit and feel; there are no tires to kick such as in buying an automobile. Customers usually must buy the service to actually experience it. Thus, they must trust a service company to deliver on its promises and conduct itself honorably.

Some services are difficult for customers to judge even after they have been performed and therefore trust plays a big role. Were all the repairs on the automobile necessary? Did the maintenance crew follow protocol in preparing an aircraft for flying? Did the marketing research firm conduct all of the specified interviews? As important as the lesson of fair play is for services in general, we believe it is even more important for these services because customers are at such an information disadvantage with the service provider.

Service companies need to make special efforts to be fair and to demonstrate fairness. Companies can use customer research to generate feedback on the fairness of their practices, actual and contemplated. Firms can attempt to communicate more openly, creatively, and regularly with customers and other stakeholders about what they do and why they do it. Companies can demonstrate fairness by improving access to relief when problems occur.

A potentially powerful strategy for demonstrating fairness is the service guarantee. If customers are dissatisfied with the service, they can invoke the guarantee and receive consideration for the burden they have endured. When executed well,[5] service guarantees can symbolize a company's commitment to fair play with customers, facilitate competitive differentiation, and force the organization to improve service quality to avoid the cost and embarrassment of frequent payouts.

Roasters and Toasters, a gourmet coffee and baked goods cafe, promotes its guarantee on menus and wall posters: "Uniquely exceptional and outstanding food and service or it's on the house." The customer defines outstanding. The cafe claims a 95 percent customer retention rate. Hampton Inn offers the night's stay free to customers who are dissatisfied with the hotel's service. Any hotel employee can implement the guarantee. The guarantee allows Hampton Inn to track customer complaints and make the necessary improvements. Hotel employee retention has improved, and nearly nine out of ten guests who invoke the guarantee indicate that they will stay at Hampton Inn again.

The lesson of fair play concerns the company's underlying value system. Does management place stakeholders' trust over short-term earnings? Does management ask the question "Is it fair?" not just the question "Is it legal?" Managers interested in delivering excellent service must also be interested in being fair to customers.

LESSON EIGHT: TEAMWORK

Service work is frequently demanding and stressful. Having many customers to service, such as on a full airline flight or in a busy bank office, can be mentally and physically exhausting. Some customers are unpleasant, cross, or worse. Control over the service is often dispersed among different organizational units that function without cooperation, frustrating contact employees' ability to effectively serve their customers. It is common for employees to be so stressed by the service role that they become less caring, less sensitive, less eager to please.

The presence of service "teammates" is an important dynamic in sustaining servers' motivation to serve. Coworkers who support each other and achieve together can be an antidote to service burnout. Team involvement can be rejuvenating, inspirational, and fun. Our research shows convincingly that service-perfor-

mance shortfalls are highly correlated with the absence of teamwork.

Service team building should not be left to chance. The chain of internal services required to offer the end service normally spans multiple functions. Companies must actively work at fostering teamwork across these functions, not just within them. This may involve frequent meetings of the functions and other communications; shared performance goals, measurements, and rewards; and cross-training employees in various facets of the service chain.

A more fundamental approach is organizing into cross-functional teams in which service providers from different parts of the service chain are grouped to serve a common set of customers. Lakeland Regional Medical Center in Lakeland, Florida, has used this approach quite successfully by organizing bedside care around teams of multiskilled practitioners. These teams are comprised of "care pairs"—a registered nurse and a cross-trained technician—supported by specialized assistance as needed. Care pairs work in care teams with other care pairs across shifts to serve the same physician's patients throughout the patients' hospital stay. Care pairs provide up to ninety percent of pre- and post-surgical services for four to six patients at a time. Intensively trained, and supported by a computer terminal in each patient's room, the care pair's range of functions includes preadmission testing and information services, admitting, charting, charging, room cleanup, patient transportation, physical therapy, respiratory care treatments, and performance of ECG procedures.

Lakeland's management refers to the new organizational approach as the "patient-focused model." Management believes the key to the model's success with patients and service providers is the continuity of care facilitated by the care team concept. Management can directly compare the classical and patient-focused models because only part of the hospital has been converted to the new system thus far. The data are striking. In a classical setting, the average Lakeland patient sees fifty-three different personnel in a four-day stay. In the patient-focused environment, the average patient see thirteen staff members. For seventy-one of seventy-two patient satisfaction measures, patients in the restructured environment ranked their experiences equal to or better than patients in the classical environment. For forty-nine of the seventy-two measures, the results are statistically significant.[6] When forty-four of the staff members involved in the original pilot project were surveyed, they reported improvements in job stress, quality of work life, perceptions of quality of care, and overall job satisfaction.[7]

LESSON NINE: EMPLOYEE RESEARCH

Employee research is as important to service improvement as customer research, for three reasons. First, employees are themselves customers of internal service, and thus are the only people who can assess internal service quality. Because internal service quality affects external service quality, measuring internal service quality is essential. Second, employees can offer insight into conditions that reduce service quality in the organization. Employees experience the company's service delivery system day after day. They see more than customers see and they see it from a different angle. Employee research helps reveal why service problems occur, and what companies might do to solve these problems.[8] Third, employee research serves as an early-warning system. Because of employees' more intensive exposure to the service delivery system, they often see the system breaking down before customers do.

First Chicago is an ardent practitioner of employee research. In addition to holding regular focus group interviews with employees, the bank systematically surveys them. In a recent year the first quarter's survey included questions such as: "Do you have what you need to do your job?" and "Does the equipment work?" The second quarter survey involved employees' attitudes toward the bank's services, prices, and communications. The third quarter survey concerned employees perceptions of internal service quality. The fourth quarter survey covered employees' satisfaction with their immediate supervisors and senior management. Employees rated managers on issues such as whether they discussed work priorities, appreciated extra effort, and were visible. The bank also operates an employee telephone hotline called "2-Talk" that is answered in the Consumer Affairs Department. Employees are encouraged to call 2-Talk whenever they receive poor service themselves, witness service problems, or have service-improvement ideas.[9]

The lesson of employee research relates directly to several other lessons. When the product is a performance, it is especially important that companies listen to the performers. This listening behavior should result in improved service system design. Listening to employees and addressing their concerns promotes teamwork between management and service personnel.

LESSON TEN: SERVANT LEADERSHIP

Improving service involves undoing what exists as much as creating what doesn't. Delivering excellent service requires a special form of leadership we call "servant leadership." Servant leaders serve the servers, inspiring and enabling them to achieve. Such leaders fundamentally believe in the capacity of people to achieve, viewing their own role as setting a direction and a standard of excellence, and giving people the tools and freedom to perform. Because these leaders believe in their people, they invest much of their personal energy coaching them and teaching them, challenging them, inspiring them, and, of course, listening to them.

The late Sam Walton, who built Wal-Mart Stores into the largest retail chain in America, was the quintessential servant leader. Walton devoted considerable time to visiting his stores, listening to the sounds of the business, removing impediments to improvement, and communicating the company's vision to Wal-Mart associates.

We do not have hard data to support our belief that servant leadership is the engine that moves organizations toward service excellence. Yet, ten years studying the subject of service quality convinces us it is so. Interviews with staff at Lakeland Regional Medical Center—from senior management to care pair personnel—are indicative of the evidence we have accumulated on the importance of servant leadership in service improvement.

Members of the Patient Focused Development Team, a middle-management group responsible for helping to drive Lakeland's restructuring, were asked to identify the keys to the effort's success. One member answered: "Top management role-modeled it for us. They spent a lot of time developing the vision and working it out." Another member responded: "Management has relinquished control and power. They know that we know what to do." A third member added: "Management provided the education to support the change. They articulated what the restructuring was and was not."

Without the energizing vision of leadership, without the direction, inspiration, and support, the direct investments in service-improvement—in technology, systems, training, and research, for example—do not produce full benefit.

A FINAL PERSPECTIVE

By now it should be clear that our ten lessons are not mutually exclusive and that they must be viewed in a holistic manner. To that end, we have constructed in Exhibit 2 a service quality ring to capture these interrelationships. Listening is positioned on the outer ring because listening has an impact on all the other lessons. Identifying the basics of service, improving service system design, recovering from service shortfalls—these

EXHIBIT 2   A Service Quality Ring

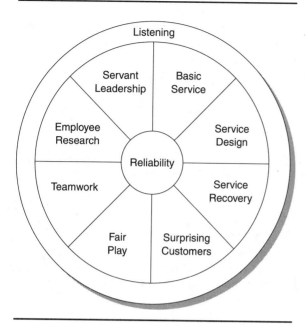

and other essentials of service quality involve listening behavior. Reliability is pictured in the center, because reliability is the core of service quality. Little else matters to customers when the service is unreliable. The sequence of the lessons is purposeful. The service system should be designed to deliver the basic service excellently. Recovery service usually provides an opportunity to surprise customers and to demonstrate fair play. Teamwork, employee research, and servant leadership are critical factors in an organization's emotional readiness to deliver quality service.

ENDNOTES

1. Details of our research are presented in five monographs published by the Marketing Science Institute, Cambridge, MA (Reports No. 84-106, 86-108, 87-100, 90-122, and 91-113). The authors gratefully acknowledge the Marketing Science Institute for supporting the research on which this article is based. Our research protocol has been to explore issues through qualitative research, model what we find, and then use quantitative research to test relationships in the model. Thus far, in five research phases, we have conducted 28 customer focus group interviews in multiple cities, thirteen customer surveys, and a case study of one of America's largest banks. We have also done personal interviews, focus group interviews, and surveys with service employees and managers. We have now conducted research in a dozen service sectors, including automobile repair, automobile insurance, property and casualty insurance, hotels, securities brokerage, and truck and tractor rental/leasing.

2. J. Kingman-Brundage, "Blueprinting for the Bottom Line," in *Service Excellence: Marketing's Impact on Performance* (Chicago: American Marketing Association, 1989), 26. This volume contains five papers on service blueprinting/mapping for readers interested in pursuing this subject.

3. J. Anton, "Why It Pays to Solicit Customer Complaints," *Telemarketing,* 7(5) November 1988. Technical Assistance Research Programs (TARP), a consulting firm specializing in the study of customer complaints, has shown that 31 percent of customers facing an average potential loss of $142 due to defective products or services still did not complaint.

4. S. Applebaum, "The Solution Channel," *Cablevision,* July 29, 1992, 26.

5. For an excellent discussion of the characteristics of an effective service guarantee, see C. W. L. Hart, "The Power of Unconditional Service Guarantees," *Harvard Business Review,* 66(4) July–August 1988, 54–62. Also see C. W. L. Hart, *Extraordinary Guarantees* (New York: American Management Association, 1993).

6. Unpublished data provided by Lakeland Regional Medical Center, Lakeland, Florida.

7. To read more about this research and to learn more about the background of the patient-focused model of health-care delivery, see P. M. Watson, et al., "Operational Restructuring: A Patient-Focused Approach," *Nursing Administration Quarterly,* 16(1) Fall 1991, 45–52.

8. In our research with employees, we have used with great success two key questions as part of a broader group of questions: 1. What is the biggest problem you face day in and day out trying to deliver a high quality of service to your customers? 2. If you were president of this company for one day, and could make only one decision to improve quality of service, what decision would you make? Answers to these two questions can be especially valuable in starting or revitalizing a service-improvement effort for the questions cut through surface issues to expose serious service impediments in the organization.

9. To read more about First Chicago's approach to employee research, see L. Cooper and B. Summers, *Getting Started in Quality* (Chicago: The First National Bank of Chicago, 1990).

ABOUT THE AUTHORS

Leonard L. Berry, who received his Ph.D. from Arizona State University, holds the J.C. Penney Chair of Retailing Studies, is a professor of marketing, and is director of the Center for Retailing Studies at Texas A&M University. He is a former national president of the American Marketing Association. His research interests are services marketing, service quality, and retailing strategy. He is the author of journal articles and books, including *Marketing Services: Competing through Quality* (The Free Press, 1991), which he wrote with A. Parasuraman.

A. Parasuraman received his D.B.A. from Indiana University and is Federated Professor of Retailing and Marketing Studies at Texas A&M University. His research interests include service-quality measurement and improvement, and services marketing strategy. In 1988 he was selected as one of the "Ten Most Influential Figures in Quality" by the editorial board of *The Quality Review,* co-published by the American Quality Foundation and the American Society for Quality Control. He has published in leading marketing journals, and is the author of a college textbook, *Marketing Research* (Addison-Wesley, 1991).

Valarie A. Zeithaml received her D. B. A. from the University of Maryland. She is the principal in Partners for Service Excellence, and was previously on the faculty at Duke University and Texas A&M University. Her research interests include services marketing and consumer perceptions of price and quality. Her articles have appeared in leading marketing journals. She is co-author (with Leonard Berry and A. Parasuraman) of *Delivering Quality Service: Balancing Customer Perceptions and Expectations* (The Free Press, 1990).

EXECUTIVE COMMENTARY

Dennis Adsit, Bull HN

Over the last few years, the primary focus of service quality improvement efforts at Bull HN has been on what Berry, et al., term "service design" and "employee research." Working these areas has yielded a number of key lessons.

SERVICE DESIGN We targeted our handling process for analysis, completing what is referred to as a "service map" of our work procedures. The hopelessly entangled picture that resulted left little doubt that we had to streamline this critical process. We then embarked on the daunting task of changing the process as well as upgrading the various information systems that support it.

In this initial part of my commentary, I would like to pass along the lessons learned in managing the transition period, the time period during which service map results are being addressed. The first lesson has to do with communication; basically, you can never do too much.

Through letters and face-to-face meetings, we told our customers we would be investing considerable time and effort as well as dollars in upgrading our services.

We promised them that as a result they would see some changes in their interactions with us when the job was finished. With respect to employees, we involved a cross-functional, multilevel team from the time we began the planning of the redesign to the final implementation. We kept employees not involved in the planning team informed through videos and various written communications. In these communications, we played it by the book, focusing primarily on the vision—how the new service delivery process would look and the benefits it would hold for customers. We even talked about the changes the improvements would bring about in the ways employees did their jobs. Along with these aspects of our vision statement, we entailed the rationale behind the changes anticipated.

Despite our good intentions and hard work, we ran into problems throughout the transition period. Chief among them was our inability to completely insulate our customers from drops in the level of service quality during the transition.

When customers called in, they sometimes experienced long hold times, or they got disconnected and had to call back because we had "dropped" their calls. As Berry, et al., point out, when this kind of unreliability occurs, your relationship with your customers is in jeopardy. Good communication with your employees is essential at this time; they can buffer the impact.

Based on our experience, we suggest that an organization about to undertake a service redesign project pay attention to three points to ensure that good employee communication takes place throughout the process. First, much has been said about the importance of vision in a change management effort. However, in the vision state, things work perfectly. What's more critical to customers and employees is the transition period. The organization and its customers need to be prepared for the possibility that the change will not be as smooth as they would like it to be. Focusing on working together to solve the problems can minimize finger pointing as well as the development of an "us vs. them" mentality.

Second, once the rollout begins, the implementation team needs to keep employees and management apprised of each milestone in the rollout. They need to know what problems are surfacing, and what is being done to fix them. Illusory or not, this gives employees a better sense that the project, while difficult, is under control. They, in turn, can more confidently represent this view to the customers.

Finally, when a system enhancement involves removing some value-added functionality, it may be viewed as a loss by employees and increase their resistance to the change effort. Global gains can often involve local losses. The organization needs to be clearer about such changes as well as about the reasons behind the loss of functionality.

The ultimate goal of a service redesign effort is to improve service quality and productivity. However, the road to improved productivity and quality can involve service interrupts, delays, miscommunications, and emotional flare-ups as a result of worn nerves. How a company treats its employees during the reengineering effort is just as important as how it treats its customers. The better informed employees are, the better they will be able to solve problems, manage their own stress, and handle frustrated customers.

EMPLOYEE RESEARCH At Bull HN, our efforts at conducting employee research take two forms: an annual employee survey, and in-depth, targeted climate assessments.

The former is primarily an upward appraisal process for managers, with many of the questions reflecting the "Servant Leadership" model discussed in the article. The survey does, however, also include some questions about teams and customers.

With any ongoing survey effort, one must vigilantly guard against the onset of employee cynicism. We have run into this throughout the life of our survey, as reflected in such comments as, "They don't really care what we think," and "Nothing ever happens as a result of these surveys anyway." The conventional wisdom is that overcoming cynicism depends on what you do with the results. We have learned, however, that minimizing negative attitudes about the survey depends not only on what we do with the results but also on other factors such as survey administration and follow-up.

Our first administration of the survey taught us a lot. We built a long, comprehensive survey. Only after surveys were mailed out, mailed back, keypunched, analyzed, and fed back to senior management were individual survey results released to managers and other employees. By this time, three to four months had elapsed from the time surveys had been completed and turned in. In the "nanosecond nineties," this much of a delay is not acceptable. It sends out a signal to employees that you are not serious about listening to them or taking their comments to heart by giving them prompt attention.

Based on the lessons learned since our first survey, we have streamlined the administration process. We cut the number of items from over one hundred to less than thirty. This drastically reduces the length of time it takes for employees to fill out the survey. The idea is to keep the "hassle factor" to a minimum. Next, we encouraged managers to focus their improvement efforts in three to five key areas. With hundreds of items, it is hard to prioritize improvements. By eliminating items and helping managers focus better, it reduces the sense that nothing is being done with the results.

Finally, from an administration standpoint, we eliminated the manual input of the results. We invested in some hardware and software that enabled employees to use their telephones to respond to the survey. This does not reduce the time it takes for employees to complete their surveys, but it means that we can have reports in the hands of managers days after the response window closes. This reassures employees that we are hustling to get back to them with what they said to us.

Once managers have their results, we work to ensure that something happens with the feedback. All managers receive detailed instructions on how to hold feedback sessions with their employees and are expected to do so. These sessions can be difficult and the managers have found the training quite helpful.

To further ensure positive action, we have also made the survey results more visible and have created more accountability for improvement. The first time we did the survey, it was anonymous. That is, an individual manager was the only one who saw his or her results. Now, managers one and two levels above an individual manager are aware of the results. This is a departure from recommendations I have seen from consultants and practices in other companies. We feel, however, that the questions that make up our survey represent our expectations for our managers, and we want to know if their employees think they are delivering against those expectations. We are currently tying management and executive bonuses, in part, to improvement scores on the survey. Managers and employees both recognize that we treat this information seriously.

Finally, in spite of the increased pressure we are putting on managers to improve, we are not leaving them on their own to figure out how to improve their scores. We are in the process of studying the impact that certain actions and behaviors of managers have on their scores. We are also investigating the relationship between this upward appraisal data and objective measures of performance. Both of these investigations are being undertaken to help managers see the link between what they do and the results (survey and financial) they achieve.

Taken together, these efforts to improve our survey administration and follow-up processes have resulted in a respectable 78% response rate and a reduction in some of the cynicism we heard after our first survey. Much more work still needs to be done, but we have passed the point where employees feel this is a meaningless exercise. After they have seen our commitment, we are seeing theirs.

Our experiences with service design and employee research have made it clear: if you want to give good service to your customers or you want feedback on the internal workings of your service delivery system, you must have a kind of "respectful mindfulness" for the people providing that service and that feedback. I am struck by how easy it can be to lose sight of this.

Dennis Adsit is Director of Human Resources and Technical Training for Bull HN's North American Customer Services business. Previously, he has served as Director of Headquarters and International Human Resources, and as Manager of Organizational Development. He holds a Ph.D. in industrial psychology from the University of Minnesota. Dr. Adsit serves on the Executive Advisory Panel for AME

John Hater, Federal Express Corporation

In 1990, Federal Express was the first company to capture the Malcolm Baldrige National Quality Award in the service category. With corporate objectives of 100 percent customer satisfaction and 100 percent service performance, Federal Express practices all of the ten lessons outlined in this article. For example, Federal Express monitors twelve statistical measures of customer satisfaction and service quality from the customer's viewpoint that are reported weekly to employees.

Of equal importance is the Federal Express top-down commitment to *employee satisfaction* that we believe is the *producer* of customer *service* and satisfaction. Our founder and CEO, Frederick W. Smith, summarized the corporate philosophy this way: "When people are placed first, they will provide the highest possible service, and profits will follow."[1] The corporate philosophy is succinctly stated: *People–Service–Profit (P–S–P)*. What this means is that employee considerations are given a high priority when developing corporate programs and policies, when acquiring and designing facilities, equipment, and systems, and when scheduling and arranging work. Of course, the needs of our customers must be met efficiently, but managers always are expected to consider their people in business decisions.

Our conclusions have been supported by substantial research such as that conducted by Schneider and Bowen, who reported high correlations (r = .56) between employee perceptions of human resource practices and customer perceptions of service. They con-

cluded that both service-related and human-resources-related practices are the source of cues visible to customers and are used by them to evaluate service quality.[2] In a 1992 study of employee climate themes, Schneider, Wheeler, and Cox found that the routines and rewards most strongly related to service passion included not only responsiveness to customers and the way service is delivered but also human resource practices (i.e., hiring procedures, training, and pay equity).[3]

LISTENING Lesson one (Listening) is accomplished through a quarterly summary of daily telephone surveys of customers, annual direct mail surveys, Federal Express Center comment cards, and the monitoring of calls between customers and employees to measure "tone" of service. "Listening" also includes an aspect of one Federal Express program in which we track employee morale and attitudes. Our Survey-Feedback-Action (SFA) program is an annual survey of all employees that functions not only as a barometer of employee well-being, but also as a management evaluation tool and a work-group problem-solving mechanism. It has a 98% participation rate. The first ten items of the survey comprise an annual subordinate review of management known as the Leadership Index. The survey results from this Index become the numerical measure that determines whether the company's annual "People" goal within the People–Service–Profit goal structure is being met. Managers' personal MBO plans include Leadership Index goals. Meeting or exceeding People goals, as well as Service and Profit goals, can qualify an individual manager for twice-yearly bonuses. Another significant aspect of this program is its consistency with the company's basic tenets: "customer satisfaction begins with employee satisfaction," "managers serve employees," and "manager as leader."

SERVANT LEADERSHIP Lesson ten, Servant Leadership, embraces the idea that leaders inspire, challenge, and coach their people to deliver excellent service. This lesson is similar to the transformational leadership model by Dr. Bernard Bass in which leaders transmit a sense of mission, stimulate learning experiences, and arouse new ways of thinking.[4] After conducting our own in-house research on the effectiveness of this model,[5] Federal Express adopted the transformational leadership factors of charismatic leadership, intellectual stimulation, and individualized consideration for its Leadership Evaluation and Awareness Process (LEAP).

The LEAP program promotes employees into management who complete a process designed to evaluate their leadership qualities, including the transformational leadership factors. LEAP begins with a class that realistically previews managerial responsibilities for candidates and is followed by a three- to six-month period during which a candidate's manager evaluates and coaches the candidate based on leadership attributes. Peer evaluations are also collected by means of a confidential assessment form. The LEAP panel evaluation integrates a situational interview with the manager's recommendation and peer assessment and culminates in an "endorsed/not endorsed" decision. It should also be noted that the LEAP peer assessment component itself is the result of listening to employees' concerns about the quality of first-line management. Since LEAP's initiation, the turnover rate among first-line managers has dropped more than 80 percent.

KEEP PEOPLE FIRST   As we strive to reach 100 percent customer satisfaction and 100 percent service performance, we should put our employees first in the design of programs, policies, facilities, equipment, and systems. Federal Express has been successful with this approach and data collected in other companies has confirmed that customers benefit from service provided by satisfied employees.

Key employee programs contribute to meeting service quality goals. Some examples are: skills and knowledge training; extensive employee communication that includes television broadcasts of live, call-in talk shows; promotion from within for all job openings; pay for performance reward systems; and an employee grievance process offering employees the right of appeal to the highest levels of management. The programs replace talk with action to keep people first. While we can only assume a connection between employee programs and customer satisfaction, the feedback from our customers is encouraging. In a recent telephone survey of customers, 95% were *completely* satisfied with their interactions with our couriers, an indicator that, for us, reinforces the connection.

ENDNOTES

1. D. L. Bohl, *Blueprints for Service Quality: The Federal Express Approach* (New York, NY: American Management Association, 1991).

2. B. Schneider and D. E. Bowen, "Employee and Customer Perceptions of Service in Banks: Replication and Extension," *Journal of Applied Psychology,* 70, 1985, 423–433.

3. B. Schneider, J. K. Wheeler, and J. F. Cox, "A Passion for Service: Using Content Analysis to Explicate Service Climate Themes," *Journal of Applied Psychology,* 77, 1992, 705–716.

4. B. M. Bass, *Leadership and Performance beyond Expectations* (New York, NY: The Free Press, 1985).

5. J. J. Hater and B. M. Bass, "Superiors' Evaluations and Subordinates' Perceptions of Transformational and Transactional Leadership," *Journal of Applied Psychology,* 73, 1988, 695–702.

John Hater, Ph.D., is Senior Industrial Psychologist at Federal Express and has worked on a variety of human resource programs, including validation of selection instruments and leadership research since 1982. He received his Ph.D. in industrial/organizational psychology from Texas Christian University. Dr. Hater serves on AME's Executive Advisory Panel.

Eric J. Vanetti, Xerox Corporation

The road to becoming a total quality company is a never-ending one; the nature of such an organization is a constantly moving target. We at Xerox embarked upon the journey in the early 1980s and to this date find ourselves working toward ever-changing goals. Along the way, the ten service quality lessons described by Berry, Parasuraman, and Zeithaml have been learned and collectively used to alter our culture, improve our work processes, and enhance our ability to meet customer requirements. As a result, I have come to believe that the business environment will be such that organizations seeking to achieve quality excellence must engage in continuous learning. Although the ten quality factors will probably remain constant, the manner in which they are applied will vary, influenced by technological change, global competition, organizational restructuring, and more demanding customer requirements.

To illustrate, I can point to a recent restructuring at Xerox which created several business divisions differentiated by product line; i.e., Printing Systems, Office Document Products, Engineering Systems, etc. The intent of the restructuring was to give these business divisions end-to-end accountability for the development, manufacturing, marketing, and sales and service of their respective product lines, all in the interest of improving quality and attending to customer needs. In addition, our internal service organization has had to redefine its service delivery strategy to work across functions and other organizations to ensure that the level of service produced meets external customer and business division requirements.

A service quality lesson that has been particularly significant to Xerox is what the authors call "servant leadership" and what we at Xerox refer to as "empowerment." Simply put, it means that managers are asked to establish a clear direction for their people, then work with them in identifying specific objectives to reach their goal. Once managers provide employees with the resources, enablers, and support required, they are expected to get out of the way! Empowerment at Xerox also means that decision-making authority and capability is pushed down to the point of customer contact. Managers are required to create an environment that encourages employees to take ownership for making business decisions relating to customers.

Our experience with servant leadership has also demonstrated the value of teamwork. Service employees are organized into self-managed work groups that are accountable for performance results, including the satisfaction and retention of customers. Once a clear vision for service delivery has been defined and communicated, it's up to the work groups to achieve it. People are recognized and rewarded, not just for individual achievement, but for work group accomplishments.

Eric J. Vanetti, Ph.D., is the Manager of Organizational Development & Research in Human Resources at Xerox Corporation. He received his Ph.D. in industrial and organizational psychology from Old Dominion University. Dr. Vanetti is a member of AME's Executive Advisory Panel.

David J. Veale, Coca-Cola

The placement of "Listening" around the Service Quality Ring developed by Berry, et al., is an important point to consider. Listening to customers and employees, keeping your ear to the ground, is the skill that makes service quality happen. If an organization cannot listen well, not much movement or development occurs. Good, accurate listening is the fundamental skill on which all other quality behaviors rely. In my experience, however, such listening is not all that common.

For example, an academic organization with which I am familiar recently invited local business leaders to a luncheon. The purpose of the meeting was to discuss improvement of the organization's program offerings. The business people responded, tossing out various possibilities for change, the most notable of which was to offer more flexibility in scheduling. After a spirited discussion, the facilitator, who happened to be the head of the organization, outlined a number of reasons why the scheduling changes suggested could not be made. Someone in the audience commented, "Who's the customer?" The subject was dropped and the meeting continued. Some time later, all of the participants received a letter from the organization thanking them for their viewpoints and noting that the conclusions reached at

the meeting seemed to indicate that the organization was on target with both its programs and schedules!

To me, this example illustrates the difference between "real" listening and "false" listening. Real listening means hearing comments about your service and trying to appreciate the customer's point of view, even thought you may not agree. False listening happens when organizations make a pretense of listening solely for the purpose of obtaining support or buy-in without any intention of following through. Thus, the false listening is used more as a public relations technique than as a service enhancement strategy.

To Coca-Cola, employee research is an important source of information because employees are not only the providers of our products but consumers as well. As a result, it is helpful to an organization to create conditions where employees who consume a service or product have easy ways to point out service problems. For example, we have a program called "Coca-Cola Cares." Every employee is asked to tell the company about any product or service problem they encounter, on or off the job. Wallet-sized cards with a special toll-free number have been distributed to employees for this purpose.

Flexibility, although not specifically mentioned as a means of achieving service quality, is implied throughout the article. The type of equipment customers want, the kinds of billing, delivery scheduling, and modes of delivery can vary widely from customer to customer. An example in the grocery marketing business is Efficient Consumer Response (ECR), a new way of conceiving the partnership between manufacturers and grocery stores with the purpose of driving out costs. Initiatives such as the Electronic Data Interchange (EDI) in which invoices, purchase orders, and even payments are made electronically, are part of the ECR strategy. Some grocery chains have the ability and commitment to move forward, while others have no intention of moving in that direction. In order to serve each of our customers in the way they expect, Coca-Cola has to have different service modalities; one service does not fit all. For a store like Wal-Mart, EDI may provide a competitive advantage, but for a mom-and-pop store, this type of service may be seen as a competitive disadvantage because of the perceived capital costs. Thus, how we provide our service can vary from customer to customer. We are flexible in the service we offer so that our customers get what they want.

Balancing the service value/price equation is another important service quality lesson to be learned. The customer associates and expects a certain level or type of service with a particular price. For example, a traveler anticipates a different level of service at a Motel 6 than at a Ritz-Carlton hotel. Either one can be a good value. However, a company can easily lose margin by providing Ritz-Carlton service at Motel 6 prices or vice versa. It's important for an organization to know what the customer's value expectations are with respect to its product/price equation.

Once the level of service and business has been established, then an organization can work on "surprising" the customer. Sometimes these surprises cost little to nothing, but can be helpful in differentiating one's product or service from a competitor's. Companies can differentiate themselves on what we refer to as "elegant negotiables," things the customer wants that cost virtually nothing to the provider. For example, one of our salespeople was looking for a venue to sponsor a rollerblade event to advertise one of our brands. In talking with a local grocery chain, he discovered it was plan-

ning to celebrate its anniversary. It had been looking around for an appropriate event at which to hold the celebration. Because we were able to link our event with the customer's anniversary, we provided them with a perceived service while saving ourselves time and money through the collaboration.

Since reading this article, I have found myself using its lessons in assessing the quality of service provided by Coca-Cola, by the vendors with whom I work, and even by the hotels I use. When problems have arisen, I've found they can usually be attributed to a problem in one of the service areas on the Service Quality Ring.

David J. Veale, Ph.D., is Manager of Training and Development for Coca-Cola Foods, a Division of the Coca-Cola Company. He also has worked for Pacific Gas and Electric Company, the Massachusetts Department of Mental Health, and State Senate. He received his Ph.D. from the University of California, Santa Cruz. Dr. Veale is a member of AME's Executive Advisory Panel.

PLANNING DEMING MANAGEMENT FOR SERVICE ORGANIZATIONS

Thomas F. Rienzo

T he word "quality" carries an almost spiritual character in globally focused, highly competitive businesses. Articles extolling the virtues and techniques of quality are *de rigueur* in current American business periodicals. Quality is a universally acknowledged factor in successful businesses. Allen F. Jacobsen, chairman of the board and chief executive officer of 3M Company, says, "I'm convinced that the winners of the '90s will be companies that make quality and customer service an obsession in every single market [in which] they operate."

Corporate America has begun an ambitious effort to improve the quality of goods and services offered by American companies. These efforts, sustained by fierce global competition, will continue. The United States Commerce Department reported a trade deficit of $4.02 billion in June 1991 with an accumulated midyear 1991 merchandise trade deficit of $30.27 billion. That is an improvement over the $48.28 billion deficit measured through the first half of 1990. Currently, negative trade balances with Japan alone exceed $3 billion per month.

Because of this, many firms in the United States are attempting to emulate successful Japanese business performances. Japan's economic success is rooted in quality; Japanese quality is rooted in W. Edwards Deming.

DEMING: A BIOGRAPHICAL SKETCH

W. Edwards Deming received his formal academic training in mathematics and physics, earning a Ph.D. from Yale in 1927. After completing his degree, he found employment in the U.S. Department of Agriculture applying statistical techniques to the effects of nitrogen on farm crops. While working there, Deming met Walter Shewhart, a statistician with Bell

Telephone Laboratories. Shewhart had created methods of statistically measuring variation in industrial processes, called control charts, that permitted workers to distinguish between random variation and special causes affecting changes in manufacturing processes. Deming was impressed. He traveled regularly to New York to study with Shewhart, whose statistical philosophy and techniques form the heart of Deming's quality seminars today.

During World War II, Deming taught numerous courses in statistical quality control, using Shewhart control charts, to improve the quality of American war production. Though successful during those years, statistical techniques faded in the United States after the war ended. American companies, which operated in a seller's market with virtually no competition, considered Deming's methods of statistical process control time-consuming and unnecessary. By 1949 they were no longer part of corporate America. Deming himself lamented that "there was nothing—not even smoke" (Walton 1986).

Deming first brought his statistical quality control techniques and management philosophy to Japan in 1947. He found the Japanese eager students. By 1951, the Deming Prize, which recognized superlative achievement in quality, was established in Japan. In 1960, Deming became the first American to receive Japan's Second Order of the Sacred Treasure award because of his great impact upon Japanese industry.

SOURCE: Thomas F. Rienzo, "Planning Deming Management for Service Organizations," *Business Horizons* (May–June, 1993): 19–29. Thomas F. Rienzo is a research engineer with Hercules Incorporated, Kalamazoo, Michigan.

Although he was an industrial superstar in Japan, Deming was not well known in the United States. He made a comfortable living as a statistical consultant, but most American business managers were not aware of his management methods, which formed the foundations of Japanese manufacturing excellence. American managers *were* aware, however, of stiff Japanese competition beginning in the 1970s. They realized that Japan was setting world quality standards for many manufactured goods.

One television show changed Deming's status in the United States. On June 24, 1980, NBC broadcast "If Japan Can . . . Why Can't We?" The final quarter hour of the show focused on Deming's contributions to Japan as well as on business improvements documented at Nashua Corporation, a U.S. company following the Deming quality philosophy. About four months before his 80th birthday, W. Edwards Deming became famous in America. Since that time his services and seminars have been in great demand throughout the world.

SYSTEM OF PROFOUND KNOWLEDGE

Deming claims that many firms cannot perform well from a long-term perspective because their managers do not know what to do. He is fond of repeating "There is no substitute for knowledge!" vigorously and frequently during his seminars.

American managers cannot provide answers to their problems because they do not know what questions to ask. William Scherkenbach (1990) claims the whole of Deming's management philosophy is directed toward asking the right questions. In Deming's view, insightful management hinges on the application of an awareness process he has labeled "profound knowledge," which consists of four components:

1. Appreciation for a system
2. Theory of variation
3. Theory of knowledge
4. Psychology

These components are interdependent and interactive. Deming created his Fourteen Points for Management to provide a method of developing and implementing profound knowledge in the workplace.

APPRECIATION FOR A SYSTEM

Deming defines a system as a series of functions or activities within an organization that work together for the aim of the organization. A system cannot function effectively without a clear aim, communicated to everyone capable of measurably affecting system operation. Complex systems, like businesses, must have full cooperation among components to accomplish their aims.

Managers are charged with the responsibility of optimizing systems; flow diagrams can help them understand what they are attempting to optimize. Figure 1 shows Deming's perspective of production viewed as a system. Deming first used this chart in 1950 while explaining his quality management theories to Japanese business leaders. Flow diagrams help clarify relationships between system components, help define connections between processes, and provide insight into interactions. A systems approach to business activities also reveals that all processes have suppliers providing inputs and customers utilizing outputs. Most companies have a large number of processes whose suppliers and customers are internal to the corporation.

THEORY OF VARIATION

Systems are most efficiently optimized by concentrating on activities as far upstream as possible. Some understanding of variation is required to accomplish optimization. Variation always exists in any process, whether it involves equipment or people. Deming insists that managers have some means of distinguishing between changes in a process occurring at random, compared with changes resulting from some special cause affecting the process.

Statistical methods can help provide that distinction. Deming says, "Management is prediction!"[1] A process in statistical control is stable; as such, it furnishes a rational basis for prediction. Methods used to assess variation in systems are described in literature involving statistical process control.

THEORY OF KNOWLEDGE

Deming is convinced that hard work and best efforts are necessary though not sufficient conditions for achieving quality or satisfying a market. His Second Theorem declares, "We are ruined by best efforts misdirected."

Many shortcomings of American business do not result from a lack of effort, but from a lack of knowledgeable theory concerning subject matter that businesses attempt to manage. Deming believes that theory is essential: "Theory leads to questions. Without questions, experience and examples teach nothing. Without questions, one can only have an example. To copy an example of success, without understanding it with the aid of theory, may lead to disaster." He also claims,

FIGURE 1   Production Viewed as a System

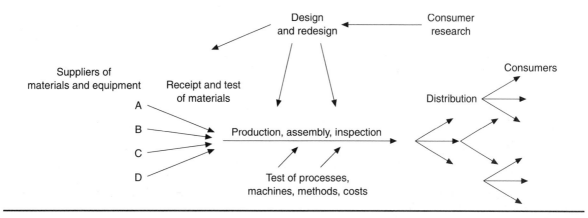

"There are no shortcuts to mastery of subject matter; there is no substitute for knowledge."

Deming expects managers to realize that they must concern themselves with issues that cannot be objectively measured. He frequently quotes Lloyd S. Nelson: "The most important figures for management are unknown and unknowable" (Deming 1986). The multiplying effect on sales attributable to happy customers, losses from annual ratings, or losses from inhibitors to pride of workmanship defies objective measurements.

PSYCHOLOGY

Psychology provides insight into human relationships and the ways in which people respond to circumstances in their lives. Deming is concerned about a knowledge of psychology in management because he sees current norms squeezing out workers' self-esteem and self-respect. He recommends eliminating a number of common management techniques that he believes are destructive, and offers suggestions for improvement (see Figure 2). Deming believes that managers place too much emphasis on extrinsic motivation, thereby missing opportunities to help people achieve real satisfaction in their work lives.

THE VALUE OF PROFOUND KNOWLEDGE

Profound knowledge is crucial to the long-term operation of business because each component brings essential insight into optimization of the organization as a holistic entity, and success in business is measured by performance of the entire company. Appreciation for a system minimizes the damaging effects of suboptimization, in which one part of a company performs well at the expense of the business system. Theory of variation

provides for recognizing a stable system in statistical control. Management is prediction, and rational prediction is possible *only* with processes in statistical control. Deming flatly rejects the contention that major threats in business result from lack of effort: they result instead from not knowing what to do. Theory of knowledge tells us what to do. Psychology helps get everyone in the organization involved in its improvement.

Profound knowledge is itself a system. Components are interdependent and interactive. The aim of profound knowledge is optimum performance. Although Deming's management methods are presented in a business environment, profound knowledge can be applied in any area of human endeavor in which people attempt to achieve a goal through a system.

THE FOURTEEN POINTS FOR MANAGEMENT

Deming's Fourteen Points provide a method to develop and implement profound knowledge in business and guide long-term business plans and goals.

POINT 1: CREATE CONSTANCY OF PURPOSE FOR IMPROVEMENT OF PRODUCT AND SERVICE Continuation of a business requires a core set of values and a purpose that do not change with time. Constancy of purpose means accepting obligations that include innovation, research, education, and continuous improvement of product and service design.

POINT 2: ADOPT THE NEW PHILOSOPHY The new philosophy seeks to optimize holistic systems rather than suboptimize components. It eschews management practices that rob people of their pride of workmanship, and seeks profound knowledge as the basis for plans and decisions.

FIGURE 2   Faulty Management Practices and Suggestions for Improvement

FAULTY PRACTICE	BETTER PRACTICE
Skills only required	*Theory of management required*
Management of outcome with immediate action when figures deviate from expectations or standards.	Work on the system to reduce failure at the source. Avoid tampering. Instead, distinguish by appropriate techniques between special causes and common causes.
The so-called merit system—actually a destroyer of people.	Institute leadership. Reward cooperation.
Incentive pay for individuals—pay based on performance. The incentive is numbers, not quality.	Put all people on regular systems of pay. Provide leadership.
Problem report and resolution. This technique often results in tampering, making things worse.	Study the system. Learn methods to minimize net economic loss.
Work standards (quota and time standards) rob people of pride of workmanship and shut off any possibility of obtaining valid data to improve process.	Provide leadership. Everyone is entitled to pride of workmanship.
MBO—Management by Numbers ("Do it. I don't care how, just do it.")	Improve the system to get better results in the future.

SOURCE: Deming notes from "Transformation for Management of Quality and Productivity," Seminar, February 19, 1991.

POINT 3: CEASE DEPENDENCE ON MASS INSPECTION Inspection to improve quality is too late, ineffective, and costly. Quality does not come from inspection, but rather from improvements in the process. No amount of inspection affects process quality.

POINT 4: END THE PRACTICE OF AWARDING BUSINESS ON THE BASIS OF PRICE TAG ALONE Price has no meaning without a measure of the quality being purchased. Reliance on price must be replaced by evaluations of the effects of purchased goods and services on the operation of all processes involved in their use. Purchasers and suppliers should move from adversarial positions to cooperative ones.

POINT 5: IMPROVE CONSTANTLY AND FOREVER THE SYSTEM OF PRODUCTION AND SERVICE Quality should be built in at the design stage, and systems should be redesigned continually for improved quality. Variation should be minimized as systems draw nearer and nearer toward operating at optimum points. Statistical tools and operational definitions (definitions determined by use in practice) can be extremely useful in implementing this point. They can provide the means with which to measure improvement.

POINT 6: INSTITUTE TRAINING Training should be based on system optimization and customer satisfaction. It should be a springboard from which workers can develop pride of workmanship. Training should provide managers and workers with the tools they will need to evaluate processes and improve systems. Deming recommends at least some training in statistical thinking so workers can appreciate variation.

POINT 7: ADOPT AND INSTITUTE LEADERSHIP Real leadership requires profound knowledge. Deming states that leaders must know the work they supervise. They must be empowered and directed to inform higher-level management about conditions that need correction. Higher-level management must act on that information. Leadership is the engine that drives systems toward optimization.

POINT 8: DRIVE OUT FEAR Deming (1986) claims that "no one can put in his best performance unless he feels secure." Fear begets misinformation, hidden agendas, and padded numbers. It may induce workers to satisfy a rule or a quota at the expense of the best interests of the company. All these consequences make system optimization very difficult.

POINT 9: BREAK DOWN BARRIERS BETWEEN STAFF AREAS This point is a direct result of an integrated, systemic view of business processes. Optimization of systems is impossible unless all components recognize their systemic function and have some feedback concerning the way their activities are affecting system performance. Interstaff teams provide the best means to break down barriers between staff areas and enhance communication.

POINT 10: ELIMINATE SLOGANS, EXHORTATIONS, AND TARGETS FOR THE WORK FORCE Deming claims that posters and exhortations are directed at the wrong people. Posters represent the hope that workers could, by some additional effort, accomplish the goals set by management. Managers must learn that the responsibility for improving the business system is theirs, not the workers'. If posters and exhortations ask people to do what the system will not allow them to do, the only result will be disillusionment and frustration.

POINT 11A: ELIMINATE NUMERICAL QUOTAS FOR THE WORK FORCE Deming views a quota as "a fortress against improvement of quality and productivity." He continues, "I have yet to see a quota that includes any trace of a system by which to help anyone do a better job" (1986). Quotas do not consider quality. They cannot provide data valuable in improving the system: they destroy pride in workmanship.

POINT 11B: ELIMINATE NUMERICAL GOALS FOR PEOPLE IN MANAGEMENT Numerical goals are set when managers do not know the capabilities of the systems they are managing. They are generally set in ignorance or, at best, on the basis of what seems reasonable by experience. Stable systems do not need numerical goals. Output will be determined by system capability. Unstable systems have no capability. There can be no basis for setting a numerical goal in an unpredictable system.

POINT 12: REMOVE BARRIERS THAT ROB PEOPLE OF PRIDE OF WORKMANSHIP This point recommends that all workers be given the tools and training they need to do a job in which they can take pride. It requires managers to listen to workers and act upon their suggestions and requests. Listening and follow-up action, which are hard work, need to be reinforced by high-level management. Some organizations seem more interested in bureaucratic procedures than their own employees.

POINT 13: ENCOURAGE EDUCATION AND SELF-IMPROVEMENT FOR EVERYONE Systems will improve as a result of applied knowledge, which is linked to education. Deming writes, "In respect to self-improvement, it is wise for anyone to bear in mind that there is no shortage of good people. Shortage exists at the high levels of knowledge; this is true in every field." Deming recommends life-long learning, whether in formal or informal settings. Committed, knowledgeable people have the best chance of optimizing systems in which they work.

POINT 14: TAKE ACTION TO ACCOMPLISH THE TRANSFORMATION If business systems are to be optimized, everyone must be involved. The leadership for this involvement rests clearly with management. Managers must show the work force that they are serious about adopting a systems view of their business. They must demonstrate their concern for worker interests, provide adequate training to measure system performance, and measure attempts to improve it.

DEMING'S FOURTEEN POINTS AS MORAL PRINCIPLES

The Fourteen Points are not a list of action items. They are more similar to a code of conduct or a value system that provides a frame of reference with which to view the world. They are similar to the Ten Commandments—statements of principles that are considerably easier to list than to implement. Implementation requires judgment and guidance. Deming preaches a philosophy of life that is very similar to that of major religions: continuous, lifelong improvement from conversion to new core beliefs. The Deming philosophy really does require a transformation in thinking. Deming is guiding firms on a pilgrimage that takes time and perseverance, and he freely admits that there is no quick fix, no instant pudding. There will be struggle and some degree of pain, but the potential rewards are tremendous.

The journey Deming proposes demands faith. He comments on innovation as an obligation of his first point (Deming 1986): "One requirement for innovation is faith that there will be a future." When he writes, "He that would run his company on visible figures alone will in time have neither company nor figures," and tells us that the most important figures for management are unknown and unknowable, he is advocating acting by faith. How else can anyone deal with what is not visible, or what is unknowable, except by faith?

APPLICATION OF THE FOURTEEN POINTS IN SERVICE INDUSTRIES

Although quality as preached by Deming and others has been seen as principally applying to the manufacturing sector, there is no question that service businesses also can benefit from adopting Deming's philosophy in their firms. Below are some examples of successful implementations of this philosophy.

WINDSOR EXPORT SUPPLY

Windsor Export Supply is a division of Ford Motor Company. Its 250 employees take orders for parts from

Ford's foreign manufacturing plants, most of which are located in South America. It also fills orders for Ford parts from customers outside the Ford organization.

Once an order is placed with Windsor, it purchases parts from Ford's North American plants, arranges shipment, and collects payment. In the early 1980s, orders began diminishing for the division in the face of stiff Japanese competition. Ford's manufacturing capacity had also grown overseas, and demand was declining for North American parts. Although Windsor was still profitable, Ford executives sought advice from Deming on improving the performance of the Windsor organization.

Windsor was the first service group at Ford to receive training in the Deming management philosophy. Ford's initial efforts with Deming focused on the factory floor. There were many barriers to pride of workmanship at Windsor. Managers were surprised to learn that white-collar service employees felt the same kind of frustrations in their jobs as blue-collar factory workers. Harry Artinian of the Ford statistical methods office noted, "If you took the white shirts and ties off those people and put them in overalls, you'd hear the same words" (Walton 1986).

Deciding what parts of the Windsor process to measure and optimize was a complicated procedure. In manufacturing, the accounting system highlights scrap, rework, and excess inventory. Those kinds of figures do not exist for service functions. The process of targeting significant inhibitors to performance at Windsor depended upon the knowledge and experience of the company's managers. The management team responsible for instituting Deming methods began with training and flow diagrams, hoping to get one good project as a consequence. Worker response was encouraging, and six projects were initiated.

One successful project involved freight auditing. Windsor would receive invoices from freight carriers through a contracted auditor, who completed the company paperwork and issued instructions for payment to the Ford accounts payable office in Oakville, Ontario. The contracted auditor was chosen to take advantage of "state-of-the-art" methods. But late payments and missing information were routine occurrences. Past due bills mounted, occasionally for months. Almost everyone involved in the system was frustrated.

The freight auditing optimization team measured elapsed time between the date Windsor received an invoice and the date Oakville issued a check. Using control charts, the team found that the system was stable with an average response time of 14 days, but as many as 35 days might pass between invoice receipt and issuance of a check. The team used cause-and-effect diagrams to identify reasons for delay. They found keypunch errors, misfiling, missing codes, and misplaced bills. Attempts to resolve those problems with the contracted auditor proved unsuccessful, so Windsor took over the auditing function, making a number of changes to correct problem areas. The final result of these efforts was a drop in average response time to six days and a reduction in the proportion of rejected bills at Oakville from 34 percent to less than 1 percent.

PARKVIEW EPISCOPAL MEDICAL CENTER

Parkview Episcopal Medical Center is one of two hospitals serving Pueblo, Colorado. Hospital Corporation of America, which manages the facility, designated it as a "role model" hospital for quality improvement. Strict limitations in revenue prompted Parkview to undertake the cultural changes associated with Deming management. Ninety-five percent of its patient base is made up of Medicare and Medicaid beneficiaries, HMO members, and the medically indigent. "With that amount of fixed payment," CEO Michael Pugh says, "It's clear that we have to do something different to survive" (Koska 1990).

Pugh was introduced to the Deming quality management philosophy for the first time in the spring of 1988. By autumn, many Parkview senior managers had received quality training. Pugh established a Quality Improvement Council of senior managers to help guide the implementation of Deming's "new philosophy." The hospital jumped on Deming Point 6, "Institute Training," with a vengeance. Quality improvement teams were formed to address hospital problems under the direction of a group of managers trained specifically to lead them. Almost all department managers attended a week-long course on statistics taught by a consultant. All hospital employees were schedule to attend a quality awareness course.

Pugh estimates that it takes two to three years to integrate Deming quality methods into organizational culture. He advises managers to expect a steep employee learning curve. As Parkview moves further into its new philosophy, Pugh notes definite improvements in employee morale. The hospital turnover rate was less than 12 percent in 1990, compared with rates of 15 to 18 percent in previous years. Cost savings are more difficult to quantify, but quality improvement teams in operating room (OR) scheduling and food service delivery provided the hospital with more than $10,000 in annual savings in each department during 1990.

Parkview's approach to surgery scheduling provides an example of its utilization of the Deming approach to quality. The hospital had a history of not meeting early morning surgery schedules; 48 percent of morning surgical procedures began late, affecting operating times for the remainder of the day. Therefore, an OR quality improvement team was formed that included nurses, technicians, and physicians. The group tracked actual causes for delays, finding two common system causes: either the surgeon was late, or the OR was not ready. The team tried to encourage surgeons to arrive on time by 1) reminding physicians that they were expected to be on time for surgeries; 2) not permitting any surgeon who was late to surgery two times in one month to schedule the first case of the day; and 3) posting the names of late doctors in the physicians' lounge.

When the team examined instances when the OR was not ready to begin surgery at the scheduled 7:30 a.m. starting time, it discovered that extensive surgeries, such as total knee or hip replacements, were most likely to start late. The OR staff, coming in at 7:00 a.m.., was unable to prepare instrumentation for extensive operations in 30 minutes. The team suggested moving starting times for major surgeries to 8:00 a.m. Leann Leuer, R. N., director of surgical services, commented, "By changing the rules a little bit we still start on time. Morale has improved because staff has more time to set up, and the surgeons aren't angry because they don't have to stand around waiting." As a result of the team's efforts, the number of late surgeries dropped from 48 to 8 percent.

GENERIC APPLICATION OF THE DEMING MANAGEMENT PHILOSOPHY

The Fourteen Points must be fully integrated into an entire business to realize the full benefits of Deming's management philosophy. However, Deming does not see this generally being done. He recognizes that statistical quality control has permeated unique processes on the shop floor, but he estimates that only about 3 percent of the benefits of his management transformation lie in this area. The big gains are in overall business strategy and company-wide systems.

Why have firms concentrated on unique shop floor processes and largely ignored company-wide systems, where Deming estimates that 97 percent of the benefits of the "new philosophy " wait to be tapped? Lack of effort is not a satisfactory explanation; in Deming's perspective, it rarely is. Many high-level American man-

agers have not moved beyond unique shop-floor quality control because they have not accepted the Fourteen Points as desirable moral principles, or because they do not know how to bring the Deming philosophy into their company systems. Generic guidelines for implementing the philosophy throughout entire organizations would be helpful for managers who accept Deming's teaching but do not know how to get beyond statistical quality control at the shop floor.

GUIDELINES FOR IMPLEMENTING DEMING MANAGEMENT

The Deming quality philosophy requires adopting a corporate culture based on his Fourteen Points for management. Because high-level managers are responsible for corporate culture, they must be the first converts to the new philosophy to provide an environment in which Deming's ideas can have lasting effects. Conversion begins at the top and travels down through the organization. Following adoption of the new philosophy, high-level managers need training in statistical thinking and the Fourteen Points. They should also create flow diagrams for systems under their authority to help them understand what they are charged with optimizing. Figure 3 presents a generic flow diagram. It is created by first considering the needs and desires of customers, then working back through business processes to suppliers. Declaration of systems aims follows with an attempt to implement the Fourteen Points in the organization. Once aims are declared, training of middle management can begin.

The Shewhart Cycle, also called the PDCA cycle, can be a helpful procedure in implementing the Fourteen Points. It is shown in Figure 4. In the cycle, changes or experiments are planned and carried out. The effects are studied to determine whether changes have improved the system or offer any insight into prediction. A number of cycle iterations may be necessary before satisfactory results are achieved.

RESPONSIBILITIES OF MANAGEMENT

The Deming philosophy must first transform upper management. Training, system diagrams, and the PDCA cycle are critical in implementing the Fourteen Points. Wherever possible, upper management should take action to improve the business system.

Once systems aims are declared, middle managers can begin learning the new philosophy. They must also be trained in statistical methods and the Fourteen Points. To better understand the systems for which they are responsible, middle managers should create flow

FIGURE 3   Generic Flow Diagram

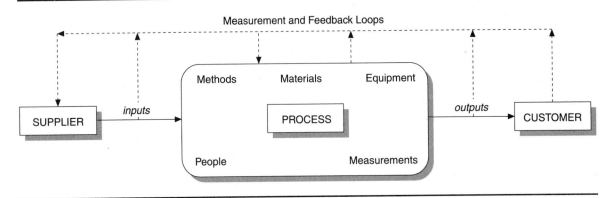

diagrams, recognizing the aims that their systems are supposed to serve. Middle managers are close enough to the front lines of their businesses that they can use their training to target the largest system inhibitors to performance facing their sections of the company.

A variety of process tools are available to aid middle managers in bringing attention to large performance inhibitors. Flow diagrams increase understanding of systems. Cause-and-effect diagrams help clarify relationships between business components. Pareto charts and histograms demonstrate frequency of occurrences. Run charts and scatter diagrams show trends in process performance. Control charts allow managers to distinguish between common process variation and special causes that need immediate attention. These tools are discussed in detail in many statistical quality control texts.

FIGURE 3   The PDCA Cycle

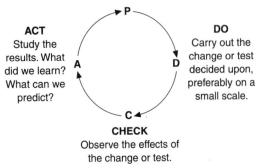

PLAN
What changes are desirable? What data are available? Are new observations needed? If yes, plan a change or test. Decide how to use observations.

ACT
Study the results. What did we learn? What can we predict?

DO
Carry out the change or test decided upon, preferably on a small scale.

CHECK
Observe the effects of the change or test.

Although middle management generally identifies significant system inhibitors to performance, lower management and non-management employees are in the best position to generate recommendations for improvement and deal with special causes that are not part of the system. One highly effective way of approaching inhibitors to performance is through interdisciplinary teams that target specific problems or opportunities.

Training is essential for the teams to function effectively. All employees should be exposed to the Deming philosophy, be informed of system aims, and learn statistical methods of measuring process performance. The PDCA cycle and process tools previously discussed are crucial ingredients for process optimization. Lower-level managers and workers can deal immediately with unique special causes outside their statistically stable systems. After study, they can also recommend ways of improving systems to upper management.

Company-wide implementation of Deming concepts, at all levels, is shown in Figure 5:

☐ Upper management is responsible for creating a corporate culture consistent with Deming's philosophy, instituting the Fourteen Points, understanding business supersystems, and declaring system aims. Upper management also must act to improve corporate business systems, often at the request of lower levels of management.

☐ Middle managers must adopt the new philosophy, understand systems for which they are responsible, implement the Fourteen Points, and target for attention significant inhibitors to performance. They too must take action to improve their business processes, frequently in response to recommendations from lower levels of management.

FIGURE 5   Implementing Deming Concepts Company-Wide

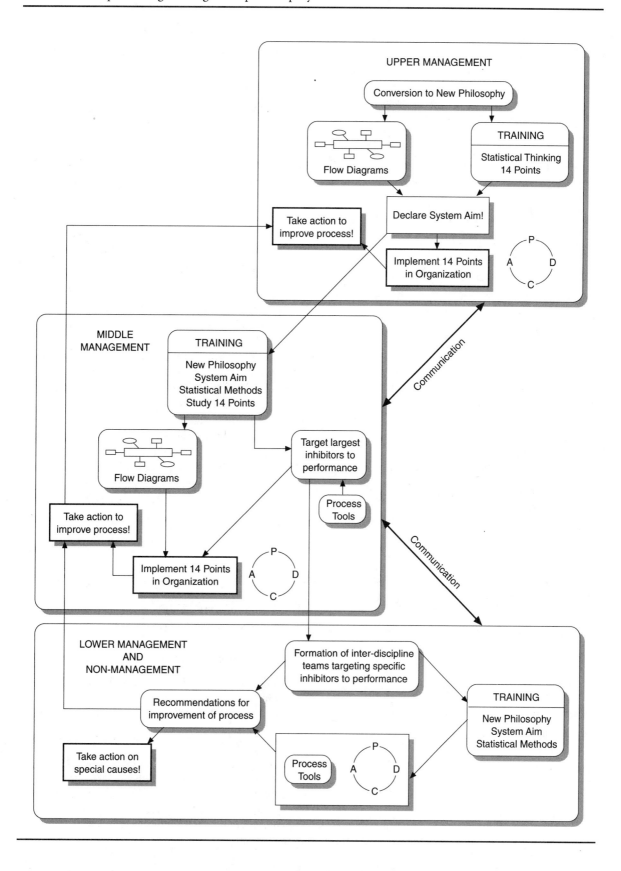

☐ Lower management and non-managerial workers must be instructed in the new philosophy and receive training to measure system performance and recognize special causes of variation. They must seek solutions to significant problems, often through interdisciplinary teams. Lower-level managers can take immediate action on special causes of process variation and recommend system changes to higher management. Deming concepts cannot be successfully applied without open communication among managerial levels.

RULES OF IMPLEMENTATION

Figure 6 lists key activities involved in instituting Deming management methods on a company-wide basis, with general rules guiding their implementation. Systems are understood beginning with customer needs and desires, but optimized beginning with suppliers. Adoption of the new philosophy is accomplished top-down, as is the identification of significant inhibitors to performance. Solutions to overcoming those inhibitors, however, are developed bottom-up. Line workers and first-line management can act on special causes of variation, but management alone can make changes to improve common cause variations inherent in the system.

Cultural change is essential in any organization attempting to adopt Deming management because its major challenge comes not in planning, but in execution. Mary Walton (1990) explains the development of a Deming quality lifestyle as a sequence of five stages:

STAGE 1: THE DECISION TO ADOPT Management recognizes that historic ways of doing business no longer produce desired results.

STAGE 2: INCUBATION   The quality message is transmitted throughout the organization, emphasizing that upper management is committed to change. Vision and mission statements are created.

STAGE 3: PLANNING AND PROMOTION Company quality needs are determined and plans are developed to introduce the quality transformation throughout the company.

STAGE 4: EDUCATION Employees are trained in statistical thinking and given tools to evaluate and improve the systems in which they work.

STAGE 5: NEVER-ENDING IMPROVEMENT Quality techniques become enmeshed in every operation of the organization. Quality becomes a part *of* business activities, not apart *from* business activities.

Continuous improvement is a never-ending journey that requires time, effort, and perseverance. Groups not truly converted to Deming's value system may well abandon the Fourteen Points when initial feelings of enthusiasm wane. The Deming philosophy is also paradoxical. Profound knowledge demands tremendous amounts of data and information, yet Deming insists that managers act on faith to manage what is invisible and unknowable.

W. Edwards Deming has preached his gospel of management transformation for more than 44 years. It is time for American companies to listen to his message.

FIGURE 6   General Rules of Implementation

Activity	*Rule of Implementation*
Understanding systems through flow diagrams	Create flow diagram by beginning with customers and work back to suppliers
Optimizing systems with the aid of flow diagrams	Begin with suppliers and work forward to customers
Adopting the new philosophy	Adopt top-down, beginning with upper management
Identifying significant system problems and opportunities, and setting priorities in seeking solutions	Identify problems and opportunities top-down, frequently starting with middle management
Seeking solutions to problems involving common causes	Solutions emerge bottom-up from teams of workers and first-line supervision
Acting to correct special cause problems	Comes from workers and first-line supervision, unless higher-level management is needed to authorize substantial monetary expenditure
Acting to correct common cause problems	Comes from management at appropriate level, after receiving recommendations from problem-solving team

NOTES

1. This and all other non-referenced Deming quotations are from his "Transformation Seminar" given at the Adam's Mark Hotel, Philadelphia, February 19–22, 1991.

REFERENCES

W. Edwards Deming, *Out of the Crisis* (Cambridge, MA: MIT Center for Advanced Engineering Study, 1986).

Lucinda Harper, "Trade Deficit Shrank in June to $4.02 Billion," *Wall Street Journal,* August 19, 1991, A2.

A. F. Jacobsen, speech, quoted in *Business America,* March 25, 1991, 4.

Mary T. Koska, "Adopting Deming's Quality Improvement Ideas: A Case Study," *Hospitals,* July 5, 1990, 58–64.

William W. Scherkenbach, *The Deming Route to Quality and Productivity: Road Maps and Roadblocks* (Rockville, MD: Mercury Press, 1990).

Mary Walton, *Deming Management at Work* (New York: Putnam Publishing Group, 1990).

Mary Walton, *The Deming Management Method* (New York: Putnam Publishing Group, 1986).

CHAPTER 13

COMPETING AS A SERVICE FIRM IV
BUILDING A CUSTOMER-FOCUSED
SERVICE ORGANIZATION

CHAPTER OVERVIEW

Chapter 3 developed the idea that the decisions made by the operating and marketing functions are interlinked. Almost everything operations decides to do has an impact on the servuction system and, hence, on the consumer; likewise, many of the decisions made by marketing affect the expectations or behavior of the consumer and the servuction system.

Because of the interactive nature of that system, any department or function that influences all or part of it will find itself interrelating with all the other functions that have influence. For example, a service business that does not delegate its personnel function to operations, as many do, will find itself with a three-cornered fight, as shown in the figure below.

Somehow, marketing always seem to lose in this fight. The purpose of this chapter is, first of all, to describe why marketing often may have less influence in service companies than in goods companies. Second, the chapter goes on to describe alternative ways of increasing customer orientation in the culture of service firms.

THE HISTORICAL WEAKNESS OF MARKETING IN SERVICE FIRMS

It is necessary to draw an important distinction between marketing orientation, the marketing function, and the marketing department. Gronroos defines the marketing orientation as follows:

> *Marketing orientation* means that a firm or organization plans its operations according to market needs. The objectives of the firm should be to satisfy customer needs rather than merely to use existing production facilities or raw materials.[1]

This *orientation,* thus, is clearly an attitude of mind that puts the customer's needs first in any trade-off. Such an orientation does not require a formally designated marketing department.

The functions of marketing in services encompass such tasks as the design of the product, pricing, and promotion. Decisions in these areas must be made in order for the organization to operate, but they need not necessarily be made by people with a marketing title, nor by individuals in a marketing department.

In a typical goods company, these distinctions are not necessary, but they are necessary in service firms where a formal marketing department may not necessarily exist. Since the product is an interactive process, it may be more appropriate to leave the different functional "decisions" to different departments.

THE TECHNOLOGY MATRIX

Figure 13.1 shows a matrix originally suggested some years ago by Maister and Lovelock.[2] One axis of the matrix relates directly to the work of Chase[3] and represents the degree of customer contact. According to Chase's ideas, the higher the level of customer contact, the higher the level of inefficiency that will be produced because of the uncertainty introduced by those consumers. This idea is based largely on the

FIGURE 13.1   The Customization/Customer-Contact Matrix

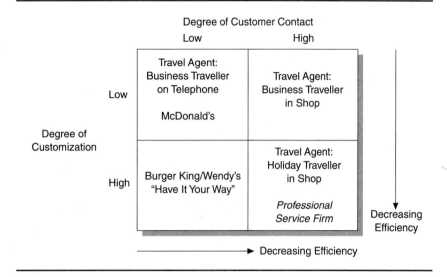

concept of an interactive system and the participation of the consumers in the process. The second axis relates to the amount of customization of the service available to consumers. Once again, we would expect the "low" state to be preferable, since it would allow the system to operate close to the ideal "production line." A number of sample systems have been introduced into the cells to illustrate how the matrix is used.

For example, a travel agency can operate in a number of cells simultaneously. Booking an airline ticket by telephone for a business traveler fits into the low/low cell. But the same organization just as well could operate in a different cell if it also maintained a shop. From within that system, both high and low customization are possible, depending on whether the customer is a business traveler wanting a ticket or a vacationer planning a multi-stop European trip.

The matrix has an ideal cell from an operations perspective: the low/low state. In that cell, the degree of customer contact is minimized so that large parts of the organization can be isolated and can run like any other manufacturing plant.[4] In that cell, also, the level of customization is minimized so that the operating system can be focused on a limited range of output and its efficiency thus can be increased.[5] However, a move into this cell can have major implications for marketing. Customers actually may be seeking contact and customization, and may be willing to pay a premium for them.

A top-quality French restaurant might fit into the high/high category. Compared to McDonald's, this is a different business with a different formula (but, interestingly, the target segment may be the same person on a very different occasion). The loss of efficiency implied by the high/high cell is compensated for by the price that can be charged.

More importantly for the purposes of this discussion, the different cells suggest alternative roles and places for the marketing departments of firms operating within them. Two contrasting examples are the provision of legal services by a traditional law firm and by Hyatt Legal Services.

Operationally, the traditional firm will fit into the high/high cell in the matrix, and we might expect little scope for operational efficiency. The firm's lawyers will be in intensive contact with the clients and will be customizing the service, client by client. Except for routine cases, there will be little scope for economies of scale.

From a marketing point of view, the product in the high/high cell often is created in the client's offices, away from the home firm of the lawyer. In such situations, it is clear that a central marketing department could have little influence over the product and that most of the marketing needs to be delegated to the field if not to the individual level. Selling is done by the consultants or professionals, so that, too, must be delegated.

The alternative is Hyatt Legal Services. Operationally, this firm represents a clear attempt to move the technology away from the inefficiency of the high/high cell toward the low/low or, at least, the high-contact/low-customization cell. By reducing the types of problems tackled, operations can be simplified and economies of scale generated. These economies, in turn, can be passed on to the customer through lower fees.

The marketing implications of such a change of technology are relatively straightforward. The service is branded in order to add value for the consumer in a market that traditionally is not heavily branded. The system depends on systematization and, from an operations point of view, implies centralization. We therefore would expect to find a strong centralized marketing department as well. Clearly, many service firms do not operate in the low/low cell of the matrix, even though they might wish to do so. For many service firms, therefore, the traditional combination of marketing functions in a marketing department breaks down. The result is that there is not a strong marketing group to drive a marketing orientation within the organization. The weakness of the marketing function is compounded by the strength of the operations group and the interlinkages between them.

THE EVOLUTIONARY PLACE OF MARKETING

All service businesses start with the kind of service formula described in Chapter 9. The up-front work necessary to create the formula requires a strong marketing unit. Once the prototype is built, however, the next problems are operational ones. Without the appropriate level of operational efficiency, the formula simply will not work.

If the firm then chooses to compete for geography (see Chapter 9), and to adopt a multi-site strategy, the formula is frozen. The role of marketing becomes one of site selection and advertising, but, if loss of focus is to be avoided, the "product" must be fixed.

By the end of the multi-site phase, the operations group is huge, while the marketing group is small and often fragmented. Only when the service firm decides it needs to begin to compete for market share with multiple services or multiple segments is marketing needed again. Before that happens, however, a lowly branch manager in such a network might receive these three memoranda on the same day:

From the Marketing Department:
We shortly will be launching a new advertising campaign based on the friendliness of our staff. This is in direct response to the increasingly competitive marketplace we face. Please ensure your staff members deliver the promises we are making.

From the Operations Department:
As you are aware, we are facing an increasingly competitive marketplace and, as a result, our profits have come under pressure. It is crucial, therefore, that we minimize waste to keep our costs under control. From today, therefore, no recruitment whatsoever will be allowed.

SERVICES IN ACTION 13.1

LA QUINTA MOTOR INNS

La Quinta Motor Inns was founded in 1968 with the establishment of two hotels in San Antonio, Texas. In the following decade, the company experienced rapid growth, and, by 1980, La Quinta had 95 units in 23 states, with a total of over 11,000 rooms. La Quinta, by offering a quality product priced consistently below the competition, achieved one of the highest occupancy rates of any hotel chain in the country.

The firm was very much led from the top. La Quinta's president took an active role in the running of the company, particularly when it came to selecting sites for new inns, a task that he regarded as a key part of the firm's marketing strategy. Each site was chosen personally by the president, and the factors that went into each site-selection decision were determined by him on the basis of experience and "gut feeling." The other important officer of the firm was the senior vice president of operations, who was personally responsible for quality and frequently made impromptu personal inspections of sites.

La Quinta employed a vice president of marketing, who was responsible to the vice president of operations. Under the vice president of marketing were three more officers: the vice president of advertising, the publicity director, and the editor of the firm's internal magazine.

The major role of the marketing department was to handle the firm's communications. Advertising and publicity were aimed at creating public awareness of the chain in a cost-effective manner. Marketing had no role in the site-selection process, which was handled by the president, or in selling; the sales director reported separately to the vice president of operations. Nor did the marketing department play any role in developing new services or making pricing decisions.

Senior management believed that marketing was, in fact, an integral function of many departments: finance (in setting prices), sales, and operations. The existence of a specific marketing department was necessary only to fulfill the communications and public-relations functions that other departments could not handle. The concept of marketing as a separate function was considered unnecessary in a firm of La Quinta's type.

The personnel of the marketing department, however, felt that they were being underutilized and that they could, in particular, provide greater inputs to operations and pricing decisions. They complained that they frequently did not know what specific services would be offered until after the service decision had been made. Marketing also considered personal opinions on the part of management to be an inadequate substitute for market research, particularly when coping with change.

From the Personnel Department:
Our staff members have become increasingly militant. This is due, in large part, to the availability of alternative employment with our new competitors. We currently are involved in a particularly delicate set of negotiations and would be grateful if you could minimize any disruptions at the local level.

These instructions obviously conflict with one another. To obey the operations department means no recruitment and therefore an increase in the work load of the contact personnel. Such an increased work load undoubtedly will spill over into labor negotiations and could be disastrous for the personnel function. Finally, the increased work load, in all probability, will have a negative effect on staff morale. Given the transparency of the service organization, this low morale will be visible to customers and will affect their satisfaction levels adversely.

When the firm is marketing oriented, the site manager will trade off the three sets of instructions, giving added weight to marketing. It should be stressed that, within service firms, it is nearly impossible to be totally marketing oriented. Customers cannot be given everything they want because of the very real constraints imposed by the operating system. Unfortunately, by now our service firm is operations dominated and oriented toward operational efficiency, and operations has line responsibility for branches. As a result, the manager throws away all but the operations department memo. The final result may be an abusive memo from the operations vice president to her counterpart in marketing. The memo would ask why marketing was sending a memorandum to the branches at all, and suggesting that, in the future, all memos be cleared with operations. This would not be personal, but would be a manifestation of the different cultures in marketing and operations. Different departments in all organizations have a tendency to develop different cultures and to move away from each other. This is a naturally occurring phenomenon that organizational theorists call *differentiation*.[6]

Organizational theorists define *differentiation* as the difference between departments in terms of goals, time behaviors, reward structures, and tasks. The original work by Lawrence and Lorsch[7] suggested that marketing had longer time horizons than manufacturing, was less rigidly and hierarchically organized, and tended to reward innovation and creativity, which were less valued in manufacturing. These findings were reviewed in the study by Langeard et al.,[8] which found differences in revenue versus cost orientation, time horizons, and motivations for change between service operations and marketing departments.

Within goods companies, such differences do not become pathological. Fortunately, in goods-producing companies, the availability of inventory allows the two departments to operate semi-autonomously, at least in the short term. Manufacturing needs to know the likely demand that marketing will create and the particular products that are needed, but once these targets are agreed upon, the two departments can operate independently. Production then can be scheduled to create inventory as it is needed. Marketing does not need to know when or how production takes place. Once inventory is available, it can be transferred formally; indeed, it is often "sold" by manufacturing to marketing. Coordination may be achieved by a planning manager or coordinator who interfaces between the two departments. Conflicts, when they arise, can be resolved only by the general manager in such organizations, who oversees the different functions.

In a service firm, the technology is different. There is very little opportunity to inventory anything, and the system itself contains no inventories; it is a real-time experience. The impact of this is that the coordination of the different functions takes place at two points in the organization—at the very top and at the very bottom. Branch managers at the bottom of an organization take a very different perspective on interfunctional trade-offs than do their general-management counterparts at the top.

THE NEED FOR MORE CUSTOMER ORIENTATION

The service firm has reached the limits of the multi-site strategy and now needs to become marketing oriented again. Alternatively, or sometimes simultaneously, the firm starts to feel threatened by serious competition. Unfortunately, most service operations find it difficult to defend against competition. Because service systems and concepts cannot be shielded from infringement, there are few barriers, other than location, to protect a service firm.

The traditional goods-marketing logic would argue that the implications for marketing are twofold. First, an increasing need for effective marketing may require closer coordination of the various marketing decisions. That coordination, in turn, may require the creation of a marketing function, either at the site level or at the head office, to collect all relevant information and generally to improve the quality of marketing decision making.

The second implication for marketing is the need to give added weight to the marketing orientation. Particularly if the organization has been operations dominated in the past, a strong marketing department may be necessary to keep the natural search for operational efficiency from predominating. Unfortunately, this denies the interrelatedness of the different functions implied by the servuction system. Marketing effectiveness generally can be bought only at the expense of operational efficiency. Moreover, neither operational nor marketing objectives can be allowed to predominate. A compromise between the two *must* be reached. A marketing department may not be the answer.[9]Indeed, the creation of a marketing department might produce nothing more than inter-departmental warfare that focuses the organization inward, precisely when it should be focusing outward. More important is the need to generate increased levels of marketing orientation. To do this requires a change in the dominant culture of the organization, away from operations and toward marketing.

BUILDING CUSTOMER ORIENTATION IN SERVICE FIRMS

Figure 13.2 presents a simple framework for considering culture change. It suggests that culture is integrally linked to and partly an outcome of three organizational components: structure, systems, and people. Structure is self-explanatory and relates to the formal reporting structures normally represented in an organization chart. Systems are a more complex area in this context, since they deal not with information-technology systems but with people-management systems for control, evaluation, promotion, and recognition. Each has both an informal and a formal component. Control systems provide individuals and groups with a score and the informal system tells them which item matters to their boss at the moment. Evaluation and promotion systems cover all the formal paraphernalia of management by objectives,

FIGURE 13.2   The Culture Framework

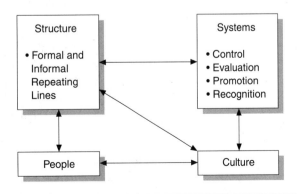

but also by the informal "What do I have to do to be a hero?" criteria. Recognition systems focus on formal and informal rewards—from company trips to lunch with the chief executive. An attempt to change to a more customer-oriented culture, therefore, can use any of four levers: structure, systems, people, or culture, separately or together.

CHANGING CULTURE THROUGH STRUCTURE

Structure can change culture. However, it is a blunt weapon since it takes years to implement an organizational change successfully, and only when implementation is successful will culture start to change. To different approaches to using the cultural lever have been tried: a marketing department as a change agent and restructuring around the servuction system model.

MARKETING DEPARTMENTS AS CHANGE AGENTS Marketing departments can be created in environments where one might not expect them to be, for their role can be merely to change the orientation of the organization by creating an advocate for the consumer.

But, as Gronross points out, there is a real danger in this approach. Gronroos suggests that, once such a department has been created, operations personnel will merely transfer responsibility for satisfying consumers to the marketing department.[10] Even worse, Lovelock and his colleagues showed that, in such a situation, there is also the likelihood that open warfare will break out between the two departments.[11]

Many of the conflicts implied by this approach have been suggested by organizational behavior theorists. Conflicts emerge in the first place because of differences in orientation between the marketing and operations departments. Operations departments, by their very nature, tend to be cost driven; their focus is on evaluating the operation to find costs to save and procedures to simplify. This outlook tends to have a short time horizon. Marketing, by comparison, is looking for enhancements that can be made to the product in order to create a competitive advantage. The creation of such an advantage is not something that firms can expect to achieve in the short term.

Coordination of such highly differentiated functions usually requires the use of nonconventional integrating mechanisms. To mesh these different perspectives and to allow the two groups to understand each other, a number of strategies have been suggested by organizational-behavior theory. Interfunctional task forces provide a classic way of forcing disparate individuals to work together, and to develop a better understanding of each other's perspective. In the same way, interfunctional transfers can create informal networks of individuals from different departments who understand and trust each other.

For example, operations managers promoted to run a marketing department will face certain initial problems. Their orientation is toward operations, but their new role requires a marketing perspective. If such a transfer can be achieved successfully, the result is usually a general manager who makes rational and clear trade-offs between operations and marketing. Moreover, it also creates a marketing person who has direct contacts in the operations group and can overcome many of the traditional barriers to change.

Once the orientation of the organization has become one of general management with a strong consumer orientation, the marketing department can shrink. For example, in the early 1980s, many professional service firms created marketing departments in this way. The departments focused on advertising, but also on research and customer-satisfaction surveys. The result was a shift in the culture of the firm and the reassertion of the primacy of the client.

RESTRUCTURING AROUND THE MODEL A number of service firms have explicitly or implicitly restructured around the servuction model. For example, one major airline has all departments who have direct customer contact report to the head of marketing. Only engineering and flight crew (pilots) report to the head of operations. Combining all customer-facing departments with the marketing group has reversed the argument from "It will cost too much; it is inefficient," to "The customer needs this; how can we make it happen?"

CHANGING CULTURE THROUGH SYSTEMS

A number of different approaches have been used. Some firms, for example, have started to give bonuses to managers at all levels based upon the firm's score in terms of customer satisfaction. Research can be tailored to measure satisfaction, if necessary, down to the branch level and managers can be rewarded for improved scores. Unfortunately, as Chapter 2 pointed out, only part of customer satisfaction is under the control of management. Expectations can be raised by competitive offerings and the satisfaction score can drop as a consequence.

An alternative approach has been to introduce revenue into branch manager targets. A major New York bank wished to change the retail branch manager orientation from considering only costs and security to considering customers first. They introduced a revenue-based performance evaluation system. For the first time, managers had to worry about where the customers come from and had to stop thinking of the customers as "people who made a mess of my branch." Early successes by a few managers produced interesting results. Up to 20 percent of managers left the company, claiming that this was not what they had been hired to do. The balance woke up the moribund central marketing group to demand help with getting more customers. The long-run result of the change in systems was an increase in customer orientation and bad debt. The managers had discovered that money is an easy product to sell and the bank had discovered it needed to revamp its credit-control function.

Planning systems also can be used to change the orientation of companies. Formal marketing planning can drive organizations through the logic of marketing and can force them to develop an understanding of consumers' needs. Such planning exercises can become "mind-numbing bureaucratic exercises," but, for the first two or three cycles, the process can become educational. This is all the more powerful if combined with training and/or direct attacks on the culture.

CHANGING CULTURE THROUGH PEOPLE

Outsiders increasingly are being brought into the marketing department of service firms to try to change the orientation. What a package-goods marketing person discovers in a service firm was described in Chapter 1. In essence, they discover the complexity of the marketing task—assuming they stay with the firm long enough.

Such an approach must be supplemented with development programs inside the firm. Cross-functional transfers and task forces were discussed earlier in the context of structure. The result of such activities is, however, the creation of a cadre of people who understand both marketing and operations. Operations people need to be trained in marketing and marketing people need to understand all the areas described in this text.

SERVICES IN ACTION 13.2

DUNFEY HOTELS

The Dunfey Hotel Corporation is not so much a hotel chain as it is four separate hotel chains managed by one group. In 1980, the company owned, leased, or managed 22 hotels in the following divisions:

☐ Dunfey Classic and Luxury Hotels, four properties in the luxury/executive end of the market, including the Ambassador East in Chicago and the Berkshire Place in New York City.

☐ Dunfey Major Meeting and Convention Hotels, seven properties in the eastern states and Texas.

☐ Dunfey Inns and Airport Hotels, nine lower-priced hotels for travelers, located in New England and Pennsylvania.

☐ International Hotels, two properties, one each in London and Paris.

Dunfey managed these diverse properties through a single management system known as the Dunfey Planning Process. A key figure in this process was the managing director, an ex-marketing employee. Under the Dunfey Planning Process, the directors of operations from each of the four groups annually submitted their proposed plans and broad strategy documents for the forthcoming year. These plans and strategies then were reviewed by the corporate planning committee, a group that included the chairman, managing director, senior controller, operations directors, and marketing director.

Rather than working in individual departmental teams, Dunfey combined the various departments into one team at the highest level. If the plans submitted by the groups were approved, the marketing director and the group of directors of operations then wrote mission statements for each group. Each mission statement set forth the desired market position for each hotel and defined the "ideal business mix," which, in turn, defined the desired customer base, room rate, and time of use. This mission statement, if approved by the planning committee, then was translated into a marketing plan for each hotel.

The role of the marketing department was to provide an interface between the central planning committee and the four hotel groups during the planning process. Marketing was charged first with providing input into the planning process at the top and then with managing the planning process as it was implemented by the individual groups. No direct advertising or selling was done by the Dunfey marketing department; each hotel was responsible for its own promotion and selling.

CHANGING CULTURE DIRECTLY

Culture-change programs are becoming increasingly popular, especially when combined with the other levers described here. These programs range from broad-scale educational activities to highly empowered process re-engineering around the consumer. Figure 13.3 provides a simple way to categorize such activities. Along one axis are the nature of groups used. Mixed groups are cross-sectional, family groups can be a department or a naturally occurring group based on a process, e.g., all individuals involved with loading a particular flight with passengers. The second axis deals with the level of empowerment envisaged. Low levels of empowerment imply that indi-

FIGURE 13.3   Categorizing Culture Change Initiatives

	Group	
	Mixed	Family
Low / Empowerment	"Putting the Customer First"	"Orientation Change"
High	"Change the Way You Work"	"Change the Way We Work"

viduals will change their behavior, but the group will have no authority to change the processes and systems of the organization. High-level empowerment implies the ability to change the organization during the event or series of events. The slogans in the cells represent the hypothetical titles of such change programs, which often involve one or more meetings.

Cell 1 refers to "putting the customer first" programs that take place in mixed groups within the organization. Drawn together in sessions, personnel are lectured to and motivated to put the customer first. Through role playing, they are en-couraged to recognize the importance of the customer and change their behavior accordingly.

These programs can be very successful, particularly when rolled through the organization quickly. This overcomes the "major problems on the return to work" syndrome. To be successful, the new behavior needs to be reinforced on the job. If managers and colleagues are not aligned, the value of the program can be wiped out within hours. New behaviors created in the sessions will be focused upon by colleagues and old habits will be reinstated quickly.

Cell 2, "orientation change," overcomes these problems by processing people in family groups that can reinforce each other on the job. Both cells, however, focus on changing attitudes and individual behaviors. Changing organizational processes and systems is not part of this type of initiative. This potentially produces role conflict as desired behaviors are stopped by the physical environment or the operating system.

"Change the way you work" in cell 3 draws on the empowerment ideas described in detail in Chapter 6. It implies active empowerment of people attending the session. They are allowed to break the rules in the context of serving their customer. However, because of the mixed group, this type of initiative is focused on the individual rather than the process-level empowerment.

Cell 4, "change the way we work," refers to initiatives that draw on many of the ideas in this book. Groups are in families and can be asked to flowchart their activities. They then can be asked to re-engineer the process to better serve the customer. The level of excitement in such groups is matched only by the anxiety of their bosses. Empowerment at this level really does place the boss in the role of coach and enabler.

SUMMARY

Many factors mean that focused, strong marketing departments exist only in certain special types of service firms. Moreover, in certain phases of the competitive strategy of the firm the role of marketing is a narrow one. The result is often a large and politically strong operations group that dominates the culture.

Marketing is needed because of strategy or competitive environment changes that result in a culture change. The marketing orientation must increase above everything else. Tools exist that enable a change culture, and marketing has an active role to play in that process.

CHAPTER 13 READING

The article provides a detailed marketing-culture instrument for performing an audit on service firms.

QUESTIONS

1. Complete the culture instrument for a firm you are familiar with. What does it tell you? Do they need to change? Why?

2. On a recent flight on Scandinavian Airlines, a passenger asked for a *London Times*. She was informed that, unfortunately, all copies were gone, and she settled for a *Wall Street Journal* instead. A few moments later, the flight attendant returned with a *Times* that was slightly crumpled. When queried, he answered that he had noticed the captain was carrying a *Times* when she came on board and that he had borrowed it for the passenger!

    a. Would such behavior be a competitive weapon in the U.S. airline business?

    b. What stops that behavior today?

    c. How would you develop an initiative in a U.S. airline to induce this kind of behavior?

3. How would you describe the role of the marketing departments in Holiday Inns, the U.S. Postal Service, and Morgan Stanley?

4. What is it in the environment of the three companies in Question 3 that dictates the nature and role of their marketing departments?

NOTES

1.   C. Gronroos, "Designing a Long-Range Marketing Strategy for Services," *Long-Range Planning*, 13 (April 1980): 36; and C. Gronroos, "Innovative Marketing Strategies and Organizational Structures for Service Firms," in L. Berry, G. L. Shostack and G. D. Upah, eds., *Emerging Perspectives in Services Marketing*, Chicago: American Marketing Association, 9–21.

2.   D. H. Maister and C. H. Lovelock, "Managing Facilitator Services," *Sloan Management Review* (Summer 1982): 19–31.

3.   R. B. Chase, "Where Does the Consumer Fit in a Service Operation?" *Harvard Business Review*, 56, no. 6 (November–December 1978): 137–142.

4.   *Ibid.*

5.   W. Skinner, "The Focused Factory," *Harvard Business Review*, 52, no. 3 (May–June 1974):113–121.

6.   P. R. Lawrence and J. Lorsch, "Differentiation and Integration in Complex Organizations," *Administrative Science Quarterly*, 12 (1967): 1–47.

7.   *Ibid.*

8.   E. Langeard, J. E. G. Bateson, C. Lovelock, and P. Eiglier, *Marketing of Services: New Insights from Consumers and Managers,* report no. 81-104 (Cambridge, MA: Marketing Science Institute), 1981.

9.   Gronroos, "Innovative Marketing Strategies," 16.

10.   Gronroos, "Designing a Long-Range Marketing Strategy," 36; Gronroos, "Innovative Marketing Strategies," 9–21.

11.   C. H. Lovelock, E. Langeard, J. E. G. Bateson, and P. Eiglier, "Some Organizational Problems Facing Marketing in the Service Sector," in J. Donnelly and W. George, eds., *Marketing of Services* (Chicago: American Marketing Association, 1981), 148–153.

WHAT KIND OF MARKETING CULTURE EXISTS IN YOUR SERVICE FIRM? AN AUDIT

Cynthia Webster

Mississippi State University

The current literature in both services marketing and organizational culture leads to the argument that an appropriate culture is one of the most important ingredients for successfully marketing services. This article discusses the meaning and importance of marketing culture and presents a 34-item instrument for assessing the marketing culture of a service firm. The dimensions and items of the audit are discussed and potential applications of the audit are outlined.

INTRODUCTION

There is now general agreement among scholars that services marketing is different, and perhaps more difficult to analyze, than goods marketing because of four well-documented features of services: intangibility, perishability, inseparability of production and consumption, and heterogeneity.[6] As these unique features have resulted in managerial problems, several strategies have been advanced as possible solutions. There has, however, been relatively little research focusing on the organizational environments or climates that are conducive to implementing the proposed solutions. This lack of attention is unfortunate, since the current literature in both services marketing and organizational culture suggests that an appropriate culture is one of the most important ingredients for successfully marketing services.

The primary purposes of this article are to explain why the marketing culture of a service firm is important, to summarize the research that has been done in this area, to present a measure of the marketing culture of a service firm, and to make suggestions on how the measure can be used.

ORGANIZATIONAL CULTURE

Many conceptualizations of culture have been written, but a common element running through them can be summarized as follows: Organizational culture refers to the unwritten, formally decreed, and what actually takes place; it is the pattern of shared values and beliefs that help individuals understand organizational functioning and thus provides them norms for behavior in the organization.[3] Thus organizational culture focuses attention on informal, hidden forces within a firm—forces that exert tremendous influence on the behavior and productivity of its employees, perhaps more so than formal, written policies or guidelines.[10]

At a basic level, human systems need some "glue," some central theme or themes around which behavior can coalesce. In the absence of such a thematic element, employees cannot know when, toward what, and how to direct their energies. Organizational culture provides this thematic coherence.

The culture of a firm has been found to be important in many other ways. For example, some researchers mention its importance as a form of control of partici-

SOURCE: Cynthia Webster, "What Kind of Marketing Culture Exists in Your Service Firm? An Audit," *The Journal of Services Marketing,* vol. 6, no. 2 (Spring 1992): 54–67.

Cynthia Webster is currently associate professor of marketing at Mississippi State University. Dr. Webster's teaching interests include both undergraduate and graduate level marketing research and consumer behavior, and her research focuses on services marketing, forecasting, and Hispanic consumption behavior. She has presented papers at several regional, national, and international conferences and has published numerous articles in marketing journals.

pants. It might also be a critical key used by strategic managers to direct the course of their organizations.[7] Some researchers feel that a firm's culture has as much or more influence on corporate effectiveness as the formal structure of jobs, authority, and technical and financial procedures. Organizational culture affects employees' behavior, a firm's ability to meet their needs and demands, and the way the firm copes with the external environment. It establishes the rationale for "do's and don'ts" of behavior.[1]

Organizational culture also has significance in terms of employee socialization. Culture emerges out of the interactions between members of a work group. This process is closely connected to what organizational behaviorists have termed "newcomer socialization"—the period during which new organization members come to "learn the ropes" or know more precisely what is expected of them and what organization membership has to offer. Thus organizational culture is also important to the prospective and new employee. A prospective employee can ask: What does it take to do well in this firm? How are good people recognized? A strong culture can help new employees do the following: (1) understand their places in a culture, since their positions there have important implications for their survival and ability to contribute in the firm, (2) determine the culture positions of other organization members, (3) understand an organization's cultural norms and values, and (4) think about what kind of culture they want to have. Likewise, human resources managers and recruitment personnel can be helped to understand the kinds of people who would flourish (or flounder) in their company's particular environment. Such an appreciation can help attract needed talent and avoid costly hiring mistakes. Moreover, current employees will show greater pride in and support for an organization whose purpose, direction, and specialness they clearly understand.[4]

The appropriate culture for a particular firm depends on the objectives and strategies being pursued by that firm. For example, a decision to compete on customer service rather than price requires an appropriate formal structure and control system which then indicates the types of people needed to accomplish the objectives. On the other hand, if a firm is competing on the basis of price, then the issue is whether this fact is understood from top management to the operational level. The firm may follow any type of strategy or have any set of beliefs. The critical point is that these beliefs be widely shared and strongly held. People throughout the firm must be able and willing to tell another when a core belief is not being followed or accepted.[7]

MARKETING CULTURE AND THE SERVICE FIRM

Some scholars have begun to recognize the importance of organizational culture in the management of the marketing function. For example, organizational culture concepts have been included in a model of selling effectiveness.[18] Growing concern for issues of implementation in marketing strategy and the development of a customer orientation within organizations is also raising questions specifically to organizational culture.

Marketing culture refers to the pattern of shared values and beliefs that help individuals understand the marketing function and provides them with norms for behavior in the firm. It refers to the importance the firm as a whole places on the marketing function. In other words, the marketing culture of a service firm refers to the way marketing "things" are done in the firm.

The concept of marketing culture should not be confused with the concept of market orientation. A firm has market orientation if it implements the marketing concept. The marketing culture is a more fundamental concept: it can focus on the marketing concept, on innovation, on technical advancement, and the like. Where the marketing concept encompasses profitability, profitability is expected to be the consequence of a strong, appropriate, and consistent marketing culture.

Some researchers have begun an analysis of the linkage between organizational culture and the marketing of services. One study focused on determining whether there are significant differences between perceptions of the importance of marketing culture of goods-producing firms and those of service firms.[14] In other words, are the dimensions of marketing culture (i.e., service quality, interpersonal relationships, selling task, organization, internal communications, and innovativeness) more important in service firms than in goods-producing firms? Although the individual dimensions of marketing culture were perceived as being relatively important for both types of firms, significantly more importance was placed on each dimension for the service firms.

One reason the marketing culture is particularly important for the service firms is that the simultaneous delivery and receipt of services brings the employees and customers physically and psychologically close.[12] The policies and procedures established for these employees have both intentional and unintentional consequences because they cannot be hidden from the customer. In other words, there is no room for quality control between the employee's behavior and the customer's "purchase." An organization's marketing culture is evident to those who are served.

Interestingly, it has been discovered that there is a significant relationship between the type of marketing culture a service firm has and its profitability and marketing effectiveness.[15,16]

THE SERVICE FIRM MARKETING CULTURE AUDIT

Although soft or qualitative techniques (such as focus-group and in-depth interviews) have traditionally been used to measure complex constructs such as personality or lifestyle, it has been proven that valid quantitative measures of complex constructs can be developed. When quantifying a construct, it is essential to be very careful, scientific, thorough, and rigorous. A leading researcher has designed a paradigm for developing measures of marketing constructs,[2] so there now exists an instrument that can be used to measure the marketing culture of a service firm.

Appendix A summarizes the steps employed in developing and purifying the service firm marketing culture scale. The result of these 19 steps was high reliabilities and relatively consistent factor structures of the measure across independent samples. These characteristics provide support for scale's trait,[11] content,[14] and construct validity through use of a well-known approach,[19] convergent validity was established for the marketing culture measure. The scale's nomological validity, another indicator of construct validity, was assessed by examination of whether the construct measured by it was empirically associated with measures of other conceptually related constructs. (Readers interested in learning more about the establishment of the scale's validity and reliability characteristics should refer to Appendix B.)

The purified marketing culture scale consists of 34 items measuring the six dimensions of the construct: service quality, interpersonal relationships, selling task, organization, internal communications, and innovativeness. Table 1 shows the resulting questionnaire to measure the marketing culture of a service firm. The six-point scale that follows each item in the actual audit could be structured to relate to either the importance of the item (as shown) or the extent to which the firm possesses that attribute. Notice that the scales are unbalanced to prevent extreme skewness of the data.[5] The way the scales would be structured would depend on the reason for the audit. For an example of the use of the audit, see Appendix C.

SUMMARY

The literature in both services marketing and organizational culture suggests that an appropriate culture or climate is one of the most important ingredients for successfully marketing services.[10] Given this importance, this article has delineated the reasons why the marketing culture of a service firm is important, summarized the research that has been done in this area, and made the first presentation of a measure of the marketing culture of a service firm.

An exploration into the culture of a firm is considered important since it has been shown that the culture:

☐ provides the central theme around which employees' behavior can coalesce

☐ is the critical key strategic managers might use to direct the course of their firm

☐ provides a pattern of shared values and beliefs, the norms for behavior, and a form of control of employees

☐ influences productivity, the manner in which the firm copes with the various aspects of the external environment, and newcomer socialization

☐ aids in hiring practices—i.e., helps in understanding the characteristics of people who would do well in the firm

☐ establishes the rationale for "do's and don'ts" of behavior[4,12,13]

It has been shown that there are significant differences in the way goods-producing and service firms perceive the importance of the marketing culture. While both kinds of firms place considerable importance on the marketing culture, the employees in service firms place significantly more importance on it.[14] It has also been discovered that there is a significant relationship between the kind of marketing culture that exists in a service firm and the profitability and marketing effectiveness of that firm.[16]

Through a recommended rigorous, scientific approach toward measuring a marketing construct, a valid and reliable instrument was developed for service firms.[2] Six components or dimensions of the construct were discovered: service quality, interpersonal relationships, selling task, organization, internal communications, and innovativeness. To measure the dimensions of marketing culture, thirty-four items were identified. This measure can be utilized by the service marketing practitioner in several different ways. The recommended utilizations follow.

TABLE 1   An Audit to Assess the Marketing Culture of a Service Firm

To Assess the Importance Placed on SERVICE QUALITY

The firm specifically defining what exceptional service is

6	5	4	3	2	1
Necessary	Very Important	Important	Somewhat Important	Of Little Importance	No Importance

The commitment of top management to providing quality service

6	5	4	3	2	1
Necessary	Very Important	Important	Somewhat Important	Of Little Importance	No Importance

Systematic, regular measurement and monitoring of employees' performance

6	5	4	3	2	1
Necessary	Very Important	Important	Somewhat Important	Of Little Importance	No Importance

Employees' focus on customer needs, desires, and attitudes

6	5	4	3	2	1
Necessary	Very Important	Important	Somewhat Important	Of Little Importance	No Importance

The belief of employees that their behavior reflects the firm's

6	5	4	3	2	1
Necessary	Very Important	Important	Somewhat Important	Of Little Importance	No Importance

For employees to meet the firm's expectations

6	5	4	3	2	1
Necessary	Very Important	Important	Somewhat Important	Of Little Importance	No Importance

For the firm to place emphasis on employees' communication skills

6	5	4	3	2	1
Necessary	Very Important	Important	Somewhat Important	Of Little Importance	No Importance

Employees' attention to detail in their work

6	5	4	3	2	1
Necessary	Very Important	Important	Somewhat Important	Of Little Importance	No Importance

To Assess the Importance Placed on INTERNAL COMMUNI-CATIONS

The firm having an approved set of policies and procedures which is made available to every employee

6	5	4	3	2	1
Necessary	Very Important	Important	Somewhat Important	Of Little Importance	No Importance

That supervisors clearly state what their expectations are of others

6	5	4	3	2	1
Necessary	Very Important	Important	Somewhat Important	Of Little Importance	No Importance

That each employee understands the mission and general objectives of the firm

6	5	4	3	2	1
Necessary	Very Important	Important	Somewhat Important	Of Little Importance	No Importance

Management's sharing of financial information with all employees

6	5	4	3	2	1
Necessary	Very Important	Important	Somewhat Important	Of Little Importance	No Importance

The encouragement of front-line service personnel to become involved in standard-setting

6	5	4	3	2	1
Necessary	Very Important	Important	Somewhat Important	Of Little Importance	No Importance

The firm to focus efforts on training and motivating employees

6	5	4	3	2	1
Necessary	Very Important	Important	Somewhat Important	Of Little Importance	No Importance

TABLE 1   An Audit to Assess the Marketing Culture of a Service Firm *(continued)*

To Assess the Importance Placed on INNOVATIVENESS

For all employees to be receptive to ideas for change

6 — Necessary   5 — Very Important   4 — Important   3 — Somewhat Important   2 — Of Little Importance   1 — No Importance

The firm keeping up with technological advances

6 — Necessary   5 — Very Important   4 — Important   3 — Somewhat Important   2 — Of Little Importance   1 — No Importance

The receptiveness of the company to change

6 — Necessary   5 — Very Important   4 — Important   3 — Somewhat Important   2 — Of Little Importance   1 — No Importance

To Assess the Importance Placed on ORGANIZATION

Each employee to be well organized

6 — Necessary   5 — Very Important   4 — Important   3 — Somewhat Important   2 — Of Little Importance   1 — No Importance

For careful planning to be characteristic of each employee's daily routine

6 — Necessary   5 — Very Important   4 — Important   3 — Somewhat Important   2 — Of Little Importance   1 — No Importance

For employees to prioritize work

6 — Necessary   5 — Very Important   4 — Important   3 — Somewhat Important   2 — Of Little Importance   1 — No Importance

For employee's work area to be well organized

6 — Necessary   5 — Very Important   4 — Important   3 — Somewhat Important   2 — Of Little Importance   1 — No Importance

Each employee to manage time well

6 — Necessary   5 — Very Important   4 — Important   3 — Somewhat Important   2 — Of Little Importance   1 — No Importance

To Assess the Importance Placed on INTERPERSONAL RELATIONSHIPS

For the company to be considerate of employee's feelings

6 — Necessary   5 — Very Important   4 — Important   3 — Somewhat Important   2 — Of Little Importance   1 — No Importance

For the firm to treat each employee as an important part of the organization

6 — Necessary   5 — Very Important   4 — Important   3 — Somewhat Important   2 — Of Little Importance   1 — No Importance

For employees to feel comfortable in giving opinions to higher management

6 — Necessary   5 — Very Important   4 — Important   3 — Somewhat Important   2 — Of Little Importance   1 — No Importance

That managers/supervisors have an "open-door" policy

6 — Necessary   5 — Very Important   4 — Important   3 — Somewhat Important   2 — Of Little Importance   1 — No Importance

Management's interaction with front-line employees

6 — Necessary   5 — Very Important   4 — Important   3 — Somewhat Important   2 — Of Little Importance   1 — No Importance

(continued)

TABLE 1   An Audit to Assess the Marketing Culture of a Service Firm *(continued)*

To Assess the Importance Placed on SELLING TASK	The firm's emphasis on hiring the right people 6 ————— 5 ————— 4 ————— 3 ————— 2 ————— 1 Necessary Very Important Important Somewhat Important Of Little Importance No Importance The firm providing skill-based training and product knowledge to front-line service providers 6 ————— 5 ————— 4 ————— 3 ————— 2 ————— 1 Necessary Very Important Important Somewhat Important Of Little Importance No Importance The encouragement of creative approaches to selling 6 ————— 5 ————— 4 ————— 3 ————— 2 ————— 1 Necessary Very Important Important Somewhat Important Of Little Importance No Importance The firm's recognition of high achievers in selling 6 ————— 5 ————— 4 ————— 3 ————— 2 ————— 1 Necessary Very Important Important Somewhat Important Of Little Importance No Importance For employees to enjoy pursuing new accounts 6 ————— 5 ————— 4 ————— 3 ————— 2 ————— 1 Necessary Very Important Important Somewhat Important Of Little Importance No Importance For the firm to reward employees, better than competing firms, with incentives to sell 6 ————— 5 ————— 4 ————— 3 ————— 2 ————— 1 Necessary Very Important Important Somewhat Important Of Little Importance No Importance For employees to aggressively pursue new business 6 ————— 5 ————— 4 ————— 3 ————— 2 ————— 1 Necessary Very Important Important Somewhat Important Of Little Importance No Importance		

MANAGER IMPLICATIONS AND RECOMMENDATIONS

Given the importance of the culture of any organization and the high level of customer contact in service firms, the effects of culture should not be left to chance. The marketing culture audit described in this study has several recommended applications.

First, it enables one to assess a service firm's marketing culture along each dimension. It can also provide an overall measure of the culture's quality in the form of an average score across all six dimensions. The manner in which the results are interpreted depends on the scaling technique used. For example, if the firm uses the scales as shown in Table 1, then a higher average means that more importance is placed on marketing culture or on a particular dimension of marketing culture. A firm can also measure the extent to which its employees believe that each dimension *does* exist and *should* exist. Both can be measured with the same type of scale, but it would range from 6 "Strongly Agree" to 1 "Strongly Disagree."

One preferred way of assessing an individual's perception of marketing culture is to compare the person's score with the score achieved by other people.[2] The process is known as "developing norms." However, norms need not be developed if one wants only to determine which of two employees is more satisfied, or to determine how a particular individual's perception has changed over time. For these comparisons, one need merely compare the raw scores.

Second, the audit can be used to determine if the employees approve or disapprove of the culture dimensions and its component items. It is important that everyone in the firm understands what top management values, but there must also be a high degree of consensus regarding a belief or norm.[7] When the audit is used to determine the level of approval/disapproval attached to each dimension, the scales might range from 6 "Approve" to 1 "Disapprove."

A third use of the audit is to segment a service firm's customers into marketing culture groups based upon the perceived importance of the various dimensions of the construct. For example, consumers who place a high degree of importance on interpersonal relations may be in one segment, and consumers who place little importance on this dimension may be in another segment. Identification of the distinguishing characteristics of each customer segment may provide the service firm with valuable insights for its marketing and promotional strategies.

Fourth, service firm managers can use the audit to compare consumers' attitudes toward their marketing culture versus that of key competitors. Here the audit should be administered to a representative sample of consumers, with the respondents indicating their perceptions of the extent to which each firm possessed a cultural characteristic. The firm conducting the study would be able to determine any differences in consumers' attitudes regarding the firms as well as where each firm's strengths and weaknesses lie.

The marketing culture audit can also be used to affect employee's behavior as well as the firm's ability to meet their needs and preferences. By examining the items on the scale, managers/decision makers can more easily decide where to focus in order to influence employees' behavior. Additionally, the specific nature of the scale helps communicate to the employees what the firm expects. On the other hand, the firm can administer the scale to employees to pinpoint areas in which they think improvement is needed.

Sixth, management might use the audit to determine if there is a gap between what employees consider to be the ideal marketing culture and what they perceive to be the firm's actual service culture. A related application of such an instrument is that of determining if there are significant discrepancies between managers' and employees' perceptions of their firm's service culture. Though the importance of culture consistency within a firm has been widely acknowledged, research[17] has found significant attitude differences among service firm employees from higher management, middle management, and ground-level employees toward the compo-

nents of actual and ideal marketing culture, and many differences in how employees actually view the marketing culture of their service firm (i.e. the actual marketing culture) and the marketing culture they would like to have (i.e., the ideal marketing culture). It should be noted that the definition of an ideal culture stems from how a firm wants to be positioned relative to key competitors along each dimension. An important implication of this research finding is that importance needs to be placed on strategies and tactics to close the gap between the actual and ideal marketing cultures. There are several recommended strategies and tactics.

The first step in bridging the gap between the actual and ideal marketing cultures is for the top management of the service firm to decide how the firm should be positioned, the specific objectives they want to meet, and the strategies that should be implemented to meet those objectives.

Second, the problem of inconsistency might be alleviated by continuous communication between marketing personnel regarding what they are trying to accomplish. They should work with operations and systems personnel as well as other nonmarketing people from the beginning, in order to gain greater support, develop a feedback loop, and ensure that everyone is working toward the same objectives.

After it is decided what the desired cultural components of the service firm are and what the structural aspects of the culture are, the philosophies and creeds should be published in recruiting brochures, employee orientation handbooks, initial indoctrination and training materials, videotapes, and other artifacts that will communicate key elements of the culture to newcomers. To help ensure that the desired marketing culture is known and understood and that all employees are working toward the same objectives, the service firm might occasionally administer the marketing culture perception audit to discover any problem areas.

APPENDIX A   Summary of Steps Employed in Developing and Purifying the Service Firm Marketing Culture Scale

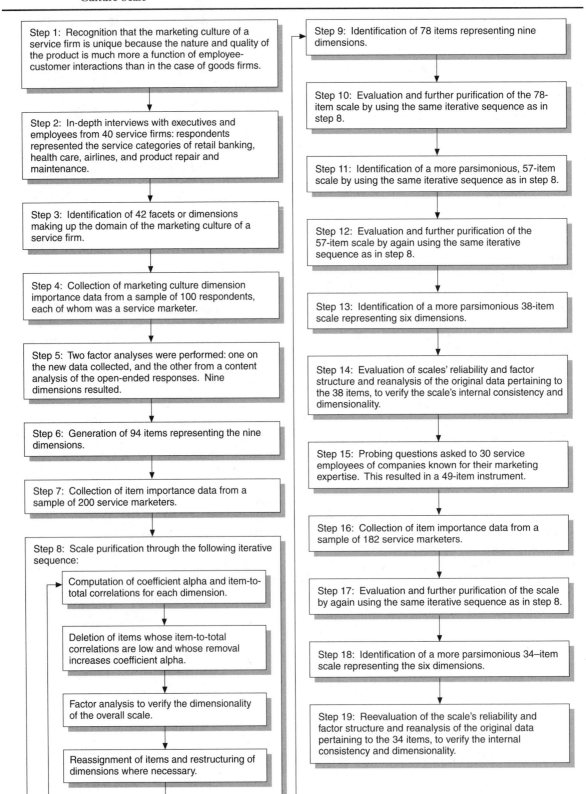

Step 1: Recognition that the marketing culture of a service firm is unique because the nature and quality of the product is much more a function of employee-customer interactions than in the case of goods firms.

Step 2: In-depth interviews with executives and employees from 40 service firms: respondents represented the service categories of retail banking, health care, airlines, and product repair and maintenance.

Step 3: Identification of 42 facets or dimensions making up the domain of the marketing culture of a service firm.

Step 4: Collection of marketing culture dimension importance data from a sample of 100 respondents, each of whom was a service marketer.

Step 5: Two factor analyses were performed: one on the new data collected, and the other from a content analysis of the open-ended responses. Nine dimensions resulted.

Step 6: Generation of 94 items representing the nine dimensions.

Step 7: Collection of item importance data from a sample of 200 service marketers.

Step 8: Scale purification through the following iterative sequence:

Computation of coefficient alpha and item-to-total correlations for each dimension.

Deletion of items whose item-to-total correlations are low and whose removal increases coefficient alpha.

Factor analysis to verify the dimensionality of the overall scale.

Reassignment of items and restructuring of dimensions where necessary.

Step 9: Identification of 78 items representing nine dimensions.

Step 10: Evaluation and further purification of the 78-item scale by using the same iterative sequence as in step 8.

Step 11: Identification of a more parsimonious, 57-item scale by using the same iterative sequence as in step 8.

Step 12: Evaluation and further purification of the 57-item scale by again using the same iterative sequence as in step 8.

Step 13: Identification of a more parsimonious 38-item scale representing six dimensions.

Step 14: Evaluation of scales' reliability and factor structure and reanalysis of the original data pertaining to the 38 items, to verify the scale's internal consistency and dimensionality.

Step 15: Probing questions asked to 30 service employees of companies known for their marketing expertise. This resulted in a 49-item instrument.

Step 16: Collection of item importance data from a sample of 182 service marketers.

Step 17: Evaluation and further purification of the scale by again using the same iterative sequence as in step 8.

Step 18: Identification of a more parsimonious 34–item scale representing the six dimensions.

Step 19: Reevaluation of the scale's reliability and factor structure and reanalysis of the original data pertaining to the 34 items, to verify the internal consistency and dimensionality.

APPENDIX B
ESTABLISHMENT OF VALIDITY AND RELIABILITY OF THE SCALE

The initial and purification steps which were taken in constructing the scale appear in Appendix A. The first step in the marketing scale purification was to administer the instrument to 30 service employees from top-management to operational-level positions. The employees were randomly chosen from companies known for their marketing expertise; e.g., A & M Pizza, Inc., dba Domino's Pizza, Federal Express, Southland Distribution Centers, and others. The respondents were presented with the instrument and asked probing questions regarding the quality of the dimensions and the items used to measure each marketing culture dimension. As a result of these in-depth interviews, additional items were added to the scale.

The resulting 49-item scale was then administered to a sample of 182 service marketers from a large metropolitan area. Respondents were asked to indicate the importance of each culture item by marking a seven-point scale ranging from "Strongly Agree" = 7 to "Strongly Disagree" = 1. Four service categories were chosen for investigation: retail banking, health care (i.e., health spas), airlines, and product repair and maintenance. Both the service firms from each industry and the person within the firm were randomly selected; respondents represented top-management, middle-management, and ground-level operational levels. The field research was conducted by trained data collectors and was completed during a three-week period. The 49-item instrument was refined by analyzing pooled data (i.e., data from all four service categories considered together). The instrument was then subjected to the computation of coefficient alpha, the values ranging from .56 to .78 across the six dimensions, which suggested that deleting certain items from some of the dimensions would improve the alpha values. The iterative sequence of computing alphas and item-to-total correlations, followed by deletion of items, was repeated several times, resulting in a set of 41 items with alpha values ranging from .68 to .85 across the six dimensions.

Examining the dimensionality of the reduced 41-item scale was the next step in this stage of scale purification and was accomplished by factor analyzing the difference scores on the items. The principal axis factoring procedure was used to extract six factors, and the resulting solution was rotated orthogonally through oblique rotation. The factor-loading matrix revealed that some items still had high loadings on more than one factor. After such items were removed from the factor-loading matrix, the original factors retained their meaningfulness since they had high correlations with the remaining items.

The deletion of some items necessitated the recomputation of alphas and item-to-total correlations and the reexamination of the factor structure of the reduced item pool. Several iterations of the sequence of analyses resulted in a final pool of 34 items representing six dimensions. The high alpha values and corrected item-to-total correlations indicated good internal consistency within each dimension. Also, the combined reliability for the 34-item scale, computed by using the formula for the reliability of linear combinations, was quite high (.94).

To further evaluate the reliabilities of the instrument, the component and total reliabilities and the corrected item-to-total correlations were calculated for each of the four subsamples. The reliabilities and item-to-total correlations were consistently high across all subsamples. The total-scale reliability was .88 or better in each of the four cases.

The high reliabilities and relatively consistent factor structures of the measure across the independent samples provide support for its "trait" validity. However, although these high reliabilities and internal consistencies are important conditions for a scale's construct validity—the extent to which a scale fully captures the underlying, unobservable construct it is intended to measure—they are not sufficient. The scale must satisfy the basic conceptual criterion of "face" or "content" validity: Does the scale appear to measure what it is intended to measure? Do the scale items capture key dimensions of the unobservable construct being measured? Assessing a scale's content validity is qualitative and involves examining two aspects: (1) the thoroughness with which the construct to be scaled and its domain have been explicated and (2) the extent to which the scale items represent the construct's domain (Parasuraman et al. 1986). The procedures used in developing the instrument satisfy both these evaluative requirements. Hence, the scale can be considered to possess content validity.

To further evaluate the marketing culture scale and its psychometric properties, data were collected pertaining to the marketing culture of four nationally known firms: a bank, a health care organization, an airline, and a repair and maintenance company. Trained field researchers in a major southwestern metropolitan area recruited an independent shopping-mall sample of 100 current or recent customers age 21 or older for each of the four firms.

Respondents were asked to provide ratings on general expectation items and on firm-specific perception items. Additionally, respondents answered several questions relating to their overall experiences with and perceptions about the firm being investigated. Responses were used in assessing the marketing culture scale's convergent validity.

Convergent validity was assessed by examining the association between the scale's scores and responses to a question in the second stage of data collection, which asked customers to rate the service firm's overall marketing culture (OVERALLMC) by checking one of four categories—excellent, good, fair, poor. The correspondence between the OVERALLMC ratings and the marketing culture scores (on each of the scale's six dimensions as well as on the total scale) was examined via one-way ANOVA. The treatment variable in the ANOVAs was OVERALLMC—with three categories instead of four because so few respondents checked "poor" that it was necessary to create a "fair/poor" category. The dependent variable was the average difference score (i.e., perception-minus-expectation score) on each marketing culture dimension as well as on the total culture scale (separate ANOVAs were conducted for each dimension and for the total scale). Significant ANOVA results were investigated further with Duncan's multiple range test to identify significant differences in the culture scores among the OVERALLMC categories.

In each of the four samples, the combined culture score for those in the "excellent" category was significantly higher (less negative) than for those in the "good" category. Furthermore, respondents in the "good" category had significantly higher combined culture score than those in the "fair/poor" category. Looking at the scores on the individual culture dimensions, the scores under "excellent" were consistently higher than those under "fair/poor"; with few exceptions, the differences were statistically significant. The strength and persistence of the linkage between the OVERALLMC categories and the culture scores across four independent samples offered strong support for the marketing culture scale's convergent validity.

The scale's "nomological" validity, another indicator of construct validity, was assessed by examining whether the construct measured by it was empirically associated with measures of other conceptually related constructs. Respondents in each sample answered two general questions that provided measures of two variables one could expect to be related conceptually to perceived marketing culture: (1) whether the respondents would recommend the service firm to a friend and (2) whether they had ever complained about the services they received from the firm. Respondents answering "yes" to the first question (RECOMMEND) and "no" to the second question (COMPLAINT) could be expected to perceive higher service quality than other respondents.

All scores under the "yes" category of RECOMMEND were higher than the corresponding scores under the "no" category. With few exceptions, the differences were statistically significant (on the basis of two-group t-tests). The scores under the "no" category of PROBLEM were consistently and, with few exceptions, significantly higher than the corresponding scores under the "yes" category. The findings provided support for the scale's nomological validity.

In summary, several different indicators, stemming from analyses of data from four independent samples, strongly suggested that the marketing culture scale is a reliable and valid measure of perceived marketing culture.

APPENDIX C
THE UTILIZATION OF THE MARKETING CULTURE AUDIT: A CASE

As a result of informal qualitative research (i.e., listening to customers' and employee's comments and complaints), the top management of Memphis-based XYZ Corporation concluded that not all the employees fully understood the importance and role that marketing played in the company. In other words, management was not convinced that all employees in each branch and from top management to operational level within each branch office fully understood which aspects of marketing were most important to the corporation and the relative importance of each dimension. The key decision makers within this service business knew that they could not achieve their corporate objectives if the employees were not working for the same goals.

By using the marketing culture audit, key management personnel decided on the importance they wanted their firm to place on each dimension of marketing culture. Next, the scale was administered to every employee in the corporation. As a result, management was able to determine: (1) the importance that the employees placed on each marketing culture dimension and specific item, (2) whether there were significant differences among top, middle, and operational-level employees regarding each culture item, (3) which dimensions of marketing culture needed attention and elaboration. XYZ Corporation then developed and implemented a communication program to instruct all of its employees about the desired marketing culture. To monitor the marketing culture of the firm, XYZ Corporation continued to administer the audit periodically.

END NOTES

1. Amsa, P., "Organizational Culture and Work Group Behavior: An Empirical Study," *Journal of Management Studies,* 23 (May 1986), 347–362.

2. Churchill, Gilbert A., Jr., "A Paradigm for Developing Better Measures of Marketing Constructs," *Journal of Marketing Research,* 16 (February 1979), 64–73.

3. Deshpande, Rohit, and Frederick E. Webster, Jr., "Organizational Culture and Marketing: Defining the Research Agenda," *Journal of Marketing,* 53 (January 1989), 3–15.

4. Downey, Stephen M., "The Relationship between Corporate Culture and Corporate Identity," *Public Relations Quarterly,* Winter 1987, pp. 7–12.

5. Kohli, Ajay K., and Bernard J. Jaworski, "Market Orientation: The Construct, Research Propositions, and Managerial Implications," *Journal of Marketing,* 54 (April 1990), 1–18.

6. Lovelock, Christopher H., "Why Marketing Management Needs to Be Different for Services," in *Marketing of Services,* ed. J. H. Donnelly and W. R. George, Chicago: American Marketing Association, 1981, pp. 5–9.

7. O'Reilly, Charles, "Corporations, Culture, and Commitment: Motivation and Social Control in Organizations," *California Management Review,* Summer 1989, pp. 9–25.

8. Parasuraman, A., "Customer-Oriented Organizational Culture: A Key to Successful Service Marketing," in *Creativity in Services Proceedings,* 4th Annual Services conference, 1986, pp. 73–77.

9. Parasuraman, A., Valarie A. Zeithaml, and Leonard L. Berry, "SERVQUAL: A Multiple-Item Scale for Measuring Customer Perceptions of Service Quality," working paper, Marketing Science Institute, Cambridge, MA, 1986.

10. Pascale, R., "Fitting New Employees into the Company Culture," *Fortune,* May 28, 1984, pp. 28–41.

11. Peter, J. Paul, "Construct Validity: A Review of Basic Issues and Marketing Practices," *Journal of Marketing Research,* 18 (May 1981), 133–145.

12. Schneider, Benjamin, "The People Make the Place," *Personnel Psychology,* 40: 3, (1987), 437–453.

13. Schneider, Benjamin, and Arnon E. Reichers, "On the Etiology of Climates," *Personnel Psychology,* 36:1, (1983), 19–39.

14. Webster, Cynthia, "Marketing Culture: Does It Differ between a Service and a Goods-Producing Firm?" *Atlantic Marketing Association Conference Proceedings,* (October 1990).

15. Webster, Cynthia, "Refinement of the Marketing Culture Scale and the Relationship between Marketing Culture and Profitability of a Service Firm," *Journal of Business Research,* (1991).

16. Webster, Cynthia, "The Effect of the Marketing Culture on the Marketing Effectiveness of a Service Firm," article currently under review for publication.

17. Webster, Cynthia, "Culture Consistency within the Service Firm: The Effects of Employee Position on Attitudes toward Marketing Firm Culture," *Journal of the Academy of Marketing Science,* (1991).

18. Weitz, Barton A., Harish Sujan, and Mita Sujan, "Knowledge, Motivation, and Adaptive Behavior: A Framework for Improving Selling Effectiveness," *Journal of Marketing,* 50 (October 1986), 174–191.

19. Zeithaml, Valarie A., A. Parasuraman, and Leonard L. Berry, "Problems and Strategies in Services Marketing," *Journal of Marketing,* 49 Spring 1986, 33–46.

INDEX